Windows Azure SQL Database Programming & Design

Kalman Toth

Windows Azure SQL Database Programming & Design

Trademark Notices

Microsoft is a trademark of Microsoft Corporation.
SQL Server 2012 is a program product of Microsoft Corporation.
SQL Server 2008 is a program product of Microsoft Corporation.
SQL Server 2005 is a program product of Microsoft Corporation.
SQL Server 2000 is a program product of Microsoft Corporation.
SQL Server Management Studio (SSMS) is a program product of Microsoft Corporation.
SQL Server Data Tools (SSDT) is a program product of Microsoft Corporation.
Microsoft Help Viewer is a program product of Microsoft Corporation.
SQL Server Analysis Services (SSAS) is a program product of Microsoft Corporation.
SQL Server Integration Services (SSIS) is a program product of Microsoft Corporation.
SQL Server Reporting Services (SSRS) is a program product of Microsoft Corporation.
SQL Azure is a program product of Microsoft Corporation.
Windows Azure SQL Database is a program product of Microsoft Corporation.
Office Visio is a program product of Microsoft Corporation.
Exam 70-461 is an exam product of Microsoft Corporation.
ORACLE is a trademark of ORACLE Corporation.
Java is a trademark of ORACLE Corporation.
DB2 is a trademark of IBM Corporation.
SYBASE is a trademark of Sybase Corporation.
McAfee is a trademark of McAfee Corporation.

Warning and Disclaimer

Every effort has been made to ensure accuracy, however, no warranty or fitness implied. The information & programs are provided on an "as is" basis.

Contents at a Glance

CHAPTER 1: master & Sample Databases 1

CHAPTER 2: Installing Azure SQL & Sample Databases 37

CHAPTER 3: Azure SQL Database Differences & Solutions 89

CHAPTER 4: Basic Structure of SELECT Statement 95

CHAPTER 5: SQL Server Management Studio 2012 113

CHAPTER 6: Fundamentals of Client-Server Computing 153

CHAPTER 7: Introduction to Relational Database Design 183

CHAPTER 8: Database Normalization 251

CHAPTER 9: Functional Database Design 261

CHAPTER 10: Advanced Database Design 289

CHAPTER 11: Mastery of Database Design 333

CHAPTER 12: New Programming Features in SS 2012 381

CHAPTER 13: Combining Tables with INNER & OUTER JOINs 397

CHAPTER 14: SELECT Statement Syntax with Examples 437

CHAPTER 15: Subqueries in SELECT Statements 499

CHAPTER 16: Modify Content - INSERT, UPDATE, DELETE & MERGE 525

CHAPTER 17: Transact-SQL Programming Review 549

CHAPTER 18: Exporting & Importing Data - On-Premises SS 2012 565

CHAPTER 19: Ensuring Data Integrity in the Enterprise 607

CHAPTER 20: Performance Optimization Techniques 637

CHAPTER 21: Advanced T-SQL Querying & Programming 663

APPENDIX A: Job Interview Questions 769

APPENDIX B: Job Interview Answers 773

INDEX of Windows Azure SQL Database Programming & Design 775

About the Author

Kalman Toth has been working with relational database technology since 1990 when one day his boss, at a commodity brokerage firm in Greenwich, Connecticut, had to leave early and gave his SQL Server login & password to Kalman along with a small SQL task. Kalman was a C/C++ developer fascinated by SQL, therefore, he studied a Transact-SQL manual 3 times from start to end "dry", without any server access. His boss was satisfied with the execution of SQL task and a few days later Kalman's dream came true: he got his very own SQL Server login. His relational database career since then includes database design, database development, database administration, OLAP architecture and Business Intelligence development. Applications included enterprise-level general ledger & financial accounting, bond funds auditing, international stock market feeds processing, broker-dealer firm risk management, derivative instruments analytics, consumer ecommerce database management for online dating, personal finance, physical fitness, diet and health. Currently he is Principal Trainer at www.sqlusa.com. His MSDN forum participation in the Transact-SQL and SQL Server Tools was rewarded with the Microsoft Community Contributor award. Kalman has a Master of Arts degree in Physics from Columbia University and a Master of Philosophy degree in Computing Science also from Columbia. Microsoft certifications in database administration, development and Business Intelligence. The dream SQL career took him across United States & Canada as well as South America & Europe. SQL also involved him in World History. At one time he worked for Deloitte & Touche on the 96th floor of World Trade Center North. On September 11, 2001, he was an RDBMS consultant at Citibank on 111 Wall Street. After escaping at 10:30 on that fateful Tuesday morning in the heavy dirt smoke, it took 10 days before he could return to his relational database development job just 1/2 mile from the nearly three thousand victims buried under steel. What Kalman loves about SQL is that the same friendly, yet powerful, commands can process 2 records or 2 million records or 200 million records the same easy way. His current interest is Artificial Intelligence. He is convinced that machine intelligence will not only replace human intelligence but surpass it million times in the near future. His hobby is flying gliders & vintage fighter planes. Accessibility: Twitter: @sqlusa http://twitter.com/sqlusa, http://www.sqlusa.com/contact2005/.

CONTENTS

CHAPTER 1: master & Sample Databases 1

AdventureWorks Series of OLTP Databases **1**
- Diagram of Person.Person & Related Tables 3
- Diagram of Sales.SalesOrderHeader and Related Tables 4

SELECT Query Basics **5**
- The Simplest SELECT Statement 5
- SELECT Query with WHERE Clause Predicate 7
- Aggregating Data with GROUP BY Query 8
- GROUP BY Query with 2 Tables & ORDER BY for Sorting 9
- LEN(), DATALENGTH(), LTRIM() & RTRIM() Functions 9
- Finding All Accessories in Production.Product Table 10
- How Can SQL Work without Looping? 11
- Single-Valued SQL Queries 11
- Data Dictionary for Tables in Sales Schema - On-Premises SS 12
- NULL Values in Tables & Query Results 13
- NULL Values Generated by Queries 14
- The SOUNDEX() Function to Check Sound Alikes 15

Building an FK-PK Diagram in AdventureWorks2012 .... **16**

AdventureWorksDWAZ2008R2 Data Warehouse Database **17**
- Diagram of a Star Schema in AdventureWorksDW2012 18

AdventureWorks2008 Sample Database **19**

AdventureWorks2012 Sample Database **20**
- Production.Product and Related Tables 21
- Descriptions of Columns in Production.Product Table 22
- Mountain Bikes in Production.Product Table 23

Prior SQL Server Sample Databases **24**

Northwind Sample Database **25**
- Diagram of Northwind Database 26

pubs Sample Database **27**
- Book Titles in pubs Database 28
- Diagram of pubs Database 29

SQL Server 2012 System Databases **30**
- Azure SQL master Database 31
- Querying System Views in master Database 32

SQL Server 2012 model Database 33
SQL Server 2012 msdb Database 34
SQL Server 2012 tempdb Database 35

CHAPTER 2: Installing Azure SQL & Sample Databases 37

SQL Azure - Enterprise in the Clouds 37
Getting Started with Azure SQL Database 39
Connecting Azure SQL Server from 2012 Management Studio 40

Installing AdventureWorks2012 for Azure SQL 41
Checking AdventureWorks2012 Tables Population 42

SS Import/Export Wizard for Migrating Data to Azure SQL 46
Creating Clustered Index 54
AdventureWorks2012 Final Tables Population 57
AdventureWorksDWAZ2008R2 Tables Population 59
AdventureWorksLTAZ2008R2 Tables Population 60

Migrate pubs & Northwind to Azure SQL Server 60
Installing instnwnd.sql Script 61
Discovering the New SQL Azure Instance 62

Connecting to 2 SQL Server Instances Simultaneously 63

Linked Server to Windows Azure SQL Database 64
T-SQL Script for Linked Server Setup in On-Premises SQL Serv er 64
Querying Azure SQL Database via Linked Server 65

SQL Server 2012 BACKUP DATABASE Command 66

Export Data-tier Application - Azure SQL 66

Import Data-tier Application 73

Deploy Data-tier Application 79

SQL Azure Books Online - BOL 84
Unsupported Transact-SQL Statements 84
Partially Supported Transact-SQL Statements 84
Windows Azure Platform Management Portal 84
Administration 84
Guidelines and Limitations 84

Installing SQL Server 2012 AdventureWorks2012 85

Installing SQL Server 2012 Northwind & pubs Databases 85

SQL Database Migration Wizard 86

CHAPTER 3: Azure SQL Database Differences & Solutions 89

Some System Views Don't Execute in master DB 89

Solution for USE dbname 89

Solution for SELECT INTO 90

Solution for 3-part Naming - Cross Database Access 90

Solution for Database BACKUP & RESTORE 90

Solution for Changing Database in SSMS Query Editor 90

Solution for SQL Server Agent 90

SQL Data Synch - Cloud Replication 91

SSMS: A transport-level error has occurred 91

Account & Billing Information 91

Azure SQL Database Management Portal 92

Query Editing & Running 92

Administration Tools 93

Design Tools 94

CHAPTER 4: Basic Structure of SELECT Statement 95

The SELECT Clause 95

SELECT with Search Expression 96

SELECT Statement with Subquery 97

Creating Delimited String List (CSV) with XML PATH 98

Logical Processing Order of the SELECT Statement 99

The TOP Clause 100

The DISTINCT Clause to Omit Duplicates 101

The CASE Conditional Expression 102

The OVER Clause 104

FROM Clause: Specifies the Data Source 105

The WHERE Clause to Filter Records (Rows) 106

The GROUP BY Clause to Aggregate Results 107

The HAVING Clause to Filter Aggregates 108

The ORDER BY Clause to Sort Results 109
The EXCEPT & INTERSECT Set Operators 109
CTE - Common Table Expression 110
Combining Results of Multiple Queries with UNION 111
TOP n by Group Query with OVER PARTITION BY 112
CHAPTER 5: SQL Server Management Studio 2012 113
SQL Server Programming, Administration & Management Tool 113
Query Editor 114
Execute All Batches in Query Editor 115
The Significance of GO in T-SQL Scripts 115
Routing Results to Grid, Text or File 118
Routing Results to Text 119
Routing Results to File 120
Saving Results in CSV Flat File Format 121
Copy & Paste Results to Excel 123
Error Handling & Debugging 125
Locating the Error Line in a Query 126
Error Message Pointing to the Wrong Line 127
Parsing a Query for Syntax Errors 128
Deferred Name Resolution Process 129
Executing Single Batch Only 130
Executing Part of a Query 131
Object Explorer 132
Context-Sensitive Right-Click Menu 133
Graphical Query Designer 134
Designing a GROUP BY Query in Query Designer 135
Graphically Editing of an Existing Query 140
Configuring Line Numbers in Query Editor 142
IntelliSense - Your Smart Assistant - OPSS2012 144
IntelliSense Guessing and Completing Object Names 145
IntelliSense Assisting with User-Defined Objects 148
IntelliSense Smart Guessing Partial Word in Middle of Object Names 149
Hovering over Red Squiggly Underline Errors for Explanation 150
Common Error: The multi-part identifier "abc" could not be bound. 151
Refreshing IntelliSense Cache for New DB Objects 152

CHAPTER 6: Fundamentals of Client-Server Computing *153*

Client - Server Relational Database Management System 153

Database Objects on Server-Side 154

Database Related Items on Client-Side 155

SQL Server Profiler to Monitor Client-Server Communications 156

Table - Database Object 157

Tables in Production Schema 158

Index - Database Object 159

Diagram of EmployeeDepartmentHistory and Related Tables 160

Index Description in Data Dictionary 161

Constraint - Database Object 162

List all PRIMARKY KEYs & FOREIGN KEYs 163

View - Database Object 164

CREATE Indexed View for Business Critical Queries 165

Graphical View Designer 166

Stored Procedure: Server-Side Program 167

Stored Procedure with Input Parameters 168

Stored Procedure Descriptions in Data Dictionary 169

Trigger: Event Fired Server-Side Program 170

Function: READ-ONLY Server-Side Program 171

User-Defined Function Descriptions in Data Dictionary 172

Sequence - Database Object - OPSS2012 173

ROW_NUMBER() & Ranking Functions 174

Dynamic SQL To Soar Beyond the Limits of Static SQL 177

Built-in System Functions 178

Local Variables & Table Variables in T-SQL 179

Constructing T-SQL Identifiers 181

The Use of [] - Square Brackets in Identifiers 182

CHAPTER 7: Introduction to Relational Database Design *183*

Logical Data Modeling 183

Physical Data Modeling **183**
Column Definitions for the FactInternetSales Table 184

Table Column Data Types **185**
Date Type max_length, precision, scale & collation_name Listing 186

U.S. Default Collation SQL_Latin1_General_CP1_CI_AS **187**

DATE & DATETIME Temporal Data Types **188**

Two Ways of Commenting in T-SQL Scripts **189**

Exploring Database Schemas **190**
SCHEMA_NAME() Function 191
Tables in HumanResources, Person & Purchasing Schemas 192

The CREATE TABLE Statement **193**
Branch Banking Database with ON DELETE CASCADE 193

Temporary Tables: Workhorses of T-SQL **196**

ALTER TABLE for Changing Table Definition **198**
Renaming Tables & Columns with sp_rename 199

DROP TABLE: A Dangerous Statement **200**

Table Constraints Inclusion in CREATE TABLE **201**

Nullability Column-Level Constraints in CREATE TABLE **202**

PRIMARY KEY & FOREIGN KEY Constraints **204**
Single Column & Composite PRIMARY KEY List with XML PATH 206

SSMS GUI Table Designer - OPSS2012 .... **207**
Basic GUI Table Design 208
CHECK Constraint Definition 209
Managing Indexes and Keys 210
Setting PRIMARY KEY with a Single Click 211
Configuring FOREIGN KEY: Declarative Referential Integrity 212
T-SQL Script Generation from GUI Table Designer 214
Generated CREATE TABLE & Related Objects Script 215

One-to-Many Relationship Implementation **217**

FOREIGN KEY Referencing A UNIQUE KEY **218**

FOREIGN KEY Relationship Without Constraint **219**

Database Diagram Design Tool in SSMS **220**

PRIMARY KEY & FOREIGN KEY as JOIN ON Keys 221

Composite & Indirect FOREIGN KEY 222

NATURAL KEY is a Must in Every Table 223

CANDIDATE KEY 224

Logical Data Modeling in Visio 225

Relational Database Design with Visio 227

AdventureWorks Database Model in Visio 228

Reverse Engineering a Database with Visio 229

Reverse Engineered Diagram of Northwind 230

Forward Engineering a Database with Visio 231

Forward Engineering from SSMS Diagram Tool 231

Generate Change Script Option 236

Scripting Single Database Object with Related Objects 238

Scripting DB Objects With Script Wizard 240

SEQUENCE Objects - On-Premises SS 2012 247

SEQUENCE Object Sharing - OPSS2012 248

Cyclical Sequence Objects 249

Getting the Source Code with sp_helptext 250

CHAPTER 8: Database Normalization *251*

The Goals of Database Normalizaton 251

Orders & Related Tables Diagram in Northwind 252

First Normal Form (1NF) 253

Second Normal Form (2NF) 254

Third Normal Form (3NF) 255

Fourth Normal Form (4NF) 256

Database Denormalizaton 257

Better Alternative to Denormalization 258

Ten Most Common Database Design Mistakes 259

Working for a Company with Messy Database Design 259

Query to List All Table Sizes in a Database 260

CHAPTER 9: Functional Database Design *261*

Types of Table Relationships 261

One-To-Many Relationship - FOREIGN KEY Reference 262

Composite PRIMARY KEY 265

Parent-Child Hierarchy 266

Hierarchical Relationship - Multi-Level with FOREIGN KEYs 267

Tree Hierarchy Representation with hierarchyid 268

Many-To-Many Relationship - Junction Table 269

Parent-Child or Master-Detail Tables Design 270

Column Descriptions of SalesOrderHeader & SalesOrderDetail Tables 271

Diagram of PurchaseOrderHeader and Related Tables 272

Multiple FOREIGN KEYs from One Table to Another 273

Parent - Multiple Children Table Design 274

LookupHeader & Lookup Tables for Storing All Lookups 275

History Table Design 277

Implementing One-To-One Relationship 278

One-To-One Relationship between publisher & pub_info Tables 279

Tables with Computed Columns 280

Building the Data Dictionary - On-Premises SS 282

GUI Data Dictionary Maintenance 282

Data Dictionary Maintenance with T-SQL Scripts 284

Lead Developer as Database Designer 286

Database Design Team at Big Budget Projects 286

Hiring Database Design Consultant where Resources Are Limited 286

Database System Solution Implementation Hierarchy 286

List All Default Constraints with Definition 287

Partitioning Query via Pure SQL - Ye Olde Way 288

CHAPTER 10: Advanced Database Design *289*

FileTable - Integrating Folders with DB - OPSS2012 289

Adding Files to FileTable Using T-SQL 294

Deleting Files from FileTable Using T-SQL 294

Data Compression: Compressed Table - OPSS 295

Data Compression: Compressed Index 301

The GUI Data Compression Wizard 302

Partitioned Table, Partition Function & Scheme - OPSS 308

The GUI Create Partition Wizard 316

Azure SQL Partition & Federation Examples 316

Columnstore Index for DW Performance - OPSS2012 317

Workaround for DBCC DROPCLEANBUFFERS 318

DATE Data Type Solves Many Problems with DATETIME 319

Database Design & Programming Standards 320

Database Design Standards 320

Identifiers 321

Principles of T-SQL Identifier Architecture 322

Stored Procedure Outline 323

User-Defined Function Outline 323

How to Create a Database with T-SQL Script 324

Adding New Column to a Table with ALTER TABLE 325

IDENTITY Column in a Table Variable 326

Partition Data By Country Query 327

Diagram of Sales.SalesPerson & Related Tables 328

Adding IDENTITY Column To Empty Table 329

SET IDENTITY INSERT tablename ON 329

DBCC CHECKIDENT Command - OPSS 330

ADD Partitioned Sequence Number to Table 331

Add ROW_NUMBER & RANK Columns to Table 332

3-Part Name Table Reference - On-Premises SQL Server 332

CHAPTER 11: Mastery of Database Design 333

The Nature of Connection Between Tables 333

Categorical Relationship 333

Information Object Belongs To Relationship 334

Exporting & Presenting XML Data from Production.ProductModel 338

Company Received an Order Relationship 341

Type Relationship 343

When to Use & Not to Use Composite PRIMARY KEYs 345

How To Design a Table 346

Table-Related Database Objects 347

Listing All PRIMARY KEYs 348

UNIQUEIDENTIFIER As PRIMARY KEY 349

List All PK & FK Columns in the Database 350

How to Get Database Object Definition Information 351

Scripting Object CREATE Definitions 351

Single Object CREATE & Other Scripts from SSMS Object Explorer 352

Searching for Database Objects in Object Explorer Details 354

OBJECT_DEFINITION() Function for Getting Source Code 355

Scripting DB Objects with PowerShell - OPSS2012 356

System Views since SQL Server 2005 357

Querying Systems Views 358

Listing All System Views 359

List of System Tables Prior to SQL Server 2005 - OPSS 361

Other Methods of Metadata Access 362

Graphical Dependency Information 362

Scripting GUI Object Change - OPSS2012 363

The sp_helpdb System Procedure - OPSS 364

The sp_help and sp_helptext System Procedures 365

Listing All CHECK Constraints in a Database 368

Creating a UDF CHECK Constraint 369

List All DEFAULT Constraint Definitions 370

Database Object-Definition from sys.sql_modules System View 371

Snowflake Schema Data Warehouse Design 373

Object Explorer Table Editor - OPSS 374

All Tables Row Count without the COUNT() Function 375

Column Properties Page - OPSS 376

Listing All Columns with PK, FK & IDENTITY Properties 377

The Collation Column Property & the COLLATE Clause 378

Listing All Database & Server Collations 379

Designing Table for Multi-Language Support with UNICODE 380

CHAPTER 12: New Programming Features in SS 2012 381

PARSE() Function 381

TRY_CONVERT() Function - OPSS2012 383

TRY_CONVERT() Usage in Adding Column to Table 384

TRY_CAST() Function 385

TRY_PARSE() Function 386

FORMAT() Function 387

CONCAT() Function 388

CHOOSE() Function 388

THROW Statement 389

IIF() Function 390

DATEFROMPARTS() & DATETIMEFROMPARTS() Functions 390

EOMONTH() Function 391

Result Set Paging with OFFSET & FETCH NEXT 392

Result Paging Stored Procedure 393

LEAD() & LAG() Functions - OPSS2012 394

FIRST_VALUE() & LAST_VALUE() - OPSS2012 395

EXEC New Option: WITH RESULT SETS 396

CHAPTER 13: Combining Tables with INNER & OUTER JOINs 397

SELECT with INNER JOIN 397

FOREIGN KEY Constraint as Base for INNER JOIN 398

Diagram of Person.Person and Related Tables 399

EQUI-JOIN BETWEEN FOREIGN KEY & PRIMARY KEY 400

Diagram of Sales.Customer and Related Tables 401

Extracting All or Partial Data from JOINed Tables 402

Table Aliases for Readability 404

Column Aliases for Readability & Presentation 404

Derived Table Alias with a List of Column Aliases 405

INNER JOIN with Additional Conditions 406

Counting Rows in JOINs....407
INNER JOIN with 3 Tables....408
INNER JOIN with Junction Table....410
NON-EQUI JOINs for Data Analytics....411
Interchangeability of ON & WHERE Predicates in INNER JOINs....412
SELF-JOIN for Analytics Within a Table....413
Applying SELF-JOIN for Numbering Result Lines....415
INNER JOIN with 5 Tables....416
Creating View as Workaround for "Too Many JOINs"....417
Non-Key INNER JOIN for Analytics....418
JOINing Tables without Relationship for Combinatorics....419
Cartesian Product....419
SQL OUTER JOIN for Inclusion of Unmatched Rows....420
LEFT JOIN: Include Unmatched Rows from Left Table....421
RIGHT JOIN - Same as LEFT with Tables Switched....422
Cardinality of OUTER JOINs....424
LEFT JOIN & RIGHT JOIN on the Same Table....425
FULL JOIN to Include All Unmatched Rows....426
CROSS JOIN for Cartesian Product....427
CROSS JOIN Generated Multiplication Table....428
INNER JOIN with 7 Tables....429
INNER JOIN with GROUP BY Subquery....430
Making Queries Readable & Results Presentable....431
A 12 Tables JOIN Query....432
Order of Tables or Predicates Does Not Matter....434
The CROSS APPLY Operator....435
Using CROSS APPLY with Columns Specified Table Alias....436
CHAPTER 14: SELECT Statement Syntax with Examples....437
Simple SELECT Statement Variations....437

Using the TOP Clause in SELECT Queries 439

Using the WHERE Clause in SELECT Queries 440

Using Literals in SELECT Queries 441

Date & Time Literals in SELECT Queries 442

ymd, dmy & mdy String Date Format Literals 443

Setting DATEFIRST with Literal 444

Language Setting - SET LANGUAGE 444

The sys.syslanguages System View 445

Determining SET Options 446

Easy SELECT Queries for Fun & Learning 447

Cardinality of DISTINCT & GROUP BY Clauses 450

Column Alias Can only Be Used in ORDER BY 451

Workarounds for Column Alias Use Restriction 451

When the Clock Strikes Midnight: datetime Behaviour 452

LEFT(), RIGHT() & SUBSTRING() String Functions 453

Transact-SQL Reserved Keywords 455

Case Sensitive Sort with Latin1_General_CS_AI 456

The ORDER BY Clause for Sorting Query Results 457

Using Column Alias in the ORDER BY Clause 458

Using Table Alias in the ORDER BY Clause 459

Easy ORDER BY Queries for Exercises 460

Using Multiple Keys in the ORDER BY Clause 466

ORDER BY in Complex Queries 467

ORDER BY with ROW_NUMBER() 468

ORDER BY Clause with CASE Conditional Expression 469

ORDER BY Clause with IIF Conditional Function 472

ORDER BY Clause with the RANK() Function 473

ORDER BY Clause with Custom Mapped Sort Sequence 474

ORDER BY Clause with Custom Alphanumeric Sort Sequence 475

Working with Synonyms 476

Date & Time Conversion To / From String 477

The CONVERT() Function with Style Number Parameter 477

String to Datetime Conversion Without Century 480

Combine Date & Time String into Datetime 481

Date and Time Internal Storage Format 481

Date & Time Operations Using System Operators & Functions 482
Extract Date Only from DATETIME Data Type 482
String Date Formats Without Time 483
DATEADD() and DATEDIFF() Functions 485
Last Date & First Date Calculations 486
BETWEEN Operator for Date Range 487
Date Validation Function ISDATE() 490
Month Sequence Generator 491
The DATEPART() Function to Decompose a Date 493
The DATENAME() Function to Get Date Part Names 494
Extract Date from Text with PATINDEX Pattern Matching 495
Last Week Calculations 497
Specific Day Calculations 498

CHAPTER 15: Subqueries in SELECT Statements 499

Subqueries 499
Non-Correlated Subqueries 500
Subquery returned more than 1 value Error 501
Correlated Subqueries 502
Correlated Subqueries with Same Table 504
CROSS APPLY with Correlated Subquery 504

Derived Tables: SELECT from SELECT 505

The UNION & UNION ALL Set Operators 506

CTE: Common Table Expression for Structured Coding 507
Multiple CTEs Query 508
Testing Common Table Expressions 509
Nested CTEs Queries 510
Testing Nested CTEs 511
Recursive CTEs for Tree Hierarchy Processing 513
Recursive Generation of Date & Month Sequences 514
Generate Month Names in Different Languages 515
Graphical Organizational Chart of AdventureWorks Cycles 516
Chain of Command Recursive Query 518
Graphical Bill of Materials for Mountain-100 Silver, 44 Bike 519

PIVOT Operator to Transform Rows Into Columns 521
Recompiling the vSalesPersonSalesByFiscalYears View 522

UNPIVOT Crosstab View Results 523

Using Subquery in Column List of SELECT 524

CHAPTER 16: Modify Content - INSERT, UPDATE, DELETE & MERGE 525

INSERT VALUES - Table Value Constructor.........525

INSERT VALUES - Ye Olde Way.........526

INSERT SELECT.........527

INSERT SELECT Literal List with UNION.........527

INSERT SELECT from Table.........528

SCOPE_IDENTITY() for Last-Inserted IDENTITY Value.........528

INSERT with Subset of Columns.........529

Capturing Last-Inserted IDENTITY Set Values with OUTPUT.........529

INSERT EXEC Stored Procedure.........530

INSERT EXEC System Procedure.........532

INSERT Only New Rows Omit the Rest.........533

DELETE - A Dangerous Operation.........534

TRUNCATE TABLE & DBCC CHECKIDENT.........535

UPDATE - A Complex Operation.........537

Checking Cardinality & Changes by UPDATE Prior to Execution.........537

ANSI Style UPDATE.........538

UPDATE from Table in Another Database - OPSS.........539

UPDATE Syntax Challenges.........540

UPDATE with INNER JOIN.........541

Capturing Affected Rows with @@ROWCOUNT.........541

UPDATE with Common Table Expression.........542

Four Methods of UPDATE with GROUP BY Query.........543

ANSI UPDATE.........543

FROM Clause UPDATE with Derived Table.........543

FROM Clause UPDATE with CTE.........544

CTE UPDATE.........544

MERGE for Combination INSERT, UPDATE or DELETE.........545

Using MERGE Instead of UPDATE.........548

CHAPTER 17: Transact-SQL Programming Review 549

IF...ELSE Conditional.........549

WHILE Looping - UPDATE in Batches.........550

WHILE Loop Usage in Cursors.........551

T-SQL Transaction **552**
DELETE from 2 Tables with TRANSACTION Control 552
Stored Procedure with Input & Output Parameters **553**
Dynamic SQL Stored Procedure to REBUILD Indexes **554**
User-Defined Functions **555**
Table-Valued Functions 555
Table-Valued Function for PRIME Numbers Generation 556
Inline Functions 557
Scalar Functions 558
Dynamic PIVOT Script **559**
INSERT, UPDATE & DELETE through a View **560**
Sensitive Data Audit Trigger **561**
Automatic Timestamp Trigger **562**
Recursive Product Assembly **563**
Percent on Base Calculation **564**
CHAPTER 18: Exporting & Importing Data - On-Premises SS 2012 .... ***565***
Saving a T-SQL Script as .sql File **565**
Executing a .sql Script File Using SQLCMD **566**
Making a T-SQL Script Rerunnable **567**
bcp Usage for Exporting & Importing Data **569**
Importing Data with the bcp Utility 570
Exporting Data with SQL Server Import and Export Wizard **571**
Importing Data with SQL Server Import and Export Wizard **585**
Exporting Database Table to Excel **595**
Exporting Data Directly into a Flat File **604**
Command Prompt Commands List by HELP **605**
CHAPTER 19: Ensuring Data Integrity in the Enterprise ***607***
Why is Data Integrity Paramount **607**
Entity Integrity **608**

How to Remove Duplicates in a Table **609**
Remove Duplicates with CTE & ROW_NUMBER OVER PARTITION BY 611
Remove Duplicates with GROUP BY 611

Domain Integrity **612**
Domain Integrity Summary Display with sp_help 613
THE COLUMNPROPERTY() Function 614

Column List Using System Views & Data Dictionary **615**

Declarative Referential Integrity **616**
FOREIGN KEY Constraints Represent the Only Connections Among Tables 619

Enterprise-Level Business Rules Enforcement **622**
Special Role of Triggers 622
Product Reorder Trigger 623
Trigger Examples In AdventureWorks2012 625

Business Intelligence in the Enterprise - On-premises Demo **627**
SSRS: Designing Complex Interactive Reports 627
SSAS: Designing Multi-Dimensional Cubes 630
Browsing Multidimensional Cube in Management Explorer 632
Excel PivotTable Report Using AS Cube Datasource 633
SSIS: Enterprise Level Data Integration 635

Full-Text Index & Full-Text Search - On-Premises SS **636**

CHAPTER 20: Performance Optimization Techniques ***637***

Optimization Basics **637**

Optimizing a Query by Reengineering **639**
Examining the Actual Execution Plan 641
Comparing Execution Plan Cost Summary Pop-ups 642
Optimizing with Multi Statements Query Using Temporary Tables 643
Optimizing with Covering Index 645

Optimizing with Indexing **646**
The Larger the Table the More Benefits of Indexing 647
Non-SARGable Predicates Force Index Scan 650
WHERE Clause SARGable Predicate Construction 651
Stored Procedure Parameter Sniffing & Prevention 652

Optimizing with MERGE **652**
Stress Testing a View with Include Client Statistics Feature 653

8 Point Optimization Guide **654**

Object Explorer GUI REBUILD Indexes - On-premises SS 2012 655
UPDATE STATISTICS on All Tables Stored Procedure 656
Blocking of a Query by Another Query 657
Activity Monitor - On-premises SS 2012 658
Operational Solutions for Performance Problems 658
Server & Database Standard Reports - On-premises SS 2012 659
Server Dashboard - On-premises SS 2012 660

Batching Large INSERT, UPDATE & DELETE 661

Database Engine Tuning Advisor - On-Premises SQL Server 662

CHAPTER 21: Advanced T-SQL Querying & Programming 663

String Pattern Matching & Parsing 663
The LIKE Operator 663
The CHARINDEX() Function 664
The PATINDEX() Function 665

Composable DML - INSERT into 2 Tables with One Statement 666

Double Assignment Operator 667

Running Total & MovingAverage Calculation 668
Running Total with Subquery - Ye Olde Way 669
Running Total with Multiple Assignment UPDATE 670

Subtotal, Total & Grand Total GROUPING Function 671

The GROUP BY Clause with GROUPING SETS 672

SELECT Top N from Each Group 673
SELECT Top N from Each Group Ye Olde Way 674

UPDATE PRIMARY KEY & Connecting FK in a Transaction 674
Disable & Enable FOREIGN KEY Constraint 674

Table-Valued Parameters 675

Creating Comma Delimited String from a Column 677
Configuring Comma Delimited Result Sets in SSMS 678

Nesting Cursors 679
Set Based Operations Equivalent Code 681

Advanced Graphical Query Designer - On-Premises SS 682
Aliasing Tables in the Diagram Pane 682
Specifying OUTER JOIN in Diagram Pane 683

Template Explorer & Browser 685

Create Inline Function Template 686

PowerShell - On-Premises SQL Server 689

PowerShell Command List 690

TRY...CATCH Block With TRANSACTION 697

SET TRANSACTION ISOLATION LEVEL Command 698

READ UNCOMMITTED Isolation Level - Dirty Reads 699

READ COMMITTED Isolation Level - Default for SQL Server 700

REPEATABLE READ Isolation Level 701

SERIALIZABLE Isolation Level 703

SNAPSHOT Isolation Level 704

Tabular Summary of Isolation Levels 705

INSERT Data Into Parent-Child Tables in One Transaction 706

ROLLBACK Does Not Roll Back Everything 707

Optimistic Concurrency Control 708

Xquery Examples 713

The query() Method 713

value() Method 715

nodes() Method 715

exist() Method 716

modify() Method 718

Insert (XML DML) 719

Delete (XML DML) 720

Working with hierarchyid Data Type 721

Orgchart Based on AdventureWorks2012 721

Inline User-Defined Function OrgChart at Any Level 722

hierarchyid System Functions 723

Sort Outline Numbering with hierarchyid 724

Dynamic SQL PIVOT 725

Date Range Programming with Datetime Column 727

4-Week 13 Month Calendar 730

DDL Trigger on DATABASE CREATE 731

Spatial Data Types: Geometry & Geography 732

The POLYGON & STLength() Functions 732

Polygon Difference & Intersection 733

Geometry Area & CIRCULARSTRING Functions 734
The geography Data Type in Map Application 736
Surveying Spatial Locations in Person.Address with TABLESAMPLE 737

Data Encryption & Decryption 738

Database Backup - On-Premises SQL Server 739
Full Database Backup with Verification 739
Full Database Backup with Datestamp in Filename 739
Backup of a Single Table 740
Setting SSMS Query Options to Include Double Quotes with Strings 741

Database Restore - On-Premises SQL Server 742
Restore of a Single Table 743

Database Maintenance Plan Wizard - On-Premises SS 745

Configure Stored Procedure As SS Agent Job & Schedule 750

BULK INSERT Command - On-Premises SQL Server 751
Format File Generation with bcp 751
Export Data with bcp Format File Option 751
Import Data with BULK INSERT Format File Option 751
Importing & Exporting Images - OPSS 753
Exporting All Images from Table 755

FOR XML Clause 757
FOR XML RAW 757
FOR XML AUTO 757
FOR XML EXPLICIT 758
FOR XML PATH 759
Concatenation Loop With XML PATH 760

Interesting T-SQL Scripts 761

Transforming Dynamic SQL Result Set into a View 764
Accessing a View from Excel 764

Querying the Database from a Client C# Program 766
C# Connection to Windows Azure SQL Database 768

APPENDIX A: Job Interview Questions 769

Selected Database Design Questions 769

Selected Database Programming Questions 770

APPENDIX B: Job Interview Answers 773

Selected Database Design Answers 773

Selected Database Programming Answers 774

INDEX of Windows Azure SQL Database Programming & Design 775

Index of the Most Important Topics.. 775

INTRODUCTION

Microsoft Windows Azure SQL Database opens new horizons in RDBMS applications by removing most of the database management & administration functions from the database owner and at the same time making database content easily available across the United States and in fact the entire World via cloud computing technologies.

Developers across the world are facing database issues daily. While they are immersed in procedural languages with loops , RDBMS forces them to think in terms of sets without loops. It takes transition. It takes training. It takes experience. Developers are exposed also to Excel worksheets or spreadsheets as they were called in the not so distant past. So if you know worksheets how hard databases can be? After all worksheets look pretty much like database tables? The big difference is connections among well-designed tables. A database is a set of connected tables which represent entities in the real world. A database can be 100 connected tables or 3000. The connection is very simple: row A in table Alpha has affiliated data with row B in table Beta. But even with 200 tables and 300 connections (FOREIGN KEY references), it takes a good amount of time to familiarize to the point of acceptable working knowledge.

The SQL language running strong after 3 decades of glorious existence. What is the difference? The basic difference is that SQL can handle large datasets in a consistent manner based on mathematical foundations. You can throw together a computer language easy: assignment statements, looping, if-then conditional, 300 library functions, and voila! Here is the new language: Mars/1, named after the red planet to be fashionable with NASA's new Mars robot. But can Mars/1 JOIN a table of 1 million rows with a table of 10 million rows in a second? The success of SQL language is so compelling that other technologies are tagged onto it like XML/XQuery which deals with semi-structured information objects.

In SQL you are thinking at a high level. In C# or Java, you are dealing with details, lots of them. That is the big difference. Why is so much of the book dedicated to database design? Why not plunge into SQL coding and sooner or later the developer will get a hang of the design? Because high level thinking requires thinking at the database design level. A farmer has 6 mules, how do we model it in the database? We design the Farmer and FarmAnimal tables, then connect them with FarmerID FOREIGN KEY in FarmAnimal referencing the FarmerID PRIMARY KEY in the Farmer table. What is the big deal about it, looks so simple? In fact, how about just calling the tables Table1 & Table2 to be more generic? Ouch... meaningful naming is the very basis of good database design. Relational database design is truly simple for simple well-understood models. The challenge starts in modeling complex objects such as financial derivative instruments, airplane passenger scheduling or social network website. When you need to add 5 new tables to a 1000 tables database and hook them in (define FOREIGN KEY references) correctly, it is a huge challenge. To begin with, some of the 5 new tables may already be redundant, but you don't know that until you understand what the 1000 tables are really storing. Frequently, learning the application area is the biggest challenge for a developer when starting a new job.

The SQL language is simple to program and read even if when touching 10 tables. Complexities are abound though. The very first one: does the SQL statement touch the right data set? 999 records and 1000 or 998? T-SQL statements are turned into Transact-SQL scripts, stored procedures, user-defined functions and triggers, server-side database objects. They can be 5 statements or 1000 statements long programs. The style of Transact-SQL programming is different from the style in procedural programming languages. There are no arrays, only tables or table variables. Typically there is no looping, only set-based operations. Error control is different. Testing & debugging is relatively simple in Transact-SQL due to the interactive environment and the magic of selecting & executing a part without recompiling the whole.

WHO THIS BOOK IS FOR

Developers, programmers and systems analysts who are new to cloud database technology. Also developers, designers and administrators, who know some SQL programming and database design, wish to expand their RDBMS design & development technology horizons on Azure SQL Database. Familiarity with other computer language is assumed. The book has lots of queries, lots of T-SQL scripts, plenty to learn. The best way to learn it is to type in the query in your own SQL Server copy and test it, examine it, change it. Wouldn't it be easier just to copy & paste it? It would but the learning value would diminish. You need to feel the SQL language in your fingers. SQL queries must "pour" out from your fingers into the keyboard. Why is that so important? After everything can be found on the web and just copy & paste? Well not exactly. If you want to be an expert, it has to be in your head not on the web. Second, when your supervisor is looking over your shoulder, "Charlie, can you tell me what is the total revenue for March?", you have to be able to type in the query without SQL forum search and provide the results to your superior promptly.

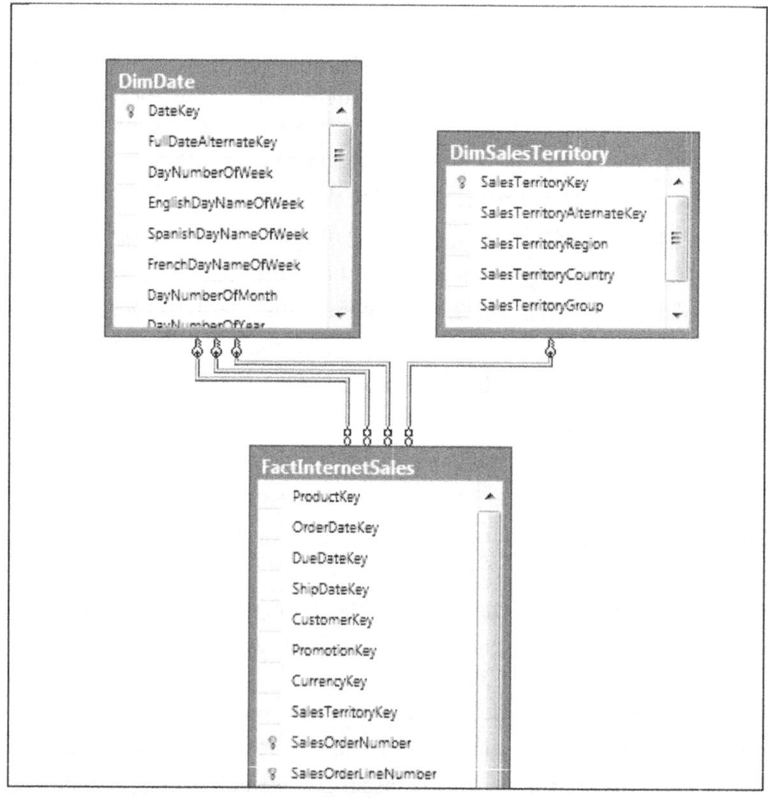

ABOUT THIS BOOK

Windows Azure SQL Database design and Transact-SQL programming. It is not a reference manual, rather learn by examples: there are over 1,400 SELECT queries in the book. Instead of imaginary tables, the book uses the SQL Server sample databases for explanations and examples: pubs (PRIMARY KEYs 9, FOREIGN KEYs 10) , Northwind (PRIMARY KEYs 13, FOREIGN KEYs 13) and the AdventureWorks family. Among them: AdventureWorks, AdventureWorks2008, AdventureWorks2012 (PRIMARY KEYs 71, FOREIGN KEYs 90), & AdventureWorksDW2012 (PRIMARY KEYs 27, FOREIGN KEYs 44). The book introduces relational database design concepts, then reinforces them again and again, not to bore the reader, rather indoctrinate with relational database design principles. Light weight SQL starts at the beginning of the book, because working with database metadata (not the content of the database, rather data which describes the database) is essential for understanding database design. By the time the reader gets to T-SQL programming, already knows basic SQL programming from the database design section of the book. The book was designed to be readable in any environment, even on the beach laptop around or no laptop in sight at all. All queries are followed by results row count and /or full/partial results listing in tabular (grid) format. For full benefits though, the reader should try out the T-SQL queries and scripts as he progresses from page to page, topic to topic. Example for SQL Server 2012 T-SQL query and results presentation.

```
SELECT          V.Name                                        AS Vendor,
                FORMAT(SUM(POH.TotalDue), 'c', 'en-US')       AS [Total Purchase],
                FORMAT(AVG(POH.TotalDue), 'c', 'en-US')       AS [Average Purchase]
FROM Purchasing.Vendor AS V
   INNER JOIN Purchasing.PurchaseOrderHeader AS POH
         ON V.VendorID = POH.VendorID
GROUP BY V.Name  ORDER BY Vendor;
-- (79 row(s) affected) - Partial results.
```

Vendor	Total Purchase	Average Purchase
Advanced Bicycles	$28,502.09	$558.86
Allenson Cycles	$498,589.59	$9,776.27
American Bicycles and Wheels	$9,641.01	$189.04
American Bikes	$1,149,489.84	$22,539.02

CONVENTIONS USED IN THIS BOOK

The Transact-SQL queries and scripts (sequence of statements) are shaded.

The number of resulting rows is displayed as a comment line: -- (79 row(s) affected) .

The results of the queries is usually displayed in grid format.

Less frequently the results are enclosed in comment markers: /*...... */ .

When a query is a trivial variation of a previous query, no result is displayed.

While the intention of the book is database design & database development, SQL Server installation and some database administration tasks are included.

Azure SQL, SQL Database & SQL Azure are shorts for the official name "Windows Azure SQL Database".

On-premises SQL Server 2012 means regular SQL Server with database storage on the server itself.

OPSS2012 is a short for On-Premises SQL Server 2012.

OPSS is a short for On-Premises SQL Server (not specific to SS 2012).

SQL Server 2012 query/feature means that currently there is no Azure SQL support for all parts of the query or SSMS feature usage.

"Apparatus Intelligentia

vincet

Humanum Intelligentia"

Dedicated to

Vint Cerf

the Father of the Internet

This page is intentionally left blank.

CHAPTER 1: master & Sample Databases

AdventureWorks Series of OLTP Databases

AdventureWorks sample On Line Transaction Processing (OLTP) database has been introduced with SQL Server 2005 to replace the previous sample database Northwind, a fictional gourmet food items distributor. The intent of the AdventureWorks sample database is to support the business operations of AdventureWorks Cycles, a fictitious mountain, touring and road bike manufacturer. The company sells through dealer network and online on the web. In addition to bikes, it sells frames and parts as well as accessories such as helmets, biking clothes and water bottles. The AdventureWorks2012 (also sample database for Azure SQL) database image of Touring-1000 Blue, 50 bike in Production.ProductPhoto table.

T-SQL query to generate the list of tables of AdventureWorks2012 in 5 columns. The core query is simple. Presenting the results in 5 columns instead of 1 column adds a bit of complexity.

```
;WITH cteTableList AS (     SELECT CONCAT(SCHEMA_NAME(schema_id), '.', name)              AS TableName,
 (( ROW_NUMBER() OVER( ORDER BY CONCAT(SCHEMA_NAME(schema_id),'.', name)) ) % 5)      AS Remainder,
 (( ROW_NUMBER() OVER( ORDER BY CONCAT(SCHEMA_NAME(schema_id),'.', name)) - 1 )/ 5)   AS Quotient
                            FROM sys.tables),
CTE AS (SELECT TableName, CASE WHEN Remainder=0 THEN 5 ELSE Remainder END AS Remainder, Quotient
        FROM cteTableList)
SELECT  MAX(CASE WHEN Remainder = 1 THEN TableName END),
        MAX(CASE WHEN Remainder = 2 THEN TableName END),
        MAX(CASE WHEN Remainder = 3 THEN TableName END),
        MAX(CASE WHEN Remainder = 4 THEN TableName END),
        MAX(CASE WHEN Remainder = 5 THEN TableName END)
FROM  CTE GROUP  BY Quotient ORDER  BY Quotient;
GO
```

The query result set in grid format: tables in AdventureWorks2012

dbo.AWBuildVersion	dbo.DatabaseLog	dbo.ErrorLog	HumanResources.Department	HumanResources.Employee

HumanResources.EmployeeDepartmentHistory	HumanResources.EmployeePayHistory	HumanResources.JobCandidate	HumanResources.Shift	Person.Address
Person.AddressType	Person.BusinessEntity	Person.BusinessEntityAddress	Person.BusinessEntityContact	Person.ContactType
Person.CountryRegion	Person.EmailAddress	Person.Password	Person.Person	Person.PersonPhone
Person.PhoneNumberType	Person.StateProvince	Production.BillOfMaterials	Production.Culture	Production.Document
Production.Illustration	Production.Location	Production.Product	Production.ProductCategory	Production.ProductCostHistory
Production.ProductDescription	Production.ProductDocument	Production.ProductInventory	Production.ProductListPriceHistory	Production.ProductModel
Production.ProductModelIllustration	Production.ProductModelProductDescriptionCulture	Production.ProductPhoto	Production.ProductProductPhoto	Production.ProductReview
Production.ProductSubcategory	Production.ScrapReason	Production.TransactionHistory	Production.TransactionHistoryArchive	Production.UnitMeasure
Production.WorkOrder	Production.WorkOrderRouting	Purchasing.ProductVendor	Purchasing.PurchaseOrderDetail	Purchasing.PurchaseOrderHeader
Purchasing.ShipMethod	Purchasing.Vendor	Sales.CountryRegionCurrency	Sales.CreditCard	Sales.Currency
Sales.CurrencyRate	Sales.Customer	Sales.PersonCreditCard	Sales.SalesOrderDetail	Sales.SalesOrderHeader
Sales.SalesOrderHeaderSalesReason	Sales.SalesPerson	Sales.SalesPersonQuotaHistory	Sales.SalesReason	Sales.SalesTaxRate
Sales.SalesTerritory	Sales.SalesTerritoryHistory	Sales.ShoppingCartItem	Sales.SpecialOffer	Sales.SpecialOfferProduct
Sales.Store	NULL	NULL	NULL	NULL

Diagram of Person.Person & Related Tables

SQL Server 2012 database diagram displays the Person.Person and related tables. PRIMARY KEYs are marked with a gold (in color display) key. The "oo-------->" line is interpreted as many-to-one relationship. For example a person (one) can have one or more (many) credit cards. The "oo" side is the table with **FOREIGN KEY** referencing the gold key side table with the **PRIMARY KEY**. The diagram tool is not supported in Azure SQL.

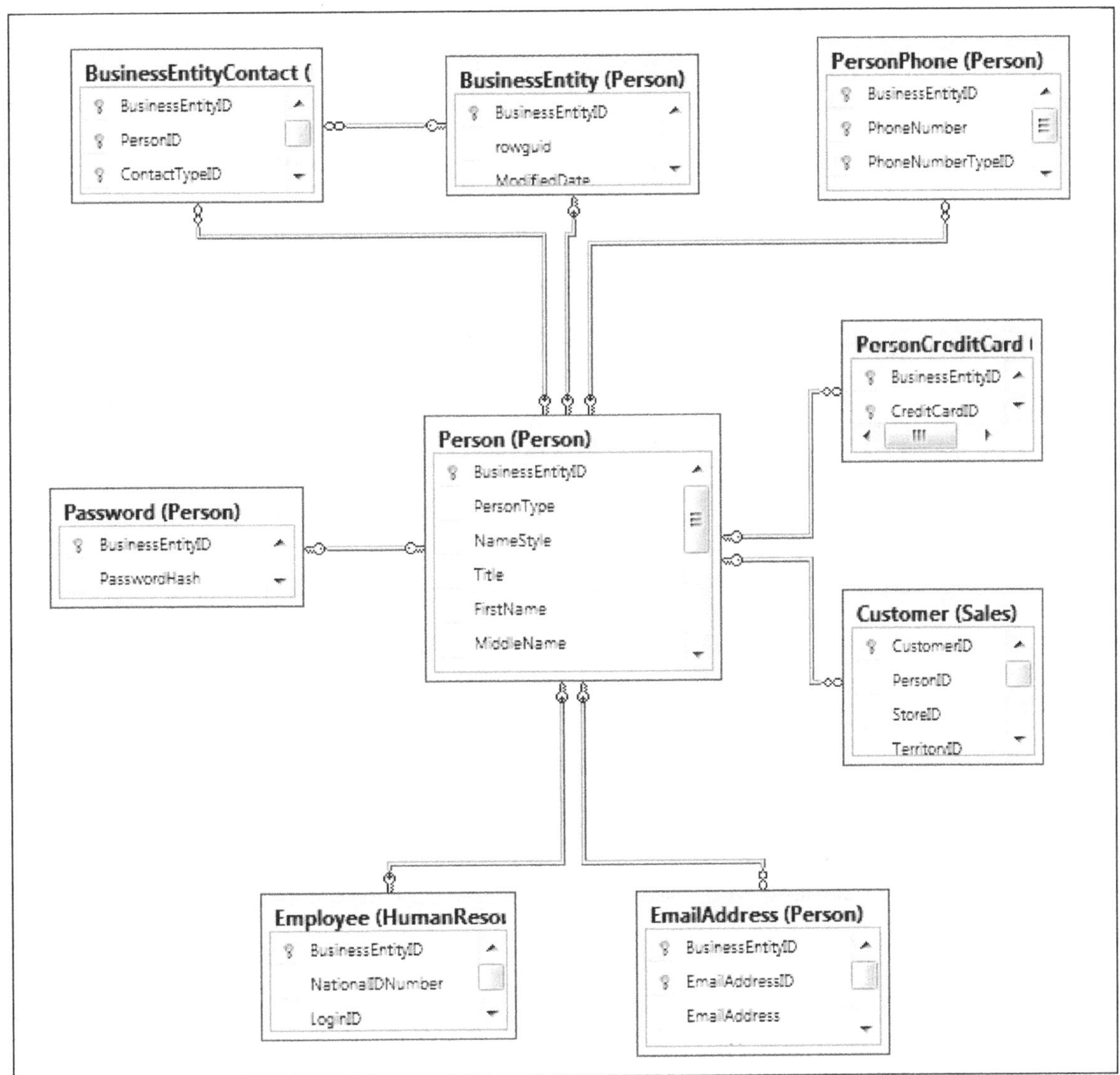

Diagram of Sales.SalesOrderHeader and Related Tables

SQL Server 2012 database diagram displays Sales.SalesOrderHeader and all tables related with **FOREIGN KEY** constraints. The SalesOrderHeader table stores the general information about each order. Line items, e.g. 5 Helmets at $30 each, are stored in the SalesOrderDetail table.

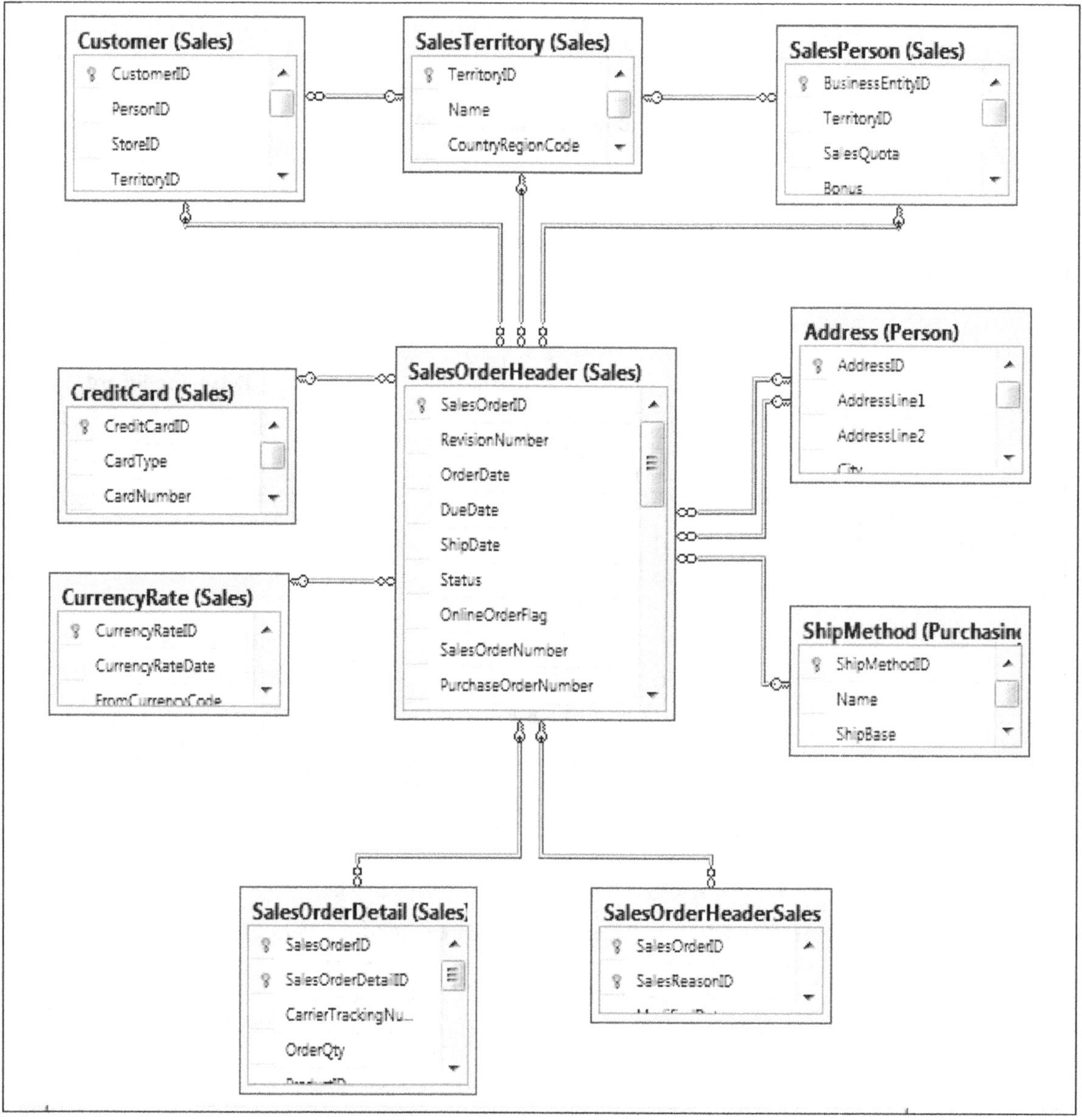

SELECT Query Basics

We have to use "light-weight" SQL (Structured Query Language) in the database design lessons. The reason is that rather difficult to discuss any database related topic without demonstration T-SQL scripts, in fact it would not make sense. **Relational database** and the **SQL language** are "married" to each other forever and ever.

The Simplest SELECT Statement

The simplest SELECT statement is "SELECT * FROM TableNameX" as demonstrated following. The "*" means wildcard inclusion of all columns in the table. Since there is no any other clause in the SELECT statement, it means also to retrieve all rows in the **table in no particular order**. Small tables which were populated in order are usually retrieved in order even though there is no ORDER BY clause. But this behaviour is purely coincidental. **Only ORDER BY clause can guarantee a sorted output.**

```
SELECT * FROM HumanResources.Department;
-- (16 row(s) affected)
```

DepartmentID	Name	GroupName	ModifiedDate
1	Engineering	Research and Development	2002-06-01 00:00:00.000
2	Tool Design	Research and Development	2002-06-01 00:00:00.000
3	Sales	Sales and Marketing	2002-06-01 00:00:00.000
4	Marketing	Sales and Marketing	2002-06-01 00:00:00.000
5	Purchasing	Inventory Management	2002-06-01 00:00:00.000
6	Research and Development	Research and Development	2002-06-01 00:00:00.000
7	Production	Manufacturing	2002-06-01 00:00:00.000
8	Production Control	Manufacturing	2002-06-01 00:00:00.000
9	Human Resources	Executive General and Administration	2002-06-01 00:00:00.000
10	Finance	Executive General and Administration	2002-06-01 00:00:00.000
11	Information Services	Executive General and Administration	2002-06-01 00:00:00.000
12	Document Control	Quality Assurance	2002-06-01 00:00:00.000
13	Quality Assurance	Quality Assurance	2002-06-01 00:00:00.000
14	Facilities and Maintenance	Executive General and Administration	2002-06-01 00:00:00.000
15	Shipping and Receiving	Inventory Management	2002-06-01 00:00:00.000
16	Executive	Executive General and Administration	2002-06-01 00:00:00.000

When tables are JOINed, SELECT * returns all the columns with all the data in the participant tables.

```
SELECT TOP 3 * FROM Sales.SalesOrderHeader H
            INNER JOIN Sales.SalesOrderDetail D
                ON H.SalesOrderID = D.SalesOrderID;
-- 121,317 rows in the JOIN
```

Query Result Set In Text Format

If no grid format available, text format can be used. While it works, it is a challenge to read it, but computer geeks are used to this kind of data dump.

```
/* SalesOrderID RevisionNumber OrderDate DueDate ShipDate Status
OnlineOrderFlag SalesOrderNumber PurchaseOrderNumber AccountNumber CustomerID
SalesPersonID TerritoryID BillToAddressID ShipToAddressID ShipMethodID CreditCardID
CreditCardApprovalCode CurrencyRateID SubTotal TaxAmt Freight TotalDue
Comment rowguid
ModifiedDate SalesOrderID SalesOrderDetailID CarrierTrackingNumber OrderQty ProductID
SpecialOfferID UnitPrice UnitPriceDiscount LineTotal rowguid ModifiedDate
------------ ------------- ----------------------- ----------------------- ----------------------- ------ -------------- -------------------
------ ------------------------ ---------------- ----------- ------------ ----------- --------------- --------------- ------------ -----------
- ---------------------- --------------- --------------------- --------------------- --------------------- --------------------- --------------
------------------------------------------------------------------------------------------------------------------ -------------------------
---------- ---------------------- ----------- ------------------ ------------------------ -------- ----------- ------------- -------------
-------- -------------------- ----------------------------------------- ------------------------------------ ----------------------
43735 3 2005-07-10 00:00:00.000 2005-07-22 00:00:00.000 2005-07-17 00:00:00.000 5 1
SO43735 NULL 10-4030-016522 16522 NULL 9 25384 25384
1 6526 1034619Vi33896 119 3578.27 286.2616 89.4568
3953.9884 NULL 98F80245-
C398-4562-BDAF-EA3E9A0DDFAC 2005-07-17 00:00:00.000 43735 391 NULL 1
749 1 3578.27 0.00 3578.270000 74838EF7-FDEB-4EB3-8978-
BA310FBA82E6 2005-07-10 00:00:00.000
43736 3 2005-07-10 00:00:00.000 2005-07-22 00:00:00.000 2005-07-17 00:00:00.000 5 1
SO43736 NULL 10-4030-011002 11002 NULL 9 20336 20336
1 1416 1135092Vi7270 119 3399.99 271.9992 84.9998
3756.989 NULL C14E29E7-
DB11-44EF-943E-143925A5A9AE 2005-07-17 00:00:00.000 43736 392 NULL 1
773 1 3399.99 0.00 3399.990000 3A0229FA-0A03-4126-
97CE-C3425968B670 2005-07-10 00:00:00.000
43737 3 2005-07-11 00:00:00.000 2005-07-23 00:00:00.000 2005-07-18 00:00:00.000 5 1
SO43737 NULL 10-4030-013261 13261 NULL 8 29772 29772
1 NULL NULL 136 3578.27 286.2616 89.4568 3953.9884
NULL 0B3E274D-E5A8-4E8C-A417-
0EAFABCFF162 2005-07-18 00:00:00.000 43737 393 NULL 1 750 1
3578.27 0.00 3578.270000 65AFCCE8-CA28-41C4-9A07-0265FB2DA5C8
2005-07-11 00:00:00.000 (3 row(s) affected) */
```

```
SELECT MatchingRows = COUNT(*) FROM Sales.SalesOrderHeader H
  INNER JOIN Sales.SalesOrderDetail D
        ON H.SalesOrderID = D.SalesOrderID;     -- INNER JOIN MatchingRows 121317
```

```
SELECT AllRowsInDetail = COUNT(*) FROM Sales.SalesOrderDetail
-- AllRowsInDetail 121317
```

SELECT Query with WHERE Clause Predicate

Query to demonstrate how can we be selective with columns, furthermore, filter returned rows (WHERE clause) and sort them (ORDER BY clause).

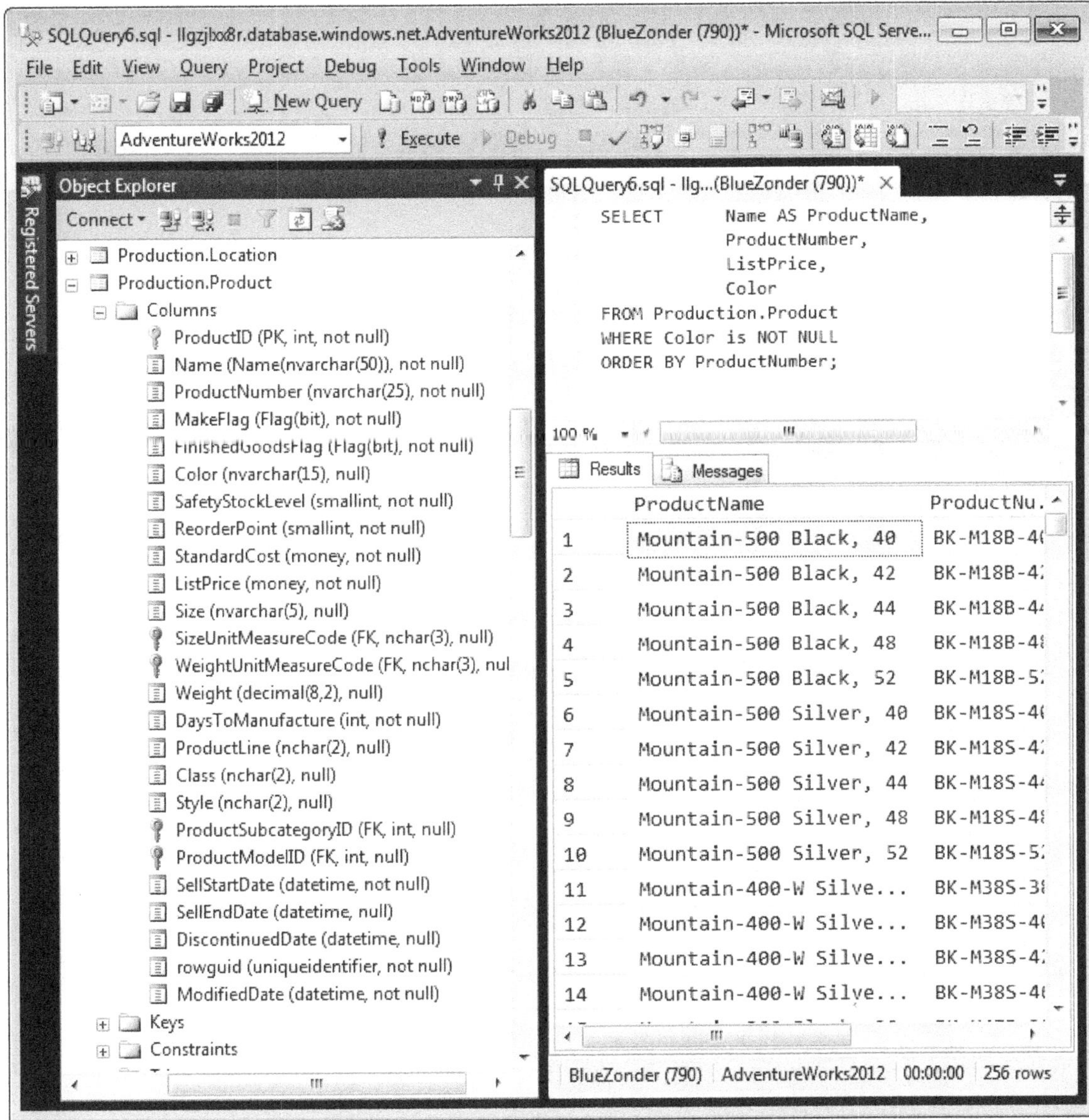
SQLQuery6.sql - Ilgzjbx8r.database.windows.net.AdventureWorks2012 (BlueZonder (790))* - Microsoft SQL Serve...
File Edit View Query Project Debug Tools Window Help
New Query
AdventureWorks2012
Execute
Debug
Object Explorer
Connect
Production.Location
Production.Product
Columns
ProductID (PK, int, not null)
Name (Name(nvarchar(50)), not null)
ProductNumber (nvarchar(25), not null)
MakeFlag (Flag(bit), not null)
FinishedGoodsFlag (Flag(bit), not null)
Color (nvarchar(15), null)
SafetyStockLevel (smallint, not null)
ReorderPoint (smallint, not null)
StandardCost (money, not null)
ListPrice (money, not null)
Size (nvarchar(5), null)
SizeUnitMeasureCode (FK, nchar(3), null)
WeightUnitMeasureCode (FK, nchar(3), nul
Weight (decimal(8,2), null)
DaysToManufacture (int, not null)
ProductLine (nchar(2), null)
Class (nchar(2), null)
Style (nchar(2), null)
ProductSubcategoryID (FK, int, null)
ProductModelID (FK, int, null)
SellStartDate (datetime, not null)
SellEndDate (datetime, null)
DiscontinuedDate (datetime, null)
rowguid (uniqueidentifier, not null)
ModifiedDate (datetime, not null)
Keys
Constraints
Registered Servers
SQLQuery6.sql - Ilg...(BlueZonder (790))*
SELECT Name AS ProductName,
ProductNumber,
ListPrice,
Color
FROM Production.Product
WHERE Color is NOT NULL
ORDER BY ProductNumber;
100 %
Results
Messages
ProductName ProductNu.
1 Mountain-500 Black, 40 BK-M18B-4(
2 Mountain-500 Black, 42 BK-M18B-4:
3 Mountain-500 Black, 44 BK-M18B-4
4 Mountain-500 Black, 48 BK-M18B-4
5 Mountain-500 Black, 52 BK-M18B-5:
6 Mountain-500 Silver, 40 BK-M18S-4(
7 Mountain-500 Silver, 42 BK-M18S-4:
8 Mountain-500 Silver, 44 BK-M18S-4
9 Mountain-500 Silver, 48 BK-M18S-4
10 Mountain-500 Silver, 52 BK-M18S-5:
11 Mountain-400-W Silve... BK-M38S-3
12 Mountain-400-W Silve... BK-M38S-4(
13 Mountain-400-W Silve... BK-M38S-4:
14 Mountain-400-W Silve... BK-M38S-4
BlueZonder (790) AdventureWorks2012 00:00:00 256 rows

Aggregating Data with GROUP BY Query

The second basic query is GROUP BY aggregation which creates a **summary** of detail data. GROUP BY query can be used to preview, review, survey , assess, and analyze data at a high level.

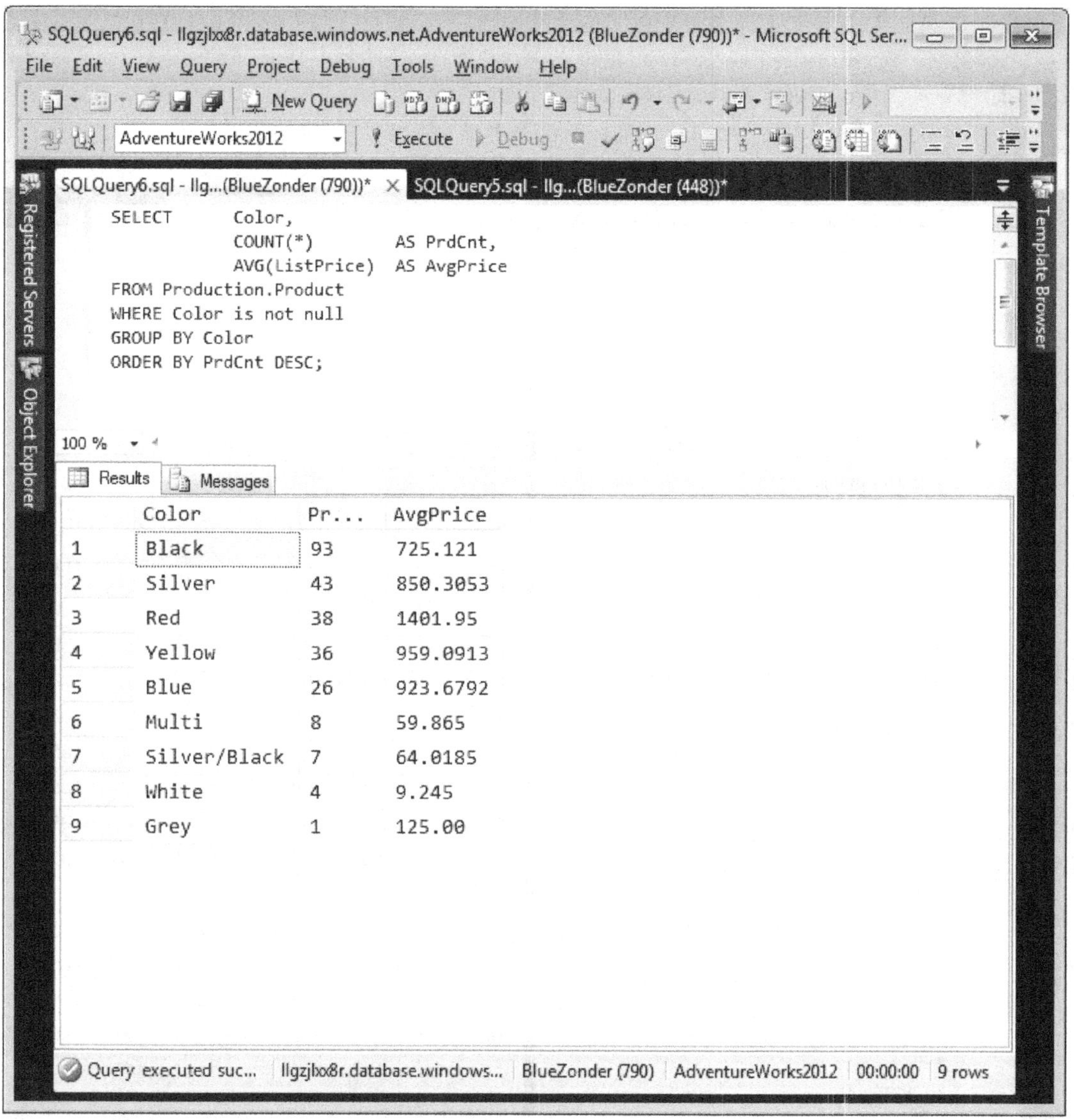
```
SELECT      Color,
            COUNT(*)        AS PrdCnt,
            AVG(ListPrice)  AS AvgPrice
FROM Production.Product
WHERE Color is not null
GROUP BY Color
ORDER BY PrdCnt DESC;
```

	Color	Pr...	AvgPrice
1	Black	93	725.121
2	Silver	43	850.3053
3	Red	38	1401.95
4	Yellow	36	959.0913
5	Blue	26	923.6792
6	Multi	8	59.865
7	Silver/Black	7	64.0185
8	White	4	9.245
9	Grey	1	125.00

NOTE

GROUP BY aggregate queries can efficiently "fingerprint" (profile) data in tables, even millions of rows. GROUP BY aggregates form the computational base of Business Intelligence.

GROUP BY Query with 2 Tables & ORDER BY for Sorting

SQL Server 2012 query JOINing two tables on matching KEYs, FOREIGN KEY to PRIMARY KEY, to combine the data contents in a consistent fashion.

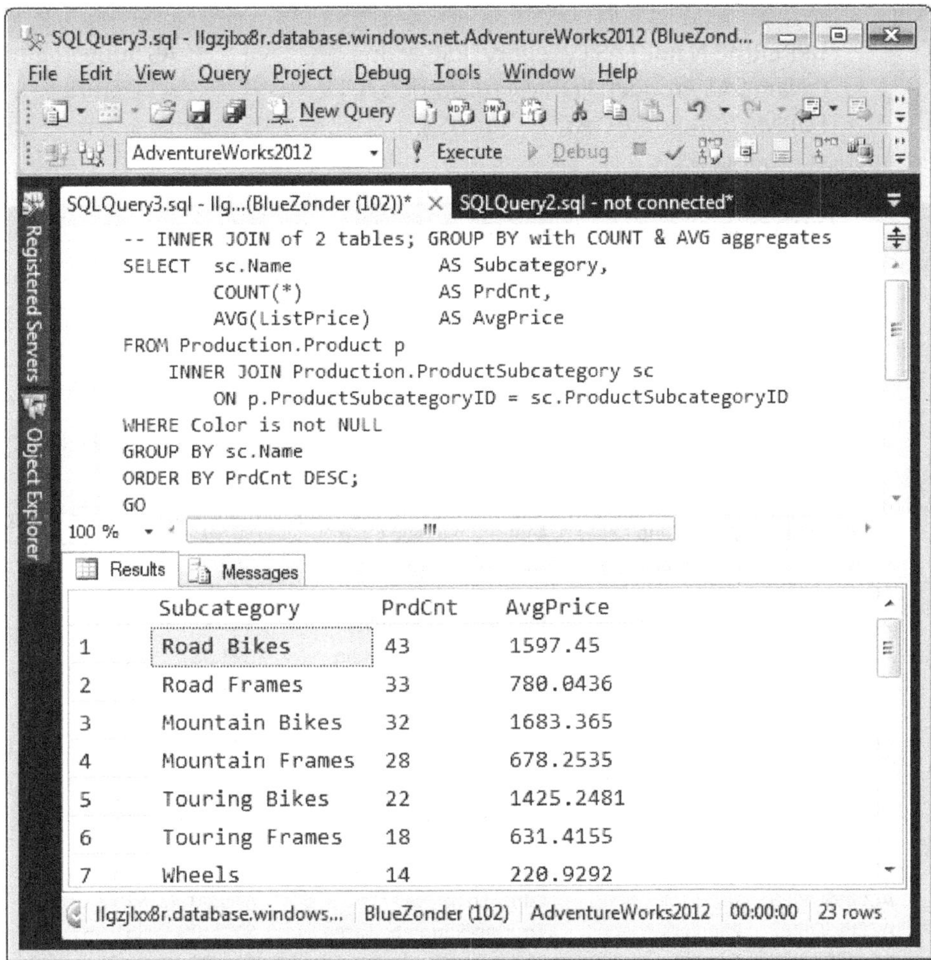
SQLQuery3.sql - llgzjlxx8r.database.windows.net.AdventureWorks2012 (BlueZond...
File Edit View Query Project Debug Tools Window Help
New Query
AdventureWorks2012
Execute Debug
SQLQuery3.sql - llg...(BlueZonder (102))*
SQLQuery2.sql - not connected*
Registered Servers
Object Explorer
-- INNER JOIN of 2 tables; GROUP BY with COUNT & AVG aggregates
SELECT sc.Name AS Subcategory,
COUNT(*) AS PrdCnt,
AVG(ListPrice) AS AvgPrice
FROM Production.Product p
INNER JOIN Production.ProductSubcategory sc
ON p.ProductSubcategoryID = sc.ProductSubcategoryID
WHERE Color is not NULL
GROUP BY sc.Name
ORDER BY PrdCnt DESC;
GO
100 %
Results
Messages
Subcategory PrdCnt AvgPrice
1 Road Bikes 43 1597.45
2 Road Frames 33 780.0436
3 Mountain Bikes 32 1683.365
4 Mountain Frames 28 678.2535
5 Touring Bikes 22 1425.2481
6 Touring Frames 18 631.4155
7 Wheels 14 220.9292
llgzjlxx8r.database.windows... BlueZonder (102) AdventureWorks2012 00:00:00 23 rows

LEN(), DATALENGTH(), LTRIM() & RTRIM() Functions

The LEN() function counts characters without the trailing spaces. DATALENGTH() counts storage bytes including trailing spaces. LTRIM() trims leading spaces, RTRIM() trims trailing spaces.

```
DECLARE @W varchar(32)= CHAR(32)+'Denver'+CHAR(32);
DECLARE @UW nvarchar(32) = CHAR(32)+N'MEGŐRZÉSE'+CHAR(32); -- UNICODE 2 bytes per character
SELECT Length=LEN(@W), DLength=DATALENGTH (@W);                                    -- 7  8
SELECT Length=LEN(@UW), DLength=DATALENGTH (@UW);                                  -- 10 22
SELECT Length=LEN(LTRIM(RTRIM(@W))), DLength=DATALENGTH (LTRIM(RTRIM(@W)));        -- 6  6
SELECT Length=LEN(LTRIM(RTRIM(@UW))), DLength=DATALENGTH (LTRIM(RTRIM(@UW)));      -- 9  18
```

Finding All Accessories in Production.Product Table

Query to list all accessories (a category) for sale.

```
USE AdventureWorks2012;
```

```
SELECT      UPPER(PC.Name) AS Category, PSC.Name              AS Subcategory,
            P.Name AS Product, FORMAT(ListPrice, 'c', 'en-US')   AS ListPrice,
            FORMAT(StandardCost, 'c', 'en-US')               AS StandardCost
FROM Production.Product AS P
   INNER JOIN Production.ProductSubcategory AS PSC
            ON PSC.ProductSubcategoryID = P.ProductSubcategoryID
   INNER JOIN Production.ProductCategory AS PC
            ON PC.ProductCategoryID = PSC.ProductCategoryID
WHERE PC.Name = 'Accessories'
ORDER BY Category, Subcategory, Product;
```

Category	Subcategory	Product	ListPrice	StandardCost
ACCESSORIES	Bike Racks	Hitch Rack - 4-Bike	$120.00	$44.88
ACCESSORIES	Bike Stands	All-Purpose Bike Stand	$159.00	$59.47
ACCESSORIES	Bottles and Cages	Mountain Bottle Cage	$9.99	$3.74
ACCESSORIES	Bottles and Cages	Road Bottle Cage	$8.99	$3.36
ACCESSORIES	Bottles and Cages	Water Bottle - 30 oz.	$4.99	$1.87
ACCESSORIES	Cleaners	Bike Wash - Dissolver	$7.95	$2.97
ACCESSORIES	Fenders	Fender Set - Mountain	$21.98	$8.22
ACCESSORIES	Helmets	Sport-100 Helmet, Black	$34.99	$13.09
ACCESSORIES	Helmets	Sport-100 Helmet, Blue	$34.99	$13.09
ACCESSORIES	Helmets	Sport-100 Helmet, Red	$34.99	$13.09
ACCESSORIES	Hydration Packs	Hydration Pack - 70 oz.	$54.99	$20.57
ACCESSORIES	Lights	Headlights - Dual-Beam	$34.99	$14.43
ACCESSORIES	Lights	Headlights - Weatherproof	$44.99	$18.56
ACCESSORIES	Lights	Taillights - Battery-Powered	$13.99	$5.77
ACCESSORIES	Locks	Cable Lock	$25.00	$10.31
ACCESSORIES	Panniers	Touring-Panniers, Large	$125.00	$51.56
ACCESSORIES	Pumps	Minipump	$19.99	$8.25
ACCESSORIES	Pumps	Mountain Pump	$24.99	$10.31
ACCESSORIES	Tires and Tubes	HL Mountain Tire	$35.00	$13.09
ACCESSORIES	Tires and Tubes	HL Road Tire	$32.60	$12.19
ACCESSORIES	Tires and Tubes	LL Mountain Tire	$24.99	$9.35
ACCESSORIES	Tires and Tubes	LL Road Tire	$21.49	$8.04
ACCESSORIES	Tires and Tubes	ML Mountain Tire	$29.99	$11.22
ACCESSORIES	Tires and Tubes	ML Road Tire	$24.99	$9.35
ACCESSORIES	Tires and Tubes	Mountain Tire Tube	$4.99	$1.87
ACCESSORIES	Tires and Tubes	Patch Kit/8 Patches	$2.29	$0.86
ACCESSORIES	Tires and Tubes	Road Tire Tube	$3.99	$1.49
ACCESSORIES	Tires and Tubes	Touring Tire	$28.99	$10.84
ACCESSORIES	Tires and Tubes	Touring Tire Tube	$4.99	$1.87

How Can SQL Work without Looping?

Looping is implicit in the SQL language. The commands are set oriented and carried out for each member of the set be it 5 or 500 millions in an unordered manner.

```
SELECT * FROM Sales.SalesOrderDetail;    (121317 row(s) affected)
```

SQL Server database engine looped through internally on all rows in SalesOrderDetail table in an unordered way. In fact the database engine may have used some ordering for efficiency, but that behaviour is a blackbox as far as programming concerned. Implicit looping makes SQL statements so simple, yet immensely powerful for information access from low level to high level.

Single-Valued SQL Queries

Single-valued SQL queries are very important because **we can use them where ever the T-SQL syntax requires a single value just by enclosing the query in parenthesis**. The next T-SQL query returns a single value, a cell from the table which is the intersection of a row and a column.

```
SELECT ListPrice FROM Production.Product  WHERE ProductID = 800;
-- (1 row(s) affected)
```

ListPrice
1120.49

The ">" comparison operator requires a single value on the right hand side so we plug in the single-valued query. The WHERE condition is evaluated for each row (implicit looping).

```
SELECT ProductID, Name AS ProductName, ListPrice
FROM Production.Product                          -- 504 rows
WHERE ListPrice > 2 *   (
                        SELECT ListPrice FROM Production.Product
                        WHERE ProductID = 800
                        )
ORDER BY ListPrice DESC, ProductName;    -- (35 row(s) affected) - Partial results.
```

ProductID	ProductName	ListPrice
750	Road-150 Red, 44	3578.27
751	Road-150 Red, 48	3578.27
752	Road-150 Red, 52	3578.27
753	Road-150 Red, 56	3578.27
749	Road-150 Red, 62	3578.27
771	Mountain-100 Silver, 38	3399.99

Data Dictionary for Tables in Sales Schema - On-Premises SS

It is not easy to understand a database with 70 tables, even harder with 2,000 tables. Documentation is very helpful, if not essential, for any database. SQL Server provides Data Dictionary facility for documenting tables and other objects in the database. Data which describes the design & structure of a database is called **metadata**.

Here is the high level documentation of tables in the Sales schema using the SQL Server 2012 fn_listextendedproperty system function.

```
SELECT
        CONCAT('Sales.', objname COLLATE DATABASE_DEFAULT)          AS TableName,
        value                                                       AS [Description]
FROM fn_listextendedproperty (NULL, 'schema', 'Sales', 'table', default, NULL, NULL)
ORDER BY TableName;
```

TableName	Description
Sales.ContactCreditCard	Cross-reference table mapping customers in the Contact table to their credit card information in the CreditCard table.
Sales.CountryRegionCurrency	Cross-reference table mapping ISO currency codes to a country or region.
Sales.CreditCard	Customer credit card information.
Sales.Currency	Lookup table containing standard ISO currencies.
Sales.CurrencyRate	Currency exchange rates.
Sales.Customer	Current customer information. Also see the Individual and Store tables.
Sales.CustomerAddress	Cross-reference table mapping customers to their address(es).
Sales.Individual	Demographic data about customers that purchase Adventure Works products online.
Sales.SalesOrderDetail	Individual products associated with a specific sales order. See SalesOrderHeader.
Sales.SalesOrderHeader	General sales order information.
Sales.SalesOrderHeaderSalesReason	Cross-reference table mapping sales orders to sales reason codes.
Sales.SalesPerson	Sales representative current information.
Sales.SalesPersonQuotaHistory	Sales performance tracking.
Sales.SalesReason	Lookup table of customer purchase reasons.
Sales.SalesTaxRate	Tax rate lookup table.
Sales.SalesTerritory	Sales territory lookup table.
Sales.SalesTerritoryHistory	Sales representative transfers to other sales territories.
Sales.ShoppingCartItem	Contains online customer orders until the order is submitted or cancelled.
Sales.SpecialOffer	Sale discounts lookup table.
Sales.SpecialOfferProduct	Cross-reference table mapping products to special offer discounts.
Sales.Store	Customers (resellers) of Adventure Works products.
Sales.StoreContact	Cross-reference table mapping stores and their employees.

BOL: **Functions (Windows Azure SQL Database)**
http://msdn.microsoft.com/en-us/library/windowsazure/ee336248.aspx

NULL Values in Tables & Query Results

NULL means no value. If so why do we capitalize it? We don't have to. Somehow, it became a custom in the RDBMS industry, nobody knows anymore how it started. Since the U.S. default collation for server and databases are case insensitive, we can just use "null" as well. **NULL value is different from empty string ('') or 0 (zero) which can be tested by the "=" or "!=" operators.** If a database table does not have a value in a cell for whatever reason, it is marked (flagged) as NULL by the database engine. When a value is entered, the NULL marking goes away. **NULL values can be tested by "IS NULL" or "IS NOT NULL" operators, but not the "=" or "!=" operators.**

The likelihood is high that the color attribute is not applicable to items like tire tube, that is the reason that some cell values were left unassigned (null).

```
SELECT TOP 5    Name                                AS ProductName,
                ProductNumber,
                ListPrice,
                Color
FROM Production.Product
WHERE Color IS NULL  ORDER BY ProductName DESC;
```

ProductName	ProductNumber	ListPrice	Color
Water Bottle - 30 oz.	WB-H098	4.99	NULL
Touring Tire Tube	TT-T092	4.99	NULL
Touring Tire	TI-T723	28.99	NULL
Touring Rim	RM-T801	0.00	NULL
Touring End Caps	EC-T209	0.00	NULL

We can do random selection as well and get a mix of products with color and null value.

```
SELECT TOP 5    Name AS ProductName,
                ProductNumber,
                ListPrice,
                Color
FROM Production.Product  ORDER BY NEWID(); -- Random sort
```

ProductName	ProductNumber	ListPrice	Color
Touring-1000 Yellow, 46	BK-T79Y-46	2384.07	Yellow
HL Spindle/Axle	SD-9872	0.00	NULL
ML Mountain Tire	TI-M602	29.99	NULL
Road-650 Red, 60	BK-R50R-60	782.99	Red
Pinch Bolt	PB-6109	0.00	NULL

NULL Values Generated by Queries

NULL values can be generated by queries as well. Typically, LEFT JOIN, RIGHT JOIN and some functions generate NULLs. The meaning of OUTER JOINs: include no-match rows from the left or right table in addition to the matching rows.

```
SELECT TOP 5
        PS.Name                 AS Category,
        P.Name                  AS ProductName,
        ProductNumber,
        ListPrice,
        Color
FROM Production.Product P
  RIGHT JOIN Production.ProductSubcategory PS
      ON    PS.ProductSubcategoryID = P.ProductSubcategoryID
            AND ListPrice >= 3500.0
ORDER BY newid();
GO
```

Category	ProductName	ProductNumber	ListPrice	Color
Road Bikes	Road-150 Red, 62	BK-R93R-62	3578.27	Red
Road Bikes	Road-150 Red, 52	BK-R93R-52	3578.27	Red
Bib-Shorts	NULL	NULL	NULL	NULL
Socks	NULL	NULL	NULL	NULL
Cranksets	NULL	NULL	NULL	NULL

Some system functions, like the brand new TRY_CONVERT(), can generate NULL values as well. If the PostalCode cannot be converted into an integer, TRY_CONVERT() returns NULL.

```
SELECT TOP 5    ConvertedZip = TRY_CONVERT(INT, PostalCode),
                AddressLine1,
                City,
                PostalCode
FROM Person.Address  ORDER by newid();
```

ConvertedZip	AddressLine1	City	PostalCode
91945	5979 El Pueblo	Lemon Grove	91945
NULL	7859 Green Valley Road	London	W1V 5RN
3220	6004 Peabody Road	Geelong	3220
NULL	6713 Eaker Way	Burnaby	V3J 6Z3
NULL	5153 Hackamore Lane	Shawnee	V8Z 4N5

The SOUNDEX() Function to Check Sound Alikes

The soundex() function is very interesting for testing different spelling of words such as names.

```
USE AdventureWorks2012;
GO
```

```
SELECT DISTINCT LastName
FROM Person.Person
WHERE soundex(LastName) = soundex('Steel');
GO
```

LastName
Seidel
Sotelo
Stahl
Steel
Steele

```
SELECT DISTINCT LastName
FROM Person.Person
WHERE soundex(LastName) = soundex('Brown');
```

LastName
Bourne
Brian
Brown
Browne
Bruno

```
SELECT DISTINCT FirstName FROM Person.Person
WHERE soundex(FirstName) = soundex('Mary');
```

FirstName
Mari
Maria
María
Mariah
Marie
Mario
Mary
Mary Lou
Mayra

Building an FK-PK Diagram in AdventureWorks2012

SQL Server 2012 **FOREIGN KEY - PRIMARY KEY** diagram of AdventureWorks2012 database with over 70 tables can be built just by adding the tables to the diagram. The FK-PK lines are automatically drawn. An FK-PK line represents a predefined referential constraint.

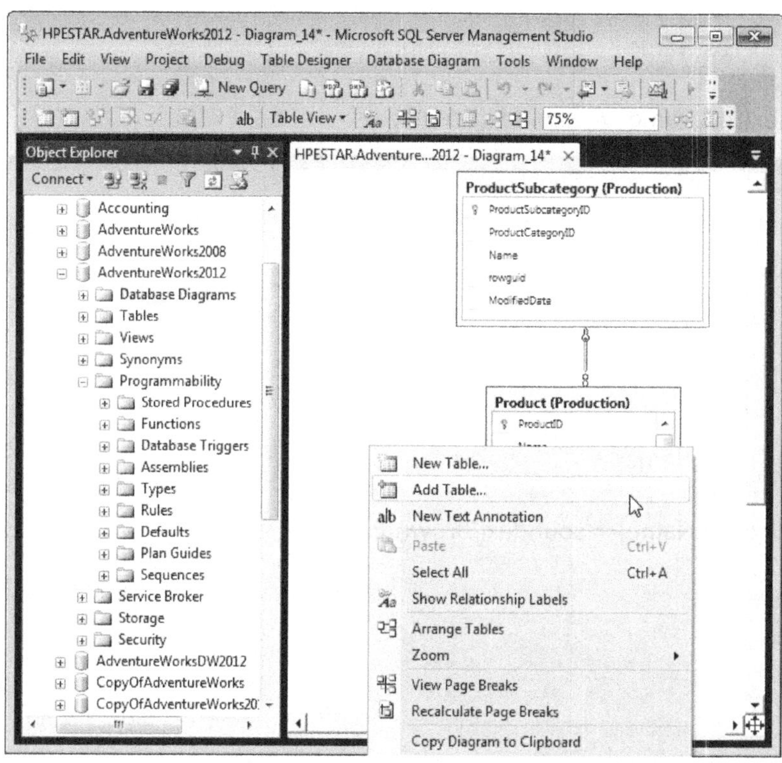

While all tables are important in a database, tables with the most connections play central roles, in a way analogous to the Sun with planets around it.

```
-- PRIMARY KEY tables with the most FOREIGN KEY references
SELECT      schema_name(o.schema_id)        AS SchemaName,
            o.name                          AS PKTable,
            count(*)                        AS FKCount
FROM sys.foreign_keys s   INNER JOIN sys.objects o   ON s.referenced_object_id = o.object_id
GROUP BY o.schema_id, o.name   HAVING count(*) >= 5   ORDER BY FKCount DESC;
```

SchemaName	PKTable	FKCount
Production	Product	14
Person	Person	7
HumanResources	Employee	6
Person	BusinessEntity	5
Sales	SalesTerritory	5

AdventureWorksDWAZ2008R2 Data Warehouse Database

AdventureWorksDW series contain second hand data only since they are Data Warehouse databases. All data originates from other sources such as the AdventureWorks OLTP database & Excel worksheets. Tables in the data warehousing database are divided into two groups: dimension tables & fact tables.

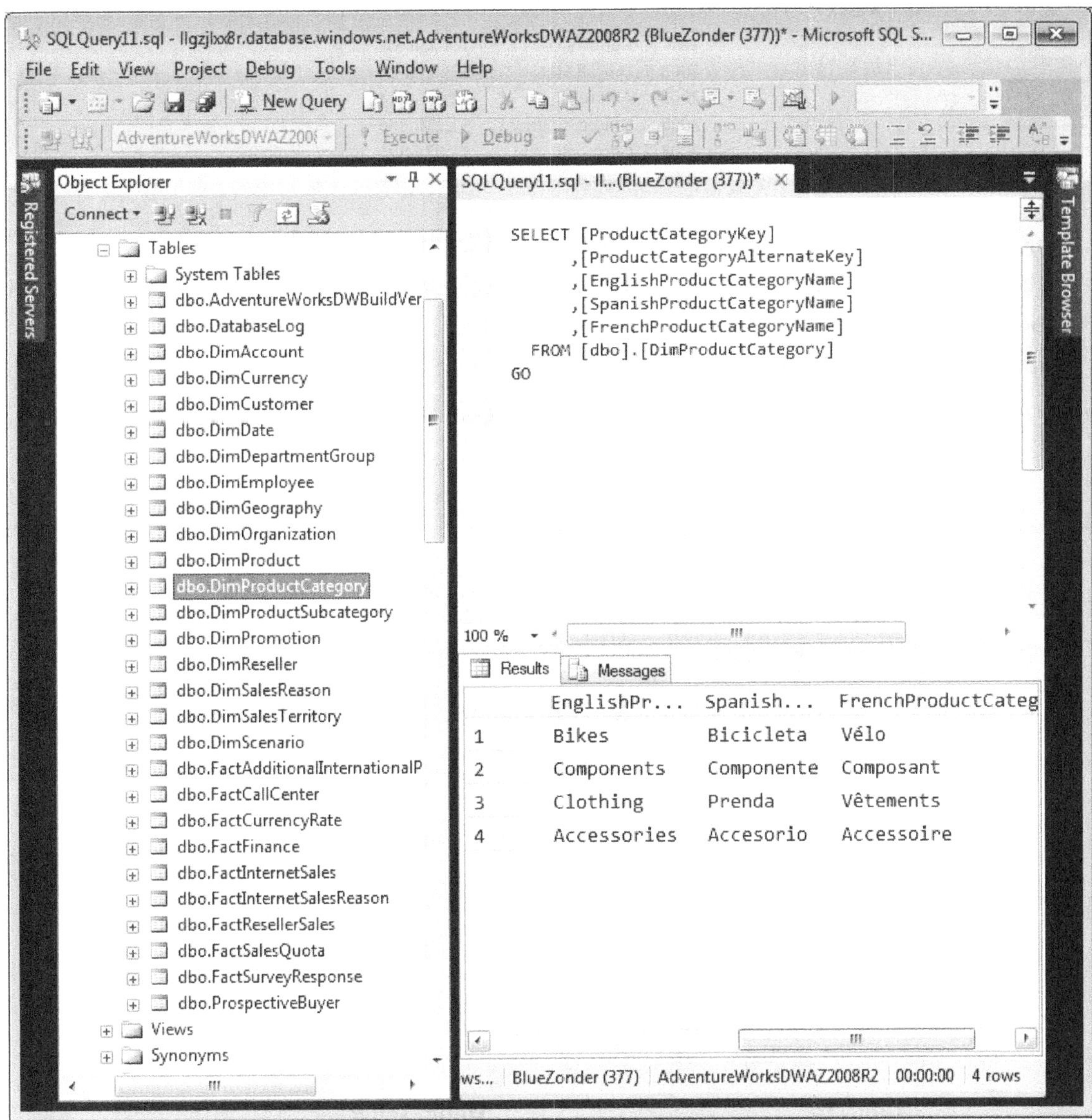

Simple Data Warehouse Query

```
SELECT          D.CalendarYear AS [Year], C.SalesTerritoryCountry AS [Country],
                FORMAT(SUM(S.SalesAmount),'c0','en-US') AS TotalSales
FROM FactInternetSales AS S  INNER JOIN DimDate AS D ON S.OrderDateKey = D.DateKey
        INNER JOIN DimSalesTerritory AS C ON S.SalesTerritoryKey = C.SalesTerritoryKey
GROUP BY D.CalendarYear, C.SalesTerritoryCountry  ORDER BY Year DESC, SUM(S.SalesAmount) DESC;
```

Year	Country	TotalSales
2008	United States	$3,324,031
2008	Australia	$2,563,884
2008	United Kingdom	$1,210,286
2008	Germany	$1,076,891
2008	France	$922,179

Diagram of a Star Schema in AdventureWorksDW2012

The high level star schema diagram in AdventureWorksDW2012 Data Warehouse database with FactResellerSales fact table and related dimension tables. The temporal dimension table DimDate plays a central role in Business Intelligence data analytics.

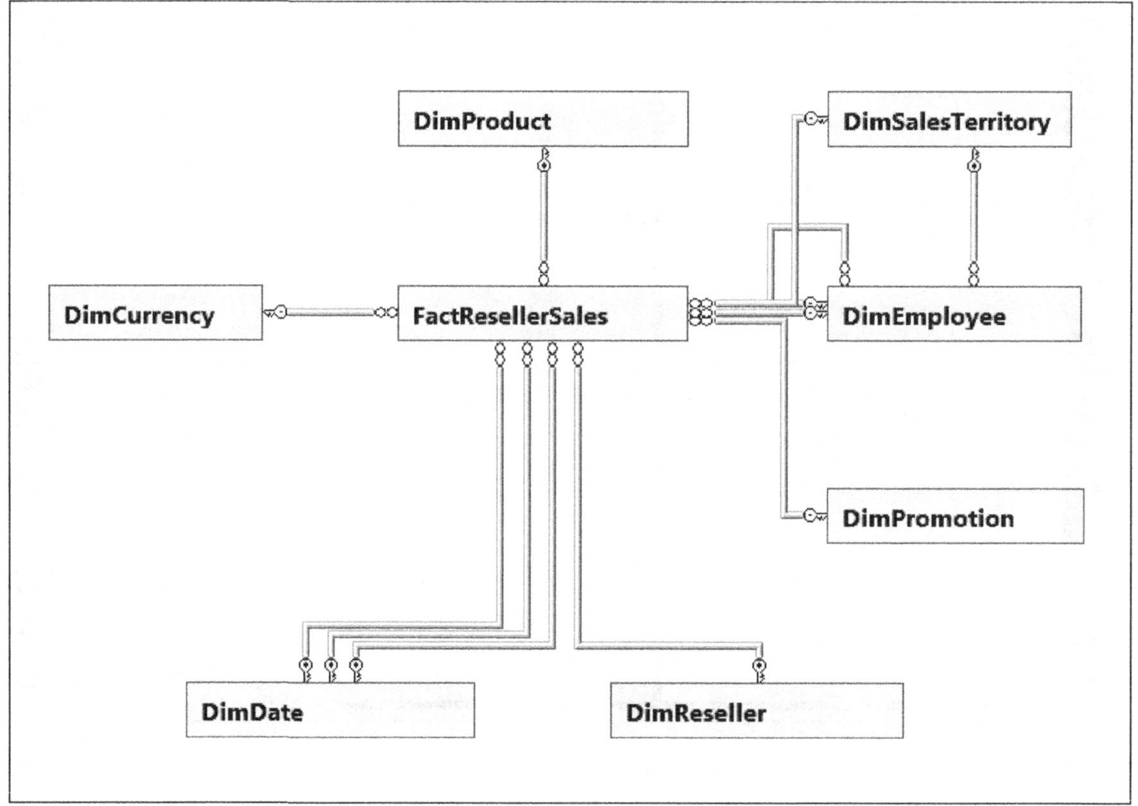

AdventureWorks2008 Sample Database

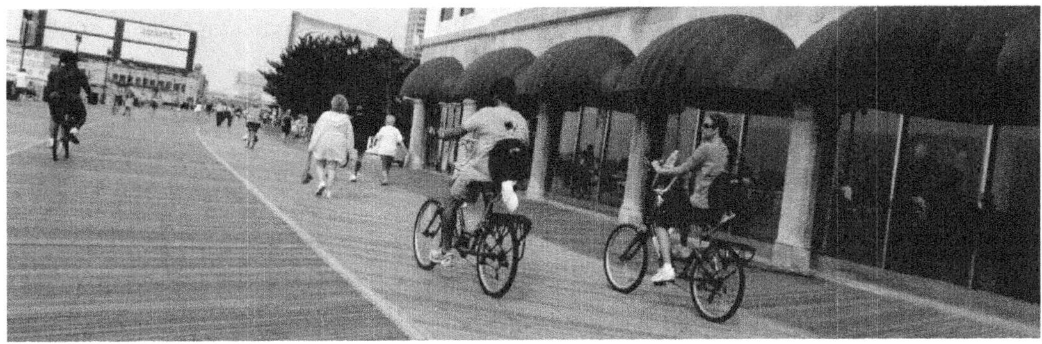

There were substantial changes made from the prior version of the sample database. Among them demonstration use of the **hierarchyid** data type which has been introduced with SS 2008 to support sophisticated tree hierarchy processing. In addition employee, customer and dealer PRIMARY KEYs are pooled together and called BusinessEntityID.

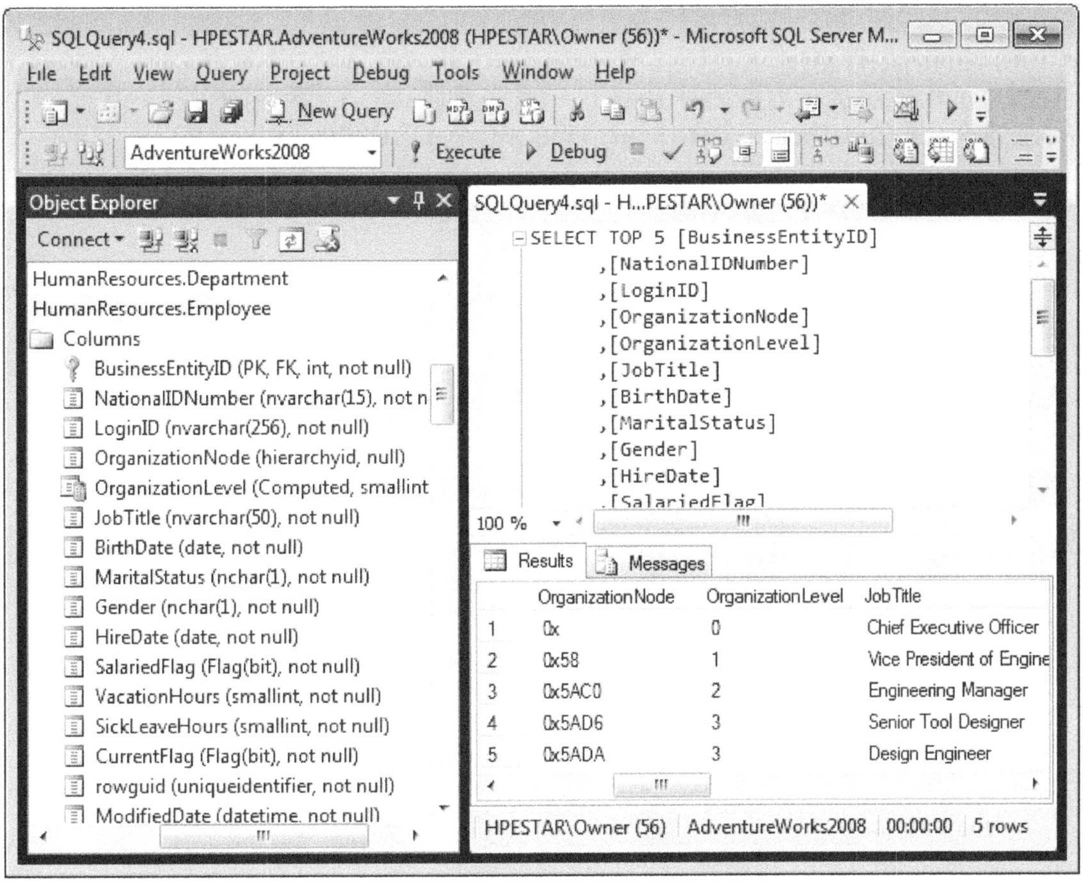

SQLQuery4.sql - HPESTAR.AdventureWorks2008 (HPESTAR\Owner (56))* - Microsoft SQL Server M...
File Edit View Query Project Debug Tools Window Help
New Query
AdventureWorks2008
Execute
Debug
Object Explorer
Connect
HumanResources.Department
HumanResources.Employee
Columns
BusinessEntityID (PK, FK, int, not null)
NationalIDNumber (nvarchar(15), not n
LoginID (nvarchar(256), not null)
OrganizationNode (hierarchyid, null)
OrganizationLevel (Computed, smallint
JobTitle (nvarchar(50), not null)
BirthDate (date, not null)
MaritalStatus (nchar(1), not null)
Gender (nchar(1), not null)
HireDate (date, not null)
SalariedFlag (Flag(bit), not null)
VacationHours (smallint, not null)
SickLeaveHours (smallint, not null)
CurrentFlag (Flag(bit), not null)
rowguid (uniqueidentifier, not null)
ModifiedDate (datetime, not null)
SQLQuery4.sql - H...PESTAR\Owner (56))*
SELECT TOP 5 [BusinessEntityID]
,[NationalIDNumber]
,[LoginID]
,[OrganizationNode]
,[OrganizationLevel]
,[JobTitle]
,[BirthDate]
,[MaritalStatus]
,[Gender]
,[HireDate]
,[SalariedFlag]
100 %
Results
Messages
OrganizationNode OrganizationLevel JobTitle
1 0x 0 Chief Executive Officer
2 0x58 1 Vice President of Engine
3 0x5AC0 2 Engineering Manager
4 0x5AD6 3 Senior Tool Designer
5 0x5ADA 3 Design Engineer
HPESTAR\Owner (56) AdventureWorks2008 00:00:00 5 rows

AdventureWorks2012 Sample Database

There were no apparent design changes made from the prior version of the sample database. A significant content change: dates were advanced 4 years. An OrderDate (Sales.SalesOrderHeader table) of 2004-02-01 in previous versions is now 2008-02-01.

The OrderDate statistics in the two sample databases.

```
USE AdventureWorks2008;
SELECT  [Year]              = YEAR(OrderDate),      OrderCount      = COUNT(*)
FROM Sales.SalesOrderHeader GROUP BY YEAR(OrderDate)  ORDER BY [Year];
```

Year	OrderCount
2001	1379
2002	3692
2003	12443
2004	13951

```
USE AdventureWorks2012;
SELECT  [Year]              = YEAR(OrderDate),      OrderCount      = COUNT(*)
FROM Sales.SalesOrderHeader GROUP BY YEAR(OrderDate)  ORDER BY [Year];
```

Year	OrderCount
2005	1379
2006	3692
2007	12443
2008	13951

Starting with SQL Server 2012, numeric figures, among others, can be formatted with the FORMAT function.

```
SELECT  [Year]              = YEAR(OrderDate),
        OrderCount          = FORMAT(COUNT(*), '###,###')
FROM Sales.SalesOrderHeader
GROUP BY YEAR(OrderDate)  ORDER BY [Year];
```

Year	OrderCount
2005	1,379
2006	3,692
2007	12,443
2008	13,951

Production.Product and Related Tables

The Product table is the "center" of the database. The reason is that AdventureWorks Cycles is a product base company selling through dealers and directly to consumers through the internet. You may wonder why are we pushing **FOREIGN KEY - PRIMARY KEY** relationship so vehemently? Because there is nothing else to a database just **well-designed tables and their connections which are FK-PK constraints.** SQL Server 2012 diagram.

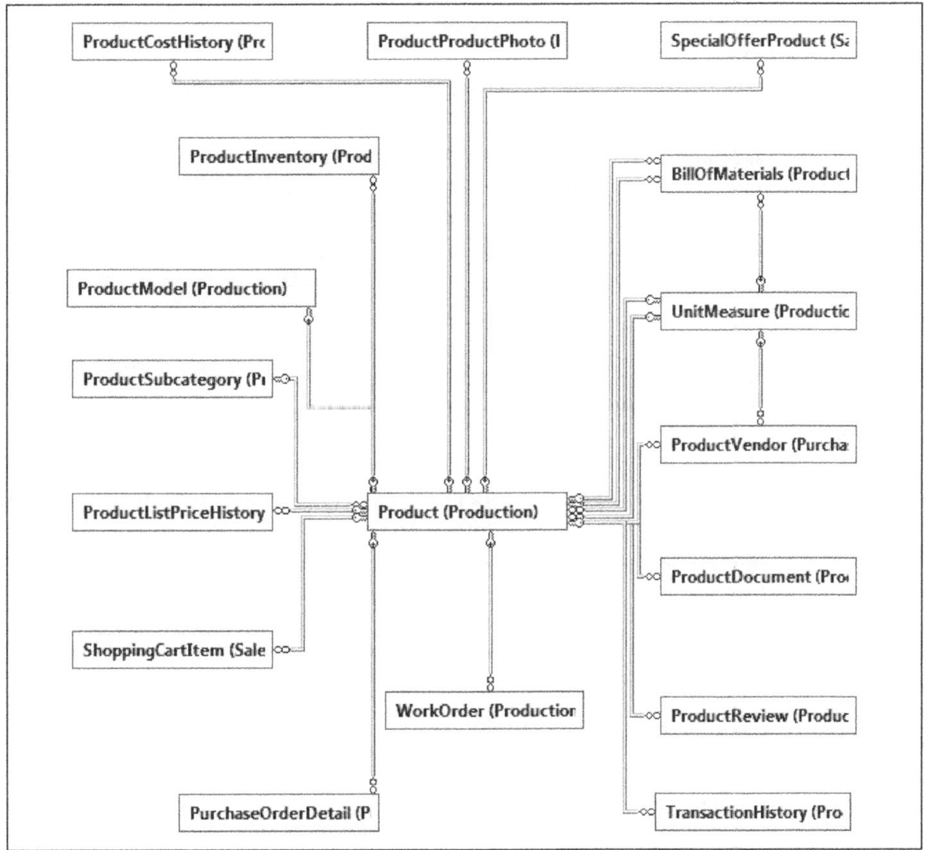

Simple OLTP query.

```
SELECT Color, WOCount=COUNT(*)  FROM Production.WorkOrder W
        INNER JOIN Production.Product P    ON W.ProductID = P.ProductID  WHERE Color != ''
GROUP BY Color ORDER BY WOCount DESC;
```

Color	WOCount
Black	18952
Silver	6620
Yellow	5231
Red	4764
Blue	2319

Descriptions of Columns in Production.Product Table

SQL Server 2012 queries to list the description of table and columns from Extended Property (data dictionary).

```
USE AdventureWorks2012;
SELECT          objname AS TableName, value   AS [Description]
FROM fn_listextendedproperty( NULL, 'schema', 'Production', 'table', 'Product', NULL, NULL);
```

TableName	Description
Product	Products sold or used in the manfacturing of sold products.

```
SELECT          'Production.Product'            AS TableName,            -- String literal
                objname                         AS ColumnName,
                value                           AS [Description]
FROM fn_listextendedproperty(   NULL, 'schema', 'Production', 'table', 'Product', 'column', default);
```

TableName	ColumnName	Description
Production.Product	ProductID	Primary key for Product records.
Production.Product	Name	Name of the product.
Production.Product	ProductNumber	Unique product identification number.
Production.Product	MakeFlag	0 = Product is purchased, 1 = Product is manufactured in-house.
Production.Product	FinishedGoodsFlag	0 = Product is not a salable item. 1 = Product is salable.
Production.Product	Color	Product color.
Production.Product	SafetyStockLevel	Minimum inventory quantity.
Production.Product	ReorderPoint	Inventory level that triggers a purchase order or work order.
Production.Product	StandardCost	Standard cost of the product.
Production.Product	ListPrice	Selling price.
Production.Product	Size	Product size.
Production.Product	SizeUnitMeasureCode	Unit of measure for Size column.
Production.Product	WeightUnitMeasureCode	Unit of measure for Weight column.
Production.Product	Weight	Product weight.
Production.Product	DaysToManufacture	Number of days required to manufacture the product.
Production.Product	ProductLine	R = Road, M = Mountain, T = Touring, S = Standard
Production.Product	Class	H = High, M = Medium, L = Low
Production.Product	Style	W = Womens, M = Mens, U = Universal
Production.Product	ProductSubcategoryID	Product is a member of this product subcategory. Foreign key to ProductSubCategory.ProductSubCategoryID.
Production.Product	ProductModelID	Product is a member of this product model. Foreign key to ProductModel.ProductModelID.
Production.Product	SellStartDate	Date the product was available for sale.
Production.Product	SellEndDate	Date the product was no longer available for sale.
Production.Product	DiscontinuedDate	Date the product was discontinued.
Production.Product	rowguid	ROWGUIDCOL number uniquely identifying the record. Used to support a merge replication sample.
Production.Product	ModifiedDate	Date and time the record was last updated.

Mountain Bikes in Production.Product Table

Query to list all mountain bikes offered for sale by AdventureWorks Cycles with category, subcategory, list price and standard cost information.

```
USE AdventureWorks2012;
SELECT  UPPER(PC.Name) AS Category, PSC.Name AS Subcategory,
        P.Name AS Product, FORMAT(ListPrice, 'c', 'en-US') AS ListPrice,
        FORMAT(StandardCost, 'c', 'en-US') AS StandardCost
FROM Production.Product AS P
  INNER JOIN Production.ProductSubcategory AS PSC
             ON PSC.ProductSubcategoryID = P.ProductSubcategoryID
  INNER JOIN Production.ProductCategory AS PC
             ON PC.ProductCategoryID = PSC.ProductCategoryID
WHERE PSC.Name = 'Mountain Bikes'
ORDER BY Category, Subcategory, Product;
```

Category	Subcategory	Product	ListPrice	StandardCost
BIKES	Mountain Bikes	Mountain-100 Black, 38	$3,374.99	$1,898.09
BIKES	Mountain Bikes	Mountain-100 Black, 42	$3,374.99	$1,898.09
BIKES	Mountain Bikes	Mountain-100 Black, 44	$3,374.99	$1,898.09
BIKES	Mountain Bikes	Mountain-100 Black, 48	$3,374.99	$1,898.09
BIKES	Mountain Bikes	Mountain-100 Silver, 38	$3,399.99	$1,912.15
BIKES	Mountain Bikes	Mountain-100 Silver, 42	$3,399.99	$1,912.15
BIKES	Mountain Bikes	Mountain-100 Silver, 44	$3,399.99	$1,912.15
BIKES	Mountain Bikes	Mountain-100 Silver, 48	$3,399.99	$1,912.15
BIKES	Mountain Bikes	Mountain-200 Black, 38	$2,294.99	$1,251.98
BIKES	Mountain Bikes	Mountain-200 Black, 42	$2,294.99	$1,251.98
BIKES	Mountain Bikes	Mountain-200 Black, 46	$2,294.99	$1,251.98
BIKES	Mountain Bikes	Mountain-200 Silver, 38	$2,319.99	$1,265.62
BIKES	Mountain Bikes	Mountain-200 Silver, 42	$2,319.99	$1,265.62
BIKES	Mountain Bikes	Mountain-200 Silver, 46	$2,319.99	$1,265.62
BIKES	Mountain Bikes	Mountain-300 Black, 38	$1,079.99	$598.44
BIKES	Mountain Bikes	Mountain-300 Black, 40	$1,079.99	$598.44
BIKES	Mountain Bikes	Mountain-300 Black, 44	$1,079.99	$598.44
BIKES	Mountain Bikes	Mountain-300 Black, 48	$1,079.99	$598.44
BIKES	Mountain Bikes	Mountain-400-W Silver, 38	$769.49	$419.78
BIKES	Mountain Bikes	Mountain-400-W Silver, 40	$769.49	$419.78
BIKES	Mountain Bikes	Mountain-400-W Silver, 42	$769.49	$419.78
BIKES	Mountain Bikes	Mountain-400-W Silver, 46	$769.49	$419.78
BIKES	Mountain Bikes	Mountain-500 Black, 40	$539.99	$294.58
BIKES	Mountain Bikes	Mountain-500 Black, 42	$539.99	$294.58
BIKES	Mountain Bikes	Mountain-500 Black, 44	$539.99	$294.58
BIKES	Mountain Bikes	Mountain-500 Black, 48	$539.99	$294.58
BIKES	Mountain Bikes	Mountain-500 Black, 52	$539.99	$294.58
BIKES	Mountain Bikes	Mountain-500 Silver, 40	$564.99	$308.22
BIKES	Mountain Bikes	Mountain-500 Silver, 42	$564.99	$308.22
BIKES	Mountain Bikes	Mountain-500 Silver, 44	$564.99	$308.22
BIKES	Mountain Bikes	Mountain-500 Silver, 48	$564.99	$308.22
BIKES	Mountain Bikes	Mountain-500 Silver, 52	$564.99	$308.22

Prior SQL Server Sample Databases

There are two other sample databases used in the releases of SQL Server: **Northwind** and **pubs**. Northwind has been introduced with SQL Server 7.0 in 1998. That SQL Server version had very short lifetime, replaced with SQL Server 2000 in year 2000. The pubs sample database originates from the time Microsoft & Sybase worked jointly on the database server project around 1990. Despite the relative simplicity of pre-2005 sample databases, they were good enough to demonstrate basic RDBMS SQL queries.

Book sales summary GROUP BY aggregation query.

```
USE pubs;
SELECT pub_name                      AS Publisher,
    au_lname                         AS Author,
    title                            AS Title,
    SUM(qty)                         AS SoldQty
FROM   authors
    INNER JOIN titleauthor
        ON authors.au_id = titleauthor.au_id
    INNER JOIN titles
        ON titles.title_id = titleauthor.title_id
    INNER JOIN publishers
        ON publishers.pub_id = titles.pub_id
    INNER JOIN sales
        ON sales.title_id = titles.title_id
GROUP  BY       pub_name,
                au_lname,
                title
ORDER BY Publisher, Author, Title;
-- (23 row(s) affected) - Partial results.
```

Publisher	Author	Title
Algodata Infosystems	Bennet	The Busy Executive's Database Guide
Algodata Infosystems	Carson	But Is It User Friendly?
Algodata Infosystems	Dull	Secrets of Silicon Valley
Algodata Infosystems	Green	The Busy Executive's Database Guide
Algodata Infosystems	Hunter	Secrets of Silicon Valley
Algodata Infosystems	MacFeather	Cooking with Computers: Surreptitious Balance Sheets
Algodata Infosystems	O'Leary	Cooking with Computers: Surreptitious Balance Sheets
Algodata Infosystems	Straight	Straight Talk About Computers
Binnet & Hardley	Blotchet-Halls	Fifty Years in Buckingham Palace Kitchens
Binnet & Hardley	DeFrance	The Gourmet Microwave

Northwind Sample Database

The Northwind database contains well-prepared sales data for a fictitious company called Northwind Traders, which imports & exports specialty gourmet foods & drinks from wholesale suppliers around the world. The company's sales offices are located in Seattle & London. Among gourmet food item products: Carnarvon Tigers, Teatime Chocolate Biscuits, Sir Rodney's Marmalade, Sir Rodney's Scones, Gustaf's Knäckebröd, Tunnbröd & Guaraná Fantástica.

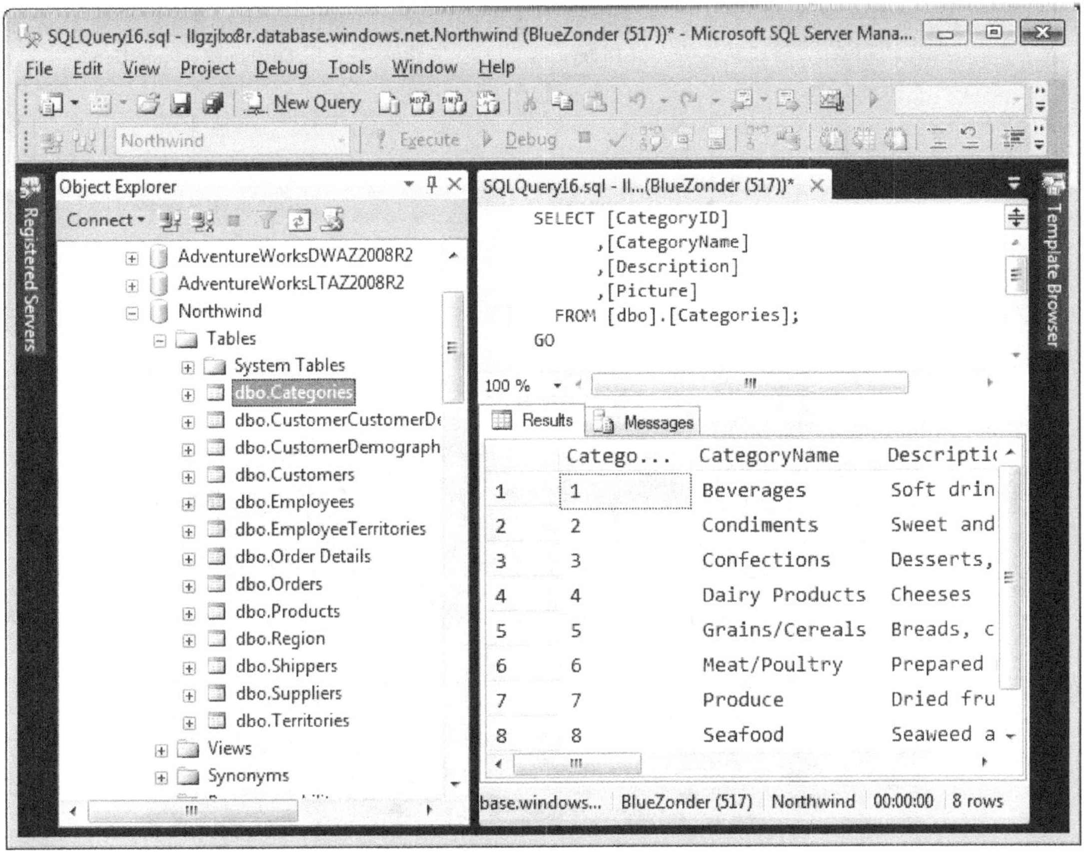

```
SELECT [CategoryID]
      ,[CategoryName]
      ,[Description]
      ,[Picture]
  FROM [dbo].[Categories];
GO
```

	Catego...	CategoryName	Descripti
1	1	Beverages	Soft drin
2	2	Condiments	Sweet and
3	3	Confections	Desserts,
4	4	Dairy Products	Cheeses
5	5	Grains/Cereals	Breads, c
6	6	Meat/Poultry	Prepared
7	7	Produce	Dried fru
8	8	Seafood	Seaweed a

Diagram of Northwind Database

The basic SQL Server 2012 diagram of Northwind database excluding a few ancillary tables. The Orders table is central since the business is wholesale distribution (reselling) of high-end food products.

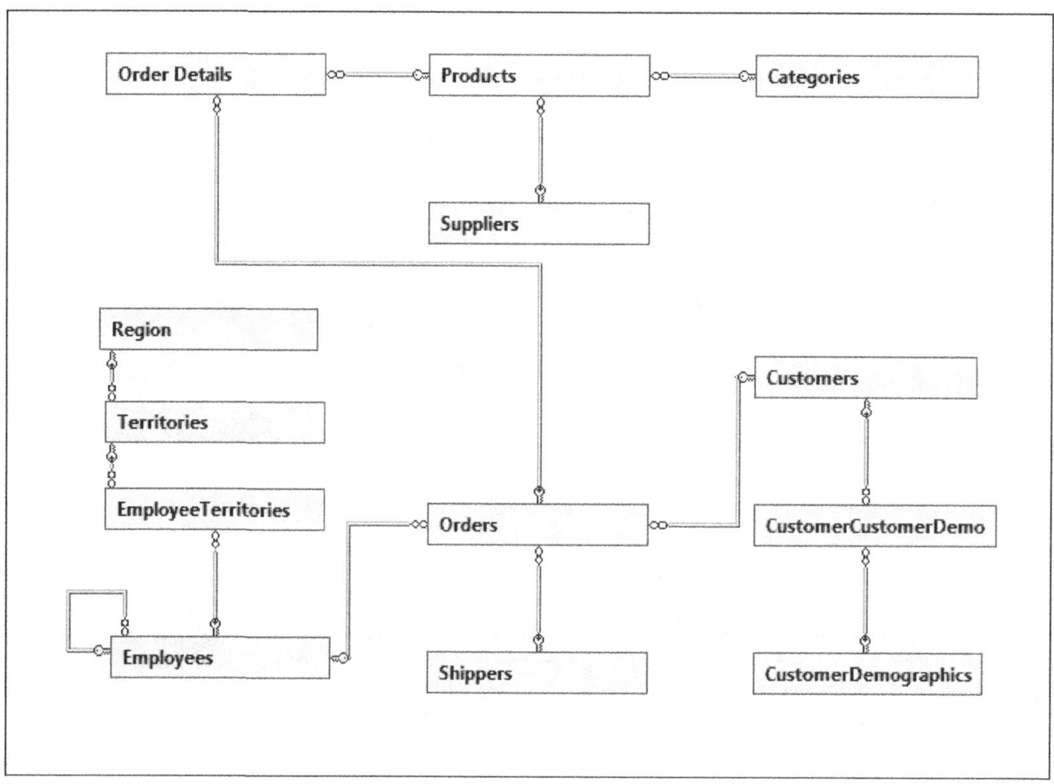

pubs Sample Database

The pubs database is a very small and simple publishing database, yet it demonstrates the main features of database design such as PRIMARY KEYs, FOREIGN KEYs, and junction table reflecting many-to-many relationship. The main entities (tables) are: (book) titles, authors, titleauthor (junction table), publishers, sales & royalties. SQL Server 2012 query.

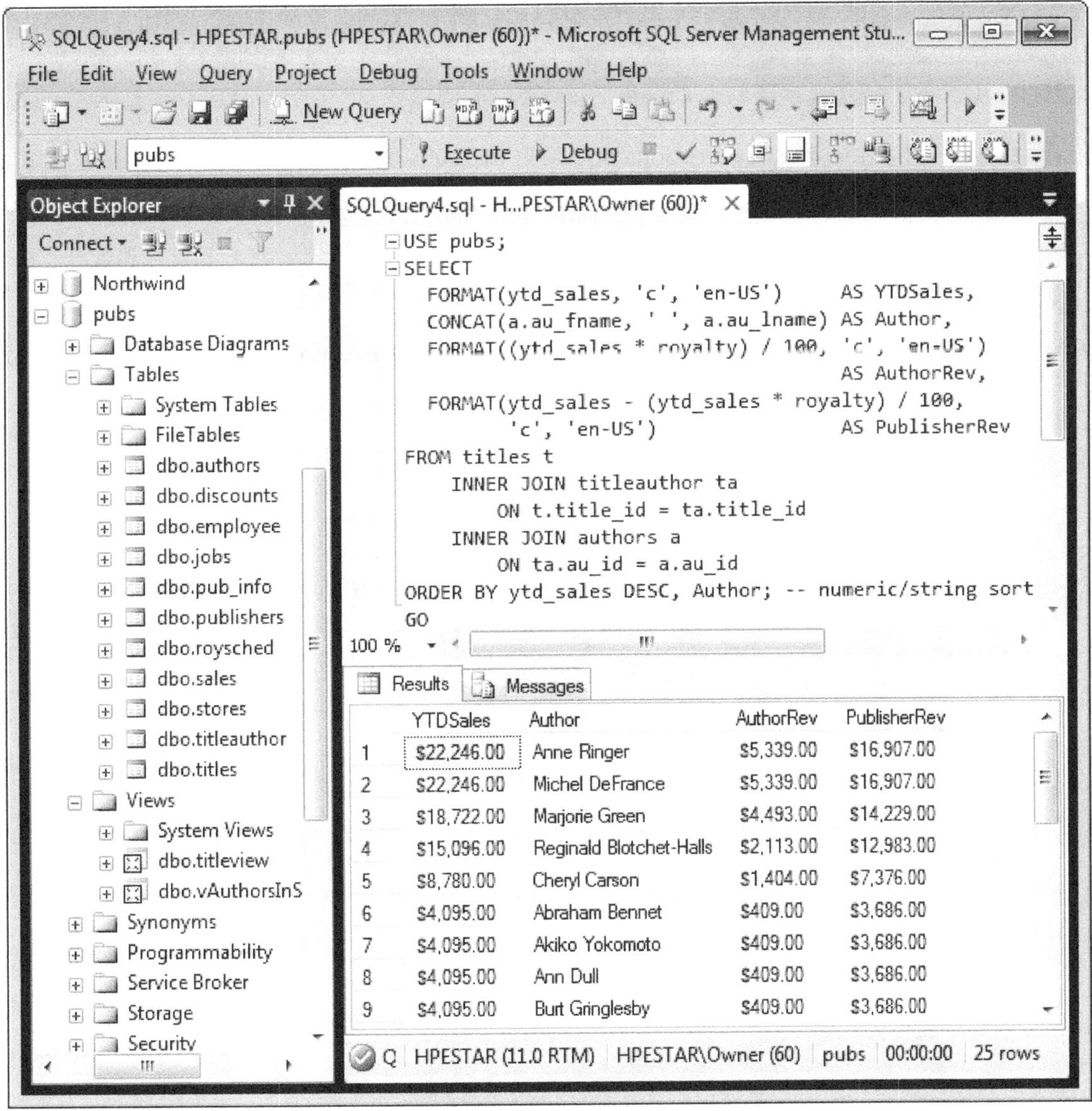

USE pubs;
SELECT
FORMAT(ytd_sales, 'c', 'en-US') AS YTDSales,
CONCAT(a.au_fname, ' ', a.au_lname) AS Author,
FORMAT((ytd_sales * royalty) / 100, 'c', 'en-US') AS AuthorRev,
FORMAT(ytd_sales - (ytd_sales * royalty) / 100, 'c', 'en-US') AS PublisherRev
FROM titles t
INNER JOIN titleauthor ta
ON t.title_id = ta.title_id
INNER JOIN authors a
ON ta.au_id = a.au_id
ORDER BY ytd_sales DESC, Author; -- numeric/string sort
GO
YTDSales Author AuthorRev PublisherRev
1 $22,246.00 Anne Ringer $5,339.00 $16,907.00
2 $22,246.00 Michel DeFrance $5,339.00 $16,907.00
3 $18,722.00 Marjorie Green $4,493.00 $14,229.00
4 $15,096.00 Reginald Blotchet-Halls $2,113.00 $12,983.00
5 $8,780.00 Cheryl Carson $1,404.00 $7,376.00
6 $4,095.00 Abraham Bennet $409.00 $3,686.00
7 $4,095.00 Akiko Yokomoto $409.00 $3,686.00
8 $4,095.00 Ann Dull $409.00 $3,686.00
9 $4,095.00 Burt Gringlesby $409.00 $3,686.00
HPESTAR (11.0 RTM) HPESTAR\Owner (60) pubs 00:00:00 25 rows

Book Titles in pubs Database

The titles table has the most interesting content in the pubs database as demonstrated by the following T-SQL query.

```
SELECT  TOP 4 title_id AS TitleID, title AS Title, type                    AS Type,
        pub_id AS PubID, FORMAT(price, 'c','en-US')                        AS Price,
        FORMAT(advance, 'c','en-US')                                       AS  Advance,
        FORMAT(royalty/100.0, 'p') AS Royalty, FORMAT(ytd_sales, 'c', 'en-US')  AS YTDSales,
        Notes
FROM dbo.titles
ORDER BY title;
```

TitleID	Title	Type	PubID	Price	Advance	Royalty	YTDSales	Notes
PC1035	But Is It User Friendly?	popular_comp	1389	$22.95	$7,000.00	16.00 %	$8,780.00	A survey of software for the naive user, focusing on the 'friendliness' of each.
PS1372	Computer Phobic AND Non-Phobic Individuals: Behavior Variations	psychology	0877	$21.59	$7,000.00	10.00 %	$375.00	A must for the specialist, this book examines the difference between those who hate and fear computers and those who don't.
BU1111	Cooking with Computers: Surreptitious Balance Sheets	business	1389	$11.95	$5,000.00	10.00 %	$3,876.00	Helpful hints on how to use your electronic resources to the best advantage.
PS7777	Emotional Security: A New Algorithm	psychology	0736	$7.99	$4,000.00	10.00 %	$3,336.00	Protecting yourself and your loved ones from undue emotional stress in the modern world. Use of computer and nutritional aids emphasized.

Diagram of pubs Database

Since pubs is a small database, the SQL Server 2012 diagram conveniently fits on a page.

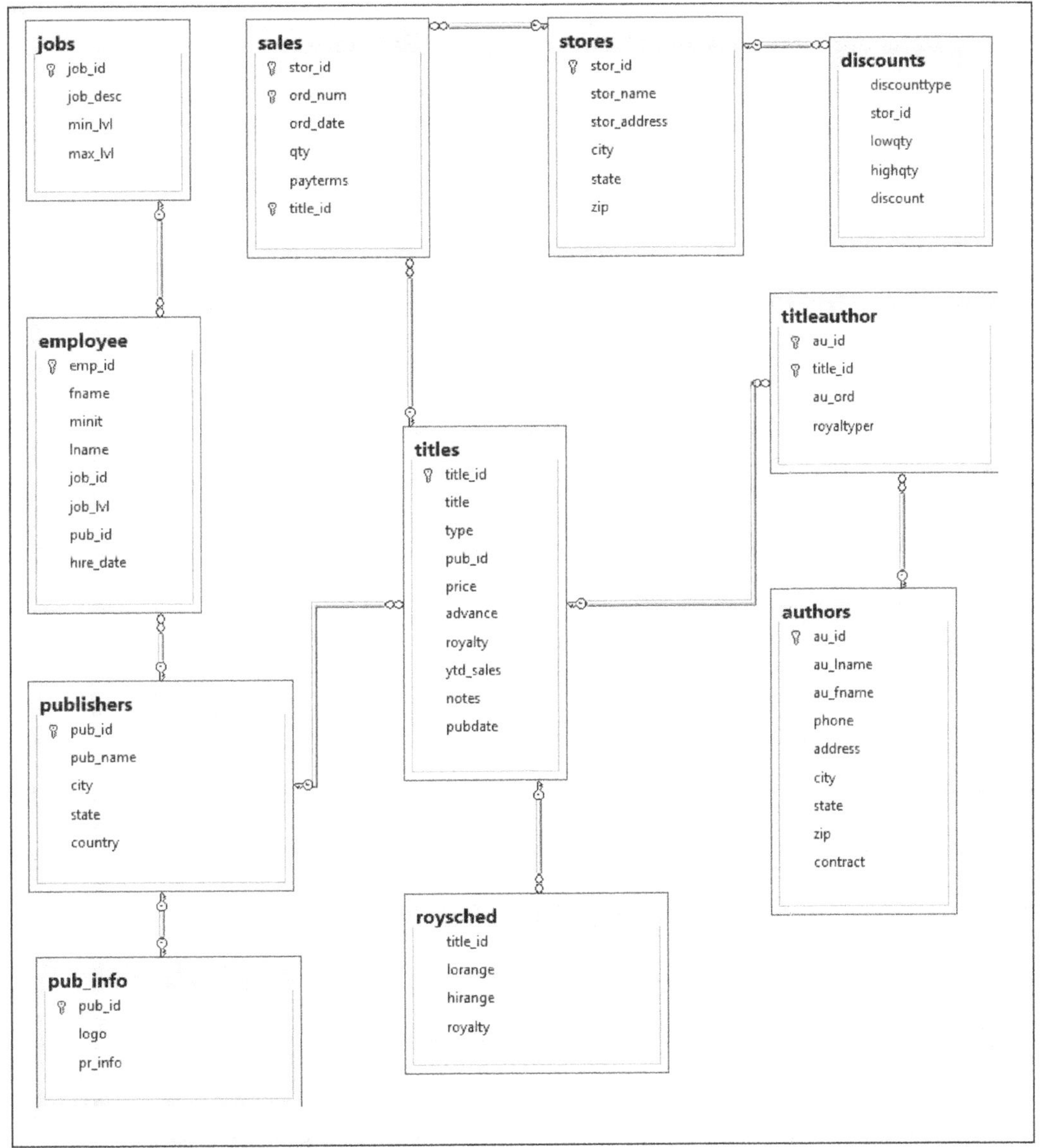

Simple JOIN on non-key columns.

```
USE pubs; SELECT p.*, a.* FROM authors AS a
INNER JOIN publishers AS p ON a.city = p.city ORDER BY p.city, a.au_lname;
```

pub_id	pub_name	city	state	country	au_id	au_lname	au_fname	phone	address	city	state	zip	contract
1389	Algodata Infosystems	Berkeley	CA	USA	409-56-7008	Bennet	Abraham	415 658-9932	6223 Bateman St.	Berkeley	CA	94705	1
1389	Algodata Infosystems	Berkeley	CA	USA	238-95-7766	Carson	Cheryl	415 548-7723	589 Darwin Ln.	Berkeley	CA	94705	1

SQL Server 2012 System Databases

The master, model, tempdb and msdb are system databases for special database server operations purposes. SSMS Object Explorer drill-down listing of system databases. **Windows Azure SQL Database server has only the master system database.**

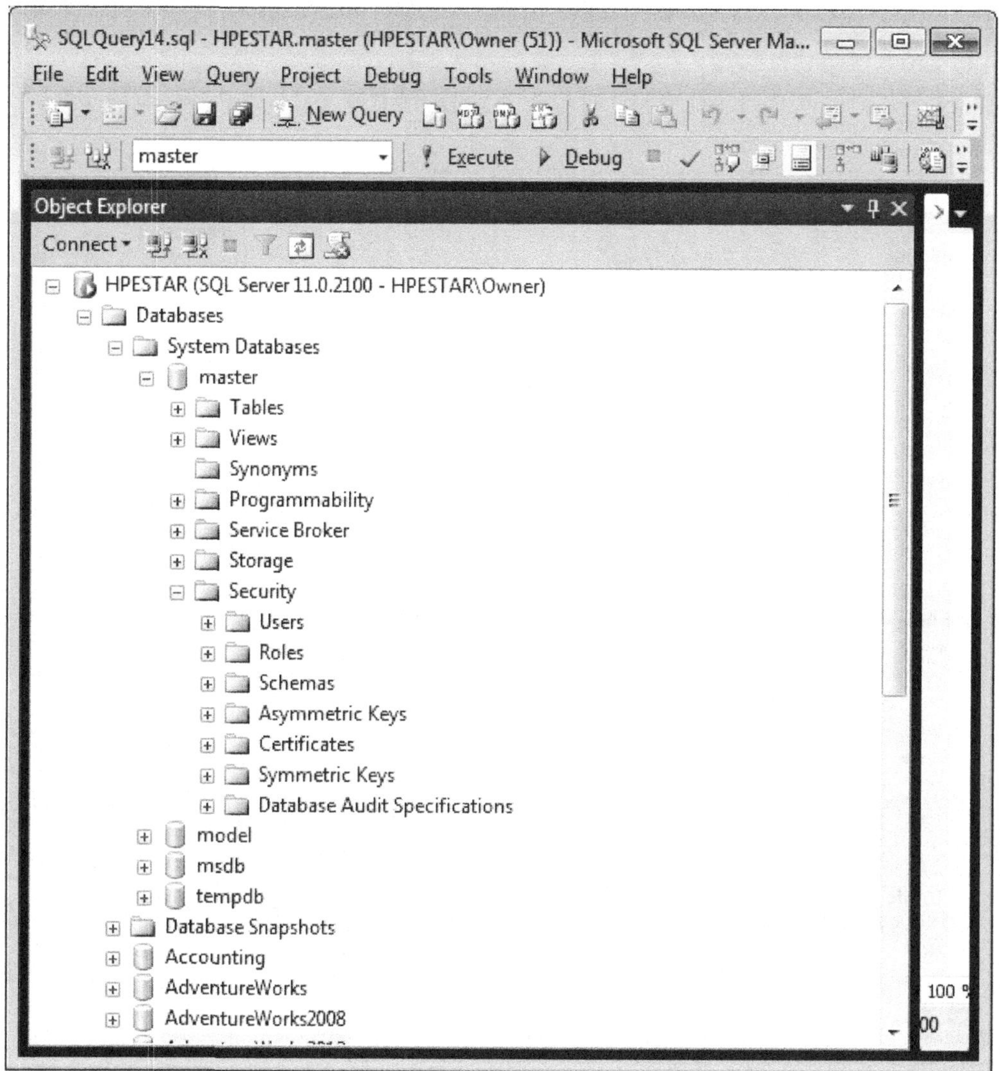

SQL Server 2012 query to create a new table in tempdb for development purposes.

```
SELECT * INTO tempdb.dbo.Product
FROM Production.Product
WHERE ListPrice > 0.0;
-- (304 row(s) affected)
```

Azure SQL master Database

The master system database is the nerve center of SQL Server. It contains tables and db objects essential for server operations. System tables are accessible only through read-only views. System tables cannot be changed by users. A subset of the system views are called Dynamic Management Views (DMV) which return server state information for monitoring the operational aspects of a SQL Server instance, diagnosing problems, and performance tuning. Dynamic Management Functions (DMF) are applied in conjunction with DMVs. SQL Server 2012 query.

```
SELECT TOP 5      ST.text,
                  EQS.*
FROM master.sys.dm_exec_query_stats AS EQS                          -- DMV
CROSS APPLY master.sys.dm_exec_sql_text(EQS.sql_handle) as ST       -- DMF
ORDER BY last_worker_time DESC;
```

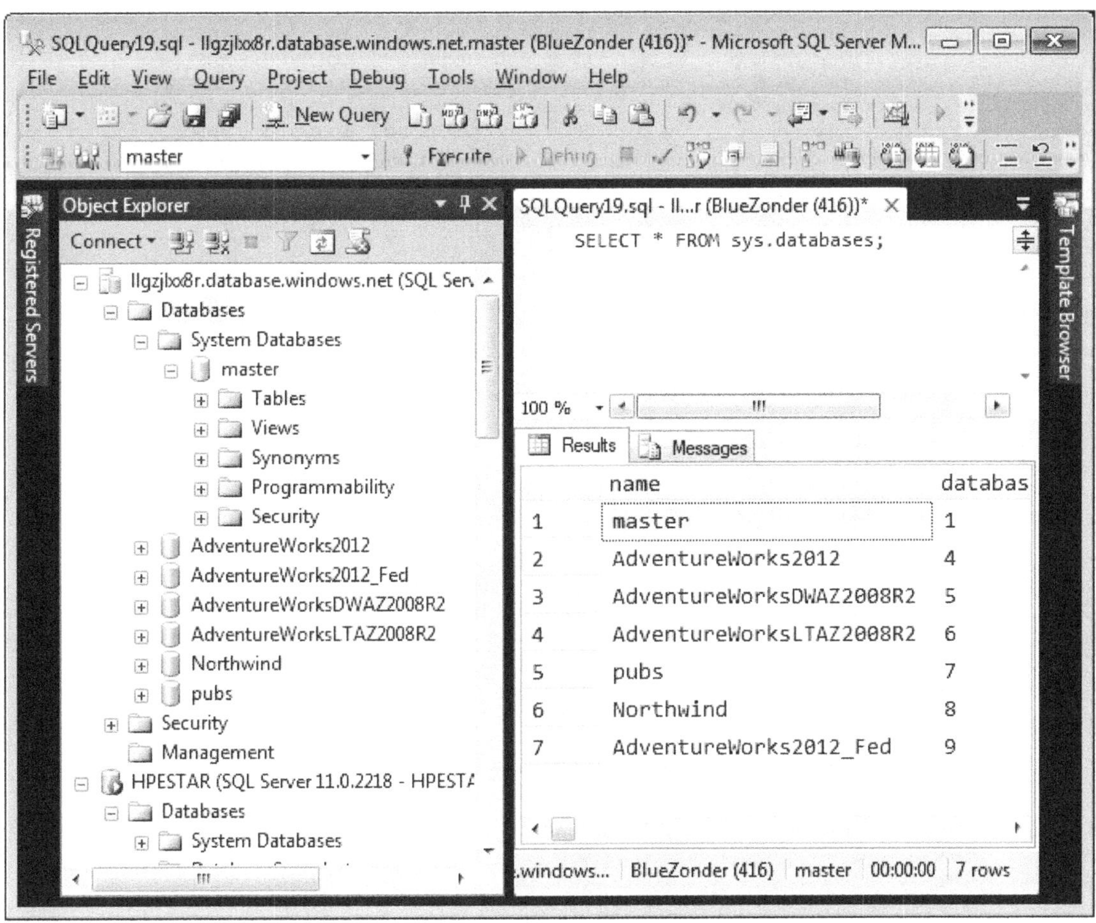

Querying System Views in master Database

```
SELECT name, object_id, schema_id  FROM sys.system_views ORDER BY name;
-- (116 row(s) affected) - Partial results.
```

name	object_id	schema_id
all_columns	-103	4
all_objects	-101	4
all_parameters	-104	4
all_sql_modules	-107	4
all_views	-102	4

```
SELECT name, type, type_desc, object_id, parent_object_id FROM sys.objects
ORDER BY type_desc, name;
```

name	type	type_desc	object_id	parent_object_id
DF__sysdac_hi__creat__32E0915F	D	DEFAULT_CONSTRAINT	853578079	805577908
DF__sysdac_hi__date___33D4B598	D	DEFAULT_CONSTRAINT	869578136	805577908
DF__sysdac_hi__date___34C8D9D1	D	DEFAULT_CONSTRAINT	885578193	805577908
DF__sysdac_in__creat__2F10007B	D	DEFAULT_CONSTRAINT	789577851	709577566
DF__sysdac_in__date___2E1BDC42	D	DEFAULT_CONSTRAINT	773577794	709577566
DF__sysdac_in__descr__2D27B809	D	DEFAULT_CONSTRAINT	757577737	709577566
PK_sysdac_history_internal	PK	PRIMARY_KEY_CONSTRAINT	821577965	805577908
PK_sysdac_instances_internal	PK	PRIMARY_KEY_CONSTRAINT	725577623	709577566
fn_sysdac_get_currentusername	FN	SQL_SCALAR_FUNCTION	661577395	0
fn_sysdac_get_username	FN	SQL_SCALAR_FUNCTION	693577509	0
fn_sysdac_is_currentuser_sa	FN	SQL_SCALAR_FUNCTION	645577338	0
fn_sysdac_is_dac_creator	FN	SQL_SCALAR_FUNCTION	629577281	0
fn_sysdac_is_login_creator	FN	SQL_SCALAR_FUNCTION	677577452	0
sp_sysdac_add_history_entry	P	SQL_STORED_PROCEDURE	949578421	0
sp_sysdac_add_instance	P	SQL_STORED_PROCEDURE	933578364	0
sp_sysdac_delete_instance	P	SQL_STORED_PROCEDURE	965578478	0
sp_sysdac_drop_database	P	SQL_STORED_PROCEDURE	997578592	0
sp_sysdac_ensure_dac_creator	P	SQL_STORED_PROCEDURE	917578307	0
sp_sysdac_rename_database	P	SQL_STORED_PROCEDURE	1013578649	0
sp_sysdac_resolve_pending_entry	P	SQL_STORED_PROCEDURE	1077578877	0
sp_sysdac_rollback_all_pending_objects	P	SQL_STORED_PROCEDURE	1109578991	0
sp_sysdac_rollback_committed_step	P	SQL_STORED_PROCEDURE	1045578763	0
sp_sysdac_rollback_pending_object	P	SQL_STORED_PROCEDURE	1093578934	0
sp_sysdac_setreadonly_database	P	SQL_STORED_PROCEDURE	1029578706	0
sp_sysdac_update_history_entry	P	SQL_STORED_PROCEDURE	1061578820	0
sp_sysdac_upgrade_instance	P	SQL_STORED_PROCEDURE	981578535	0
UQ_sysdac_history_internal	UQ	UNIQUE_CONSTRAINT	837578022	805577908
UQ_sysdac_instances_internal	UQ	UNIQUE_CONSTRAINT	741577680	709577566
sysdac_history_internal	U	USER_TABLE	805577908	0
sysdac_instances_internal	U	USER_TABLE	709577566	0
bandwidth_usage	V	VIEW	533576939	0
database_connection_stats	V	VIEW	1173579219	0
database_firewall_rules	V	VIEW	517576882	0
database_usage	V	VIEW	549576996	0
dm_database_copies	V	VIEW	1141579105	0
dm_operation_status	V	VIEW	1493580359	0
event_log	V	VIEW	1157579162	0
firewall_rules	V	VIEW	501576825	0
resource_stats	V	VIEW	597577167	0
resource_usage	V	VIEW	565577053	0
sql_logins	V	VIEW	485576768	0
sysdac_instances	V	VIEW	901578250	0

SQL Server 2012 model Database

Not in Windows Azure SQL Database. The model database serves as prototype for a new database. The model database is also the prototype for tempdb when the SQL Server instance started. Upon server shutdown or restart everything is wiped out of tempdb, it starts with a clean slate as a copy of the model database. Therefore we should only place objects into the tempdb can be purged any time.

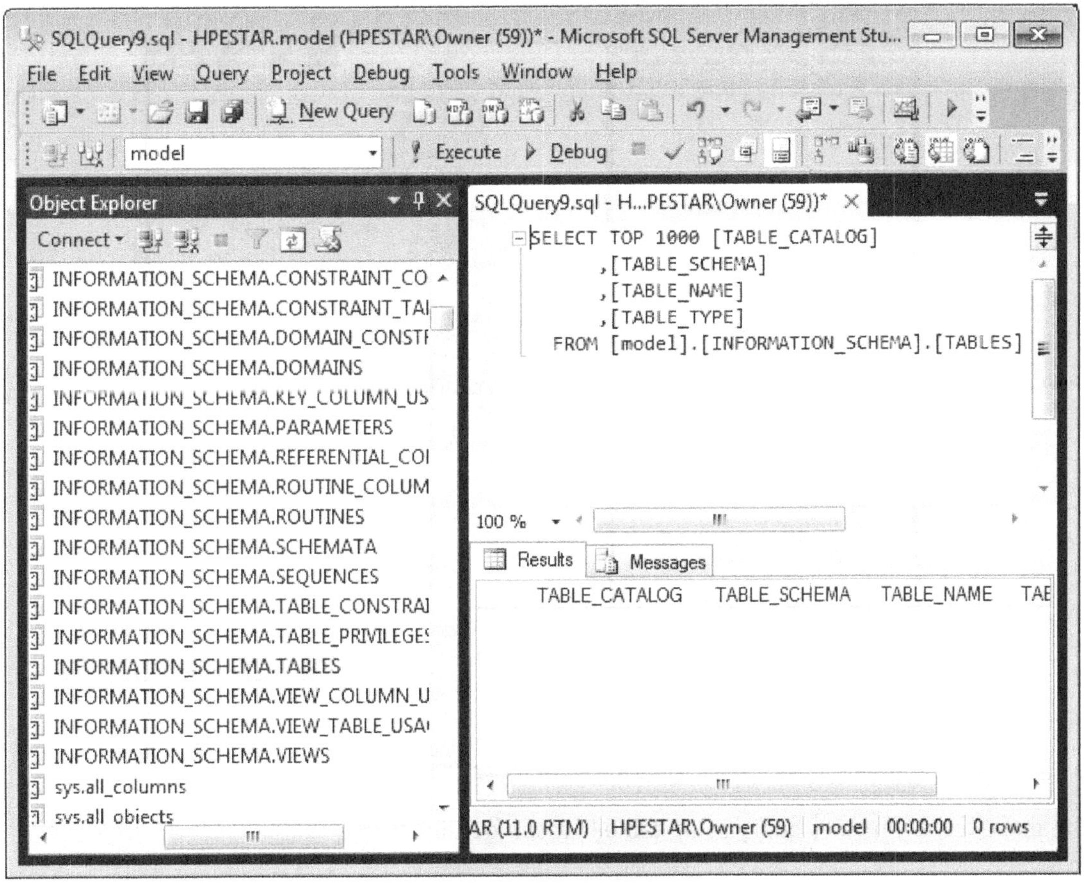

SQLQuery9.sql - HPESTAR.model (HPESTAR\Owner (59))* - Microsoft SQL Server Management Stu...
File Edit View Query Project Debug Tools Window Help
New Query
model
Execute Debug
Object Explorer
Connect
INFORMATION_SCHEMA.CONSTRAINT_CO
INFORMATION_SCHEMA.CONSTRAINT_TAI
INFORMATION_SCHEMA.DOMAIN_CONSTI
INFORMATION_SCHEMA.DOMAINS
INFORMATION_SCHEMA.KEY_COLUMN_US
INFORMATION_SCHEMA.PARAMETERS
INFORMATION_SCHEMA.REFERENTIAL_COI
INFORMATION_SCHEMA.ROUTINE_COLUM
INFORMATION_SCHEMA.ROUTINES
INFORMATION_SCHEMA.SCHEMATA
INFORMATION_SCHEMA.SEQUENCES
INFORMATION_SCHEMA.TABLE_CONSTRAI
INFORMATION_SCHEMA.TABLE_PRIVILEGE
INFORMATION_SCHEMA.TABLES
INFORMATION_SCHEMA.VIEW_COLUMN_U
INFORMATION_SCHEMA.VIEW_TABLE_USA
INFORMATION_SCHEMA.VIEWS
sys.all_columns
sys.all_objects
SQLQuery9.sql - H...PESTAR\Owner (59))*
SELECT TOP 1000 [TABLE_CATALOG]
,[TABLE_SCHEMA]
,[TABLE_NAME]
,[TABLE_TYPE]
FROM [model].[INFORMATION_SCHEMA].[TABLES]
100 %
Results
Messages
TABLE_CATALOG TABLE_SCHEMA TABLE_NAME TAE
AR (11.0 RTM) HPESTAR\Owner (59) model 00:00:00 0 rows

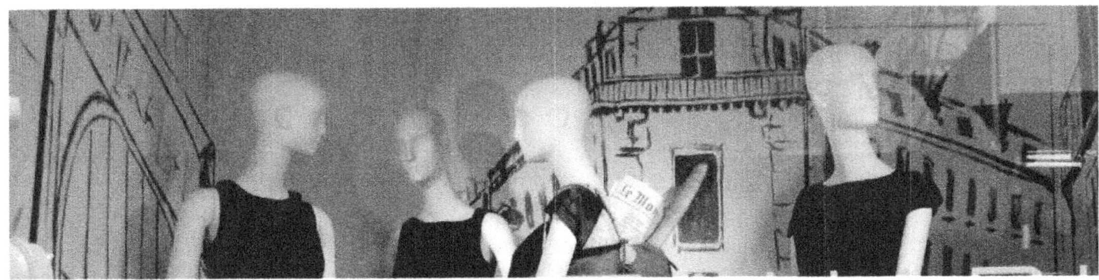

SQL Server 2012 msdb Database

Not in Windows Azure SQL Database. The msdb database is used for server internal operations such as support for SQL Server Agent job scheduling facility or keeping track of database the all important backups and restores.

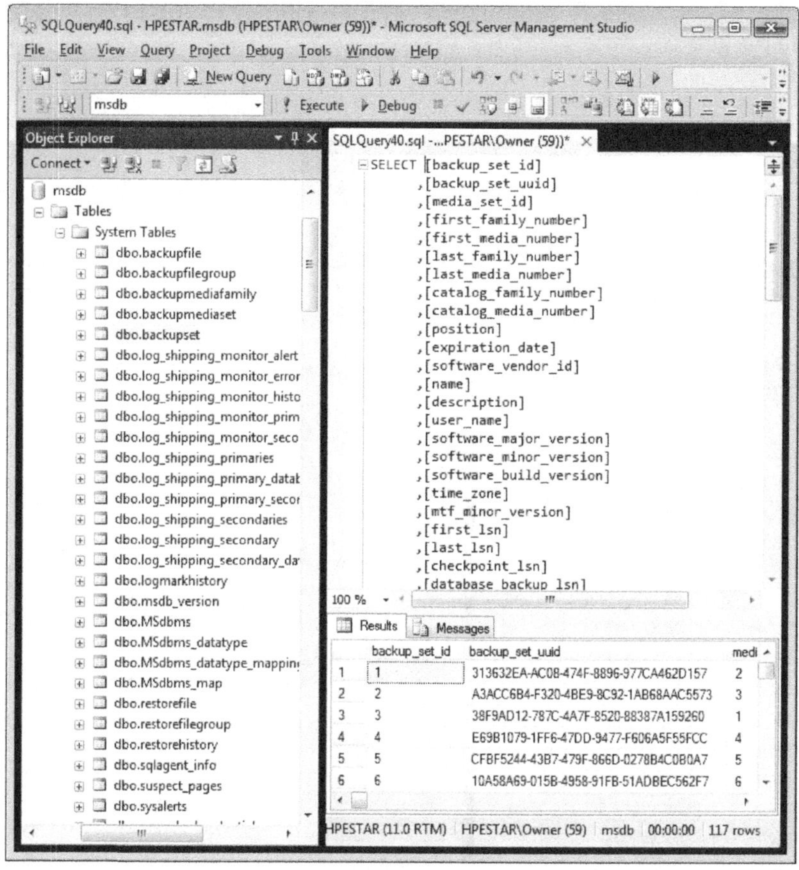

Database backup history query using table in msdb database.

```
SELECT   s.name AS Name, CONVERT(DATE,MAX(b.backup_finish_date)) AS LastGoodBackup,
         b.type AS Type
FROM master.dbo.sysdatabases AS s
LEFT OUTER JOIN msdb.dbo.backupset AS b ON s.name = b.database_name
GROUP BY s.name, b.type ORDER BY Name, Type;
```

Name	LastGoodBackup	Type
Accounting	2016-11-29	D
AdventureWorks	2016-11-29	D
AdventureWorks2008	2016-11-29	D
AdventureWorks2012	2016-11-29	D

SQL Server 2012 tempdb Database

Not in Windows Azure SQL Database. The tempdb serves as temporary database for system operations such as sorting. Temporary tables (#temp1) and global temporary tables (##globaltemp1) are stored in the tempdb as well. "Permanent" tables can be created in tempdb with a short lifetime which lasts till shutdown or restart.

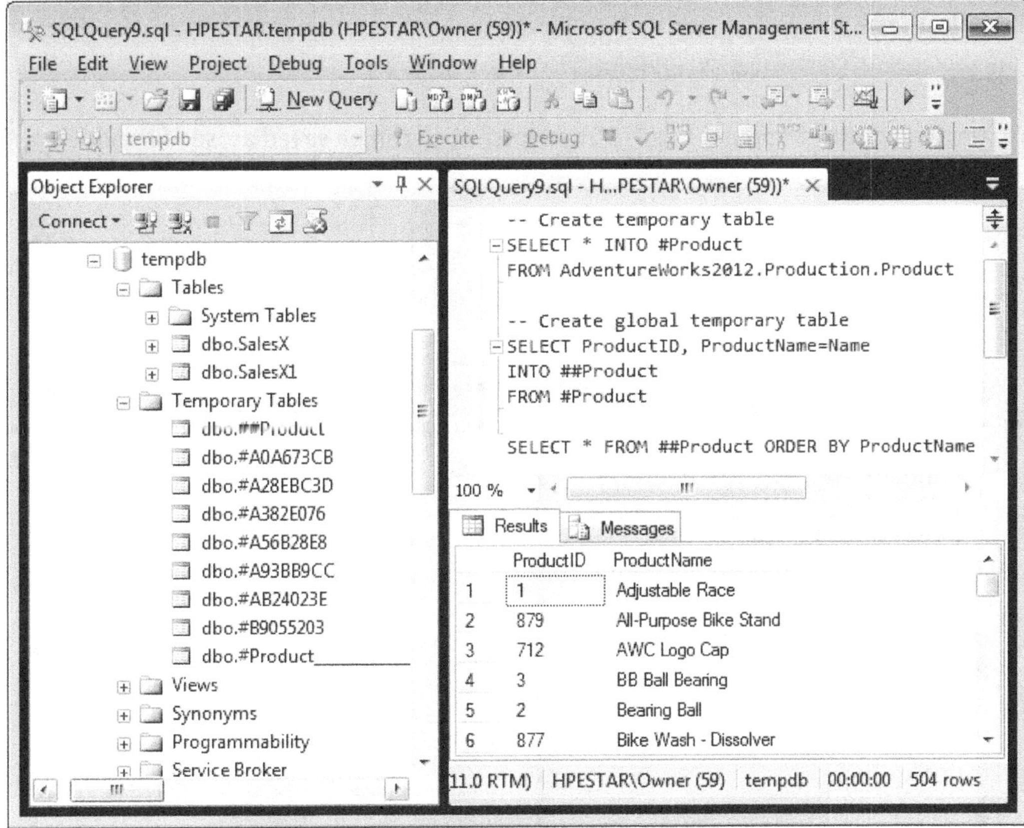

Sudden Death in tempdb When Server Restarts - On-Premises SQL Server

Even though a temporary table and a global temporary table are created and queried in the context setting for AdventureWorks2012 database, they are placed into tempdb automatically. Same consideration when a temporary table is created from a stored procedure which is compiled in an application database. Upon server restart everything is wiped out of tempdb, rebirth follows as a copy of model db. We should not place anything into tempdb we cannot afford to lose. tempdb is also used by SQL Server engine for operations such as version control, sorting and more. SQL Server 2012 demo.

Instead of GUI & mouse, **use T-SQL scripts** which can be saved as .sql disk files.

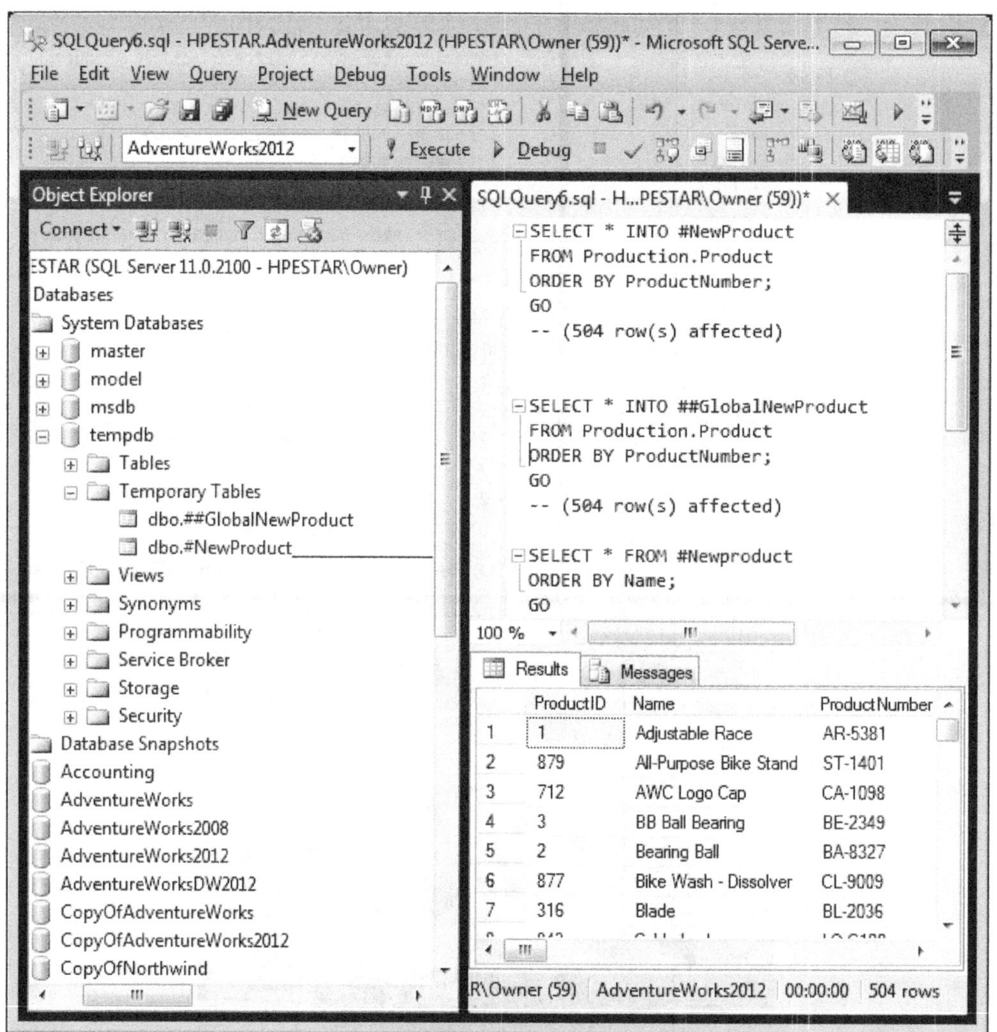

CHAPTER 2: Installing Azure SQL & Sample Databases

SQL Azure - Enterprise in the Clouds

Microsoft Windows Azure account is available at:

Windows Azure portal http://www.windowsazure.com/en-us/ Your **Windows Azure SQL Database** management portal https://yourazuresqlserver.database.windows.net

At the time of writing this book, there is a 90-day free trial package available which includes an SQL database. Credit card is required for an Azure account. One form of verification: a code is sent to your mobile phone.

Creating Database Using the Azure Portal

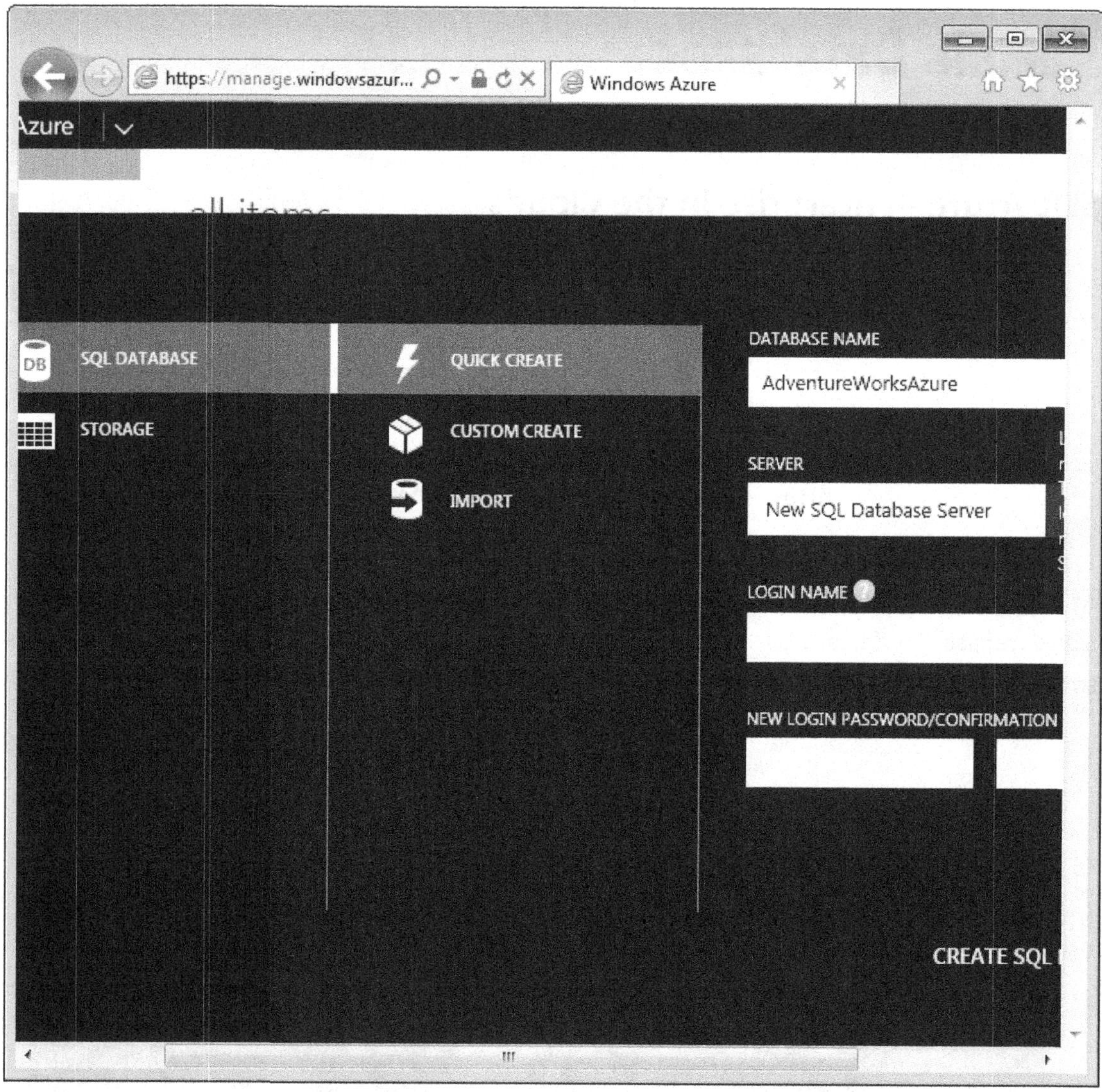

Database can also be created from a Command Prompt utility, SQLCMD, an application program and SQL Server Management Studio. Connection to Windows Azure SQL Database server required and permission to create a database.

Getting Started with Azure SQL Database

Basic configuration has to be done online such as setting Azure SQL server login & password, and setting up firewall rules so you can use Management Studio and other client software from your computer. The configuration processes are automated to a large degree and user-friendly. The best part: once you are finished with configuration, you can continue with the "friendly skies" from the friendly Management Studio environment.

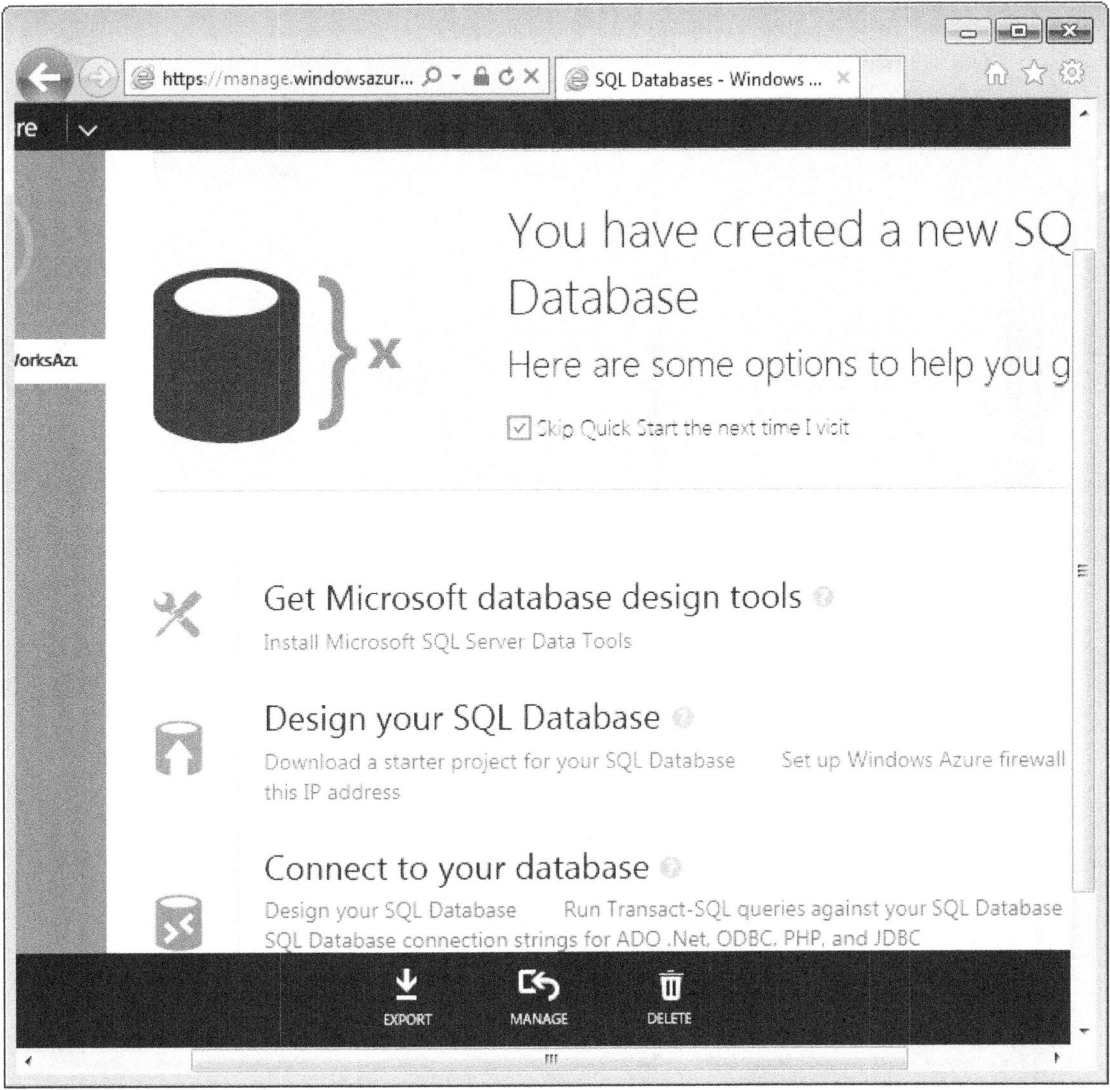

Connecting Azure SQL Server from 2012 Management Studio

You can connect to the Azure SQL Server after setting up a firewall rule for your computer IP using the regular dialog box with SQL Server authentication. The server name is: yourazureserver.database.windows.net. The login & password is what you configured on Azure. Some server & login information has been blanked out on the following screenshot. The Azure T-SQL is different from SQL Server 2012 T-SQL

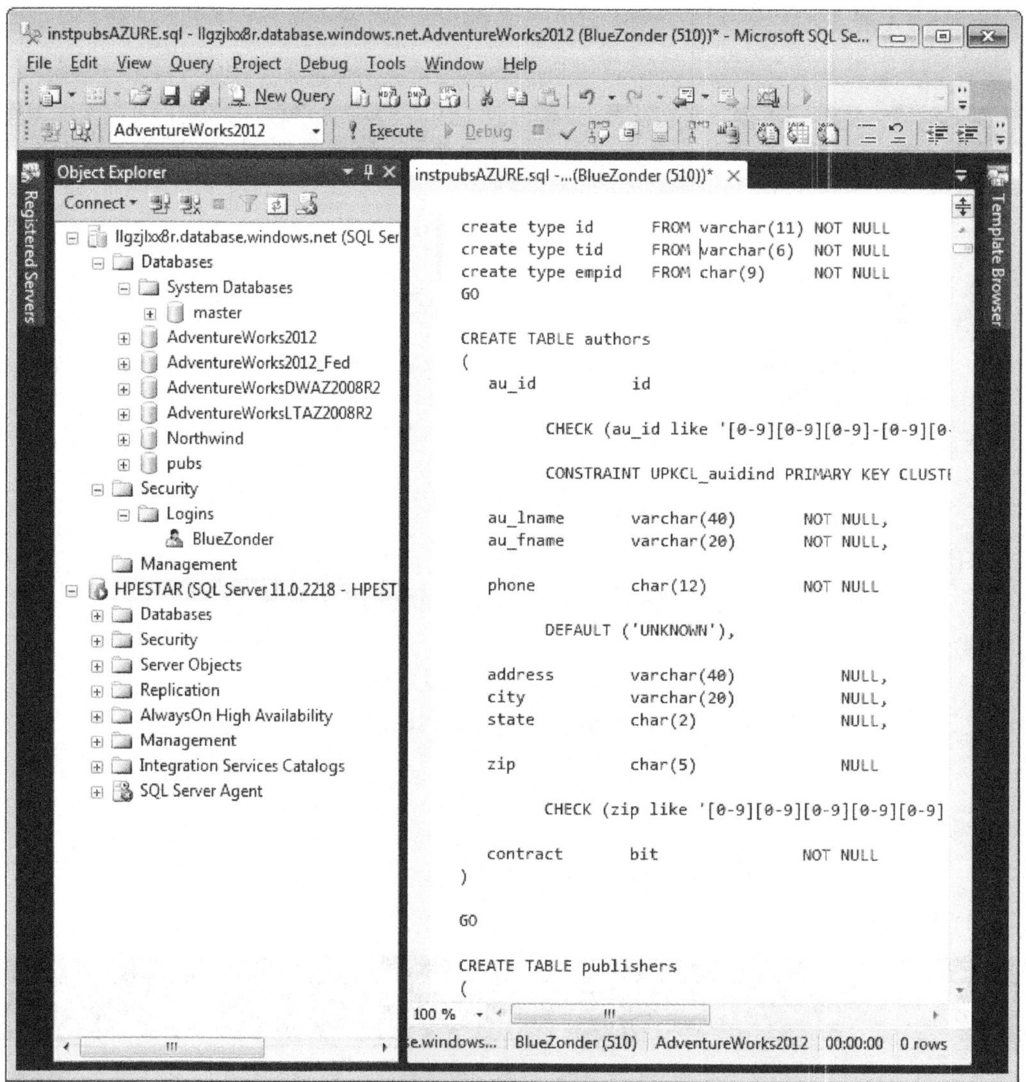

We can get SQL Azure version information by a SELECT:

```
select @@version  -- Microsoft SQL Azure (RTM) - 11.0.2065.0 Aug 29 2012 18:41:07
```

Installing AdventureWorks2012 for Azure SQL

There is a special download site for SQL Azure AdventureWorks sample databases

Download site: **Adventure Works for Azure SQL Database**
http://msftdbprodsamples.codeplex.com/releases/view/37304

Download 2 files:

- AdventureWorks2012ForWindowsAzureSQLDatabase
- AdventureWorks2008R2AZ.zip

Download site: **.NET Framework 4 or higher**
http://msdn.microsoft.com/en-us/vstudio/aa4961

Unzip the zipped files into a directory. In the same directory using Command Prompt run the following command in AdventureWorks directory:

```
CreateAdventureWorksForSQLAzure.cmd yourserverid.database.windows.net
yourserverlogin yourpassword
```

This is going to upload the sample AdventureWorks2012 database into the Azure server using bcp. It takes a few minutes, maybe even an hour if the internet connection is slow. A few tables were created on Azure SQL database but did not populate. The reason of population failure for the Sales.Customer table: it has a computed column AccountNumber.

```
[AccountNumber]  AS (isnull('AW'+[dbo].[ufnLeadingZeros]([CustomerID]),'')),
```

We shall use SQL Server (SSIS) Import/Export Wizard to transfer the data from SQL Server 2012 AdventureWorks2012 database. Similar upload process for AdventureWorks2012_Fed:

```
CreateAdventureWorksForSQLAzure_Fed yourserverid.database.windows.net
yourserverlogin yourpassword
```

Commands to upload AdventureWorksDWAZ2008R2 database in DW folder & AdventureWorksLTAZ2008R2 database in LT folder.

```
buildawdwaz.cmd tcp:YOURAZURESERVER.database.windows.net YOURLOGIN
YOURPASSWORD
```

```
buildawltaz.cmd tcp:YOURAZURESERVER.database.windows.net YOURLOGIN  YOURPASSWORD
```

Checking AdventureWorks2012 Tables Population

We can use database metadata, cursor WHILE loop and dynamic SQL to get the row count for each table.

```
DECLARE @SchemaName SYSNAME, @TableName  SYSNAME,  @TableType  varchar(12);
DECLARE @SQL NVARCHAR(MAX);

CREATE TABLE #Population
 (        TableName    VARCHAR(256),
          TableType    varchar(12),
          [Population] INT   );

DECLARE curTablesAndViews CURSOR FAST_FORWARD FOR
          SELECT TABLE_SCHEMA,  TABLE_NAME,  TABLE_TYPE
          FROM   INFORMATION_SCHEMA.TABLES   WHERE  TABLE_TYPE = 'BASE TABLE';

OPEN curTablesAndViews;

FETCH NEXT FROM curTablesAndViews INTO @SchemaName, @TableName, @TableType;

WHILE ( @@FETCH_STATUS = 0 )   BEGIN
    SELECT @SQL = CONCAT('INSERT #Population SELECT ''',
               @SchemaName, '.', @TableName, ''',''',
               @TableType, ''', COUNT(*) as Population ',
               'FROM [', @SchemaName, '].[', @TableName, ']');

    PRINT @SQL -- debugging
    EXEC SP_EXECUTESQL        @SQL;

    FETCH NEXT FROM curTablesAndViews INTO @SchemaName, @TableName, @TableType;
  END

CLOSE curTablesAndViews;
DEALLOCATE curTablesAndViews;

-- Return the list of rows counts
SELECT *  FROM   #Population  ORDER  BY [Population] DESC;
GO

DROP TABLE #Population;
```

Azure SQL AdventureWorks2012 Tables Population after Upload

Note: Sales.Customer table was populated by SS Import/Export Wizard execution.

TableName	TableType	Population
Sales.SalesOrderDetail	BASE TABLE	121317
Production.TransactionHistory	BASE TABLE	113443
Production.TransactionHistoryArchive	BASE TABLE	89253
Production.WorkOrderRouting	BASE TABLE	67131
Sales.SalesOrderHeader	BASE TABLE	31465
Person.BusinessEntity	BASE TABLE	20777
Person.Password	BASE TABLE	19972
Person.PersonPhone	BASE TABLE	19972
Person.Person	BASE TABLE	19972
Person.EmailAddress	BASE TABLE	19972
Sales.Customer	BASE TABLE	19820
Person.Address	BASE TABLE	19614
Person.BusinessEntityAddress	BASE TABLE	19614
Sales.PersonCreditCard	BASE TABLE	19118
Sales.CreditCard	BASE TABLE	19118
Sales.CurrencyRate	BASE TABLE	13532
Purchasing.PurchaseOrderDetail	BASE TABLE	8845
Purchasing.PurchaseOrderHeader	BASE TABLE	4012
Production.BillOfMaterials	BASE TABLE	2679
Production.ProductInventory	BASE TABLE	1069
Person.BusinessEntityContact	BASE TABLE	909
Production.ProductDescription	BASE TABLE	762
Production.ProductModelProductDescriptionCulture	BASE TABLE	762
Sales.Store	BASE TABLE	701
Sales.SpecialOfferProduct	BASE TABLE	538
Production.Product	BASE TABLE	504
Production.ProductProductPhoto	BASE TABLE	504
Purchasing.ProductVendor	BASE TABLE	460
Production.ProductListPriceHistory	BASE TABLE	395
Production.ProductCostHistory	BASE TABLE	395
HumanResources.EmployeePayHistory	BASE TABLE	316
HumanResources.EmployeeDepartmentHistory	BASE TABLE	296
HumanResources.Employee	BASE TABLE	290
Person.CountryRegion	BASE TABLE	238
Person.StateProvince	BASE TABLE	181
Sales.SalesPersonQuotaHistory	BASE TABLE	163
Production.ProductModel	BASE TABLE	128

Sales.CountryRegionCurrency	BASE TABLE	109
Sales.Currency	BASE TABLE	105
Purchasing.Vendor	BASE TABLE	104
Production.ProductPhoto	BASE TABLE	101
Production.UnitMeasure	BASE TABLE	38
Production.ProductSubcategory	BASE TABLE	37
Production.ProductDocument	BASE TABLE	32
Sales.SalesTaxRate	BASE TABLE	29
Person.ContactType	BASE TABLE	20
Sales.SalesTerritoryHistory	BASE TABLE	17
Sales.SalesPerson	BASE TABLE	17
HumanResources.Department	BASE TABLE	16
Sales.SpecialOffer	BASE TABLE	16
Production.ScrapReason	BASE TABLE	16
Production.Location	BASE TABLE	14
Production.Document	BASE TABLE	13
HumanResources.JobCandidate	BASE TABLE	13
Sales.SalesTerritory	BASE TABLE	10
Sales.SalesReason	BASE TABLE	10
Production.Culture	BASE TABLE	8
Production.Illustration	BASE TABLE	5
Purchasing.ShipMethod	BASE TABLE	5
Production.ProductCategory	BASE TABLE	4
Production.ProductReview	BASE TABLE	4
Person.PhoneNumberType	BASE TABLE	3
Sales.ShoppingCartItem	BASE TABLE	3
HumanResources.Shift	BASE TABLE	3
dbo.AWBuildVersion	BASE TABLE	1
dbo.DatabaseLog	BASE TABLE	0
dbo.ErrorLog	BASE TABLE	0
Sales.SalesOrderHeaderSalesReason	BASE TABLE	0
Person.AddressType	BASE TABLE	0
Production.ProductModelIllustration	BASE TABLE	0
Production.WorkOrder	BASE TABLE	0

We shall populate the last 4 tables with SS Import/Export Wizard from SS 2012 (Earth-based) AdventureWorks2012 database. Full-text index is not supported, therefore a stored procedure using full-text search must be dropped:

```
DROP PROCEDURE [dbo].[uspSearchCandidateResumes]
```

Command Prompt Window with Upload Command

Command Prompt

```
F:\UTIL\Microsoft\Azure>cd sampledb

F:\UTIL\Microsoft\Azure\sampledb>dir
 Volume in drive F is Secondary HDD
 Volume Serial Number is 96F5-D46B

 Directory of F:\UTIL\Microsoft\Azure\sampledb

01/06/2013  03:27 PM    <DIR>          .
01/06/2013  03:27 PM    <DIR>          ..
01/06/2013  03:27 PM    <DIR>          AdventureWorks
01/06/2013  03:27 PM    <DIR>          AdventureWorks2008R2AZ
01/05/2013  03:17 AM        11,069,693 AdventureWorks2008R2AZ.zip
01/05/2013  03:16 AM        21,383,740 AdventureWorks2012ForSQLAzure.zip
01/06/2013  03:27 PM    <DIR>          AdventureWorks_Federated
01/06/2013  03:27 PM    <DIR>          Data
02/02/2012  02:06 PM             7,168 ExecuteSQL.exe
02/14/2012  10:13 AM            34,644 ReadMe.htm
               4 File(s)     32,495,245 bytes
               6 Dir(s)  1,582,238,818,304 bytes free

F:\UTIL\Microsoft\Azure\sampledb>cd adventureworks

F:\UTIL\Microsoft\Azure\sampledb\AdventureWorks>CreateAdventureWorksForSQLAzure.
cmd yourserverid.database.windows.net yourserverlogin yourpassword
```

Upload in Progress

Note: the error messages are due to the repeat execution of the upload utility.

Command Prompt - CreateAdventureWorksForSQLAzure.cmd llgzjlx8r.database.windows.net Blue...

```
1000 rows sent to SQL Server. Total sent: 7000
1000 rows sent to SQL Server. Total sent: 8000
1000 rows sent to SQL Server. Total sent: 9000
1000 rows sent to SQL Server. Total sent: 10000
1000 rows sent to SQL Server. Total sent: 11000
1000 rows sent to SQL Server. Total sent: 12000
1000 rows sent to SQL Server. Total sent: 13000
1000 rows sent to SQL Server. Total sent: 14000
1000 rows sent to SQL Server. Total sent: 15000
1000 rows sent to SQL Server. Total sent: 16000
1000 rows sent to SQL Server. Total sent: 17000
1000 rows sent to SQL Server. Total sent: 18000
1000 rows sent to SQL Server. Total sent: 19000
1000 rows sent to SQL Server. Total sent: 20000
SQLState = 23000, NativeError = 2627
Error = [Microsoft][SQL Server Native Client 11.0][SQL Server]Violation of PRIMA
RY KEY constraint 'PK_BusinessEntity_BusinessEntityID'. Cannot insert duplicate
key in object 'Person.BusinessEntity'. The duplicate key value is (1).
SQLState = 01000, NativeError = 3621
Warning = [Microsoft][SQL Server Native Client 11.0][SQL Server]The statement ha
s been terminated.

BCP copy in failed
Populating Person.ContactType
```

SS Import/Export Wizard for Migrating Data to Azure SQL

We will populate empty Azure tables from SS tables. SSMS Object Explorer view of the cloud and Earth (on-premises) servers.

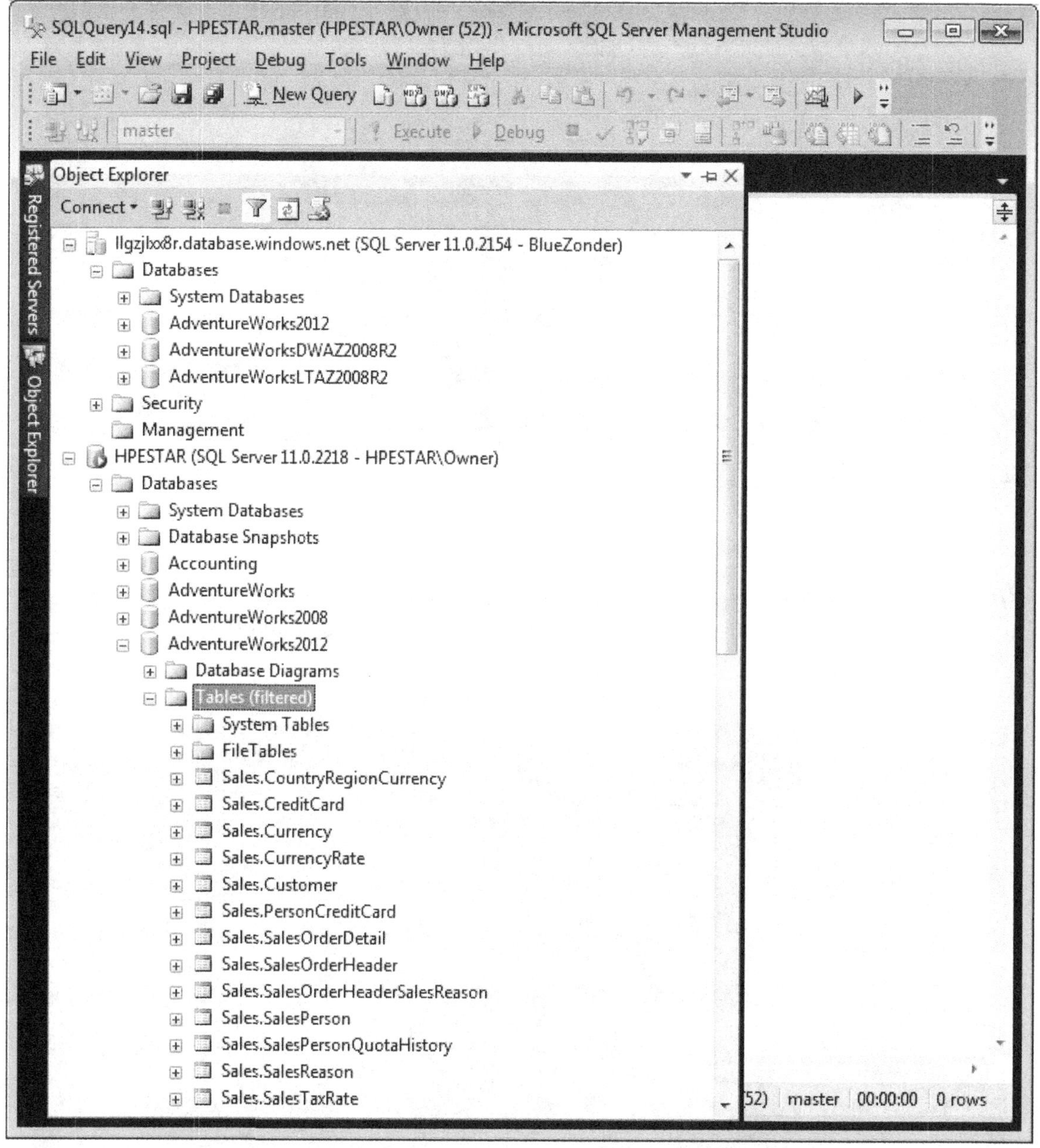

Launching the SS Import/Export Wizard

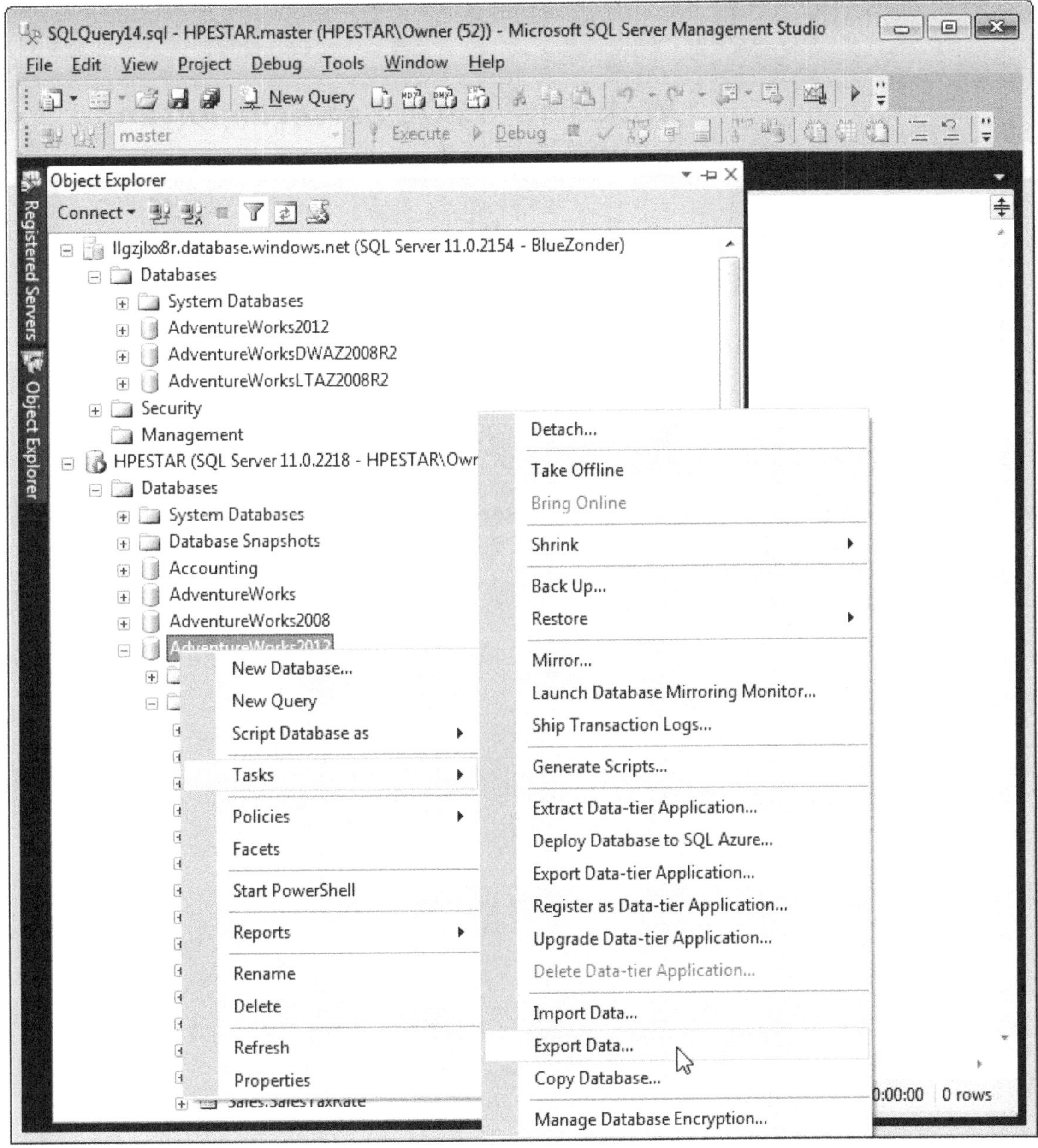

SQL Server Import/Export Wizard Welcome Page

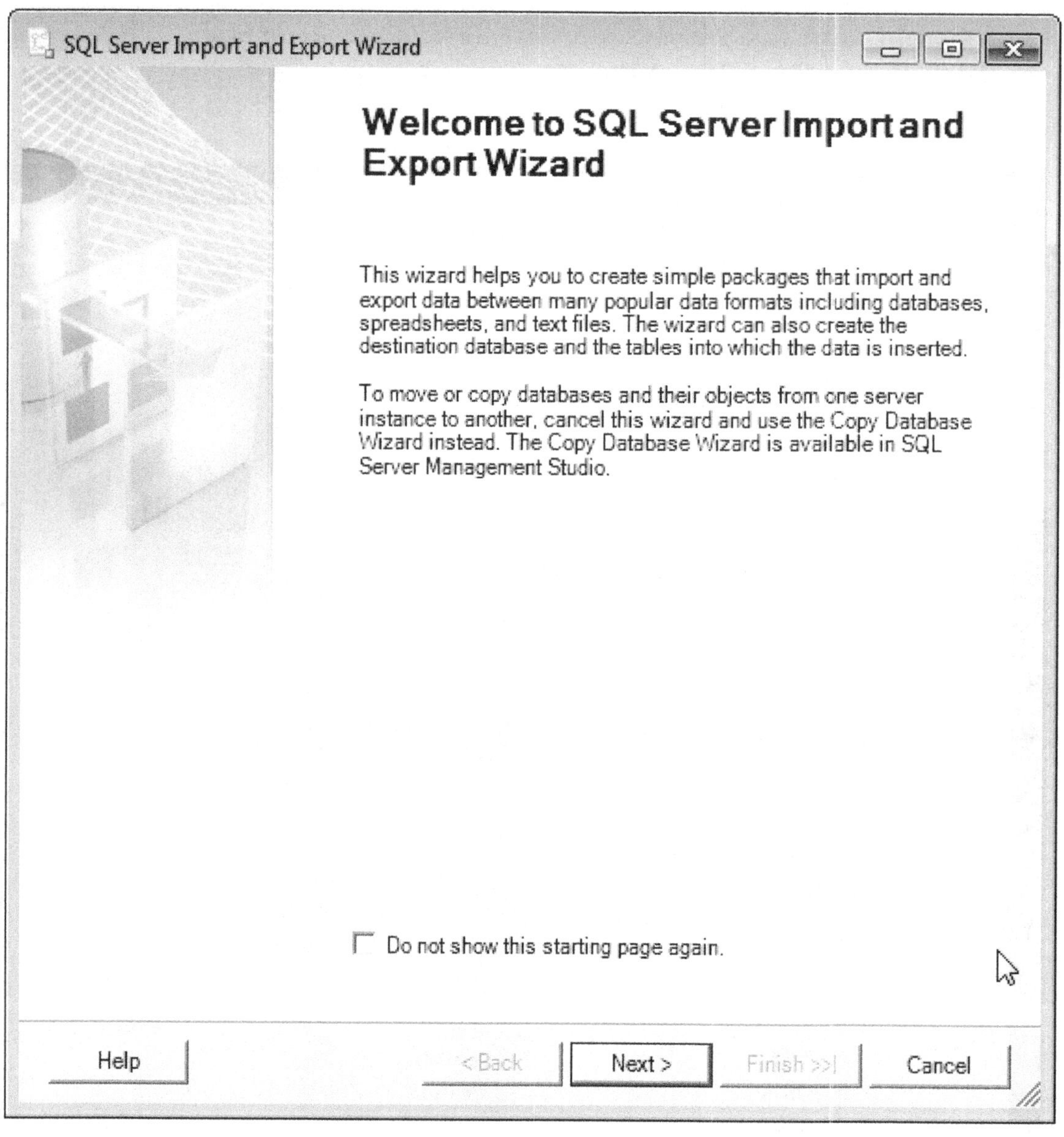

Data Source Page with Automatic Fillin Values

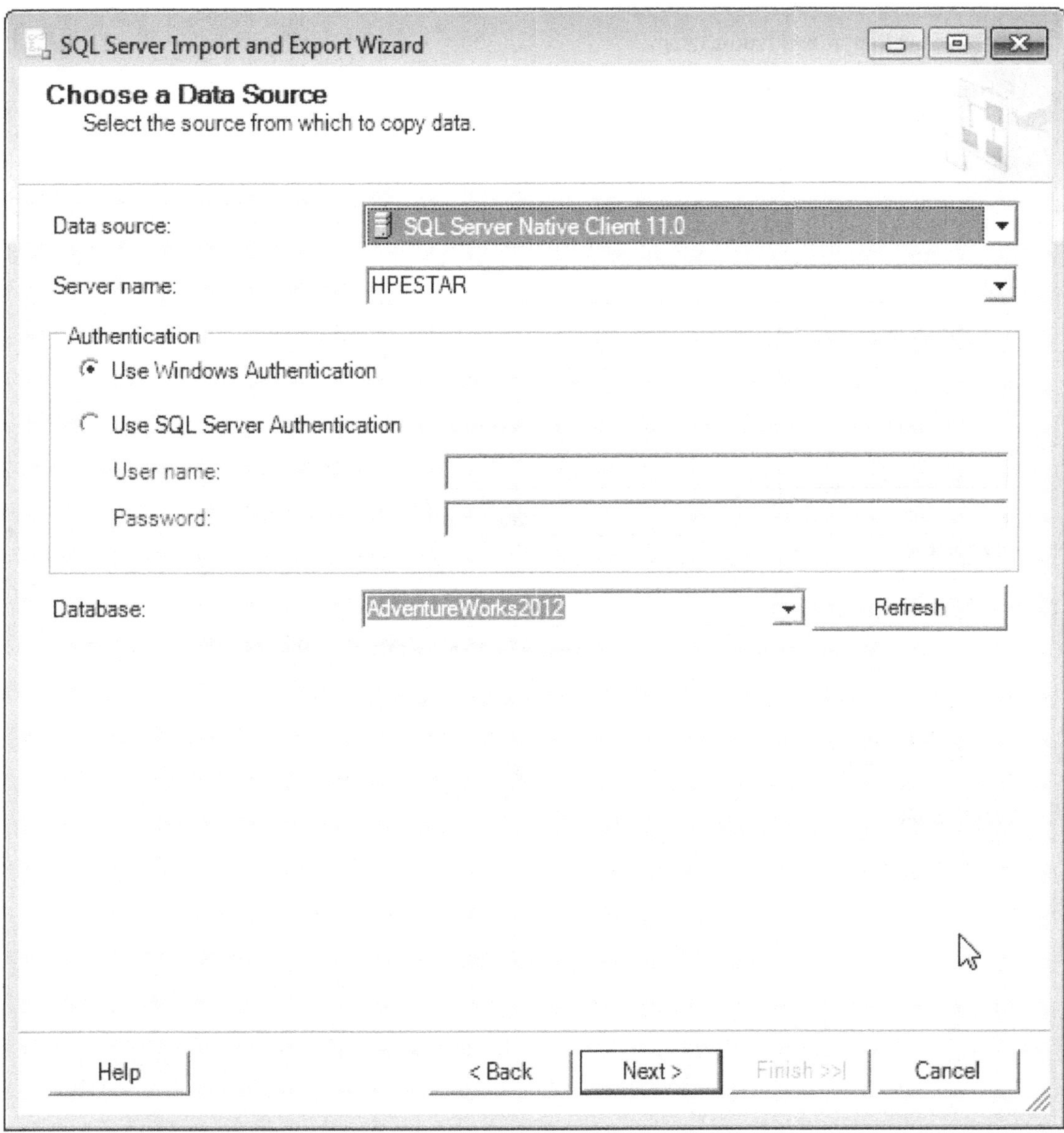

Destination Page - Azure SQL Database

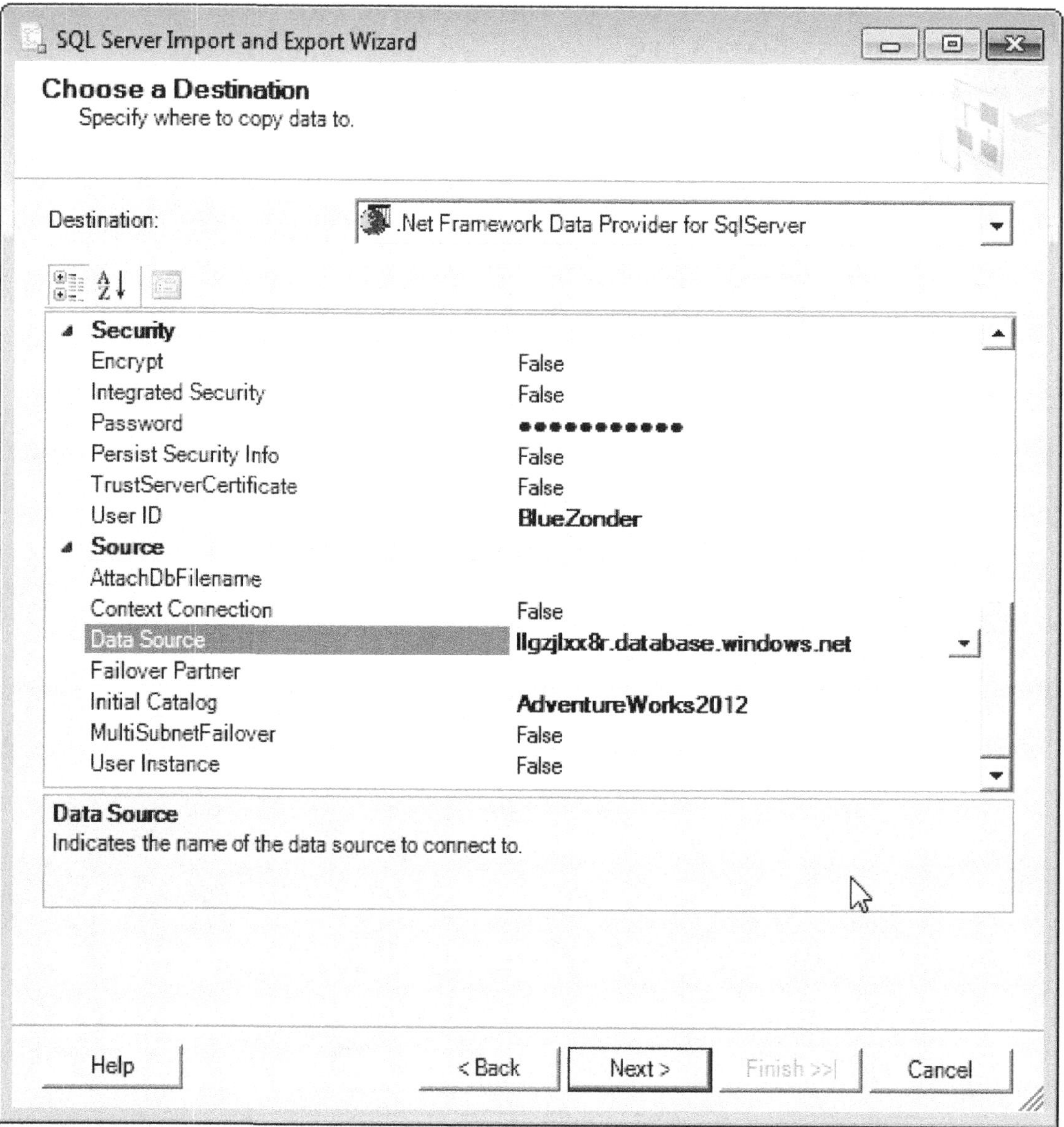

Choose Table Copy or Query Results Copy

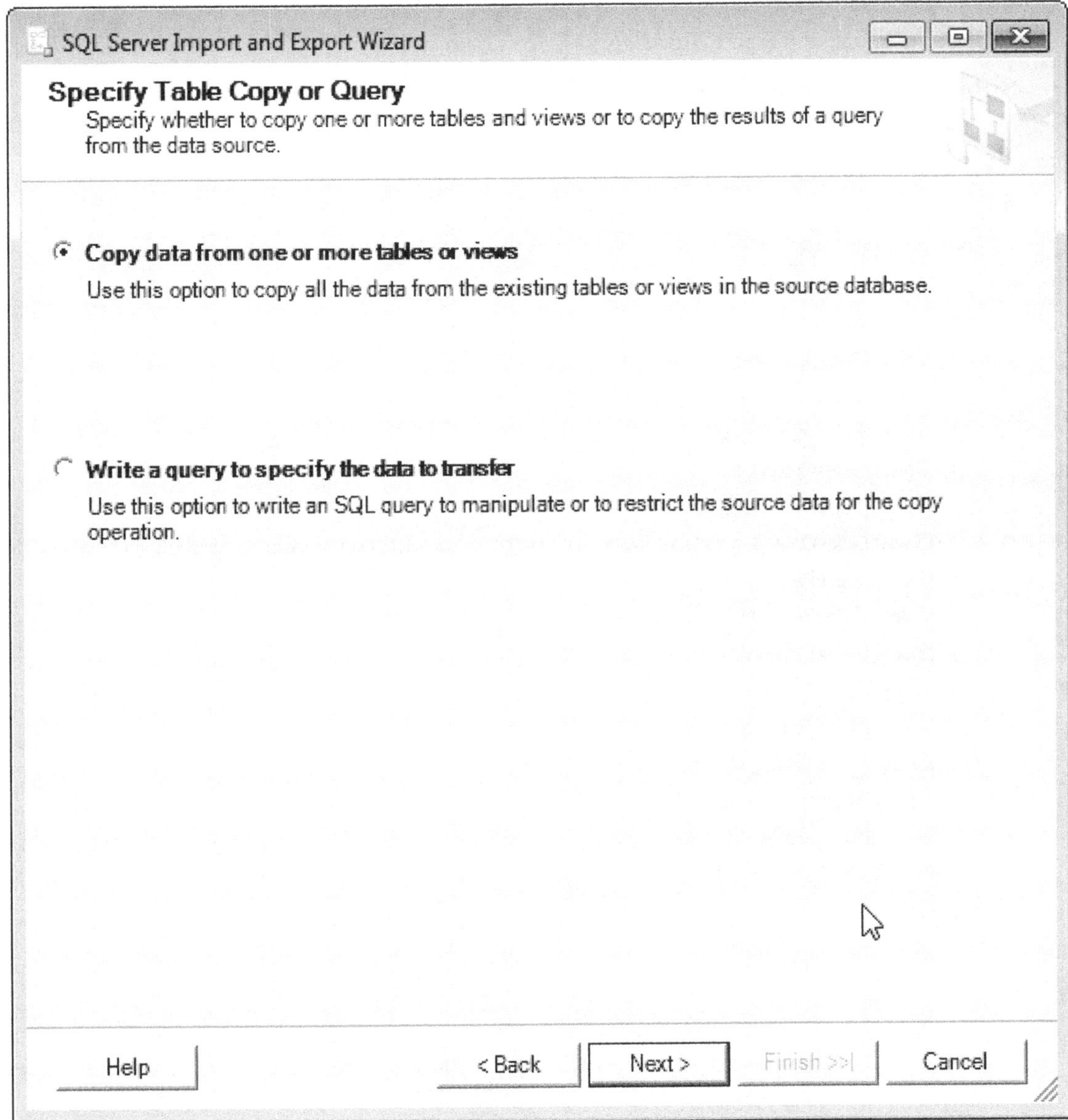

Choose Table to Copy

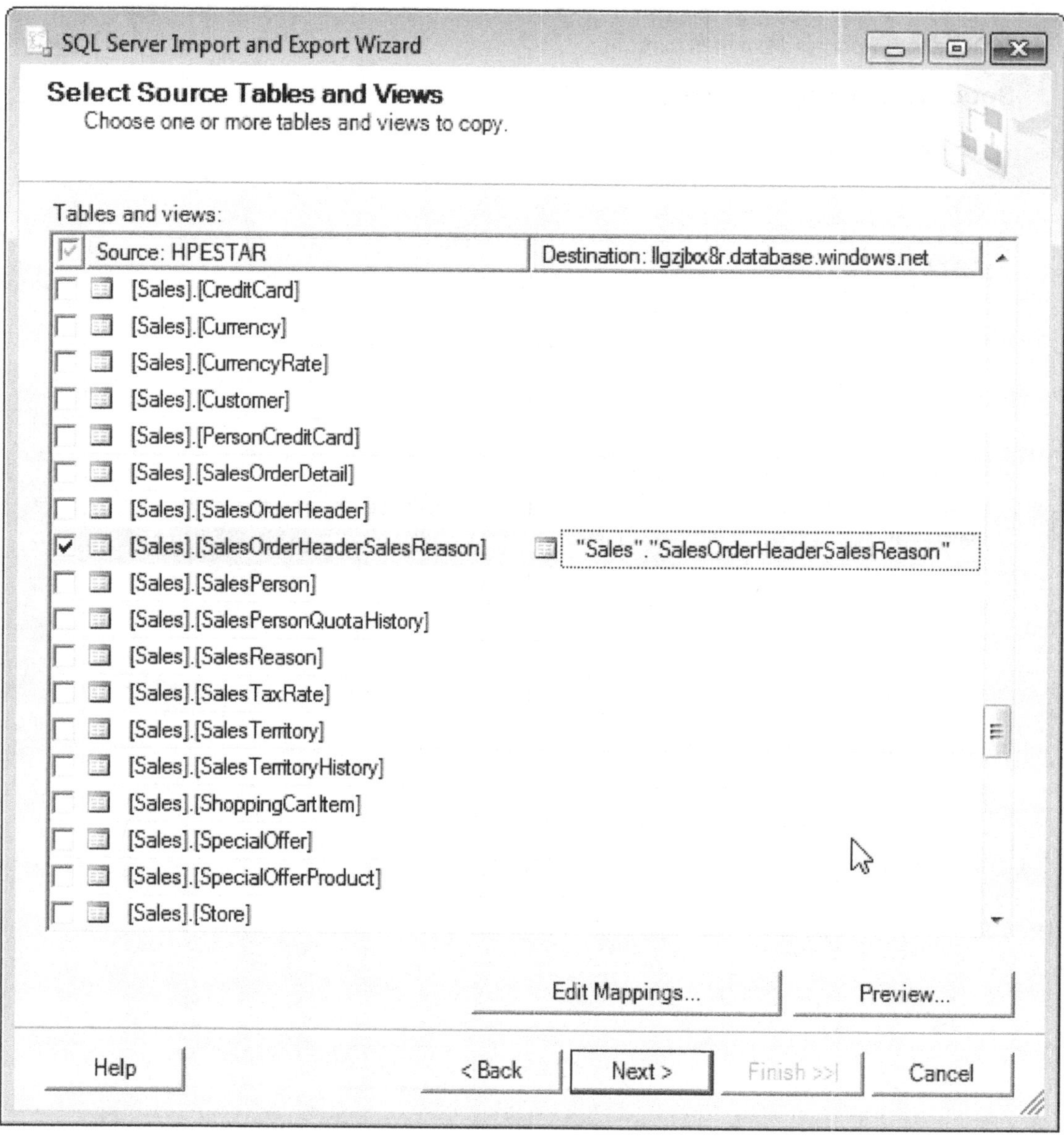

Column Mapping & Preview Data Pages - No Change

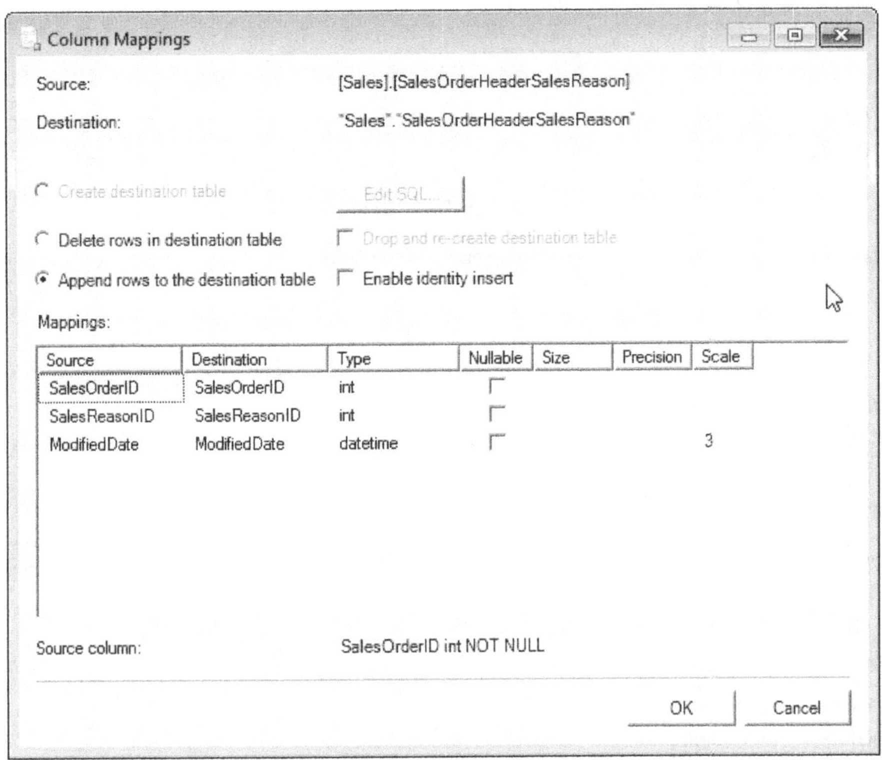
Column Mappings
Source:
[Sales].[SalesOrderHeaderSalesReason]
Destination:
"Sales"."SalesOrderHeaderSalesReason"
Create destination table
Edit SQL...
Delete rows in destination table
Drop and re-create destination table
Append rows to the destination table
Enable identity insert
Mappings:
Source
Destination
Type
Nullable
Size
Precision
Scale
SalesOrderID
SalesOrderID
int
SalesReasonID
SalesReasonID
int
ModifiedDate
ModifiedDate
datetime
3
Source column:
SalesOrderID int NOT NULL
OK
Cancel

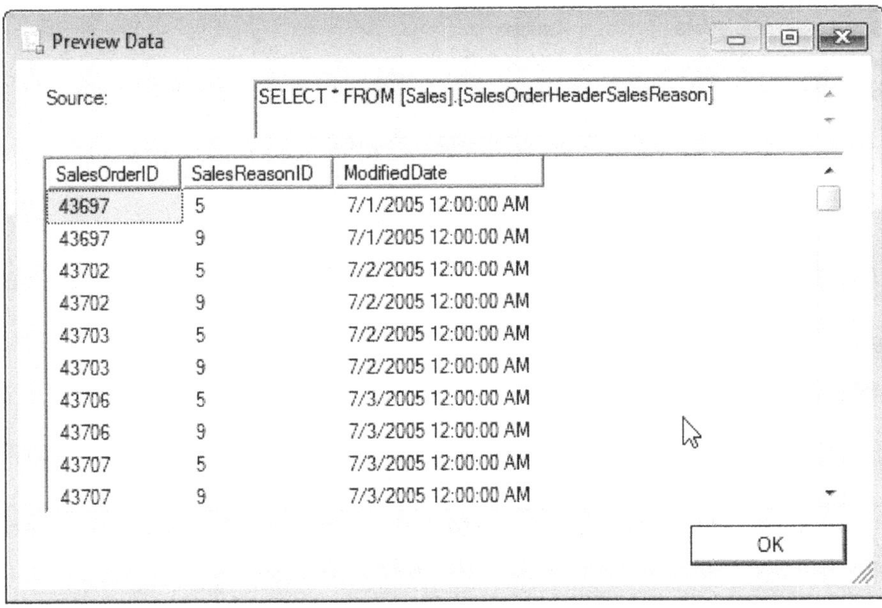
Preview Data
Source:
SELECT * FROM [Sales].[SalesOrderHeaderSalesReason]
SalesOrderID
SalesReasonID
ModifiedDate
43697 5 7/1/2005 12:00:00 AM
43697 9 7/1/2005 12:00:00 AM
43702 5 7/2/2005 12:00:00 AM
43702 9 7/2/2005 12:00:00 AM
43703 5 7/2/2005 12:00:00 AM
43703 9 7/2/2005 12:00:00 AM
43706 5 7/3/2005 12:00:00 AM
43706 9 7/3/2005 12:00:00 AM
43707 5 7/3/2005 12:00:00 AM
43707 9 7/3/2005 12:00:00 AM
OK

A Computed Column Must Be Mapped with IGNORE

The following page is nor related to the current table transfer, it is just an explanation using the Production.Workorder table tranfer process.

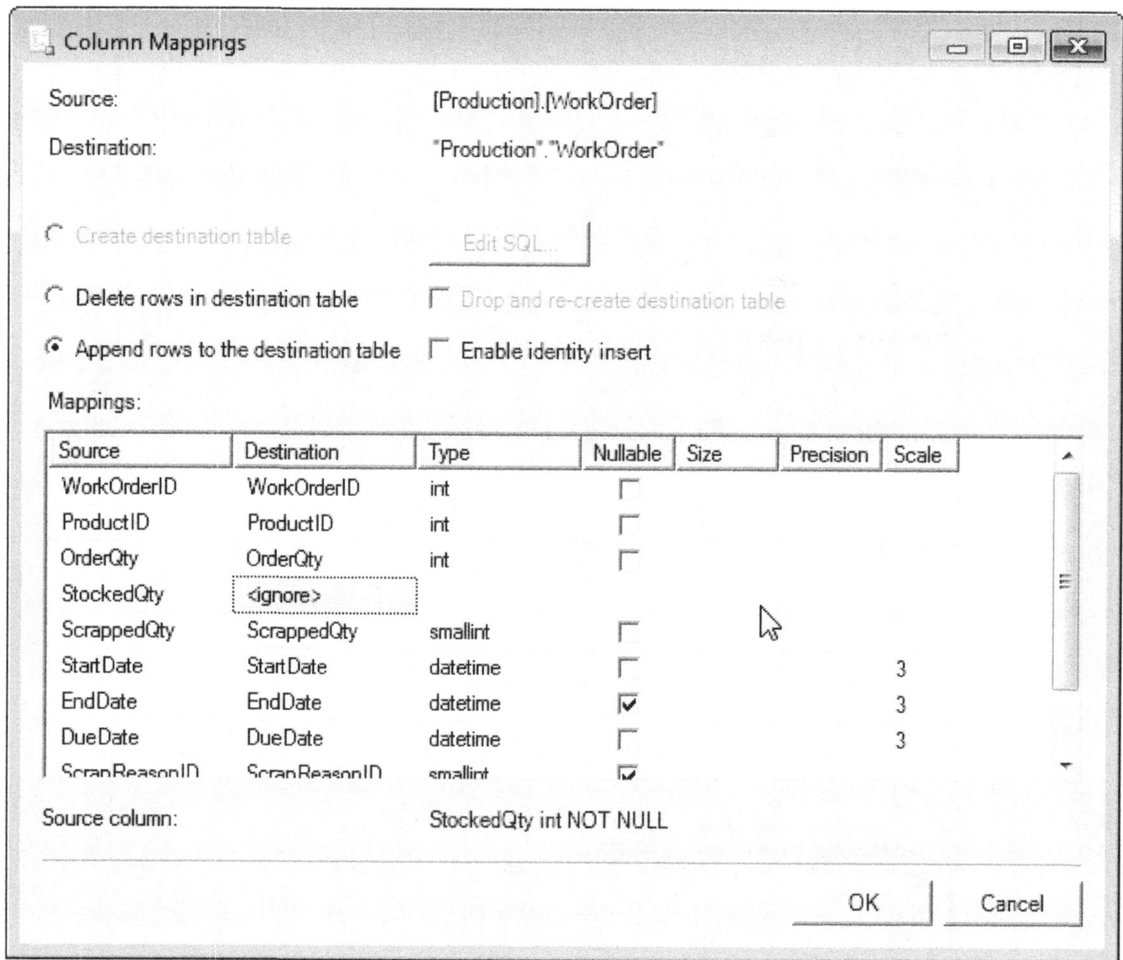

Creating Clustered Index

Create clustered index by script:

```
CREATE CLUSTERED INDEX idxDBLog on databaselog(PostTime, DatabaseUser, Event);
```

A table can only have 1 clustered index and 0 to many nonclustered indexes. Clustered index is a requirement in SQL Azure, exception temporary tables.

Save & Run Options Page

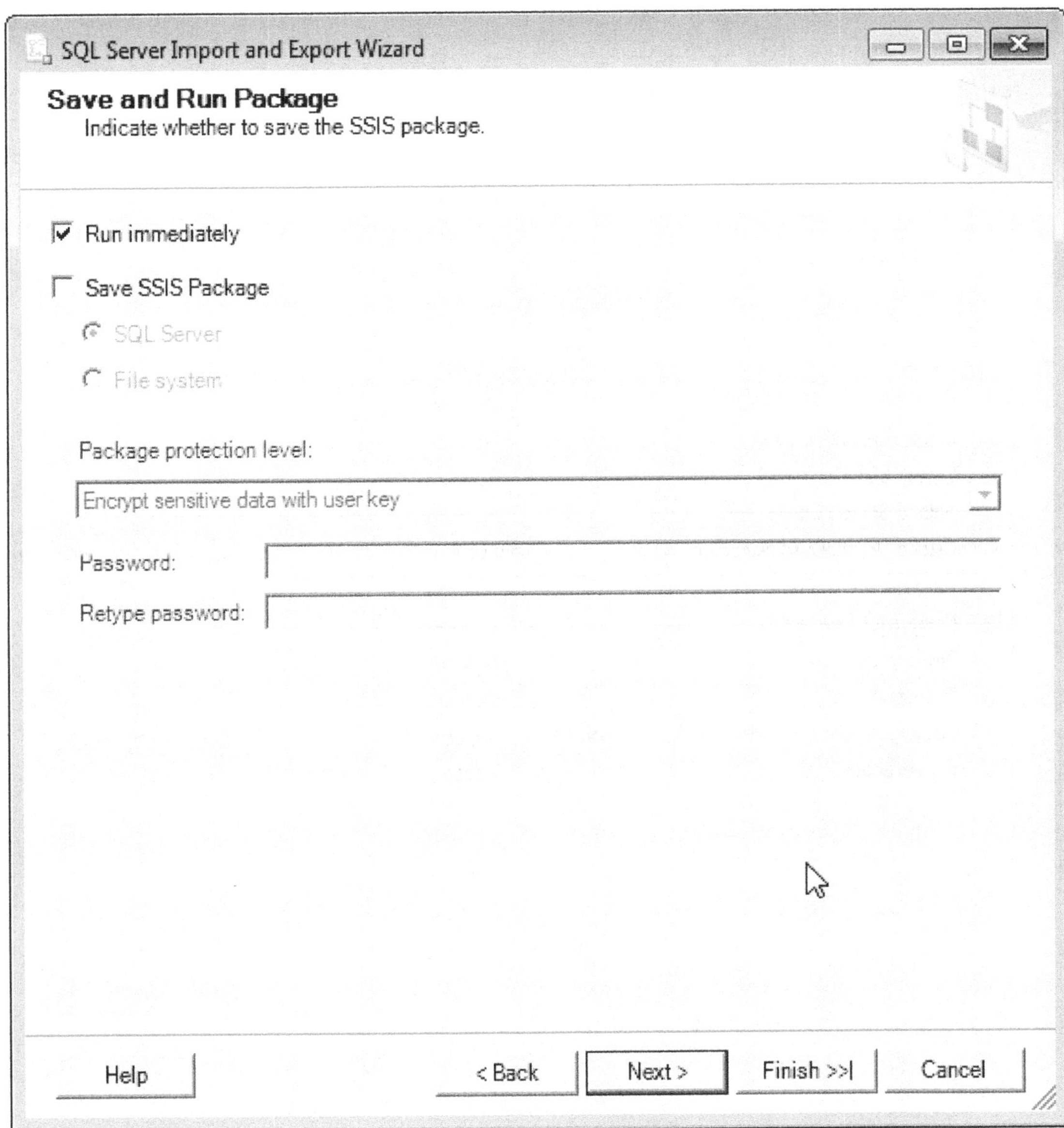

Finish & Execution Page

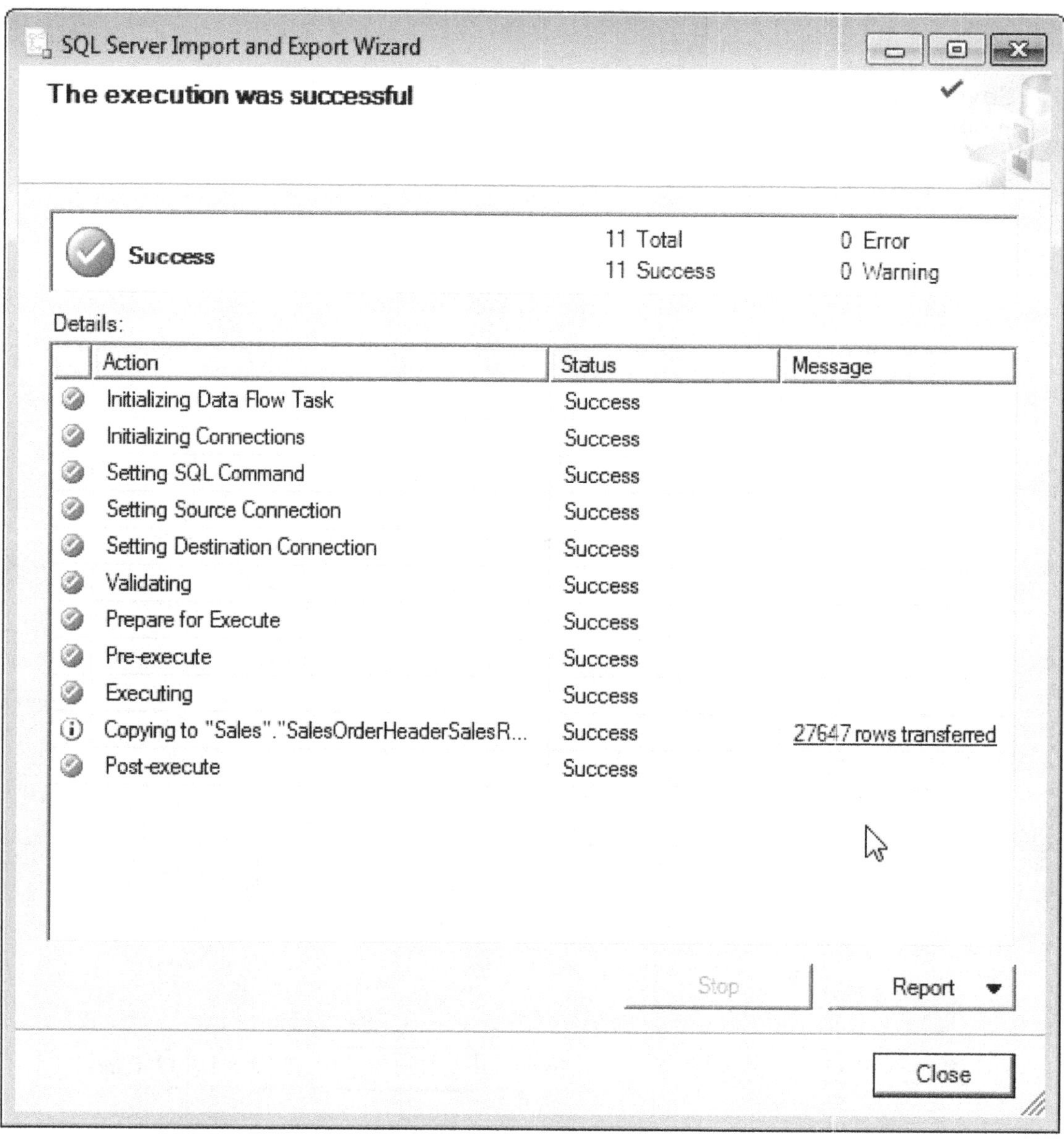

AdventureWorks2012 Final Tables Population

Most of the tables were populated by the upload utility, the rest by SQL Server Import and Export Wizard.

TableName	TableType	Population
Sales.SalesOrderDetail	BASE TABLE	121317
Production.TransactionHistory	BASE TABLE	113443
Production.TransactionHistoryArchive	BASE TABLE	89253
Production.WorkOrder	BASE TABLE	72591
Production.WorkOrderRouting	BASE TABLE	67131
Sales.SalesOrderHeader	BASE TABLE	31465
Sales.SalesOrderHeaderSalesReason	BASE TABLE	27647
Person.BusinessEntity	BASE TABLE	20777
Person.Password	BASE TABLE	19972
Person.Person	BASE TABLE	19972
Person.PersonPhone	BASE TABLE	19972
Person.EmailAddress	BASE TABLE	19972
Sales.Customer	BASE TABLE	19820
Person.Address	BASE TABLE	19614
Person.BusinessEntityAddress	BASE TABLE	19614
Sales.PersonCreditCard	BASE TABLE	19118
Sales.CreditCard	BASE TABLE	19118
Sales.CurrencyRate	BASE TABLE	13532
Purchasing.PurchaseOrderDetail	BASE TABLE	8845
Purchasing.PurchaseOrderHeader	BASE TABLE	4012
Production.BillOfMaterials	BASE TABLE	2679
Production.ProductInventory	BASE TABLE	1069
Person.BusinessEntityContact	BASE TABLE	909
Production.ProductDescription	BASE TABLE	762
Production.ProductModelProductDescriptionCulture	BASE TABLE	762
Sales.Store	BASE TABLE	701
Sales.SpecialOfferProduct	BASE TABLE	538
Production.Product	BASE TABLE	504
Production.ProductProductPhoto	BASE TABLE	504
Purchasing.ProductVendor	BASE TABLE	460
Production.ProductListPriceHistory	BASE TABLE	395
Production.ProductCostHistory	BASE TABLE	395
HumanResources.EmployeePayHistory	BASE TABLE	316
HumanResources.EmployeeDepartmentHistory	BASE TABLE	296
HumanResources.Employee	BASE TABLE	290

Person.CountryRegion	BASE TABLE	238
Person.StateProvince	BASE TABLE	181
Sales.SalesPersonQuotaHistory	BASE TABLE	163
Production.ProductModel	BASE TABLE	128
Sales.CountryRegionCurrency	BASE TABLE	109
Sales.Currency	BASE TABLE	105
Purchasing.Vendor	BASE TABLE	104
Production.ProductPhoto	BASE TABLE	101
Production.UnitMeasure	BASE TABLE	38
Production.ProductSubcategory	BASE TABLE	37
Production.ProductDocument	BASE TABLE	32
Sales.SalesTaxRate	BASE TABLE	29
Person.ContactType	BASE TABLE	20
Sales.SalesPerson	BASE TABLE	17
Sales.SalesTerritoryHistory	BASE TABLE	17
HumanResources.Department	BASE TABLE	16
Sales.SpecialOffer	BASE TABLE	16
Production.ScrapReason	BASE TABLE	16
Production.Location	BASE TABLE	14
Production.Document	BASE TABLE	13
HumanResources.JobCandidate	BASE TABLE	13
Sales.SalesTerritory	BASE TABLE	10
Sales.SalesReason	BASE TABLE	10
Production.Culture	BASE TABLE	8
Production.ProductModelIllustration	BASE TABLE	7
Person.AddressType	BASE TABLE	6
Production.Illustration	BASE TABLE	5
Purchasing.ShipMethod	BASE TABLE	5
Production.ProductCategory	BASE TABLE	4
Production.ProductReview	BASE TABLE	4
Person.PhoneNumberType	BASE TABLE	3
Sales.ShoppingCartItem	BASE TABLE	3
HumanResources.Shift	BASE TABLE	3
dbo.AWBuildVersion	BASE TABLE	1
dbo.DatabaseLog	BASE TABLE	0
dbo.ErrorLog	BASE TABLE	0

AdventureWorksDWAZ2008R2 Tables Population

The upload utility worked without error.

TableName	TableType	Population
dbo.FactInternetSalesReason	BASE TABLE	63877
dbo.FactResellerSales	BASE TABLE	60253
dbo.FactInternetSales	BASE TABLE	59800
dbo.FactFinance	BASE TABLE	39019
dbo.DimCustomer	BASE TABLE	18301
dbo.FactAdditionalInternationalProductDescription	BASE TABLE	15018
dbo.FactCurrencyRate	BASE TABLE	14123
dbo.FactSurveyResponse	BASE TABLE	2700
dbo.ProspectiveBuyer	BASE TABLE	2039
dbo.DimDate	BASE TABLE	1177
dbo.DimReseller	BASE TABLE	695
dbo.DimGeography	BASE TABLE	649
dbo.DimProduct	BASE TABLE	600
dbo.DimEmployee	BASE TABLE	294
dbo.FactSalesQuota	BASE TABLE	162
dbo.FactCallCenter	BASE TABLE	119
dbo.DimCurrency	BASE TABLE	104
dbo.DimAccount	BASE TABLE	99
dbo.DimProductSubcategory	BASE TABLE	37
dbo.DimPromotion	BASE TABLE	16
dbo.DimOrganization	BASE TABLE	14
dbo.DimSalesTerritory	BASE TABLE	11
dbo.DimSalesReason	BASE TABLE	10
dbo.DimDepartmentGroup	BASE TABLE	7
dbo.DimProductCategory	BASE TABLE	4
dbo.DimScenario	BASE TABLE	3
dbo.AdventureWorksDWBuildVersion	BASE TABLE	1
dbo.DatabaseLog	BASE TABLE	0

AdventureWorksLTAZ2008R2 Tables Population

The upload did not have any error.

TableName	TableType	Population
SalesLT.Customer	BASE TABLE	839
SalesLT.ProductDescription	BASE TABLE	755
SalesLT.ProductModelProductDescription	BASE TABLE	755
SalesLT.SalesOrderDetail	BASE TABLE	537
SalesLT.Address	BASE TABLE	446
SalesLT.CustomerAddress	BASE TABLE	413
SalesLT.Product	BASE TABLE	293
SalesLT.ProductModel	BASE TABLE	127
SalesLT.ProductCategory	BASE TABLE	41
SalesLT.SalesOrderHeader	BASE TABLE	32
dbo.BuildVersion	BASE TABLE	1
dbo.ErrorLog	BASE TABLE	0

Migrate pubs & Northwind to Azure SQL Server

First download the sample databases.

Download Center: **Northwind and pubs Sample Databases for SQL Server 2000**
http://www.microsoft.com/en-us/download/details.aspx?id=23654

Paste instpubs.sql script into a Query Editor window. It requires manual fixes to make it work. For example, adding PRIMARY KEY with clustered index to some tables prior to population or sp_addtype had to be replaced with CREATE TYPE.

pubs tables population

TableName	TableType	Population
dbo.roysched	BASE TABLE	86
dbo.employee	BASE TABLE	43
dbo.jobs	BASE TABLE	28
dbo.titleauthor	BASE TABLE	25
dbo.authors	BASE TABLE	23
dbo.sales	BASE TABLE	21
dbo.titles	BASE TABLE	18
dbo.pub_info	BASE TABLE	8
dbo.publishers	BASE TABLE	8
dbo.stores	BASE TABLE	6
dbo.discounts	BASE TABLE	3

Installing instnwnd.sql Script

Similarly converting the script, the biggest change was adding PRIMARY KEY with clustered index to some (secondary) tables.

Northwind tables population

TableName	TableType	Population
dbo.Order Details	BASE TABLE	2155
dbo.Orders	BASE TABLE	830
dbo.Customers	BASE TABLE	91
dbo.Products	BASE TABLE	77
dbo.Territories	BASE TABLE	53
dbo.EmployeeTerritories	BASE TABLE	49
dbo.Suppliers	BASE TABLE	29
dbo.Employees	BASE TABLE	9
dbo.Categories	BASE TABLE	8
dbo.Region	BASE TABLE	4
dbo.Shippers	BASE TABLE	3
dbo.CustomerCustomerDemo	BASE TABLE	0
dbo.CustomerDemographics	BASE TABLE	0

Discovering the New SQL Azure Instance

We can start probing the new SQL Server instance in Query Editor & Object Explorer.

```
SELECT @@VERSION;
-- Microsoft SQL Azure (RTM) - 11.0.2154.0 ....
```

```
SELECT @@SERVERNAME;
-- llgzjlxx8r
```

```
-- SS Version, Level (service pack), Edition
SELECT    CONCAT ('Microsoft SQL Azure ',convert(varchar, SERVERPROPERTY('ProductVersion') ), ' -- ',
          convert(varchar, SERVERPROPERTY('ProductLevel') ), ' -- ',convert(varchar, SERVERPROPERTY('Edition') ));
-- Microsoft SQL Azure 11.0.2295.0 -- RTM -- SQL Azure
```

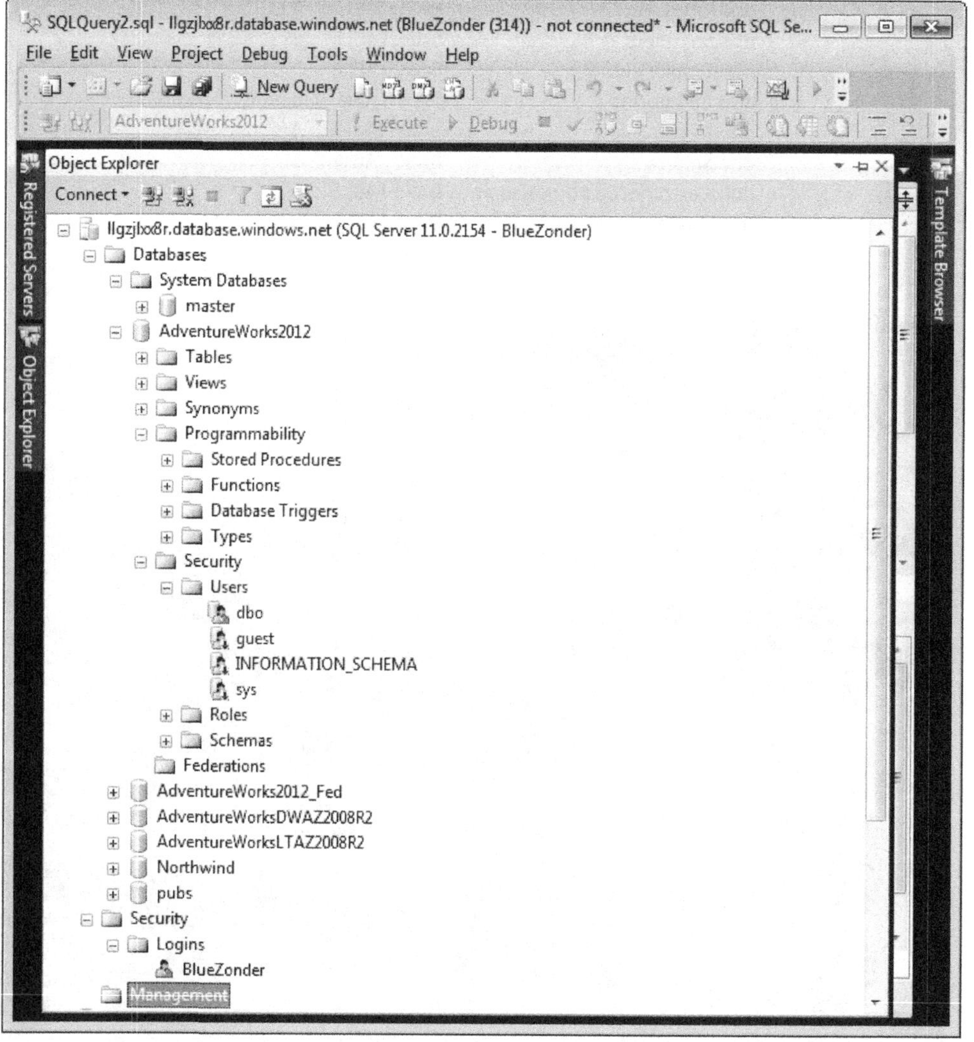

Connecting to 2 SQL Server Instances Simultaneously

SSMS Object Explorer support multiple SS instances connections. Warning: **Production, QA and Development SS instances may look similar, an opportunity to get confused and carry out actions on the wrong server**. Best prevention: **take regular database backups and connect only to one SQL Server instance at one time**.

The first connection is the SQL Azure instance, the second is the SQL Server default instance.

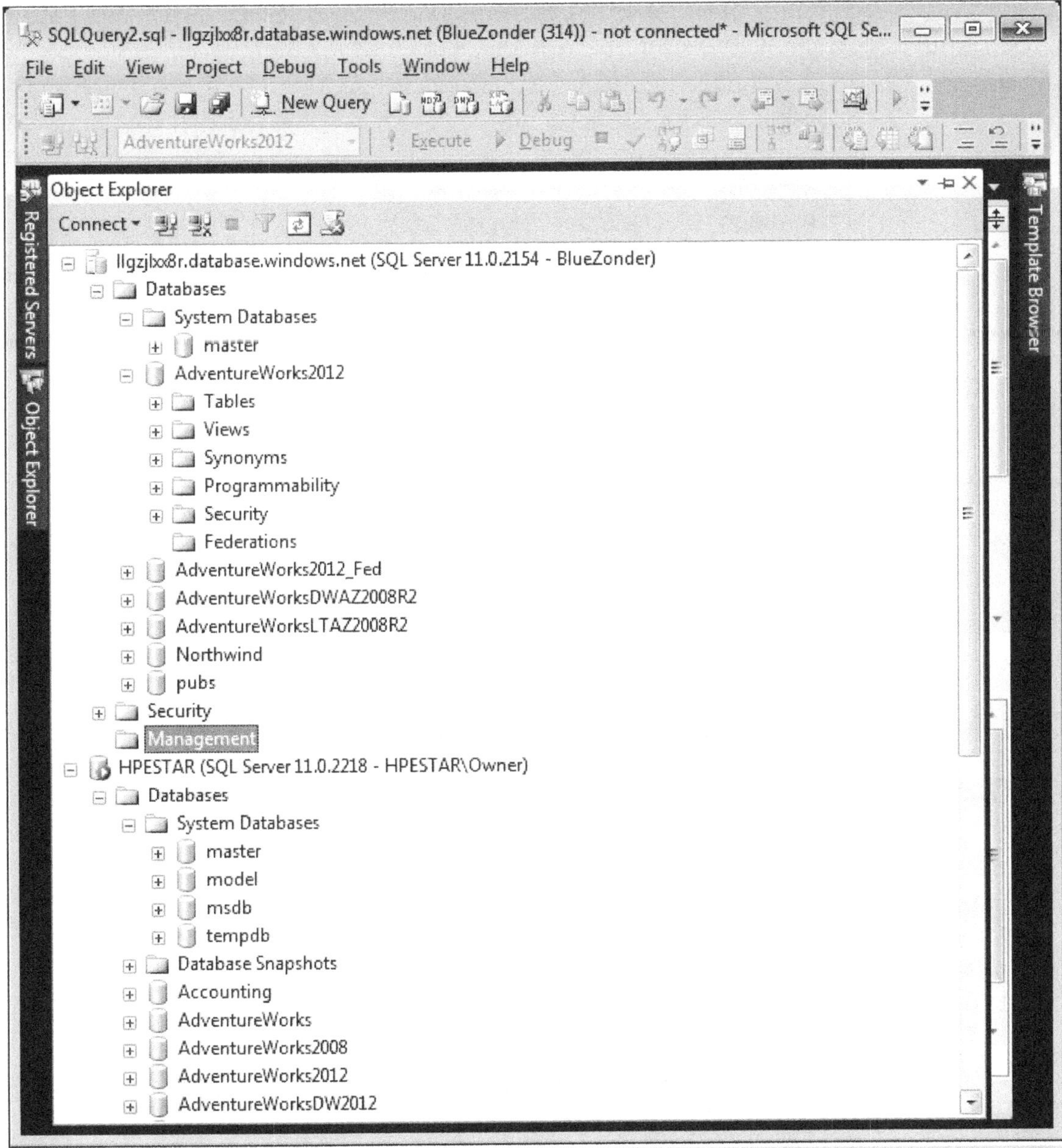

Linked Server to Windows Azure SQL Database

Windows Azure SQL Database server can be configured as linked server from a on-premises SQL Server 2012 (not supported the reverse way). First we have to setup a system DSN.

1. Control Panel, System & Security, Administrative Tools, Data Sources(ODBC), System DSN

2. Add SQL Server Native Client 11.0, "AzureDSN", yourserver. database.windows.net,1433

3. SQL Server authentication: yourazuresqllogin, yourazuresqlpassword

4. Enter default database AdventureWorks2012, Test connection & click "OK"

T-SQL Script for Linked Server Setup in On-Premises SQL Serv er

```
USE master;                    -- Linked server to Windows Azure SQL Database
EXEC master.dbo.sp_addlinkedserver @server = N'ALPHA_AZURE',
@srvproduct=N'Microsoft OLE DB Provider for ODBC Driver',
@provider=N'MSDASQL', @datasrc='AzureDSN', @location='localhost',
@catalog='AdventureWorks2012';

EXEC master.dbo.sp_addlinkedsrvlogin @rmtsrvname=N'ALPHA_AZURE', @useself=N'False',
@locallogin=NULL, @rmtuser='yourazuresqllogin', @rmtpassword='yourazuresqlpassword';
```

Querying Azure SQL Database via Linked Server

The queries are executed on-premises SQL Server. The data is from Azure SQL Database.

Blog: **Linked Server and Distributed Queries against Windows Azure SQL Database**
http://blogs.msdn.com/b/windowsazure/archive/2012/09/19/announcing-updates-to-windows-azure-sql-database.aspx

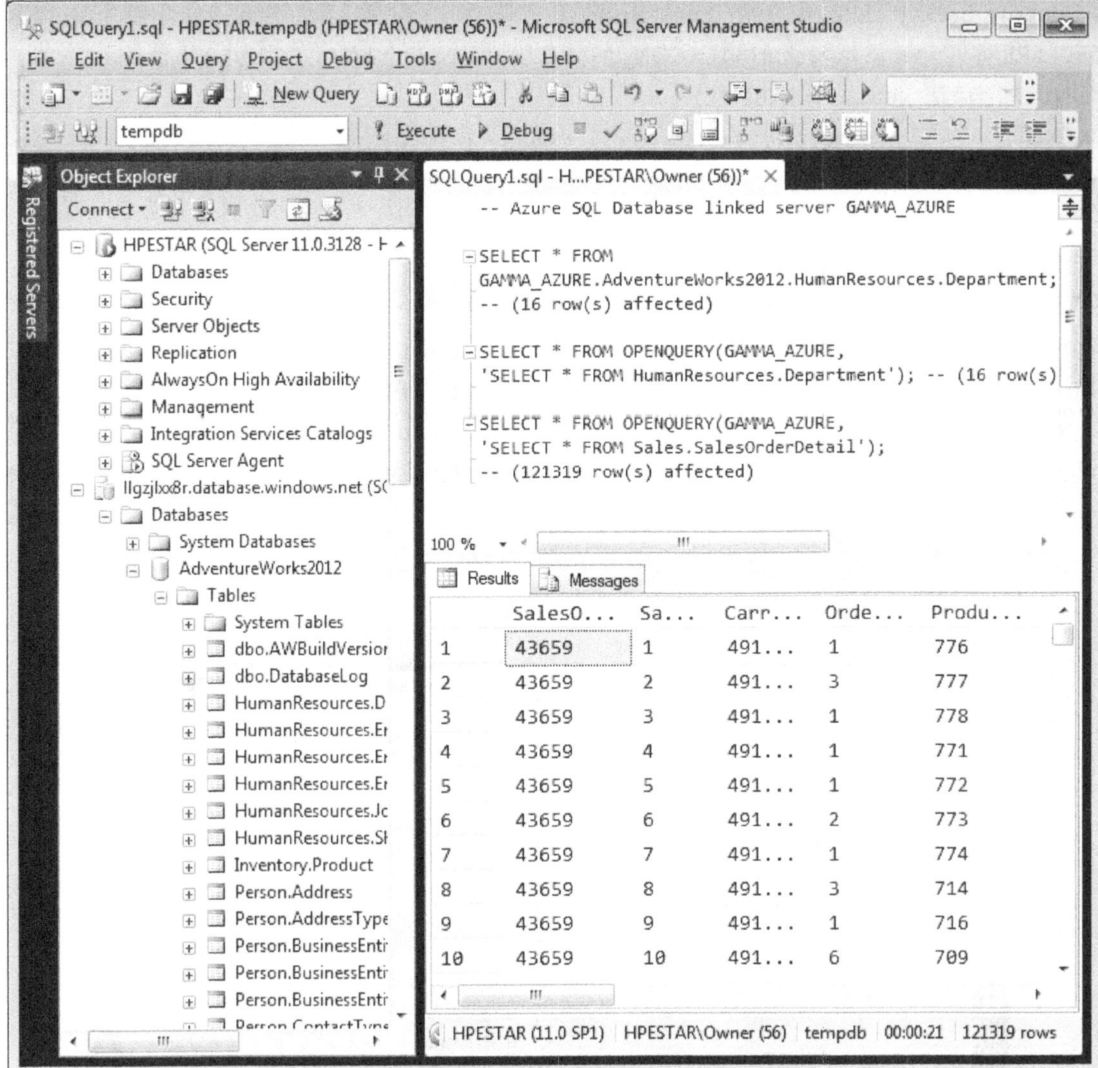

Note: At the time of book writing some table queries returned errors. Example: HumanResources. Shift table with time(7) data type.

SQL Server 2012 BACKUP DATABASE Command

SQL Server 2012 database backup command; the backup filename can be changed at will to reflect the backup date.

```
BACKUP DATABASE [AdventureWorks2012] TO  DISK = N'F:\data\backup\AW20161023.bak';
```

```
-- Dynamic backup filename with datestamp
DECLARE @Filename nvarchar(64) = CONCAT(N'F:\data\backup\AW', CONVERT(varchar,
CONVERT(DATE, getdate())),'.bak');
BACKUP DATABASE [AdventureWorks2012] TO  DISK = @Filename;
-- AW2018-08-23.bak
```

Export Data-tier Application - Azure SQL

The export file (.bacpac) includes both the definitions of the objects in the database and all of the data in the tables. Export launching sequence. Windows Azure SQL Database Import / Export operations can copy databases between Windows Azure SQL Database servers, or can migrate databases between the SQL Server Database Engine and Windows Azure SQL Database.

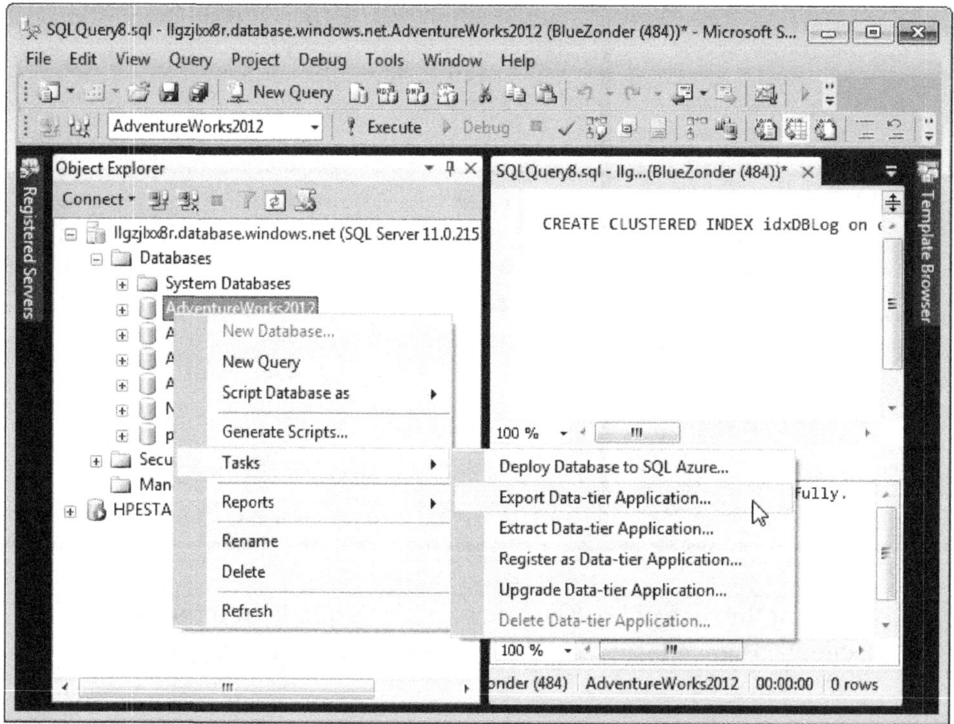

Introduction Page

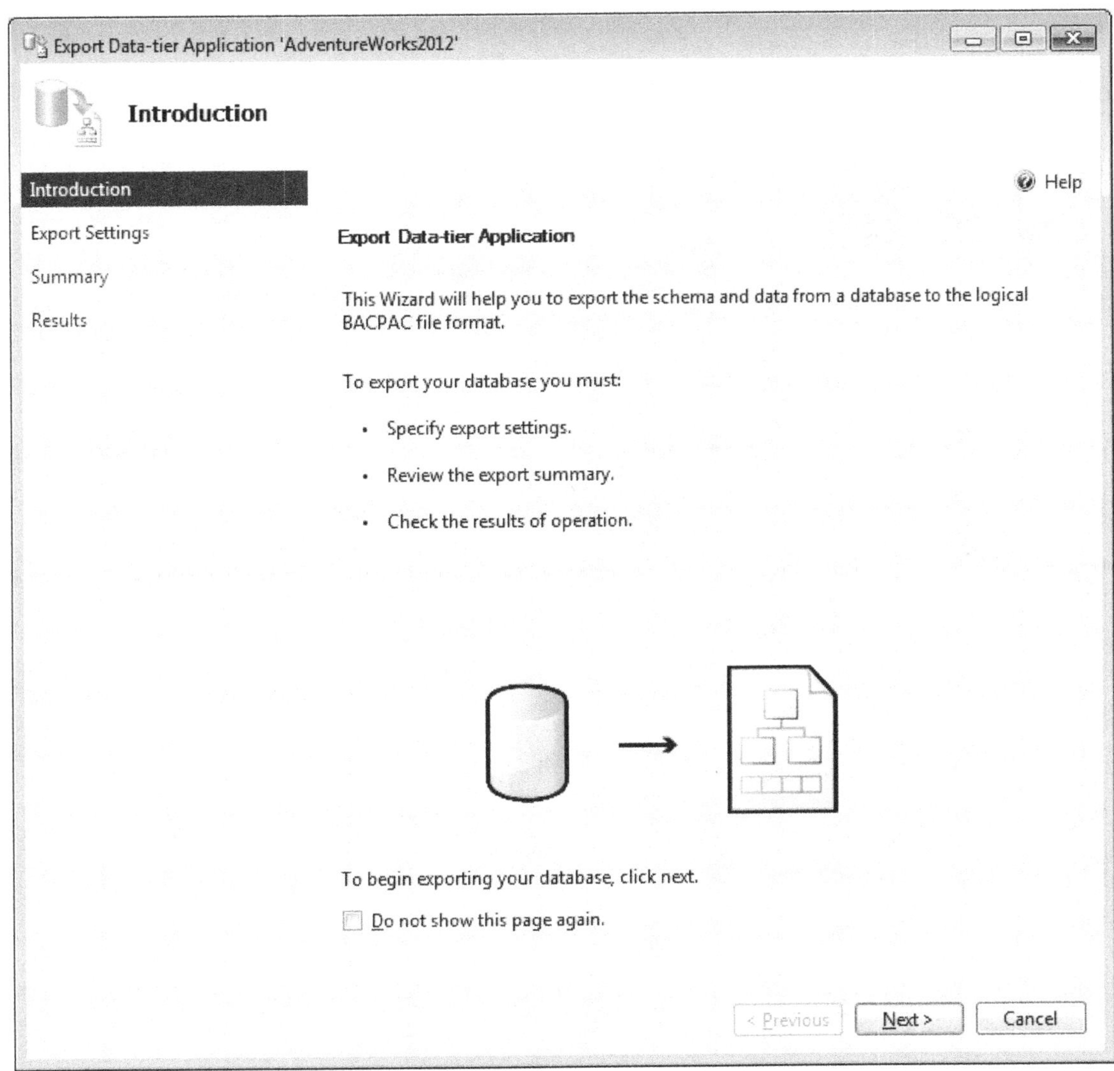

Export Settings

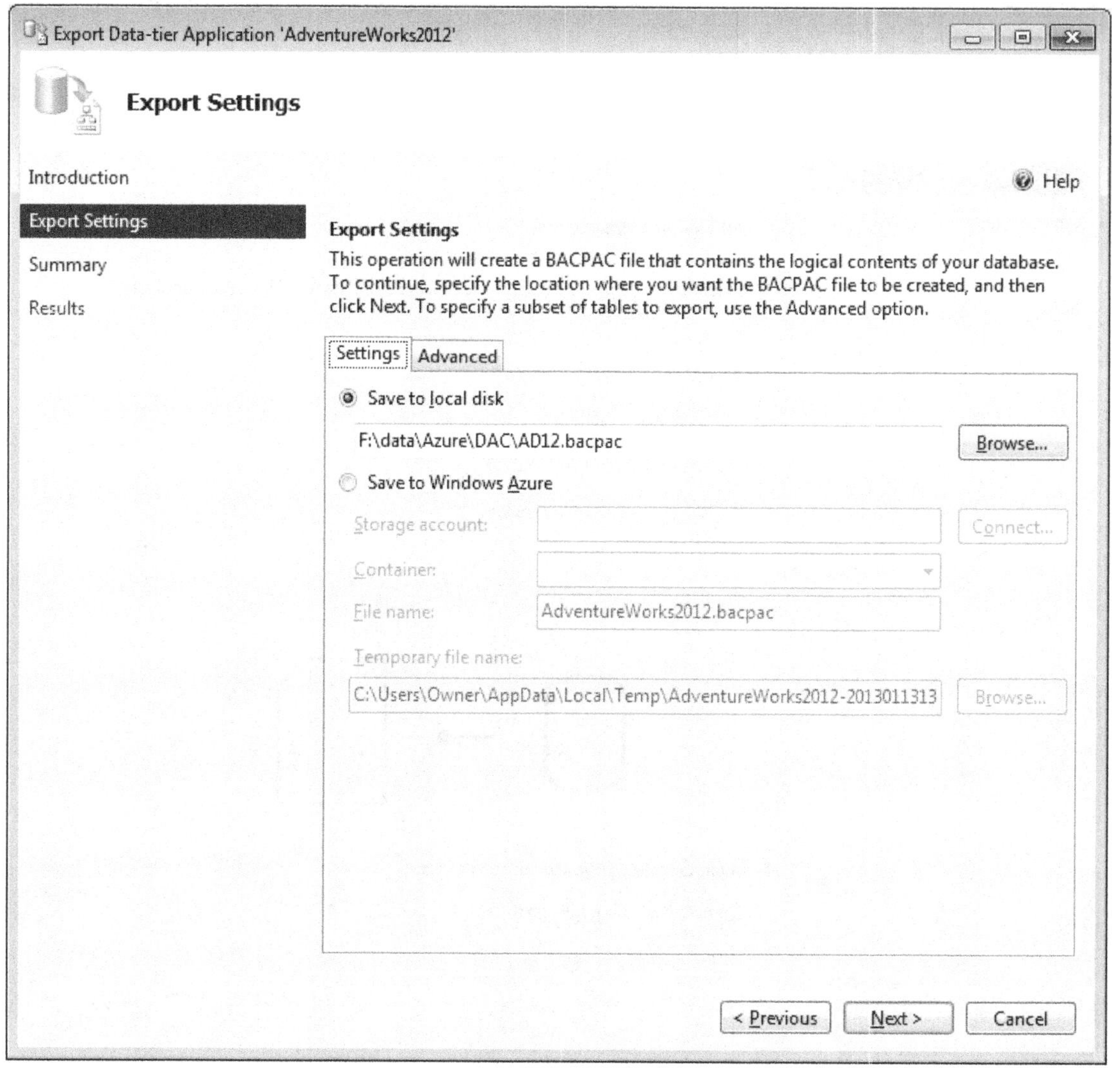

Advanced Export Settings

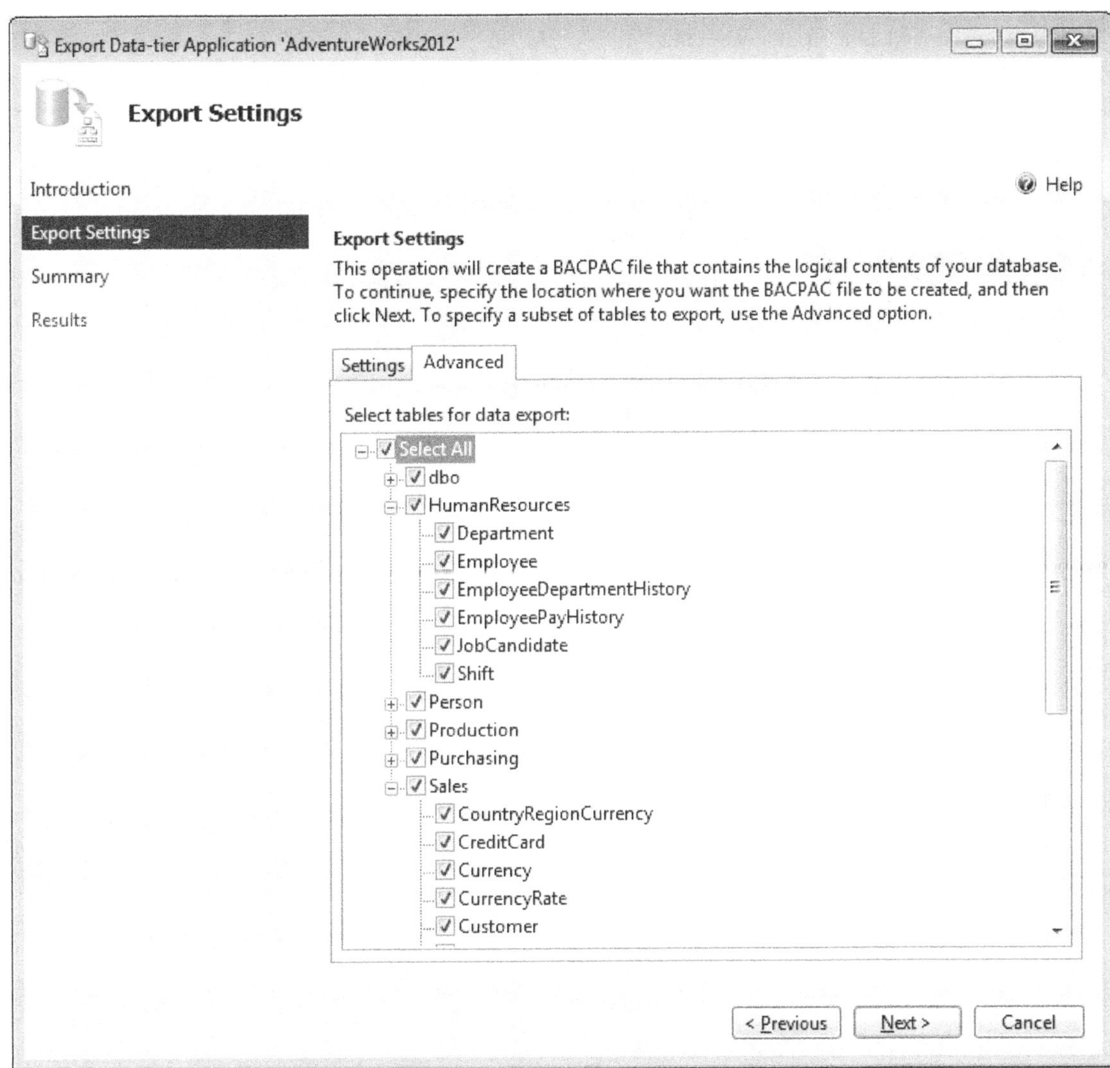

Summary

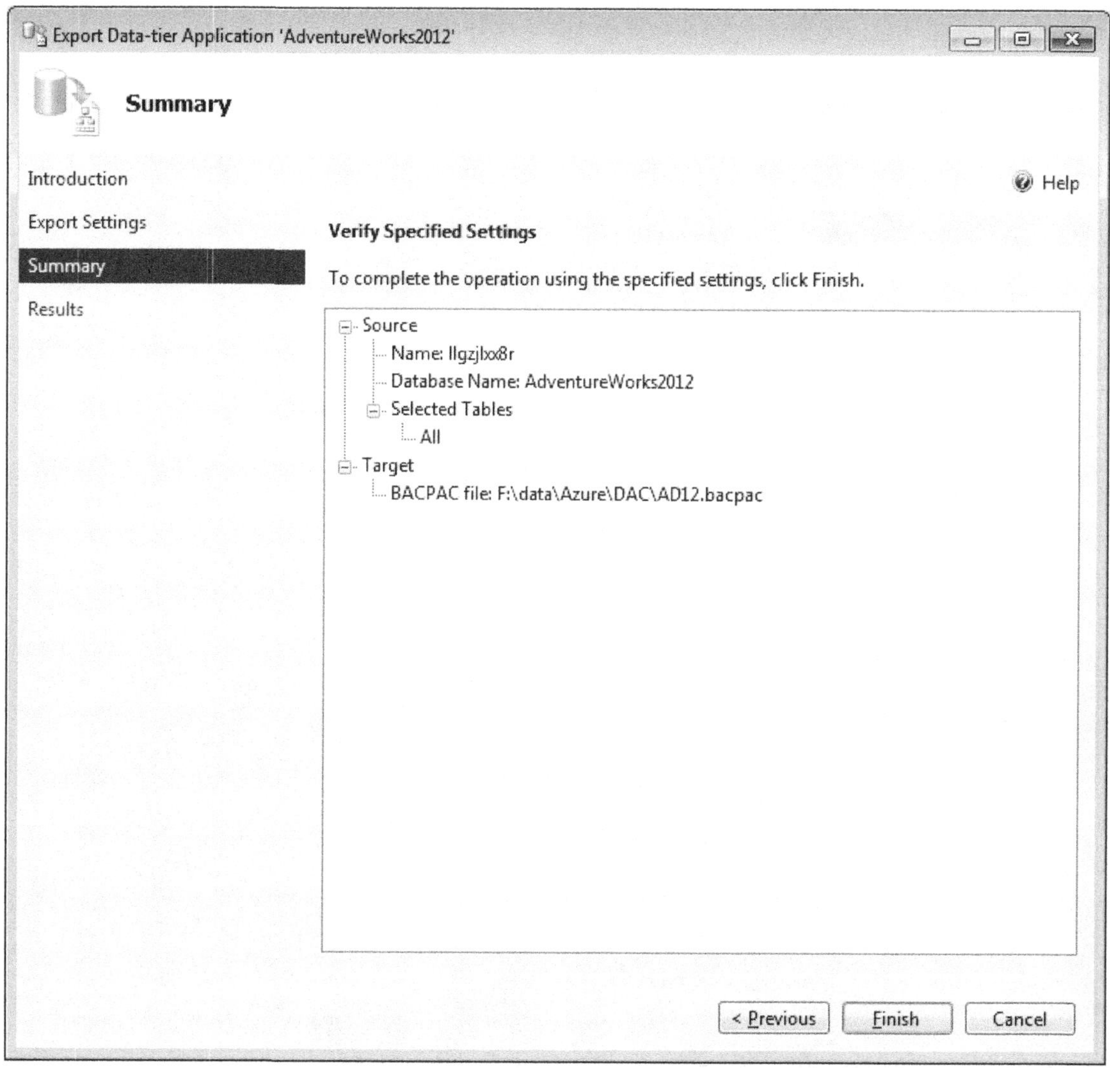
Export Data-tier Application 'AdventureWorks2012'
Summary
Introduction
Export Settings
Summary
Results
Help
Verify Specified Settings
To complete the operation using the specified settings, click Finish.
Source
Name: llgzjlxx8r
Database Name: AdventureWorks2012
Selected Tables
All
Target
BACPAC file: F:\data\Azure\DAC\AD12.bacpac
< Previous
Finish
Cancel

Progress

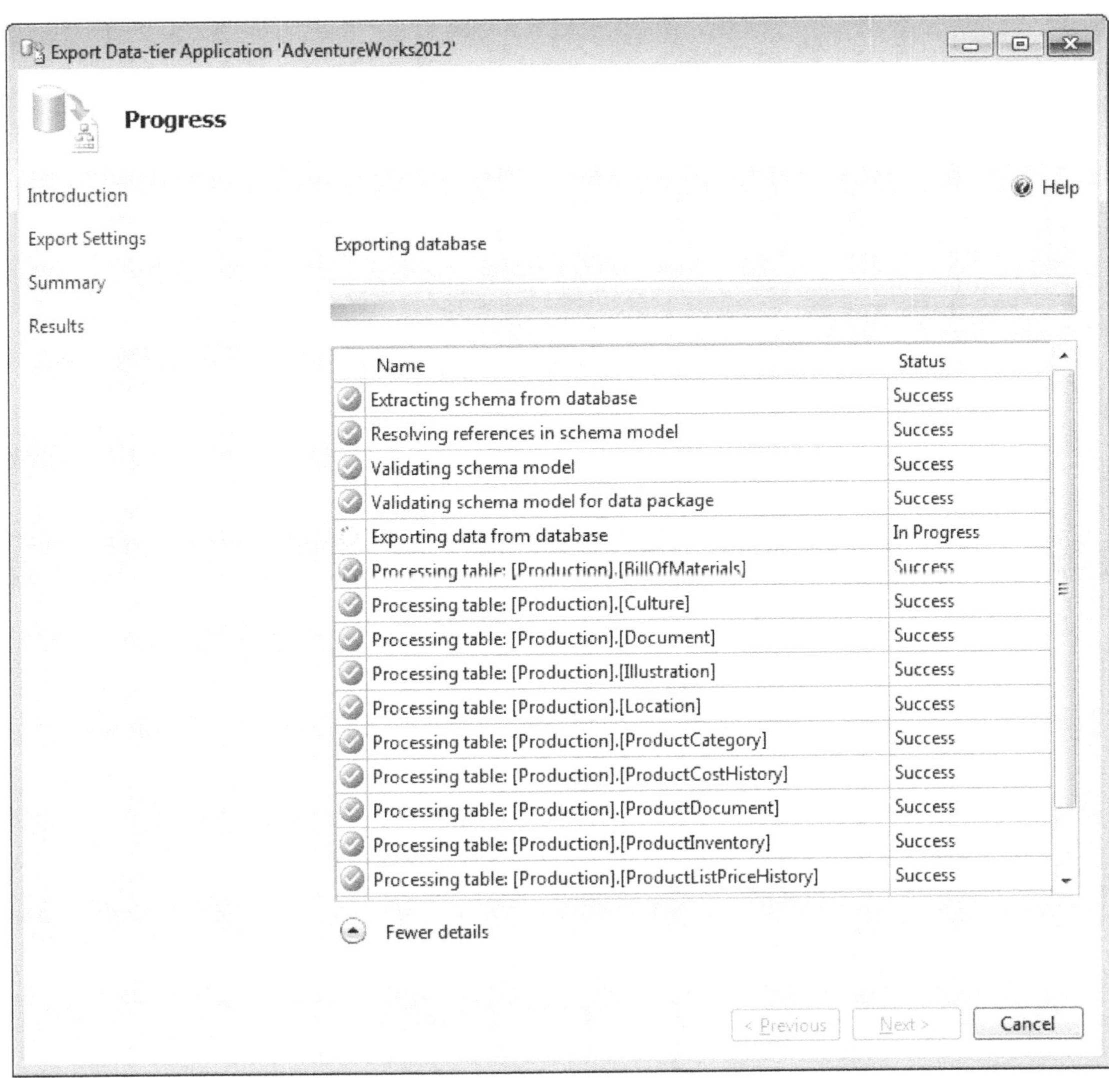
Export Data-tier Application 'AdventureWorks2012'
Progress
Introduction
Export Settings
Summary
Results
Help
Exporting database
Name
Status
Extracting schema from database
Success
Resolving references in schema model
Success
Validating schema model
Success
Validating schema model for data package
Success
Exporting data from database
In Progress
Processing table: [Production].[BillOfMaterials]
Success
Processing table: [Production].[Culture]
Success
Processing table: [Production].[Document]
Success
Processing table: [Production].[Illustration]
Success
Processing table: [Production].[Location]
Success
Processing table: [Production].[ProductCategory]
Success
Processing table: [Production].[ProductCostHistory]
Success
Processing table: [Production].[ProductDocument]
Success
Processing table: [Production].[ProductInventory]
Success
Processing table: [Production].[ProductListPriceHistory]
Success
Fewer details
< Previous
Next >
Cancel

Operation Complete - Elapsed Time 2 Minutes

Summary:

Name	Result
Processing table: [Sales].[Customer]	Success
Processing table: [HumanResources].[JobCandidate]	Success
Processing table: [Production].[ProductModel]	Success
Processing table: [Sales].[SalesPerson]	Success
Processing table: [Sales].[SalesTerritory]	Success
Processing table: [Sales].[SalesOrderHeader]	Success
Processing table: [Production].[ProductDescription]	Success
Processing table: [Production].[ProductModelProductDescriptionCultu...	Success
Processing table: [Production].[Product]	Success
Processing table:.[AWBuildVersion]	Success
Processing table:.[DatabaseLog]	Success
Processing table:.[ErrorLog]	Success
Processing table: [HumanResources].[EmployeePayHistory]	Success
Processing table: [Person].[BusinessEntity]	Success
Processing table: [Person].[Password]	Success

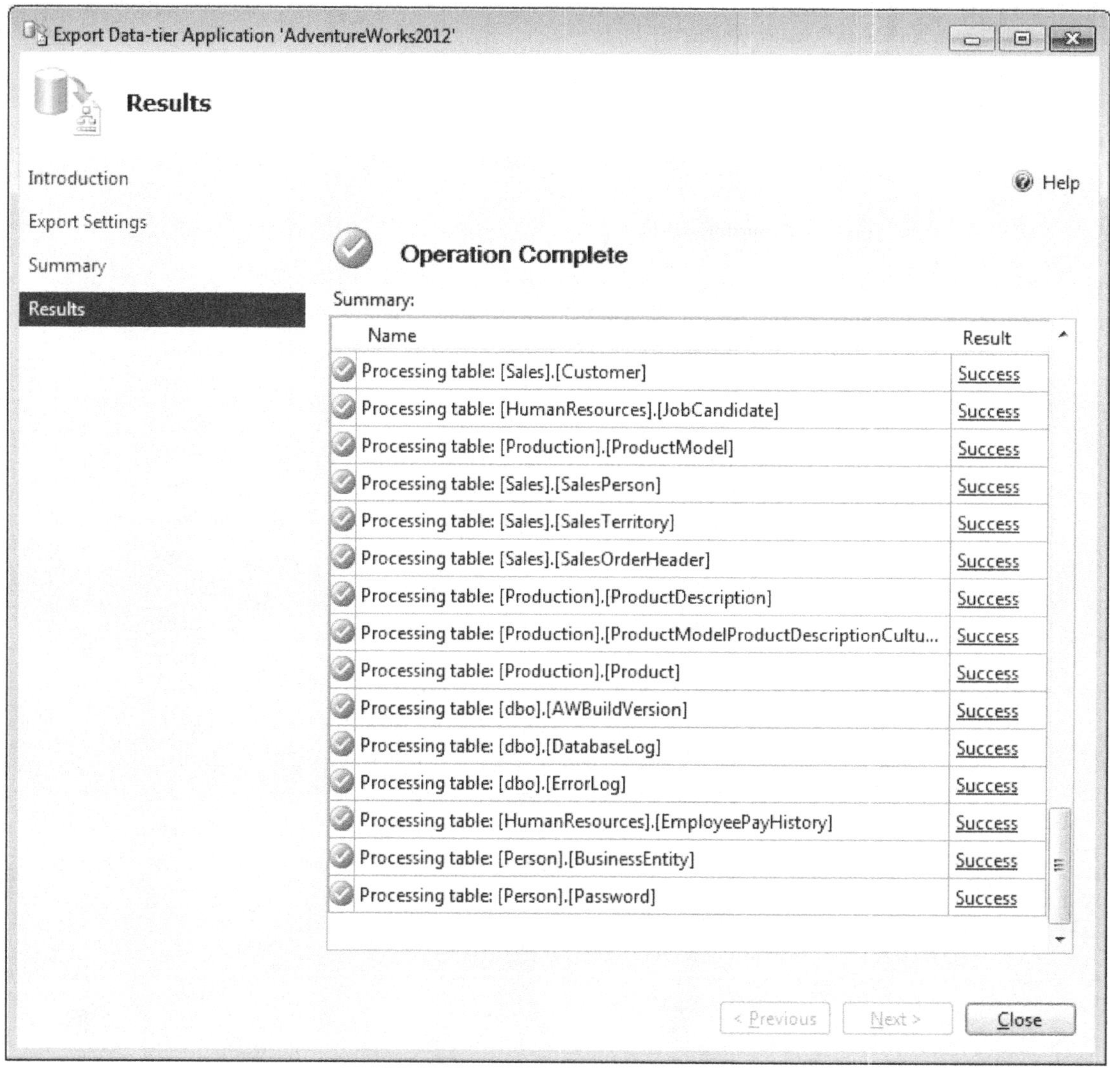

Import Data-tier Application

Import recreates the database from the .bacpac file.

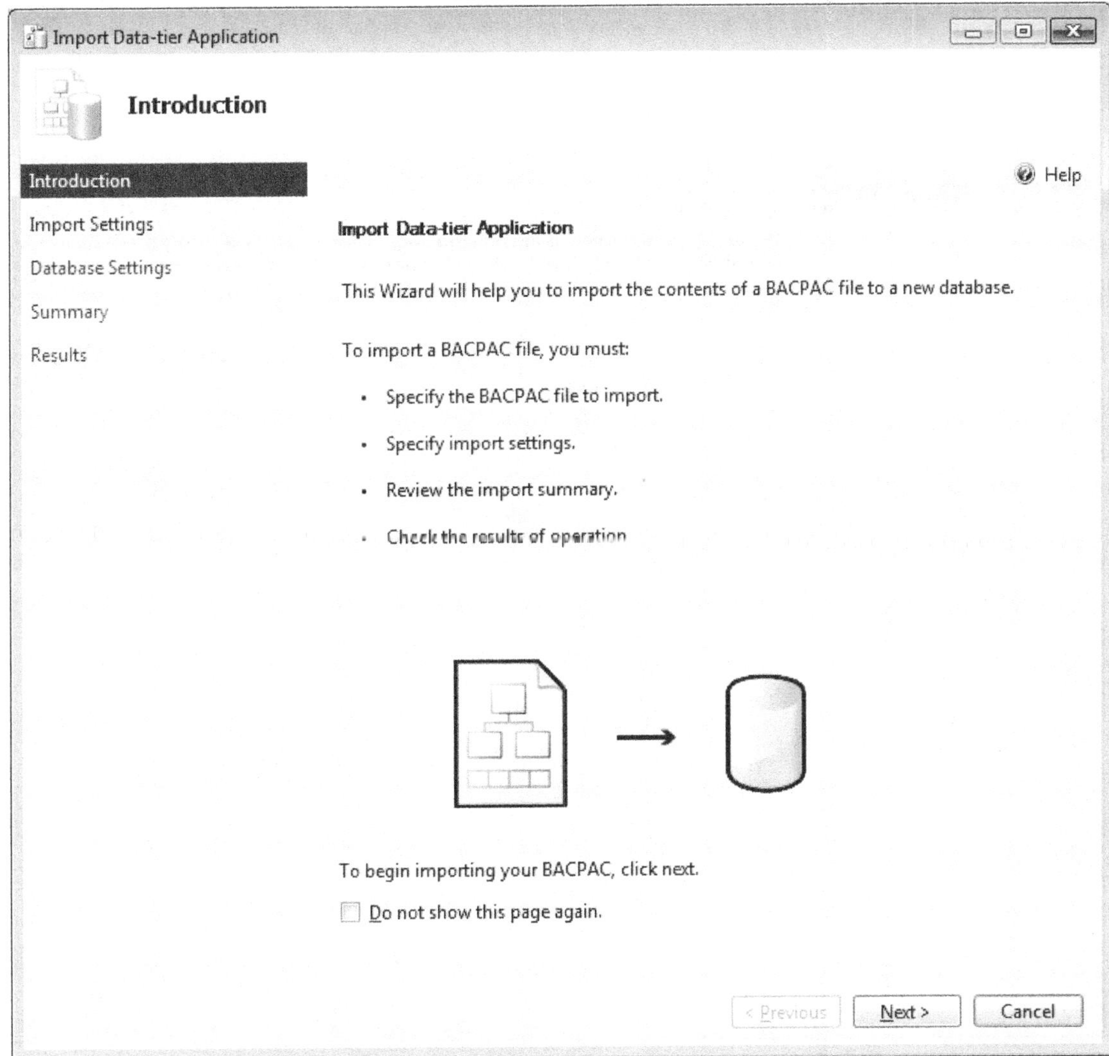

Import Settings

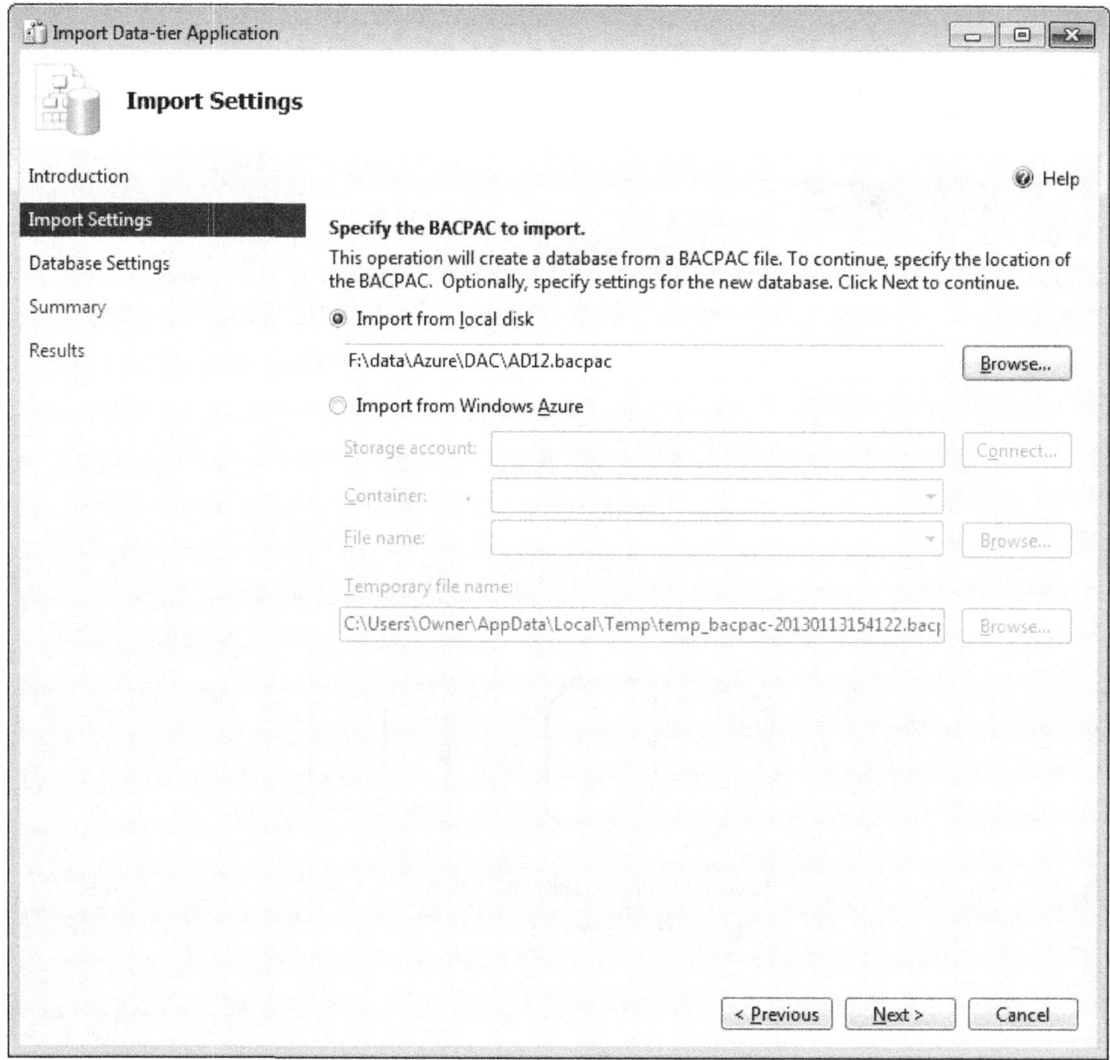

Database Settings

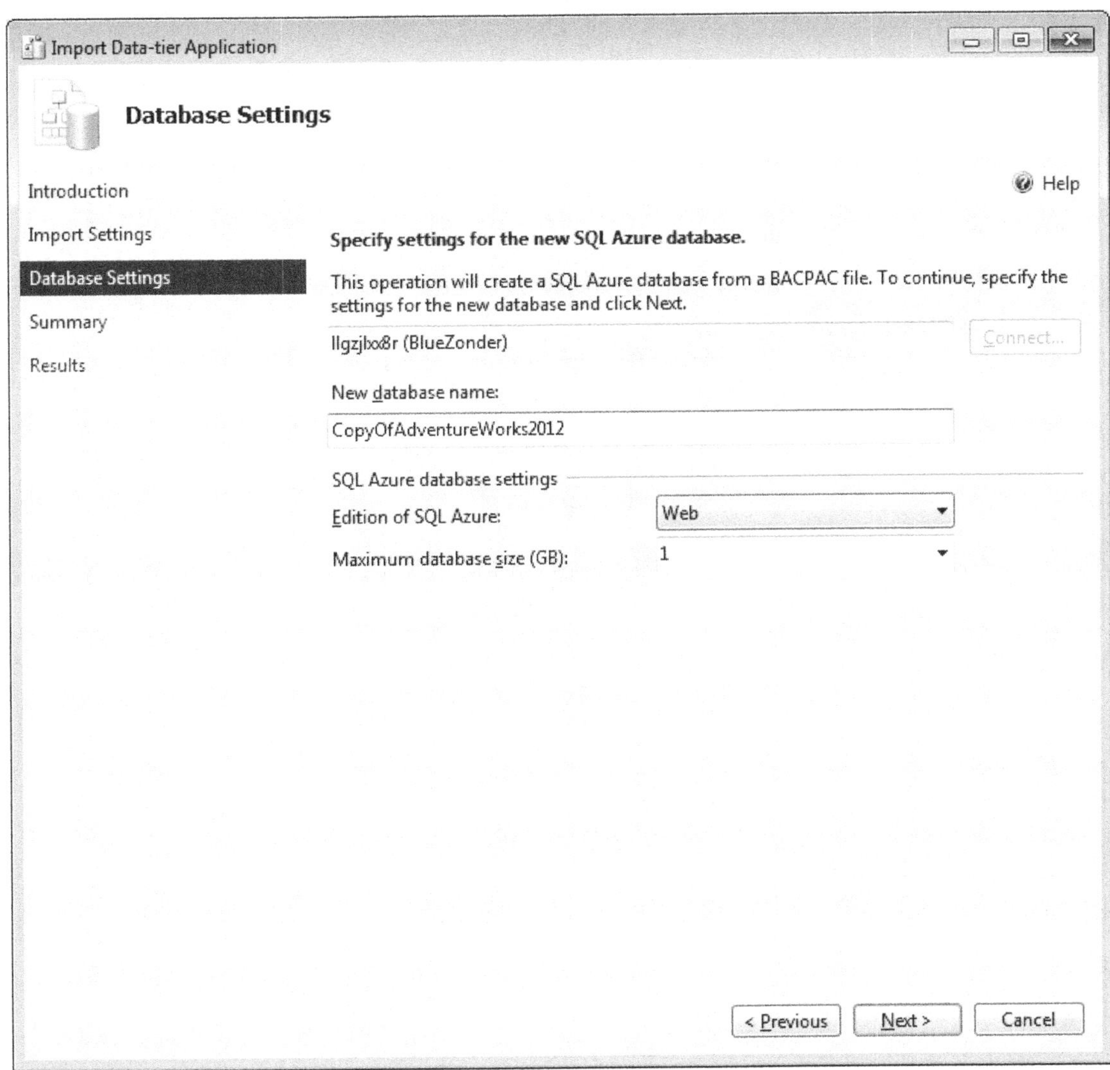

Summary

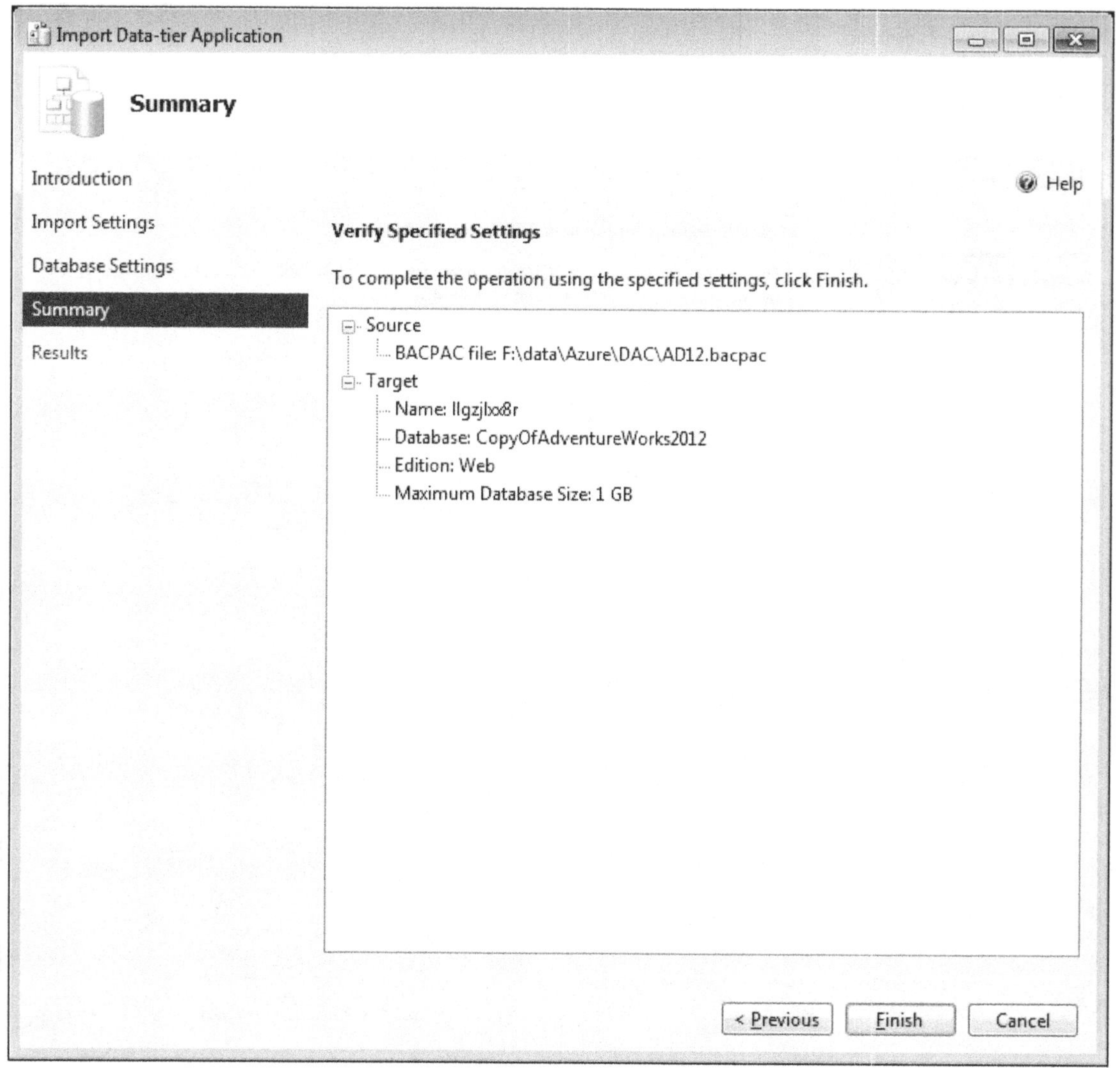
Import Data-tier Application
Summary
Introduction
Import Settings
Database Settings
Summary
Results
Help
Verify Specified Settings
To complete the operation using the specified settings, click Finish.
Source
BACPAC file: F:\data\Azure\DAC\AD12.bacpac
Target
Name: llgzjlxx8r
Database: CopyOfAdventureWorks2012
Edition: Web
Maximum Database Size: 1 GB
< Previous
Finish
Cancel

Importing Progress

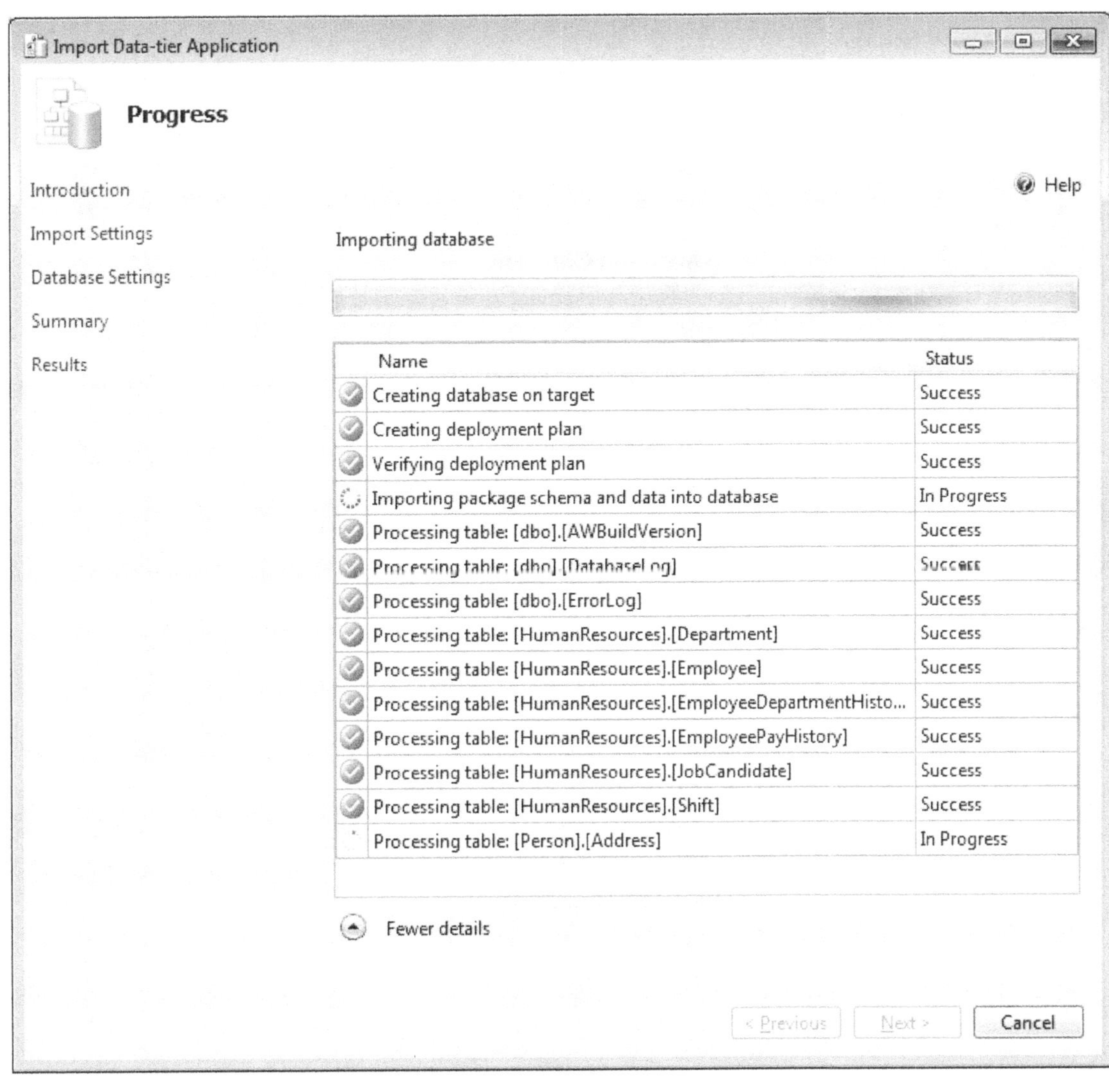
Creating deployment plan	Success
Verifying deployment plan	Success
Importing package schema and data into database	In Progress
Processing table:.[AWBuildVersion]	Success
Processing table:.[DatabaseLog]	Success
Processing table:.[ErrorLog]	Success
Processing table: [HumanResources].[Department]	Success
Processing table: [HumanResources].[Employee]	Success
Processing table: [HumanResources].[EmployeeDepartmentHisto...	Success
Processing table: [HumanResources].[EmployeePayHistory]	Success
Processing table: [HumanResources].[JobCandidate]	Success
Processing table: [HumanResources].[Shift]	Success
Processing table: [Person].[Address]	In Progress

Fewer details

< Previous | Next > | Cancel

CHAPTER 2: Installing Azure SQL & Sample Databases

Operation Complete - Elapsed Time 20 Minutes

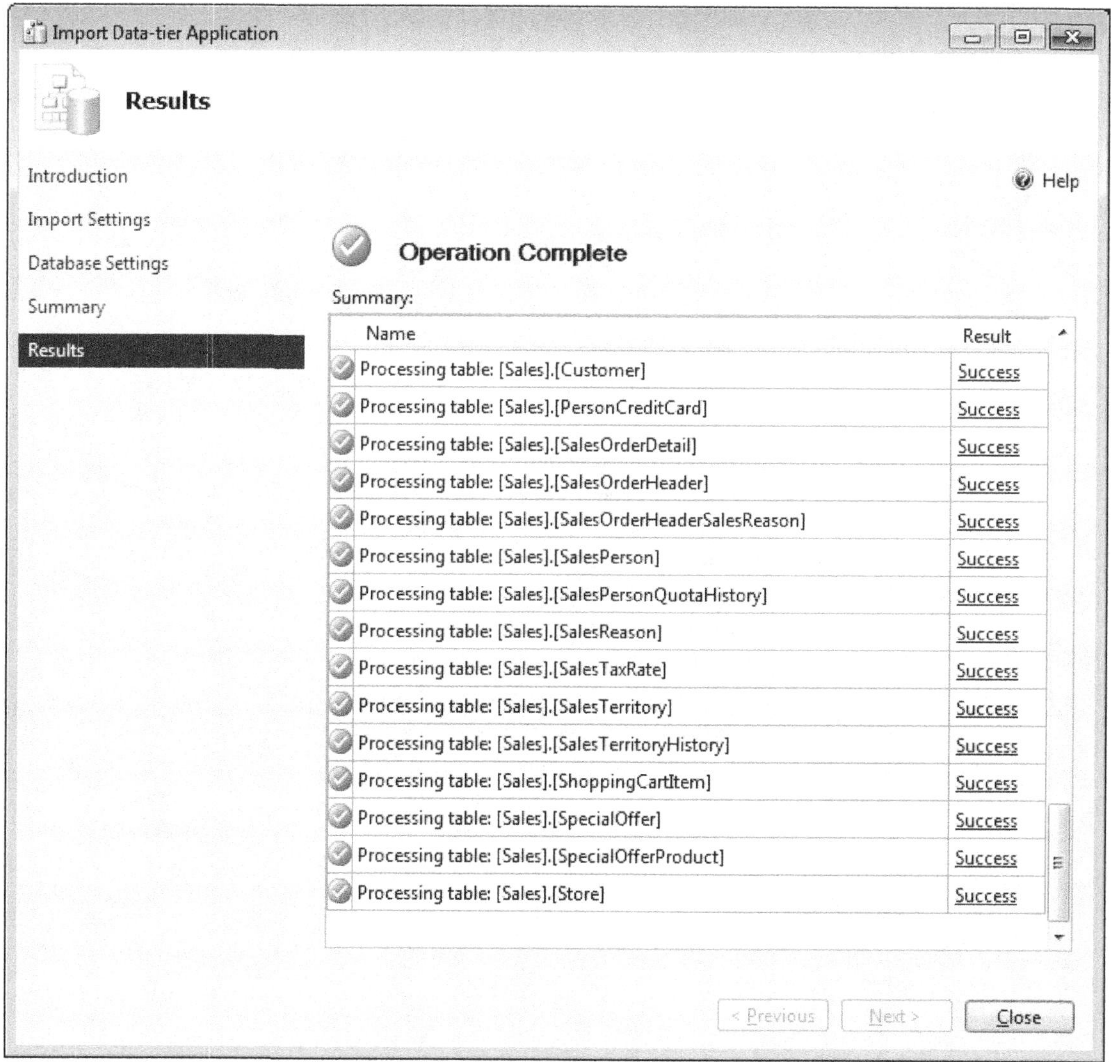

Deploy Data-tier Application

A data-tier application (DAC) is an entity that contains all of the database & SQL Server instance objects used by an application. The DAC package file can be generated by Visual Studio, SSMS Extract Data-tier Application or some utilities.

MSDN Articles
Understanding Data-tier Applications http://msdn.microsoft.com/en-us/library/ee240739(v=sql.105).aspx **Deploying Data-tier Applications** http://msdn.microsoft.com/en-us/library/ee210580(v=sql.105).aspx

The deployment file type is .dacpac.

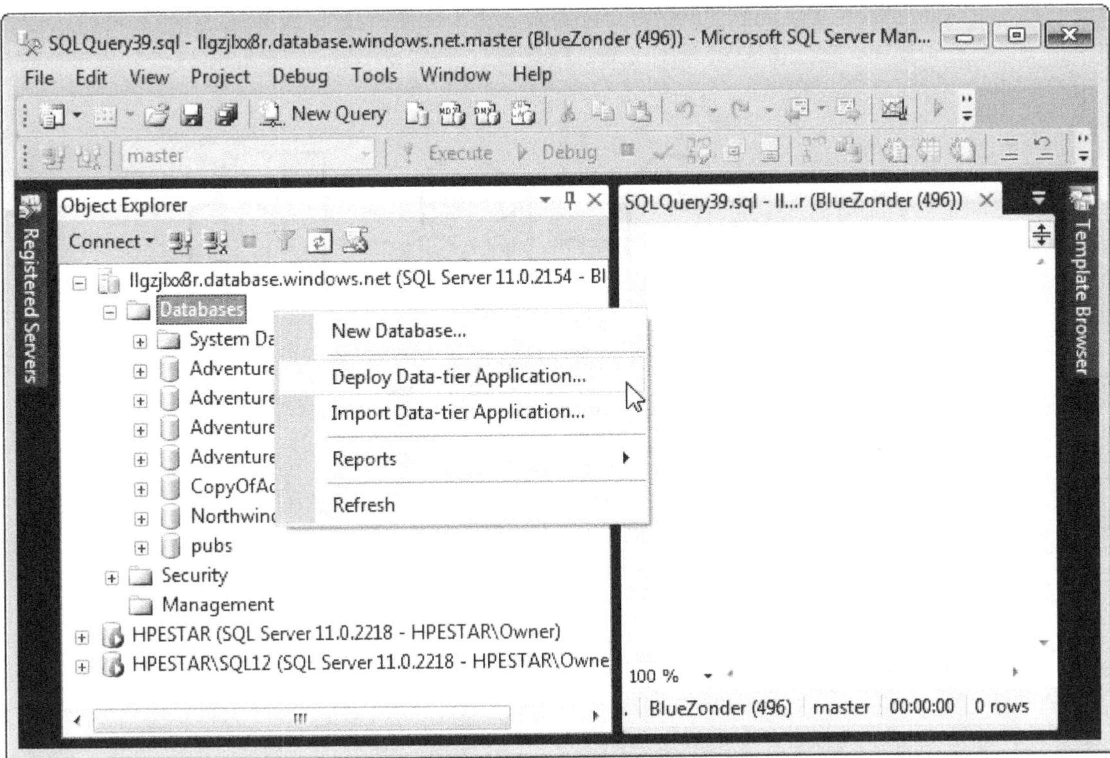

The Introduction Page Explains the Process

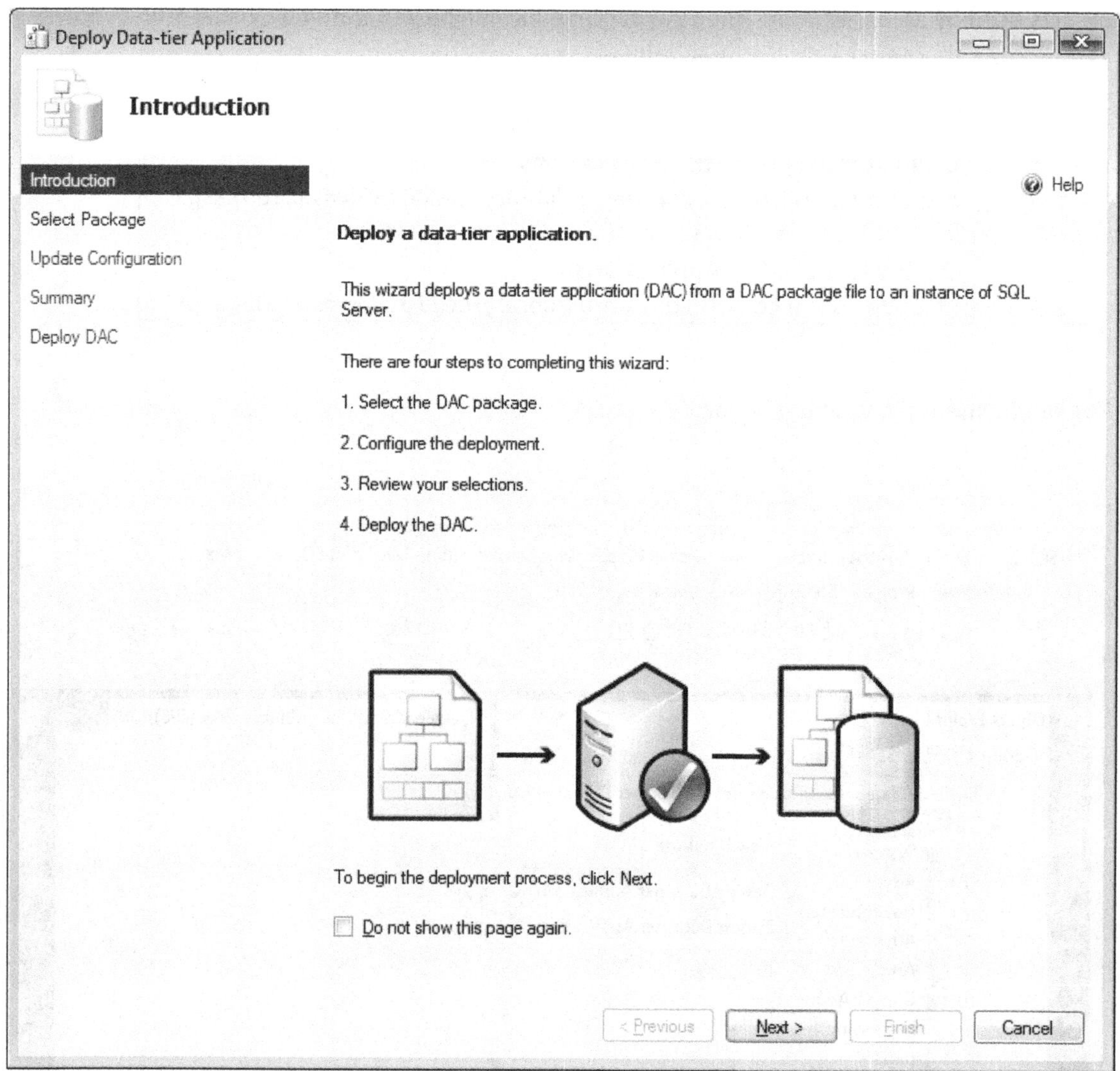

Select the DAC Package to Deploy

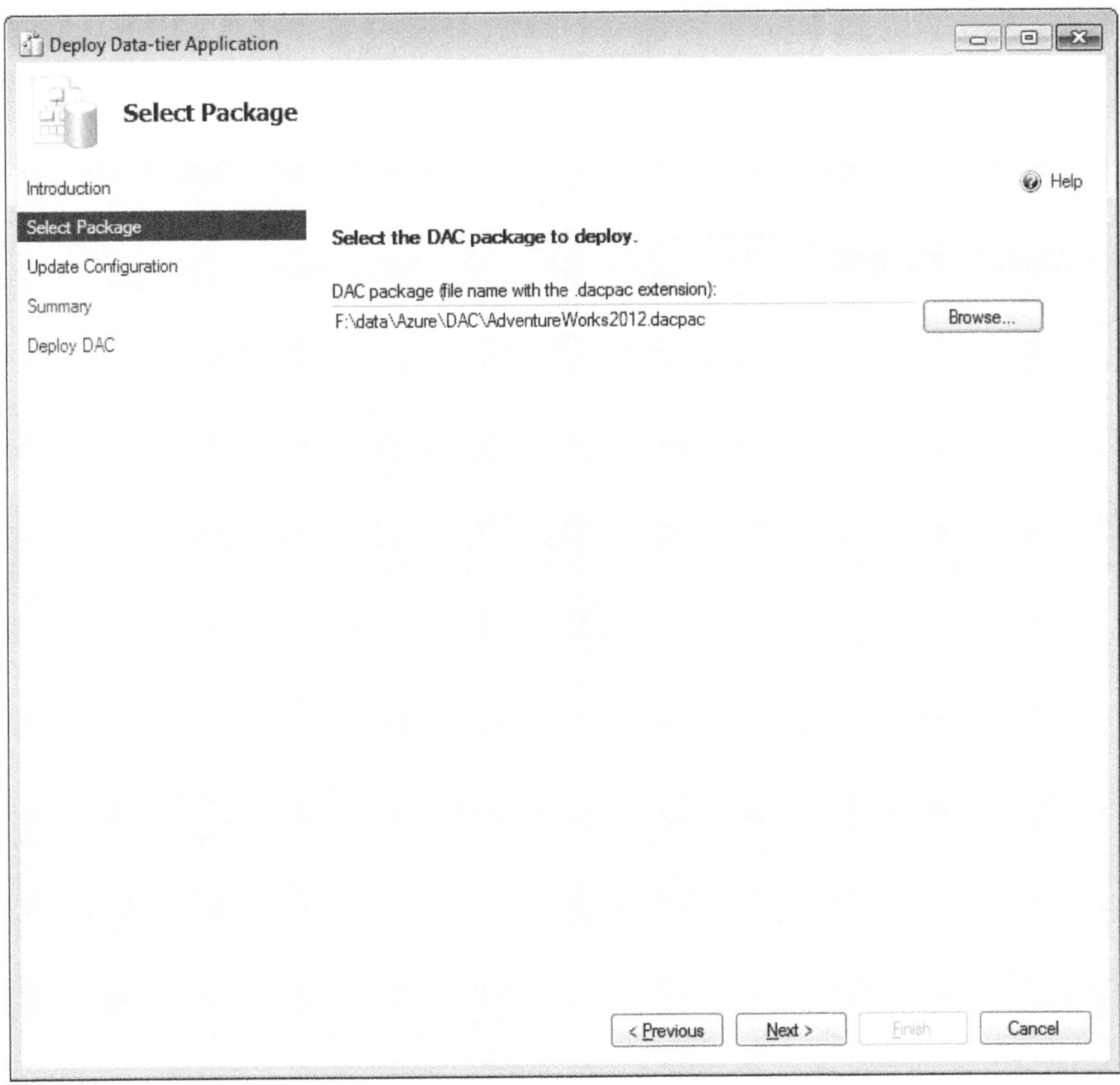

Configure the Database Deployment Properties

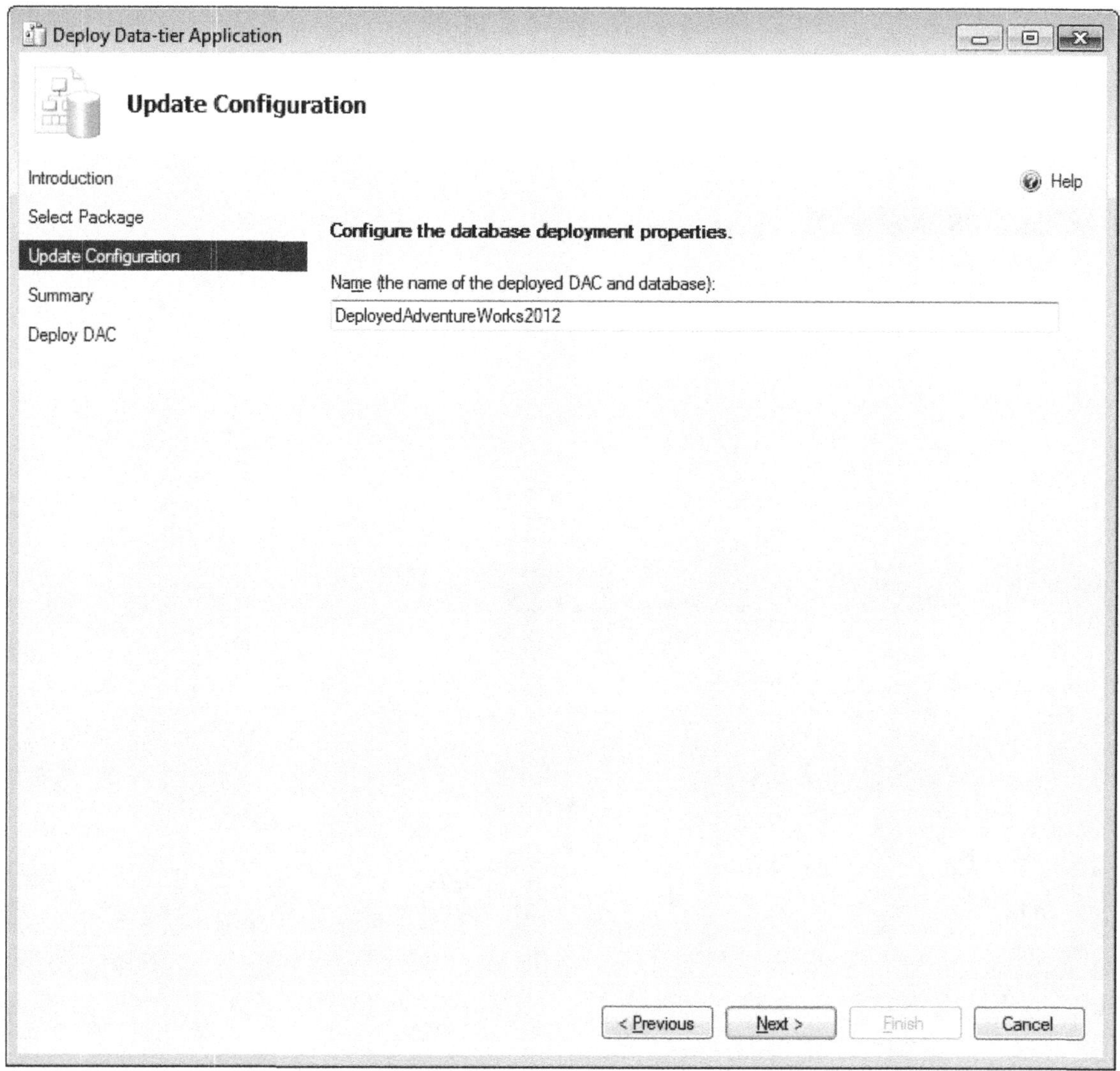

Summary screen follows. Click Finish to start processing.

Object Explorer View After Deployment - Runtime around 1 minute

All tables are empty in deployed database. All objects are defined.

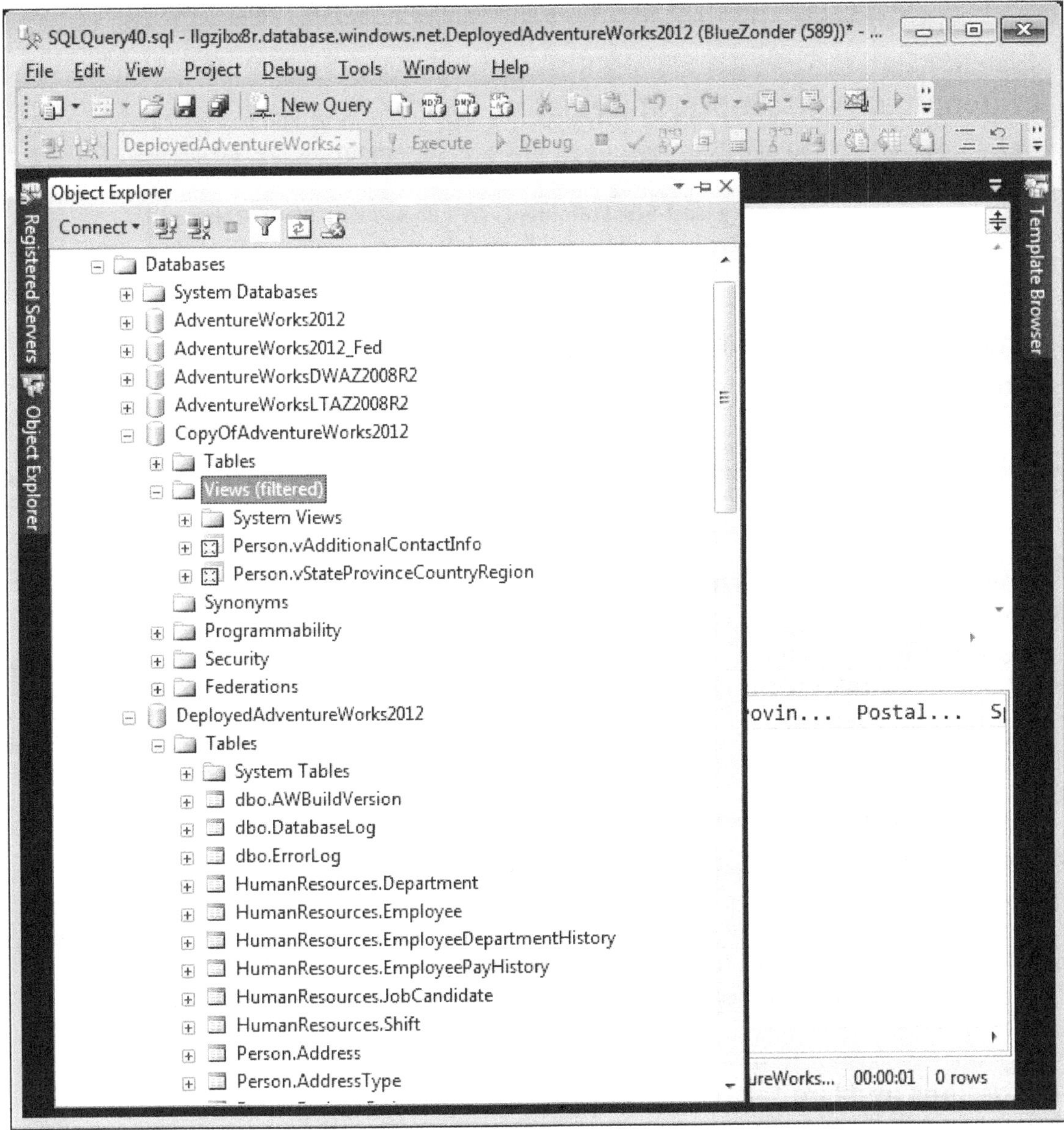

SQL Azure Books Online - BOL

Books Online is available on the web.

Windows Azure SQL Database http://msdn.microsoft.com/en-us/library/windowsazure/ee336279.aspx

Unsupported Transact-SQL Statements

A very important section of BOL on unsupported T-SQL statements.

Unsupported Transact-SQL Statements (Windows Azure SQL Database) http://msdn.microsoft.com/en-us/library/windowsazure/ee336253.aspx

Partially Supported Transact-SQL Statements

Another very important section of BOL on partially supported T-SQL statements.

Partially Supported Transact-SQL Statements (Windows Azure SQL Database) http://msdn.microsoft.com/en-us/library/windowsazure/ee336267.aspx

Windows Azure Platform Management Portal

Windows Azure web management portal.

Windows Azure Platform Management Portal http://msdn.microsoft.com/en-us/library/windowsazure/gg467325.aspx

Administration

Managing Azure SQL server & databases on management portal, migration and trouble-shooting.

Administration (Windows Azure SQL Database) http://msdn.microsoft.com/en-us/library/windowsazure/ff394116.aspx

Guidelines and Limitations

Guidelines and Limitations page has very important information about SQL Azure.

Guidelines and Limitations (Windows Azure SQL Database) http://msdn.microsoft.com/en-us/library/windowsazure/ff394102.aspx

Installing SQL Server 2012 AdventureWorks2012

AdventureWorks2012 and other related databases can be installed from the following webpage:
http://msftdbprodsamples.codeplex.com/releases/view/55330

Community Projects & Samples from the Start Menu will bring up the following site:
http://sqlserversamples.codeplex.com/

Installing SQL Server 2012 Northwind & pubs Databases

Northwind and pubs Sample Databases for SQL Server 2000
http://www.microsoft.com/en-us/download/details.aspx?displaylang=en&id=23654

SQL Database Migration Wizard

Download site information.

SQL Database Migration Wizard v3.9.10 & v4.0.13 http://sqlazuremw.codeplex.com/

Start the **SQLAzureMW** application in the download folder.

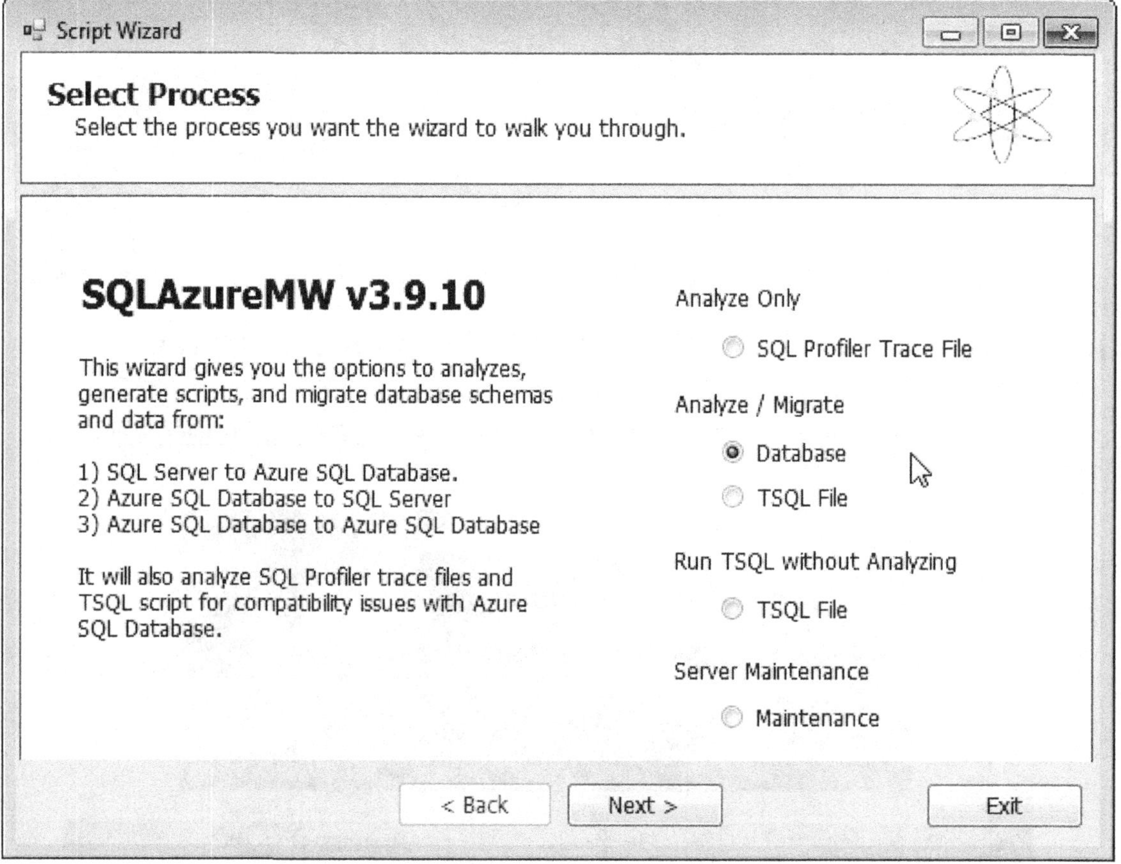

Connecting to Source Server & Database

Connect to Source (on-premises) Server using dialog pop-up and specify database (AdventureWorks).

Select source objects

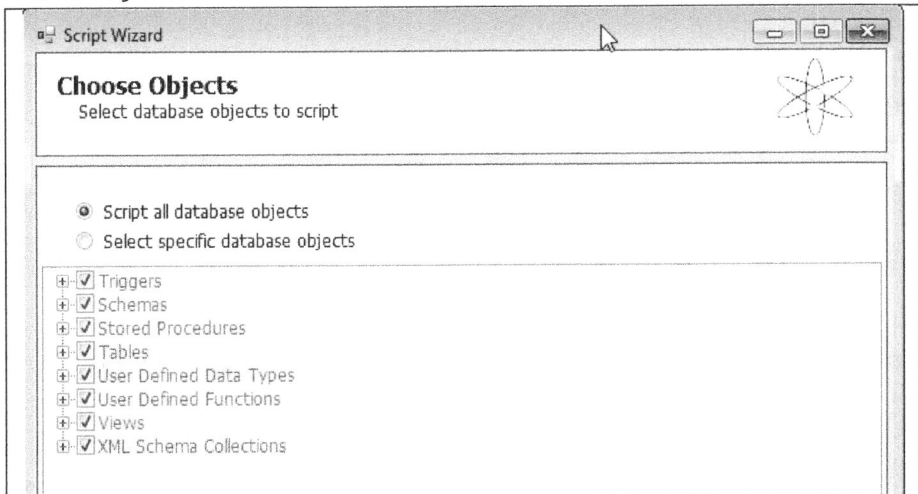

Scripting Summary

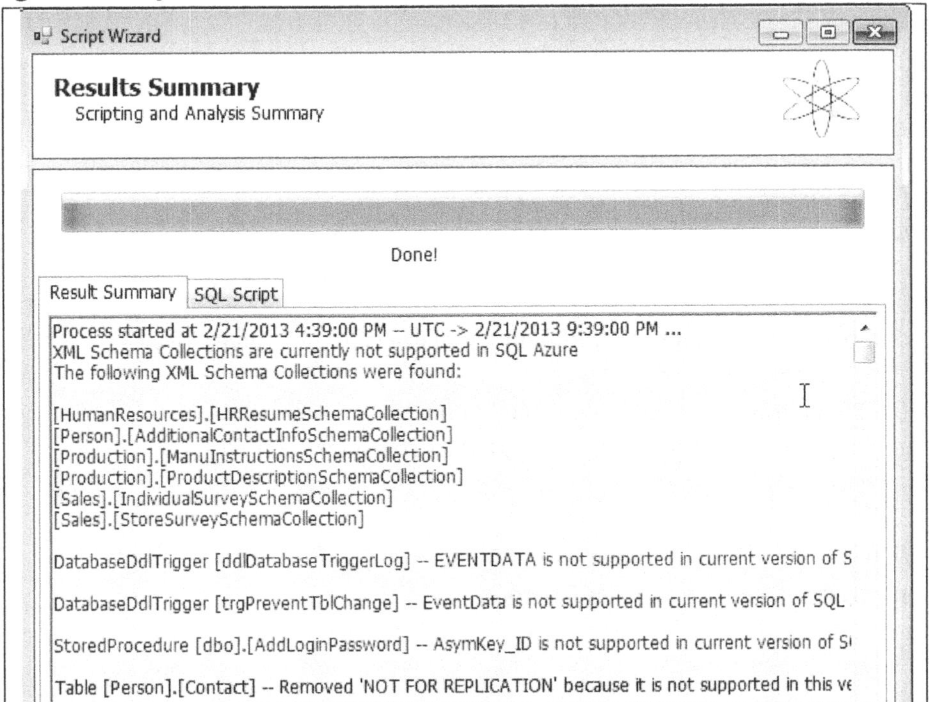

Connecting to Azure SQL Server and Starting the Upload

Connect to target Windows Azure SQL Database server. Usual dialog pop-up for server connection. Choose CREATE DATABASE at next window. New database name is AdventureWorks. Processing the scripts - uploading db objects and content.

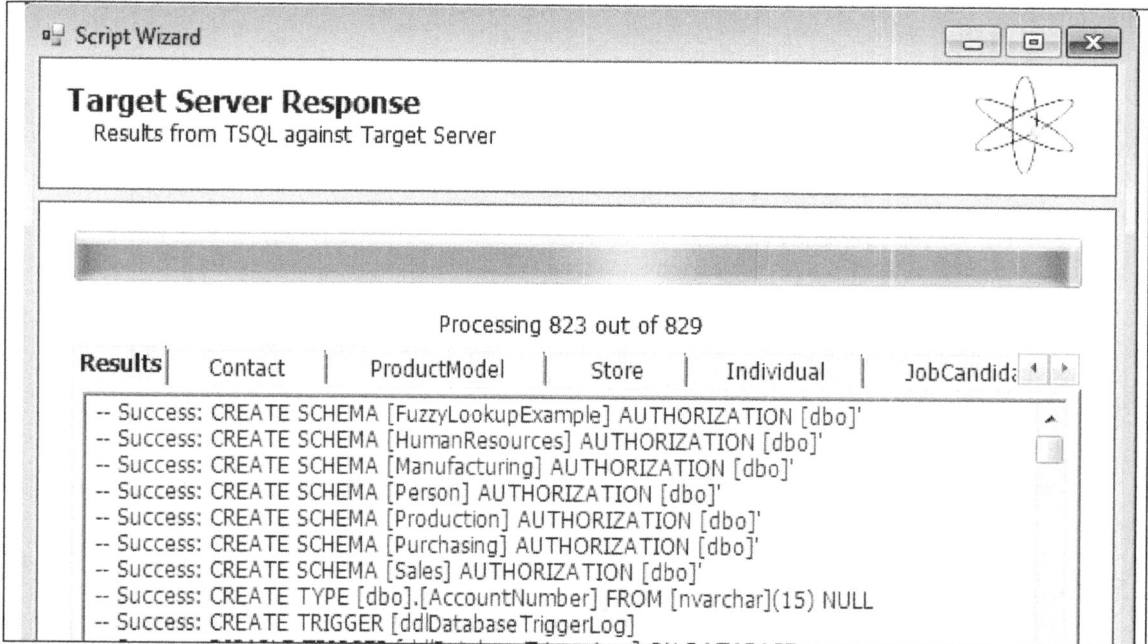
Script Wizard
Target Server Response
Results from TSQL against Target Server
Processing 823 out of 829
Results
Contact
ProductModel
Store
Individual
-- Success: CREATE SCHEMA [FuzzyLookupExample] AUTHORIZATION [dbo]'
-- Success: CREATE SCHEMA [HumanResources] AUTHORIZATION [dbo]'
-- Success: CREATE SCHEMA [Manufacturing] AUTHORIZATION [dbo]'
-- Success: CREATE SCHEMA [Person] AUTHORIZATION [dbo]'
-- Success: CREATE SCHEMA [Production] AUTHORIZATION [dbo]'
-- Success: CREATE SCHEMA [Purchasing] AUTHORIZATION [dbo]'
-- Success: CREATE SCHEMA [Sales] AUTHORIZATION [dbo]'
-- Success: CREATE TYPE [dbo].[AccountNumber] FROM [nvarchar](15) NULL
-- Success: CREATE TRIGGER [ddlDatabaseTriggerLog]

One of the bcp upload command log entries.

```
2/21/2016 4:55:14 PM
 --> Uploading data to PurchaseOrderHeader
 --> BCP Command: bcp.exe "AdventureWorks.Purchasing.PurchaseOrderHeader" in
"c:\SQLAzureMW\BCPData\Purchasing.PurchaseOrderHeader.dat" -E -w -b 10000 -a 16384 -q -S
llgzjlxx8r.database.windows.net -U "BlueZonder@llgzjlxx8r" -P "yyyyyyyyyyy"
*************************
2/21/2016 4:55:55 PM --> Copied 4000 of 4000 (100%)
Clock Time (ms.) Total    : 1498   Average : (2670.23 rows per sec.)
```

There were a few bcp upload errors. They need to be corrected inidividually either by using SQL Server Import/Export Wizard or other ETL tools.

.

CHAPTER 3: Azure SQL Database Differences & Solutions

Some System Views Don't Execute in master DB

Some of the system views give error in master db while work OK in application db. Currently, there is no way of telling which works which not.

```
-- In master db
SELECT * FROM sys.dm_exec_query_stats;
/*  Msg 297, Level 16, State 1, Line 1
The user does not have permission to perform this action.   */
```

```
-- In AdventureWorks2012
SELECT * FROM sys.dm_exec_query_stats;
-- (7 row(s) affected)
```

Solution for USE dbname

USE dbname works only for the current database in the current connection. For a different database, a new connection must be opened. Current database is AdventureWorks2012, open a new connection for Northwind.

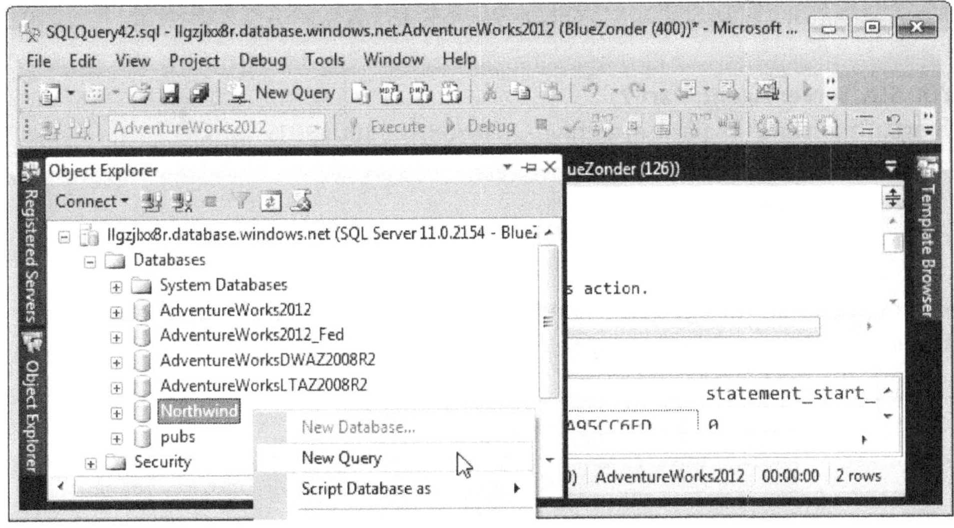

Solution for SELECT INTO

CREATE TABLE first, then INSERT SELECT. Alternative, use the SS Import/Export Wizard.

Solution for 3-part Naming - Cross Database Access

Use the SS Import/Export Wizard or similar data transfer tool.

Solution for Database BACKUP & RESTORE

If the database is not use, Export/Import Data-tier Application is similar to SQL Server 2012 BACKUP & RESTORE commands. However, if the database is in use, Export/Import will not handle transactional consistency.

MSDN Blog: **Data backup strategies for Windows and SQL Azure**
http://blogs.msdn.com/b/davidmcg/archive/2011/09/29/data-backup-strategies-for-windows-and-sql-azure.aspx

Solution for Changing Database in SSMS Query Editor

When connection is established to the master database, the drop-down window can be used to change database. It cannot be used for another change, a new connection must be open.

Solution for SQL Server Agent

SQL Server Agent is not supported in Azure SQL. There is no msdb system database.

Blogs: **I Miss You SQL Server Agent: Part 1**
http://blogs.msdn.com/b/sqlazure/archive/2010/07/30/10044271.aspx

I Miss You SQL Server Agent: Part 2
http://blogs.msdn.com/b/sqlazure/archive/2010/08/02/10045012.aspx

Linked Servers to SQL Azure
http://blogs.msdn.com/b/sqlcat/archive/2011/03/08/linked-servers-to-sql-azure.aspx

Build your own SQL Server Agent for Windows Azure SQL Database with the Scheduler
http://fabriccontroller.net/blog/posts/build-your-own-sql-server-agent-for-windows-azure-sql-database-with-the-scheduler/

SQL Data Synch - Cloud Replication

SQL Data Synch synchronizes selected data through a Windows Azure SQL Database instance. SQL Data Sync supports synchronizations within or across Windows Azure data centers. SQL Data Sync also supports hybrid configurations of Windows Azure SQL Database instances and Enterprise(on-premises) SQL Server databases. SQL Data Synch is in a way similar to SQL Server Replication in functionality, however, it is technologically different since it is based on

Articles: **SQL Data Sync**
http://msdn.microsoft.com/en-us/library/hh456371.aspx

SQL Data Sync Overview
http://social.technet.microsoft.com/wiki/contents/articles/1821.sql-data-sync-overview.aspx

SSMS: A transport-level error has occurred

The entire error message:

Msg 10053, Level 20, State 0, Line 0

A transport-level error has occurred when sending the request to the server. (provider: TCP Provider, error: 0 - An established connection was aborted by the software in your host machine.)

This is the message when in an SSMS timed-out connection query or script execution attempted. SSMS is trying to reestablish the connection in the background which may take seconds. Execution then should succeed when the execute icon is clicked.

Account & Billing Information

Two system views provide detail usage data for billing: sys.database_usage & sys.bandwidth_usage.

BOL: **Accounts and Billing in Windows Azure SQL Database**
http://msdn.microsoft.com/en-us/library/windowsazure/ee621788.aspx

Azure SQL Database Management Portal

The management portal can be accessed using a special URL:

https://yourservername.database.windows.net

Login and password required, database name is optional.

Query Editing & Running

A simplified version of SSMS Query Editor on-line.

```
SELECT P.Name AS ProductName, L.Name AS Location,
       SUM(PI.Quantity) AS QtyOnHand
FROM Production.Product AS P
    INNER JOIN Production.ProductInventory AS PI ON P.ProductID = PI.ProductID
    INNER JOIN Production.Location AS L ON PI.LocationID = L.LocationID
GROUP BY P.Name, L.Name ORDER BY ProductName, Location ;
```

Messages Results

1 1069 Row(s)

ProductName	Location	QtyOnHand
Adjustable Race	Miscellaneous Storage	324
Adjustable Race	Subassembly	353
Adjustable Race	Tool Crib	408
All-Purpose Bike Stand	Finished Goods Storage	144

Management icons:

- "Open" loads a query file from local disk.
- "Save as" saves query into a folder.
- "Actual Plan" displays actual execution plan as graphical chart.
- "Estimated Plan" displays estimated execution plan.

Administration Tools

Summary information is displayed and new database can be created.

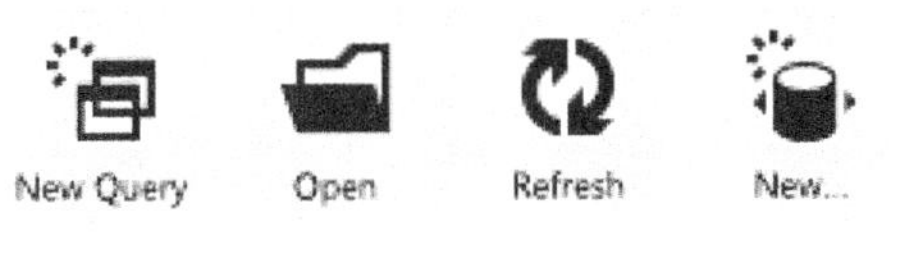

Database Properties

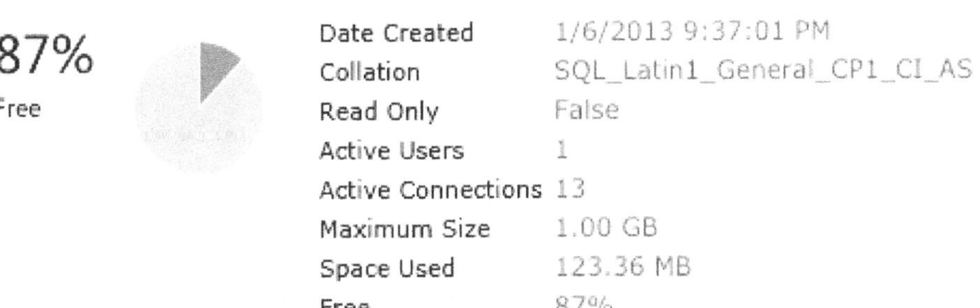

The **Query Performance** page displays performance related information and statistics on executed queries.

Summary Query Performance

Query	Run Count	CPU ms/sec	Duration ms/sec	Physical Reads/se	Logical Writes/se	Logical Reads/s
SELECT P.Name AS ProductName, L.Name AS	1	0	0	0	0	0
SELECT database_ic		0	0	0	0	0
select is_federation		0	0	0	0	0
SELECT CAST((sele		0	0	0	0	0
SELECT CAST((sele		0	0	0	0	0
SELECT CAST((sele		0	0	0	0	0
SELECT CAST((select SUBSTRING(text,eq1.sta	1	0	0	0	0	0

```
SELECT P.Name AS ProductName,...
    SUM(PI.Quantity) AS QtyOnHand
FROM Production.Product AS P
  INNER JOIN...
  INNER JOIN Production.Location...
GROUP BY P.Name, L.Name ORDER...
```

Design Tools

Design tools allow editing/creating/dropping of tables, views and stored procedures. Dependency information can also be displayed in graphical format.

Tables Views Stored Procedures

Search by table name

Schema Name ▲	Table Name ▲	Table Size	Row Count		
Sales	CurrencyRate	1.15 MB	13532	Edit	Dependencies
Sales	Customer	2.18 MB	19820		
Sales	PersonCreditCard	480.00 KB	19118		
Sales	SalesOrderDetail	15.30 MB	121319		
Sales	SalesOrderHeader	7.91 MB	31466	Edit	Dependencies

Dependency subgraph for Sales.SalesOrderHeader table.

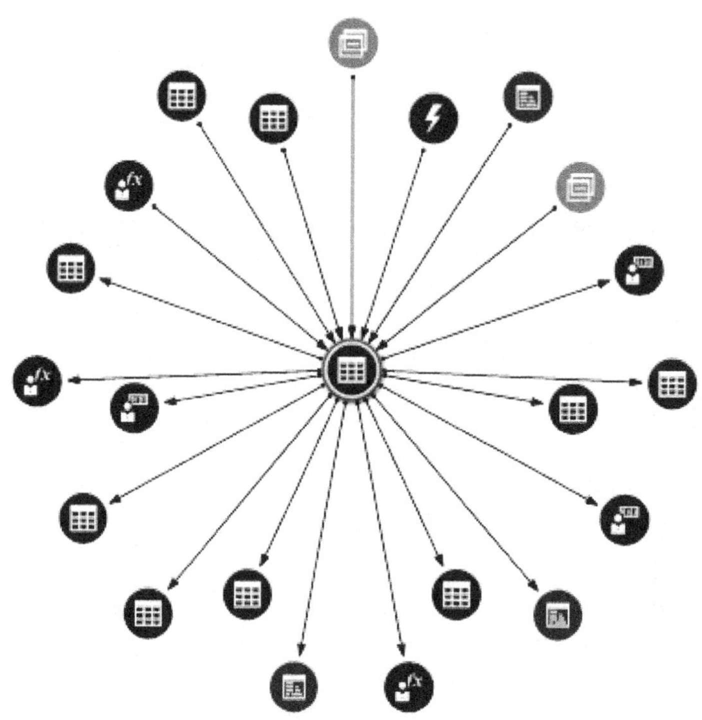

CHAPTER 4: Basic Structure of SELECT Statement

The SELECT Clause

All queries are executed in the context of **AdventureWorks2012 Azure SQL Database** unless otherwise indicated.

The SELECT clause is the only required clause in a SELECT statement, all the other clauses are optional. The SELECT columns can be literals (constants), expressions, table columns and even subqueries. Lines can be commented with "--".

```
SELECT 15 * 15;                                  -- 225
```

```
SELECT Today = convert(DATE, getdate());              -- 2016-07-27    -- getdate() T-SQL only
SELECT Today = convert(DATE, CURRENT_TIMESTAMP);  -- 2016-07-27    -- ANSI SQL
```

```
SELECT          Color,
                ProdCnt                 = COUNT(*),
                AvgPrice                = FORMAT(AVG(ListPrice),'c','en-US')
FROM Production.Product p
WHERE Color is not null
GROUP BY Color   HAVING count(*) > 10  ORDER BY AvgPrice DESC;
```

Color	ProdCnt	AvgPrice
Yellow	36	$959.09
Blue	26	$923.68
Silver	43	$850.31
Black	93	$725.12
Red	38	$1,401.95

```
-- Equivalent with column aliases on the right
SELECT          Color,
                COUNT(*)                              AS ProdCnt,
                FORMAT(AVG(ListPrice),'c','en-US')    AS AvgPrice
FROM Production.Product p  WHERE Color is not null
GROUP BY Color HAVING count(*) > 10  ORDER BY AvgPrice DESC;
GO
```

SELECT with Search Expression

SELECT statement can have complex expressions for text or numbers as demonstrated in the next T-SQL query for finding the street name in AddressLine1 column.

```
SELECT AddressID,
       SUBSTRING(AddressLine1, CHARINDEX(' ', AddressLine1+' ', 1) +1,
       CHARINDEX(' ', AddressLine1+' ', CHARINDEX(' ', AddressLine1+' ', 1) +1) -
       CHARINDEX(' ', AddressLine1+' ', 1) -1)                    AS StreetName,
       AddressLine1,
       City
FROM Person.Address
WHERE ISNUMERIC (LEFT(AddressLine1,1))=1
  AND City = 'Seattle'
ORDER BY AddressLine1;
-- (141 row(s) affected)- Partial results.
```

AddressID	StreetName	AddressLine1	City
13079	boulevard	081, boulevard du Montparnasse	Seattle
859	Oak	1050 Oak Street	Seattle
110	Slow	1064 Slow Creek Road	Seattle
113	Ravenwood	1102 Ravenwood	Seattle
95	Bradford	1220 Bradford Way	Seattle
32510	Steven	1349 Steven Way	Seattle
118	Balboa	136 Balboa Court	Seattle
32519	Mazatlan	137 Mazatlan	Seattle
25869	Calle	1386 Calle Verde	Seattle
114	Yorba	1398 Yorba Linda	Seattle
15657	Book	151 Book Ct	Seattle
105	Stillman	1619 Stillman Court	Seattle
18002	Carmel	1635 Carmel Dr	Seattle
19813	Acardia	1787 Acardia Pl.	Seattle
16392	Orchid	1874 Orchid Ct	Seattle
18053	Green	1883 Green View Court	Seattle
13035	Mt.	1887 Mt. Diablo St	Seattle
29864	Valley	1946 Valley Crest Drive	Seattle
13580	Hill	2030 Hill Drive	Seattle
106	San	2144 San Rafael	Seattle

```
-- Search for Crest in the middle of AddessLine1
SELECT * FROM Person.Address
WHERE AddressLine1 LIKE '% Crest %';
-- (21 row(s) affected)
```

SELECT Statement with Subquery

Two Northwind category images, Beverages & Dairy Products, from the dbo.Categories table.

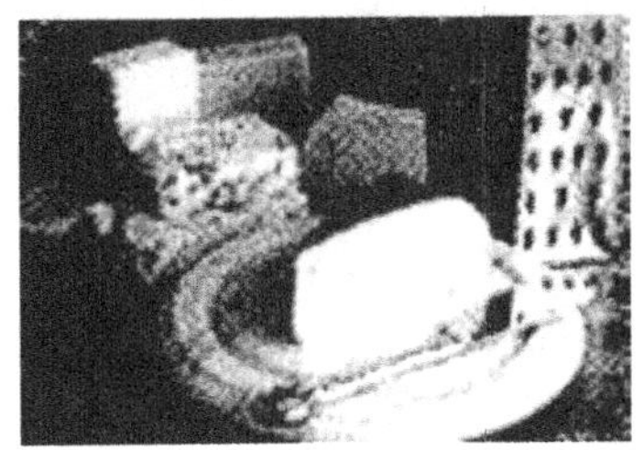

The following SELECT statement involves a subquery which is called a derived table. It also demonstrates that INNER JOIN can be performed with a GROUP BY subquery as well not only with another table or view.

```
USE Northwind;  -- Change context: Right click on Northwind in OE; Click on New Query
SELECT          c.CategoryName                          AS Category,
                cnum.NoOfProducts                       AS CatProdCnt,
                p.ProductName                           AS Product,
                FORMAT(p.UnitPrice,'c', 'en-US')        AS UnitPrice
 FROM    Categories c
                INNER JOIN Products p         ON c.CategoryID = p.CategoryID
                INNER JOIN (    SELECT          c.CategoryID,
                                                NoOfProducts = count(* )
                                FROM    Categories c
                                        INNER JOIN Products p
                                        ON c.CategoryID = p.CategoryID
                                GROUP BY c.CategoryID
                           ) cnum                               -- derived table
                        ON c.CategoryID = cnum.CategoryID
ORDER BY Category, Product;       -- (77 row(s) affected) - Partial results.
```

Category	CatProdCnt	Product	UnitPrice
Dairy Products	10	Mozzarella di Giovanni	$34.80
Dairy Products	10	Queso Cabrales	$21.00
Dairy Products	10	Queso Manchego La Pastora	$38.00
Dairy Products	10	Raclette Courdavault	$55.00
Grains/Cereals	7	Filo Mix	$7.00
Grains/Cereals	7	Gnocchi di nonna Alice	$38.00
Grains/Cereals	7	Gustaf's Knäckebröd	$21.00
Grains/Cereals	7	Ravioli Angelo	$19.50
Grains/Cereals	7	Singaporean Hokkien Fried Mee	$14.00
Grains/Cereals	7	Tunnbröd	$9.00

Creating Delimited String List (CSV) with XML PATH

The XML PATH clause , the text() function and correlated subquery is used to create a comma delimited string within the SELECT columns. Note: it cannot be done using traditional (without XML) SQL single statement, it can be done with multiple SQL statements only. STUFF() string function is applied to replace the leading comma with an empty string.

```
SELECT Territory          = st.[Name],
       SalesYTD =  FORMAT(floor(SalesYTD), 'c', 'en-US'), -- currency format
       SalesStaffAssignmentHistory =

         STUFF((SELECT CONCAT(', ', c.FirstName, SPACE(1), c.LastName)      AS [text()]
                FROM   Person.Person c
                INNER JOIN Sales.SalesTerritoryHistory sth
                ON c.BusinessEntityID = sth.BusinessEntityID
                WHERE  sth.TerritoryID =  st.TerritoryID
                ORDER  BY StartDate
                FOR XML Path ('')), 1, 1, SPACE(0))

FROM   Sales.SalesTerritory st
ORDER  BY st.SalesYTD DESC;
GO
```

Territory	SalesYTD	SalesStaffAssignmentHistory
Southwest	$10,510,853.00	Linda Mitchell, Shu Ito
Northwest	$7,887,186.00	Pamela Ansman-Wolfe, David Campbell, Tete Mensa-Annan
Canada	$6,771,829.00	Garrett Vargas, José Saraiva, Jae Pak
Australia	$5,977,814.00	Lynn Tsoflias
United Kingdom	$5,012,905.00	José Saraiva
France	$4,772,398.00	Ranjit Varkey Chudukatil
Germany	$3,805,202.00	Rachel Valdez
Central	$3,072,175.00	Jillian Carson, Michael Blythe
Southeast	$2,538,667.00	Tsvi Reiter
Northeast	$2,402,176.00	Michael Blythe, Jillian Carson

```
-- Comma delimited list of column names
SELECT CONCAT(',', c.name)  AS [text()]
FROM  sys.columns c   WHERE c.[object_id] = OBJECT_ID('Purchasing.PurchaseOrderDetail')
ORDER BY column_id FOR XML PATH('');
```

Logical Processing Order of the SELECT Statement

The results from the previous step will be available to the next step. The logical processing order for a SELECT statement is the following. Actual processing by the database engine may be different due to performance and other considerations.

1.	FROM
2.	ON
3.	JOIN
4.	WHERE
5.	GROUP BY
6.	WITH CUBE or WITH ROLLUP
7.	HAVING
8.	SELECT
9.	DISTINCT
10.	ORDER BY
11.	TOP

As an example, it is logical to filter with the WHERE clause prior to applying GROUP BY. It is also logical to sort when the final result set is available.

```
SELECT Color, COUNT(*) AS ColorCount  FROM Production.Product
WHERE Color is not NULL  GROUP BY Color ORDER BY ColorCount DESC;
```

Color	ColorCount
Black	93
Silver	43
Red	38
Yellow	36
Blue	26
Multi	8
Silver/Black	7
White	4
Grey	1

The TOP Clause

The TOP clause filters results according the sorting specified in an ORDER BY clause, otherwise random filtering takes place.

Simple TOP usage to return 10 rows only.

```
SELECT TOP 10 SalesOrderID, OrderDate,  TotalDue
FROM Sales.SalesOrderHeader  ORDER BY TotalDue DESC;
```

SalesOrderID	OrderDate	TotalDue
51131	2007-07-01 00:00:00.000	187487.825
55282	2007-10-01 00:00:00.000	182018.6272
46616	2006-07-01 00:00:00.000	170512.6689
46981	2006-08-01 00:00:00.000	166537.0808
47395	2006-09-01 00:00:00.000	165028.7482
47369	2006-09-01 00:00:00.000	158056.5449
47355	2006-09-01 00:00:00.000	145741.8553
51822	2007-08-01 00:00:00.000	145454.366
44518	2005-11-01 00:00:00.000	142312.2199
51858	2007-08-01 00:00:00.000	140042.1209

TOP function usage: not known in advance how many rows will be returned due to "TIES".

```
SELECT   TOP 1 WITH TIES  coalesce(Color, 'N/A')                  AS Color,
                FORMAT(ListPrice, 'c', 'en-US')                   AS ListPrice,
                Name                                              AS ProductName,
                ProductID
FROM     Production.Product
ORDER BY ROW_NUMBER()  OVER(PARTITION BY Color ORDER BY ListPrice DESC);
```

.

Color	ListPrice	ProductName	ProductID
N/A	$229.49	HL Fork	804
Black	$3,374.99	Mountain-100 Black, 38	775
Red	$3,578.27	Road-150 Red, 62	749
Silver	$3,399.99	Mountain-100 Silver, 38	771
Blue	$2,384.07	Touring-1000 Blue, 46	966
Grey	$125.00	Touring-Panniers, Large	842
Multi	$89.99	Men's Bib-Shorts, S	855
Silver/Black	$80.99	HL Mountain Pedal	937
White	$9.50	Mountain Bike Socks, M	709
Yellow	$2,384.07	Touring-1000 Yellow, 46	954

The DISTINCT Clause to Omit Duplicates

The DISTINCT clause returns only unique results, omitting duplicates in the result set.

```
USE AdventureWorks2012;
SELECT DISTINCT Color FROM Production.Product
WHERE Color is not NULL
ORDER BY Color;
GO
```

Color
Black
Blue
Grey
Multi
Red
Silver
Silver/Black
White
Yellow

```
SELECT DISTINCT ListPrice
FROM Production.Product
 WHERE ListPrice > 0.0
ORDER BY ListPrice DESC;
GO
-- (102 row(s) affected) - Partial results.
```

ListPrice
3578.27
3399.99
3374.99
2443.35

```
-- Using DISTINCT in COUNT - NULL is counted
SELECT          COUNT(*)                        AS TotalRows,
                COUNT(DISTINCT Color)           AS ProductColors,
                COUNT(DISTINCT Size)            AS ProductSizes
FROM Production.Product;
```

TotalRows	ProductColors	ProductSizes
504	9	18

The CASE Conditional Expression

The CASE conditional expression evaluates to a **single value of the same data type**, therefore **it can be used anywhere in a query where a single value is required.**

```
SELECT      CASE ProductLine
                WHEN 'R' THEN 'Road'
                WHEN 'M' THEN 'Mountain'
                WHEN 'T' THEN 'Touring'
                WHEN 'S' THEN 'Other'
                ELSE 'Parts'
            END                         AS Category,
            Name                        AS ProductName,
            ProductNumber
FROM Production.Product
ORDER BY ProductName;
GO -- (504 row(s) affected) - Partial results.
```

Category	ProductName	ProductNumber
Touring	Touring-3000 Blue, 62	BK-T18U-62
Touring	Touring-3000 Yellow, 44	BK-T18Y-44
Touring	Touring-3000 Yellow, 50	BK-T18Y-50
Touring	Touring-3000 Yellow, 54	BK-T18Y-54
Touring	Touring-3000 Yellow, 58	BK-T18Y-58
Touring	Touring-3000 Yellow, 62	BK-T18Y-62
Touring	Touring-Panniers, Large	PA-T100
Other	Water Bottle - 30 oz.	WB-H098
Mountain	Women's Mountain Shorts, L	SH-W890-L

Query to return different result sets for repeated execution due to newid().

```
USE Northwind;  -- Execute in a Northwind connection
SELECT  TOP 3 CompanyName,   City=CONCAT(City, ', ', Country),         PostalCode,
        [IsNumeric] =  CASE     WHEN PostalCode like '[0-9][0-9][0-9][0-9][0-9]'
                                THEN '5-Digit Numeric'   ELSE 'Other'  END
FROM    dbo.Suppliers
ORDER BY NEWID();                       -- random sort
GO
```

CompanyName	City	PostalCode	IsNumeric
PB Knäckebröd AB	Göteborg, Sweden	S-345 67	Other
Gai pâturage	Annecy, France	74000	5-Digit Numeric
Heli Süßwaren GmbH & Co. KG	Berlin, Germany	10785	5-Digit Numeric

Same query as above expanded with ROW_NUMBER() and another CASE expression column.

```
SELECT      ROW_NUMBER() OVER (ORDER BY Name)               AS RowNo,
            CASE ProductLine
             WHEN 'R' THEN 'Road'
             WHEN 'M' THEN 'Mountain'
             WHEN 'T' THEN 'Touring'
             WHEN 'S' THEN 'Other'
             ELSE 'Parts'
            END                                       AS Category,
            Name                                      AS ProductName,
            CASE WHEN Color is null THEN 'N/A'
                    ELSE Color END                    AS Color,
            ProductNumber
FROM Production.Product   ORDER BY ProductName;
-- (504 row(s) affected) - Partial results.
```

RowNo	Category	ProductName	Color	ProductNumber
1	Parts	Adjustable Race	N/A	AR-5381
2	Mountain	All-Purpose Bike Stand	N/A	ST-1401
3	Other	AWC Logo Cap	Multi	CA-1098
4	Parts	BB Ball Bearing	N/A	BE-2349
5	Parts	Bearing Ball	N/A	BA-8327

Performance Note

Limit results output with the TOP clause when appropriate. Returning huge result sets from SQL Azure database takes time and **cost factor** may be involved.

Testing PostalCode with ISNUMERIC and generating a flag with CASE expression.

```
SELECT  TOP (4) AddressID,   City,    PostalCode                              AS Zip,
          CASE WHEN ISNUMERIC(PostalCode) = 1 THEN 'Y'  ELSE 'N'  END    AS IsZipNumeric
FROM    Person.Address  ORDER BY NEWID();
```

AddressID	City	Zip	IsZipNumeric
16704	Paris	75008	Y
26320	Grossmont	91941	Y
27705	Matraville	2036	Y
18901	Kirkby	KB9	N

The OVER Clause

The OVER clause defines the partitioning and sorting of a rowset (intermediate result set) preceding the application of an associated window function, such as ranking. Window functions are also dubbed as ranking functions.

```
USE AdventureWorks2012;
-- Query with three different OVER clauses
SELECT  ROW_NUMBER() OVER ( ORDER BY SalesOrderID, ProductID)               AS RowNum
        ,SalesOrderID, ProductID, OrderQty
        ,RANK() OVER(PARTITION BY SalesOrderID ORDER BY OrderQty DESC)      AS Ranking
        ,SUM(OrderQty) OVER(PARTITION BY SalesOrderID)                      AS TotalQty
        ,AVG(OrderQty) OVER(PARTITION BY SalesOrderID)                      AS AvgQty
        ,COUNT(OrderQty) OVER(PARTITION BY SalesOrderID)  AS "Count"  -- T-SQL keyword, use "" or []
        ,MIN(OrderQty) OVER(PARTITION BY SalesOrderID)                      AS "Min"
        ,MAX(OrderQty) OVER(PARTITION BY SalesOrderID)                      AS "Max"
FROM Sales.SalesOrderDetail
WHERE SalesOrderID BETWEEN 61190 AND 61199
ORDER BY RowNum;
-- (143 row(s) affected) - Partial results.
```

RowNum	SalesOrderID	ProductID	OrderQty	Ranking	TotalQty	AvgQty	Count	Min	Max
1	61190	707	4	13	159	3	40	1	17
2	61190	708	3	18	159	3	40	1	17
3	61190	711	5	8	159	3	40	1	17
4	61190	712	12	2	159	3	40	1	17
5	61190	714	3	18	159	3	40	1	17
6	61190	715	5	8	159	3	40	1	17
7	61190	716	5	8	159	3	40	1	17
8	61190	858	4	13	159	3	40	1	17
9	61190	859	7	6	159	3	40	1	17
10	61190	864	8	4	159	3	40	1	17
11	61190	865	3	18	159	3	40	1	17
12	61190	870	9	3	159	3	40	1	17
13	61190	876	4	13	159	3	40	1	17
14	61190	877	5	8	159	3	40	1	17
15	61190	880	1	34	159	3	40	1	17
16	61190	881	5	8	159	3	40	1	17
17	61190	883	2	26	159	3	40	1	17
18	61190	884	17	1	159	3	40	1	17
19	61190	885	3	18	159	3	40	1	17
20	61190	886	1	34	159	3	40	1	17
21	61190	889	2	26	159	3	40	1	17
22	61190	892	4	13	159	3	40	1	17
23	61190	893	3	18	159	3	40	1	17
24	61190	895	1	34	159	3	40	1	17

FROM Clause: Specifies the Data Source

The FROM clause specifies the source data sets for the query such as tables, views, derived tables and table-valued functions. Typically the tables are JOINed together. The most common JOIN is INNER JOIN which is based on equality between FOREIGN KEY and PRIMARY KEY values in the two tables.

PERFORMANCE NOTE
All FOREIGN KEYs should be indexed. PRIMARY KEYs are indexed automatically with unique index.

```
USE AdventureWorks2012;
GO
SELECT
 ROW_NUMBER() OVER(ORDER BY SalesYTD DESC)                                AS RowNo,
 ROW_NUMBER() OVER(PARTITION BY PostalCode ORDER BY SalesYTD DESC)    AS SeqNo,
              CONCAT(p.FirstName, SPACE(1), p.LastName)               AS SalesStaff,
              FORMAT(s.SalesYTD,'c','en-US')                           AS YTDSales,
              City,
              a.PostalCode                                             AS ZipCode
FROM Sales.SalesPerson AS s
  INNER JOIN Person.Person AS p
    ON s.BusinessEntityID = p.BusinessEntityID
  INNER JOIN Person.Address AS a
    ON a.AddressID = p.BusinessEntityID
WHERE TerritoryID IS NOT NULL    AND SalesYTD <> 0 ORDER BY ZipCode, SeqNo;
```

RowNo	SeqNo	SalesStaff	YTDSales	City	ZipCode
1	1	Linda Mitchell	$4,251,368.55	Issaquah	98027
3	2	Michael Blythe	$3,763,178.18	Issaquah	98027
4	3	Jillian Carson	$3,189,418.37	Issaquah	98027
8	4	Tsvi Reiter	$2,315,185.61	Issaquah	98027
12	5	Garrett Vargas	$1,453,719.47	Issaquah	98027
14	6	Pamela Ansman-Wolfe	$1,352,577.13	Issaquah	98027
2	1	Jae Pak	$4,116,871.23	Renton	98055
5	2	Ranjit Varkey Chudukatil	$3,121,616.32	Renton	98055
6	3	José Saraiva	$2,604,540.72	Renton	98055
7	4	Shu Ito	$2,458,535.62	Renton	98055
9	5	Rachel Valdez	$1,827,066.71	Renton	98055
10	6	Tete Mensa-Annan	$1,576,562.20	Renton	98055
11	7	David Campbell	$1,573,012.94	Renton	98055
13	8	Lynn Tsoflias	$1,421,810.92	Renton	98055

The WHERE Clause to Filter Records (Rows)

The WHERE clause filters the rows generated by the query. Only rows satisfying (TRUE) the WHERE clause predicates are returned.

> PERFORMANCE NOTE
> All columns in WHERE clause should be indexed.

```
USE AdventureWorks2012;
```

String equal match predicate - equal is TRUE, not equal is FALSE.

```
SELECT ProductID, Name, ListPrice, Color
FROM Production.Product  WHERE Name = 'Mountain-100 Silver, 38' ;
```

ProductID	Name	ListPrice	Color
771	Mountain-100 Silver, 38	3399.99	Silver

```
-- Function equality predicate
SELECT * FROM Sales.SalesOrderHeader WHERE YEAR(OrderDate) = 2008;
-- (13951 row(s) affected)
```

> **PERFORMANCE NOTE**
> **When a column is used as a parameter in a function (e.g. YEAR(OrderDate)), index (if any) usage is voided. Instead of random SEEK, all rows are SCANned in the table. The predicate is not SARGable.**

```
-- String wildcard match predicate
SELECT ProductID, Name, ListPrice, Color
FROM Production.Product  WHERE Name LIKE ('%touring%');
```

```
-- Integer range predicate
SELECT ProductID, Name, ListPrice, Color
FROM Production.Product  WHERE ProductID >= 997 ;
```

```
-- Double string wildcard match predicate
SELECT ProductID, Name, ListPrice, Color
FROM Production.Product  WHERE Name LIKE ('%bike%')  AND Name LIKE ('%44%');
```

```
-- String list match predicate
SELECT ProductID, Name, ListPrice, Color  FROM Production.Product
WHERE Name IN ('Mountain-100 Silver, 44', 'Mountain-100 Black, 44');
```

The GROUP BY Clause to Aggregate Results

The GROUP BY clause is applied to partition the rows and calculate aggregate values. An extremely powerful way of looking at the data from a summary point of view.

```
SELECT
        V.Name                                          AS Vendor,
        FORMAT(SUM(TotalDue), 'c', 'en-US')             AS TotalPurchase,
        A.City,
        SP.Name                                         AS State,
        CR.Name                                         AS Country
FROM Purchasing.Vendor AS V
  INNER JOIN Person.BusinessEntityAddress AS VA
        ON VA.BusinessEntityID = V.BusinessEntityID
  INNER JOIN Person.Address AS A
        ON A.AddressID = VA.AddressID
  INNER JOIN Person.StateProvince AS SP
        ON SP.StateProvinceID =  A.StateProvinceID
  INNER JOIN Person.CountryRegion AS CR
        ON CR.CountryRegionCode = SP.CountryRegionCode
  INNER JOIN Purchasing.PurchaseOrderHeader POH
        ON POH.VendorID = V.BusinessEntityID
GROUP BY  V.Name, A.City, SP.Name, CR.Name
ORDER BY SUM(TotalDue) DESC,  Vendor;   -- TotalPurchase does a string sort instead of numeric
GO
-- (86 row(s) affected) - Partial results.
```

Vendor	TotalPurchase	City	State	Country
Superior Bicycles	$5,034,266.74	Lynnwood	Washington	United States
Professional Athletic Consultants	$3,379,946.32	Burbank	California	United States
Chicago City Saddles	$3,347,165.20	Daly City	California	United States
Jackson Authority	$2,821,333.52	Long Beach	California	United States
Vision Cycles, Inc.	$2,777,684.91	Glendale	California	United States
Sport Fan Co.	$2,675,889.22	Burien	Washington	United States
Proseware, Inc.	$2,593,901.31	Lebanon	Oregon	United States
Crowley Sport	$2,472,770.05	Chicago	Illinois	United States
Greenwood Athletic Company	$2,472,770.05	Lemon Grove	Arizona	United States
Mitchell Sports	$2,424,284.37	Everett	Washington	United States
First Rate Bicycles	$2,304,231.55	La Mesa	New Mexico	United States
Signature Cycles	$2,236,033.80	Coronado	California	United States
Electronic Bike Repair & Supplies	$2,154,773.37	Tacoma	Washington	United States
Vista Road Bikes	$2,090,857.52	Salem	Oregon	United States
Victory Bikes	$2,052,173.62	Issaquah	Washington	United States
Bicycle Specialists	$1,952,375.30	Lake Oswego	Oregon	United States

The HAVING Clause to Filter Aggregates

The HAVING clause is similar to the WHERE clause filtering but applies to GROUP BY aggregates.

```
SELECT
            V.Name                                      AS Vendor,
            FORMAT(SUM(TotalDue), 'c', 'en-US')         AS TotalPurchase,
            A.City,
            SP.Name                                     AS State,
            CR.Name                                     AS Country
FROM Purchasing.Vendor AS V
  INNER JOIN Person.BusinessEntityAddress AS VA
            ON VA.BusinessEntityID = V.BusinessEntityID
  INNER JOIN Person.Address AS A
            ON A.AddressID = VA.AddressID
  INNER JOIN Person.StateProvince AS SP
            ON SP.StateProvinceID =   A.StateProvinceID
  INNER JOIN Person.CountryRegion AS CR
            ON CR.CountryRegionCode = SP.CountryRegionCode
 INNER JOIN Purchasing.PurchaseOrderHeader POH
            ON POH.VendorID = V.BusinessEntityID
GROUP BY  V.Name, A.City, SP.Name, CR.Name

HAVING SUM(TotalDue) < $26000    -- HAVING clause predicate

ORDER BY SUM(TotalDue) DESC,  Vendor;;
```

Vendor	TotalPurchase	City	State	Country
Speed Corporation	$25,732.84	Anacortes	Washington	United States
Gardner Touring Cycles	$25,633.64	Altadena	California	United States
National Bike Association	$25,513.90	Sedro Woolley	Washington	United States
Australia Bike Retailer	$25,060.04	Bellingham	Washington	United States
WestAmerica Bicycle Co.	$25,060.04	Houston	Texas	United States
Ready Rentals	$23,635.06	Kirkland	Washington	United States
Morgan Bike Accessories	$23,146.99	Albany	New York	United States
Continental Pro Cycles	$22,960.07	Long Beach	California	United States
American Bicycles and Wheels	$9,641.01	West Covina	California	United States
Litware, Inc.	$8,553.32	Santa Cruz	California	United States
Business Equipment Center	$8,497.80	Everett	Montana	United States
Bloomington Multisport	$8,243.95	West Covina	California	United States
International	$8,061.10	Salt Lake City	Utah	United States
Wide World Importers	$8,025.60	Concord	California	United States
Midwest Sport, Inc.	$7,328.72	Detroit	Michigan	United States
Wood Fitness	$6,947.58	Philadelphia	Pennsylvania	United States
Metro Sport Equipment	$6,324.53	Lebanon	Oregon	United States
Burnett Road Warriors	$5,779.99	Corvallis	Oregon	United States
Lindell	$5,412.57	Lebanon	Oregon	United States
Consumer Cycles	$3,378.17	Torrance	California	United States
Northern Bike Travel	$2,048.42	Anacortes	Washington	United States

The ORDER BY Clause to Sort Results

The ORDER BY clause sorts the result set. It guarantees ordering according to the columns or expressions listed from major to minor keys. Unique ordering requires a set of keys which generate unique data rows. The major key, YEAR(HireDate), in the first example is not sufficient for uniqueness.

```
USE AdventureWorks2012;          -- Sort on 2 keys
SELECT BusinessEntityID AS EmployeeID, JobTitle, HireDate
FROM HumanResources.Employee  ORDER BY YEAR(HireDate) DESC, EmployeeID;
-- (290 row(s) affected) - Partial results.
```

EmployeeID	JobTitle	HireDate
285	Pacific Sales Manager	2007-04-15

```
-- Sort on CASE conditional expression
SELECT   BusinessEntityID AS SalesStaffID, CONCAT(LastName, ', ', FirstName) AS FullName,
         CASE CountryRegionName WHEN 'United States' THEN TerritoryName
                  ELSE '' END AS TerritoryName, CountryRegionName
FROM Sales.vSalesPerson   WHERE TerritoryName IS NOT NULL          -- view
ORDER BY CASE WHEN CountryRegionName != 'United States' THEN  CountryRegionName
                  ELSE TerritoryName  END;        -- (14 row(s) affected) - Partial results.
```

SalesStaffID	FullName	TerritoryName	CountryRegionName
286	Tsoflias, Lynn		Australia

The EXCEPT & INTERSECT Set Operators

The EXCEPT operator & the INTERSECT operator require the column lists are compatible for the comparison. **SELECT INTO workaround: create Prod1 & Prod2. Script out Production.Product. Perform the following changes for Prod1 CREATE TABLE (similarly for Prod2):**

```
CREATE TABLE dbo.Prod1( [ProductID] [int]  NOT NULL,
......
 CONSTRAINT [PK_Product_ProductID1] PRIMARY KEY CLUSTERED
......
-- Populate the two tables with 400 random(newid()) picks from the Product table
INSERT Prod1 SELECT TOP (400) * FROM Production.Product ORDER BY NEWID();
INSERT Prod2 SELECT TOP (400) * FROM Production.Product ORDER BY NEWID();

-- EXCEPT SET OPERATOR - no match rows
SELECT * FROM PROD1 EXCEPT SELECT * FROM PROD2;  -- (81 row(s) affected)

-- INTERSECT SET OPERATOR - matching rows
SELECT * FROM PROD1 INTERSECT SELECT * FROM PROD2;  -- (319 row(s) affected)
```

CTE - Common Table Expression

CTE helps with structured programming by the definition of named subqueries at the beginning of the query. It supports nesting and recursion.

```
USE AdventureWorks2012;    -- Testing CTE
WITH CTE (SalesPersonID, NumberOfOrders, MostRecentOrderDate)
   AS (          SELECT SalesPersonID, COUNT(*), CONVERT(date, MAX(OrderDate))
                 FROM Sales.SalesOrderHeader
                 GROUP BY SalesPersonID  )
SELECT * FROM CTE;                              -- (18 row(s) affected) - Partial results.
```

SalesPersonID	NumberOfOrders	MostRecentOrderDate
284	39	2004-05-01
278	234	2004-06-01
281	242	2004-06-01

hierarchyid Function is Used to Obtain Manager's ID

```
;WITH CTE (SalesPersonID, NumberOfOrders, MostRecentOrderDate)
   AS ( SELECT SalesPersonID, COUNT(*), CONVERT(date, MAX(OrderDate))
        FROM Sales.SalesOrderHeader   GROUP BY SalesPersonID      )
-- Start of outer (main) query
 SELECT        E.BusinessEntityID                     AS Employee,
               OE.NumberOfOrders                      AS EmpOrders,
               OE.MostRecentOrderDate                 AS EmpLastOrder,
               EE.BusinessEntityID                    AS Manager,
               OM.NumberOfOrders                      AS MgrOrders,
               OM.MostRecentOrderDate                 AS MgrLastOrder
 FROM   HumanResources.Employee AS E
        INNER JOIN CTE AS OE                   ON E.BusinessEntityID = OE.SalesPersonID
                  INNER JOIN HumanResources.Employee EE
                    ON E.OrganizationNode.GetAncestor(1) = EE.OrganizationNode
        LEFT OUTER JOIN CTE AS OM              ON EE.BusinessEntityID = OM.SalesPersonID
ORDER BY E.BusinessEntityID;                   -- (17 row(s) affected) - Partial results.
```

EmployeeID	EmpOrders	EmpLastOrder	ManagerID	MgrOrders	MgrLastOrder
268	48	2004-06-01	273	NULL	NULL
275	450	2004-06-01	268	48	2004-06-01
276	418	2004-06-01	268	48	2004-06-01
277	473	2004-06-01	268	48	2004-06-01
278	234	2004-06-01	268	48	2004-06-01

Combining Results of Multiple Queries with UNION

UNION and UNION ALL (no duplicates elimination) operators can be used to **stack result sets from two or more queries into a single result set**. SQL Server 2012 query.

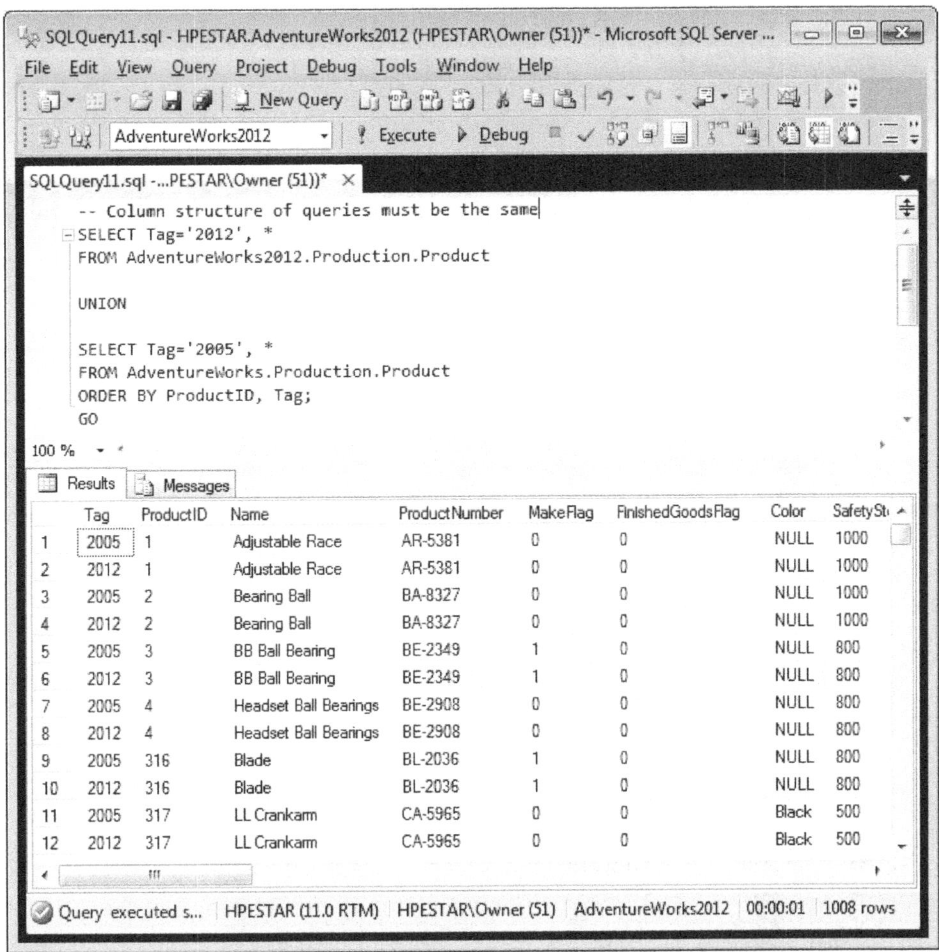

	Tag	ProductID	Name	ProductNumber	MakeFlag	FinishedGoodsFlag	Color	SafetySt
1	2005	1	Adjustable Race	AR-5381	0	0	NULL	1000
2	2012	1	Adjustable Race	AR-5381	0	0	NULL	1000
3	2005	2	Bearing Ball	BA-8327	0	0	NULL	1000
4	2012	2	Bearing Ball	BA-8327	0	0	NULL	1000
5	2005	3	BB Ball Bearing	BE-2349	1	0	NULL	800
6	2012	3	BB Ball Bearing	BE-2349	1	0	NULL	800
7	2005	4	Headset Ball Bearings	BE-2908	0	0	NULL	800
8	2012	4	Headset Ball Bearings	BE-2908	0	0	NULL	800
9	2005	316	Blade	BL-2036	1	0	NULL	800
10	2012	316	Blade	BL-2036	1	0	NULL	800
11	2005	317	LL Crankarm	CA-5965	0	0	Black	500
12	2012	317	LL Crankarm	CA-5965	0	0	Black	500

SQL Server 2012 query. SQL Azure requires the transfer of DimCustomer table from AdventureWorksDW2012 database to AdventureWorks2012 (with SSIS for example).

```
-- Combining data from OLTP & data warehouse databases
SELECT FirstName,LastName, 0 AS TotalChildren
FROM Person.Person
UNION ALL
SELECT FirstName,LastName, TotalChildren
FROM AdventureWorksDW2012..DimCustomer;
```

TOP n by Group Query with OVER PARTITION BY

OVER PARTITION BY method is very convenient for TOP n by group selection. List of top 3 orders placed by resellers (customers of AdventureWorks Cycles). SQL Server 2012 query.

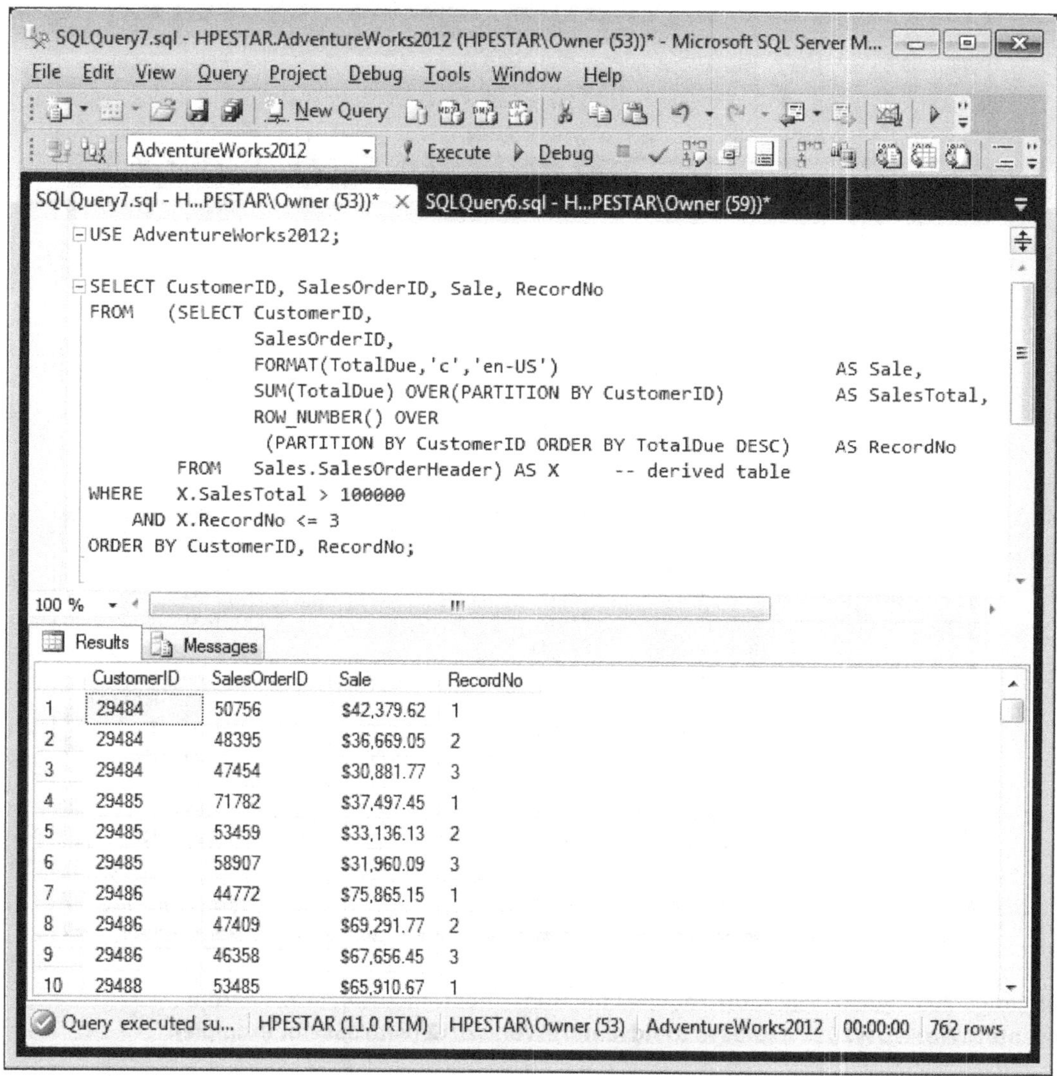

```
USE AdventureWorks2012;

SELECT CustomerID, SalesOrderID, Sale, RecordNo
FROM   (SELECT CustomerID,
               SalesOrderID,
               FORMAT(TotalDue,'c','en-US')                              AS Sale,
               SUM(TotalDue) OVER(PARTITION BY CustomerID)               AS SalesTotal,
               ROW_NUMBER() OVER
                (PARTITION BY CustomerID ORDER BY TotalDue DESC)         AS RecordNo
        FROM   Sales.SalesOrderHeader) AS X     -- derived table
WHERE   X.SalesTotal > 100000
    AND X.RecordNo <= 3
ORDER BY CustomerID, RecordNo;
```

	CustomerID	SalesOrderID	Sale	RecordNo
1	29484	50756	$42,379.62	1
2	29484	48395	$36,669.05	2
3	29484	47454	$30,881.77	3
4	29485	71782	$37,497.45	1
5	29485	53459	$33,136.13	2
6	29485	58907	$31,960.09	3
7	29486	44772	$75,865.15	1
8	29486	47409	$69,291.77	2
9	29486	46358	$67,656.45	3
10	29488	53485	$65,910.67	1

Query executed su... | HPESTAR (11.0 RTM) | HPESTAR\Owner (53) | AdventureWorks2012 | 00:00:00 | 762 rows

```
-- SQL Azure: Row numbering by partitioning view results
SELECT  ROW_NUMBER() OVER(PARTITION BY PhoneNumberType ORDER BY SalesYTD DESC) RN,
        CONCAT(FirstName, ' ', LastName) as Name, ROUND(SalesYTD,2,1) AS YTDSales,
        PhoneNumberType
FROM Sales.vSalesPerson
ORDER BY PhoneNumberType, RN; -- (17 row(s) affected)
```

CHAPTER 5: SQL Server Management Studio 2012

SQL Server Programming, Administration & Management Tool

SQL Server Management Studio (SSMS) is a GUI (Graphical User Interface) tool for accessing, configuring, managing, administering, and developing all major components of SQL Server with the exception of Business Intelligence components: SSAS (Analysis Services), SSRS (Reporting Services) & SSIS (Integration Services). The two main environments in SSMS: Object Explorer and Query Editor. Object Explorer is used to access servers, databases and db objects. Query Editor is to develop and execute queries. SSMS is used by a DBA (Data Base Administrator) for administrative and programming functions. SSMS can also be used by a database developer to develop application related db objects such as stored procedures, functions and triggers. Some developers prefer to stay in Visual Studio environment which has features to support database development albeit not as extensive as Management Studio. A typical screen display of Management Studio. SQL Server 2012 query.

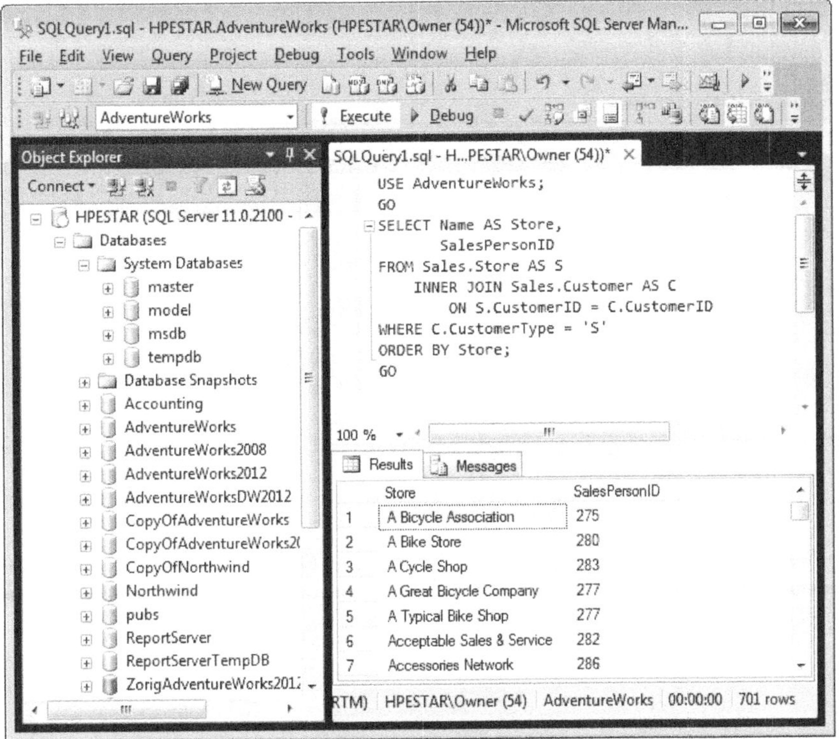

Query Editor

The Query Editor is used to type in queries, edit them and submit them for execution by the server. Queries can also be loaded from a disk file, typically with .sql extension. In addition to textual query development, a number of special tools available such as graphical query designer, debugger, execution plan display and query analysis by the Database Engine Tuning Advisor. IntelliSense provides contextual assistance with SQL syntax checking and guessing object names in a drop-down menu based on the typed prefix. SQL Server 2012 query.

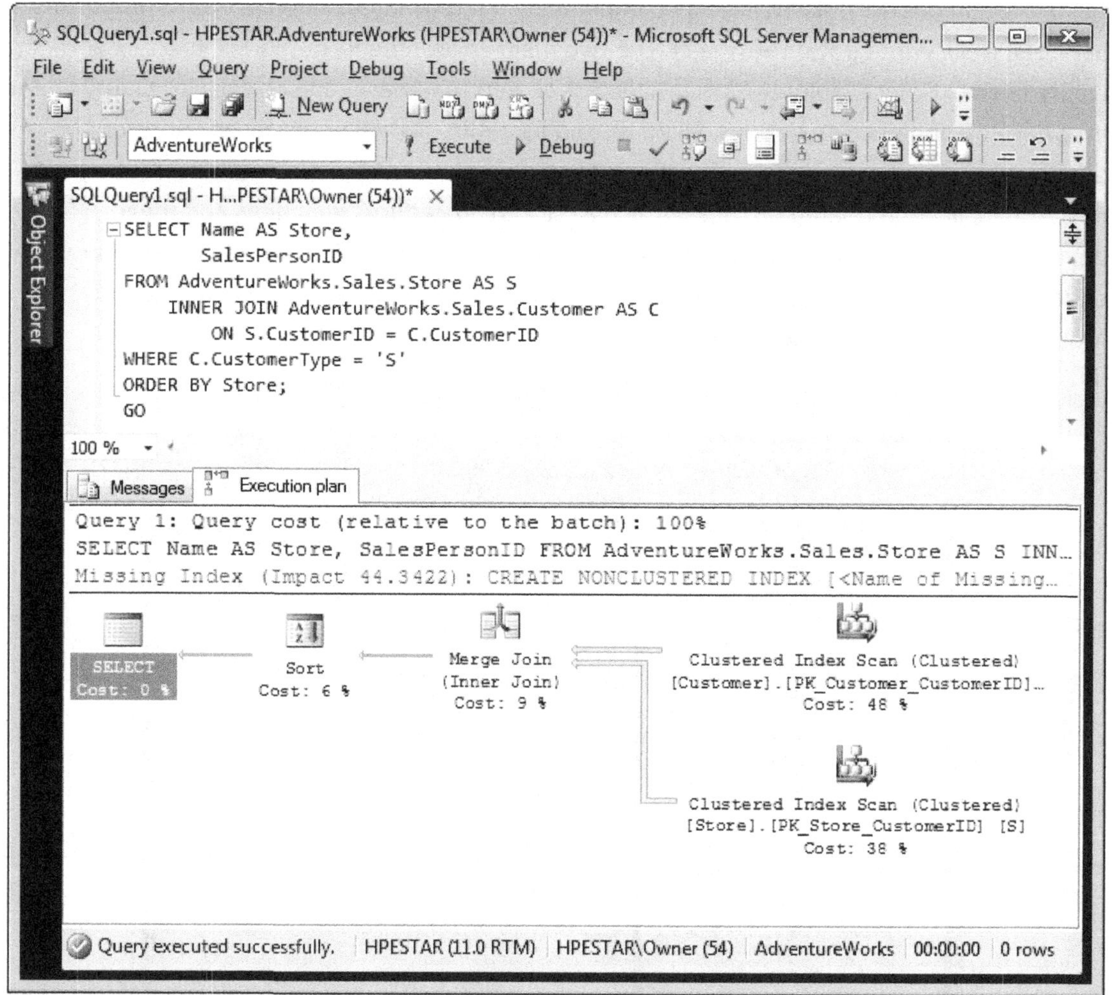

Execute All Batches in Query Editor

The entire content of the Query Editor is executed when we click on the Execute button. Batches typically separated by "GO" on a separate line. SQL Server 2012 query.

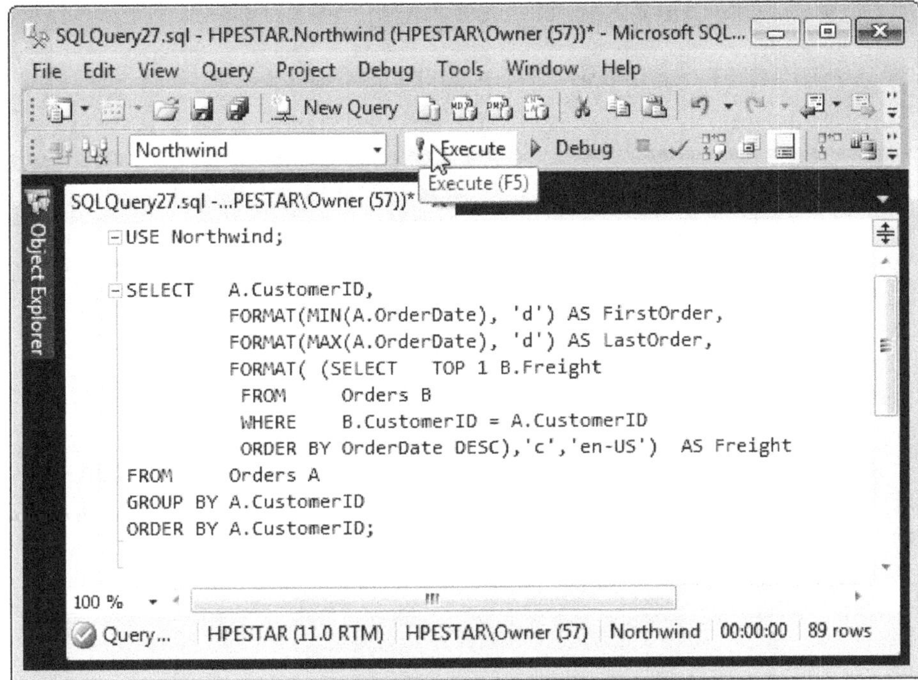

SQLQuery27.sql - HPESTAR.Northwind (HPESTAR\Owner (57))* - Microsoft SQL...
File Edit View Query Project Debug Tools Window Help
New Query
Northwind
Execute
Debug
Execute (F5)
Object Explorer
SQLQuery27.sql -...PESTAR\Owner (57))*
USE Northwind;
SELECT A.CustomerID,
FORMAT(MIN(A.OrderDate), 'd') AS FirstOrder,
FORMAT(MAX(A.OrderDate), 'd') AS LastOrder,
FORMAT((SELECT TOP 1 B.Freight
FROM Orders B
WHERE B.CustomerID = A.CustomerID
ORDER BY OrderDate DESC),'c','en-US') AS Freight
FROM Orders A
GROUP BY A.CustomerID
ORDER BY A.CustomerID;
100 %
Query...
HPESTAR (11.0 RTM)
HPESTAR\Owner (57)
Northwind
00:00:00
89 rows

The Significance of GO in T-SQL Scripts

"GO" is not transmitted to SQL Server. "GO" indicates the end of batch to the client software such as SSMS. "GO" also indicates the end of a logical unit to the human reader. Certain statements must be the first line, or have "GO" preceding them. SQL Azure scripts.

```
USE AdventureWorks2012;
CREATE FUNCTION Z () RETURNS TABLE AS
RETURN  SELECT * FROM Production.ProductSubcategory;
GO
/* A fatal scripting error occurred. Incorrect syntax was encountered while parsing GO.   */
```

```
USE AdventureWorks2012;
GO
CREATE FUNCTION Z () RETURNS TABLE AS RETURN SELECT * FROM
Production.ProductSubcategory;
GO
-- Command(s) completed successfully.
```

Results Pane contains result rows of the query. It is currently set to Grid format.

SQL Server 2012 query.

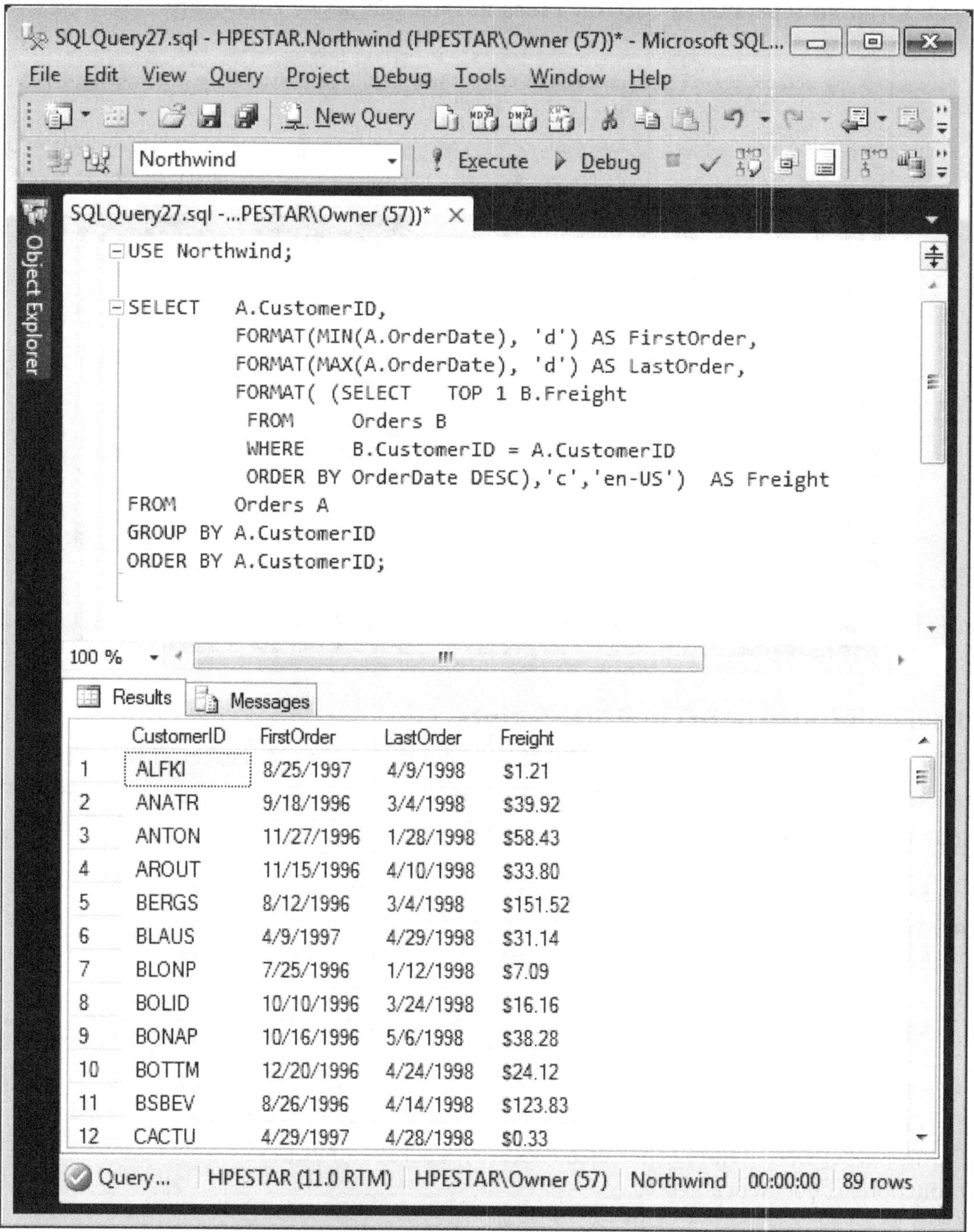
SQLQuery27.sql - HPESTAR.Northwind (HPESTAR\Owner (57))* - Microsoft SQL...
File Edit View Query Project Debug Tools Window Help
New Query
Northwind
Execute
Debug
Object Explorer
SQLQuery27.sql -...PESTAR\Owner (57))*
USE Northwind;
SELECT A.CustomerID,
FORMAT(MIN(A.OrderDate), 'd') AS FirstOrder,
FORMAT(MAX(A.OrderDate), 'd') AS LastOrder,
FORMAT((SELECT TOP 1 B.Freight
FROM Orders B
WHERE B.CustomerID = A.CustomerID
ORDER BY OrderDate DESC),'c','en-US') AS Freight
FROM Orders A
GROUP BY A.CustomerID
ORDER BY A.CustomerID;
100 %
Results
Messages
CustomerID FirstOrder LastOrder Freight
1 ALFKI 8/25/1997 4/9/1998 $1.21
2 ANATR 9/18/1996 3/4/1998 $39.92
3 ANTON 11/27/1996 1/28/1998 $58.43
4 AROUT 11/15/1996 4/10/1998 $33.80
5 BERGS 8/12/1996 3/4/1998 $151.52
6 BLAUS 4/9/1997 4/29/1998 $31.14
7 BLONP 7/25/1996 1/12/1998 $7.09
8 BOLID 10/10/1996 3/24/1998 $16.16
9 BONAP 10/16/1996 5/6/1998 $38.28
10 BOTTM 12/20/1996 4/24/1998 $24.12
11 BSBEV 8/26/1996 4/14/1998 $123.83
12 CACTU 4/29/1997 4/28/1998 $0.33
Query... HPESTAR (11.0 RTM) HPESTAR\Owner (57) Northwind 00:00:00 89 rows

The Messages Pane gets the row count values, warning & error messages as well as the output of the PRINT & RAISERROR statements if any.

The client software also gets the same messages following SQL Server 2012 query execution.

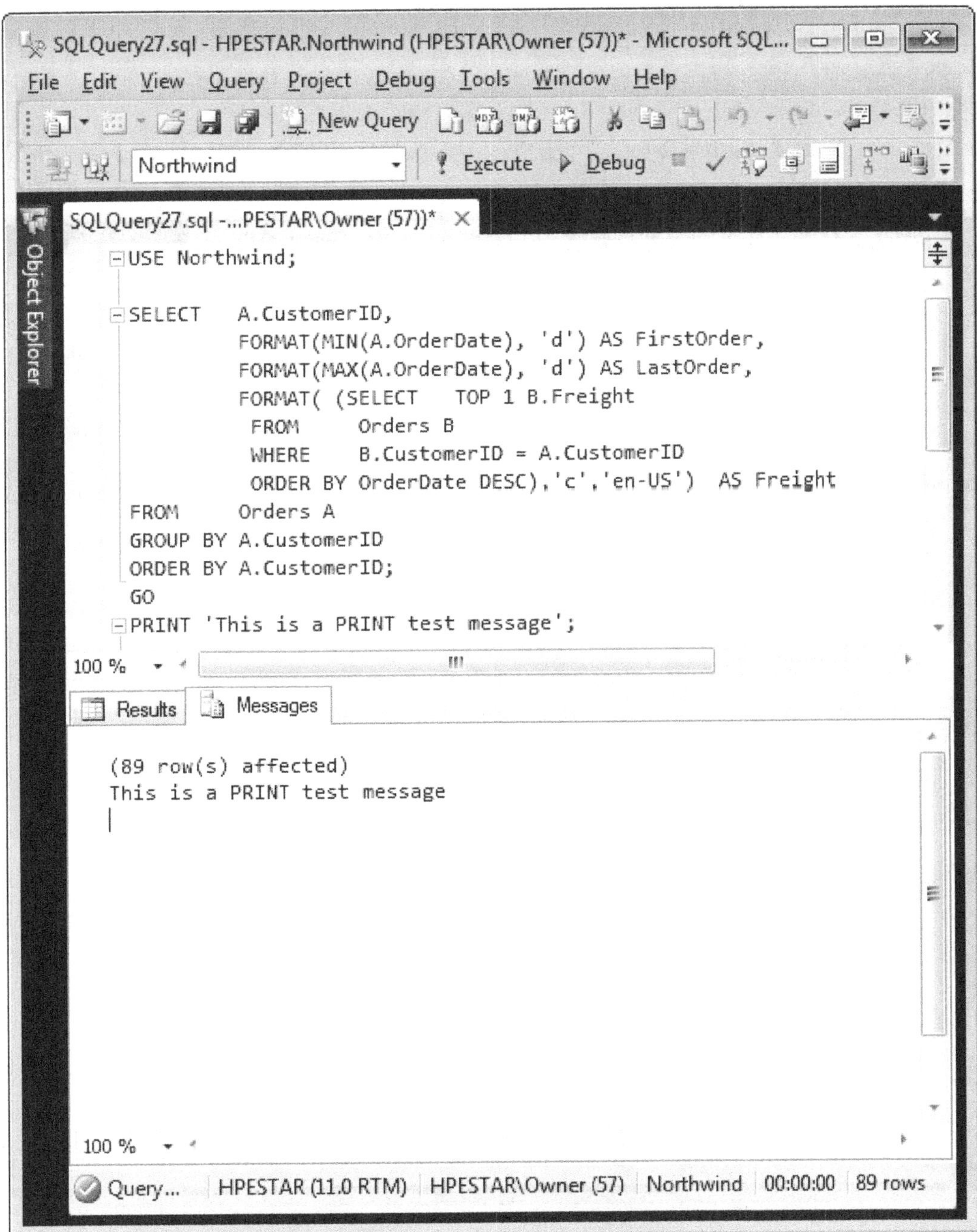

Routing Results to Grid, Text or File

Results can be routed to Grid, Text or File from the right-click menu or the Query drop-down menu.

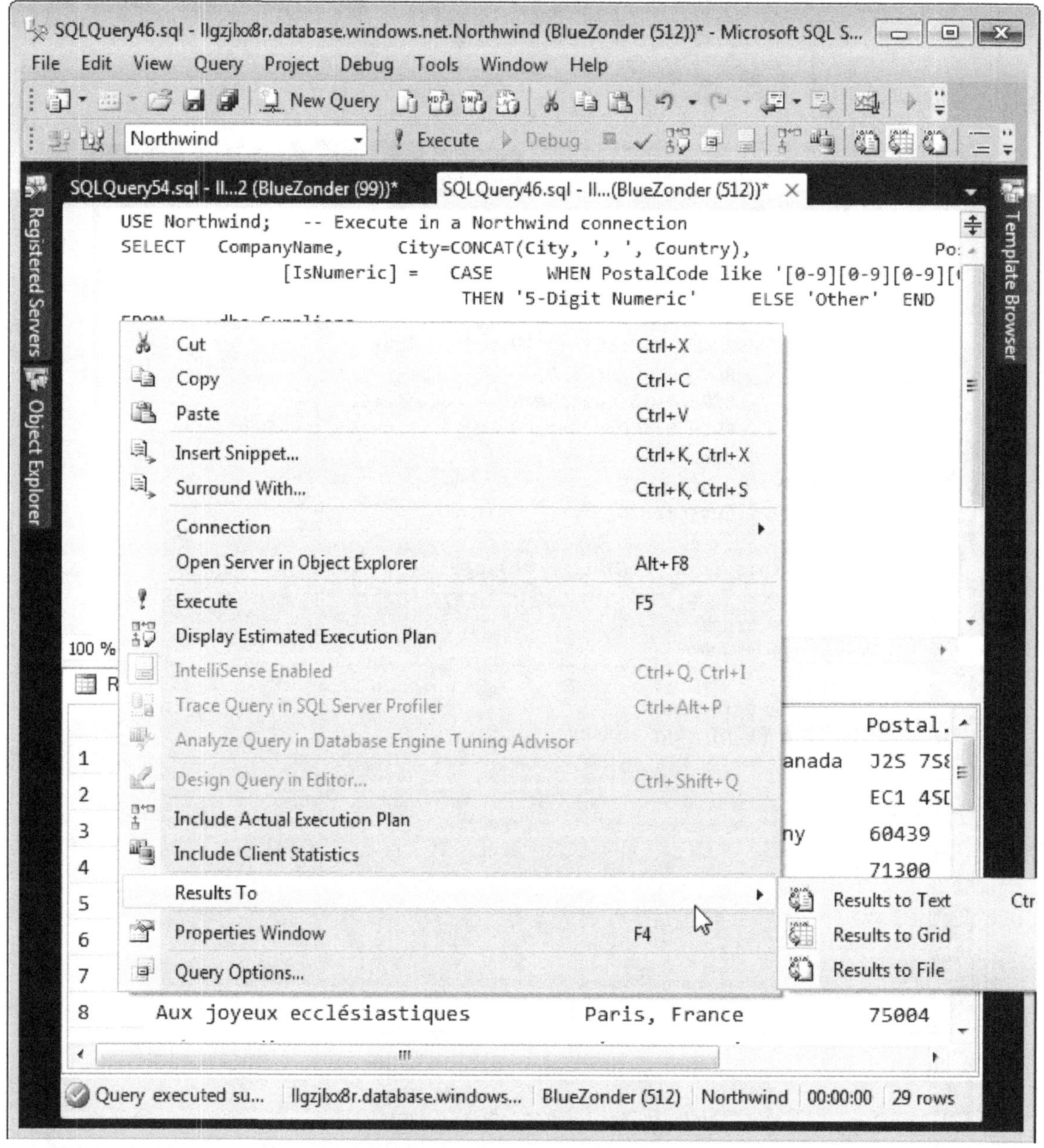

Routing Results to Text

The following screen window image displays results in text format. Messages also come to the Results window, following the results rows.

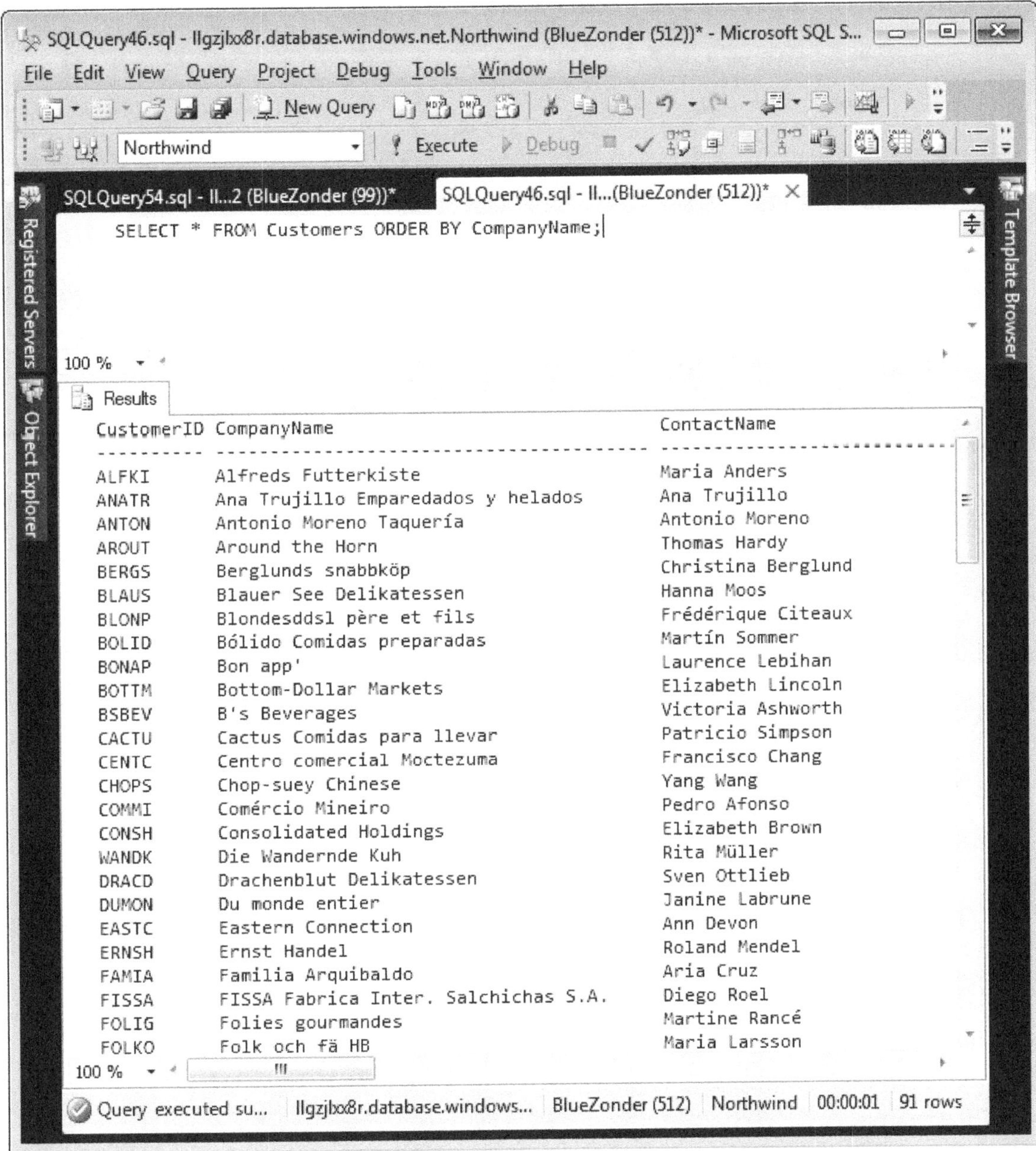
SQLQuery46.sql - llgzjbx8r.database.windows.net.Northwind (BlueZonder (512))* - Microsoft SQL S...
File Edit View Query Project Debug Tools Window Help
New Query
Northwind
Execute Debug
SQLQuery54.sql - Il...2 (BlueZonder (99))*
SQLQuery46.sql - Il...(BlueZonder (512))*
Registered Servers
Object Explorer
Template Browser
SELECT * FROM Customers ORDER BY CompanyName;
100 %
Results
CustomerID CompanyName ContactName
ALFKI Alfreds Futterkiste Maria Anders
ANATR Ana Trujillo Emparedados y helados Ana Trujillo
ANTON Antonio Moreno Taquería Antonio Moreno
AROUT Around the Horn Thomas Hardy
BERGS Berglunds snabbköp Christina Berglund
BLAUS Blauer See Delikatessen Hanna Moos
BLONP Blondesddsl père et fils Frédérique Citeaux
BOLID Bólido Comidas preparadas Martín Sommer
BONAP Bon app' Laurence Lebihan
BOTTM Bottom-Dollar Markets Elizabeth Lincoln
BSBEV B's Beverages Victoria Ashworth
CACTU Cactus Comidas para llevar Patricio Simpson
CENTC Centro comercial Moctezuma Francisco Chang
CHOPS Chop-suey Chinese Yang Wang
COMMI Comércio Mineiro Pedro Afonso
CONSH Consolidated Holdings Elizabeth Brown
WANDK Die Wandernde Kuh Rita Müller
DRACD Drachenblut Delikatessen Sven Ottlieb
DUMON Du monde entier Janine Labrune
EASTC Eastern Connection Ann Devon
ERNSH Ernst Handel Roland Mendel
FAMIA Familia Arquibaldo Aria Cruz
FISSA FISSA Fabrica Inter. Salchichas S.A. Diego Roel
FOLIG Folies gourmandes Martine Rancé
FOLKO Folk och fä HB Maria Larsson
100 %
Query executed su... llgzjbx8r.database.windows... BlueZonder (512) Northwind 00:00:01 91 rows

Routing Results to File

When the routing option is file, the file save window pops up upon query execution.

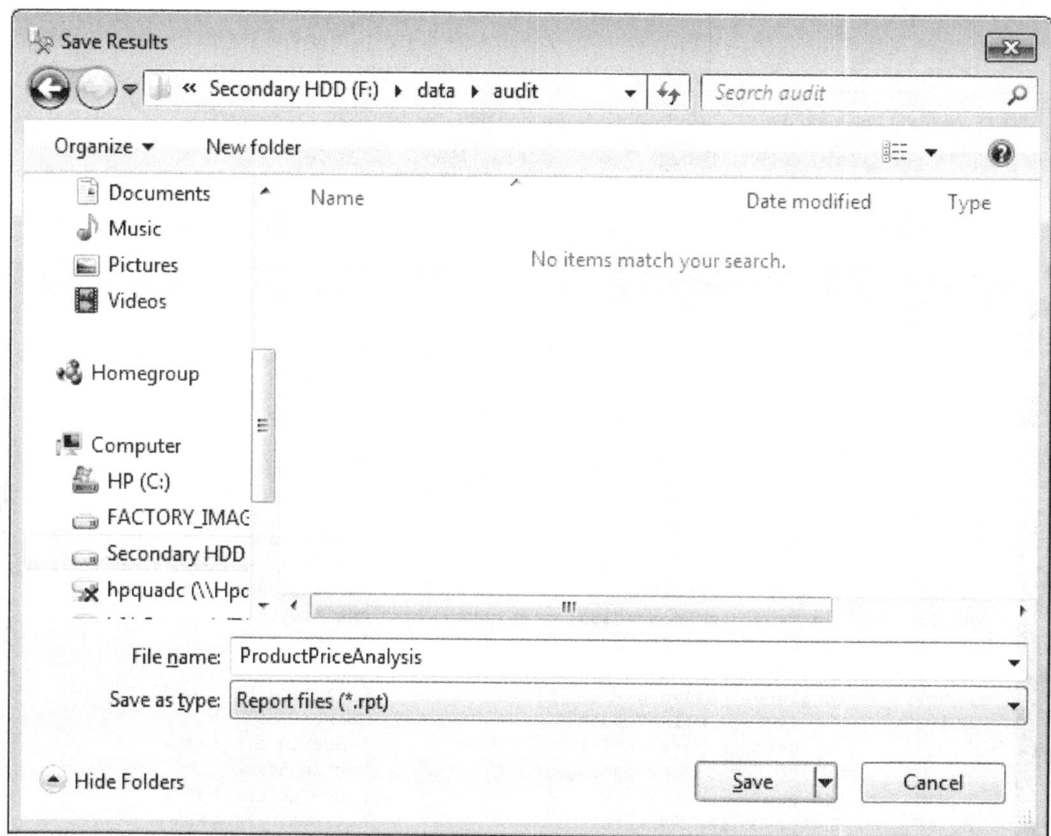

Part of the file in Notepad.

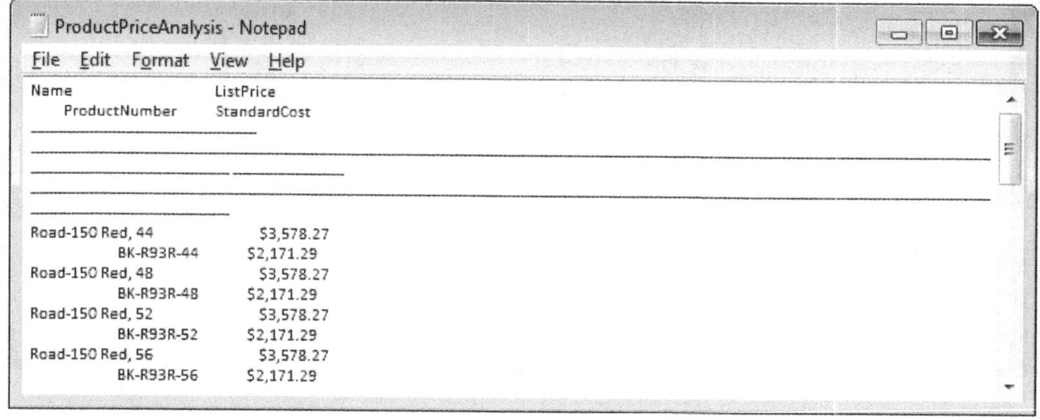


```
Name                                    ListPrice
          ProductNumber                 StandardCost

Road-150 Red, 44                             $3,578.27
                   BK-R93R-44             $2,171.29
Road-150 Red, 48                             $3,578.27
                   BK-R93R-48             $2,171.29
Road-150 Red, 52                             $3,578.27
                   BK-R93R-52             $2,171.29
Road-150 Red, 56                             $3,578.27
                   BK-R93R-56             $2,171.29
```

Saving Results in CSV Flat File Format

Results can also be saved in CSV (comma separated values) format which can be read by Excel and other software. SQL Server 2012 query.

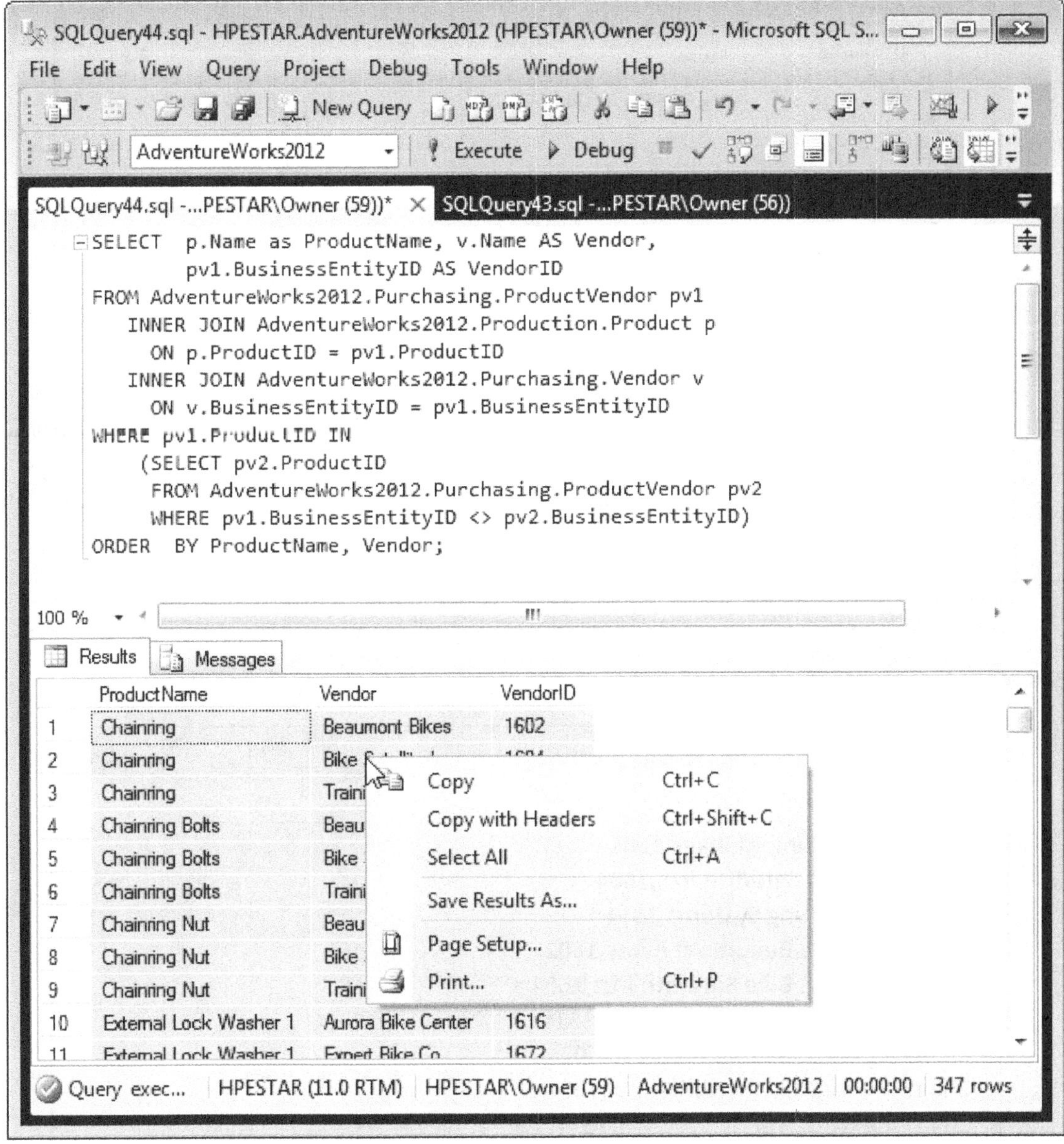

The saving file dialog box is configured automatically to csv saving.

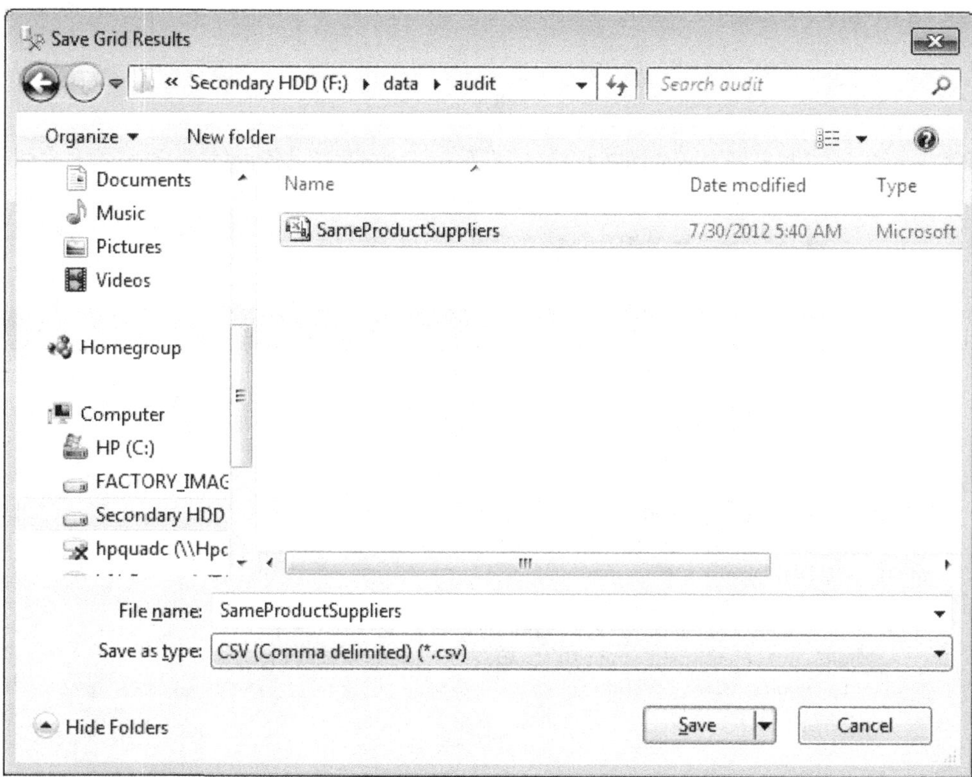

Part of the file in Notepad window.

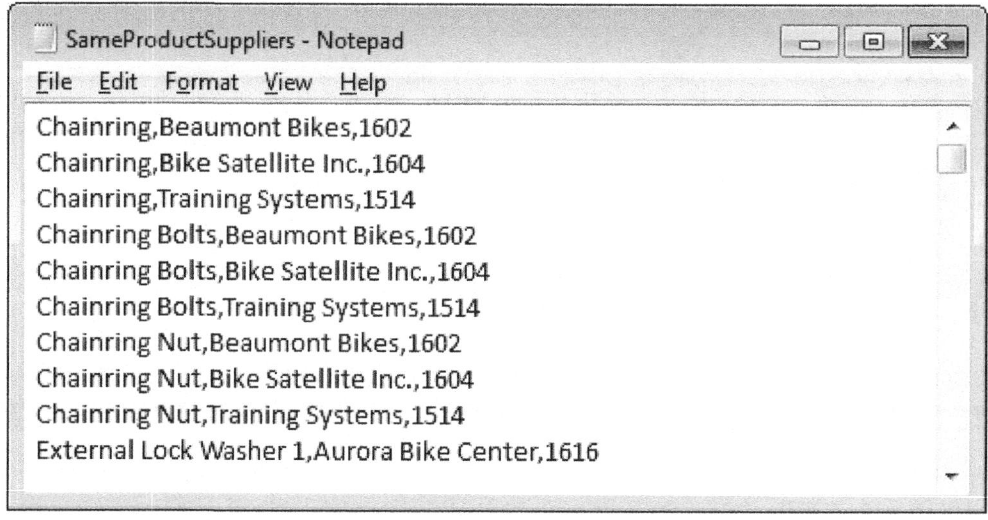


```
Chainring,Beaumont Bikes,1602
Chainring,Bike Satellite Inc.,1604
Chainring,Training Systems,1514
Chainring Bolts,Beaumont Bikes,1602
Chainring Bolts,Bike Satellite Inc.,1604
Chainring Bolts,Training Systems,1514
Chainring Nut,Beaumont Bikes,1602
Chainring Nut,Bike Satellite Inc.,1604
Chainring Nut,Training Systems,1514
External Lock Washer 1,Aurora Bike Center,1616
```

Copy & Paste Results to Excel

Using the copy / copy with headers option in SSMS result window, the query results can simply be pasted into an Excel worksheet. Excel may do implicit conversions on some columns. SQL Server 2012 query.

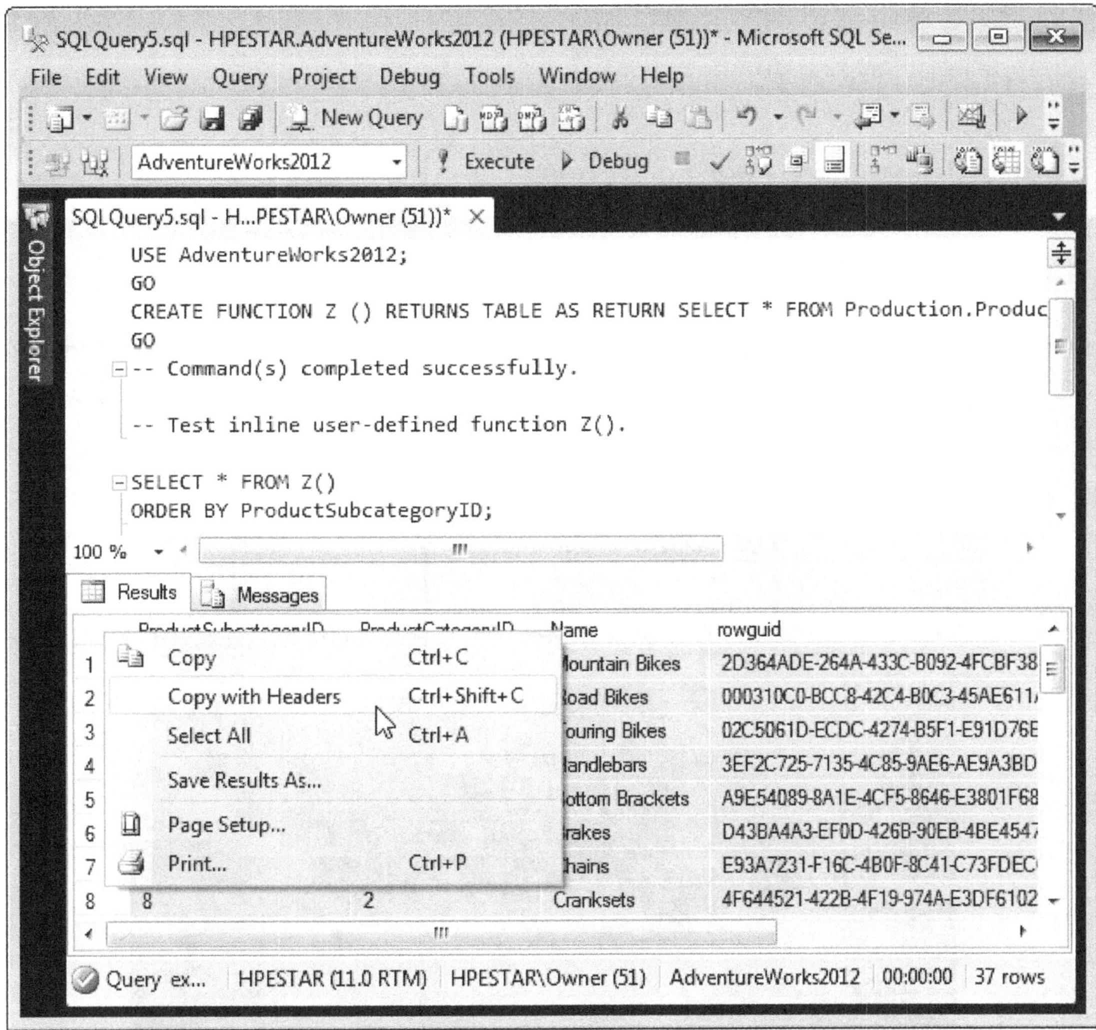

After pasting into an Excel worksheet some formatting may be necessary such as for datetime columns.

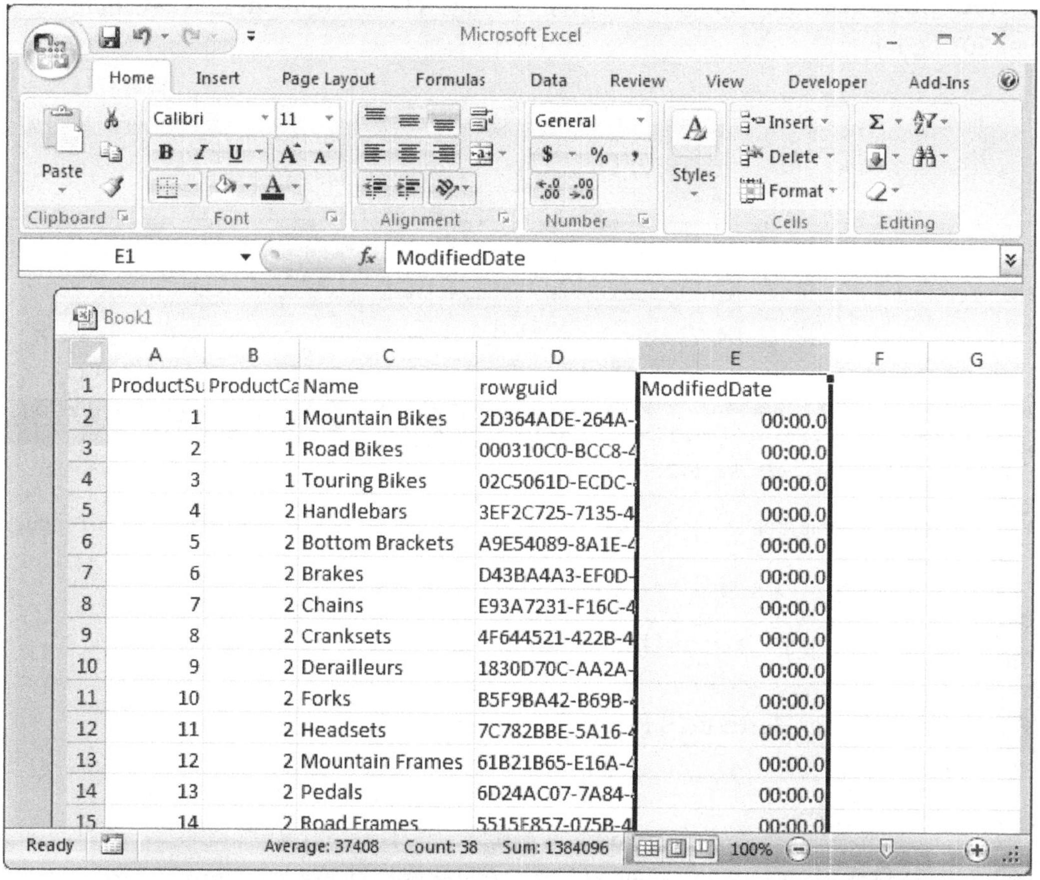

Microsoft Excel — Book1

E1 | *fx* ModifiedDate

	A	B	C	D	E
1	ProductSu	ProductCa	Name	rowguid	ModifiedDate
2	1	1	Mountain Bikes	2D364ADE-264A-	00:00.0
3	2	1	Road Bikes	000310C0-BCC8-4	00:00.0
4	3	1	Touring Bikes	02C5061D-ECDC-	00:00.0
5	4	2	Handlebars	3EF2C725-7135-4	00:00.0
6	5	2	Bottom Brackets	A9E54089-8A1E-4	00:00.0
7	6	2	Brakes	D43BA4A3-EF0D-	00:00.0
8	7	2	Chains	E93A7231-F16C-4	00:00.0
9	8	2	Cranksets	4F644521-422B-4	00:00.0
10	9	2	Derailleurs	1830D70C-AA2A-	00:00.0
11	10	2	Forks	B5F9BA42-B69B-	00:00.0
12	11	2	Headsets	7C782BBE-5A16-	00:00.0
13	12	2	Mountain Frames	61B21B65-E16A-4	00:00.0
14	13	2	Pedals	6D24AC07-7A84-	00:00.0
15	14	2	Road Frames	5515F857-075B-4	00:00.0

Ready Average: 37408 Count: 38 Sum: 1384096 100%

Error Handling & Debugging

Error handling and debugging is a major part of database development work. When there is an error, it is displayed in the Messages area (or returned to the application client software) which automatically becomes active. In the following example, we introduced an invalid column name which resulted in error. The error message line reference starts with the top line of the batch which is the first line after the first "GO" which indicates a new batch. The red wave-underlining comes from optional IntelliSense and not related to the execution attempt error message. IntelliSense gives warning ahead of time if it detects a potential error. Simple errors can be corrected with help from the error message. Complex errors may required web search and/or examining the query in parts. SQL Server 2012 query.

SQLQuery27.sql - HPESTAR.Northwind (HPESTAR\Owner (57))* - Microsoft SQL Server Man...
File Edit View Query Project Debug Tools Window Help
New Query
Northwind
Execute
Debug
SQLQuery27.sql -...PESTAR\Owner (57))*
Object Explorer
USE Northwind;
GO
SELECT A.CustomerIDzzzz,
FORMAT(MIN(A.OrderDate), 'd') AS FirstOrder,
FORMAT(MAX(A.OrderDate), 'd') AS LastOrder,
FORMAT((SELECT TOP 1 B.Freight
FROM Orders B
WHERE B.CustomerID = A.CustomerID
ORDER BY OrderDate DESC),'c','en-US') AS Freight
FROM Orders A
GROUP BY A.CustomerID
ORDER BY A.CustomerID;
GO
PRINT 'This is a PRINT test message';
GO
100 %
Results
Msg 207, Level 16, State 1, Line 1
Invalid column name 'CustomerIDzzzz'.
This is a PRINT test message
100 %
Query completed wi...
HPESTAR (11.0 RTM)
HPESTAR\Owner (57)
Northwind
00:00:00
0 rows

Locating the Error Line in a Query

Position the cursor on the error and double click. The error line will be highlighted. This method does not work for all errors. SQL Server 2012 query.

SQLQuery54.sql - HPESTAR.AdventureWorks2012 (HPESTAR\Owner (61))* - Microsoft SQL S...
File Edit View Query Project Debug Tools Window Help
New Query
AdventureWorks2012
Execute
Debug
SQLQuery54.sql -...PESTAR\Owner (61))*
SQLQuery53.sql -...PESTAR\Owner (59))*
USE AdventureWorks2012;
WITH cteLastSalaryChange
AS (SELECT BusinessEntityID AS EmployeeID,
Maxi(RateChangeDate) AS ChangeDate
FROM HumanResources.EmployeePayHistory
GROUP BY BusinessEntityID),
cteLastSalary
AS (SELECT eph.BusinessEntityID AS EmployeeID,
Rate
FROM HumanResources.EmployeePayHistory eph
INNER JOIN cteLastSalaryChange lsc
ON lsc.EmployeeID = eph.BusinessEntityID
AND lsc.ChangeDate = eph.RateChangeDate)
-- SELECT * FROM cteLastSalary -- for testing & debugging
SELECT TOP 1 FORMAT(Rate, 'c', 'en-US') AS SecondHighestPayRate
FROM (SELECT TOP 2 Rate
FROM cteLastSalary
ORDER BY Rate DESC) a -- Derived table
ORDER BY Rate ASC;
100 %
Messages
Msg 195, Level 15, State 10, Line 6
'Maxi' is not a recognized built-in function name.
100 %
Query comple...
HPESTAR (11.0 RTM)
HPESTAR\Owner (61)
AdventureWorks2012
00:00:00
0 rows

Error Message Pointing to the Wrong Line

For some errors, the first line of the query (3) is returned by the database engine not the actual error line (13). The error message is still very helpful though in this instance. SQL Server 2012 query.

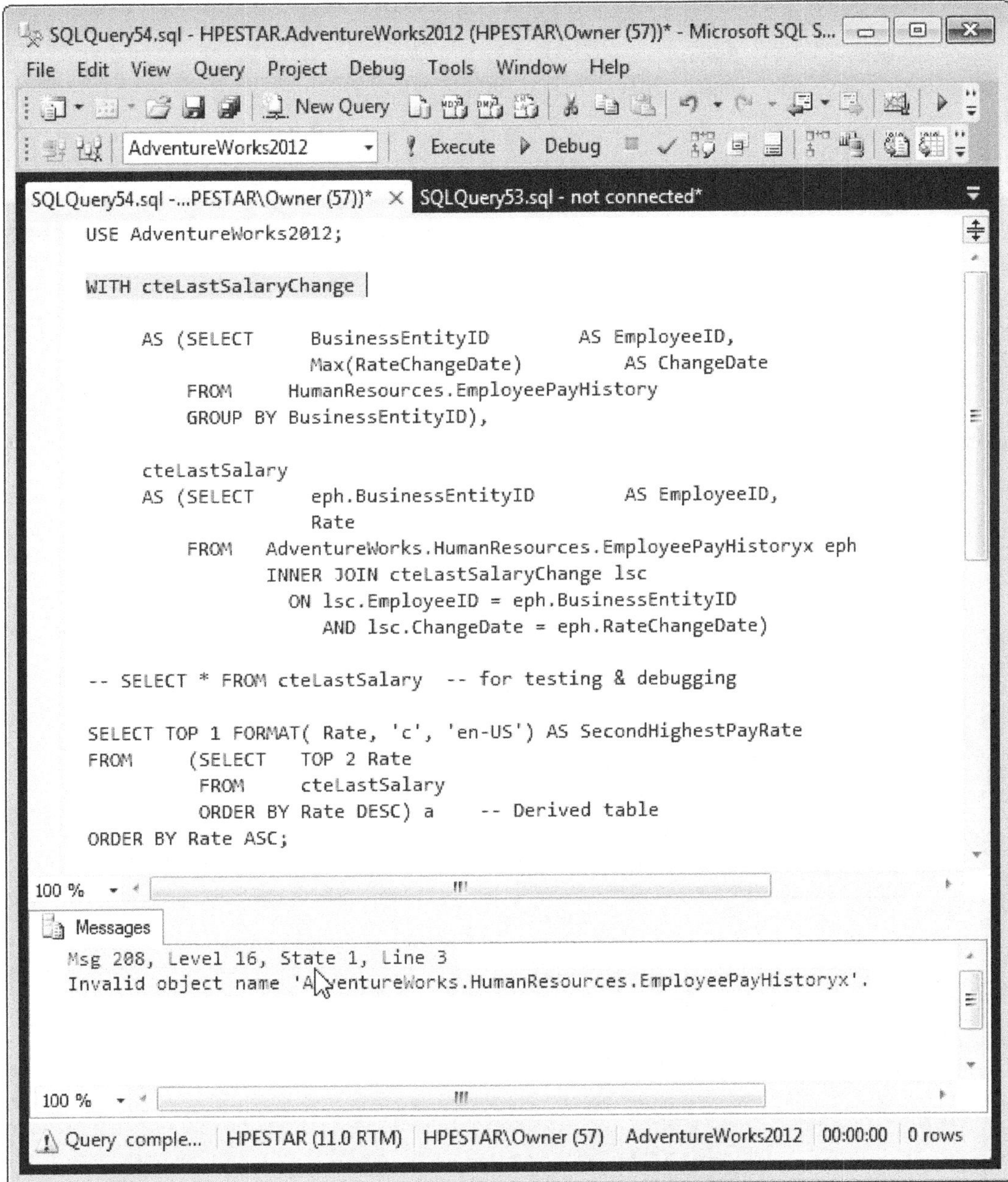

```
USE AdventureWorks2012;

WITH cteLastSalaryChange

    AS (SELECT    BusinessEntityID       AS EmployeeID,
                  Max(RateChangeDate)        AS ChangeDate
        FROM     HumanResources.EmployeePayHistory
        GROUP BY BusinessEntityID),

    cteLastSalary
    AS (SELECT    eph.BusinessEntityID       AS EmployeeID,
                  Rate
        FROM    AdventureWorks.HumanResources.EmployeePayHistoryx eph
                INNER JOIN cteLastSalaryChange lsc
                  ON lsc.EmployeeID = eph.BusinessEntityID
                    AND lsc.ChangeDate = eph.RateChangeDate)

-- SELECT * FROM cteLastSalary  -- for testing & debugging

SELECT TOP 1 FORMAT( Rate, 'c', 'en-US') AS SecondHighestPayRate
FROM     (SELECT   TOP 2 Rate
          FROM     cteLastSalary
          ORDER BY Rate DESC) a    -- Derived table
ORDER BY Rate ASC;
```

```
Msg 208, Level 16, State 1, Line 3
Invalid object name 'AdventureWorks.HumanResources.EmployeePayHistoryx'.
```

Parsing a Query for Syntax Errors

A query (or one or more batches) can be parsed for syntax errors. Parsing catches syntax errors such as using "ORDER" instead of "ORDER BY" for sorting. SQL Server 2012 query.

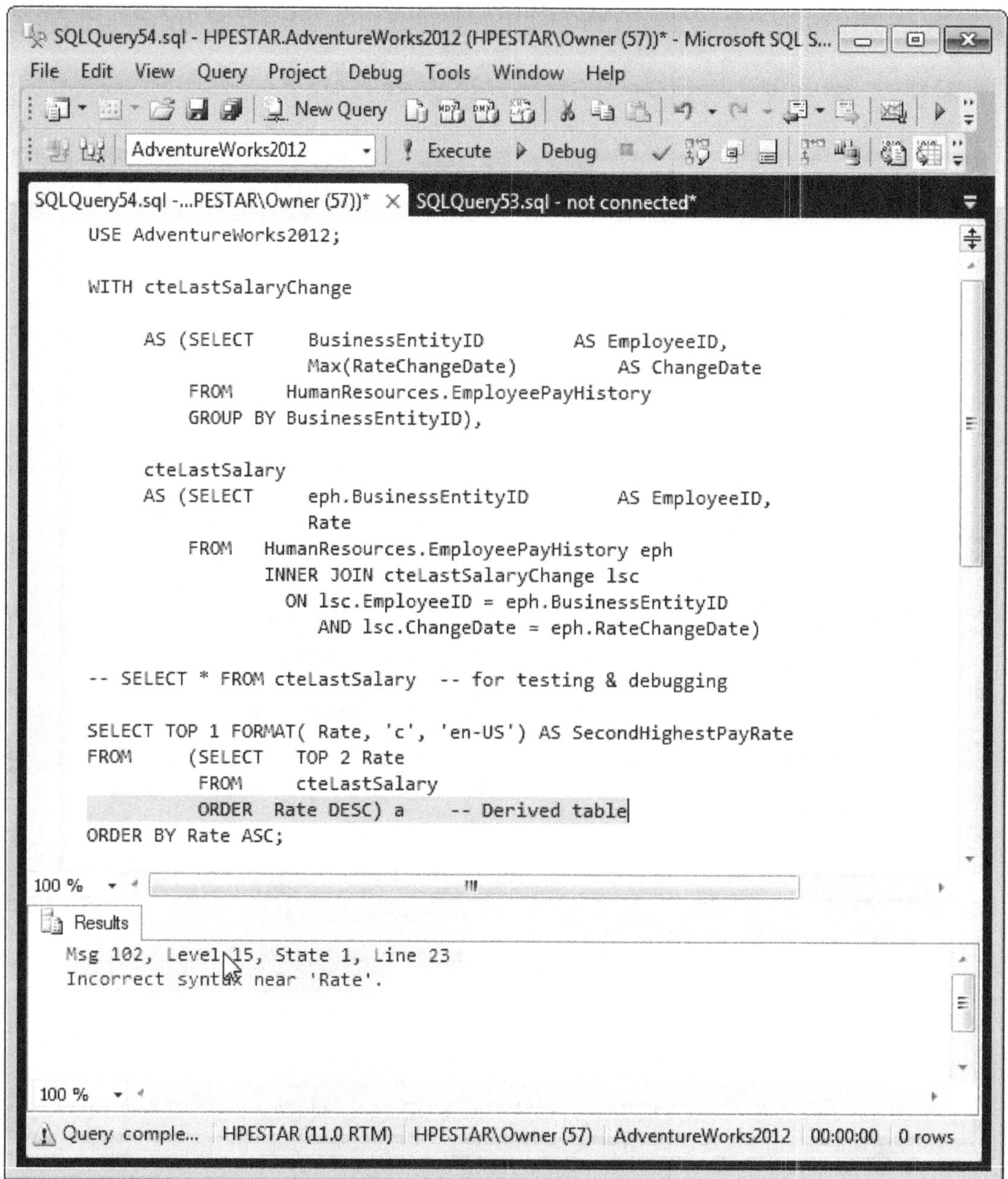

```
USE AdventureWorks2012;

WITH cteLastSalaryChange

     AS (SELECT     BusinessEntityID         AS EmployeeID,
                    Max(RateChangeDate)          AS ChangeDate
         FROM     HumanResources.EmployeePayHistory
         GROUP BY BusinessEntityID),

     cteLastSalary
     AS (SELECT     eph.BusinessEntityID         AS EmployeeID,
                    Rate
         FROM    HumanResources.EmployeePayHistory eph
                INNER JOIN cteLastSalaryChange lsc
                  ON lsc.EmployeeID = eph.BusinessEntityID
                     AND lsc.ChangeDate = eph.RateChangeDate)

-- SELECT * FROM cteLastSalary  -- for testing & debugging

SELECT TOP 1 FORMAT( Rate, 'c', 'en-US') AS SecondHighestPayRate
FROM     (SELECT   TOP 2 Rate
          FROM     cteLastSalary
          ORDER  Rate DESC) a     -- Derived table
ORDER BY Rate ASC;
```

```
Msg 102, Level 15, State 1, Line 23
Incorrect syntax near 'Rate'.
```

Deferred Name Resolution Process

Deferred Name Resolution Process: Only syntax errors are caught when parsed, not execution (runtime) errors as shown in the following demo which has an invalid table reference (EmployeePayHistoryx). Similarly, **stored procedures can be compiled without errors with invalid table references**. A table need not exist for stored procedure compilation, only for execution. SQL Server 2012 query.

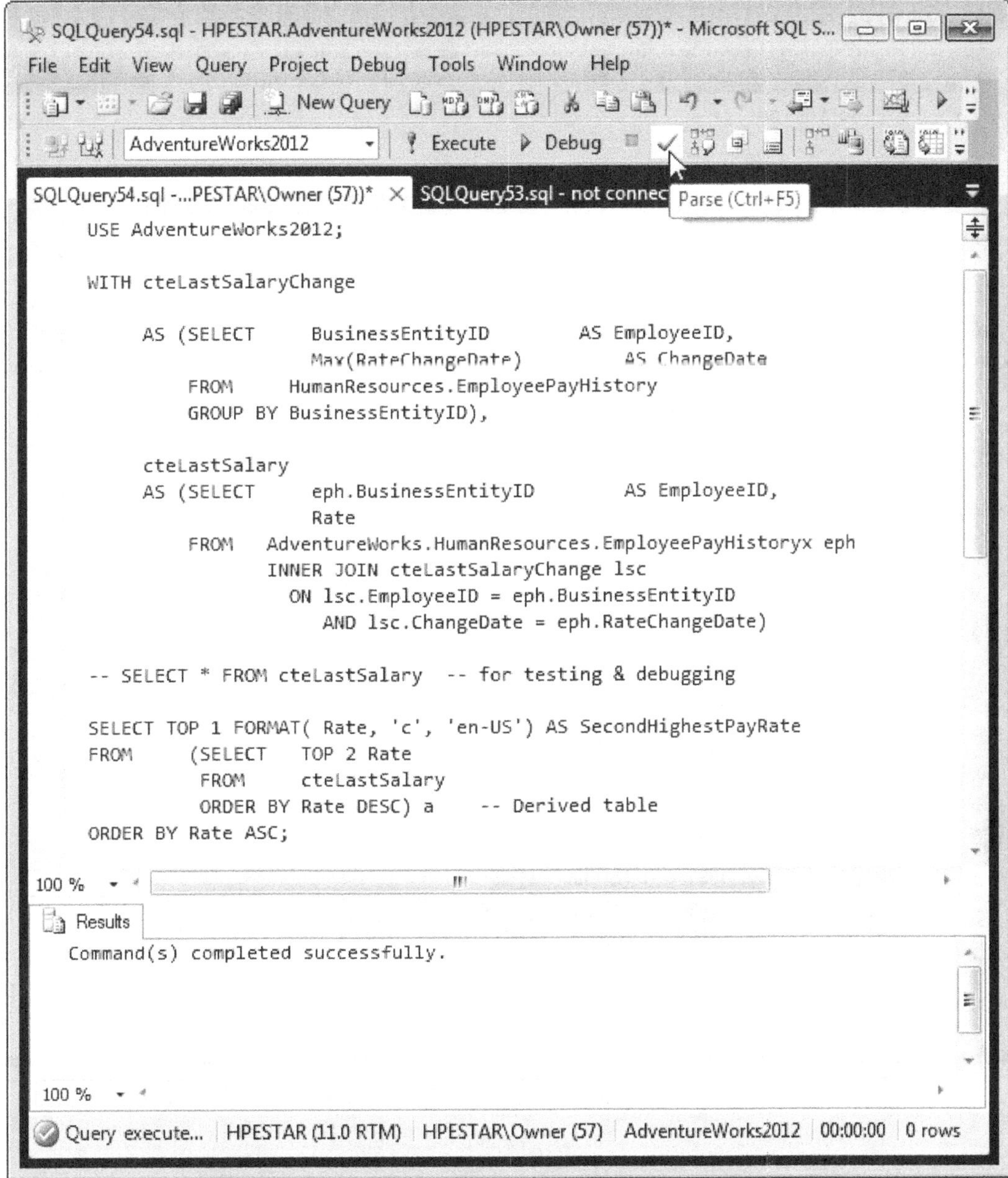

Executing Single Batch Only

A single batch can be executed by selecting (highlighting) it and clicking on Execute. SQL Server 2012 query.

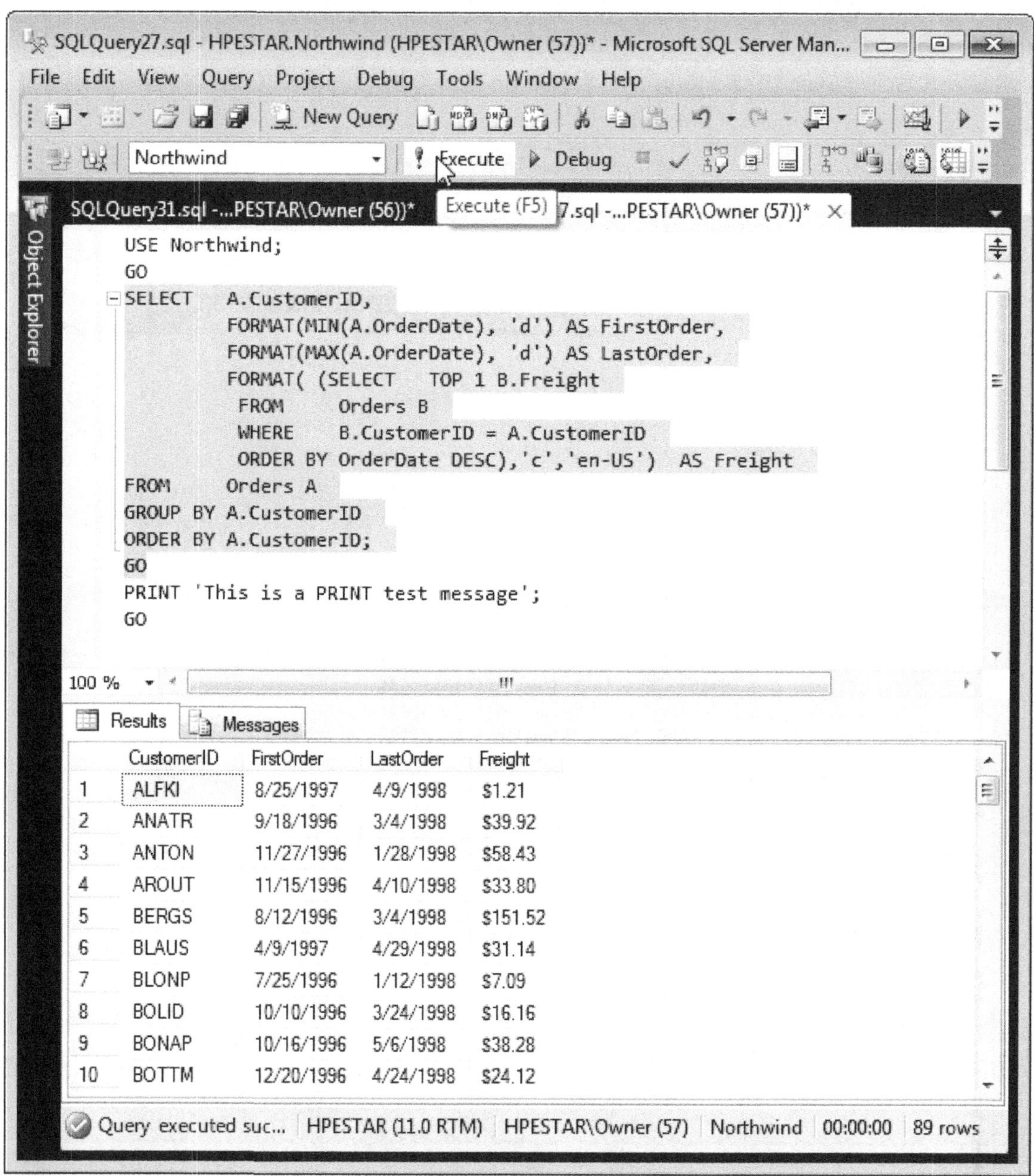

Executing Part of a Query

A part of a query can be executed as long as it is a valid query, otherwise error results. The query part has to be selected (highlighted) and the Execute button has to be pushed. The selected part of the query is considered a batch which is sent to the server. In this example, we executed the subquery (inner query) in the WHERE clause predicate. SQL Server 2012 query.

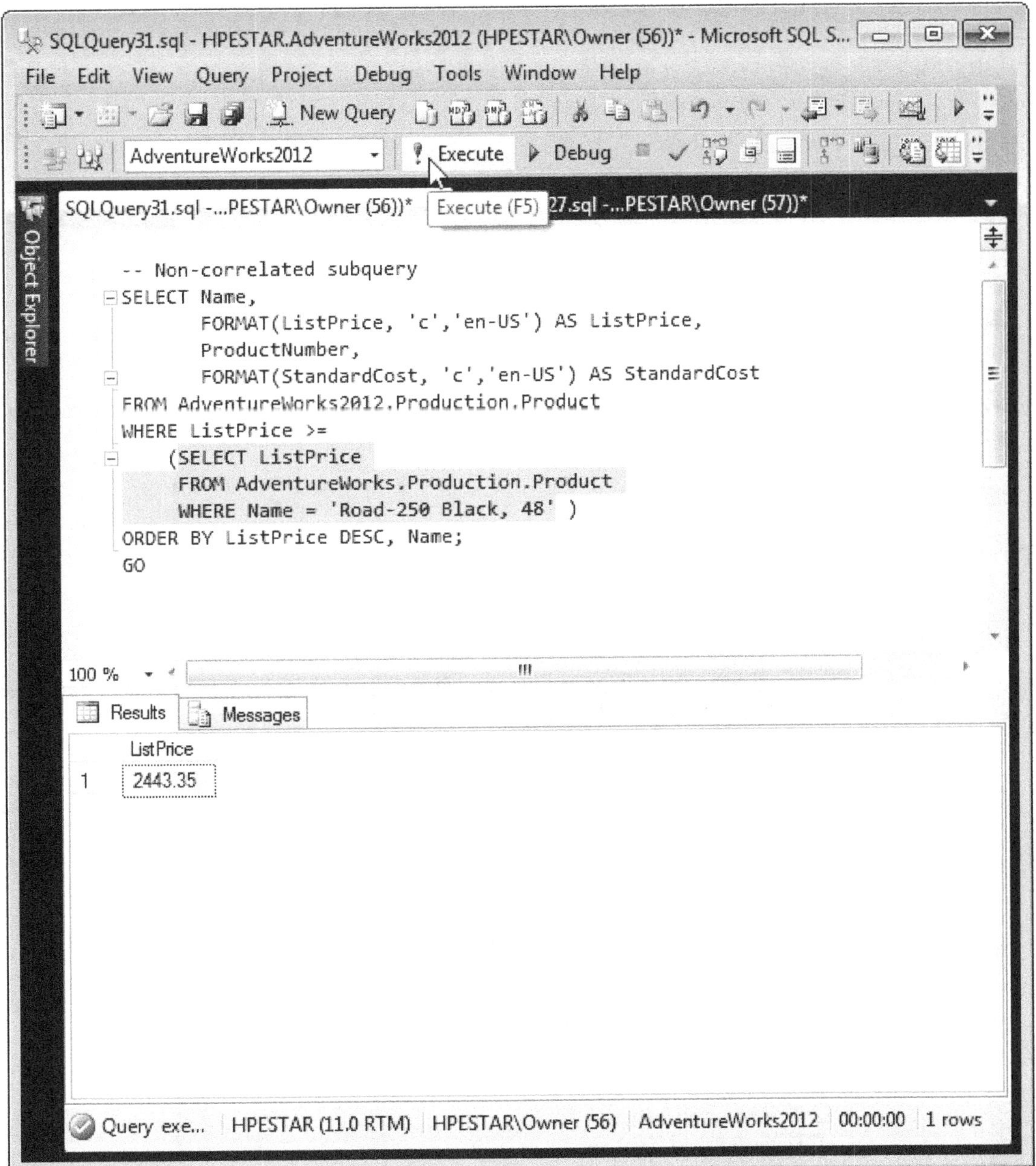
SQLQuery31.sql - HPESTAR.AdventureWorks2012 (HPESTAR\Owner (56))* - Microsoft SQL S...
File Edit View Query Project Debug Tools Window Help
New Query
AdventureWorks2012
Execute
Debug
Object Explorer
SQLQuery31.sql -...PESTAR\Owner (56))*
Execute (F5)
27.sql -...PESTAR\Owner (57))*
-- Non-correlated subquery
SELECT Name,
FORMAT(ListPrice, 'c','en-US') AS ListPrice,
ProductNumber,
FORMAT(StandardCost, 'c','en-US') AS StandardCost
FROM AdventureWorks2012.Production.Product
WHERE ListPrice >=
(SELECT ListPrice
FROM AdventureWorks.Production.Product
WHERE Name = 'Road-250 Black, 48')
ORDER BY ListPrice DESC, Name;
GO
100 %
Results
Messages
ListPrice
1
2443.35
Query exe...
HPESTAR (11.0 RTM)
HPESTAR\Owner (56)
AdventureWorks2012
00:00:00
1 rows

Object Explorer

SSMS Object Explorer functions as:

- A tree-based directory of all database objects
- A launching base for graphical user-interface tools
- An access way to object properties

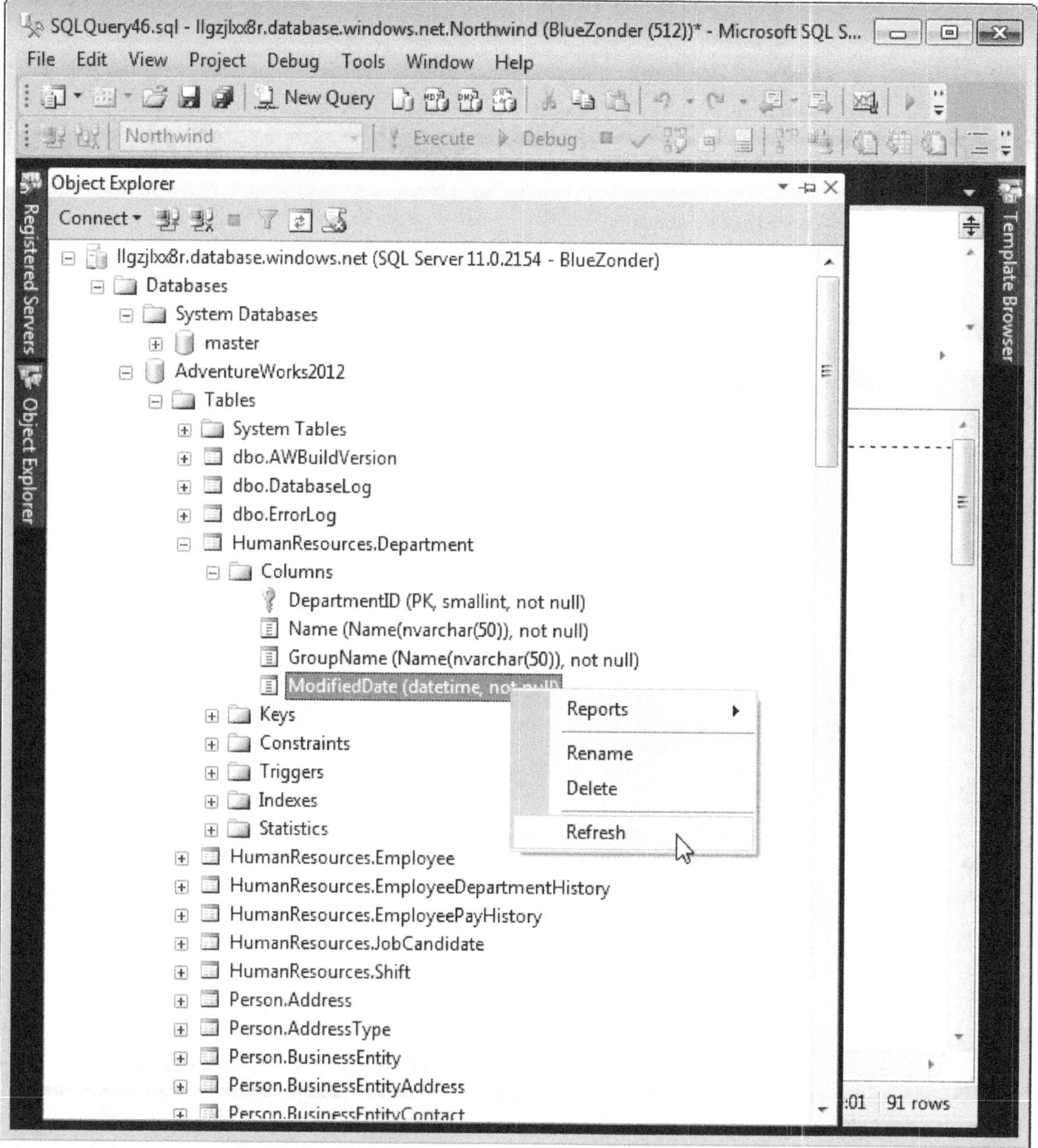

Context-Sensitive Right-Click Menu

Based on what object the cursor is on, right-click menu changes accordingly, it is context-sensitive. In the following demo the cursor is on table object when we right click on the mouse.

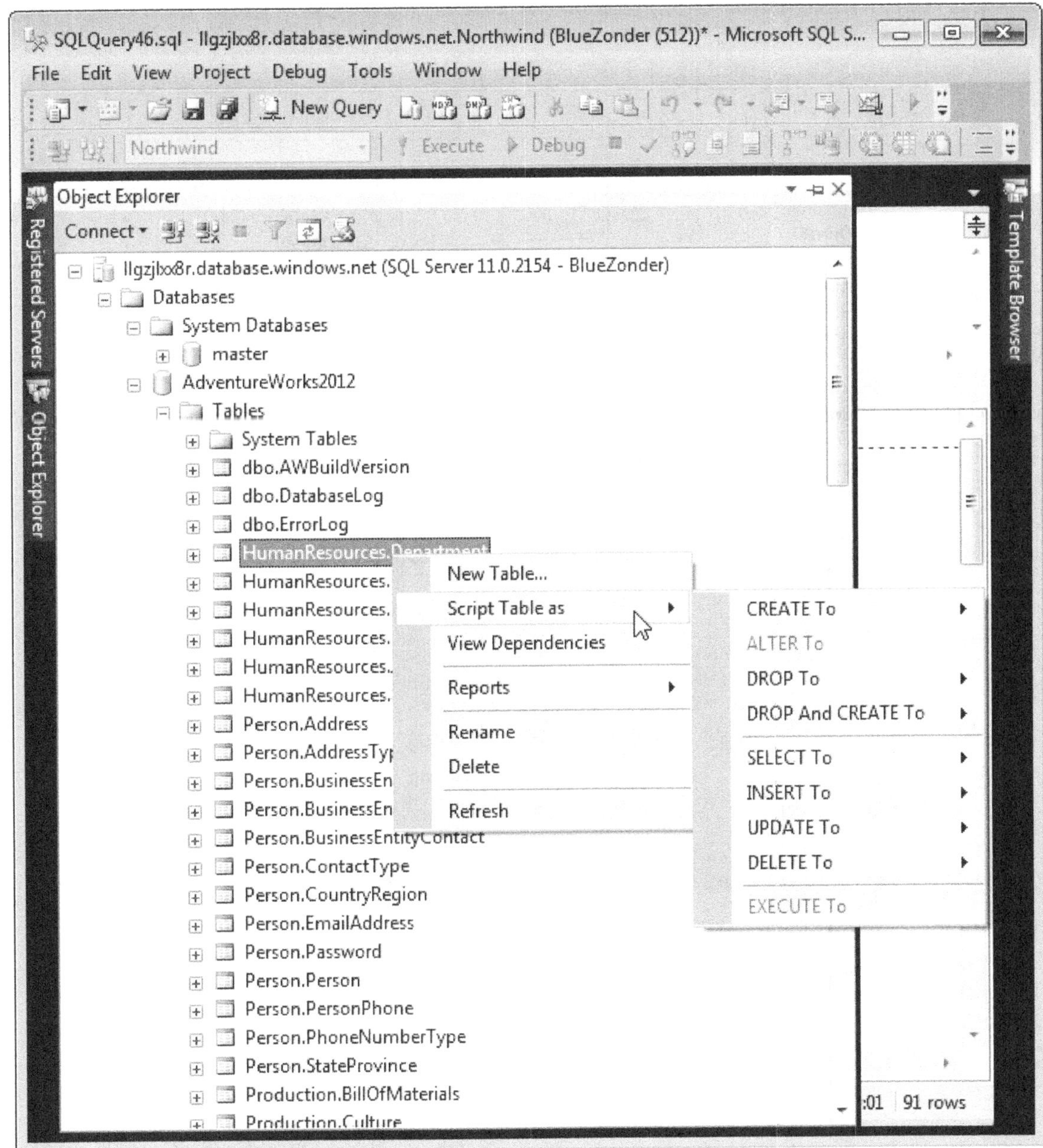

Graphical Query Designer

The graphical query designer is **not supported in Azure SQL**. The Design Query in Editor entry on the Query drop-down menu launches the graphical Query Designer which can be used to design the query with GUI method and the T-SQL SELECT code will be generated automatically upon completion. SQL Server 2012 query.

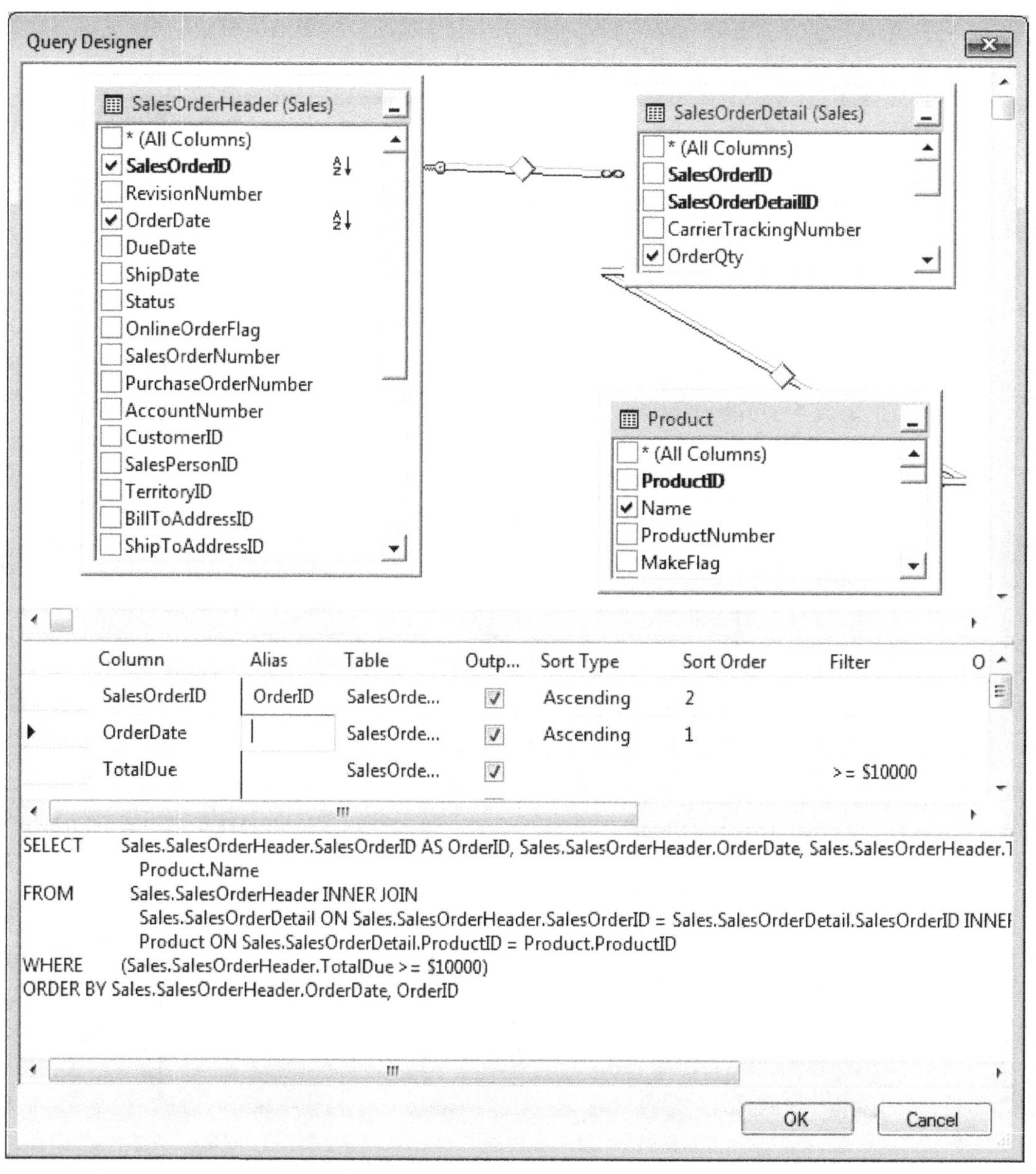

Designing a GROUP BY Query in Query Designer

Query Designer can be used to design from simple to complex queries. It can also serve as a starter query for a more complex query. It is really easy to get the tables JOINs graphically. SQL Server 2012 query.

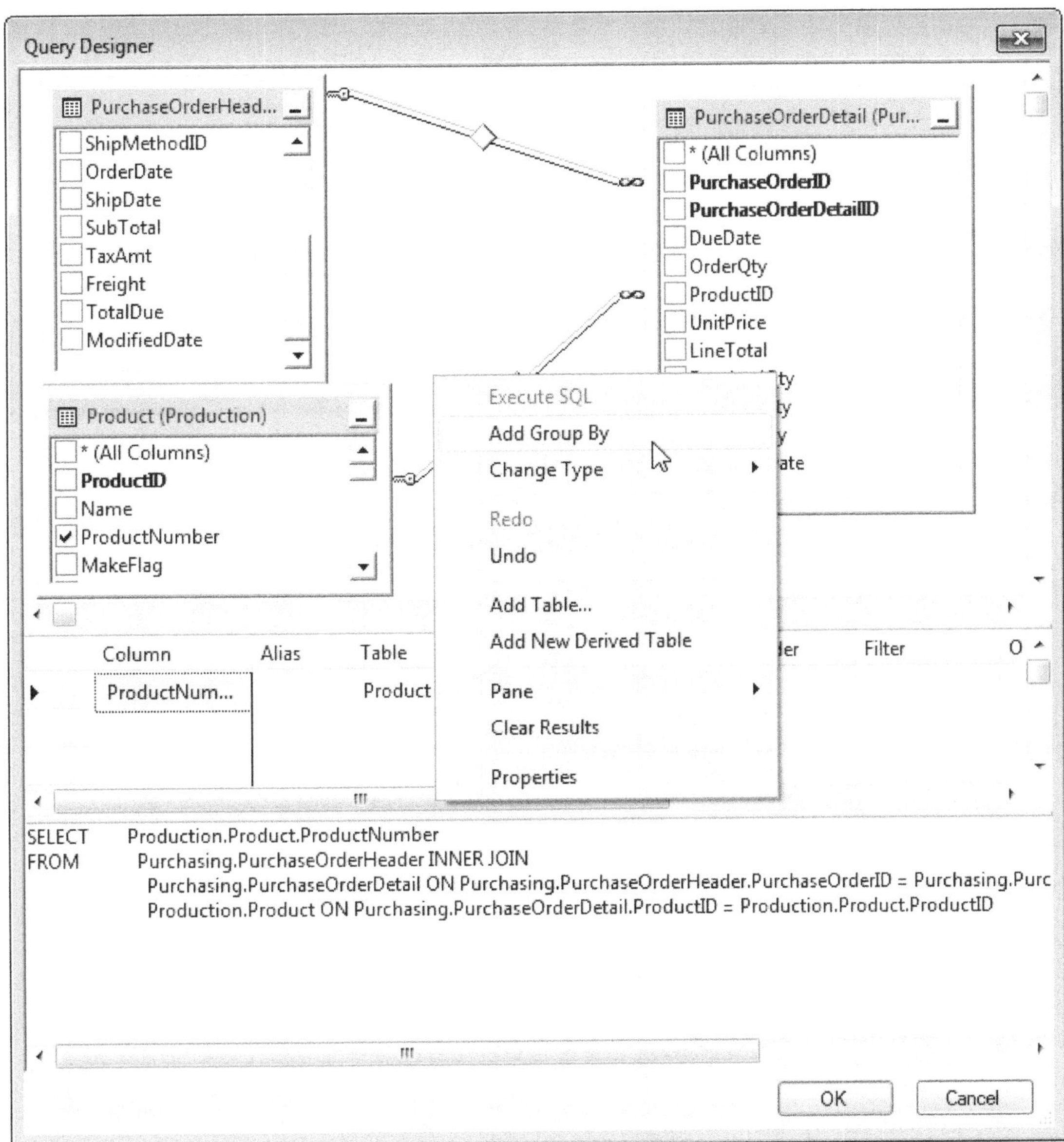

The Production.Product.Name column will also be configured as GROUP BY (drop-down default).

<u>SQL Server 2012 query.</u>

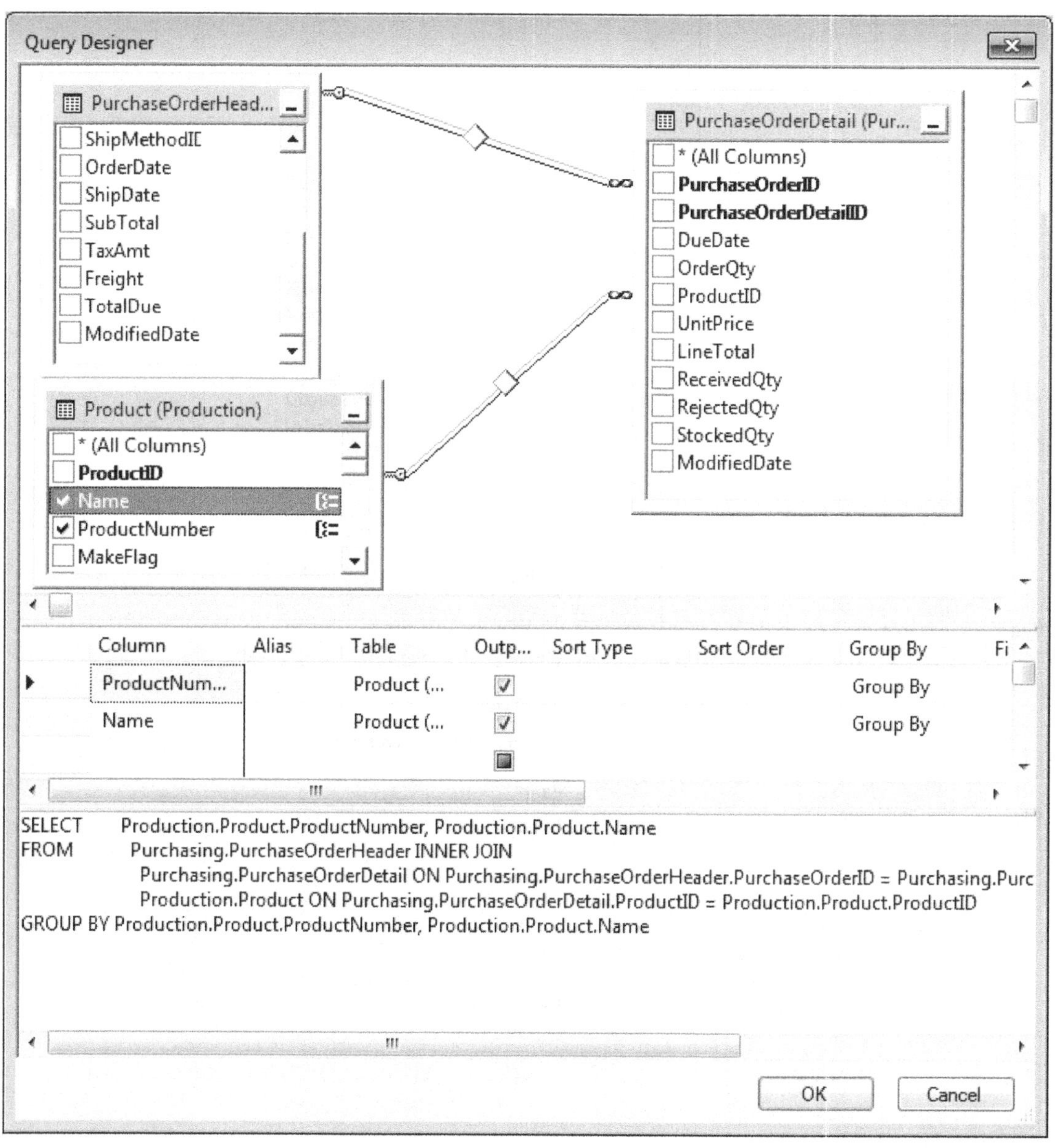

We add the TotalDue column and change the summary function to "SUM" from "Group by" and configure sorting on the first column.

SQL Server 2012 query.

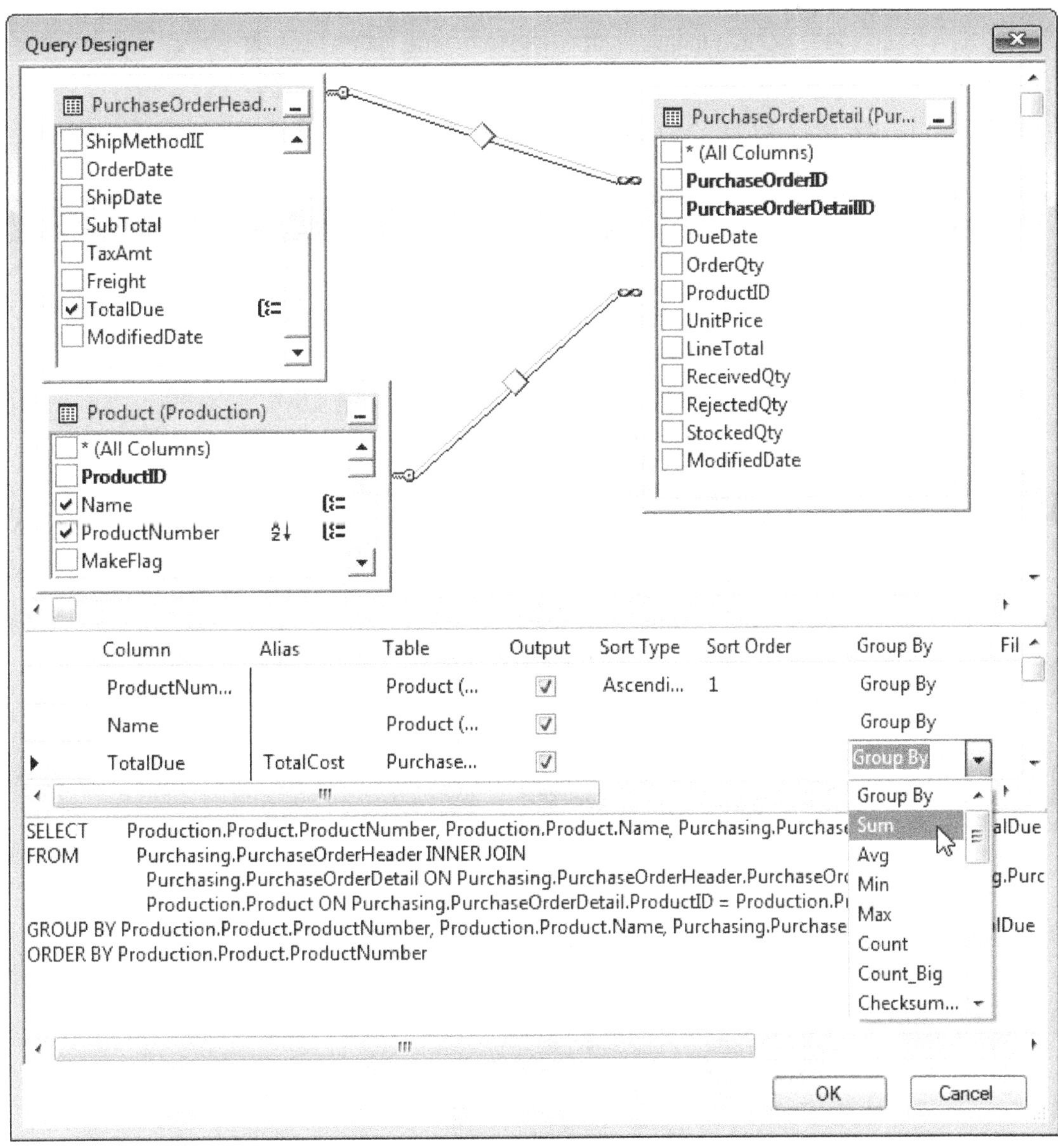

After pressing OK, the query is moved into the Query Editor window. Frequently it requires reformatting.

SQL Server 2012 query.

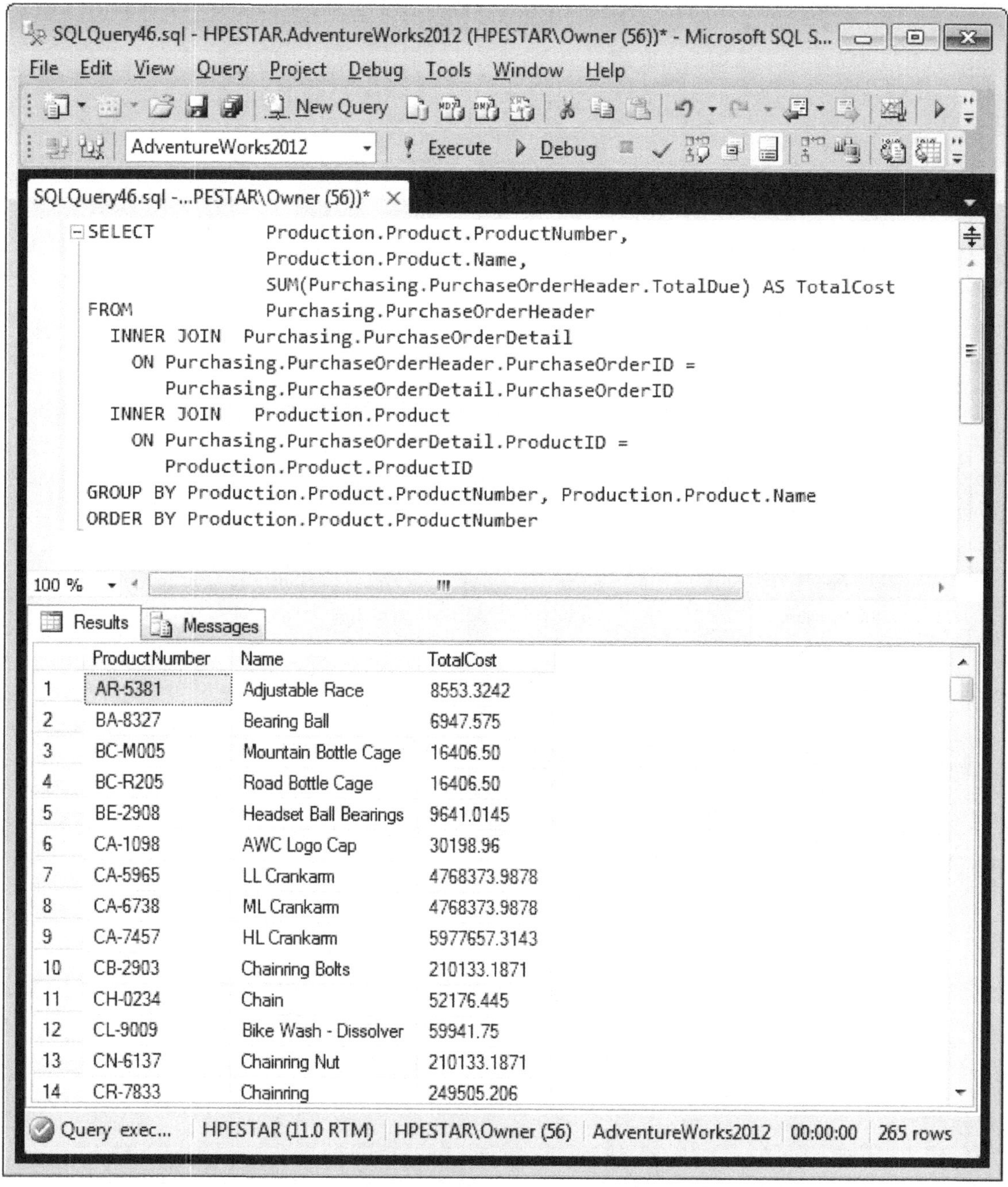
SQLQuery46.sql - HPESTAR.AdventureWorks2012 (HPESTAR\Owner (56))* - Microsoft SQL S...
File Edit View Query Project Debug Tools Window Help
New Query
AdventureWorks2012
Execute
Debug
SQLQuery46.sql -...PESTAR\Owner (56))*
SELECT Production.Product.ProductNumber,
Production.Product.Name,
SUM(Purchasing.PurchaseOrderHeader.TotalDue) AS TotalCost
FROM Purchasing.PurchaseOrderHeader
INNER JOIN Purchasing.PurchaseOrderDetail
ON Purchasing.PurchaseOrderHeader.PurchaseOrderID =
Purchasing.PurchaseOrderDetail.PurchaseOrderID
INNER JOIN Production.Product
ON Purchasing.PurchaseOrderDetail.ProductID =
Production.Product.ProductID
GROUP BY Production.Product.ProductNumber, Production.Product.Name
ORDER BY Production.Product.ProductNumber
100 %
Results
Messages
ProductNumber Name TotalCost
1 AR-5381 Adjustable Race 8553.3242
2 BA-8327 Bearing Ball 6947.575
3 BC-M005 Mountain Bottle Cage 16406.50
4 BC-R205 Road Bottle Cage 16406.50
5 BE-2908 Headset Ball Bearings 9641.0145
6 CA-1098 AWC Logo Cap 30198.96
7 CA-5965 LL Crankarm 4768373.9878
8 CA-6738 ML Crankarm 4768373.9878
9 CA-7457 HL Crankarm 5977657.3143
10 CB-2903 Chainring Bolts 210133.1871
11 CH-0234 Chain 52176.445
12 CL-9009 Bike Wash - Dissolver 59941.75
13 CN-6137 Chainring Nut 210133.1871
14 CR-7833 Chainring 249505.206
Query exec... HPESTAR (11.0 RTM) HPESTAR\Owner (56) AdventureWorks2012 00:00:00 265 rows

The only remaining issue with the query is the 3-part column references which is hard to read. We can change the query for readability improvement by using table aliases.

SQL Server 2012 query.

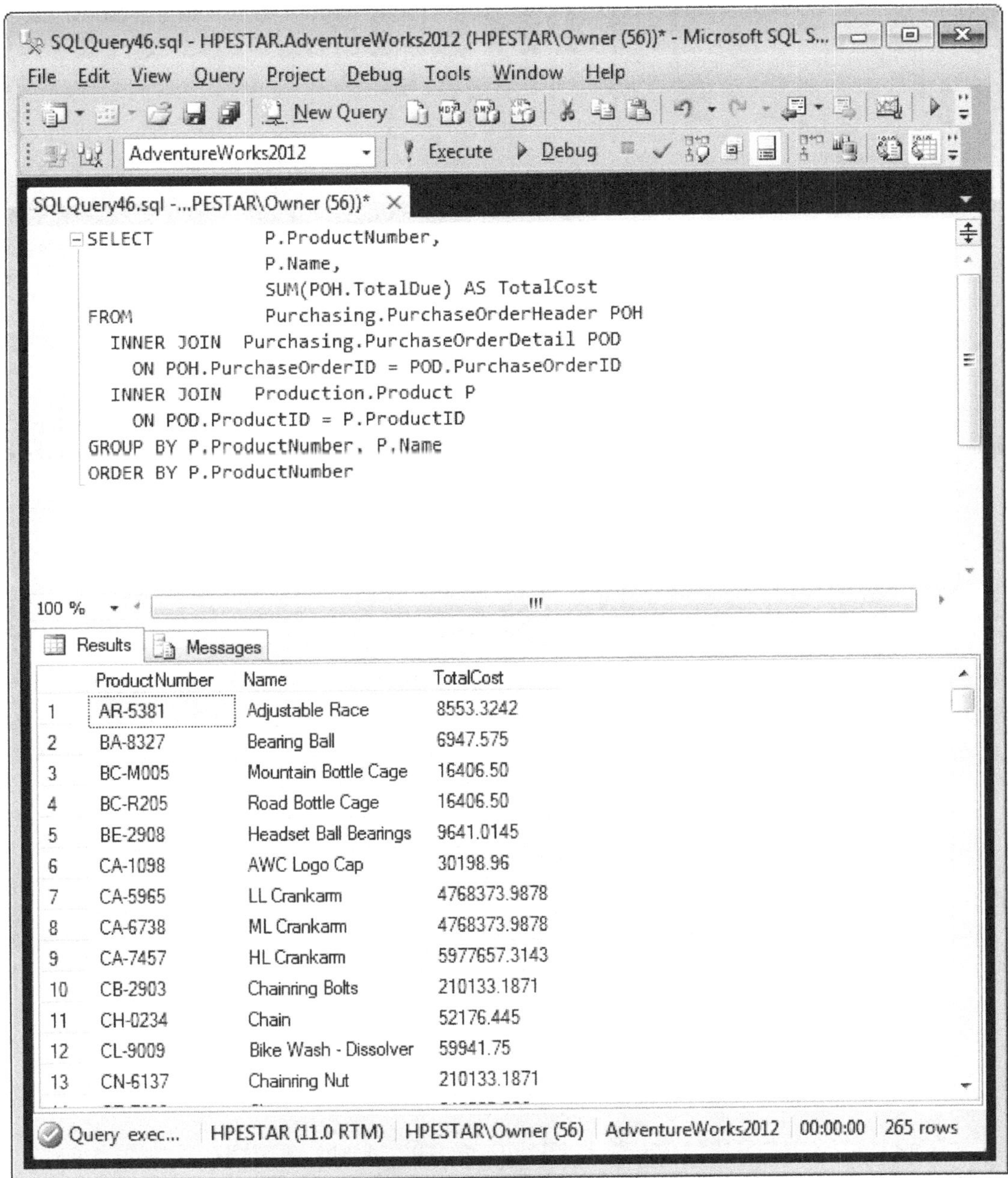

```
SELECT          P.ProductNumber,
                P.Name,
                SUM(POH.TotalDue) AS TotalCost
FROM            Purchasing.PurchaseOrderHeader POH
  INNER JOIN  Purchasing.PurchaseOrderDetail POD
    ON POH.PurchaseOrderID = POD.PurchaseOrderID
  INNER JOIN   Production.Product P
    ON POD.ProductID = P.ProductID
GROUP BY P.ProductNumber, P.Name
ORDER BY P.ProductNumber
```

	ProductNumber	Name	TotalCost
1	AR-5381	Adjustable Race	8553.3242
2	BA-8327	Bearing Ball	6947.575
3	BC-M005	Mountain Bottle Cage	16406.50
4	BC-R205	Road Bottle Cage	16406.50
5	BE-2908	Headset Ball Bearings	9641.0145
6	CA-1098	AWC Logo Cap	30198.96
7	CA-5965	LL Crankarm	4768373.9878
8	CA-6738	ML Crankarm	4768373.9878
9	CA-7457	HL Crankarm	5977657.3143
10	CB-2903	Chainring Bolts	210133.1871
11	CH-0234	Chain	52176.445
12	CL-9009	Bike Wash - Dissolver	59941.75
13	CN-6137	Chainring Nut	210133.1871

Graphically Editing of an Existing Query

An existing query, exception certain complex queries, can be uploaded into the Graphical Query Designer the following way: select (highlight) the query and right-click for the drop-down menu; click on Design Query in Editor. SQL Server 2012 query.

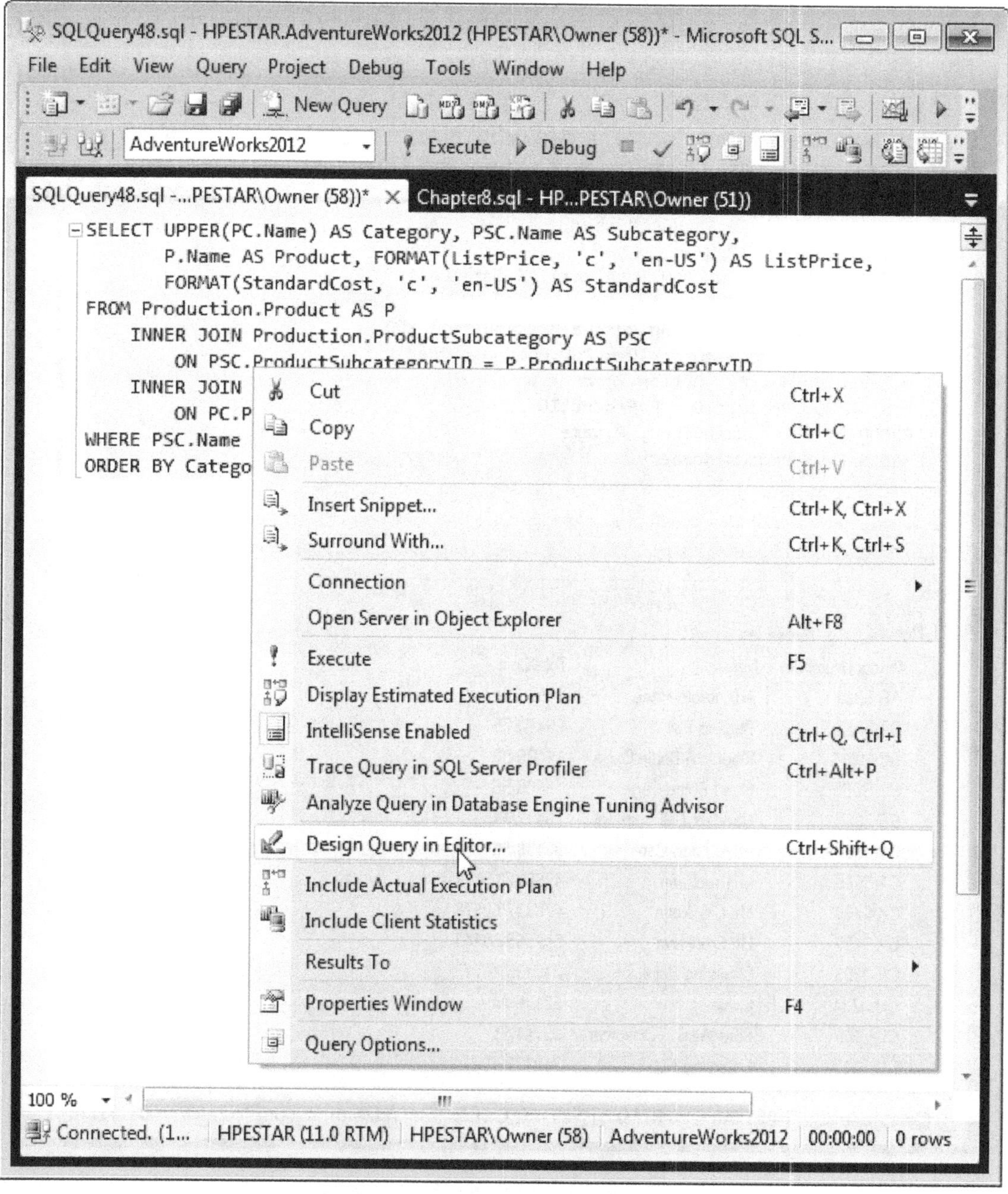

Following screen image shows the query in the Graphical Query Designer after some manual beautifying such as moving the tables for better display.

The query can be edited graphically and upon clicking on "OK", the query text is updated in the Query Editor window. SQL Server 2012 query.

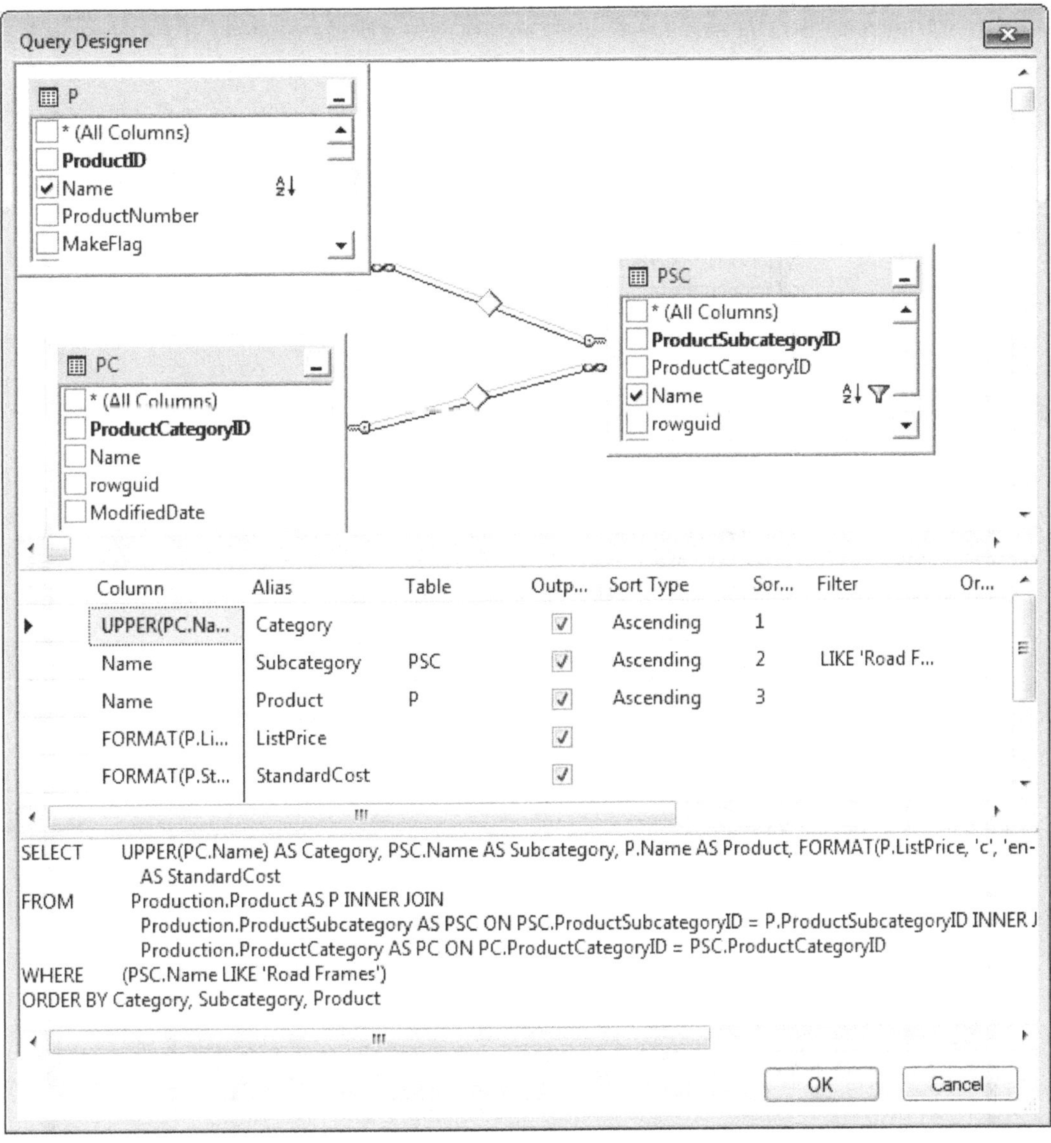

Configuring Line Numbers in Query Editor

Partially supported in Azure SQL. Line numbering is an option which is off by default. Line numbers are helpful to find errors in large queries or T-SQL scripts (a sequence of T-SQL statements) when the error references a line number. Following is an example an error which includes the line number.

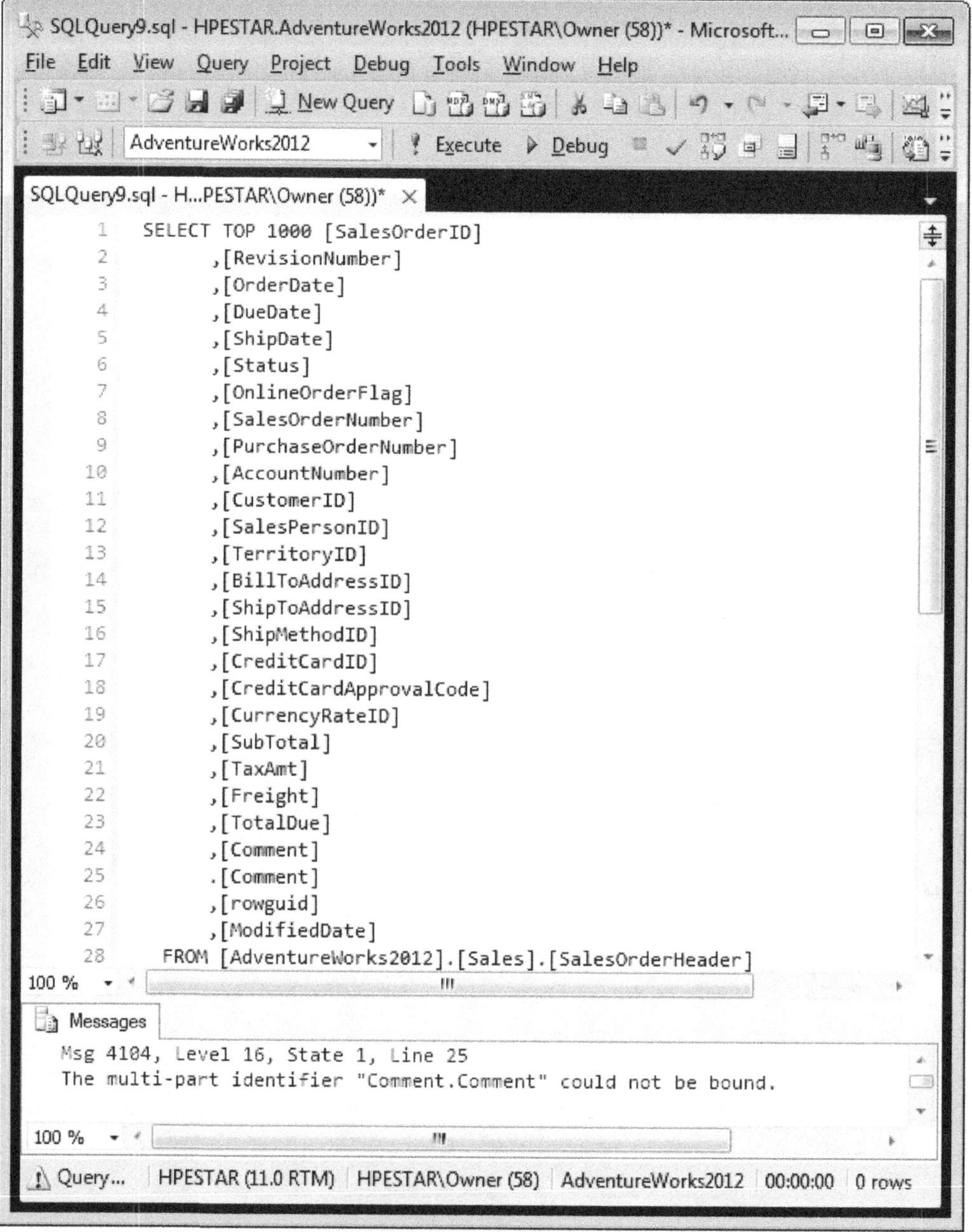

The Display Line Numbers option in the query editor can be activated from Options.

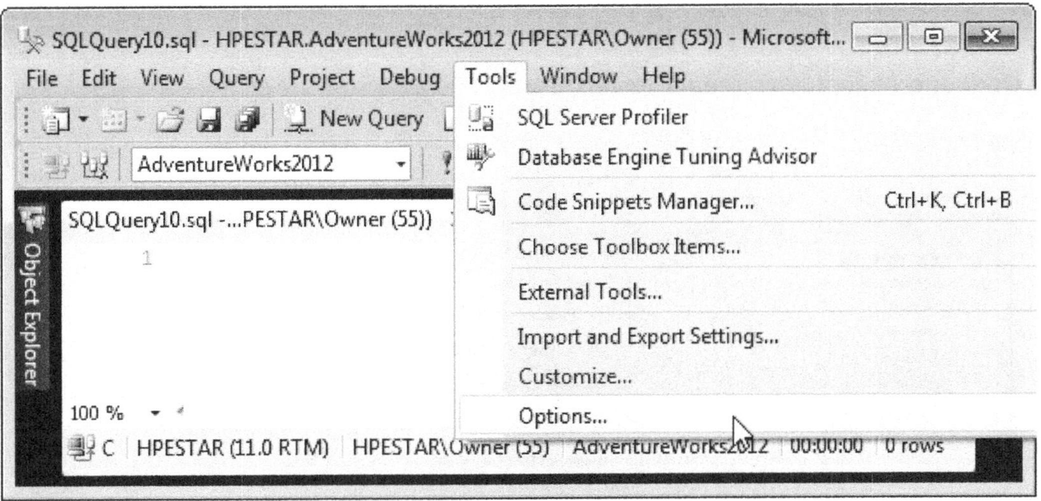

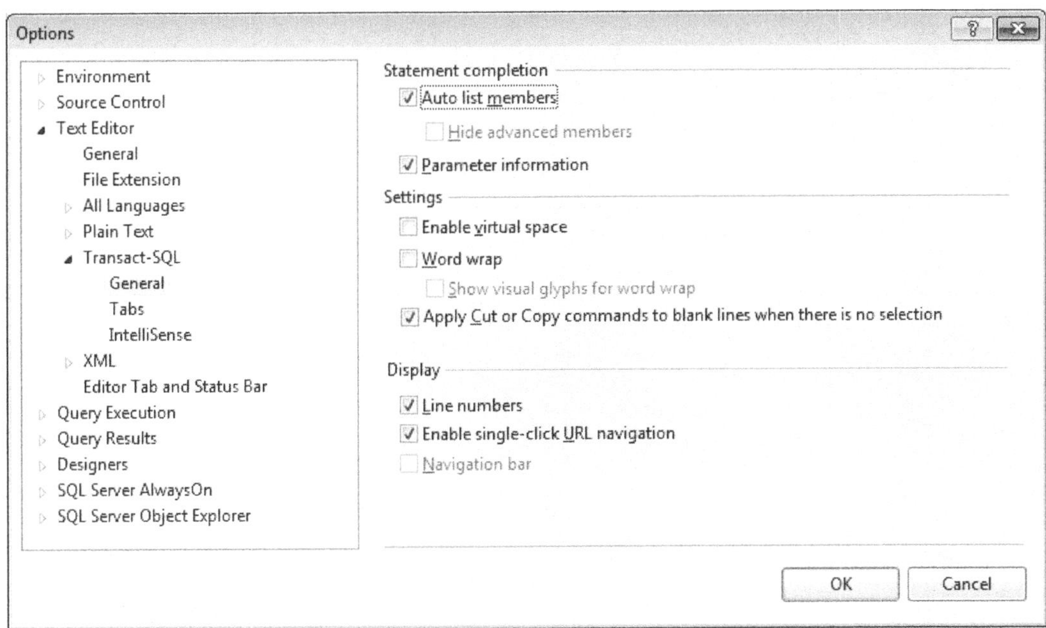

IntelliSense - Your Smart Assistant - OPSS2012

IntelliSense is not suppoted in Azure SQL. IntelliSense is a smart agent in Query Editor. It helps completing long object names and pointing out potential errors by red wave-lining (squiggly) them.

The Options configuration screen for IntelliSense.

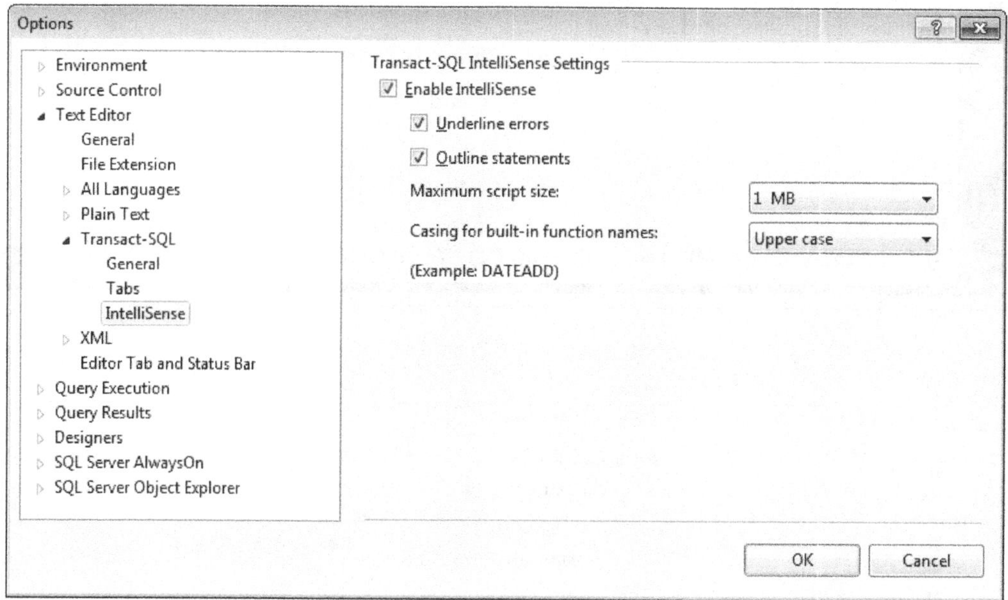

Underlining with red wave-line potential errors such as misspelling of a column name.

```
SELECT TOP 1000 [BillOfMaterialsID]
      ,[ProductAssemblyID]
      ,[ComponentID]
      ,[StartDate]
      ,[EndDate]
      ,[UnitMeasureCodex]
      ,[BOMLevel]
      ,[PerAssemblyQty]
      ,[ModifiedDate]
  FROM [AdventureWorks2012].[Production].[BillOfMaterials]
```

100 %

IntelliSense Guessing and Completing Object Names

Screenshots show IntelliSense in action when typing queries.

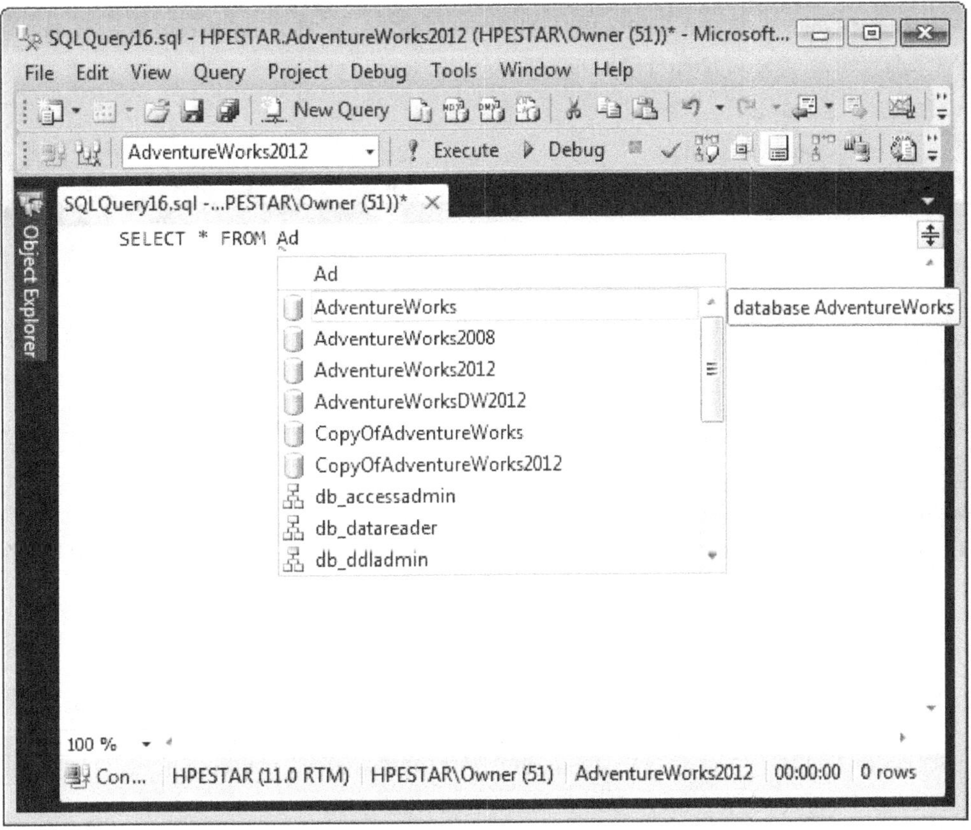

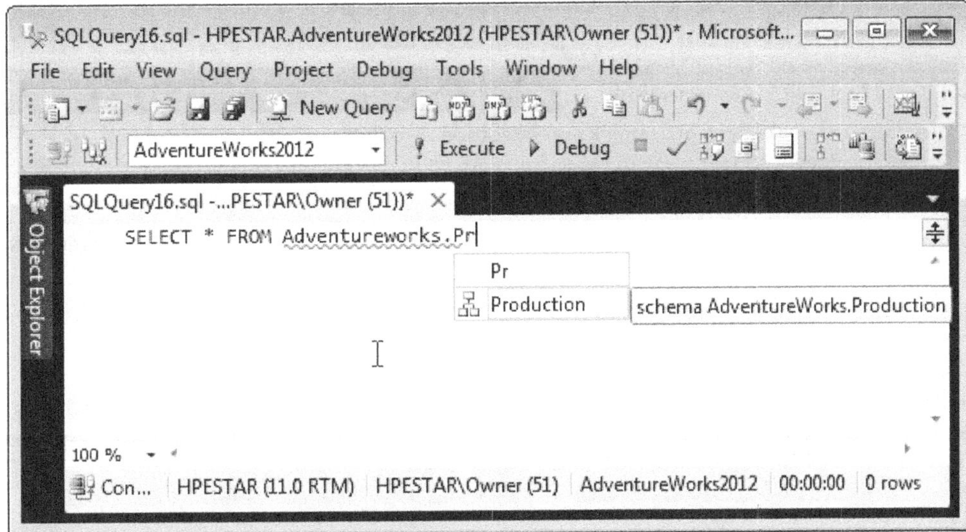

IntelliSense drop-down menu for "Prod".

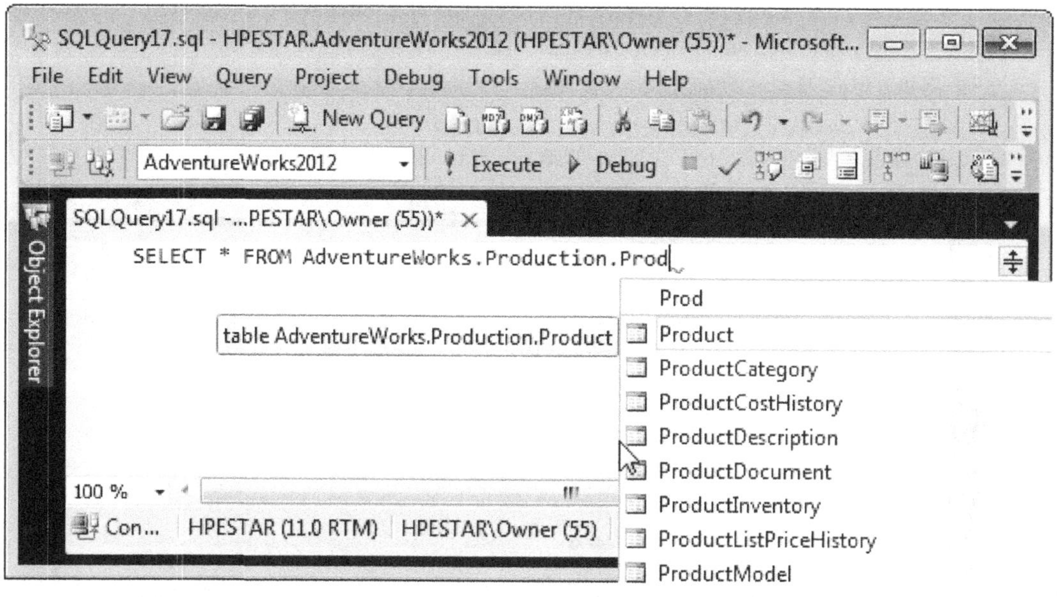

IntelliSense drop-down menu for "ProductS".

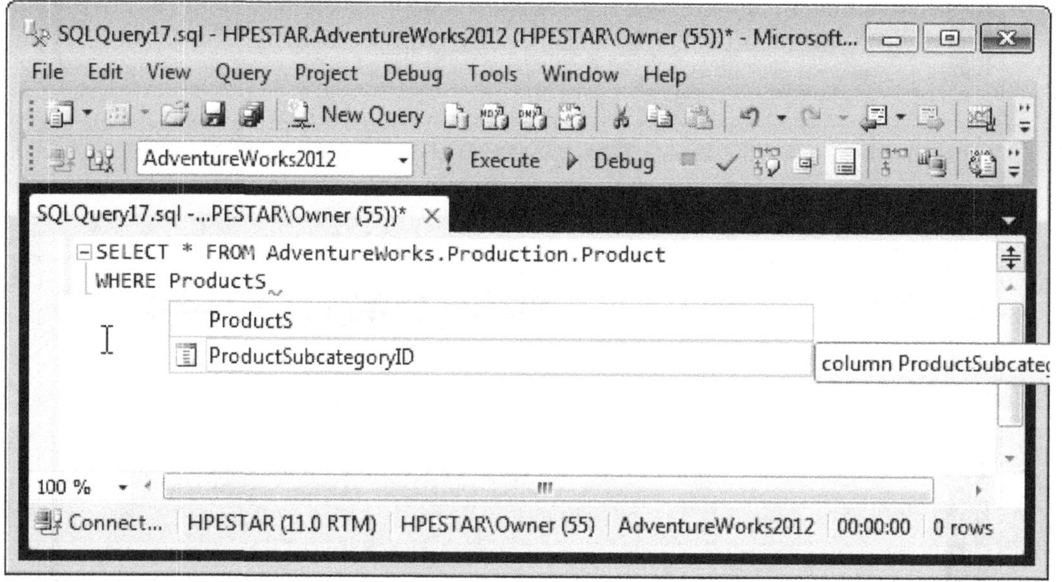

IntelliSense completion assistance for "ProductN"

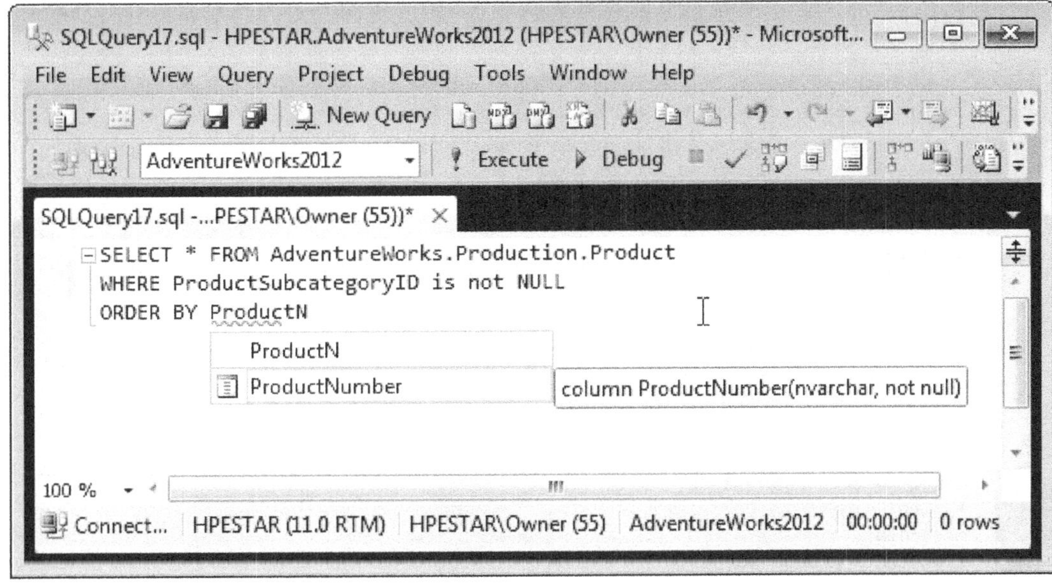

IntelliSense completion assistance for "Produ"

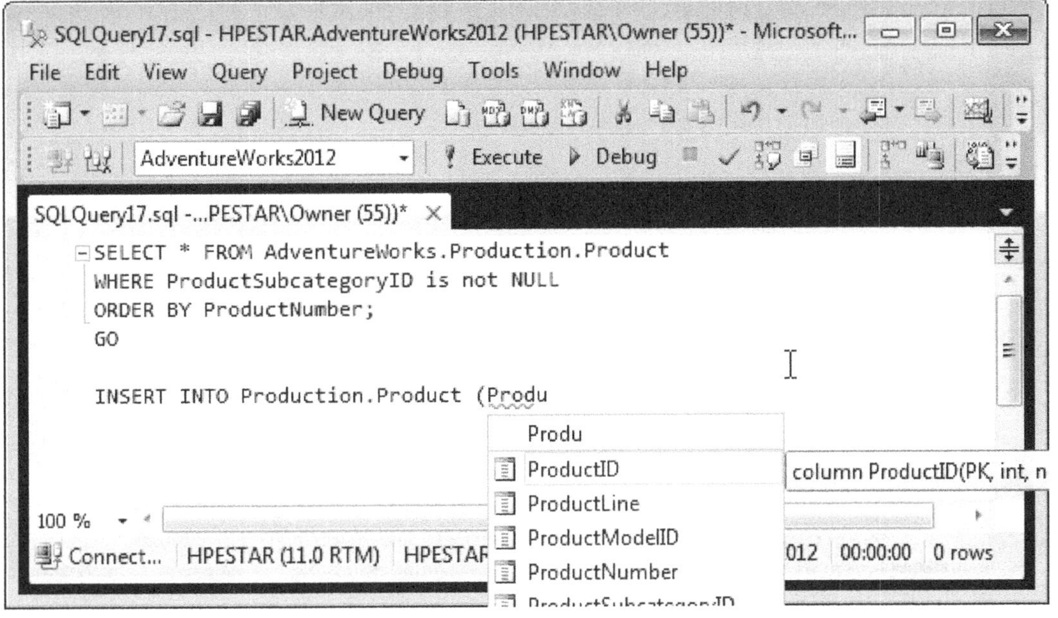

IntelliSense Assisting with User-Defined Objects

IntelliSense helps out with a user-defined stored procedure execution.

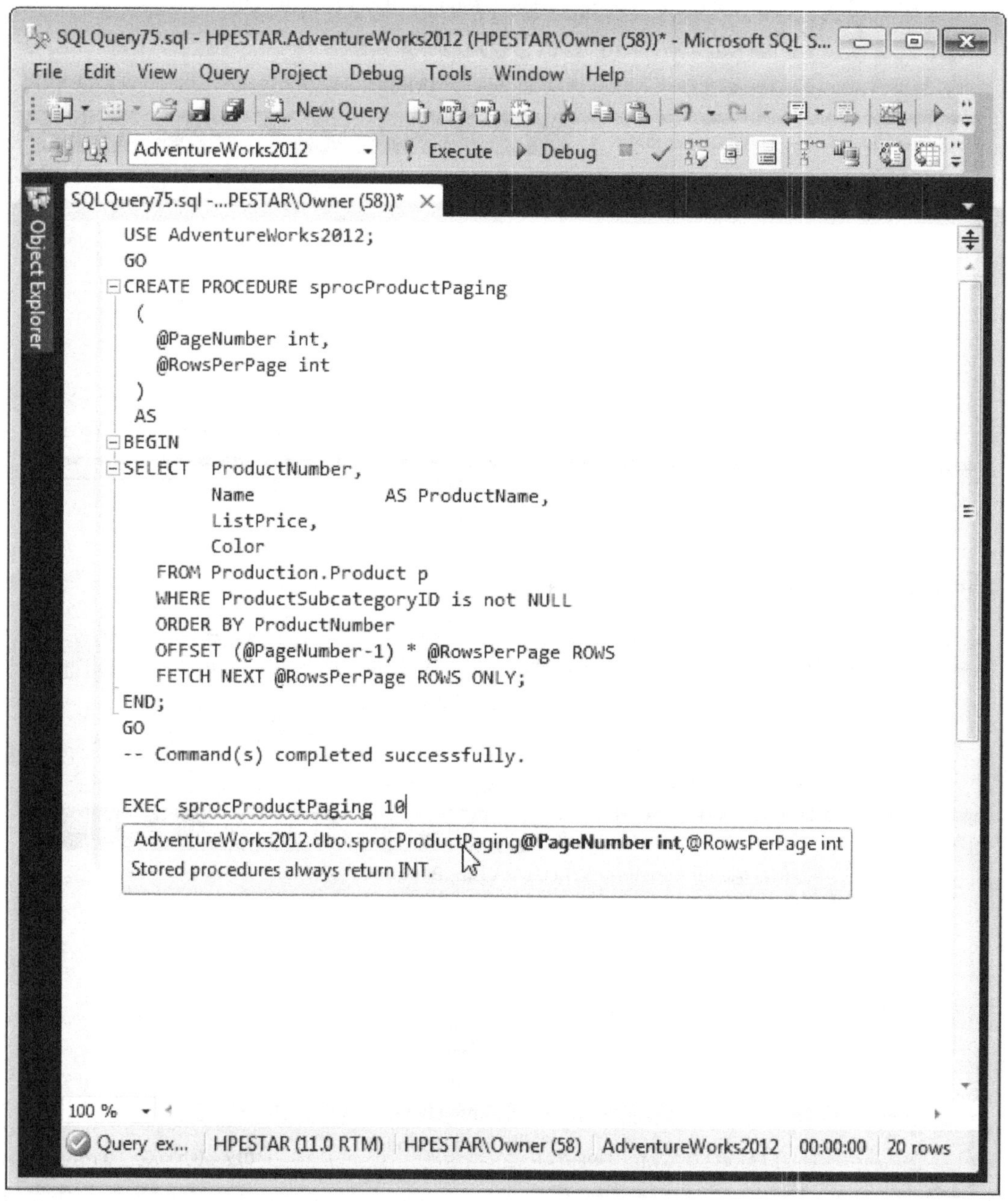
SQLQuery75.sql - HPESTAR.AdventureWorks2012 (HPESTAR\Owner (58))* - Microsoft SQL S...
File Edit View Query Project Debug Tools Window Help
New Query
AdventureWorks2012
Execute
Debug
SQLQuery75.sql -...PESTAR\Owner (58))*
Object Explorer
USE AdventureWorks2012;
GO
CREATE PROCEDURE sprocProductPaging
(
@PageNumber int,
@RowsPerPage int
)
AS
BEGIN
SELECT ProductNumber,
Name AS ProductName,
ListPrice,
Color
FROM Production.Product p
WHERE ProductSubcategoryID is not NULL
ORDER BY ProductNumber
OFFSET (@PageNumber-1) * @RowsPerPage ROWS
FETCH NEXT @RowsPerPage ROWS ONLY;
END;
GO
-- Command(s) completed successfully.
EXEC sprocProductPaging 10
AdventureWorks2012.dbo.sprocProductPaging@PageNumber int,@RowsPerPage int
Stored procedures always return INT.
100 %
Query ex...
HPESTAR (11.0 RTM)
HPESTAR\Owner (58)
AdventureWorks2012
00:00:00
20 rows

IntelliSense Smart Guessing Partial Word in Middle of Object Names

You don't have to remember how an object name starts. You just have to remember some part of the name. Looking for the system view associated with "waits".

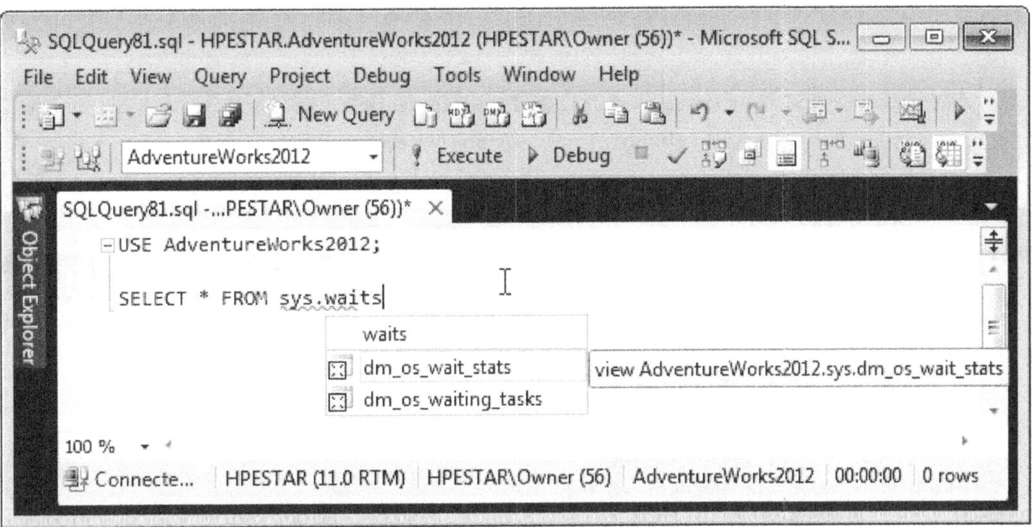

Looking for the SalesOrderHeader table but only remembering "head".

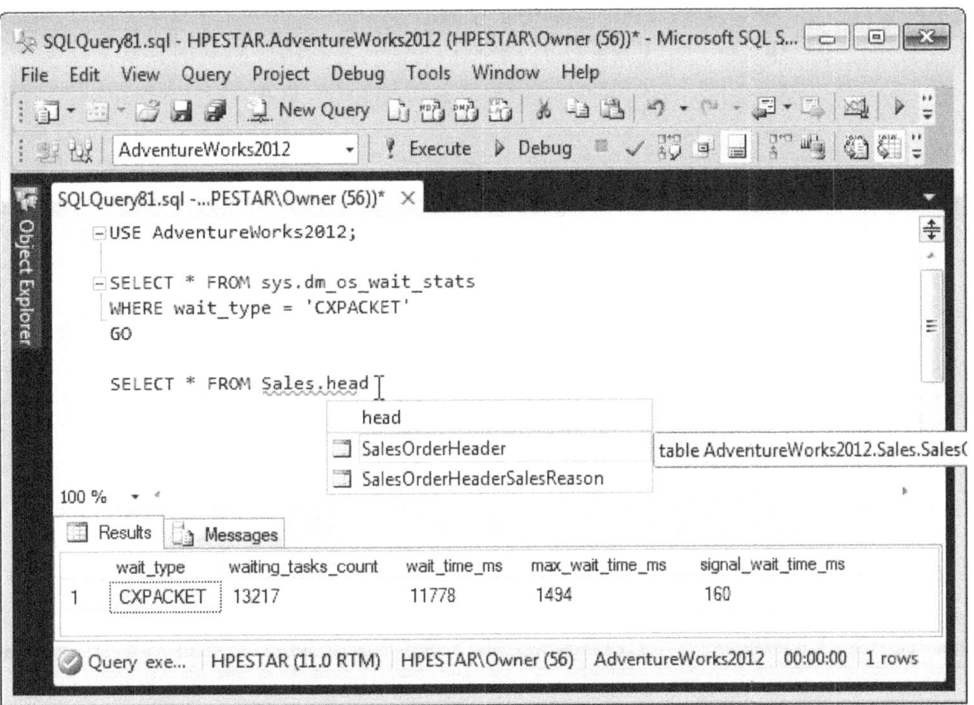

Hovering over Red Squiggly Underline Errors for Explanation

IntelliSense red wave (squiggly) underlining of errors which is caused, actually, by a single invalid table reference.

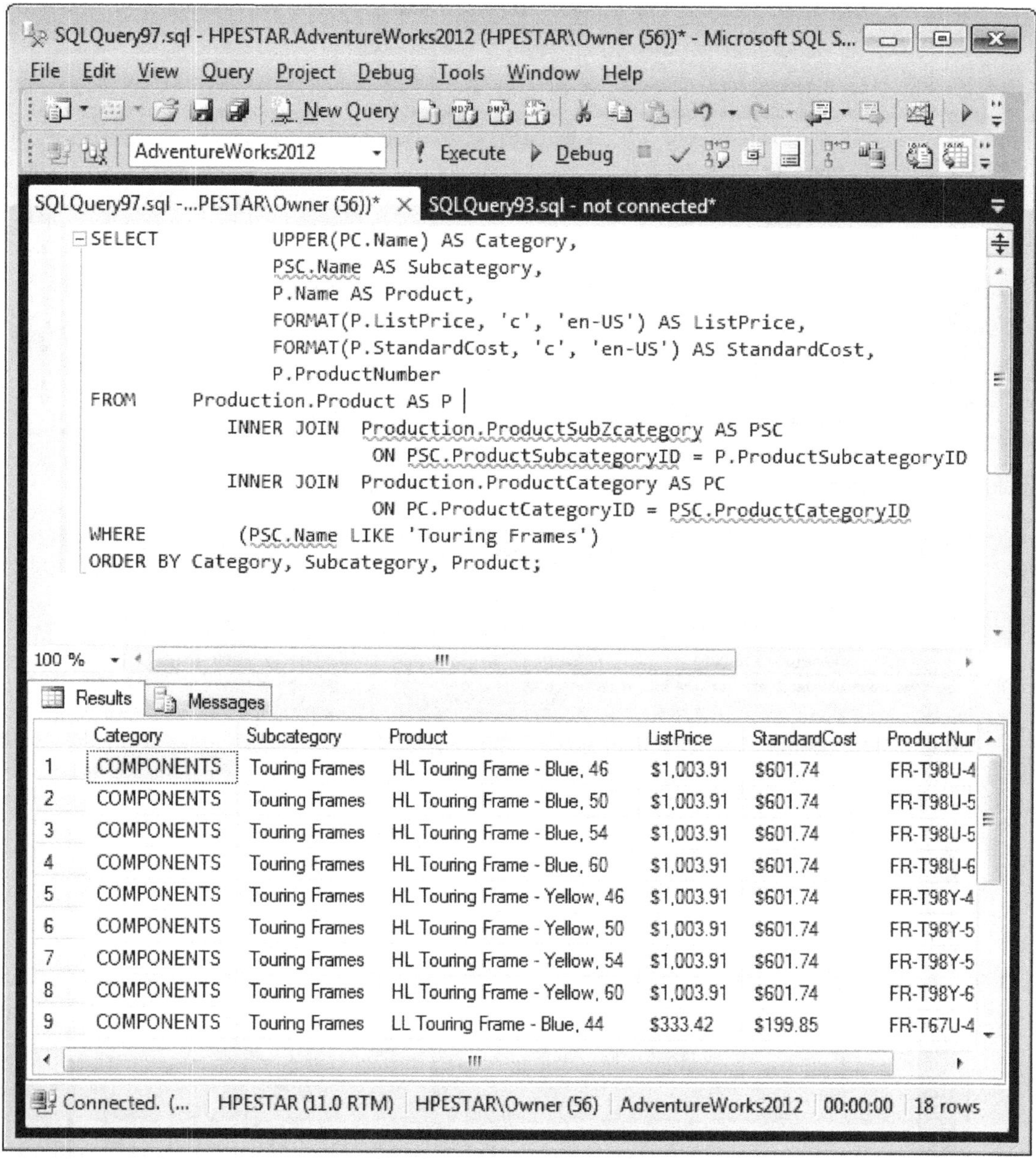
SQLQuery97.sql - HPESTAR.AdventureWorks2012 (HPESTAR\Owner (56))* - Microsoft SQL S...
File Edit View Query Project Debug Tools Window Help
New Query
AdventureWorks2012
Execute
Debug
SQLQuery97.sql -...PESTAR\Owner (56))*
SQLQuery93.sql - not connected*
SELECT UPPER(PC.Name) AS Category,
PSC.Name AS Subcategory,
P.Name AS Product,
FORMAT(P.ListPrice, 'c', 'en-US') AS ListPrice,
FORMAT(P.StandardCost, 'c', 'en-US') AS StandardCost,
P.ProductNumber
FROM Production.Product AS P
INNER JOIN Production.ProductSubZcategory AS PSC
ON PSC.ProductSubcategoryID = P.ProductSubcategoryID
INNER JOIN Production.ProductCategory AS PC
ON PC.ProductCategoryID = PSC.ProductCategoryID
WHERE (PSC.Name LIKE 'Touring Frames')
ORDER BY Category, Subcategory, Product;
100 %
Results
Messages
Category Subcategory Product ListPrice StandardCost ProductNur
1 COMPONENTS Touring Frames HL Touring Frame - Blue, 46 $1,003.91 $601.74 FR-T98U-4
2 COMPONENTS Touring Frames HL Touring Frame - Blue, 50 $1,003.91 $601.74 FR-T98U-5
3 COMPONENTS Touring Frames HL Touring Frame - Blue, 54 $1,003.91 $601.74 FR-T98U-5
4 COMPONENTS Touring Frames HL Touring Frame - Blue, 60 $1,003.91 $601.74 FR-T98U-6
5 COMPONENTS Touring Frames HL Touring Frame - Yellow, 46 $1,003.91 $601.74 FR-T98Y-4
6 COMPONENTS Touring Frames HL Touring Frame - Yellow, 50 $1,003.91 $601.74 FR-T98Y-5
7 COMPONENTS Touring Frames HL Touring Frame - Yellow, 54 $1,003.91 $601.74 FR-T98Y-5
8 COMPONENTS Touring Frames HL Touring Frame - Yellow, 60 $1,003.91 $601.74 FR-T98Y-6
9 COMPONENTS Touring Frames LL Touring Frame - Blue, 44 $333.42 $199.85 FR-T67U-4
Connected. (... HPESTAR (11.0 RTM) HPESTAR\Owner (56) AdventureWorks2012 00:00:00 18 rows

Common Error: The multi-part identifier "abc" could not be bound.

Hovering over the first error results in an explanation pop-up. This is a distant error, the kind usually the hardest to solve, because, actually, it is a secondary error caused by the primary error which is located on a different line. In this instance, there are few lines difference only, but in a large stored procedure the difference can be 200 lines as an example.

```
PSC.Name AS Subcategory,
```

The multi-part identifier "PSC.Name" could not be bound.

Hovering over the second error yields the cause of all errors: "ProductSubZcategory".

```
Production.ProductSubZcategory AS PSC
```

Invalid object name 'Production.ProductSubZcategory'.

The remaining error messages are all "multi-part..." caused by the solitary invalid table reference.

```
PSC.ProductSubcategoryID = P.ProductSubcategoryID
```

The multi-part identifier "PSC.ProductSubcategoryID" could not be bound.

After fixing the table name, all errors are gone.

```
SELECT          UPPER(PC.Name)                                  AS Category,
                PSC.Name                                        AS Subcategory,
                P.Name                                          AS Product,
                FORMAT(P.ListPrice, 'c', 'en-US')               AS ListPrice,
                FORMAT(P.StandardCost, 'c', 'en-US')            AS StandardCost,
                P.ProductNumber
FROM      Production.Product AS P
            INNER JOIN  Production.ProductSubcategory AS PSC
                          ON PSC.ProductSubcategoryID = P.ProductSubcategoryID
            INNER JOIN  Production.ProductCategory AS PC
                          ON PC.ProductCategoryID = PSC.ProductCategoryID
WHERE        (PSC.Name LIKE 'Touring Frames')
ORDER BY Category, Subcategory, Product;
```

Refreshing IntelliSense Cache for New DB Objects

IntelliSense cache is not updated real-time. If new objects are created in another connection (session), they will not be seen until exit SSMS/reenter or IntelliSense cache is updated. No red-wave underline for the **newly created object SOD** in the same connection.

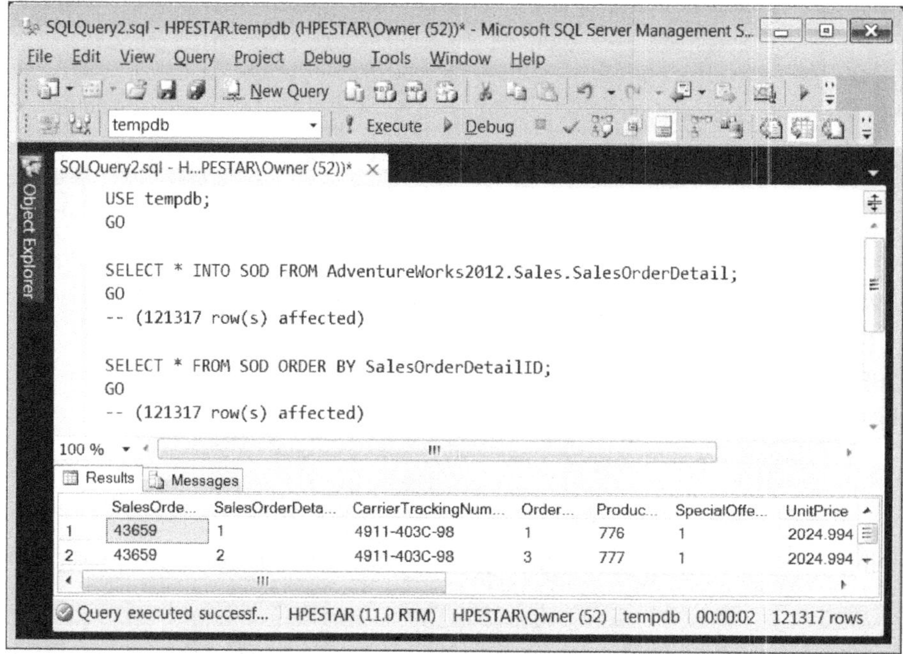

In another connection, the query works, but there are red squiggly underlining for the new table & column. **After refreshing local cache on Edit drop-down menu, the red squiggly goes away.**

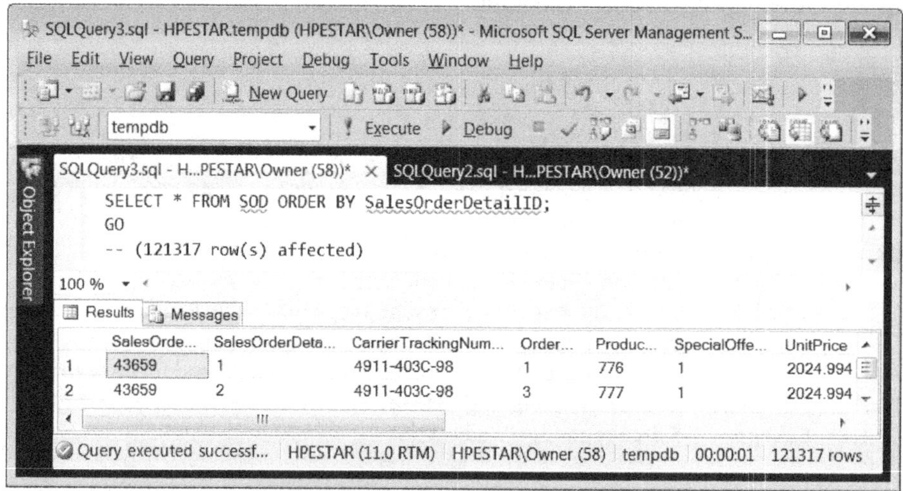

CHAPTER 6: Fundamentals of Client-Server Computing

Client - Server Relational Database Management System

The "server" is SQL Server, operating on a powerful hardware platform, managing databases and related items. The client is application software. The real client is naturally a human user who runs the application software. Automated software which uses the database for one thing or another is also considered a "client". The client computer, in the next room or thousands of miles away, is connected to the server through communications link. The client software sends a request, a query, to SQL Server, after execution the server returns the results to the client. An example for a query sent by the client to the server:

```
SELECT ListPrice FROM Production.Product WHERE ProductID = 800;
```

SQL Server executes the query and returns "1120.49" to the client with a flag indicating successful query execution. A tempting analogy is a restaurant: kitchen is the server, patrons are the clients and the communications / delivery done by waiters & waitresses.

Screenshot displays SQL Server (highlighted) along with other related software such as SQL Server Agent (job scheduling facility) , SSIS (data transformation & transfer), SSRS (Reporting), SSAS (OLAP Cube) and other auxiliary software.

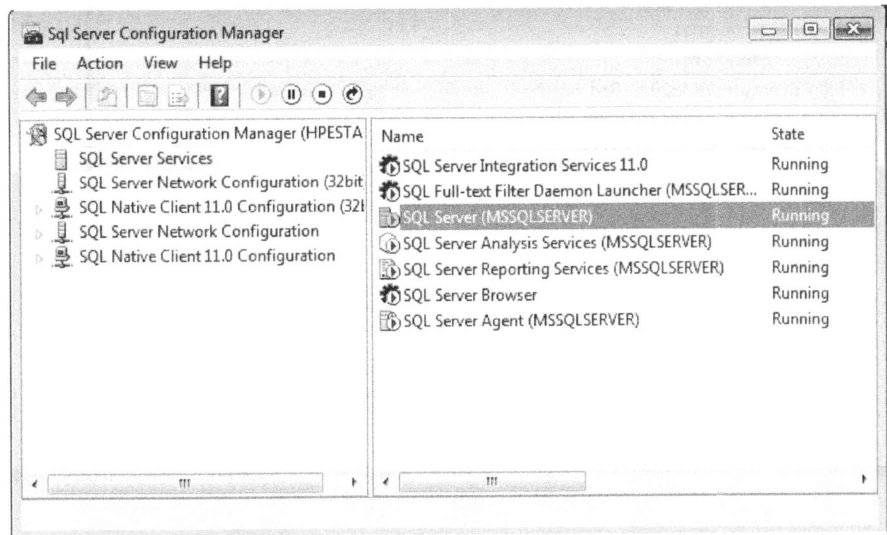

Database Objects on Server-Side

Screenshot of Object Explorer displays almost all important database objects with the exception of constraints, table triggers and indexes.

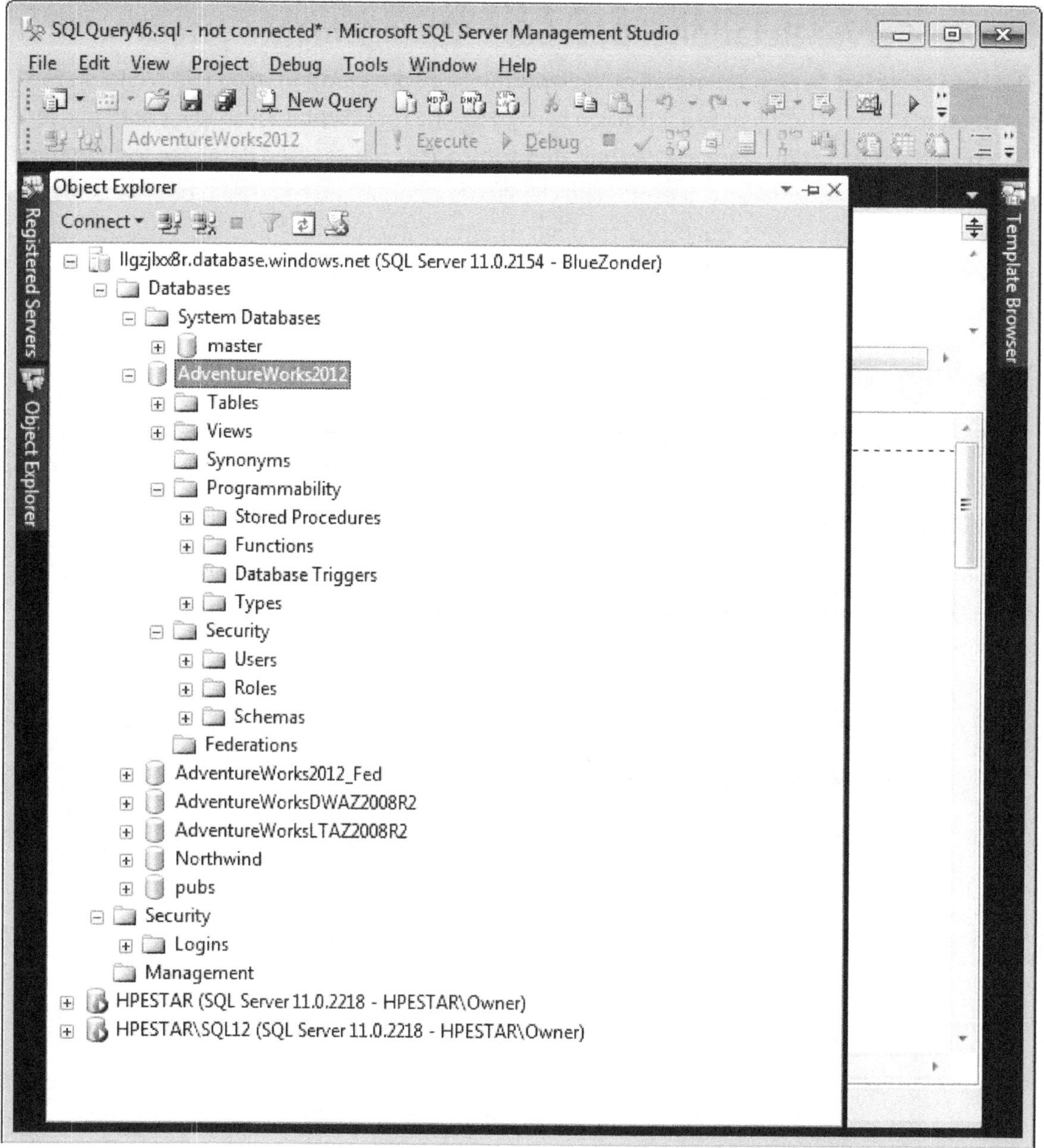

Database Related Items on Client-Side

On the client side the following items:

- Azure SQL client libraries to access the server and database
- SQL queries imbedded in application programs
- Stored procedure calls imbedded in application software

Queries by themselves are not database object. To make them database objects we have to build stored procedures, functions or views around them.

BOL Articles
Windows Azure SQL Database Data Access
http://msdn.microsoft.com/en-us/library/windowsazure/ee336239.aspx
How to: Connect to Windows Azure SQL Database Using ADO.NET
http://msdn.microsoft.com/en-us/library/windowsazure/ee336243.aspx

The following code segment illustrates database connection and query from ASP to Inventory database. In ANSI SQL terminology catalog means database.

```
' Connect
<%
Dim StrConnInventory
Dim ConnInventory
StrConnInventory = " Provider=SQLNCLI10;Password=myPassword;User ID=[username]@[servername];
Initial Catalog=dbname; Data Source=tcp:[servername].database.windows.net;"
Set ConnInventory = Server.CreateObject("ADODB.Connection")
ConnInventory.ConnectionTimeout = 4000
ConnInventory.CommandTimeout = 4000
ConnInventory.Open StrConnInventory
' Query
Dim YourQuery As String = "SELECT Name, Price FROM Product"
 Dim YourCommand As New SqlCommand(YourQuery)
 YourCommand.Connection = ConnInventory
 YourConnection.Open()
 YourCommand.ExecuteNonQuery()
 Response.Write(YourCommand)
 YourCommand.Connection.Close()
%>
' Disconnect
<%
ConnInventory.Close
Set ConnInventory = Nothing
%>
```

SQL Server Profiler to Monitor Client-Server Communications

SQL Server Profiler is not supported by Azure SQL. The Azure management portal has performance oriented tools such as Summary Query Performance report.

MSDN Blog: **CloudTip #14-How do I get SQL Profiler info from SQL Azure?**
http://blogs.msdn.com/b/benko/archive/2012/05/19/cloudtip-14-how-do-i-get-sql-profiler-info-from-sql-azure.aspx

SQL Server Profiler, a tool in SSMS, has two modes of operations: interactive GUI and silent T-SQL script based operation. The simplest use of the Profiler is to check what queries are sent to the server (SQL Server) from the client and how long does processing take (duration). The client software sending the queries is SSMS. Even though SSMS appears as the "face of SQL Server", it is only a client software. SQL Server 2012 query.

```
USE pubs;          SELECT * FROM titles;
```

```
USE Northwind;
SELECT * FROM Products ORDER BY ProductName;
```

```
USE AdventureWorks2012;
GO
SELECT * FROM Sales.SalesOrderHeader WHERE OrderDate='20080201';
```

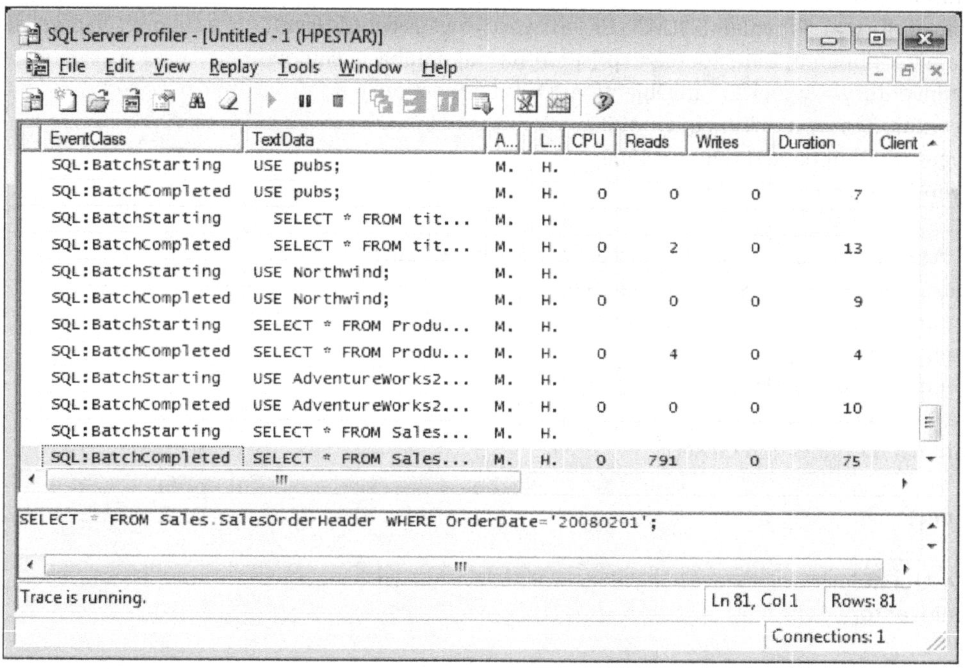

Table - Database Object

A database table holds data in tabular format by rows and columns. The main method of connecting tables is FOREIGN KEY referencing PRIMARY KEY. A set of connected tables makes up the database. Screenshot displays the structure and partial content of Northwind database Products table.

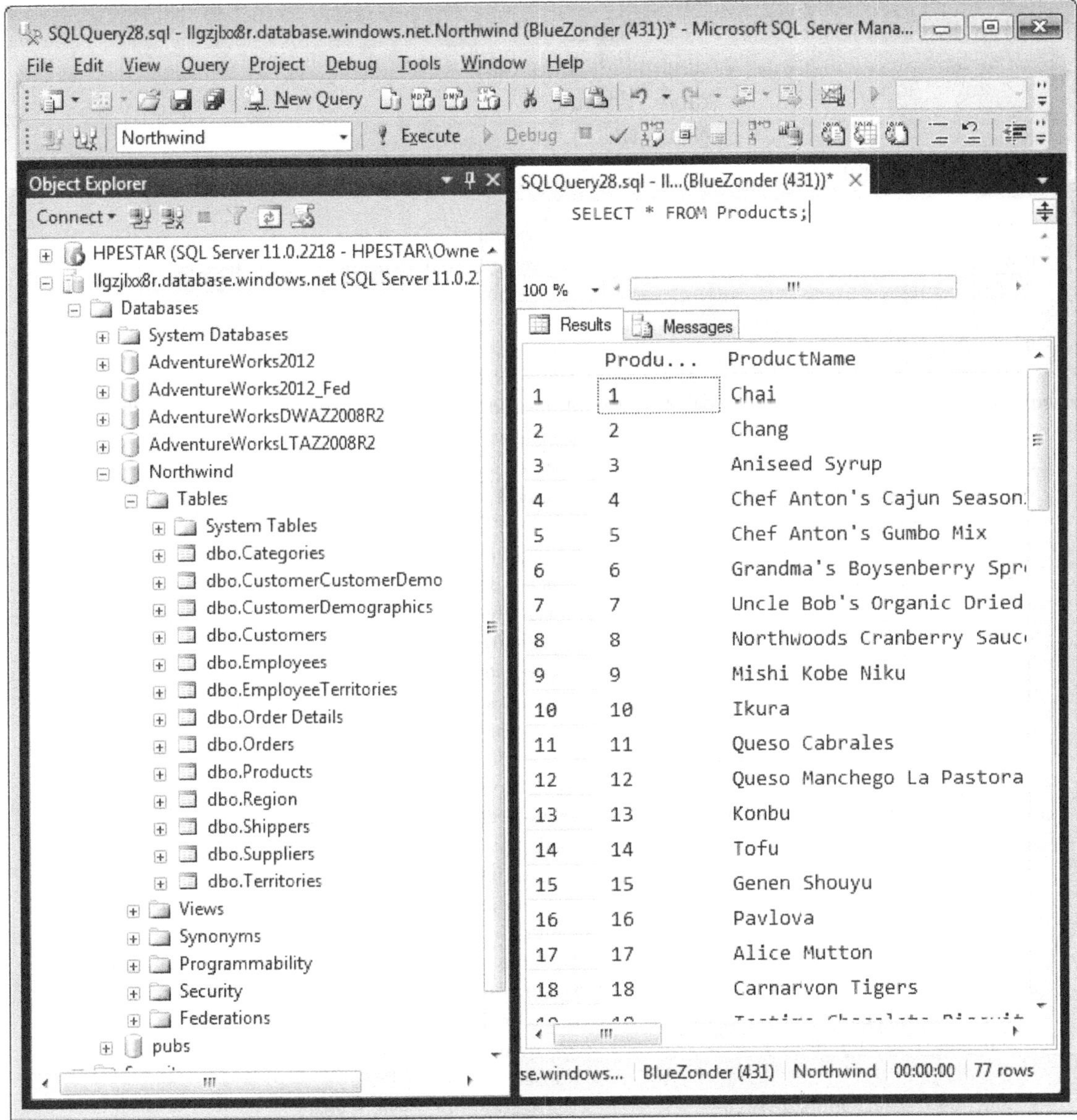

Tables in Production Schema

The listing and data dictionary description of tables in AdventureWorks2012 Production schema. SQL Server 2012 query.

```
USE AdventureWorks2012;
SELECT  CONCAT('Production.', objname COLLATE DATABASE_DEFAULT) AS TableName,
        value                                                   AS [Description]
FROM fn_listextendedproperty (          NULL,
                              'schema', 'Production',
                              'table', default,
                               NULL, NULL)
ORDER BY TableName;
```

TableName	Description
Production.BillOfMaterials	Items required to make bicycles and bicycle subassemblies. It identifies the hierarchical relationship between a parent product and its components.
Production.Culture	Lookup table containing the languages in which some AdventureWorks data is stored.
Production.Document	Product maintenance documents.
Production.Illustration	Bicycle assembly diagrams.
Production.Location	Product inventory and manufacturing locations.
Production.Product	Products sold or used in the manfacturing of sold products.
Production.ProductCategory	High-level product categorization.
Production.ProductCostHistory	Changes in the cost of a product over time.
Production.ProductDescription	Product descriptions in several languages.
Production.ProductDocument	Cross-reference table mapping products to related product documents.
Production.ProductInventory	Product inventory information.
Production.ProductListPriceHistory	Changes in the list price of a product over time.
Production.ProductModel	Product model classification.
Production.ProductModelIllustration	Cross-reference table mapping product models and illustrations.
Production.ProductModelProductDescriptionCulture	Cross-reference table mapping product descriptions and the language the description is written in.
Production.ProductPhoto	Product images.
Production.ProductProductPhoto	Cross-reference table mapping products and product photos.
Production.ProductReview	Customer reviews of products they have purchased.
Production.ProductSubcategory	Product subcategories. See ProductCategory table.
Production.ScrapReason	Manufacturing failure reasons lookup table.
Production.TransactionHistory	Record of each purchase order, sales order, or work order transaction year to date.
Production.TransactionHistoryArchive	Transactions for previous years.
Production.UnitMeasure	Unit of measure lookup table.
Production.WorkOrder	Manufacturing work orders.
Production.WorkOrderRouting	Work order details.

Index - Database Object

An index on a table is a B-tree based structure which speeds up random searches. **Typically PRIMARY KEY (automatic), FOREIGN KEY and WHERE clause columns have indexes.** If the index is constructed on more than one column, it is called **composite index**. If all the columns in a query are in the index, it is called **covering index**. The "script index as" option produces the PRIMARY KEY ALTER TABLE script. PK automatically creates a unique index, clustered is default.

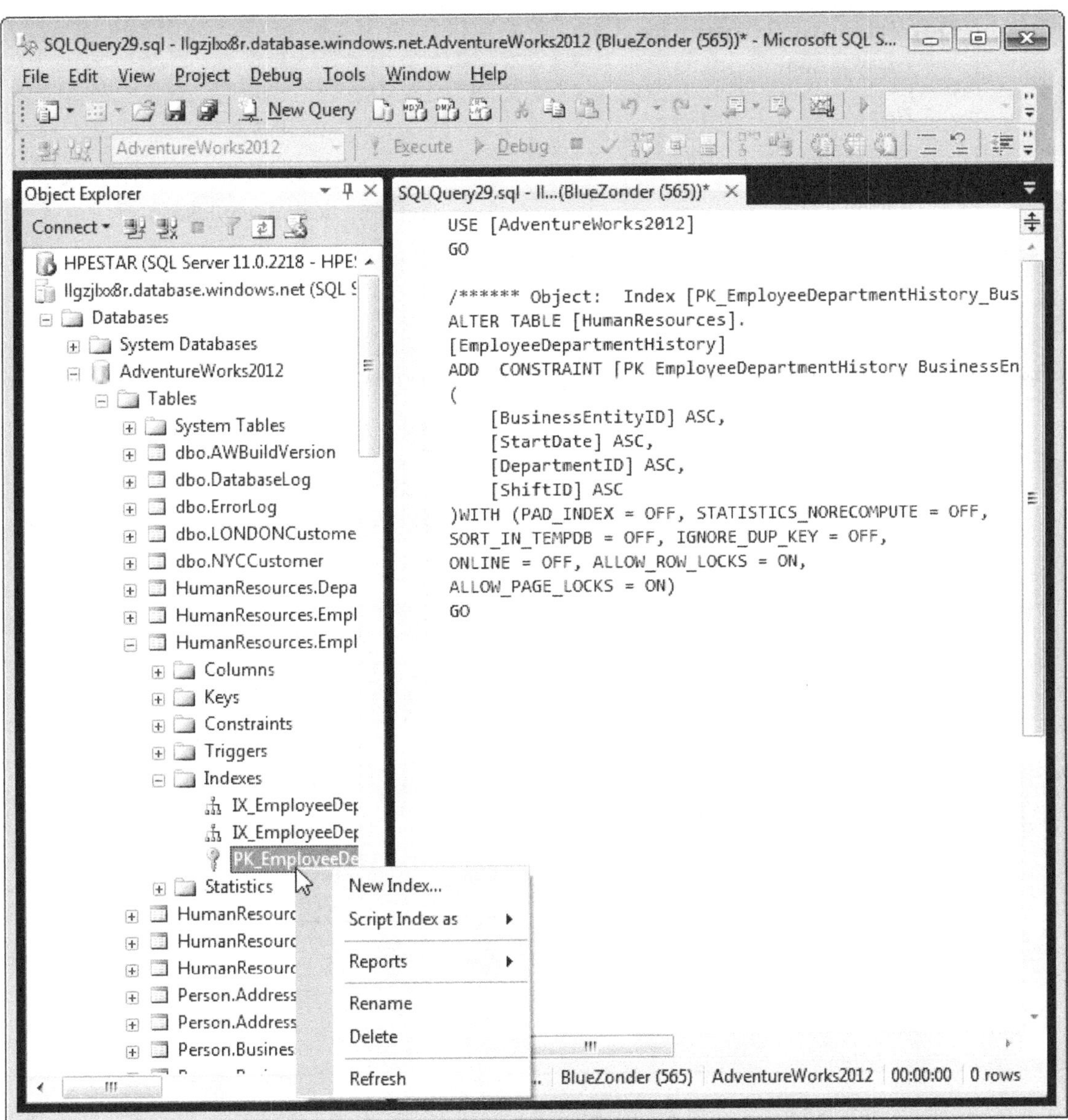

Diagram of EmployeeDepartmentHistory and Related Tables

EmployeeDepartmentHistory is a simple junction table with three FOREIGN KEYs to the Employee, Shift and Department tables respectively. SQL Server 2012 diagram.

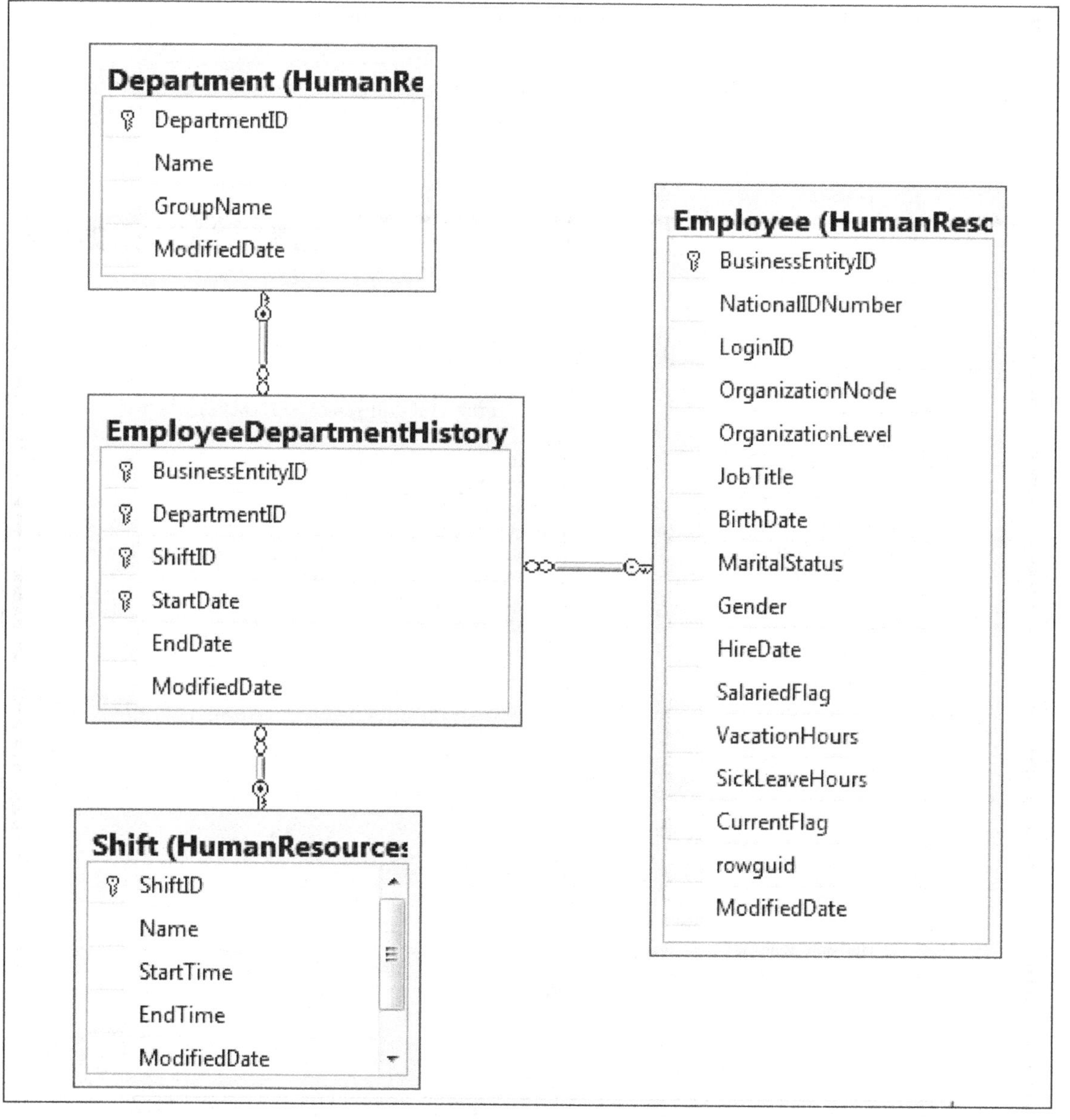

Index Description in Data Dictionary

The fn_listextendedproperty function is not supported in Azure SQL. The indexes listing for Product, SalesOrderHeader & SalesOrderDetail tables. SQL Server 2012 query.

```
USE AdventureWorks2012;

SELECT  objtype                          AS ObjectType,
        'Sales.SalesOrderHeader'         AS TableName,
        objname                          AS ObjectName,
        value                            AS [Description]
FROM fn_listextendedproperty (NULL, 'schema', 'Sales', 'table', 'SalesOrderHeader', 'index', default)

UNION

SELECT objtype, 'Sales.SalesOrderDetail', objname, value
FROM fn_listextendedproperty (NULL, 'schema', 'Sales', 'table', 'SalesOrderDetail', 'index', default)

UNION

SELECT objtype, 'Production.Product', objname,  value
FROM fn_listextendedproperty (NULL, 'schema', 'Production', 'table', 'Product', 'index', default)
ORDER BY TableName;
GO
```

ObjectType	TableName	ObjectName	Description
INDEX	Production.Product	AK_Product_Name	Unique nonclustered index.
INDEX	Production.Product	AK_Product_ProductNumber	Unique nonclustered index.
INDEX	Production.Product	AK_Product_rowguid	Unique nonclustered index. Used to support replication samples.
INDEX	Production.Product	PK_Product_ProductID	Clustered index created by a primary key constraint.
INDEX	Sales.SalesOrderDetail	AK_SalesOrderDetail_rowguid	Unique nonclustered index. Used to support replication samples.
INDEX	Sales.SalesOrderDetail	IX_SalesOrderDetail_ProductID	Nonclustered index.
INDEX	Sales.SalesOrderDetail	PK_SalesOrderDetail_SalesOrderID_SalesOrderDetailID	Clustered index created by a primary key constraint.
INDEX	Sales.SalesOrderHeader	AK_SalesOrderHeader_rowguid	Unique nonclustered index. Used to support replication samples.
INDEX	Sales.SalesOrderHeader	AK_SalesOrderHeader_SalesOrderNumber	Unique nonclustered index.
INDEX	Sales.SalesOrderHeader	IX_SalesOrderHeader_CustomerID	Nonclustered index.
INDEX	Sales.SalesOrderHeader	IX_SalesOrderHeader_SalesPersonID	Nonclustered index.
INDEX	Sales.SalesOrderHeader	PK_SalesOrderHeader_SalesOrderID	Clustered index created by a primary key constraint.

Constraint - Database Object

The PRIMARY KEY constraint ensures that each row has a unique ID. The FOREIGN KEY constraint ensures that the FK points to (references) a valid PK. CHECK constraint enforces formulas (check clauses) defined for a column such as OrderQty > 0. If the formula evaluates to TRUE, the CHECK constraint satisfied, otherwise ERROR condition is generated by the database engine. SSMS screenshot shows a CHECK constraints listing query and results in the AdventureWorks2012 database.

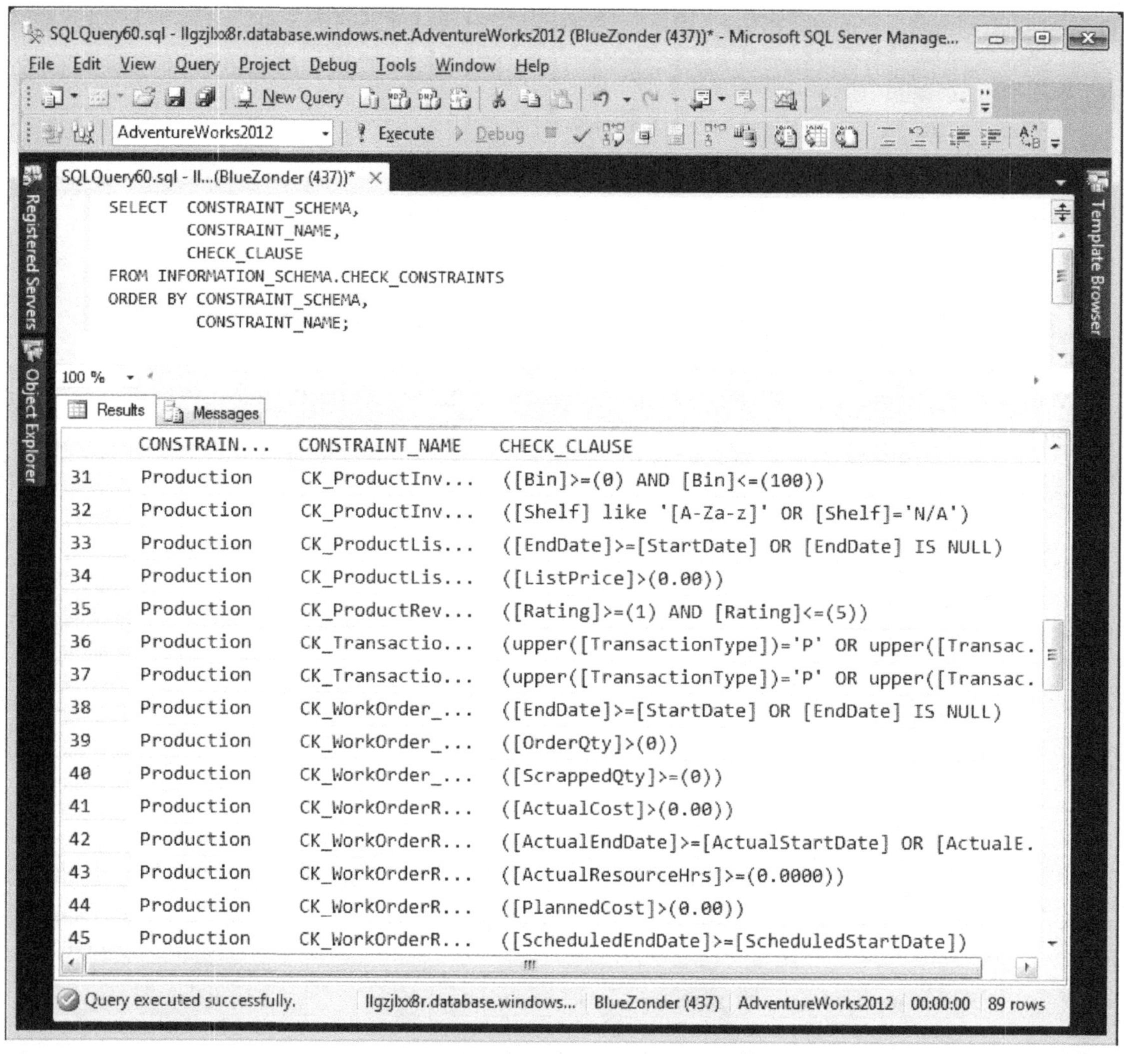

SQLQuery60.sql - llgzjbx8r.database.windows.net.AdventureWorks2012 (BlueZonder (437))* - Microsoft SQL Server Manage...
File Edit View Query Project Debug Tools Window Help
New Query
AdventureWorks2012
Execute Debug
SQLQuery60.sql - Il...(BlueZonder (437))*
SELECT CONSTRAINT_SCHEMA,
CONSTRAINT_NAME,
CHECK_CLAUSE
FROM INFORMATION_SCHEMA.CHECK_CONSTRAINTS
ORDER BY CONSTRAINT_SCHEMA,
CONSTRAINT_NAME;
100 %
Results
Messages
CONSTRAIN... CONSTRAINT_NAME CHECK_CLAUSE
31 Production CK_ProductInv... ([Bin]>=(0) AND [Bin]<=(100))
32 Production CK_ProductInv... ([Shelf] like '[A-Za-z]' OR [Shelf]='N/A')
33 Production CK_ProductLis... ([EndDate]>=[StartDate] OR [EndDate] IS NULL)
34 Production CK_ProductLis... ([ListPrice]>(0.00))
35 Production CK_ProductRev... ([Rating]>=(1) AND [Rating]<=(5))
36 Production CK_Transactio... (upper([TransactionType])='P' OR upper([Transac.
37 Production CK_Transactio... (upper([TransactionType])='P' OR upper([Transac.
38 Production CK_WorkOrder_... ([EndDate]>=[StartDate] OR [EndDate] IS NULL)
39 Production CK_WorkOrder_... ([OrderQty]>(0))
40 Production CK_WorkOrder_... ([ScrappedQty]>=(0))
41 Production CK_WorkOrderR... ([ActualCost]>(0.00))
42 Production CK_WorkOrderR... ([ActualEndDate]>=[ActualStartDate] OR [ActualE.
43 Production CK_WorkOrderR... ([ActualResourceHrs]>=(0.0000))
44 Production CK_WorkOrderR... ([PlannedCost]>(0.00))
45 Production CK_WorkOrderR... ([ScheduledEndDate]>=[ScheduledStartDate])
Query executed successfully.
llgzjbx8r.database.windows...
BlueZonder (437)
AdventureWorks2012
00:00:00
89 rows
Registered Servers
Object Explorer
Template Browser

List all PRIMARKY KEYs & FOREIGN KEYs

Query to retrieve all PRIMARY KEYs & FOREIGN KEYs in the database based on INFORMATION_SCHEMA views.

```
SELECT          CONCAT(c.table_schema, '.', c.table_name)          AS TableName,
                column_name                                        AS ColumnName,
                constraint_type                                    AS KeyConstraint
FROM   information_schema.table_constraints pk
    INNER JOIN information_schema.key_column_usage c
        ON c.table_name = pk.table_name
          AND c.constraint_name = pk.constraint_name
ORDER  BY       KeyConstraint,
                TableName,
                ColumnName;
-- (194 row(s) affected) - Partial results.
```

TableName	ColumnName	KeyConstraint
Sales.SalesOrderHeaderSalesReason	SalesOrderID	FOREIGN KEY
Sales.SalesOrderHeaderSalesReason	SalesReasonID	FOREIGN KEY
Sales.SalesPerson	BusinessEntityID	FOREIGN KEY
Sales.SalesPerson	TerritoryID	FOREIGN KEY
Sales.SalesPersonQuotaHistory	BusinessEntityID	FOREIGN KEY
Sales.SalesTaxRate	StateProvinceID	FOREIGN KEY
Sales.SalesTerritory	CountryRegionCode	FOREIGN KEY
Sales.SalesTerritoryHistory	BusinessEntityID	FOREIGN KEY
Sales.SalesTerritoryHistory	TerritoryID	FOREIGN KEY
Sales.ShoppingCartItem	ProductID	FOREIGN KEY
Sales.SpecialOfferProduct	ProductID	FOREIGN KEY
Sales.SpecialOfferProduct	SpecialOfferID	FOREIGN KEY
Sales.Store	BusinessEntityID	FOREIGN KEY
Sales.Store	SalesPersonID	FOREIGN KEY
dbo.AWBuildVersion	SystemInformationID	PRIMARY KEY
dbo.DatabaseLog	DatabaseLogID	PRIMARY KEY
dbo.ErrorLog	ErrorLogID	PRIMARY KEY
HumanResources.Department	DepartmentID	PRIMARY KEY
HumanResources.Employee	BusinessEntityID	PRIMARY KEY
HumanResources.EmployeeDepartmentHistory	BusinessEntityID	PRIMARY KEY
HumanResources.EmployeeDepartmentHistory	DepartmentID	PRIMARY KEY
HumanResources.EmployeeDepartmentHistory	ShiftID	PRIMARY KEY
HumanResources.EmployeeDepartmentHistory	StartDate	PRIMARY KEY
HumanResources.EmployeePayHistory	BusinessEntityID	PRIMARY KEY
HumanResources.EmployeePayHistory	RateChangeDate	PRIMARY KEY

View - Database Object

A SELECT query, with some restrictions, can be repackaged as view and thus become a server-side object, a coveted status, from "homeless" to "mansion". The creation of view is very simple, basically a name assignment is required as shown in the following demonstration. As soon as the CREATE VIEW statement is executed successfully the query, unknown to the SQL Server so far, becomes an "official" SQL Server database object, stored in the database. A view, a virtual table, can be used just like a table in SELECT queries. A note about the query: **the column aliases FirstAuthor and SecondAuthor cannot be used in the WHERE clause, only in the ORDER BY clause if present.**

SELECT results from views require ORDER BY if sorting is desired. There is no way around it.

```
USE pubs;
GO
```

```
CREATE VIEW vAuthorsInSameCity
AS
SELECT          FirstAuthor      = CONCAT(au1.au_fname,' ', au1.au_lname),
                SecondAuthor     = CONCAT(au2.au_fname,' ', au2.au_lname),
                FirstCity        = au1.city,
                SecondCity       = au2.city
FROM     authors au1
      INNER JOIN authors au2
       ON au1.city = au2.city
WHERE    CONCAT(au1.au_fname,' ', au1.au_lname) < CONCAT(au2.au_fname,' ', au2.au_lname)
GO
```

```
SELECT * FROM vAuthorsInSameCity
ORDER BY FirstAuthor, SecondAuthor
GO
-- (13 row(s) affected) - Partial results.
```

FirstAuthor	SecondAuthor	FirstCity	SecondCity
Abraham Bennet	Cheryl Carson	Berkeley	Berkeley
Albert Ringer	Anne Ringer	Salt Lake City	Salt Lake City
Ann Dull	Sheryl Hunter	Palo Alto	Palo Alto
Dean Straight	Dirk Stringer	Oakland	Oakland
Dean Straight	Livia Karsen	Oakland	Oakland
Dean Straight	Marjorie Green	Oakland	Oakland
Dean Straight	Stearns MacFeather	Oakland	Oakland
Dirk Stringer	Livia Karsen	Oakland	Oakland

CREATE Indexed View for Business Critical Queries

An indexed view is stored like a table unlike a standard view which is a virtual table with a query that is evaluated upon view invocation. Performance is the main benefit of an indexed view, but it comes at a cost: it slows down INSERTs and other operations in the underlying tables.

```
IF OBJECT_ID ('Sales.vSalesByDateByProduct', 'V') IS NOT NULL DROP VIEW Sales.vSalesByDateByProduct ;
GO
CREATE VIEW Sales.vSalesByDateByProduct WITH SCHEMABINDING  AS
  SELECT OrderDate, ProductNumber, SUM(LineTotal) AS TotalSales, COUNT_BIG(*) AS Items
  FROM Sales.SalesOrderDetail AS sod INNER JOIN Sales.SalesOrderHeader AS soh
    ON soh.SalesOrderID = sod.SalesOrderID   INNER JOIN Production.Product p ON sod.ProductID=p.ProductID
    GROUP BY OrderDate, ProductNumber;
GO
CREATE UNIQUE CLUSTERED INDEX idxVSalesCI ON Sales.vSalesByDateByProduct (OrderDate, ProductNumber);
GO
SELECT * FROM Sales.vSalesByDateByProduct ORDER BY OrderDate, ProductNumber;
GO  -- (26878 row(s) affected) - Partial results.
```

OrderDate	ProductNumber	TotalSales	Items
2005-07-01 00:00:00.000	BK-M82B-38	44549.868000	7
2005-07-01 00:00:00.000	BK-M82B-42	32399.904000	8
2005-07-01 00:00:00.000	BK-M82B-44	46574.862000	7
2005-07-01 00:00:00.000	BK-M82B-48	40499.880000	9
2005-07-01 00:00:00.000	BK-M82S-38	20399.940000	4
2005-07-01 00:00:00.000	BK-M82S-42	10199.970000	5
2005-07-01 00:00:00.000	BK-M82S-44	38759.886000	12
2005-07-01 00:00:00.000	BK-M82S-48	14279.958000	6
2005-07-01 00:00:00.000	BK-R50B-44	5452.965700	8
2005-07-01 00:00:00.000	BK-R50B-52	12164.308100	14
2005-07-01 00:00:00.000	BK-R50B-58	12583.767000	10
2005-07-01 00:00:00.000	BK-R50B-60	4614.047900	5
2005-07-01 00:00:00.000	BK-R50B-62	699.098200	1
2005-07-01 00:00:00.000	BK-R50R-44	18456.191600	14
2005-07-01 00:00:00.000	BK-R50R-48	8389.178000	10
2005-07-01 00:00:00.000	BK-R50R-52	5872.424600	7
2005-07-01 00:00:00.000	BK-R50R-60	18036.732700	14
2005-07-01 00:00:00.000	BK-R50R-62	7969.719100	8
2005-07-01 00:00:00.000	BK-R68R-44	12247.116000	8
2005-07-01 00:00:00.000	BK-R68R-52	40240.524000	16

Graphical View Designer

A view can be designed graphically or an existing view altered by using the Design option on the View drop-down menu in SSMS Object Explorer. First we create a view, then enter the graphical view designer to take a look. SQL Server 2012 feature.

```
USE [Northwind];
GO
CREATE VIEW [dbo].[ListOfProducts] AS
SELECT Categories.CategoryName as Category, ProductName, CompanyName AS Supplier
FROM Categories          INNER JOIN Products  ON Categories.CategoryID = Products.CategoryID
                         INNER JOIN Suppliers  ON Suppliers.SupplierID = Products.SupplierID
WHERE (((Products.Discontinued)=0));
GO
```

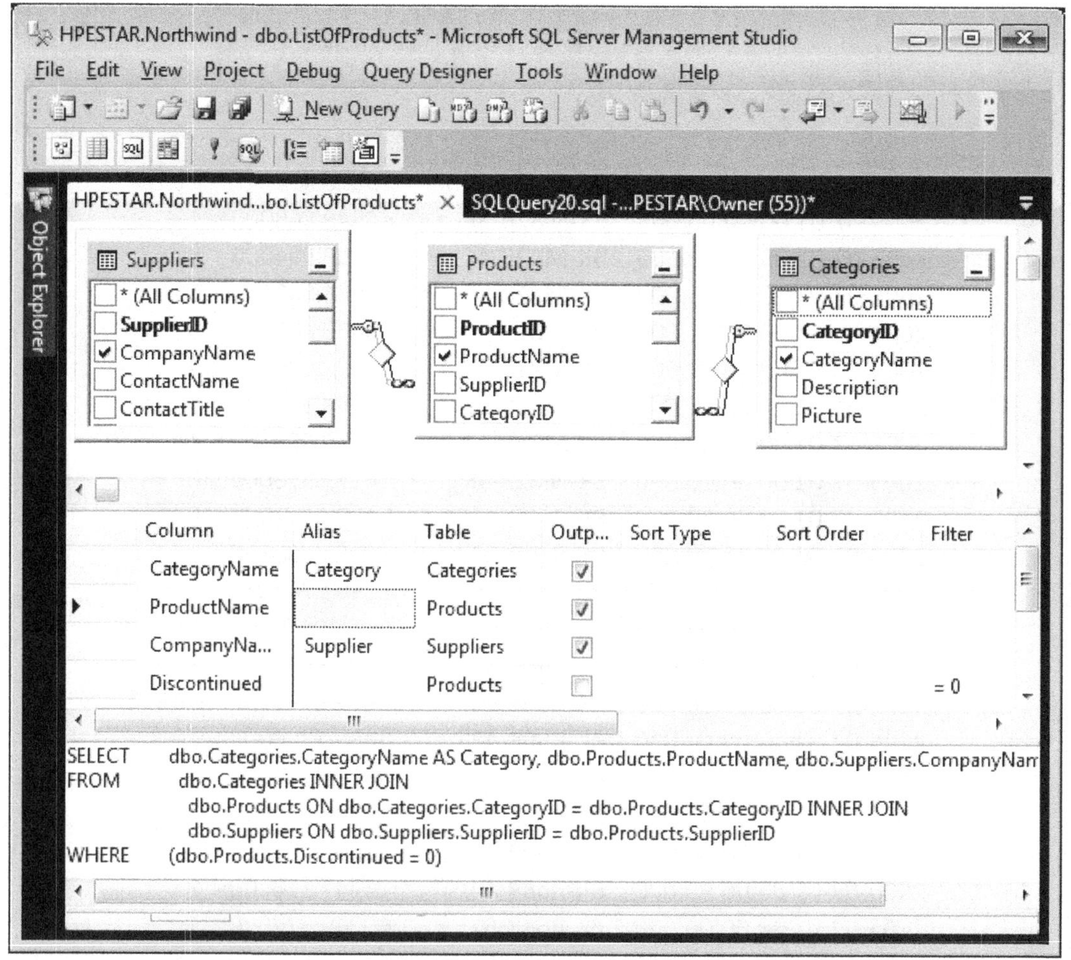

Stored Procedure: Server-Side Program

Stored procedures are T-SQL programs with optional input/output parameters. They vary from very simply to extremely complex. Following is the query which we will transform into a stored procedure, a server-side database object. Typical stored procedure returns table-like results to the client application software just like a SELECT query. That is though not a requirement.

```
USE AdventureWorks2012;
GO
SELECT      P.Name                  AS Product,
            L.Name                  AS [Inventory Location],
            SUM(PI.Quantity)        AS [Qty Available]
FROM Production.Product AS P
   INNER JOIN Production.ProductInventory AS PI
            ON P.ProductID = PI.ProductID
   INNER JOIN Production.Location AS L
            ON PI.LocationID = L.LocationID
  INNER JOIN Production.ProductSubcategory SC
            ON P.ProductSubcategoryID = SC.ProductSubcategoryID
WHERE SC.Name = 'Touring Bikes'
GROUP BY P.Name, L.Name
ORDER BY P.Name;
GO
-- (44 row(s) affected) - Partial results.
```

Product	Inventory Location	Qty Available
Touring-1000 Blue, 46	Final Assembly	86
Touring-1000 Blue, 46	Finished Goods Storage	99
Touring-1000 Blue, 50	Final Assembly	81
Touring-1000 Blue, 50	Finished Goods Storage	67
Touring-1000 Blue, 54	Final Assembly	60
Touring-1000 Blue, 54	Finished Goods Storage	73
Touring-1000 Blue, 60	Final Assembly	99
Touring-1000 Blue, 60	Finished Goods Storage	30
Touring-1000 Yellow, 46	Final Assembly	83
Touring-1000 Yellow, 46	Finished Goods Storage	65
Touring-1000 Yellow, 50	Final Assembly	62
Touring-1000 Yellow, 50	Finished Goods Storage	75
Touring-1000 Yellow, 54	Final Assembly	40
Touring-1000 Yellow, 54	Finished Goods Storage	35
Touring-1000 Yellow, 60	Final Assembly	100

Stored Procedure with Input Parameters

To make the stored procedure even more useful, we replace the literal 'Touring Bikes' with an input parameter.

```
CREATE PROC uspProductInventoryLocation @Subcategory nvarchar(50)
AS
BEGIN
SELECT		P.Name				AS Product,
		L.Name				AS [Inventory Location],
		SUM(PI.Quantity)		AS [Qty Available]
FROM Production.Product AS P
   INNER JOIN Production.ProductInventory AS PI
		ON P.ProductID = PI.ProductID
   INNER JOIN Production.Location AS L
		ON PI.LocationID = L.LocationID
  INNER JOIN Production.ProductSubcategory SC
		ON P.ProductSubcategoryID = SC.ProductSubcategoryID
WHERE SC.Name = @Subcategory
GROUP BY P.Name, L.Name
ORDER BY P.Name;
END
GO
```

```
-- Execute stored procedure with parameter
EXEC uspProductInventoryLocation 'Touring Bikes';
-- (44 row(s) affected)
```

```
EXEC uspProductInventoryLocation 'Mountain Bikes';		-- (64 row(s) affected) - Partial results.
```

Product	Inventory Location	Qty Available
Mountain-100 Black, 38	Final Assembly	56
Mountain-100 Black, 38	Finished Goods Storage	99
Mountain-100 Black, 42	Final Assembly	116
Mountain-100 Black, 42	Finished Goods Storage	78
Mountain-100 Black, 44	Final Assembly	100
Mountain-100 Black, 44	Finished Goods Storage	49
Mountain-100 Black, 48	Final Assembly	65
Mountain-100 Black, 48	Finished Goods Storage	88
Mountain-100 Silver, 38	Final Assembly	100
Mountain-100 Silver, 38	Finished Goods Storage	49
Mountain-100 Silver, 42	Final Assembly	65
Mountain-100 Silver, 42	Finished Goods Storage	88
Mountain-100 Silver, 44	Final Assembly	75
Mountain-100 Silver, 44	Finished Goods Storage	83
Mountain-100 Silver, 48	Final Assembly	102

Stored Procedure Descriptions in Data Dictionary

Query to list stored procedure descriptions in selected schemas. SQL Server 2012 query.

```
USE AdventureWorks2012;
```

```
SELECT
        CONCAT('dbo.', objname COLLATE DATABASE_DEFAULT)        AS SprocName,
        value                                                   AS [Description]
FROM fn_listextendedproperty (NULL, 'schema', 'dbo', 'procedure', default, NULL, NULL)
WHERE LEN(convert(nvarchar(max),value)) > 4
UNION
SELECT
        CONCAT('dbo.', objname COLLATE DATABASE_DEFAULT),
        value
FROM fn_listextendedproperty (NULL, 'schema', 'HumanResources', 'procedure', default, NULL, NULL)
ORDER BY SprocName;
```

SprocName	Description
dbo.uspGetBillOfMaterials	Stored procedure using a recursive query to return a multi-level bill of material for the specified ProductID.
dbo.uspGetEmployeeManagers	Stored procedure using a recursive query to return the direct and indirect managers of the specified employee.
dbo.uspGetManagerEmployees	Stored procedure using a recursive query to return the direct and indirect employees of the specified manager.
dbo.uspGetWhereUsedProductID	Stored procedure using a recursive query to return all components or assemblies that directly or indirectly use the specified ProductID.
dbo.uspLogError	Logs error information in the ErrorLog table about the error that caused execution to jump to the CATCH block of a TRY...CATCH construct. Should be executed from within the scope of a CATCH block otherwise it will return without inserting error information.
dbo.uspPrintError	Prints error information about the error that caused execution to jump to the CATCH block of a TRY...CATCH construct. Should be executed from within the scope of a CATCH block otherwise it will return without printing any error information.
dbo.uspUpdateEmployeeHireInfo	Updates the Employee table and inserts a new row in the EmployeePayHistory table with the values specified in the input parameters.
dbo.uspUpdateEmployeeLogin	Updates the Employee table with the values specified in the input parameters for the given BusinessEntityID.
dbo.uspUpdateEmployeePersonalInfo	Updates the Employee table with the values specified in the input parameters for the given EmployeeID.

Trigger: Event Fired Server-Side Program

Trigger is like a stored procedure with four differences:

- Trigger is fired by an event such as table insert not by a call like a stored procedure.
- Trigger has the deleted (old row copy) and inserted (new row copy) tables available.
- Trigger does not have input/output parameter option.
- Trigger never returns table-like results.

Trigger to synchronize data in StateTaxFreeBondArchive table if data is inserted or updated in the StateTaxFreeBond table.

```
CREATE TRIGGER trgFillInMissingCouponRate

ON [dbo].StateTaxFreeBond

FOR INSERT,UPDATE

AS

BEGIN

    UPDATE StateTaxFreeBondArchive

        SET CouponRate = isnull(i.CouponRate,m.CouponRate)

    FROM StateTaxFreeBondArchive m

        INNER JOIN inserted i

            ON m.MBCID = i.MBCID

END
GO
```

Once a trigger is compiled, it is active and working silently in the background whenever insert, update or delete event fires it up.

It is important to note that there is a downside to the trigger "stealth" operation: if a trigger is dropped , it may not be noticed as part of the day-to-day operation. This behaviour is unlike stored procedure whereby if dropped, it causes error in the calling application software which can be noticed by users.

Function: READ-ONLY Server-Side Program

A user-defined function is also a program like a stored procedure, however, **no database change can be performed within a function, read only**. The database can be changed both in a trigger and a stored procedure. The following T-SQL script demonstrates the creation and use of a table-valued user-defined function. The other function type is scalar-valued, returns only a single value.

```
CREATE FUNCTION dbo.ufnSplitCommaDelimitedIntegerString (@NumberList nvarchar(max))
RETURNS @SplitList TABLE (  Element INT )
AS
 BEGIN
   DECLARE @Pointer    int,
        @Element nvarchar(32)
   SET @NumberList = LTRIM(RTRIM(@NumberList))
   IF ( RIGHT(@NumberList, 1) != ',' )
    SET @NumberList=@NumberList + ','
   SET @Pointer = CHARINDEX(',', @NumberList, 1)
   IF REPLACE(@NumberList, ',', '') <> ''
    BEGIN
      WHILE ( @Pointer > 0 )
       BEGIN
         SET @Element = LTRIM(RTRIM(LEFT(@NumberList, @Pointer - 1)))
         IF ( @Element <> '' )
          INSERT INTO @SplitList
          VALUES      (CONVERT(int, @Element))
         SET @NumberList = RIGHT(@NumberList,
                  LEN(@NumberList) - @Pointer  )
         SET @Pointer = CHARINDEX(',', @NumberList, 1)
       END
    END
   RETURN
 END;
GO
SELECT * FROM  dbo.ufnSplitCommaDelimitedIntegerString ('1, 2, 4, 8, 16, 32, 64, 128, 256');
```

Element
1
2
4
8
16
32
64
128
256

User-Defined Function Descriptions in Data Dictionary

Query to list user-defined function descriptions in the default "dbo" schema. "dbo" stands for database owner, a database role. SQL Server 2012 query.

```
USE AdventureWorks2012;
GO

SELECT
        CONCAT('dbo.', objname COLLATE DATABASE_DEFAULT)          AS UDFName,
        value                                                      AS [Description]
FROM fn_listextendedproperty (NULL, 'schema', 'dbo', 'function', default, NULL, NULL)
WHERE LEN(convert(nvarchar(max),value)) > 4
ORDER BY UDFName;
GO
```

UDFName	Description
dbo.ufnGetAccountingEndDate	Scalar function used in the uSalesOrderHeader trigger to set the starting account date.
dbo.ufnGetAccountingStartDate	Scalar function used in the uSalesOrderHeader trigger to set the ending account date.
dbo.ufnGetContactInformation	Table value function returning the first name, last name, job title and contact type for a given contact.
dbo.ufnGetDocumentStatusText	Scalar function returning the text representation of the Status column in the Document table.
dbo.ufnGetProductDealerPrice	Scalar function returning the dealer price for a given product on a particular order date.
dbo.ufnGetProductListPrice	Scalar function returning the list price for a given product on a particular order date.
dbo.ufnGetProductStandardCost	Scalar function returning the standard cost for a given product on a particular order date.
dbo.ufnGetPurchaseOrderStatusText	Scalar function returning the text representation of the Status column in the PurchaseOrderHeader table.
dbo.ufnGetSalesOrderStatusText	Scalar function returning the text representation of the Status column in the SalesOrderHeader table.
dbo.ufnGetStock	Scalar function returning the quantity of inventory in LocationID 6 (Miscellaneous Storage)for a specified ProductID.
dbo.ufnLeadingZeros	Scalar function used by the Sales.Customer table to help set the account number

Sequence - Database Object - OPSS2012

Not supported in Azure SQL. The INT IDENTITY(1,1) function commonly used as **SURROGATE PRIMARY KEY** is limited to the host table. Sequence object, new in SQL Server 2012, can be shared by tables and programs. T-SQL script to demonstrate how two tables can share an integer sequence.

```
USE AdventureWorks2012;
GO
CREATE SEQUENCE CustomerSequence as INT
START WITH 1  INCREMENT BY 1;
GO
CREATE TABLE LONDONCustomer
 (
	CustomerID	INT PRIMARY KEY,
	Name		NVARCHAR(64) UNIQUE,
	ModifiedDate	DATE default (CURRENT_TIMESTAMP)	);
GO
CREATE TABLE NYCCustomer
 (
	CustomerID	INT PRIMARY KEY,
	Name		NVARCHAR(64) UNIQUE,
	ModifiedDate	DATE default (CURRENT_TIMESTAMP)	);
GO
INSERT NYCCustomer (CustomerID, Name)
VALUES
	(NEXT VALUE FOR CustomerSequence, 'Richard Blackstone'),
	(NEXT VALUE FOR CustomerSequence, 'Anna Smithfield');
GO
SELECT * FROM NYCCustomer;
```

CustomerID	Name	ModifiedDate
1	Richard Blackstone	2016-07-18
2	Anna Smithfield	2016-07-18

```
INSERT LONDONCustomer (CustomerID, Name)
VALUES
	(NEXT VALUE FOR CustomerSequence, 'Kevin Lionheart'),
	(NEXT VALUE FOR CustomerSequence, 'Linda Wakefield');
GO

SELECT * FROM LONDONCustomer;
```

CustomerID	Name	ModifiedDate
3	Kevin Lionheart	2016-07-18
4	Linda Wakefield	2016-07-18

ROW_NUMBER() & Ranking Functions

Ranking functions (window functions), introduced with SQL Server 2005, provide sequencing and ranking items in a partition or all. ROW_NUMBER() (sequence) function is the most used.

```
SELECT  CustomerID,
        CONVERT(date, OrderDate)                              AS OrderDate,
        RANK() OVER (  PARTITION BY CustomerID
                       ORDER BY OrderDate DESC)               AS RankNo
FROM   Sales.SalesOrderHeader
ORDER  BY CustomerID,   RankNo;
GO
-- (31465 row(s) affected) - Partial results.
```

CustomerID	OrderDate	RankNo
11014	2007-11-01	1
11014	2007-09-24	2
11015	2007-07-22	1
11016	2007-08-13	1
11017	2008-04-16	1
11017	2007-07-05	2
11017	2005-07-15	3
11018	2008-04-26	1
11018	2007-07-20	2
11018	2005-07-20	3
11019	2008-07-15	1
11019	2008-07-14	2
11019	2008-06-12	3
11019	2008-06-02	4
11019	2008-06-01	5
11019	2008-04-28	6
11019	2008-04-19	7
11019	2008-03-22	8
11019	2008-03-11	9
11019	2008-02-23	10
11019	2008-01-24	11
11019	2007-11-26	12
11019	2007-11-09	13
11019	2007-10-30	14
11019	2007-09-14	15
11019	2007-09-05	16
11019	2007-08-16	17
11020	2007-07-02	1

Partition data by CustomerID and rank it OrderDate DESC (most recent orders first).

```
SELECT *
FROM  (SELECT CustomerID,
         CONVERT(date, OrderDate)          AS OrderDate,
         RANK() OVER (
           PARTITION BY CustomerID
           ORDER BY OrderDate DESC)        AS RankNo
     FROM  Sales.SalesOrderHeader) x -- derived table
WHERE RankNo BETWEEN 1 AND 4
ORDER BY CustomerID;
GO
-- (29383 row(s) affected) - Partial results.
```

CustomerID	OrderDate	RankNo
11675	2007-08-13	1
11675	2006-04-27	2
11676	2008-06-11	1
11676	2008-02-21	2
11677	2008-06-02	1
11677	2008-03-24	2
11677	2008-03-17	3
11677	2008-03-07	4
11678	2007-08-09	1
11678	2006-04-12	2
11679	2008-06-01	1
11679	2008-04-15	2
11680	2008-07-22	1
11680	2008-03-04	2
11681	2008-05-28	1
11681	2007-09-08	2
11682	2008-06-11	1
11682	2008-03-08	2
11683	2007-08-11	1
11683	2006-04-07	2
11684	2008-06-14	1
11684	2008-01-02	2
11685	2008-06-15	1
11685	2007-09-12	2
11686	2007-10-26	1
11686	2007-09-09	2
11687	2007-12-23	1
11687	2007-10-14	2
11688	2007-08-18	1
11688	2006-04-04	2
11689	2008-03-05	1
11689	2008-02-27	2

Query to compare RANK, DENSE_RANK and NTILE.

```
USE AdventureWorks2012;

SELECT c.AccountNumber                                AS CustAccount,
    FLOOR(h.SubTotal / 1000)                          AS [SubTotal (Thousands $)],
    ROW_NUMBER() OVER(
      ORDER BY FLOOR(h.SubTotal /1000) DESC)          AS RowNumber,
    RANK()  OVER(
      ORDER BY FLOOR(h.SubTotal /1000) DESC)          AS Rank,
    DENSE_RANK()   OVER(
      ORDER BY FLOOR(h.SubTotal /1000) DESC)          AS DenseRank,
    NTILE(5)   OVER(
      ORDER BY FLOOR(h.SubTotal /1000) DESC)          AS NTile
FROM   Sales.Customer c
    INNER JOIN Sales.SalesOrderHeader h
          ON c.CustomerID = h.CustomerID
    INNER JOIN Sales.SalesTerritory t
          ON h.TerritoryID = t.TerritoryID
WHERE  t.Name = 'Germany'
        AND OrderDate >= '20070101' AND OrderDate  <  DATEADD(mm, 1, '20070101' )
        AND SubTotal > 1.0
ORDER  BY RowNumber;
```

CustAccount	SubTotal (Thousands $)	RowNumber	Rank	DenseRank	NTile
AW00016538	2.00	1	1	1	1
AW00012276	2.00	2	1	1	1
AW00016552	2.00	3	1	1	1
AW00016821	2.00	4	1	1	1
AW00016567	2.00	5	1	1	2
AW00016603	2.00	6	1	1	2
AW00016540	2.00	7	1	1	2
AW00016587	2.00	8	1	1	2
AW00012275	2.00	9	1	1	3
AW00016565	2.00	10	1	1	3
AW00012291	2.00	11	1	1	3
AW00016572	2.00	12	1	1	4
AW00016824	2.00	13	1	1	4
AW00016549	2.00	14	1	1	4
AW00019030	1.00	15	15	2	5
AW00019035	1.00	16	15	2	5
AW00019034	1.00	17	15	2	5

Dynamic SQL To Soar Beyond the Limits of Static SQL

Static (regular) T-SQL syntax does not accept variables at all places in a query. With dynamic SQL we can overcome the limitation. Dynamic SQL script uses table list metadata from the INFORMATION_SCHEMA.TABLES system view to build a COUNT() query for all tables. COUNT(*) returns 4 bytes integer. For large values COUNT_BIG() returns an 8 bytes integer.

```
DECLARE @SQL nvarchar(max) = '', @Schema sysname, @Table sysname;
SELECT TOP 20 @SQL = CONCAT(@SQL , 'SELECT "',QUOTENAME(TABLE_SCHEMA),'.',
        QUOTENAME(TABLE_NAME),'"',
        '= COUNT(*) FROM ', QUOTENAME(TABLE_SCHEMA),'.',QUOTENAME(TABLE_NAME) , ';',
        CHAR(10))
FROM INFORMATION_SCHEMA.TABLES
WHERE TABLE_TYPE='BASE TABLE';
PRINT @SQL;            -- Test & debug - Partial results.
```

```
SELECT "[Production].[BillOfMaterials]"= COUNT(*) FROM [Production].[BillOfMaterials];
SELECT "[Production].[Culture]"= COUNT(*) FROM [Production].[Culture];
SELECT "[Production].[Document]"= COUNT(*) FROM [Production].[Document];
SELECT "[Production].[Illustration]"= COUNT(*) FROM [Production].[Illustration];
SELECT "[Production].[Location]"= COUNT(*) FROM [Production].[Location];
SELECT "[Production].[ProductCategory]"= COUNT(*) FROM [Production].[ProductCategory];
SELECT "[Production].[ProductCostHistory]"= COUNT(*) FROM [Production].[ProductCostHistory];
SELECT "[Production].[ProductDocument]"= COUNT(*) FROM [Production].[ProductDocument];
SELECT "[Production].[ProductInventory]"= COUNT(*) FROM [Production].[ProductInventory];
SELECT "[Production].[ProductListPriceHistory]"= COUNT(*) FROM
[Production].[ProductListPriceHistory];
```

```
EXEC sp_executesql @SQL  -- Dynamic SQL query execution
-- Partial results.
```

[Production].[ScrapReason]
16

[HumanResources].[Shift]
3

[Production].[ProductCategory]
4

[Purchasing].[ShipMethod]
5

Built-in System Functions

SQL Server T-SQL language has a large collection of system functions such as date & time, string and math function. The nested REPLACE string function can be used to remove unwanted characters from a string.

```
DECLARE @text nvarchar(128) = '#1245! $99^@';
SELECT REPLACE(REPLACE(REPLACE(REPLACE(REPLACE(REPLACE(REPLACE(REPLACE(REPLACE(@text,
            '!',''),'@',''),'#',''),'$',''),'%',''),'^',''),'&',''),'*',''),' ','');      -- 124599
```

All the system functions (exception hierarchyid) are listed in SSMS Object Explorer under the Programmability tab.

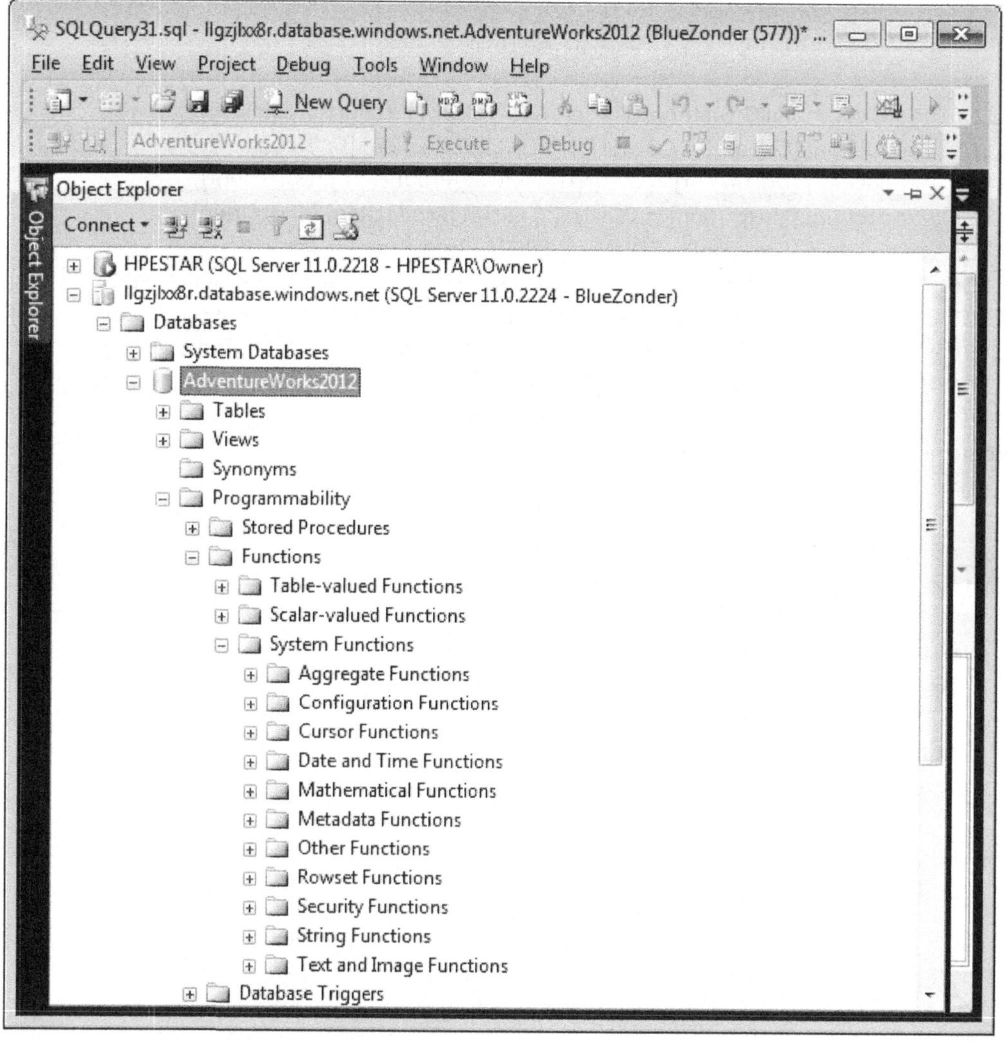

Local Variables & Table Variables in T-SQL

Local variables with different data types have scope of a batch or a stored procedure/trigger/function. Note that a "GO" in T-SQL script indicates end of batch, therefore the end of scope for local variables. Table variable is a virtual table with similar scope to local variable. Script to demonstrate local and table variables.

```
DECLARE @i INT;  SET @i = 999;

SELECT @i + @i;
-- 1998

SELECT @i = 555;  -- assignment
SELECT @i + @i;
GO
-- 1110
```

```
DECLARE @i INT = 999;                    -- new in SQL Server 2008
SET @i += 1;                             -- new in SQL Server 2008

SELECT @i;
GO
-- 1000
```

```
DECLARE @OrderShipperJunction TABLE                    -- Table variable
 (
   ShipperID             SMALLINT IDENTITY ( 1, 1 ) PRIMARY KEY,
   ShipperName           NVARCHAR(64),
   PurchaseOrderID       INT,
   ShipDate              DATE DEFAULT (CURRENT_TIMESTAMP),
   FreightCost           SMALLMONEY
 ) ;
INSERT @OrderShipperJunction
     (ShipperName,
      PurchaseOrderID,
      FreightCost)
VALUES('Custom Motor Bike Distributor',      11111,      177.34)

SELECT * FROM   @OrderShipperJunction
GO
```

ShipperID	ShipperName	PurchaseOrderID	ShipDate	FreightCost
1	Custom Motor Bike Distributor	11111	2016-07-18	177.34

Metadata Visibility Through System Views

The system views provide SQL Server and database metadata which can be used just for viewing in SSMS Object Explorer or programmatically in T-SQL scripts. The system views are based on system tables which are no longer accessible since SQL Server 2005. The system view sys.objects contains all the basic info on each and every user objects in the database with the exception of indexes. Query to retrieve partial data form sys.objects system view.

```
select
   s.name                          as [Schema],
   o.name                          as [Name],
   o.type_desc                     as [Type],
   o.create_date                   as CreateDate
from   sys.objects o
         inner join sys.schemas s
            on s.schema_id = o.schema_id
where is_ms_shipped = 0
order by [Type], [Schema], [Name]
-- (722 row(s) affected)  -  Partial results.
```

Schema	Name	Type	CreateDate
HumanResources	Department	USER_TABLE	2012-03-14 13:14:19.267
HumanResources	Employee	USER_TABLE	2012-03-14 13:14:19.303
HumanResources	EmployeeDepartmentHistory	USER_TABLE	2012-03-14 13:14:19.313
HumanResources	EmployeePayHistory	USER_TABLE	2012-03-14 13:14:19.320
HumanResources	JobCandidate	USER_TABLE	2012-03-14 13:14:19.337
HumanResources	Shift	USER_TABLE	2012-03-14 13:14:19.593
Person	Address	USER_TABLE	2012-03-14 13:14:19.140
Person	AddressType	USER_TABLE	2012-03-14 13:14:19.150
Person	BusinessEntity	USER_TABLE	2012-03-14 13:14:19.183
Person	BusinessEntityAddress	USER_TABLE	2012-03-14 13:14:19.190
Person	BusinessEntityContact	USER_TABLE	2012-03-14 13:14:19.197
Person	ContactType	USER_TABLE	2012-03-14 13:14:19.207
Person	CountryRegion	USER_TABLE	2012-03-14 13:14:19.220
Person	EmailAddress	USER_TABLE	2012-03-14 13:14:19.290
Person	Password	USER_TABLE	2012-03-14 13:14:19.350
Person	Person	USER_TABLE	2012-03-14 13:14:19.357
Person	PersonPhone	USER_TABLE	2012-03-14 13:14:19.370
Person	PhoneNumberType	USER_TABLE	2012-03-14 13:14:19.377
Person	StateProvince	USER_TABLE	2012-03-14 13:14:19.623
Production	BillOfMaterials	USER_TABLE	2012-03-14 13:14:19.170
Production	Culture	USER_TABLE	2012-03-14 13:14:19.237

Constructing T-SQL Identifiers

Identifiers are the names given to SQL Server & database objects such as linked servers, tables, views or stored procedures.

Very simple rule: **do not include any special character in an identifier other than single underscore (_). Double underscore in an identifier inevitably leads to confusion, loss of database developer productivity.**

Creating good identifiers helps with productivity in database development, administration and maintenance. Using names AccountsPayable1 and AccountsPayable2 as variations for AccountsPayable is not good because the 1,2 suffixes are meaningless. On the other hand AccountsPayableLondon & AccountsPayableNYC are good, meaningful names. The list of identifiers can be enumerated from sys.objects.

```
SELECT name FROM sys.objects   ORDER BY name; -- (820 row(s) affected)
```

Selected results with comments.

Identifier(name)	Style Comment
Account	single word
AddressType	double words CamelCase style
BillOfMaterials	CamelCase (also known as Pascal case)
BusinessEntityContact	CamelCase
CK__ImageStore__67152DD3	double underscore separator, CK prefix for CHECK CONSTRAINT
CK_Document_Status	single underscore separator
CK_EmployeeDepartmentHistory_EndDate	mixed - CamelCase and underscore
DF__ImageStor__is_sy__75634D2A	database engine (system) generated name
sp_creatediagram	old-fashioned, sp prefix for system procedure
syscscolsegments	old-fashioned with abbreviations
ufnGetProductDealerPrice	Hungarian naming, ufn stands for user(-defined) function
vSalesPersonSalesByFiscalYears	Hungarian naming, v prefix is for view

The Use of [] - Square Brackets in Identifiers

Each identifier can be enclosed in square brackets, but not required. If the identifier is the same as a T-SQL reserved keyword, then it is required. Square brackets are also required when the identifier includes a special character such as space. In ANSI SQL double quotes are used like in "Order Details" table. **Double quotes can become very confusing when single quotes are present in the query**. The use of brackets is demonstrated in the following T-SQL script.

```
USE Northwind;
```

```
-- Syntax error without brackets since table name has space
SELECT * FROM Order Details;
/* ERROR
Msg 156, Level 15, State 1, Line 3
Incorrect syntax near the keyword 'Order'.
*/
```

```
-- Valid statement with brackets around table name
SELECT * FROM [Order Details];
-- (2155 row(s) affected)
```

```
-- Create and populate table with SELECT INTO
-- Error since ORDER is a reserved keyword
SELECT * INTO Order FROM Orders;
/* ERROR
Msg 156, Level 15, State 1, Line 1
Incorrect syntax near the keyword 'Order'.
*/
```

```
-- With brackets, query is valid
SELECT * INTO [Order] FROM Orders;
-- (830 row(s) affected)
```

When a database object is scripted out in SSMS Object Explore, the identifiers are surrounded with square brackets even when not needed as shown in the following demonstration.

```
CREATE TABLE [dbo].[Order Details](
	[OrderID] [int] NOT NULL,
	[ProductID] [int] NOT NULL,
	[UnitPrice] [money] NOT NULL,
	[Quantity] [smallint] NOT NULL,
	[Discount] [real] NOT NULL,
 CONSTRAINT [PK_Order_Details] PRIMARY KEY CLUSTERED
 (	[OrderID] ASC,
	[ProductID] ASC));
```

CHAPTER 7: Introduction to Relational Database Design

Logical Data Modeling

Logical data modeling is the first step in database design. The task can be carried out by systems analysts, subject-matter experts, database designers or lead database developers. Small budget projects usually settle for an experienced database developer in the design role. The database design team spends time with the future users (stakeholders) of the database to find out the expectations and requirements for the new database. As soon as the design team has some basic idea of functional requirements, the iterative process continues with discussing entities (corresponds to tables in the database) and their relationships with the users. For example the Order entity has many to many relationship to the Product entity. A Product occurs in many orders, and an Order may hold many products.

Physical Data Modeling

Physical Data Modeling is the process of translating the logical data model into actual database tables and related objects such as PRIMARY KEY and FOREIGN KEY constraints. If a software tool was used to design the logical data model then the forward engineering feature can be applied to generate SQL scripts to create tables and related database objects. **An important step in this process is the design of indexes to support SQL query performance**. Example for Data Warehouse dimension table implementation.

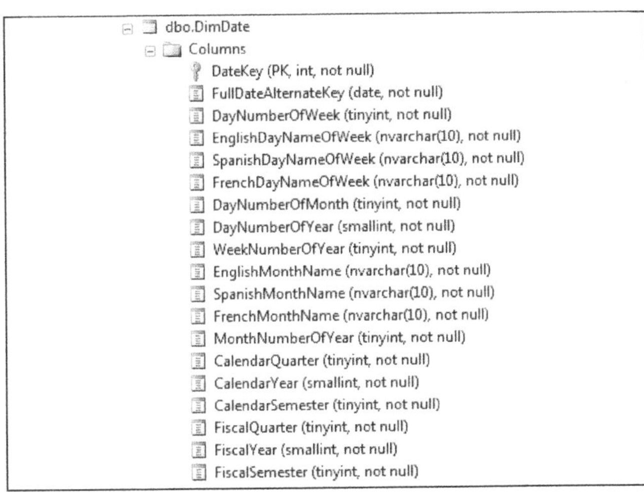

Column Definitions for the FactInternetSales Table

Table columns for a fact table in AdventureWorksDWAZ2008R2 database. PK stands for PRIMARY KEY, FK for FOREGN KEY. The PRIMARY KEY is a composite of 2 columns: SalesOrderNumber and SalesOrderLineNumber.

The screen image is from SSMS Object Explorer.

```
dbo.FactInternetSales
  Columns
    ProductKey (int, not null)
    OrderDateKey (int, not null)
    DueDateKey (int, not null)
    ShipDateKey (int, not null)
    CustomerKey (int, not null)
    PromotionKey (int, not null)
    CurrencyKey (int, not null)
    SalesTerritoryKey (int, not null)
    SalesOrderNumber (PK, nvarchar(20), not null)
    SalesOrderLineNumber (PK, tinyint, not null)
    RevisionNumber (tinyint, not null)
    OrderQuantity (smallint, not null)
    UnitPrice (money, not null)
    ExtendedAmount (money, not null)
    UnitPriceDiscountPct (float, not null)
    DiscountAmount (float, not null)
    ProductStandardCost (money, not null)
    TotalProductCost (money, not null)
    SalesAmount (money, not null)
    TaxAmt (money, not null)
    Freight (money, not null)
    CarrierTrackingNumber (nvarchar(25), null)
    CustomerPONumber (nvarchar(25), null)
```

Table Column Data Types

Exact Numerics

bigint	8 byte signed integer -- Exact Numerics
bit	Boolean
decimal	5 - 17 bytes decimal number with variable precision
int	4 byte signed integer
money	8 byte with ten-thousandth accuracy
numeric	Same as decimal
smallint	2 byte signed integer
smallmoney	4 byte with ten-thousandth accuracy
tinyint	1 byte signed integer

Approximate Numerics

float	4 - 8 byte floating point -- Approximate Numerics
real	4 byte floating point

Date and Time

date	3 byte date only
datetime	8 byte date & time
datetime2	6 - 8 byte date & time
datetimeoffset	10 byte date & time with time zone
smalldatetime	4 byte date & time
time	5 byte time only

Character Strings

char	Fixed length ASCII character storage - 1 byte for each character -- Character String
text	Variable-length ASCII data with a maximum string length of 2^31-1 (deprecated)
varchar	Variable length ASCII character storage

Unicode Character Strings

nchar	Fixed length UNICODE character storage - 2 bytes for each character
ntext	Variable-length UNICODE data with a maximum string length of 2^30-1 (deprecated)
nvarchar	Variable length UNICODE character storage

Binary Strings

binary	Fixed-length binary data with maximum storage size of 2^31-1 bytes -- Binary String
image	Variable-length binary data with maximum storage size of 2^31-1 bytes (deprecated)
varbinary	Variable-length binary data with maximum storage size of 2^31-1 bytes

Other Data Types

cursor	Contains a reference to a cursor - not for column use
hierarchyid	Represents a position in a tree hierarchy, typically a few bytes up to 892 bytes
sql_variant	Stores values of various SQL Server data types, maximum length of 8016 bytes
table	Store a result set for processing at a later time, not for columns
timestamp	8 byte generated binary number, mechanism for version-stamping table rows
uniqueidentifier	16 byte GUID - Globally Unique Identifier
xml	Stores XML data up to 2GB in size

Date Type max_length, precision, scale & collation_name Listing

Database metadata on data types can be found in types system view.

```
SELECT          name, system_type_id, max_length, precision, scale,
                isnull(collation_name, SPACE(0)) AS collation_name
FROM sys.types WHERE schema_id = 4 ORDER BY name;
```

name	system_type_id	max_length	precision	scale	collation_name
bigint	127	8	19	0	
binary	173	8000	0	0	
bit	104	1	1	0	
char	175	8000	0	0	SQL_Latin1_General_CP1_CI_AS
date	40	3	10	0	
datetime	61	8	23	3	
datetime2	42	8	27	7	
datetimeoffset	43	10	34	7	
decimal	106	17	38	38	
float	62	8	53	0	
geography	240	-1	0	0	
geometry	240	-1	0	0	
hierarchyid	240	892	0	0	
image	34	16	0	0	
int	56	4	10	0	
money	60	8	19	4	
nchar	239	8000	0	0	SQL_Latin1_General_CP1_CI_AS
ntext	99	16	0	0	SQL_Latin1_General_CP1_CI_AS
numeric	108	17	38	38	
nvarchar	231	8000	0	0	SQL_Latin1_General_CP1_CI_AS
real	59	4	24	0	
smalldatetime	58	4	16	0	
smallint	52	2	5	0	
smallmoney	122	4	10	4	
sql_variant	98	8016	0	0	
sysname	231	256	0	0	SQL_Latin1_General_CP1_CI_AS
text	35	16	0	0	SQL_Latin1_General_CP1_CI_AS
time	41	5	16	7	
timestamp	189	8	0	0	
tinyint	48	1	3	0	
uniqueidentifier	36	16	0	0	
varbinary	165	8000	0	0	
varchar	167	8000	0	0	SQL_Latin1_General_CP1_CI_AS
xml	241	-1	0	0	

Azure SQL Data Types Summary Page

BOL: **Data Types (Windows Azure SQL Database)**
http://msdn.microsoft.com/en-us/library/windowsazure/ee336233.aspx

U.S. Default Collation SQL_Latin1_General_CP1_CI_AS

```
SELECT SERVERPROPERTY('Collation'); -- SQL_Latin1_General_CP1_CI_AS
```

Interpretation:

- SQL collation not Windows
- Latin 1 alphabet
- Code page 1 for sorting
- Case insensitive
- Accent sensitive

SQL_Latin1_General_CP1_CI_AS is the default collation of SQL Server 2012 in the United States. Only a handful of experts around the world really understand collations. Collation is a column level property. Server and database collations are only defaults. To change the collation of a column, use ALTER TABLE. The easiest fix in most collation error cases is placing COLLATE DATABASE_DEFAULT following the right most operator. There are a number of articles on the web which deal extensively with collations.

```
CREATE TABLE Product1 (ProductID INT PRIMARY KEY, Name nvarchar(50), ListPrice money);
```

```
INSERT Product1
SELECT ProductID, Name, ListPrice FROM Production.Product;
GO -- (504 row(s) affected)
```

```
ALTER TABLE Product1 ALTER COLUMN Name nvarchar(50) COLLATE SQL_Latin1_General_CP1_CS_AS null;
GO -- (504 row(s) affected)
```

```
SELECT * FROM Production.Product P INNER JOIN Product1 P1        ON P.Name = P1.Name;
/* Msg 468, Level 16, State 9, Line 2
Cannot resolve the collation conflict between "SQL_Latin1_General_CP1_CS_AS"
and "SQL_Latin1_General_CP1_CI_AS" in the equal to operation. */
```

```
SELECT * FROM Production.Product P INNER JOIN Product1 P1
        ON P.Name = P1.Name COLLATE DATABASE_DEFAULT;  -- (504 row(s) affected).
```

DATE & DATETIME Temporal Data Types

DATE data type has been introduced with SQL Server 2008. DATETIME on the other hand is around since the inception of SQL Server. A good deal of programming effort goes into supporting hundreds of different string date & time formats. Each country has its own string date formats adding more to the general confusion. As an example in the United States the mdy string date format is used. In the United Kingdom, the dmy format is used. When one looks at a date like 10/11/2015, it is not apparent which date format is it. In a globalized world the data flows freely from one country to another, frequently without adequate documentation, hence the loss of database developer productivity as related to date & time data issues. **Best to use the ISO string date formats 'YYYYMMDD' or 'YYYY-MM-DD'.** List of century (CCYY or YYYY) datetime conversions styles (stylenumber >= 100).

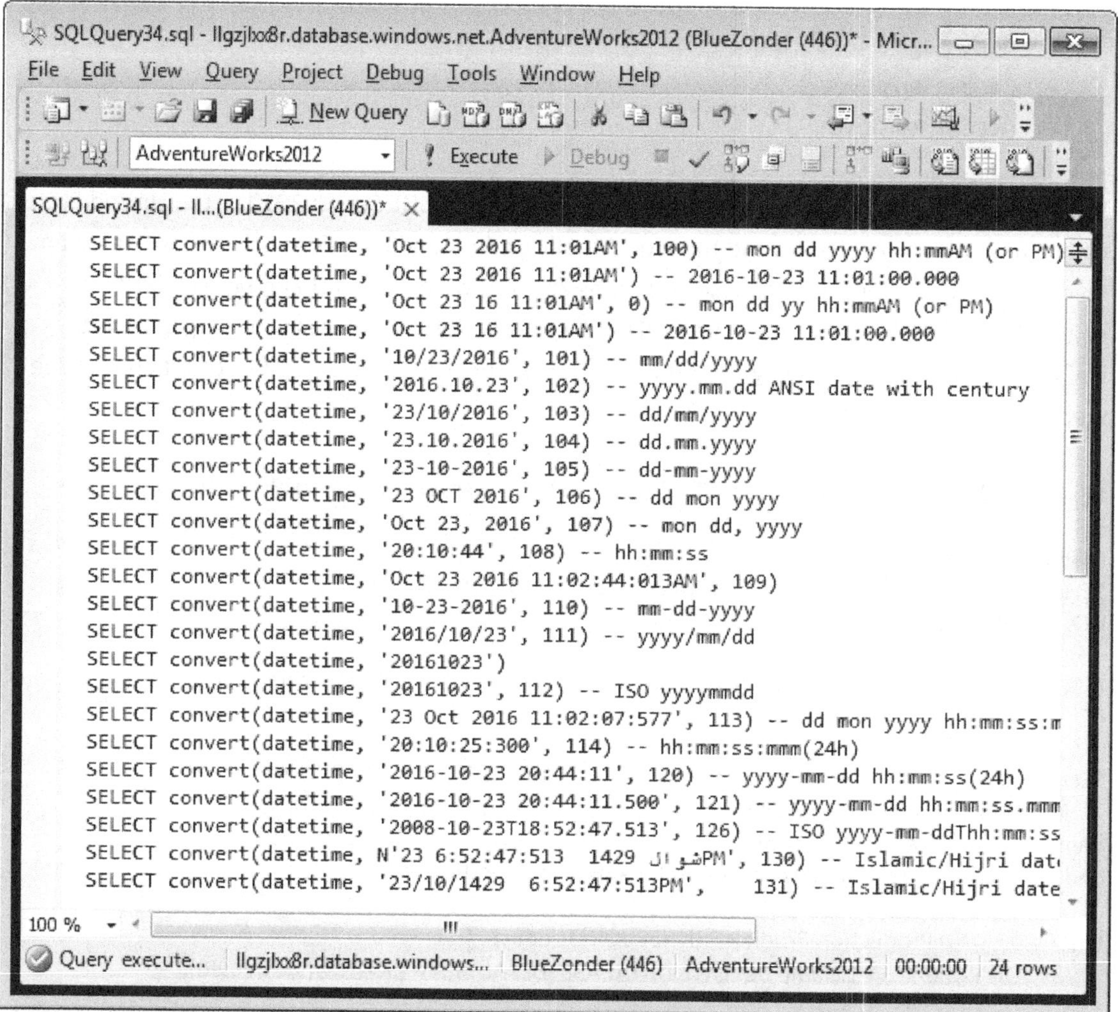

SQLQuery34.sql - llgzjbx8r.database.windows.net.AdventureWorks2012 (BlueZonder (446))* - Micr...
File Edit View Query Project Debug Tools Window Help
New Query
AdventureWorks2012
Execute
Debug
SQLQuery34.sql - ll...(BlueZonder (446))*
SELECT convert(datetime, 'Oct 23 2016 11:01AM', 100) -- mon dd yyyy hh:mmAM (or PM)
SELECT convert(datetime, 'Oct 23 2016 11:01AM') -- 2016-10-23 11:01:00.000
SELECT convert(datetime, 'Oct 23 16 11:01AM', 0) -- mon dd yy hh:mmAM (or PM)
SELECT convert(datetime, 'Oct 23 16 11:01AM') -- 2016-10-23 11:01:00.000
SELECT convert(datetime, '10/23/2016', 101) -- mm/dd/yyyy
SELECT convert(datetime, '2016.10.23', 102) -- yyyy.mm.dd ANSI date with century
SELECT convert(datetime, '23/10/2016', 103) -- dd/mm/yyyy
SELECT convert(datetime, '23.10.2016', 104) -- dd.mm.yyyy
SELECT convert(datetime, '23-10-2016', 105) -- dd-mm-yyyy
SELECT convert(datetime, '23 OCT 2016', 106) -- dd mon yyyy
SELECT convert(datetime, 'Oct 23, 2016', 107) -- mon dd, yyyy
SELECT convert(datetime, '20:10:44', 108) -- hh:mm:ss
SELECT convert(datetime, 'Oct 23 2016 11:02:44:013AM', 109)
SELECT convert(datetime, '10-23-2016', 110) -- mm-dd-yyyy
SELECT convert(datetime, '2016/10/23', 111) -- yyyy/mm/dd
SELECT convert(datetime, '20161023')
SELECT convert(datetime, '20161023', 112) -- ISO yyyymmdd
SELECT convert(datetime, '23 Oct 2016 11:02:07:577', 113) -- dd mon yyyy hh:mm:ss:m
SELECT convert(datetime, '20:10:25:300', 114) -- hh:mm:ss:mmm(24h)
SELECT convert(datetime, '2016-10-23 20:44:11', 120) -- yyyy-mm-dd hh:mm:ss(24h)
SELECT convert(datetime, '2016-10-23 20:44:11.500', 121) -- yyyy-mm-dd hh:mm:ss.mmm
SELECT convert(datetime, '2008-10-23T18:52:47.513', 126) -- ISO yyyy-mm-ddThh:mm:ss
SELECT convert(datetime, N'23 6:52:47:513 1429 شوالPM', 130) -- Islamic/Hijri dat
SELECT convert(datetime, '23/10/1429 6:52:47:513PM', 131) -- Islamic/Hijri date
100 %
Query execute... llgzjbx8r.database.windows... BlueZonder (446) AdventureWorks2012 00:00:00 24 rows

Two Ways of Commenting in T-SQL Scripts

Line comment is prefixed by "--". Multiple lines comment has to be enclosed with "/*" and "*/".

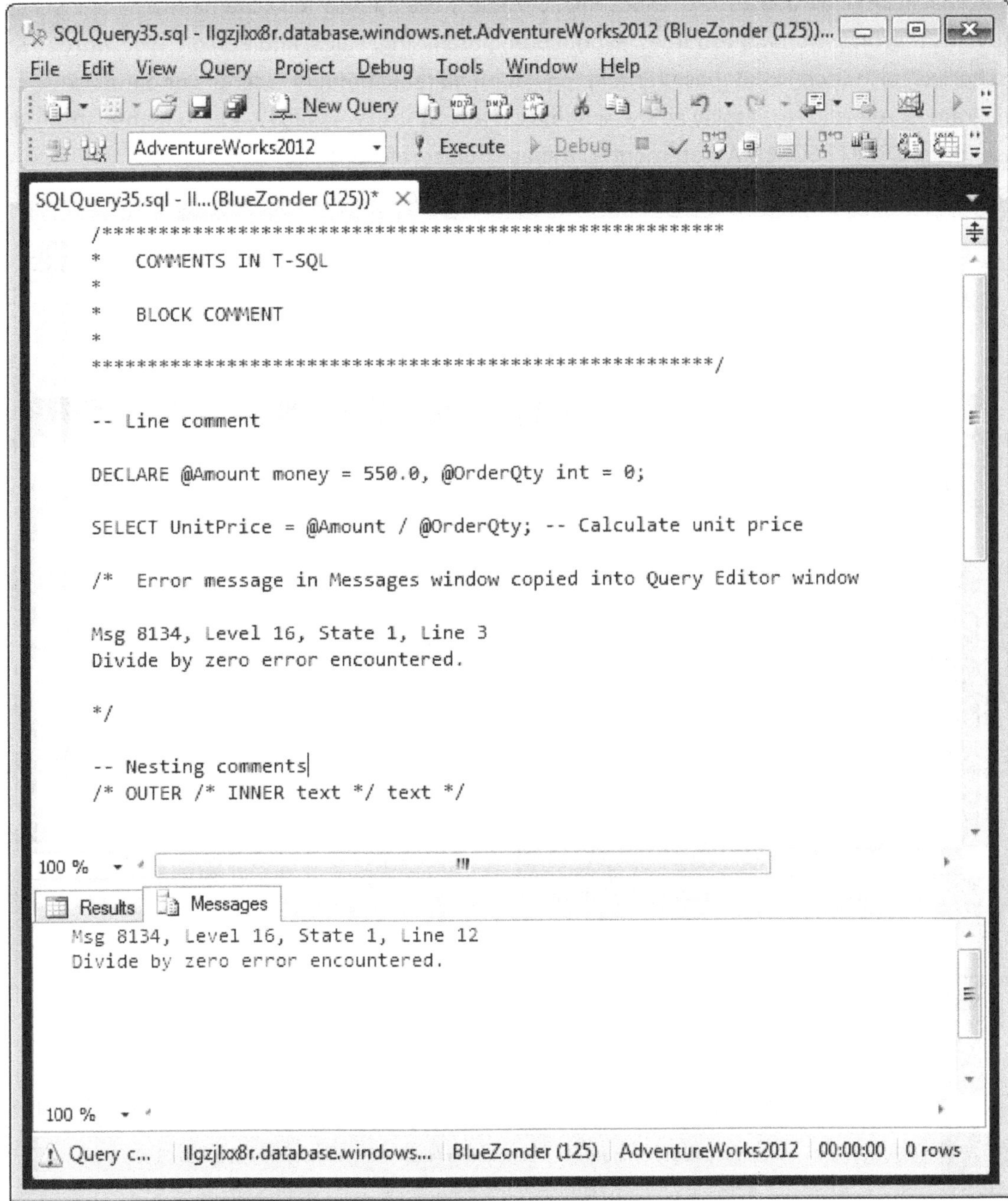
SQLQuery35.sql - llgzjlxx8r.database.windows.net.AdventureWorks2012 (BlueZonder (125))...
File Edit View Query Project Debug Tools Window Help
New Query
AdventureWorks2012
Execute
Debug
SQLQuery35.sql - ll...(BlueZonder (125))*
/***
*   COMMENTS IN T-SQL
*
*   BLOCK COMMENT
*
***/
-- Line comment
DECLARE @Amount money = 550.0, @OrderQty int = 0;
SELECT UnitPrice = @Amount / @OrderQty; -- Calculate unit price
/* Error message in Messages window copied into Query Editor window
Msg 8134, Level 16, State 1, Line 3
Divide by zero error encountered.
*/
-- Nesting comments
/* OUTER /* INNER text */ text */
100 %
Results
Messages
Msg 8134, Level 16, State 1, Line 12
Divide by zero error encountered.
100 %
Query c...
llgzjlxx8r.database.windows...
BlueZonder (125)
AdventureWorks2012
00:00:00
0 rows

Exploring Database Schemas

A schema - introduced in SQL Server 2005 - is a single-level container of database objects to replace database object "owner" in previous SQL Server versions. **The default schema is "dbo", database owner**. Schemas can be used for functional separation of objects which may be essential in large databases with thousands of tables. The application schemas in AdventureWorks: HumanResources, Production, Purchasing, Sales, and Person. The word "schemas" also used in database terminology to mean table definition scripts or database diagram. Screenshot to display all the schemas in AdventureWorks2012 and to demonstrate the use of the CREATE SCHEMA statement. Database object reference in Azure SQL is: "schemaname.objectname" like "Sales.SalesOrderheader".

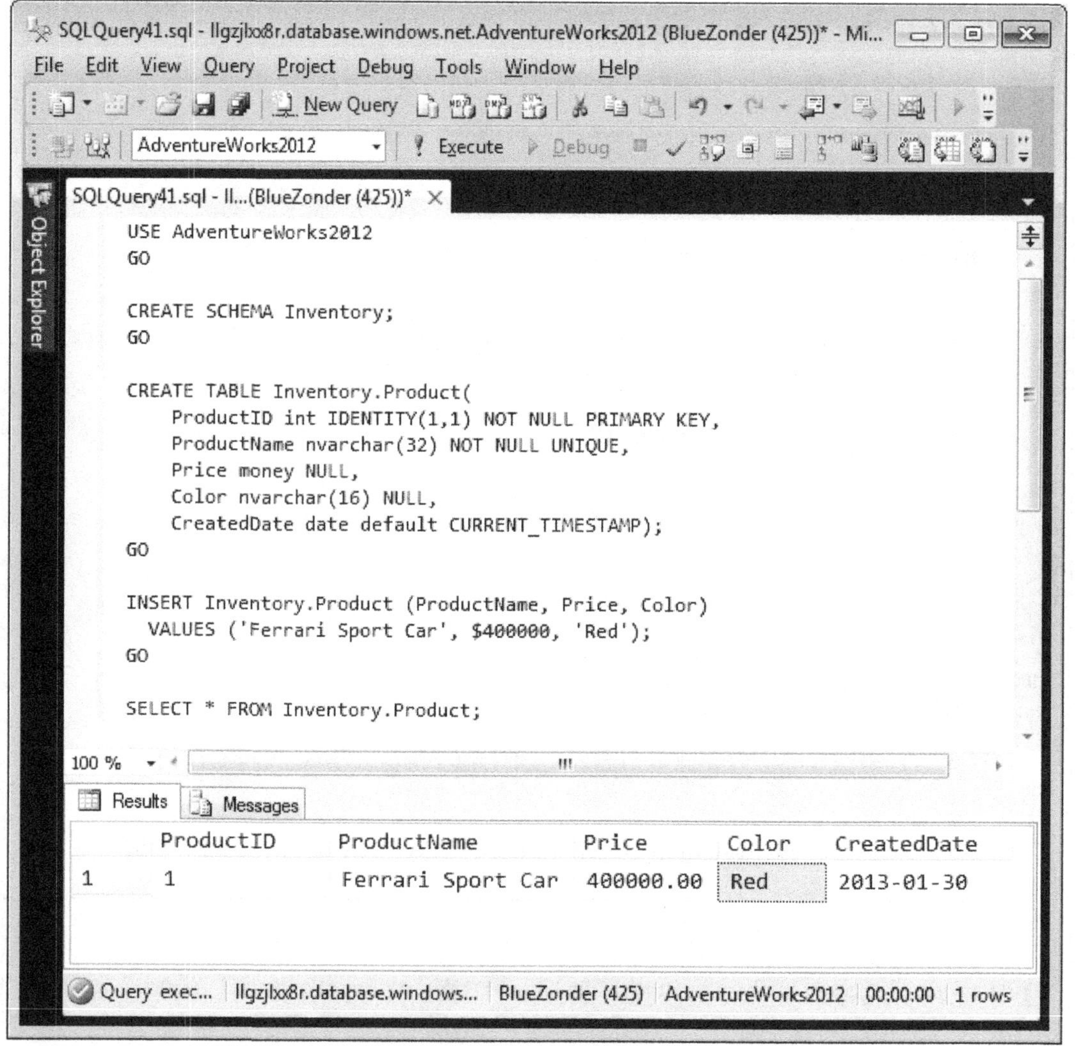
SQLQuery41.sql - llgzjlx8r.database.windows.net.AdventureWorks2012 (BlueZonder (425))* - Mi...
File Edit View Query Project Debug Tools Window Help
New Query
AdventureWorks2012
Execute
Debug
Object Explorer
SQLQuery41.sql - ll...(BlueZonder (425))*
USE AdventureWorks2012
GO
CREATE SCHEMA Inventory;
GO
CREATE TABLE Inventory.Product(
ProductID int IDENTITY(1,1) NOT NULL PRIMARY KEY,
ProductName nvarchar(32) NOT NULL UNIQUE,
Price money NULL,
Color nvarchar(16) NULL,
CreatedDate date default CURRENT_TIMESTAMP);
GO
INSERT Inventory.Product (ProductName, Price, Color)
VALUES ('Ferrari Sport Car', $400000, 'Red');
GO
SELECT * FROM Inventory.Product;
100 %
Results
Messages
ProductID ProductName Price Color CreatedDate
1 1 Ferrari Sport Car 400000.00 Red 2013-01-30
Query exec... llgzjlx8r.database.windows... BlueZonder (425) AdventureWorks2012 00:00:00 1 rows

SCHEMA_NAME() Function

The SCHEMA_NAME() function can be used to obtain the name of a schema based on the schema_id parameter. Query to list all 3 database objects with the name "Product" in 3 different schemas.

```
SELECT          CONCAT(SCHEMA_NAME(schema_id),'.',name) as ObjectName,
                name, object_id, schema_id, type, type_desc
FROM sys.objects
WHERE name = 'Product' ORDER BY ObjectName;
```

ObjectName	name	object_id	schema_id	type	type_desc
dbo.Product	Product	264388011	1	U	USER_TABLE
Inventory.Product	Product	1533964541	11	U	USER_TABLE
Production.Product	Product	1973582069	7	U	USER_TABLE

T-SQL query to display all the schemas in

```
SELECT s.*,  p.name as PrincipalName   FROM sys.schemas s
 INNER JOIN sys.database_principals p    ON s.principal_id = p.principal_id
ORDER BY principal_id, s.name;
```

name	schema_id	principal_id	PrincipalName
dbo	1	1	dbo
HumanResources	5	1	dbo
Inventory	10	1	dbo
Person	6	1	dbo
Production	7	1	dbo
Purchasing	8	1	dbo
Sales	9	1	dbo
guest	2	2	guest
INFORMATION_SCHEMA	3	3	INFORMATION_SCHEMA
sys	4	4	sys
db_owner	16384	16384	db_owner
db_accessadmin	16385	16385	db_accessadmin
db_securityadmin	16386	16386	db_securityadmin
db_ddladmin	16387	16387	db_ddladmin
db_backupoperator	16389	16389	db_backupoperator
db_datareader	16390	16390	db_datareader
db_datawriter	16391	16391	db_datawriter
db_denydatareader	16392	16392	db_denydatareader
db_denydatawriter	16393	16393	db_denydatawriter
name	schema_id	principal_id	PrincipalName

Tables in HumanResources, Person & Purchasing Schemas

Query to list tables in the above schemas with data dictionary description. SQL Server 2012 query.

```
USE AdventureWorks2012;
SELECT  CONCAT('Purchasing.', objname COLLATE DATABASE_DEFAULT)       AS TableName,
        value                                                         AS [Description]
FROM fn_listextendedproperty (NULL, 'schema', 'Purchasing', 'table', default, NULL, NULL)
UNION
SELECT  CONCAT('Person.', objname COLLATE DATABASE_DEFAULT)           AS TableName,
        value                                                         AS [Description]
FROM fn_listextendedproperty (NULL, 'schema', 'Person', 'table', default, NULL, NULL)
UNION
SELECT  CONCAT('HumanResources.', objname COLLATE DATABASE_DEFAULT) AS TableName,
        value                                                         AS [Description]
FROM fn_listextendedproperty (NULL, 'schema', 'HumanResources', 'table', default, NULL, NULL)
ORDER BY TableName;
```

TableName	Description
HumanResources.Department	Lookup table containing the departments within the Adventure Works Cycles company.
HumanResources.Employee	Employee information such as salary, department, and title.
HumanResources.EmployeeDepartmentHistory	Employee department transfers.
HumanResources.EmployeePayHistory	Employee pay history.
HumanResources.JobCandidate	Résumés submitted to Human Resources by job applicants.
HumanResources.Shift	Work shift lookup table.
Person.Address	Street address information for customers, employees, and vendors.
Person.AddressType	Types of addresses stored in the Address table.
Person.BusinessEntity	Source of the ID that connects vendors, customers, and employees with address and contact information.
Person.BusinessEntityAddress	Cross-reference table mapping customers, vendors, and employees to their addresses.
Person.BusinessEntityContact	Cross-reference table mapping stores, vendors, and employees to people
Person.ContactType	Lookup table containing the types of business entity contacts.
Person.CountryRegion	Lookup table containing the ISO standard codes for countries and regions.
Person.EmailAddress	Where to send a person email.
Person.Password	One way hashed authentication information
Person.Person	Human beings involved with AdventureWorks: employees, customer contacts, and vendor contacts.
Person.PersonPhone	Telephone number and type of a person.
Person.PhoneNumberType	Type of phone number of a person.
Person.StateProvince	State and province lookup table.
Purchasing.ProductVendor	Cross-reference table mapping vendors with the products they supply.
Purchasing.PurchaseOrderDetail	Individual products associated with a specific purchase order. See PurchaseOrderHeader.
Purchasing.PurchaseOrderHeader	General purchase order information. See PurchaseOrderDetail.
Purchasing.ShipMethod	Shipping company lookup table.
Purchasing.Vendor	Companies from whom Adventure Works Cycles purchases parts or other goods.

The CREATE TABLE Statement

Creates a table based on column name, data type & size specifications. Constraint and default information can be included as well, or alternately given as a separate ALTER TABLE statement.

Branch Banking Database with ON DELETE CASCADE

T-SQL script to create basic banking application tables. Preceding the first CREATE TABLE, we execute a CREATE SCHEMA to group the tables within one schema.

```
USE AdventureWorks2012;
GO
```

```
CREATE SCHEMA Banking;
GO
```

```
CREATE TABLE Banking.Branch
 (
   BranchID     INT IDENTITY ( 1, 1 ),
   BranchName   CHAR(32) NOT NULL UNIQUE,
   BranchCity   CHAR(32) NOT NULL,
   Assets       MONEY NOT NULL,
   ModifiedDate DATETIME DEFAULT (getdate()),
   PRIMARY KEY ( BranchID ),
 );

CREATE TABLE Banking.Account
 (
   AccountID     INT IDENTITY ( 1, 1 ) UNIQUE,
   BranchID      INT NOT NULL,
   AccountNumber CHAR(20) NOT NULL UNIQUE,
   AccountType   CHAR(12) NOT NULL CONSTRAINT ATC CHECK (AccountType IN ('C', 'S')),
   Balance       MONEY NOT NULL,
   ModifiedDate  DATETIME DEFAULT (getdate()),
   PRIMARY KEY ( AccountID ),
   FOREIGN KEY ( BranchID ) REFERENCES Banking.Branch(BranchID) ON DELETE   CASCADE
 );
```

```
-- T-SQL script continued

CREATE TABLE Banking.[Transaction]
 (
   TransactionID INT IDENTITY ( 1, 1 ) PRIMARY KEY,
   AccountID     INT NOT NULL,
   TranType      CHAR(1),
   Amount        MONEY,
   ModifiedDate  DATETIME DEFAULT (getdate()),
   UNIQUE ( AccountID, ModifiedDate),
   FOREIGN KEY ( AccountID ) REFERENCES Banking.Account(AccountID) ON DELETE   CASCADE
 );

CREATE TABLE Banking.Customer
 (
   CustomerID   INT IDENTITY ( 1, 1 ) PRIMARY KEY,
   Name         CHAR(32) NOT NULL,
   SSNo         CHAR(9) NOT NULL UNIQUE,
   [Type]       CHAR(20) NOT NULL,
   Street       VARCHAR(32) NOT NULL,
   City         CHAR(32) NOT NULL,
   [State]      CHAR(32) NOT NULL,
   Zip          CHAR(10) NOT NULL,
   Country      CHAR(32) NOT NULL,
   ModifiedDate DATETIME DEFAULT (getdate())
  );

CREATE TABLE Banking.Loan
 (
   LoanID       INT IDENTITY ( 1, 1 ) PRIMARY KEY,
   BranchID     INT NOT NULL REFERENCES Banking.Branch(BranchID) ON DELETE   CASCADE,
   LoanNumber   CHAR(20) NOT NULL UNIQUE,
   LoanType     VARCHAR(30) NOT NULL,
   Amount       MONEY NOT NULL,
   ModifiedDate DATETIME DEFAULT (getdate())
 );
```

-- T-SQL script continued

```
CREATE TABLE Banking.Depositor
 (
   CustomerID   INT NOT NULL,
   AccountID    INT NOT NULL,
   ModifiedDate DATETIME DEFAULT (getdate()),
   PRIMARY KEY ( CustomerID, AccountID ),
   FOREIGN KEY ( AccountID ) REFERENCES Banking.Account(AccountID) ON DELETE   CASCADE,
   FOREIGN KEY ( CustomerID ) REFERENCES Banking.Customer(CustomerID)
 );

CREATE TABLE Banking.Borrower
 (
   CustomerID   INT NOT NULL,
   LoanID       INT NOT NULL,
   ModifiedDate DATETIME DEFAULT (getdate()),
   PRIMARY KEY ( CustomerID, LoanID ),
   FOREIGN KEY ( CustomerID ) REFERENCES Banking.Customer(CustomerID),
   FOREIGN KEY ( LoanID ) REFERENCES Banking.Loan(LoanID)
 );
```

Temporary Tables: Workhorses of T-SQL

So much so that they even have their own database in SQL Server 2012: tempdb. **There is no tempdb in Azure SQL.** Temporary tables (example: #Product1) can be applied in queries just like permanent tables. The difference is:

- Temporary tables visible only in the connection.

- Temporary tables have limited life.

There are two versions:

- Temporary tables (#tempA) are multi-user automatically, cannot be shared among connections.

- Global temporary tables (##gtempB) is single-user, can be shared among connections.

Global temporary tables are not supported in Azure SQL.

Temporary tables can be created by CREATE TABLE or SELECT INTO (SQL Server 2012) methods. **Temporary table do not require clustered index in Azure SQL.**

```
USE AdventureWorks2012;
GO
-- Command(s) completed successfully.
```

```
-- Create temporary table with CREATE TABLE
CREATE TABLE #Product (
        ProductID INT,
        ProductName nvarchar(50),
        ListPrice money,
        Color varchar(16)
);
GO
-- Command(s) completed successfully.
```

```
INSERT INTO #Product
SELECT  ProductID,
        Name,
        ListPrice,
        Color
FROM Production.Product ORDER BY Name;
GO --(504 row(s) affected)
```

Temporary Tables Are Handy When Developing Scripts Or Stored Procedures

```
SELECT TOP 10 * FROM #Product
ORDER BY ProductName;
GO
```

ProductID	ProductName	ListPrice	Color
1	Adjustable Race	0.00	NULL
879	All-Purpose Bike Stand	159.00	NULL
712	AWC Logo Cap	8.99	Multi
3	BB Ball Bearing	0.00	NULL
2	Bearing Ball	0.00	NULL
877	Bike Wash - Dissolver	7.95	NULL
316	Blade	0.00	NULL
843	Cable Lock	25.00	NULL
952	Chain	20.24	Silver
324	Chain Stays	0.00	NULL

```
DROP TABLE #Product;
GO
```

```
CREATE TABLE #ProductA( ProductID int, ProductName nvarchar(50), ListPrice smallmoney,
                    StandardCost smallmoney, Color nvarchar(15));
INSERT INTO #ProductA
SELECT ProductID, ProductName = Name, ListPrice, StandardCost, Color
FROM Production.Product  ORDER BY ProductName;
GO  -- (504 row(s) affected)
```

```
SELECT TOP 10 * FROM #ProductA
ORDER BY ProductName;
```

ProductID	ProductName	ListPrice	StandardCost	Color
1	Adjustable Race	0.00	0.00	NULL
879	All-Purpose Bike Stand	159.00	59.466	NULL
712	AWC Logo Cap	8.99	6.9223	Multi
3	BB Ball Bearing	0.00	0.00	NULL
2	Bearing Ball	0.00	0.00	NULL
877	Bike Wash - Dissolver	7.95	2.9733	NULL
316	Blade	0.00	0.00	NULL
843	Cable Lock	25.00	10.3125	NULL
952	Chain	20.24	8.9866	Silver
324	Chain Stays	0.00	0.00	NULL

```
DROP TABLE #ProductA;
GO
```

ALTER TABLE for Changing Table Definition

An empty table can easily be altered by ALTER TABLE. A populated table change (alter) may require additional operations such as data conversion to the new column data type. Generally increasing the size of a column is a safe change even if the table is populated. If we were to change size from 25 to 10, truncation may occur (data loss), for which we would have to plan by examining what will be lost if any. When decreasing string column size, we can use the LEFT function to truncate the string. T-SQL script to increase the size of a column from 25 to 32, then decrease it 9.

```
USE CopyOfAdventureWorks2012;
-- Sales.SalesOrderDetail columns
/*Name     Policy Health State
SalesOrderID (PK, FK, int, not null)
SalesOrderDetailID (PK, int, not null)
CarrierTrackingNumber (nvarchar(25), null)  .....  */
```

```
-- Increase column size of CarrierTrackingNumber
ALTER TABLE Sales.SalesOrderDetail    ALTER COLUMN CarrierTrackingNumber nvarchar(32)  null;
```

```
/* Columns after ALTER TABLE
Name       Policy Health State
SalesOrderID (PK, FK, int, not null)
SalesOrderDetailID (PK, int, not null)
CarrierTrackingNumber (nvarchar(32), null)  .....          */
```

```
SELECT TOP (1) SalesOrderID, CarrierTrackingNumber FROM  Sales.SalesOrderDetail ORDER BY SalesOrderID;
```

SalesOrderID	CarrierTrackingNumber
43659	4911-403C-98

We shall now decrease the size to 9 characters, but first truncate the extra characters. Without the UPDATE, the following error happens.

```
/* Msg 8152, Level 16, State 13, Line 1 String or binary data would be truncated. The statement has been terminated.*/
```

```
UPDATE Sales.SalesOrderDetail SET CarrierTrackingNumber = LEFT (CarrierTrackingNumber,9);
-- (121317 row(s) affected)
```

```
-- Decrease column size of CarrierTrackingNumber
ALTER TABLE Sales.SalesOrderDetail    ALTER COLUMN CarrierTrackingNumber nvarchar(9)  null;
-- Command(s) completed successfully.
```

```
SELECT TOP (1) SalesOrderID, CarrierTrackingNumber FROM  Sales.SalesOrderDetail  ORDER BY SalesOrderID;
```

SalesOrderID	CarrierTrackingNumber
43659	4911-403C

Renaming Tables & Columns with sp_rename

The system stored procedure sp_rename can be used to rename tables, columns and other user-created database objects.

```
-- Create table for testing
CREATE TABLE Department(
        DepartmentID smallint  NOT NULL PRIMARY KEY,
        Name dbo.Name NOT NULL,
        GroupName dbo.Name NOT NULL,
        ModifiedDate datetime NOT NULL);
GO
```

```
INSERT Department SELECT * FROM HumanResources.Department;
GO
-- (16 row(s) affected)
```

```
SELECT TOP 1 * FROM Department;
GO
```

DepartmentID	Name	GroupName	ModifiedDate
1	Engineering	Research and Development	2002-06-01 00:00:00.000

```
-- Rename table column
EXEC sp_rename "Department.Name", "Department";
GO
```

```
SELECT TOP 1 * FROM Department;
GO
```

DepartmentID	Department	GroupName	ModifiedDate
1	Engineering	Research and Development	2002-06-01 00:00:00.000

```
-- Rename table
EXEC sp_rename "dbo.Department", "ProfitCenter"
GO
```

```
SELECT * FROM ProfitCenter;
GO
```

DepartmentID	Department	GroupName	ModifiedDate
1	Engineering	Research and Development	2002-06-01 00:00:00.000

```
DROP TABLE tempdb.dbo.ProfitCenter;
GO
```

DROP TABLE: A Dangerous Statement

The DROP TABLE statement is to delete a table, including content, for good. It is a very dangerous statement which we don't want to execute accidentally. Therefore, if appropriate we should comment it out in a T-SQL script to prevent unintentional execution.

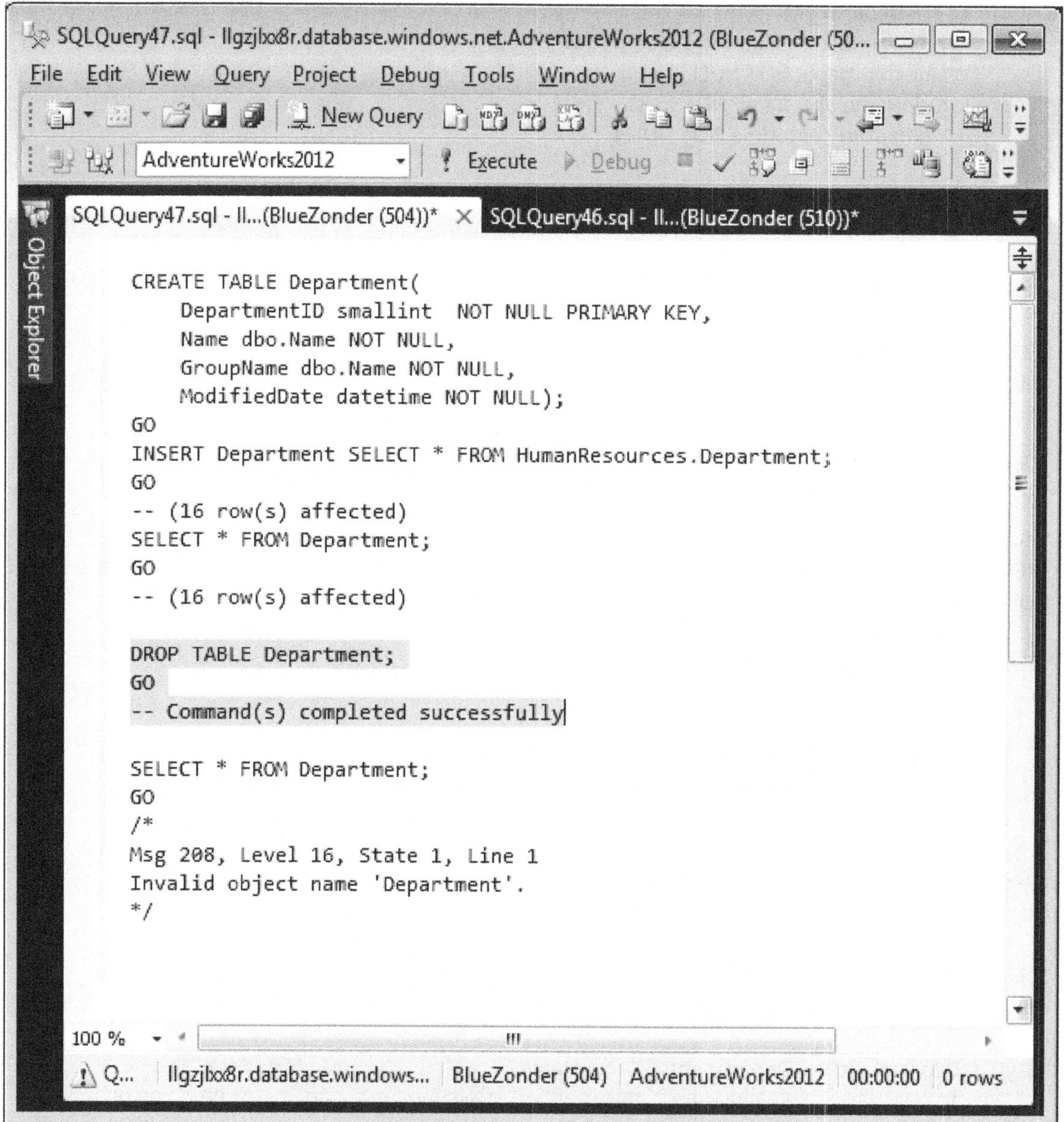
SQLQuery47.sql - llgzjbx8r.database.windows.net.AdventureWorks2012 (BlueZonder (50...
File Edit View Query Project Debug Tools Window Help
New Query
AdventureWorks2012
Execute
Debug
SQLQuery47.sql - ll...(BlueZonder (504))*
SQLQuery46.sql - ll...(BlueZonder (510))*
Object Explorer
CREATE TABLE Department(
DepartmentID smallint NOT NULL PRIMARY KEY,
Name dbo.Name NOT NULL,
GroupName dbo.Name NOT NULL,
ModifiedDate datetime NOT NULL);
GO
INSERT Department SELECT * FROM HumanResources.Department;
GO
-- (16 row(s) affected)
SELECT * FROM Department;
GO
-- (16 row(s) affected)
DROP TABLE Department;
GO
-- Command(s) completed successfully
SELECT * FROM Department;
GO
/*
Msg 208, Level 16, State 1, Line 1
Invalid object name 'Department'.
*/
100 %
Q...
llgzjbx8r.database.windows...
BlueZonder (504)
AdventureWorks2012
00:00:00
0 rows

Table Constraints Inclusion in CREATE TABLE

Table constraints are user-defined database objects that restricts the behaviors of columns. PRIMARY KEY, UNIQUE KEY, FOREIGN KEY, or CHECK constraint, or a DEFAULT constraint can be included in the CREATE TABLE statement on the same line as the column or added as a separate line. In the definition of the Banking.Branch table UNIQUE and DEFAULT constraints are included in the same line while the PRIMARY KEY constraint has its own line at the end of column list. In the definition of Banking.Loan table, the PRIMARY KEY constraint is included with the column definition. FOREIGN KEY constraint definition can include ON DELETE CASCADE action option, meaning if the PRIMARY KEY is deleted all FOREIGN KEYs in the table referencing it should also be deleted.

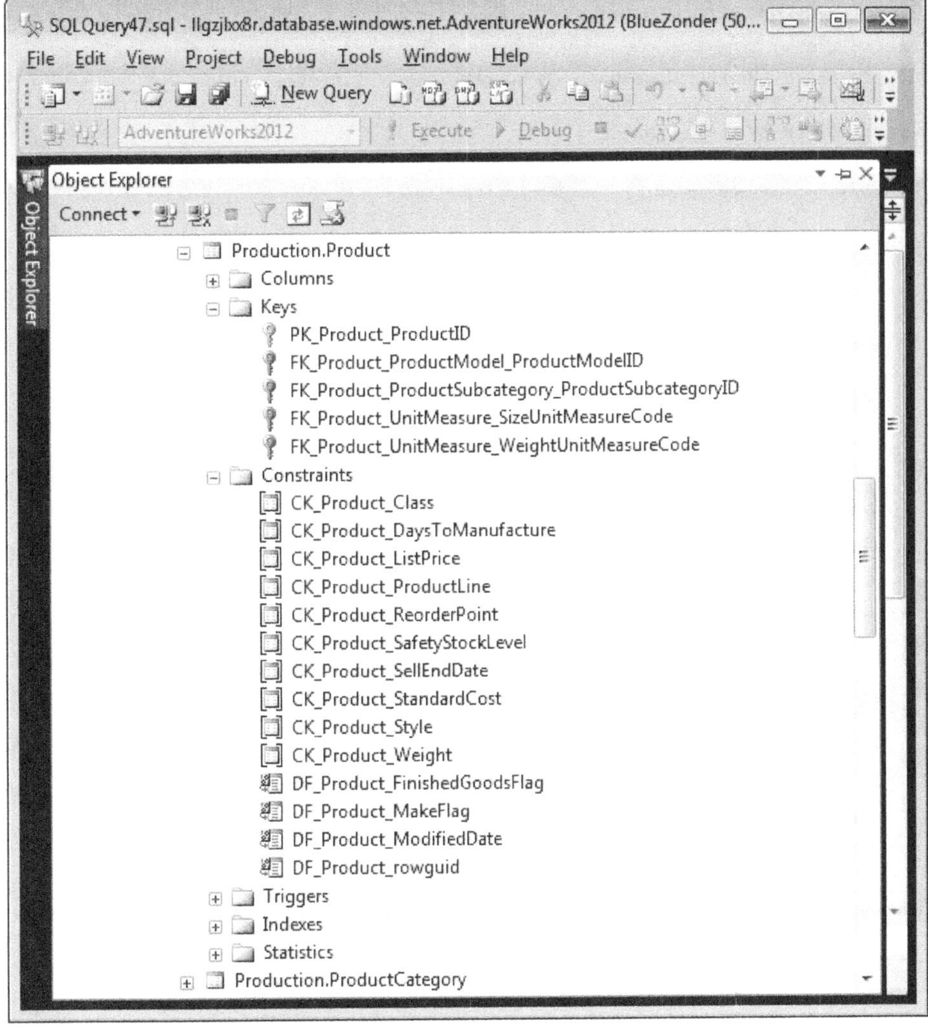

Nullability Column-Level Constraints in CREATE TABLE

The default is NULL, the column can contain NULL entries, the column is nullable. We have to specifically declare NOT NULL on the column line in CREATE TABLE if we want to add the cardinality constraint to the column. The NULL / NOT NULL constraint cannot be declared on a separate line. In the Production.Product table the Color column is nullable. The ListPrice column is not nullable instead has 0.0 price where there is no price.

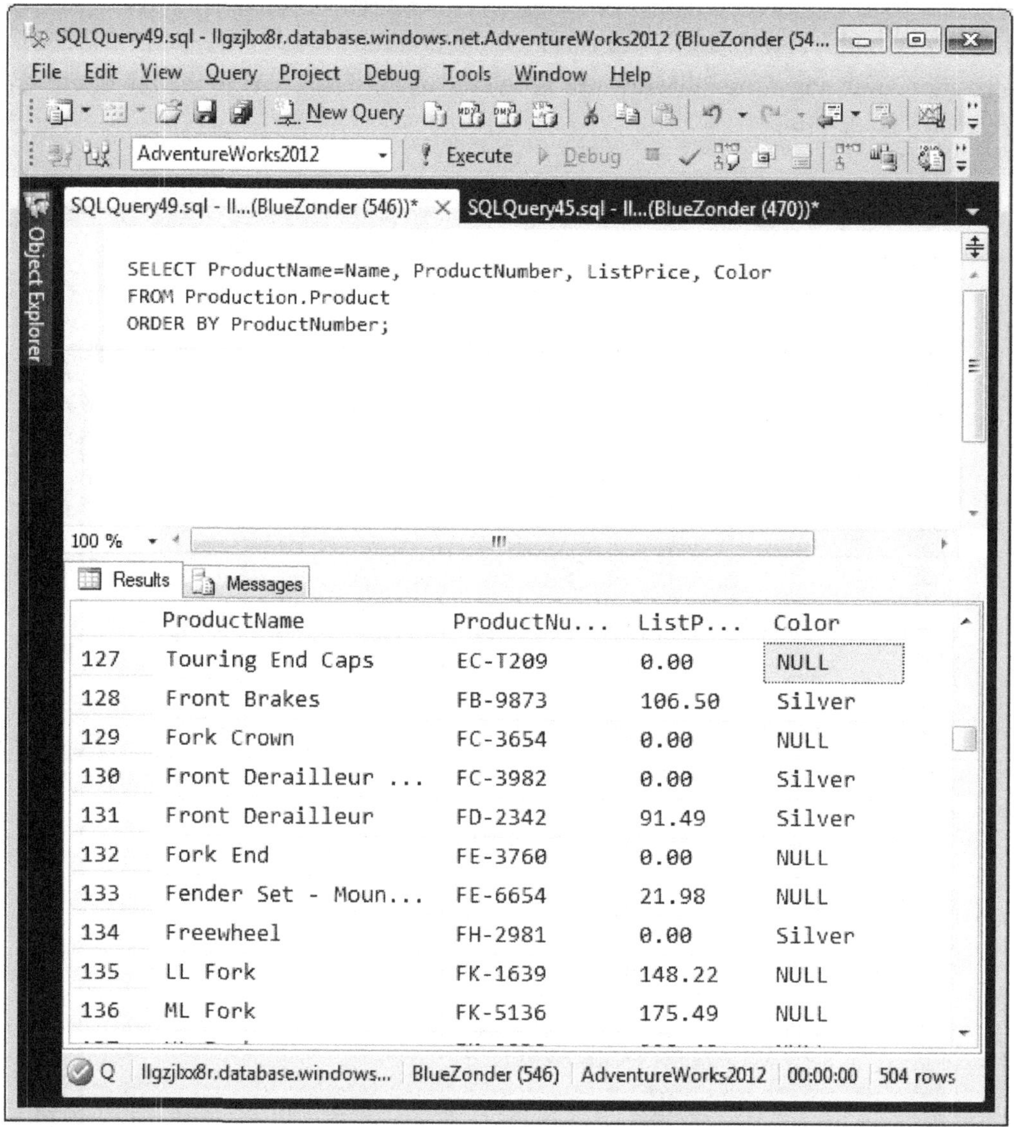

PRIMARY KEY constraint on a column automatically implies NOT NULL

The UNIQUE KEY CONSTRAINT allows only one NULL entry in a column since two or more NULL entries would not be unique. Demonstration script:

```
CREATE TABLE Product     (  ProductID INT UNIQUE,
                            ProductName varchar(64) PRIMARY KEY
                         );
```

```
INSERT Product (ProductName) VALUES ('Mobile Phone xZing');
-- (1 row(s) affected)
```

```
-- One NULL is OK in ProductID column
-- Second NULL insert attempt errors out

INSERT Product (ProductName) VALUES ('Motor Bike');

/* Msg 2627, Level 14, State 1, Line 7
Violation of UNIQUE KEY constraint 'UQ__Product__B40CC6ECDF4DC6D3'.
Cannot insert duplicate key in object 'dbo.Product'.
The duplicate key value is (<NULL>).
The statement has been terminated. */
```

```
-- NULL value in PRIMARY KEY column not allowed

INSERT Product (ProductID) VALUES (2);

/* Msg 515, Level 16, State 2, Line 2
Cannot insert the value NULL into column
'ProductName', table 'tempdb.dbo.Product';
column does not allow nulls. INSERT fails.
The statement has been terminated. */
```

```
SELECT * FROM Product;
```

ProductID	ProductName
NULL	Mobile Phone xZing

The PRIMARY KEY constraint is a combination of UNIQUE and NOT NULL constraints.

PRIMARY KEY & FOREIGN KEY Constraints

The PRIMARY KEY constraint is to ensure a referenceable unique address for each row in a table. PK column value cannot be NULL. The underlying mechanism to carry out the enforcement action is a unique index which is clustered by default but in can be nonclustered. PRIMARY KEY constraint can be considered as a UNIQUE constraint with NOT NULL on the column. The typical PRIMARY KEY is the SURROGATE PRIMARY KEY INT IDENTITY(1,1) column. There can only be one PRIMARY KEY defined per table. A PRIMARY KEY can consist of multiple columns, a composite PRIMARY KEY. A PRIMARY KEY (also index) cannot be based on part of a column. Production.ProductSubcategory table PRIMARY KEY setup.

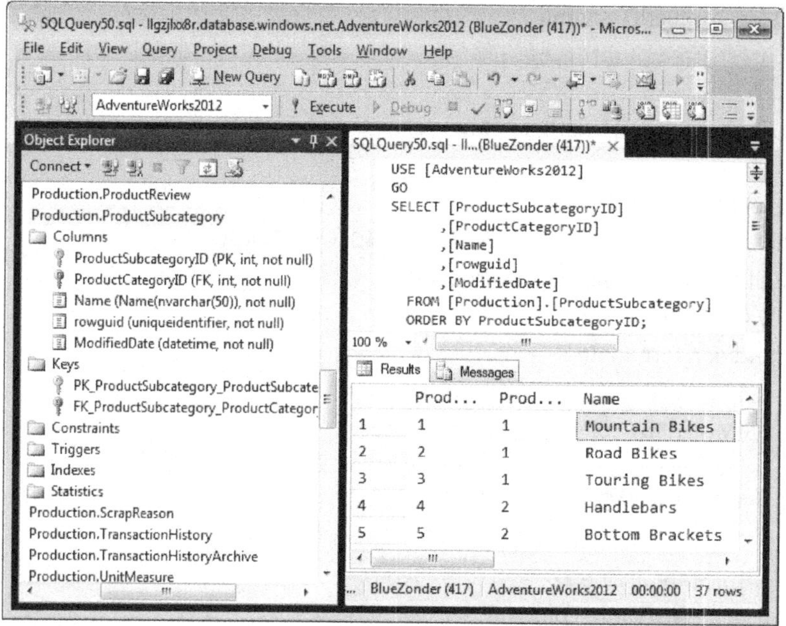

The ProductSubcategoryID is the PRIMARY KEY constraint. It is an INT IDENTITY(1,1) surrogate key. ProductCategoryID is a FOREIGN KEY referencing the Production.ProductCategory table ProductCategoryID column. "Name" is the NATURAL KEY. rowguid (used in replication) & ModifiedDate are row maintenance columns. The NATURAL KEY column Name has NOT NULL constraint and unique index defined. As such it can serve as PRIMARY KEY for the table, but we shall see why a meaningless integer number (INT IDENTITY) is better for PRIMARY KEY. Related to this topic: A heap is a table without a clustered index. The implication is if we choose nonclustered PRIMARY KEY, we have to define a clustered index on other column(s) so that the database engine can work with the table as normal. Clustered index speeds up range searches.

The SURROGATE PRIMARY KEY should not be exposed to end-users, it is for programming use only.

FOREIGN KEY constraint requires that the referenced PK value exists.

FOREIGN KEY column is nullable. FOREIGN KEY can be named differently from the referenced PRIMARY KEY, although for readability purposes usually the same. **Multiple FK columns can reference the same PK column**. In such a case only one FK column can have the same name as the PK column. Invalid FK reference results in error.

```
USE [AdventureWorks2012]
GO
```

```
INSERT INTO Production.ProductSubcategory
        (ProductCategoryID
        ,Name)
   VALUES
        (99
        ,'Inner Tube')
```

```
/*
Msg 547, Level 16, State 0, Line 2
The INSERT statement conflicted with the FOREIGN KEY constraint
"FK_ProductSubcategory_ProductCategory_ProductCategoryID".
The conflict occurred in database "AdventureWorks2012",
table "Production.ProductCategory", column 'ProductCategoryID'.
The statement has been terminated.
*/
```

DELETE attempt on a referenced PRIMARY KEY will give an error unless DELETE CASCADE is defined on the FK:

```
DELETE FROM Production.ProductSubcategory
WHERE ProductSubCategoryID = 4
GO
```

```
/* Msg 547, Level 16, State 0, Line 1
The DELETE statement conflicted with the REFERENCE constraint
"FK_Product_ProductSubcategory_ProductSubcategoryID".
The conflict occurred in database "AdventureWorks2012",
table "Production.Product", column 'ProductSubcategoryID'.
The statement has been terminated. */
```

Single Column & Composite PRIMARY KEY List with XML PATH

Query to form delimited list for composite PRIMARY KEY columns. STUFF function deletes the leading comma.

```
-- Show composite PRIMARY KEYs as a comma-delimited list
USE AdventureWorks2012;
SELECT  K.TABLE_SCHEMA,
        T.TABLE_NAME,
        PK_COLUMN_NAMES =
                STUFF(( SELECT
                                CONCAT(', ',    KK.COLUMN_NAME)            AS [text()]
                                FROM   INFORMATION_SCHEMA.KEY_COLUMN_USAGE kk
                        WHERE  K.CONSTRAINT_NAME = KK.CONSTRAINT_NAME
                                ORDER BY  KK.ORDINAL_POSITION
                                FOR XML Path ('')), 1, 1, '')
FROM    INFORMATION_SCHEMA.TABLE_CONSTRAINTS T
  INNER JOIN    INFORMATION_SCHEMA.KEY_COLUMN_USAGE K
        ON T.CONSTRAINT_NAME = K.CONSTRAINT_NAME
WHERE           T.CONSTRAINT_TYPE = 'PRIMARY KEY'
                AND K.ORDINAL_POSITION = 1
ORDER BY        K.TABLE_SCHEMA,
                T.TABLE_NAME;
-- (71 row(s) affected) - Partial results
```

TABLE_SCHEMA	TABLE_NAME	PK_COLUMN_NAMES
dbo	AWBuildVersion	SystemInformationID
dbo	DatabaseLog	DatabaseLogID
dbo	ErrorLog	ErrorLogID
HumanResources	Department	DepartmentID
HumanResources	Employee	BusinessEntityID
HumanResources	EmployeeDepartmentHistory	BusinessEntityID, StartDate, DepartmentID, ShiftID
HumanResources	EmployeePayHistory	BusinessEntityID, RateChangeDate
HumanResources	JobCandidate	JobCandidateID
HumanResources	Shift	ShiftID
Person	Address	AddressID
Person	AddressType	AddressTypeID
Person	BusinessEntity	BusinessEntityID
Person	BusinessEntityAddress	BusinessEntityID, AddressID, AddressTypeID
Person	BusinessEntityContact	BusinessEntityID, PersonID, ContactTypeID
Person	ContactType	ContactTypeID
Person	CountryRegion	CountryRegionCode
Person	EmailAddress	BusinessEntityID, EmailAddressID
Person	Password	BusinessEntityID
Person	Person	BusinessEntityID
Person	PersonPhone	BusinessEntityID, PhoneNumber, PhoneNumberTypeID

SSMS GUI Table Designer - OPSS2012

SSMS Object Explorer includes a GUI Table Designer which can be launched the following ways for new or existing table from the right-click drop-down menus. Azure SQL generates a template to CREATE TABLE. SQL Server 2012 version enters the inteactive GUI table designer.

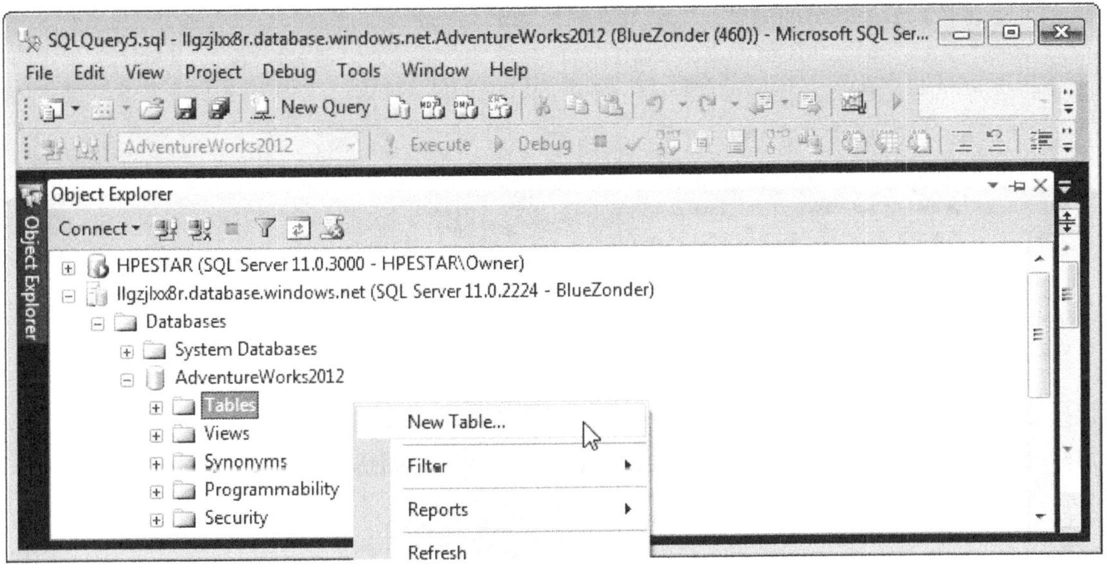

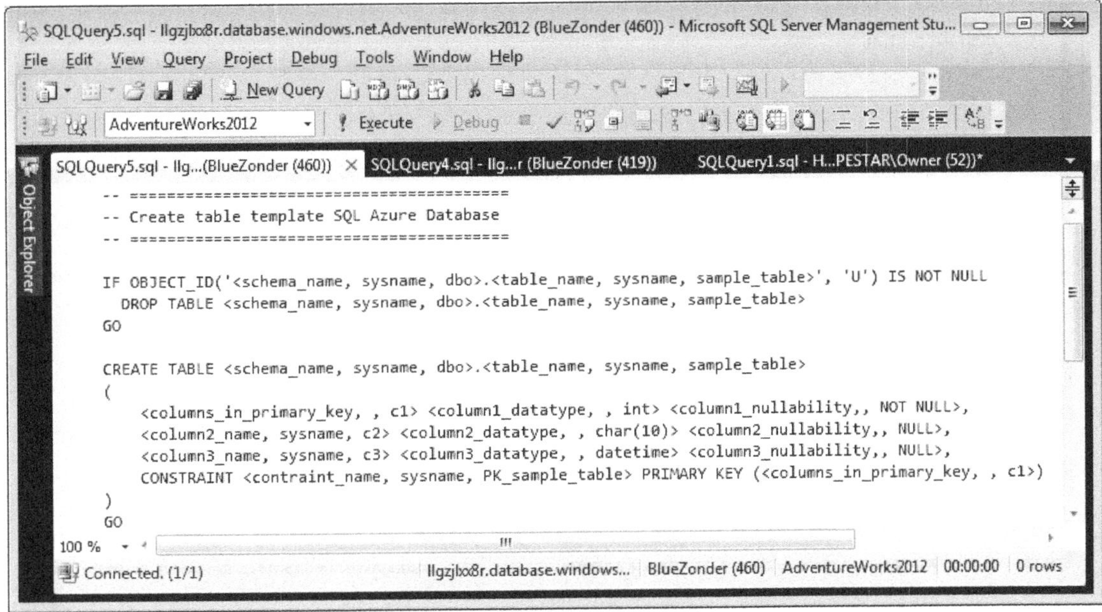

Basic GUI Table Design

The Table Designer provides line-by-line row design including all properties (bottom of dialog box) such as defaults, computed columns, identity and so on. SQL Server 2012 feature.

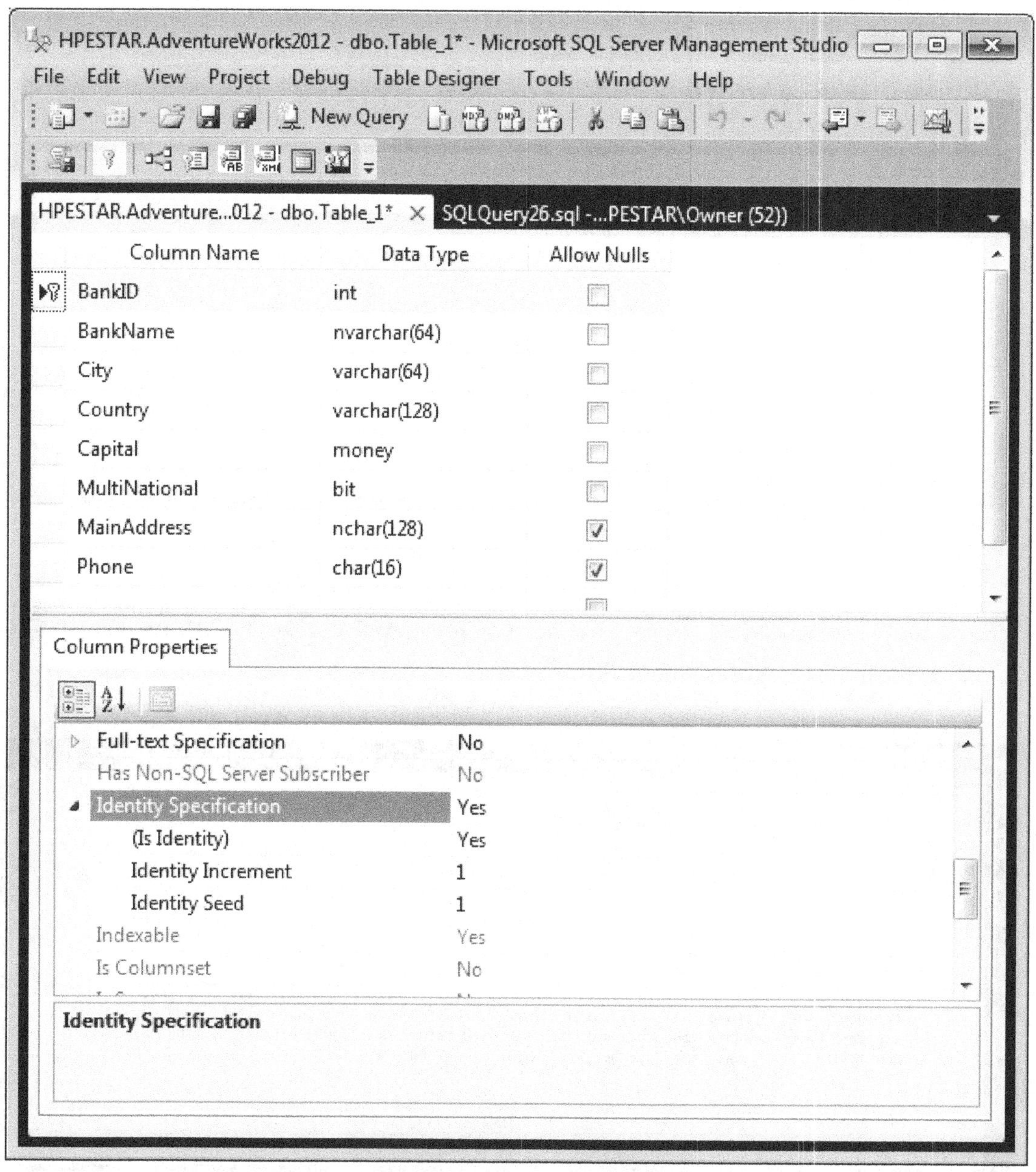

CHECK Constraint Definition

CHECK Constraint design window can be launched from toolbox icon: Manage Check Constraints or right-click drop-down menu. We create a constraint on Capital to be greater or equal to $5 billion. SQL Server 2012 feature.

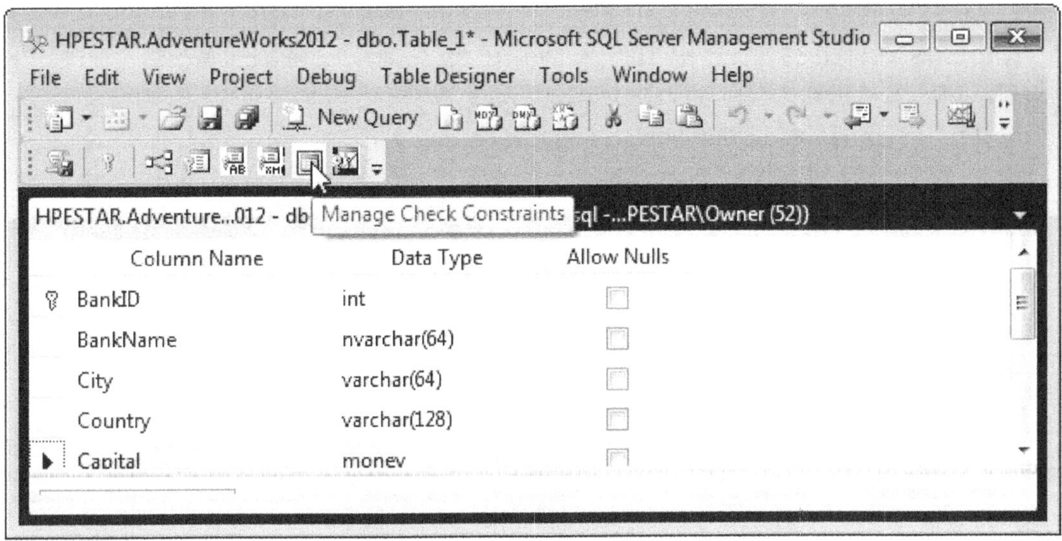

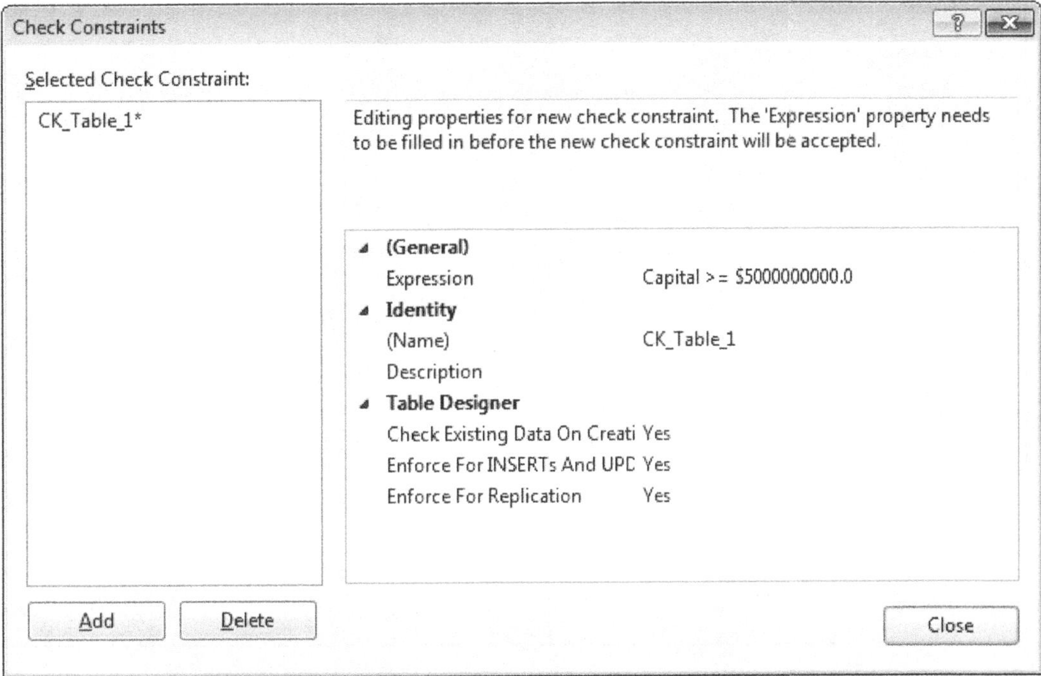

Managing Indexes and Keys

The Manage Indexes and Keys window can be launched by toolbox icon or right-click menu. We add UNIQUE KEY property to the BankName column. SQL Server 2012 feature.

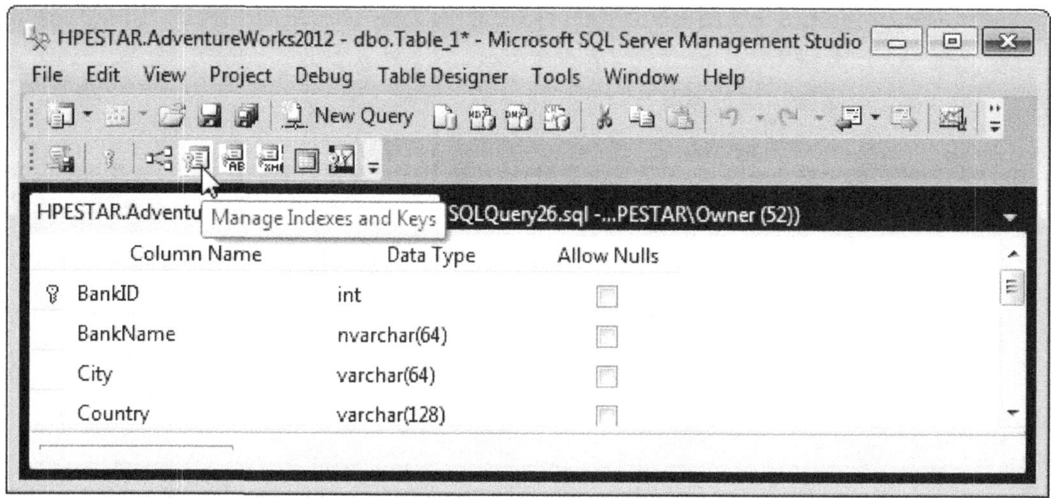

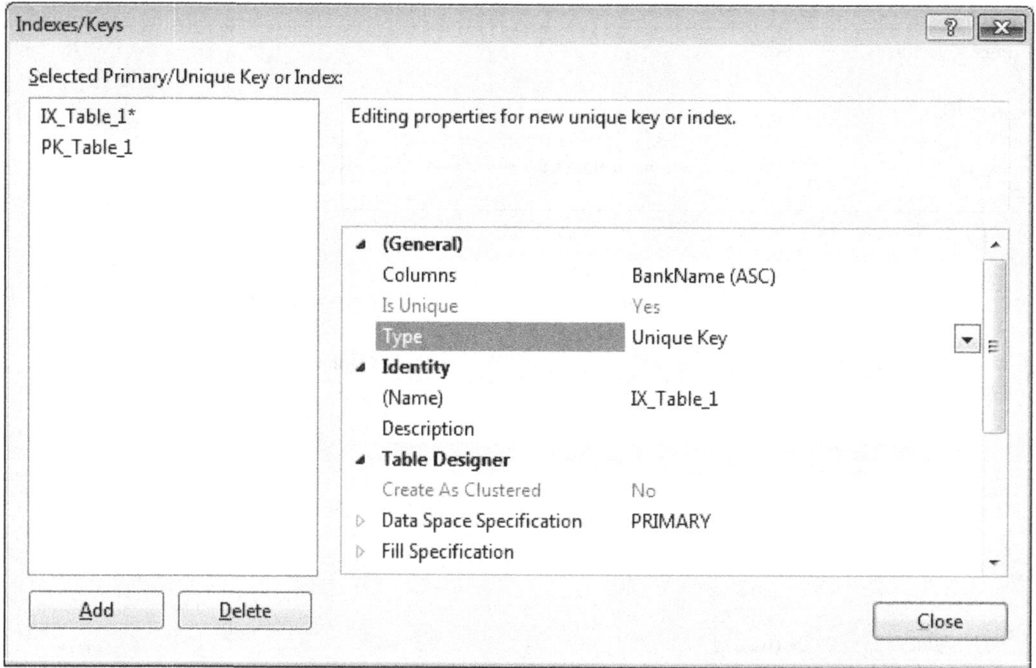

Setting PRIMARY KEY with a Single Click

PRIMARY KEY can simply be configured just by clicking on the gold key icon. A PRIMARY KEY constraint is created automatically. SQL Server 2012 feature.

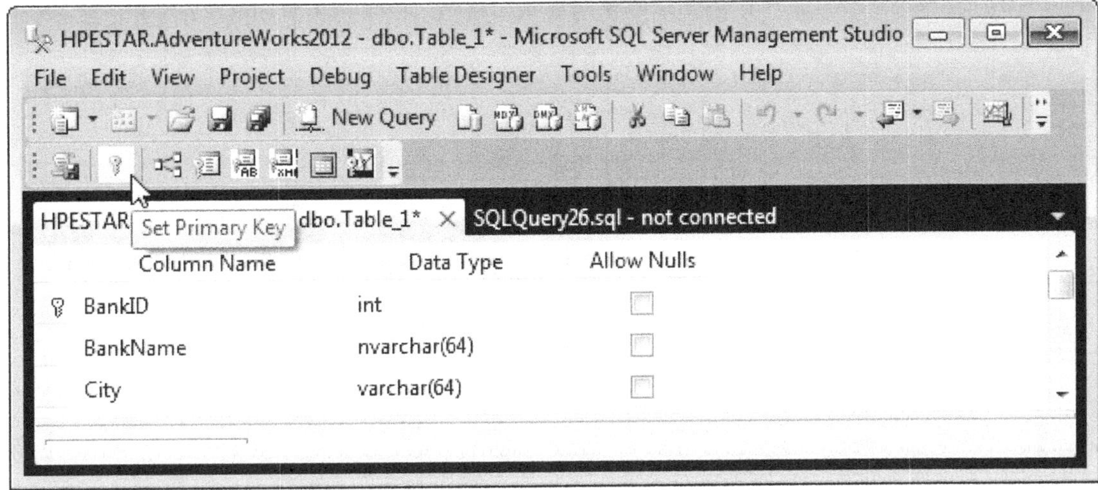

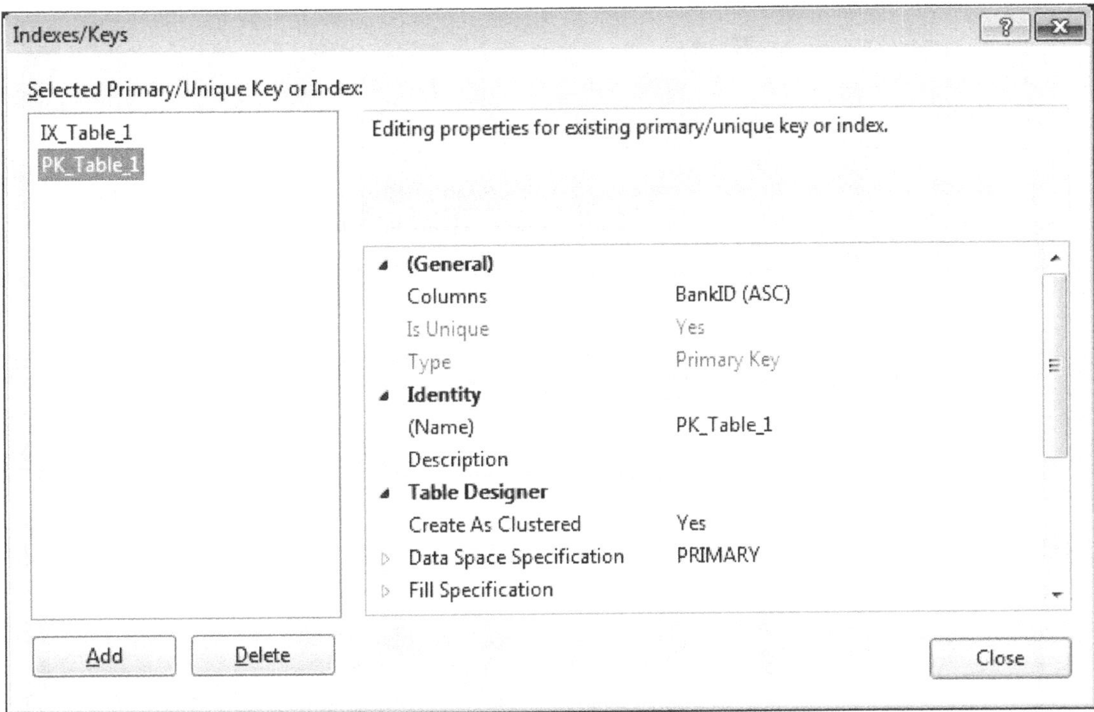

Configuring FOREIGN KEY: Declarative Referential Integrity

The Relationships facility can be used to create a FOREIGN KEY link (constraint). NOTE: demo only, BusinessEntityID column in the demo table has no relationship to AdventureWorks tables. <u>SQL Server 2012 feature.</u>

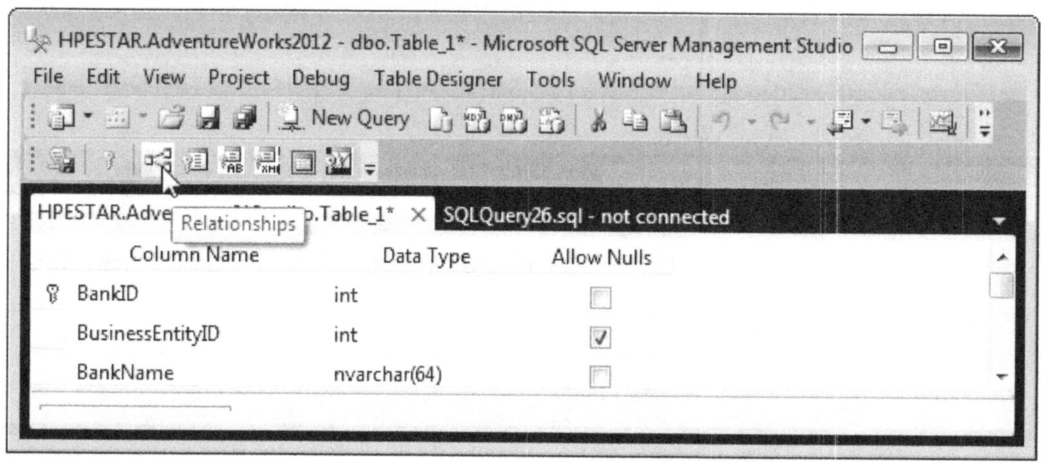

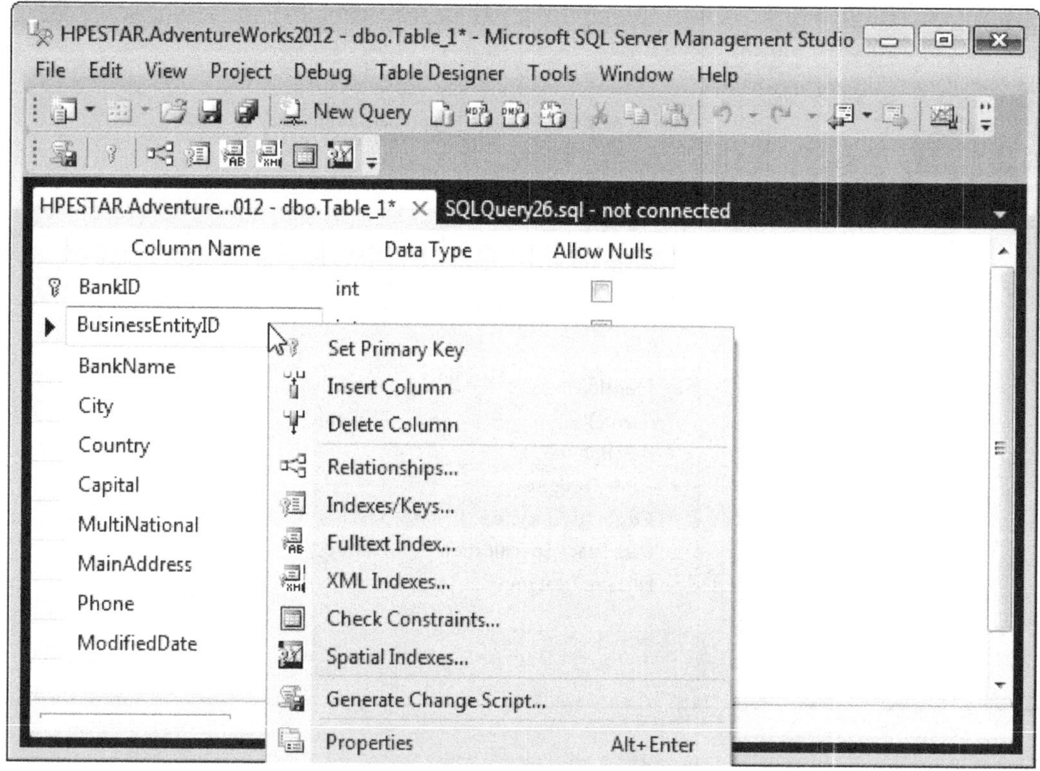

Tables And Columns Specific Tab Is To Define Mapping From FK To PK

SQL Server 2012 feature.

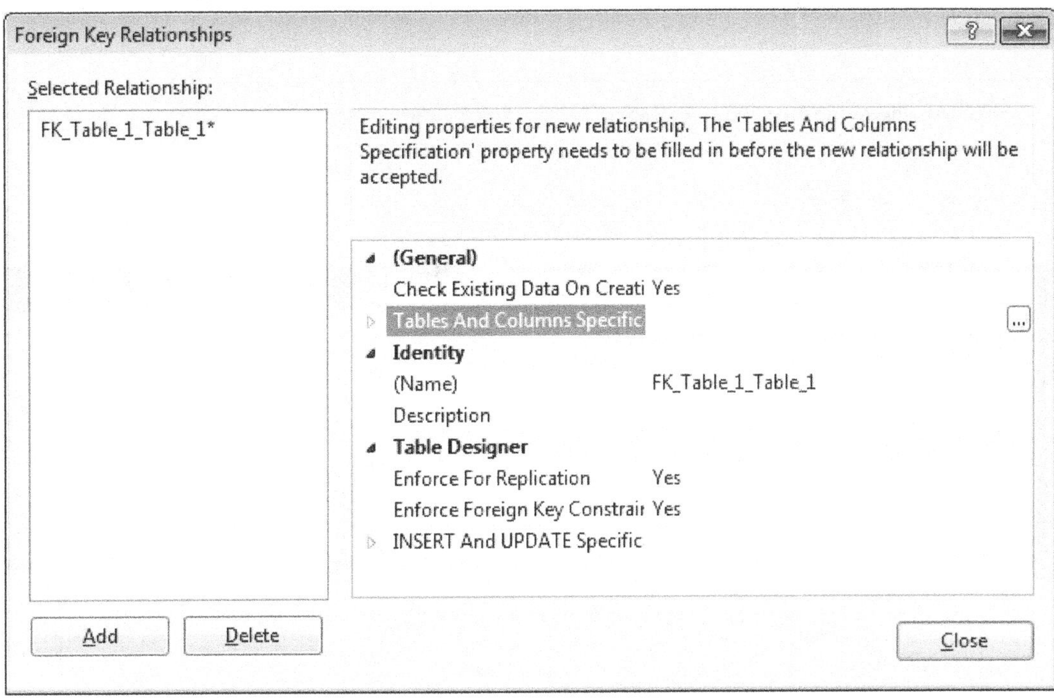

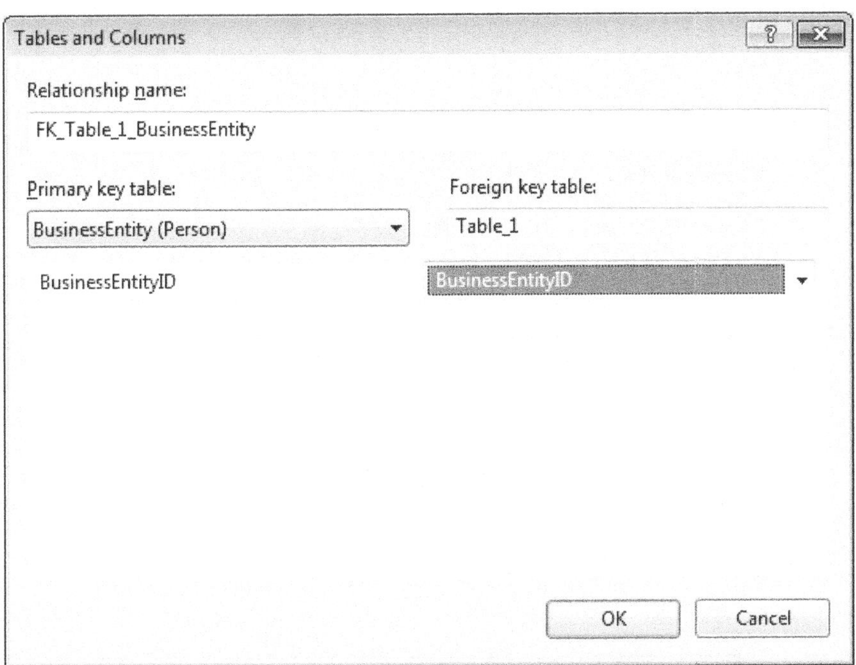

T-SQL Script Generation from GUI Table Designer

T-SQL code can be generated any time prior to saving the changes. SQL Server 2012 feature.

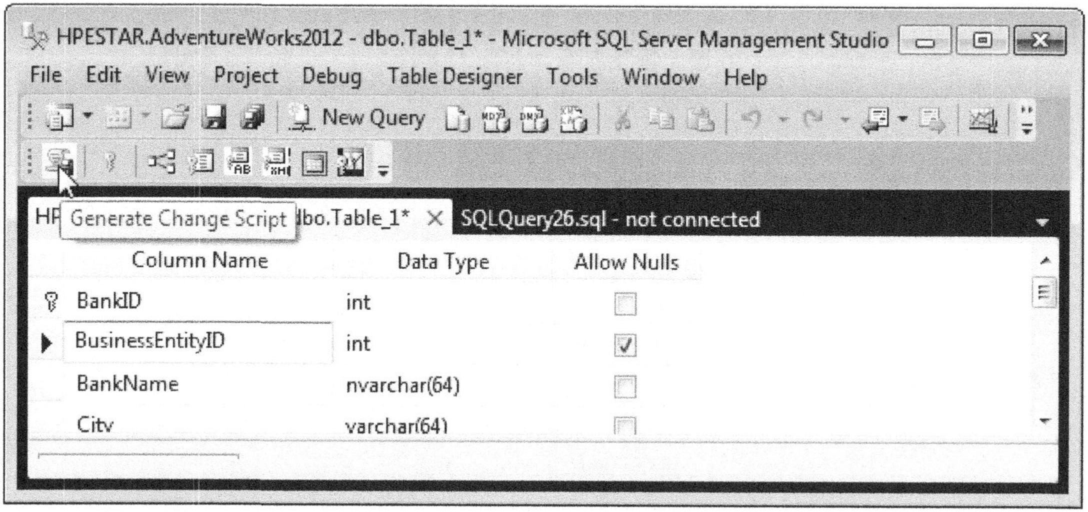
HPESTAR.AdventureWorks2012 - dbo.Table_1* - Microsoft SQL Server Management Studio
File Edit View Project Debug Table Designer Tools Window Help
New Query
Generate Change Script
dbo.Table_1*
SQLQuery26.sql - not connected
Column Name
Data Type
Allow Nulls
BankID
int
BusinessEntityID
int
BankName
nvarchar(64)
City
varchar(64)

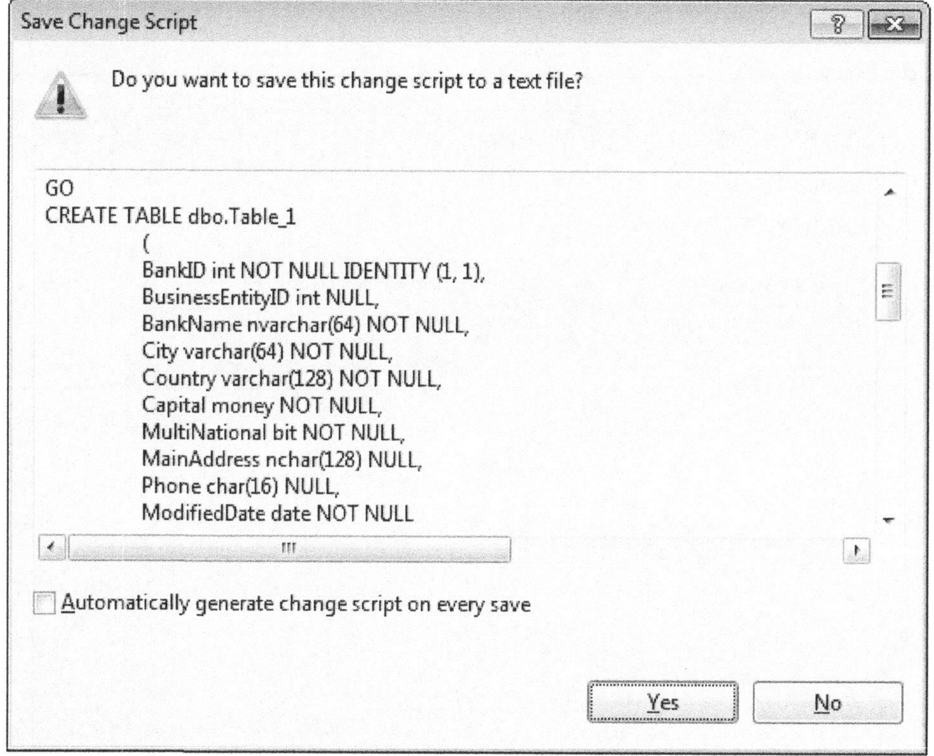
Save Change Script
Do you want to save this change script to a text file?
GO
CREATE TABLE dbo.Table_1
(
BankID int NOT NULL IDENTITY (1, 1),
BusinessEntityID int NULL,
BankName nvarchar(64) NOT NULL,
City varchar(64) NOT NULL,
Country varchar(128) NOT NULL,
Capital money NOT NULL,
MultiNational bit NOT NULL,
MainAddress nchar(128) NULL,
Phone char(16) NULL,
ModifiedDate date NOT NULL
Automatically generate change script on every save
Yes
No

Generated CREATE TABLE & Related Objects Script

Code generated by the Table Designer. SQL Server 2012 feature.

```
/* To prevent any potential data loss issues, you should review this script in detail before running it
outside the context of the database designer.*/
BEGIN TRANSACTION
SET QUOTED_IDENTIFIER ON
SET ARITHABORT ON
SET NUMERIC_ROUNDABORT OFF
SET CONCAT_NULL_YIELDS_NULL ON
SET ANSI_NULLS ON
SET ANSI_PADDING ON
SET ANSI_WARNINGS ON
COMMIT
BEGIN TRANSACTION
GO
CREATE TABLE dbo.Table_1
	(
	BankID int NOT NULL IDENTITY (1, 1),
	BusinessEntityID int NULL,
	BankName nvarchar(64) NOT NULL,
	City varchar(64) NOT NULL,
	Country varchar(128) NOT NULL,
	Capital money NOT NULL,
	MultiNational bit NOT NULL,
	MainAddress nchar(128) NULL,
	Phone char(16) NULL,
	ModifiedDate date NOT NULL
	)  ON [PRIMARY]
GO
ALTER TABLE dbo.Table_1 ADD CONSTRAINT
	CK_Table_1 CHECK (Capital >= $5000000000.0)
GO
ALTER TABLE dbo.Table_1 ADD CONSTRAINT
	DF_Table_1_ModifiedDate DEFAULT CURRENT_TIMESTAMP FOR ModifiedDate
GO
ALTER TABLE dbo.Table_1 ADD CONSTRAINT
	PK_Table_1 PRIMARY KEY CLUSTERED
	(
	BankID
	) WITH( STATISTICS_NORECOMPUTE = OFF, IGNORE_DUP_KEY = OFF, ALLOW_ROW_LOCKS = ON,
ALLOW_PAGE_LOCKS = ON) ON [PRIMARY]

GO
```

```
-- T-SQL script continues

ALTER TABLE dbo.Table_1 ADD CONSTRAINT
	IX_Table_1 UNIQUE NONCLUSTERED
	(
	BankName
	) WITH( STATISTICS_NORECOMPUTE = OFF, IGNORE_DUP_KEY = OFF, ALLOW_ROW_LOCKS = ON,
ALLOW_PAGE_LOCKS = ON) ON [PRIMARY]

GO
ALTER TABLE dbo.Table_1 ADD CONSTRAINT
	FK_Table_1_Table_1 FOREIGN KEY
	(
	BankID
	) REFERENCES dbo.Table_1
	(
	BankID
	) ON UPDATE  NO ACTION
	 ON DELETE  NO ACTION

GO
ALTER TABLE dbo.Table_1 SET (LOCK_ESCALATION = TABLE)
GO
COMMIT
```

Upon Exit or Save, a name can be assigned to the table. In this instance, the Table_1 is changed to MultiNationalBank. The Table Designer automatically replaces all the "Table_1" occurrences in the script with "MultiNationalBank".

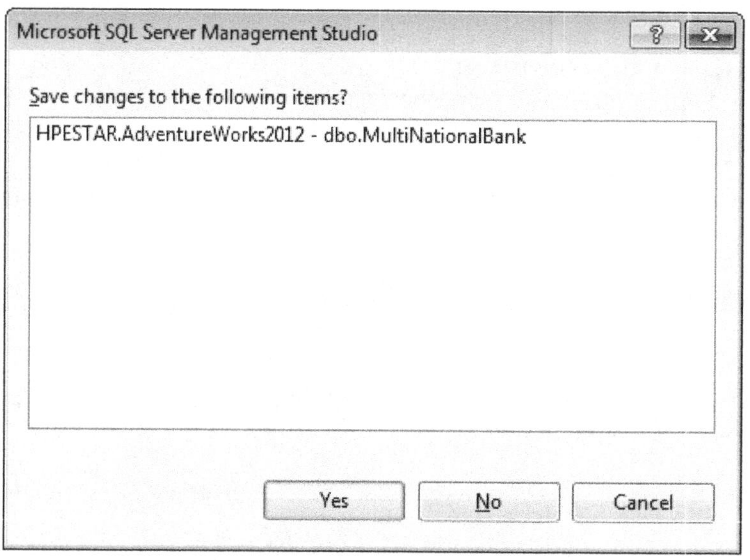

One-to-Many Relationship Implementation

The cardinality of relationship implemented with PRIMARY KEY & FOREIGN KEY constraints is one-to-many. Many FKs can reference a single PK value. In the following demo, many products map to a single subcategory value 'Touring Bike'. The matching is not done on the name between tables, rather on the surrogate PK value 3.

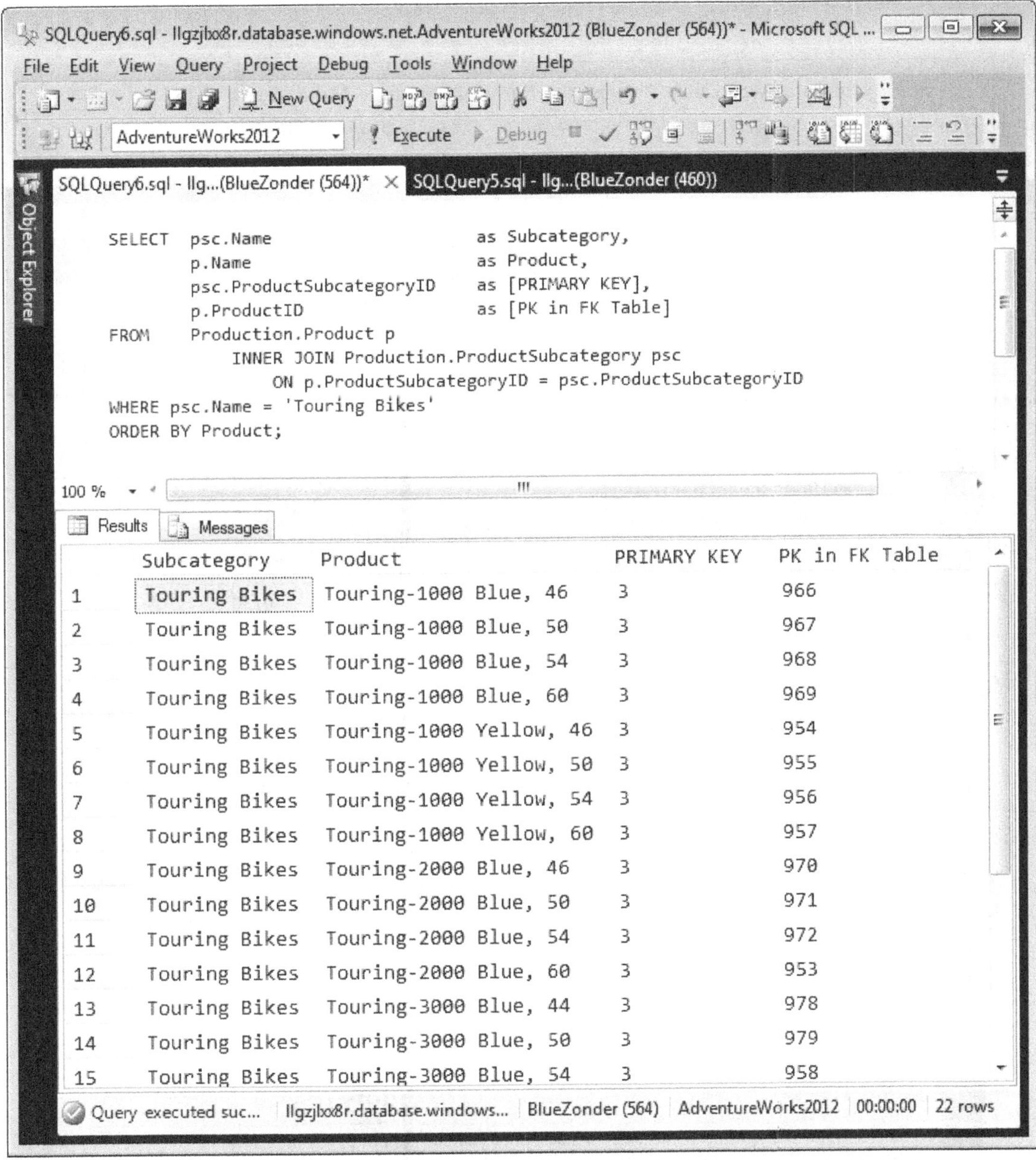
SQLQuery6.sql - llgzjbx8r.database.windows.net.AdventureWorks2012 (BlueZonder (564))* - Microsoft SQL ...
File Edit View Query Project Debug Tools Window Help
New Query
AdventureWorks2012
Execute
Debug
SQLQuery6.sql - llg...(BlueZonder (564))*
SQLQuery5.sql - llg...(BlueZonder (460))
Object Explorer
SELECT psc.Name as Subcategory,
p.Name as Product,
psc.ProductSubcategoryID as [PRIMARY KEY],
p.ProductID as [PK in FK Table]
FROM Production.Product p
INNER JOIN Production.ProductSubcategory psc
ON p.ProductSubcategoryID = psc.ProductSubcategoryID
WHERE psc.Name = 'Touring Bikes'
ORDER BY Product;
100 %
Results
Messages
Query executed suc...
llgzjbx8r.database.windows...
BlueZonder (564)
AdventureWorks2012
00:00:00
22 rows

	Subcategory	Product	PRIMARY KEY	PK in FK Table
1	Touring Bikes	Touring-1000 Blue, 46	3	966
2	Touring Bikes	Touring-1000 Blue, 50	3	967
3	Touring Bikes	Touring-1000 Blue, 54	3	968
4	Touring Bikes	Touring-1000 Blue, 60	3	969
5	Touring Bikes	Touring-1000 Yellow, 46	3	954
6	Touring Bikes	Touring-1000 Yellow, 50	3	955
7	Touring Bikes	Touring-1000 Yellow, 54	3	956
8	Touring Bikes	Touring-1000 Yellow, 60	3	957
9	Touring Bikes	Touring-2000 Blue, 46	3	970
10	Touring Bikes	Touring-2000 Blue, 50	3	971
11	Touring Bikes	Touring-2000 Blue, 54	3	972
12	Touring Bikes	Touring-2000 Blue, 60	3	953
13	Touring Bikes	Touring-3000 Blue, 44	3	978
14	Touring Bikes	Touring-3000 Blue, 50	3	979
15	Touring Bikes	Touring-3000 Blue, 54	3	958

FOREIGN KEY Referencing A UNIQUE KEY

A FOREIGN KEY can reference a UNIQUE KEY or UNIQUE index column in another table in addition to the PRIMARY KEY. In the following demonstration a FOREIGN KEY is created from ProdNumber column pointing to Production.Product ProductNumber (UNIQUE index) column. SQL Server 2012 feature.

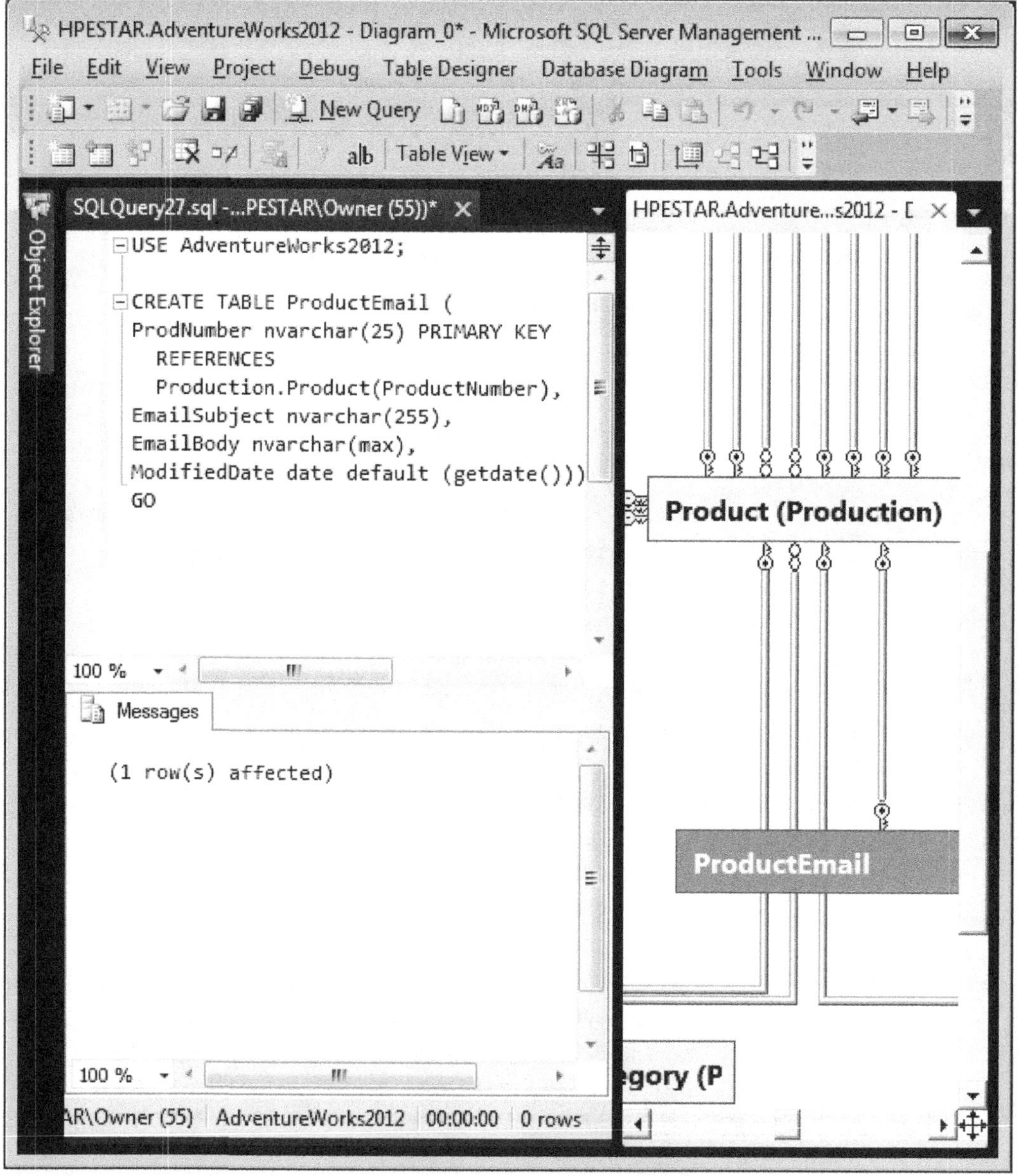

FOREIGN KEY Relationship Without Constraint

A table can have a FOREIGN KEY which is not supported by server-side constraint. In such instance the client-side application software has to ensure that the relationship is valid. Generally it is undesirable. **Whatever can be done on the server-side should be done there because it is more efficient development wise, maintenance wise and performance wise.** Demonstration to remove the FK constraint on the ProductID column in the [Order Details] table of the CopyOfNorthwind database. SQL Server 2012 demo.

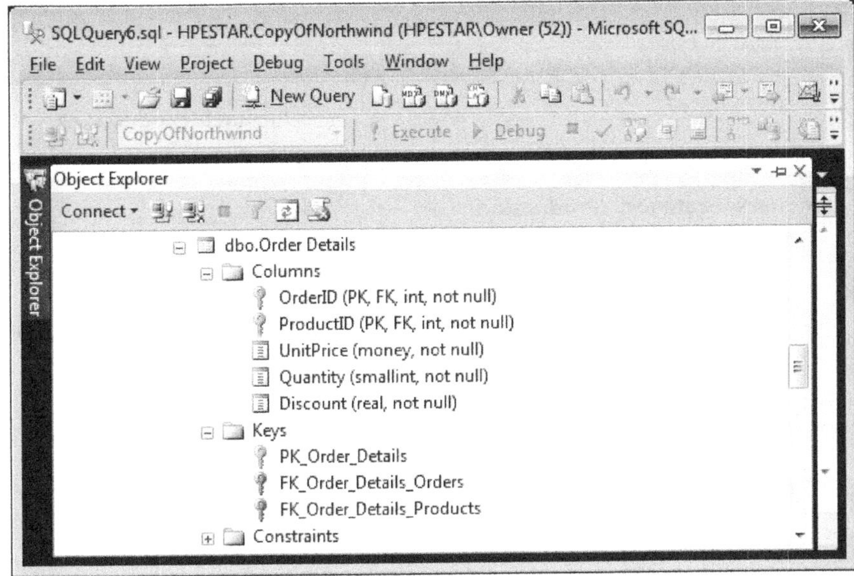

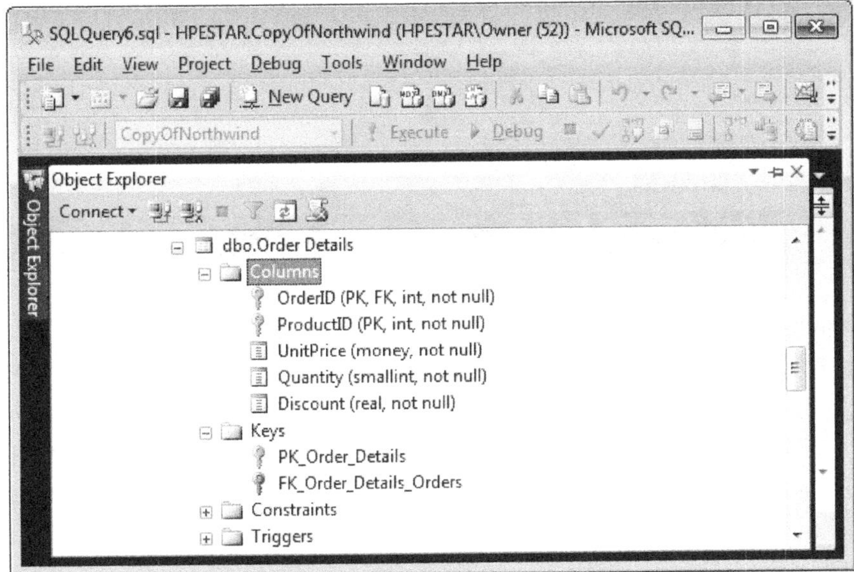

Database Diagram Design Tool in SSMS

Management Studio Object Explorer includes a diagramming tool for tables and their relationships with each other. While not as sophisticated as independent database design tools, it is excellent for working with a small number of tables. SQL Server 2012 feature.

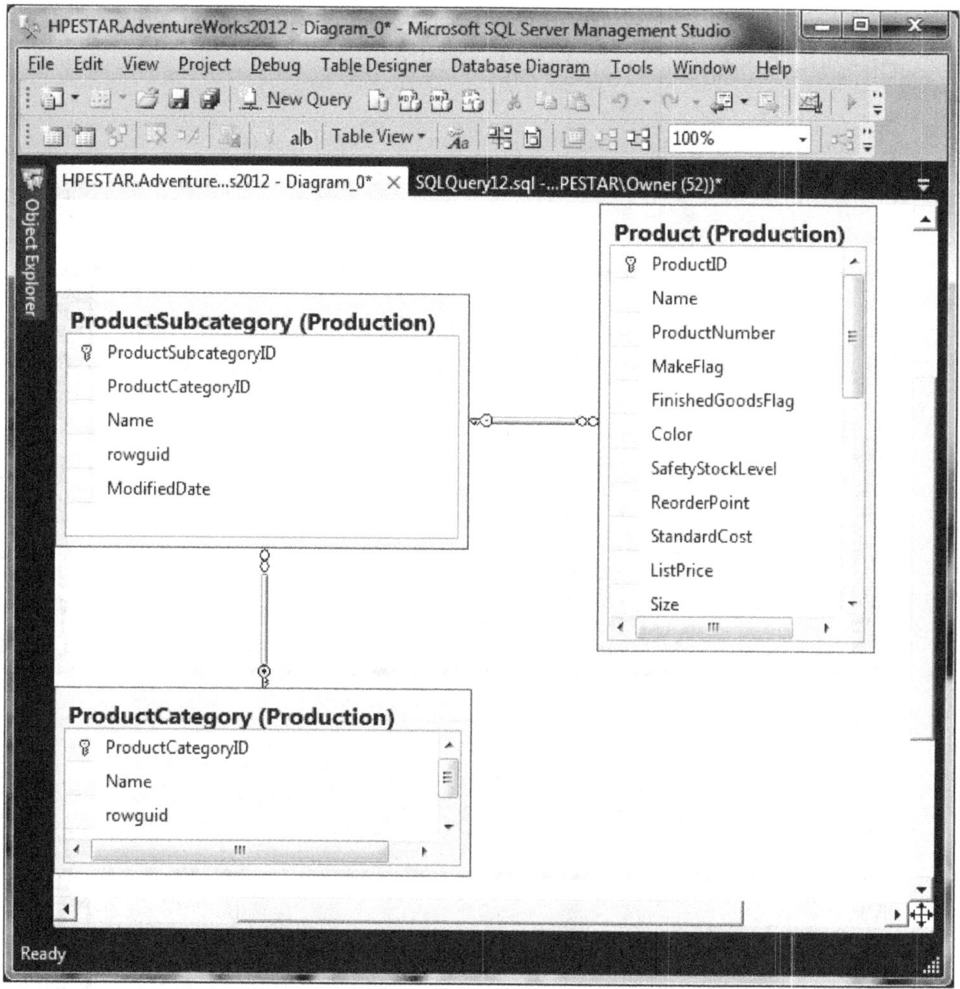

The diagramming tool has both reverse engineering and forward engineering features. **Reverse engineering**: it creates a diagram based on table and PK/FK constraints definitions. **Forward engineering**: it can change table and constraint setup in the database based on diagram changes. The Gold Key (PRIMARY KEY symbol) end of the connection line points to the PRIMARY KEY table, while the double "o" (infinite symbol in mathematics, here meaning many) end to the FOREIGN KEY table.

PRIMARY KEY & FOREIGN KEY as JOIN ON Keys

When we need data from two related tables we have to JOIN the tables. The typical JOIN keys are the PRIMARY KEY and FOREIGN KEY. In the following demonstration, we want to display the subcategory for each Touring Bike product from the Product table. Since the 'Touring Bike' subcategory value is in the ProductSubcategory table, we have to JOIN it to the Product table. The JOIN keys are: ProductSubcategoryID PRIMARY KEY in the ProductSubcategory table and ProductSubcategoryID FOREIGN KEY in the Product table. Naming the FK same as the PK is helpful with readability, therefore developer productivity.

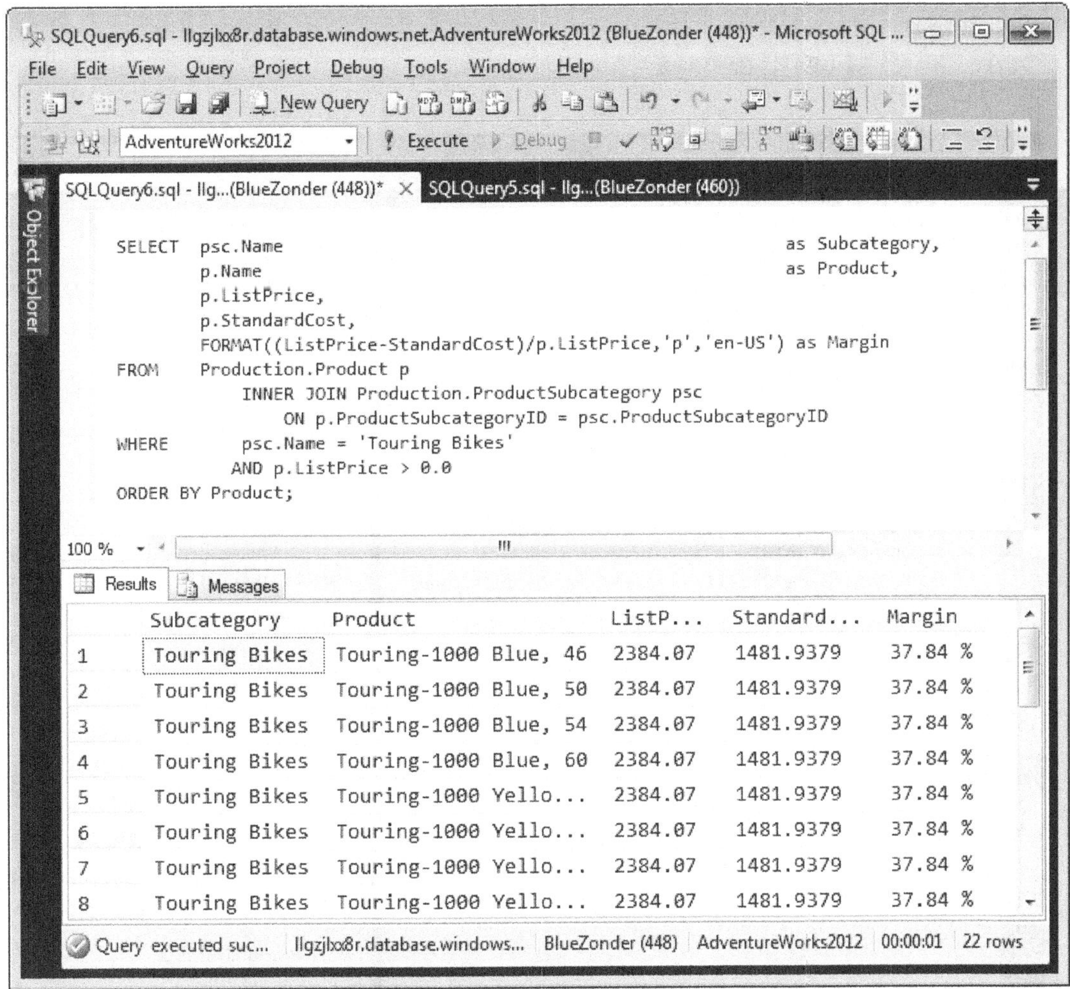

The Margin column is calculated with an expression. It is also formatted as percentage with US English culture.

Composite & Indirect FOREIGN KEY

A composite (more than one column) PRIMARY KEY requires matching composite FOREIGN KEY references. In the Sales.SalesOrderDetail table SpecialOfferID & ProductID constitute a composite FOREIGN KEY which references the SpecialOfferProduct table composite PRIMARY KEY. Thus ProductID indirectly references the Production.Product table. SQL Server 2012 feature.

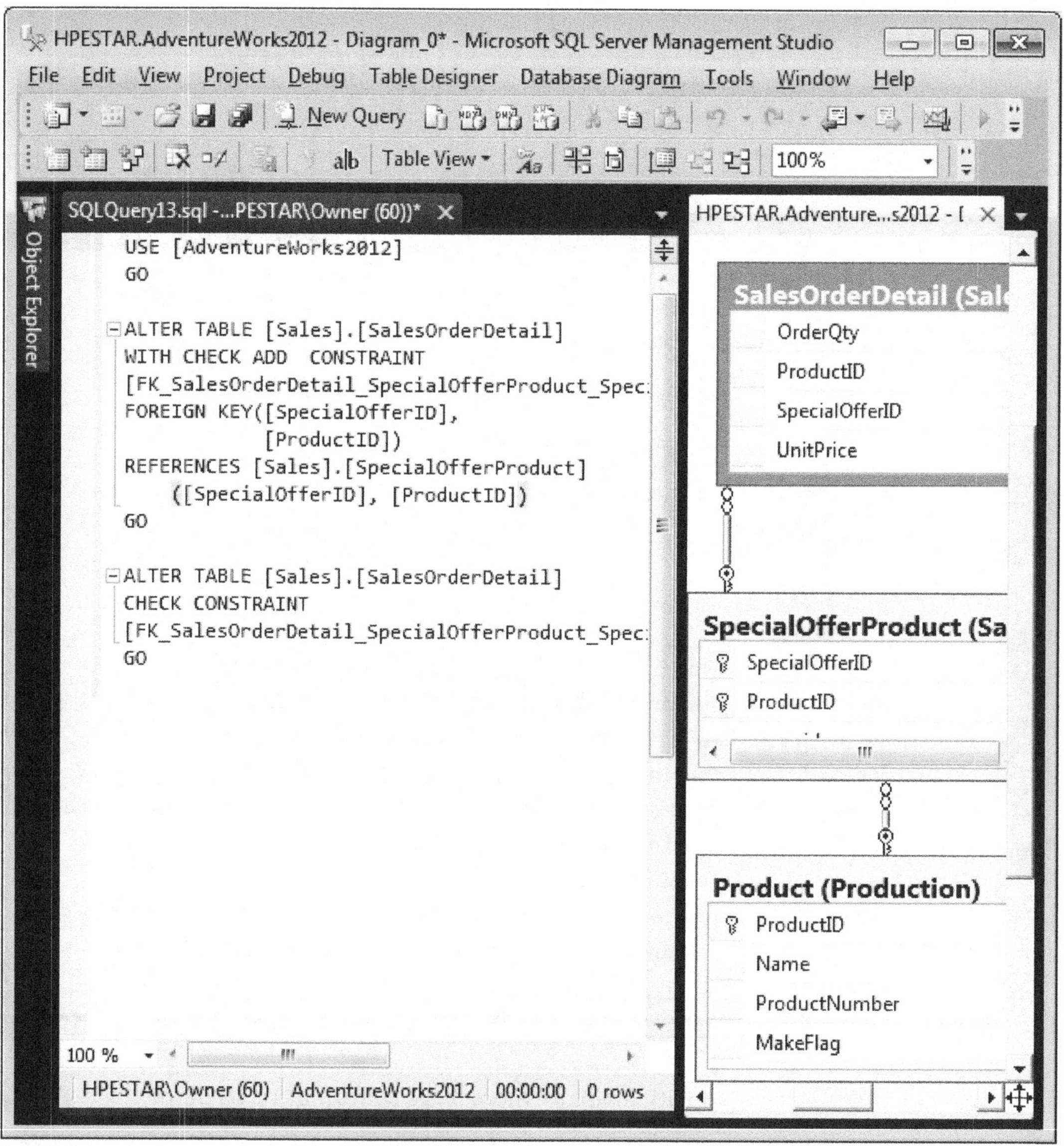

NATURAL KEY is a Must in Every Table

NATURAL KEY is a unique key which can serve as PRIMARY KEY for identifying data. A product name is a natural key in a product table. A product number is also a NATURAL KEY in a product table. Note that product "number" should better be called product identification since it is frequently not a number rather it is alphanumeric like: AB342BL where BL stands for blue. The Name and ProductNumber columns are NATURAL KEYs in the Production.Product table. **Every table should have a NATURAL KEY**. If it does not, there is a definition problem. Naturally, test tables, work tables and staging tables are exceptions to this rule.

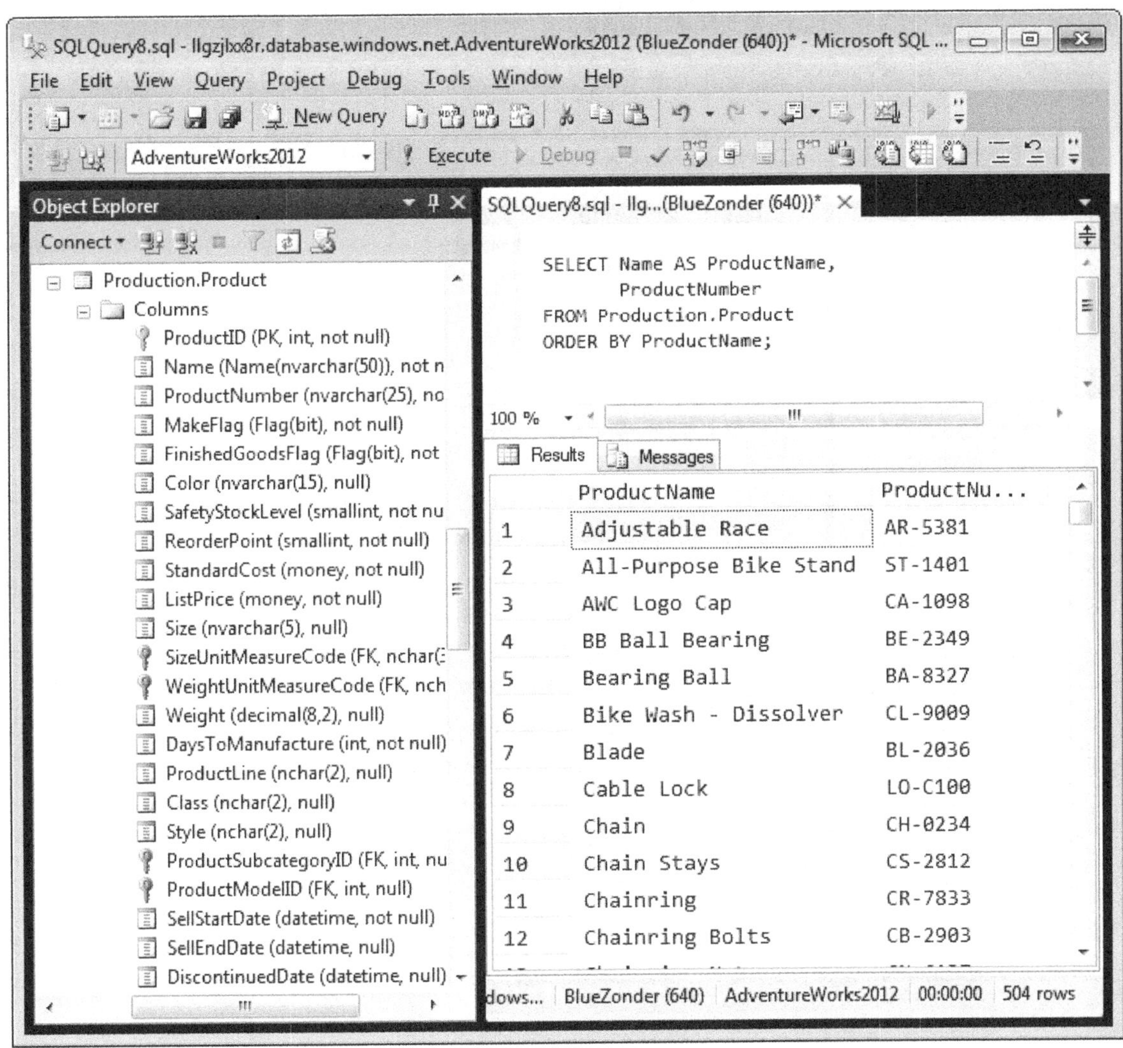

CANDIDATE KEY

A CANDIDATE KEY can be any column or a combination of columns that can qualify as UNIQUE KEY in a table with no NULL value. The ProductID, Name, ProductNumber, rowguid (16 byte random value like FA3C65CD-0A22-47E3-BDF6-53F1DC138C43, hyphens are for readability) are all CANDIDATE KEYs in the Production.Product table. Only one of them can be the PRIMARY KEY. In this instance the selected PRIMARY KEY is ProductID, a SURROGATE (to NATURAL KEY) INT IDENTITY (1,1) PRIMARY KEY.

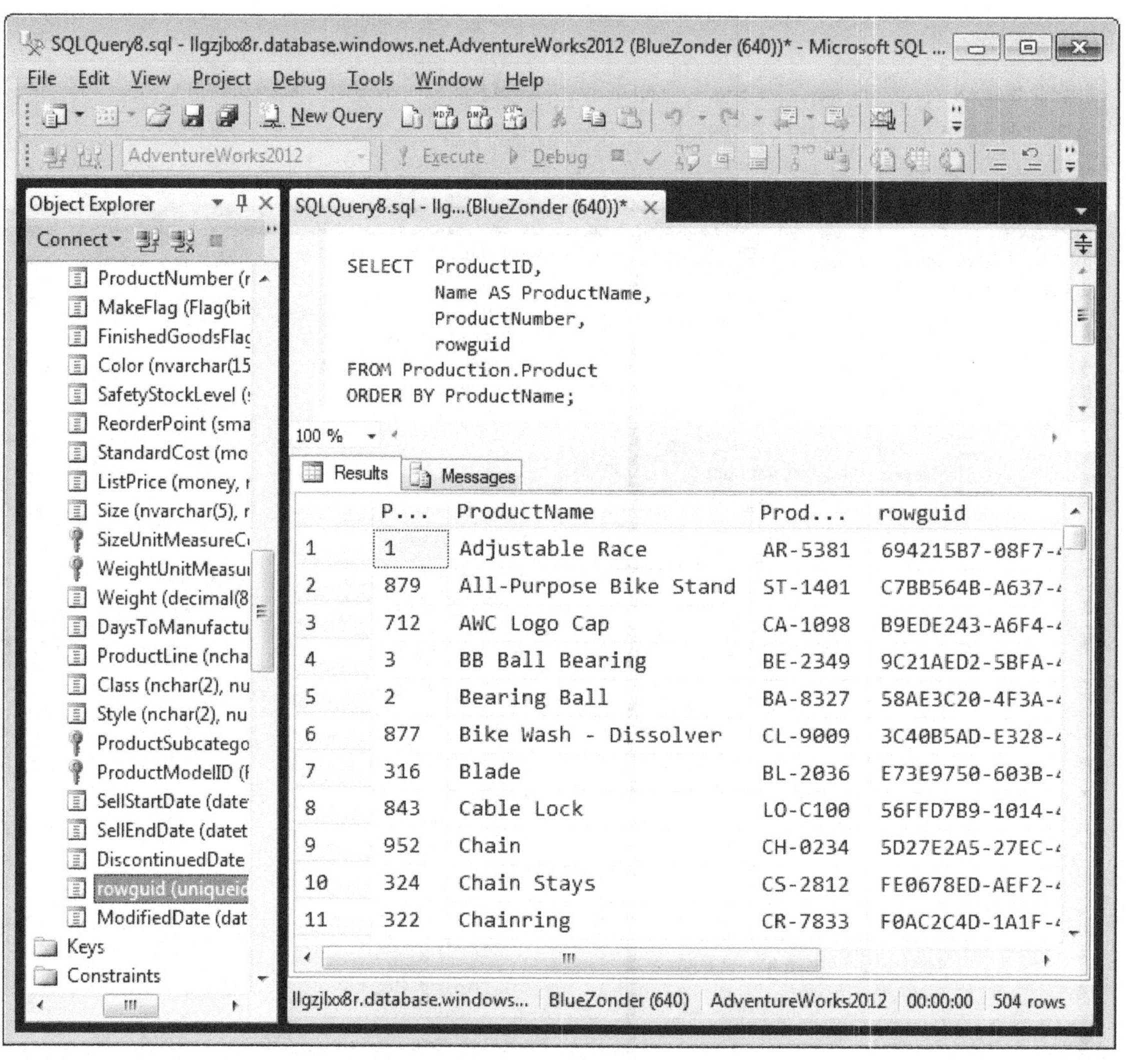

```
SELECT  ProductID,
        Name AS ProductName,
        ProductNumber,
        rowguid
FROM Production.Product
ORDER BY ProductName;
```

	P...	ProductName	Prod...	rowguid
1	1	Adjustable Race	AR-5381	694215B7-08F7-...
2	879	All-Purpose Bike Stand	ST-1401	C7BB564B-A637-...
3	712	AWC Logo Cap	CA-1098	B9EDE243-A6F4-...
4	3	BB Ball Bearing	BE-2349	9C21AED2-5BFA-...
5	2	Bearing Ball	BA-8327	58AE3C20-4F3A-...
6	877	Bike Wash - Dissolver	CL-9009	3C40B5AD-E328-...
7	316	Blade	BL-2036	E73E9750-603B-...
8	843	Cable Lock	LO-C100	56FFD7B9-1014-...
9	952	Chain	CH-0234	5D27E2A5-27EC-...
10	324	Chain Stays	CS-2812	FE0678ED-AEF2-...
11	322	Chainring	CR-7833	F0AC2C4D-1A1F-...

Logical Data Modeling in Visio

The following screenshots demonstrate logical / conceptual data modeling in Visio using the ORM diagram tool.

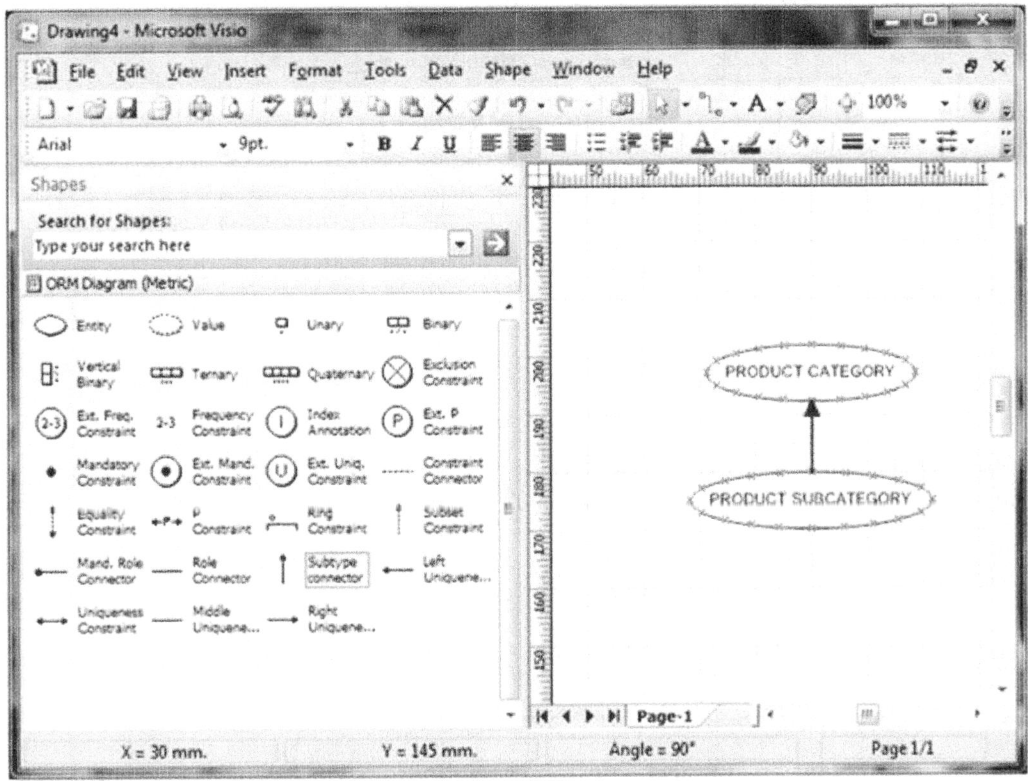

Following is the actual implementation of the above relationship.

```
CREATE TABLE [Production].[ProductCategory](
	[ProductCategoryID] [int] IDENTITY(1,1) PRIMARY KEY,
	[Name] [dbo].[Name] NOT NULL,
	[rowguid] [uniqueidentifier]  NOT NULL,
	[ModifiedDate] [datetime] NOT NULL		);

CREATE TABLE [Production].[ProductSubcategory](
	[ProductSubcategoryID] [int] IDENTITY(1,1) PRIMARY KEY,
	[ProductCategoryID] [int] NOT NULL REFERENCES
Production.ProductCategory(ProductCategoryID),
	[Name] [dbo].[Name] NOT NULL,
	[rowguid] [uniqueidentifier]  NOT NULL,
	[ModifiedDate] [datetime] NOT NULL		);
```

Branch Banking Conceptual Diagram Preparation In Visio ORM Diagram Tool

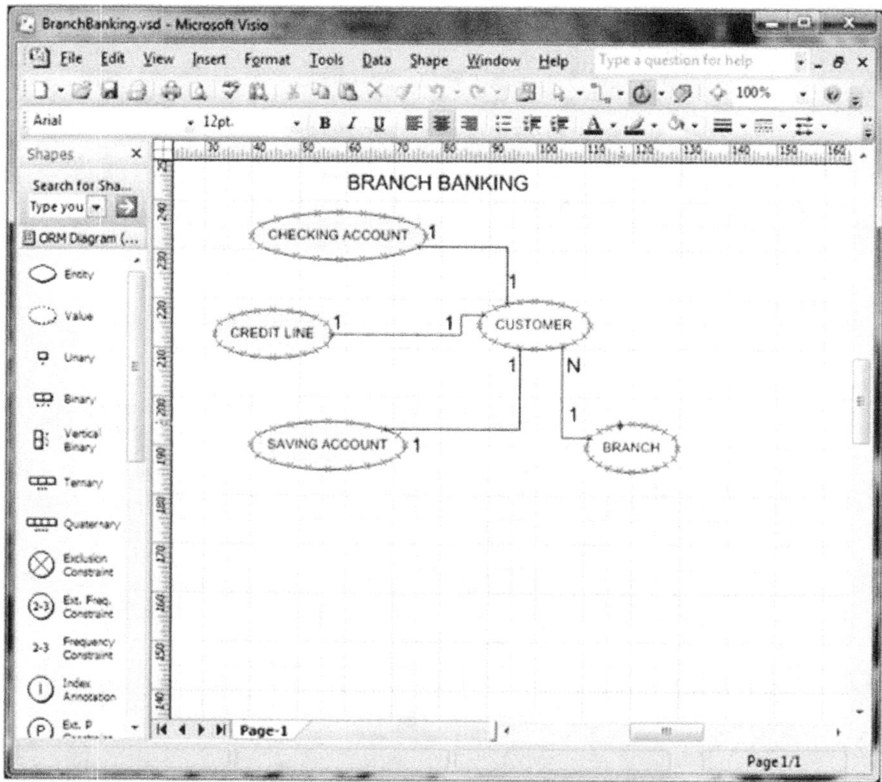

The actual implementation of Branch - Customer relationship.

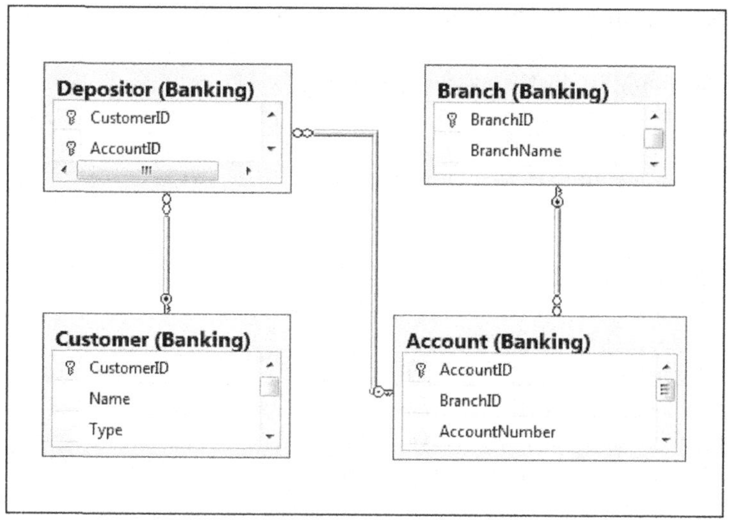

Relational Database Design with Visio

Office Visio can be used for physical database modeling and design. Another widely used database modeling tool is ERWIN.

A sample database design diagram in Visio. Lines represent FOREIGN KEY constraints, arrowheads point to the referenced table.

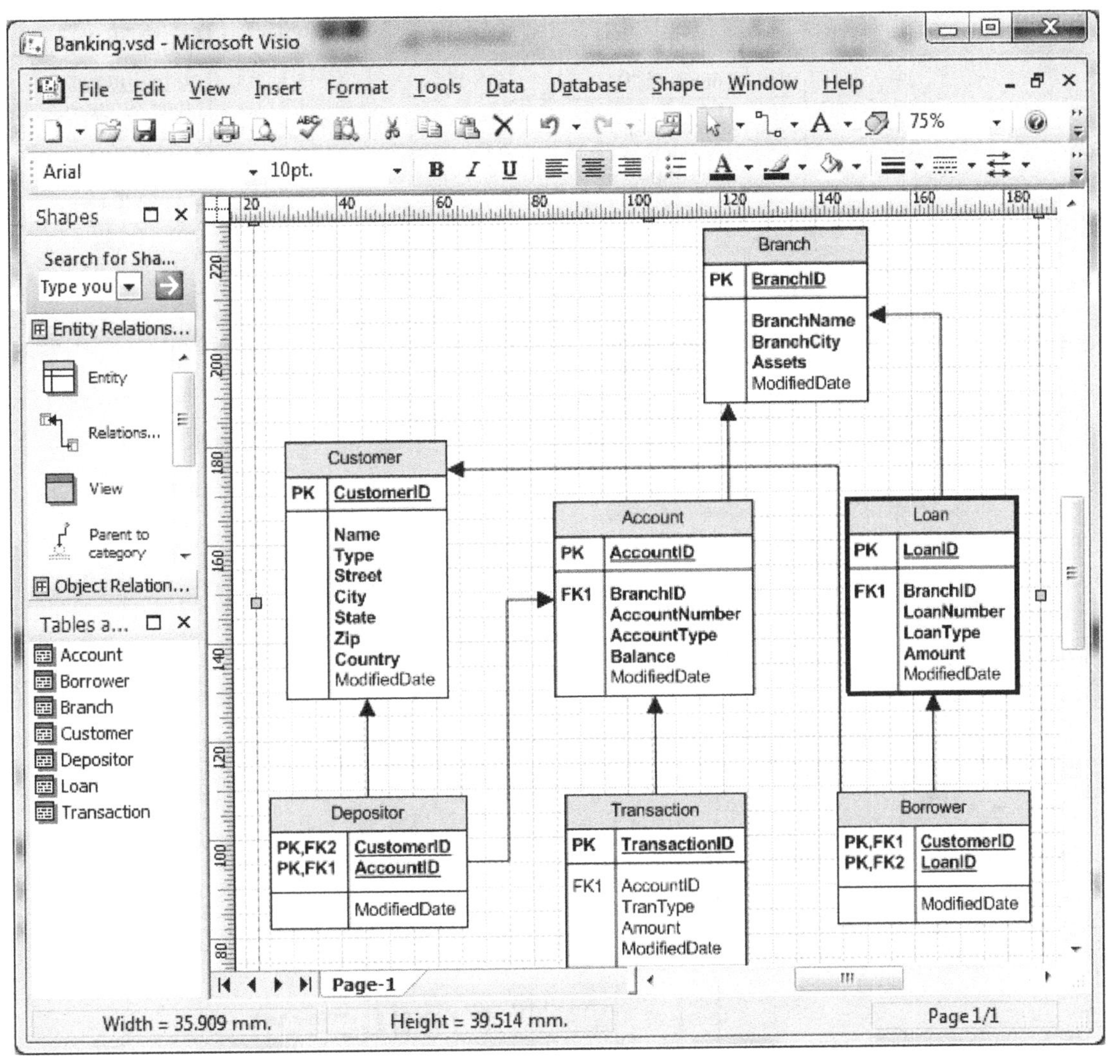

AdventureWorks Database Model in Visio

A segment of the AdventureWorks database design model in Visio. U indicates UNIQUE KEY or unique index.

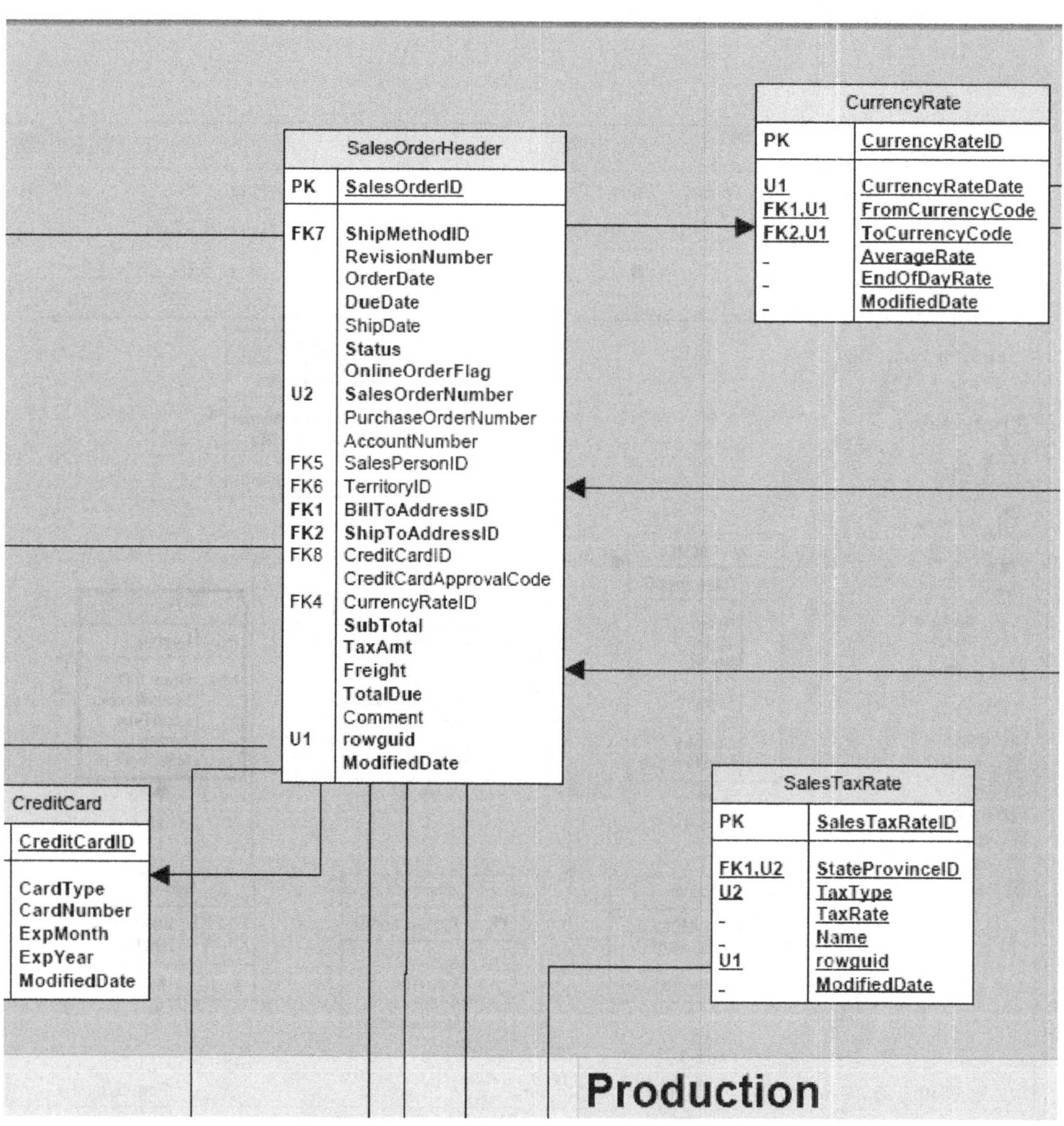

Reverse Engineering a Database with Visio

Visio can reverse engineer a database. Based on PRIMARY KEY & FOREIGN KEY constraints and table definitions, it can construct a database diagram automatically. Here are the first and an intermediate steps.

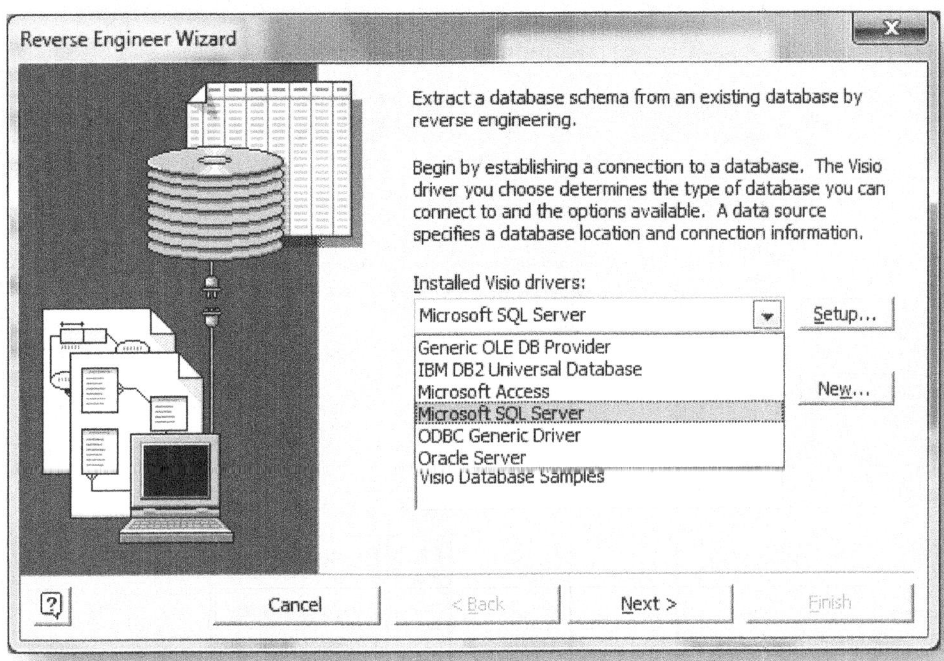

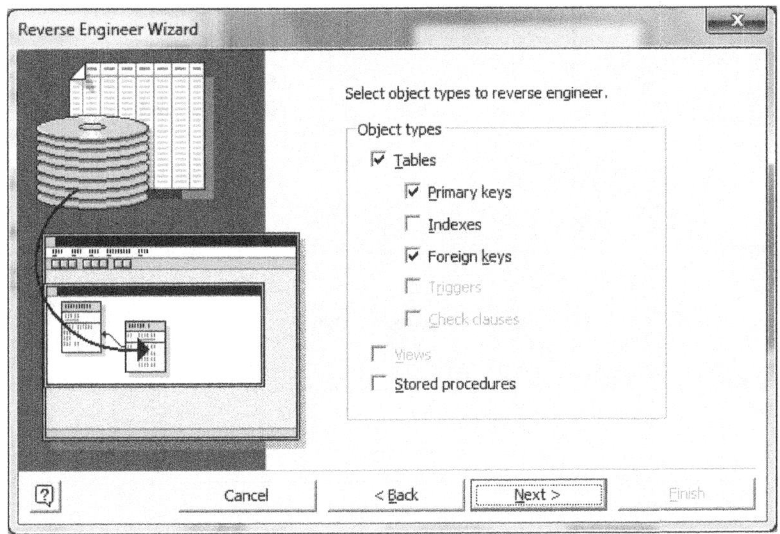

Reverse Engineered Diagram of Northwind

A section display from the reverse engineered diagram of Northwind sample database(not clear why "Discontinued" displays in bold):

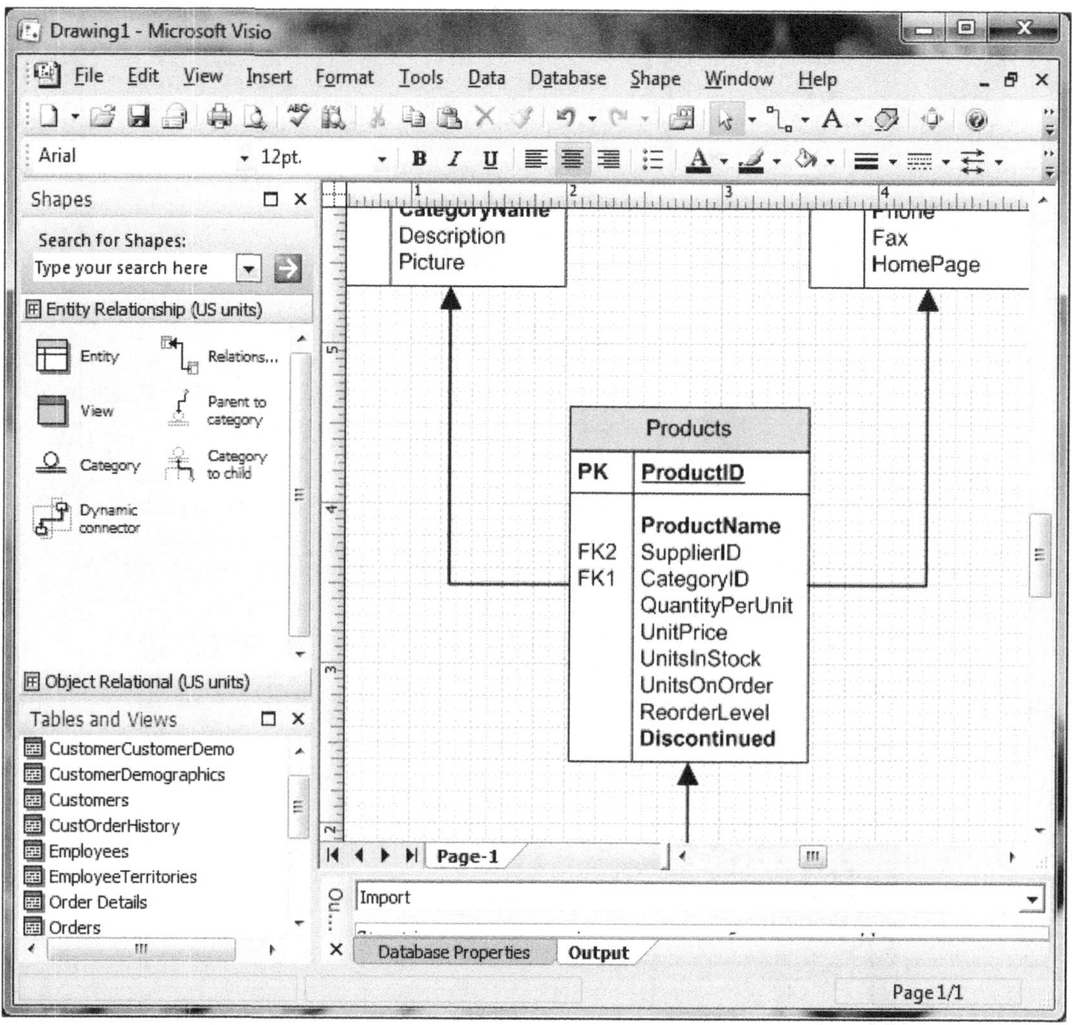

Forward Engineering a Database with Visio

Visio product itself does not have forward engineering feature. Alberto Ferrari developed an Office Addin for generating database scripts from a Visio database model diagram: Visio Forward Engineer Addin for Office 2010 (http://sqlblog.com/blogs/alberto_ferrari/archive/2010/04/16/visio-forward-engineer-addin-for-office-2010.aspx).

Codeplex blog post and free download for the same: Visio Forward Engineer Addin (http://forwardengineer.codeplex.com/).

Forward Engineering from SSMS Diagram Tool

The Database Diagram Tool in SSMS Object Explorer support graphical design and forward engineering. SQL Server 2012 feature.

Screenshot to show the creation of a new table "Automobile" in the Diagram Tool.

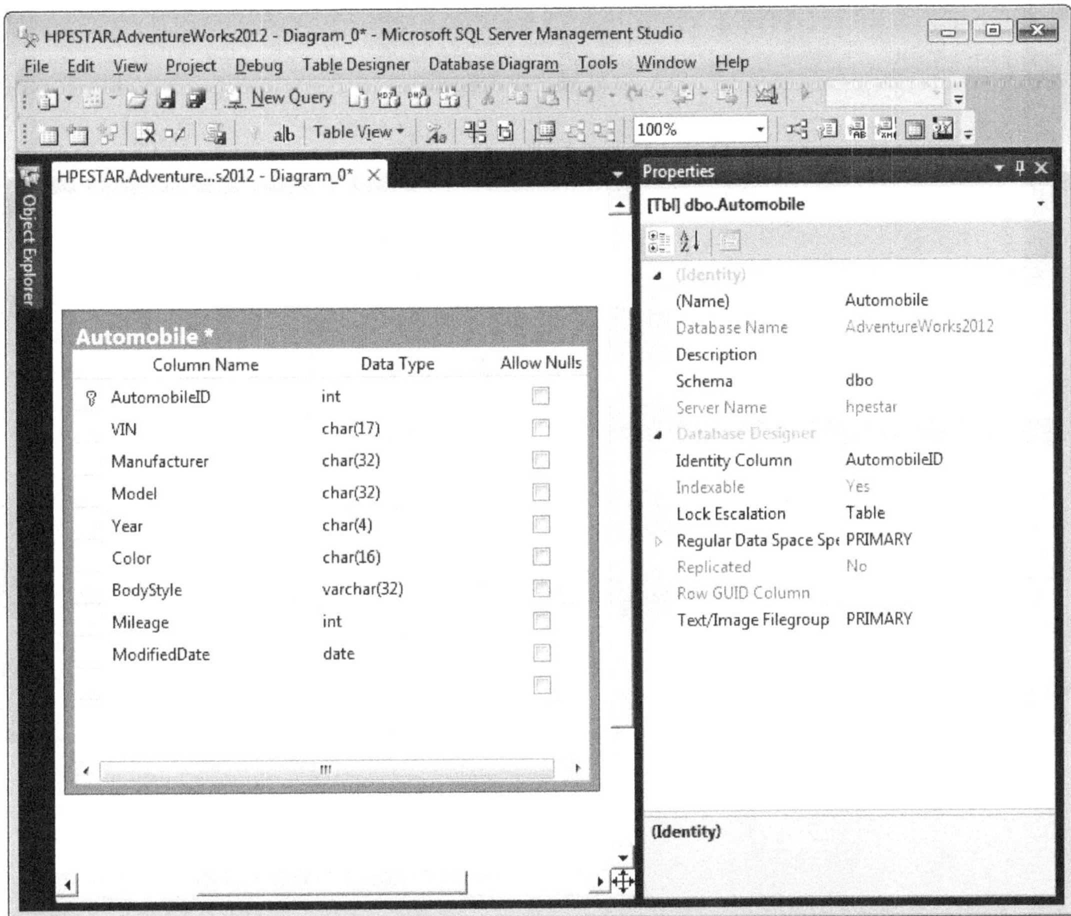

The Properties Dialog Box Allows The Individual Configuration Of Each Column

The Right Click drop-down menu has options to Add Indexes/Keys, Add XML Indexes, Add Spatial Indexes, Add Fulltext Indexes, Delete Tables from Database (DANGEROUS!), CHECK constraint and other table related database objects. . SQL Server 2012 feature.

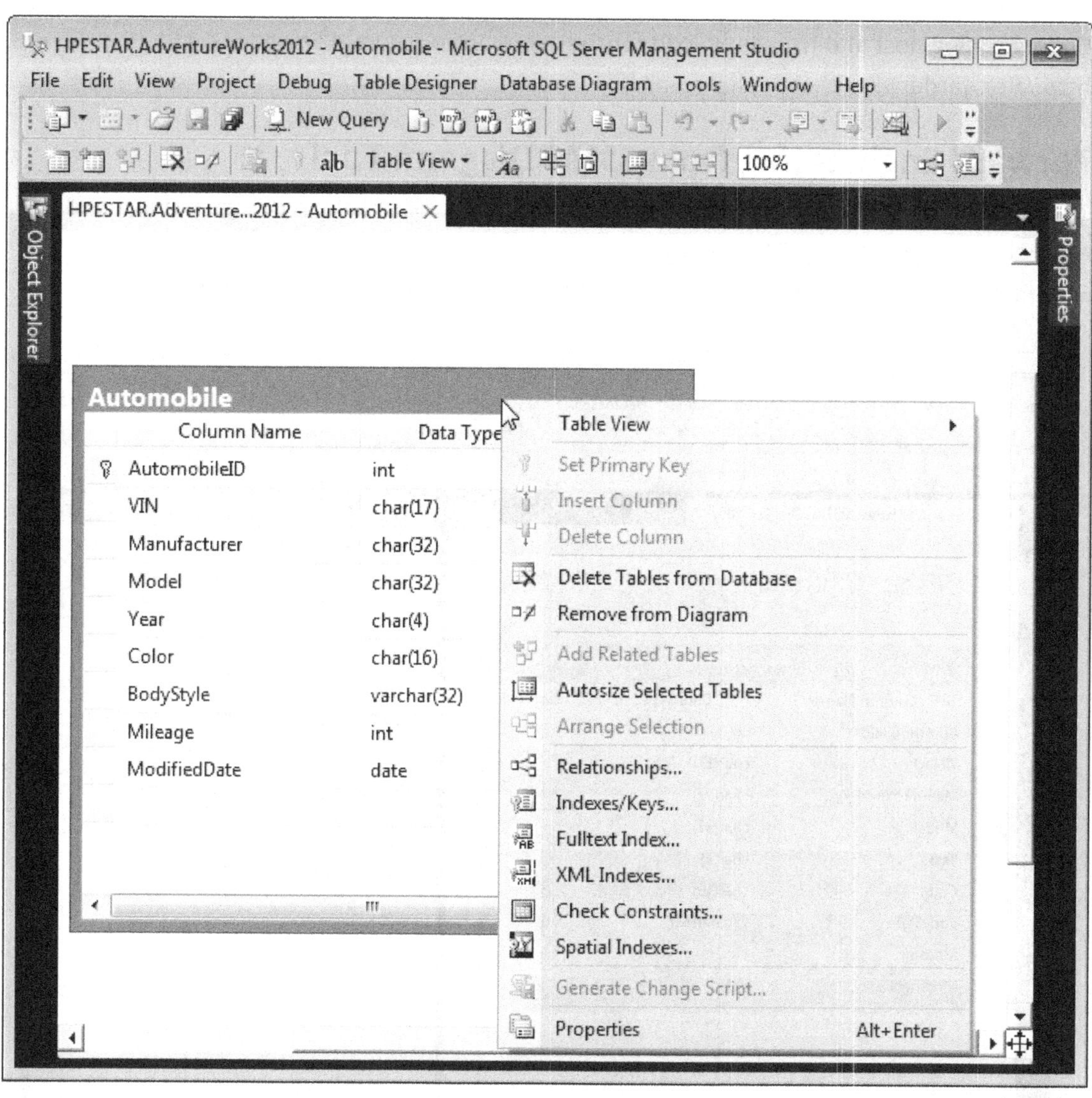

Forward Engineering Can Be Initiated By Exiting / Saving The Diagram

The save option dialog box activates automatically upon exit. . SQL Server 2012 feature.

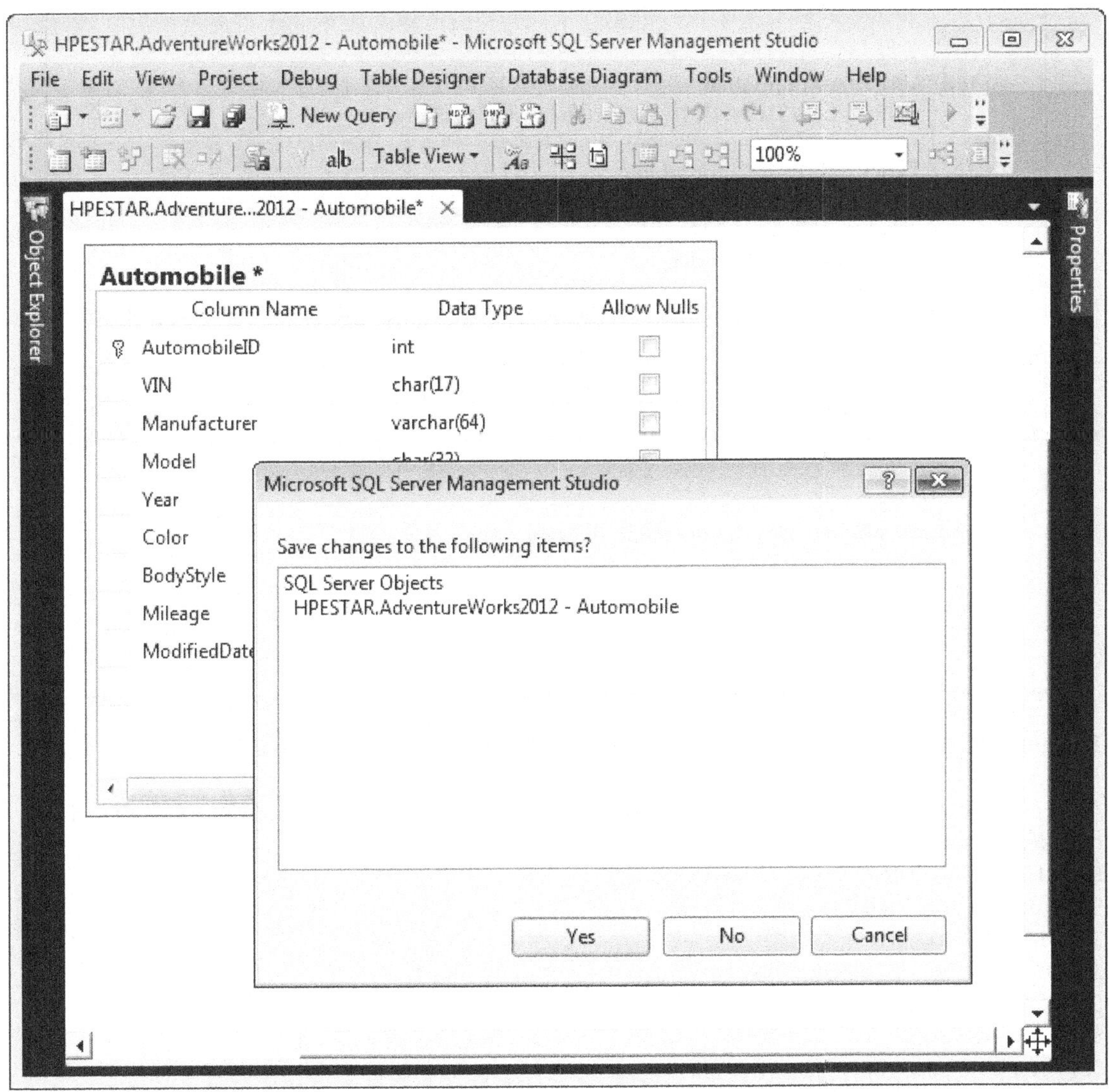

Save Change Script Panel Pops Up With The Generated T-SQL Change Script

SQL Server 2012 feature.

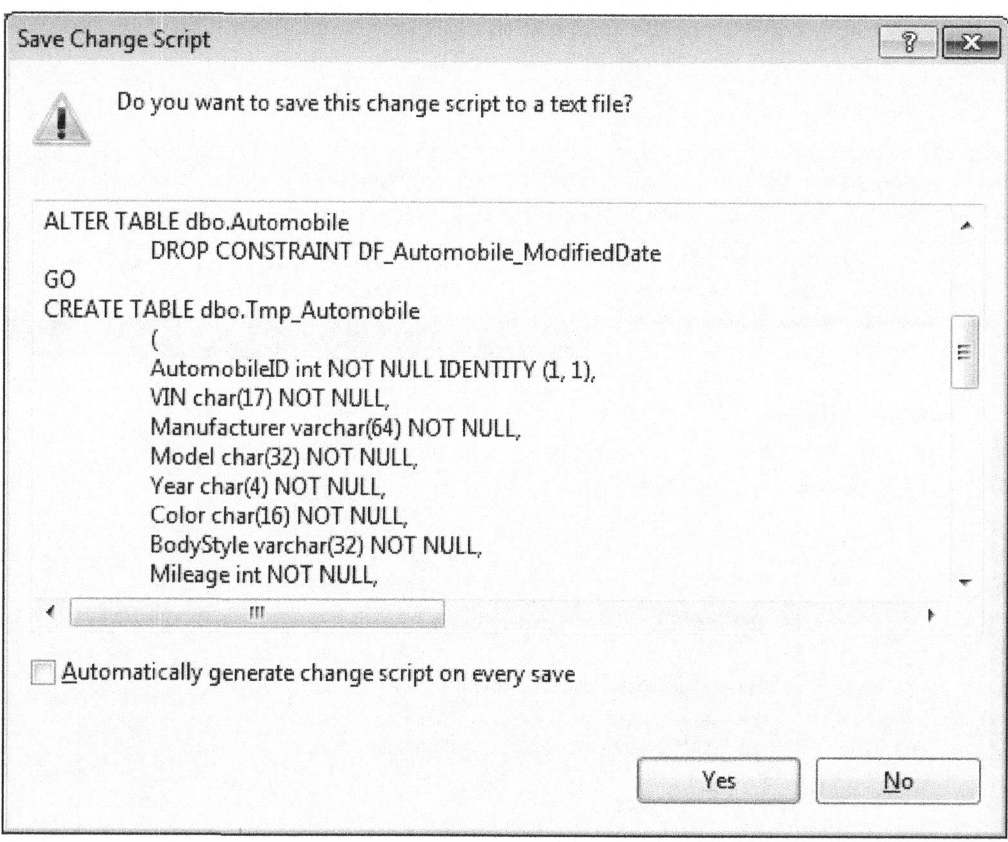
Save Change Script
Do you want to save this change script to a text file?
ALTER TABLE dbo.Automobile
DROP CONSTRAINT DF_Automobile_ModifiedDate
GO
CREATE TABLE dbo.Tmp_Automobile
(
AutomobileID int NOT NULL IDENTITY (1, 1),
VIN char(17) NOT NULL,
Manufacturer varchar(64) NOT NULL,
Model char(32) NOT NULL,
Year char(4) NOT NULL,
Color char(16) NOT NULL,
BodyStyle varchar(32) NOT NULL,
Mileage int NOT NULL,
Automatically generate change script on every save
Yes
No

The generated T-SQL change script for changing Manufacturer data type to varchar(64).

```
/* To prevent any potential data loss issues, you should review this script in detail before running it
outside the context of the database designer.*/
BEGIN TRANSACTION
SET QUOTED_IDENTIFIER ON
SET ARITHABORT ON
SET NUMERIC_ROUNDABORT OFF
SET CONCAT_NULL_YIELDS_NULL ON
SET ANSI_NULLS ON
SET ANSI_PADDING ON
SET ANSI_WARNINGS ON
COMMIT
BEGIN TRANSACTION
GO
```

```
-- T-SQL script continued

ALTER TABLE dbo.Automobile
	DROP CONSTRAINT DF_Automobile_ModifiedDate
GO


CREATE TABLE dbo.Tmp_Automobile	(

	AutomobileID int NOT NULL IDENTITY (1, 1),
	VIN char(17) NOT NULL,
	Manufacturer varchar(64) NOT NULL,
	Model char(32) NOT NULL,
	Year char(4) NOT NULL,
	Color char(16) NOT NULL,
	BodyStyle varchar(32) NOT NULL,
	Mileage int NOT NULL,
	ModifiedDate date NOT NULL )  ON [PRIMARY]
GO
ALTER TABLE dbo.Tmp_Automobile SET (LOCK_ESCALATION = TABLE)
GO
ALTER TABLE dbo.Tmp_Automobile ADD CONSTRAINT
	DF_Automobile_ModifiedDate DEFAULT (getdate()) FOR ModifiedDate
GO
SET IDENTITY_INSERT dbo.Tmp_Automobile ON
GO
IF EXISTS(SELECT * FROM dbo.Automobile)
	EXEC('INSERT INTO dbo.Tmp_Automobile (AutomobileID, VIN, Manufacturer, Model, Year,
Color, BodyStyle, Mileage, ModifiedDate)
		SELECT AutomobileID, VIN, CONVERT(varchar(64), Manufacturer), Model, Year, Color,
BodyStyle, Mileage, ModifiedDate FROM dbo.Automobile WITH (HOLDLOCK TABLOCKX)')
GO
SET IDENTITY_INSERT dbo.Tmp_Automobile OFF
GO
DROP TABLE dbo.Automobile
GO
EXECUTE sp_rename N'dbo.Tmp_Automobile', N'Automobile', 'OBJECT'
GO
ALTER TABLE dbo.Automobile ADD CONSTRAINT
	PK_Automobile PRIMARY KEY CLUSTERED
	(  AutomobileID
	) WITH( STATISTICS_NORECOMPUTE = OFF, IGNORE_DUP_KEY = OFF, ALLOW_ROW_LOCKS = ON,
ALLOW_PAGE_LOCKS = ON) ON [PRIMARY]
GO
COMMIT
```

Generate Change Script Option

Forward Engineering can also be initiated by the Generate Change Script option. The same option can be used when making any changes to the Diagram using the Diagram Tool. SQL Server 2012 feature.

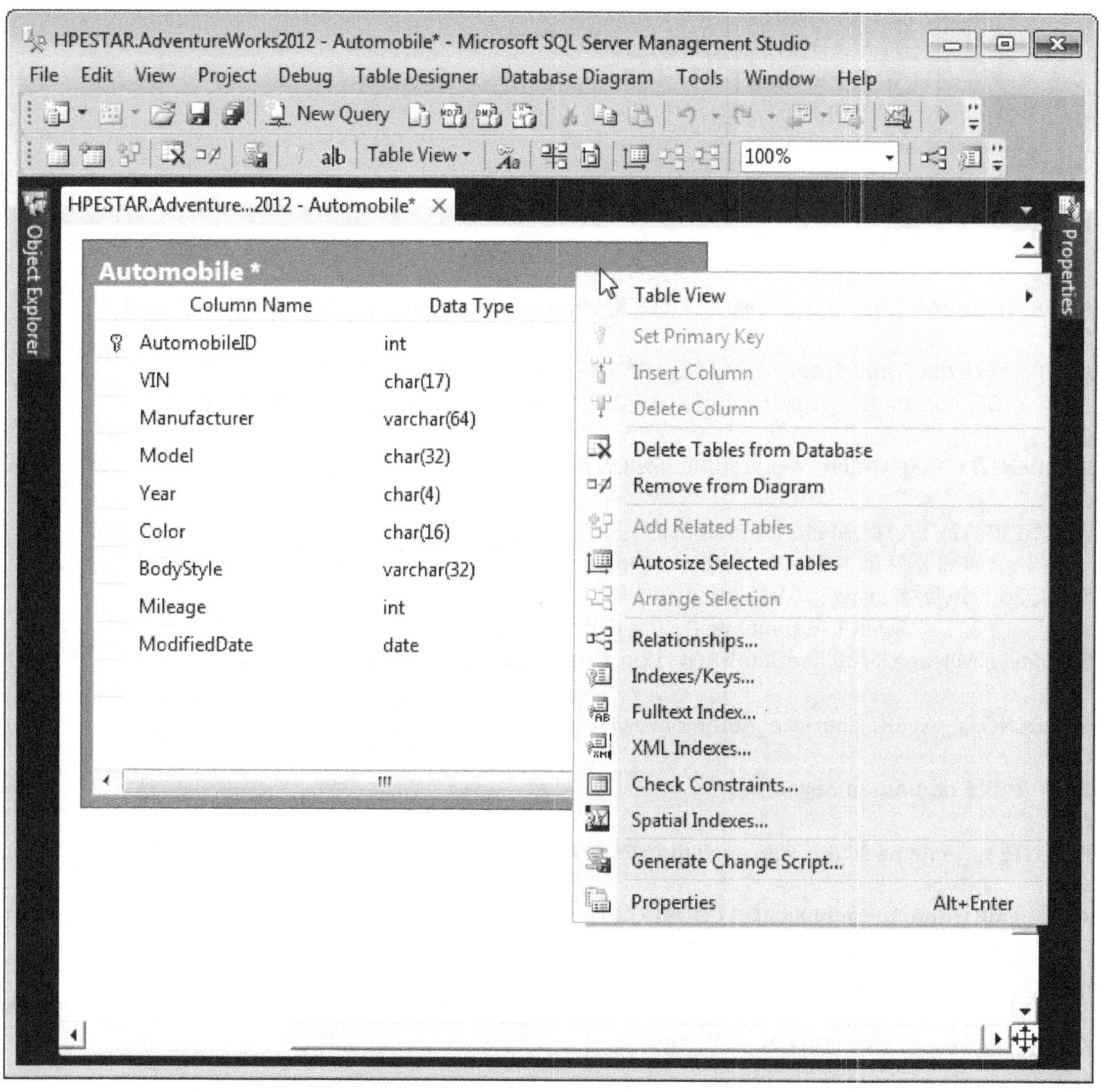

The Generated Script Of The Automobile Table By The Diagram Tool

SQL Server 2012 feature. "ON [PRIMARY]" is not supported in Azure SQL.

```
USE [AdventureWorks2012]
GO

/****** Object:  Table [dbo].[Automobile]    Script Date: 7/22/2016 11:20:17 AM ******/
SET ANSI_NULLS ON
GO

SET QUOTED_IDENTIFIER ON
GO

SET ANSI_PADDING ON
GO

CREATE TABLE [dbo].[Automobile](
	[AutomobileID] [int] IDENTITY(1,1) NOT NULL,
	[VIN] [char](17) NOT NULL,
	[Manufacturer] [char](32) NOT NULL,
	[Model] [char](32) NOT NULL,
	[Year] [char](4) NOT NULL,
	[Color] [char](16) NOT NULL,
	[BodyStyle] [varchar](32) NOT NULL,
	[Mileage] [int] NOT NULL,
	[ModifiedDate] [date] NOT NULL,
 CONSTRAINT [PK_Automobile] PRIMARY KEY CLUSTERED
(
	[AutomobileID] ASC
)WITH (PAD_INDEX = OFF, STATISTICS_NORECOMPUTE = OFF, IGNORE_DUP_KEY = OFF,
ALLOW_ROW_LOCKS = ON, ALLOW_PAGE_LOCKS = ON) ON [PRIMARY]
) ON [PRIMARY]

GO

SET ANSI_PADDING ON
GO

ALTER TABLE [dbo].[Automobile] ADD  CONSTRAINT [DF_Automobile_ModifiedDate]
DEFAULT (getdate()) FOR [ModifiedDate]
GO
```

Scripting Single Database Object with Related Objects

The scripting feature works only through the graphical user interface (GUI) in SSMS Object Explorer. **There is no command to script a table.** Start with Right Click on the Banking.Account table.

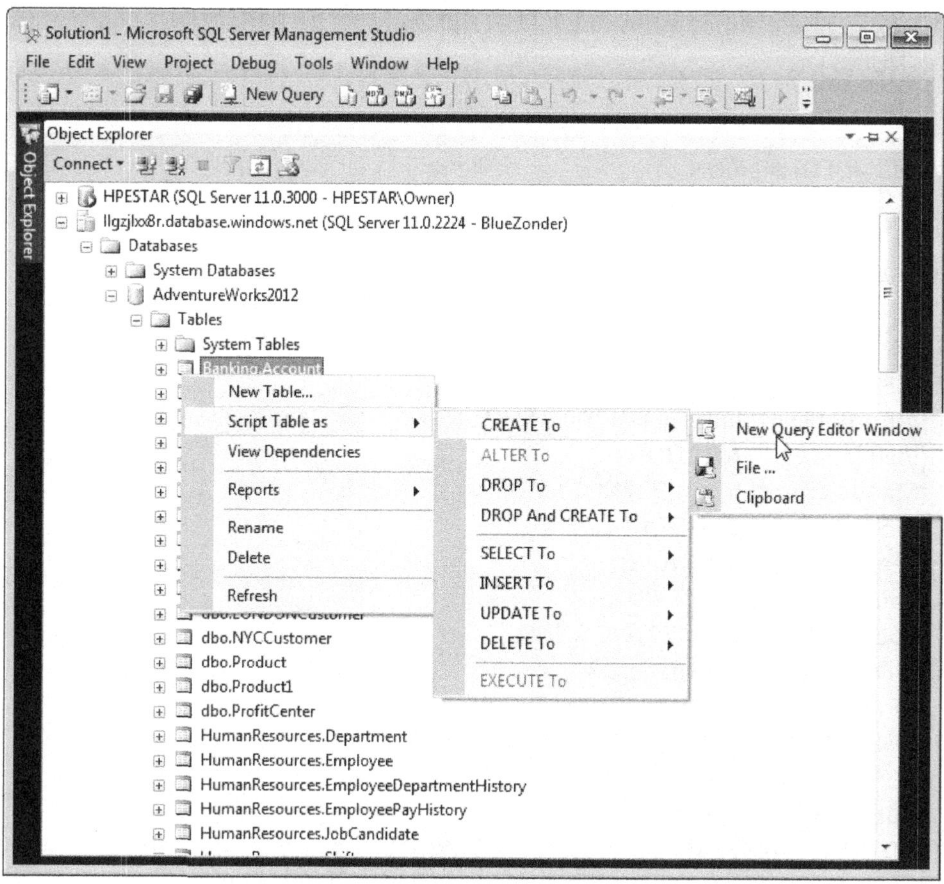

Generated script for the Banking.Account table and related objects.

```
USE [AdventureWorks2012]
GO
SET ANSI_NULLS ON
GO
SET QUOTED_IDENTIFIER ON
GO
SET ANSI_PADDING ON
GO
```

-- T-SQL script continued

```
CREATE TABLE [Banking].[Account](
	[AccountID] [int] IDENTITY(1,1) NOT NULL,
	[BranchID] [int] NOT NULL,
	[AccountNumber] [char](20) NOT NULL,
	[AccountType] [char](12) NOT NULL,
	[Balance] [money] NOT NULL,
	[ModifiedDate] [datetime] NULL,
PRIMARY KEY CLUSTERED
(	[AccountID] ASC
)WITH (PAD_INDEX = OFF, STATISTICS_NORECOMPUTE = OFF, IGNORE_DUP_KEY = OFF,
ALLOW_ROW_LOCKS = ON, ALLOW_PAGE_LOCKS = ON),
UNIQUE NONCLUSTERED
(
	[AccountID] ASC
)WITH (PAD_INDEX = OFF, STATISTICS_NORECOMPUTE = OFF, IGNORE_DUP_KEY = OFF,
ALLOW_ROW_LOCKS = ON, ALLOW_PAGE_LOCKS = ON),
UNIQUE NONCLUSTERED
(	[AccountNumber] ASC
)WITH (PAD_INDEX = OFF, STATISTICS_NORECOMPUTE = OFF, IGNORE_DUP_KEY = OFF,
ALLOW_ROW_LOCKS = ON, ALLOW_PAGE_LOCKS = ON)
)
GO

SET ANSI_PADDING OFF
GO

ALTER TABLE [Banking].[Account] ADD  DEFAULT (getdate()) FOR [ModifiedDate]
GO

ALTER TABLE [Banking].[Account]  WITH CHECK ADD FOREIGN KEY([BranchID])
REFERENCES [Banking].[Branch] ([BranchID])
ON DELETE CASCADE
GO

ALTER TABLE [Banking].[Account]  WITH CHECK ADD  CONSTRAINT [ATC] CHECK
(([AccountType]='S' OR [AccountType]='C'))
GO

ALTER TABLE [Banking].[Account] CHECK CONSTRAINT [ATC]
GO
```

Scripting DB Objects With Script Wizard

The Script Wizard is a sophisticated tool for scripting out multiple objects, in fact all objects can be scripted in a single setup and execution. The generated script can be saved to single/multiple files, new query window or the Clipboard. The launching sequence of menus starts with Right Click on the database.

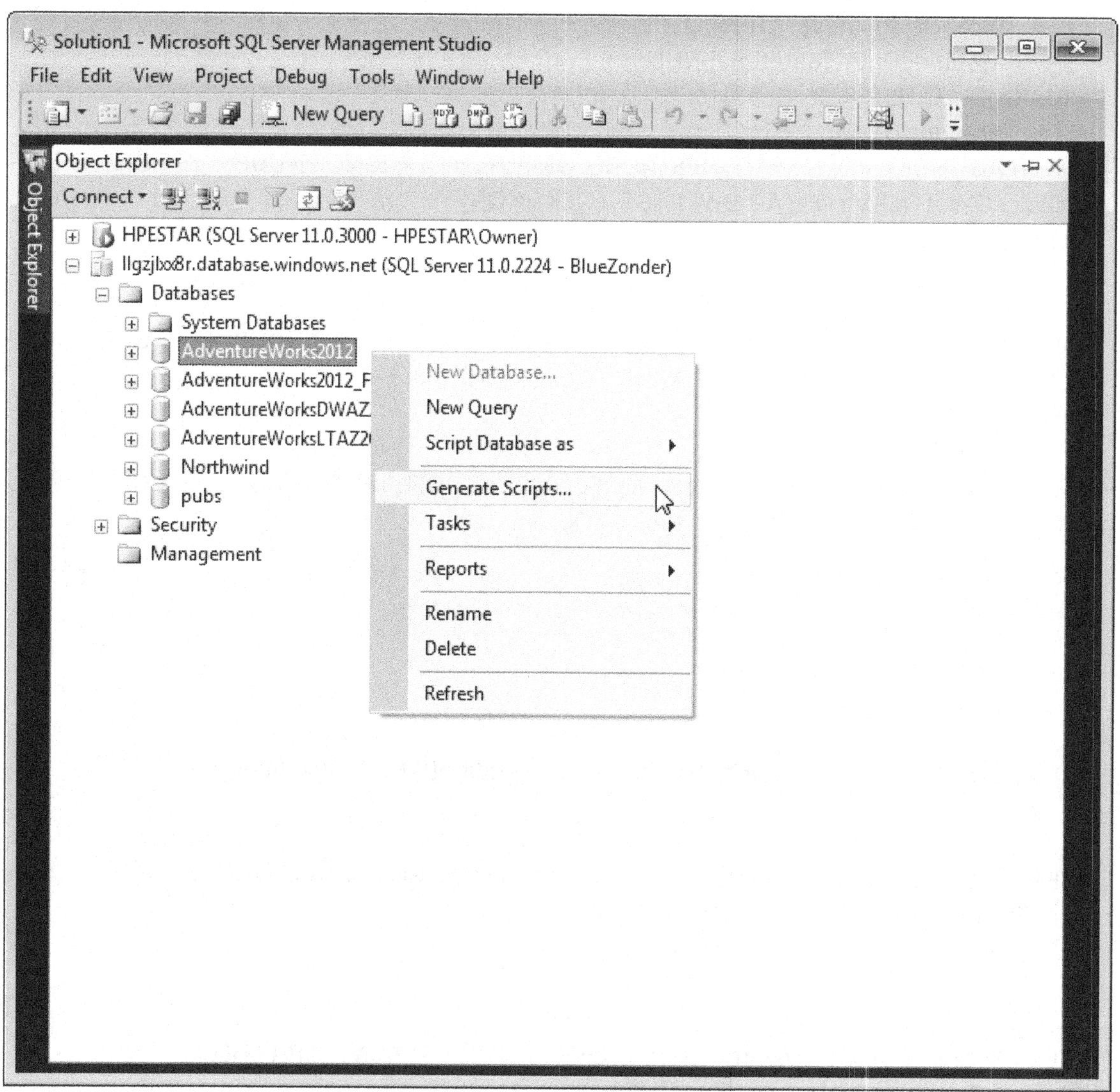

Script Wizard Optional Description Page

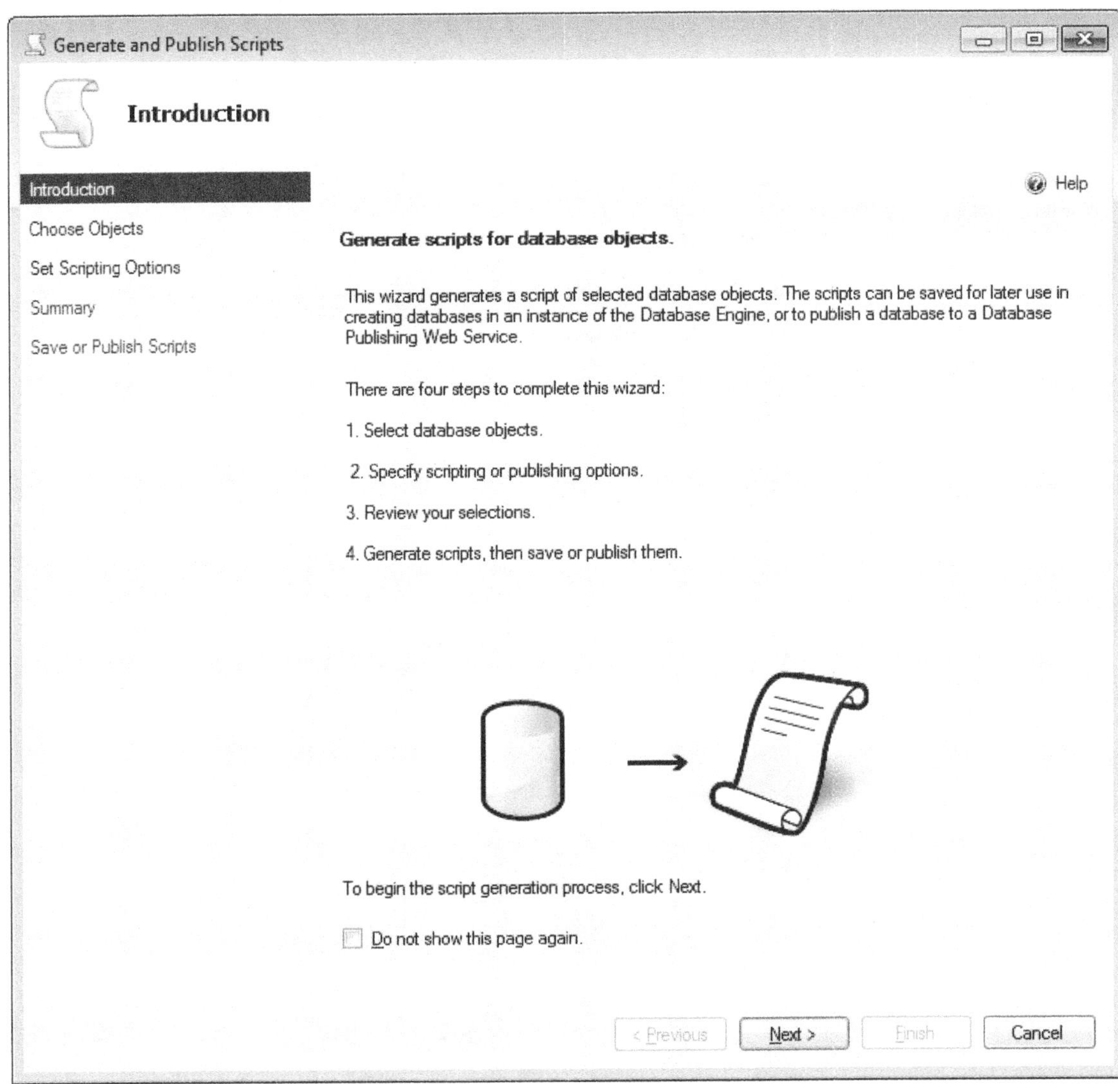

Object Selection Panel For Scripting

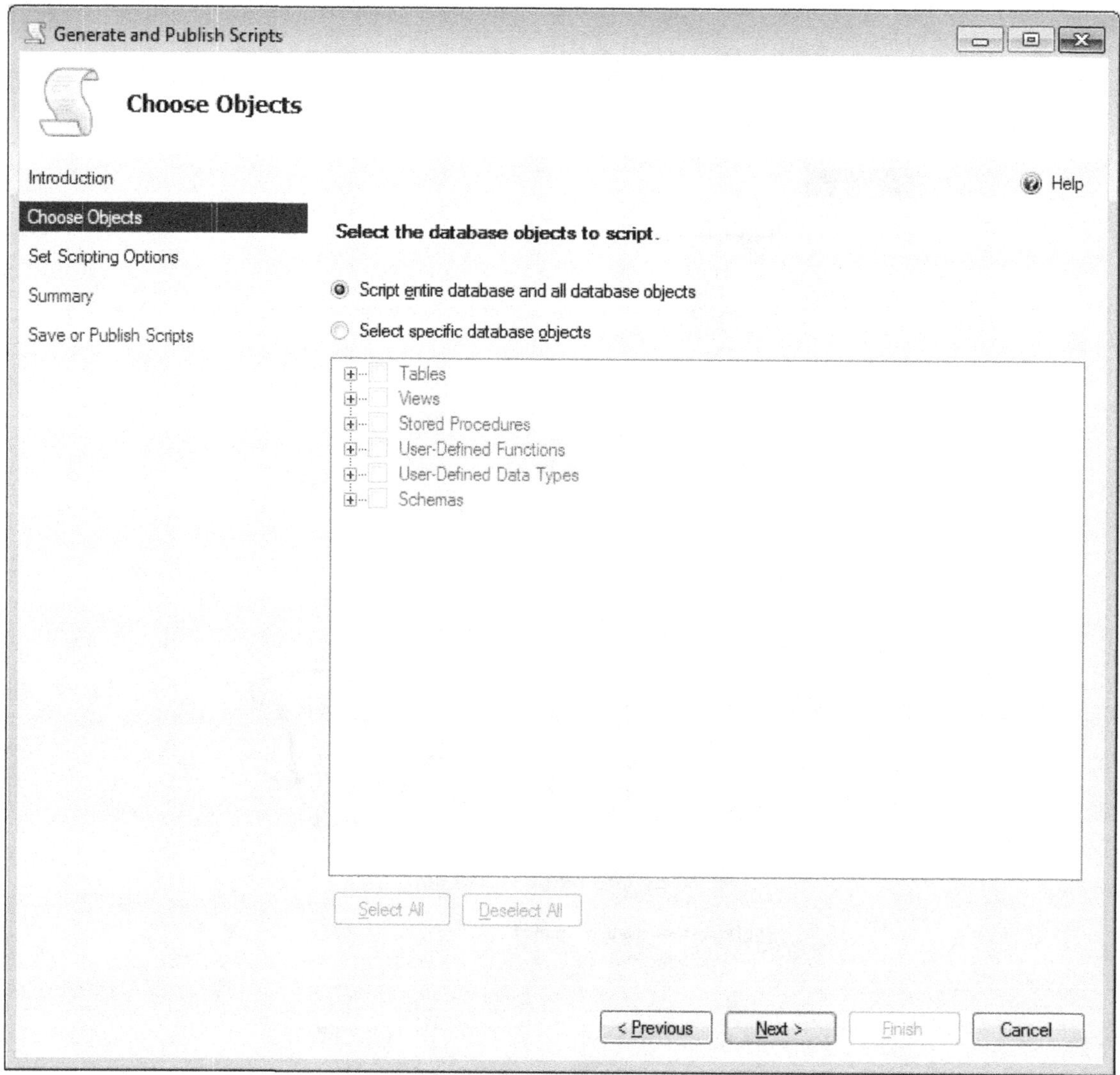

Choosing a Table for Scripting

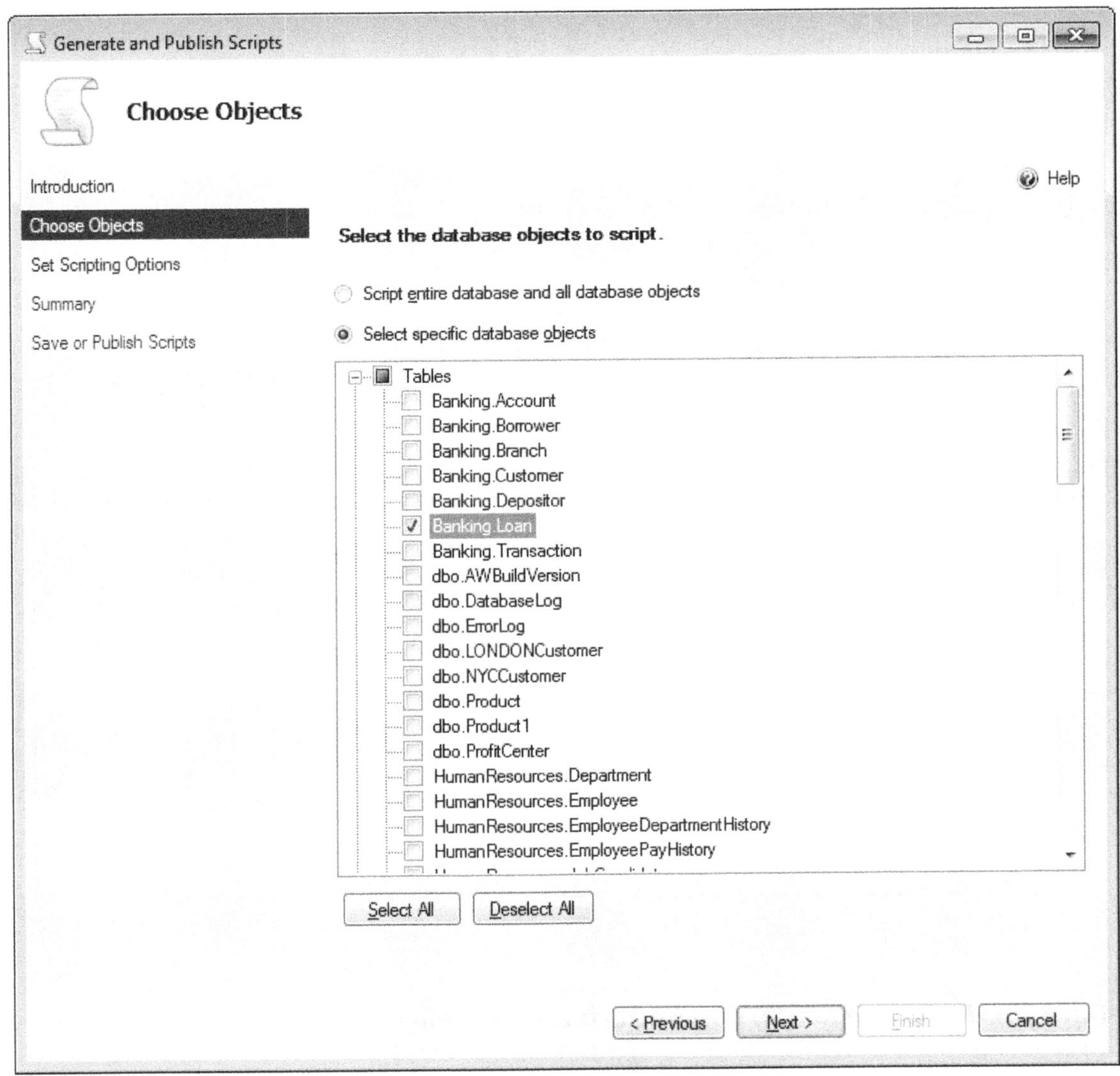

Advance Scripting Options

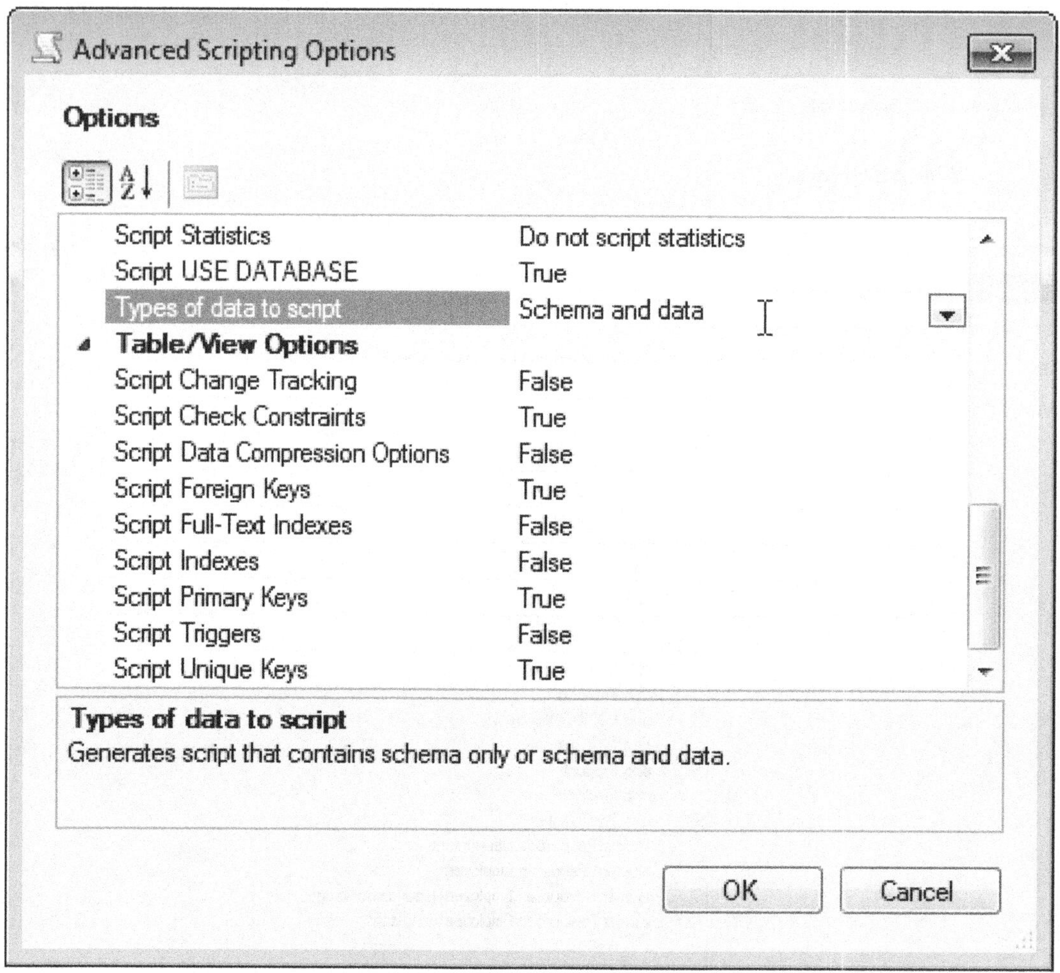

Data (INSERT Statements) Can Be Scripted As Well

Data only
Schema and data
Schema only

A number of options can be set for generation, including scripting of related objects.

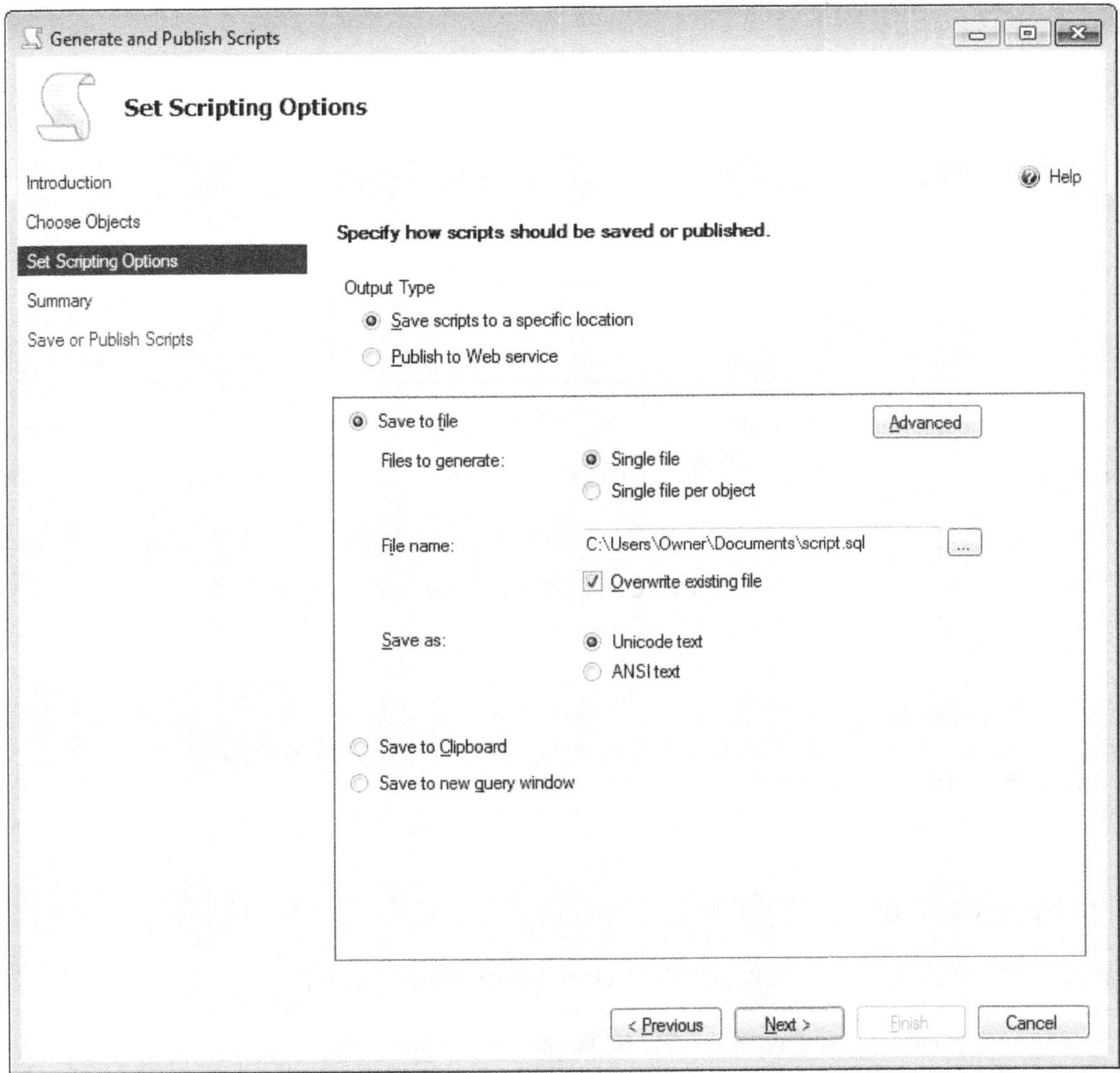

The script generated by the Script Wizard for the Banking.Loan table and related objects

```
USE [AdventureWorks2012]
GO
/****** Object:  Table [Banking].[Loan]    Script Date: 2/1/2016 7:55:28 AM ******/
SET ANSI_NULLS ON
GO
SET QUOTED_IDENTIFIER ON
GO
SET ANSI_PADDING ON
GO

CREATE TABLE [Banking].[Loan](
	[LoanID] [int] IDENTITY(1,1) NOT NULL,
	[BranchID] [int] NOT NULL,
	[LoanNumber] [char](20) NOT NULL,
	[LoanType] [varchar](30) NOT NULL,
	[Amount] [money] NOT NULL,
	[ModifiedDate] [datetime] NULL,
PRIMARY KEY CLUSTERED
(
	[LoanID] ASC
)WITH (PAD_INDEX = OFF, STATISTICS_NORECOMPUTE = OFF, IGNORE_DUP_KEY = OFF,
ALLOW_ROW_LOCKS = ON, ALLOW_PAGE_LOCKS = ON),
UNIQUE NONCLUSTERED
(
	[LoanNumber] ASC
)WITH (PAD_INDEX = OFF, STATISTICS_NORECOMPUTE = OFF, IGNORE_DUP_KEY = OFF,
ALLOW_ROW_LOCKS = ON, ALLOW_PAGE_LOCKS = ON)
)

GO
SET ANSI_PADDING OFF
GO
ALTER TABLE [Banking].[Loan] ADD  DEFAULT (getdate()) FOR [ModifiedDate]
GO
ALTER TABLE [Banking].[Loan]  WITH CHECK ADD FOREIGN KEY([BranchID])
REFERENCES [Banking].[Branch] ([BranchID])
ON DELETE CASCADE
GO
```

SEQUENCE Objects - On-Premises SS 2012

Sequence objects are new in SQL Server 2012. They are similar to the INT IDENTITY(1,1) sequence, however, there is a big difference: they don't "live" inside a table. They are table independent database objects. T-SQL demonstration script displays the flexibility of the new method for sequence number management.

```
-- Create a sequence object similar to INT IDENTITY(1,1)
CREATE SEQUENCE seqPurchaseOrder
AS INT
START WITH 1   INCREMENT BY 1;
GO
```

```
SELECT NEXT VALUE FOR seqPurchaseOrder;
GO 50
/* 1 2 3 .... 50 */
```

```
SELECT NEXT VALUE FOR seqPurchaseOrder;
GO
-- 51
```

```
SELECT NextOrderNo = NEXT VALUE FOR seqPurchaseOrder;
-- 52
```

```
SELECT NEXT VALUE FOR seqPurchaseOrder as NextOrderNo;
-- 54
```

```
EXEC sp_help seqPurchaseOrder;
```

Name	Owner	Type	Created_datetime
seqPurchaseOrder	dbo	sequence object	2016-06-27 09:14:32.940

```
DECLARE @List TABLE (id int identity(1,1) primary key, i int);
INSERT @List(i) SELECT NEXT VALUE FOR seqPurchaseOrder;
INSERT @List(i) SELECT NEXT VALUE FOR seqPurchaseOrder;
INSERT @List(i) SELECT NEXT VALUE FOR seqPurchaseOrder;
INSERT @List(i) SELECT NEXT VALUE FOR seqPurchaseOrder;
INSERT @List(i) VALUES (NEXT VALUE FOR seqPurchaseOrder);
SELECT * FROM @List
```

id	i
1	55
2	56
3	57
4	58
5	59

SEQUENCE Object Sharing - OPSS2012

SEQUENCE is visible in other connections/session as well not only now but until it exists.

Create a new connection to test NEXT VALUE for seqPurchaseOrder.

```
-- Check current value
SELECT current_value
FROM sys.sequences
WHERE name = 'seqPurchaseOrder';
-- 58
```

```
-- Check metadata
SELECT name, object_id, schema_name(schema_id) as SchemaName, type
FROM sys.sequences;
```

name	object_id	SchemaName	type
seqPurchaseOrder	1338487847	dbo	SO

```
DECLARE @List TABLE (id int identity(1,1) primary key,
            i int default (NEXT VALUE FOR seqPurchaseOrder));
INSERT @List(i) DEFAULT VALUES;
INSERT @List(i) DEFAULT VALUES;
INSERT @List(i) DEFAULT VALUES;
INSERT @List(i) DEFAULT VALUES;
INSERT @List(i)DEFAULT VALUES;
SELECT * FROM @List
```

id	i
1	59
2	60
3	61
4	62
5	63

```
DROP SEQUENCE seqPurchaseOrder;
GO
```

```
SELECT NEXT VALUE FOR seqPurchaseOrder;
```

/* Error Message: Msg 208, Level 16, State 1, Line 2

Invalid object name 'seqPurchaseOrder'. */

Cyclical Sequence Objects

We can create cyclical sequence objects as well for enumerating cyclical temporal objects such as weekdays or months.

```
CREATE SEQUENCE seqCycleSeven
AS TINYINT
START WITH 1  INCREMENT BY 1  MINVALUE  1   MAXVALUE  7  CYCLE
GO
```

```
CREATE TABLE #Weekdays ( ID INT IDENTITY(1,1) PRIMARY KEY, Weekday nchar(20));
GO
```

```
-- Populate table with days progressing by addition of cycle number to current day
INSERT INTO #Weekdays
SELECT DATENAME(dw, dateadd(dd,NEXT VALUE for seqCycleSeven,CURRENT_TIMESTAMP));
GO 20
```

```
SELECT * FROM #Weekdays ORDER BY ID;
GO
```

ID	Weekday
1	Tuesday
2	Wednesday
3	Thursday
4	Friday
5	Saturday
6	Sunday
7	Monday
8	Tuesday
9	Wednesday
10	Thursday
11	Friday
12	Saturday
13	Sunday
14	Monday
15	Tuesday
16	Wednesday
17	Thursday
18	Friday
19	Saturday
20	Sunday

```
DROP SEQUENCE seqCycleSeven;  DROP TABLE #Weekdays;
```

Getting the Source Code with sp_helptext

The sp_helptext system procedure can be applied to get the source code for some objects, but not all. **Table source code can only be obtained with GUI scripting in Object Explorer.**

```
EXEC sp_helptext 'sp_who'
GO
-- Command(s) completed successfully. - 94 rows - Partial results.
```

```
CREATE PROCEDURE sys.Sp_who --- 1995/11/28 15:48
 @loginame SYSNAME = NULL --or 'active'
AS
  DECLARE @spidlow  INT,
      @spidhigh INT,
      @spid    INT,
      @sid     VARBINARY(85)

  SELECT @spidlow = 0,
      @spidhigh = 32767

  IF ( @loginame IS NOT NULL
     AND Upper(@loginame COLLATE latin1_general_ci_as) = 'ACTIVE' )
   BEGIN
     SELECT spid,
         ecid,
         status,
         loginame=Rtrim(loginame),
         hostname,
         blk=CONVERT(CHAR(5), blocked),
         dbname = CASE
                WHEN dbid = 0 THEN NULL
                WHEN dbid <> 0 THEN Db_name(dbid)
               END,
         cmd,
         request_id
     FROM   sys.sysprocesses_ex
     WHERE  spid >= @spidlow
         AND spid <= @spidhigh
         AND Upper(cmd) <> 'AWAITING COMMAND'

     RETURN ( 0 )
   END
```

CHAPTER 8: Database Normalization

The Goals of Database Normalizaton

Database normalization is the design technique of logically organizing data in a database:

- Data should uniquely be addressable in a database by table, row and column identification - like x, y, z coordinates in 3D space.
- Data redundancy (storing the same data in more than one table) should be avoided.
- Data dependency (a property is fully dependent on the PRIMARY KEY) should ensure that a piece of data gets into the right table or if there is none, a new one is created.

The first goal is relatively easy to achieve yet data duplication in a table is a constant issue plaguing database installations. The second goal is simple as well yet it conflicts with deep-seated human insecurity of not seeing all the data together. The third goal on the other hand requires careful design considerations, it can be challenging for complex data relationships or if the database designer is not familiar with the application. If an OLTP database with many data access points is not normalized, the result is inefficiency in database application development and maintenance which can be quite costly to a company for years to come. Metadata query to list all FOREIGN KEYs in Northwind followed by a high level database diagram.

```
use Northwind;
select     fkschema = fk.constraint_schema,  fktable = fk.table_name, fkcolumn = fk.column_name,
           pkcolumn = pk.column_name,   pktable = pk.table_name, pkschema = pk.table_schema,
           fkname = rc.constraint_name
from  information_schema.referential_constraints rc
           inner join information_schema.key_column_usage fk
                      on fk.constraint_name = rc.constraint_name
           inner join information_schema.key_column_usage pk
                      on pk.constraint_name = rc.unique_constraint_name
where   fk.ordinal_position = pk.ordinal_position
order by fkschema, fktable, fkcolumn;
go
```

fkschema	fktable	fkcolumn	pkcolumn	pktable	pkschema	fkname
dbo	CustomerCustomerDemo	CustomerID	CustomerID	Customers	dbo	FK_CustomerCustomerDemo_Customers
dbo	CustomerCustomerDemo	CustomerTypeID	CustomerTypeID	CustomerDemographics	dbo	FK_CustomerCustomerDemo
dbo	Employees	ReportsTo	EmployeeID	Employees	dbo	FK_Employees_Employees
dbo	EmployeeTerritories	EmployeeID	EmployeeID	Employees	dbo	FK_EmployeeTerritories_Employees
dbo	EmployeeTerritories	TerritoryID	TerritoryID	Territories	dbo	FK_EmployeeTerritories_Territories
dbo	Order Details	OrderID	OrderID	Orders	dbo	FK_Order_Details_Orders
dbo	Order Details	ProductID	ProductID	Products	dbo	FK_Order_Details_Products
dbo	Orders	CustomerID	CustomerID	Customers	dbo	FK_Orders_Customers
dbo	Orders	EmployeeID	EmployeeID	Employees	dbo	FK_Orders_Employees
dbo	Orders	ShipVia	ShipperID	Shippers	dbo	FK_Orders_Shippers
dbo	Products	CategoryID	CategoryID	Categories	dbo	FK_Products_Categories
dbo	Products	SupplierID	SupplierID	Suppliers	dbo	FK_Products_Suppliers
dbo	Territories	RegionID	RegionID	Region	dbo	FK_Territories_Region

Orders & Related Tables Diagram in Northwind

The database diagram clearly shows the central role of the Orders table at a company which is a reseller not a manufacturer. SQL Server 2012 feature.

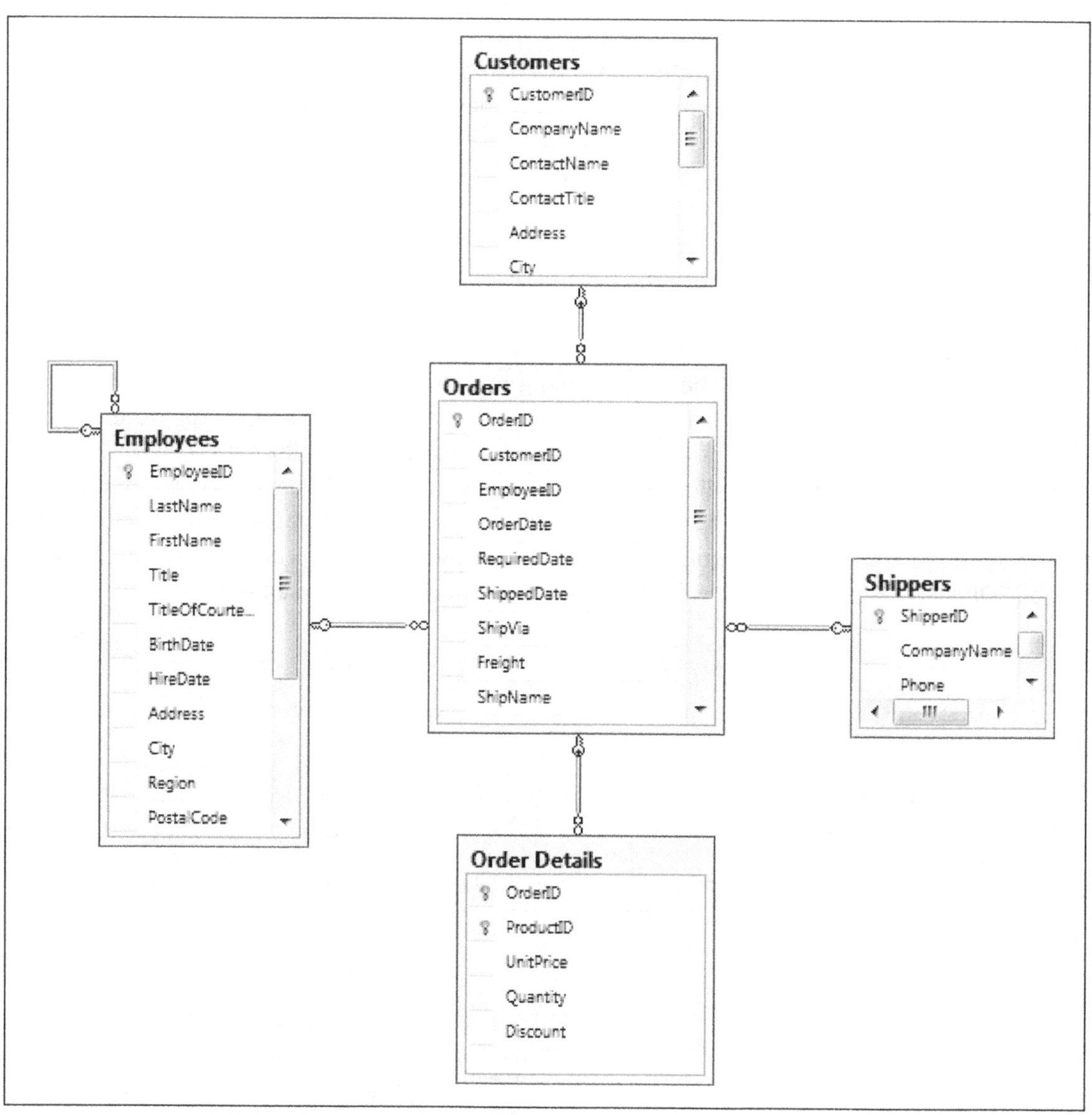

First Normal Form (1NF)

The first normal form establishes RDBMS basics. The rules make common sense.

- Each group of related data (entity) should have its own table (no piggybacking data).
- Each column should be identified with a unique name in a table.
- Each row should be identified with a unique column or set of columns (PRIMARY KEY).

Selected tables (entities) in Northwind database.

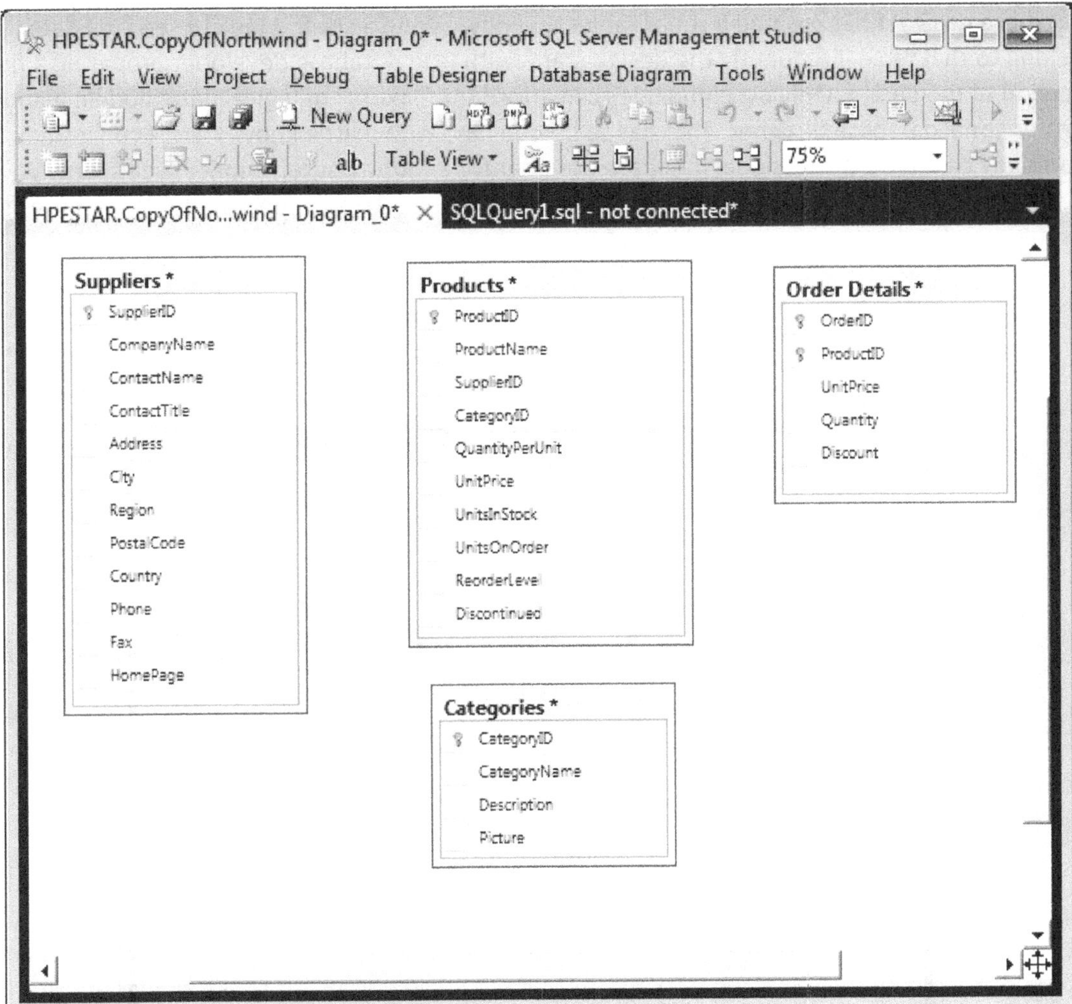

Second Normal Form (2NF)

The Second Normal Form addresses the issue of piggybacking data on a related table.

- Tables are in First Normal Form.
- Remove subsets of data that apply to multiple rows of a table and create a separate table for them.
- Create relationships between these new tables and their predecessors through the use of FOREIGN KEYs.

The tacit assumption here that there was no logical data modeling or that had a mistake. The database designer has created a set of tables and now taking a second look to see if all data belong to that table. Frequently the design starts with lead database developer preparing a first version of the design. Only big companies can afford the "luxury" of logical data modeling and professional database designer. That has to be qualified with a little known fact. Even a small company can hire a professional database designer for a month, surely money well spent. Categories table can easily piggyback on the Products table. Being a separate table increases the usefulness, flexibility and expandability of the design.

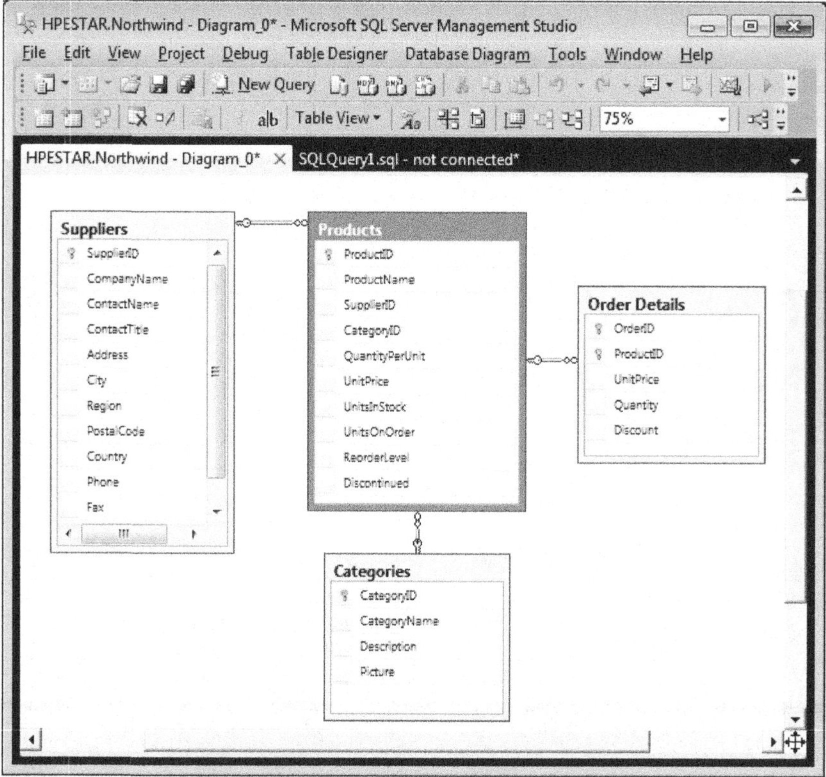

Third Normal Form (3NF)

The Third Normal Form addresses the issue of storing the data in the appropriate table.

- Tables are in Second Normal Form.
- Remove columns that are not dependent upon the PRIMARY KEY and move them to the correct table.

The royalty and ytd_sales columns are not fully dependent on the title_id PRIMARY KEY. In fact royalty schedule is specified in the roysched table and the dependency includes quantity sold. A view (virtual table) can be setup to return the current royalties based on books sold and the royalty schedule. A more appropriate table for ytd_sales would be saleshist (SalesHistory). The inclusion of the time dependent dynamic ytd_sales column is suspicious right off the bat since all the other columns are static.

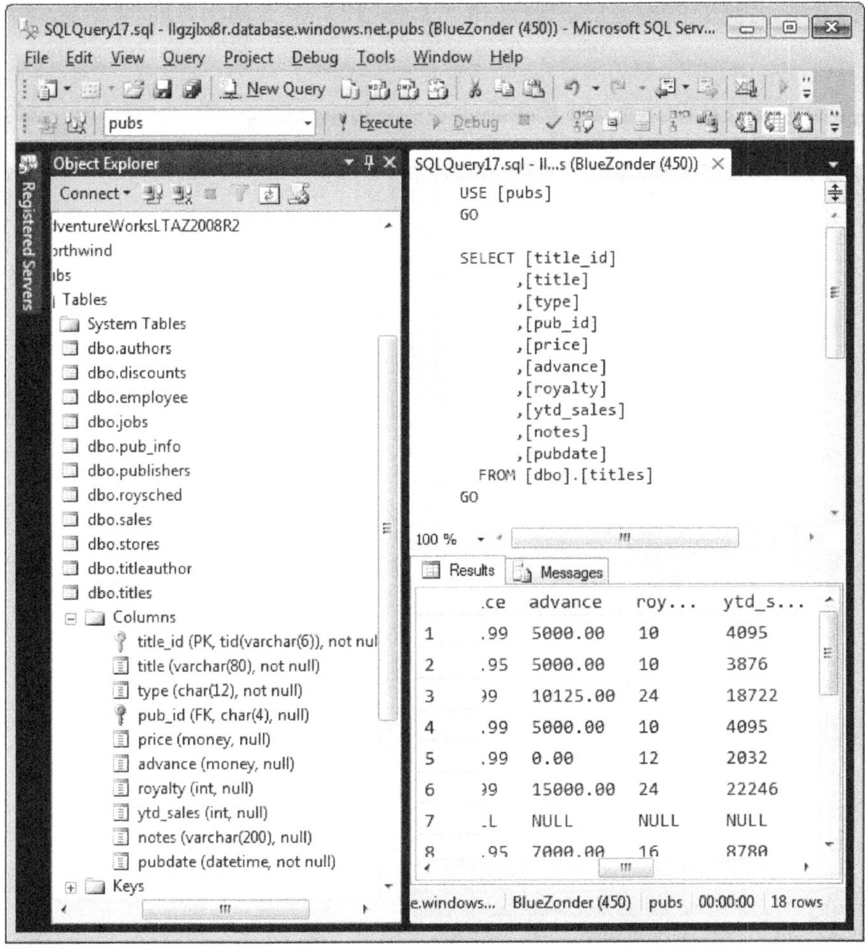

Fourth Normal Form (4NF)

The Fourth Normal Form addresses the issue of subtle data dependency:

- Tables are in Third Normal Form.
- A relation should not have multi-valued dependencies.

If we look at "Road-650 Black, 44" and "Road-650 Red, 44" bikes in Production.Product we see that they are the same bike with different color. So it would be sufficient to store only a single row "Road-650, 44" and setup a junction table between the Product table and the (new) Color table to indicate the color variations and other dependent information. We can see that the color occurs in 3 columns: Name, ProductNumber (first letter of color) and Color. By doing 4NF normalization we can remove the color reference from the Name and ProductNumber columns.

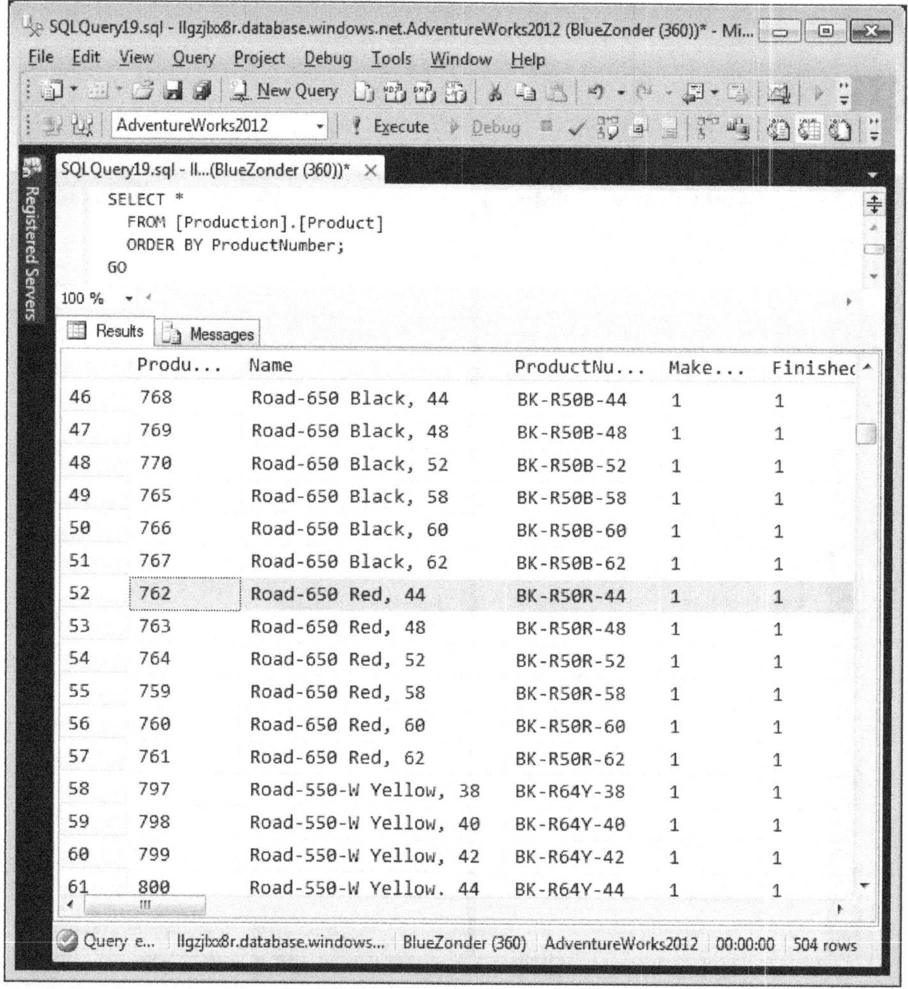

Database Denormalizaton

Logging, history, audit, auxiliary, and data warehouse tables need not be normalized. OLTP database denormalization is a technique to reduce the number of tables in a normalized OLTP database. The author personally disagrees with this process: why would you go into the trouble and expense of creating a normalized database and then ruin it? Regardless of the author's opinion, denormalization is an accepted notion in the database industry. Too many tables require too many JOINs, that is the underlying justification. The trouble with this process is two-fold:

- There is no guideline when to stop with denormalization, 10% table reduction, 50%?
- Also, there are no guidelines as to which tables to eliminate when denormalizing.

If you eliminate too many tables you may just end up with a messy database instead of the original neat & efficient 3NF database thus creating a potential disaster for your employer. Typically you would look at the small static tables as candidates for elimination which are not FOREIGN KEY referenced from many tables. There are precise guidelines how to achieve a normalized database. It is a scientific process. Denormalization is not. Performance is another reason mentioned for denormalization, but that is generally not a valid claim. There are much better ways to achieve good performance than denormalizing a well-designed database system. Hypothetically, let's take a look at low population tables in AdventureWorks2012, as candidates for denormalization.

```
SELECT TOP(10) * FROM (SELECT distinct concat(schema_name(schema_id),'.',name) as TableName,
                                    row_count as Rows
FROM sys.dm_db_partition_stats ps inner join sys.objects o on ps.object_id = o.object_id ) X ORDER BY Rows ASC;
```

TableName	Rows
Person.PhoneNumberType	3
HumanResources.Shift	3
Sales.ShoppingCartItem	3
Production.ProductCategory	4
Production.ProductReview	4
Production.Illustration	5
Purchasing.ShipMethod	5
Person.AddressType	6

Tables like PhoneNumberType, Shift, Shipmethod and SalesReason can likely be eliminated without dire consequences. However, why ruin a well-designed 3NF database such as AdventureWorks2012 just to decrease the number of JOINs with one or two? Is it annoying to have 10 JOINs in a query? Not really. That is how SQL works. Is SQL Server going to be much faster with 8 JOINs as opposed to 10 JOINs? No, there is no such a rule in query optimization.

Technet Article: **Optimizing the Database Design by Denormalizing**
http://technet.microsoft.com/en-us/library/cc505841.aspx

Better Alternative to Denormalization

The best alternative is to use views for frequently used queries to avoid building JOINs again and again. The results of SELECT from a view must be sorted with ORDER BY just like the case for tables. There is no way around it. Demonstration of the powerful method.

```
USE AdventureWorks;
SELECT
        V.Name                                  AS Vendor,
        CONCAT(C.LastName, ', ', C.FirstName)   AS Contact,
        CT.Name                                 AS Title
FROM Person.Contact AS C
  INNER JOIN Purchasing.VendorContact VC
        ON C.ContactID = VC.ContactID
  INNER JOIN Person.ContactType CT
        ON CT.ContactTypeID = VC.ContactTypeID
  INNER JOIN Purchasing.Vendor V
        ON V.VendorID = VC.VendorID
ORDER BY Vendor, Contact;  -- (156 row(s) affected)
GO
```

```
CREATE VIEW vVendorContact
AS
SELECT
        V.Name                                  AS Vendor,
        CONCAT(C.LastName, ', ', C.FirstName)   AS Contact,
        CT.Name                                 AS Title
FROM Person.Contact AS C
  INNER JOIN Purchasing.VendorContact VC    ON C.ContactID = VC.ContactID
  INNER JOIN Person.ContactType CT          ON CT.ContactTypeID = VC.ContactTypeID
  INNER JOIN Purchasing.Vendor V            ON V.VendorID = VC.VendorID
GO
```

```
SELECT TOP 5 * FROM vVendorContact ORDER BY Vendor, Contact;
```

Vendor	Contact	Title
A. Datum Corporation	Pellow, Frank	Assistant Sales Agent
A. Datum Corporation	Wilkie, Jay	Sales Agent
A. Datum Corporation	Yu, Wei	Sales Manager
Advanced Bicycles	Moeller, Jonathan	Sales Associate
Advanced Bicycles	Wilson, James	Sales Manager

We have created from the 4 tables JOIN, a very simple to use, very easy to remember view.

Ten Most Common Database Design Mistakes

Along his database career the author found the following list of common design issues:

- Not involving systems analysts and/or subject matter experts in conceptual design.
- Not employing accomplished database designer / lead developer to implement 3NF design standards.
- Oversizing columns; Missing /wrong indexes.
- Not having NATURAL KEY (UNIQUE KEY) in addition to INT IDENTITY SURROGATE PRIMARY KEY.
- Poor documentation & lack of naming convention for the project.
- Not using PRIMARY KEY, FOREIGN KEY, UNIQUE , CHECK & DEFAULT constraints to protect data integrity.
- Using client programs for data management instead of **server side** stored procedures, functions & views.
- Using triggers to fix design or client software problems.
- Not following the solution implementation hierarchy: constraints > stored procedures > triggers > client SW.
- Lack of formal Quality Assurance process.

Working for a Company with Messy Database Design

In your career you may work for companies with proper 3NF design databases, companies with messy databases or somewhere in the middle. It is a joy to work in 3NF environment. On the other hand, if the database is badly designed, or more accurately lacks design, you have to be careful in criticizing it because you can pick up enemies quickly or even get fired. Badly designed database usually becomes an IT department political issue instead of remaining a technical issue. Most companies don't want to invest in redesigning the database properly. In such a situation you have to accept working with poorly designed databases, enjoy your nice paycheck and wait for an opportunity when new tables or database is needed to create proper 3NF design.

Query to List All Table Sizes in a Database

T-SQL script to list all table sizes in AdventureWorks2012 database. Note: the tables are uniquely named in AdventureWorks databases, so there are no duplicates if the schema name is not used. This assumption though not true generally. Objects can be named the same in different schemas. SQL Server 2012 query.

```
declare @TableSpace table (TableName sysname, RowsK varchar(32), -- table variable
          ReservedMB varchar(32), DataMB varchar(32),
           IndexMB varchar(32), UnusedMB varchar(32));

insert @TableSpace
exec sp_MSforeachtable @command1="exec sp_spaceused '?';"  -- undocumented system procedure

update @TableSpace set RowsK = CONVERT(varchar,  1+convert(int, RowsK)/1024)
update @TableSpace set ReservedMB = CONVERT(varchar,
                    1+convert(int,LEFT(ReservedMB, charindex(' K', ReservedMB,-1)))/1024);
update @TableSpace set DataMB = CONVERT(varchar,
                    1+convert(int,LEFT(DataMB, charindex(' K', DataMB,-1)))/1024);
update @TableSpace set IndexMB = CONVERT(varchar,
                    convert(int,LEFT(IndexMB, charindex(' K', IndexMB,-1)))/1024);
update @TableSpace set UnusedMB = CONVERT(varchar,
                    convert(int,LEFT(UnusedMB, charindex(' K', UnusedMB,-1)))/1024);

select * from @TableSpace order by convert(int,DataMB) desc;
go
-- (71 row(s) affected) -- Partial results.
```

TableName	RowsK	ReservedMB	DataMB	IndexMB	UnusedMB
Person	20	84	30	51	2
SalesOrderDetail	119	18	10	6	1
DatabaseLog	2	7	7	0	0
TransactionHistory	111	11	7	3	0
WorkOrderRouting	66	8	6	1	0
SalesOrderHeader	31	9	6	2	0
WorkOrder	71	7	5	2	0
TransactionHistoryArchive	88	9	5	3	0
ProductPhoto	1	3	3	0	0
Address	20	6	3	2	0
CreditCard	19	3	2	0	0
EmailAddress	20	4	2	1	0
Password	20	2	2	0	0
PersonPhone	20	3	2	0	0
SalesTerritory	1	1	1	0	0
PhoneNumberType	1	1	1	0	0
Product	1	1	1	0	0
SalesTerritoryHistory	1	1	1	0	0
SalesPersonQuotaHistory	1	1	1	0	0
Employee	1	1	1	0	0

CHAPTER 9: Functional Database Design

Types of Table Relationships

The most frequent relationship is one-to-many (or many-to-one) indicating many FOREIGN KEY references to a single PRIMARY KEY table row. Example: Products & ProductCategories; A product category may have 50 different products. The next most popular one is many-to-many relationship indicating that a single row in Table Alpha can reference multiple rows in Table Beta. Example: Classes & Students at a college; A class may have 20 students and a student may take 5 different classes. In the following pubs table relationship diagram we can see:

- many-to-many relationship (oo - oo connectors): titleauthor table
- one-to-one relationship (2 gold keys): publishers & pub_info tables
- one-to-many: the remaining relationships

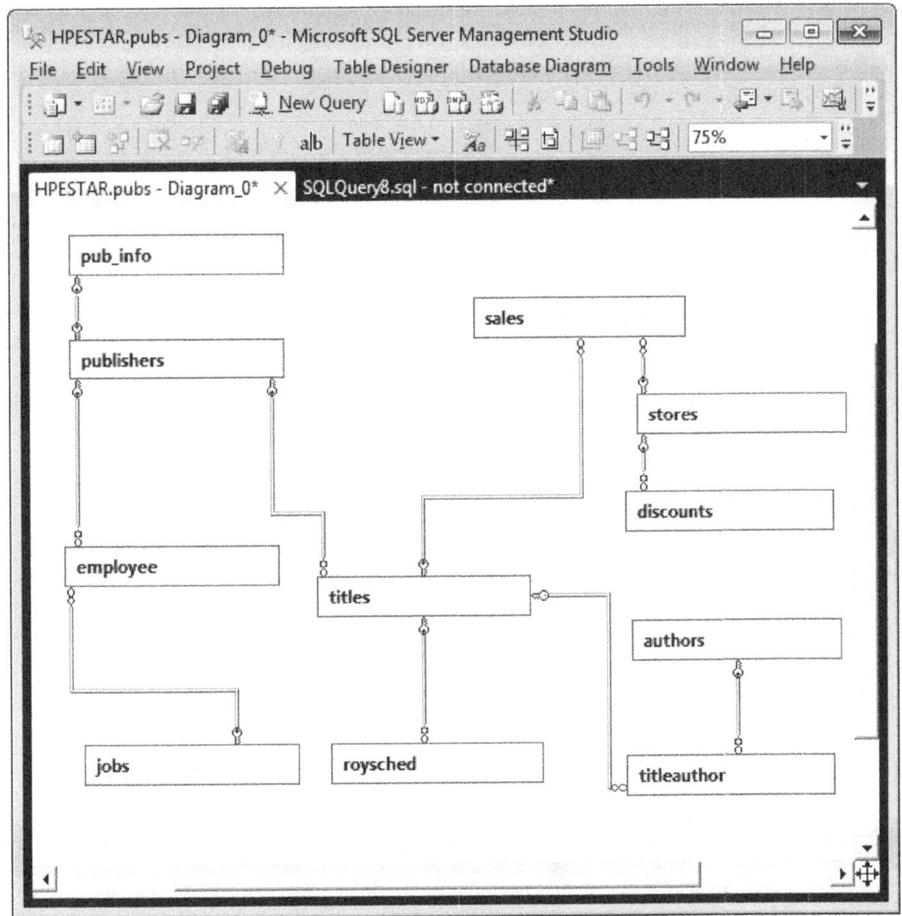

One-To-Many Relationship - FOREIGN KEY Reference

Northwind example shows that each product belongs to a category. CategoryID column in the Products table (FOREIGN KEY) references CategoryID in Categories table (PRIMARY KEY). One category can have 0 to many products. FK name can be different from PK name. However, if possible, PK name is the best choice for FK name. When multiple FK-s referencing the same PK, we have to choose different names for FK-s.

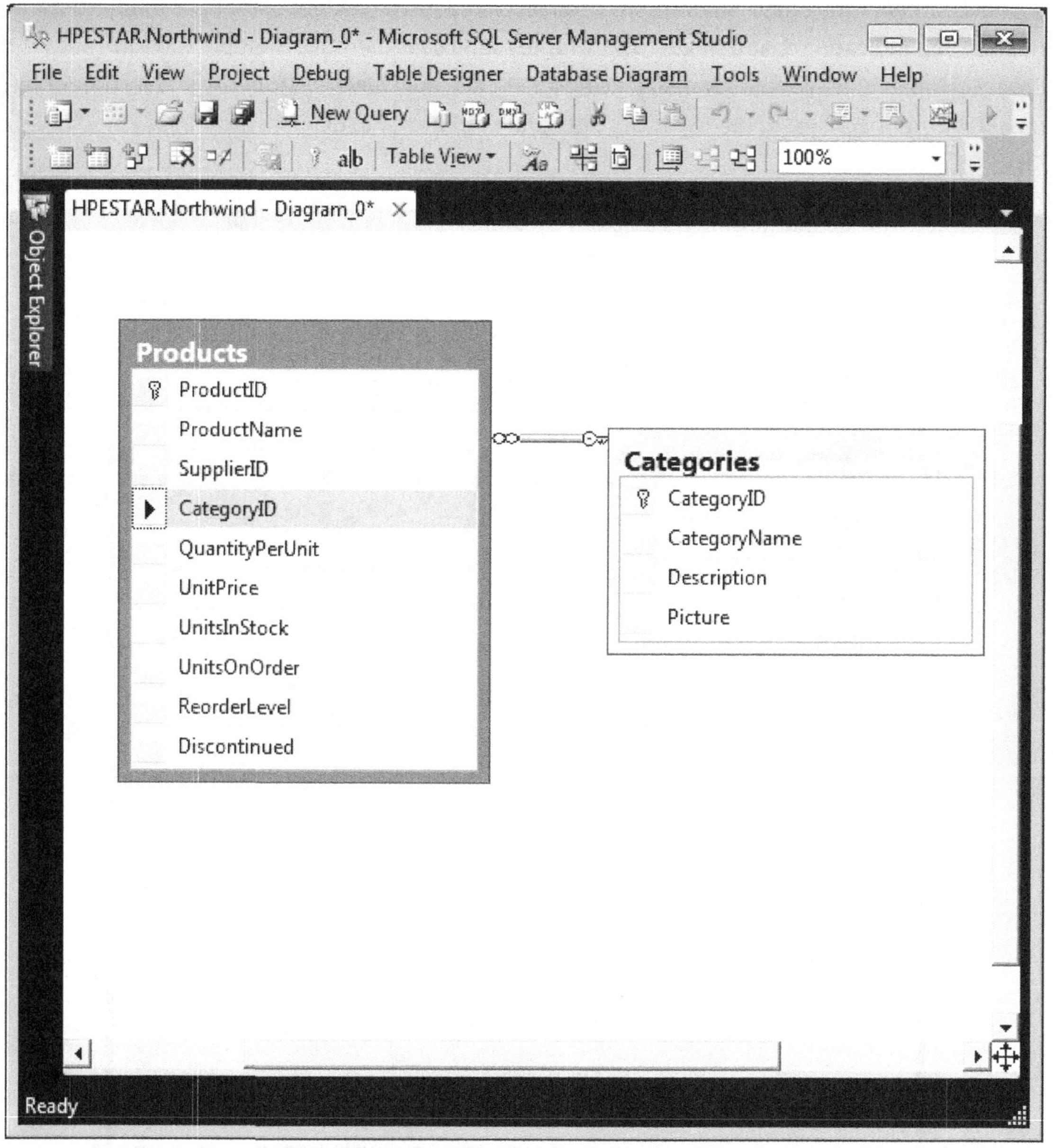

CategoryID in the Products table is a FOREIGN KEY (a pointer) to a PRIMARY KEY in the Categories table

Therefore, we can safely JOIN the two tables using the two ON KEYs.

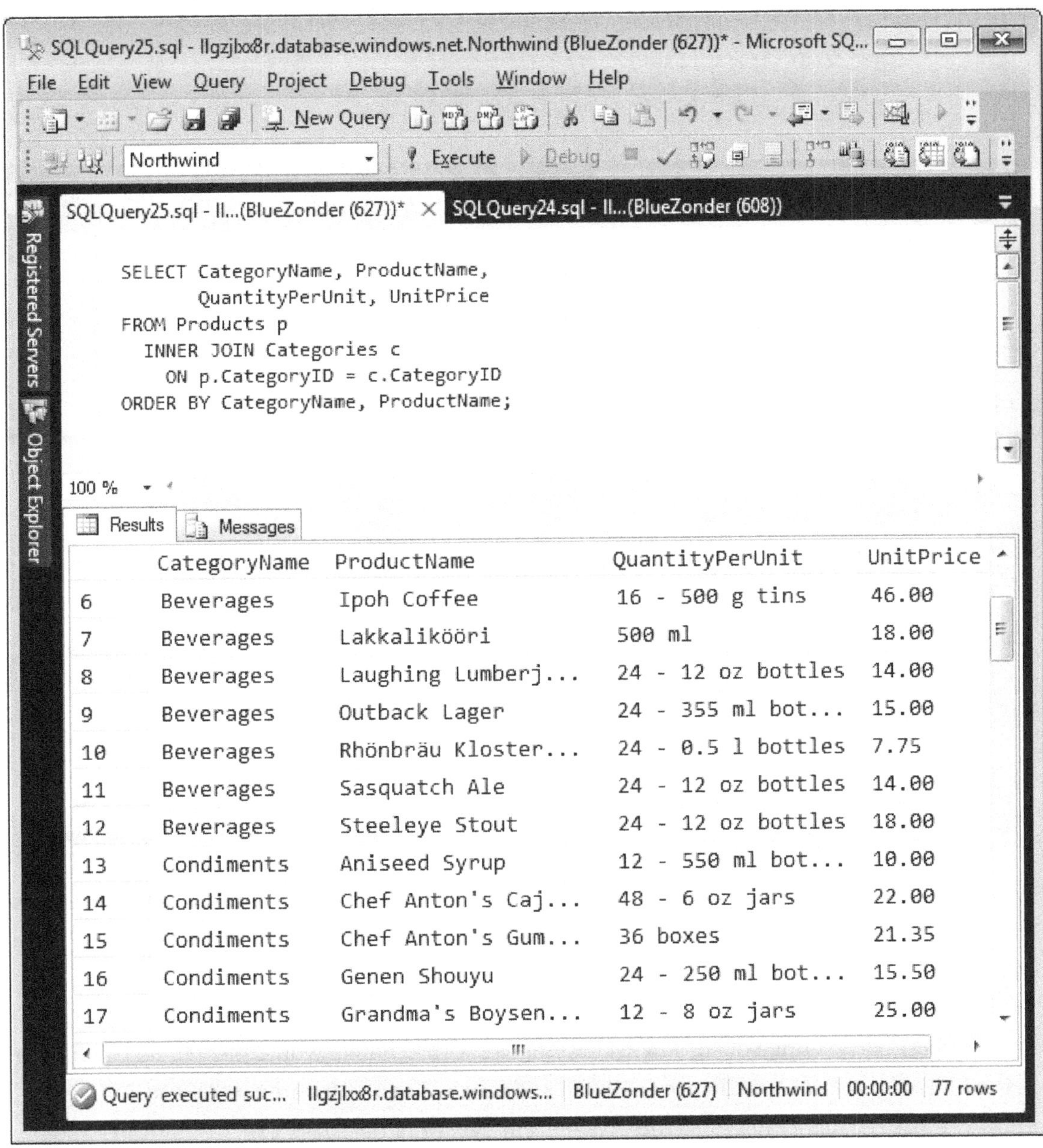

	CategoryName	ProductName	QuantityPerUnit	UnitPrice
6	Beverages	Ipoh Coffee	16 - 500 g tins	46.00
7	Beverages	Lakkalikööri	500 ml	18.00
8	Beverages	Laughing Lumberj...	24 - 12 oz bottles	14.00
9	Beverages	Outback Lager	24 - 355 ml bot...	15.00
10	Beverages	Rhönbräu Kloster...	24 - 0.5 l bottles	7.75
11	Beverages	Sasquatch Ale	24 - 12 oz bottles	14.00
12	Beverages	Steeleye Stout	24 - 12 oz bottles	18.00
13	Condiments	Aniseed Syrup	12 - 550 ml bot...	10.00
14	Condiments	Chef Anton's Caj...	48 - 6 oz jars	22.00
15	Condiments	Chef Anton's Gum...	36 boxes	21.35
16	Condiments	Genen Shouyu	24 - 250 ml bot...	15.50
17	Condiments	Grandma's Boysen...	12 - 8 oz jars	25.00

The PRIMARY KEY and FOREIGN KEY should not be exposed to the database application user

The Business Intelligence consumer needs meaningful information not meaningless numbers. The software engineer can see the PK and FK values as part of his work.

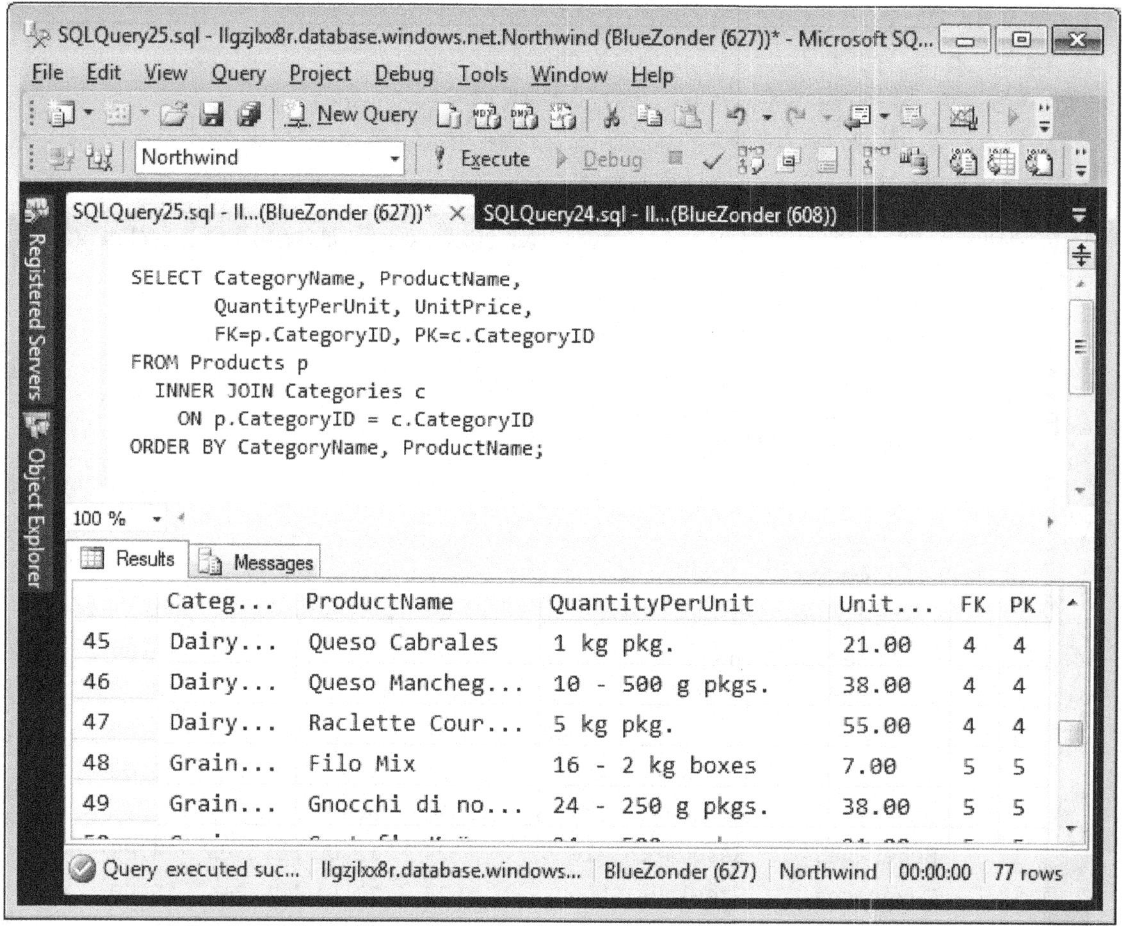

```
SELECT CategoryName, ProductName,
       QuantityPerUnit, UnitPrice,
       FK=p.CategoryID, PK=c.CategoryID
FROM Products p
  INNER JOIN Categories c
    ON p.CategoryID = c.CategoryID
ORDER BY CategoryName, ProductName;
```

	Categ...	ProductName	QuantityPerUnit	Unit...	FK	PK
45	Dairy...	Queso Cabrales	1 kg pkg.	21.00	4	4
46	Dairy...	Queso Mancheg...	10 - 500 g pkgs.	38.00	4	4
47	Dairy...	Raclette Cour...	5 kg pkg.	55.00	4	4
48	Grain...	Filo Mix	16 - 2 kg boxes	7.00	5	5
49	Grain...	Gnocchi di no...	24 - 250 g pkgs.	38.00	5	5

We could make the NATURAL KEY ProductName a PRIMARY KEY in the Products table. However, that is a string field (column) nvarchar(40) which can be 80 bytes in size (each UNICODE character is 2 bytes). That would present increased space use and decreased performance in JOINs. It would also present increased maintenance cost if we have to change a product name, for example, "Ravioli Angelo" to "Ravioli Los Angeles". The change would have to be performed in the PRIMARY KEY table and each FOREIGN KEY table. The 4-byte integer SURROGATE PRIMARY KEY ProductID solves all the problems above. Minimal space use, fast in JOINs and since a meaningless number (a database pointer), we never have to change it. If the ProductName changes, it is just a single UPDATE in the PRIMARY KEY table.

Composite PRIMARY KEY

A composite PRIMARY KEY consists of two or more columns. Junction tables typically apply composite PRIMARY KEYs. An example is the Production.ProductProductPhoto junction table.

> ProductID (PK, FK, int, not null)
> ProductPhotoID (PK, FK, int, not null)
> Primary (Flag(bit), not null)
> ModifiedDate (datetime, not null

The PRIMARY KEY is the composite of two FOREIGN KEYs: ProductID and ProductPhotoID.

T-SQL script definition of the above composite PRIMARY KEY.

```
USE [AdventureWorks2012];
GO

ALTER TABLE [Production].[ProductProductPhoto]
ADD  CONSTRAINT [PK_ProductProductPhoto_ProductID_ProductPhotoID]
PRIMARY KEY NONCLUSTERED
(
        [ProductID] ASC,
        [ProductPhotoID] ASC
);
```

A FOREIGN KEY referencing a composite PRIMARY KEY must have the same column structure. Query to display all the data in the table.

```
SELECT  ProductID
        ,ProductPhotoID
        ,[Primary]
        ,ModifiedDate
 FROM Production.ProductProductPhoto;
-- (504 row(s) affected) - Partial results.
```

ProductID	ProductPhotoID	Primary	ModifiedDate
813	1	1	2006-06-01 00:00:00.000
814	1	1	2006-06-01 00:00:00.000
815	160	1	2006-06-01 00:00:00.000
816	160	1	2006-06-01 00:00:00.000
817	160	1	2006-06-01 00:00:00.000
818	160	1	2006-06-01 00:00:00.000

> NOTE
> Use composite UNIQUE KEY and INT SURROGATE PRIMARY KEY in base tables.
> Composite PRIMARY KEY requires composite FOREIGN KEY!

Parent-Child Hierarchy

When an employee's record includes the manager's ID, it is called self-reference since the manager is an employee also. A simple organizational chart (tree structure) can be established by self-referencing FOREIGN KEYs.

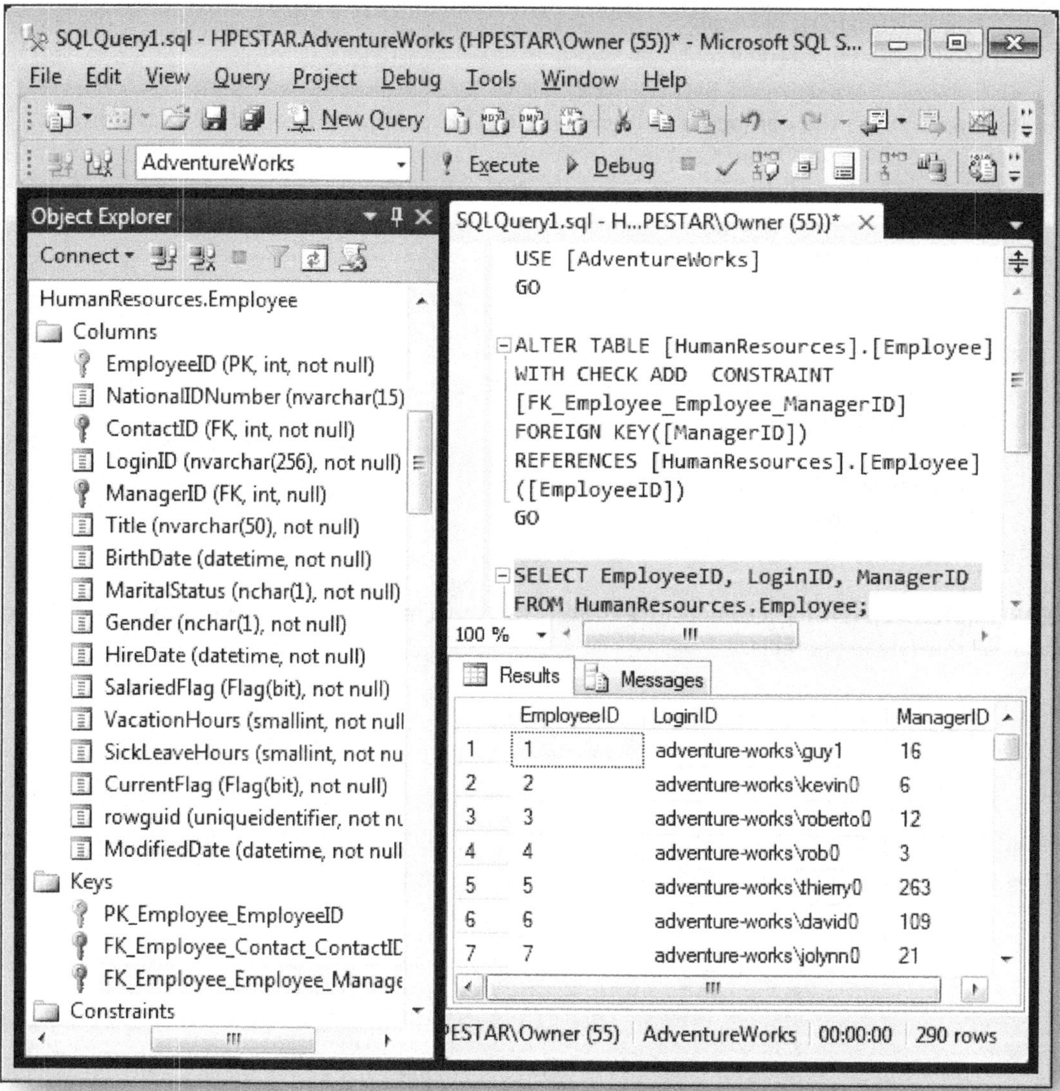

Reading the table: david0 is the supervisor of kevin0, and roberto0 is the supervisor of rob0.

Hierarchical Relationship - Multi-Level with FOREIGN KEYs

Product, ProductSubcategory and ProductCategory in AdventureWorks represent multi-level hierarchy which can be implemented with FOREIGN KEYs. To get the hierarchical information, we need to INNER JOIN the tables on the FOREIGN KEYS and PRIMARY KEYS. Column aliases are used to create meaningful column names from the 3 "Name"-s.

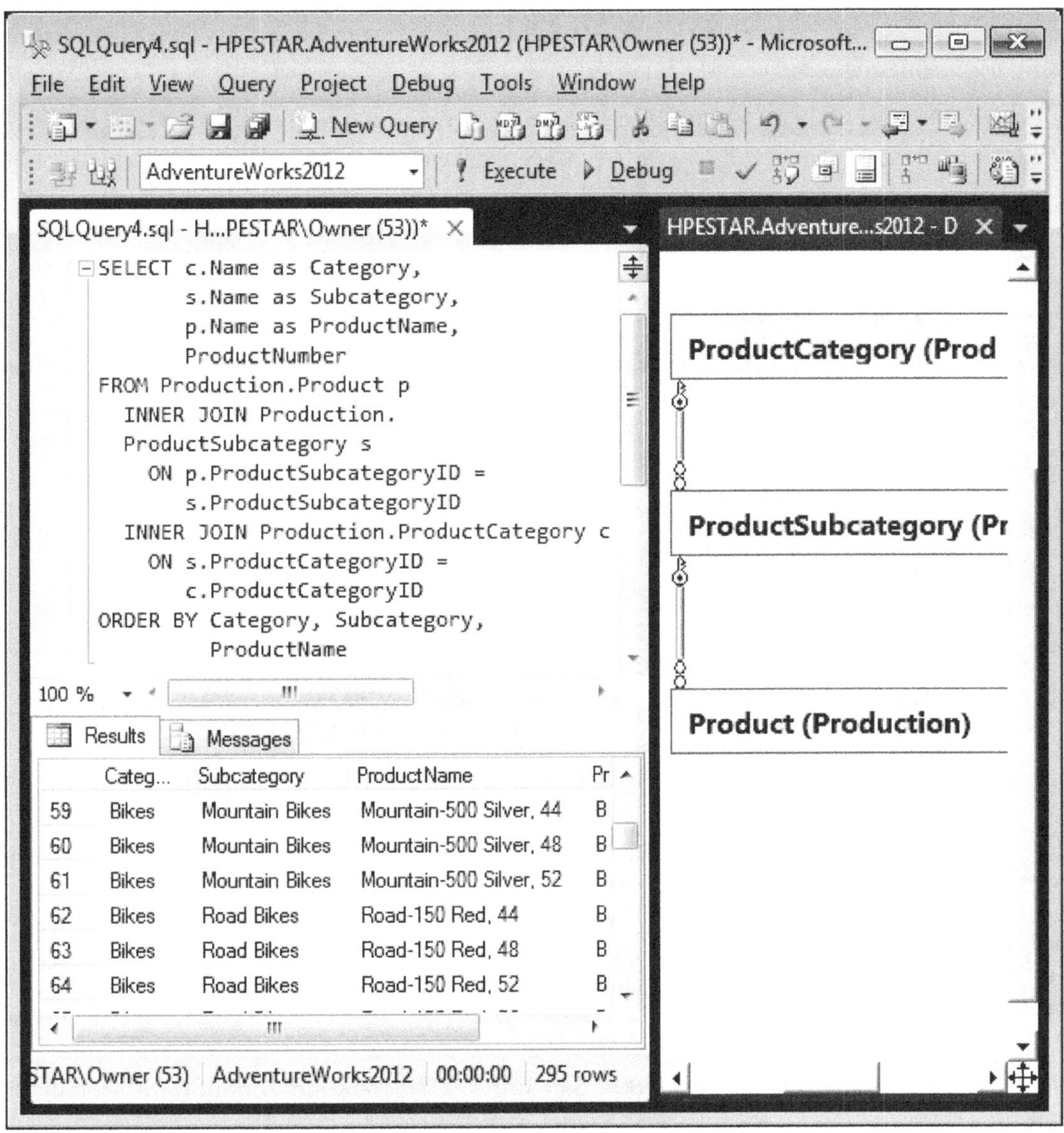

Tree Hierarchy Representation with hierarchyid

An alternate to using self-referencing FOREIGN KEY is the application of hierarchyid data type introduced with SQL Server 2008.

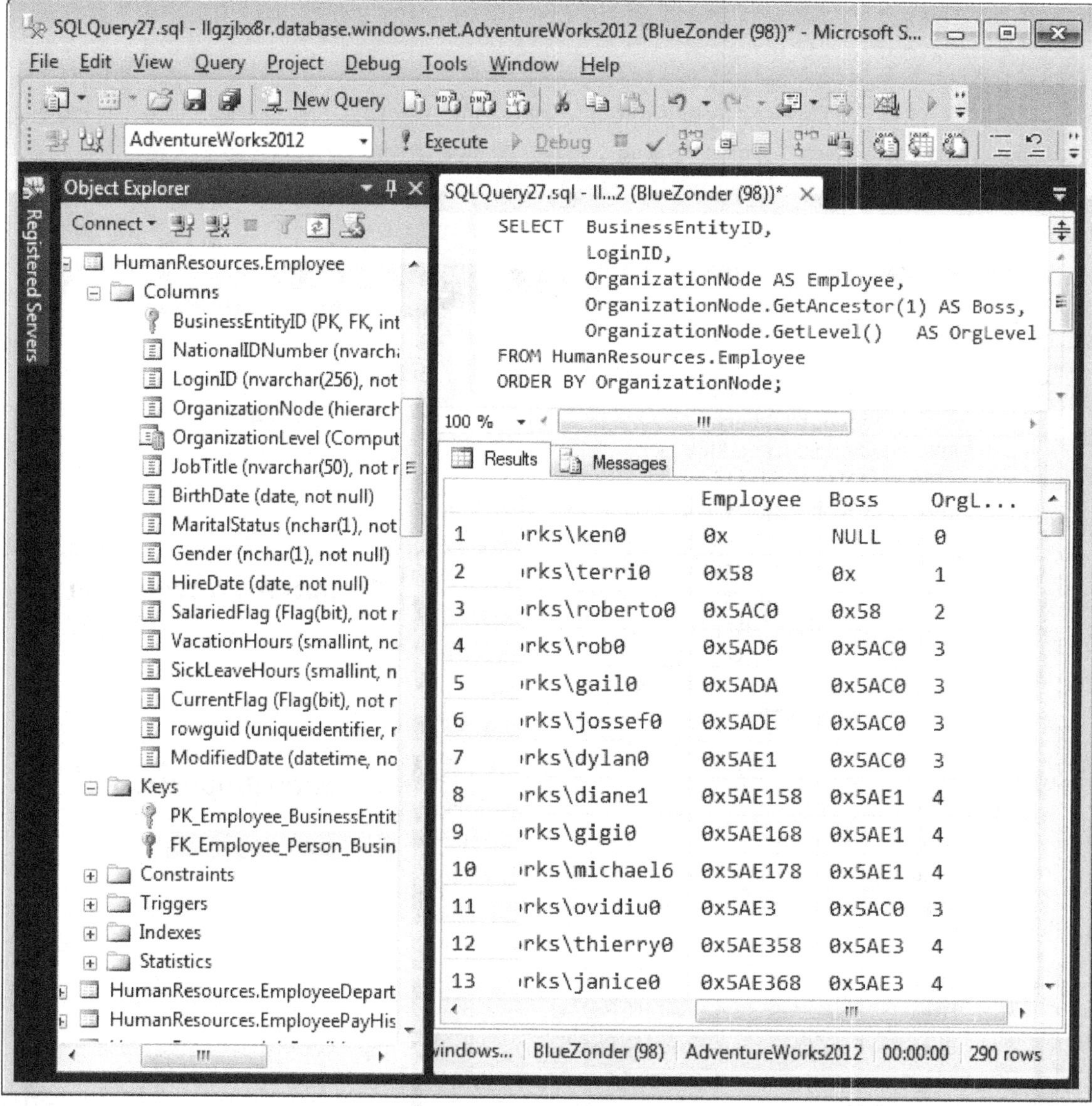

We can read from the table that ken0 (Ken Sanchez, CEO) is the supervisor of terri0 who in turn is the supervisor of roberto0 who is the supervisor of rob0.

Many-To-Many Relationship - Junction Table

Junction tables have many names, most popular among them are junction table, cross-reference table and bridge table. The titleauthor table in the pubs database is a junction table: a title (book) can have many authors and an author can write many titles. The PRIMARY KEY is a composite of two FOREIGN KEYs referencing the titles and authors tables.

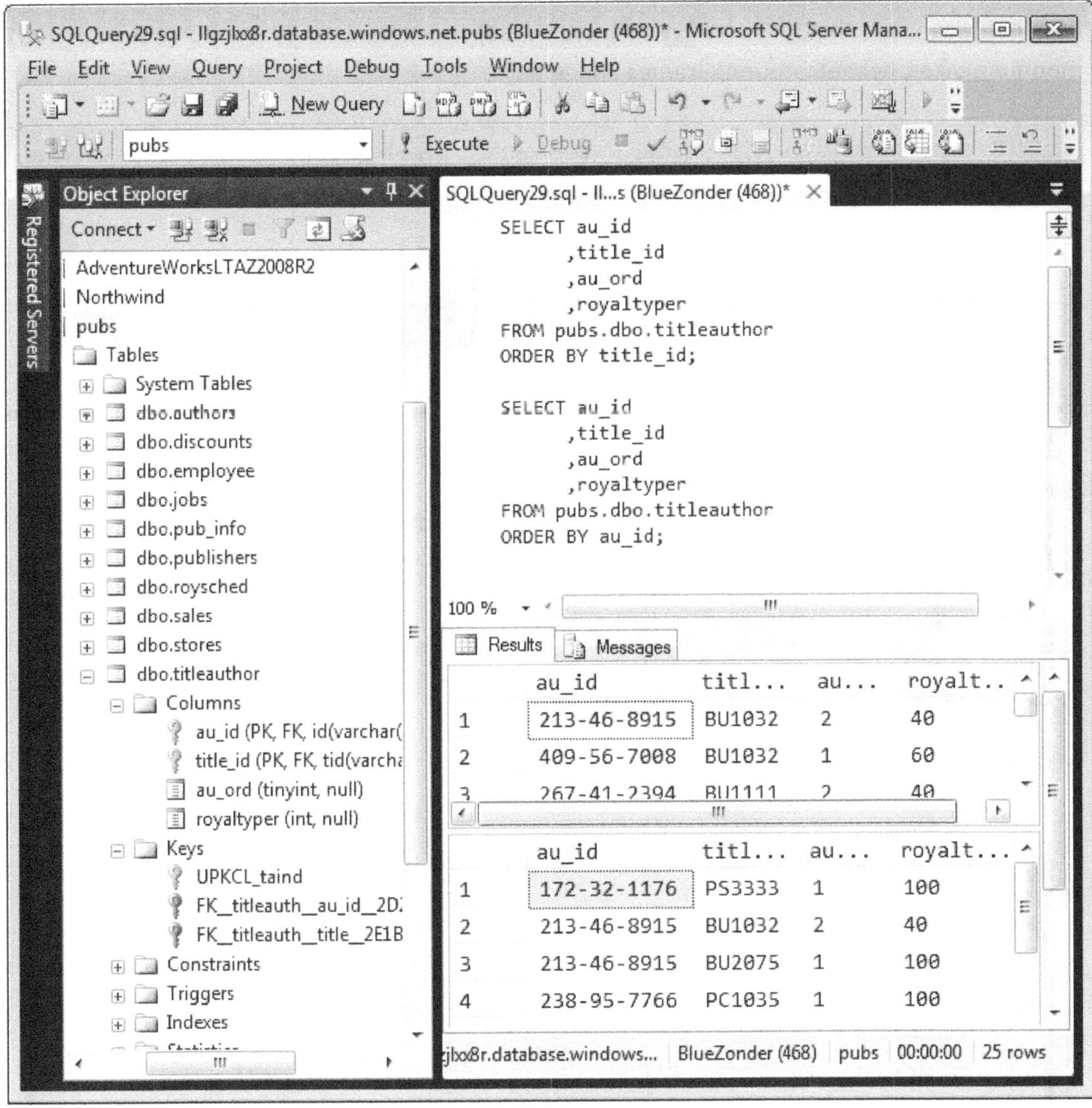

Reading the author - title junction table: book title PC8888 has multiple (two) authors, while author 486-29-1786 wrote multiple (two) books.

Parent-Child or Master-Detail Tables Design

In the AdventureWorks series of sample databases, Sales.SalesOrderHeader and Sales.SalesOrderDetail tables are implemented as master-detail tables. Similarly for Purchasing.PurchaseOrderHeader and Purchasing.PurchaseOrderDetail. The PRIMARY KEY of SalesOrderHeader is SalesOrderID (INT IDENTITY(1,1)). The PRIMARY KEY of SalesOrderDetail is composite of SalesOrderID FOREIGN KEY and SalesOrderDetailID (INT IDENTITY(1,1)). The business meaning is that an order from a bicycle reseller can have many line items such mountain bikes, helmets, touring frames and jerseys.

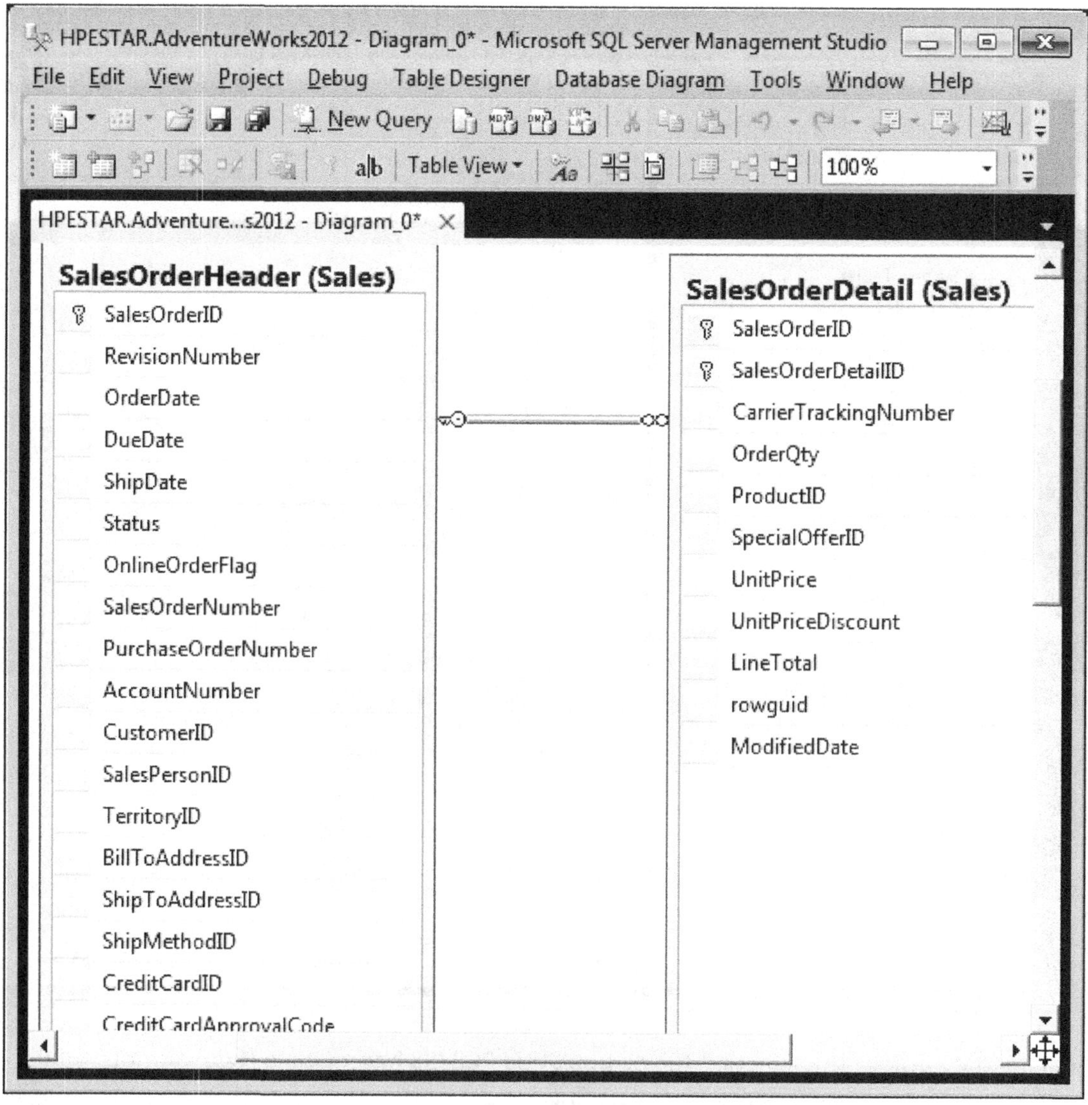

Column Descriptions of SalesOrderHeader & SalesOrderDetail Tables

UNION query to lists the column descriptions for the above master-detail tables from the data dictionary. SQL Server 2012 query.

```
SELECT 'Sales.SalesOrderHeader' AS TableName, objname     AS ColumnName,
       value                                               AS [Description]
FROM fn_listextendedproperty (NULL, 'schema', 'Sales', 'table', 'SalesOrderHeader', 'Column', default)

UNION

SELECT 'Sales.SalesOrderDetail' AS TableName, objname     AS ColumnName,
       value                                               AS [Description]
FROM fn_listextendedproperty (NULL, 'schema', 'Sales', 'table', 'SalesOrderDetail', 'Column', default)

ORDER BY TableName DESC, ColumnName;
```

TableName	ColumnName	Description
Sales.SalesOrderHeader	AccountNumber	Financial accounting number reference.
Sales.SalesOrderHeader	BillToAddressID	Customer billing address. Foreign key to Address.AddressID.
Sales.SalesOrderHeader	Comment	Sales representative comments.
Sales.SalesOrderHeader	CreditCardApprovalCode	Approval code provided by the credit card company.
Sales.SalesOrderHeader	CreditCardID	Credit card identification number. Foreign key to CreditCard.CreditCardID.
Sales.SalesOrderHeader	CurrencyRateID	Currency exchange rate used. Foreign key to CurrencyRate.CurrencyRateID.
Sales.SalesOrderHeader	CustomerID	Customer identification number. Foreign key to Customer.BusinessEntityID.
Sales.SalesOrderHeader	DueDate	Date the order is due to the customer.
Sales.SalesOrderHeader	Freight	Shipping cost.
Sales.SalesOrderHeader	ModifiedDate	Date and time the record was last updated.
Sales.SalesOrderHeader	OnlineOrderFlag	0 = Order placed by sales person. 1 = Order placed online by customer.
Sales.SalesOrderHeader	OrderDate	Dates the sales order was created.
Sales.SalesOrderHeader	PurchaseOrderNumber	Customer purchase order number reference.
Sales.SalesOrderHeader	RevisionNumber	Incremental number to track changes to the sales order over time.
Sales.SalesOrderHeader	rowguid	ROWGUIDCOL number uniquely identifying the record. Used to support a merge replication sample.
Sales.SalesOrderHeader	SalesOrderID	Primary key.
Sales.SalesOrderHeader	SalesOrderNumber	Unique sales order identification number.
Sales.SalesOrderHeader	SalesPersonID	Sales person who created the sales order. Foreign key to SalesPerson.BusinessEntityID.
Sales.SalesOrderHeader	ShipDate	Date the order was shipped to the customer.
Sales.SalesOrderHeader	ShipMethodID	Shipping method. Foreign key to ShipMethod.ShipMethodID.
Sales.SalesOrderHeader	ShipToAddressID	Customer shipping address. Foreign key to Address.AddressID.
Sales.SalesOrderHeader	Status	Order current status. 1 = In process; 2 = Approved; 3 = Backordered; 4 = Rejected; 5 = Shipped; 6 = Cancelled
Sales.SalesOrderHeader	SubTotal	Sales subtotal. Computed as SUM(SalesOrderDetail.LineTotal)for the appropriate SalesOrderID.
Sales.SalesOrderHeader	TaxAmt	Tax amount.
Sales.SalesOrderHeader	TerritoryID	Territory in which the sale was made. Foreign key to SalesTerritory.SalesTerritoryID.
Sales.SalesOrderHeader	TotalDue	Total due from customer. Computed as Subtotal + TaxAmt + Freight.
Sales.SalesOrderDetail	CarrierTrackingNumber	Shipment tracking number supplied by the shipper.
Sales.SalesOrderDetail	LineTotal	Per product subtotal. Computed as UnitPrice * (1 - UnitPriceDiscount) * OrderQty.
Sales.SalesOrderDetail	ModifiedDate	Date and time the record was last updated.
Sales.SalesOrderDetail	OrderQty	Quantity ordered per product.
Sales.SalesOrderDetail	ProductID	Product sold to customer. Foreign key to Product.ProductID.
Sales.SalesOrderDetail	rowguid	ROWGUIDCOL number uniquely identifying the record. Used to support a merge replication sample.
Sales.SalesOrderDetail	SalesOrderDetailID	Primary key. One incremental unique number per product sold.
Sales.SalesOrderDetail	SalesOrderID	Primary key. Foreign key to SalesOrderHeader.SalesOrderID.
Sales.SalesOrderDetail	SpecialOfferID	Promotional code. Foreign key to SpecialOffer.SpecialOfferID.
Sales.SalesOrderDetail	UnitPrice	Selling price of a single product.
Sales.SalesOrderDetail	UnitPriceDiscount	Discount amount.

Diagram of PurchaseOrderHeader and Related Tables

Database diagram to display the special relationship to the child table PurchaseOrderDetail and PK-FK relationships to other tables.

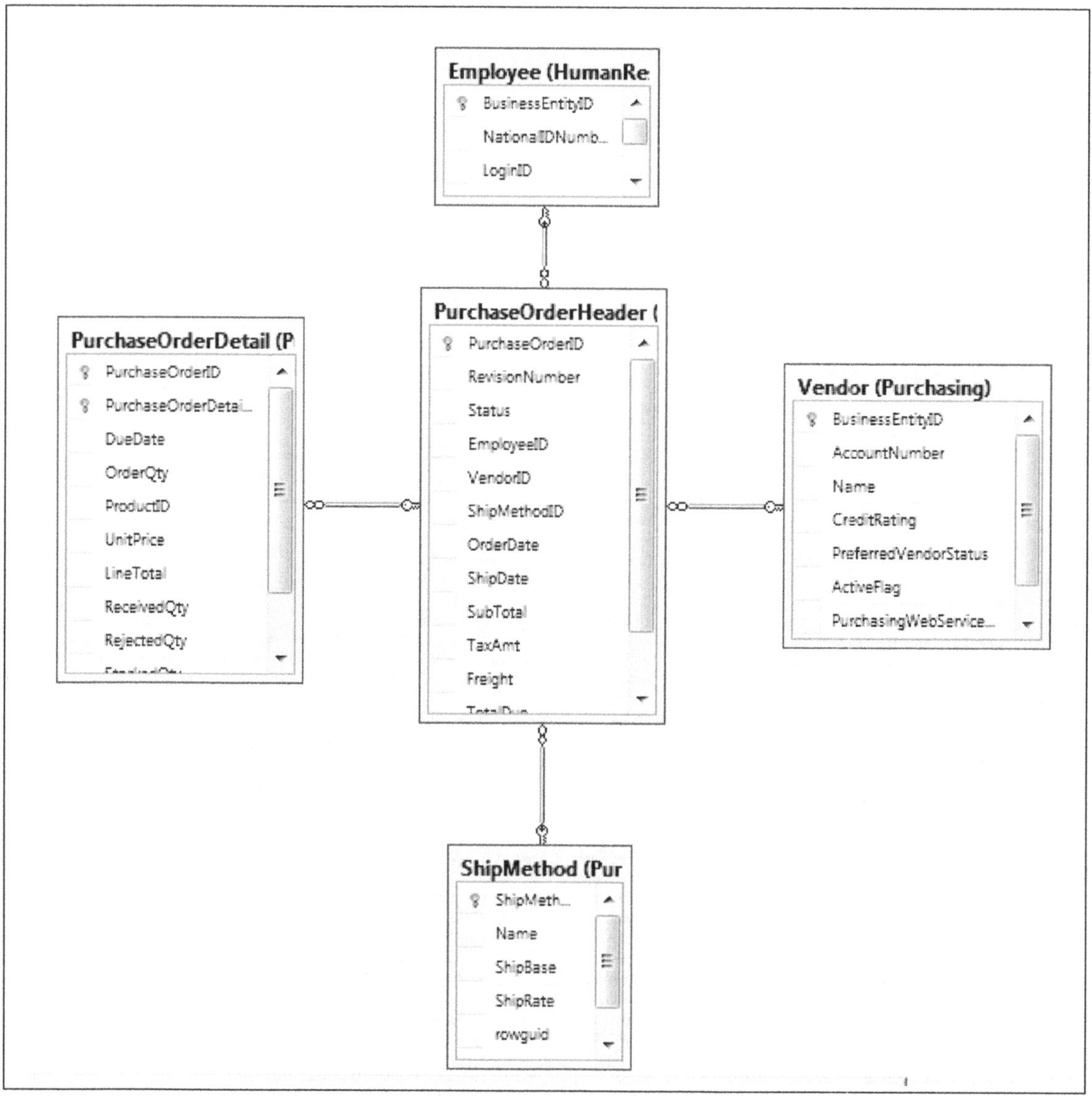

Multiple FOREIGN KEYs from One Table to Another

Database diagram to illustrate the double FOREIGN KEYs from BillOfMaterials table to the Product table. The FOREIGN KEYs are named **ComponentID and ProductAssemblyID**. In the Product table **SizeUnitMeasureCode & WeightUnitMeasureCode** are double FOREIGN KEYs to the UnitMeasure table.

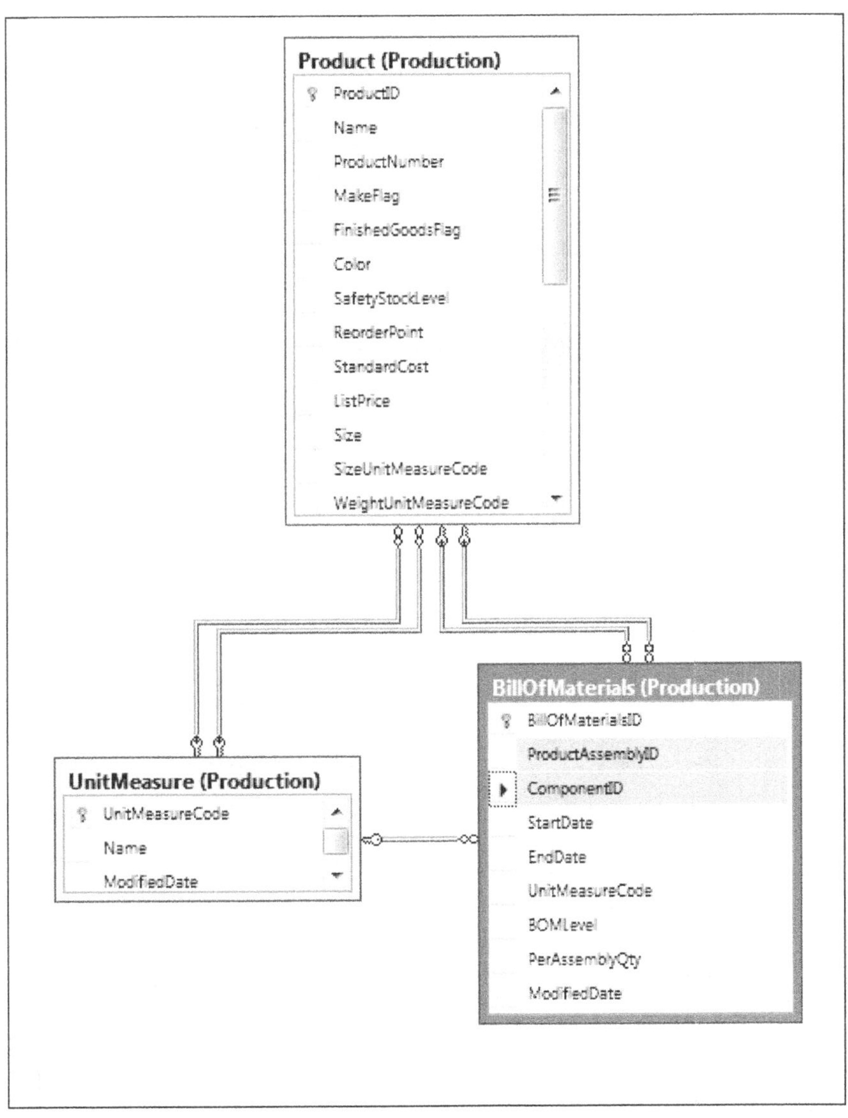

Parent - Multiple Children Table Design

Database design & diagram to represent a parent table with two children table. Notice that in the children table the PRIMARY KEY is a FOREIGN KEY simultaneously.

```
CREATE TABLE Security  (
    Symbol              CHAR(7)  PRIMARY KEY,
    SecurityName        NVARCHAR(64),
    CUSIP               CHAR(9),
    ModifiedDate        DATETIME DEFAULT (CURRENT_TIMESTAMP)    );
```

```
CREATE TABLE Stock  (
    Symbol              CHAR(7)  PRIMARY KEY REFERENCES Security ON DELETE CASCADE,
    AuthShares          BIGINT,
    IssuedShares        BIGINT,
    ClosingPrice        DECIMAL(14, 2),
    ModifiedDate        DATETIME DEFAULT (CURRENT_TIMESTAMP)    );
```

```
CREATE TABLE Bond   (
    Symbol              CHAR(7)  PRIMARY KEY REFERENCES Security ON DELETE CASCADE,
    Rate                DECIMAL(14, 6),
    FaceValue           DECIMAL(14, 2),
    MaturityDate        DATE,
    ClosingPrice        DECIMAL(14, 2),
    ModifiedDate        DATETIME DEFAULT (CURRENT_TIMESTAMP)    );
```

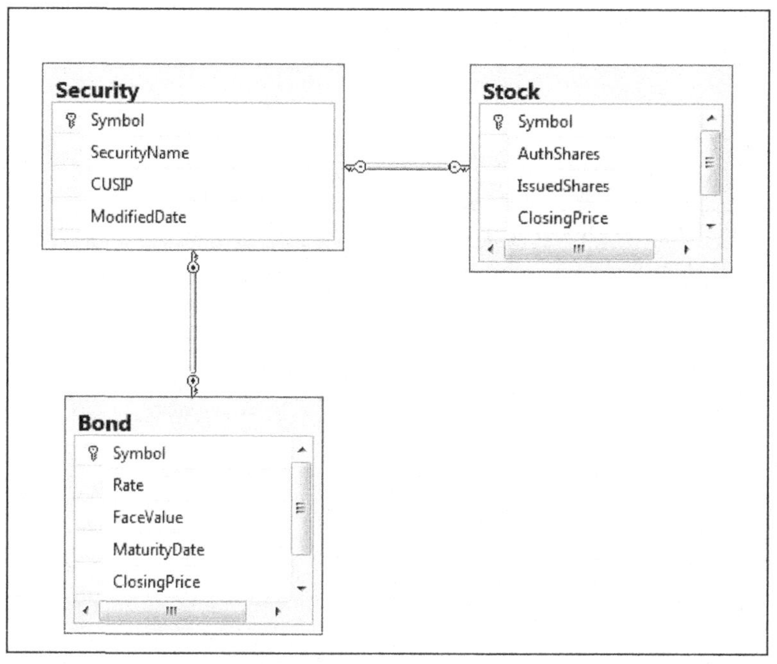

LookupHeader & Lookup Tables for Storing All Lookups

T-SQL script to demonstrate a simple implementation of LookupHeader & Lookup (detail) tables to prevent database "pollution" by many small lookup (code/translate) tables with similar structure.

```
USE AdventureWorks2012;
```

```
CREATE TABLE LookupHeader
 (
	LookupHeaderID		INT IDENTITY(1, 1)		PRIMARY KEY,
	[Type]			VARCHAR(80)			UNIQUE,
	ModifiedDate		DATETIME			default ( CURRENT_TIMESTAMP)
 );
go
```

```
CREATE TABLE Lookup
 (
	LookupID		INT IDENTITY(1,1) PRIMARY KEY nonclustered,
	LookupHeaderID		INT NOT NULL REFERENCES LookupHeader(LookupHeaderID),
	Code			VARCHAR(6) NOT NULL,
	[Description]		VARCHAR(255),
	ModifiedDate		DATETIME default ( CURRENT_TIMESTAMP)
 );
go
```

```
-- composite PRIMARY KEY
ALTER TABLE dbo.Lookup
	ADD CONSTRAINT uq_lookup UNIQUE CLUSTERED ( LookupHeaderID, Code );
go
```

```
INSERT LookupHeader  ([Type]) VALUES ('Country');
INSERT LookupHeader  ([Type]) VALUES ('Department');
```

```
SELECT * FROM   LookupHeader ;
go
```

LookupHeaderID	Type	ModifiedDate
1	Country	2016-08-08 07:34:59.077
2	Department	2016-08-08 07:34:59.113

```
-- Populate department code
INSERT INTO LookUp (LookupHeaderID, Code, Description)  VALUES	(2,  '1', 'Human Resources');
INSERT INTO LookUp (LookupHeaderID, Code, Description)  VALUES	(2,  '2', 'Accounting');
INSERT INTO LookUp (LookupHeaderID, Code, Description)  VALUES	(2,  '3', 'Engineering');
GO
```

```
-- T-SQL script continued

-- Populate country code lookup
INSERT INTO LookUp (LookupHeaderID, Code, Description)
SELECT 1, [CountryRegionCode],[Name]
FROM [Person].[CountryRegion]
ORDER BY CountryRegionCode;
go
```

```
-- Check lookup table content
SELECT * FROM   Lookup ORDER  BY LookupHeaderID, Code;
```

Partial display of the Lookup table content.

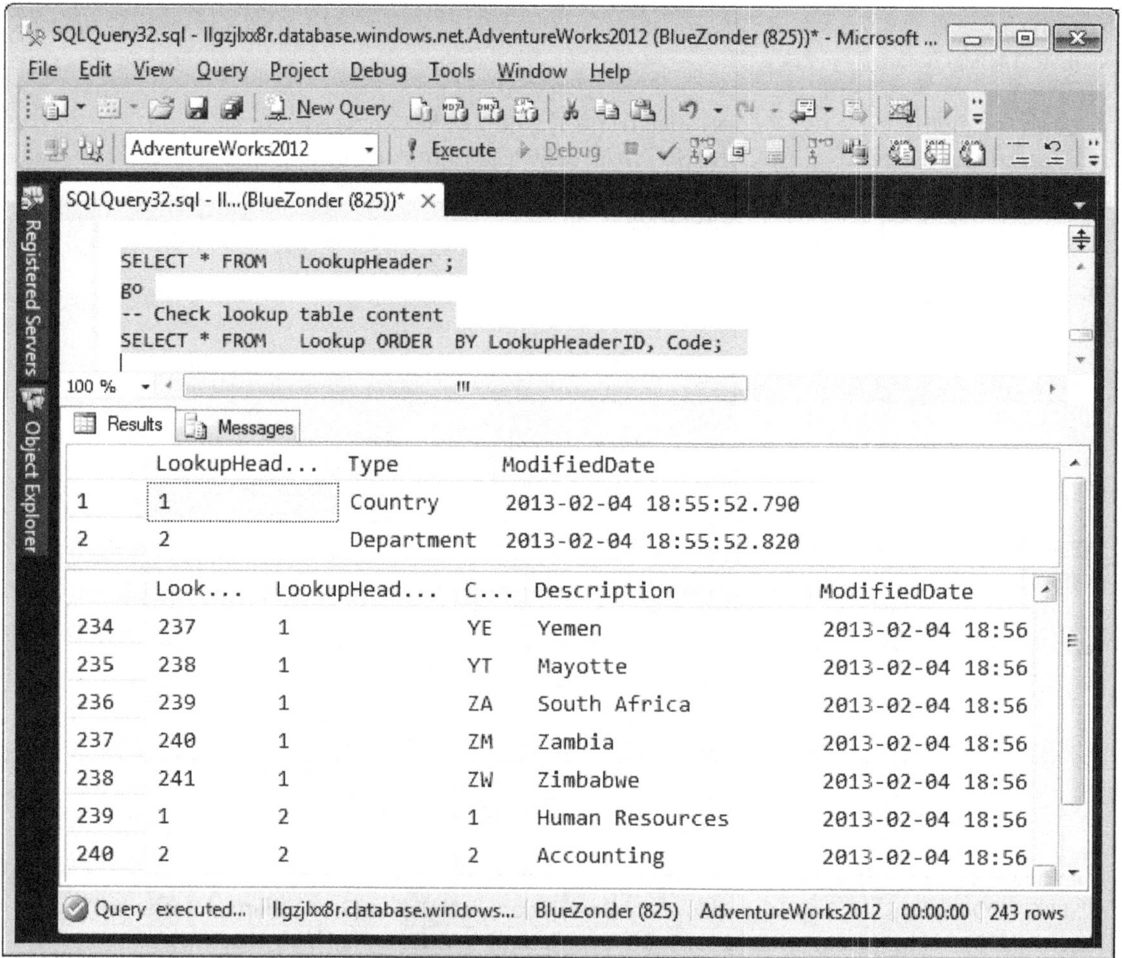

History Table Design

AdventureWorks2012 EmployeeDepartmentHistory table follows the career of an employee from department to department each with StartDate and EndDate. If EndDate is NULL, that is the employee's current department. For employee ID 250 (BusinessEntityID) the current department is 5. The PRIMARY KEY is composite of BusinessEntityID (employee ID), DepartmentID, ShiftID and StartDate. The first 3 columns in the PRIMARY KEY are FOREIGN KEYs also. BusinessEntityID references (points to) the Employee table, DepartmentID the Department table and ShiftID the Shift table.

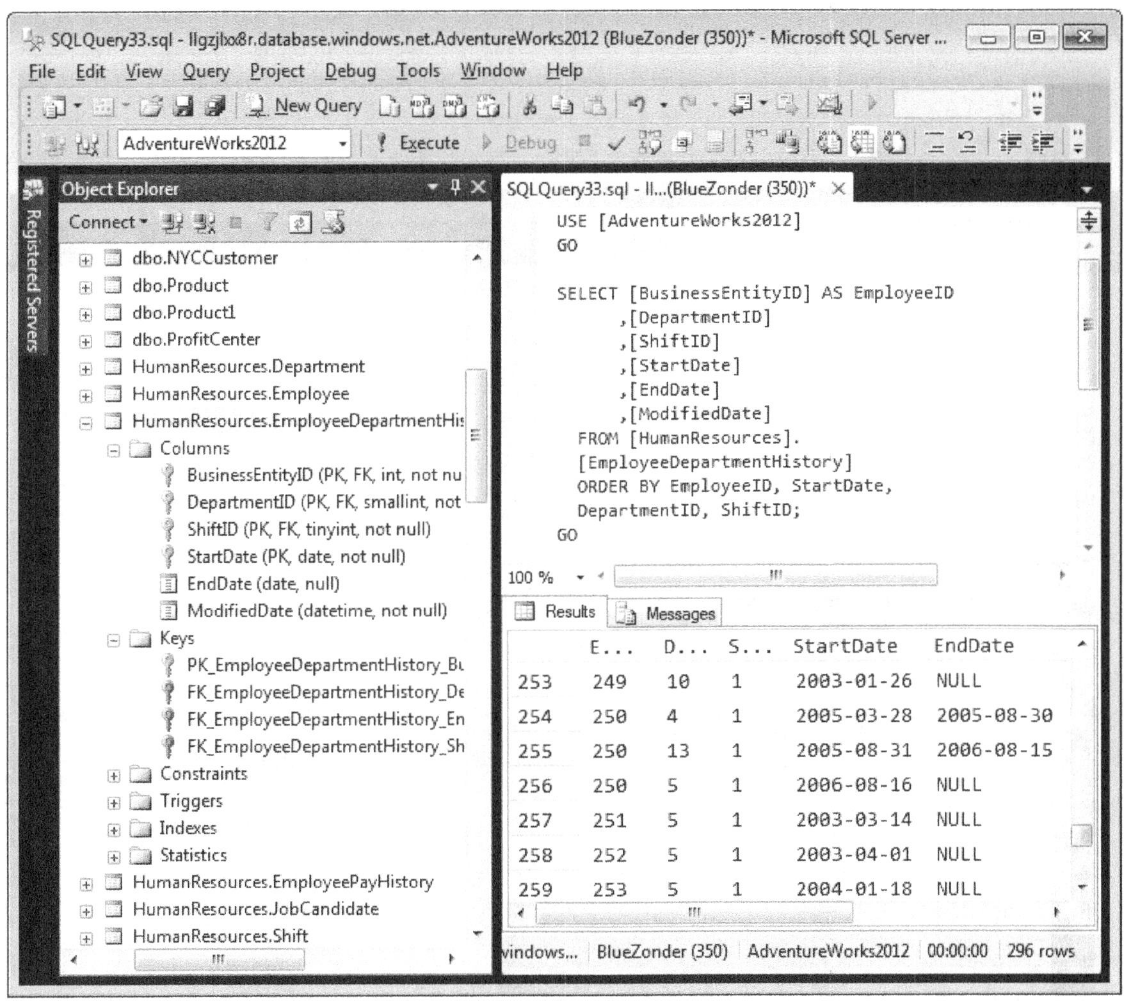

Implementing One-To-One Relationship

In a one-to-one relationship, a row in the main table can have no more than one matching row in the secondary table, and vice versa. **A one-to-one relationship requires that both of the related columns are primary keys.** One-to-one relationship tables are not very common because most of the time a single table is used. Nonetheless, we might use a one-to-one relationship tables to: Vertically partition a table with many columns; Vertically divide a table to a narrow and wide part for performance reasons - example: email header & email body; Isolate sensitive columns in a table for security reasons; Store information that applies only to a subset of the main table thus avoiding lots of NULLs in the rows. Demonstration to show the one-to-one relationship between Product and ProductInventory tables.

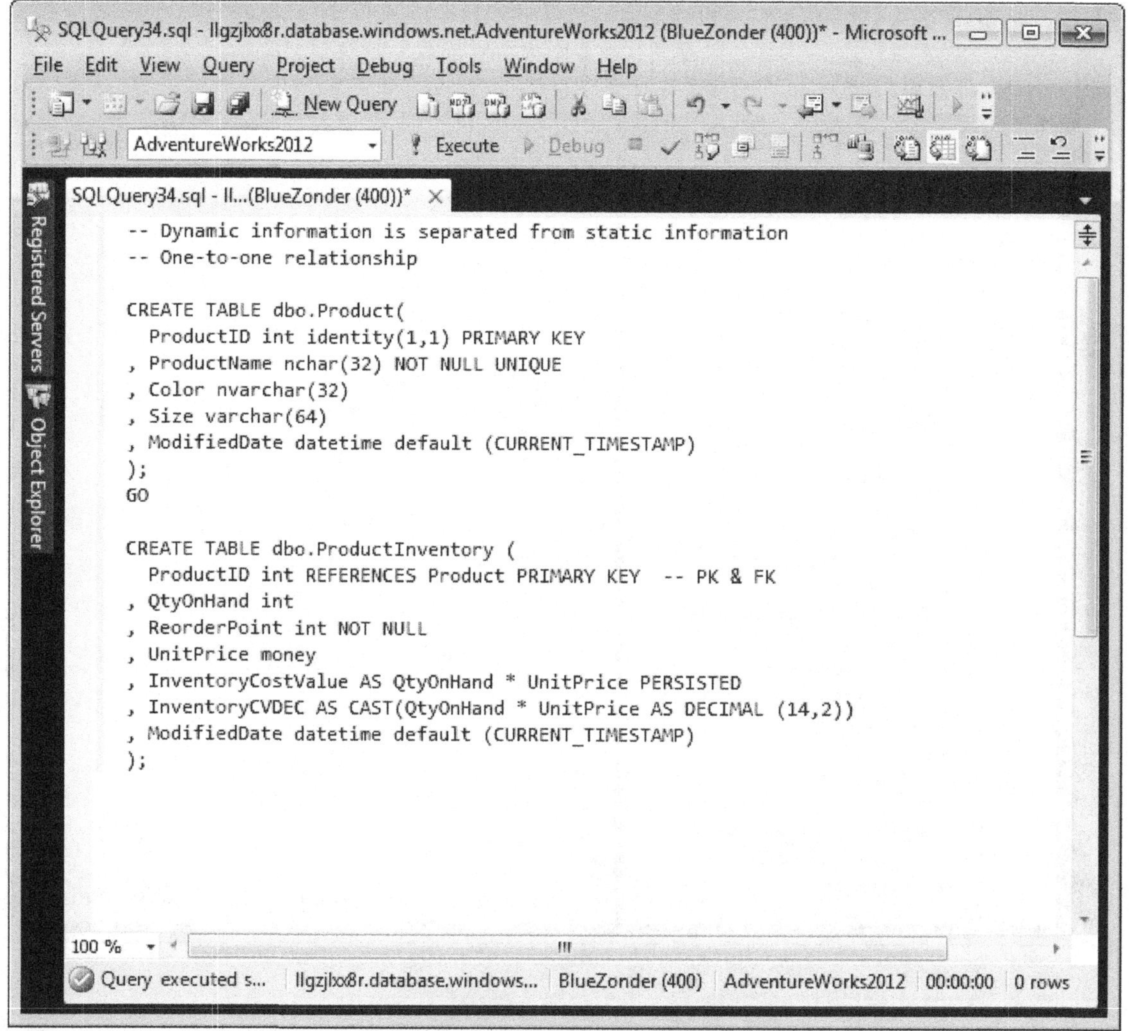


```
-- Dynamic information is separated from static information
-- One-to-one relationship

CREATE TABLE dbo.Product(
  ProductID int identity(1,1) PRIMARY KEY
, ProductName nchar(32) NOT NULL UNIQUE
, Color nvarchar(32)
, Size varchar(64)
, ModifiedDate datetime default (CURRENT_TIMESTAMP)
);
GO

CREATE TABLE dbo.ProductInventory (
  ProductID int REFERENCES Product PRIMARY KEY  -- PK & FK
, QtyOnHand int
, ReorderPoint int NOT NULL
, UnitPrice money
, InventoryCostValue AS QtyOnHand * UnitPrice PERSISTED
, InventoryCVDEC AS CAST(QtyOnHand * UnitPrice AS DECIMAL (14,2))
, ModifiedDate datetime default (CURRENT_TIMESTAMP)
);
```

One-To-One Relationship between publisher & pub_info Tables

The intent of the database designer was to separate the bulk data (logo image, PR description) from the regular size columns which likely are more frequently used as well. The implementation: pub_id in pub_info table is PRIMARY KEY and FOREIGN KEY to publishers pub_id.

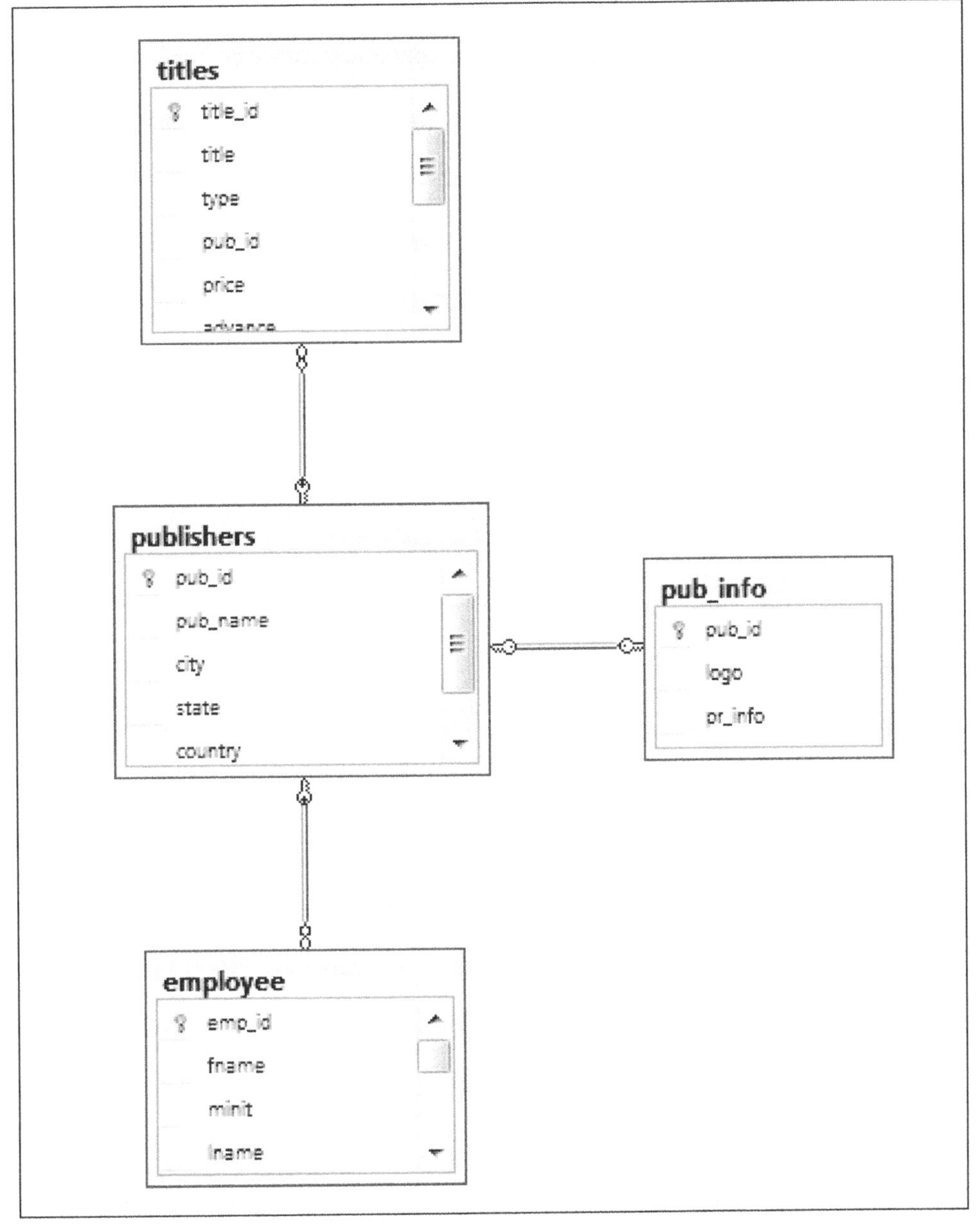

Tables with Computed Columns

A column can be automatically generated by a formula/expression involving other columns. The generation is "on the fly" when needed. To persist the column the PERSISTED property must be used. That is a requirement for some use such as indexing. All computed columns can be listed by a simple query.

```
SELECT object_name(object_id) as TableName, name AS ComputedColumn,
        definition AS Expression FROM sys.computed_columns ORDER BY name;
```

The demonstration introduces 2 computed columns into the ProductInventory table.

```
USE AdventureWorks2012;
```

```
CREATE TABLE dbo.Product (
        ProductID int identity(1,1) PRIMARY KEY
        , ProductName nchar(32) NOT NULL UNIQUE
        , Color nvarchar(32)
        , Size varchar(64)
        , ModifiedDate datetime default (CURRENT_TIMESTAMP) );
```

```
-- Table with two computed columns
CREATE TABLE dbo.ProductInventory (
        ProductID int REFERENCES Product(ProductID) PRIMARY KEY
        , QtyOnHand int
        , ReorderPoint int NOT NULL
        , UnitPrice money
        , InventoryCostValue AS QtyOnHand * UnitPrice PERSISTED
        , InventoryCVDEC AS CAST(QtyOnHand * UnitPrice AS DECIMAL(14,0))
        , ModifiedDate datetime default (CURRENT_TIMESTAMP) );
GO
```

```
INSERT Product(ProductName, Color, Size) SELECT 'MusicMobile', 'White', '2" x 3"';
INSERT Product(ProductName, Color, Size) SELECT 'ReaderMobile',  'Black', '5" x 9"';
INSERT Product(ProductName, Color, Size) SELECT 'PhoneMobile',  'Blue', '2 1/2" x 4"';
INSERT Product(ProductName, Color, Size) SELECT 'DELTA laptop', 'Gray', '12" x 16" x 2"';
GO
```

```
SELECT * from dbo.Product;
```

ProductID	ProductName	Color	Size	ModifiedDate
1	MusicMobile	White	2" x 3"	2016-07-08 10:05:53.943
2	ReaderMobile	Black	5" x 9"	2016-07-08 10:05:53.947
3	PhoneMobile	Blue	2 1/2" x 4"	2016-07-08 10:05:53.947
4	DELTA laptop	Gray	12" x 16" x 2"	2016-07-08 10:05:53.947

```
-- T-SQL script continued

INSERT ProductInventory (ProductID, QtyOnHand, ReorderPoint, UnitPrice)  SELECT 1, 105, 30, $99.99;
INSERT ProductInventory (ProductID, QtyOnHand, ReorderPoint, UnitPrice)  SELECT 2, 105, 40, $299.99;
INSERT ProductInventory (ProductID, QtyOnHand, ReorderPoint, UnitPrice)  SELECT 3, 208, 30, $399.99;
INSERT ProductInventory (ProductID, QtyOnHand, ReorderPoint, UnitPrice)  SELECT 4, 103, 30, $599.99;
GO
```

```
SELECT * FROM ProductInventory;
GO
```

ProductID	QtyOnHand	ReorderPoint	UnitPrice	InventoryCostValue	InventoryCVDEC
1	105	30	99.99	10498.95	10499
2	105	40	299.99	31498.95	31499
3	208	30	399.99	83197.92	83198
4	103	30	599.99	61798.97	61799

Combination query with INNER JOIN and formatting.

```
SELECT          ProductName                                   AS [Product Name],
                QtyOnHand                                     AS [Quantity On Hand],
                ReorderPoint                                  AS [Reorder Point],
                FORMAT(UnitPrice,'c','en-US')                 AS [Unit Price],
                FORMAT(InventoryCostValue, 'c','en-US')       AS [ Inventory Cost Value],
                FORMAT(InventoryCVDEC, 'c','en-US')           AS [Inventory Cost Rounded]
FROM Product P
        INNER JOIN ProductInventory PI
                ON P.ProductID = PI.ProductID
ORDER BY ProductName;
GO
```

Product Name	Quantity On Hand	Reorder Point	Unit Price	Inventory Cost Value	Inventory Cost Rounded
DELTA laptop	103	30	$599.99	$61,798.97	$61,799.00
MusicMobile	105	30	$99.99	$10,498.95	$10,499.00
PhoneMobile	208	30	$399.99	$83,197.92	$83,198.00
ReaderMobile	105	40	$299.99	$31,498.95	$31,499.00

```
-- Cleanup - FOREIGN KEY table must be dropped first
DROP TABLE tempdb.dbo.ProductInventory;
DROP TABLE tempdb.dbo.Product;
```

Building the Data Dictionary - On-Premises SS

The best way to build the data dictionary is the same time when the database objects are created. It can also be done in the final phases of the database development project when changes are rare to the object designs.

GUI Data Dictionary Maintenance

As an example, right click on a table column name and choose Properties.

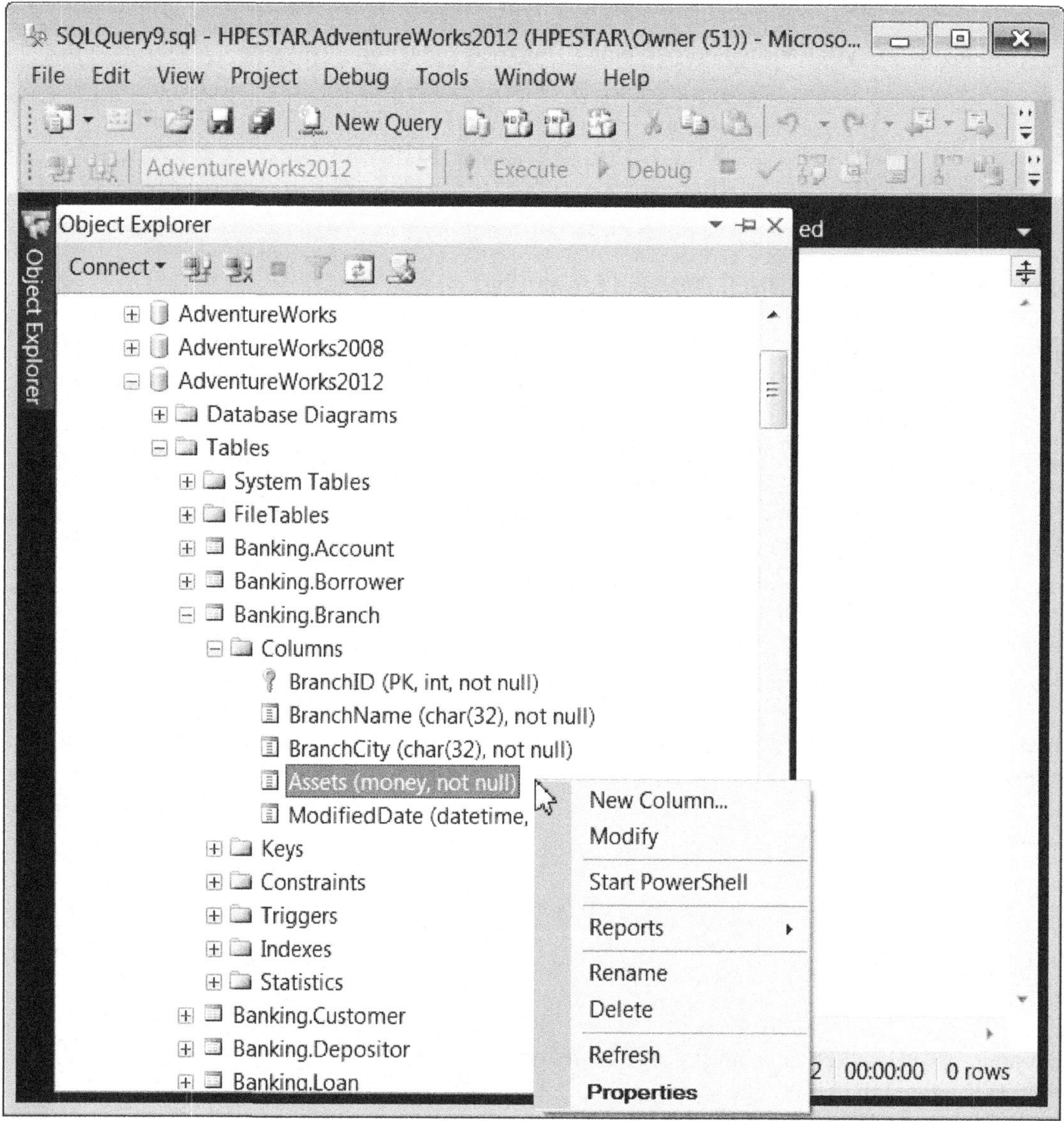

Extended Properties page can be used for Data Dictionary entry

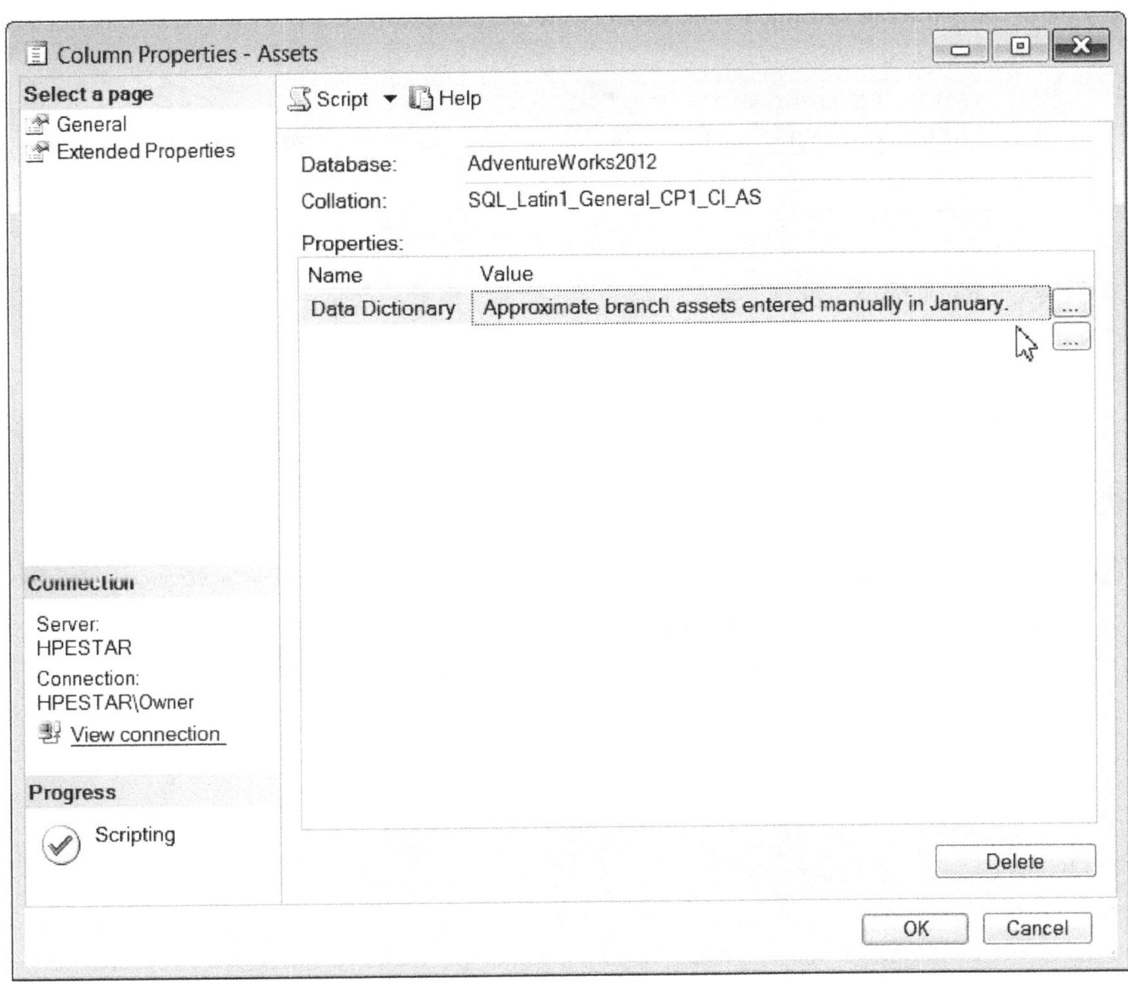

Check the new entry in the Data Dictionary with a query.

```
SELECT *
FROM fn_listextendedproperty (NULL, 'schema', 'Banking', 'table', 'Branch', 'Column', NULL);
GO
```

objtype	objname	name	value
COLUMN	Assets	Data Dictionary	Approximate branch assets entered manually in January.

Data Dictionary Maintenance with T-SQL Scripts

The advantage of using T-SQL scripts for Data Dictionary maintenance is that the script can be saved as a .sql file and rerun when necessary as is or after editing.

BOL: **AdventureWorks Data Dictionary**
http://msdn.microsoft.com/en-us/library/ms124438(v=sql.100).aspx

```
USE [AdventureWorks2012];
```

```
-- Delete Data Dictionary entry
EXEC sys.sp_dropextendedproperty @name=N'Data Dictionary' ,
        @level0type=N'SCHEMA',@level0name=N'Banking',
        @level1type=N'TABLE',@level1name=N'Branch',
        @level2type=N'COLUMN',@level2name=N'Assets';
GO
```

```
-- Add Data Dictionary entry
EXEC sys.sp_addextendedproperty @name=N'Data Dictionary',
        @value=N'Approximate branch assets entered manually in January each year.' ,
        @level0type=N'SCHEMA',@level0name=N'Banking', @level1type=N'TABLE',
        @level1name=N'Branch', @level2type=N'COLUMN',@level2name=N'Assets';
GO
```

```
-- Check new Data Dictionary entry
SELECT *
FROM fn_listextendedproperty (NULL, 'schema', 'Banking', 'table', 'Branch', 'Column', NULL);
```

objtype	objname	name	value
COLUMN	Assets	Data Dictionary	Approximate branch assets entered manually in January each year.

```
-- Data Dictionary entry for BranchName
EXEC sys.sp_addextendedproperty @name=N'Data Dictionary',
        @value=N'Name of the branch. Updated by supervisor only.' ,
        @level0type=N'SCHEMA',@level0name=N'Banking', @level1type=N'TABLE',
        @level1name=N'Branch', @level2type=N'COLUMN',@level2name=N'BranchName';
GO
```

Updating an Existing Data Dictionary Entry

```
-- Update Data Dictionary entry
EXEC sys.sp_updateextendedproperty @name=N'Data Dictionary',
@value=N'Approximate branch assets entered in January each year by an automated process.' ,
@level0type=N'SCHEMA',@level0name=N'Banking',
@level1type=N'TABLE',@level1name=N'Branch',
@level2type=N'COLUMN',@level2name=N'Assets'
GO
```

```
SELECT *
FROM fn_listextendedproperty (NULL, 'schema', 'Banking', 'table', 'Branch', 'Column', NULL);
GO
```

objtype	objname	name	value
COLUMN	Assets	Data Dictionary	Approximate branch assets entered in January each year by an automated process.

```
-- Data Dictionary entry for BranchCity
EXEC sys.sp_addextendedproperty @name=N'Data Dictionary',
        @value=N'City & State where branch is located.' ,
        @level0type=N'SCHEMA',@level0name=N'Banking', @level1type=N'TABLE',
        @level1name=N'Branch', @level2type=N'COLUMN',@level2name=N'BranchCity';
GO
```

```
-- Listing all Data Dictionary entries for table
SELECT *
FROM fn_listextendedproperty (NULL, 'schema', 'Banking', 'table', 'Branch', 'Column', NULL)
ORDER BY objname;
```

objtype	objname	name	value
COLUMN	Assets	Data Dictionary	Approximate branch assets entered in January each year by an automated process.
COLUMN	BranchCity	Data Dictionary	City & State where branch is located.
COLUMN	BranchName	Data Dictionary	Name of the branch. Updated by supervisor only.

Lead Developer as Database Designer

A senior database developer should be able to design a modest business application database. The reason is that he worked with a number of databases so well-familiar with the concept of 3NF relational database design. Naturally if the lead developer is not familiar with the business, then it is rather difficult, there is a steep learning curve. But then it is difficult also for a professional database designer. Getting a systems analyst on board is the best approach to work with the database designer.

Database Design Team at Big Budget Projects

Large companies for important projects may setup the following design team:

- 1-2 database designers
- 1-3 systems analysts
- 1-4 subject matter experts

Hiring Database Design Consultant where Resources Are Limited

Even a small company or a small project at large company should consider hiring a professional database designer on a consulting basis for a month or so to design the database. A well-designed 3NF database may reduce development from 50 man-months to 35 man-months, thus the payback may start before the project is completed. The payback continues after production deployment due to lower cost of future application software development and database maintenance. Once this author was consulting in stored procedure development at a small organization which was the fund raiser for a Connecticut seminary. Only one full-time manager/dba/developer, with consultants help. Quite shockingly, the database was excellent 3NF design. Only big-budget places can afford such a good 3NF design so goes the common wisdom. The manager explained that he hired a consultant expert database designer for a month. An excellent choice indeed.

Database System Solution Implementation Hierarchy

Frequently solutions can be implemented more than one way in a relational database system. For example, the constraint OrderQty > 0 can be implemented as CHECK constraint, stored procedure, trigger and as code in application software. There are great advantages to implement a solution at the lowest possible level of the following hierarchy.

- Table design
- Constraint
- Stored procedure
- Trigger
- Client software

List All Default Constraints with Definition

T-SQL metadata query to enumerate all column defaults with definition using a system view.

```
SELECT  SCHEMA_NAME(schema_id)                          AS SCHEMA_NAME,
        OBJECT_NAME(PARENT_OBJECT_ID)                   AS TABLE_NAME,
        COL_NAME (PARENT_OBJECT_ID, PARENT_COLUMN_ID)   AS COLUMN_NAME,
        Definition                                      AS DEFAULT_DEFINITION,
        NAME                                            AS DEFAULT_CONSTRAINT_NAME
FROM SYS.DEFAULT_CONSTRAINTS
ORDER BY 1, 2; -- column numbers
-- (166 row(s) affected) - Partial results.
```

SCHEMA_NAME	TABLE_NAME	COLUMN_NAME	DEFAULT_DEFINITION	DEFAULT_CONSTRAINT_NAME
dbo	AWBuildVersion	ModifiedDate	(getdate())	DF_AWBuildVersion_ModifiedDate
dbo	ErrorLog	ErrorTime	(getdate())	DF_ErrorLog_ErrorTime
HumanResources	Department	ModifiedDate	(getdate())	DF_Department_ModifiedDate
HumanResources	Employee	SalariedFlag	((1))	DF_Employee_SalariedFlag
HumanResources	Employee	VacationHours	((0))	DF_Employee_VacationHours
HumanResources	Employee	SickLeaveHours	((0))	DF_Employee_SickLeaveHours
HumanResources	Employee	CurrentFlag	((1))	DF_Employee_CurrentFlag
HumanResources	Employee	rowguid	(newid())	DF_Employee_rowguid
HumanResources	Employee	ModifiedDate	(getdate())	DF_Employee_ModifiedDate
HumanResources	EmployeeDepartmentHistory	ModifiedDate	(getdate())	DF_EmployeeDepartmentHistory_ModifiedDate
HumanResources	EmployeePayHistory	ModifiedDate	(getdate())	DF_EmployeePayHistory_ModifiedDate
HumanResources	JobCandidate	ModifiedDate	(getdate())	DF_JobCandidate_ModifiedDate
HumanResources	Shift	ModifiedDate	(getdate())	DF_Shift_ModifiedDate
Person	Address	rowguid	(newid())	DF_Address_rowguid
Person	Address	ModifiedDate	(getdate())	DF_Address_ModifiedDate
Person	AddressType	rowguid	(newid())	DF_AddressType_rowguid
Person	AddressType	ModifiedDate	(getdate())	DF_AddressType_ModifiedDate
Person	BusinessEntity	rowguid	(newid())	DF_BusinessEntity_rowguid
Person	BusinessEntity	ModifiedDate	(getdate())	DF_BusinessEntity_ModifiedDate

The sp_helpconstraints system procedure to list all constraints (including default) on a table.

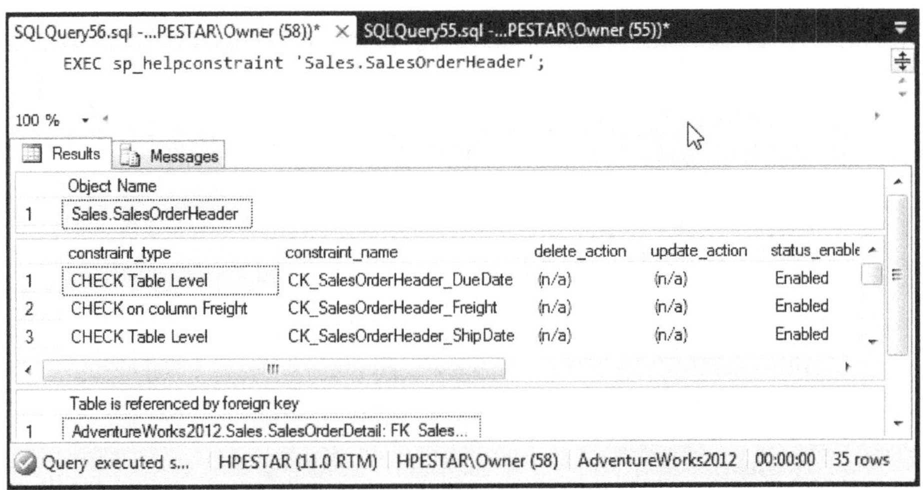

Partitioning Query via Pure SQL - Ye Olde Way

Add new sequence numbering column for subsets(partition by OrderID) with standard SQL only. Note that the old way is not very efficient, the ROW_NUMBER() OVER PARTITION is better performing.

```
USE Northwind;
SELECT  OD.OrderID,
        SeqNo                                                          AS LineItem,
        OD.ProductID,
        UnitPrice,
        Quantity                                                       AS Qty,
        CONVERT(NUMERIC(3, 2), Discount)                               AS Discount,
        CONVERT(NUMERIC(12, 2), UnitPrice * Quantity * ( 1.0 - Discount ))  AS LineTotal
FROM  [Order Details] OD
    INNER JOIN (SELECT count(*) SeqNo,  a.OrderID,  a.ProductID
          FROM  [Order Details] A
              INNER JOIN [Order Details] B
                  ON A.ProductID >= B.ProductID   AND A.OrderID = B.OrderID
          GROUP  BY A.OrderID,
                A.ProductID) a
        ON OD.OrderID = a.OrderID
          AND OD.ProductID = a.ProductID
WHERE  OD.OrderID < 10300
ORDER  BY OD.OrderID,  OD.ProductID, SeqNo;
-- (140 row(s) affected) - Partial results.
```

OrderID	LineItem	ProductID	UnitPrice	Qty	Discount	LineTotal
10255	1	2	15.20	20	0.00	304.00
10255	2	16	13.90	35	0.00	486.50
10255	3	36	15.20	25	0.00	380.00
10255	4	59	44.00	30	0.00	1320.00
10256	1	53	26.20	15	0.00	393.00
10256	2	77	10.40	12	0.00	124.80
10257	1	27	35.10	25	0.00	877.50
10257	2	39	14.40	6	0.00	86.40
10257	3	77	10.40	15	0.00	156.00
10258	1	2	15.20	50	0.20	608.00
10258	2	5	17.00	65	0.20	884.00
10258	3	32	25.60	6	0.20	122.88
10259	1	21	8.00	10	0.00	80.00
10259	2	37	20.80	1	0.00	20.80
10260	1	41	7.70	16	0.25	92.40
10260	2	57	15.60	50	0.00	780.00
10260	3	62	39.40	15	0.25	443.25

CHAPTER 10: Advanced Database Design

FileTable - Integrating Folders with DB - OPSS2012

Storing large number of binary files such as images was a challenge until SQL Server 2012: FileTable integrates files in a folder into the database, yet keep them accessible at Windows file system level. In the past, there were two solutions:

- Keep only the filenames in the database table.
- Keep both the filenames and binary file objects (varbinary(max)) in the table.

Using the first method, the files were not backed up with the database since they were not part of the database. Applying the second method, the binary objects were in the database, but as a deadweight, since not much can be done with them. FileTable is the best of both worlds: files are backed up / restored with the database, yet they remain visible at the file system level. So if a new file is dropped (copied) into the folder, it becomes visible to SQL Server instantaneously. FileTable requires the FILESTREAM feature as shown on the Server Properties dialog box.

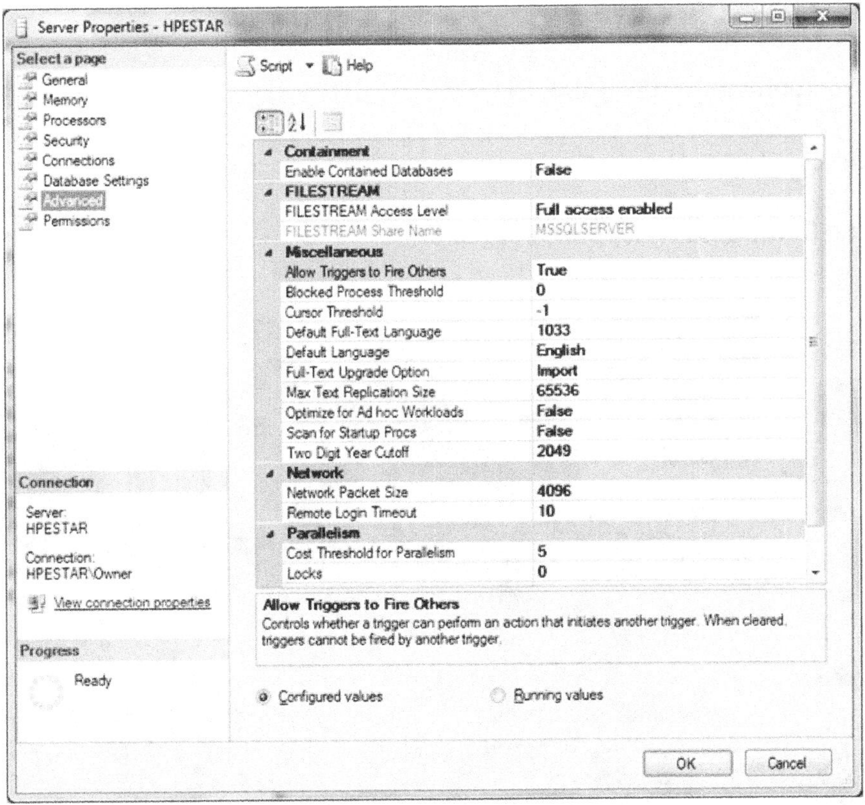

The CREATE TABLE statement for a FileTable

```
-- Create FileTable  -- new to SQL Server 2012
CREATE TABLE ImageStore
AS FileTable
   WITH (
        FileTable_Directory = 'ImageStore',
        FileTable_Collate_Filename = database_default
        );
GO
-- (1 row(s) affected)
```

We can determine the FileTable folder name which is visible at the file system level the following way.

```
SELECT DBName=DB_NAME ( database_id ), directory_name
   FROM sys.database_filestream_options
        WHERE directory_name is not null;
GO
```

DBName	directory_name
AdventureWorks2012	FSDIR

FileTable directory(path):

\\YOURSERVER\MSSQLSERVER\FSDIR\ImageStore

The dialog box for database options setup as related to FILESTREAM

"hpestar" is the name of the SQL Server instance (default instance, same name as the computer).

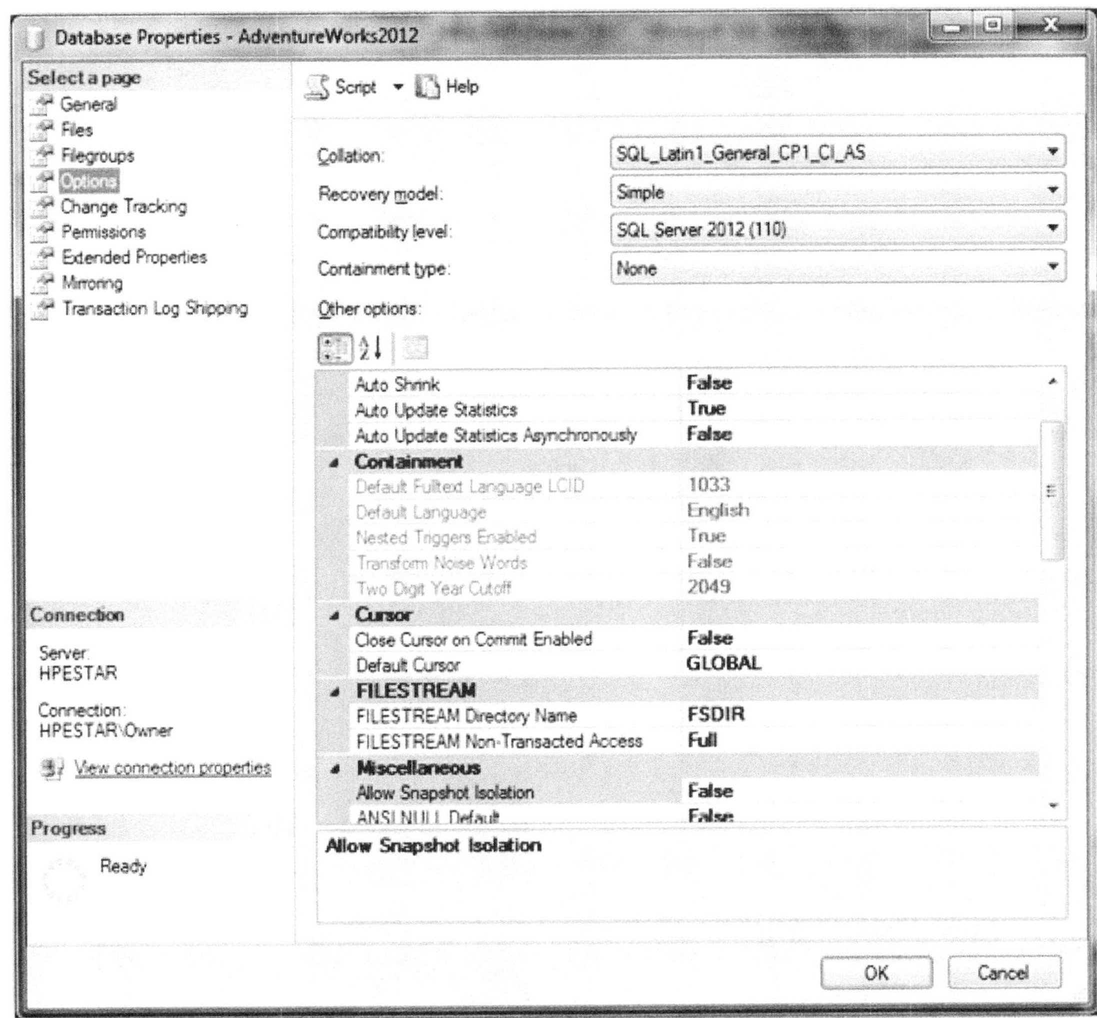

The FileTable folder is currently empty.

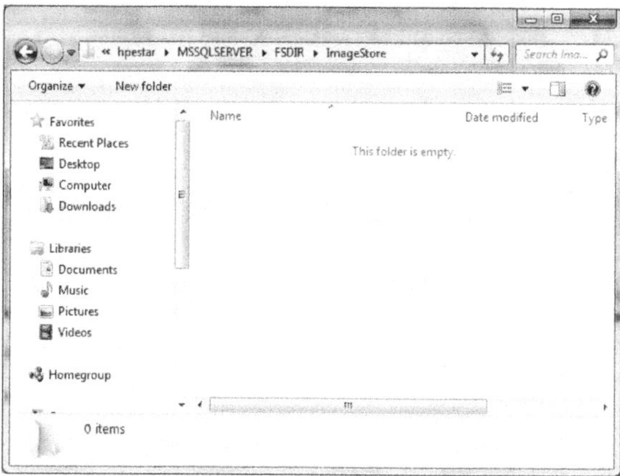

We shall now copy 3 photos in the ImageStore folder using Windows Copy & Paste operation.

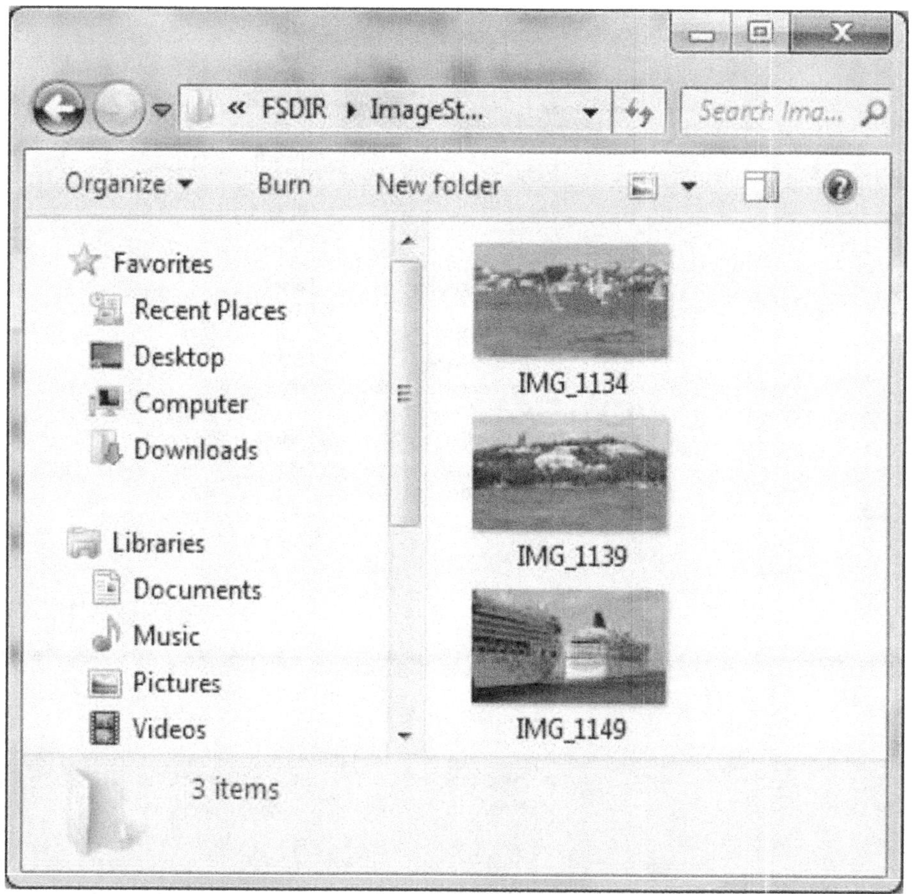

The photos are "visible" from the database side as well.

The INSERT, UPDATE and DELETE commands are operational on FileTable, however, a new column cannot be added as demonstrated in the following script:

```
SELECT * FROM ImageStore;
GO
UPDATE ImageStore SET name='RollerCoaster.jpg'
WHERE stream_id='E73EA731-AAAA-E111-9078-D8D3857FC43E';
GO
SELECT * FROM ImageStore;
```

Adding Files to FileTable Using T-SQL

There are two T-SQL methods available.

```
-- Adding files from T-SQL - method 1 xp_cmdshell copy
EXEC xp_cmdshell 'copy "C:\photo\000Test\xBermuda.jpg"
"\\HPESTAR\mssqlserver\FSDIR\ImageStore\xBermuda.jpg"'
GO
```

```
-- Adding files from T-SQL - method 2 OPENROWSET
INSERT INTO [dbo].[ImageStore] ([name],[file_stream])
SELECT 'Bermuda9.jpg', * FROM
    OPENROWSET(BULK N'C:\photo\2012\BERMUDA\BERMUDA\IMG_1154.jpg', SINGLE_BLOB)
                AS FileUpload
```

Deleting Files from FileTable Using T-SQL

```
SELECT * FROM ImageStore
GO
```

```
DELETE ImageStore
WHERE stream_id = '62F55342-ABAA-E111-9078-D8D3857FC43E'
GO
```

```
SELECT * FROM ImageStore
GO
```

```
-- Column(s) cannot be added to a FileTable
ALTER TABLE ImageStore
ADD AddDate smalldatetime NULL
CONSTRAINT AddDateDflt
DEFAULT CURRENT_TIMESTAMP WITH VALUES ;
GO
/* Msg 33422, Level 16, State 1, Line 2
The column 'AddDate' cannot be added to table 'ImageStore' as it is a FileTable.
Adding columns to the fixed schema of a FileTable object is not permitted.
*/
```

```
DROP TABLE ImageStore
GO
```

Data Compression: Compressed Table - OPSS

Azure SQL Database Blog: **Compression for Speed and Cost Savings**
http://blogs.msdn.com/b/sqlazure/archive/2010/09/02/10057355.aspx
Article: **Compressed UTF-8 Strings in SQL Azure**
http://joelfillmore.com/compressed-utf-8-strings-in-sql-azure/

The table compression option has been introduced with SQL Server 2008. Data is compressed inside a database table, and it reduces the size of the table. Performance benefit in addition to space saving: "reads" reduction; queries need to read fewer pages from the disk. Sufficient CPU resources are required for the SQL Server instance to compress and decompress table data, when data is read (SELECT) or written (INSERT, UPDATE, MERGE). Analysis is required to ensure that table compression has no adverse effect on business critical query performance. Data compression may not be available in all editions of SQL Server. In the demonstration, first we create a new table for testing.

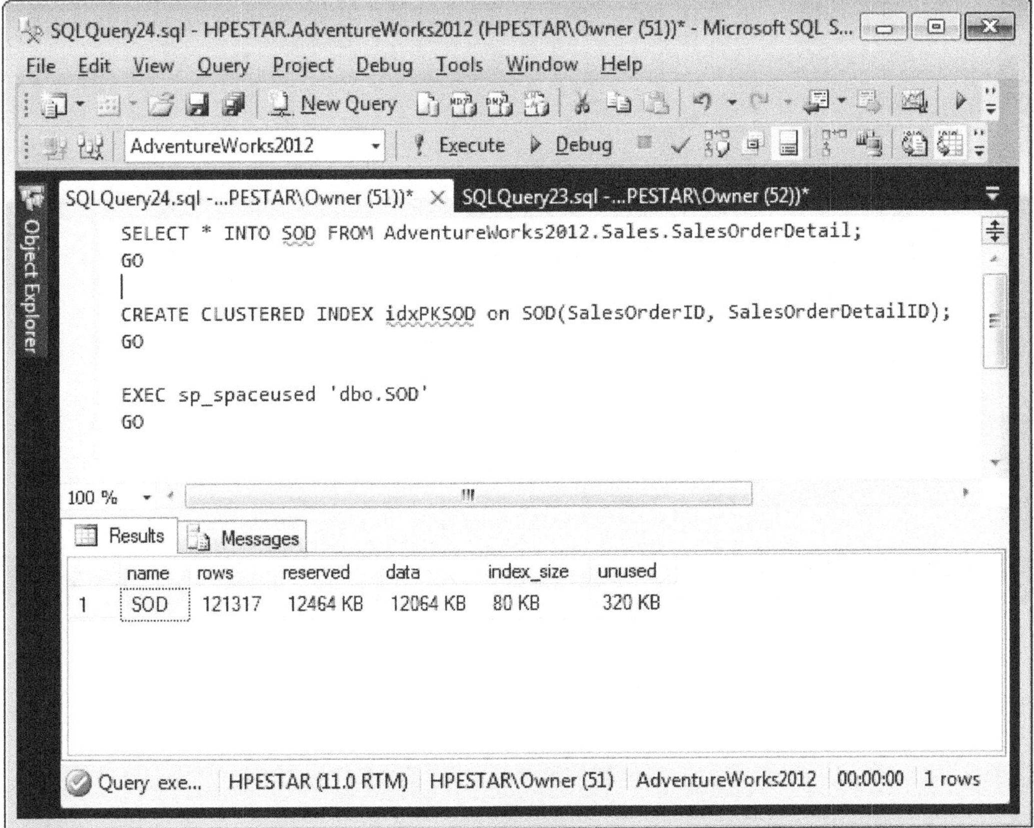

Switching to PAGE-LEVEL Compression

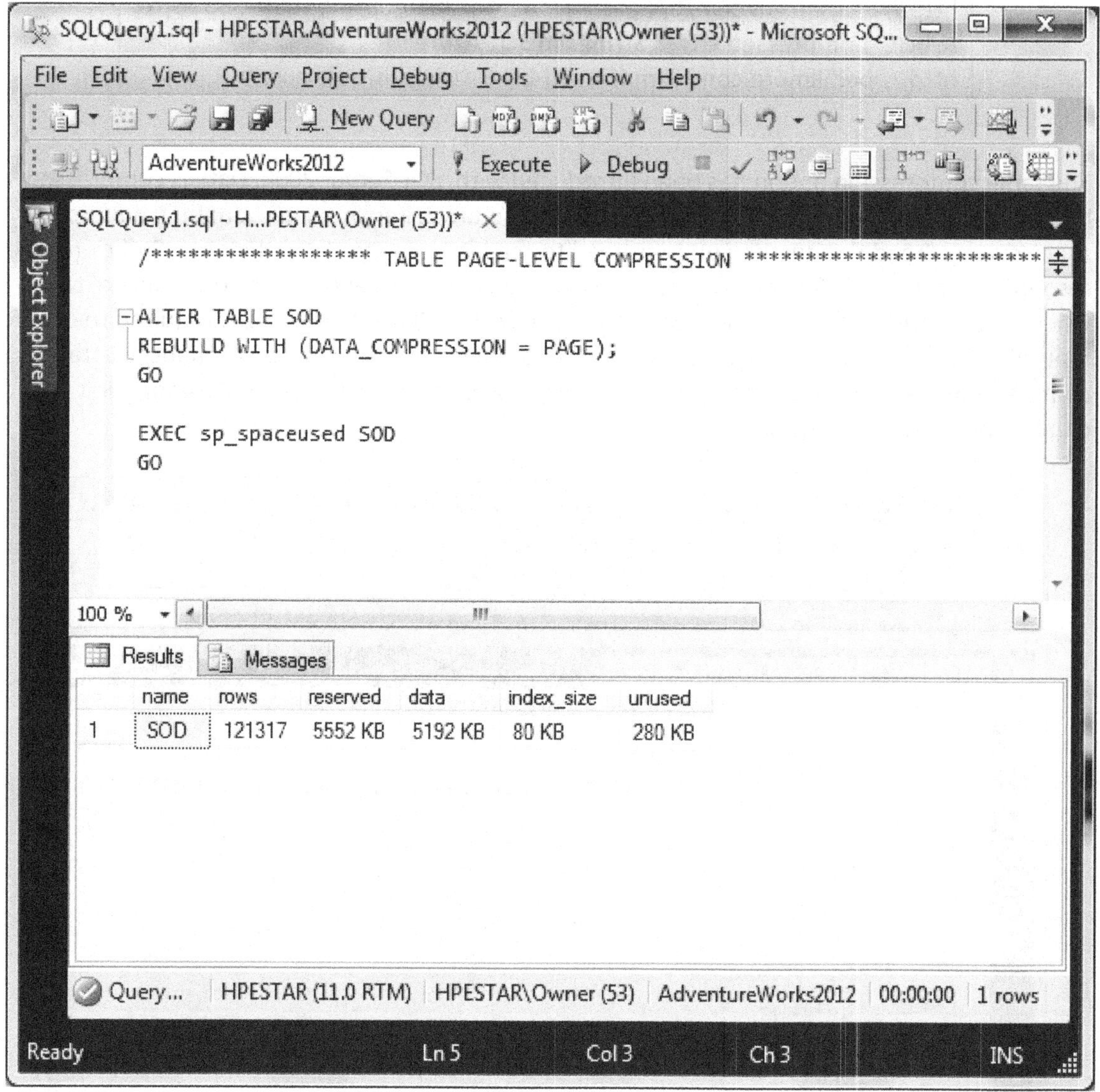

Data storage size decreased from around 12 MB to around 5 MB.

Testing ROW-LEVEL Compression

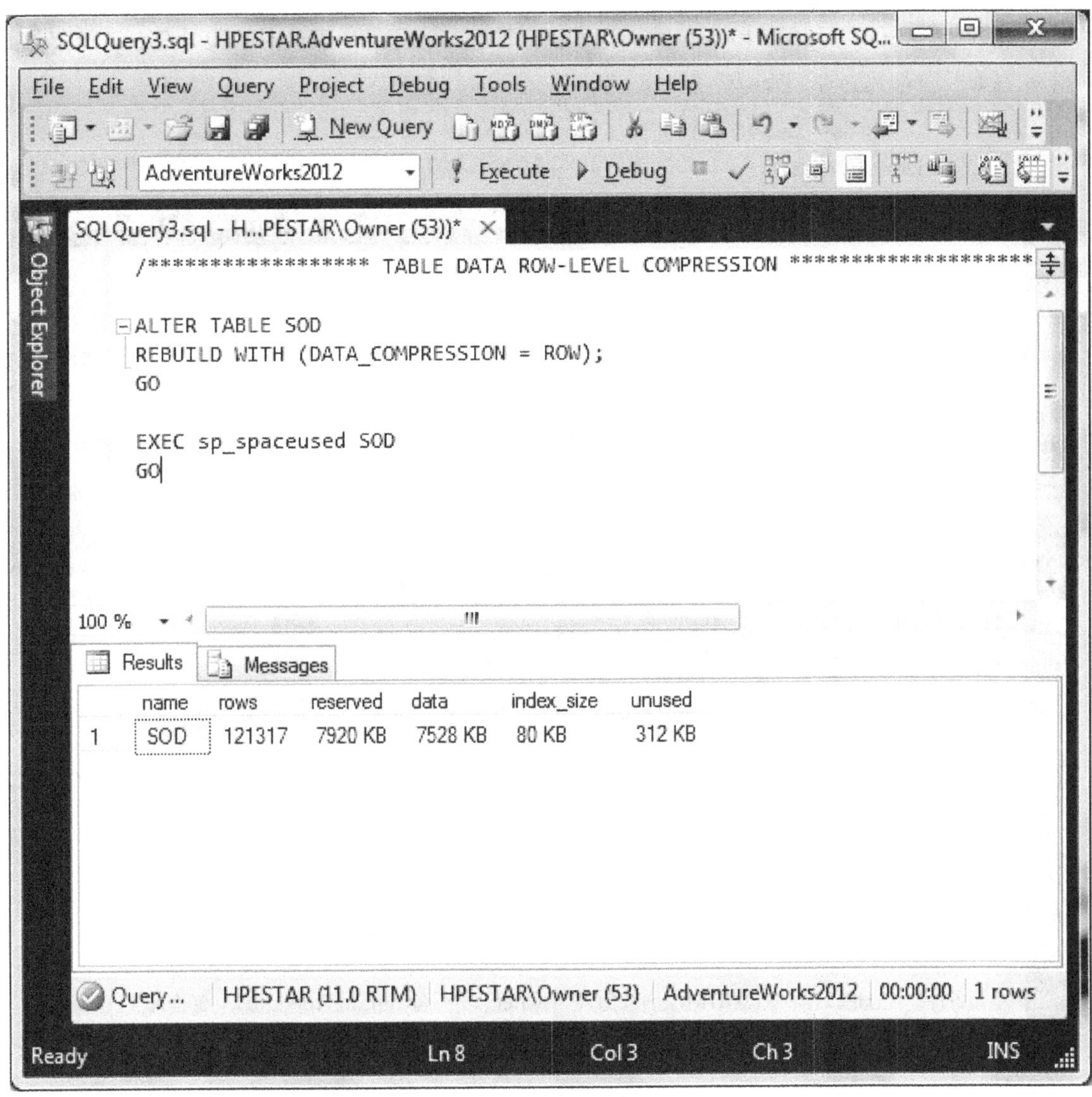

We can see the space reduction from 12MB to around 7.5MB.

Space reduction can be estimated with a system stored procedure.

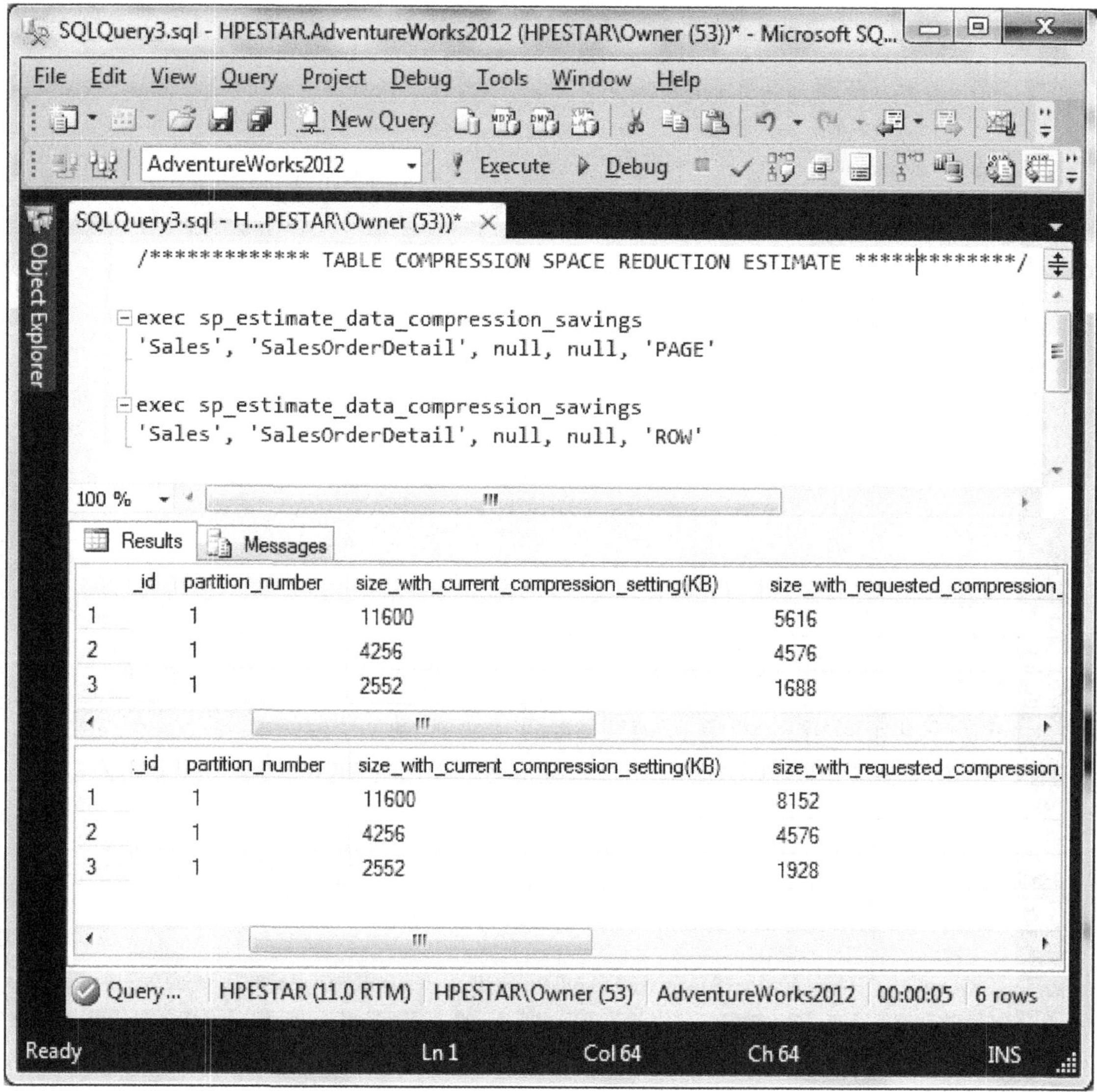

Careful and extensive considerations are required to decide to apply row, page or no compression to a table.

Query To Check How Many Rows Are Stored In An 8K Page In The Original Non-Compressed Table

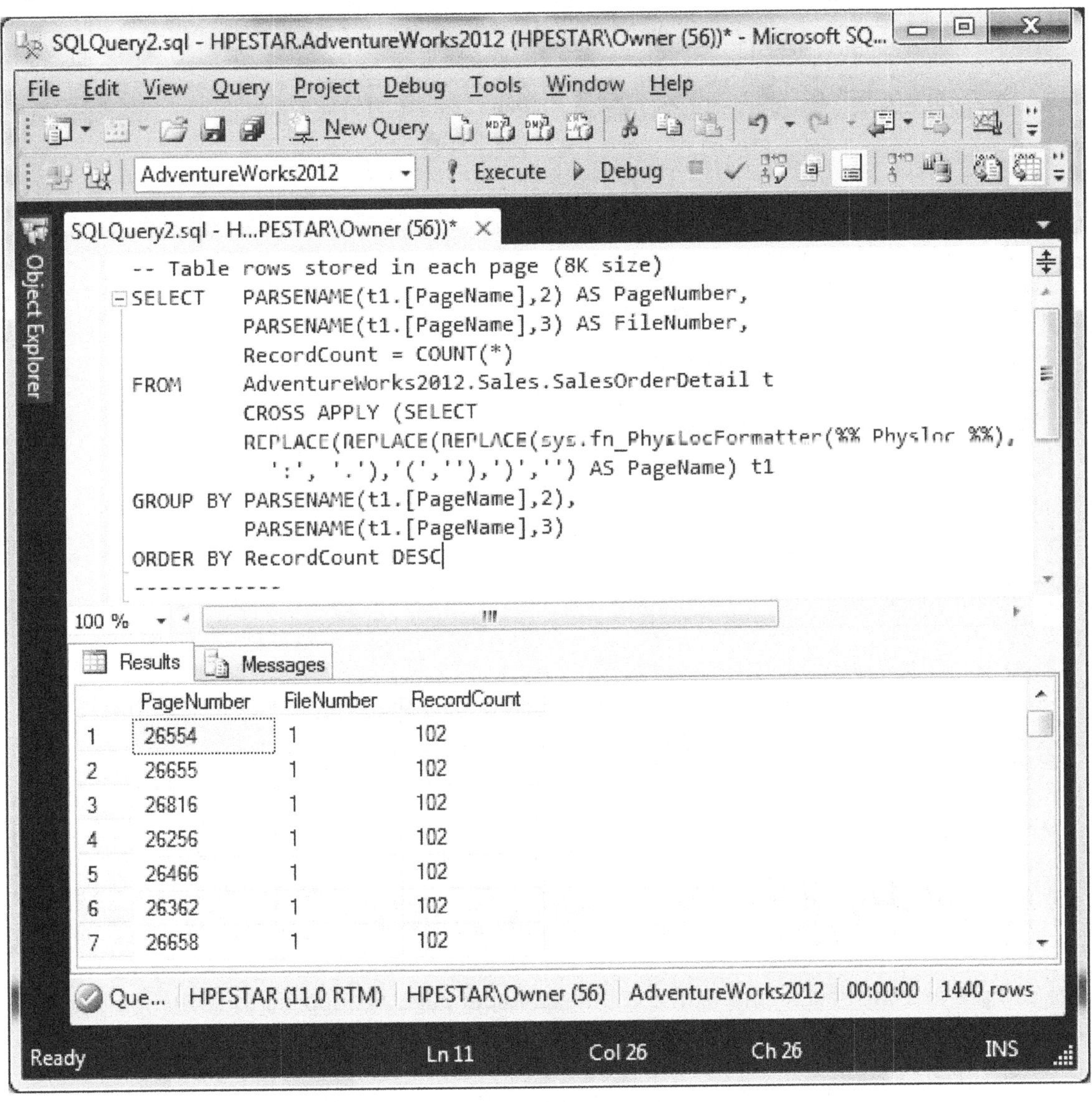

```
-- Table rows stored in each page (8K size)
SELECT   PARSENAME(t1.[PageName],2) AS PageNumber,
         PARSENAME(t1.[PageName],3) AS FileNumber,
         RecordCount = COUNT(*)
FROM     AdventureWorks2012.Sales.SalesOrderDetail t
         CROSS APPLY (SELECT
         REPLACE(REPLACE(REPLACE(sys.fn_PhysLocFormatter(%% Physloc %%),
           ':', '.'),'(',''),')','') AS PageName) t1
GROUP BY PARSENAME(t1.[PageName],2),
         PARSENAME(t1.[PageName],3)
ORDER BY RecordCount DESC
------------
```

	PageNumber	FileNumber	RecordCount
1	26554	1	102
2	26655	1	102
3	26816	1	102
4	26256	1	102
5	26466	1	102
6	26362	1	102
7	26658	1	102

Query to check the same for the compressed table SOD

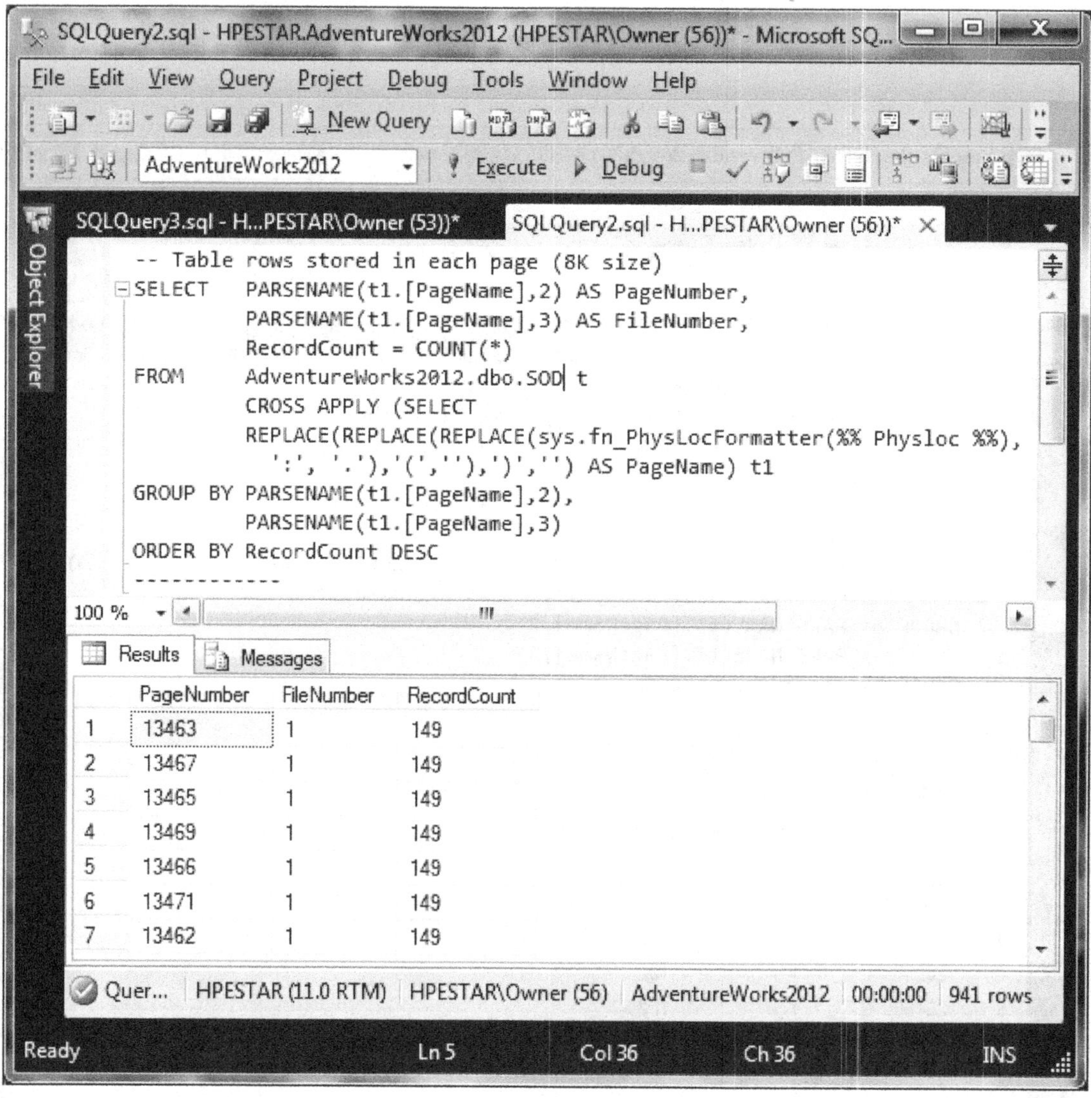

```
-- Table rows stored in each page (8K size)
SELECT   PARSENAME(t1.[PageName],2) AS PageNumber,
         PARSENAME(t1.[PageName],3) AS FileNumber,
         RecordCount = COUNT(*)
FROM     AdventureWorks2012.dbo.SOD t
         CROSS APPLY (SELECT
         REPLACE(REPLACE(REPLACE(sys.fn_PhysLocFormatter(%% Physloc %%),
           ':', '.'),'(',''),')','') AS PageName) t1
GROUP BY PARSENAME(t1.[PageName],2),
         PARSENAME(t1.[PageName],3)
ORDER BY RecordCount DESC
------------
```

	PageNumber	FileNumber	RecordCount
1	13463	1	149
2	13467	1	149
3	13465	1	149
4	13469	1	149
5	13466	1	149
6	13471	1	149
7	13462	1	149

We can see that the best record (rows) count is 149 per page as opposed to 102 when the rows are not compressed. Since compression and decompression are processing intensive, we are trading CPU load vs. disk load. Which one to choose? PAGE compression is the true compression with maximum space saving. Choose PAGE compression for best disk IO reduction. As mentioned earlier careful preparation is required to make sure there are no undesirable side effects.

Data Compression: Compressed Index

Index can also be compressed. The following script creates and compresses an index with included columns.

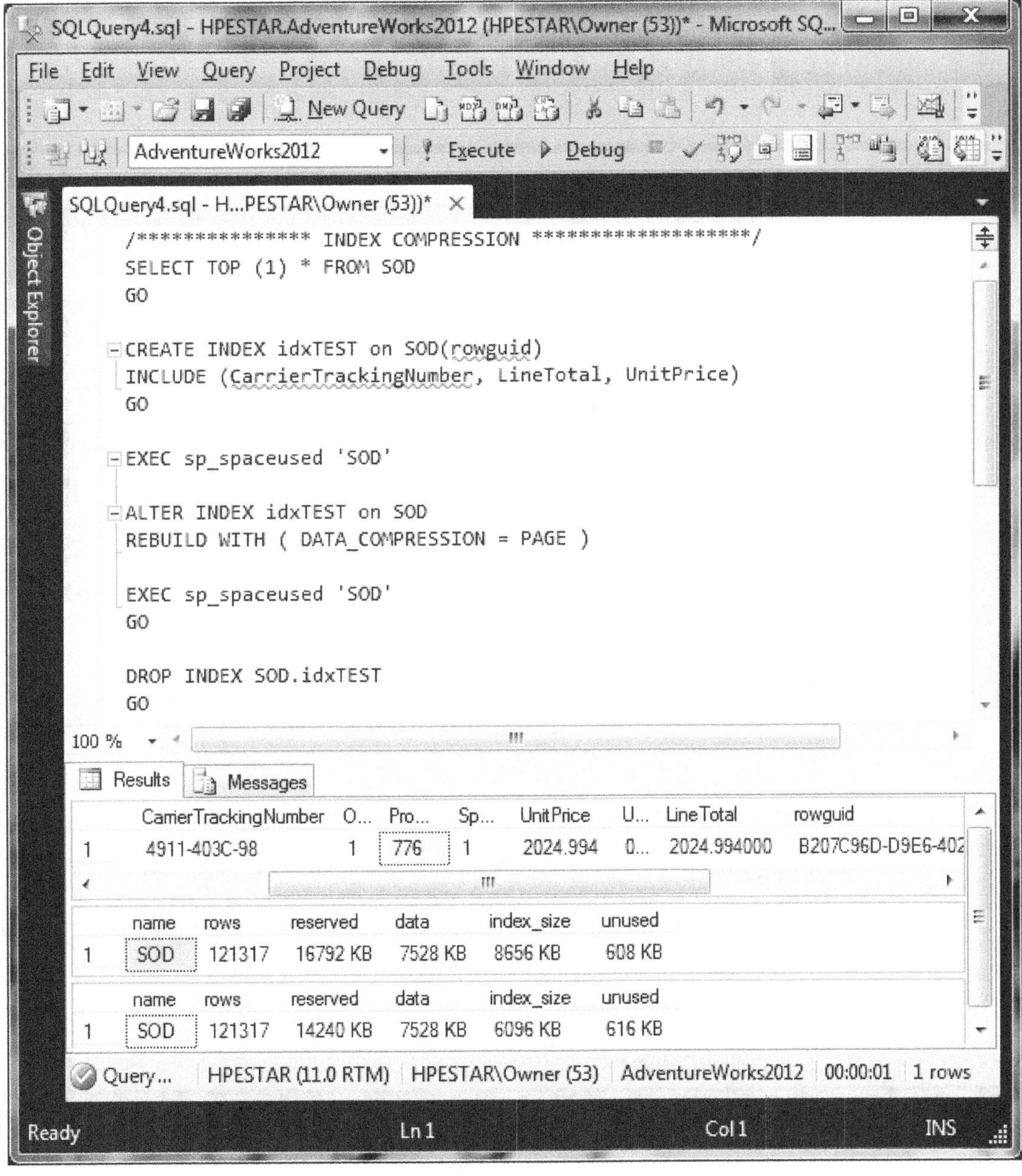
SQLQuery4.sql - HPESTAR.AdventureWorks2012 (HPESTAR\Owner (53))* - Microsoft SQ...
File Edit View Query Project Debug Tools Window Help
New Query
AdventureWorks2012
Execute Debug
Object Explorer
SQLQuery4.sql - H...PESTAR\Owner (53))*
/*************** INDEX COMPRESSION ******************/
SELECT TOP (1) * FROM SOD
GO
CREATE INDEX idxTEST on SOD(rowguid)
INCLUDE (CarrierTrackingNumber, LineTotal, UnitPrice)
GO
EXEC sp_spaceused 'SOD'
ALTER INDEX idxTEST on SOD
REBUILD WITH (DATA_COMPRESSION = PAGE)
EXEC sp_spaceused 'SOD'
GO
DROP INDEX SOD.idxTEST
GO
100 %
Results
Messages
CarrierTrackingNumber O... Pro... Sp... UnitPrice U... LineTotal rowguid
1 4911-403C-98 1 776 1 2024.994 0... 2024.994000 B207C96D-D9E6-402
name rows reserved data index_size unused
1 SOD 121317 16792 KB 7528 KB 8656 KB 608 KB
name rows reserved data index_size unused
1 SOD 121317 14240 KB 7528 KB 6096 KB 616 KB
Query... HPESTAR (11.0 RTM) HPESTAR\Owner (53) AdventureWorks2012 00:00:01 1 rows
Ready Ln 1 Col 1 INS

We can observe the index size reduction. Note that index_size includes all indexes.

The GUI Data Compression Wizard

The wizard can be started with Right Click on the table in SSMS Object Explorer.

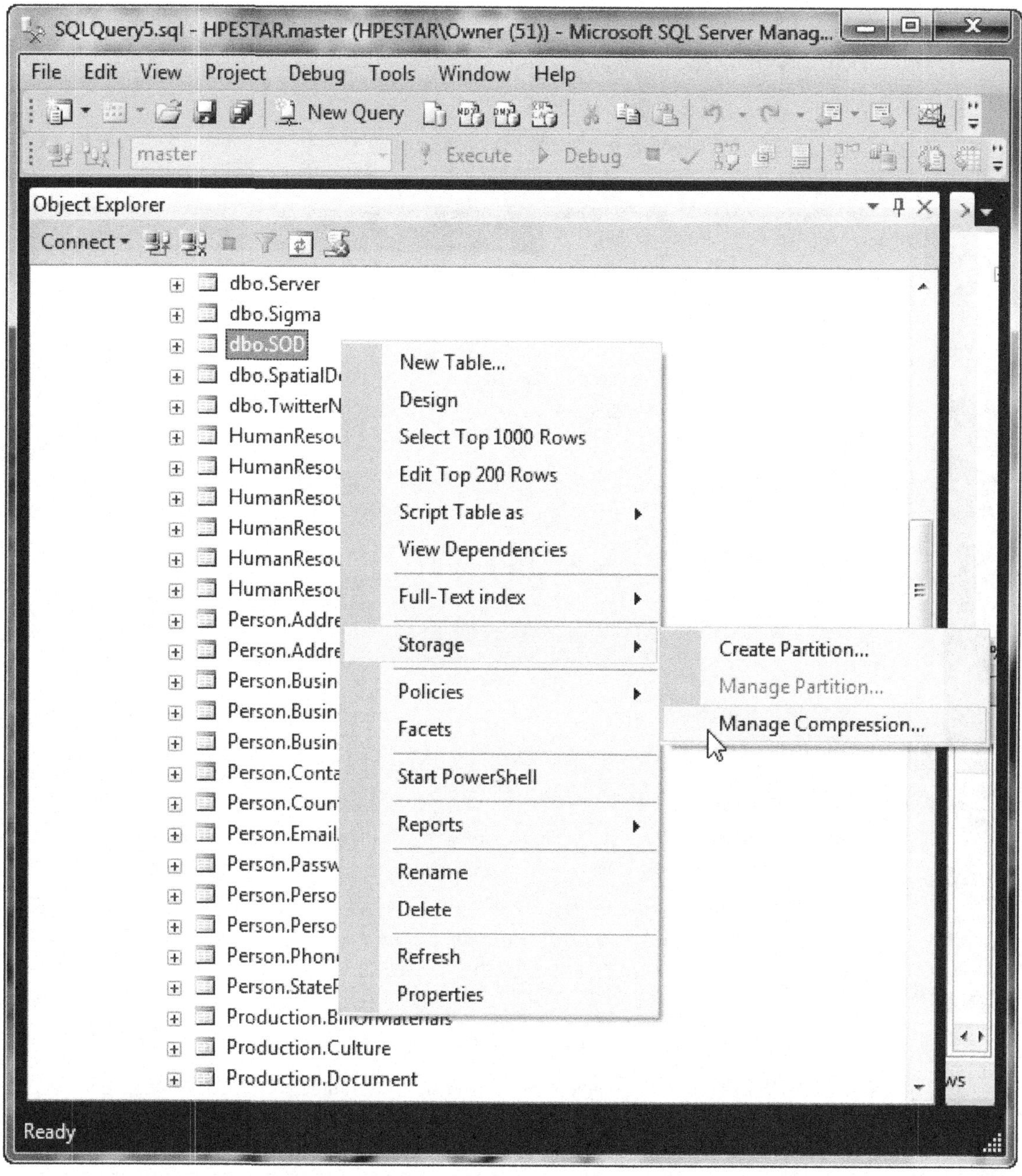

Space Saving Calculation Wizard Page

The figures include table & indexes total size.

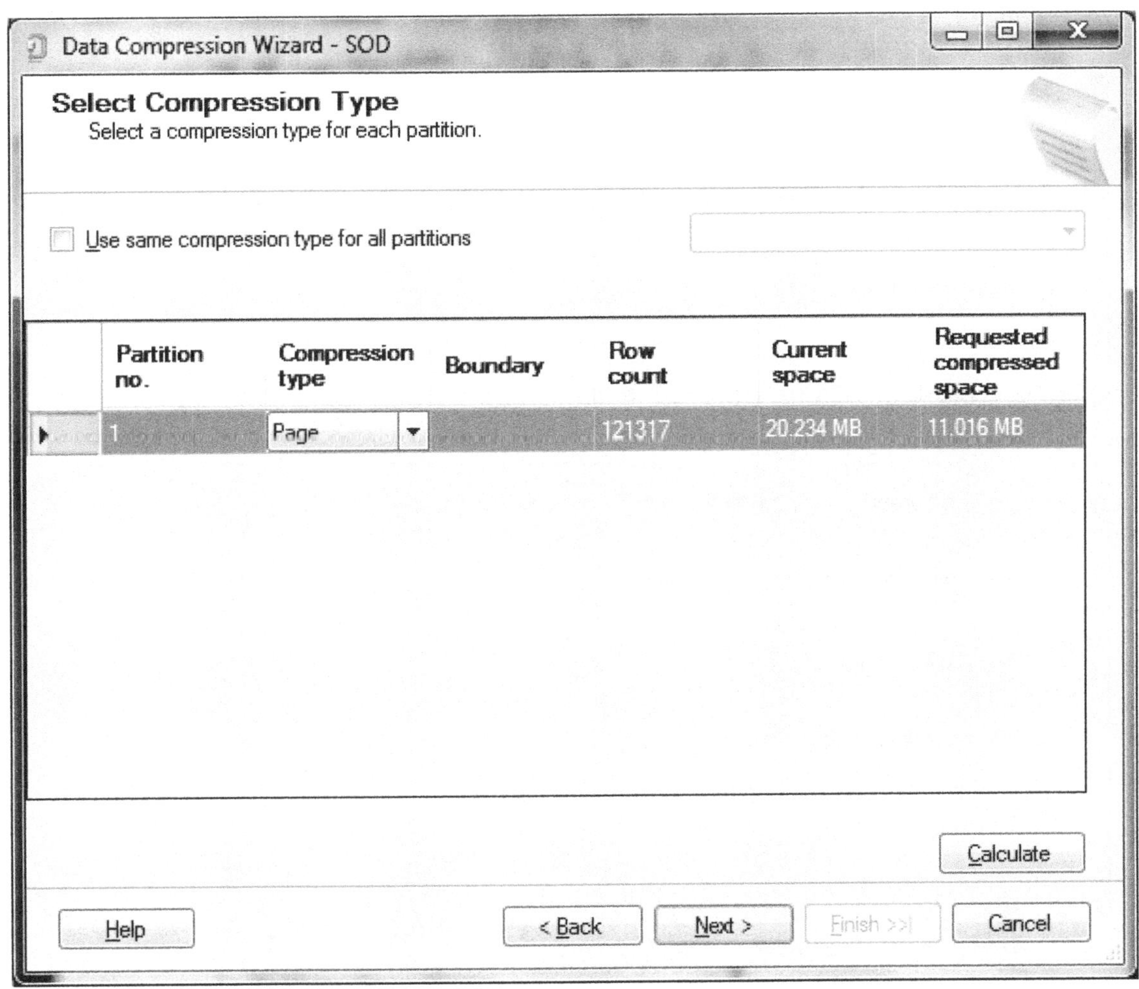

Output Panel Offers Scripting And Execution Options

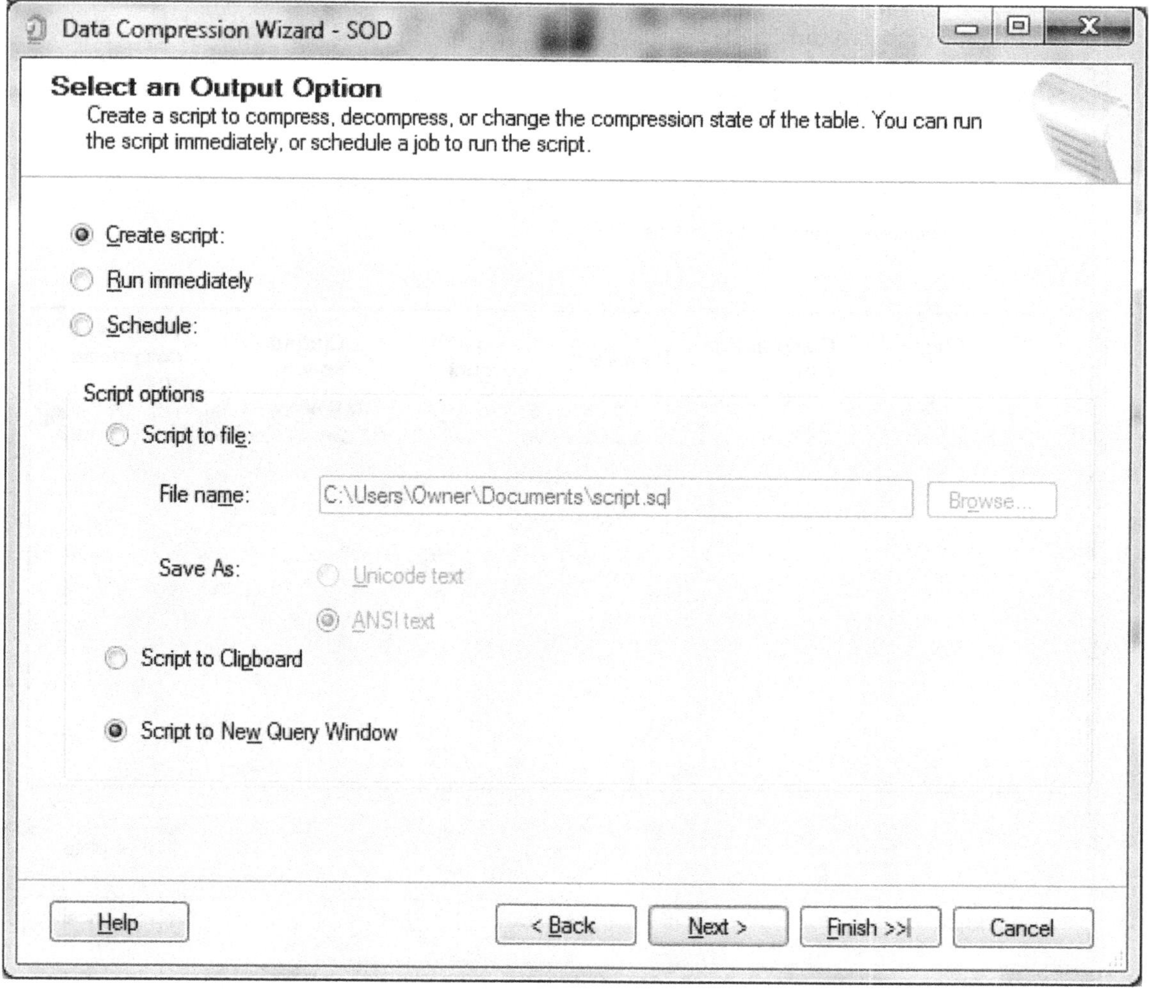

Testing the generated script with the sp_spaceused system stored procedure

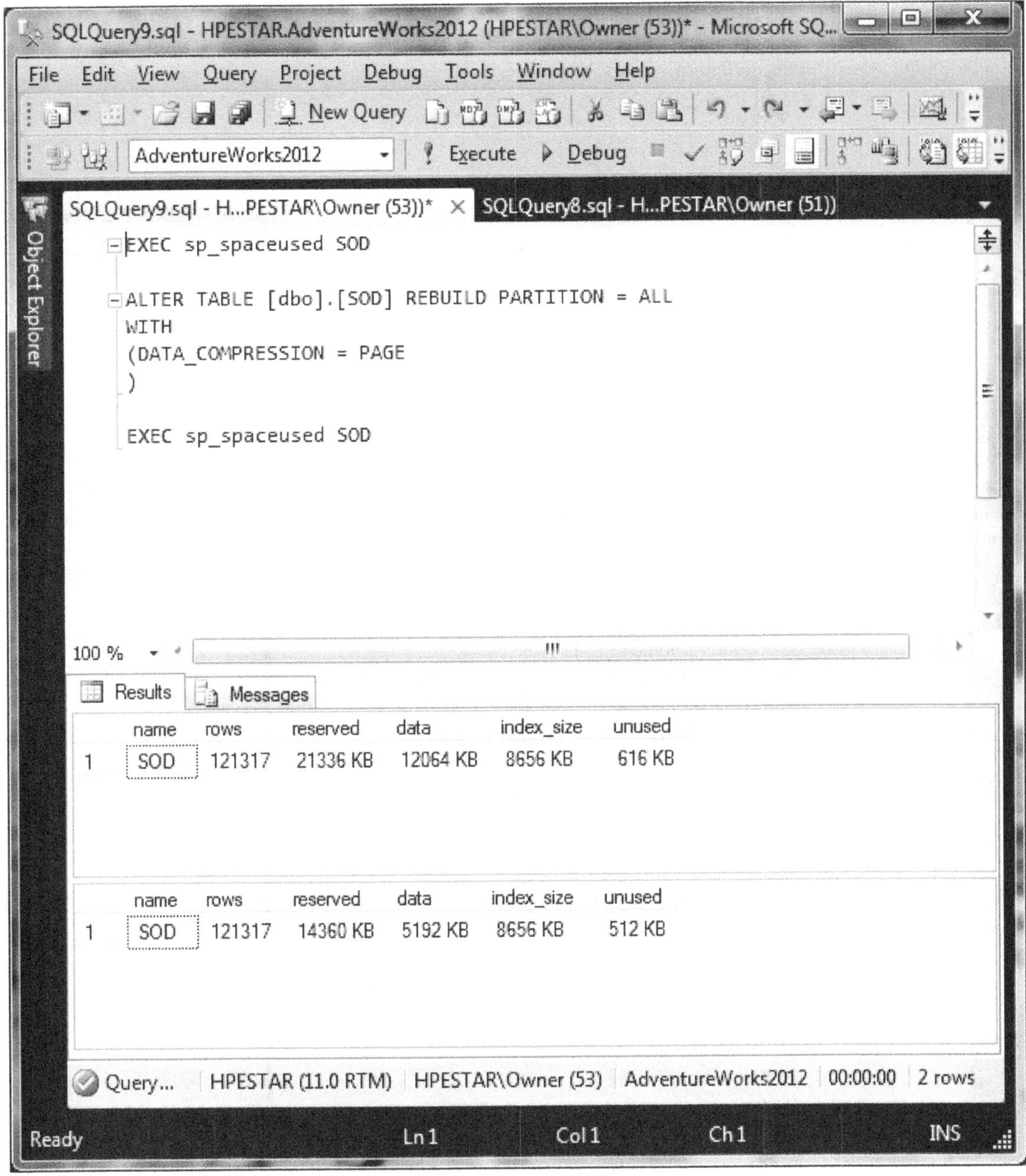

Indexes Can Be Compressed With The Wizard As Well

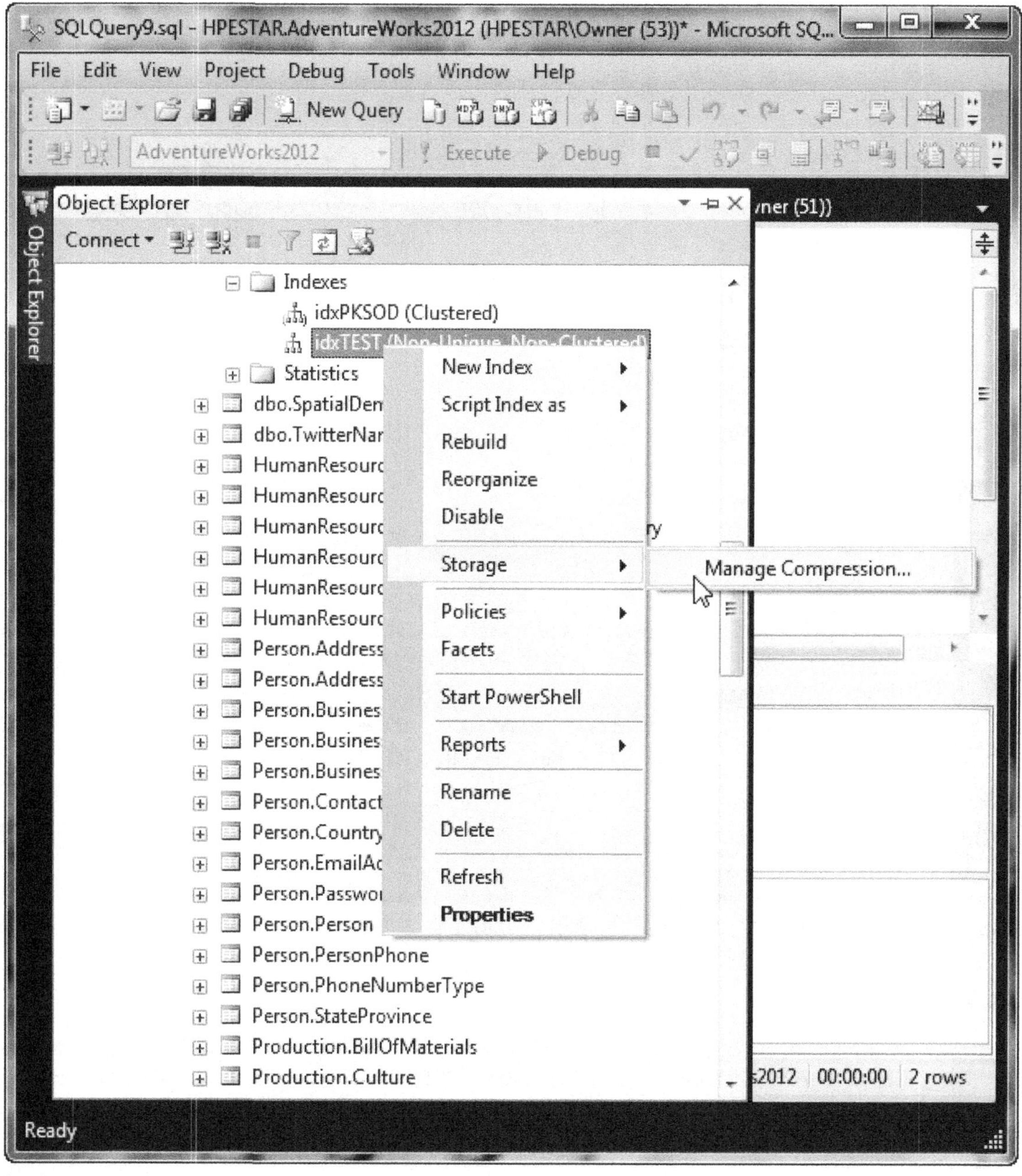

The generated script follows with measurement before and after index compression.

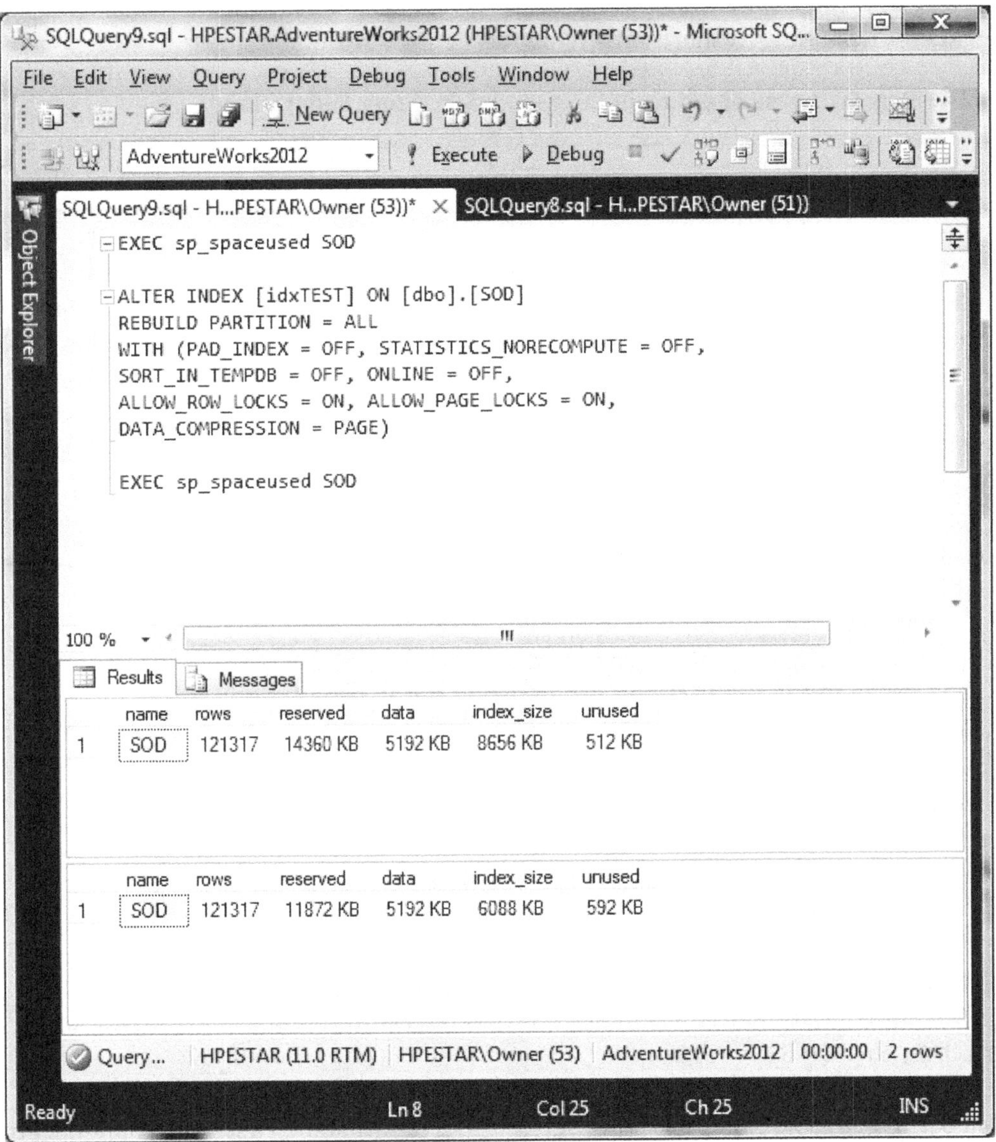

We can observe that the index size has been reduced from 8656KB to 6088 KB.

Articles

Data Compression: Strategy, Capacity Planning and Best Practices
http://msdn.microsoft.com/en-us/library/dd894051(v=sql.100).aspx
Data Compression http://msdn.microsoft.com/en-us/library/cc280449.aspx

Partitioned Table, Partition Function & Scheme - OPSS

Technet Article: **How to Shard with Windows Azure SQL Database**
http://social.technet.microsoft.com/wiki/contents/articles/1926.how-to-shard-with-windows-azure-sql-database.aspx
MSDN Blog: **Database Sharding in the Cloud: SQL Azure Federations**
http://blogs.msdn.com/b/lukad/archive/2011/12/27/database-sharding-in-the-cloud-sql-azure-federations.aspx

When data is stored from New York, Chicago, Houston, London and Hong Kong operations in a table, it makes you wonder if the server trips over NYC data when looking for London information. Analogous, 95% of the time in a typical business the last 30 days data may be accessed in a table, yet the dominant storage is for the 5% access of the 5 years prior data. The solution is logical: partition the data according to a usage-based scheme. Partitioning can improve performance, the scalability and manageability of large tables and tables that have varying query access patterns. **Gains with partitioning is not automatic.** Careful design studies are necessary for a successful table partitioning implementation.

In order to carry out a demonstration, first we create a copy of AdventureWorks2012 database from a backup file.

```
/* RESTORE script to create a new copy of AdventureWorks2012
  * Folder  FS1 should exist; FSBeta should not exist; AW12 should exist
  * Folder Backup should exist */
USE [master];
BACKUP DATABASE [AdventureWorks2012] TO  DISK = N'C:\Data\Backup\AW12.bak'
```

```
RESTORE DATABASE [CopyOfAdventureWorks2012]
FROM  DISK = N'C:\Data\Backup\AW12.bak'
WITH  FILE = 1,  MOVE N'FSAlpha' TO N'F:\data\FS1\FSBeta',
MOVE N'AdventureWorks2012_Data' TO N'F:\AW12\xAdventureWorks2012_Data.mdf',
MOVE N'AdventureWorks2012_Log' TO N'F:\AW12\xAdventureWorks2012_log.ldf',
NOUNLOAD,  STATS = 5
```

We will partition a table with SalesOrderDetail subset information. First a partition function is created.

```
USE CopyOfAdventureWorks2012;
GO
CREATE PARTITION FUNCTION pfSOD (int)
AS RANGE LEFT FOR VALUES (1, 20000, 40000, 60000, 80000, 150000) ;
```

The next step is to test the partition function to make sure it works as intended.

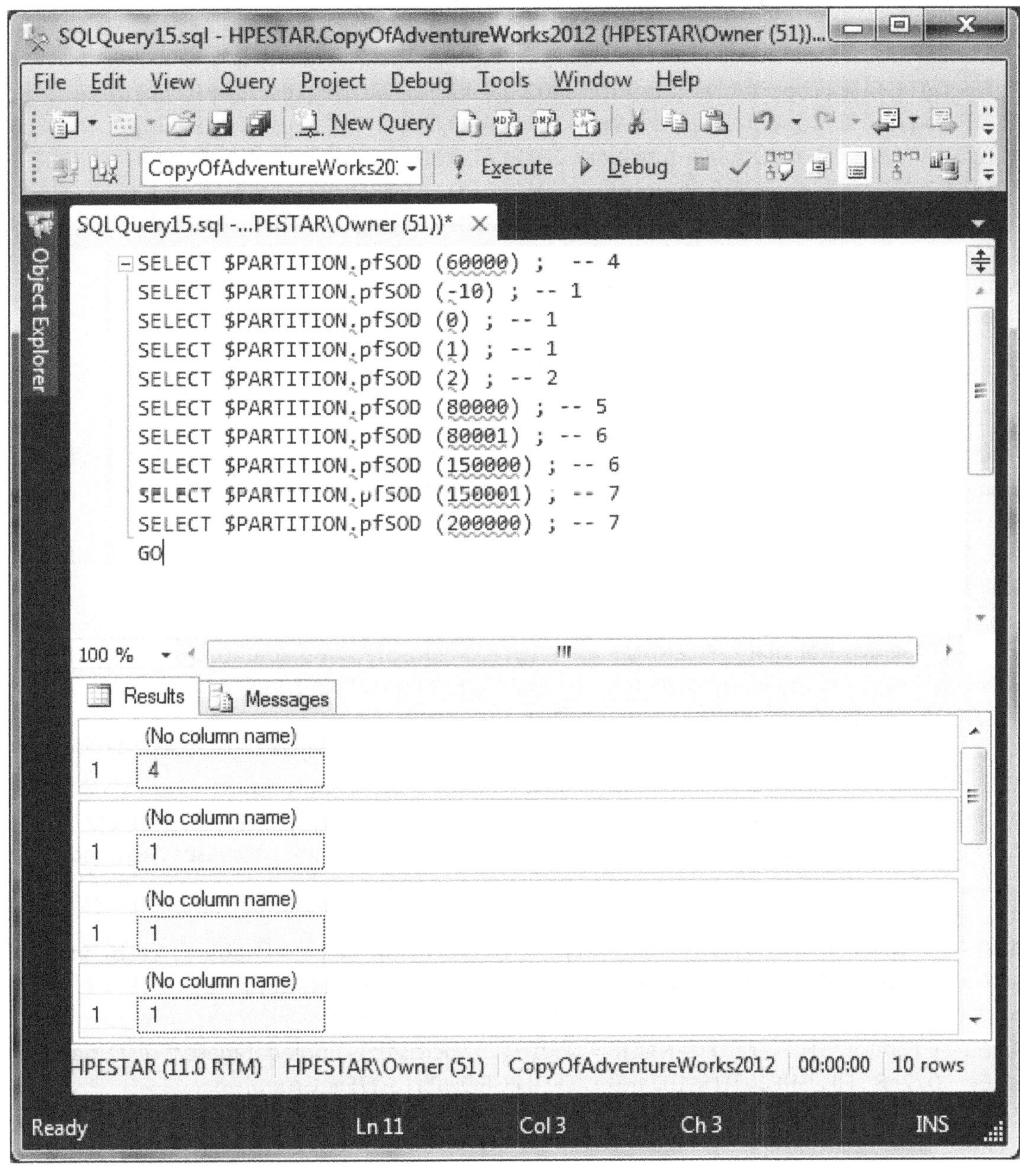
SQLQuery15.sql - HPESTAR.CopyOfAdventureWorks2012 (HPESTAR\Owner (51))...
File Edit View Query Project Debug Tools Window Help
New Query
CopyOfAdventureWorks20:
Execute
Debug
Object Explorer
SQLQuery15.sql -...PESTAR\Owner (51))*
SELECT $PARTITION.pfSOD (60000) ; -- 4
SELECT $PARTITION.pfSOD (-10) ; -- 1
SELECT $PARTITION.pfSOD (0) ; -- 1
SELECT $PARTITION.pfSOD (1) ; -- 1
SELECT $PARTITION.pfSOD (2) ; -- 2
SELECT $PARTITION.pfSOD (80000) ; -- 5
SELECT $PARTITION.pfSOD (80001) ; -- 6
SELECT $PARTITION.pfSOD (150000) ; -- 6
SELECT $PARTITION.pfSOD (150001) ; -- 7
SELECT $PARTITION.pfSOD (200000) ; -- 7
GO
100 %
Results
Messages
(No column name)
1 4
(No column name)
1 1
(No column name)
1 1
(No column name)
1 1
HPESTAR (11.0 RTM)
HPESTAR\Owner (51)
CopyOfAdventureWorks2012
00:00:00
10 rows
Ready
Ln 11
Col 3
Ch 3
INS

T-SQL scripts to create FILEGROUPs for the partitions

```
USE [master]
GO
```

```
ALTER DATABASE [CopyOfAdventureWorks2012] ADD FILEGROUP [Test1FileGroup]
ALTER DATABASE [CopyOfAdventureWorks2012] ADD FILEGROUP [Test2FileGroup]
ALTER DATABASE [CopyOfAdventureWorks2012] ADD FILEGROUP [Test3FileGroup]
ALTER DATABASE [CopyOfAdventureWorks2012] ADD FILEGROUP [Test4FileGroup]
ALTER DATABASE [CopyOfAdventureWorks2012] ADD FILEGROUP [Test5FileGroup]
ALTER DATABASE [CopyOfAdventureWorks2012] ADD FILEGROUP [Test6FileGroup]
ALTER DATABASE [CopyOfAdventureWorks2012] ADD FILEGROUP [Test7FileGroup]
GO
```

```
ALTER DATABASE [CopyOfAdventureWorks2012]
ADD FILE ( NAME = N'Test1', FILENAME = N'F:\UTIL\Microsoft\sampledatabases\Test1.ndf' ,
SIZE = 3072KB , FILEGROWTH = 1024KB ) TO FILEGROUP [Test1FileGroup]
ALTER DATABASE [CopyOfAdventureWorks2012]
ADD FILE ( NAME = N'Test2', FILENAME = N'F:\UTIL\Microsoft\sampledatabases\Test2.ndf' ,
SIZE = 3072KB , FILEGROWTH = 1024KB ) TO FILEGROUP [Test2FileGroup]
ALTER DATABASE [CopyOfAdventureWorks2012]
ADD FILE ( NAME = N'Test3', FILENAME = N'F:\UTIL\Microsoft\sampledatabases\Test3.ndf' ,
SIZE = 3072KB , FILEGROWTH = 1024KB ) TO FILEGROUP [Test3FileGroup]
ALTER DATABASE [CopyOfAdventureWorks2012]
ADD FILE ( NAME = N'Test4', FILENAME = N'F:\UTIL\Microsoft\sampledatabases\Test4.ndf' ,
SIZE = 3072KB , FILEGROWTH = 1024KB ) TO FILEGROUP [Test4FileGroup]
ALTER DATABASE [CopyOfAdventureWorks2012]
ADD FILE ( NAME = N'Test5', FILENAME = N'F:\UTIL\Microsoft\sampledatabases\Test5.ndf' ,
SIZE = 3072KB , FILEGROWTH = 1024KB ) TO FILEGROUP [Test5FileGroup]
ALTER DATABASE [CopyOfAdventureWorks2012]
ADD FILE ( NAME = N'Test6', FILENAME = N'F:\UTIL\Microsoft\sampledatabases\Test6.ndf' ,
SIZE = 3072KB , FILEGROWTH = 1024KB ) TO FILEGROUP [Test6FileGroup]
ALTER DATABASE [CopyOfAdventureWorks2012]
ADD FILE ( NAME = N'Test7', FILENAME = N'F:\UTIL\Microsoft\sampledatabases\Test7.ndf' ,
SIZE = 3072KB , FILEGROWTH = 1024KB ) TO FILEGROUP [Test7FileGroup]
GO
```

T-SQL scripts to create a partition scheme, a partitioned table and populate the new table with INSERT SELECT

```
USE CopyOfAdventureWorks2012;
GO
```

```
CREATE PARTITION SCHEME psSOD
AS PARTITION pfSOD
TO (Test1FileGroup, Test2FileGroup, Test3FileGroup, Test4FileGroup,
Test5FileGroup, Test6FileGroup, Test7FileGroup) ;
GO
```

```
CREATE TABLE SODPartitioned   (col1 int, col2 char(30))  ON psSOD (col1) ;
GO
```

```
insert SODPartitioned
select     SalesOrderDetailID, 'Unit Price: '+convert(varchar,UnitPrice)
from Sales.SalesOrderDetail;
GO
```

```
insert SODPartitioned
select SalesOrderDetailID+1,  'Unit Price: '+convert(varchar,UnitPrice+1)
from Sales.SalesOrderDetail;
GO
```

```
insert SODPartitioned select SalesOrderDetailID+2,  'Unit Price: '+convert(varchar,UnitPrice+2)
from Sales.SalesOrderDetail;
```

Query To Check The Data Distribution Within The Partitions

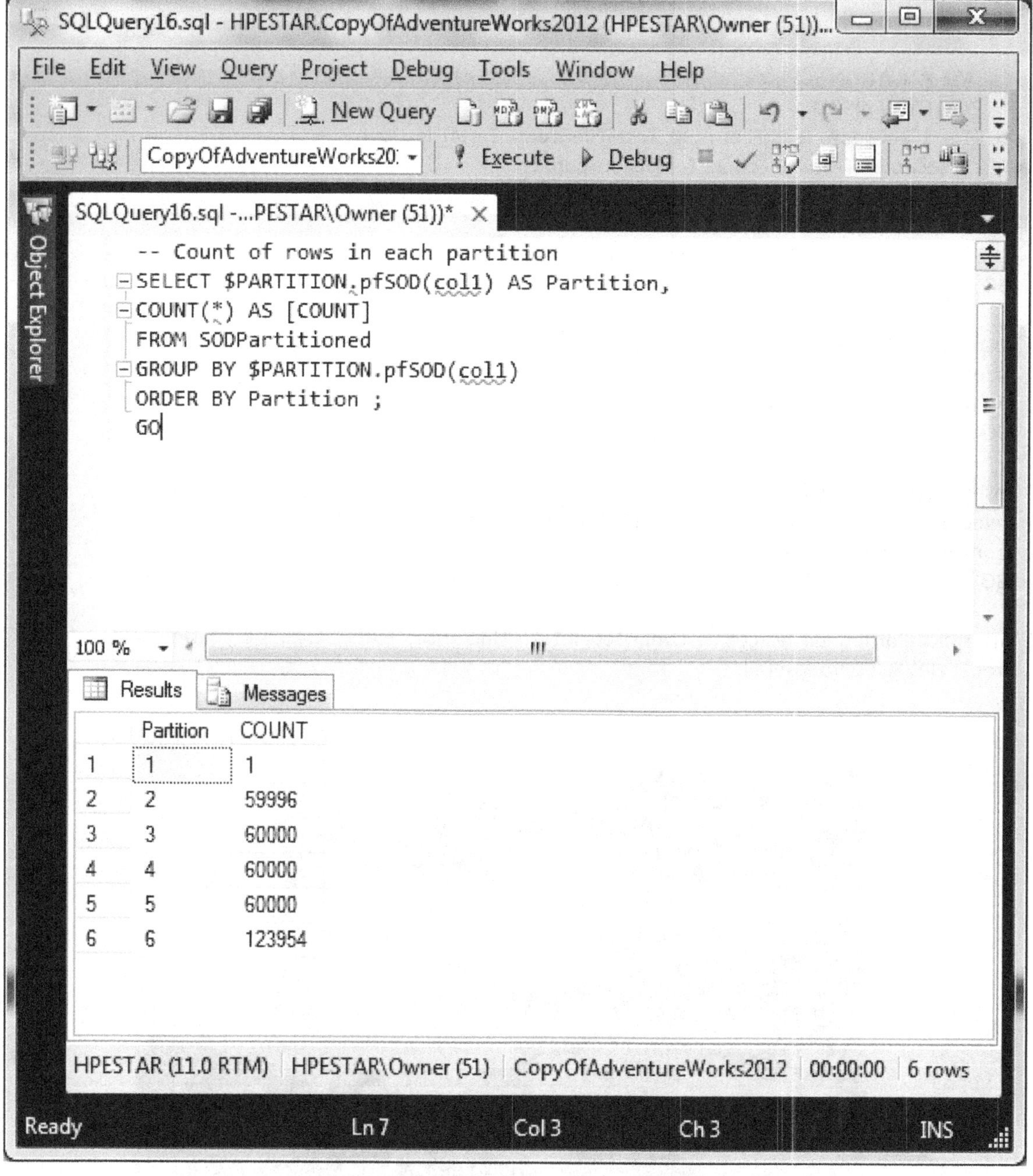

A few more counting queries to check entire table and a single partition population

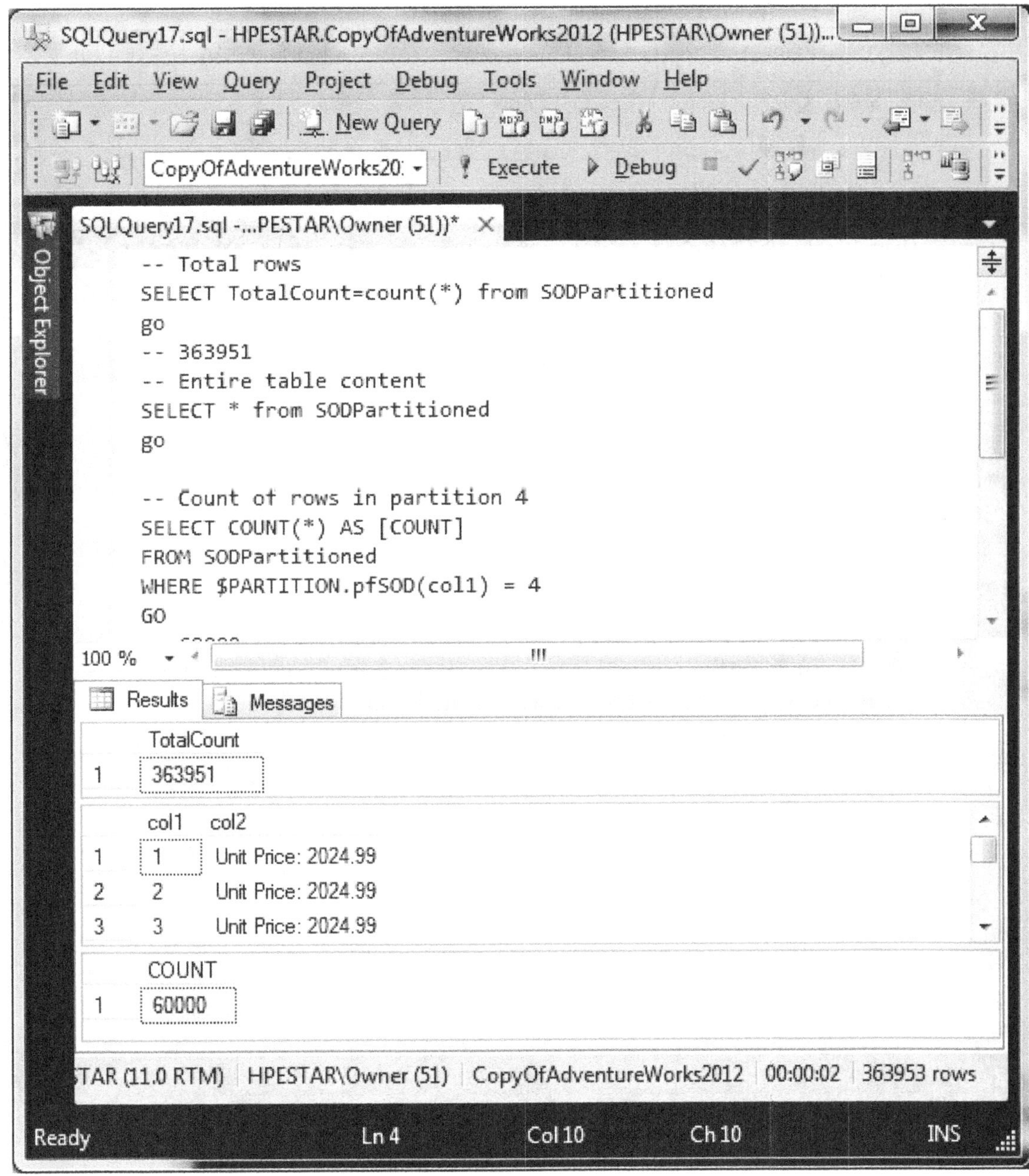
SQLQuery17.sql - HPESTAR.CopyOfAdventureWorks2012 (HPESTAR\Owner (51))...
File Edit View Query Project Debug Tools Window Help
New Query
CopyOfAdventureWorks20
Execute Debug
SQLQuery17.sql -...PESTAR\Owner (51))*
Object Explorer
-- Total rows
SELECT TotalCount=count(*) from SODPartitioned
go
-- 363951
-- Entire table content
SELECT * from SODPartitioned
go
-- Count of rows in partition 4
SELECT COUNT(*) AS [COUNT]
FROM SODPartitioned
WHERE $PARTITION.pfSOD(col1) = 4
GO
100 %
Results
Messages
TotalCount
1 363951
col1 col2
1 1 Unit Price: 2024.99
2 2 Unit Price: 2024.99
3 3 Unit Price: 2024.99
COUNT
1 60000
TAR (11.0 RTM) HPESTAR\Owner (51) CopyOfAdventureWorks2012 00:00:02 363953 rows
Ready Ln 4 Col 10 Ch 10 INS

System views with "partition" prefix contain metadata on partitions.

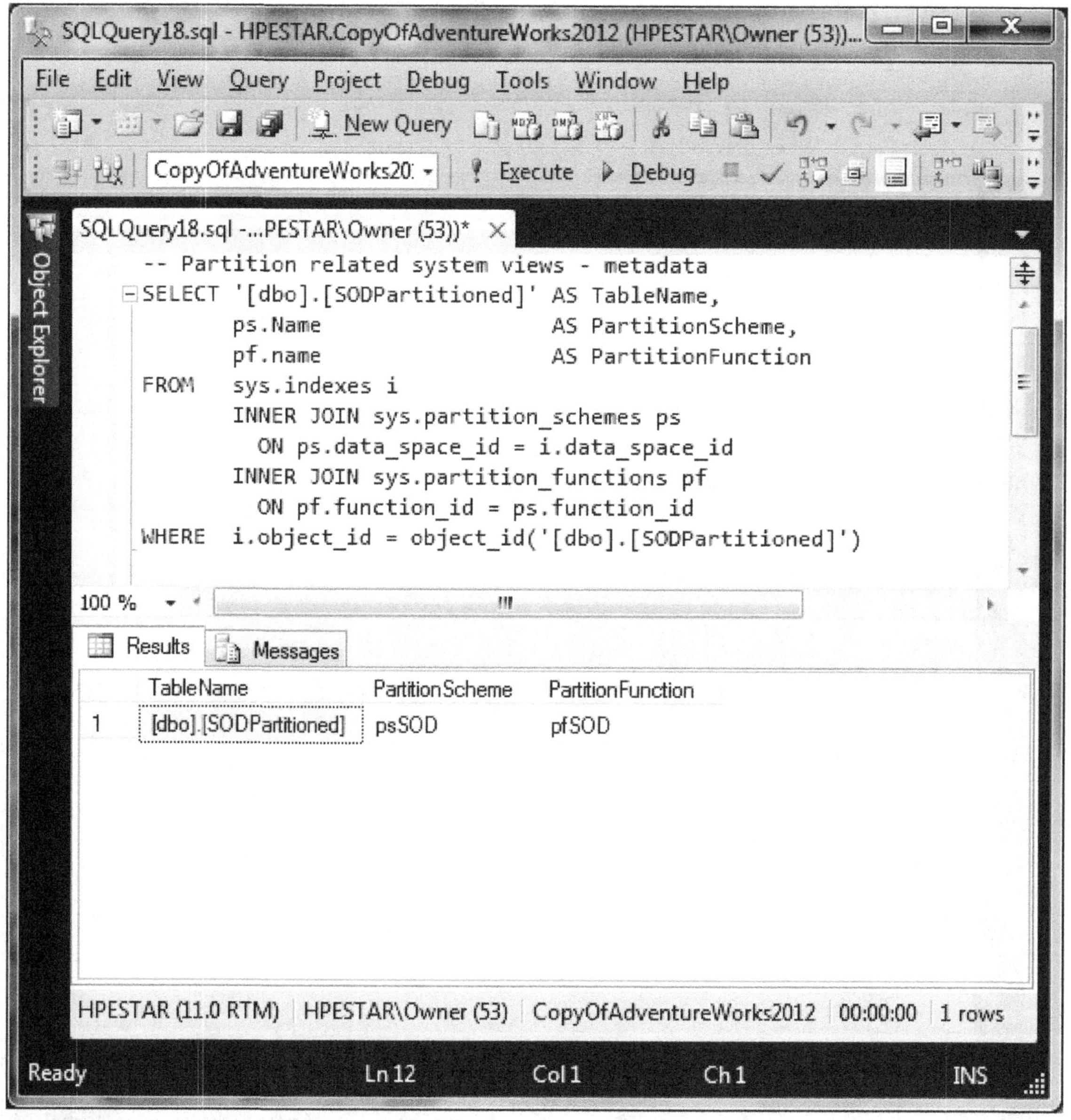
SQLQuery18.sql - HPESTAR.CopyOfAdventureWorks2012 (HPESTAR\Owner (53))...
File Edit View Query Project Debug Tools Window Help
New Query
CopyOfAdventureWorks20
Execute Debug
Object Explorer
SQLQuery18.sql -...PESTAR\Owner (53))*
-- Partition related system views - metadata
SELECT '[dbo].[SODPartitioned]' AS TableName,
ps.Name AS PartitionScheme,
pf.name AS PartitionFunction
FROM sys.indexes i
INNER JOIN sys.partition_schemes ps
ON ps.data_space_id = i.data_space_id
INNER JOIN sys.partition_functions pf
ON pf.function_id = ps.function_id
WHERE i.object_id = object_id('[dbo].[SODPartitioned]')
100 %
Results
Messages
TableName PartitionScheme PartitionFunction
1 [dbo].[SODPartitioned] psSOD pfSOD
HPESTAR (11.0 RTM) HPESTAR\Owner (53) CopyOfAdventureWorks2012 00:00:00 1 rows
Ready Ln 12 Col 1 Ch 1 INS

In the following example, we partition for "UK", "US" and other countries.

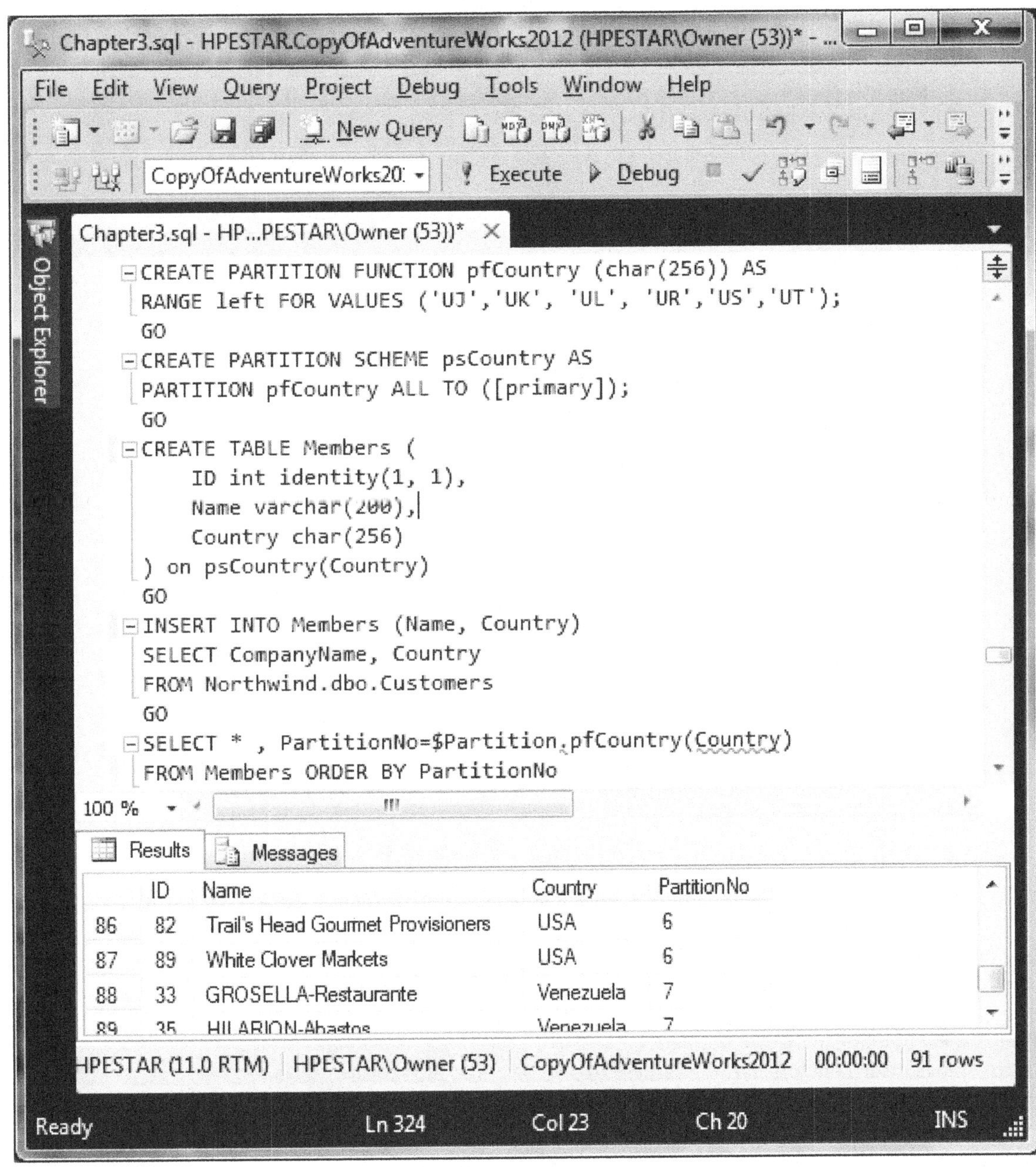
Chapter3.sql - HPESTAR.CopyOfAdventureWorks2012 (HPESTAR\Owner (53))* - ...
File Edit View Query Project Debug Tools Window Help
New Query
CopyOfAdventureWorks20:
Execute
Debug
Object Explorer
Chapter3.sql - HP...PESTAR\Owner (53))*
CREATE PARTITION FUNCTION pfCountry (char(256)) AS
RANGE left FOR VALUES ('UJ','UK', 'UL', 'UR','US','UT');
GO
CREATE PARTITION SCHEME psCountry AS
PARTITION pfCountry ALL TO ([primary]);
GO
CREATE TABLE Members (
ID int identity(1, 1),
Name varchar(200),
Country char(256)
) on psCountry(Country)
GO
INSERT INTO Members (Name, Country)
SELECT CompanyName, Country
FROM Northwind.dbo.Customers
GO
SELECT * , PartitionNo=$Partition.pfCountry(Country)
FROM Members ORDER BY PartitionNo
100 %
Results
Messages
ID Name Country PartitionNo
86 82 Trail's Head Gourmet Provisioners USA 6
87 89 White Clover Markets USA 6
88 33 GROSELLA-Restaurante Venezuela 7
HPESTAR (11.0 RTM)
HPESTAR\Owner (53)
CopyOfAdventureWorks2012
00:00:00
91 rows
Ready
Ln 324
Col 23
Ch 20
INS

The GUI Create Partition Wizard

SSMS Object Explorer Create Partition Wizard provides GUI environment for partition design and setup.

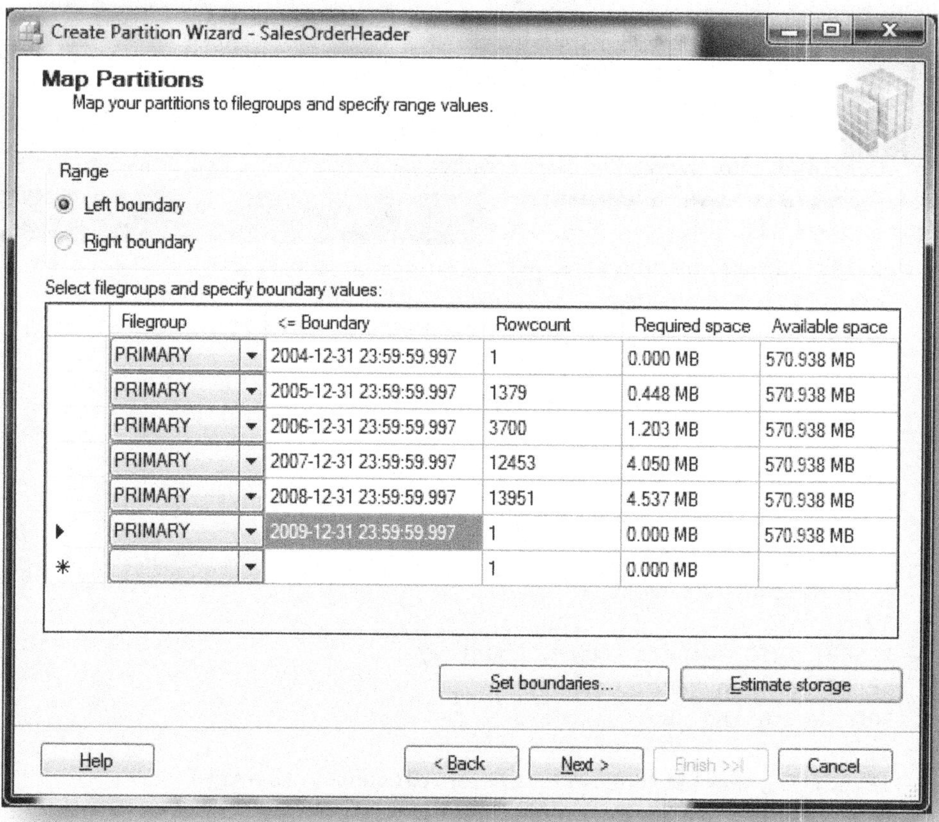

Azure SQL Partition & Federation Examples

Azure SQL Partition & Federation are different technology from SQL Server 2012 table partitioning.

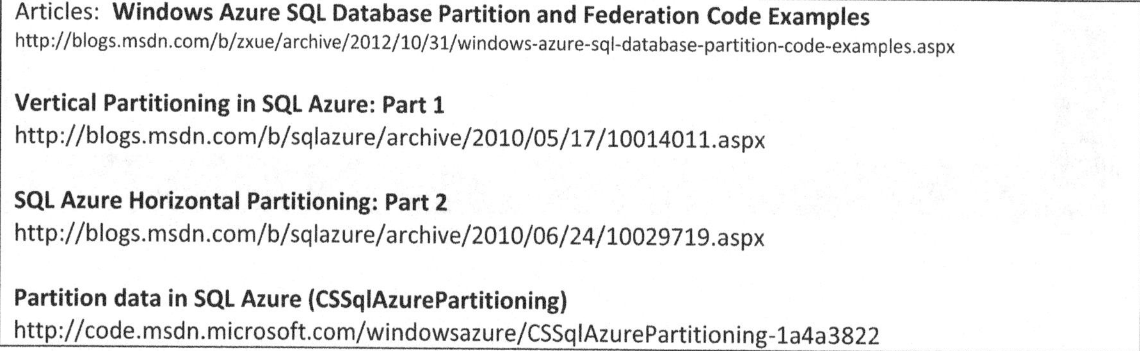

Articles: **Windows Azure SQL Database Partition and Federation Code Examples**
http://blogs.msdn.com/b/zxue/archive/2012/10/31/windows-azure-sql-database-partition-code-examples.aspx

Vertical Partitioning in SQL Azure: Part 1
http://blogs.msdn.com/b/sqlazure/archive/2010/05/17/10014011.aspx

SQL Azure Horizontal Partitioning: Part 2
http://blogs.msdn.com/b/sqlazure/archive/2010/06/24/10029719.aspx

Partition data in SQL Azure (CSSqlAzurePartitioning)
http://code.msdn.microsoft.com/windowsazure/CSSqlAzurePartitioning-1a4a3822

Columnstore Index for DW Performance - OPSS2012

Columnstore index for static tables, new to SQL Server 2012, is designed for Data Warehouse performance enhancement. The first script is a timing script for a GROUP BY summary query, and the second script is the creation of the columnstore index.

```
-- Timing before creating Columnstore index (5th timing)
USE AdventureWorksDW2012;
dbcc dropcleanbuffers;
declare @start datetime = getdate()
SELECT SalesTerritoryKey, SUM(ExtendedAmount) AS SalesByTerritory
FROM FactResellerSales     GROUP BY SalesTerritoryKey;
select [Timing]=datediff(millisecond, @Start, getdate());
GO 5
-- 190 msec
```

```
CREATE NONCLUSTERED COLUMNSTORE INDEX [idxColStoreResellerSales]
ON [FactResellerSales]
(
   [ProductKey],
   [OrderDateKey],
   [ShipDateKey],
   [EmployeeKey],
   [PromotionKey],
   [CurrencyKey],
   [SalesTerritoryKey],
   [SalesOrderNumber],
   [SalesOrderLineNumber],
   [OrderQuantity],
   [UnitPrice],
   [ExtendedAmount],
   [UnitPriceDiscountPct],
   [DiscountAmount],
   [ProductStandardCost],
   [TotalProductCost],
   [SalesAmount],
   [TaxAmt],
   [Freight],
   [CarrierTrackingNumber],
   [CustomerPONumber],
   [OrderDate],
   [DueDate],
   [ShipDate]
);
```

Checking the same query after creating the index.

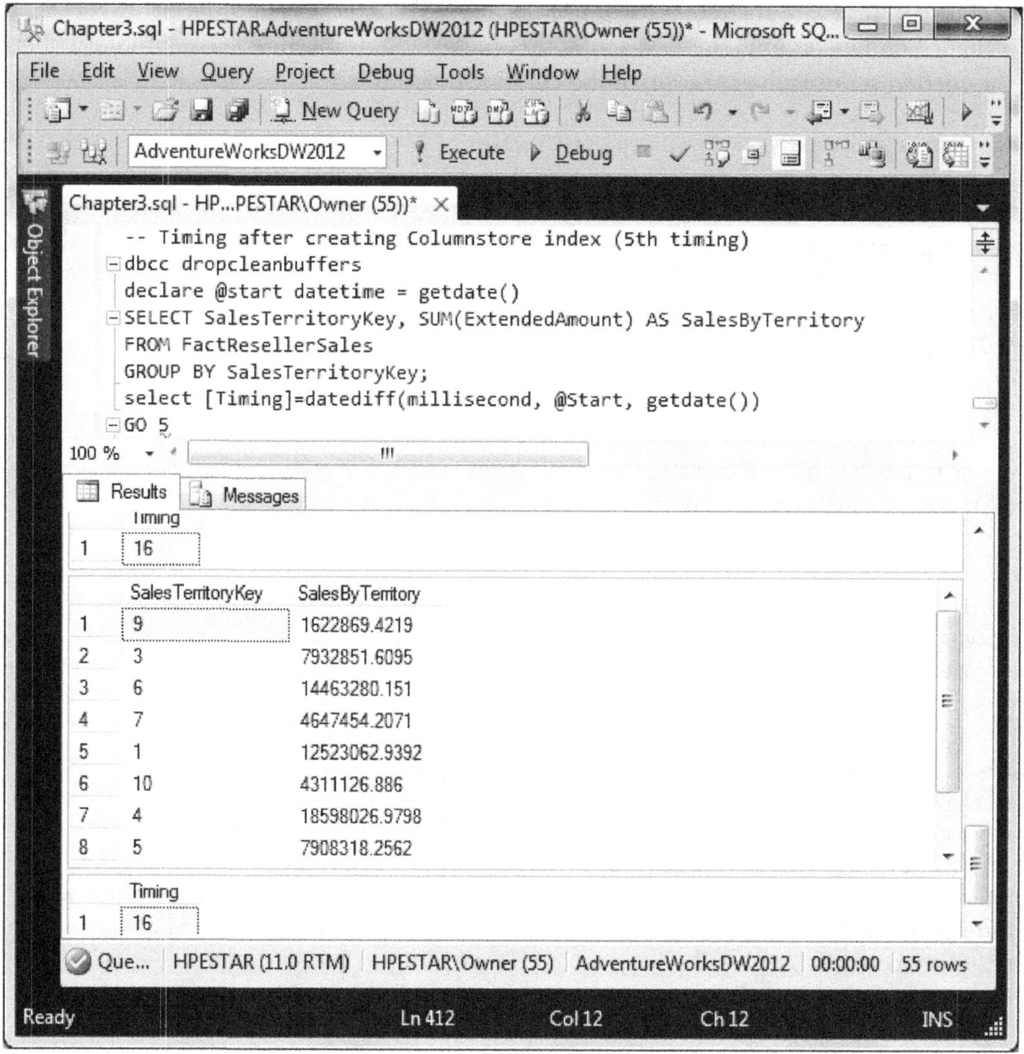

The performance gain on this particular query: from 190 msec to 16 msec. Generally columnstore index leads to significant query performance improvement in Data Warehouse environment.

Workaround for DBCC DROPCLEANBUFFERS

Best to takeperformance measurements at various time of the day, save results and average. Query return should be small, otherwise web transfer time variation will invalidate Azure SQL performance timing.

DATE Data Type Solves Many Problems with DATETIME

DATE columns should be DATE type (3 bytes) not DATETIME type (8 bytes) with exception when time is needed for the record such as credit card or online banking transaction.

Example: Sales.Customer table create with one computed column which has unique index defined on AccountNumber(computed).

```
CREATE TABLE Sales.Customer(
        CustomerID int IDENTITY(1,1) PRIMARY KEY,
        PersonID int                    REFERENCES Person.Person,
        StoreID int                     REFERENCES Sales.Store,
        TerritoryID int                 REFERENCES Sales.SalesTerritory,
        AccountNumber AS (isnull('AW'+dbo.ufnLeadingZeros(CustomerID),'')) ,
        RowGuid uniqueidentifier ROWGUIDCOL NOT NULL default (newid()),
        ModifiedDate DATE NOT NULL default (CURRENT_TIMESTAMP));
```

```
SELECT TOP 2 * FROM Sales.Customer ORDER BY AccountNumber;
```

CustomerID	PersonID	StoreID	TerritoryID	AccountNumber	rowguid	ModifiedDate
1	NULL	934	1	AW00000001	3F5AE95E-B87D-4AED-95B4-C3797AFCB74F	2008-10-13
2	NULL	1028	1	AW00000002	E552F657-A9AF-4A7D-A645-C429D6E02491	2008-10-13

Pad with Leading Zeros

Padding with leading zeros is a frequent business requirement. The ufnLeadingZeros() scalar-valued user-defined function converts the number into a string and pads it with leading zeros. The new **FORMAT command** can be utilized as well for leading zeros.

```
SELECT [dbo].[ufnLeadingZeros] (999);   -- 00000999
```

```
-- T-SQL script to pad with leading zeros
USE AdventureWorks2012;  DECLARE @Len tinyint=8;
SELECT   BusinessEntityID AS EmployeeID,   Rate,
         RIGHT(REPLICATE('0',@Len) + CAST(Rate AS VARCHAR(20)),@Len) AS PaddedRate
FROM   HumanResources.EmployeePayHistory;
```

EmployeeID	Rate	PaddedRate
1	125.50	00125.50
2	63.4615	00063.46
3	43.2692	00043.27

```
SELECT TOP(1) FORMAT(ProductID, '00000') FROM Production.Product;  -- 00980
SELECT FORMAT(999, '00000'); -- 00999
```

Database Design & Programming Standards

Standards have multiple purposes:

- Increase the productivity of the database developer.
- Increase the productivity of the project team.
- Decrease future maintenance cost of the RDBMS system.

Standards are about communications among project team members and among future software engineers who will come in contact with the work done presently by the software project team. Software standards are simple ordinary rules which should be followed. It is like when you turn on the left-turn signal in your car, the driver behind you anticipates you slowing down and making the next left turn. The situation is a little bit different though with software standards: there is no enforcing authority like the state authority in case of traffic rules. Many times argument can break out within the project team: "I like it this way", "it is really stupid to do it that way", "database expert Q says to do it this way in a blog" and so on. The following standards are pretty reasonable, and are based on industry acceptance, albeit not universal acceptance. The project manager has to enlist the support of all of the project team members for successful standards implementation. Database Design & Programming Standards to aid in optimal usability of SQL Server schema, scripts and stored procedures, user defined functions developed for applications by defining a reasonable, consistent and effective coding style. The identifier segment of the standard will formalize naming conventions. Without standards, database design, function, stored procedure and script development may become sloppy and unreadable, resulting in diminished productivity, usability, reusability, maintainability and extendibility.

Database Design Standards

Base design is normalized to 3NF or higher. History, log, Data Warehouse and reporting tables, containing second-hand data, need not be normalized. Similar considerations for staging and lookup tables. Each OLTP table has the following layout:

```
TableNameID (PRIMARY KEY) - commonly int identity(1,1) SURROGATE PRIMARY KEY
TableNameAlphaID (FOREIGN KEY if any)
TableNameBetaID (FOREIGN KEY if any)
natural-key column(s)
non-key columns
row maintenance columns
 RowGuid          uniqueidentifier
 IsActive         maintenance flag (bit 0 = not active, 1 = active)
 CreateDate       maintenance date (datetime if necessary)
 ModifiedDate     maintenance date (datetime if necessary)
 ModifiedByUser   last user who modified the record
```

Identifiers

CamelCase (Pascal case) naming convention: OrderDetail, ShippingCompany

With prefix example: vInvoiceHistory (view - Hungarian naming after Charles Simonyi)

Old-style naming example: sales_order_detail

Space usage is not a good idea in identifier: confusing & forces square brackets or double quotation marks use (delimited identifier).

Using spaces example: [sales order detail]

PREFIX ASSIGNMENT

Primary Key Clustered	pk
Primary Key Nonclustered	pknc
Index Clustered	idxc
Index Nonclustered	idxnc
Foreign Key	fk
Unique Constraint	uq
Check Constraint	chk
Column Default	dflt
Synonym	syn

Passed Parameter @p (input/output parameter) or @ - Example: @pStartDate, @StartDate

Local Variable @ - Example: @WeekOfTransaction

Table usually no prefix; exception large number of tables

Reporting table	rpt
Log table	log
History table	hist or arch
Date Warehouse table	dw, dim, fact
Common Table Expression	cte
View	v or view
User Defined Scalar Function	udf or fns or ufn or fn
User Defined Table Function	udf or fnt or ufn or fn
Stored Procedure	usp, sproc, or none

Principles of T-SQL Identifier Architecture

Each word in the naming must be functional. The first word must be the highest level category or action indicator. Examples for stored procedure names:

uspAccountPayableSummary
uspInsertAccountPayableTransaction
uspUpdateStockPrice
sprocInsertInventoryItem
sprocAccountReceivableSummary
AccountReceivableMonthly

Commonly accepted or easily understood abbreviations are allowed. Examples for business abbreviations usage in view naming:

vAPSummary
vAPDetail
vARSummary
vARMonthly
vGLTrialBalance

AdventureWorks2012 long stored procedure and view names.

```
SELECT name, type FROM sys.objects WHERE LEN(name) > 20 AND type in ('V', 'P') ORDER BY name;
```

name	type
uspGetBillOfMaterials	P
uspGetEmployeeManagers	P
uspGetManagerEmployees	P
uspGetWhereUsedProductID	P
uspSearchCandidateResumes	P
uspUpdateEmployeeHireInfo	P
uspUpdateEmployeeLogin	P
uspUpdateEmployeePersonalInfo	P
vAdditionalContactInfo	V
vEmployeeDepartmentHistory	V
vJobCandidateEducation	V
vJobCandidateEmployment	V
vProductAndDescription	V
vProductModelCatalogDescription	V
vProductModelInstructions	V
vSalesPersonSalesByFiscalYears	V
vStateProvinceCountryRegion	V
vStoreWithDemographics	V

Stored Procedure Outline

```
use {DatabaseName};
if (objectProperty(object_id('{schema}.{ProcedureName}'),
'IsProcedure') is not null)
    drop procedure {schema}.{ProcedureName}
go

create procedure {schema}.{ProcedureName}
  [{parameter}  {data type}]....
as
/*****************************************************************
* PROCEDURE: {ProcedureName}
* PURPOSE: {brief procedure description}
* NOTES: {special set up or requirements, etc.}
* CREATED:  {developer name} {date}
* LAST MODIFIED: {developer name} {date}

* DATE         AUTHOR              DESCRIPTION
---------------------------------------------------------------
* {date}       {developer} {brief modification description}
*****************************************************************/
BEGIN
[declare {variable name} {data type}....
[{set session}] e.g. SET NOCOUNT ON
[{initialize variables}]

{body of procedure - comment only what is not obvious}

return (Value if any)

{error handler}
return (Value if any)
END
 go
```

User-Defined Function Outline

Similar to stored procedure outline

How to Create a Database with T-SQL Script

Database can be created by the CREATE DATABASE command. Limited currently 149 databases. Create new Inventory DB.

BOL: **CREATE DATABASE (Windows Azure SQL Database)**
http://msdn.microsoft.com/en-us/library/windowsazure/ee336274.aspx

```
USE master;
GO
CREATE DATABASE Inventory;
GO   -- Command(s) completed successfully.
```

SQL Server 2012 script.

```
USE master;
GO
```

```
-- F:\DB\DATA\ folder should exist
CREATE DATABASE [Finance]   ON  PRIMARY  ( NAME = N'Finance_Data',
FILENAME = N'F:\DB\DATA\Finance.mdf' , SIZE = 217152KB ,
MAXSIZE = UNLIMITED, FILEGROWTH = 16384KB )
LOG ON  ( NAME = N'Finance_Log',  FILENAME = N'F:\DB\DATA\Finance_1.ldf' ,
SIZE = 67584KB , MAXSIZE = 2048GB , FILEGROWTH = 16384KB )
GO
```

```
-- SQL compatibility level 110 is SQL Server 2012
ALTER DATABASE [Finance] SET COMPATIBILITY_LEVEL = 110
GO
```

```
USE Finance;   -- SQL select into table create
SELECT * INTO POH FROM Purchasing.PurchaseOrderHeader;
GO
```

```
-- SQL select query for 3 random records
SELECT TOP (3) * FROM POH ORDER BY NEWID()
GO
```

PurchaseOrderID	RevisionNumber	Status	EmployeeID	VendorID
3506	1	4	261	1666
233	1	4	257	1578
84	1	3	261	1654

Adding New Column to a Table with ALTER TABLE

It happens quite often that a table in production for years needs a new column. While adding a new column to a populated table is relatively simple, there is a downside: application software needs to be retested to make sure it still works with the new table. One offending statement is "SELECT * FROM". The application software was programmed, let's say for example, 6 columns, after the addition SELECT * is sending 7 columns which causes error in the application. T-SQL scripts to demonstrate the addition of a new column to a table for sequencing or other purposes.

```
USE AdventureWorks2012;
```

```
CREATE TABLE #Product (NewProductID INT, ProductID INT, Name nvarchar(50),
        ProductNumber nvarchar(25), ListPrice money, Color nvarchar(15));
```

```
INSERT INTO #Product
SELECT NewProductID = ROW_NUMBER()   OVER (  ORDER BY ProductID),
            ProductID, Name, ProductNumber, ListPrice, Color
FROM   Production.Product
GO
```

```
ALTER TABLE #Product ADD CountryOfOrigin nvarchar(32) not null DEFAULT ('USA');
GO
-- Command(s) completed successfully.
```

```
SELECT          ProductID,
                Name                          AS ProductName,
                ProductNumber,
                ListPrice,
                COALESCE(Color,'')            AS Color,
                CountryOfOrigin
FROM   #Product  ORDER BY ProductName;
GO
```

ProductID	ProductName	ProductNumber	ListPrice	Color	CountryOfOrigin
1	Adjustable Race	AR-5381	0.00		USA
879	All-Purpose Bike Stand	ST-1401	159.00		USA
712	AWC Logo Cap	CA-1098	8.99	Multi	USA
3	BB Ball Bearing	BE-2349	0.00		USA
2	Bearing Ball	BA-8327	0.00		USA
877	Bike Wash - Dissolver	CL-9009	7.95		USA
316	Blade	BL-2036	0.00		USA
843	Cable Lock	LO-C100	25.00		USA
952	Chain	CH-0234	20.24	Silver	USA
324	Chain Stays	CS-2812	0.00		USA
322	Chainring	CR-7833	0.00	Black	USA
320	Chainring Bolts	CB-2903	0.00	Silver	USA

```
DROP TABLE #Product;     -- Cleanup
```

IDENTITY Column in a Table Variable

Using IDENTITY function for row numbering in new column with table variable. Statements must be in one batch, that is the scope of table variable.

```
DECLARE @Product TABLE
 (
   ID        INT IDENTITY(1, 1),    -- new column
   ProductID  int,
   ProductName varchar(64),
   ListPrice  money,
   Color      varchar(32)
 );

INSERT @Product
     (ProductID,
      ProductName,
      ListPrice,
      Color)
SELECT ProductID,
     Name,
     ListPrice,
     Color
FROM  Production.Product
WHERE  ListPrice > 0
     AND Color IS NOT NULL
ORDER BY Name;

SELECT TOP(7) *
FROM  @Product
ORDER BY ID;
GO
```

ID	ProductID	ProductName	ListPrice	Color
1	712	AWC Logo Cap	8.99	Multi
2	952	Chain	20.24	Silver
3	866	Classic Vest, L	63.50	Blue
4	865	Classic Vest, M	63.50	Blue
5	864	Classic Vest, S	63.50	Blue
6	948	Front Brakes	106.50	Silver
7	945	Front Derailleur	91.49	Silver

Note: the above "GO" (ending the batch) terminated the scope of @Product table variable.

```
SELECT TOP(7) *  FROM  @Product ;
/* Msg 1087, Level 15, State 2, Line 1     Must declare the table variable "@Product"  */
```

Partition Data By Country Query

Partition sales data by country and sequence sales staff from best to worst. NOTE: **ROW_NUMBER() is only sequencing; to rank with ties use the RANK() function.**

```
CREATE TABLE #SalesPersonRank(SalesPerson nvarchar(110),
        Country nvarchar(50),   [Row Number] bigint, SalesYTD nvarchar(50));
```

```
INSERT #SalesPersonRank
SELECT CONCAT(LastName,', ', FirstName)                 AS SalesPerson,
        CountryRegionName                                AS Country,
        ROW_NUMBER()  OVER(
                        PARTITION BY CountryRegionName
                        ORDER BY SalesYTD DESC)          AS 'Row Number',
        FORMAT( SalesYTD, 'c', 'en-US')                  AS SalesYTD
FROM   Sales.vSalesPerson   WHERE  TerritoryName IS NOT NULL    AND SalesYTD <> 0;
```

```
-- Add new column StarRank, which is 1 "*" for each $1,000,000 of sales
ALTER TABLE #SalesPersonRank ADD StarRank varchar(32) NOT NULL DEFAULT ('');
--Command(s) completed successfully.
```

```
-- New column empty so far, population follows with UPDATE
UPDATE #SalesPersonRank SET StarRank =
REPLICATE ('*', FLOOR(CONVERT(Money, REPLACE(SalesYTD,',','')) / 1000000.0));
-- (14 row(s) affected)
```

```
SELECT *  FROM   #SalesPersonRank   ORDER  BY Country,     [Row Number];
```

SalesPerson	Country	Row Number	SalesYTD	StarRank
Tsoflias, Lynn	Australia	1	$1,421,810.92	*
Saraiva, José	Canada	1	$2,604,540.72	**
Vargas, Garrett	Canada	2	$1,453,719.47	*
Varkey Chudukatil, Ranjit	France	1	$3,121,616.32	***
Valdez, Rachel	Germany	1	$1,827,066.71	*
Pak, Jae	United Kingdom	1	$4,116,871.23	****
Mitchell, Linda	United States	1	$4,251,368.55	****
Blythe, Michael	United States	2	$3,763,178.18	***
Carson, Jillian	United States	3	$3,189,418.37	***
Ito, Shu	United States	4	$2,458,535.62	**
Reiter, Tsvi	United States	5	$2,315,185.61	**
Mensa-Annan, Tete	United States	6	$1,576,562.20	*
Campbell, David	United States	7	$1,573,012.94	*
Ansman-Wolfe, Pamela	United States	8	$1,352,577.13	*

```
DROP TABLE #SalesPersonRank;
```

Diagram of Sales.SalesPerson & Related Tables

The sales staff is crucial in any business organization. It is reflected on the following diagram.

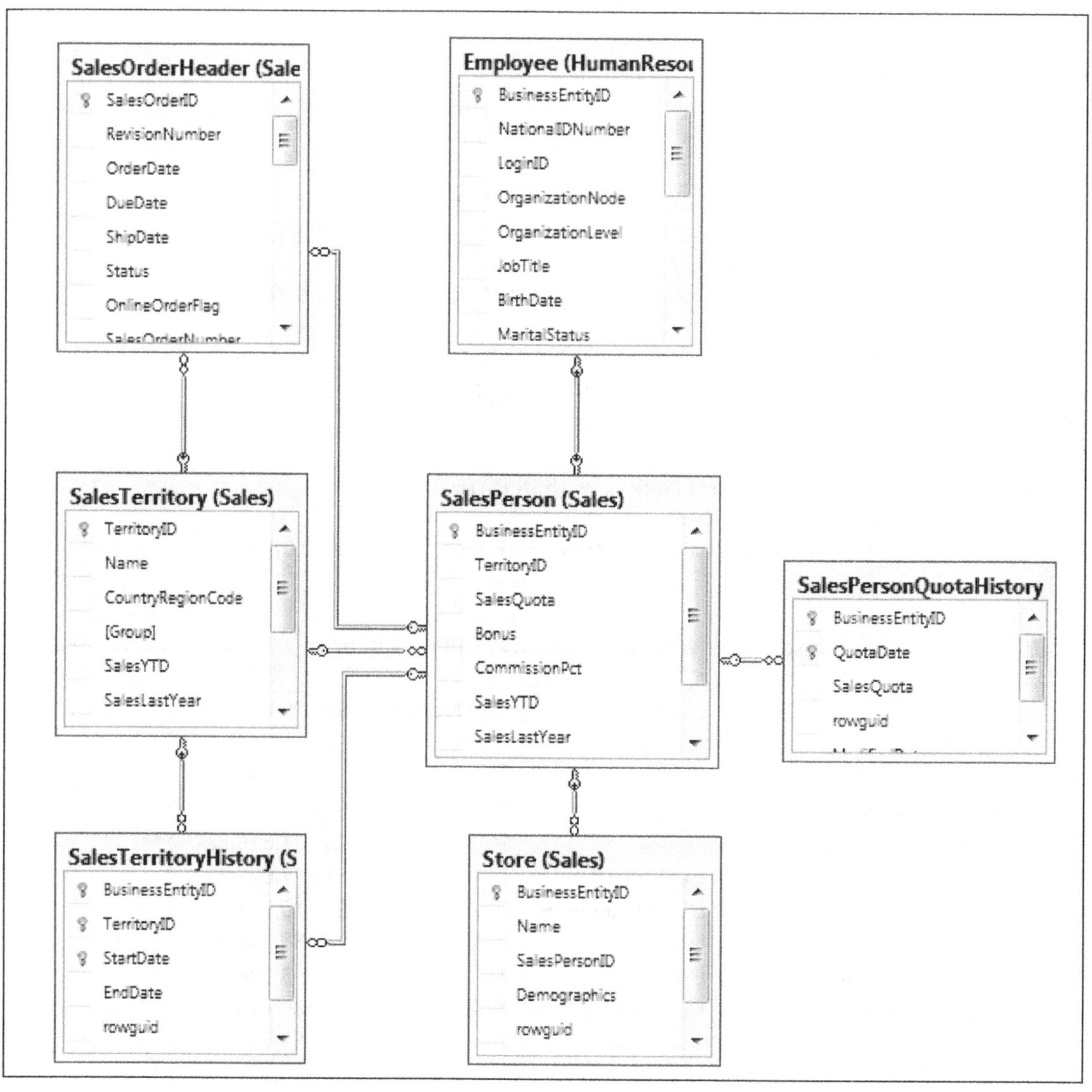

Adding IDENTITY Column To Empty Table

Add IDENTITY column to a table for sequential unique numbering (autonumber).

```
CREATE TABLE Department
 (
   Name       varchar(32)  UNIQUE,
   GroupName    varchar(256),
   ModifiedDate date default (CURRENT_TIMESTAMP)
 );
GO -- Command(s) completed successfully.
```

```
-- Add new IDENTITY column
ALTER TABLE Department    ADD DepartmentID smallint IDENTITY(1, 1) PRIMARY KEY;
GO
-- Command(s) completed successfully.
```

```
-- Only one identity column per table
ALTER TABLE Department
 ADD SecondIdentity smallint IDENTITY(1, 1);
GO
/* Msg 2744, Level 16, State 2, Line 1
Multiple identity columns specified for table 'Department'. Only one identity  column per table is allowed.
*/
```

```
INSERT INTO Department ( DepartmentID, Name, Groupname) VALUES (17, 'Student Affairs', 'Executive');
/* Msg 544, Level 16, State 1, Line 1
Cannot insert explicit value for identity column in table 'Department'  when IDENTITY_INSERT is set to
OFF. */
```

SET IDENTITY INSERT tablename ON

```
-- SQL identity insert enabled
SET IDENTITY_INSERT Department ON;
```

```
INSERT INTO Department ( DepartmentID, Name, Groupname) VALUES (17, 'Student Affairs', 'Executive');
-- (1 row(s) affected)
```

```
-- SQL identity insert disabled (default)
SET IDENTITY_INSERT Department OFF;
GO
```

DBCC CHECKIDENT Command - OPSS

DBCC CHECKIDENT can be used to check and reseed IDENTITY parameters.

```
DBCC CHECKIDENT('Production.Product');
/*Checking identity information: current identity value '999', current column value '999'.
DBCC execution completed. If DBCC printed error messages, contact your system administrator. */
```

```
-- SQL reseeding identity column; reset identity column
DBCC CHECKIDENT ("dbo.Department", RESEED, 999);
/*Checking identity information: current identity value '17'.
DBCC execution completed. If DBCC printed error messages, contact your system administrator. */
```

```
INSERT INTO Department (Name, Groupname) VALUES ( 'Alumni Affairs', 'Executive');
```

```
SELECT * FROM Department;
```

Name	GroupName	ModifiedDate	DepartmentID
Student Affairs	Executive	2016-07-19	17
Alumni Affairs	Executive	2016-07-19	1000

```
-- Add more records to table with INSERT SELECT
INSERT INTO Department (Name, Groupname)
SELECT Name, GroupName  FROM HumanResources.Department;
```

```
SELECT * FROM Department ORDER BY DepartmentID;
```

Name	GroupName	ModifiedDate	DepartmentID
Student Affairs	Executive	2012-07-19	17
Alumni Affairs	Executive	2012-07-19	1000
Engineering	Research and Development	2012-07-19	1001
Tool Design	Research and Development	2012-07-19	1002
Sales	Sales and Marketing	2012-07-19	1003
Marketing	Sales and Marketing	2012-07-19	1004
Purchasing	Inventory Management	2012-07-19	1005
Research and Development	Research and Development	2012-07-19	1006
Production	Manufacturing	2012-07-19	1007
Production Control	Manufacturing	2012-07-19	1008
Human Resources	Executive General and Administration	2012-07-19	1009
Finance	Executive General and Administration	2012-07-19	1010
Information Services	Executive General and Administration	2012-07-19	1011
Document Control	Quality Assurance	2012-07-19	1012
Quality Assurance	Quality Assurance	2012-07-19	1013
Facilities and Maintenance	Executive General and Administration	2012-07-19	1014
Shipping and Receiving	Inventory Management	2012-07-19	1015
Executive	Executive General and Administration	2012-07-19	1016

```
DROP TABLE tempdb.dbo.Department;
```

ADD Partitioned Sequence Number to Table

Partition table by subcategory (ProductSubcategoryID) by applying ROW_NUMBER for sequencing within each partition.

```
CREATE TABLE #ProductsByCategory( RowID bigint NULL, SubCategory nvarchar(50) NOT NULL,
        ProductName nvarchar(50) NOT NULL, ProductNumber nvarchar(25) NOT NULL,
        Color nvarchar(15) NULL, ListPrice money NOT NULL);
GO
```

```
INSERT INTO #ProductsByCategory
SELECT ROW_NUMBER()   OVER ( PARTITION BY p.ProductSubcategoryID
                             ORDER BY ProductID)          AS RowID,
    ps.Name                                               AS SubCategory,
    p.Name                                                AS ProductName,
    ProductNumber,  Color,    ListPrice
FROM  Production.Product p
    INNER JOIN Production.ProductSubcategory ps
        ON p.ProductSubcategoryID = ps.ProductSubcategoryID ;
```

```
-- Add new column for display in currency format
ALTER TABLE #ProductsByCategory ADD Dollar varchar(32) not null DEFAULT ('');
GO -- Command(s) completed successfully.
```

```
-- Populate new column with UPDATE
UPDATE #ProductsByCategory SET Dollar = FORMAT(ListPrice, 'c', 'en-US');
GO -- (295 row(s) affected)
```

```
SELECT * FROM #ProductsByCategory ORDER BY Subcategory, RowID;
```

RowID	SubCategory	ProductName	ProductNumber	Color	ListPrice	Dollar
1	Bib-Shorts	Men's Bib-Shorts, S	SB-M891-S	Multi	89.99	$89.99
2	Bib-Shorts	Men's Bib-Shorts, M	SB-M891-M	Multi	89.99	$89.99
3	Bib-Shorts	Men's Bib-Shorts, L	SB-M891-L	Multi	89.99	$89.99
1	Bike Racks	Hitch Rack - 4-Bike	RA-H123	NULL	120.00	$120.00
1	Bike Stands	All-Purpose Bike Stand	ST-1401	NULL	159.00	$159.00
1	Bottles and Cages	Water Bottle - 30 oz.	WB-H098	NULL	4.99	$4.99
2	Bottles and Cages	Mountain Bottle Cage	BC-M005	NULL	9.99	$9.99
3	Bottles and Cages	Road Bottle Cage	BC-R205	NULL	8.99	$8.99
1	Bottom Brackets	LL Bottom Bracket	BB-7421	NULL	53.99	$53.99
2	Bottom Brackets	ML Bottom Bracket	BB-8107	NULL	101.24	$101.24
3	Bottom Brackets	HL Bottom Bracket	BB-9108	NULL	121.49	$121.49
1	Brakes	Rear Brakes	RB-9231	Silver	106.50	$106.50
2	Brakes	Front Brakes	FB-9873	Silver	106.50	$106.50
1	Caps	AWC Logo Cap	CA-1098	Multi	8.99	$8.99
1	Chains	Chain	CH-0234	Silver	20.24	$20.24

```
-- Cleanup
DROP TABLE #ProductsByCategory
```

Add ROW_NUMBER & RANK Columns to Table

Add row number and rank number to Product table create without partitioning and rank (dense ranking) high price items to low price items.

```
CREATE TABLE #RankedProduct ( ROWID bigint NULL,
        RANKID bigint NULL, Price money NOT NULL, ProductID int NOT NULL,
        Name nvarchar(50) NOT NULL,  ProductNumber nvarchar(25) NOT NULL,
        MakeFlag bit NOT NULL,  FinishedGoodsFlag bit NOT NULL, Color nvarchar(15) NULL );
GO
```

```
INSERT INTO #RankedProduct
SELECT ROW_NUMBER() OVER( ORDER BY Name ASC)                    AS ROWID,
    DENSE_RANK() OVER( ORDER BY ListPrice DESC)                 AS RANKID,
    ListPrice                                                   AS Price,
   ProductID, Name, ProductNumber, MakeFlag, FinishedGoodsFlag, Color
FROM   Production.Product  ORDER  BY  RANKID, ROWID;
```

```
SELECT * FROM   tempdb.dbo.RankedProduct;
GO -- (504 row(s) affected) - Partial results.
```

ROWID	RANKID	Price	ProductID	Name	ProductNumber	MakeFlag	FinishedGoodsFlag	Color
376	1	3578.27	750	Road-150 Red, 44	BK-R93R-44	1	1	Red
377	1	3578.27	751	Road-150 Red, 48	BK-R93R-48	1	1	Red
378	1	3578.27	752	Road-150 Red, 52	BK-R93R-52	1	1	Red
379	1	3578.27	753	Road-150 Red, 56	BK-R93R-56	1	1	Red
380	1	3578.27	749	Road-150 Red, 62	BK-R93R-62	1	1	Red
332	2	3399.99	771	Mountain-100 Silver, 38	BK-M82S-38	1	1	Silver
333	2	3399.99	772	Mountain-100 Silver, 42	BK-M82S-42	1	1	Silver
334	2	3399.99	773	Mountain-100 Silver, 44	BK-M82S-44	1	1	Silver

```
DROP TABLE tempdb.dbo.RankedProduct;
GO
```

3-Part Name Table Reference - On-Premises SQL Server

The above script can be executed from any database on this SQL Server instance when we are using three-part name (databasename.schemaname.tablename) as table reference. Referencing a table on a linked server requires 4-part name. Double dot in table reference means default value between dots. Example:

[LONDONPROD1].TranMaster..OnlineOrderDetail is equivalent to
[LONDONPROD1].TranMaster.dbo.OnlineOrderDetail .

CHAPTER 11: Mastery of Database Design

The Nature of Connection Between Tables

There is only **one kind of connection between tables** which is defined as FOREIGN KEY **references** the PRIMARY KEY or UNIQUE KEY. Nonetheless, the application functional meaning of the connections can be many, for example, star schema in a data warehouse.

Categorical Relationship

```
USE AdventureWorks2012;
```

```
CREATE TABLE Production.ProductSubcategoryTest(
	ProductSubcategoryID int IDENTITY(1,1) PRIMARY KEY,
	ProductCategoryID int NOT NULL
		REFERENCES Production.ProductCategory(ProductCategoryID),
	Name dbo.Name NOT NULL,
	rowguid uniqueidentifier  NOT NULL DEFAULT( NEWID() ),
	ModifiedDate datetime NOT NULL DEFAULT( CURRENT_TIMESTAMP ));
-- (1 row(s) affected)
```

Based on the naming, with the help of our Human Intelligence, we conclude the connection is **categorization**, from subcategory to (super)category. The example clearly illustrates the importance of good naming in database design. SQL Server would work equally well with Table1 and Table2, but that would make the design practically unreadable.

The connection between Production.Product and Production.ProductSubcategory is also categorization at the bottom level of the Product --> Subcategory --> Category hierarchy.

```
ALTER TABLE Production.Product
	WITH CHECK
	ADD  CONSTRAINT FK_Product_ProductSubcategory_ProductSubcategoryID
	FOREIGN KEY(ProductSubcategoryID)
	REFERENCES Production.ProductSubcategory (ProductSubcategoryID)
GO
```

Information Object Belongs To Relationship

Since we are working with information in the data processing industry, it may not come as a big surprise that frequently we are dealing with information object rather than real world objects. The products in the AdventureWorks2012 database have information objects associated with them: photos, documents and reviews for example. The relationship is many information objects to one product.

.

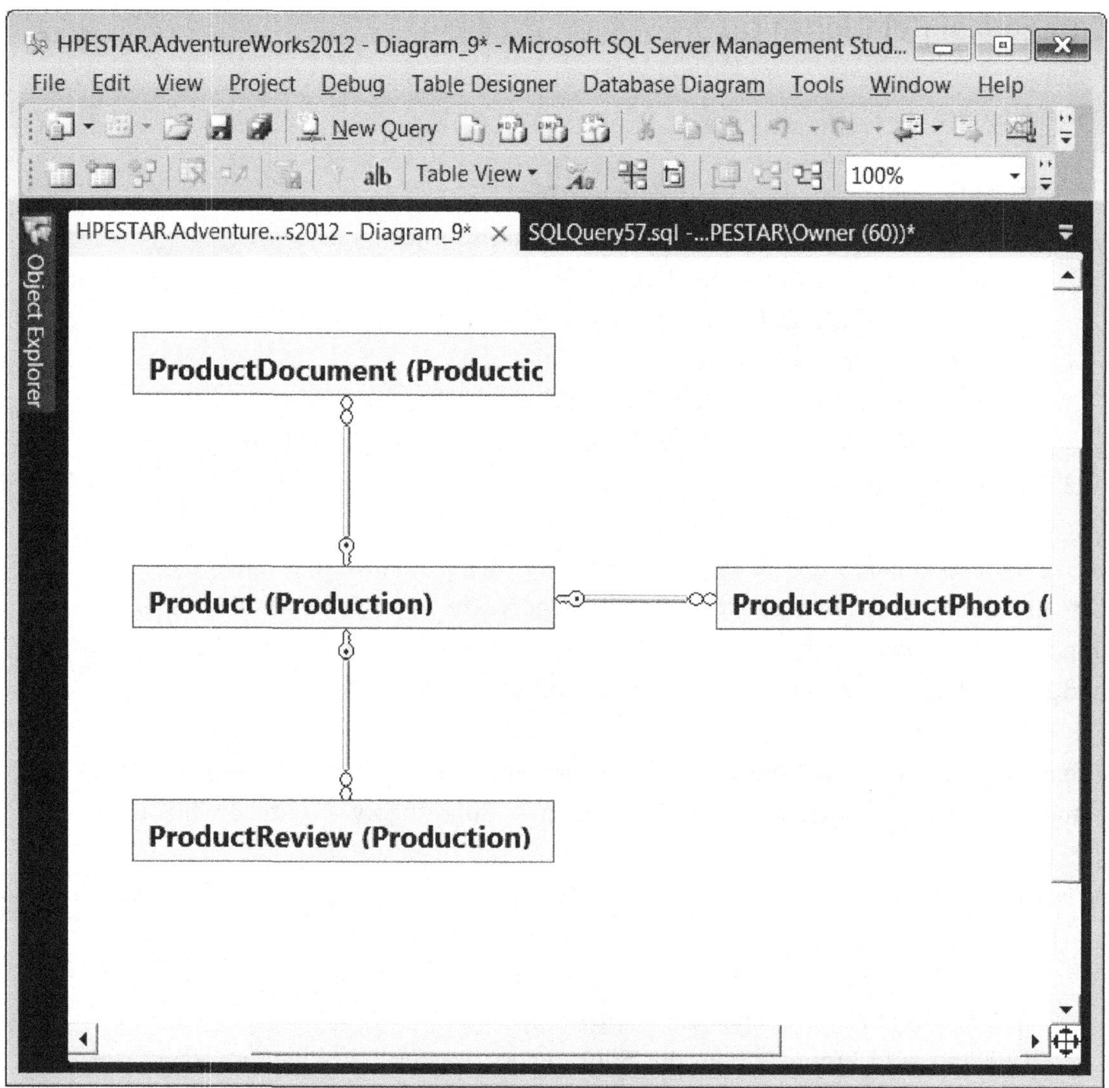

Checking Out Information Objects

Let's take a look at the ProductReview table. The information object is customer review about a product.

```
SELECT  P.Name                              AS ProductName,
        R.ReviewerName,
         LEFT(R.Comments,256)               AS Comments
FROM Production.ProductReview R
        INNER JOIN Production.Product P
                ON P.ProductID = R.ProductID
ORDER BY        ProductName,
                ReviewerName;
GO
```

ProductName	ReviewerName	Comments
HL Mountain Pedal	David	A little on the heavy side, but overall the entry/exit is easy in all conditions. I've used these pedals for more than 3 years and I've never had a problem. Cleanup is easy. Mud and sand don't get trapped. I would like them even better if there was a w
HL Mountain Pedal	Jill	Maybe it's just because I'm new to mountain biking, but I had a terrible time getting use to these pedals. In my first outing, I wiped out trying to release my foot. Any suggestions on ways I can adjust the pedals, or is it just a learning curve thing?
Mountain Bike Socks, M	John Smith	I can't believe I'm singing the praises of a pair of socks, but I just came back from a grueling 3-day ride and these socks really helped make the trip a blast. They're lightweight yet really cushioned my feet all day. The reinforced toe is nearly bulle
Road-550-W Yellow, 40	Laura Norman	The Road-550-W from Adventure Works Cycles is everything it's advertised to be. Finally, a quality bike that is actually built for a woman and provides control and comfort in one neat package. The top tube is shorter, the suspension is weight-tuned and th

The Bike Photo Information Object

The digital bike photo is stored in binary format in the Production.ProductPhoto table. Visualization requires Reporting Services report or external graphics software. SSMS cannot display the image, only the binary content.

```
SELECT          P.Name                                      AS ProductName,
                PP.ThumbnailPhotoFilename,
                PP.LargePhotoFilename
FROM Production.ProductProductPhoto PPP
        INNER JOIN Production.Product P
                ON P.ProductID = PPP.ProductID
        INNER JOIN Production.ProductPhoto PP
                ON PPP.ProductPhotoID = PP.ProductPhotoID
WHERE P.Name = 'Road-550-W Yellow, 40'
ORDER BY        ProductName;
GO
```

ProductName	ThumbnailPhotoFilename	LargePhotoFilename
Road-550-W Yellow, 40	racer02_yellow_f_small.gif	racer02_yellow_f_large.gif

The photo of the yellow road bike.

XML Diagram Object

The AdventureWorks2012 sample database includes a number of XML data type columns. These columns cannot be displayed in a formatted fashion using Management Studio, rather they require special software for formatting or visualization.

```
SELECT Diagram FROM Production.Illustration WHERE IllustrationID = 4;
-- Partial results
```


```
<Canvas>
  <!-- Layer 1/<Path> -->
  <Path StrokeThickness="0.500000" Stroke="#ff656565" StrokeMiterLimit="1.000000" Fill="#ff656565" Data="F1 M 111.049805,46.655762 L 114.526367,48.509766 L 112.671875,52.911621 L 109.694336,51.374512 L 111.049805,46.655762 Z" />
  <!-- Layer 1/<Path> -->
  <Path StrokeThickness="1.202600" Stroke="#ff989898" StrokeMiterLimit="1.000000" Data="F1 M 155.380859,314.981934" />
  <!-- Layer 1/<Path> -->
  <Path StrokeThickness="1.000000" Stroke="#ff000000" StrokeMiterLimit="1.000000" Data="F1 M 88.621094,132.691406 C 88.621094,132.691406 89.542969,135.905762 88.029785,130.630371 C 86.841797,126.486328 88.501953,126.418457 91.141113,125.661621 C 93.777832,124.904785 116.826172,118.705566 120.486328,117.249512 C 124.144531,115.791504 125.061523,117.566406 125.819336,120.205566 C 126.576172,122.842285 126.205078,121.554688 126.205078,121.554688 L 122.169922,123.121582 L 164.131836,264.715332 L 161.495117,268.324707 L 163.008789,273.599121 L 141.530273,279.757324 L 139.910156,274.105957 L 134.900391,272.280762 L 93.264160,131.816406 L 88.621094,132.691406 Z">
   <Path.Fill>
    <LinearGradientBrush MappingMode="Absolute" StartPoint="87.639160,198.240234" EndPoint="164.131836,198.240234">
     <LinearGradientBrush.GradientStops>
      <GradientStop Offset="0.000000" Color="#ffffffff" />
      <GradientStop Offset="0.258800" Color="#fffcfcfc" />
      <GradientStop Offset="0.396200" Color="#fff4f4f4" />
```


The diagram can be visualized by special XAML software.

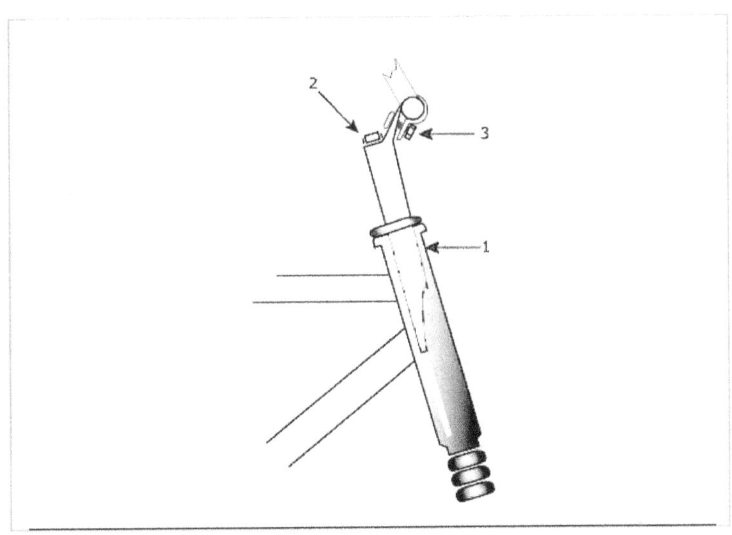

Exporting & Presenting XML Data from Production.ProductModel

XML columns contain semi-structured data. There is no general software which can make the XML data presentable. Each XML data requires specialized software for presentation. The Production.ProductModel table contains 2 XML columns. We export one cell from the first XML column, CatalogDescription, using bcp into an xhtml fil. SQL Server 2012 feature.

```
bcp "SELECT CatalogDescription FROM Production.ProductModel WHERE ProductModelID=19"
queryout f:\data\xml\Product19.xhtml -c -t -S yourserver -T
```

```
Command Prompt
Microsoft Windows [Version 6.1.7601]
Copyright (c) 2009 Microsoft Corporation.  All rights reserved.

C:\Users\Owner>bcp "SELECT CatalogDescription FROM AdventureWorks2012.Production
.ProductModel WHERE ProductModelID=19" queryout f:\data\xml\Product19.xhtml -c -
t -S HPESTAR -T

Starting copy...

1 rows copied.
Network packet size (bytes): 4096
Clock Time (ms.) Total     : 32      Average : (31.25 rows per sec.)

C:\Users\Owner>_
```

When we double click on the new .xhtml file, the information appears in a presentable format without the XML tags.

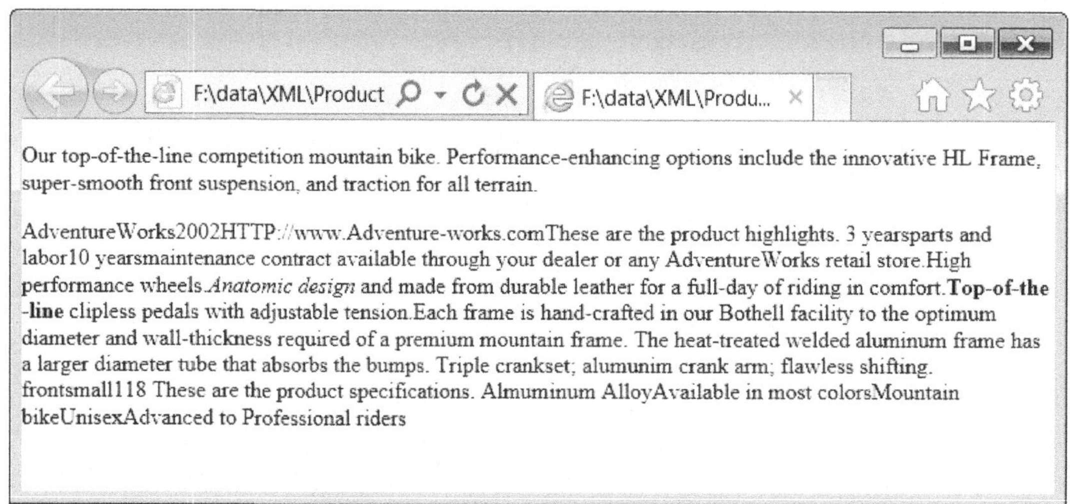

Product, ProductPhoto & ProductProductPhoto Tables Diagram

The ProductProductPhoto is a junction table representing many to many relationship between the Product and ProductPhoto. A product may have many photos and a photo may belong to many products.

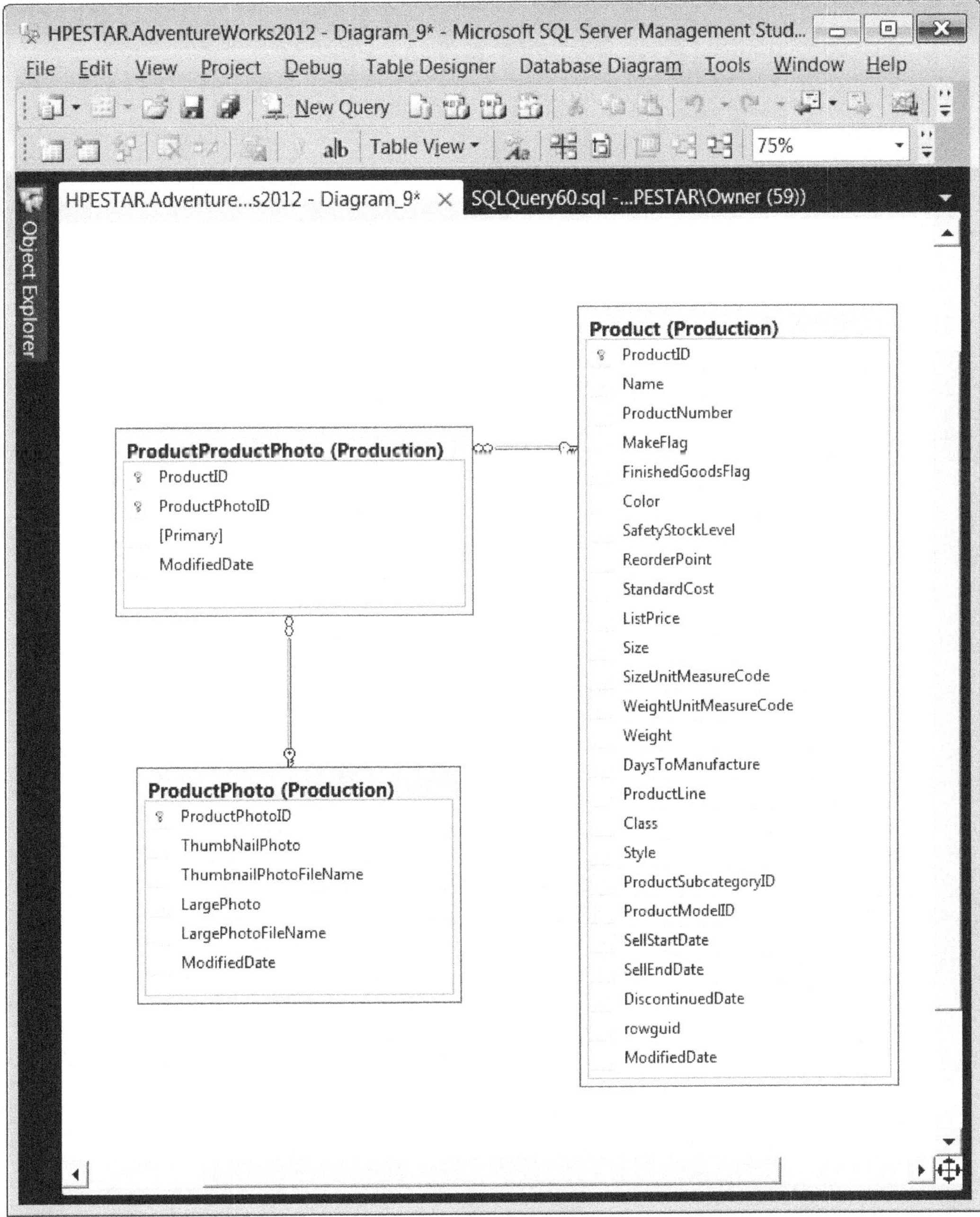

Graphical Query Design Using the Product & Photo Tables

The good database design lends itself to easy query building with Query Designer. To alias a table requires right click on the table and setting the Alias property. SQL Server 2012 feature.

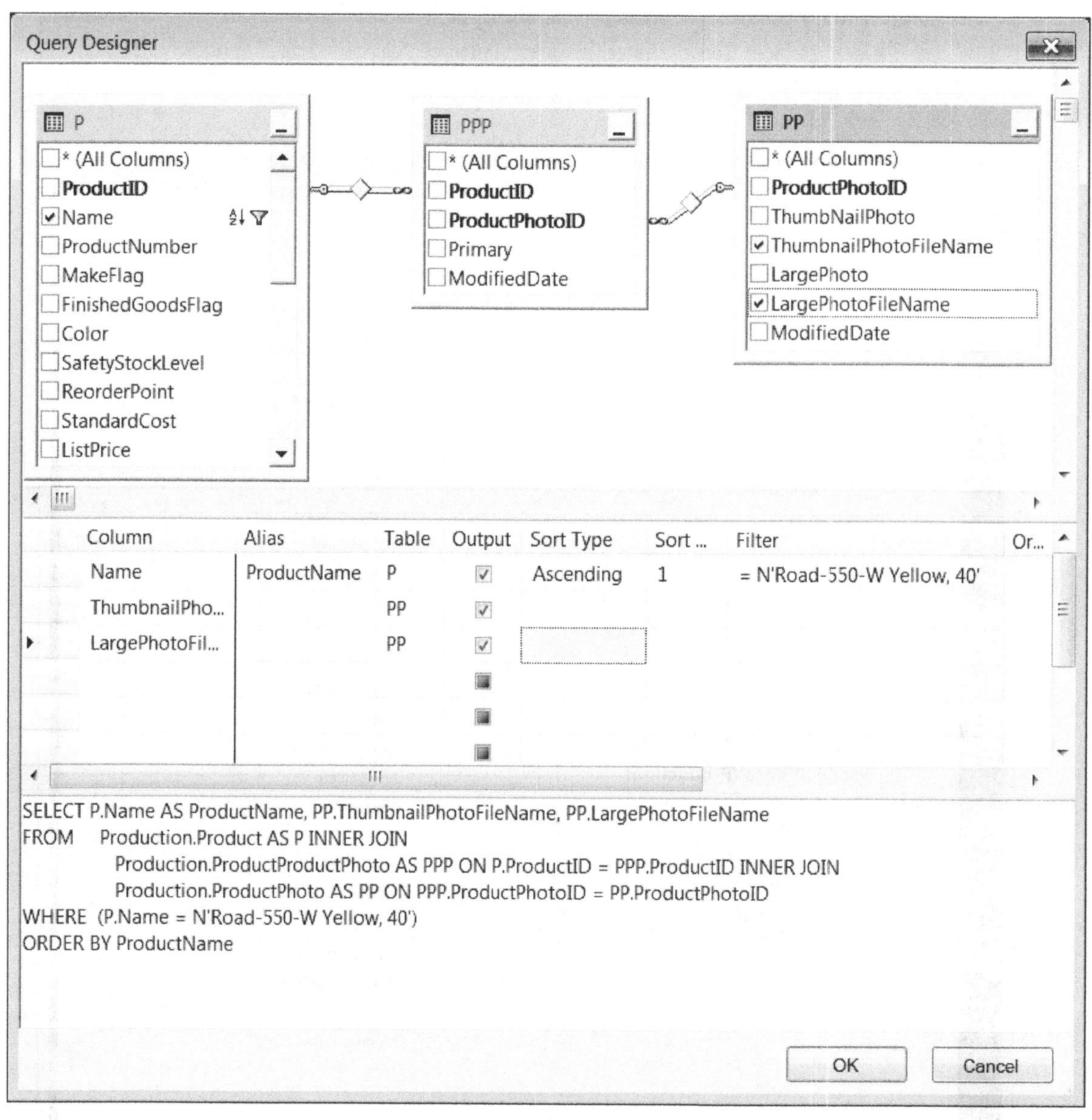

Company Received an Order Relationship

Vendor is a company supplying parts or finished product to AdventureWorks Cycles. Here is the relationship diagram. The purchase order to vendor FOREIGN KEY means a sale for the vendor. The detail to header FOREIGN KEY means the detail belongs to the header.

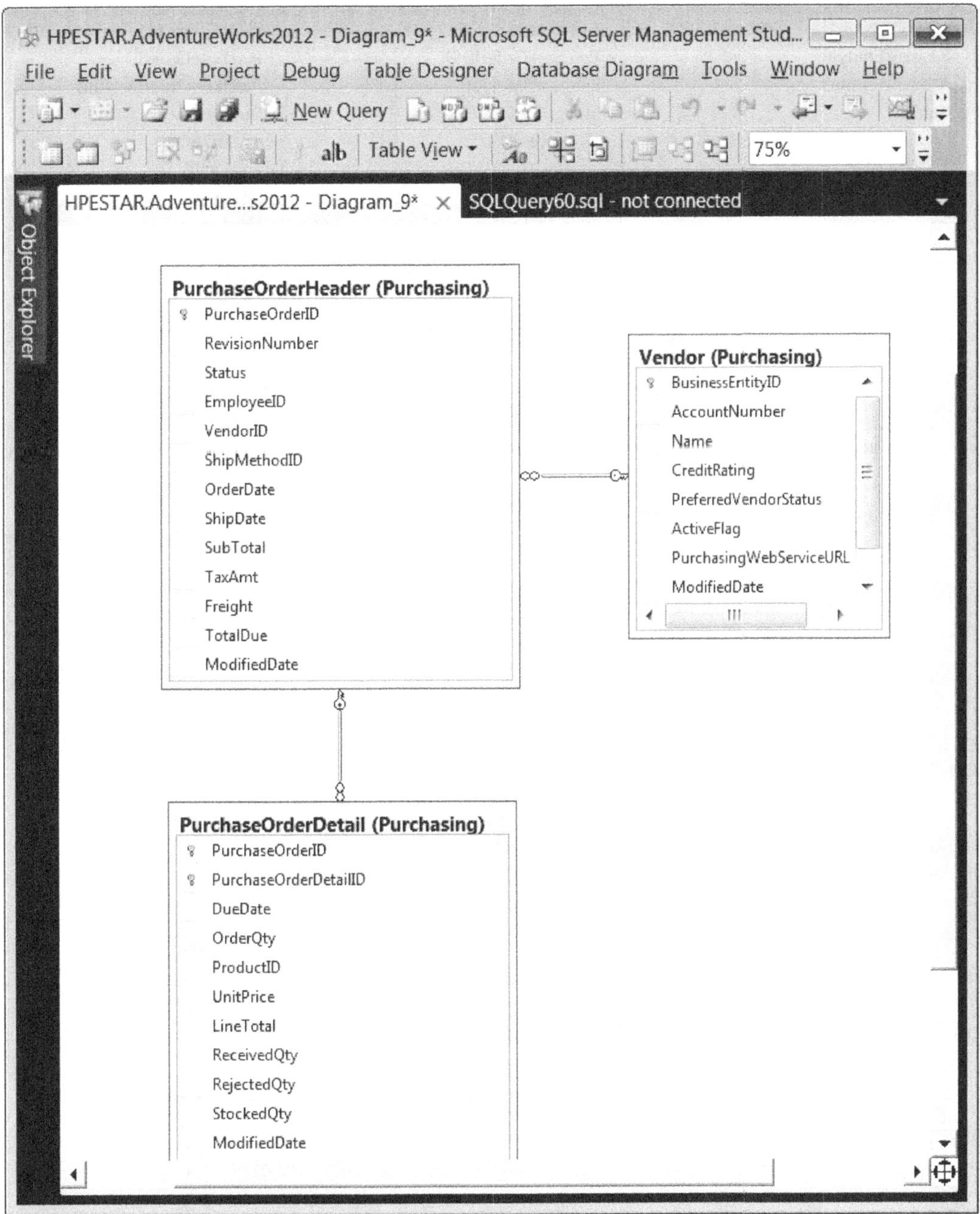

Querying the Vendor & Purchase Order Tables

The query list all purchase orders issued by AdventureWorks Cycles on a particular day.

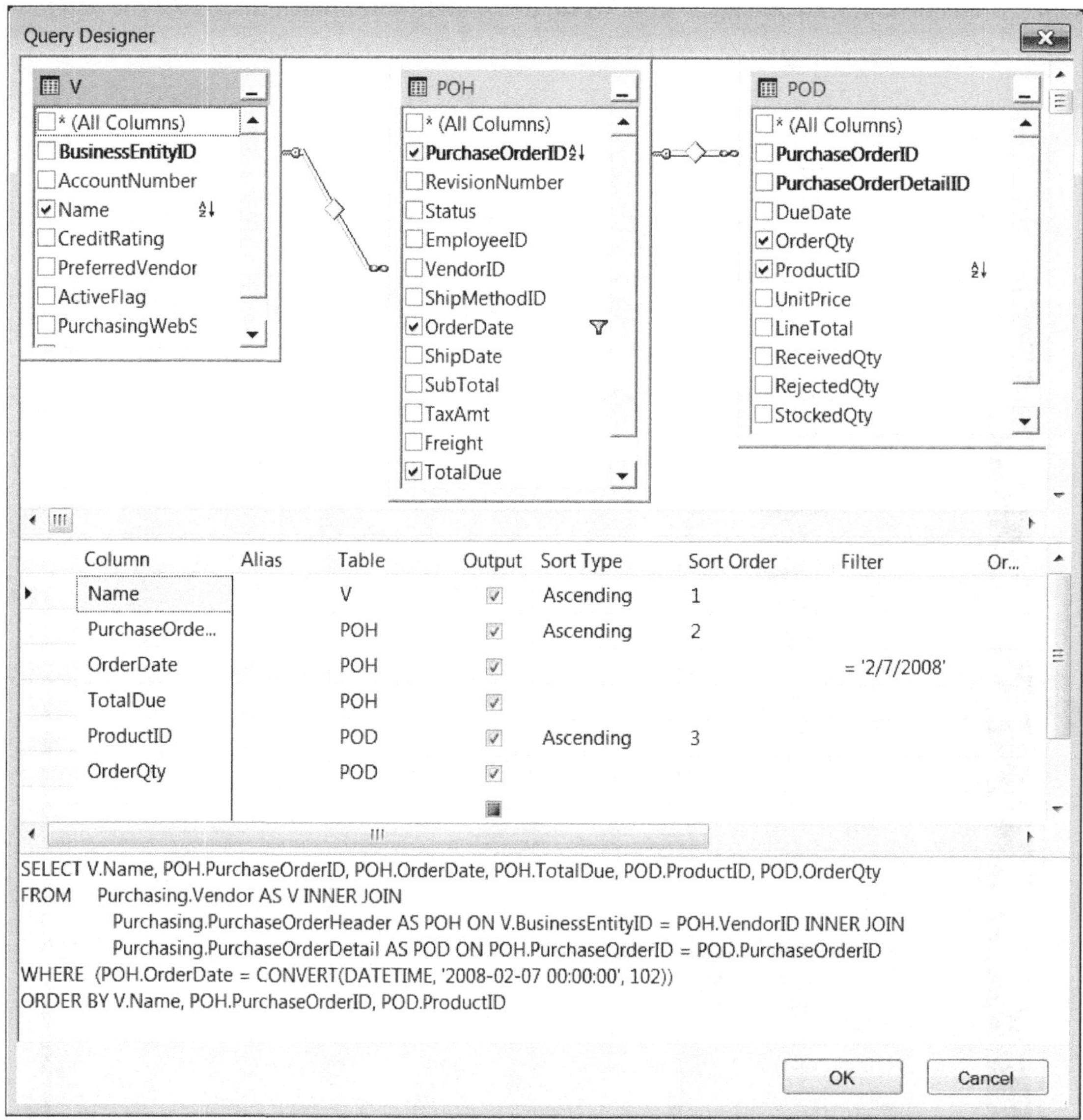

Upon execution the query returns 34 rows. Partial results.

Name	PurchaseOrderID	OrderDate	TotalDue	ProductID	OrderQty
Advanced Bicycles	1641	2008-02-07 00:00:00.000	555.9106	369	3
Allenson Cycles	1642	2008-02-07 00:00:00.000	9776.2665	530	550
American Bicycles and Wheels	1643	2008-02-07 00:00:00.000	189.0395	4	3

Type Relationship

A very frequent FOREIGN KEY representing an attribute of an object. For example a celebrity is a singer, actor, fashion model, writer, talk show host, sports figure and so on.

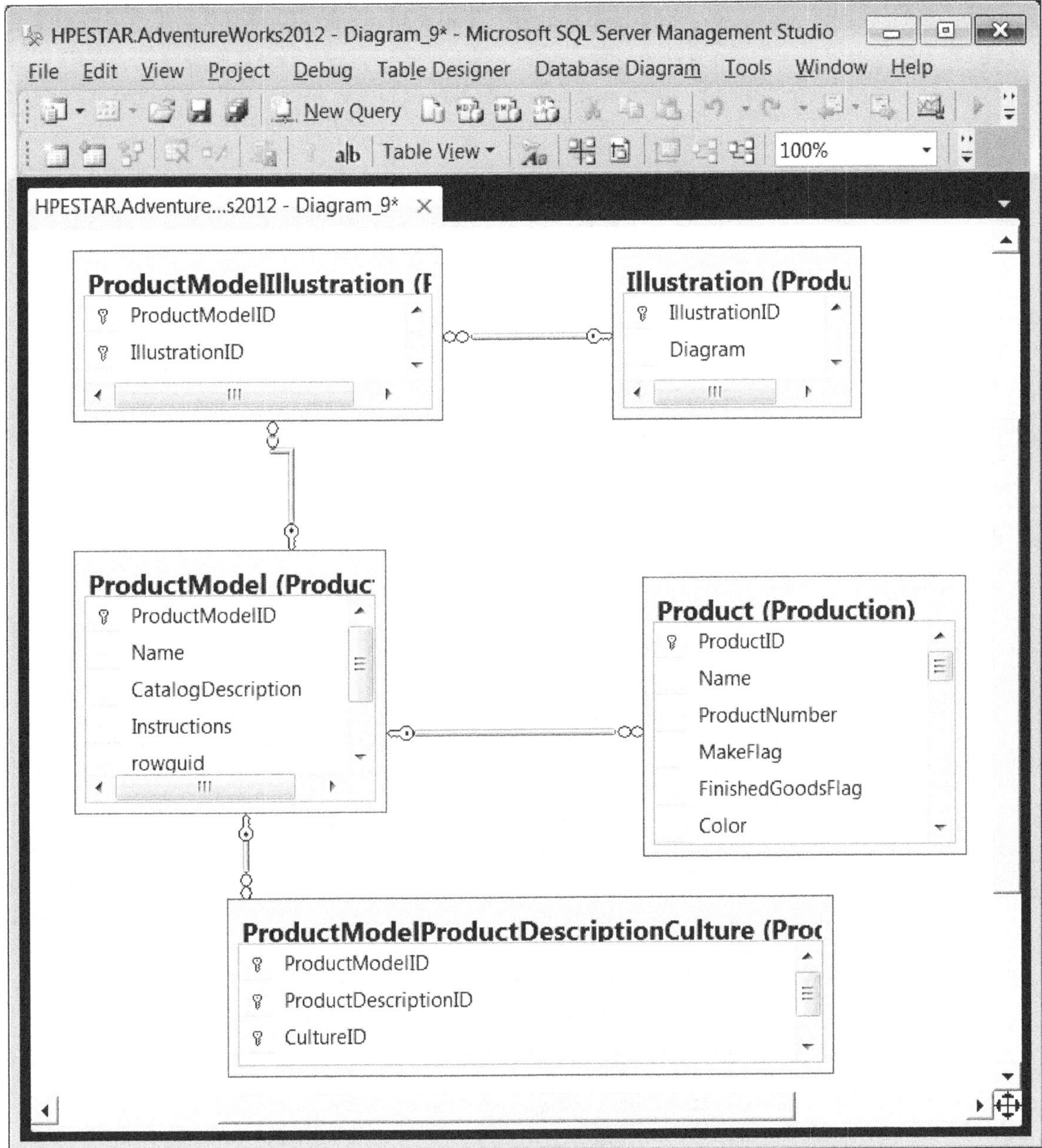

Obtaining Model Information for a Bike

We use the graphical query designer to see Model information for high-priced bikes.

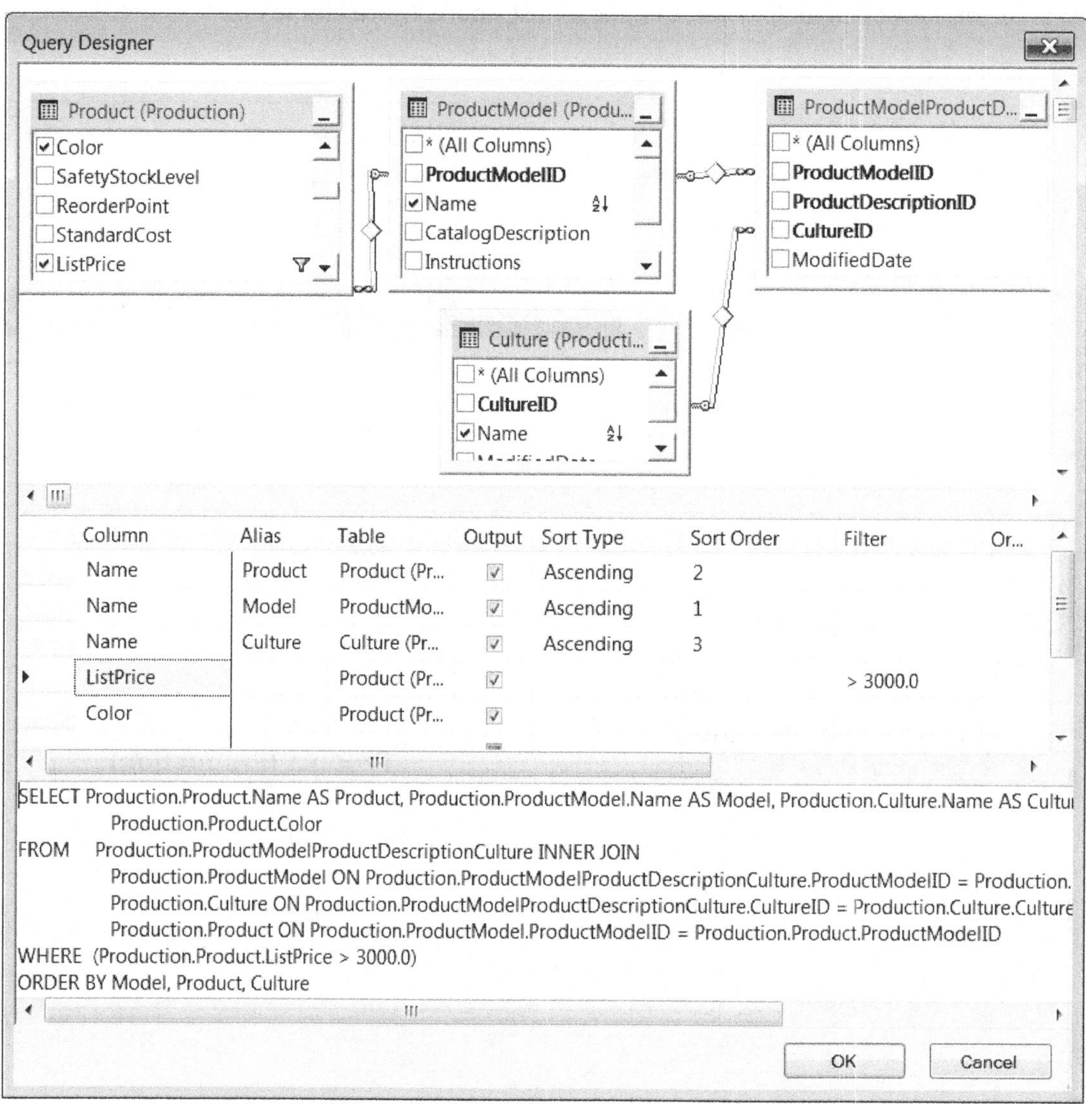

Partial results from the generated query.

Product	Model	Culture	ListPrice	Color
Mountain-100 Silver, 48	Mountain-100	English	3399.99	Silver
Mountain-100 Silver, 48	Mountain-100	French	3399.99	Silver
Mountain-100 Silver, 48	Mountain-100	Hebrew	3399.99	Silver
Mountain-100 Silver, 48	Mountain-100	Thai	3399.99	Silver
Road-150 Red, 44	Road-150	Arabic	3578.27	Red
Road-150 Red, 44	Road-150	Chinese	3578.27	Red

When to Use & Not to Use Composite PRIMARY KEYs

A composite PRIMARY KEY can be used in a junction table if it is unlikely that FOREIGN KEY reference needed from other tables. AdventureWorks2012 example of composite PRIMARY KEY with 4 columns in a junction table.

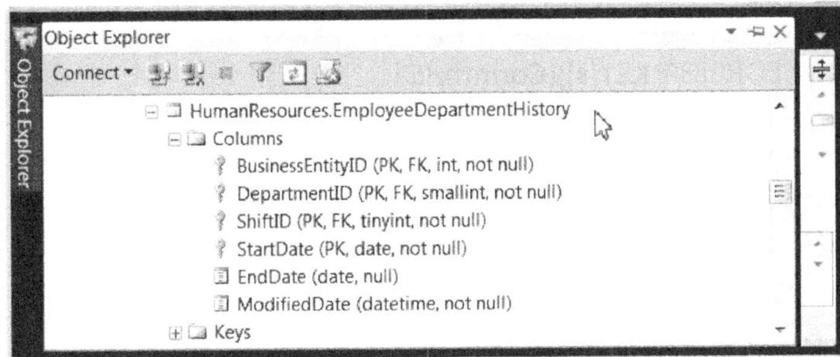

Composite PRIMARY KEY should not be used if FOREIGN KEY reference is necessary today or in the future: ineffective to have FOREIGN KEYs consisting of multiple columns & subtle violation of 3NF rules by duplication of PK table content in other tables as FKs. **The bottom line: COMPOSITE PRIMARY KEYs should not be used in regular tables.** Instead of the composite PRIMARY KEY design:

```
CREATE TABLE AlbumSong(
 AlbumTitle NVARCHAR(64) not null,
 DiskNo INTEGER  not null,
 TrackNo INTEGER  not null,
 PRIMARY KEY (AlbumTitle, DiskNo, TrackNo),
 Song NVARCHAR(128) not null,
 ModifiedDate DATE default(CURRENT_TIMESTAMP));
```

Design with **SURROGATE PRIMARY KEY** and apply composite **UNIQUE KEY** constraint:

```
CREATE TABLE AlbumSong(
 AlbumSongID INT IDENTITY(1,1) PRIMARY KEY NONCLUSTERED,
 AlbumTitle NVARCHAR(64) not null,
 DiskNo INTEGER  not null,
 TrackNo INTEGER  not null,
 UNIQUE CLUSTERED (AlbumTitle, DiskNo, TrackNo),
 Song NVARCHAR(128) not null,
 ModifiedDate DATE default(CURRENT_TIMESTAMP));
```

Where to place the clustered index should be based on performance considerations.

How To Design a Table

It is very important that we follow in order. Rules are with reference to the Celebrity table.

- Identify the NATURAL KEY column(s) (LastName, FirstName) & set it as UNIQUE (KEY)
- Design the non-key columns (BirthDate, BirthPlace, NameAtBirth)
- Design the row maintenance columns (CreatedDate)
- Configure the FOREIGN KEY(s) (CountryID)
- Configure the IDENTITY SURROGATE PRIMARY KEY (CelebrityID)

```
CREATE TABLE Profession (
	ProfessionID TINYINT IDENTITY(1,1) PRIMARY KEY,
	Name varchar(50) NOT NULL UNIQUE,
	CreatedDate DATETIME DEFAULT(CURRENT_TIMESTAMP) );
```

```
CREATE TABLE Country (
	ID TINYINT IDENTITY(1,1) PRIMARY KEY,
	Name varchar(128) NOT NULL UNIQUE,
	CreatedDate DATETIME DEFAULT(CURRENT_TIMESTAMP) );
```

```
CREATE TABLE Celebrity(
	CelebrityID SMALLINT IDENTITY(1,1) PRIMARY KEY nonclustered,
	CountryID TINYINT REFERENCES Country(ID),
	LastName nvarchar(40) NOT NULL CHECK( LEN(LastName) > 4),
	FirstName nvarchar(40),
	UNIQUE clustered (LastName, FirstName),
	BirthDate DATE NOT NULL,
	BirthPlace nvarchar(50),
	NameAtBirth nvarchar(60),
	CreatedDate DATETIME DEFAULT(CURRENT_TIMESTAMP) );
```

```
CREATE TABLE CelebrityProfessionXref(
	CelebrityID SMALLINT NOT NULL REFERENCES Celebrity(CelebrityID),
	ProfessionID TINYINT NOT NULL REFERENCES Profession(ProfessionID),
	PRIMARY KEY (CelebrityID, ProfessionID),
	CreatedDate DATETIME DEFAULT(CURRENT_TIMESTAMP) );
```

Without NATURAL KEY we don't have a table. The NATURAL KEY can be set as UNIQUE KEY or PRIMARY KEY. We can tentatively move the clustered index away from the PRIMARY KEY (default), however, final decision point is when we identify the business critical queries. Clustered index is helpful with range query performance.

Table-Related Database Objects

Table is the content object in a database. It has a number of supporting objects to keep the content accurate and accessible. The list of database object types in sys.objects system view.

```
SELECT SeqNo=ROW_NUMBER() OVER (ORDER BY type_desc),
     *
FROM ( SELECT DISTINCT type, type_desc
               FROM sys.objects ) x
ORDER BY SeqNo;
```

SeqNo	type	type_desc
1	C	CHECK_CONSTRAINT
2	D	DEFAULT_CONSTRAINT
3	F	FOREIGN_KEY_CONSTRAINT
4	IT	INTERNAL_TABLE
5	PK	PRIMARY_KEY_CONSTRAINT
6	SO	SEQUENCE_OBJECT
7	SQ	SERVICE_QUEUE
8	IF	SQL_INLINE_TABLE_VALUED_FUNCTION
9	FN	SQL_SCALAR_FUNCTION
10	P	SQL_STORED_PROCEDURE
11	TF	SQL_TABLE_VALUED_FUNCTION
12	TR	SQL_TRIGGER
13	S	SYSTEM_TABLE
14	TT	TYPE_TABLE
15	UQ	UNIQUE_CONSTRAINT
16	U	USER_TABLE
17	V	VIEW

Indexes have their own system view.

```
SELECT          OBJECT_NAME(object_ID)        AS TableName,
                name                          AS IndexName,
                index_id,
                type_desc
FROM sys.indexes  ORDER BY TableName, index_id;
-- (333 row(s) affected) - Partial Results
```

TableName	IndexName	index_id	type_desc
Address	PK_Address_AddressID	1	CLUSTERED
Address	AK_Address_rowguid	2	NONCLUSTERED
Address	IX_Address_AddressLine1_AddressLine2_City_StateProvinceID_PostalCode	3	NONCLUSTERED
Address	IX_Address_StateProvinceID	4	NONCLUSTERED

Listing All PRIMARY KEYs

Getting database object information can start in sys.objects system view.

```
SELECT SCHEMA_NAME(schema_id)              AS SchemaName,
       OBJECT_NAME(parent_object_id)       AS TableName,
       name                                AS PKName
FROM sys.objects WHERE type = 'PK'
ORDER BY SchemaName, TableName;
GO
```

SchemaName	TableName	PKName
dbo	AWBuildVersion	PK_AWBuildVersion_SystemInformationID
dbo	DatabaseLog	PK_DatabaseLog_DatabaseLogID
dbo	ErrorLog	PK_ErrorLog_ErrorLogID
HumanResources	Department	PK_Department_DepartmentID
HumanResources	Employee	PK_Employee_BusinessEntityID
HumanResources	EmployeeDepartmentHistory	PK_EmployeeDepartmentHistory_BusinessEntityID_StartDate_DepartmentID
HumanResources	EmployeePayHistory	PK_EmployeePayHistory_BusinessEntityID_RateChangeDate
HumanResources	JobCandidate	PK_JobCandidate_JobCandidateID
HumanResources	Shift	PK_Shift_ShiftID
Person	Address	PK_Address_AddressID
Person	AddressType	PK_AddressType_AddressTypeID
Person	BusinessEntity	PK_BusinessEntity_BusinessEntityID
Person	BusinessEntityAddress	PK_BusinessEntityAddress_BusinessEntityID_AddressID_AddressTypeID
Person	BusinessEntityContact	PK_BusinessEntityContact_BusinessEntityID_PersonID_ContactTypeID
Person	ContactType	PK_ContactType_ContactTypeID
Person	CountryRegion	PK_CountryRegion_CountryRegionCode
Person	EmailAddress	PK_EmailAddress_BusinessEntityID_EmailAddressID
Person	Password	PK_Password_BusinessEntityID
Person	Person	PK_Person_BusinessEntityID
Person	PersonPhone	PK_PersonPhone_BusinessEntityID_PhoneNumber_PhoneNumberTypeID
Person	PhoneNumberType	PK_PhoneNumberType_PhoneNumberTypeID
Person	StateProvince	PK_StateProvince_StateProvinceID
Production	BillOfMaterials	PK_BillOfMaterials_BillOfMaterialsID
Production	Culture	PK_Culture_CultureID
Production	Document	PK_Document_DocumentNode
Production	Illustration	PK_Illustration_IllustrationID
Production	Location	PK_Location_LocationID
Production	Product	PK_Product_ProductID
Production	ProductCategory	PK_ProductCategory_ProductCategoryID
Production	ProductCostHistory	PK_ProductCostHistory_ProductID_StartDate
Production	ProductDescription	PK_ProductDescription_ProductDescriptionID
Production	ProductDocument	PK_ProductDocument_ProductID_DocumentNode
Production	ProductInventory	PK_ProductInventory_ProductID_LocationID
Production	ProductListPriceHistory	PK_ProductListPriceHistory_ProductID_StartDate
Production	ProductModel	PK_ProductModel_ProductModelID
Production	ProductModelIllustration	PK_ProductModelIllustration_ProductModelID_IllustrationID
Production	ProductModelProductDescriptionCulture	PK_ProductModelProductDescriptionCulture_ProductModelID_ProductDescriptionID_CultureID
Production	ProductPhoto	PK_ProductPhoto_ProductPhotoID
Production	ProductProductPhoto	PK_ProductProductPhoto_ProductID_ProductPhotoID
Production	ProductReview	PK_ProductReview_ProductReviewID
Production	ProductSubcategory	PK_ProductSubcategory_ProductSubcategoryID
Production	ScrapReason	PK_ScrapReason_ScrapReasonID
Production	TransactionHistory	PK_TransactionHistory_TransactionID
Production	TransactionHistoryArchive	PK_TransactionHistoryArchive_TransactionID
Production	UnitMeasure	PK_UnitMeasure_UnitMeasureCode
Production	WorkOrder	PK_WorkOrder_WorkOrderID
Production	WorkOrderRouting	PK_WorkOrderRouting_WorkOrderID_ProductID_OperationSequence
Purchasing	ProductVendor	PK_ProductVendor_ProductID_BusinessEntityID
Purchasing	PurchaseOrderDetail	PK_PurchaseOrderDetail_PurchaseOrderID_PurchaseOrderDetailID
Purchasing	PurchaseOrderHeader	PK_PurchaseOrderHeader_PurchaseOrderID
Purchasing	ShipMethod	PK_ShipMethod_ShipMethodID
Purchasing	Vendor	PK_Vendor_BusinessEntityID
Sales	CountryRegionCurrency	PK_CountryRegionCurrency_CountryRegionCode_CurrencyCode
Sales	CreditCard	PK_CreditCard_CreditCardID

Sales	Currency	PK_Currency_CurrencyCode
Sales	CurrencyRate	PK_CurrencyRate_CurrencyRateID
Sales	Customer	PK_Customer_CustomerID
Sales	PersonCreditCard	PK_PersonCreditCard_BusinessEntityID_CreditCardID
Sales	SalesOrderDetail	PK_SalesOrderDetail_SalesOrderID_SalesOrderDetailID
Sales	SalesOrderHeader	PK_SalesOrderHeader_SalesOrderID
Sales	SalesOrderHeaderSalesReason	PK_SalesOrderHeaderSalesReason_SalesOrderID_SalesReasonID
Sales	SalesPerson	PK_SalesPerson_BusinessEntityID
Sales	SalesPersonQuotaHistory	PK_SalesPersonQuotaHistory_BusinessEntityID_QuotaDate
Sales	SalesReason	PK_SalesReason_SalesReasonID
Sales	SalesTaxRate	PK_SalesTaxRate_SalesTaxRateID
Sales	SalesTerritory	PK_SalesTerritory_TerritoryID
Sales	SalesTerritoryHistory	PK_SalesTerritoryHistory_BusinessEntityID_StartDate_TerritoryID
Sales	ShoppingCartItem	PK_ShoppingCartItem_ShoppingCartItemID
Sales	SpecialOffer	PK_SpecialOffer_SpecialOfferID
Sales	SpecialOfferProduct	PK_SpecialOfferProduct_SpecialOfferID_ProductID
Sales	Store	PK_Store_BusinessEntityID

UNIQUEIDENTIFIER As PRIMARY KEY

For most applications INT IDENTITY(1,1) (SURROGATE) PRIMARY KEY is the perfect choice. However, some enterprise applications require the generation of a random rowid without any reference to a database. For those, UNIQUEIDENTIFIER can be used with NEWID() or NEWSEQUENTIALID() fill. **The latter is faster but not completely random therefore should not be used for secure applications.** INT IDENTITY() is fastest of the three (not in following test). SQL Server 2012 script.

```
USE tempdb; SET NOCOUNT ON;
DECLARE @MaxCount Int = 100000,@START DATETIME,@END DATETIME, @i INT
CREATE TABLE TESTID ( ID UNIQUEIDENTIFIER DEFAULT NEWID() PRIMARY KEY,
-- CREATE TABLE TESTID ( ID UNIQUEIDENTIFIER DEFAULT NEWSEQUENTIALID() PRIMARY KEY,
COL1 CHAR(256) DEFAULT 'Everglades', COL2 CHAR(256) DEFAULT 'Everglades',
COL3 CHAR(256) DEFAULT 'Everglades', COL4 CHAR(256) DEFAULT 'Everglades',
COL5 CHAR(256) DEFAULT 'Everglades', COL6 CHAR(256) DEFAULT 'Everglades',
COL7 CHAR(256) DEFAULT 'Everglades', COL8 CHAR(256) DEFAULT 'Everglades',
COL9 CHAR(256) DEFAULT 'Everglades', COL10 CHAR(256) DEFAULT 'Everglades');
SELECT TOP(0) * INTO #Result FROM TESTID;
DBCC DROPCLEANBUFFERS;  SET @START = GETDATE(); SET @i = 1;
WHILE (@i < @MaxCount)  BEGIN INSERT TESTID DEFAULT VALUES; SET @i += 1; END
INSERT #Result SELECT t1.* FROM TESTID t1 INNER JOIN TESTID t2 ON t1.ID=t2.ID
SELECT  DATEDIFF(ms,@START,GETDATE());  DROP TABLE #Result; DROP TABLE TESTID;
```

```
-- Test with newid(): 22,436 msec
-- Test with newid(): 14,866 msec
-- Test with newid(): 14,576 msec
```

```
-- Test with newsequentialid(): 12,126 msec
-- Test with newsequentialid(): 11,290 msec
-- Test with newsequentialid(): 10,713 msec
```

List All PK & FK Columns in the Database

We can use INFORMATION_SCHEMA metadata system views for the task. The position indicates the placement of the column within a composite key.

```
USE AdventureWorks2012;
SELECT k.table_schema                         AS SchemaName,
       k.table_name                           AS  TableName,
       k.column_name                          AS ColumnName,
       k.ordinal_position                     AS Position,
       c.constraint_type                      AS KeyConstraint
FROM   information_schema.table_constraints c
   INNER JOIN information_schema.key_column_usage k
     ON c.table_name = k.table_name
       AND c.constraint_name = k.constraint_name
ORDER BY SchemaName, TableName, KeyConstraint DESC, Position, ColumnName;
GO
-- (194 row(s) affected) - Partial results
```

SchemaName	TableName	ColumnName	Position	KeyConstraint
HumanResources	Department	DepartmentID	1	PRIMARY KEY
HumanResources	Employee	BusinessEntityID	1	PRIMARY KEY
HumanResources	Employee	BusinessEntityID	1	FOREIGN KEY
HumanResources	EmployeeDepartmentHistory	BusinessEntityID	1	PRIMARY KEY
HumanResources	EmployeeDepartmentHistory	StartDate	2	PRIMARY KEY
HumanResources	EmployeeDepartmentHistory	DepartmentID	3	PRIMARY KEY
HumanResources	EmployeeDepartmentHistory	ShiftID	4	PRIMARY KEY
HumanResources	EmployeeDepartmentHistory	BusinessEntityID	1	FOREIGN KEY
HumanResources	EmployeeDepartmentHistory	DepartmentID	1	FOREIGN KEY
HumanResources	EmployeeDepartmentHistory	ShiftID	1	FOREIGN KEY
HumanResources	EmployeePayHistory	BusinessEntityID	1	PRIMARY KEY
HumanResources	EmployeePayHistory	RateChangeDate	2	PRIMARY KEY
HumanResources	EmployeePayHistory	BusinessEntityID	1	FOREIGN KEY
HumanResources	JobCandidate	JobCandidateID	1	PRIMARY KEY
HumanResources	JobCandidate	BusinessEntityID	1	FOREIGN KEY
HumanResources	Shift	ShiftID	1	PRIMARY KEY
Person	Address	AddressID	1	PRIMARY KEY
Person	Address	StateProvinceID	1	FOREIGN KEY
Person	AddressType	AddressTypeID	1	PRIMARY KEY
Person	BusinessEntity	BusinessEntityID	1	PRIMARY KEY
Person	BusinessEntityAddress	BusinessEntityID	1	PRIMARY KEY
Person	BusinessEntityAddress	AddressID	2	PRIMARY KEY
Person	BusinessEntityAddress	AddressTypeID	3	PRIMARY KEY
Person	BusinessEntityAddress	AddressID	1	FOREIGN KEY
Person	BusinessEntityAddress	AddressTypeID	1	FOREIGN KEY
Person	BusinessEntityAddress	BusinessEntityID	1	FOREIGN KEY
Person	BusinessEntityContact	BusinessEntityID	1	PRIMARY KEY
Person	BusinessEntityContact	PersonID	2	PRIMARY KEY
Person	BusinessEntityContact	ContactTypeID	3	PRIMARY KEY
Person	BusinessEntityContact	BusinessEntityID	1	FOREIGN KEY
Person	BusinessEntityContact	ContactTypeID	1	FOREIGN KEY
Person	BusinessEntityContact	PersonID	1	FOREIGN KEY
Person	ContactType	ContactTypeID	1	PRIMARY KEY

How to Get Database Object Definition Information

There are alternate ways of getting object definition metadata.

Scripting Object CREATE Definitions

This is the easiest and most reliable way. Start with a right click on the object in Object Explorer to get the drop-down menu.

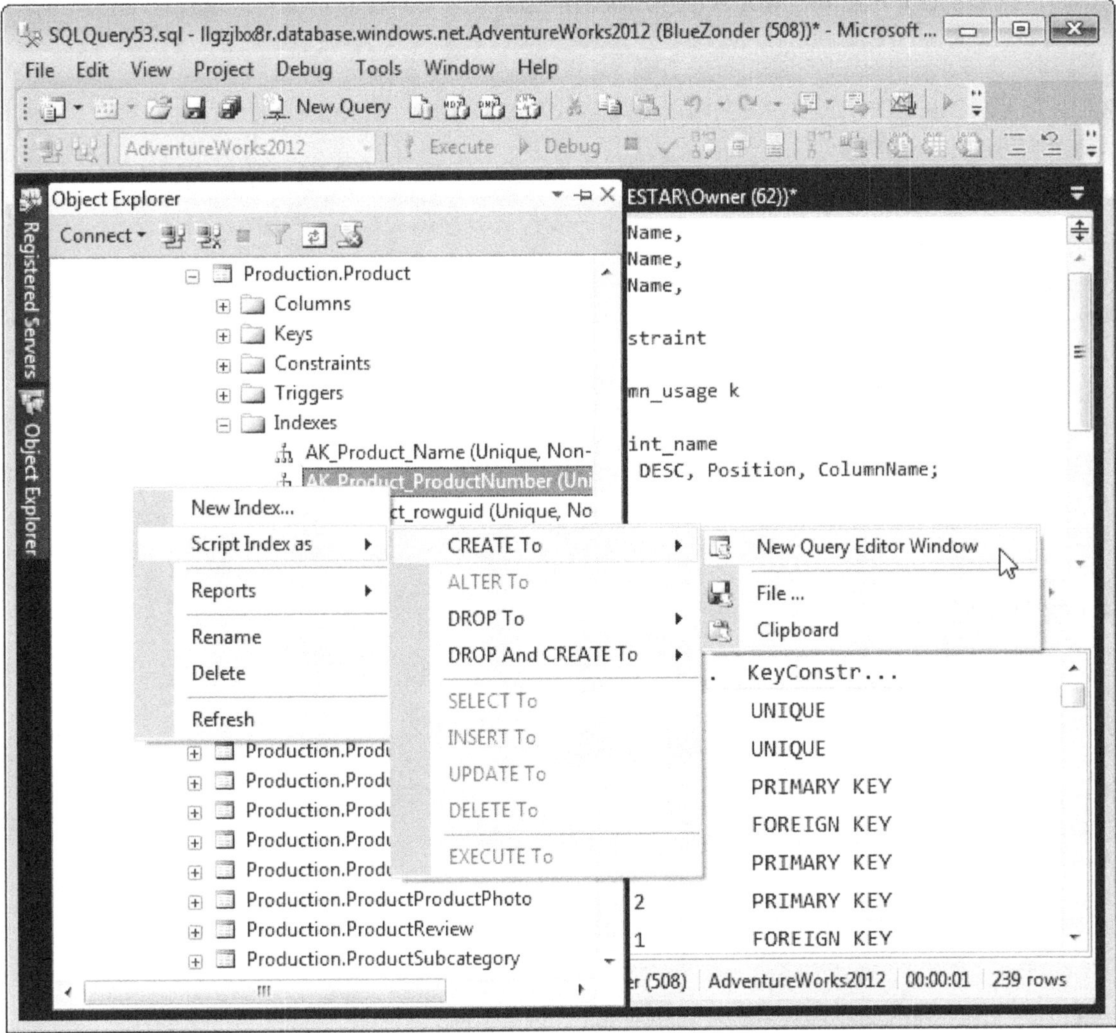

Single Object CREATE & Other Scripts from SSMS Object Explorer

Some of the scripts are generated complete. Others are just templates which require completion and testing.

Index CREATE Script

```
USE [AdventureWorks2012]
GO
```

```
/****** Object:  Index [AK_Product_ProductNumber]
Script Date: 2/5/2016 8:05:58 PM ******/

CREATE UNIQUE NONCLUSTERED INDEX [AK_Product_ProductNumber]
ON [Production].[Product]
(
	[ProductNumber] ASC
)WITH (PAD_INDEX = OFF,
STATISTICS_NORECOMPUTE = OFF,
SORT_IN_TEMPDB = OFF,
IGNORE_DUP_KEY = OFF,
DROP_EXISTING = OFF,
ONLINE = OFF,
ALLOW_ROW_LOCKS = ON,
ALLOW_PAGE_LOCKS = ON)
GO
```

Index DROP Script

```
/****** Object:  Index [IX_EmployeeDepartmentHistory_ShiftID]    Script Date: ..... ******/
DROP INDEX [IX_EmployeeDepartmentHistory_ShiftID] ON
[HumanResources].[EmployeeDepartmentHistory]
GO
```

View DELETE Script

```
USE [AdventureWorks2012]
GO

DELETE FROM [Person].[vStateProvinceCountryRegion]
      WHERE <Search Conditions,,>
GO
```

View UPDATE Script

```
USE [AdventureWorks2012]
GO
UPDATE [Production].[vProductAndDescription]
  SET [ProductID] = <ProductID, int,>
    ,[Name] = <Name, Name,>
    ,[ProductModel] = <ProductModel, Name,>
    ,[CultureID] = <CultureID, nchar(6),>
    ,[Description] = <Description, nvarchar(400),>
 WHERE <Search Conditions,,>
GO
```

Inline Table-Valued User-Defined Function ALTER Script

```
USE [AdventureWorks2012]
GO
/****** Object:  UserDefinedFunction [Sales].[ufnStaffSalesByFiscalYear]    Script Date: ...... ******/
SET ANSI_NULLS ON
GO
SET QUOTED_IDENTIFIER ON
GO
ALTER FUNCTION [Sales].[ufnStaffSalesByFiscalYear] (@OrderYear INT)
RETURNS TABLE  AS
RETURN
SELECT
     CONVERT(date, soh.OrderDate)                                             AS OrderDate
    ,CONCAT(p.FirstName, ' ', COALESCE(p.MiddleName, ''), ' ', p.LastName)    AS FullName
    ,e.JobTitle
    ,st.Name                                                                  AS SalesTerritory
    ,FORMAT(soh.SubTotal, 'c', 'en-US')                                       AS SalesAmount
    ,YEAR(DATEADD(mm, 6, soh.OrderDate))                                      AS FiscalYear
FROM Sales.SalesPerson sp
    INNER JOIN Sales.SalesOrderHeader soh
          ON sp.BusinessEntityID = soh.SalesPersonID
    INNER JOIN Sales.SalesTerritory st
          ON sp.TerritoryID = st.TerritoryID
    INNER JOIN HumanResources.Employee e
          ON soh.SalesPersonID = e.BusinessEntityID
    INNER JOIN Person.Person p
          ON p.BusinessEntityID = sp.BusinessEntityID
WHERE               soh.OrderDate >= datefromparts(@OrderYear, 1, 1)
            AND soh.OrderDate < dateadd(yy,1, datefromparts(@OrderYear, 1, 1));
GO
```

Searching for Database Objects in Object Explorer Details

We start by positioning on AdventureWorks2012 in Object Explorer. We activate the Object Explorer Details window from the Views tab. Enter the keyword or wildcard in the search box and press the Enter key.

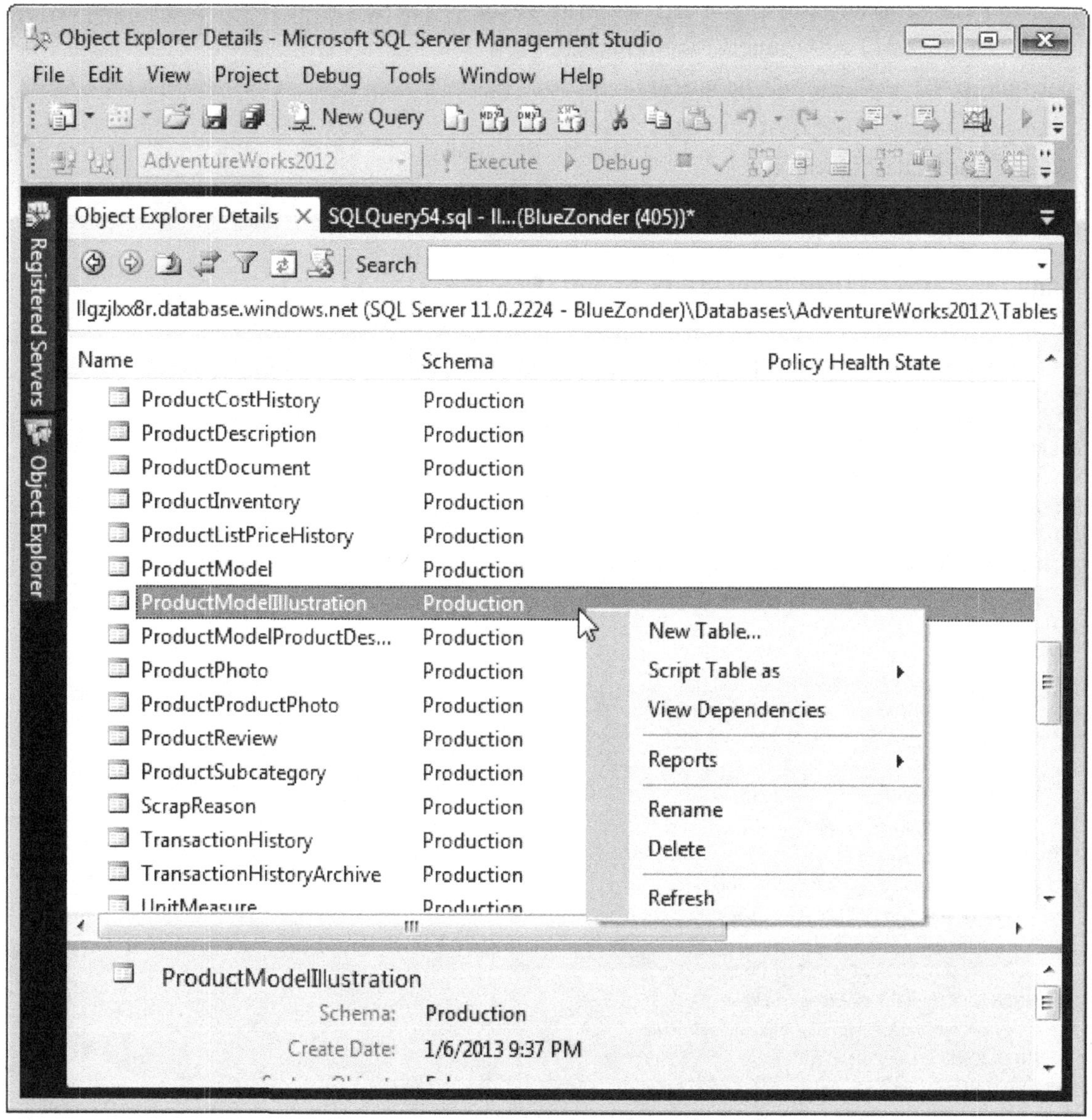

OBJECT_DEFINITION() Function for Getting Source Code

The OBJECT_DEFINITIION() function can be used to retrieve the database object definition source text for some objects such as view, stored procedure, trigger & function.

```
SELECT OBJECT_DEFINITION(object_id('INFORMATION_SCHEMA.TABLES'));
```

```
CREATE VIEW INFORMATION_SCHEMA.TABLES
AS
SELECT
        DB_NAME()                               AS TABLE_CATALOG,
        s.name                                  AS TABLE_SCHEMA,
        o.name                                  AS TABLE_NAME,
        CASE o.type
                WHEN 'U' THEN 'BASE TABLE'
                WHEN 'V' THEN 'VIEW'
        END                                     AS TABLE_TYPE
FROM
        sys.objects o LEFT JOIN sys.schemas s
        ON s.schema_id = o.schema_id
WHERE
                        o.type IN ('U', 'V')
```

```
SELECT OBJECT_DEFINITION(object_id('Sales.vSalesPersonSalesByFiscalYears'));
```

```
CREATE VIEW [Sales].[vSalesPersonSalesByFiscalYears] AS
SELECT    pvt.[SalesPersonID]
  ,pvt.[FullName]
  ,pvt.[JobTitle]
  ,pvt.[SalesTerritory]
  ,pvt.[2006]
  ,pvt.[2007]
  ,pvt.[2008]
FROM (SELECT      soh.[SalesPersonID]
    ,p.[FirstName] + ' ' + COALESCE(p.[MiddleName], '') + ' ' + p.[LastName] AS [FullName]
    ,e.[JobTitle]
    ,st.[Name] AS [SalesTerritory]
    ,soh.[SubTotal]
    ,YEAR(DATEADD(m, 6, soh.[OrderDate])) AS [FiscalYear]
  FROM [Sales].[SalesPerson] sp
    INNER JOIN [Sales].[SalesOrderHeader] soh
    ON sp.[BusinessEntityID] = soh.[SalesPersonID]
    INNER JOIN [Sales].[SalesTerritory] st
    ON sp.[TerritoryID] = st.[TerritoryID]
    INNER JOIN [HumanResources].[Employee] e
    ON soh.[SalesPersonID] = e.[BusinessEntityID]
                INNER JOIN [Person].[Person] p
                ON p.[BusinessEntityID] = sp.[BusinessEntityID]  ) AS soh
PIVOT (
  SUM([SubTotal])
  FOR [FiscalYear]
  IN ([2006], [2007], [2008])
) AS pvt;
```

Scripting DB Objects with PowerShell - OPSS2012

PowerShell script can be used to script database object including tables. Scripting tables in the Purchasing schema of AdventureWorks2012 sample database. In all Command Prompt scripts the lines must be without carriage return or new line breaks (CR/NL).

```
sqlps
Set-Location SQLSERVER:\SQL\HPESTAR\DEFAULT\Databases\AdventureWorks2012\Tables;
ForEach ($item in Get-ChildItem  | Where-Object { $_.Schema -eq "Purchasing" })
{$item.Script()}
```

```
Command Prompt - sqlps
C:\Users\Owner>sqlps
Microsoft SQL Server PowerShell
Version 11.0.2100.60
Microsoft Corp. All rights reserved.

PS SQLSERVER:\> Set-Location SQLSERVER:\SQL\HPESTAR\DEFAULT\Databases\AdventureW
orks2012\Tables;
PS SQLSERVER:\SQL\HPESTAR\DEFAULT\Databases\AdventureWorks2012\Tables> ForEach (
$item in Get-ChildItem  | Where-Object { $_.Schema -eq "Purchasing" }) {$item.Sc
ript()}
SET ANSI_NULLS ON
SET QUOTED_IDENTIFIER ON
CREATE TABLE [Purchasing].[ProductVendor](
        [ProductID] [int] NOT NULL,
        [BusinessEntityID] [int] NOT NULL,
        [AverageLeadTime] [int] NOT NULL,
        [StandardPrice] [money] NOT NULL,
        [LastReceiptCost] [money] NULL,
        [LastReceiptDate] [datetime] NULL,
        [MinOrderQty] [int] NOT NULL,
        [MaxOrderQty] [int] NOT NULL,
        [OnOrderQty] [int] NULL,
        [UnitMeasureCode] [nchar](3) COLLATE SQL_Latin1_General_CP1_CI_AS NOT NU
LL,
        [ModifiedDate] [datetime] NOT NULL
```

Instead of the console the scripting output can be piped to a .sql file.

```
ForEach ($item in Get-ChildItem  | Where-Object { $_.Schema -eq "Purchasing" }) {$item.Script()
| Out-File "f:data\sql\PurchasingTables.sql" -Append }
```

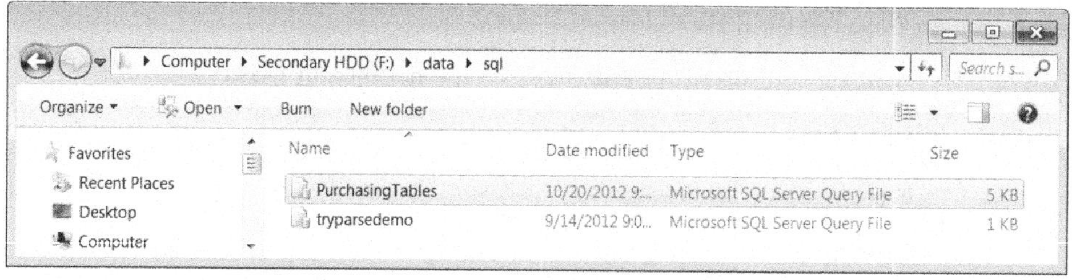

System Views since SQL Server 2005

SQL Server 2005 has introduced a large collection, 400 in SS 2012, of system views providing detail metadata and operational data which was not available before. As an example, the full-text index & full-text search functionalities have a number of supporting system views. The system tables are no longer accessible. System views cannot be altered or updated. **System views are read only**. The head of systems views list.

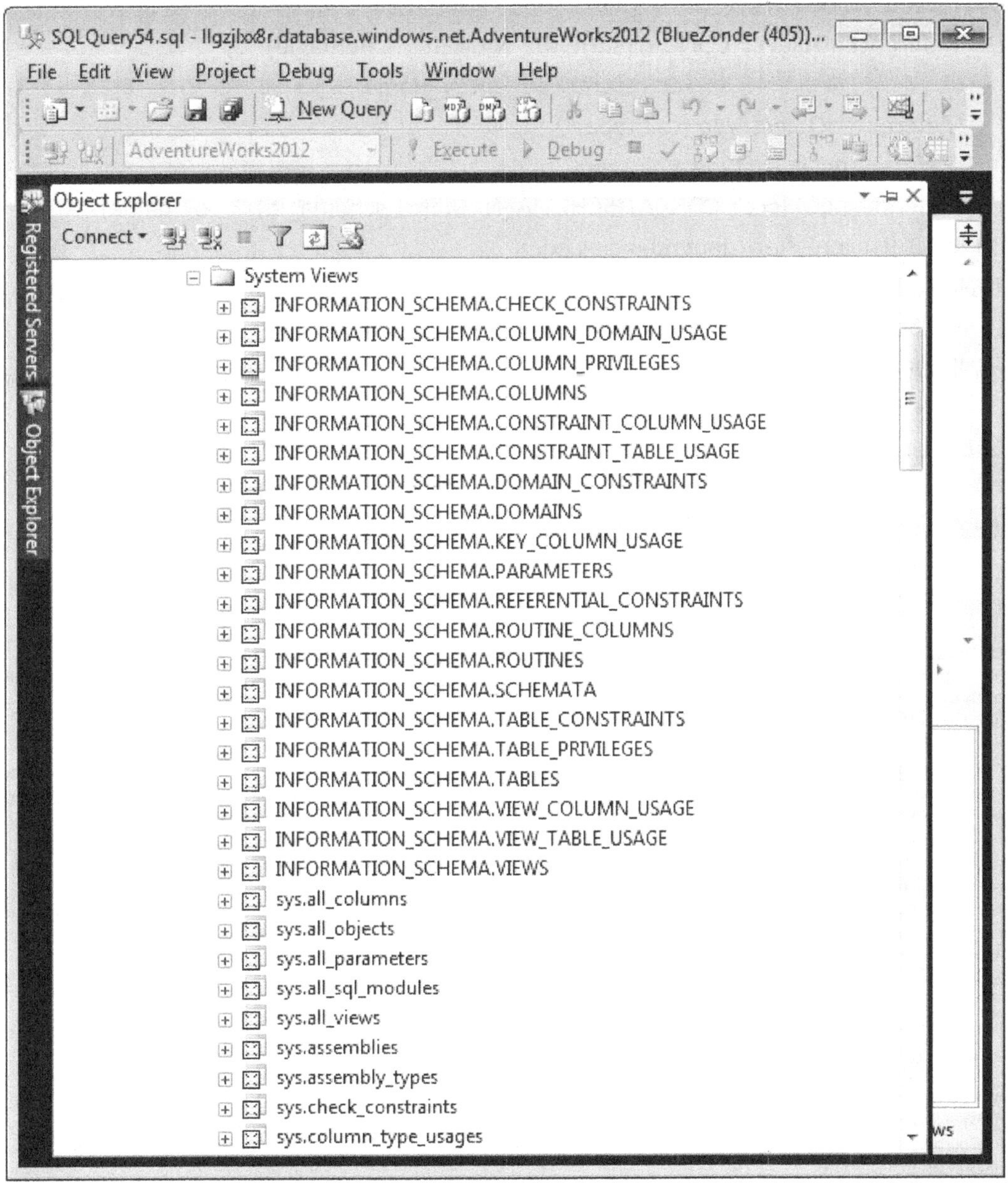

Querying Systems Views

Querying system views is not a trivial task. Frequently a group of tables involved and a Dynamic Management Function (DMF) CROSS APPLY may be necessary for useful results.

Download site for SQL Server 2008 R2 System Views Map: *http://www.microsoft.com/en-us/download/details.aspx?id=722* .

```
USE AdventureWorks2012;
SELECT ReferencedObject = CONCAT(SCHEMA_NAME(o2.schema_id), '.',
                                 ed.referenced_entity_name),
        ReferencedObjectType = o2.type,
        ReferencingObjectType = o1.type,
        ReferencingObject = CONCAT(SCHEMA_NAME(o1.schema_id), '.', o1.name)
FROM   sys.sql_expression_dependencies ed
    INNER JOIN sys.objects o1
        ON ed.referencing_id = o1.object_id
    INNER JOIN sys.objects o2
        ON ed.referenced_id = o2.object_id
WHERE  o1.type IN ( 'P', 'TR', 'V', 'TF' )
ORDER  BY       ReferencedObjectType, ReferencedObject, ReferencingObject;
-- (163 row(s) affected) - Partial results
```

ReferencedObject	ReferencedObjectType	ReferencingObjectType	ReferencingObject
HumanResources.Department	U	V	HumanResources.vEmployeeDepartment
HumanResources.Department	U	V	HumanResources.vEmployeeDepartmentHistory
HumanResources.Employee	U	TF	dbo.ufnGetContactInformation
HumanResources.Employee	U	P	dbo.uspGetEmployeeManagers
HumanResources.Employee	U	P	dbo.uspGetManagerEmployees
HumanResources.Employee	U	P	HumanResources.uspUpdateEmployeeHireInfo
HumanResources.Employee	U	P	HumanResources.uspUpdateEmployeeLogin
HumanResources.Employee	U	P	HumanResources.uspUpdateEmployeePersonalInfo
HumanResources.Employee	U	V	HumanResources.vEmployee
HumanResources.Employee	U	V	HumanResources.vEmployeeDepartment
HumanResources.Employee	U	V	HumanResources.vEmployeeDepartmentHistory
HumanResources.Employee	U	V	Sales.vSalesPerson
HumanResources.Employee	U	V	Sales.vSalesPersonSalesByFiscalYears
HumanResources.EmployeeDepartmentHistory	U	V	HumanResources.vEmployeeDepartment
HumanResources.EmployeeDepartmentHistory	U	V	HumanResources.vEmployeeDepartmentHistory
HumanResources.EmployeePayHistory	U	P	HumanResources.uspUpdateEmployeeHireInfo
HumanResources.JobCandidate	U	P	dbo.uspSearchCandidateResumes
HumanResources.JobCandidate	U	V	HumanResources.vJobCandidate
HumanResources.JobCandidate	U	V	HumanResources.vJobCandidateEducation
HumanResources.JobCandidate	U	V	HumanResources.vJobCandidateEmployment

Listing All System Views

Since SQL Server 2005 system tables are off limits, replaced by system views, 400 in SQL Server 2012 and 119 in Azure SQL.

```
;WITH cteTableList AS (      SELECT CONCAT(SCHEMA_NAME(schema_id), '.', name)              AS TableName,
  (( ROW_NUMBER() OVER( ORDER BY CONCAT(SCHEMA_NAME(schema_id),'.', name)) ) % 3)        AS Remainder,
  (( ROW_NUMBER() OVER( ORDER BY CONCAT(SCHEMA_NAME(schema_id),'.', name)) - 1 )/ 3)     AS Quotient
                         FROM sys.system_views),
CTE AS (SELECT TableName, CASE WHEN Remainder=0 THEN 3 ELSE Remainder END AS Remainder, Quotient
        FROM cteTableList)
SELECT  MAX(CASE WHEN Remainder = 1 THEN TableName END),
        MAX(CASE WHEN Remainder = 2 THEN TableName END),
        MAX(CASE WHEN Remainder = 3 THEN TableName END)
FROM  CTE GROUP  BY Quotient ORDER  BY Quotient;
```

INFORMATION_SCHEMA.CHECK_CONSTRAINTS	INFORMATION_SCHEMA.COLUMN_DOMAIN_USAGE	INFORMATION_SCHEMA.COLUMN_PRIVILEGES
INFORMATION_SCHEMA.COLUMNS	INFORMATION_SCHEMA.CONSTRAINT_COLUMN_USAGE	INFORMATION_SCHEMA.CONSTRAINT_TABLE_USAGE
INFORMATION_SCHEMA.DOMAIN_CONSTRAINTS	INFORMATION_SCHEMA.DOMAINS	INFORMATION_SCHEMA.KEY_COLUMN_USAGE
INFORMATION_SCHEMA.PARAMETERS	INFORMATION_SCHEMA.REFERENTIAL_CONSTRAINTS	INFORMATION_SCHEMA.ROUTINE_COLUMNS
INFORMATION_SCHEMA.ROUTINES	INFORMATION_SCHEMA.SCHEMATA	INFORMATION_SCHEMA.TABLE_CONSTRAINTS
INFORMATION_SCHEMA.TABLE_PRIVILEGES	INFORMATION_SCHEMA.TABLES	INFORMATION_SCHEMA.VIEW_COLUMN_USAGE
INFORMATION_SCHEMA.VIEW_TABLE_USAGE	INFORMATION_SCHEMA.VIEWS	sys.all_columns
sys.all_objects	sys.all_parameters	sys.all_sql_modules
sys.all_views	sys.assemblies	sys.assembly_types
sys.check_constraints	sys.column_type_usages	sys.columns
sys.computed_columns	sys.database_permissions	sys.database_principals
sys.database_role_members	sys.databases	sys.default_constraints
sys.dm_continuous_copy_status	sys.dm_db_index_usage_stats	sys.dm_db_missing_index_details
sys.dm_db_missing_index_group_stats	sys.dm_db_missing_index_groups	sys.dm_db_objects_impacted_on_version_change
sys.dm_db_partition_stats	sys.dm_db_wait_stats	sys.dm_exec_cached_plans
sys.dm_exec_connections	sys.dm_exec_procedure_stats	sys.dm_exec_query_memory_

		grants
sys.dm_exec_query_stats	sys.dm_exec_requests	sys.dm_exec_sessions
sys.dm_exec_trigger_stats	sys.dm_tran_active_transaction s	sys.dm_tran_database_transa ctions
sys.dm_tran_locks	sys.dm_tran_session_transactio ns	sys.dm_xe_database_session_ event_actions
sys.dm_xe_database_sessio n_events	sys.dm_xe_database_session_o bject_columns	sys.dm_xe_database_session_ targets
sys.dm_xe_database_sessio ns	sys.event_notification_event_ty pes	sys.event_notifications
sys.event_session_actions	sys.event_session_events	sys.event_session_fields
sys.event_session_targets	sys.event_sessions	sys.events
sys.federated_table_colum ns	sys.federation_distributions	sys.federation_member_distri butions
sys.federation_members	sys.federations	sys.foreign_key_columns
sys.foreign_keys	sys.identity_columns	sys.index_columns
sys.indexes	sys.key_constraints	sys.numbered_procedure_par ameters
sys.numbered_procedures	sys.objects	sys.parameter_type_usages
sys.parameters	sys.plan_guides	sys.procedures
sys.schemas	sys.spatial_index_tessellations	sys.spatial_indexes
sys.spatial_reference_syste ms	sys.sql_expression_dependenci es	sys.sql_modules
sys.stats	sys.stats_columns	sys.synonyms
sys.syscharsets	sys.syscolumns	sys.syscursorrefs
sys.syscursors	sys.sysdatabases	sys.syslanguages
sys.sysobjects	sys.sysreferences	sys.system_columns
sys.system_objects	sys.system_parameters	sys.system_sql_modules
sys.system_views	sys.systypes	sys.sysusers
sys.table_types	sys.tables	sys.trigger_event_types
sys.trigger_events	sys.triggers	sys.types
sys.views	sys.xml_schema_collections	NULL

List of System Tables Prior to SQL Server 2005 - OPSS

Some of the system tables were updatable in SQL Server 2000 and previous versions. SS 2005 introduced system views which are not updatable and barred access to system tables.

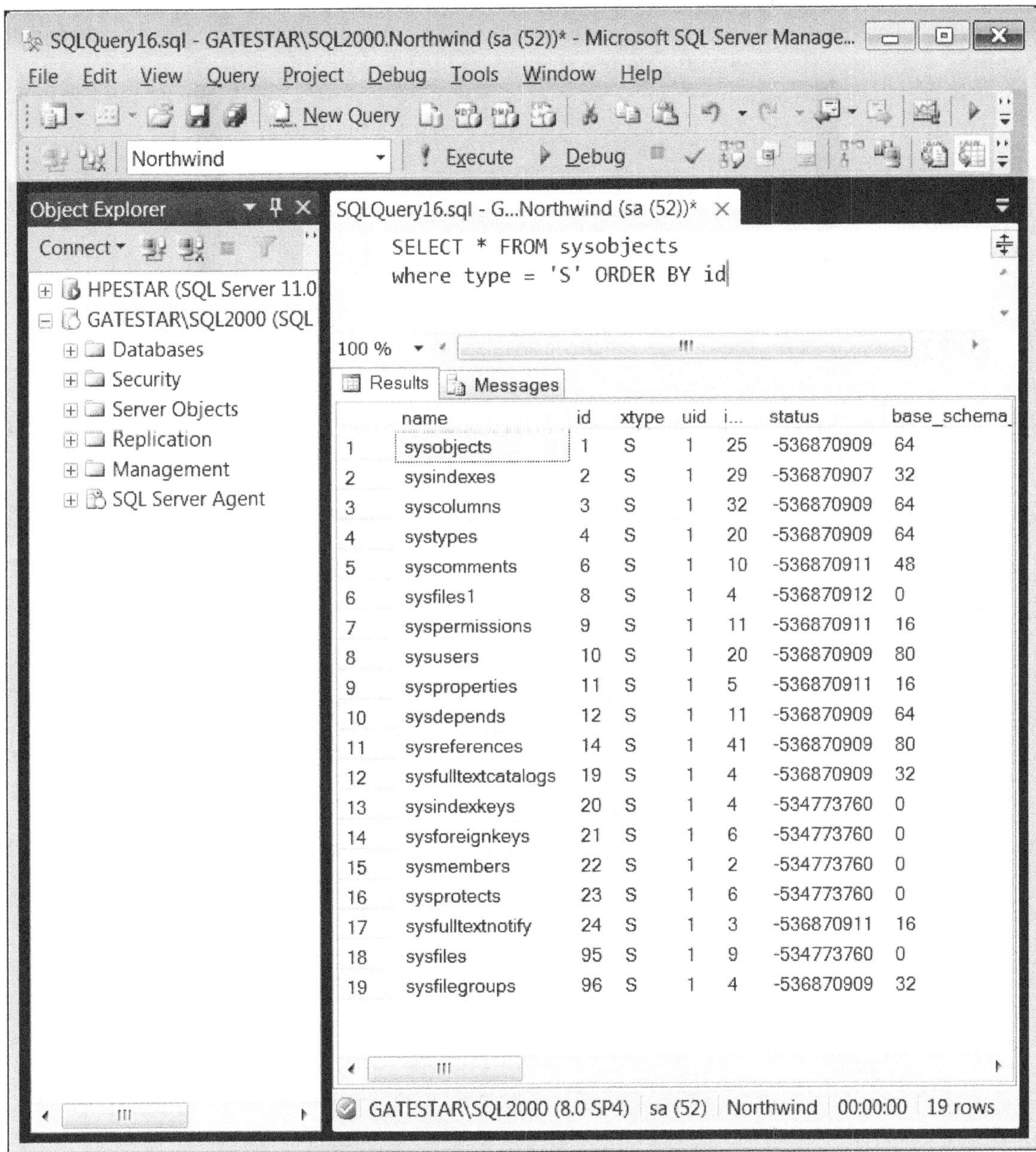

	name	id	xtype	uid	i...	status	base_schema_
1	sysobjects	1	S	1	25	-536870909	64
2	sysindexes	2	S	1	29	-536870907	32
3	syscolumns	3	S	1	32	-536870909	64
4	systypes	4	S	1	20	-536870909	64
5	syscomments	6	S	1	10	-536870911	48
6	sysfiles1	8	S	1	4	-536870912	0
7	syspermissions	9	S	1	11	-536870911	16
8	sysusers	10	S	1	20	-536870909	80
9	sysproperties	11	S	1	5	-536870911	16
10	sysdepends	12	S	1	11	-536870909	64
11	sysreferences	14	S	1	41	-536870909	80
12	sysfulltextcatalogs	19	S	1	4	-536870909	32
13	sysindexkeys	20	S	1	4	-534773760	0
14	sysforeignkeys	21	S	1	6	-534773760	0
15	sysmembers	22	S	1	2	-534773760	0
16	sysprotects	23	S	1	6	-534773760	0
17	sysfulltextnotify	24	S	1	3	-536870911	16
18	sysfiles	95	S	1	9	-534773760	0
19	sysfilegroups	96	S	1	4	-536870909	32

Other Methods of Metadata Access

Graphical Dependency Information

Object dependencies can be launched by a right click on the object.

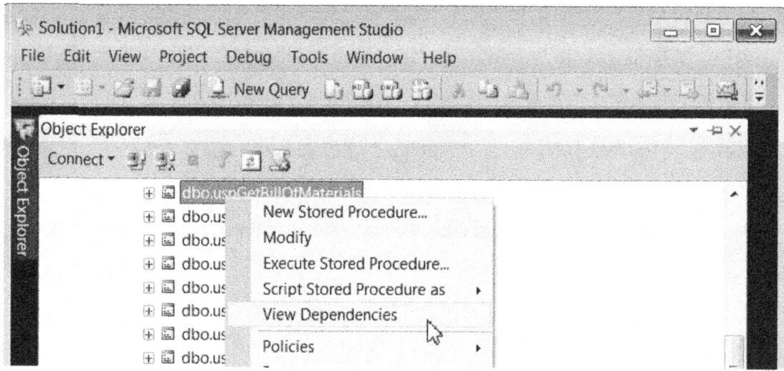

The dependency chart for the uspGetBillOfMaterials stored procedure.

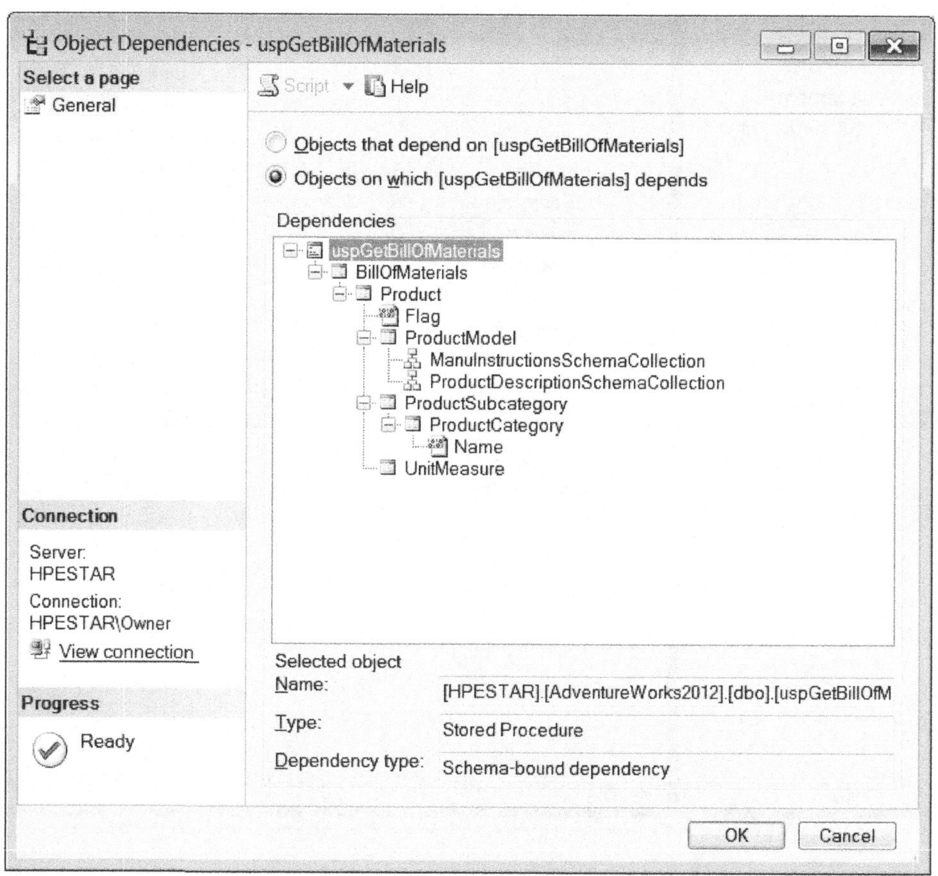

Scripting GUI Object Change - OPSS2012

Most of the dialog panels have scripting options. In fact we don't even have to perform the action, we can just script it and execute the script in a (new) connection. The advantage of this approach that the generated script can be modified and saved for future use or reference. We start an index change with right click and properties.

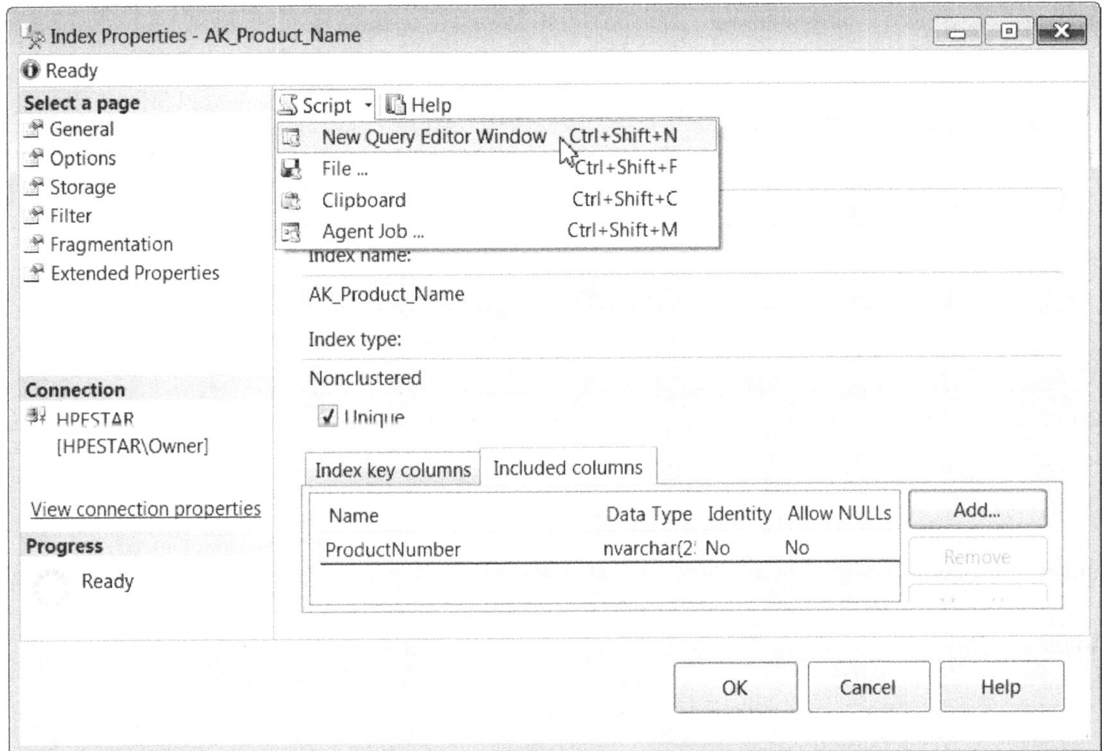

The generated script.

```
USE [AdventureWorks2012]
GO
SET ANSI_PADDING ON
GO
CREATE UNIQUE NONCLUSTERED INDEX [AK_Product_Name] ON [Production].[Product] (
[Name] ASC )
INCLUDE (        [ProductNumber]) WITH (PAD_INDEX = OFF, STATISTICS_NORECOMPUTE = OFF,
SORT_IN_TEMPDB = OFF,
IGNORE_DUP_KEY = OFF, DROP_EXISTING = ON, ONLINE = OFF, ALLOW_ROW_LOCKS = ON,
ALLOW_PAGE_LOCKS = ON, FILLFACTOR = 85) ON [PRIMARY]
GO
```

The sp_helpdb System Procedure - OPSS

The sp_helpdb system procedure returns information on all or a specified database.

```
EXEC sp_helpdb;
-- Partial results
```

Accounting	3.88 MB	HPESTAR\Owner	17	May 24 2012	Status=ONLINE, Updateability=READ_WRITE, UserAccess=MULTI_USER, Recovery=FULL, Version=706, Collation=SQL_Latin1_General_CP1_CI_AS, SQLSortOrder=52, IsAutoCreateStatistics, IsAutoUpdateStatistics, IsFullTextEnabled	110
AdventureWorks	213.94 MB	HPESTAR\Owner	16	May 24 2012	Status=ONLINE, Updateability=READ_WRITE, UserAccess=MULTI_USER, Recovery=SIMPLE, Version=706, Collation=SQL_Latin1_General_CP1_CI_AS, SQLSortOrder=52, IsAnsiNullsEnabled, IsAnsiPaddingEnabled, IsAnsiWarningsEnabled, IsArithmeticAbortEnabled, IsAutoCreateStatistics, IsAutoUpdateStatistics, IsFullTextEnabled, IsNullConcat, IsQuotedIdentifiersEnabled, IsRecursiveTriggersEnabled	90

```
EXEC sp_helpdb AdventureWorks2012;
```

name	db_size	owner	dbid	created	status	compatibility_level
AdventureWorks2012	3118.38 MB	sa	7	May 19 2012	Status=ONLINE, Updateability=READ_WRITE, UserAccess=MULTI_USER, Recovery=SIMPLE, Version=706, Collation=SQL_Latin1_General_CP1_CI_AS, SQLSortOrder=52, IsAnsiNullsEnabled, IsAnsiPaddingEnabled, IsAnsiWarningsEnabled, IsArithmeticAbortEnabled, IsAutoCreateStatistics, IsAutoUpdateStatistics, IsFullTextEnabled, IsNullConcat, IsQuotedIdentifiersEnabled	110

The sp_help and sp_helptext System Procedures

The sp_help and sp_helptext provides database metadata in various formats including multiple result sets.

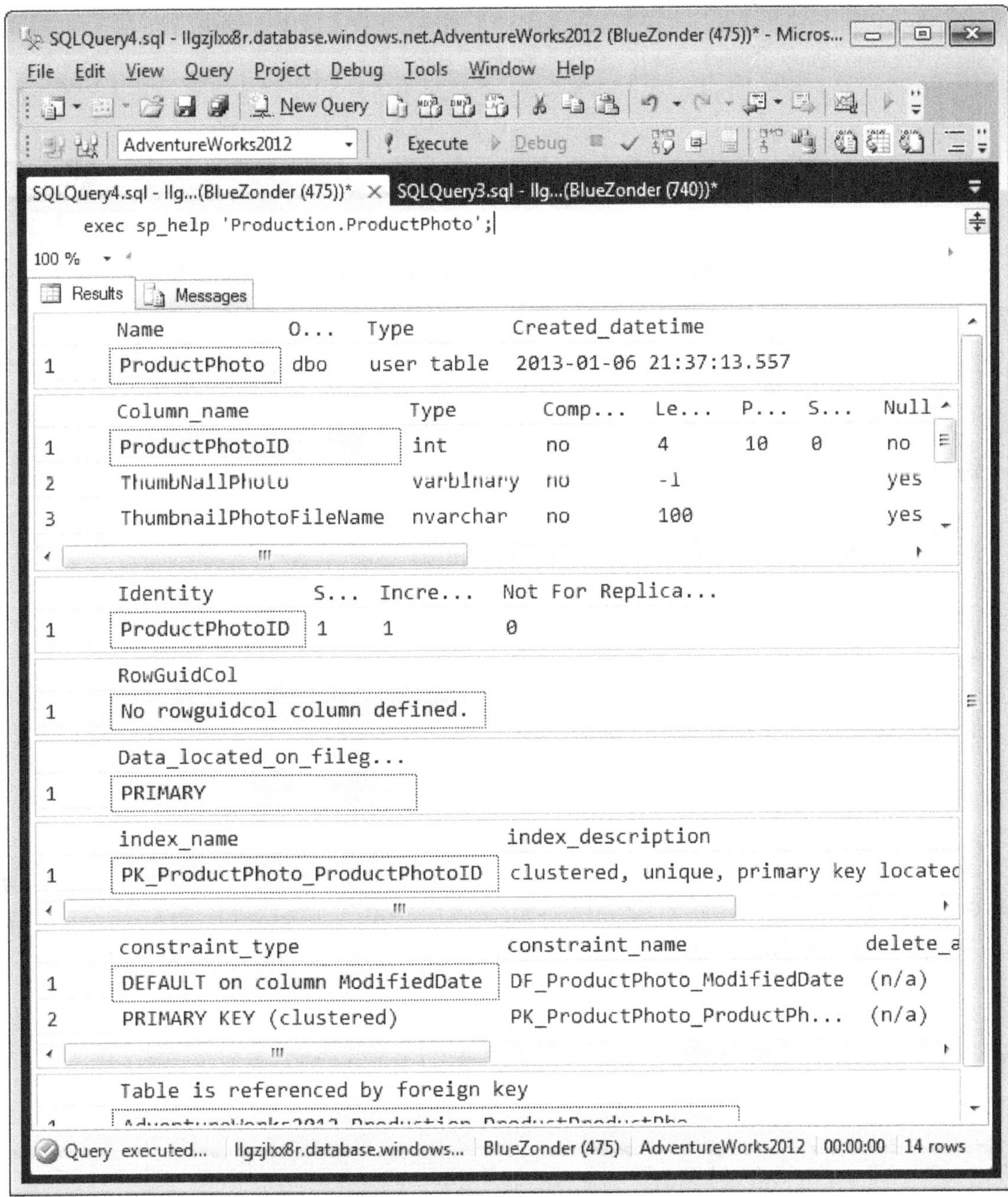

Using sp_helptext for Obtaining Definition

sp_helptext works only for some database objects. Table definition cannot be obtained by command, any command.

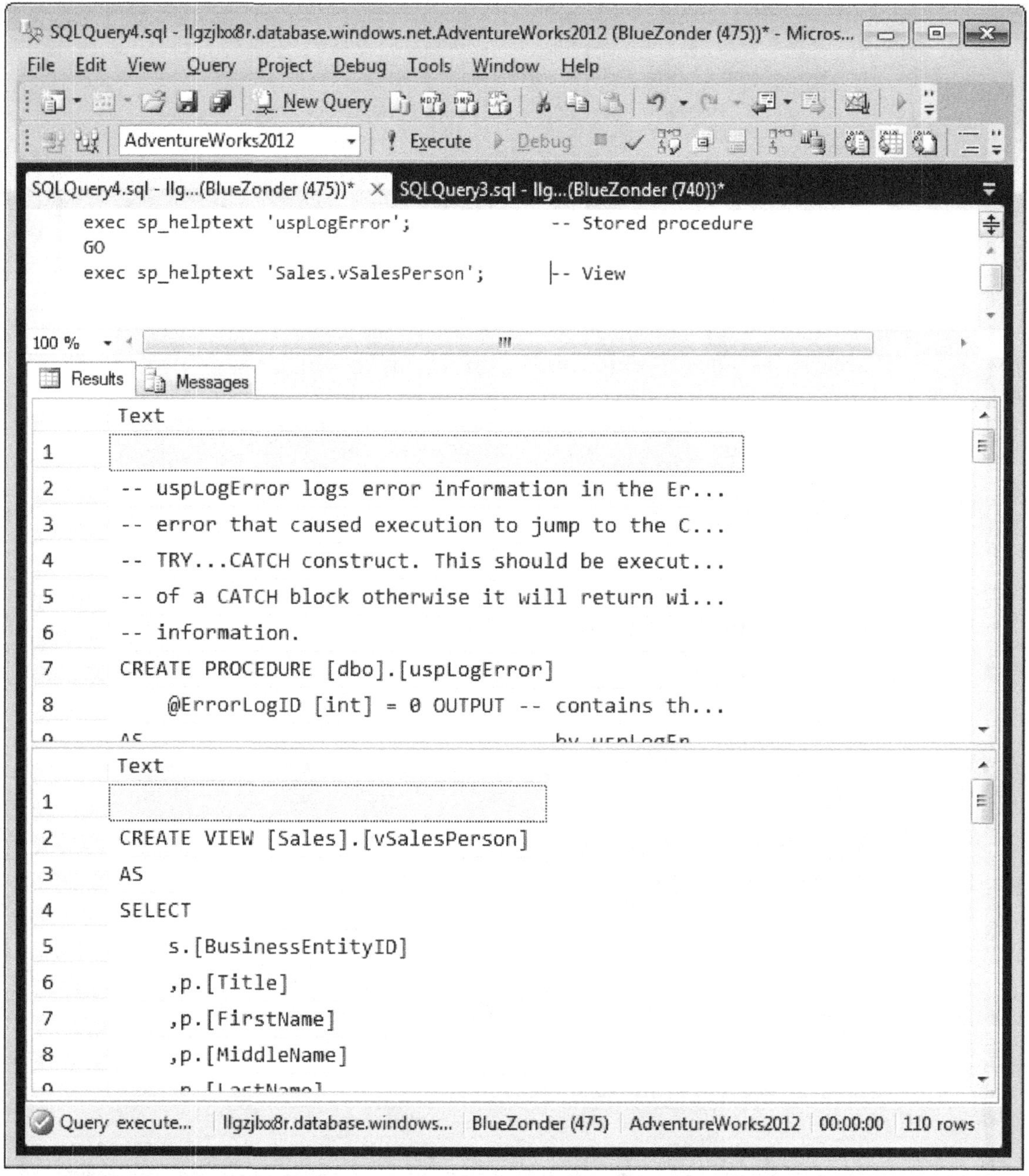

List of sp_helpx System Procedures

Following list is from the master database System Stored Procedures. Filter is set on sp_help.

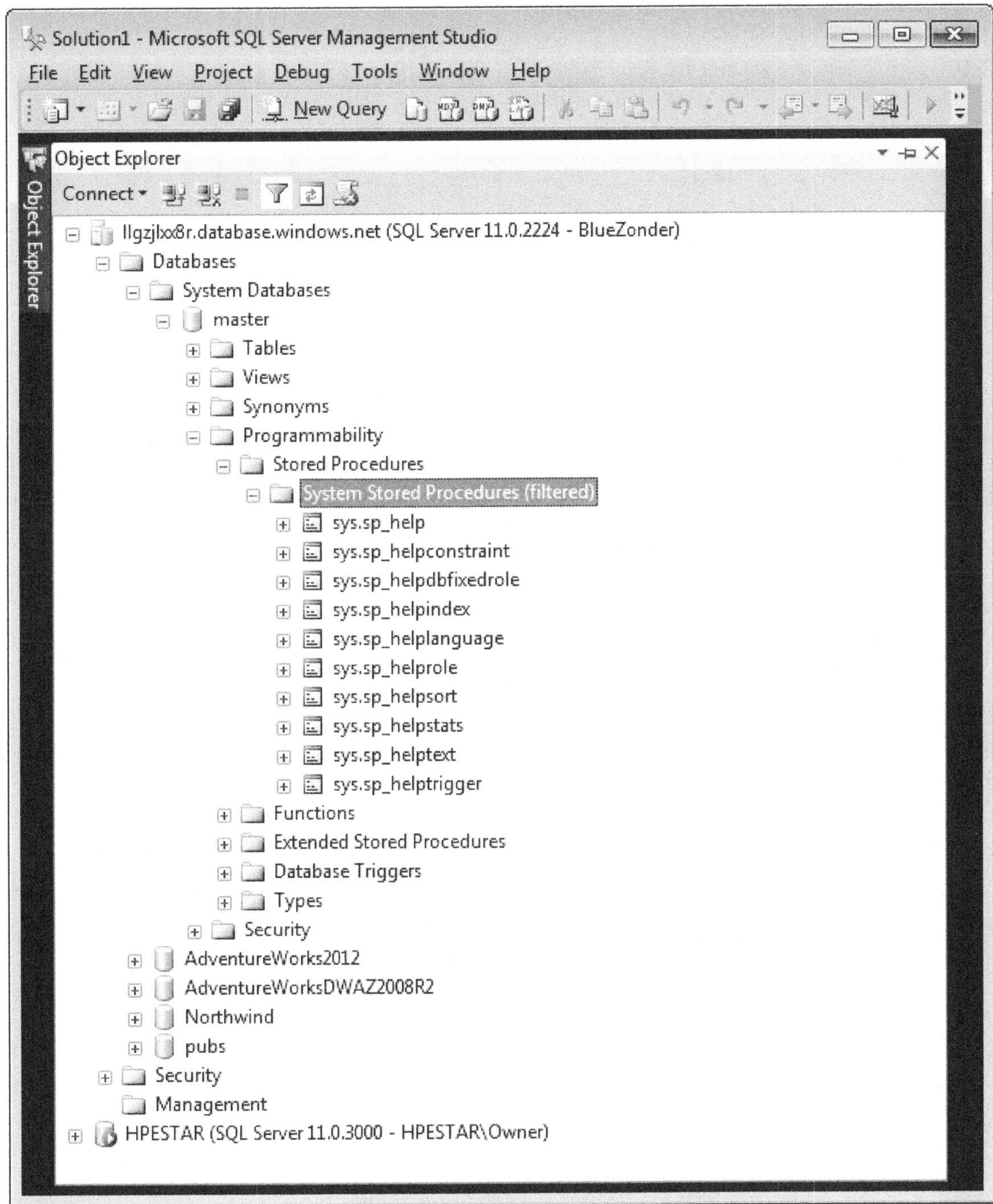

Listing All CHECK Constraints in a Database

We can use INFORMATION_SCHEMA views to perform this task.

```
USE AdventureWorks2012;
GO
```

```
SELECT          cc.CONSTRAINT_SCHEMA                AS SCHEMA_NAME,
                 TABLE_NAME,
                COLUMN_NAME,
                CHECK_CLAUSE,
                cc.CONSTRAINT_NAME
FROM    INFORMATION_SCHEMA.CHECK_CONSTRAINTS cc
                INNER JOIN INFORMATION_SCHEMA.CONSTRAINT_COLUMN_USAGE c
                        ON cc.CONSTRAINT_NAME = c.CONSTRAINT_NAME
ORDER BY        SCHEMA_NAME,
                TABLE_NAME,
                COLUMN_NAME;
-- (105 row(s) affected) - Partial results.
```

SCHEMA_NAME	TABLE_NAME	COLUMN_NAME	CHECK_CLAUSE	CONSTRAINT_NAME
HumanResources	Employee	BirthDate	([BirthDate]>='1930-01-01' AND [BirthDate]<=dateadd(year,(-18),getdate()))	CK_Employee_BirthDate
HumanResources	Employee	Gender	(upper([Gender])='F' OR upper([Gender])='M')	CK_Employee_Gender
HumanResources	Employee	HireDate	([HireDate]>='1996-07-01' AND [HireDate]<=dateadd(day,(1),getdate()))	CK_Employee_HireDate
HumanResources	Employee	MaritalStatus	(upper([MaritalStatus])='S' OR upper([MaritalStatus])='M')	CK_Employee_MaritalStatus
HumanResources	Employee	SickLeaveHours	([SickLeaveHours]>=(0) AND [SickLeaveHours]<=(120))	CK_Employee_SickLeaveHours
HumanResources	Employee	VacationHours	([VacationHours]>=(-40) AND [VacationHours]<=(240))	CK_Employee_VacationHours
HumanResources	EmployeeDepartmentHistory	EndDate	([EndDate]>=[StartDate] OR [EndDate] IS NULL)	CK_EmployeeDepartmentHistory_EndDate
HumanResources	EmployeeDepartmentHistory	StartDate	([EndDate]>=[StartDate] OR [EndDate] IS NULL)	CK_EmployeeDepartmentHistory_EndDate
HumanResources	EmployeePayHistory	PayFrequency	([PayFrequency]=(2) OR [PayFrequency]=(1))	CK_EmployeePayHistory_PayFrequency
HumanResources	EmployeePayHistory	Rate	([Rate]>=(6.50) AND [Rate]<=(200.00))	CK_EmployeePayHistory_Rate
Person	Person	EmailPromotion	([EmailPromotion]>=(0) AND [EmailPromotion]<=(2))	CK_Person_EmailPromotion

Creating a UDF CHECK Constraint

UDF CHECK constraint relies on a user-defined function for logic rather than the simple constraint expression. Demonstration script creates a test table with UDF check constraint. **UDF CHECK constraint may have performance problems for multi-row events such as single statement INSERT of 100 records.**

```
USE AdventureWorks2012;
CREATE TABLE dbo.Person( BusinessEntityID int PRIMARY KEY, FirstName nvarchar(50) NOT NULL,
        LastName nvarchar(50) NOT NULL, Email varchar(64) NULL);
INSERT dbo.Person
SELECT TOP 10    P.BusinessEntityID, FirstName, LastName,    -- Create test table
                 Email=convert(varchar(64),EmailAddress)
FROM Person.Person P INNER JOIN Person.EmailAddress E  ON E.BusinessEntityID = P.BusinessEntityID;
GO  -- (10 row(s) affected)
-- Create user-defined function (UDF) for checking
CREATE FUNCTION ufnEmailValidityCheck (@Email varchar(64))
RETURNS BIT  AS
BEGIN
IF EXISTS(SELECT 1 WHERE
   CHARINDEX('.',@Email,CHARINDEX('@',@Email))-CHARINDEX('@',@Email)>1
   AND CHARINDEX('.',REVERSE(LTRIM(RTRIM(@Email)))) > 2
   AND CHARINDEX('@',LTRIM(@Email)) > 2) RETURN(1)
RETURN (0)
END;
GO
 -- Create UDF check constraint
ALTER TABLE [dbo].[Person]  WITH CHECK
ADD CONSTRAINT [EmailCheck] CHECK (   dbo.ufnEmailValidityCheck (Email) = 1);
GO
 -- SQL check constraint violated missing . (period)
INSERT Person (BusinessEntityID, FirstName, LastName, Email)
VALUES (100000, 'Elvis', 'Presley', 'elvispresley@thekingcom');
/*  Msg 547, Level 16, State 0, Line 5
The INSERT statement conflicted with the CHECK constraint "EmailCheck".
The conflict occurred in database "tempdb", table "dbo.Person", column 'Email'.*/
 -- SQL check constraint met
INSERT Person (BusinessEntityID, FirstName, LastName, Email)
VALUES (100000, 'Elvis', 'Presley', 'elvispresley@theking.com');
GO   -- (1 row(s) affected)
 SELECT * FROM Person ORDER BY Email;  -- Partial results.
```

BusinessEntityID	FirstName	LastName	Email
8	Diane	Margheim	diane1@adventure-works.com
7	Dylan	Miller	dylan0@adventure-works.com
100000	Elvis	Presley	elvispresley@theking.com

List All DEFAULT Constraint Definitions

We can use system views to carry out the task.

```
USE AdventureWorks2012;
```

```
SELECT
  SCHEMA_NAME(o.schema_id)          AS SchemaName,
  o.name                            AS TableName,
  c.name                            AS ColumnName,
  d.definition                      AS DefaultDefinition,
  d.name                            AS ConstraintName
FROM sys.default_constraints d
       INNER JOIN sys.columns c
              ON d.parent_object_id = c.object_id
              AND d.parent_column_id = c.column_id
       INNER JOIN sys.objects o
              ON o.object_id = c.object_id
ORDER BY SchemaName, TableName, ColumnName;
-- (152 row(s) affected) - Partial results.
```

SchemaName	TableName	ColumnName	DefaultDefinition	ConstraintName
dbo	AWBuildVersion	ModifiedDate	(getdate())	DF_AWBuildVersion_ModifiedDate
dbo	ErrorLog	ErrorTime	(getdate())	DF_ErrorLog_ErrorTime
HumanResources	Department	ModifiedDate	(getdate())	DF_Department_ModifiedDate
HumanResources	Employee	CurrentFlag	((1))	DF_Employee_CurrentFlag
HumanResources	Employee	ModifiedDate	(getdate())	DF_Employee_ModifiedDate
HumanResources	Employee	rowguid	(newid())	DF_Employee_rowguid
HumanResources	Employee	SalariedFlag	((1))	DF_Employee_SalariedFlag
HumanResources	Employee	SickLeaveHours	((0))	DF_Employee_SickLeaveHours
HumanResources	Employee	VacationHours	((0))	DF_Employee_VacationHours
HumanResources	EmployeeDepartmentHistory	ModifiedDate	(getdate())	DF_EmployeeDepartmentHistory_ModifiedDate
HumanResources	EmployeePayHistory	ModifiedDate	(getdate())	DF_EmployeePayHistory_ModifiedDate
HumanResources	JobCandidate	ModifiedDate	(getdate())	DF_JobCandidate_ModifiedDate
HumanResources	Shift	ModifiedDate	(getdate())	DF_Shift_ModifiedDate
Person	Address	ModifiedDate	(getdate())	DF_Address_ModifiedDate
Person	Address	rowguid	(newid())	DF_Address_rowguid
Person	AddressType	ModifiedDate	(getdate())	DF_AddressType_ModifiedDate
Person	AddressType	rowguid	(newid())	DF_AddressType_rowguid
Person	BusinessEntity	ModifiedDate	(getdate())	DF_BusinessEntity_ModifiedDate
Person	BusinessEntity	rowguid	(newid())	DF_BusinessEntity_rowguid
Person	BusinessEntityAddress	ModifiedDate	(getdate())	DF_BusinessEntityAddress_ModifiedDate
Person	BusinessEntityAddress	rowguid	(newid())	DF_BusinessEntityAddress_rowguid
Person	BusinessEntityContact	ModifiedDate	(getdate())	DF_BusinessEntityContact_ModifiedDate
Person	BusinessEntityContact	rowguid	(newid())	DF_BusinessEntityContact_rowguid
Person	ContactType	ModifiedDate	(getdate())	DF_ContactType_ModifiedDate
Person	CountryRegion	ModifiedDate	(getdate())	DF_CountryRegion_ModifiedDate

Database Object-Definition from sys.sql_modules System View

The sys.sql_modules systems view contains definition for stored procedures, triggers, functions and views. Prior to SQL Server 2005 the sys.syscomments table was used to obtain object definition source code.

```
USE AdventureWorks2012;
GO
```

```
SELECT object_id, LEFT(definition,64) AS DefinitionPrefix
FROM sys.SQL_Modules ORDER BY object_id;
GO
-- (52 row(s) affected) - Partial results.
```

object_id	DefinitionPrefix
7671075	CREATE VIEW [Sales].[vStoreWithContacts] AS SELECT s.[
23671132	CREATE VIEW [Sales].[vStoreWithAddresses] AS SELECT s.
39671189	CREATE VIEW [Purchasing].[vVendorWithContacts] AS SELECT
55671246	CREATE VIEW [Purchasing].[vVendorWithAddresses] AS SELECT
71671303	CREATE FUNCTION [dbo].[ufnGetAccountingStartDate]() RETURNS [
87671360	CREATE FUNCTION [dbo].[ufnGetAccountingEndDate]() RETURNS [da
103671417	CREATE FUNCTION [dbo].[ufnGetContactInformation](@PersonID int
119671474	CREATE FUNCTION [dbo].[ufnGetProductDealerPrice](@ProductI
135671531	CREATE FUNCTION [dbo].[ufnGetProductListPrice](@ProductID [int
151671588	CREATE FUNCTION [dbo].[ufnGetProductStandardCost](@ProductID [

Retrieving the Full Definition of a Stored Procedure

```
SELECT          schema_name(schema_id)              AS SchemaName,
                object_Name(m.object_ID)            AS ObjectName,
                definition                          AS ObjectDefinition
FROM   sys.SQL_Modules m
  INNER JOIN sys.objects o      ON m.object_id=o.object_id
WHERE  object_Name(m.object_ID) = 'uspGetBillOfMaterials'
GO
```

```
SchemaName        ObjectName              ObjectDefinition
dbo          uspGetBillOfMaterials        CREATE PROCEDURE [dbo].[uspGetBillOfMaterials]
   @StartProductID [int],
   @CheckDate [datetime]
AS
BEGIN
   SET NOCOUNT ON;

   -- Use recursive query to generate a multi-level Bill of Material (i.e. all level 1
   -- components of a level 0 assembly, all level 2 components of a level 1 assembly)
   -- The CheckDate eliminates any components that are no longer used in the product on this date.
   WITH [BOM_cte]([ProductAssemblyID], [ComponentID], [ComponentDesc], [PerAssemblyQty], [StandardCost], [ListPrice],
[BOMLevel], [RecursionLevel]) -- CTE name and columns
   AS (
      SELECT b.[ProductAssemblyID], b.[ComponentID], p.[Name], b.[PerAssemblyQty], p.[StandardCost], p.[ListPrice], b.[BOMLevel],
0 -- Get the initial list of components for the bike assembly
      FROM [Production].[BillOfMaterials] b
         INNER JOIN [Production].[Product] p
         ON b.[ComponentID] = p.[ProductID]
      WHERE b.[ProductAssemblyID] = @StartProductID
         AND @CheckDate >= b.[StartDate]
         AND @CheckDate <= ISNULL(b.[EndDate], @CheckDate)
      UNION ALL
      SELECT b.[ProductAssemblyID], b.[ComponentID], p.[Name], b.[PerAssemblyQty], p.[StandardCost], p.[ListPrice], b.[BOMLevel],
[RecursionLevel] + 1 -- Join recursive member to anchor
      FROM [BOM_cte] cte
         INNER JOIN [Production].[BillOfMaterials] b
         ON b.[ProductAssemblyID] = cte.[ComponentID]
         INNER JOIN [Production].[Product] p
         ON b.[ComponentID] = p.[ProductID]
      WHERE @CheckDate >= b.[StartDate]
         AND @CheckDate <= ISNULL(b.[EndDate], @CheckDate)
      )
   -- Outer select from the CTE
   SELECT b.[ProductAssemblyID], b.[ComponentID], b.[ComponentDesc], SUM(b.[PerAssemblyQty]) AS [TotalQuantity] ,
b.[StandardCost], b.[ListPrice], b.[BOMLevel], b.[RecursionLevel]
   FROM [BOM_cte] b
   GROUP BY b.[ComponentID], b.[ComponentDesc], b.[ProductAssemblyID], b.[BOMLevel], b.[RecursionLevel], b.[StandardCost],
b.[ListPrice]
   ORDER BY b.[BOMLevel], b.[ProductAssemblyID], b.[ComponentID]     OPTION (MAXRECURSION 25)
END;
```

Snowflake Schema Data Warehouse Design

If the following DW design were Star Schema, the DimProduct would be a flat dimension including DimProductSubcategory and DimProductCategory. In Snowflake Schema the dimension tables follow 3NF relational design.

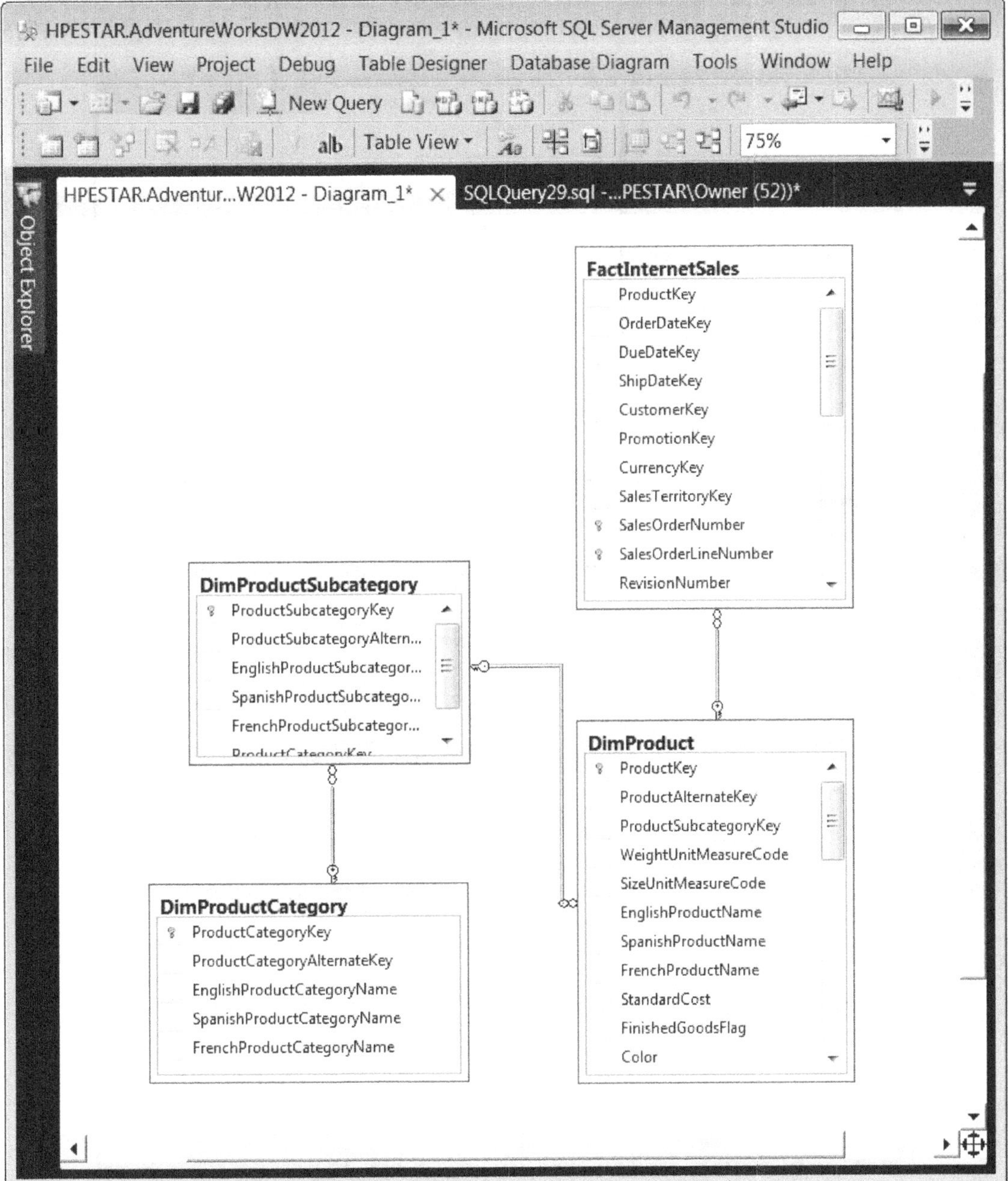

Object Explorer Table Editor - OPSS

A table editor is available for directly editing data in a table. It is designed for limited use. First we create a test table, Department, then we launch the editor.

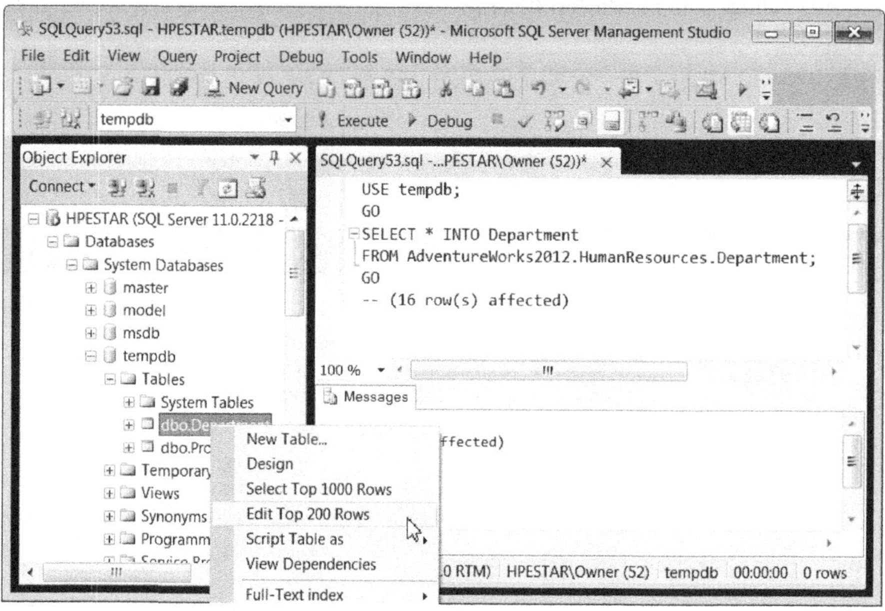

We added row 17 just by typing it in, then investigated the right click drop-down menu.

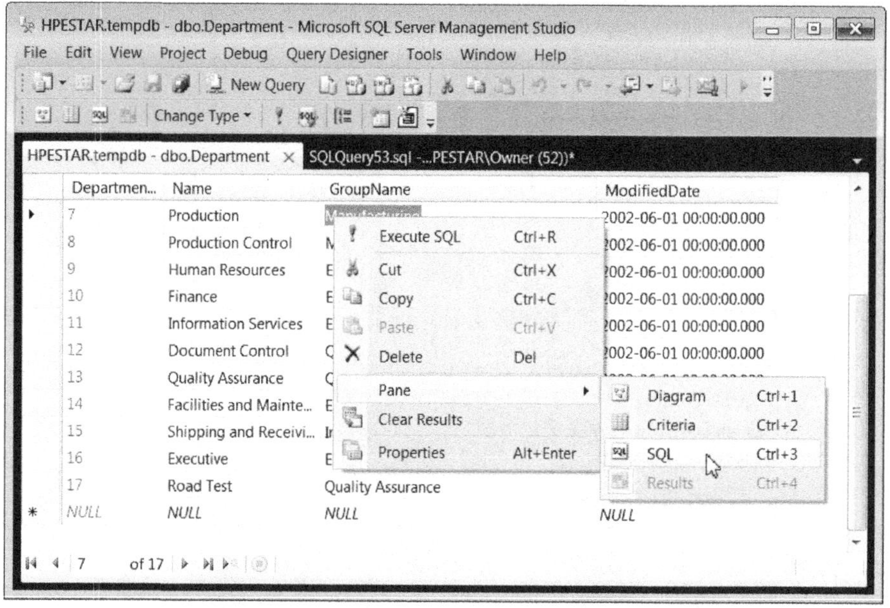

All Tables Row Count without the COUNT() Function

Here is quick way to get a row count, not exact like COUNT(*) but really fast.

```
USE AdventureWorks2012;
```

```
SELECT * FROM
(SELECT
        distinct
        concat(schema_name(schema_id),'.',name)          as TableName,
        row_count                                        as Rows
FROM sys.dm_db_partition_stats ps
        inner join sys.objects o
                on ps.object_id = o.object_id
) X  -- derived table
ORDER BY Rows DESC;
GO
-- (71 row(s) affected) -- Partial results.
```

TableName	Rows
Sales.SalesOrderDetail	121,317
Production.TransactionHistory	113,443
Production.TransactionHistoryArchive	89,253
Production.WorkOrder	72,591
Production.WorkOrderRouting	67,131
Sales.SalesOrderHeader	31,465
Sales.SalesOrderHeaderSalesReason	27,647
Person.BusinessEntity	20,777
Person.EmailAddress	19,972
Person.Password	19,972
Person.Person	19,972
Person.PersonPhone	19,972
Sales.Customer	19,820
Person.Address	19,614
Person.BusinessEntityAddress	19,614
Sales.CreditCard	19,118
Sales.PersonCreditCard	19,118
Sales.CurrencyRate	13,532
Purchasing.PurchaseOrderDetail	8,845
Purchasing.PurchaseOrderHeader	4,012
Production.BillOfMaterials	2,679
dbo.DatabaseLog	1,597
Production.ProductInventory	1,069
Person.BusinessEntityContact	909
Production.ProductDescription	762

Column Properties Page - OPSS

Object Explorer right click on a column launches the column properties page. Production.Product table ProductNumber column properties. No changes can be performed on this page. To change the table, we have to launch the table designer.

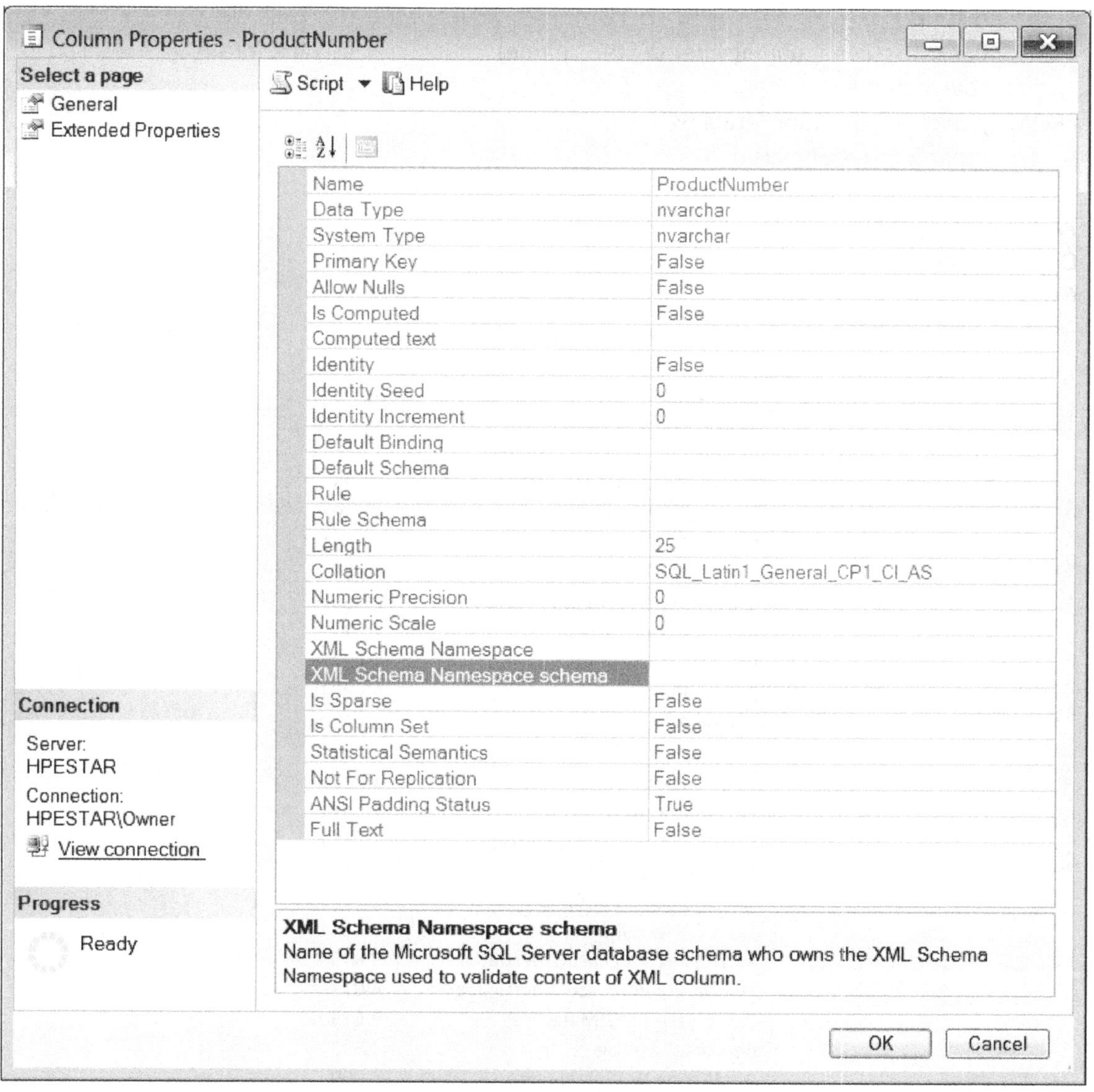

Listing All Columns with PK, FK & IDENTITY Properties

There are various ways for retrieving column properties including the COLUMNPROPERTY() function.

```
USE AdventureWorks2012;
```

```
SELECT c.TABLE_CATALOG                                                    AS DatabaseName,
    c.TABLE_SCHEMA                                                        AS SchemaName,
    c.TABLE_NAME                                                          AS TableName,
    c.COLUMN_NAME                                                         AS ColumnName,
    Columnproperty(Object_id(CONCAT(c.TABLE_SCHEMA,'.',c.TABLE_NAME)),
                    c.COLUMN_NAME, 'ISIDENTITY')                          AS IsIdentity,
    CASE
     WHEN CONSTRAINT_NAME IN (SELECT NAME
                    FROM   sys.objects
                    WHERE  TYPE = 'PK') THEN 1
     ELSE 0    END                                                        AS IsPrimaryKey,
    CASE
     WHEN CONSTRAINT_NAME IN (SELECT NAME
                    FROM   sys.objects
                    WHERE  TYPE = 'F') THEN 1
     ELSE 0    END                                                        AS IsForeignKey
FROM   INFORMATION_SCHEMA.TABLES t
    INNER JOIN INFORMATION_SCHEMA.COLUMNS c
        ON c.TABLE_CATALOG = t.TABLE_CATALOG
         AND c.TABLE_SCHEMA = t.TABLE_SCHEMA
         AND c.TABLE_NAME = t.TABLE_NAME
    LEFT JOIN INFORMATION_SCHEMA.KEY_COLUMN_USAGE u
        ON c.TABLE_CATALOG = u.TABLE_CATALOG
         AND c.TABLE_SCHEMA = u.TABLE_SCHEMA
         AND c.TABLE_NAME = u.TABLE_NAME
         AND c.COLUMN_NAME = u.COLUMN_NAME
WHERE  TABLE_TYPE = 'BASE TABLE'
ORDER  BY SchemaName,    TableName,    c.ORDINAL_POSITION;
GO
-- (534 row(s) affected) - Partial results.
```

DatabaseName	SchemaName	TableName	ColumnName	IsIdentity	IsPrimaryKey	IsForeignKey
AdventureWorks2012	Person	EmailAddress	BusinessEntityID	0	0	1
AdventureWorks2012	Person	EmailAddress	BusinessEntityID	0	1	0
AdventureWorks2012	Person	EmailAddress	EmailAddressID	1	1	0
AdventureWorks2012	Person	EmailAddress	EmailAddress	0	0	0

The Collation Column Property & the COLLATE Clause

Each text column requires the collation property. The server & databases also have collation property as defaults only. When the database collation is changed, the actual column collations remain the same. New table columns will inherit the database default collation. New databases inherit the server collation. A column collation can be changed with ALTER TABLE. To change all text collations in a database may prove to be a big task.

```
USE AdventureWorks2012;
CREATE TABLE Product (ProductID INT PRIMARY KEY, Name nvarchar(50), ListPrice money);
GO
INSERT INTO Product  SELECT ProductID, Name, ListPrice  FROM Production.Product;
-- (504 row(s) affected)
```

```
ALTER TABLE Product ALTER COLUMN Name nvarchar(50)
                COLLATE SQL_Latin1_General_CP1_CS_AS null;
-- Command(s) completed successfully.
```

Text operations with different collations result in error.

```
SELECT COUNT(*) FROM Product p
                    INNER JOIN Production.Product aw12
                        ON p.Name = aw12.Name;
GO
```

```
/*  Msg 468, Level 16, State 9, Line 3
Cannot resolve the collation conflict between "SQL_Latin1_General_CP1_CI_AS" and
"SQL_Latin1_General_CP1_CS_AS" in the equal to operation.    */
```

We can correct it in the query with the COLLATE clause. We can use a specific collation on one side of the expression, or the easy to remember DATABASE_DEFAULT.

```
SELECT COUNT(*) FROM Product p
                    INNER JOIN Production.Product aw12
                        ON p.Name = aw12.Name COLLATE DATABASE_DEFAULT;
-- 504
```

Restoring the original column collation.

```
ALTER TABLE Product alter column ProductName varchar(40)
                COLLATE SQL_Latin1_General_CP1_CI_AS null;
```

Listing All Database & Server Collations

Database collations can be enumerated by a query, while there is special function for server collations. QUOTENAME() function forms proper object names.

```
USE AdventureWorks2012;
GO
```

```
SELECT CONCAT(QUOTENAME(s.name), '.', QUOTENAME(t.name),
              '.', QUOTENAME(c.name))                    AS ColumnName,
              c.collation_name                           AS Collation
FROM sys.schemas s
  INNER JOIN sys.tables t
    ON t.schema_id = s.schema_id
  INNER JOIN sys.columns c
    ON c.object_id = t.object_id
WHERE collation_name is not null
ORDER BY ColumnName;
-- (104 row(s) affected) - Partial results.
```

ColumnName	Collation
[HumanResources].[Employee].[NationalIDNumber]	SQL_Latin1_General_CP1_CI_AS
[HumanResources].[Shift].[Name]	SQL_Latin1_General_CP1_CI_AS
[Person].[Address].[AddressLine1]	SQL_Latin1_General_CP1_CI_AS
[Person].[Address].[AddressLine2]	SQL_Latin1_General_CP1_CI_AS

All server collations can be obtained from a table-valued system function.

```
use master;
select  name                                   AS Name,
        COLLATIONPROPERTY(name, 'CodePage')    AS CodePage,
        LEFT(description,80)                   AS Description
from sys.fn_HelpCollations() order by Name;
-- (2397 row(s) affected) - Partial results;
```

Name	CodePage	Description
Modern_Spanish_CS_AS_KS_WS	1252	Modern-Spanish, case-sensitive, accent-sensitive, kanatype-sensitive, width-sens
Modern_Spanish_CS_AS_WS	1252	Modern-Spanish, case-sensitive, accent-sensitive, kanatype-insensitive, width-se
Mohawk_100_BIN	1252	Mohawk-100, binary sort
Mohawk_100_BIN2	1252	Mohawk-100, binary code point comparison sort
Mohawk_100_CI_AI	1252	Mohawk-100, case-insensitive, accent-insensitive, kanatype-insensitive, width-in

Designing Table for Multi-Language Support with UNICODE

Let's script the DimProductSubcategory table from AdventureWorks2012 to demonstrate multi-language support. nvarchar data type is for UNICODE data with each character 2 bytes. It has sufficient capacity to hold even Chinese, Japanese and Korean letters among others.

```
CREATE TABLE dbo.DimProductSubcategory(
	ProductSubcategoryKey int IDENTITY(1,1) NOT NULL,
	ProductSubcategoryAlternateKey int NULL,
	EnglishProductSubcategoryName nvarchar(50) NOT NULL,
	SpanishProductSubcategoryName nvarchar(50) NOT NULL,
	FrenchProductSubcategoryName nvarchar(50) NOT NULL,
	ProductCategoryKey int NULL,
	CONSTRAINT PK_DimProductSubcategory_ProductSubcategoryKey
		PRIMARY KEY CLUSTERED (ProductSubcategoryKey ASC),
	CONSTRAINT AK_DimProductSubcategory_ProductSubcategoryAlternateKey
		UNIQUE NONCLUSTERED (ProductSubcategoryAlternateKey ASC ) );
```

Since there are no COLLATE clauses for the English, Spanish & French names, the collation is the database default. The DATABASEPROPERTYEX() function can be used to retrieve it.

```
USE AdventureWorksDWAZ2008R2;
SELECT DATABASEPROPERTYEX('AdventureWorksDWAZ2008R2', 'Collation');
-- SQL_Latin1_General_CP1_CI_AS
```

To get a Spanish language sort, we have to add the COLLATE clause to the ORDER BY clause.

```
SELECT * FROM DimProductSubcategory
ORDER BY SpanishProductSubcategoryName COLLATE Modern_Spanish_CI_AS_WS;
-- (37 row(s) affected) - Partial results.
```

ProductSubcategoryKey	ProductSubcategoryAlternateKey	EnglishProductSubcategoryName	SpanishProductSubcategoryName	FrenchProductSubcategoryName	ProductCategoryKey
4	4	Handlebars	Barra	Barre d'appui	2
2	2	Road Bikes	Bicicleta de carretera	Vélo de route	1
1	1	Mountain Bikes	Bicicleta de montaña	VTT	1
3	3	Touring Bikes	Bicicleta de paseo	Vélo de randonnée	1
8	8	Cranksets	Bielas	Pédalier	2
36	36	Pumps	Bomba	Pompe	4

Find all collations for a culture.

```
SELECT name, description = LEFT(description, 60) FROM   sys.fn_HelpCollations()
WHERE  name LIKE '%german%'  ORDER BY name;  -- (36 row(s) affected)
```

CHAPTER 12: New Programming Features in SS 2012

PARSE() Function

T-SQL script to demonstrate the use of the PARSE() function. The culture parameter provides support for languages & countries beyond the CONVERT() function available in past versions.

```
-- PARSE() returns the result of expression translated to requested data type - String to datetime
SELECT PARSE('SAT, 13 December 2014' AS datetime USING 'en-US') AS [Date&Time];
-- 2014-12-13 00:00:00.000

SELECT PARSE('Saturday, 13 December 2014' AS datetime USING 'en-US') AS [Date&Time];
-- 2014-12-13 00:00:00.000

SELECT PARSE('Saturday 13 December 2014' AS datetime USING 'en-US') AS [Date&Time];
-- 2014-12-13 00:00:00.000

SELECT PARSE('Saturday December 13 2014' AS datetime USING 'en-US') AS [Date&Time];
-- 2014-12-13 00:00:00.000

SELECT PARSE('Saturday December 13, 2014' AS datetime USING 'en-US') AS [Date&Time];
-- 2014-12-13 00:00:00.000

-- Inconsistent string date
SELECT PARSE('Monday, 13 December 2014' AS datetime USING 'en-US') AS [Date&Time];
/*Msg 9819, Level 16, State 1, Line 1
Error converting string value 'Monday, 13 December 2014' into data type datetime using culture 'en-US'*/

-- German culture
SELECT PARSE('Samstag December 13, 2014' AS datetime USING 'DE') AS [Date&Time];
-- 2014-12-13 00:00:00.000

-- Spanish
SELECT PARSE('Sábado December 13, 2014' AS datetime USING 'ES') AS [Date&Time];
-- 2014-12-13 00:00:00.000

-- Hungarian
SELECT PARSE('Szombat December 13, 2014' AS datetime USING 'HU') AS [Date&Time];
-- 2014-12-13 00:00:00.000

SELECT PARSE('Cumartesi December 13, 2014' AS datetime USING 'TR') AS [Date&Time]; -- Turkish
```

PARSE() Function Usage for Currency Conversion

```
-- German culture - Euro currency conversion
SELECT PARSE('€9999,95' AS money USING 'DE') AS Currency;
-- 9999.95
```

```
SELECT PARSE('€9999,95' AS money USING 'de-DE') AS Currency;
-- 9999.95
```

```
-- Italian culture - Euro currency conversion
SELECT PARSE('€9999,95' AS money USING 'IT') AS Currency;
-- 9999.95
```

```
-- Netherland culture - Euro currency conversion
SELECT PARSE('€9999,95' AS money USING 'NL') AS Currency;
-- 9999.95
```

```
-- Slovakian culture - Euro currency conversion
SELECT PARSE('€9999,95' AS money USING 'SK') AS Currency;
-- 9999.95
```

```
-- United States - Euro is not US currency
SELECT PARSE('€9999,95' AS money USING 'US') AS Currency;
/*
Msg 9818, Level 16, State 1, Line 1
The culture parameter 'US' provided in the function call is not supported.
*/
```

```
-- Italian
SELECT CONVERT(DECIMAL (12,0), PARSE('€99999,95' AS money USING 'IT')) AS DecimalValue;
-- 100000
```

```
-- PARSE with variable parameters
DECLARE @AMOUNT AS VARCHAR(12) = '$9999.00';   DECLARE @CULTURE AS CHAR(5) = 'EN-US';
SELECT DOLLAR = PARSE(@AMOUNT AS MONEY USING @CULTURE) ;
GO
-- 9999.00
```

```
-- PARSE invalid data
DECLARE @AMOUNT AS VARCHAR(12) = '$9999A.00';   DECLARE @CULTURE AS CHAR(5) = 'EN-US';
SELECT DOLLAR = PARSE(@AMOUNT AS MONEY USING @CULTURE);
GO
/*
Msg 9819, Level 16, State 1, Line 4
Error converting string value '$9999A.00' into data type money using culture 'EN-US'.
 */
```

TRY_CONVERT() Function - OPSS2012

The TRY_CONVERT() function augments the CONVERT function to handle invalid data without giving an error. **It is a revolutionary new feature which makes invalid data handling significantly easier in T-SQL.**

```
-- CONVERT returns error on invalid data
SELECT [City]
          ,[PostalCode]
          ,CONVERT(INT, PostalCode)
 FROM Person.Address
 ORDER BY PostalCode;
/* Msg 245, Level 16, State 1, Line 1
Conversion failed when converting the nvarchar value '7L' to data type int.
*/
```

```
--  TRY_CONVERT() returns NULL for invalid data
SELECT DISTINCT [City]
          ,[PostalCode]
          ,TRY_CONVERT(INT, PostalCode) AS INTValue
 FROM Person.Address
 ORDER BY PostalCode;
```

City	PostalCode	INTValue
Union Gap	98903	98903
Ellensburg	98926	98926
Spokane	99202	99202
Kennewick	99337	99337
Walla Walla	99362	99362
Stoke-on-Trent	AS23	NULL
Birmingham	B29 6SL	NULL
Cambridge	BA5 3HX	NULL
W. York	BD1 4SJ	NULL
London	C2H 7AU	NULL
Cambridge	CB4 4BZ	NULL
Billericay	CM11	NULL

```
-- String date conversion to date data type
SET DATEFORMAT dmy;  -- US date format
SELECT TRY_CONVERT(date, '31/12/2016') AS Result;
-- 2016-12-31
```

```
-- Invalid date
SELECT TRY_CONVERT(date, '12/31/2016') AS Result;
-- NULL
GO
```

TRY_CONVERT() Usage in Adding Column to Table

Add new column as sequential row number (rowid) to table using the identity(int,1,1) function. SQL Server 2012 script.

NOTE

The IDENTITY values usually follow the ORDER BY specifications sequentially, but there is no guarantee. If ordering is important, create an empty table first with IDENTITY column and populate it with INSERT SELECT ORDER BY.

```
USE tempdb;

SELECT TRY_CONVERT(int, [SalesOrderID]) AS [NewSalesOrderID],   -- disable IDENTITY inheritance
     *
INTO  SOH
FROM  AdventureWorks.Sales.SalesOrderHeader  ORDER BY OrderDate,  CustomerID;
GO
-- (31465 row(s) affected)
```

```
-- Take out duplicate SalesOrderID with the IDENTITY property
ALTER TABLE SOH DROP COLUMN SalesOrderID;
GO
```

```
-- Rename NewSalesOrderID to SalesOrderID
EXEC sp_rename 'dbo.SOH.NewSalesOrderID', 'SalesOrderID';
GO
```

```
-- Add IDENTITY function as new first column  for sequence generation - sequential ID
SELECT RowNumber = IDENTITY(INT, 1, 1),      *
INTO  #SOH  FROM  SOH  ORDER BY OrderDate,  CustomerID;
GO
```

```
SELECT * INTO  SalesOrderHeader  FROM  #SOH ;  -- Create a permanent table
GO
SELECT TOP (5) *  FROM  SalesOrderHeader  ORDER BY RowNumber ;
GO
```

RowNumber	SalesOrderID	RevisionNumber	OrderDate	DueDate	ShipDate
1	43676	1	2001-07-01 00:00:00.000	2001-07-13 00:00:00.000	2001-07-08 00:00:00.000
2	43695	1	2001-07-01 00:00:00.000	2001-07-13 00:00:00.000	2001-07-08 00:00:00.000
3	43674	1	2001-07-01 00:00:00.000	2001-07-13 00:00:00.000	2001-07-08 00:00:00.000
4	43660	1	2001-07-01 00:00:00.000	2001-07-13 00:00:00.000	2001-07-08 00:00:00.000
5	43672	1	2001-07-01 00:00:00.000	2001-07-13 00:00:00.000	2001-07-08 00:00:00.000

```
DROP TABLE SOH ;
DROP TABLE #SOH ;
DROP TABLE tempdb.dbo.SalesOrderHeader ;
```

TRY_CAST() Function

The TRY_CAST() function augments the CAST function to handle invalid data without giving an error. **It is a revolutionary new feature which makes invalid data handling significantly easier in T-SQL.**

```
-- CONVERT returns error on invalid data
SELECT [City]
            ,[PostalCode]
            ,CONVERT(INT, PostalCode)
 FROM Person.Address
 ORDER BY PostalCode;
/* Msg 245, Level 16, State 1, Line 1
Conversion failed when converting the nvarchar value '7L' to data type int.
*/
```

```
--  TRY_CAST() returns NULL for invalid data
SELECT DISTINCT [City]
            ,[PostalCode]
            ,TRY_CAST(PostalCode AS INT) AS INTValue
 FROM Person.Address
 ORDER BY PostalCode;
```

City	PostalCode	INTValue
Union Gap	98903	98903
Ellensburg	98926	98926
Spokane	99202	99202
Kennewick	99337	99337
Walla Walla	99362	99362
Stoke-on-Trent	AS23	NULL
Birmingham	B29 6SL	NULL
Cambridge	BA5 3HX	NULL
W. York	BD1 4SJ	NULL
London	C2H 7AU	NULL
Cambridge	CB4 4BZ	NULL
Billericay	CM11	NULL

```
-- String date conversion to date data type
SET DATEFORMAT dmy;  -- US date format
SELECT TRY_CAST('31/12/2016' as date) AS Result;
-- 2016-12-31
```

```
-- Invalid date in dmy setting
SELECT TRY_CAST('12/31/2016' as date) AS Result;
-- NULL
```

TRY_PARSE() Function

The TRY_PARSE() function returns NULL instead of error in case of invalid data. T-SQL script to demonstrate the various uses of TRY_PARSE.

```
--  TRY_PARSE() parses or returns NULL if cast fails
SELECT TRY_PARSE('Monday, 13 December 2014' AS datetime USING 'en-US') AS [Date&Time];
-- NULL
```

```
SELECT TRY_PARSE('SAT, 13 December 2014' AS datetime USING 'en-US') AS [Date&Time];
-- 2014-12-13 00:00:00.000
```

```
-- Using the new feature with CASE Conditional.
SELECT CASE WHEN TRY_PARSE('Monday, 13 December 2014' AS datetime USING 'en-US') is NULL
        THEN (SELECT CONVERT(datetime, '19000101'))
    ELSE  (SELECT PARSE('Monday, 13 December 2014' AS datetime USING 'en-US')) END;
-- 1900-01-01 00:00:00.000
```

```
-- TRY_PARSE with variable parameters and IIF conditional
DECLARE @AMOUNT AS VARCHAR(12) = '$9999.00', @CULTURE AS CHAR(5) = 'EN-US';

SELECT RESULT = IIF(TRY_PARSE(@AMOUNT AS MONEY USING @CULTURE) IS NOT NULL
                                        ,PARSE(@AMOUNT AS MONEY USING @CULTURE) ,-1.0);
-- 9999.0000
```

```
DECLARE @AMOUNT AS VARCHAR(12) = '$9999A.00'; DECLARE @CULTURE AS CHAR(5) = 'EN-US';

SELECT RESULT = IIF(TRY_PARSE(@AMOUNT AS MONEY USING @CULTURE) IS NOT NULL
                                        ,PARSE(@AMOUNT AS MONEY USING @CULTURE) ,-1.0);
-- -1.0000
```

```
DECLARE @AMOUNT AS VARCHAR(12) = '$9999A.00', @CULTURE AS CHAR(5) = 'EN-US';

SELECT RESULT = IIF(TRY_PARSE(@AMOUNT AS MONEY USING @CULTURE) IS NOT NULL
                                        ,PARSE(@AMOUNT AS MONEY USING @CULTURE) ,NULL);
GO
-- NULL
```

```
-- Note the multiplication by 100 using the German culture
DECLARE @AMOUNT AS VARCHAR(12) = '€77777.00'; DECLARE @CULTURE AS CHAR(5) = 'de-DE';

SELECT RESULT = IIF(TRY_PARSE(@AMOUNT AS MONEY USING @CULTURE) IS NOT NULL
                                        ,PARSE(@AMOUNT AS MONEY USING @CULTURE) ,NULL);
GO
-- 7777700.00
```

FORMAT() Function

FORMAT() function is borrowed from the .NET languages. It augments the CONVERT function. T-SQL scripts to demonstrate some of the functionalities.

SELECT FORMAT(1111.22,'c','en-us');	$1,111.22
SELECT FORMAT(1111.22,'c','en-gb');	£1,111.22
SELECT FORMAT(1111.22,'c','de');	1.111,22 €
SELECT FORMAT(1111.22,'c','it');	€ 1.111,22
SELECT FORMAT(1111.22,'c','hu');	1 111,22 Ft
SELECT FORMAT(1111.22,'c','tr');	1.111,22 TL
SELECT FORMAT(1111.22,'c','es');	1.111,22 €
SELECT FORMAT(1111.22,'c','nl');	1.111,22 €
SELECT FORMAT(1111.22,'c','pl');	1 111,22 zł
SELECT FORMAT(1111.22,'c','ru');	1 111,22p.
SELECT FORMAT(1111.22,'c','se');	kr 1 111,22

```
DECLARE @culture char(2)='fr' ; SELECT FORMAT(1111.22, 'c', @culture); -- 1 111,22 €
```

```
SELECT FORMAT(1111.22,'c','gr');   /* Msg 9818, Level 16, State 1, Line 1
The culture parameter 'gr' provided in the function call is not supported.  */
```

```
SELECT FORMAT ( getdate(), 'yyyy/MM/dd hh:mm:ss tt', 'en-US' );      -- 2016/06/03 09:56:44 AM
SELECT FORMAT ( getdate(), 'MMM dd, yyyy hh:mm:ss tt', 'en-US' );    -- Jun 03, 2016 09:57:45 AM
```

```
SELECT FORMAT ( getdate(), 'y', 'en-US' ) ;          -- July, 2016
SELECT FORMAT ( getdate(), 'M', 'en-US' ) ;          -- July 10
SELECT FORMAT ( getdate(), 'd', 'en-US' ) ;          -- 7/10/2016
```

```
-- Percent formatting
SELECT TOP (4) ProductNumber, ListPrice, StandardCost, Markup = FORMAT(ListPrice / StandardCost, 'p', 'en-us')
FROM Production.Product  WHERE ListPrice > 0.0  ORDER BY ProductNumber;
```

ProductNumber	ListPrice	StandardCost	Markup
BB-7421	53.99	23.9716	225.22 %
BB-8107	101.24	44.9506	225.22 %
BB-9108	121.49	53.9416	225.22 %
BC-M005	9.99	3.7363	267.37 %

CONCAT() Function

The CONCAT() function concatenates two or more strings. Previously the + operator was the only available way to concatenate. **NOTE: CONCAT treats NULL as an empty string, this is different from the + operator concatenation.** T-SQL scripts to demonstrate usage.

```
-- Using + string concatenation operator
SELECT 'New'+SPACE(1)+'York'+SPACE(1)+'City' ;        -- New York City
```

```
-- Using the new CONCAT() function
SELECT CONCAT('New', SPACE(1),'York', SPACE(1), 'City'); -- New York City
```

```
-- Concatenating string columns with CONCAT()
SELECT CONCAT(FirstName, ' ', LastName) AS FullName
FROM Person.Person
ORDER by FullName;
/* FullName
...
Blake Wright
Blake Young
Bob Alan
Bob Chapman
Bob Fernandez ... /
```

CHOOSE() Function

The CHOOSE() function returns an item from a list of values as specified by an index. T-SQL scripts to demonstrate usage.

```
SELECT CHOOSE ( 3, 'NYC', 'LA', 'Chicago', 'Houston' ) AS City;
-- Chicago
```

```
SELECT CHOOSE ( 3, 'one', 'two', 'three', 'four', 'five' ) AS Number;
-- three
```

```
DECLARE @weekday as tinyint=6;
SELECT CHOOSE(@weekday, 'Sunday', 'Monday', 'Tuesday', 'Wednesday', 'Thursday', 'Friday', 'Saturday');
-- Friday
```

```
-- Random weekday selection using newid() and rand() functions
DECLARE @weekday as tinyint=Round(Rand(Cast(Newid() AS VARBINARY)) * 6+1,0);
SELECT CHOOSE(@weekday, 'Sunday', 'Monday', 'Tuesday', 'Wednesday', 'Thursday', 'Friday', 'Saturday');
GO 10
-- Friday  Sunday  Tuesday .....
```

THROW Statement

The THROW statement passes the error incurred in TRY - CATCH to the application. Demonstration T-SQL script follows.

```
CREATE TABLE Alpha
(
        ID INT PRIMARY KEY
);
GO
```

```
BEGIN TRY
  INSERT Alpha(ID) VALUES(7);
  INSERT Alpha(ID) VALUES(7); -- Force error by attempting duplicate insert
END TRY
BEGIN CATCH
  PRINT 'In CATCH';
 -- The error message encountered will be passed down to the client software application
  THROW;
END CATCH;
/*
In CATCH

Msg 2627, Level 14, State 1, Line 7
Violation of PRIMARY KEY constraint 'PK__Alpha__3214EC272A076B44'. Cannot insert
duplicate key in object 'dbo.Alpha'. The duplicate key value is (1).
*/
```

```
-- No THROW catch  - Error message not materialized
BEGIN TRY
  INSERT Alpha(ID) VALUES(7);
END TRY
BEGIN CATCH
  PRINT 'In CATCH';
END CATCH;
/*
(0 row(s) affected)
In CATCH.
*/
```

```
-- Cleanup
DROP TABLE Alpha
GO
```

IIF() Function

The IIF() function returns one of two values based on a condition. Here is a T-SQL demonstration script.

```
SELECT TOP 10  ProductID, ListPrice,
               IIF ( Color is not null, Color, 'N/A' ) AS [Color]
FROM Production.Product
ORDER BY ProductID DESC;
GO
```

ProductID	ListPrice	Color
999	539.99	Black
998	539.99	Black
997	539.99	Black
996	121.49	N/A
995	101.24	N/A
994	53.99	N/A
993	539.99	Black
992	539.99	Black
991	539.99	Black
990	539.99	Black

DATEFROMPARTS() & DATETIMEFROMPARTS() Functions

The DATEFROMPARTS() & DATETIMEFROMPARTS() functions generate date / datetime value from date parts. Demonstration T-SQL script.

```
SELECT DATEFROMPARTS ( 2016, 10, 23 ) AS RealDate;
GO
-- 2016-10-23
```

```
SELECT DATETIMEFROMPARTS ( 2016, 10, 23, 10, 10, 10, 500 ) AS RealDateTime;
GO
-- 2016-10-23 10:10:10.500
```

```
DECLARE @Year smallint = 2016, @Month tinyint = 10, @Day tinyint = 23;
SELECT DATEFROMPARTS(@Year, @Month, @Day);
GO
-- 2016-10-23
```

EOMONTH() Function

The EOMONTH() function returns the last day of the month for the given input date parameter.

T-SQL script to demonstrate usage.

```
SELECT EOMONTH('20140201') -- 2014-02-28
```

```
SELECT EOMONTH('20160201') -- 2016-02-29
GO
```

```
-- Future/past months optional parameter
DECLARE    @anydate DATE = '20161023';
SELECT
        CurrentMonthEnd         = EOMONTH(@anydate),
        NextMonthEnd            = EOMONTH(@anydate,  1),
        PrevMonthEnd            = EOMONTH(@anydate, -1);
GO
```

CurrentMonthEnd	NextMonthEnd	PrevMonthEnd
2016-10-31	2016-11-30	2016-09-30

```
-- Span 12 months of last day of month by using the sequence from spt_values
DECLARE    @anydate DATE = '20161023';
SELECT  TOP 12   LastDayOfMonth= EOMONTH(@anydate, number)
FROM master.dbo.spt_values WHERE type = 'P'  ORDER BY number;
GO
```

LastDayOfMonth
2016-10-31
2016-11-30
2016-12-31
2017-01-31
2017-02-28
2017-03-31
2017-04-30
2017-05-31
2017-06-30
2017-07-31
2017-08-31
2017-09-30

Result Set Paging with OFFSET & FETCH NEXT

Frequently a query produces a large results set. On the client side usually it has to be presented in small segments such as 20 lines at a time.

```
USE AdventureWorks2012;

SELECT ProductNumber, Name, ListPrice, Color
FROM Production.Product  ORDER BY ProductNumber
         OFFSET 0 ROWS    FETCH NEXT 10 ROWS ONLY;
-- (10 row(s) affected)
```

ProductNumber	Name	ListPrice	Color
AR-5381	Adjustable Race	0.00	NULL
BA-8327	Bearing Ball	0.00	NULL
BB-7421	LL Bottom Bracket	53.99	NULL
BB-8107	ML Bottom Bracket	101.24	NULL
BB-9108	HL Bottom Bracket	121.49	NULL
BC-M005	Mountain Bottle Cage	9.99	NULL
BC-R205	Road Bottle Cage	8.99	NULL
BE-2349	BB Ball Bearing	0.00	NULL
BE-2908	Headset Ball Bearings	0.00	NULL
BK-M18B-40	Mountain-500 Black, 40	539.99	Black

```
SELECT ProductNumber, Name, ListPrice, Color
FROM Production.Product  ORDER BY ProductNumber
         OFFSET 10 ROWS    FETCH NEXT 10 ROWS ONLY;
-- (10 row(s) affected)
```

ProductNumber	Name	ListPrice	Color
BK-M18B-42	Mountain-500 Black, 42	539.99	Black
BK-M18B-44	Mountain-500 Black, 44	539.99	Black
BK-M18B-48	Mountain-500 Black, 48	539.99	Black
BK-M18B-52	Mountain-500 Black, 52	539.99	Black
BK-M18S-40	Mountain-500 Silver, 40	564.99	Silver
BK-M18S-42	Mountain-500 Silver, 42	564.99	Silver
BK-M18S-44	Mountain-500 Silver, 44	564.99	Silver
BK-M18S-48	Mountain-500 Silver, 48	564.99	Silver
BK-M18S-52	Mountain-500 Silver, 52	564.99	Silver
BK-M38S-38	Mountain-400-W Silver, 38	769.49	Silver

```
SELECT ProductNumber, Name, ListPrice, Color
FROM Production.Product   ORDER BY ProductNumber OFFSET 500 ROWS    FETCH NEXT 10 ROWS ONLY;
-- (4 row(s) affected)
```

ProductNumber	Name	ListPrice	Color
VE-C304-L	Classic Vest, L	63.50	Blue
VE-C304-M	Classic Vest, M	63.50	Blue
VE-C304-S	Classic Vest, S	63.50	Blue
WB-H098	Water Bottle - 30 oz.	4.99	NULL

Result Paging Stored Procedure

The OFFSET FETCH functionality can be wrapped into a stored procedure.

```
USE AdventureWorks2012;
GO
```

```
CREATE PROCEDURE sprocProductPaging   (   @PageNumber int,    @RowsPerPage int  )
AS
BEGIN
SELECT          ProductNumber,
                Name AS ProductName,
                ListPrice,
                Color
  FROM Production.Product p
  WHERE ProductSubcategoryID is not NULL
  ORDER BY ProductNumber
  OFFSET (@PageNumber-1) * @RowsPerPage ROWS
  FETCH NEXT @RowsPerPage ROWS ONLY;
END;
GO
-- Command(s) completed successfully.
```

```
EXEC sprocProductPaging 10, 20
GO
-- (20 row(s) affected)
```

ProductNumber	ProductName	ListPrice	Color
FR-T67Y-44	LL Touring Frame - Yellow, 44	333.42	Yellow
FR-T67Y-50	LL Touring Frame - Yellow, 50	333.42	Yellow
FR-T67Y-54	LL Touring Frame - Yellow, 54	333.42	Yellow
FR-T67Y-58	LL Touring Frame - Yellow, 58	333.42	Yellow
FR-T67Y-62	LL Touring Frame - Yellow, 62	333.42	Yellow
FR-T98U-46	HL Touring Frame - Blue, 46	1003.91	Blue
FR-T98U-50	HL Touring Frame - Blue, 50	1003.91	Blue
FR-T98U-54	HL Touring Frame - Blue, 54	1003.91	Blue
FR-T98U-60	HL Touring Frame - Blue, 60	1003.91	Blue
FR-T98Y-46	HL Touring Frame - Yellow, 46	1003.91	Yellow
FR-T98Y-50	HL Touring Frame - Yellow, 50	1003.91	Yellow
FR-T98Y-54	HL Touring Frame - Yellow, 54	1003.91	Yellow
FR-T98Y-60	HL Touring Frame - Yellow, 60	1003.91	Yellow
FW-M423	LL Mountain Front Wheel	60.745	Black
FW-M762	ML Mountain Front Wheel	209.025	Black
FW-M928	HL Mountain Front Wheel	300.215	Black
FW-R623	LL Road Front Wheel	85.565	Black
FW-R762	ML Road Front Wheel	248.385	Black
FW-R820	HL Road Front Wheel	330.06	Black
FW-T905	Touring Front Wheel	218.01	Black

LEAD() & LAG() Functions - OPSS2012

THE LEAD() & LAG() analytical functions belong to the **OVER** family of functions.

```
USE AdventureWorks2012;
GO
 SELECT
          SalesOrderID,
          OrderQty,
          FORMAT(LineTotal, 'c', 'en-US')                                   AS LineTotal,
          LEAD(SalesOrderDetailID) OVER (ORDER BY SalesOrderDetailID )      AS [LEAD],
          SalesOrderDetailID                                                AS SODID,
          LAG(SalesOrderDetailID) OVER (ORDER BY SalesOrderDetailID  )      AS [LAG]
 FROM Sales.SalesOrderDetail sod
 WHERE SalesOrderID IN    (SELECT SalesOrderID FROM Sales.SalesOrderHeader
                           WHERE TotalDue >= 180000)
 ORDER BY SalesOrderDetailID;
--(111 row(s) affected) - Partial results.
```

SalesOrderID	OrderQty	LineTotal	LEAD	SODID	LAG
51131	11	$337.57	36817	36816	NULL
51131	12	$368.25	36818	36817	36816
51131	9	$5,421.11	36819	36818	36817
51131	2	$400.10	36820	36819	36818
51131	15	$200.76	36821	36820	36819
51131	2	$567.90	36822	36821	36820
51131	6	$8,582.65	36823	36822	36821
51131	4	$1,135.80	36824	36823	36822
51131	16	$12,206.44	36825	36824	36823
51131	8	$4,818.77	36826	36825	36824

.....

SalesOrderID	OrderQty	LineTotal	LEAD	SODID	LAG
55282	2	$76.20	55443	55442	55441
55282	4	$1,781.64	55444	55443	55442
55282	10	$146.94	55445	55444	55443
55282	3	$600.16	55446	55445	55444
55282	3	$1,807.04	55447	55446	55445
55282	28	$800.10	55448	55447	55446
55282	15	$18,685.15	55449	55448	55447
55282	8	$239.95	55450	55449	55448
55282	3	$1,336.23	55451	55450	55449
55282	7	$33.39	NULL	55451	55450

FIRST_VALUE() & LAST_VALUE() - OPSS2012

The FIRST_VALUE() and LAST_VALUE() analytic functions can be applied in conjunction with the OVER clause.

```
USE AdventureWorks2012;
GO
;WITH CTE AS
        (SELECT   PSC.Name AS Subcategory,
 FIRST_VALUE(P.Name) OVER (PARTITION BY PSC.Name ORDER BY ListPrice ASC) AS LeastExpensive,
        MIN(ListPrice) OVER (PARTITION BY PSC.Name ORDER BY ListPrice ASC)          AS LowPrice,
 LAST_VALUE(P.Name)  OVER (PARTITION BY PSC.Name ORDER BY ListPrice ASC) AS MostExpensive,
        MAX(ListPrice) OVER (PARTITION BY PSC.Name ORDER BY ListPrice ASC)          AS HighPrice,
        ROW_NUMBER() OVER (PARTITION BY PSC.Name ORDER BY ListPrice DESC)       AS RN
        FROM Production.Product P
        INNER JOIN Production.ProductSubcategory PSC
                ON P.ProductSubcategoryID = PSC.ProductSubcategoryID)
SELECT * FROM CTE WHERE RN = 1 ORDER BY Subcategory;
```

Subcategory	LeastExpensive	LowPrice	MostExpensive	HighPrice	RN
Bib-Shorts	Men's Bib-Shorts, S	89.99	Men's Bib-Shorts, L	89.99	1
Bike Racks	Hitch Rack - 4-Bike	120.00	Hitch Rack - 4-Bike	120.00	1
Bike Stands	All-Purpose Bike Stand	159.00	All-Purpose Bike Stand	159.00	1
Bottles and Cages	Water Bottle - 30 oz.	4.99	Mountain Bottle Cage	9.99	1
Bottom Brackets	LL Bottom Bracket	53.99	HL Bottom Bracket	121.49	1
Brakes	Rear Brakes	106.50	Front Brakes	106.50	1
Caps	AWC Logo Cap	8.99	AWC Logo Cap	8.99	1
Chains	Chain	20.24	Chain	20.24	1
Cleaners	Bike Wash - Dissolver	7.95	Bike Wash - Dissolver	7.95	1
Cranksets	LL Crankset	175.49	HL Crankset	404.99	1
Derailleurs	Front Derailleur	91.49	Rear Derailleur	121.46	1
Fenders	Fender Set - Mountain	21.98	Fender Set - Mountain	21.98	1
Forks	LL Fork	148.22	HL Fork	229.49	1
Gloves	Half-Finger Gloves, S	24.49	Full-Finger Gloves, L	37.99	1
Handlebars	LL Road Handlebars	44.54	HL Mountain Handlebars	120.27	1
Headsets	LL Headset	34.20	HL Headset	124.73	1
Helmets	Sport-100 Helmet, Blue	34.99	Sport-100 Helmet, Black	34.99	1
Hydration Packs	Hydration Pack - 70 oz.	54.99	Hydration Pack - 70 oz.	54.99	1
Jerseys	Long-Sleeve Logo Jersey, S	49.99	Short-Sleeve Classic Jersey, XL	53.99	1
Lights	Taillights - Battery-Powered	13.99	Headlights - Weatherproof	44.99	1
Locks	Cable Lock	25.00	Cable Lock	25.00	1
Mountain Bikes	Mountain-500 Black, 40	539.99	Mountain-100 Silver, 48	3399.99	1
Mountain Frames	LL Mountain Frame - Black, 40	249.79	HL Mountain Frame - Silver, 46	1364.50	1
Panniers	Touring-Panniers, Large	125.00	Touring-Panniers, Large	125.00	1
Pedals	LL Mountain Pedal	40.49	Touring Pedal	80.99	1
Pumps	Minipump	19.99	Mountain Pump	24.99	1
Road Bikes	Road-750 Black, 44	539.99	Road-150 Red, 56	3578.27	1
Road Frames	LL Road Frame - Black, 44	337.22	HL Road Frame - Red, 58	1431.50	1
Saddles	LL Mountain Seat/Saddle	27.12	HL Touring Seat/Saddle	52.64	1
Shorts	Men's Sports Shorts, S	59.99	Women's Mountain Shorts, L	69.99	1
Socks	Racing Socks, M	8.99	Mountain Bike Socks, L	9.50	1
Tights	Women's Tights, S	74.99	Women's Tights, L	74.99	1
Tires and Tubes	Patch Kit/8 Patches	2.29	HL Mountain Tire	35.00	1
Touring Bikes	Touring-3000 Blue, 44	742.35	Touring-1000 Blue, 60	2384.07	1
Touring Frames	LL Touring Frame - Blue, 50	333.42	HL Touring Frame - Yellow, 60	1003.91	1
Vests	Classic Vest, S	63.50	Classic Vest, L	63.50	1
Wheels	LL Mountain Front Wheel	60.745	HL Road Rear Wheel	357.06	1

EXEC New Option: WITH RESULT SETS

The WITH RESULT SETS clause can be used to remap the result set of a stored procedure or system procedure execution.

```
USE AdventurWork2012;
GO
```

```
CREATE PROC sprocProd AS SELECT ProductID, Name, ProductNumber, ListPrice FROM
Production.Product;
GO
```

```
EXEC sprocProd
 WITH RESULT SETS
 (
  (
  ID INT,
  ProductName NVARCHAR(50),
  ProdNo NVARCHAR(20),
  Price SMALLMONEY
  )
);-- (145 row(s) affected) - Partial results.
```

ID	ProductName	ProdNo	Price
1	Adjustable Race	AR-5381	0.00
2	Bearing Ball	BA-8327	0.00
3	BB Ball Bearing	BE-2349	0.00
4	Headset Ball Bearings	BE-2908	0.00
316	Blade	BL-2036	0.00
317	LL Crankarm	CA-5965	0.00
318	ML Crankarm	CA-6738	0.00
319	HL Crankarm	CA-7457	0.00
320	Chainring Bolts	CB-2903	0.00
321	Chainring Nut	CN-6137	0.00
322	Chainring	CR-7833	0.00
323	Crown Race	CR-9981	0.00
324	Chain Stays	CS-2812	0.00
325	Decal 1	DC-8732	0.00
326	Decal 2	DC-9824	0.00
327	Down Tube	DT-2377	0.00
328	Mountain End Caps	EC-M092	0.00
329	Road End Caps	EC-R098	0.00
330	Touring End Caps	EC-T209	0.00
331	Fork End	FE-3760	0.00

CHAPTER 13: Combining Tables with INNER & OUTER JOINs

SELECT with INNER JOIN

The SELECT statement is used to retrieve data from table(s). An INNER JOIN is a join in which the values in the columns being joined are compared using a comparison operator. Inner join also known as equi-join when equality condition is applied. Equi-join: PRIMARY KEY (table a) = FOREIGN KEY (table b). SQL Server 2012 feature.

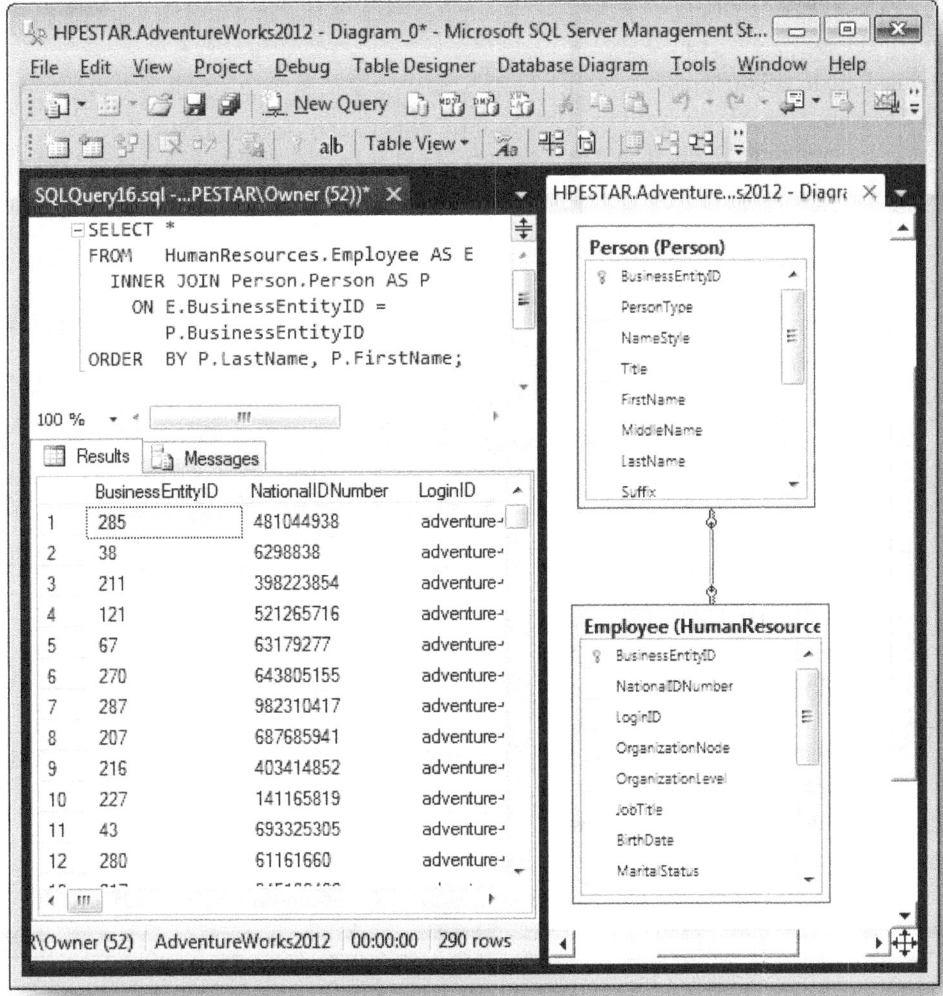

FOREIGN KEY Constraint as Base for INNER JOIN

The INNER JOIN is based on HumanResources.Employee.BusinessEntityID (PRIMARY KEY) is a FOREIGN KEY to Person.Person.BusinessEntityID. The Employee table is in one-to-one relationship with a subset of the Person table. SQL Server 2012 feature.

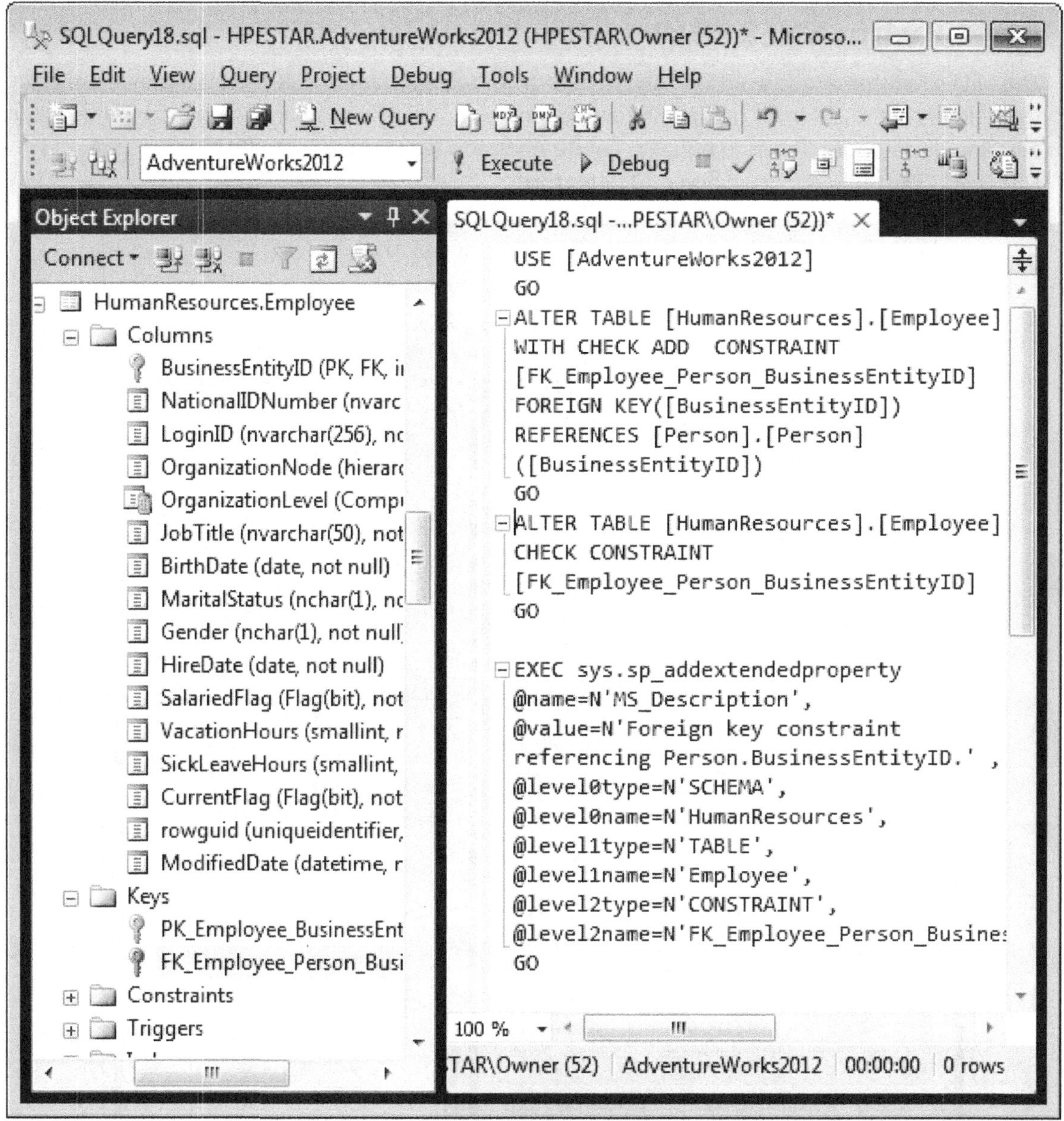

Diagram of Person.Person and Related Tables

The population of Person.Person includes all employees, contacts, and customers, therefore a key table in the database.

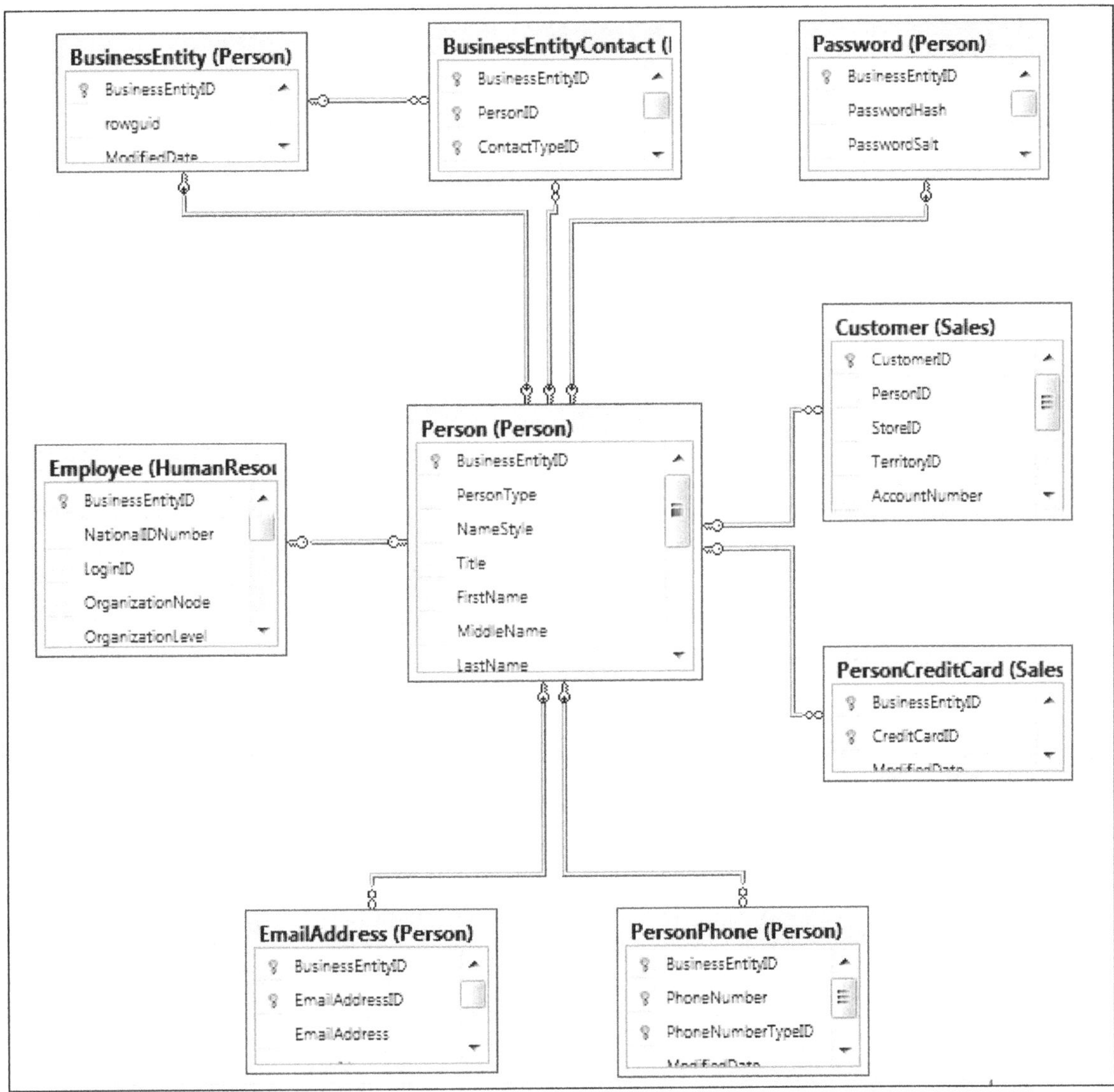


```
-- INNER JOIN ON PRIMARY KEY & FOREIGN KEY
SELECT * FROM Person.Person AS P
            INNER JOIN Person.PersonPhone AS PH
                  ON P.BusinessEntityID = PH.BusinessEntityID;
-- (19972 row(s) affected)
```

EQUI-JOIN BETWEEN FOREIGN KEY & PRIMARY KEY

EQUI JOIN means the equality operator is used to match the left and right keys. The reason for the popularity: the goal of most query is to gather information from related tables records (rows). Query to demonstrate why are 3 tables necessary to get a meaningful business report with just a few columns.

```
USE AdventureWorks;
GO
```

```
SELECT          CONCAT(LastName, ', ', FirstName)          AS Consumer,
                EmailAddress,
                Phone,
                CU.AccountNumber,
                C.ContactID,
                I.CustomerID
FROM Person.Contact AS C
   INNER JOIN Sales.Individual AS I
      ON C.ContactID = I.ContactID
   INNER JOIN Sales.Customer AS CU
      ON I.CustomerID = CU.CustomerID
WHERE CU.CustomerType = 'I'
ORDER BY LastName, FirstName ;
GO
-- (18484 row(s) affected) - Partial results.
```

Consumer	EmailAddress	Phone	AccountNumber	ContactID	CustomerID
Pal, Yolanda	yolanda11@adventure-works.com	1 (11) 500 555-0110	AW00023748	2837	23748
Palit, Punya	punya0@adventure-works.com	164-555-0118	AW00017574	14759	17574
Parker, Adam	adam29@adventure-works.com	808-555-0157	AW00018228	14771	18228
Parker, Alex	alex26@adventure-works.com	613-555-0123	AW00029252	14783	29252
Parker, Alexandra	alexandra50@adventure-works.com	974-555-0142	AW00016866	8977	16866
Parker, Allison	allison30@adventure-works.com	750-555-0124	AW00026501	9021	26501
Parker, Amanda	amanda51@adventure-works.com	978-555-0167	AW00018081	8985	18081
Parker, Amber	amber7@adventure-works.com	1 (11) 500 555-0198	AW00023959	8999	23959
Parker, Andrea	andrea23@adventure-works.com	612-555-0113	AW00020091	8461	20091
Parker, Angel	angel21@adventure-works.com	815-555-0120	AW00014273	14779	14273
Parker, Bailey	bailey28@adventure-works.com	604-555-0112	AW00019529	9007	19529
Parker, Blake	blake44@adventure-works.com	432-555-0151	AW00015008	3413	15008
Parker, Caleb	caleb28@adventure-works.com	593-555-0116	AW00026318	14760	26318
Parker, Carlos	carlos25@adventure-works.com	937-555-0143	AW00020676	14778	20676
Parker, Charles	charles43@adventure-works.com	266-555-0118	AW00021267	4105	21267
Parker, Chloe	chloe5@adventure-works.com	360-555-0121	AW00027480	8965	27480
Parker, Connor	connor28@adventure-works.com	936-555-0177	AW00028839	14763	28839
Parker, Courtney	courtney5@adventure-works.com	266-555-0176	AW00017612	9002	17612
Parker, Dalton	dalton42@adventure-works.com	535-555-0190	AW00013064	3722	13064
Parker, Devin	devin40@adventure-works.com	897-555-0155	AW00011684	4192	11684
Parker, Eduardo	eduardo41@adventure-works.com	131-555-0192	AW00012939	4269	12939

Diagram of Sales.Customer and Related Tables

Customer is the source of revenue for any business. Therefore, proper table design is paramount.

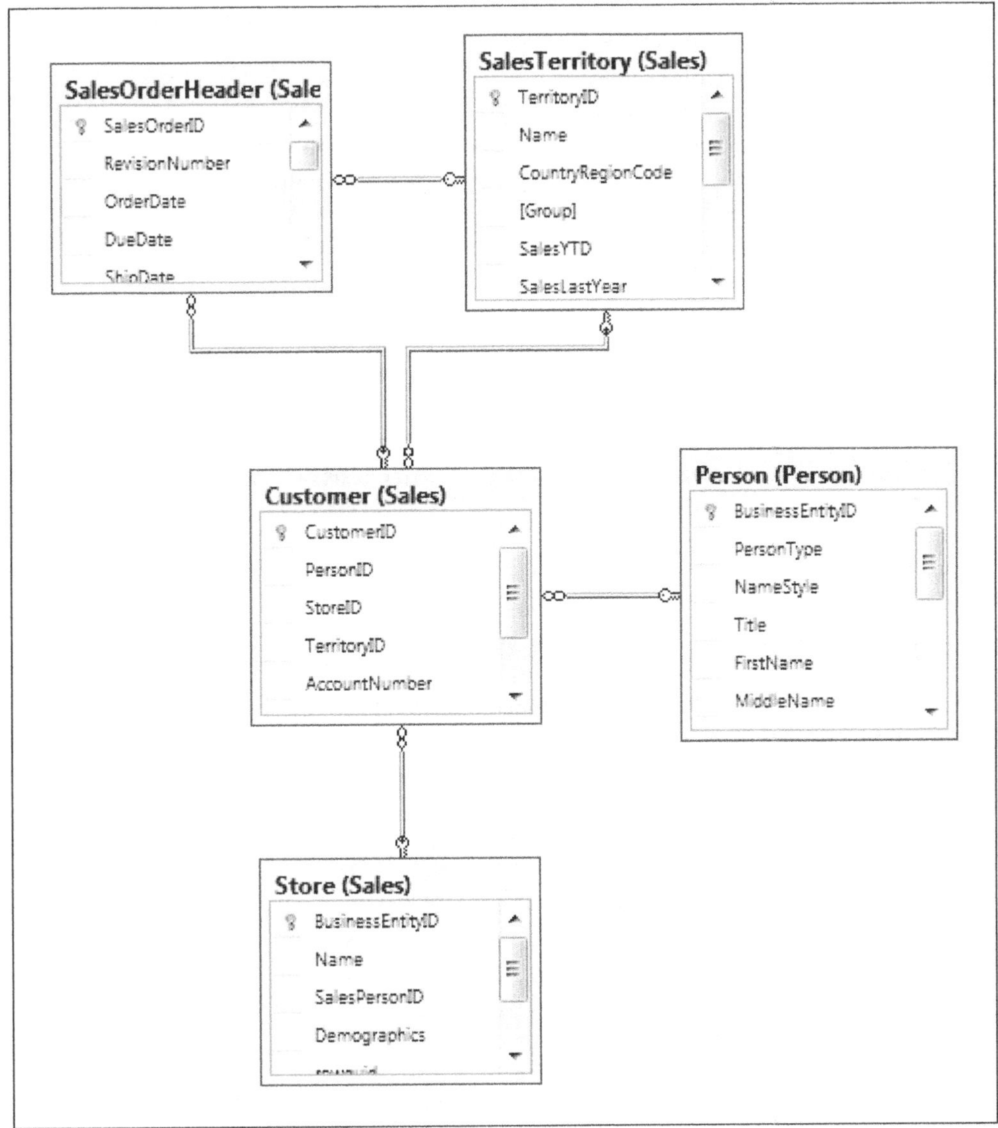


```
-- INNER JOIN ON PRIMARY KEY & FOREIGN KEY - NOTE: PK & FK named differently
SELECT * FROM Sales.Store AS S
                INNER JOIN Sales.Customer AS C   ON S.BusinessEntityID = C.StoreID;
-- (1336 row(s) affected)
```

Extracting All or Partial Data from JOINed Tables

T-SQL scripts to demonstrate how to JOIN two tables and extract all or subset of the information.

```
USE AdventureWorks2012;
```

```
-- SELECT all columns from the JOINed tables
SELECT *
FROM   HumanResources.Employee                   AS E     -- E is a table alias
    INNER JOIN Person.Person                     AS P     -- P is a table alias
        ON E.BusinessEntityID = P.BusinessEntityID
ORDER  BY P.LastName;
-- (290 row(s) affected)  - Partial results.
```

FirstName	MiddleName	LastName
Syed	E	Abbas
Kim	B	Abercrombie
Hazem	E	Abolrous
Pilar	G	Ackerman
Jay	G	Adams

```
SELECT E.*                          -- SELECT Employee columns from the JOINed tables
FROM   HumanResources.Employee AS E
    INNER JOIN Person.Person AS P    ON E.BusinessEntityID = P.BusinessEntityID
ORDER  BY P.LastName;
--  Partial results.
```

JobTitle	BirthDate	MaritalStatus	Gender
Pacific Sales Manager	1969-02-11	M	M
Production Technician - WC60	1961-01-14	M	F
Quality Assurance Manager	1971-11-27	S	M
Shipping and Receiving Supervisor	1966-10-11	S	M

```
-- SELECT Person columns from the JOINed tables
SELECT P.* FROM   HumanResources.Employee AS E
                  INNER JOIN Person.Person AS P     ON E.BusinessEntityID = P.BusinessEntityID
ORDER  BY P.LastName;
-- Partial results.
```

BusinessEntityID	PersonType
285	SP
38	EM
211	EM

SELECT All Columns From The Joined Tables Using Table Alias And Wildcard

```
SELECT E.*, P.*
FROM   HumanResources.Employee                    AS E      -- E is a table alias
    INNER JOIN Person.Person                      AS P      -- P is a table alias
        ON E.BusinessEntityID = P.BusinessEntityID
ORDER  BY P.LastName;
-- Same results as SELECT * FROM
```

```
-- Count JOINed rows
SELECT count(*)
FROM   HumanResources.Employee AS E
    INNER JOIN Person.Person AS P
        ON E.BusinessEntityID = P.BusinessEntityID
-- 290
```

```
-- Vertically output reduction: eliminate columns from the available pool
SELECT   E.BusinessEntityID                 AS EmployeeID,   -- column alias
         E.JobTitle,
         P.FirstName,
         P.LastName
FROM   HumanResources.Employee AS E
    INNER JOIN Person.Person AS P   ON E.BusinessEntityID = P.BusinessEntityID
ORDER  BY P.LastName;
-- (290 row(s) affected) - Partial results.
```

EmployeeID	JobTitle	FirstName	LastName
285	Pacific Sales Manager	Syed	Abbas
38	Production Technician - WC60	Kim	Abercrombie
211	Quality Assurance Manager	Hazem	Abolrous
121	Shipping and Receiving Supervisor	Pilar	Ackerman

```
-- Create a new output column from the available pool of columns
SELECT   E.BusinessEntityID                          AS EmployeeID,
         E.JobTitle,
         CONCAT(P.FirstName, ' ', P.LastName)        AS NAME
FROM   HumanResources.Employee AS E
    INNER JOIN Person.Person AS P     ON E.BusinessEntityID = P.BusinessEntityID
ORDER  BY P.LastName;
-- (290 row(s) affected) - Partial results.
```

EmployeeID	JobTitle	NAME
285	Pacific Sales Manager	Syed Abbas
38	Production Technician - WC60	Kim Abercrombie
211	Quality Assurance Manager	Hazem Abolrous
121	Shipping and Receiving Supervisor	Pilar Ackerman

Table Aliases for Readability

The table alias serves as shorthand for table name to improve the **readability of queries**. It should be as short as possible and as meaningful as possible when we have to use a few letters. The next T-SQL query applies four table aliases: c, soh, sod, p.

```
USE AdventureWorks;
SELECT DISTINCT SalesPerson = CONCAT(c.FirstName,SPACE(1), c.LastName)
FROM   Person.Contact c
    INNER JOIN Sales.SalesOrderHeader soh
      ON soh.SalesPersonId = c.ContactID
    INNER JOIN Sales.SalesOrderDetail sod
      ON soh.SalesOrderId = sod.SalesOrderId
    INNER JOIN Production.Product p
      ON sod.ProductID = p.ProductID      AND p.Name LIKE ('%Touring Frame%');
GO /*     SalesPerson
          Carla Eldridge
          Carol Elliott
          Gail Erickson  ....*/
```

Column Aliases for Readability & Presentation

The column alias serves as a meaningful column name either replacing a column name or filling in when there is no column name. In the previous example the = sign was used to establish the column alias. Alternate setting follows applying "AS" (it can be skipped) after the column. If the alias has spaces it has to be included in square brackets like [Bond Sales] or double quotes.

```
USE AdventureWorks;
SELECT DISTINCT  CONCAT(c.FirstName,' ', c.LastName)                    AS SalesPerson
FROM   Person.Contact c
    INNER JOIN Sales.SalesOrderHeader soh
      ON soh.SalesPersonId = c.ContactID
    INNER JOIN Sales.SalesOrderDetail sod
      ON soh.SalesOrderId = sod.SalesOrderId
    INNER JOIN Production.Product p
      ON sod.ProductID = p.ProductID   AND p.Name LIKE ('%Touring Frame%');
-- (17 row(s) affected) - Partial results.
```

SalesPerson
Carla Eldridge
Carol Elliott
Gail Erickson
Gary Drury
Janeth Esteves
Jauna Elson
John Emory

Derived Table Alias with a List of Column Aliases

Optionally column alias list can be specified for derived tables just like in CTE definition. T-SQL query demonstrates nested derived tables with table-column aliases (P & J).

```
SELECT DISTINCT ProdID, ProdName, ProdPrice, OrderQuantity
FROM    (
            SELECT   ID, ProductName, Price,              -- Derived table columns
                     OrderQty                             -- SOD column
            FROM Sales.SalesOrderDetail SOD
              INNER JOIN
                     (SELECT ProductID, Name, ListPrice
                      FROM Production.Product
                     ) P(ID, ProductName, Price)                  -- inner derived table
                ON SOD.ProductID = P.ID
        ) J (ProdID, ProdName, ProdPrice, OrderQuantity)          -- outer derived table
ORDER BY ProdPrice DESC, ProdName;
-- (2667 row(s) affected) - Partial results.
```

ProdID	ProdName	ProdPrice	OrderQuantity
750	Road-150 Red, 44	3578.27	3
750	Road-150 Red, 44	3578.27	6
750	Road-150 Red, 44	3578.27	1
750	Road-150 Red, 44	3578.27	4
750	Road-150 Red, 44	3578.27	2
750	Road-150 Red, 44	3578.27	5
751	Road-150 Red, 48	3578.27	6
751	Road-150 Red, 48	3578.27	3
751	Road-150 Red, 48	3578.27	2
751	Road-150 Red, 48	3578.27	5
751	Road-150 Red, 48	3578.27	4
751	Road-150 Red, 48	3578.27	1
752	Road-150 Red, 52	3578.27	5
752	Road-150 Red, 52	3578.27	3
752	Road-150 Red, 52	3578.27	6
752	Road-150 Red, 52	3578.27	1
752	Road-150 Red, 52	3578.27	4
752	Road-150 Red, 52	3578.27	2
753	Road-150 Red, 56	3578.27	6
753	Road-150 Red, 56	3578.27	3

INNER JOIN with Additional Conditions

The ON clause of a JOIN can include additional conditions as the following demonstration shows. The INNER JOIN is still based on FOREIGN KEY relationship, but only a subset of records (rows) returned due to the additional conditions, or JOIN predicates. The first query returns the distinct set of cases where the Selling Price was below the ListPrice for ProductID 800 which is a yellow road bike. The second query covers the remaining range where the Selling Price was equal or above the ListPrice.

```
USE AdventureWorks2012;
SELECT DISTINCT( P.ProductID ),
        ProductName = P.Name,              -- column alias
        P.ListPrice,
        SOD.UnitPrice AS 'Selling Price'   -- column alias
FROM  Sales.SalesOrderDetail AS SOD        -- table alias
   INNER JOIN  Production.Product AS P     -- table alias
    ON SOD.ProductID = P.ProductID
     AND SOD.UnitPrice < P.ListPrice              -- JOIN predicate
     AND  P.ProductID = 800;                      -- JOIN predicate
```

ProductID	ProductName	ListPrice	Selling Price
800	Road-550-W Yellow, 44	1120.49	600.2625
800	Road-550-W Yellow, 44	1120.49	672.294
800	Road-550-W Yellow, 44	1120.49	1000.4375

```
SELECT DISTINCT( P.ProductID ),
        ProductName = P.Name,
        P.ListPrice,
        SOD.UnitPrice AS 'Selling Price'
FROM  Sales.SalesOrderDetail AS SOD
   INNER JOIN  Production.Product AS P
    ON SOD.ProductID = P.ProductID
     AND SOD.UnitPrice >= P.ListPrice
     AND  P.ProductID BETWEEN 800 AND 900
ORDER BY ProductName;
-- (26 row(s) affected) - Partial results.
```

ProductID	ProductName	ListPrice	Selling Price
879	All-Purpose Bike Stand	159.00	159.00
877	Bike Wash - Dissolver	7.95	7.95
866	Classic Vest, L	63.50	63.50
865	Classic Vest, M	63.50	63.50
864	Classic Vest, S	63.50	63.50
878	Fender Set - Mountain	21.98	21.98
860	Half-Finger Gloves, L	24.49	24.49
859	Half-Finger Gloves, M	24.49	24.49
858	Half-Finger Gloves, S	24.49	24.49
876	Hitch Rack - 4-Bike	120.00	120.00

Counting Rows in JOINs

As the T-SQL script following shows, the basic FOREIGN KEY based JOIN returns 121,317 rows which is all the rows in Sales.SalesOrderDetail table. The additional condition P.ProductID = 800 selects a subset of 495 rows which is then divided between the < and >= conditions.

```
USE AdventureWorks2012;
SELECT Rows = count(*)
FROM   Sales.SalesOrderDetail AS SOD
    INNER JOIN  Production.Product AS P    ON SOD.ProductID = P.ProductID
-- 121317
```

```
SELECT Rows = count(*)
FROM   Sales.SalesOrderDetail AS SOD
    INNER JOIN  Production.Product AS P   ON SOD.ProductID = P.ProductID   AND P.ProductID = 800;
-- 495
```

```
SELECT Rows = count(*)
FROM   Sales.SalesOrderDetail AS SOD
    INNER JOIN  Production.Product AS P
     ON SOD.ProductID = P.ProductID
       AND SOD.UnitPrice < P.ListPrice
       AND P.ProductID = 800;
-- 285
```

```
SELECT Rows = count(*)
FROM   Sales.SalesOrderDetail AS SOD
    INNER JOIN  Production.Product AS P
     ON SOD.ProductID = P.ProductID
       AND SOD.UnitPrice >= P.ListPrice
       AND P.ProductID = 800;
-- 210
```

```
SELECT COUNT(P.ProductID)
FROM   Sales.SalesOrderDetail AS SOD
    INNER JOIN  Production.Product AS P
     ON SOD.ProductID = P.ProductID
       AND SOD.UnitPrice >= P.ListPrice
       AND  P.ProductID BETWEEN 800 AND 900;
-- 21085
```

```
SELECT COUNT(DISTINCT P.ProductID)
FROM   Sales.SalesOrderDetail AS SOD
    INNER JOIN  Production.Product AS P
     ON SOD.ProductID = P.ProductID   AND SOD.UnitPrice >= P.ListPrice
         AND  P.ProductID BETWEEN 800 AND 900;
```

INNER JOIN with 3 Tables

T-SQL query to demonstrate JOINing three tables. Due to the application of the FORMAT function, column name is lost. Therefore we have to alias the formatted column with the original column name or something else. Both INNER JOINs are based on FOREIGN KEY relationships. PV.ProductID is an FK to the Production.Product table, and the PV.VendorID is an FK to the Purchasing.Vendor table. The Purchasing.ProductVendor table is a junction table representing many-to-many relationships between products and vendors: a vendor may supply many products (see Beaumont Bikes in results) and a product may be supplied by many vendors (see Chainring in results).

```
USE AdventureWorks;
GO
SELECT          P.ProductNumber,
                P.Name                                      AS Product,
                V.Name                                      AS Vendor,
                FORMAT (PV.LastReceiptCost, 'c', 'en-US')   AS LastReceiptCost
FROM Production.Product AS P
  INNER JOIN Purchasing.ProductVendor AS PV
        ON P.ProductID = PV.ProductID
  INNER JOIN Purchasing.Vendor AS V
        ON V.VendorID = PV.VendorID
ORDER BY Product;
GO
-- (406 row(s) affected) - Partial results.
```

ProductNumber	Product	Vendor	LastReceiptCost
AR-5381	Adjustable Race	Litware, Inc.	$50.26
BA-8327	Bearing Ball	Wood Fitness	$41.92
CH-0234	Chain	Varsity Sport Co.	$15.74
CR-7833	Chainring	Beaumont Bikes	$25.42
CR-7833	Chainring	Bike Satellite Inc.	$26.37
CR-7833	Chainring	Training Systems	$28.70
CB-2903	Chainring Bolts	Beaumont Bikes	$47.47
CB-2903	Chainring Bolts	Bike Satellite Inc.	$45.37
CB-2903	Chainring Bolts	Training Systems	$49.64
CN-6137	Chainring Nut	Beaumont Bikes	$42.80
CN-6137	Chainring Nut	Bike Satellite Inc.	$40.49
CN-6137	Chainring Nut	Training Systems	$44.32
RA-7490	Cone-Shaped Race	Midwest Sport, Inc.	$44.22
CR-9981	Crown Race	Business Equipment Center	$50.26
RA-2345	Cup-Shaped Race	Bloomington Multisport	$48.76
DC-8732	Decal 1	SUPERSALES INC.	$0.21
DC-9824	Decal 2	SUPERSALES INC.	$0.21
LE-6000	External Lock Washer 1	Pro Sport Industries	$41.24
LE-6000	External Lock Washer 1	Aurora Bike Center	$43.27
LE-6000	External Lock Washer 1	Expert Bike Co	$41.17

T-SQL Query To Return All Road Frames Offered For Sale By AdventureWorks Cycles

```
USE AdventureWorks2012;
SELECT          UPPER(PC.Name)          AS Category,   PSC.Name                        AS Subcategory,
                P.Name          AS Product,   FORMAT(ListPrice, 'c', 'en-US')          AS ListPrice,
                FORMAT(StandardCost, 'c', 'en-US')                                     AS StandardCost
FROM Production.Product AS P
   INNER JOIN Production.ProductSubcategory AS PSC
                ON PSC.ProductSubcategoryID = P.ProductSubcategoryID
   INNER JOIN Production.ProductCategory AS PC
                ON PC.ProductCategoryID = PSC.ProductCategoryID
WHERE PSC.Name like 'Road Frames'  ORDER BY Category, Subcategory, Product;
```

Category	Subcategory	Product	ListPrice	StandardCost
COMPONENTS	Road Frames	HL Road Frame - Black, 44	$1,431.50	$868.63
COMPONENTS	Road Frames	HL Road Frame - Black, 48	$1,431.50	$868.63
COMPONENTS	Road Frames	HL Road Frame - Black, 52	$1,431.50	$868.63
COMPONENTS	Road Frames	HL Road Frame - Black, 58	$1,431.50	$1,059.31
COMPONENTS	Road Frames	HL Road Frame - Black, 62	$1,431.50	$868.63
COMPONENTS	Road Frames	HL Road Frame - Red, 44	$1,431.50	$868.63
COMPONENTS	Road Frames	HL Road Frame - Red, 48	$1,431.50	$868.63
COMPONENTS	Road Frames	HL Road Frame - Red, 52	$1,431.50	$868.63
COMPONENTS	Road Frames	HL Road Frame - Red, 56	$1,431.50	$868.63
COMPONENTS	Road Frames	HL Road Frame - Red, 58	$1,431.50	$1,059.31
COMPONENTS	Road Frames	HL Road Frame - Red, 62	$1,431.50	$868.63
COMPONENTS	Road Frames	LL Road Frame - Black, 44	$337.22	$204.63
COMPONENTS	Road Frames	LL Road Frame - Black, 48	$337.22	$204.63
COMPONENTS	Road Frames	LL Road Frame - Black, 52	$337.22	$204.63
COMPONENTS	Road Frames	LL Road Frame - Black, 58	$337.22	$204.63
COMPONENTS	Road Frames	LL Road Frame - Black, 60	$337.22	$204.63
COMPONENTS	Road Frames	LL Road Frame - Black, 62	$337.22	$204.63
COMPONENTS	Road Frames	LL Road Frame - Red, 44	$337.22	$187.16
COMPONENTS	Road Frames	LL Road Frame - Red, 48	$337.22	$187.16
COMPONENTS	Road Frames	LL Road Frame - Red, 52	$337.22	$187.16
COMPONENTS	Road Frames	LL Road Frame - Red, 58	$337.22	$187.16
COMPONENTS	Road Frames	LL Road Frame - Red, 60	$337.22	$187.16
COMPONENTS	Road Frames	LL Road Frame - Red, 62	$337.22	$187.16
COMPONENTS	Road Frames	ML Road Frame - Red, 44	$594.83	$352.14
COMPONENTS	Road Frames	ML Road Frame - Red, 48	$594.83	$352.14
COMPONENTS	Road Frames	ML Road Frame - Red, 52	$594.83	$352.14
COMPONENTS	Road Frames	ML Road Frame - Red, 58	$594.83	$352.14
COMPONENTS	Road Frames	ML Road Frame - Red, 60	$594.83	$352.14
COMPONENTS	Road Frames	ML Road Frame-W - Yellow, 38	$594.83	$360.94
COMPONENTS	Road Frames	ML Road Frame-W - Yellow, 40	$594.83	$360.94
COMPONENTS	Road Frames	ML Road Frame-W - Yellow, 42	$594.83	$360.94
COMPONENTS	Road Frames	ML Road Frame-W - Yellow, 44	$594.83	$360.94
COMPONENTS	Road Frames	ML Road Frame-W - Yellow, 48	$594.83	$360.94

INNER JOIN with Junction Table

Three tables INNER JOIN includes the titleauthor junction table which represent many-to-many relationship. All JOINs are EQUI-JOINs with FOREIGN KEYs and PRIMARY KEYs.

```
USE pubs;

SELECT      FORMAT(ytd_sales, 'c', 'en-US')                              AS YTDSales,
            CONCAT(au.au_fname, ' ', au.au_lname)                        AS Author,
            FORMAT((ytd_sales * royalty) / 100,'c','en-US')              AS AuthorRev,
            FORMAT((ytd_sales - (ytd_sales * royalty) / 100),'c','en-US') AS PublisherRev
FROM titles t
      INNER JOIN titleauthor ta
            ON t.title_id = ta.title_id
      INNER JOIN authors au
            ON ta.au_id = au.au_id
ORDER BY    YTDSales DESC,          -- Major sort key
            Author ASC;             -- Minor sort key
GO
```

YTDSales	Author	AuthorRev	PublisherRev
$8,780.00	Cheryl Carson	$1,404.00	$7,376.00
$4,095.00	Abraham Bennet	$409.00	$3,686.00
$4,095.00	Akiko Yokomoto	$409.00	$3,686.00
$4,095.00	Ann Dull	$409.00	$3,686.00
$4,095.00	Burt Gringlesby	$409.00	$3,686.00
$4,095.00	Dean Straight	$409.00	$3,686.00
$4,095.00	Marjorie Green	$409.00	$3,686.00
$4,095.00	Michael O'Leary	$409.00	$3,686.00
$4,095.00	Sheryl Hunter	$409.00	$3,686.00
$4,072.00	Johnson White	$407.00	$3,665.00
$375.00	Livia Karsen	$37.00	$338.00
$375.00	Stearns MacFeather	$37.00	$338.00
$375.00	Sylvia Panteley	$37.00	$338.00
$3,876.00	Michael O'Leary	$387.00	$3,489.00
$3,876.00	Stearns MacFeather	$387.00	$3,489.00
$3,336.00	Charlene Locksley	$333.00	$3,003.00
$22,246.00	Anne Ringer	$5,339.00	$16,907.00
$22,246.00	Michel DeFrance	$5,339.00	$16,907.00
$2,045.00	Albert Ringer	$245.00	$1,800.00
$2,045.00	Anne Ringer	$245.00	$1,800.00
$2,032.00	Innes del Castillo	$243.00	$1,789.00
$18,722.00	Marjorie Green	$4,493.00	$14,229.00
$15,096.00	Reginald Blotchet-Halls	$2,113.00	$12,983.00
$111.00	Albert Ringer	$11.00	$100.00
NULL	Charlene Locksley	NULL	NULL

NON-EQUI JOINs for Data Analytics

We can use not equal operators in JOIN predicates as demonstrated in the next query. The second predicate in the JOIN is less than JOIN.

```
USE AdventureWorks2012;
GO
-- List of "red" products sold at a discount
SELECT DISTINCT          p.ProductNumber,
                         p.Name                                  AS ProductName,
                         FORMAT(p.ListPrice,'c','en-US')         AS ListPrice,
                         FORMAT(sod.UnitPrice,'c','en-US')       AS SellPrice
FROM Sales.SalesOrderDetail AS sod
   INNER JOIN Production.Product AS p
         ON sod.ProductID = p.ProductID
          AND sod.UnitPrice < p.ListPrice
WHERE Color = 'Red'
ORDER BY p.ProductNumber;
--(86 row(s) affected) - Partial results.
```

ProductNumber	ProductName	ListPrice	SellPrice
BK-R50R-44	Road-650 Red, 44	$782.99	$234.90
BK-R50R-44	Road-650 Red, 44	$782.99	$419.46
BK-R50R-44	Road-650 Red, 44	$782.99	$430.64
BK-R50R-44	Road-650 Red, 44	$782.99	$454.13
BK-R50R-44	Road-650 Red, 44	$782.99	$469.79
BK-R50R-44	Road-650 Red, 44	$782.99	$563.75
BK-R50R-44	Road-650 Red, 44	$782.99	$699.10
BK-R50R-48	Road-650 Red, 48	$782.99	$419.46
BK-R50R-48	Road-650 Red, 48	$782.99	$430.64
BK-R50R-48	Road-650 Red, 48	$782.99	$454.13
BK-R50R-48	Road-650 Red, 48	$782.99	$469.79
BK-R50R-48	Road-650 Red, 48	$782.99	$563.75

To resolve the duplicate issue which makes DISTINCT usage necessary, we have to include the SalesOrderID column.

```
SELECT                   p.ProductNumber,
                         p.Name                                  AS ProductName,
                         FORMAT(p.ListPrice,'c','en-US')         AS ListPrice,
                         FORMAT(sod.UnitPrice,'c','en-US')       AS SellPrice,
                         sod.SalesOrderID
FROM Sales.SalesOrderDetail AS sod
   INNER JOIN Production.Product AS p
         ON sod.ProductID = p.ProductID
          AND sod.UnitPrice < p.ListPrice
WHERE Color = 'Red'   ORDER BY p.ProductNumber;
-- (8408 row(s) affected)
```

Interchangeability of ON & WHERE Predicates in INNER JOINs

We can freely place the predicates to either the ON clause or the WHERE clause in an INNER JOIN. This is not true for OUTER JOINs such as LEFT JOINs.

```
USE AdventureWorks2012;
-- List of "blue" products sold at a discount
SELECT DISTINCT  p.ProductNumber, p.Name                              AS ProductName,
                 FORMAT(p.ListPrice,'c','en-US')                      AS ListPrice,
                 FORMAT(sod.UnitPrice,'c','en-US')                    AS SellPrice
FROM Sales.SalesOrderDetail AS sod
   INNER JOIN Production.Product AS p
         ON sod.ProductID = p.ProductID
          AND sod.UnitPrice < p.ListPrice
WHERE Color = 'Blue'  ORDER BY p.ProductNumber;
--(57 row(s) affected)
```

```
SELECT DISTINCT  p.ProductNumber, p.Name                              AS ProductName,
                 FORMAT(p.ListPrice,'c','en-US')                      AS ListPrice,
                 FORMAT(sod.UnitPrice,'c','en-US')                    AS SellPrice
FROM Sales.SalesOrderDetail AS sod
   INNER JOIN Production.Product AS p
         ON sod.ProductID = p.ProductID
          AND sod.UnitPrice < p.ListPrice
         AND Color = 'Blue'
ORDER BY p.ProductNumber;
--(57 row(s) affected)
```

```
SELECT DISTINCT  p.ProductNumber, p.Name                              AS ProductName,
                 FORMAT(p.ListPrice,'c','en-US')                      AS ListPrice,
                 FORMAT(sod.UnitPrice,'c','en-US')                    AS SellPrice
FROM Sales.SalesOrderDetail AS sod
   INNER JOIN Production.Product AS p
   ON sod.ProductID = p.ProductID
WHERE sod.UnitPrice < p.ListPrice    AND Color = 'Blue'  ORDER BY p.ProductNumber;
--(57 row(s) affected)
```

```
-- Old-style INNER JOIN with table list and WHERE clause
SELECT DISTINCT  p.ProductNumber, p.Name                              AS ProductName,
                 FORMAT(p.ListPrice,'c','en-US')                      AS ListPrice,
                 FORMAT(sod.UnitPrice,'c','en-US')                    AS SellPrice
FROM Sales.SalesOrderDetail AS sod,  Production.Product AS p
WHERE sod.ProductID = p.ProductID
          AND sod.UnitPrice < p.ListPrice
         AND Color = 'Blue'
ORDER BY p.ProductNumber;          --(57 row(s) affected)
```

SELF-JOIN for Analytics Within a Table

When a table is JOINed to itself, it is a called a self-join. The purpose of such a JOIN is to examine data relations within the table. The Production.Product table is self-joined to itself on the ProductSubcategoryID FOREIGN KEY(not on a PRIMARY KEY), a many-to-many JOIN. Subsequently, we made the query "friendlier" by using subcategory names as opposed to ID-s.

```
SELECT DISTINCT P1.ProductSubcategoryID,
                P1.ListPrice                    AS ListPrice1,
                P2.ListPrice                    AS ListPrice2
FROM   Production.Product P1
 INNER JOIN Production.Product P2
  ON P1.ProductSubcategoryID = P2.ProductSubcategoryID
  AND P1.ListPrice < P2.ListPrice
  AND P1.ListPrice < $15
  AND P2.ListPrice < $15;
```

ProductSubcategoryID	ListPrice1	ListPrice2
23	8.99	9.50
28	4.99	8.99
28	4.99	9.99
28	8.99	9.99
37	2.29	3.99
37	2.29	4.99
37	3.99	4.99

```
SELECT DISTINCT PS.Name AS Subcategory,
                P1.ListPrice    AS ListPrice1,
                P2.ListPrice    AS ListPrice2
FROM   Production.ProductSubcategory PS
    INNER JOIN Production.Product P1
        ON PS.ProductSubcategoryID = P1.ProductSubcategoryID
    INNER JOIN Production.Product P2
        ON P1.ProductSubcategoryID = P2.ProductSubcategoryID
         AND P1.ListPrice < P2.ListPrice                    -- To prevent duplicate processing
         AND P1.ListPrice < $15
         AND P2.ListPrice < $15;
```

Subcategory	ListPrice1	ListPrice2
Bottles and Cages	4.99	8.99
Bottles and Cages	4.99	9.99
Bottles and Cages	8.99	9.99
Socks	8.99	9.50
Tires and Tubes	2.29	3.99
Tires and Tubes	2.29	4.99
Tires and Tubes	3.99	4.99

T-SQL SELF-JOIN Query Lists The Competing Suppliers For Each Product Purchased From Vendor

Since the ProductID in the ProductVendor table is part of a composite PRIMARY KEY, we can conclude that it is a many-to-many JOIN.

```
SELECT DISTINCT
                    Vendor = V.[Name],
                    P1.BusinessEntityID,
                    Product = P.[Name],
                    P1.ProductID
FROM   Production.Product P
    INNER JOIN Purchasing.ProductVendor P1
         ON P.ProductID = P1.ProductID
    INNER JOIN Purchasing.Vendor V
         ON P1.BusinessEntityID = V.BusinessEntityID
    INNER JOIN Purchasing.ProductVendor P2
         ON P1.ProductID = P2.ProductID
WHERE  P1.BusinessEntityID <> P2.BusinessEntityID
ORDER  BY Product, Vendor
-- (347 row(s) affected) - Partial results.
```

Vendor	BusinessEntityID	Product	ProductID
Beaumont Bikes	1602	Chainring	322
Bike Satellite Inc.	1604	Chainring	322
Training Systems	1514	Chainring	322
Beaumont Bikes	1602	Chainring Bolts	320
Bike Satellite Inc.	1604	Chainring Bolts	320
Training Systems	1514	Chainring Bolts	320
Beaumont Bikes	1602	Chainring Nut	321
Bike Satellite Inc.	1604	Chainring Nut	321
Training Systems	1514	Chainring Nut	321
Aurora Bike Center	1616	External Lock Washer 1	409
Expert Bike Co	1672	External Lock Washer 1	409
Pro Sport Industries	1686	External Lock Washer 1	409
Aurora Bike Center	1616	External Lock Washer 2	411
Pro Sport Industries	1686	External Lock Washer 2	411
Aurora Bike Center	1616	External Lock Washer 3	403
Expert Bike Co	1672	External Lock Washer 3	403
Pro Sport Industries	1686	External Lock Washer 3	403
Aurora Bike Center	1616	External Lock Washer 4	404
Expert Bike Co	1672	External Lock Washer 4	404
Pro Sport Industries	1686	External Lock Washer 4	404
Aurora Bike Center	1616	External Lock Washer 5	406
Expert Bike Co	1672	External Lock Washer 5	406
Pro Sport Industries	1686	External Lock Washer 5	406
Aurora Bike Center	1616	External Lock Washer 6	408
Expert Bike Co	1672	External Lock Washer 6	408

Applying SELF-JOIN for Numbering Result Lines

T-SQL script to demonstrate how SELF-JOIN can be used for numbering lines in query results. Note that in these days we would use **ROW_NUMBER()** function which has been introduced with SQL Server 2005.

```
USE Northwind ;
GO
```

```
SELECT   OD.OrderID,
               SeqNo                                          AS LineItem,
               OD.ProductID,
               FORMAT(UnitPrice,'c','en-US')                  AS UnitPrice,
               Quantity,
               FORMAT(Discount, 'p')                          AS Discount
FROM     [Order Details] OD
  INNER JOIN (SELECT   count(* ) AS SeqNo,
             a.OrderID,
             a.ProductID
        FROM     [Order Details] A
             INNER JOIN [Order Details] B
               ON A.ProductID >= B.ProductID                          -- Prevent duplicates
                 AND A.OrderID = B.OrderID
        GROUP BY A.OrderID,    A.ProductID) a
      ON OD.OrderID = a.OrderID
        AND OD.ProductID = a.ProductID
WHERE    OD.OrderID < 10400
ORDER BY          OD.OrderID,
                  LineItem
-- (405 row(s) affected) - Partial results.
```

Vendor	AddressLine1	AddressLine2	City	State	Country
A. Datum Corporation	2596 Big Canyon Road		New York	New York	United States
Advanced Bicycles	7995 Edwards Ave.		Lynnwood	Washington	United States
Allenson Cycles	4659 Montoya		Altadena	California	United States
American Bicycles and Wheels	1667 Warren Street		West Covina	California	United States
American Bikes	7179 Montana		Torrance	California	United States
Anderson's Custom Bikes	9 Guadalupe Dr.		Burbank	California	United States
Aurora Bike Center	65 Park Glen Court		Port Orchard	Washington	United States
Australia Bike Retailer	28 San Marino Ct.		Bellingham	Washington	United States
Beaumont Bikes	2472 Alexander Place		West Covina	Idaho	United States
Bergeron Off-Roads	9830 May Way		Mill Valley	Montana	United States
Bicycle Specialists	1286 Cincerto Circle		Lake Oswego	Oregon	United States
Bike Satellite Inc.	2141 Delaware Ct.		Downey	Tennessee	United States
Bloomington Multisport	218 Fall Creek Road		West Covina	California	United States
Burnett Road Warriors	5807 Churchill Dr.		Corvallis	Oregon	United States
Business Equipment Center	6061 St. Paul Way		Everett	Montana	United States
Capital Road Cycles	628 Muir Road		Los Angeles	California	United States
Carlson Specialties	2313 B Southampton Rd		Missoula	Montana	United States
Chicago City Saddles	3 Gehringer Drive		Daly City	California	United States
Chicago Rent-All	15 Pear Dr.		Newport Beach	California	United States
Circuit Cycles	1 Mt. Dell Drive		Portland	Oregon	United States

INNER JOIN with 5 Tables

It takes accessing five tables to get the vendor name & address information in AdventureWorks. In fact this is the main complaint against 3NF relational database design: too many JOINs required to extract data. True, but the benefits of 3NF design are overwhelming. A way to overcome the "too many JOINs" issue is creating views which are pre-canned SELECT queries.

```
USE AdventureWorks;
GO
```

```
SELECT V.Name                           AS Vendor,
    A.AddressLine1,
    isnull(A.AddressLine2, '')          AS AddressLine2,
    A.City,
    SP.Name                             AS State,
    CR.Name                     AS Country
FROM   Purchasing.Vendor AS V
    INNER JOIN Purchasing.VendorAddress AS VA
        ON VA.VendorID = V.VendorID
    INNER JOIN Person.Address AS A
        ON A.AddressID = VA.AddressID
    INNER JOIN Person.StateProvince AS SP
        ON SP.StateProvinceID = A.StateProvinceID
    INNER JOIN Person.CountryRegion AS CR
        ON CR.CountryRegionCode = SP.CountryRegionCode
ORDER  BY Vendor;
GO
-- (104 row(s) affected) - Partial results.
```

Vendor	AddressLine1	AddressLine2	City	State	Country
A. Datum Corporation	2596 Big Canyon Road		New York	New York	United States
Advanced Bicycles	7995 Edwards Ave.		Lynnwood	Washington	United States
Allenson Cycles	4659 Montoya		Altadena	California	United States
American Bicycles and Wheels	1667 Warren Street		West Covina	California	United States
American Bikes	7179 Montana		Torrance	California	United States
Anderson's Custom Bikes	9 Guadalupe Dr.		Burbank	California	United States
Aurora Bike Center	65 Park Glen Court		Port Orchard	Washington	United States
Australia Bike Retailer	28 San Marino Ct.		Bellingham	Washington	United States
Beaumont Bikes	2472 Alexander Place		West Covina	Idaho	United States
Bergeron Off-Roads	9830 May Way		Mill Valley	Montana	United States
Bicycle Specialists	1286 Cincerto Circle		Lake Oswego	Oregon	United States
Bike Satellite Inc.	2141 Delaware Ct.		Downey	Tennessee	United States
Bloomington Multisport	218 Fall Creek Road		West Covina	California	United States
Burnett Road Warriors	5807 Churchill Dr.		Corvallis	Oregon	United States
Business Equipment Center	6061 St. Paul Way		Everett	Montana	United States
Capital Road Cycles	628 Muir Road		Los Angeles	California	United States

Creating View as Workaround for "Too Many JOINs"

It is so simple to create a view, that counterproductive if not done for queries which are used again and again. Given that large database systems may have a great number of views, meaningful long names are paremount.

```
-- No implicit ORDER BY can be included in a view - no trick around it either
CREATE VIEW vVendorAddress  AS
SELECT V.Name                        AS Vendor,
    A.AddressLine1,
    isnull(A.AddressLine2, '')       AS AddressLine2,
    A.City,
    SP.Name                          AS State,
    CR.Name                AS Country
FROM   Purchasing.Vendor AS V
    INNER JOIN Purchasing.VendorAddress AS VA     ON VA.VendorID = V.VendorID
    INNER JOIN Person.Address AS A                ON A.AddressID = VA.AddressID
    INNER JOIN Person.StateProvince AS SP         ON SP.StateProvinceID = A.StateProvinceID
    INNER JOIN Person.CountryRegion AS CR        ON CR.CountryRegionCode = SP.CountryRegionCode
ORDER  BY Vendor;
GO  /* Msg 1033, Level 15, State 1, Procedure vVendorAddress, Line 18
The ORDER BY clause is invalid in views, inline functions, derived tables, subqueries, and common table
expressions, unless TOP, OFFSET or FOR XML is also specified.  */
```

```
CREATE VIEW vVendorAddress  AS
SELECT V.Name                        AS Vendor,
    A.AddressLine1,
    isnull(A.AddressLine2, '')       AS AddressLine2,
    A.City,
    SP.Name                          AS State,
    CR.Name                AS Country
FROM   Purchasing.Vendor AS V
    INNER JOIN Purchasing.VendorAddress AS VA     ON VA.VendorID = V.VendorID
    INNER JOIN Person.Address AS A                ON A.AddressID = VA.AddressID
    INNER JOIN Person.StateProvince AS SP         ON SP.StateProvinceID = A.StateProvinceID
    INNER JOIN Person.CountryRegion AS CR        ON CR.CountryRegionCode = SP.CountryRegionCode
GO
```

```
SELECT TOP 5 * FROM vVendorAddress ORDER BY Vendor;
```

Vendor	AddressLine1	AddressLine2	City	State	Country
A. Datum Corporation	2596 Big Canyon Road		New York	New York	United States
Advanced Bicycles	7995 Edwards Ave.		Lynnwood	Washington	United States
Allenson Cycles	4659 Montoya		Altadena	California	United States
American Bicycles and Wheels	1667 Warren Street		West Covina	California	United States
American Bikes	7179 Montana		Torrance	California	United States

Non-Key INNER JOIN for Analytics

So far we have seen INNER JOINs based on FOREIGN KEY to PRIMARY equality relationships. The next INNER JOIN is based on the equality of the first 5 letters of last names. It is also a SELF-JOIN. In addition to the last name part equality, two more conditions are reducing the result set. The < condition is intended to reduce duplicates and the first letter of last name is 'S' limits the query results further. This is a many-to-many JOIN.

```
USE AdventureWorks2012;

SELECT  DISTINCT
    CONCAT( A.FirstName, space(1), A.LastName)     AS Person,
    CONCAT( B.FirstName, space(1), B.LastName)     AS LastNameNeighbor
FROM   Person.Person A
    INNER JOIN  Person.Person B
      ON LEFT(A.LastName, 5) = LEFT(B.LastName, 5)
        AND A.LastName < B.LastName
        AND LEFT(A.LastName, 1) = 'S'
ORDER  BY          Person,
                   LastNameNeighbor;
-- (169 row(s) affected) - Partial results.
```

Person	LastNameNeighbor
Abigail Smith	Lorrin Smith-Bates
Adriana Smith	Lorrin Smith-Bates
Alexander Smith	Lorrin Smith-Bates
Alexandra Smith	Lorrin Smith-Bates
Alexis Smith	Lorrin Smith-Bates
Allen Smith	Lorrin Smith-Bates
Alyssa Smith	Lorrin Smith-Bates
Andre Smith	Lorrin Smith-Bates
Andrew Smith	Lorrin Smith-Bates
Arthur Smith	Lorrin Smith-Bates
Ashley Smith	Lorrin Smith-Bates
Austin Smith	Lorrin Smith-Bates
Barry Srini	Sethu Srinivasan
Ben Smith	Lorrin Smith-Bates
Benjamin Smith	Lorrin Smith-Bates
Beth Srini	Sethu Srinivasan
Brandon Smith	Lorrin Smith-Bates
Brandy Srini	Sethu Srinivasan
Brett Srini	Sethu Srinivasan
Brianna Smith	Lorrin Smith-Bates

JOINing Tables without Relationship for Combinatorics

SQL Server will execute such a JOIN on any pair of compatible columns as demonstrated by the next T-SQL query. Note this is only a demo, there is no business meaning to it unless the combinatorial results are useful for some application. A more practical example in the pubs database matching author city with publisher city using a JOIN. SQL Server 2012 query.

```
USE Northwind;   -- Cross database JOIN query
SELECT   P.ProductID,
         P.ProductName               AS NorthwindProduct,
         PP.Name                     AS AWProduct
FROM dbo.Products P
         INNER JOIN AdventureWorks2008.Production.Product PP     ON P.ProductID = PP.ProductID
ORDER BY P.ProductID;
```

ProductID	NorthwindProduct	AWProduct
1	Chai	Adjustable Race
2	Chang	Bearing Ball
3	Aniseed Syrup	BB Ball Bearing
4	Chef Anton's Cajun Seasoning	Headset Ball Bearings

Cartesian Product

When all rows in one table combined with all rows of another table it is called a Cartesian product. The cardinality of such a JOIN is (Table 1 Rows) x (Table 2 Rows).

```
-- Old-fashioned no JOIN predicate 2-table query - Cardinality 4x4 = 16
SELECT Category1 = A.Name, Category2 = B.Name
FROM Production.ProductCategory A, Production.ProductCategory B ORDER BY Category1, Category2;
```

```
-- Equivalent CROSS JOIN
SELECT Category1 = A.Name, Category2 = B.Name
FROM Production.ProductCategory A  CROSS JOIN Production.ProductCategory B
ORDER BY Category1, Category2;
```

Category1	Category2
Accessories	Accessories
Accessories	Bikes
Accessories	Clothing
Accessories	Components
Bikes	Accessories
Bikes	Bikes
Bikes	Clothing
Bikes	Components
Clothing	Accessories
Clothing	Bikes
Clothing	Clothing
Clothing	Components
Components	Accessories
Components	Bikes
Components	Clothing
Components	Components

SQL OUTER JOIN for Inclusion of Unmatched Rows

We have seen that INNER JOINs return rows only when there is at least one row from both tables that satisfies the join condition or conditions such as FOREIGN KEY matching the referenced PRIMARY KEY. Inner join queries do not return the rows that do not meet the ON condition with a row from the other table.

OUTER JOINs, however, return all rows from one or both tables in the JOIN. All rows are returned from the left table in a LEFT OUTER JOIN (including non-matching rows), and all rows are returned from the right table in a RIGHT OUTER JOIN. All rows from both tables are returned in a FULL OUTER JOIN. LEFT OUTER JOIN is totally equivalent to RIGHT OUTER JOIN. LEFT OUTER JOIN is mostly used by programmers in countries where the writing is left to right. **RIGHT OUTER JOIN is typically used by developers in countries where the writing is right to left**. **The non-matching rows in an OUTER JOIN are returned with NULL value fields**, therefore, they can be distinquished from the matching rows with a null test.

The following are synonyms:

LEFT JOIN - LEFT OUTER JOIN

RIGHT JOIN - RIGHT OUTER JOIN

FULL JOIN - FULL OUTER JOIN

The legacy syntax for outer joins *= (left join) or =* (right join) is not supported anymore. T-SQL example script lists products (left table) even if they are not being sold such as assembly parts.

```
USE AdventureWorks2012;
SELECT          P.Name,         SOD.SalesOrderID,
                CASE    WHEN SalesOrderID is null THEN 'Non-matching'
                        ELSE 'Matching' END                 AS JoinInfo
FROM   Production.Product P
    LEFT OUTER JOIN Sales.SalesOrderDetail SOD     ON P.ProductID = SOD.ProductID
ORDER  BY P.Name;  -- (121555 row(s) affected)  - Partial results.
```

Name	SalesOrderID	JoinInfo
Adjustable Race	NULL	Non-matching
All-Purpose Bike Stand	51179	Matching
All-Purpose Bike Stand	51488	Matching
All-Purpose Bike Stand	51520	Matching
All-Purpose Bike Stand	51558	Matching
All-Purpose Bike Stand	51882	Matching
All-Purpose Bike Stand	51903	Matching
All-Purpose Bike Stand	51970	Matching
All-Purpose Bike Stand	52010	Matching
All-Purpose Bike Stand	52032	Matching

LEFT JOIN: Include Unmatched Rows from Left Table

In the LEFT JOIN example, the Vendor table is LEFT JOINed to the PurchaseOrderHeader table to find out which vendors did not supply anything. The LEFT JOIN is based on FOREIGN KEY relationship.

```
USE AdventureWorks2012;

SELECT Vendor = V.Name
FROM   Purchasing.Vendor V
    LEFT JOIN Purchasing.PurchaseOrderHeader POH
        ON V.BusinessEntityID = POH.VendorID
WHERE  POH.VendorID IS NULL                -- Test if POH columns are null
ORDER by Vendor;   -- (18 row(s) affected) - Partial results.
```

Vendor
A. Datum Corporation
Cycling Master
Electronic Bike Co.
GMA Ski & Bike
Holiday Skate & Cycle
Illinois Trek & Clothing

T-SQL query to check which pedal products for sale were reviewed and which ones not.

```
SELECT  p.Name              AS ProductName,
        ProductNumber,
        pr.ProductReviewID,
        pr.ReviewerName,
        pr.Rating
FROM Production.Product p
   LEFT JOIN Production.ProductReview pr
        ON p.ProductID = pr.ProductID
WHERE p.ProductSubcategoryID is not null    AND p.Name like '%pedal%'  ORDER BY ProductNumber;
-- (8 row(s) affected)
```

ProductName	ProductNumber	ProductReviewID	ReviewerName	Rating
LL Mountain Pedal	PD-M282	NULL	NULL	NULL
ML Mountain Pedal	PD-M340	NULL	NULL	NULL
HL Mountain Pedal	PD-M562	2	David	4
HL Mountain Pedal	PD-M562	3	Jill	2
LL Road Pedal	PD-R347	NULL	NULL	NULL
ML Road Pedal	PD-R563	NULL	NULL	NULL
HL Road Pedal	PD-R853	NULL	NULL	NULL
Touring Pedal	PD-T852	NULL	NULL	NULL

RIGHT JOIN - Same as LEFT with Tables Switched

The RIGHT JOIN is totally equivalent, including performance, to the corresponding LEFT JOIN. RIGHT JOIN is more frequently used in countries where they write right to left.

```
USE AdventureWorks2012;

SELECT Vendor = V.Name
FROM   Purchasing.PurchaseOrderHeader POH
    RIGHT JOIN Purchasing.Vendor V
      ON V.BusinessEntityID = POH.VendorID
WHERE  POH.VendorID IS NULL
ORDER by Vendor;
-- (18 row(s) affected) - Partial results.
```

Vendor
A. Datum Corporation
Cycling Master
Electronic Bike Co.
GMA Ski & Bike
Holiday Skate & Cycle

T-SQL RIGHT JOIN examples progress toward a query to provide users with a good report.

```
USE AdventureWorks2012;

SELECT ST.Name AS  Territory,
    SP.BusinessEntityID
FROM   Sales.SalesTerritory ST
    RIGHT OUTER JOIN Sales.SalesPerson SP
      ON ST.TerritoryID = SP.TerritoryID;
-- (17 row(s) affected)
```

```
SELECT   isnull(ST.Name, ' ')                          AS Territory,
         SP.BusinessEntityID,
         CONCAT (C.FirstName, ' ', C.LastName)         AS Name
FROM   Sales.SalesTerritory ST
    RIGHT OUTER JOIN Sales.SalesPerson SP
      ON ST.TerritoryID = SP.TerritoryID
    INNER JOIN Person.Person C
      ON SP.BusinessEntityID = C.BusinessEntityID;
-- (17 row(s) affected)
```

Add a WHERE condition filter on Sales.SalesPerson SalesYTD column

The NULLs indicate the no match rows in the RIGHT OUTER JOIN.

```
SELECT  ST.CountryRegionCode,
        ST.Name                                      AS Territory,
        SP.BusinessEntityID                          AS EmployeeID,
        CONCAT(C.FirstName, ' ', C.LastName )        AS Name
FROM    Sales.SalesTerritory ST
    RIGHT OUTER JOIN Sales.SalesPerson SP
     ON ST.TerritoryID = SP.TerritoryID
    INNER JOIN Person.Person C
     ON SP.BusinessEntityID = C.BusinessEntityID
WHERE SP.SalesYTD > 1000.0
ORDER BY        CountryRegionCode,
                Territory;
GO
-- (17 row(s) affected)
```

CountryRegionCode	Territory	EmployeeID	Name
NULL	NULL	274	Stephen Jiang
NULL	NULL	285	Syed Abbas
NULL	NULL	287	Amy Alberts
AU	Australia	286	Lynn Tsoflias
CA	Canada	278	Garrett Vargas
CA	Canada	282	José Saraiva
DE	Germany	288	Rachel Valdez
FR	France	290	Ranjit Varkey Chudukatil
GB	United Kingdom	289	Jae Pak
US	Central	277	Jillian Carson
US	Northeast	275	Michael Blythe
US	Northwest	283	David Campbell
US	Northwest	284	Tete Mensa-Annan
US	Northwest	280	Pamela Ansman-Wolfe
US	Southeast	279	Tsvi Reiter
US	Southwest	276	Linda Mitchell
US	Southwest	281	Shu Ito

```
-- Counting the RIGHT JOIN  match rows using a ProductSubcategory column
SELECT COUNT( S.Name)
FROM Production.ProductSubcategory S RIGHT JOIN Production.Product P
  ON S.ProductSubcategoryID = P.ProductSubcategoryID;
-- 295
```

Cardinality of OUTER JOINs

The number of rows returned in an OUTER JOIN is equal to the matching rows plus the non-matching rows from either or both tables. **To identify the non-matching rows (the ones with the NULLs) in an outer join we have to choose a not-nullable column like the PRIMARY KEY column.** T-SQL script demonstrates the cardinality involved with a LEFT JOIN.

```
USE AdventureWorks2012;
```

```
-- Rows in LEFT JOIN
SELECT Rows = count(*)
FROM   Production.Product P
    LEFT OUTER JOIN Sales.SalesOrderDetail SOD
            ON P.ProductID = SOD.ProductID
-- 121555
```

```
-- Rows in right table
SELECT Rows = count(*)
FROM Sales.SalesOrderDetail
-- 121317
```

```
-- Non-matching rows in left table
SELECT Rows = count(*)
FROM   Production.Product P
    LEFT OUTER JOIN Sales.SalesOrderDetail SOD
            ON P.ProductID = SOD.ProductID
WHERE SalesOrderID is NULL
-- 238
```

```
-- Right table rows + non-matching left table rows = rows returned by left join
SELECT 121317 + 238
-- 121555
```

Since the count queries are single valued, we can do the following summation.

```
SELECT (SELECT Rows = count(*)  FROM Sales.SalesOrderDetail )
+
(SELECT Rows = count(*)
FROM   Production.Product P
    LEFT OUTER JOIN Sales.SalesOrderDetail SOD
            ON P.ProductID = SOD.ProductID
WHERE SalesOrderID is NULL);
GO  -- 121555
```

LEFT JOIN & RIGHT JOIN on the Same Table

LEFT JOIN & RIGHT JOIN can be combined on the same table to keep all rows from that table even if they don't match the other two tables. The Production.Product table has a FOREIGN KEY referencing the ProductSubcategory table and another FOREIGN KEY referencing the UnitMeasure table.

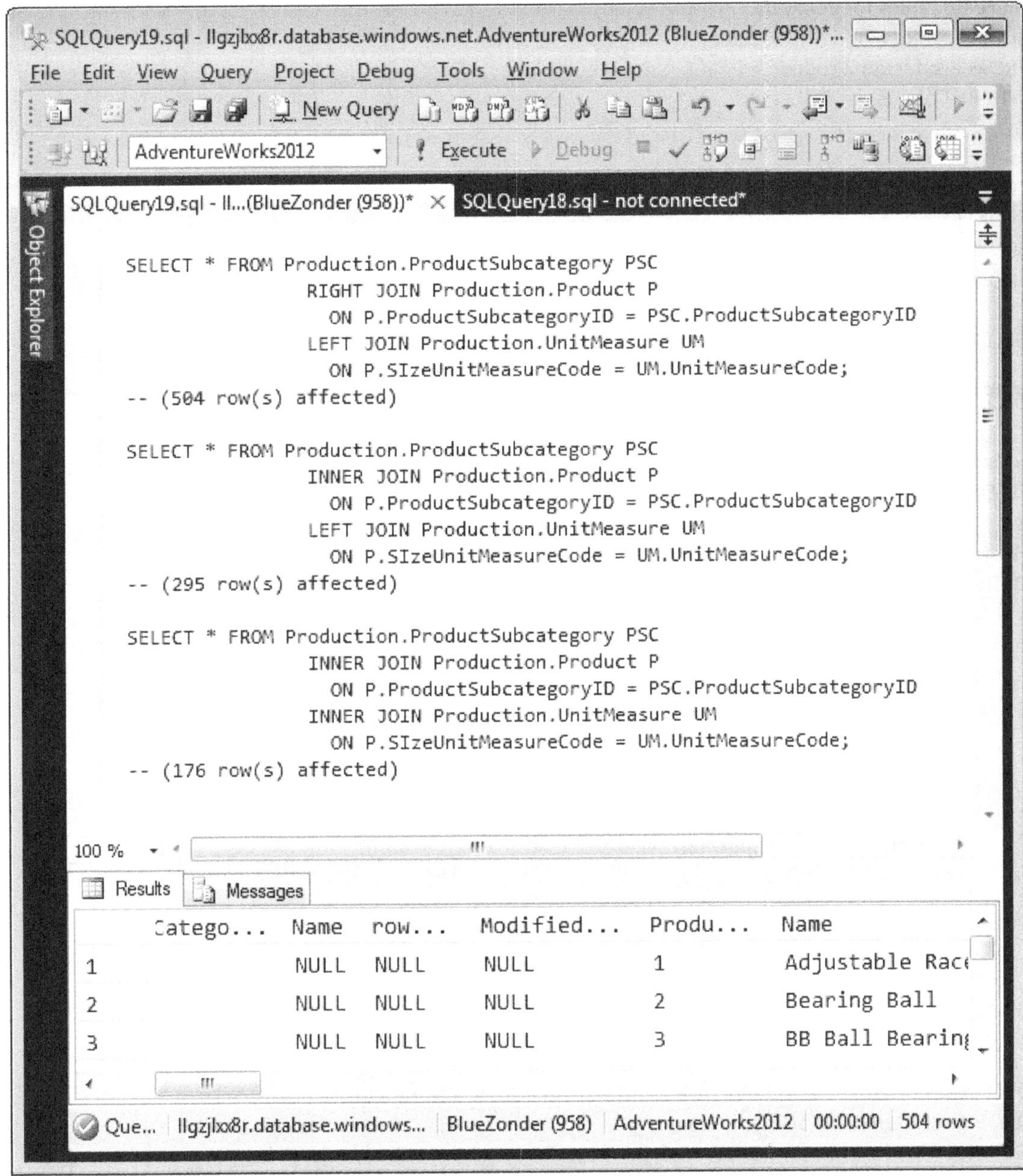

SQLQuery19.sql - llgzjlxx8r.database.windows.net.AdventureWorks2012 (BlueZonder (958))*...
File Edit View Query Project Debug Tools Window Help
New Query
AdventureWorks2012
Execute Debug
SQLQuery19.sql - ll...(BlueZonder (958))*
SQLQuery18.sql - not connected*
Object Explorer
SELECT * FROM Production.ProductSubcategory PSC
RIGHT JOIN Production.Product P
ON P.ProductSubcategoryID = PSC.ProductSubcategoryID
LEFT JOIN Production.UnitMeasure UM
ON P.SIzeUnitMeasureCode = UM.UnitMeasureCode;
-- (504 row(s) affected)
SELECT * FROM Production.ProductSubcategory PSC
INNER JOIN Production.Product P
ON P.ProductSubcategoryID = PSC.ProductSubcategoryID
LEFT JOIN Production.UnitMeasure UM
ON P.SIzeUnitMeasureCode = UM.UnitMeasureCode;
-- (295 row(s) affected)
SELECT * FROM Production.ProductSubcategory PSC
INNER JOIN Production.Product P
ON P.ProductSubcategoryID = PSC.ProductSubcategoryID
INNER JOIN Production.UnitMeasure UM
ON P.SIzeUnitMeasureCode = UM.UnitMeasureCode;
-- (176 row(s) affected)
100 %
Results
Messages
Catego... Name row... Modified... Produ... Name
1 NULL NULL NULL 1 Adjustable Race
2 NULL NULL NULL 2 Bearing Ball
3 NULL NULL NULL 3 BB Ball Bearing
Que... llgzjlxx8r.database.windows... BlueZonder (958) AdventureWorks2012 00:00:00 504 rows

FULL JOIN to Include All Unmatched Rows

The operation FULL JOIN combines LEFT JOIN and RIGHT JOIN, therefore it does not matter which is the left table or right table, it is a fully symmetrical set operation. T-SQL script demonstrates FULL OUTER JOIN.

```
USE tempdb;
-- Create tables for demo
SELECT distinct Color INTO Color
FROM Production.Product
WHERE Color is not null;
GO
```

```
SELECT ID=IDENTITY(int, 1, 1), * INTO NormalColor
FROM Color;
SELECT ID=IDENTITY(int, 1, 1), Color=CONCAT('Light', Color)  INTO LightColor
FROM Color;
```

```
DELETE NormalColor WHERE Color = 'Red';
```

```
DELETE LightColor WHERE Color = 'LightBlue';
```

```
-- Demo tables ready - full join query
SELECT   NormalColor        = n.Color,
         LightColor         = l.Color
FROM   NormalColor n        FULL OUTER JOIN LightColor l     ON n.ID = l.ID
ORDER BY NormalColor;
```

NormalColor	LightColor
NULL	LightRed
Black	LightBlack
Blue	NULL
Grey	LightGrey
Multi	LightMulti
Silver	LightSilver
Silver/Black	LightSilver/Black
White	LightWhite
Yellow	LightYellow

```
DROP TABLE  tempdb.dbo.Color; DROP TABLE tempdb.dbo.NormalColor;
DROP TABLE tempdb.dbo.LightColor;
GO
```

CROSS JOIN for Cartesian Product

A CROSS JOIN with no connecting columns for joining produces a Cartesian product: combines all rows of the left table with all rows of the right tables. If the left table has x rows and the right table y rows, the CROSS JOIN is going to have x*y rows. That is called Cartesian explosion as it happens sometimes unintentionally in database development. In fact, a huge CROSS JOIN can bring SQL Server "to its knees", overwhelming CPU and disk resources. On the same note, no matter how powerful is the hardware platform, a bad runaway query can make SQL Server unresponsive to normal queries from other connections. T-SQL script to demonstrate CROSS JOIN.

```
USE AdventureWorks2012;
```

```
-- Cardinality of CROSS JOIN
SELECT count(*) from HumanResources.Employee;          -- 290
SELECT count(*) from HumanResources.Department;        -- 16
SELECT 16 * 290;                                       -- 4640
```

```
SELECT        E.BusinessEntityID          AS EMPLOYEEID,
              D.Name                      AS DEPARTMENT
FROM  HumanResources.Employee E  CROSS JOIN HumanResources.Department D
ORDER BY      EMPLOYEEID,     DEPARTMENT;
-- (4640 row(s) affected) - Partial results.
```

EMPLOYEEID	DEPARTMENT
1	Production Control
1	Purchasing
1	Quality Assurance
1	Research and Development
1	Sales
1	Shipping and Receiving
1	Tool Design
2	Document Control
2	Engineering
2	Executive
2	Facilities and Maintenance
2	Finance
2	Human Resources
2	Information Services
2	Marketing
2	Production

CROSS JOIN Generated Multiplication Table

A CROSS JOIN can be used to create combinatorical results. In the next example, a multiplication table is created using a CROSS JOIN which is also a SELF-JOIN. CTE stands for Common Table Expression, which can be used as a table in SELECT and other queries. The master database spt_values table is used to get a sequence of numbers. The ".." in the table reference means: use the default schema which is "dbo".

```
; WITH cteNumber                                    -- cte for numbers 1 to 10
   AS (SELECT NUMBER
      FROM   master..spt_values
      WHERE  TYPE = 'P'
            AND NUMBER BETWEEN 1 AND 10)
SELECT MULTIPLICATION=CONCAT( ltrim(str(B.NUMBER)) , ' * '
               , ltrim(str(A.NUMBER)) , ' = '
               , ltrim(str(A.NUMBER * B.NUMBER)) )
FROM   cteNumber A   CROSS JOIN cteNumber B;
-- (100 row(s) affected) - Partial results.
```

MULTIPLICATION
1 * 1 = 1
1 * 2 = 2
1 * 3 = 3
1 * 4 = 4
1 * 5 = 5
1 * 6 = 6
1 * 7 = 7
1 * 8 = 8
1 * 9 = 9
1 * 10 = 10
2 * 1 = 2
2 * 2 = 4
2 * 3 = 6
2 * 4 = 8
2 * 5 = 10
2 * 6 = 12
2 * 7 = 14
2 * 8 = 16
2 * 9 = 18
2 * 10 = 20
3 * 1 = 3
3 * 2 = 6
3 * 3 = 9
3 * 4 = 12
3 * 5 = 15

INNER JOIN with 7 Tables

T-SQL query lists AdventureWorks Cycles retail (web) customers with total purchase amount and order dates. The name & address displays multiple times if a customer did multiple purchases. Generally, that is undesirable, and requires end-user report design considerations how to resolve it. The sorting uses Sales.SalesOrderHeader OrderDate which is datetime data type, instead of the mdy format string report date. mdy string format dates do not sort in chronological order.

```
USE AdventureWorks;
GO
```

```
SELECT CONCAT(C.LastName, ', ', C.FirstName)              AS CustomerName,
          A.City,
          SP.Name                                          AS State,
          CR.Name                                          AS Country,
          A.PostalCode,
          FORMAT(SOH.TotalDue, 'c','en-US')                AS SalesAmount,
          FORMAT(SOH.OrderDate,'d')                        AS OrderDate
FROM Person.Contact AS C
   INNER JOIN Sales.Individual AS I
          ON C.ContactID = I.ContactID
   INNER JOIN Sales.CustomerAddress AS CA
          ON CA.CustomerID = I.CustomerID
   INNER JOIN Person.Address AS A
          ON A.AddressID = CA.AddressID
   INNER JOIN Person.StateProvince SP
          ON SP.StateProvinceID = A.StateProvinceID
   INNER JOIN Person.CountryRegion CR
          ON CR.CountryRegionCode = SP.CountryRegionCode
   INNER JOIN Sales.SalesOrderHeader SOH
          ON C.ContactID = SOH.CustomerID
ORDER BY CustomerName, soh.OrderDate ;
-- (16493 row(s) affected)  - Partial results.
```

CustomerName	City	State	Country	PostalCode	SalesAmount	OrderDate
Adams, Aaron	Downey	California	United States	90241	$734.70	3/4/2004
Adams, Adam	Newport Beach	California	United States	92625	$2,566.12	4/16/2004
Adams, Alex	Lake Oswego	Oregon	United States	97034	$2,410.63	3/18/2003
Adams, Alex	Lake Oswego	Oregon	United States	97034	$1,293.38	12/9/2003
Adams, Alex	Lake Oswego	Oregon	United States	97034	$2,643.12	2/1/2004
Adams, Angel	Burlingame	California	United States	94010	$865.20	5/24/2003
Adams, Angel	Burlingame	California	United States	94010	$2,597.81	3/1/2004
Adams, Carlos	Langford	British Columbia	Canada	V9	$44.18	6/28/2004
Adams, Connor	Westminster	British Columbia	Canada	V3L 1H4	$183.74	4/14/2004
Adams, Elijah	Seattle	Washington	United States	98104	$8.04	11/2/2003

INNER JOIN with GROUP BY Subquery

We have to make the GROUP BY subquery into a derived table first. Subsequently, we can apply it just like any other table in a query.

```
USE AdventureWorks2012;
GO
```

```
SELECT  Subcategory = Name,
        Color,
        ColorCount,
        AvgListPrice
FROM  (
        SELECT ProductSubcategoryID,                          -- grouping column
        Color = COALESCE(Color, 'N/A'),                       -- grouping column with transformation
        ColorCount = COUNT(*),                                -- aggregate function
        AvgListPrice = AVG(COALESCE(ListPrice, 0.0))          -- aggregate function
        FROM   Production.Product
        GROUP  BY      ProductSubcategoryID,
                       Color) x                               -- derived table (subquery)
    INNER JOIN Production.ProductSubcategory psc
        ON psc.ProductSubcategoryID = x.ProductSubcategoryID
ORDER  BY Subcategory,
        Color;
GO
-- (48 row(s) affected) - Partial results.
```

Subcategory	Color	ColorCount	AvgListPrice
Bib-Shorts	Multi	3	89.990000
Bike Racks	N/A	1	120.000000
Bike Stands	N/A	1	159.000000
Bottles and Cages	N/A	3	7.990000
Bottom Brackets	N/A	3	92.240000
Brakes	Silver	2	106.500000
Caps	Multi	1	8.990000
Chains	Silver	1	20.240000
Cleaners	N/A	1	7.950000
Cranksets	Black	3	278.990000
Derailleurs	Silver	2	106.475000
Fenders	N/A	1	21.980000

Making Queries Readable & Results Presentable

A database developer has to make a query readable for productivity gain in development and ease of maintenance. At the same time the results must be readable to the user. The next query with results demonstrates how to achieve both objectives.

```
USE AdventureWorks2012;
GO
```

```
SELECT PC.Name                                          AS Category,
       PSC.Name                                         AS Subcategory,
       PM.Name                                          AS Model,
       P.Name                                           AS ProductName,
       FORMAT(ListPrice,'c','en-US')                    AS Price
FROM Production.Product AS P
   INNER JOIN Production.ProductModel AS PM
         ON PM.ProductModelID = P.ProductModelID
   INNER JOIN Production.ProductSubcategory AS PSC
         ON PSC.ProductSubcategoryID = P.ProductSubcategoryID
   INNER JOIN Production.ProductCategory AS PC
         ON PC.ProductCategoryID = PSC.ProductCategoryID
ORDER BY Category, Subcategory, ProductName;
GO
-- (295 row(s) affected) - Partial results.
```

The confusing 4 "Name" columns are clarified by well-chosen column aliases. The meaningful column aliases are used in the ORDER BY clause even though not required. To help the user, the list price is currency formatted.

Category	Subcategory	Model	ProductName	Price
Accessories	Bike Racks	Hitch Rack - 4-Bike	Hitch Rack - 4-Bike	$120.00
Accessories	Bike Stands	All-Purpose Bike Stand	All-Purpose Bike Stand	$159.00
Accessories	Bottles and Cages	Mountain Bottle Cage	Mountain Bottle Cage	$9.99
Accessories	Bottles and Cages	Road Bottle Cage	Road Bottle Cage	$8.99
Accessories	Bottles and Cages	Water Bottle	Water Bottle - 30 oz.	$4.99
Accessories	Cleaners	Bike Wash	Bike Wash - Dissolver	$7.95
Accessories	Fenders	Fender Set - Mountain	Fender Set - Mountain	$21.98
Accessories	Helmets	Sport-100	Sport-100 Helmet, Black	$34.99
Accessories	Helmets	Sport-100	Sport-100 Helmet, Blue	$34.99
Accessories	Helmets	Sport-100	Sport-100 Helmet, Red	$34.99

A 12 Tables JOIN Query

The next query JOINs 11 tables, some of the tables occur more than once in the query.

```
USE AdventureWorks;
```

```
DECLARE        @Year int,
               @Month int

SET @Year      = 2004;
SET @Month     = 1;

SELECT SOH.SalesOrderNumber                         AS SON,
    SOH.PurchaseOrderNumber                         AS PO,
    S.Name                                          AS Store,
    CONVERT(VARCHAR, SOH.OrderDate, 110)            AS OrderDate,
    CONVERT(VARCHAR, SOH.ShipDate, 110)             AS ShipDate,
    FORMAT(TotalDue,'c','en-US')                    AS [Total Due],
    CONCAT(C.FirstName,' ',C.LastName)              AS SalesStaff,
    SM.Name                                         AS ShpngMethod,
    BA.AddressLine1                                 AS BlngAddress1,
    Isnull(BA.AddressLine2, '')                     AS BlngAddress2,
    BA.City                                         AS BlngCity,
    BSP.Name                                        AS BlngStateProvince,
    BA.PostalCode                                   AS BlngPostalCode,
    BCR.Name                                        AS BlngCountryRegion,
    SA.AddressLine1                                 AS ShpngAddress1,
    Isnull(SA.AddressLine2, '')                     AS ShpngAddress2,
    SA.City                                         AS ShpngCity,
    SSP.Name                                        AS ShpngStateProvince,
    SA.PostalCode                                   AS ShpngPostalCode,
    SCR.Name                                        AS ShpngCountryRegion,
    CONCAT(CC.FirstName,' ',CC.LastName)            AS CustomerContact,
    CC.Phone                                        AS CustomerPhone,
    SOH.AccountNumber
FROM   Person.Address SA
    INNER JOIN Person.StateProvince SSP
        ON SA.StateProvinceID = SSP.StateProvinceID
    INNER JOIN Person.CountryRegion SCR
        ON SSP.CountryRegionCode = SCR.CountryRegionCode
    INNER JOIN Sales.SalesOrderHeader SOH
        INNER JOIN Person.Contact CC
            ON SOH.ContactID = CC.ContactID
        INNER JOIN Person.Address BA
            INNER JOIN Person.StateProvince BSP
                ON BA.StateProvinceID = BSP.StateProvinceID
            INNER JOIN Person.CountryRegion BCR
```

-- T-SQL query continued

```
                    ON BSP.CountryRegionCode =
                        BCR.CountryRegionCode
               ON SOH.BillToAddressID = BA.AddressID
          ON SA.AddressID = SOH.ShipToAddressID
     INNER JOIN Person.Contact C
          INNER JOIN HumanResources.Employee E
               ON C.ContactID = E.ContactID
          ON SOH.SalesPersonID = E.EmployeeID
     INNER JOIN Purchasing.ShipMethod SM
          ON SOH.ShipMethodID = SM.ShipMethodID
     INNER JOIN Sales.Store S
          ON SOH.CustomerID = S.CustomerID
WHERE  SOH.OrderDate >= datefromparts(@Year, @month, 1)
     AND  SOH.OrderDate < dateadd(mm,1,datefromparts(@Year, @month, 1))
ORDER  BY Store,   OrderDate DESC;
GO
-- (96 row(s) affected) - Partial results.
```

SON	PO	Store	OrderDate	ShipDate	Total Due	SalesStaff	ShpngMethod	BlngAddress1
SO61257	PO3741176337	Activity Center	01-01-2004	01-08-2004	$12,764.08	Tsvi Reiter	CARGO TRANSPORT 5	Factory Stores Of America
SO61256	PO1421187796	All Cycle Shop	01-01-2004	01-08-2004	$201.08	Tete Mensa-Annan	CARGO TRANSPORT 5	25111 228th St Sw
SO61251	PO6380165323	All Seasons Sports Supply	01-01-2004	01-08-2004	$2,863.30	Michael Blythe	CARGO TRANSPORT 5	Ohms Road
SO61263	PO5452121402	Amalgamated Parts Shop	01-01-2004	01-08-2004	$39,103.04	Rachel Valdez	CARGO TRANSPORT 5	Brunnenstr 422
SO61227	PO10730172247	Area Bike Accessories	01-01-2004	01-08-2004	$75,916.89	Shu Ito	CARGO TRANSPORT 5	6900 Sisk Road
SO61187	PO13978135025	Basic Bike Company	01-01-2004	01-08-2004	$72.92	David Campbell	CARGO TRANSPORT 5	15 East Main
SO61190	PO12441157171	Best Cycle Store	01-01-2004	01-08-2004	$49,337.61	Rachel Valdez	CARGO TRANSPORT 5	Berliner Platz 45
SO61221	PO15399128383	Best o' Bikes	01-01-2004	01-08-2004	$5,872.73	Michael Blythe	CARGO TRANSPORT 5	250880 Baur Blvd
SO61173	PO522171689	Better Bike Shop	01-01-2004	01-08-2004	$38,511.29	Tsvi Reiter	CARGO TRANSPORT 5	42525 Austell Road
SO61254	PO4872176154	Bicycle Exporters	01-01-2004	01-08-2004	$10,665.06	Rachel Valdez	CARGO TRANSPORT 5	Hellweg 4934
SO61243	PO7859152962	Bike Dealers Association	01-01-2004	01-08-2004	$18,976.48	Shu Ito	CARGO TRANSPORT 5	9952 E. Lohman Ave.
SO61250	PO4930183869	Bikes for Kids and Adults	01-01-2004	01-08-2004	$3,852.87	Jae Pak	CARGO TRANSPORT 5	9900 Ronson Drive
SO61209	PO11484136165	Casual Bicycle Store	01-01-2004	01-08-2004	$37,314.33	Jillian Carson	CARGO TRANSPORT 5	Westside Plaza
SO61204	PO15312134209	Citywide Service and Repair	01-01-2004	01-08-2004	$29,797.18	Jae Pak	CARGO TRANSPORT 5	Box 99354 300 Union Street
SO61192	PO10092119585	Classic Cycle Store	01-01-2004	01-08-2004	$3,691.57	Jillian Carson	CARGO TRANSPORT 5	630 Oldgate Lane

Order of Tables or Predicates Does Not Matter

Frequent question: does the order of tables matter in a JOIN? Should I put BETWEEN predicate before LIKE predicate? Valid syntax variations do not matter. The database engine translates the query to an internal form prior to creating an execution plan. Thus the different variations get translated to the same internal form. The only way we have some control over the database engine if we rewrite a single statement complex query to a multi-statements script.

Nondeterministic CTE

CTE is evaluated for every reference, therefore it may return different results if certain functions are used such as newid(), thus yielding a nondeterministic CTE.

```
;WITH CTE AS (SELECT Random = NEWID()),
CTE1 AS (SELECT * FROM CTE),
CTE2 AS (SELECT * FROM CTE),
CTE3 AS (SELECT * FROM CTE),
CTE4 AS (SELECT * FROM CTE),
CTE5 AS (SELECT * FROM CTE)
SELECT * FROM CTE1
UNION ALL
SELECT * FROM CTE2
UNION ALL
SELECT * FROM CTE3
UNION ALL
SELECT * FROM CTE4
UNION ALL
SELECT * FROM CTE5
UNION ALL
SELECT * FROM CTE
UNION ALL
SELECT * FROM CTE
UNION ALL
SELECT * FROM CTE;
```

Random
08D45FE2-52C6-4E15-83A3-0B2F27837887
D6A094E6-0C8A-43E4-B6C4-8821F6EE8E73
281A5852-3D9A-4F2A-99FA-F60EE28FD2E0
C327ED19-5C03-4D9B-A8E8-6ACABAA08F1C
80DDE508-A6AA-4F2B-AB2F-CEEF7EC5E163
5F611B03-46F4-4EED-A8E0-76020527899D
FF8DAE17-65F6-4D80-8AF5-29EBAEBD2FEB
CF342DC9-4CF9-46FD-87F0-3213106C447D

The CROSS APPLY Operator

The APPLY (CROSS APPLY & OUTER APPLY) operators were introduced with SQL Server 2005. The CROSS APPLY operator merges rows from tables (or views) with rows from table-valued function, a form of JOIN.

```
USE AdventureWorks2012;
SELECT
        q.last_execution_time                       AS LastRun,
        t.TEXT                                      AS QueryText,
        q.sql_handle                                AS SQLHandle
FROM    sys.dm_exec_query_stats AS q                                -- system view
                CROSS APPLY
                sys.dm_exec_sql_text(q.sql_handle) AS t             -- table-valued system function
WHERE LEFT(t.TEXT,8)='SELECT *'  ORDER BY LastRun DESC;
```

LastRun	QueryText
2016-08-01 14:46:12.537	SELECT * FROM Sales.SalesOrderHeader
2016-08-01 14:44:54.257	SELECT * FROM Production.Product
2016-08-01 13:29:25.213	SELECT * FROM sys.dm_os_wait_stats
2016-08-01 09:36:57.980	select * from sys.sysforeignkeys s
2016-08-01 09:36:39.077	select * from sysforeignkeys s

```
-- Return the top N purchase order by amount - inline table-valued function
CREATE FUNCTION dbo.ufnGetTopNPurchases(@VendorID AS INT, @N AS INT)
RETURNS TABLE  AS
RETURN
 SELECT TOP ( @N ) *    FROM Purchasing.PurchaseOrderHeader
 WHERE VendorID = @VendorID    ORDER BY TotalDue DESC;
GO   -- Command(s) completed successfully.
```

```
-- List the top 5 highest purchases from vendors
SELECT  V.VendorID,
        P.PurchaseOrderID,
        FORMAT(P.TotalDue, 'c','en-US')     AS TotalDue
FROM    Purchasing.Vendor AS V  CROSS APPLY  dbo.ufnGetTopNPurchases(V.VendorID, 5) AS P
ORDER BY  V.VendorID, TotalDue DESC
-- (395 row(s) affected) - Partial results.
```

VendorID	PurchaseOrderID	TotalDue
74	325	$1,654.75
74	1727	$855.22
74	2517	$855.22
74	3307	$855.22
74	167	$785.61

Using CROSS APPLY with Columns Specified Table Alias

A regular table alias would result in error in the following delimited string list query. Table alias with column(s) specifications "o(list)" works, the table alias is "o", it has one column "list".

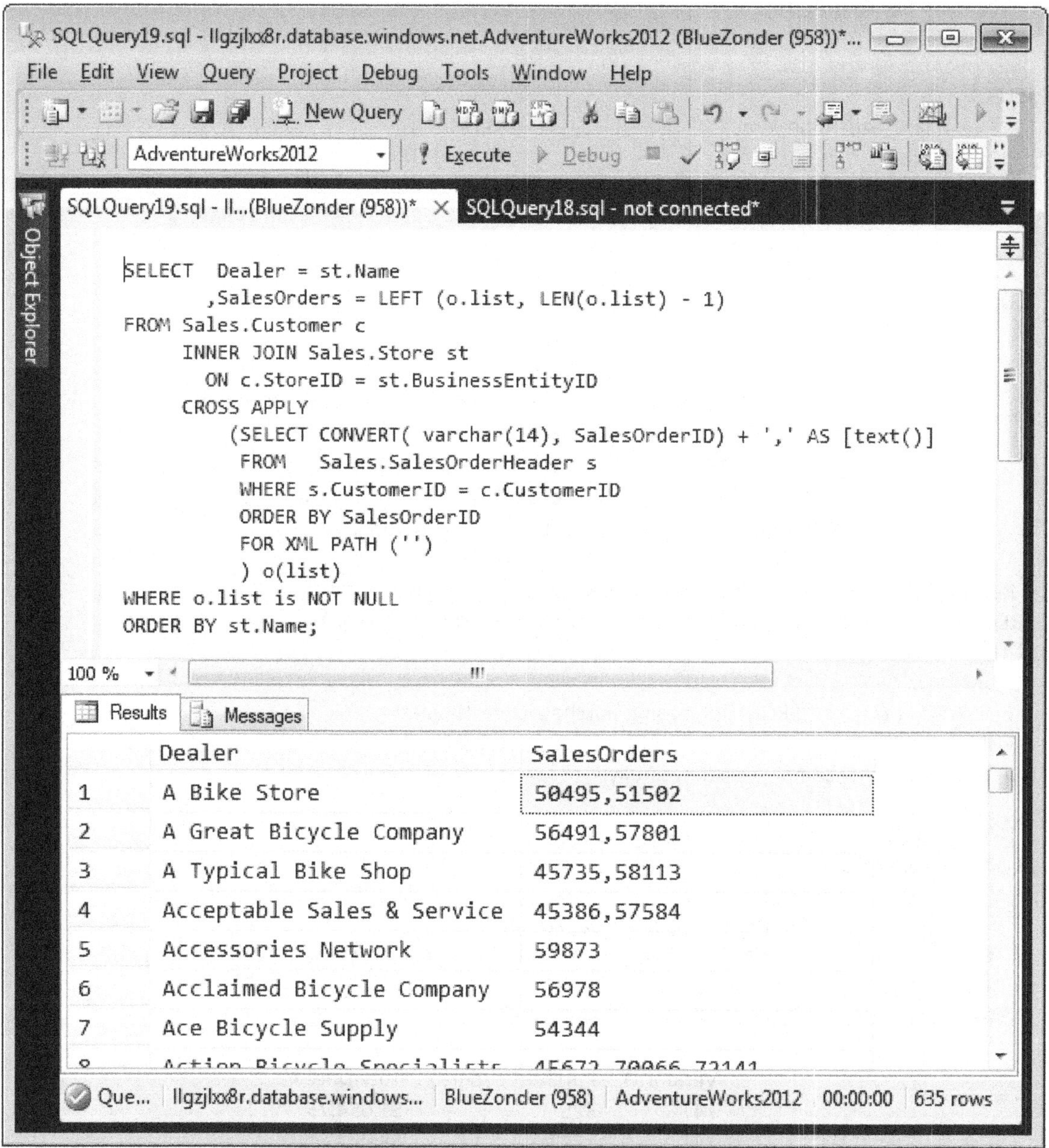

```
SELECT  Dealer = st.Name
       ,SalesOrders = LEFT (o.list, LEN(o.list) - 1)
FROM Sales.Customer c
     INNER JOIN Sales.Store st
       ON c.StoreID = st.BusinessEntityID
     CROSS APPLY
         (SELECT CONVERT( varchar(14), SalesOrderID) + ',' AS [text()]
          FROM   Sales.SalesOrderHeader s
          WHERE s.CustomerID = c.CustomerID
          ORDER BY SalesOrderID
          FOR XML PATH ('')
          ) o(list)
WHERE o.list is NOT NULL
ORDER BY st.Name;
```

	Dealer	SalesOrders
1	A Bike Store	50495,51502
2	A Great Bicycle Company	56491,57801
3	A Typical Bike Shop	45735,58113
4	Acceptable Sales & Service	45386,57584
5	Accessories Network	59873
6	Acclaimed Bicycle Company	56978
7	Ace Bicycle Supply	54344

CHAPTER 14: SELECT Statement Syntax with Examples

Simple SELECT Statement Variations

SELECT is the most famous statement in the SQL language. It is used to query tables, and generate reports for users. Although SQL Server Reporting Services and other 3rd party packages available for reporting purposes, frequently reports are generated straight from the database with SELECT queries. The next query returns all rows, all columns sorted on DepartmentID.

```
USE AdventureWorks2012;
```

```
SELECT * FROM   HumanResources.Department  ORDER BY DepartmentID;
-- (16 row(s) affected)
```

DepartmentID	Name	GroupName	ModifiedDate
1	Engineering	Research and Development	1998-06-01 00:00:00.000
2	Tool Design	Research and Development	1998-06-01 00:00:00.000
3	Sales	Sales and Marketing	1998-06-01 00:00:00.000
4	Marketing	Sales and Marketing	1998-06-01 00:00:00.000
5	Purchasing	Inventory Management	1998-06-01 00:00:00.000
6	Research and Development	Research and Development	1998-06-01 00:00:00.000
7	Production	Manufacturing	1998-06-01 00:00:00.000
8	Production Control	Manufacturing	1998-06-01 00:00:00.000
9	Human Resources	Executive General and Administration	1998-06-01 00:00:00.000
10	Finance	Executive General and Administration	1998-06-01 00:00:00.000
11	Information Services	Executive General and Administration	1998-06-01 00:00:00.000
12	Document Control	Quality Assurance	1998-06-01 00:00:00.000
13	Quality Assurance	Quality Assurance	1998-06-01 00:00:00.000
14	Facilities and Maintenance	Executive General and Administration	1998-06-01 00:00:00.000
15	Shipping and Receiving	Inventory Management	1998-06-01 00:00:00.000
16	Executive	Executive General and Administration	1998-06-01 00:00:00.000

Since the time part of ModifiedDate is not being used, and that makes business sense, we can format it just as date.)

```
SELECT TOP (3) DepartmentID, Name, GroupName, CONVERT(DATE, ModifiedDate) AS ModifiedDate
FROM   HumanResources.Department  ORDER BY DepartmentID;
-- (16 row(s) affected)
```

DepartmentID	Name	GroupName	ModifiedDate
1	Engineering	Research and Development	1998-06-01
2	Tool Design	Research and Development	1998-06-01
3	Sales	Sales and Marketing	1998-06-01

SELECT query with sort on EnglishProductName in DESCending order

ASCending sort is the default.

```
USE AdventureWorksDW2012
GO
```

```
SELECT   *
FROM     DimProduct
ORDER BY EnglishProductName DESC
GO
-- (606 row(s) affected) - Partial results.
```

EnglishProductName	SpanishProductName	FrenchProductName	StandardCost
Women's Tights, S	Mallas para mujer, P	Collants pour femmes, taille S	30.9334
Women's Tights, M	Mallas para mujer, M	Collants pour femmes, taille M	30.9334
Women's Tights, L	Mallas para mujer, G	Collants pour femmes, taille L	30.9334
Women's Mountain Shorts, S			26.1763
Women's Mountain Shorts, M			26.1763
Women's Mountain Shorts, L			26.1763
Water Bottle - 30 oz.			1.8663
Touring-Panniers, Large	Cesta de paseo, grande	Sacoches de vélo de randonnée, grande capacité	51.5625
Touring-3000 Yellow, 62	Paseo: 3000, amarilla, 62	Vélo de randonnée 3000 jaune, 62	461.4448
Touring-3000 Yellow, 58	Paseo: 3000, amarilla, 58	Vélo de randonnée 3000 jaune, 58	461.4448

The next query sorts on the SpanishProductName column in ascending order.

```
SELECT   *
FROM     DimProduct
ORDER BY SpanishProductName ASC
GO
-- (606 row(s) affected) - Partial results.
```

EnglishProductName	SpanishProductName
HL Crankset	Bielas GA
LL Crankset	Bielas GB
ML Crankset	Bielas GM
Mountain Pump	Bomba de montaña
Cable Lock	Cable antirrobo
Chain	Cadena
Mountain Bike Socks,	Calcetines para bicicleta de montaña, G

Sorting on FrenchProductName, if empty, use EnglishProductName.

```
SELECT   * FROM     DimProduct ORDER BY FrenchProductName, EnglishProductName;
GO
```

Using the TOP Clause in SELECT Queries

The TOP clause limits the number of rows returned as specified in the TOP expression according the sorted order if any. In the following query, the sorting is based on a major key (LastName) and a minor key (FirstName).

```
USE AdventureWorks2012
GO
```

```
SELECT  TOP 100 *
FROM    Person.Person ORDER BY LastName, FirstName
-- (100 row(s) affected) - Partial results.
```

BusinessEntityID	PersonType	Title	FirstName	LastName	EmailPromotion
285	SP	Mr.	Syed	Abbas	0
293	SC	Ms.	Catherine	Abel	1
295	SC	Ms.	Kim	Abercrombie	0
2170	GC	NULL	Kim	Abercrombie	2
38	EM	NULL	Kim	Abercrombie	2
211	EM	NULL	Hazem	Abolrous	0
2357	GC	NULL	Sam	Abolrous	1
297	SC	Sr.	Humberto	Acevedo	2
291	SC	Mr.	Gustavo	Achong	2
299	SC	Sra.	Pilar	Ackerman	0

The total population of the Person.Person table is 19,972 rows.

```
SELECT  * FROM   Person.Person ORDER BY LastName, FirstName
-- (19972 row(s) affected)
```

We can also count the rows applying the COUNT function.

```
SELECT  RowsCount = count(*)  FROM   Person.Person
-- 19972
```

When counting, it is safe to count the PRIMARY KEY (ProductID) values.

```
SELECT  RowsCount = count(ProductID)  FROM   Production.Product;
-- 504
```

```
SELECT  RowsCount = count(Color)  FROM   Production.Product;     -- 256
```

Using the WHERE Clause in SELECT Queries

The WHERE clause filters the rows to be returned according the one or more predicates. The next T-SQL scripts demonstrate simple WHERE clause predicates, including multiple WHERE conditions.

```
-- Last name starts with S
SELECT *
FROM    Person.Person
WHERE   LEFT(LastName,1) = 'S'
ORDER BY LastName;
-- (2130 row(s) affected)
```

```
-- First name is Shelly
SELECT  *
FROM    Person.Person
WHERE   FirstName = 'Shelly'
ORDER BY LastName;
-- (1 row(s) affected)
```

```
-- First name is John
SELECT  *
FROM    Person.Person
WHERE   FirstName = 'John'
ORDER BY LastName;
-- (58 row(s) affected)
```

```
-- First name John, last name starts with S - Multiple WHERE conditions
SELECT  *
FROM    Person.Person
WHERE   FirstName = 'John'
        AND LEFT(LastName,1) = 'S'
ORDER BY LastName ;
-- (2 row(s) affected)
```

```
-- Last name starts with S OR first name starts with J
SELECT  *
FROM    Person.Person
WHERE   LEFT(FirstName,1) = 'J'   OR LEFT(LastName,1) = 'S'
ORDER BY LastName;
-- (4371 row(s) affected)
```

```
-- Last name starts with S AND first name starts with J
SELECT  *
FROM    Person.Person  WHERE    LEFT(FirstName,1) = 'J'    AND LEFT(LastName,1) = 'S'
ORDER BY LastName;    -- (221 row(s) affected)
```

Using Literals in SELECT Queries

Literals or constants are used commonly in T-SQL queries, also as defaults for columns, local variables, and parameters. The format of a literal depends on the data type of the value it represents. The database engine may perform implicit conversion to match data types. Explicit conversion of literals can be achieved with the CONVERT or CAST functions. T-SQL scripts demonstrate literal use in WHERE clause predicates.

```
USE AdventureWorks2012;
-- Integer literal  in WHERE clause predicate
SELECT * FROM Production.Product
WHERE ProductID = 800;
-- (1 row(s) affected)
```

```
-- String literal in WHERE clause predicate
SELECT * FROM Production.Product WHERE Color = 'Blue';
-- (26 row(s) affected)
```

```
USE AdventureWorksDW2012;
-- UNICODE (2 bytes per character) string literal
SELECT * FROM DimProduct
WHERE SpanishProductName = N'Jersey clásico de manga corta, G';
-- (1 row(s) affected)
```

```
-- UNICODE string literal
SELECT * FROM DimProduct
WHERE FrenchProductName = N'Roue arrière de vélo de randonnée';
-- (1 row(s) affected)
```

```
USE AdventureWorks2012;
-- Money literal in WHERE clause predicate
SELECT * FROM Production.Product
WHERE ListPrice > = $2000.0;
-- (35 row(s) affected)
```

```
-- Floating point literal with implicit conversion to MONEY
SELECT * FROM Production.Product  WHERE ListPrice > = 2.000E+3;
-- (35 row(s) affected)
```

```
-- Hex (binary) literal
SELECT * FROM Production.Product  WHERE rowguid >= 0x23D89CEE9F444F3EB28963DE6BA2B737
-- (302 row(s) affected)
```

```
-- The rest of the 504 products
SELECT * FROM Production.Product  WHERE rowguid < 0x23D89CEE9F444F3EB28963DE6BA2B737
-- (202 row(s) affected)
```

Date & Time Literals in SELECT Queries

Date and time literals appear to come from an infinite pool. Every country has tens of string date & time variations. Despite the many external string representation, **date, datetime, datetime, time, smalldatetime** and other temporal data types have unique, well-defined representation within the database engine.

ymd date literal format is the cleanest. There is eternal confusion about the North American mdy string date format and the European dmy string date format. The date and time format with "T" separator (last one) is the ISO date time format literal. ANSI Date literal - YYYYMMDD - the best choice since it work in any country.

CONVERT or CAST Date Time Literal	Result
SELECT [Date] = CAST('20160228' AS date)	2016-02-28
SELECT [Datetime] = CAST('20160228' AS datetime)	2016-02-28 00:00:00.000
SELECT [SmallDatetime] = CAST('20160228' AS smalldatetime)	2016-02-28 00:00:00
SELECT [Datetime] = CONVERT(datetime,'2016-02-28')	2016-02-28 00:00:00.000
SELECT [Datetime2] = CONVERT(datetime2,'2016-02-28')	2016-02-28 00:00:00.0000000
SELECT [Datetime] = CONVERT(datetime, '20160228')	2016-02-28 00:00:00.000
SELECT [Datetime2] = CONVERT(datetime2,'20160228')	2016-02-28 00:00:00.0000000
SELECT [Datetime] = CAST('Mar 15, 2016' AS datetime)	2016-03-15 00:00:00.000
SELECT [Datetime2] = CAST('Mar 15, 2016' AS datetime2)	2016-03-15 00:00:00.0000000
SELECT [Date] = CAST('Mar 15, 2016' AS date)	2016-03-15
SELECT CAST('16:40:31' AS datetime)	1900-01-01 16:40:31.000
SELECT CAST('16:40:31' AS time)	16:40:31.0000000
SELECT [Datetime] = CAST('Mar 15, 2016 12:07:34.444' AS datetime)	2016-03-15 12:07:34.443
SELECT [Datetime2] = CAST('Mar 15, 2016 12:07:34.4445555' AS datetime2)	2016-03-15 12:07:34.4445555
SELECT [Datetime] = CAST('2016-03-15T12:07:34.513' AS datetime)	2016-03-15 12:07:34.513

ymd, dmy & mdy String Date Format Literals

Date and time string literals are the least understood part of the T-SQL language by database developers. It is a constant source of confusion and frustration, in addition huge economic cost of lost programmer's productivity. ymd, dmy & mdy are the main string date formats. Some countries use ydm format. Setting dateformat overrides the implicit setting by language.

The basic principles:

- **There is only one DATETIME data type internal format**, independent where SQL Server is operated: New York, London, Amsterdam, Berlin, Moscow, Hong Kong, Singapore, Tokyo, Melbourne or Rio de Janeiro.
- There are hundreds of national string date & time formats which have nothing to do with SQL Server.
- String date must be properly converted to DATETIME format.

```
SET DATEFORMAT ymd
SELECT convert(datetime,'16/05/08')                    -- 2016-05-08 00:00:00.000
```

```
-- Setting DATEFORMAT to UK-Style (European)
SET DATEFORMAT dmy
SELECT convert(datetime,'20/05/16')                    -- 2016-05-20 00:00:00.000
```

```
-- Setting DATEFORMAT to US-Style
SET DATEFORMAT mdy
SELECT convert(datetime,'05/20/16')                    -- 2016-05-20 00:00:00.000
SELECT convert(datetime,'05/20/2016')                  -- 2016-05-20 00:00:00.000
```

Interestingly we can achieve the same implicit conversion action by setting language.

```
-- Setting DATEFORMAT ymd  via language
SET LANGUAGE Japanese;  SELECT convert(datetime,'16/05/08') ;        -- 2016-05-08 00:00:00.000
```

```
-- Setting DATEFORMAT to UK-Style (European) via language
SET LANGUAGE British;  SELECT convert(datetime,'20/05/16');          -- 2016-05-20 00:00:00.000
SELECT convert(datetime,'05/20/16');
/* Msg 242, Level 16, State 3, Line 3
The conversion of a varchar data type to a datetime data type resulted in an out-of-range value.  */
```

```
-- Setting DATEFORMAT to US-Style via language
SET LANGUAGE English;  SELECT convert(datetime,'05/20/16');          -- 2016-05-20 00:00:00.000
SELECT convert(datetime,'05/20/2016');                 -- 2016-05-20 00:00:00.000
SELECT convert(datetime,'20/05/2016');
/* Msg 242, Level 16, State 3, Line 4
The conversion of a varchar data type to a datetime data type resulted in an out-of-range value.  */
```

Setting DATEFIRST with Literal

DATEFIRST indicates the first day of the week which may vary by country, culture or business. The next T-SQL script demonstrates how it can be set by integer literal 1-7. It overrides the implicit setting by language. @@DATEFIRST is a system (SQL Server database engine) variable.

```
SET DATEFIRST 7 -- Sunday as first day of the week
SELECT DATEPART(dw, '20160315');                    -- 3
SELECT DATENAME(dw, '20160315');                    -- Tuesday
SELECT @@DATEFIRST                                  -- 7
```

```
SET DATEFIRST 1 -- Monday as first day of the week
SELECT DATEPART(dw, '20160315');                    -- 2
SELECT DATENAME(dw, '20160315');                    -- Tuesday
SELECT @@DATEFIRST                                  -- 1
```

Language Setting - SET LANGUAGE

DATEFIRST is tied to the language setting, just the like the date format (ymd, dmy, or mdy).

```
SET LANGUAGE us_english
SELECT DATEPART(dw, '20160315');                    -- 3
SELECT DATENAME(dw, '20160315');                    -- Tuesday
SELECT @@DATEFIRST                                  -- 7
```

```
SET LANGUAGE german
SELECT DATEPART(dw, '20160315');                    -- 2
SELECT DATENAME(dw, '20160315');                    -- Dienstag
SELECT @@DATEFIRST                                  -- 1
```

```
SET LANGUAGE british
SELECT DATEPART(dw, '20160315');                    -- 2
SELECT DATENAME(dw, '20160315');                    -- Tuesday
SELECT @@DATEFIRST                                  -- 1
```

```
SET LANGUAGE hungarian
SELECT DATEPART(dw, '20160315');                    -- 2
SELECT DATENAME(dw, '20160315');                    -- kedd
SELECT @@DATEFIRST                                  -- 1
```

```
SET LANGUAGE spanish
SELECT DATEPART(dw, '20160315');                    -- 2
SELECT DATENAME(dw, '20160315');                    -- Martes
SELECT @@DATEFIRST                                  -- 1
```

The sys.syslanguages System View

The syslanguages table contains not only language related information, but date related settings as well.

```
SELECT
        langid,
        dateformat,
        datefirst,
        name                                            AS native_language,
        alias                                           AS english,
        left(shortmonths, 15)                           AS shortmonths,
        left(days,15)                                   AS days
FROM sys.syslanguages
ORDER BY langid;
GO
-- (34 row(s) affected)  -  Partial results.
```

langid	dateformat	datefirst	native_language	english	shortmonths	days
0	mdy	7	us_english	English	Jan,Feb,Mar,Apr	Monday,Tuesday,
1	dmy	1	Deutsch	German	Jan,Feb,Mär,Apr	Montag,Dienstag
2	dmy	1	Français	French	janv,févr,mars,	lundi,mardi,mer
3	ymd	7	日本語	Japanese	01,02,03,04,05,	月曜日,火曜日,水曜日,木曜日
4	dmy	1	Dansk	Danish	jan,feb,mar,apr	mandag,tirsdag,
5	dmy	1	Español	Spanish	Ene,Feb,Mar,Abr	Lunes,Martes,Mi
6	dmy	1	Italiano	Italian	gen,feb,mar,apr	lunedì,martedì,
7	dmy	1	Nederlands	Dutch	jan,feb,mrt,apr	maandag,dinsdag
8	dmy	1	Norsk	Norwegian	jan,feb,mar,apr	mandag,tirsdag,
9	dmy	7	Português	Portuguese	jan,fev,mar,abr	segunda-feira,t
10	dmy	1	Suomi	Finnish	tammi,helmi,maa	maanantai,tiist
11	ymd	1	Svenska	Swedish	jan,feb,mar,apr	måndag,tisdag,o
12	dmy	1	čeština	Czech	I,II,III,IV,V,V	pondělí,úterý,s
13	ymd	1	magyar	Hungarian	jan,febr,márc,á	hétfő,kedd,szer
14	dmy	1	polski	Polish	I,II,III,IV,V,V	poniedziałek,wt
15	dmy	1	română	Romanian	Ian,Feb,Mar,Apr	luni,marţi,mier
16	ymd	1	hrvatski	Croatian	sij,vel,ožu,tra	ponedjeljak,uto
17	dmy	1	slovenčina	Slovak	I,II,III,IV,V,V	pondelok,utorok
18	dmy	1	slovenski	Slovenian	jan,feb,mar,apr	ponedeljek,tore
19	dmy	1	ελληνικά	Greek	Ιαν,Φεβ,Μαρ,Απρ	Δευτέρα,Τρίτη,Τ
20	dmy	1	български	Bulgarian	януари,февруари	понеделник,втор
21	dmy	1	русский	Russian	янв,фев,мар,апр	понедельник,вто
22	dmy	1	Türkçe	Turkish	Oca,Şub,Mar,Nis	Pazartesi,Salı,
23	dmy	1	British	British English	Jan,Feb,Mar,Apr	Monday,Tuesday,
24	dmy	1	eesti	Estonian	jaan,veebr,märt	esmaspäev,teisi
25	ymd	1	latviešu	Latvian	jan,feb,mar,apr	pirmdiena,otrdi
26	ymd	1	lietuvių	Lithuanian	sau,vas,kov,bal	pirmadienis,ant
27	dmy	7	Português (Brasil)	Brazilian	Jan,Fev,Mar,Abr	Segunda-Feira,T
28	ymd	7	繁體中文	Traditional Chinese	01,02,03,04,05,	星期一,星期二,星期三,星期四
29	ymd	7	한국어	Korean	01,02,03,04,05,	월요일,화요일,수요일,목요일
30	ymd	7	简体中文	Simplified Chinese	01,02,03,04,05,	星期一,星期二,星期三,星期四
31	dmy	1	Arabic	Arabic	Jan,Feb,Mar,Apr	Monday,Tuesday,
32	dmy	7	ไทย	Thai	ม.ค.,ก.พ.,มี.ค.	จันทร์,อังคาร,พ
33	dmy	1	norsk (bokmål)	Bokmål	jan,feb,mar,apr	mandag,tirsdag,

Determining SET Options

The DBCC USEROPTIONS command is not supported in Azure SQL. @@OPTIONS system variable and the sys.dm_exec_sessions DMV can be used to determine options settings.

```
-- Check an option setting
SELECT CONCAT('isolation level ', CASE transaction_isolation_level
          WHEN 0 THEN 'unspecified'
          WHEN 1 THEN 'read uncommitted'
          WHEN 2 THEN 'read committed'
          WHEN 3 THEN 'repeatable read'
          WHEN 4 THEN 'serializable'
          WHEN 5 THEN 'snapshot' END) AS transaction_isolation_level
FROM sys.dm_exec_sessions
where session_id = @@SPID;
GO
-- isolation level read committed
```

```
-- SET isolation level option
SET transaction isolation level serializable;
```

```
-- Determine some of the options
SELECT text_size, language, date_format, date_first,
          CASE WHEN quoted_identifier = 1 THEN 'SET' ELSE '' END AS [quoted_identifier]
FROM sys.dm_exec_sessions
where session_id = @@SPID;
GO
```

text_size	language	date_format	date_first	quoted_identifier
2147483647	us_english	mdy	7	SET

```
-- Change Query Results to Text
SELECT * FROM sys.dm_exec_sessions where session_id = @@SPID;
```

```
session_id login_time   host_name   program_name    host_process_id client_version client_interface_name
 security_id   login_name      nt_domain nt_user_name      status   context_info    cpu_time
 memory_usage total_scheduled_time total_elapsed_time endpoint_id last_request_start_time
last_request_end_time
 reads   writes  logical_reads   is_user_process text_size  language   date_format date_first quoted_identifier
 arithabort ansi_null_dflt_on ansi_defaults ansi_warnings ansi_padding ansi_nulls concat_null_yields_null
 transaction_isolation_level lock_timeout deadlock_priority row_count  prev_error  original_security_id
 original_login_name      last_successful_logon   last_unsuccessful_logon unsuccessful_logons  group_id
 database_id authenticating_database_id open_transaction_count is_filtered
........
```

Easy SELECT Queries for Fun & Learning

T-SQL scripts to demonstrate simple, easy-to-read SELECT query variations. Important note: alias column names cannot be reused in successive computed columns by expressions or anywhere else in the query except the ORDER BY clause.

```
-- Datetime range with string literal date
SELECT  * FROM   Person.Person
WHERE   ModifiedDate <= '2002-08-09 00:00:00.000'  ORDER BY LastName;
-- (38 row(s) affected)
```

NOTE

The string literal above looks like datetime, but it is not. It is only a string literal. The database engine will try to convert it to datetime data type at runtime (implicit conversion), and if successful the query will be executed.
The syntax of the following query is OK, however, it will fail at execution time.

```
SELECT  * FROM   Person.Person  WHERE   ModifiedDate <= 'New York City'  ORDER BY LastName;
/* Msg 241, Level 16, State 1, Line 1 Conversion failed when converting date and/or time from character
string. */
```

```
-- Complimentary (remaining) datetime range specified again with string literal
SELECT * FROM   Person.Person  WHERE   ModifiedDate > '2002-08-09 00:00:00.000'  ORDER BY
LastName;
-- (19934 row(s) affected)
```

```
-- Total rows in Person.Person
SELECT ( 38 + 19934 ) AS TotalRows;   -- 19972
```

```
SELECT count(* ) FROM  Person.Person -- 19972
```

```
SELECT TableRows = count(* ),  Calc = 38 + 19934  FROM  Person.Person; -- 19972     19972
```

```
-- Get prefix left of comma or entire string if there is no comma present
SELECT TOP 4                                                              ProductNumber,
        LEFT(Name, COALESCE(NULLIF(CHARINDEX(',',Name)-1,-1),LEN(Name)))  AS NamePrefix,
        Name                                                              AS ProductName
FROM Production.Product   WHERE CHARINDEX(',',Name) > 0
ORDER BY ProductName;
```

ProductNumber	NamePrefix	ProductName
VE-C304-L	Classic Vest	Classic Vest, L
VE-C304-M	Classic Vest	Classic Vest, M
VE-C304-S	Classic Vest	Classic Vest, S
GL-F110-L	Full-Finger Gloves	Full-Finger Gloves, L

NULL refers to no information available. Note: "=" and "!=" operators are not used with NULL; "IS" or "IS NOT" operators are applicable.

```
SELECT *
FROM    Person.Person
WHERE   AdditionalContactInfo IS NOT NULL
ORDER BY LastName;
-- (10 row(s) affected)
```

```
SELECT *
FROM    Person.Person
WHERE   AdditionalContactInfo IS NULL
ORDER BY LastName;
-- (19962 row(s) affected)
```

```
SELECT   DISTINCT FirstName
FROM    Person.Person
ORDER BY FirstName;     -- (1018 row(s) affected)
```

```
-- Summary revenue by product, interesting sort
USE AdventureWorks2012;
GO
SELECT  TOP 10 p.Name                                          AS ProductName,
  FORMAT(SUM(((OrderQty * UnitPrice) * (1.0 - UnitPriceDiscount))),'c','en-US') AS SubTotal
FROM Production.Product AS p
INNER JOIN Sales.SalesOrderDetail AS sod
ON p.ProductID = sod.ProductID
GROUP BY p.Name
ORDER BY REVERSE(p.Name);
```

ProductName	SubTotal
Water Bottle - 30 oz.	$28,654.16
Hydration Pack - 70 oz.	$105,826.42
LL Mountain Frame - Black, 40	$1,198.99
ML Mountain Frame - Black, 40	$14,229.41
Mountain-300 Black, 40	$501,648.88
Mountain-500 Black, 40	$101,734.12
LL Mountain Frame - Silver, 40	$69,934.28
ML Mountain Frame-W - Silver, 40	$195,826.39
Mountain-500 Silver, 40	$145,089.43
Mountain-400-W Silver, 40	$323,703.82

DISTINCT & GROUP BY operations are generally "expensive".

```
SELECT   DISTINCT LastName FROM    Person.Person ORDER BY LastName;  -- (1206 row(s) affected)
```

```
-- LastName popularity descending
SELECT LastName,      Frequency = count(* )
FROM     Person.Person
GROUP BY LastName
ORDER BY Frequency DESC;
GO
```

LastName	Frequency
Diaz	211
Hernandez	188
Sanchez	175
Martinez	173
Torres	172
Martin	171
Perez	170
Gonzalez	169
Lopez	168
Rodriguez	166

```
-- Sort on column not in SELECT list - Note: demo only, confusing to end user
SELECT   LastName
FROM     Person.Person
ORDER BY FirstName;
-- (19972 row(s) affected)
```

```
-- Sort on column not in SELECT list
SELECT   Name = CONCAT(LastName, ', ', FirstName )
FROM     Person.Person
ORDER BY LastName;
-- (19972 row(s) affected)
```

```
-- Sort on column alias
SELECT   Name = CONCAT(LastName, ', ', FirstName )
FROM     Person.Person
ORDER BY Name;
-- (19972 row(s) affected)
```

```
SELECT   CONCAT(LastName, ', ', FirstName ) AS FullName
FROM     Person.Person
WHERE    LastName >= 'K'  ORDER BY LastName;
-- (12057 row(s) affected)
```

The NULLIF Function Actually Creates A NULL

```
SELECT   CONCAT(LastName, ', ', FirstName )  AS FullName
FROM     Person.Person  WHERE    LastName < 'K'  ORDER BY LastName;
-- (7915 row(s) affected)
```

```
-- Cardinality check
SELECT Difference= ((count(*)) - (12057 + 7915)) FROM  Person.Person; -- 0
```

```
-- Using the NULLIF function in counting
-- Count of all list prices - no NULLs in column
SELECT COUNT(ListPrice) FROM   Production.Product
-- 504
```

```
-- Counts only when ListPrice != 0 - does not count NULLs (ListPrice = 0.0)
SELECT COUNT(NULLIF(ListPrice,0.0)) FROM   Production.Product
-- 304
```

```
SELECT COUNT(ListPrice)   FROM   Production.Product   WHERE ListPrice = 0;
-- 200
```

Cardinality of DISTINCT & GROUP BY Clauses

The cardinality of DISTINCT and the cardinality of GROUP BY are the same with the same column(s).

```
-- FirstName by popularity descending
SELECT FirstName,
          Freq = count(* )
FROM     Person.Person
GROUP BY FirstName
ORDER BY Freq DESC;
-- (1018 row(s) affected)
```

FirstName	Freq
Richard	103
Katherine	99
Marcus	97
James	97
Jennifer	96
Dalton	93
Lucas	93
Alexandra	93
Morgan	92
Seth	92

```
SELECT   DISTINCT FirstName  FROM    Person.Person  ORDER BY FirstName;  -- (1018 row(s) affected)
```

Column Alias Can only Be Used in ORDER BY

Column aliases cannot be used in other computed columns (expressions), neither in the WHERE clause or GROUP BY clause.

```
SELECT  TableRows = count(* ),
        Calculated = 38 + 19934,
        Difference = (count(*) - 38 - 19934)
FROM  Person.Person;
```

TableRows	Calculated	Difference
19972	19972	0

Workarounds for Column Alias Use Restriction

There is a simple workaround for recycling column aliases in other clauses than just the ORDER BY: make the query into a derived table (x) and include it in an outer query. Similarly, CTEs can be used instead of derived tables.

```
-- Derived table workaround
SELECT TableRows, Calculated, Difference = TableRows - Calculated
FROM (
        SELECT  TableRows = count(* ),     Calculated = 38 + 19934,
        FROM  Person.Person
        ) x ;  -- Derived table
GO
```

TableRows	Calculated	Difference
19972	19972	0

```
-- CTE workaround
;WITH CTE AS (
        SELECT  TableRows = count(* ),     Calculated = 38 + 19934
        FROM  Person.Person)
-- Outer query
SELECT TableRows, Calculated, Difference = TableRows - Calculated
FROM CTE;
```

TableRows	Calculated	Difference
19972	19972	0

When the Clock Strikes Midnight: datetime Behaviour

This is one of the most troublesome issues in T-SQL programming (midnight bug, Cinderella syndrom): the predicate YYYYMMDD (date string literal) = DatetimeColumn does not include the entire day, only records with time at midnight: 00:00:00.000 .

```
USE AdventureWorks2012;

-- Note: only midnight 2003-08-09 included
-- Even a second after midnight is not included like 2003-08-09 00:00:01.000
SELECT  *
FROM    Person.Person
WHERE       ModifiedDate BETWEEN '2002-08-09 00:00:00.000'
            AND '2003-08-09 00:00:00.000'
ORDER BY LastName;
GO
-- (396 row(s) affected)
```

```
-- Entire day of 2003-08-09 included
-- The count same as before because no records after midnight 2003-08-09
SELECT  *
FROM    Person.Person
WHERE      ModifiedDate >= '2002-08-09 00:00:00.000'
           AND ModifiedDate <  '2003-08-10 00:00:00.000'
ORDER BY LastName;
GO
-- (396 row(s) affected)
```

LEFT(), RIGHT() & SUBSTRING() String Functions

```
SELECT   FirstCharOfFirstName = LEFT(FirstName,1),                    -- column alias
         FirstCharOfLastName  = LEFT(LastName,1),                     -- column alias
        LastCharOfLastName  = RIGHT(LastName,1),                      -- column alias
         FullName = CONCAT(FirstName, SPACE(1), LastName) ,           -- column alias
         *                                                            -- wild card, all columns
FROM     Person.Person
WHERE   SUBSTRING(FirstName,1,1) = 'J'
      AND SUBSTRING (LastName,1,1) = 'S'
      AND (RIGHT(LastName,1) = 'H' OR RIGHT(LastName,1) = 'Z')
ORDER BY LastName;
-- (59 row(s) affected) - Partial result.
```

FirstCharOfFirstName	FirstCharOfLastName	LastCharOfLastName	FullName	BusinessEntityID
J	S	z	Jacqueline Sanchez	8975
J	S	z	Jada Sanchez	9499
J	S	z	Jade Sanchez	9528
J	S	z	Janelle Sanchez	18590
J	S	z	Jared Sanchez	15266
J	S	z	Jarrod Sanchez	2948
J	S	z	Jay Sanchez	10298
J	S	z	Jennifer Sanchez	20440
J	S	z	Jeremiah Sanchez	15292
J	S	z	Jermaine Sanchez	8040

```
-- Sort on first column
SELECT BusinessEntityID, JobTitle, SUBSTRING(JobTitle, 5, 7)  AS MiddleOfJobTitle
FROM   HumanResources.Employee
WHERE  BirthDate <= '1960-12-31'     -- date literal (constant)
ORDER BY 1;
-- (27 row(s) affected) - Partial results.
```

BusinessEntityID	JobTitle	MiddleOfJobTitle
5	Design Engineer	gn Engi
6	Design Engineer	gn Engi
12	Tool Designer	Design
15	Design Engineer	gn Engi
23	Marketing Specialist	eting S
27	Production Supervisor - WC60	uction

```
-- String functions usage in formatting
DECLARE @SSN char(9) = '123456789';
SELECT SSN=CONCAT(LEFT(@SSN,3),'-', SUBSTRING(@SSN,4,2),'-', RIGHT(@SSN,4));
-- 123-45-6789
```

ASCII value range is 0-127. Extended ASCII: 128-255. Size is 8-bit, one byte.

```
SELECT TOP 5    ProductNumber,
                SUBSTRING(ProductNumber,9,1)         AS MiddleSubstring,
                ASCII(SUBSTRING(ProductNumber,9,1))   AS ASCIIValue
FROM Production.Product
WHERE LEN(ProductNumber) > 8
ORDER BY Name;                          - OK syntax, but does not make sense
```

ProductNumber	MiddleSubstring	ASCIIValue
VE-C304-L	L	76
VE-C304-M	M	77
VE-C304-S	S	83
GL-F110-L	L	76
GL-F110-M	M	77

NOTE

Table columns and columns by expressions (computed) can be mixed in a query at will.

```
-- Computed (expressions) & table columns
SELECT FirstCharOfFirstName = LEFT(FirstName,1),          -- string expression
       FirstCharOfLastName  = LEFT(LastName,1),           -- string expression
       FullName = CONCAT(LastName, ', ', FirstName ),     -- string expression
       SquareOfID = SQUARE(BusinessEntityID),             -- math expression
       *                                                  -- wild card, all table columns
FROM   Person.Person
WHERE  LEFT(FirstName,1) = 'J'
   AND LEFT(LastName,2) = 'Sm'
ORDER BY FullName;
-- (14 row(s) affected)  - Partial results.
```

FirstCharOfFirstName	FirstCharOfLastName	FullName	SquareOfID	BusinessEntityID
J	S	Smith, Jacob	348680929	18673
J	S	Smith, James	308986084	17578
J	S	Smith, Jasmine	129572689	11383
J	S	Smith, Jeff	3139984	1772
J	S	Smith, Jennifer	122699929	11077
J	S	Smith, Jeremiah	20511841	4529
J	S	Smith, Jessica	145829776	12076
J	S	Smith, John	332041284	18222
J	S	Smith, Jonathan	312228900	17670
J	S	Smith, Jose	300710281	17341
J	S	Smith, Joseph	357474649	18907
J	S	Smith, Joshua	351825049	18757
J	S	Smith, Julia	121616784	11028
J	S	Smith, Justin	324900625	18025

Transact-SQL Reserved Keywords

List of reserved keywords in SQL Server 2012 Transact-SQL. Keywords can only be used as delimited identifiers such as [Inner] or "Order".

ADD	EXTERNAL	PROCEDURE
ALL	FETCH	PUBLIC
ALTER	FILE	RAISERROR
AND	FILLFACTOR	READ
ANY	FOR	READTEXT
AS	FOREIGN	RECONFIGURE
ASC	FREETEXT	REFERENCES
AUTHORIZATION	FREETEXTTABLE	REPLICATION
BACKUP	FROM	RESTORE
BEGIN	FULL	RESTRICT
BETWEEN	FUNCTION	RETURN
BREAK	GOTO	REVERT
BROWSE	GRANT	REVOKE
BULK	GROUP	RIGHT
BY	HAVING	ROLLBACK
CASCADE	HOLDLOCK	ROWCOUNT
CASE	IDENTITY	ROWGUIDCOL
CHECK	IDENTITY_INSERT	RULE
CHECKPOINT	IDENTITYCOL	SAVE
CLOSE	IF	SCHEMA
CLUSTERED	IN	SECURITYAUDIT
COALESCE	INDEX	SELECT
COLLATE	INNER	SEMANTICKEYPHRASETABLE
COLUMN	INSERT	SEMANTICSIMILARITYDETAILSTABLE
COMMIT	INTERSECT	SEMANTICSIMILARITYTABLE
COMPUTE	INTO	SESSION_USER
CONSTRAINT	IS	SET
CONTAINS	JOIN	SETUSER
CONTAINSTABLE	KEY	SHUTDOWN
CONTINUE	KILL	SOME
CONVERT	LEFT	STATISTICS
CREATE	LIKE	SYSTEM_USER
CROSS	LINENO	TABLE
CURRENT	LOAD	TABLESAMPLE
CURRENT_DATE	MERGE	TEXTSIZE
CURRENT_TIME	NATIONAL	THEN
CURRENT_TIMESTAMP	NOCHECK	TO
CURRENT_USER	NONCLUSTERED	TOP
CURSOR	NOT	TRAN
DATABASE	NULL	TRANSACTION
DBCC	NULLIF	TRIGGER
DEALLOCATE	OF	TRUNCATE
DECLARE	OFF	TRY_CONVERT
DEFAULT	OFFSETS	TSEQUAL
DELETE	ON	UNION
DENY	OPEN	UNIQUE
DESC	OPENDATASOURCE	UNPIVOT
DISK	OPENQUERY	UPDATE
DISTINCT	OPENROWSET	UPDATETEXT
DISTRIBUTED	OPENXML	USE
DOUBLE	OPTION	USER
DROP	OR	VALUES
DUMP	ORDER	VARYING
ELSE	OUTER	VIEW
END	OVER	WAITFOR
ERRLVL	PERCENT	WHEN
ESCAPE	PIVOT	WHERE
EXCEPT	PLAN	WHILE
EXEC	PRECISION	WITH
EXECUTE	PRIMARY	WITHIN GROUP
EXISTS	PRINT	WRITETEXT
EXIT	PROC	

Case Sensitive Sort with Latin1_General_CS_AI

For case sensitive sort on a column with case insensitive collation, we have use a case sensitive (CS) collation such as Latin1_General_CS_AI.

```
-- CASE INSENSITIVE sort using default collation
SELECT lname FROM
        (SELECT TOP 5 UPPER (LastName) AS lname FROM Person.Person ORDER BY FirstName) x
UNION ALL   SELECT lname FROM
        (SELECT TOP 5 LOWER (LastName) AS lname FROM Person.Person ORDER BY FirstName) y
ORDER BY lname;
-- ADAMS, adams, alexander, ALEXANDER, leonetti, LEONETTI, WRIGHT, WRIGHT, wright, wright
```

```
-- CASE SENSITIVE sort using %CS% collation
SELECT lname FROM ( SELECT lname FROM
   (SELECT TOP 5 UPPER (LastName) AS lname FROM Person.Person ORDER BY FirstName) x
   UNION ALL  SELECT lname FROM
   (SELECT TOP 5 LOWER (LastName) AS lname FROM Person.Person ORDER BY FirstName) y  ) z
ORDER BY lname COLLATE Latin1_General_CS_AI;
-- adams,ADAMS,alexander,ALEXANDER,leonetti,LEONETTI,wright,wright,WRIGHT,WRIGHT
```

The ORDER BY Clause for Sorting Query Results

The ORDER BY clause is located at the very end of the query. In fact the sorting itself takes place after the query executed and generated **an unordered result set**. Although frequently, especially for small sets, the results appear to be sorted, **only an ORDER BY clause can guarantee proper sorting**. INSERT, UPDATE, DELETE & MERGE statement do not support sorting, **the database engine performs all set operations unordered**. T-SQL scripts demonstrate the many variations of the ORDER BY clause.

```
USE AdventureWorks2012;
GO
```

```
-- A column can be used for sorting even though not explicitly used in the SELECT list
SELECT *
FROM   Production.Product
ORDER  BY Name ASC;
GO
```

```
-- Sort on the second column, whatever it may be
SELECT *
FROM   Production.Product
ORDER  BY 2 DESC;
GO
```

```
-- ASCending is the default sort order, it is not necessary to use
SELECT  Name AS ProductName,
        *
FROM   Production.Product
ORDER  BY ProductName ASC;
GO
```

```
SELECT  TOP (10) Name AS ProductName,              *
FROM   Production.Product   ORDER  BY 1 ASC;
```

ProductName	ProductID	Name	ProductNumber	MakeFlag	FinishedGoodsFlag	Color	SafetyStockLevel
Adjustable Race	1	Adjustable Race	AR-5381	0	0	NULL	1000
All-Purpose Bike Stand	879	All-Purpose Bike Stand	ST-1401	0	1	NULL	4
AWC Logo Cap	712	AWC Logo Cap	CA-1098	0	1	Multi	4
BB Ball Bearing	3	BB Ball Bearing	BE-2349	1	0	NULL	800
Bearing Ball	2	Bearing Ball	BA-8327	0	0	NULL	1000
Bike Wash - Dissolver	877	Bike Wash - Dissolver	CL-9009	0	1	NULL	4
Blade	316	Blade	BL-2036	1	0	NULL	800
Cable Lock	843	Cable Lock	LO-C100	0	1	NULL	4
Chain	952	Chain	CH-0234	0	1	Silver	500
Chain Stays	324	Chain Stays	CS-2812	1	0	NULL	1000

Using Column Alias in the ORDER BY Clause

Column alias can be used in an ORDER BY clause. In fact, it should be used to make the query more readable.

```
-- ProductName is a column alias, it can only be used in the ORDER BY clause, not anywhere before
SELECT ProductName = Name, *
FROM Production.Product
WHERE ProductName like '%glove%'
ORDER BY ProductName ASC ;
GO
/* ERROR
Msg 207, Level 16, State 1, Line 3
Invalid column name 'ProductName'.
*/
```

```
-- The TOP clause uses the ORDER BY sorting to select the 5 rows
SELECT TOP (5) ProductName = Name, *
FROM Production.Product
WHERE Name like '%glove%'
ORDER BY ProductName ASC ;
```

ProductName	ProductID	Name	ProductNumber	MakeFlag	FinishedGoodsFlag	Color	SafetyStockLevel
Full-Finger Gloves, L	863	Full-Finger Gloves, L	GL-F110-L	0	1	Black	4
Full-Finger Gloves, M	862	Full-Finger Gloves, M	GL-F110-M	0	1	Black	4
Full-Finger Gloves, S	861	Full-Finger Gloves, S	GL-F110-S	0	1	Black	4
Half-Finger Gloves, L	860	Half-Finger Gloves, L	GL-H102-L	0	1	Black	4
Half-Finger Gloves, M	859	Half-Finger Gloves, M	GL-H102-M	0	1	Black	4

```
-- Descending sort on name which is string data type
SELECT TOP (10) ProductName = Name, *
FROM Production.Product
WHERE Name like '%road%'
ORDER BY ProductName DESC ;
```

.

ProductName	ProductID	Name	ProductNumber	MakeFlag	FinishedGoodsFlag	Color	SafetyStockLevel
Road-750 Black, 58	977	Road-750 Black, 58	BK-R19B-58	1	1	Black	100
Road-750 Black, 52	999	Road-750 Black, 52	BK-R19B-52	1	1	Black	100
Road-750 Black, 48	998	Road-750 Black, 48	BK-R19B-48	1	1	Black	100
Road-750 Black, 44	997	Road-750 Black, 44	BK-R19B-44	1	1	Black	100
Road-650 Red, 62	761	Road-650 Red, 62	BK-R50R-62	1	1	Red	100
Road-650 Red, 60	760	Road-650 Red, 60	BK-R50R-60	1	1	Red	100
Road-650 Red, 58	759	Road-650 Red, 58	BK-R50R-58	1	1	Red	100
Road-650 Red, 52	764	Road-650 Red, 52	BK-R50R-52	1	1	Red	100
Road-650 Red, 48	763	Road-650 Red, 48	BK-R50R-48	1	1	Red	100
Road-650 Red, 44	762	Road-650 Red, 44	BK-R50R-44	1	1	Red	100

Using Table Alias in the ORDER BY Clause

Unlike the column alias, table alias can be used anywhere in the query within the scope of the alias.

```
-- Using table alias in ORDER BY
SELECT P.*
FROM   Production.Product P
ORDER  BY P.Name ASC;
GO
```

ProductID	Name	ProductNumber	MakeFlag	FinishedGoodsFlag	Color	SafetyStockLevel
958	Touring-3000 Blue, 54	BK-T18U-54	1	1	Blue	100
959	Touring-3000 Blue, 58	BK-T18U-58	1	1	Blue	100
960	Touring-3000 Blue, 62	BK-T18U-62	1	1	Blue	100
961	Touring-3000 Yellow, 44	BK-T18Y-44	1	1	Yellow	100
962	Touring-3000 Yellow, 50	BK-T18Y-50	1	1	Yellow	100
963	Touring-3000 Yellow, 54	BK-T18Y-54	1	1	Yellow	100
964	Touring-3000 Yellow, 58	BK-T18Y-58	1	1	Yellow	100
965	Touring-3000 Yellow, 62	BK-T18Y-62	1	1	Yellow	100
842	Touring-Panniers, Large	PA-T100	0	1	Grey	4
870	Water Bottle - 30 oz.	WB-H098	0	1	NULL	4
869	Women's Mountain Shorts, L	SH-W890-L	0	1	Black	4
868	Women's Mountain Shorts, M	SH-W890-M	0	1	Black	4
867	Women's Mountain Shorts, S	SH-W890-S	0	1	Black	4
854	Women's Tights, L	TG-W091-L	0	1	Black	4
853	Women's Tights, M	TG-W091-M	0	1	Black	4
852	Women's Tights, S	TG-W091-S	0	1	Black	4

```
-- Specific column list instead of all (*)
SELECT  Name,
        ProductNumber,
        ListPrice AS PRICE
FROM   Production.Product  P
ORDER  BY P.Name ASC;
GO
```

```
SELECT          Name,
                ProductNumber,
                ListPrice AS PRICE
FROM   Production.Product  P
ORDER  BY P.ListPrice DESC;
```

```
-- Equivalent to above with column alias usage
SELECT          Name,
                ProductNumber,
                ListPrice AS PRICE
FROM   Production.Product  P ORDER  BY PRICE DESC;
```

Easy ORDER BY Queries for Exercises

T-SQL scripts demonstrate easily readable queries with sorted result sets.

```
USE pubs ;
```

```
SELECT TYPE,   AvgPrice=FORMAT(AVG(price) , 'c', 'en-US')
FROM   titles WHERE  royalty = 10 GROUP  BY TYPE ORDER  BY TYPE ;
```

TYPE	AvgPrice
business	$17.31
popular_comp	$20.00
psychology	$14.14
trad_cook	$17.97

```
SELECT              type = type,
                    AvgPrice = FORMAT(AVG(price),'c', 'en-US')
FROM   titles  WHERE  royalty = 10  GROUP  BY type  ORDER  BY AvgPrice;
```

type	AvgPrice
psychology	$14.14
business	$17.31
trad_cook	$17.97
popular_comp	$20.00

```
SELECT   type                                   AS [type],
         FORMAT(AVG(price),'c', 'en-US')       AS AvgPrice
FROM   titles   GROUP  BY [type]  ORDER  BY [type] desc;
```

type	AvgPrice
UNDECIDED	NULL
trad_cook	$15.96
psychology	$13.50
popular_comp	$21.48
mod_cook	$11.49
business	$13.73

An Aggregate Function Can Be Used in an ORDER BY Clause

The NULL related warning message can be turned off: SET ANSI_WARNINGS OFF; alternately ISNULL function can be used in the query.

```
SELECT TYPE, AVG(price) Avg FROM titles  GROUP  BY TYPE ORDER  BY AVG(price);
/* Warning: Null value is eliminated by an aggregate or other SET operation.
(6 row(s) affected) */
```

Eliminate NULL in result with COALESCE or ISNULL functions

```
SELECT [type] = type,
       AvgPrice = COALESCE(FORMAT(AVG(price),'c', 'en-US') ,'')
FROM   titles  GROUP  BY [type]  ORDER  BY [type] desc;
```

type	AvgPrice
UNDECIDED	
trad_cook	$15.96
psychology	$13.50
popular_comp	$21.48
mod_cook	$11.49
business	$13.73

```
SELECT          pub_name                              Publisher,
                FORMAT(AVG(price),'c', 'en-US')       AvgPrice
FROM   titles
    INNER JOIN publishers
      ON  titles.pub_id = publishers.pub_id
GROUP  BY pub_name
ORDER  BY pub_name;
```

Publisher	AvgPrice
Algodata Infosystems	$18.98
Binnet & Hardley	$15.41
New Moon Books	$9.78

```
SELECT TOP(3) * FROM   titles ORDER  BY title;
```

title_id	title	type	pub_id	price	advance	royalty	ytd_sales	notes	pubdate
PC1035	But Is It User Friendly?	popular_comp	1389	22.95	7000.00	16	8780	A survey of software for the naive user, focusing on the 'friendliness' of each.	1991-06-30 00:00:00.000
PS1372	Computer Phobic AND Non-Phobic Individuals: Behavior Variations	psychology	0877	21.59	7000.00	10	375	A must for the specialist, this book examines the difference between those who hate and fear computers and those who don't.	1991-10-21 00:00:00.000
BU1111	Cooking with Computers: Surreptitious Balance Sheets	business	1389	11.95	5000.00	10	3876	Helpful hints on how to use your electronic resources to the best advantage.	1991-06-09 00:00:00.000

```
SELECT TOP(3) *  FROM   publishers  ORDER  BY pub_name;
```

pub_id	pub_name	city	state	country
1389	Algodata Infosystems	Berkeley	CA	USA
0877	Binnet & Hardley	Washington	DC	USA
1622	Five Lakes Publishing	Chicago	IL	USA

Sorting Products by Attributes

```
USE Northwind;

SELECT          UnitsInStock,
                ProductID,
                ProductName,
                QuantityPerUnit,
                FORMAT( UnitPrice, 'c', 'en-US') AS UnitPrice  -- Column alias is same as column
FROM   dbo.Products WHERE  UnitsInStock BETWEEN 15 AND 25  ORDER  BY UnitsInStock;
```

UnitsInStock	ProductID	ProductName	QuantityPerUnit	UnitPrice
15	7	Uncle Bob's Organic Dried Pears	12 - 1 lb pkgs.	$30.00
15	26	Gumbär Gummibärchen	100 - 250 g bags	$31.23
15	48	Chocolade	10 pkgs.	$12.75
15	70	Outback Lager	24 - 355 ml bottles	$15.00
17	38	Côte de Blaye	12 - 75 cl bottles	$263.50
17	43	Ipoh Coffee	16 - 500 g tins	$46.00
17	62	Tarte au sucre	48 pies	$49.30
17	2	Chang	24 - 12 oz bottles	$19.00
19	60	Camembert Pierrot	15 - 300 g rounds	$34.00
20	24	Guaraná Fantástica	12 - 355 ml cans	$4.50
20	35	Steeleye Stout	24 - 12 oz bottles	$18.00
20	51	Manjimup Dried Apples	50 - 300 g pkgs.	$53.00
21	54	Tourtière	16 pies	$7.45
21	56	Gnocchi di nonna Alice	24 - 250 g pkgs.	$38.00
22	11	Queso Cabrales	1 kg pkg.	$21.00
22	64	Wimmers gute Semmelknödel	20 bags x 4 pieces	$33.25
24	13	Konbu	2 kg box	$6.00
24	63	Vegie-spread	15 - 625 g jars	$43.90
25	19	Teatime Chocolate Biscuits	10 boxes x 12 pieces	$9.20

```
-- A second key is necessary for unique ordering
SELECT  TOP(8)  UnitsInStock,
                ProductID,
                ProductName,
                QuantityPerUnit,
                FORMAT( UnitPrice, 'c', 'en-US') AS UnitPrice
FROM   dbo.Products
WHERE  UnitsInStock BETWEEN 15 AND 25 ORDER  BY UnitsInStock, ProductName;
```

UnitsInStock	ProductID	ProductName	QuantityPerUnit	UnitPrice
15	48	Chocolade	10 pkgs.	$12.75
15	26	Gumbär Gummibärchen	100 - 250 g bags	$31.23
15	70	Outback Lager	24 - 355 ml bottles	$15.00
15	7	Uncle Bob's Organic Dried Pears	12 - 1 lb pkgs.	$30.00
17	2	Chang	24 - 12 oz bottles	$19.00
17	38	Côte de Blaye	12 - 75 cl bottles	$263.50
17	43	Ipoh Coffee	16 - 500 g tins	$46.00
17	62	Tarte au sucre	48 pies	$49.30

Changing WHERE condition changes the cardinality of result set

```
SELECT          UnitsInStock,
                ProductID,
                ProductName,
                QuantityPerUnit,
                FORMAT( UnitPrice, 'c', 'en-US')          AS UnitPrice
FROM  dbo.Products
WHERE  UnitsInStock = 15 or UnitsInStock =  25  -- same as UnitsInStock IN (15, 25)
ORDER  BY UnitsInStock, ProductName;
```

UnitsInStock	ProductID	ProductName	QuantityPerUnit	UnitPrice
15	48	Chocolade	10 pkgs.	$12.75
15	26	Gumbär Gummibärchen	100 - 250 g bags	$31.23
15	70	Outback Lager	24 - 355 ml bottles	$15.00
15	7	Uncle Bob's Organic Dried Pears	12 - 1 lb pkgs.	$30.00
25	19	Teatime Chocolate Biscuits	10 boxes x 12 pieces	$9.20

```
SELECT  TOP(7)  UnitsInStock,
                ProductID,
                ProductName,
                QuantityPerUnit,
                FORMAT( UnitPrice, 'c', 'en-US')          AS UnitPrice
FROM  dbo.Products  ORDER  BY UnitsInStock DESC, ProductName ASC;
```

UnitsInStock	ProductID	ProductName	QuantityPerUnit	UnitPrice
125	75	Rhönbräu Klosterbier	24 - 0.5 l bottles	$7.75
123	40	Boston Crab Meat	24 - 4 oz tins	$18.40
120	6	Grandma's Boysenberry Spread	12 - 8 oz jars	$25.00
115	55	Pâté chinois	24 boxes x 2 pies	$24.00
113	61	Sirop d'érable	24 - 500 ml bottles	$28.50
112	33	Geitost	500 g	$2.50
112	36	Inlagd Sill	24 - 250 g jars	$19.00

```
SELECT  TOP(5)  UnitsInStock, ProductID, ProductName,       QuantityPerUnit,
                FORMAT( UnitPrice, 'c', 'en-US') AS UnitPrice
FROM  dbo.Products
WHERE  UnitsInStock > 15   AND UnitsInStock < 25  ORDER  BY UnitsInStock DESC, ProductName ASC;
```

UnitsInStock	ProductID	ProductName	QuantityPerUnit	UnitPrice
24	13	Konbu	2 kg box	$6.00
24	63	Vegie-spread	15 - 625 g jars	$43.90
22	11	Queso Cabrales	1 kg pkg.	$21.00
22	64	Wimmers gute Semmelknödel	20 bags x 4 pieces	$33.25
21	56	Gnocchi di nonna Alice	24 - 250 g pkgs.	$38.00

The "Tricky" BETWEEN & NOT BETWEEN Operators

They are very English-like, but results should be verified to make sure they work as intended.

```
SELECT   TOP(5)   UnitsInStock, ProductID, ProductName,        QuantityPerUnit,
                  FORMAT( UnitPrice, 'c', 'en-US') AS UnitPrice
FROM   dbo.Products
WHERE  UnitsInStock BETWEEN 15 AND 25
ORDER  BY UnitsInStock DESC, ProductName ASC;
GO
```

UnitsInStock	ProductID	ProductName	QuantityPerUnit	UnitPrice
25	19	Teatime Chocolate Biscuits	10 boxes x 12 pieces	$9.20
24	13	Konbu	2 kg box	$6.00
24	63	Vegie-spread	15 - 625 g jars	$43.90
22	11	Queso Cabrales	1 kg pkg.	$21.00
22	64	Wimmers gute Semmelknödel	20 bags x 4 pieces	$33.25

```
SELECT   TOP(5)   UnitsInStock, ProductID, ProductName,        QuantityPerUnit,
                  FORMAT( UnitPrice, 'c', 'en-US') AS UnitPrice
FROM   dbo.Products
WHERE  UnitsInStock NOT BETWEEN 15 AND 25
ORDER  BY UnitsInStock DESC, ProductName ASC;
```

UnitsInStock	ProductID	ProductName	QuantityPerUnit	UnitPrice
125	75	Rhönbräu Klosterbier	24 - 0.5 l bottles	$7.75
123	40	Boston Crab Meat	24 - 4 oz tins	$18.40
120	6	Grandma's Boysenberry Spread	12 - 8 oz jars	$25.00
115	55	Pâté chinois	24 boxes x 2 pies	$24.00
113	61	Sirop d'érable	24 - 500 ml bottles	$28.50

```
SELECT              Orders.OrderID,
                    Shippers.*
FROM   Shippers
    INNER JOIN Orders
      ON ( Shippers.ShipperID = Orders.ShipVia )
ORDER  BY Orders.OrderID;
GO
-- (830 row(s) affected) - Partial results.
```

OrderID	ShipperID	CompanyName	Phone
10248	3	Federal Shipping	(503) 555-9931
10249	1	Speedy Express	(503) 555-9831
10250	2	United Package	(503) 555-3199
10251	1	Speedy Express	(503) 555-9831
10252	2	United Package	(503) 555-3199
10253	2	United Package	(503) 555-3199

A second key is frequently required in sorting exception is PRIMARY KEY column.

```
SELECT  OrderID,
        ProductID,
        FORMAT( UnitPrice, 'c', 'en-US')            AS UnitPrice,
        Quantity,
        Discount
FROM  [Order Details]  ORDER  BY OrderID ASC, ProductID ASC;
GO
-- (2155 row(s) affected) - Partial results.
```

OrderID	ProductID	UnitPrice	Quantity	Discount
10248	11	$14.00	12	0
10248	42	$9.80	10	0
10248	72	$34.80	5	0
10249	14	$18.60	9	0
10249	51	$42.40	40	0
10250	41	$7.70	10	0
10250	51	$42.40	35	0.15
10250	65	$16.80	15	0.15

```
-- Sort keys are different from expression column EmployeeName
SELECT  CONCAT(LastName,', ', FirstName)  AS EmployeeName ,
        Title, City, Country
FROM  dbo.Employees ORDER  BY LastName,  FirstName ASC;
```

EmployeeName	Title	City	Country
Buchanan, Steven	Sales Manager	London	UK
Callahan, Laura	Inside Sales Coordinator	Seattle	USA
Davolio, Nancy	Sales Representative	Seattle	USA
Dodsworth, Anne	Sales Representative	London	UK
Fuller, Andrew	Vice President, Sales	Tacoma	USA
King, Robert	Sales Representative	London	UK
Leverling, Janet	Sales Representative	Kirkland	USA
Peacock, Margaret	Sales Representative	Redmond	USA
Suyama, Michael	Sales Representative	London	UK

```
-- Equivalent sort
SELECT TOP(3)     CONCAT(LastName,', ', FirstName) AS EmployeeName ,     Title, City, Country
FROM  dbo.Employees  ORDER  BY EmployeeName ASC;
```

EmployeeName	Title	City	Country
Buchanan, Steven	Sales Manager	London	UK
Callahan, Laura	Inside Sales Coordinator	Seattle	USA
Davolio, Nancy	Sales Representative	Seattle	USA

Using Multiple Keys in the ORDER BY Clause

If a single sort key does not result in unique ordering, multiple keys can be used. In the next example the Price (major) key is based on a column which is not unique. If we add Name as a second (minor) key, unique ordering will be guaranteed since Name is a unique column, it has a unique index and not null. It's worth noting if Name would allow nulls, we would need a third key for unique ordering.

```
-- Single key sort
SELECT  P.Name,
        P.ProductNumber,
        P.ListPrice                AS PRICE
FROM   Production.Product  P
WHERE  P.ProductLine = 'R'   AND P.DaysToManufacture < 4    ORDER  BY  P. ListPrice DESC;
```

Name	ProductNumber	PRICE
HL Road Frame - Black, 58	FR-R92B-58	1431.50
HL Road Frame - Red, 58	FR-R92R-58	1431.50
HL Road Frame - Red, 62	FR-R92R-62	1431.50
HL Road Frame - Red, 44	FR-R92R-44	1431.50
HL Road Frame - Red, 48	FR-R92R-48	1431.50
HL Road Frame - Red, 52	FR-R92R-52	1431.50
HL Road Frame - Red, 56	FR-R92R-56	1431.50
HL Road Frame - Black, 62	FR-R92B-62	1431.50
HL Road Frame - Black, 44	FR-R92B-44	1431.50
HL Road Frame - Black, 48	FR-R92B-48	1431.50
HL Road Frame - Black, 52	FR-R92B-52	1431.50
ML Road Frame-W - Yellow, 40	FR-R72Y-40	594.83

```
-- Double key sort - PRICE is the major key, Name is the minor key
SELECT  P.Name,
        P.ProductNumber,
        P.ListPrice                AS PRICE
FROM   Production.Product  P
WHERE  P.ProductLine = 'R'   AND P.DaysToManufacture < 4   ORDER  BY  PRICE DESC, Name;
```

Name	ProductNumber	PRICE
HL Road Frame - Black, 44	FR-R92B-44	1431.50
HL Road Frame - Black, 48	FR-R92B-48	1431.50
HL Road Frame - Black, 52	FR-R92B-52	1431.50
HL Road Frame - Black, 58	FR-R92B-58	1431.50
HL Road Frame - Black, 62	FR-R92B-62	1431.50
HL Road Frame - Red, 44	FR-R92R-44	1431.50
HL Road Frame - Red, 48	FR-R92R-48	1431.50
HL Road Frame - Red, 52	FR-R92R-52	1431.50
HL Road Frame - Red, 56	FR-R92R-56	1431.50
HL Road Frame - Red, 58	FR-R92R-58	1431.50
HL Road Frame - Red, 62	FR-R92R-62	1431.50
ML Road Frame - Red, 44	FR-R72R-44	594.83

ORDER BY in Complex Queries

An ORDER BY can be in a complex query and/or ORDER BY can be complex itself. T-SQL scripts demonstrate complex ORDER BY usage.

```
-- We cannot tell just by query inspection if the second key is sufficient for unique ordering or not
-- If we inspect the result set it becomes obvious that we need a third key at least (SalesOrderID unsorted)
SELECT  ProductName           = P.Name,
        NonDiscountSales      = ( OrderQty * UnitPrice ),
        Discounts             = ( ( OrderQty * UnitPrice ) * UnitPriceDiscount ) ,
        SalesOrderID
FROM  Production.Product P
    INNER JOIN Sales.SalesOrderDetail SOD
        ON P.ProductID = SOD.ProductID
ORDER BY        ProductName DESC,
                NonDiscountSales DESC;
GO
```

ProductName	NonDiscountSales	Discounts	SalesOrderID
Women's Tights, S	1049.86	104.986	47355
Women's Tights, S	824.89	41.2445	46987
Women's Tights, S	783.6455	39.1823	47400
Women's Tights, S	742.401	37.1201	50206
Women's Tights, S	701.1565	35.0578	46993
Women's Tights, S	701.1565	35.0578	46671
Women's Tights, S	701.1565	35.0578	50688
Women's Tights, S	701.1565	35.0578	49481
Women's Tights, S	659.912	32.9956	48295
Women's Tights, S	659.912	32.9956	46967
Women's Tights, S	618.6675	30.9334	46652
Women's Tights, S	608.9188	12.1784	46672
Women's Tights, S	608.9188	12.1784	47365
Women's Tights, S	565.4246	11.3085	47004
Women's Tights, S	565.4246	11.3085	50663

NOTE

Even though SELECT DISTINCT results may appear to be sorted, **only ORDER BY clause can guarantee sort**. This holds true for any kind of SELECT statement, simple or complex.

```
SELECT DISTINCT JobTitle  FROM  HumanResources.Employee ;
```

```
SELECT DISTINCT JobTitle  FROM  HumanResources.Employee ORDER  BY JobTitle;
```

ORDER BY with ROW_NUMBER()

T-SQL queries demonstrate sorting with not matching and matching ROW_NUMBER() sequence number.

```
SELECT
  ROW_NUMBER()  OVER( PARTITION BY CountryRegionName  ORDER BY SalesYTD ASC) AS SeqNo,
  CountryRegionName AS Country,  FirstName,  LastName,  JobTitle,
  FORMAT(SalesYTD, 'c', 'en-US') AS SalesYTD,
  FORMAT(SalesLastYear, 'c', 'en-US') AS SalesLastYear
FROM  Sales.vSalesPerson            ORDER  BY JobTitle,   SalesYTD DESC;
```

SeqNo	Country	FirstName	LastName	JobTitle	SalesYTD	SalesLastYear
2	United States	Amy	Alberts	European Sales Manager	$519,905.93	$0.00
3	United States	Stephen	Jiang	North American Sales Manager	$559,697.56	$0.00
1	United States	Syed	Abbas	Pacific Sales Manager	$172,524.45	$0.00
11	United States	Linda	Mitchell	Sales Representative	$4,251,368.55	$1,439,156.03
1	United Kingdom	Jae	Pak	Sales Representative	$4,116,871.23	$1,635,823.40
10	United States	Michael	Blythe	Sales Representative	$3,763,178.18	$1,750,406.48
9	United States	Jillian	Carson	Sales Representative	$3,189,418.37	$1,997,186.20
1	France	Ranjit	Varkey Chudukatil	Sales Representative	$3,121,616.32	$2,396,539.76
2	Canada	José	Saraiva	Sales Representative	$2,604,540.72	$2,038,234.65
8	United States	Shu	Ito	Sales Representative	$2,458,535.62	$2,073,506.00
7	United States	Tsvi	Reiter	Sales Representative	$2,315,185.61	$1,849,640.94
1	Germany	Rachel	Valdez	Sales Representative	$1,827,066.71	$1,307,949.79
6	United States	Tete	Mensa-Annan	Sales Representative	$1,576,562.20	$0.00
5	United States	David	Campbell	Sales Representative	$1,573,012.94	$1,371,635.32
1	Canada	Garrett	Vargas	Sales Representative	$1,453,719.47	$1,620,276.90
1	Australia	Lynn	Tsoflias	Sales Representative	$1,421,810.92	$2,278,548.98
4	United States	Pamela	Ansman-Wolfe	Sales Representative	$1,352,577.13	$1,927,059.18

```
-- ROW_NUMBER() ORDER BY in synch with sort ORDER BY
SELECT  ROW_NUMBER()  OVER(  ORDER BY JobTitle, SalesYTD DESC) AS SeqNo,
    CountryRegionName AS Country,  FirstName,  LastName,  JobTitle,
    FORMAT(SalesYTD, 'c', 'en-US') AS SalesYTD,  FORMAT(SalesLastYear, 'c', 'en-US') AS SalesLastYear
FROM  Sales.vSalesPerson  ORDER  BY       SeqNo;
```

SeqNo	Country	FirstName	LastName	JobTitle	SalesYTD	SalesLastYear
1	United States	Amy	Alberts	European Sales Manager	$519,905.93	$0.00
2	United States	Stephen	Jiang	North American Sales Manager	$559,697.56	$0.00
3	United States	Syed	Abbas	Pacific Sales Manager	$172,524.45	$0.00
4	United States	Linda	Mitchell	Sales Representative	$4,251,368.55	$1,439,156.03
5	United Kingdom	Jae	Pak	Sales Representative	$4,116,871.23	$1,635,823.40
6	United States	Michael	Blythe	Sales Representative	$3,763,178.18	$1,750,406.48
7	United States	Jillian	Carson	Sales Representative	$3,189,418.37	$1,997,186.20
8	France	Ranjit	Varkey Chudukatil	Sales Representative	$3,121,616.32	$2,396,539.76
9	Canada	José	Saraiva	Sales Representative	$2,604,540.72	$2,038,234.65
10	United States	Shu	Ito	Sales Representative	$2,458,535.62	$2,073,506.00
11	United States	Tsvi	Reiter	Sales Representative	$2,315,185.61	$1,849,640.94
12	Germany	Rachel	Valdez	Sales Representative	$1,827,066.71	$1,307,949.79
13	United States	Tete	Mensa-Annan	Sales Representative	$1,576,562.20	$0.00
14	United States	David	Campbell	Sales Representative	$1,573,012.94	$1,371,635.32
15	Canada	Garrett	Vargas	Sales Representative	$1,453,719.47	$1,620,276.90
16	Australia	Lynn	Tsoflias	Sales Representative	$1,421,810.92	$2,278,548.98
17	United States	Pamela	Ansman-Wolfe	Sales Representative	$1,352,577.13	$1,927,059.18

ORDER BY Clause with CASE Conditional Expression

Sort by LastName, MiddleName if exists else FirstName, and FirstName in case MiddleName is used.

```
USE AdventureWorks2012;

SELECT          FirstName,
                COALESCE(MiddleName, '')        AS MName,  -- ISNULL can also be used
                LastName,
                AddressLine1,
                COALESCE(AddressLine2, '')      AS Addr2,
                City,
                SP.Name                         AS [State],
                CR.Name                         AS Country,
                C.CustomerID
FROM   Person.Person AS P
    INNER JOIN Sales.Customer AS C
        ON P.BusinessEntityID = C.PersonID
    INNER JOIN Person.BusinessEntityAddress BEA
         ON BEA.BusinessEntityID = P.BusinessEntityID
    INNER JOIN Person.Address AS A
        ON A.AddressID = BEA.AddressID
    INNER JOIN Person.StateProvince SP
        ON SP.StateProvinceID = A.StateProvinceID
    INNER JOIN Person.CountryRegion CR
        ON CR.CountryRegionCode = SP.CountryRegionCode
ORDER  BY LastName,
      CASE
       WHEN MiddleName != '' THEN MiddleName
       ELSE FirstName
      END,
      FirstName;
-- (18508 row(s) affected) - Partial results.
```

FirstName	MName	LastName	AddressLine1	Addr2	City	State	Country	CustomerID
Chloe	A	Adams	3001 N. 48th Street		Marysville	Washington	United States	19410
Eduardo	A	Adams	4283 Meaham Drive		San Diego	California	United States	25292
Kaitlyn	A	Adams	3815 Berry Dr.		Westminster	British Columbia	Canada	11869
Mackenzie	A	Adams	9639 Ida Drive		Langford	British Columbia	Canada	14640
Sara	A	Adams	7503 Hill Drive		Milwaukie	Oregon	United States	16986
Adam		Adams	9381 Bayside Way		Newport Beach	California	United States	13323
Amber		Adams	9720 Morning Glory Dr.		Brisbane	Queensland	Australia	26746
Angel		Adams	9556 Lyman Rd.		Burlingame	California	United States	18504
Aaron	B	Adams	4116 Stanbridge Ct.		Downey	California	United States	28866
Noah	B	Adams	6738 Wallace Dr.		El Cajon	California	United States	16977
Bailey		Adams	1817 Adobe Drive		Kirkland	Washington	United States	13280
Ben		Adams	1534 Land Ave		Bremerton	Washington	United States	28678
Alex	C	Adams	237 Bellwood Dr.		Lake Oswego	Oregon	United States	21139
Courtney	C	Adams	6089 Santa Fe Dr.		Torrance	California	United States	18075
Ian	C	Adams	7963 Elk Dr	#4	Versailles	Yveline	France	29422

Special Sorting, Like United States On Top Of The Country Pop-Up List

It requires CASE or IIF conditional expression.

```
-- Major sort key is Color if not null, else product name
-- Minor sort on ProductNumber
SELECT ProductID,
    ProductNumber,
    Name AS ProductName,
    FORMAT(ListPrice, 'c', 'en-US')  AS ListPrice,
    Color
FROM   Production.Product
WHERE  Name LIKE ( '%Road%' )
ORDER  BY          CASE
                            WHEN Color IS NULL THEN Name
                            ELSE Color
                   END,
                   ProductNumber DESC;
-- (103 row(s) affected) - Partial results.
```

ProductID	ProductNumber	ProductName	ListPrice	Color
768	BK-R50B-44	Road-650 Black, 44	$782.99	Black
977	BK-R19B-58	Road-750 Black, 58	$539.99	Black
999	BK-R19B-52	Road-750 Black, 52	$539.99	Black
998	BK-R19B-48	Road-750 Black, 48	$539.99	Black
997	BK-R19B-44	Road-750 Black, 44	$539.99	Black
813	HB-R956	HL Road Handlebars	$120.27	NULL
512	RM-R800	HL Road Rim	$0.00	NULL
519	SA-R522	HL Road Seat Assembly	$196.92	NULL
913	SE-R995	HL Road Seat/Saddle	$52.64	NULL
933	TI-R982	HL Road Tire	$32.60	NULL
811	HB-R504	LL Road Handlebars	$44.54	NULL
510	RM-R436	LL Road Rim	$0.00	NULL
517	SA-R127	LL Road Seat Assembly	$133.34	NULL
911	SE-R581	LL Road Seat/Saddle	$27.12	NULL
931	TI-R092	LL Road Tire	$21.49	NULL
812	HB-R720	ML Road Handlebars	$61.92	NULL
511	RM-R600	ML Road Rim	$0.00	NULL
518	SA-R430	ML Road Seat Assembly	$147.14	NULL
912	SE-R908	ML Road Seat/Saddle	$39.14	NULL
932	TI-R628	ML Road Tire	$24.99	NULL
717	FR-R92R-62	HL Road Frame - Red, 62	$1,431.50	Red
706	FR-R92R-58	HL Road Frame - Red, 58	$1,431.50	Red
721	FR-R92R-56	HL Road Frame - Red, 56	$1,431.50	Red

T-SQL queries demonstrate complex sorting with the CASE expression usage.

CASE expression returns a SINGLE SCALAR VALUE of the same data type.

```
SELECT  SellStartDate,
        SellEndDate,
        *
FROM  Production.Product
WHERE  Name LIKE ( '%mountain%' )
ORDER  BY CASE
                WHEN SellEndDate IS NULL THEN SellStartDate
                ELSE SellEndDate
        END DESC, Name;
GO
-- (94 row(s) affected) -Partial results.
```

SellStartDate	SellEndDate	ProductID	Name	ProductNumber
2007-07-01 00:00:00.000	NULL	986	Mountain-500 Silver, 44	BK-M18S-44
2007-07-01 00:00:00.000	NULL	987	Mountain-500 Silver, 48	BK-M18S-48
2007-07-01 00:00:00.000	NULL	988	Mountain-500 Silver, 52	BK-M18S-52
2007-07-01 00:00:00.000	NULL	869	Women's Mountain Shorts, L	SH-W890-L
2007-07-01 00:00:00.000	NULL	868	Women's Mountain Shorts, M	SH-W890-M
2007-07-01 00:00:00.000	NULL	867	Women's Mountain Shorts, S	SH-W890-S
2006-07-01 00:00:00.000	2007-06-30 00:00:00.000	817	HL Mountain Front Wheel	FW-M928
2006-07-01 00:00:00.000	2007-06-30 00:00:00.000	825	HL Mountain Rear Wheel	RW-M928
2006-07-01 00:00:00.000	2007-06-30 00:00:00.000	815	LL Mountain Front Wheel	FW-M423
2006-07-01 00:00:00.000	2007-06-30 00:00:00.000	823	LL Mountain Rear Wheel	RW-M423
2006-07-01 00:00:00.000	2007-06-30 00:00:00.000	814	ML Mountain Frame - Black, 38	FR-M63B-38
2006-07-01 00:00:00.000	2007-06-30 00:00:00.000	830	ML Mountain Frame - Black, 40	FR-M63B-40

```
-- 2 keys descending sort
SELECT          PRODUCTNAME   = P.Name,
                SALETOTAL     = ( OrderQty * UnitPrice ),
                NETSALETOTAL  = ( ( OrderQty - RejectedQty ) * UnitPrice )
FROM  Production.Product P
    INNER JOIN Purchasing.PurchaseOrderDetail SOD
        ON P.ProductID = SOD.ProductID
ORDER  BY PRODUCTNAME  DESC,  SALETOTAL DESC;

-- Column alias sorting of GROUP BY aggregation results
SELECT [YEAR]=YEAR(OrderDate), Orders = COUNT(*)
FROM Sales.SalesOrderHeader
GROUP BY YEAR(OrderDate)  ORDER BY [YEAR];
```

YEAR	Orders
2005	1379
2006	3692
2007	12443
2008	13951

ORDER BY Clause with IIF Conditional Function

Sort by LastName, MiddleName if exists else FirstName, and FirstName in case MiddleName is used.

```
USE AdventureWorks2012;

SELECT          FirstName,
                COALESCE(MiddleName, '')        AS MName,  -- ISNULL can also be used
                LastName,
                AddressLine1,
                COALESCE(AddressLine2, '')      AS Addr2,
                City,
                SP.Name                         AS [State],
                CR.Name                         AS Country,
                C.CustomerID
FROM    Person.Person AS P
    INNER JOIN Sales.Customer AS C
        ON P.BusinessEntityID = C.PersonID
          INNER JOIN Person.BusinessEntityAddress BEA
              ON BEA.BusinessEntityID = P.BusinessEntityID
    INNER JOIN Person.Address AS A
        ON A.AddressID = BEA.AddressID
    INNER JOIN Person.StateProvince SP
        ON SP.StateProvinceID = A.StateProvinceID
    INNER JOIN Person.CountryRegion CR
        ON CR.CountryRegionCode = SP.CountryRegionCode
ORDER  BY       LastName,
                IIF( MiddleName != '',
                        MiddleName,                     -- TRUE condition return value
                        FirstName),                     -- FALSE condition return value
                FirstName;
GO
-- (18508 row(s) affected) -Partial results.
```

FirstName	MName	LastName	AddressLine1	Addr2	City	State	Country	CustomerID
Chloe	A	Adams	3001 N. 48th Street		Marysville	Washington	United States	19410
Eduardo	A	Adams	4283 Meaham Drive		San Diego	California	United States	25292
Kaitlyn	A	Adams	3815 Berry Dr.		Westminster	British Columbia	Canada	11869
Mackenzie	A	Adams	9639 Ida Drive		Langford	British Columbia	Canada	14640
Sara	A	Adams	7503 Hill Drive		Milwaukie	Oregon	United States	16986
Adam		Adams	9381 Bayside Way		Newport Beach	California	United States	13323
Amber		Adams	9720 Morning Glory Dr.		Brisbane	Queensland	Australia	26746
Angel		Adams	9556 Lyman Rd.		Burlingame	California	United States	18504
Aaron	B	Adams	4116 Stanbridge Ct.		Downey	California	United States	28866
Noah	B	Adams	6738 Wallace Dr.		El Cajon	California	United States	16977
Bailey		Adams	1817 Adobe Drive		Kirkland	Washington	United States	13280
Ben		Adams	1534 Land Ave		Bremerton	Washington	United States	28678
Alex	C	Adams	237 Bellwood Dr.		Lake Oswego	Oregon	United States	21139
Courtney	C	Adams	6089 Santa Fe Dr.		Torrance	California	United States	18075
Ian	C	Adams	7963 Elk Dr	#4	Versailles	Yveline	France	29422

ORDER BY Clause with the RANK() Function

T-SQL query demonstrates the combination of CASE expression and RANK() function in an ORDER BY clause. Note that while such a complex sort is technically impressive, ultimately it has to make sense to the user, the Business Intelligence consumer.

```
-- SQL complex sorting
USE AdventureWorks2012;

SELECT          BusinessEntityID,
                FirstName,
                LastName,
                COALESCE(Title, '') AS Title
FROM   Person.Person
WHERE  LEFT(FirstName, 1) = 'M'
ORDER  BY CASE
                WHEN LEFT(LastName, 1) = 'A' THEN RANK()
                        OVER( ORDER BY CONCAT(FirstName, SPACE(1), LastName))
                WHEN LEFT(LastName, 1) = 'M' THEN RANK()
                        OVER( ORDER BY CONCAT(LastName,', ', FirstName), Title)
                WHEN LEFT(LastName, 1) = 'U' THEN RANK()
                        OVER(  ORDER BY CONCAT(LastName,', ', FirstName)  DESC)
                ELSE RANK()
                        OVER( ORDER BY LastName ASC, FirstName DESC)
    END;
```

BusinessEntityID	FirstName	LastName	Title
9500	Mackenzie	Adams	
10144	Mackenzie	Allen	
10128	Madeline	Allen	
11708	Madison	Alexander	
11527	Madison	Anderson	
19872	Morgan	Bailey	
8059	Michelle	Bailey	
8080	Melissa	Bailey	
18291	Megan	Bailey	
8070	Mariah	Bailey	
2432	Maria	Bailey	
14378	Marcus	Bailey	
8063	Makayla	Bailey	
8032	Mackenzie	Bailey	
9521	Morgan	Baker	
3320	Miguel	Baker	
15437	Mason	Baker	
9546	Mary	Baker	
1082	Mary	Baker	
9539	Maria	Baker	

ORDER BY Clause with Custom Mapped Sort Sequence

Typically we rely on alphabets or numbers for sorting. What if, for example, we don't want United States way down on a website drop-down menu, rather than on the top with Canada and United Kingdom just above "lucky" Australia? We have to do custom mapping for such a sort in the ORDER BY clause.

```
USE AdventureWorks2012;
SELECT          AddressLine1,
                City,
                SP.StateProvinceCode            AS State,
                PostalCode,
                CR.Name                         AS  Country
FROM   Person.[Address] A
    INNER JOIN Person.StateProvince SP          ON A.StateProvinceID = SP.StateProvinceID
    INNER JOIN Person.CountryRegion CR          ON SP.CountryRegionCode = CR.CountryRegionCode
ORDER  BY (     CASE    WHEN CR.Name = 'United States' THEN 0
                        WHEN CR.Name = 'Canada' THEN 1
                        WHEN CR.Name = 'United Kingdom' THEN 2   ELSE 3  END ),
                Country,
                City,
                AddressLine1;
-- (19614 row(s) affected) - Partial results.
```

AddressLine1	City	State	PostalCode	Country
9355 Armstrong Road	York	ENG	YO15	United Kingdom
939 Vista Del Diablo	York	ENG	YO15	United Kingdom
9458 Flame Drive	York	ENG	YO15	United Kingdom
9557 Steven Circle	York	ENG	Y03 4TN	United Kingdom

Sorting on the Last Word of a String

```
CREATE TABLE #People (BusinessEnityID INT PRIMARY KEY, FullName nvarchar(100));
INSERT INTO #People
SELECT BusinessEntityID, FULLNAME = CONCAT(FirstName , SPACE(1), LastName )
FROM   Person.Person ORDER  BY BusinessEntityID ;
```

```
SELECT *   FROM   #People
ORDER  BY REVERSE(LEFT(REVERSE(FullName), charindex(' ', REVERSE(FullName) + ' '  ) - 1)),
          FullName ;
GO -- (19972 row(s) affected) - Partial results.
```

BusinessEntityID	FULLNAME
285	Syed Abbas
293	Catherine Abel
295	Kim Abercrombie

ORDER BY Clause with Custom Alphanumeric Sort Sequence

A frequent requirement is custom sorting on alphanumeric field (column). The next T-SQL query demonstrates special alphanumeric sorting.

```
USE AdventureWorks2012;

SELECT AddressLine1,
                isnull(AddressLine2, '')      AS Addressline2,
                City,
                SP.StateProvinceCode          AS State,
                PostalCode,
                CR.Name                       AS Country
FROM   Person.[Address] A
    INNER JOIN Person.StateProvince SP
     ON A.StateProvinceID = SP.StateProvinceID
    INNER JOIN Person.CountryRegion CR
     ON SP.CountryRegionCode = CR.CountryRegionCode
ORDER  BY (     CASE
                        WHEN Ascii([AddressLine1]) BETWEEN 65 AND 90 THEN 0 -- Upper case alpha
                        WHEN Ascii([AddressLine1]) BETWEEN 48 AND 57 THEN 1 -- Digits
                        ELSE 2
                END ),
                AddressLine1,
                City;
GO
-- (19614 row(s) affected) - Partial results.
```

AddressLine1	Addressline2	City	State	PostalCode	Country
Zur Lindung 46		Leipzig	NW	04139	Germany
Zur Lindung 6		Saarlouis	SL	66740	Germany
Zur Lindung 6		Solingen	NW	42651	Germany
Zur Lindung 609		Sulzbach Taunus	SL	66272	Germany
Zur Lindung 7		Berlin	HE	14129	Germany
Zur Lindung 7		Neunkirchen	SL	66578	Germany
Zur Lindung 764		Paderborn	HH	33041	Germany
Zur Lindung 78		Berlin	HH	10791	Germany
Zur Lindung 787		München	NW	80074	Germany
00, rue Saint-Lazare		Dunkerque	59	59140	France
02, place de Fontenoy		Verrieres Le Buisson	91	91370	France
035, boulevard du Montparnasse		Verrieres Le Buisson	91	91370	France
081, boulevard du Montparnasse		Saint-Denis	93	93400	France
081, boulevard du Montparnasse		Seattle	WA	98104	United States
084, boulevard du Montparnasse		Les Ulis	91	91940	France
1 Corporate Center Drive		Miami	FL	33127	United States
1 Mt. Dell Drive		Portland	OR	97205	United States
1 Smiling Tree Court	Space 55	Los Angeles	CA	90012	United States
1, allée des Princes		Courbevoie	92	92400	France

Working with Synonyms

A synonym is a shorthand name for a longer name including multi-part names. **While prefix like "sn" or "syn" is not required, it is a good practice since otherwise a synonym can be confused with a (real) table for example, leading to loss of DBA or developer productivity.**

```
USE AdventureWorks2012;
GO
```

```
-- Create synonyms for a 2-part names
CREATE SYNONYM synProd  FOR Production.Product;
CREATE SYNONYM synCust  FOR Sales.Customer;
```

```
-- SQL Server 2012 feature - Create a synonym for 4-part name linked server
CREATE SYNONYM synCustLDNAW12  FOR
        [LONDONPROD8].AdventureWorks2012.Sales.Customer;
GO -- Command(s) completed successfully.
```

```
-- Query the Customer tables by using the synonyms
SELECT * FROM synProd ORDER BY Name;                    -- (504 row(s) affected)
SELECT * FROM synCust ORDER BY AccountNumber;           -- (19820 row(s) affected)
GO
```

```
-- Delete a synonym
DROP SYNONYM synCust;  -- Command(s) completed successfully.
GO
```

```
-- Enumerating all synonyms in database
SELECT  name                                 AS "Name"
        ,base_object_name                    AS "Definition"
        ,PARSENAME(base_object_name, 4)      AS "Server"
        ,PARSENAME(base_object_name, 3)      AS "Database"
        ,PARSENAME(base_object_name, 2)      AS "Schema"
        ,PARSENAME(base_object_name, 1)      AS "Object"
 FROM sys.synonyms ORDER BY Definition;
GO
```

Name	Definition	Server	Database	Schema	Object
synProd	[Production].[Product]	NULL	NULL	Production	Product
synCust	[Sales].[Customer]	NULL	NULL	Sales	Customer

Date & Time Conversion To / From String

While there are only a few internal representation of date and time, string representations are many, even not deterministic since they may change from one country to another such as weekday and month names. T-SQL scripts demonstrate the myriad of date and time conversion possibilities.

The CONVERT() Function with Style Number Parameter

```
-- String source  format: mon dd yyyy hh:mmAM (or PM)
-- 100 is the style number parameter for CONVERT
SELECT [Date&Time] = convert(datetime, 'Oct 23 2020 11:01AM', 100)
```

Date&Time
2020-10-23 11:01:00.000

```
-- Default without style number
SELECT convert(datetime, 'Oct 23 2020 11:01AM')          -- 2020-10-23 11:01:00.000
```

```
-- Without century (yy) string date conversion with style number 0
-- Input format: mon dd yy hh:mmAM (or PM)
SELECT [Date&Time] = convert(datetime, 'Oct 23 20 11:01AM', 0)
```

Date&Time
2020-10-23 11:01:00.000

```
-- Default without style number
SELECT convert(datetime, 'Oct 23 20 11:01AM')          -- 2020-10-23 11:01:00.000
```

Convert string date & time to datetime (8-bytes internal representation) data type.

```
SELECT convert(datetime, '10/23/2016', 101)          -- mm/dd/yyyy

SELECT convert(datetime, '2016.10.23', 102)          -- yyyy.mm.dd ANSI date with century

SELECT convert(datetime, '23/10/2016', 103)          -- dd/mm/yyyy

SELECT convert(datetime, '23.10.2016', 104)-- dd.mm.yyyy

SELECT convert(datetime, '23-10-2016', 105)          -- dd-mm-yyyy

-- mon (month) types are nondeterministic conversions, dependent on language setting.
SELECT convert(datetime, '23 OCT 2016', 106)          -- dd mon yyyy
```

String Datetime Formats With "Mon" Are Nondeterministic, Language Dependent

```
SELECT [Date&Time] = convert(datetime, 'Oct 23, 2016', 107)  -- mon dd, yyyy
```

Date&Time
2016-10-23 00:00:00.000

```
SELECT [Date&Time ]=convert(datetime, '20:10:44', 108)        -- hh:mm:ss
```

Date&Time
1900-01-01 20:10:44.000

```
SELECT [Date&Time ]=convert(datetime, 'Oct 23 2016 11:02:44:013AM', 109) -- mon dd yyyy hh:mm:ss:mmmAM (or PM)
```

Date&Time
2016-10-23 11:02:44.013

```
SELECT convert(datetime, '10-23-2016', 110)                   -- mm-dd-yyyy
SELECT convert(datetime, '2016/10/23', 111)                   -- yyyy/mm/dd
```

```
-- YYYYMMDD ISO date format works at any language setting - international standard
SELECT [Date&Time ]=convert(datetime, '20161023')
```

Date&Time
2016-10-23 00:00:00.000

```
SELECT [Date&Time ]=convert(datetime, '20161023', 112)      -- ISO yyyymmdd
```

Date&Time
2016-10-23 00:00:00.000

```
SELECT [Date&Time ]=convert(datetime, '23 Oct 2016 11:02:07:577', 113) -- dd mon yyyy hh:mm:ss:mmm
```

Date&Time
2016-10-23 11:02:07.577

```
SELECT [Date&Time ]=convert(datetime, '20:10:25:300', 114)            -- hh:mm:ss:mmm(24h)
```

Date&Time
1900-01-01 20:10:25.300

```
SELECT [Date&Time ]=convert(datetime, '2016-10-23 20:44:11', 120)   -- yyyy-mm-dd hh:mm:ss(24h)
```

Date&Time
2016-10-23 20:44:11.000

Style 126 Is ISO 8601 Format: International Standard; Works With Any Language Setting

```
SELECT [Date&Time ]=convert(datetime, '2018-10-23T18:52:47.513', 126) -- yyyy-mm-ddThh:mm:ss(.mmm)
```

Date&Time
2018-10-23 18:52:47.513

```
SELECT [Date&Time ]=convert(datetime, '2016-10-23 20:44:11.500', 121)         -- yyyy-mm-dd hh:mm:ss.mmm
```

Date&Time
2016-10-23 20:44:11.500

```
--  Islamic / Hijri date conversion

SELECT CONVERT(nvarchar(32), convert(datetime,'2016-10-23'), 130);
-- 22 محرم 1438 12:00:00:000AM

SELECT [Date&Time ]=convert(datetime, N'23 شوال  1441  6:52:47:513PM', 130)
```

Date&Time
2020-06-14 18:52:47.513

```
SELECT [Date&Time ]=convert(datetime, '23/10/1441  6:52:47:513PM',    131)
```

Date&Time
2020-06-14 18:52:47.513

```
-- Convert DDMMYYYY format to datetime with intermediate conversion using STUFF().

SELECT STUFF(STUFF('31012016',3,0,'-'),6,0,'-');
-- 31-01-2016

SELECT [Date&Time ]=convert(datetime, STUFF(STUFF('31012016',3,0,'-'),6,0,'-'), 105)
```

Date&Time
2016-01-31 00:00:00.000

```
-- Equivalent
SELECT STUFF(STUFF('31012016',3,0,'/'),6,0,'/');   -- 31/01/2016
SELECT [Date&Time ]=convert(datetime, STUFF(STUFF('31012016',3,0,'/'),6,0,'/'), 103)
```

String to Datetime Conversion Without Century

String to datetime conversion without century - some exceptions. Nondeterministic means language setting (also regional setting) dependent such as Mar/Mär/mars/márc .

```
SELECT [Date&Time ]=convert(datetime, 'Oct 23 16 11:02:44AM')          -- Default
```

Date&Time
2016-10-23 11:02:44.000

SELECT convert(datetime, '10/23/16', 1)	mm/dd/yy	U.S.
SELECT convert(datetime, '16.10.23', 2)	yy.mm.dd	ANSI
SELECT convert(datetime, '23/10/16', 3)	dd/mm/yy	UK/FR
SELECT convert(datetime, '23.10.16', 4)	dd.mm.yy	German
SELECT convert(datetime, '23-10-16', 5)	dd-mm-yy	Italian
SELECT convert(datetime, '23 OCT 16', 6)	dd mon yy	non-det.
SELECT convert(datetime, 'Oct 23, 16', 7)	mon dd, yy	non-det.
SELECT convert(datetime, '20:10:44', 8)	hh:mm:ss	
SELECT convert(datetime, 'Oct 23 16 11:02:44:013AM', 9)	Default with msec	
SELECT convert(datetime, '10-23-16', 10)	mm-dd-yy	U.S.
SELECT convert(datetime, '16/10/23', 11)	yy/mm/dd	Japan
SELECT convert(datetime, '161023', 12)	yymmdd	ISO
SELECT convert(datetime, '23 Oct 16 11:02:07:577', 13)	dd mon yy hh:mm:ss:mmm EU dflt	
SELECT convert(datetime, '20:10:25:300', 14)	hh:mm:ss:mmm(24h)	
SELECT convert(datetime, '2016-10-23 20:44:11',20)	yyyy-mm-dd hh:mm:ss(24h) ODBC can.	
SELECT convert(datetime, '2016-10-23 20:44:11.500', 21)	yyyy-mm-dd hh:mm:ss.mmm ODBC	

Combine Date & Time String into Datetime

```
DECLARE @DateTimeValue varchar(32), @DateValue char(8), @TimeValue char(6)
SELECT @DateValue = '20200718',          @TimeValue = '211920'
SELECT          @DateTimeValue =
                CONCAT(
                convert(varchar, convert(datetime, @DateValue), 111),
                ' ', substring(@TimeValue, 1, 2) , ':', substring(@TimeValue, 3, 2) , ':',
substring(@TimeValue, 5, 2) )

SELECT   DateInput = @DateValue, TimeInput = @TimeValue,  DateTimeOutput = @DateTimeValue;
GO
```

DateInput	TimeInput	DateTimeOutput
20200718	211920	2020/07/18 21:19:20

```
SELECT DATETIMEFROMPARTS (2020, 07, 1, 21, 01, 20, 700)        -- New in SQL Server 2012
SELECT TIMEFROMPARTS (21, 01, 20, 0, 0)                        -- 21:01:20
```

Date and Time Internal Storage Format

DATETIME 8 bytes internal storage structure:

- 1st 4 bytes: number of days after the base date 1900-01-01
- 2nd 4 bytes: number of clock-ticks (3.33 milliseconds) since midnight

```
SELECT CONVERT(binary(8), CURRENT_TIMESTAMP);
```

Hex
0x0000A09C00F23CE1

DATE 3 bytes internal storage structure:

- 3 bytes integer: number of days after the first date 0001-01-01
- Note: hex byte order reversed

SMALLDATETIME 4 bytes internal storage structure

- 1st 2 bytes: number of days after the base date 1900-01-01
- 2nd 2 bytes: number of minutes since midnight

```
SELECT Hex=CONVERT(binary(4), convert(smalldatetime, getdate()));
```

Hex
0xA09C0375

Date & Time Operations Using System Operators & Functions

```
-- Conversion from hex (binary) to datetime value
DECLARE @dtHex binary(8)= 0x00009966002d3344;  DECLARE @dt datetime = @dtHex;
SELECT @dt;   -- 2007-07-09 02:44:34.147
```

```
-- SQL convert seconds to HH:MM:SS -
DECLARE  @Seconds INT;  SET @Seconds = 20000 ;
SELECT HH = @Seconds / 3600, MM = (@Seconds%3600) / 60, SS = (@Seconds%60) ;
```

HH	MM	SS
5	33	20

Extract Date Only from DATETIME Data Type

```
DECLARE @Now datetime = CURRENT_TIMESTAMP -- getdate()

SELECT  DateAndTime             = @Now      -- Date portion and Time portion
        ,DateString             = REPLACE(LEFT(CONVERT (varchar, @Now, 112),10),' ','-')
        ,[Date]                 = CONVERT(DATE, @Now)  -- SQL Server 2008 and on - date part
        ,Midnight1              = dateadd(day, datediff(day,0, @Now), 0)
        ,Midnight2              = CONVERT(DATETIME,CONVERT(int, @Now))
        ,Midnight3              = CONVERT(DATETIME,CONVERT(BIGINT,@Now) &
(POWER(Convert(bigint,2),32)-1));
```

DateAndTime	DateString	Date	Midnight1	Midnight2	Midnight3
2020-07-28 15:01:51.960	20200728	2020-07-28	2020-07-28 00:00:00.000	2020-07-29 00:00:00.000	2020-07-29 00:00:00.000

```
-- Compare today with database dates
SELECT          TOP (10)  OrderDate = CONVERT(date, OrderDate),
                Today = CONVERT(date, getdate()),
                DeltaDays = DATEDIFF(DD, OrderDate, getdate())
FROM Sales.SalesOrderHeader  ORDER BY NEWID();  -- random sort
```

OrderDate	Today	DeltaDays
2008-01-15	2012-08-10	1669
2006-07-14	2012-08-10	2219
2008-07-05	2012-08-10	1497
2008-03-01	2012-08-10	1623
2007-10-01	2012-08-10	1775
2007-01-15	2012-08-10	2034
2008-05-27	2012-08-10	1536
2008-04-18	2012-08-10	1575
2008-04-25	2012-08-10	1568
2006-12-17	2012-08-10	2063

String Date Formats Without Time

```
-- String date format yyyy/mm/dd from datetime
SELECT CONVERT(VARCHAR(10), GETDATE(), 111) AS [YYYY/MM/DD] ;
```

YYYY/MM/DD
2012/07/28

```
SELECT CONVERT(VARCHAR(10), GETDATE(), 112) AS [YYYYMMDD];
```

YYYYMMDD
20120728

```
SELECT REPLACE(CONVERT(VARCHAR(10), GETDATE(), 111),'/',' ') AS [YYYY MM DD];
```

YYYY MM DD
2020 07 28

```
-- Converting to special (non-standard) date formats: DD-MMM-YY
SELECT UPPER(REPLACE(CONVERT(VARCHAR,GETDATE(),6),' ','-')) AS CustomDate;
```

CustomDate
28-JUL-20

```
-- SQL convert date string to datetime - time set to 00:00:00.000 or 12:00AM

PRINT CONVERT(datetime,'07-10-2020',110) ;            -- Jul 10 2020 12:00AM
PRINT CONVERT(datetime,'2020/07/10',111) ;            -- Jul 10 2020 12:00AM
PRINT CONVERT(datetime,'20200710',  112);             -- Jul 10 2020 12:00AM
GO
```

```
-- SQL Server cast string to date / datetime
DECLARE @DateValue char(8) = '20200718'

SELECT [Date] = CAST (@DateValue AS datetime);
GO
```

Date
2020-07-18 00:00:00.000

String date to string date conversion with nested CONVERT

```
SELECT CONVERT(varchar, CONVERT(datetime, '20140508'), 100) AS StringDate;
```

StringDate
May 8 2014 12:00AM

```
-- T-SQL convert date to integer
DECLARE @Date datetime;  SET @Date = getdate();
SELECT DateAsInteger = CAST (CONVERT(varchar,@Date,112) as INT);
GO
```

DateAsInteger
20120728

```
-- SQL Server convert integer to datetime
DECLARE @iDate int = 20151225;
SELECT IntegerToDatetime = CAST(convert(varchar,@iDate) as datetime)
GO
```

IntegerToDatetime
2015-12-25 00:00:00.000

```
-- Alternates: date-only datetime values

SELECT [DATE-ONLY]=CONVERT(DATETIME, FLOOR(CONVERT(FLOAT, GETDATE())));

SELECT [DATE-ONLY]=CONVERT(DATETIME, FLOOR(CONVERT(MONEY, GETDATE())));

SELECT [DATE-ONLY]=CONVERT(DATETIME, CONVERT(DATE, GETDATE()));
```

```
-- CAST string to datetime
-- String date preparation, length is 10 characters
SELECT CONVERT(varchar, GETDATE(), 101), LEN (CONVERT(varchar, GETDATE(), 101))
--        07/28/2018       10
```

```
SELECT [DATE-ONLY]=CAST(CONVERT(varchar, GETDATE(), 101) AS DATETIME);
```

DATE-ONLY
2018-07-28 00:00:00.000

DATEADD() and DATEDIFF() Functions

```
-- T-SQL strip time from date
SELECT getdate() AS [DateTime], dateadd(dd, datediff(dd, 0, getdate()), 0) [DateOnly];
```

DateTime	DateOnly
2012-07-28 17:24:07.300	2012-07-28 00:00:00.000

```
-- First day of current month
SELECT dateadd(month, datediff(month, 0, getdate()), 0)  AS FirstDayOfCurrentMonth;
SELECT dateadd(dd,1, EOMONTH(getdate(),-1));  -- New to SQL Server 2012
```

FirstDayOfCurrentMonth
2020-07-01 00:00:00.000

```
 -- 15th day of current month
SELECT dateadd(day,14,dateadd(month, datediff(month,0,getdate()),0))
                                                        AS MiddleOfCurrentMonth;
SELECT dateadd(dd,15, EOMONTH(getdate(),-1));  -- New to SQL Server 2012
```

MiddleOfCurrentMonth
2012-07-15 00:00:00.000

```
-- First Monday of current month
SELECT   dateadd(day, (9-datepart(weekday,
         dateadd(month, datediff(month, 0, getdate()), 0)))%7,
         dateadd(month, datediff(month, 0, getdate()), 0))  AS [First Monday Of Current Month];
GO
```

First Monday Of Current Month
2012-07-02 00:00:00.000

```
-- Next Monday calculation from the reference date which was a Monday
DECLARE @Now datetime = GETDATE();
DECLARE @NextMonday datetime = dateadd(dd, ((datediff(dd, '19000101', @Now)
                    / 7) * 7) + 7, '19000101');
SELECT [Now]=@Now, [Next Monday]=@NextMonday;
GO
```

Now	Next Monday
2012-07-28 17:35:29.657	2012-07-30 00:00:00.000

Last Date & First Date Calculations

```
-- Last Friday of current month

SELECT   dateadd(day, -7+(6-datepart(weekday,

          dateadd(month, datediff(month, 0, getdate())+1, 0)))%7,

          dateadd(month, datediff(month, 0, getdate())+1, 0)) ;
```

```
-- First day of next month

SELECT dateadd(month, datediff(month, 0, getdate())+1, 0) ;
SELECT DATEADD(DD, 1, EOMONTH(getdate(),0));  -- 2016-04-01
```

```
-- 15th of next month

SELECT dateadd(day,14, dateadd(month, datediff(month, 0, getdate())+1, 0));
```

```
-- First Monday of next month

SELECT   dateadd(day, (9-datepart(weekday,
         dateadd(month, datediff(month, 0, getdate())+1, 0)))%7,
         dateadd(month, datediff(month, 0, getdate())+1, 0));
```

```
-- Next 12 months start & end - EOMONTH is new to SQL Server 2012
SELECT TOP 12
         DATEADD(DD,1, EOMONTH(getdate(),number-1))     AS Start,
         EOMONTH(getdate(),number)                      AS [End]
FROM master.dbo.spt_values   -- get integer sequence
WHERE type='P'  ORDER BY number;
GO
```

Start	End
2016-08-01	2016-08-31
2016-09-01	2016-09-30
2016-10-01	2016-10-31
2016-11-01	2016-11-30
2016-12-01	2016-12-31
2017-01-01	2017-01-31
2017-02-01	2017-02-28
2017-03-01	2017-03-31
2017-04-01	2017-04-30
2017-05-01	2017-05-31
2017-06-01	2017-06-30
2017-07-01	2017-07-31

BETWEEN Operator for Date Range

Date time range SELECT using the using >= and < operators. Count Sales Orders for date range 2007 OCT-NOV.

```
DECLARE  @StartDate DATETIME,  @EndDate DATETIME
SET @StartDate = convert(DATETIME,'10/01/2007',101)
SET @EndDate   = convert(DATETIME,'11/30/2007',101)
SELECT @StartDate, @EndDate
-- 2007-10-01 00:00:00.000  2007-11-30 00:00:00.000
SELECT dateadd(DAY,1,@EndDate),     dateadd(ms,-3,dateadd(DAY,1,@EndDate))
-- 2007-12-01 00:00:00.000  2007-11-30 23:59:59.997

SELECT [Sales Orders for 2007 OCT-NOV] = COUNT(* )
FROM   Sales.SalesOrderHeader
WHERE  OrderDate >= @StartDate
       AND OrderDate < dateadd(DAY,1,@EndDate)
```

Sales Orders for 2007 OCT-NOV
3668

Equivalent date range query using BETWEEN comparison. It requires a bit of trick programming. 23.59.59.997 is the last available time in a day.

```
SELECT [Sales Orders for 2007 OCT-NOV] = COUNT(* )
FROM   Sales.SalesOrderHeader
WHERE   OrderDate BETWEEN @StartDate
        AND dateadd(ms,-3, dateadd(DAY, 1, @EndDate))
GO
```

Sales Orders for 2007 OCT-NOV
3668

The BETWEEN operator can be used with string dates as well. Note: anything after midnight on 2004-02-10 is not included.

```
USE AdventureWorks2012;
SELECT POs=COUNT(*) FROM Purchasing.PurchaseOrderHeader
WHERE OrderDate BETWEEN '20080201' AND '20080210'
GO
```

POs
108

BETWEEN Dates Without Time: Entire 2004-02-10 Day Included This Fashion

```
SELECT POs=COUNT(*) FROM Purchasing.PurchaseOrderHeader
WHERE datediff(dd,0,OrderDate)
        BETWEEN datediff(dd,0,'20080201 12:11:39') AND datediff(dd,0,'20080210 14:33:19')
```

POs
108

The datetime range BETWEEN is equivalent to >=...AND....<= operators.

```
SELECT POs=COUNT(*) FROM Purchasing.PurchaseOrderHeader
WHERE OrderDate  BETWEEN '2008-02-01 00:00:00.000' AND '2008-02-10  00:00:00.000'
```

POs
108

Orders with datetime OrderDate-s of

'2008-02-10 00:00:01.000'	1 second after midnight (start of day at 12:00AM)
'2008-02-10 00:01:00.000'	1 minute after midnight
'2008-02-10 01:00:00.000'	1 hour after midnight
'2008-02-10 23:00:00.000'	23 hours after midnight

would not included in the preceding two queries. Only datetime OrderDate of '2008-02-10 00:00:00.000' would be included. That would be OK if the time part is not used. But even in that case and order can be entered accidentally with a time part, that would throw off the count.

To include the entire day of 2008-02-10, move the day up by one and use the < operator:

```
SELECT POs=COUNT(*) FROM Purchasing.PurchaseOrderHeader
WHERE OrderDate >= '20080201' AND OrderDate < '20080211';
```

POs
108

The reason we cannot detect a difference is due to lack of data passed midnight on 2008-02-11.

```
SELECT  [PurchaseOrderID], [RevisionNumber], [Status],
        [EmployeeID], [VendorID], [ShipMethodID], [OrderDate]
FROM [Purchasing].[PurchaseOrderHeader] WHERE PurchaseOrderID = 1665;
```

PurchaseOrderID	RevisionNumber	Status	EmployeeID	VendorID	ShipMethodID	OrderDate
1665	0	4	261	43	5	2008-02-10 00:00:00.000

Advance the datetime one second from midnight, the BETWEEN datetime query is not going to count it

```
UPDATE [Purchasing].[PurchaseOrderHeader]
        SET OrderDate = '2008-02-10 00:00:01.000'
WHERE PurchaseOrderID = 1665;  -- (1 row(s) affected)
```

This is the current value for OrderDate datetime.

PurchaseOrderID	RevisionNumber	Status	EmployeeID	VendorID	ShipMethodID	OrderDate
1665	0	4	261	43	5	2008-02-10 00:00:01.000

The following queries are not going to count this passed midnight record any more.

```
SELECT POs=COUNT(*) FROM Purchasing.PurchaseOrderHeader
WHERE OrderDate BETWEEN '2008-02-01 00:00:00.000' AND '2008-02-10  00:00:00.000'
```

POs
107

```
USE AdventureWorks; SELECT POs=COUNT(*) FROM Purchasing.PurchaseOrderHeader
WHERE OrderDate BETWEEN '20080201' AND '20080210'
```

POs
107

While the query we designed specifically for a case like this will count it correctly.

```
SELECT POs=COUNT(*) FROM Purchasing.PurchaseOrderHeader
WHERE OrderDate >= '20080201' AND OrderDate < '20080211'
```

POs
108

We restore the data to its original value.

```
UPDATE [Purchasing].[PurchaseOrderHeader]
        SET OrderDate = '2008-02-10 00:00:00.000'
WHERE PurchaseOrderID = 1665;     -- (1 row(s) affected)
```

Date Validation Function ISDATE()

```
DECLARE @StringDate varchar(32);
SET @StringDate = '2011-03-15 18:50';
IF EXISTS( SELECT * WHERE ISDATE(@StringDate) = 1)
   PRINT 'VALID DATE: ' + @StringDate
ELSE
   PRINT 'INVALID DATE: ' + @StringDate;
```

```
VALID DATE: 2011-03-15 18:50
```

```
DECLARE @StringDate varchar(32) ;
SET @StringDate = '20112-03-15 18:50';
IF EXISTS( SELECT * WHERE ISDATE(@StringDate) = 1)
   PRINT 'VALID DATE: ' + @StringDate
ELSE  PRINT 'INVALID DATE: ' + @StringDate;
GO
```

```
INVALID DATE: 20112-03-15 18:50
```

First and Last Day of Date Periods

Calculating date periods markers is a very important task in T-SQL programming, especially related to reporting queries.

```
DECLARE @Date DATE = '20161023';  SELECT ReferenceDate   = @Date;

SELECT FirstDayOfYear  = CONVERT(DATE, dateadd(yy, datediff(yy,0, @Date),0));

SELECT LastDayOfYear   = CONVERT(DATE, dateadd(yy, datediff(yy,0, @Date)+1,-1));

SELECT FDofSemester = CONVERT(DATE, dateadd(qq,((datediff(qq,0,@Date)/2)*2),0));

SELECT LastDayOfSemester  = CONVERT(DATE, dateadd(qq,((datediff(qq,0,@Date)/2)*2)+2,-1));

SELECT FirstDayOfQuarter  = CONVERT(DATE, dateadd(qq, datediff(qq,0, @Date),0));

SELECT LastDayOfQuarter = CONVERT(DATE, dateadd(qq, datediff(qq,0,@Date)+1,-1));
```

LastDayOfQuarter
2016-12-31

The brand-new EOMonth() function simplifies month start/end formulas

```
SELECT LastDayOfMonth = EOMonth (@Date);  -- New in SQL Server 2012

SELECT FirstDayOfMonth = CONVERT(DATE, dateadd(mm, datediff(mm,0, @Date),0));

SELECT LastDayOfMonth  = CONVERT(DATE, dateadd(mm, datediff(mm,0, @Date)+1,-1));

SELECT FirstDayOfWeek  = CONVERT(DATE, dateadd(wk, datediff(wk,0, @Date),0));

SELECT LastDayOfWeek   = CONVERT(DATE, dateadd(wk, datediff(wk,0, @Date)+1,-1));
GO
```

Month Sequence Generator

Sometimes date based data may have gaps missing months. For reporting purposes we may want to include all months from start date to end date. To do that we have to generate a continuous sequence of months, and use it to fill in the gaps. Calendar table can also be used for such a task.

```
DECLARE @Date date = '2000-01-01';
WITH cteSequence ( SeqNo) as
( SELECT 0  UNION ALL SELECT SeqNo + 1 FROM cteSequence WHERE SeqNo < 1000)
SELECT MonthStart=dateadd(MM, SeqNo, @Date)
FROM  cteSequence   WHERE dateadd(MM, SeqNo, @Date) <= CURRENT_TIMESTAMP
ORDER BY MonthStart
OPTION ( MAXRECURSION 0);  -- (158 row(s) affected) - Partial results.
```

MonthStart
2000-01-01
2000-02-01
2000-03-01
2000-04-01
2000-05-01
2000-06-01
2000-07-01
2000-08-01
2000-09-01
2000-10-01
2000-11-01
2000-12-01
2001-01-01
2001-02-01

Selected U.S. & International Date Styles

The U.S. date style is m/d/y.

```
DECLARE @DateTimeValue varchar(32) = '10/23/2016';

SELECT StringDate=@DateTimeValue,   [SSMS-Style] = CONVERT(datetime, @DatetimeValue);

SELECT @DateTimeValue = '10/23/2016 23:01:05';

SELECT StringDate = @DateTimeValue,  [SSMS-Style] = CONVERT(datetime, @DatetimeValue);
GO
```

StringDate	SSMS-Style
10/23/2016	2016-10-23 00:00:00.000

StringDate	SSMS-Style
10/23/2016 23:01:05	2016-10-23 23:01:05.000

The UK or British/French style is dmy.

```
DECLARE @DateTimeValue varchar(32) = '23/10/16 23:01:05';

SELECT StringDate = @DateTimeValue,  [SSMS-Style] = CONVERT(datetime, @DatetimeValue, 3);

 SELECT @DateTimeValue = '23/10/2016 04:01 PM';

SELECT StringDate = @DateTimeValue,  [SSMS-Style] = CONVERT(datetime, @DatetimeValue, 103);
GO
```

The German style is dmy as well with a new twist to it: period instead of slash.

```
DECLARE @DateTimeValue varchar(32)  = '23.10.16 23:01:05';
SELECT StringDate = @DateTimeValue,  [SSMS -Style] = CONVERT(datetime, @DatetimeValue, 4);
 SELECT @DateTimeValue = '23.10.2016 04:01 PM';
SELECT StringDate = @DateTimeValue,  [SSMS -Style] = CONVERT(datetime, @DatetimeValue, 104);
GO
```

```
-- Nondeterministic month name (mon)
SET LANGUAGE Spanish; SELECT CONVERT(varchar, getdate(), 100);      -- Ago 10 2018  4:43PM
SET LANGUAGE Turkish; SELECT CONVERT(varchar, getdate(), 100);      -- Agu 10 2018  4:44PM
SET LANGUAGE Polish; SELECT CONVERT(varchar, getdate(), 100);       -- VIII 10 2018  4:46PM
SET LANGUAGE Hungarian; SELECT CONVERT(varchar, getdate(), 100);    -- aug 10 2018  4:46PM
SET LANGUAGE Russian; SELECT CONVERT(nvarchar, getdate(), 100);     -- авг 10 2018  4:47PM
```

The DATEPART() Function to Decompose a Date

The DATEPART() function returns a part of a date.

```
DECLARE @dt datetime = getdate();
SELECT DATEPART(YEAR, @dt)          AS YYYY,
       DATEPART(MONTH, @dt)         AS MM,
       DATEPART(DAY, @dt)           AS DD;
```

YYYY	MM	DD
2016	7	29

```
USE Northwind;  SELECT  *  FROM dbo.Orders
WHERE DATEPART(YEAR, OrderDate)              = '1996'  AND
      DATEPART(MONTH,OrderDate)              = '07'    AND
      DATEPART(DAY, OrderDate)               = '10'
```

```
/*OrderID    CustomerID    EmployeeID    OrderDate    RequiredDate    ShippedDate
      ShipVia  Freight  ShipName    Shipaddress    ShipCity ShipRegion    ShipPostalCode
      ShipCountry
10253   HANAR  3    1996-07-10 00:00:00.000  1996-07-24 00:00:00.000  1996-07-16 00:00:00.000
      2    58.17    Hanari Carnes    Rua do Paço, 67   Rio de Janeiro    RJ    05454-876
      Brazil  */
```

Alternate syntax for DATEPART.

```
USE Northwind;  SELECT * FROM dbo.Orders
WHERE       YEAR(OrderDate)      = 1996      AND
            MONTH(OrderDate)     =  07       AND
            DAY(OrderDate)       =  10
GO
```

```
-- Additional datepart parameters including Julian date
DECLARE @dt datetime = getdate();
SELECT DATEPART(DAY, @dt)                  AS DD,
       DATEPART(WEEKDAY, @dt)              AS WD,
       DATEPART(DAYOFYEAR, @dt)            AS JulianDate,
       DATEPART(WEEK, @dt)                 AS Week,
       DATEPART(ISO_WEEK, @dt)             AS ISOWeek,
       DATEPART(HOUR, @dt)                 AS HH;
```

DD	WD	JulianDate	Week	ISOWeek	HH
10	5	223	33	32	17

The DATENAME() Function to Get Date Part Names

The DATENAME() function can be used to find out the words for months and weekdays.

```
SELECT DayName=DATENAME(weekday, OrderDate), SalesPerWeekDay = COUNT(*)
FROM Sales.SalesOrderHeader
GROUP BY DATENAME(weekday, OrderDate), DATEPART(weekday,OrderDate)
ORDER BY DATEPART(weekday,OrderDate);
```

DayName	SalesPerWeekDay
Sunday	4482
Monday	4591
Tuesday	4346
Wednesday	4244
Thursday	4483
Friday	4444
Saturday	4875

DATENAME application for month names

```
SELECT MonthName=DATENAME(month, OrderDate), SalesPerMonth = COUNT(*)
FROM Sales.SalesOrderHeader
GROUP BY DATENAME(month, OrderDate), MONTH(OrderDate) ORDER BY MONTH(OrderDate);
```

MonthName	SalesPerMonth
January	2483
February	2686
March	2750
April	2740
May	3154
June	3079
July	2094
August	2411
September	2298
October	2282
November	2474
December	3014

```
SELECT DATENAME(MM,dateadd(MM,7,-1)) -- July - Month name from month number
```

Extract Date from Text with PATINDEX Pattern Matching

```
USE tempdb;
go
```

```
CREATE TABLE InsiderTransaction (
    InsiderTransactionID int identity primary key,
    TradeDate datetime,
    TradeMsg varchar(256),
    ModifiedDate datetime default (getdate()) );
```

```
-- Populate table with dummy data
INSERT InsiderTransaction (TradeMsg)
VALUES ('INSIDER TRAN QABC Hammer, Bruce D. CSO 09-02-08 Buy 2,000 6.10');
INSERT InsiderTransaction (TradeMsg)
VALUES ('INSIDER TRAN QABC Schmidt, Steven CFO 08-25-08 Buy 2,500 6.70') ;
INSERT InsiderTransaction (TradeMsg)
VALUES ('INSIDER TRAN QABC  Hammer, Bruce D. CSO  08-20-08 Buy 3,000 8.59');
INSERT InsiderTransaction (TradeMsg)
VALUES ('INSIDER TRAN QABC Walters,  Jeff CTO 08-15-08  Sell 5,648 8.49');
INSERT InsiderTransaction (TradeMsg)
VALUES  ('INSIDER TRAN  QABC  Walters, Jeff CTO   08-15-08 Option Exercise 5,648 2.15');
INSERT InsiderTransaction (TradeMsg)
VALUES('INSIDER TRAN QABC Hammer, Bruce D. CSO 07-31-08  Buy 5,000 8.05');
INSERT InsiderTransaction (TradeMsg)
VALUES('INSIDER TRAN QABC Lennot, Mark  Director  08-31-07 Buy 1,500 9.97');
INSERT InsiderTransaction (TradeMsg)
VALUES('INSIDER TRAN QABC  O''Neal, Linda COO  08-01-08 Sell 5,000 6.50');
```

Pattern match for MM-DD-YY using the PATINDEX string function to extract dates from stock trade message text.

```
SELECT   InsiderTransactionID ,       substring(TradeMsg,
         patindex('%[01][0-9]-[0123][0-9]-[0-9][0-9]%', TradeMsg),8) AS TradeDate
FROM InsiderTransaction  WHERE  patindex('%[01][0-9]-[0123][0-9]-[0-9][0-9]%', TradeMsg) > 0;
```

InsiderTransactionID	TradeDate
1	09-02-08
2	08-25-08
3	08-20-08
4	08-15-08
5	08-15-08
6	07-31-08
7	08-31-07
8	08-01-08

Valid Ranges for Date & Time Data Types

- DATE (3 bytes) date range:
- January 1, 1 through December 31, 9999 A.D.

- SMALLDATETIME (4 bytes) date range:
- January 1, 1900 through June 6, 2079

- DATETIME (8 bytes) date range:
- January 1, 1753 through December 31, 9999

- DATETIME2 (6-8 bytes) date range:
- January 1, 1 A.D. through December 31, 9999 A.D.

Smalldatetime has limited range. The statement below will give a date range error.

```
SELECT CONVERT(smalldatetime, '2110-01-01')
/* Msg 242, Level 16, State 3, Line 1
The conversion of a varchar data type to a smalldatetime data type
resulted in an out-of-range value. */
```

```
-- Date Columbus discovers America
SELECT CONVERT(datetime, '14921012');
/* Msg 242, Level 16, State 3, Line 2
The conversion of a varchar data type to a datetime data type resulted in an out-of-range value. */
```

```
SELECT CONVERT(datetime2, '14921012');    -- 1492-10-10 00:00:00.0000000
```

```
SELECT CONVERT(date, '14921012');                    -- 1492-10-12
```

Last Week Calculations

```
-- SQL last Friday - Implied string to datetime conversions in dateadd & datediff
DECLARE @BaseFriday CHAR(8), @LastFriday datetime, @LastMonday datetime;
SET @BaseFriday = '19000105';
SELECT   @LastFriday = dateadd(dd,
         (datediff (dd, @BaseFriday, CURRENT_TIMESTAMP) / 7) * 7, @BaseFriday) ;
SELECT [Last Friday] = @LastFriday ;
```

Last Friday
2012-07-27 00:00:00.000

```
-- Last Monday (last week's Monday)
SELECT   @LastMonday=dateadd(dd,  (datediff (dd, @BaseFriday,
         CURRENT_TIMESTAMP) / 7) * 7 - 4, @BaseFriday)
SELECT [Last Monday]= @LastMonday;
```

Last Monday
2012-07-23 00:00:00.000

```
-- Last week - SUN - SAT
SELECT          [Last Week] = CONCAT(CONVERT(varchar,dateadd(day, -1, @LastMonday), 101), ' - ',
                CONVERT(varchar, dateadd(day, 1,  @LastFriday), 101))
```

Last Week
07/22/2012 - 07/28/2012

```
-- Next 10 weeks including this one; SUN - SAT
WITH CTE ( Number) AS (SELECT 1 UNION ALL SELECT Number + 1  FROM CTE  WHERE Number < 1000)
SELECT    TOP 10    [ Week] = CONCAT(CONVERT(varchar,dateadd(day, -1+number*7, @LastMonday), 101), ' - ',
                    CONVERT(varchar, dateadd(day, 1+number*7,  @LastFriday), 101))
FROM CTE OPTION ( MAXRECURSION 0);
```

Week
08/05/2012 - 08/11/2012
08/12/2012 - 08/18/2012
08/19/2012 - 08/25/2012
08/26/2012 - 09/01/2012
09/02/2012 - 09/08/2012
09/09/2012 - 09/15/2012
09/16/2012 - 09/22/2012
09/23/2012 - 09/29/2012
09/30/2012 - 10/06/2012
10/07/2012 - 10/13/2012

Specific Day Calculations

```
-- First day of current month
SELECT dateadd(month, datediff(month, 0, getdate()), 0);
```

```
-- 15th day of current month
SELECT dateadd(day,14,dateadd(month,datediff(month,0,getdate()),0));
```

```
-- First Monday of current month
SELECT   dateadd(day, (9-datepart(weekday,
         dateadd(month, datediff(month, 0, getdate()), 0)))%7,
         dateadd(month, datediff(month, 0, getdate()), 0)) ;
```

```
-- Next Monday calculation from the reference date which was a Monday
DECLARE @Now datetime = GETDATE();
DECLARE @NextMonday datetime = dateadd(dd, ((datediff(dd, '19000101', @Now)  / 7) * 7) + 7,
'19000101');
SELECT [Now]=@Now, [Next Monday]=@NextMonday;
```

```
-- Last Friday of current month
SELECT   dateadd(day, -7+(6-datepart(weekday,
         dateadd(month, datediff(month, 0, getdate())+1, 0)))%7,
         dateadd(month, datediff(month, 0, getdate())+1, 0)) ;
```

```
-- First day of next month
SELECT dateadd(month, datediff(month, 0, getdate())+1, 0);
```

```
-- 15th of next month
SELECT dateadd(day,14, dateadd(month, datediff(month, 0, getdate())+1, 0));
```

```
-- First Monday of next month
SELECT   dateadd(day, (9-datepart(weekday,
         dateadd(month, datediff(month, 0, getdate())+1, 0)))%7,
          dateadd(month, datediff(month, 0, getdate())+1, 0))  AS NextMonthMonday;
```

NextMonthMonday
2012-08-06 00:00:00.000

CHAPTER 15: Subqueries in SELECT Statements

Subqueries

Subquery ("inner query") is query within a query which is called the "outer query".

When a subquery involves columns form the outer query, it is called correlated subquery.

When a subquery has a table alias, it is called a derived table.

With SQL Server 2005 a new kind of subquery was introduced: Common Table Expression (CTE). A query can have one or more CTEs. If they are related, they are called nested CTEs. CTEs support recursion.

Correlated subquery is used to retrieve the last freight cost for the customer.

```
-- Correlated subquery - it has reference to an outer query column: A.CustomerID
USE Northwind;

SELECT  A.CustomerID,
    FORMAT(MIN(A.OrderDate), 'd')                           AS FirstOrder,
    FORMAT(MAX(A.OrderDate), 'd')                           AS LastOrder,
    FORMAT( (SELECT  TOP 1 B.Freight
            FROM    Orders B
            WHERE   B.CustomerID = A.CustomerID
            ORDER BY OrderDate DESC),'c','en-US')           AS LastFreight
FROM    Orders A
GROUP BY A.CustomerID ORDER BY A.CustomerID; -- (89 row(s) affected) - Partial results.
```

CustomerID	FirstOrder	LastOrder	LastFreight
ALFKI	8/25/1997	4/9/1998	$1.21
ANATR	9/18/1996	3/4/1998	$39.92
ANTON	11/27/1996	1/28/1998	$58.43
AROUT	11/15/1996	4/10/1998	$33.80
BERGS	8/12/1996	3/4/1998	$151.52
BLAUS	4/9/1997	4/29/1998	$31.14
BLONP	7/25/1996	1/12/1998	$7.09
BOLID	10/10/1996	3/24/1998	$16.16
BONAP	10/16/1996	5/6/1998	$38.28
BOTTM	12/20/1996	4/24/1998	$24.12
BSBEV	8/26/1996	4/14/1998	$123.83
CACTU	4/29/1997	4/28/1998	$0.33

Non-Correlated Subqueries

In the next query, the inner query is not linked to the outer query at all (no outer column is used in the inner query). The implication is that the inner query can be executed by itself. The inner query needs to return a single value in this instance due to the ">=" operator. If it were to return multiple values, error would result.

```
-- Non-correlated subquery
SELECT          Name,
                FORMAT(ListPrice, 'c','en-US')          AS ListPrice,
                ProductNumber,
                FORMAT(StandardCost, 'c','en-US')       AS StandardCost
FROM Production.Product
WHERE ListPrice >=
                        (SELECT ListPrice
                         FROM Production.Product
                        WHERE Name = 'Road-250 Black, 48' )

ORDER BY ListPrice DESC, Name;
GO
```

Name	ListPrice	ProductNumber	StandardCost
Road-150 Red, 44	$3,578.27	BK-R93R-44	$2,171.29
Road-150 Red, 48	$3,578.27	BK-R93R-48	$2,171.29
Road-150 Red, 52	$3,578.27	BK-R93R-52	$2,171.29
Road-150 Red, 56	$3,578.27	BK-R93R-56	$2,171.29
Road-150 Red, 62	$3,578.27	BK-R93R-62	$2,171.29
Mountain-100 Silver, 38	$3,399.99	BK-M82S-38	$1,912.15
Mountain-100 Silver, 42	$3,399.99	BK-M82S-42	$1,912.15
Mountain-100 Silver, 44	$3,399.99	BK-M82S-44	$1,912.15
Mountain-100 Silver, 48	$3,399.99	BK-M82S-48	$1,912.15
Mountain-100 Black, 38	$3,374.99	BK-M82B-38	$1,898.09
Mountain-100 Black, 42	$3,374.99	BK-M82B-42	$1,898.09
Mountain-100 Black, 44	$3,374.99	BK-M82B-44	$1,898.09
Mountain-100 Black, 48	$3,374.99	BK-M82B-48	$1,898.09
Road-250 Black, 44	$2,443.35	BK-R89B-44	$1,554.95
Road-250 Black, 48	$2,443.35	BK-R89B-48	$1,554.95
Road-250 Black, 52	$2,443.35	BK-R89B-52	$1,554.95
Road-250 Black, 58	$2,443.35	BK-R89B-58	$1,554.95
Road-250 Red, 44	$2,443.35	BK-R89R-44	$1,518.79
Road-250 Red, 48	$2,443.35	BK-R89R-48	$1,518.79
Road-250 Red, 52	$2,443.35	BK-R89R-52	$1,518.79
Road-250 Red, 58	$2,443.35	BK-R89R-58	$1,554.95

Subquery returned more than 1 value Error

The following query fails. The reason: the ">=" requires a single value on the right side. The subquery returns 46 values.

```
-- Non-correlated subquery
SELECT          Name,
                FORMAT(ListPrice, 'c','en-US')           AS ListPrice,
                ProductNumber,
                FORMAT(StandardCost, 'c','en-US')        AS StandardCost
FROM Production.Product
WHERE ListPrice >=
  (SELECT ListPrice
   FROM Production.Product
   WHERE Name LIKE 'Road%' )
ORDER BY ListPrice DESC, Name;
GO
/* Msg 512, Level 16, State 1, Line 3
Subquery returned more than 1 value. This is not permitted when the subquery follows =, !=, <, <= , >, >=
or when the subquery is used as an expression. */
```

If we change the WHERE clause predicate operator from ">=" to "IN" then the query will execute correctly since the IN operator works with a set of values on the right side.

```
-- Non-correlated subquery
SELECT   Name,
         FORMAT(ListPrice, 'c','en-US')           AS ListPrice,
         ProductNumber,
         FORMAT(StandardCost, 'c','en-US')        AS StandardCost
FROM Production.Product
WHERE ListPrice IN
         (SELECT ListPrice
          FROM  Production.Product  WHERE Name LIKE 'Road%' )
ORDER BY ListPrice DESC, Name;
-- (253 row(s) affected)  -- Partial results.
```

Name	ListPrice	ProductNumber	StandardCost
AWC Logo Cap	$8.99	CA-1098	$6.92
Racing Socks, L	$8.99	SO-R809-L	$3.36
Racing Socks, M	$8.99	SO-R809-M	$3.36
Road Bottle Cage	$8.99	BC-R205	$3.36
Road-650 Black, 44	$782.99	BK-R50B-44	$486.71
Road-650 Black, 48	$782.99	BK-R50B-48	$486.71
Road-650 Black, 52	$782.99	BK-R50B-52	$486.71

Correlated Subqueries

In a correlated subquery there is a reference to an outer query column. In other words, the subquery by itself cannot be executed due to the correlation. In the next query, the inner query references soh.SalesOrderID column from the outer query in the WHERE clause predicate which is like an EQUI-JOIN.

```
SELECT          soh.SalesOrderID,
                FORMAT (soh.OrderDate, 'yyyy-MM-dd')                    AS OrderDate,

                ( SELECT FORMAT(MAX(sod.UnitPrice),'c','en-US')
                  FROM   Sales.SalesOrderDetail AS sod
                  WHERE  soh.SalesOrderID = sod.SalesOrderID )          AS MaxUnitPrice,

                FORMAT(TotalDue, 'c', 'en-US')                          AS TotalDue
FROM     Sales.SalesOrderHeader AS soh
ORDER BY MaxUnitPrice DESC, SalesOrderID;      -- (31465 row(s) affected) - Partial results.
```

SalesOrderID	OrderDate	MaxUnitPrice	TotalDue
51087	2007-07-01	$953.63	$2,721.27
51099	2007-07-01	$953.63	$5,276.64
51119	2007-07-01	$953.63	$2,040.14
51173	2007-07-01	$953.63	$1,457.54
51701	2007-08-01	$953.63	$2,634.93
51798	2007-08-01	$953.63	$907.09
51805	2007-08-01	$953.63	$907.09
51808	2007-08-01	$953.63	$1,827.45
51861	2007-08-01	$953.63	$11,762.43
53489	2007-09-01	$953.63	$1,814.18

The next query with correlated subquery list sales staff with 0.015 commission rate.

```
SELECT CONCAT(p.LastName,', ', p.FirstName) AS SalesPerson, e.BusinessEntityID AS EmployeeID
FROM Person.Person AS p
                INNER JOIN HumanResources.Employee AS e
                        ON e.BusinessEntityID = p.BusinessEntityID
WHERE 0.015 IN  (SELECT CommissionPct   FROM Sales.SalesPerson sp
                        WHERE e.BusinessEntityID = sp.BusinessEntityID)  ORDER BY SalesPerson;
```

SalesPerson	EmployeeID
Carson, Jillian	277
Mitchell, Linda	276
Saraiva, José	282

Single-Valued Correlated Subqueries

The query syntax determines if we can use a single-valued subquery or multiple-valued. A subquery can be the argument of a function.

```
USE AdventureWorks2012;
```

```
-- Single value subquery in SELECT list
SELECT   SOH.SalesOrderID                                      AS SOID,
         CONVERT(DATE,SOH.OrderDate)                           AS OrderDate,
         FORMAT(SOH.Subtotal,'c0','en-US')                     AS Subtotal,
         (SELECT MAX(SOD.UnitPrice)
          FROM Sales.SalesOrderDetail AS SOD
          WHERE SOH.SalesOrderID=SOD.SalesOrderID)             AS MaxUnitPrice
FROM Sales.SalesOrderHeader SOH    ORDER BY SOID;
--(31467 row(s) affected) - Partial results.
```

SOID	OrderDate	Subtotal	MaxUnitPrice
43659	2005-07-01	$20,566	2039.994
43660	2005-07-01	$1,294	874.794

```
-- Make the subquery the argument of the FORMAT function
SELECT   TOP (10)            SOH.SalesOrderID                      AS SOID,
                             CONVERT(DATE,SOH.OrderDate)           AS OrderDate,
                             FORMAT(SOH.Subtotal,'c0','en-US')     AS Subtotal,
                             FORMAT(
      (SELECT MAX(SOD.UnitPrice)
      FROM Sales.SalesOrderDetail AS SOD
      WHERE SOH.SalesOrderID=SOD.SalesOrderID)
                             ,'c2','en-US')                        AS MaxUnitPrice
FROM Sales.SalesOrderHeader SOH   ORDER BY SOID;
```

SOID	OrderDate	Subtotal	MaxUnitPrice
43659	2005-07-01	$20,566	$2,039.99
43660	2005-07-01	$1,294	$874.79
43661	2005-07-01	$32,726	$2,039.99
43662	2005-07-01	$28,833	$2,146.96
43663	2005-07-01	$419	$419.46
43664	2005-07-01	$24,433	$2,039.99
43665	2005-07-01	$14,353	$2,039.99
43666	2005-07-01	$5,056	$2,146.96
43667	2005-07-01	$6,107	$2,039.99
43668	2005-07-01	$35,944	$2,146.96

Correlated Subqueries with Same Table

In a correlated subquery, we can use a table from the outer query. In such a case table alias usage is required. In the next query with correlated subquery which lists same part suppliers, the ProductVendor table is referenced by both the outer query and inner query, therefore table alias is required.

```
SELECT          p.Name                          AS ProductName,
                v.Name                          AS Vendor,
                pv1.BusinessEntityID            AS VendorID
FROM Purchasing.ProductVendor pv1
   INNER JOIN Production.Product p ON p.ProductID = pv1.ProductID
   INNER JOIN Purchasing.Vendor v  ON v.BusinessEntityID = pv1.BusinessEntityID
WHERE pv1.ProductID IN     (        SELECT pv2.ProductID
                                    FROM Purchasing.ProductVendor pv2
                                    WHERE pv1.BusinessEntityID <> pv2.BusinessEntityID)
ORDER  BY ProductName, Vendor;             -- (347 row(s) affected) - Partial results.
```

ProductName	Vendor	VendorID
Internal Lock Washer 7	Aurora Bike Center	1616
Internal Lock Washer 7	Pro Sport Industries	1686
Internal Lock Washer 8	Aurora Bike Center	1616
Internal Lock Washer 8	Pro Sport Industries	1686
Internal Lock Washer 9	Aurora Bike Center	1616
Internal Lock Washer 9	Pro Sport Industries	1686

CROSS APPLY with Correlated Subquery

The CROSS APPLY operator can connect tables with correlated subqueries as demonstrated following, INNER JOIN would not work in this case.

```
USE AdventureWorks2012;    DECLARE @Year INT = 2007, @Month INT = 2;
SELECT    s.Name                                                  AS Customer,
          FORMAT(SalesAmount.OrderTotal,'c','en-US')              AS [Total Sales]
FROM    Sales.Customer AS c  INNER JOIN Sales.Store AS s   ON s.BusinessEntityID = c.StoreID
     CROSS APPLY (          SELECT    soh.CustomerId,   Sum(sod.LineTotal) AS OrderTotal
                            FROM    Sales.SalesOrderHeader AS soh
                  INNER JOIN Sales.SalesOrderDetail AS sod
                                ON sod.SalesOrderId = soh.SalesOrderId
                            WHERE  soh.CustomerId = c.CustomerID
                            AND OrderDate > = DATEFROMPARTS(@Year, @Month, 1)
                            AND OrderDate <  DATEADD(mm, 1, DATEFROMPARTS(@Year, @Month, 1))
                            GROUP BY soh.CustomerId)              AS SalesAmount
ORDER BY Customer;          -- (10 row(s) affected) - Partial results.
```

Customer	Total Sales
Bicycle Exporters	$782.99
First Center	$1,000.44
Metro Cycle Shop	$782.99
Mountain Emporium	$782.99

Derived Tables: SELECT from SELECT

A non-correlated subquery can be made into a derived table by enclosing it in parenthesis and assigning a table alias, such as "CAT" in the following example. It can then be used like a regular table for example in JOINs.

```
USE Northwind;

SELECT  c.CategoryName  AS Category,
        p.ProductName,    p.UnitPrice,    CAT.NoOfProducts
FROM    Categories c
     INNER JOIN Products p
       ON c.CategoryID = p.CategoryID
     INNER JOIN
                        (SELECT  c.CategoryID,
                                 NoOfProducts = count(* )
                        FROM     Categories c
                          INNER JOIN Products p1
                                 ON c.CategoryID = p1.CategoryID
                        GROUP BY c.CategoryID)                        AS CAT

       ON c.CategoryID = CAT.CategoryID
ORDER BY Category;
-- (77 row(s) affected)  - Partial results.
```

Category	ProductName	UnitPrice
Dairy Products	Raclette Courdavault	55.00
Dairy Products	Camembert Pierrot	34.00
Dairy Products	Gudbrandsdalsost	36.00
Dairy Products	Flotemysost	21.50
Dairy Products	Mozzarella di Giovanni	34.80
Grains/Cereals	Gustaf's Knäckebröd	21.00
Grains/Cereals	Tunnbröd	9.00
Grains/Cereals	Singaporean Hokkien Fried Mee	14.00
Grains/Cereals	Filo Mix	7.00
Grains/Cereals	Gnocchi di nonna Alice	38.00
Grains/Cereals	Ravioli Angelo	19.50

Results from the subquery (derived table).

CategoryID	NoOfProducts
1	12
2	12
3	13
4	10
5	7
6	6
7	5
8	12

The UNION & UNION ALL Set Operators

UNION (distinct, duplicates eliminated) and UNION ALL (duplicates allowed) merge two or more sets of data into one set. Important points to remember about UNION:

- First SELECT column list establishes column names and data types; if INTO used it goes here
- Subsequent SELECTs must match the column structure; column names can be any; NULL if no data
- ORDER BY goes at the very end with the last SELECT

T-SQL UNION query merges data from different countries into a single result set.

```
USE NorthWind;
SELECT  ContactName,
        CompanyName,
        City,
        Country,
        Phone
FROM  Customers
WHERE  Country IN ( 'USA', 'Canada' )
-- (16 row(s) affected)
UNION
SELECT  ContactName,
        CompanyName             AS Company,
        City,     Country,
        Phone                   AS Telephone
FROM  Customers
WHERE  Country IN ( 'Germany', 'France' )
-- (22 row(s) affected)
UNION
SELECT  ContactName             AS Contact,
        CompanyName,     City,  Country,
        Phone                   AS Telephone
FROM  Customers
WHERE  Country IN ( 'Brazil', 'Spain' )
-- (14 row(s) affected)
ORDER  BY CompanyName,    ContactName ASC;
-- (52 row(s) affected)  - Partial results.
```

ContactName	CompanyName	City	Country	Phone
Maria Anders	Alfreds Futterkiste	Berlin	Germany	030-0074321
Hanna Moos	Blauer See Delikatessen	Mannheim	Germany	0621-08460
Frédérique Citeaux	Blondesddsl père et fils	Strasbourg	France	88.60.15.31
Martín Sommer	Bólido Comidas preparadas	Madrid	Spain	(91) 555 22 82

CTE: Common Table Expression for Structured Coding

Common Table Expression is new in SQL Server 2005. It is similar to derived tables in one aspect with a difference: it is defined at the very beginning of a the query, above the main(outer) query. In addition, CTEs can be nested and defined as recursive.

```
USE AdventureWorks2012;
```

```
WITH CTE (ManagerNode, StaffCount)
AS
(
    SELECT          OrganizationNode.GetAncestor(1),
                    COUNT(*)
    FROM HumanResources.Employee AS e
    GROUP BY OrganizationNode.GetAncestor(1)
)

SELECT              CONCAT(LEFT(FirstName,1), '. ', LastName)            AS Manager,
                    e.JobTitle,
                    StaffCount
FROM CTE s
        INNER JOIN HumanResources.Employee e
                    ON s.ManagerNode = e.OrganizationNode
        INNER JOIN Person.Person c
                    ON c.BusinessEntityID = e.BusinessEntityID
ORDER BY Manager;
```

Manager	Title	StaffCount
A. Alberts	European Sales Manager	3
A. Hill	Production Supervisor - WC10	7
A. Wright	Master Scheduler	4
B. Diaz	Production Supervisor - WC40	12
B. Welcker	Vice President of Sales	3
C. Kleinerman	Maintenance Supervisor	4
C. Petculescu	Production Supervisor - WC10	5
C. Randall	Production Supervisor - WC30	6
D. Bradley	Marketing Manager	8
D. Hamilton	Production Supervisor - WC40	6
D. Liu	Accounts Manager	7
D. Miller	Research and Development Manager	3
E. Gubbels	Production Supervisor - WC20	10
G. Altman	Facilities Manager	2
H. Abolrous	Quality Assurance Manager	2

Multiple CTEs Query

A query can have multiple CTEs, they can even be nested (CTE has reference to previous CTE). The two CTEs in the following query are first name and last name frequencies.

```
USE AdventureWorks2012;

WITH cteLastNameFreq

   AS (SELECT      LastName          AS [LastNames],
                   count(* )         AS [LNFrequency]
       FROM    Person.Person
       GROUP BY LastName),

   cteFirstNameFreq
   AS (SELECT      FirstName         AS [FirstNames],
                   count(* )         AS [FNFrequency]
      FROM    Person.Person
      GROUP BY FirstName)

SELECT   CONCAT(rtrim(FirstName), ' ', rtrim(LastName))       AS [Name],
                   isnull(Title,'')                           AS [Title] ,
                   f.FNFrequency,
                   l.LNFrequency
FROM     Person.Person c
      INNER JOIN cteFirstNameFreq AS f
        ON c.FirstName = f.FirstNames
      INNER JOIN cteLastNameFreq AS l
        ON c.LastName = l.LastNames
WHERE    LastName LIKE 'P%' ORDER BY [Name];
-- (1187 row(s) affected) - Partial results;
```

Name	Title	FNFrequency	LNFrequency
Aaron Patterson		56	117
Aaron Perez		56	170
Aaron Perry		56	122
Aaron Phillips		56	80
Aaron Powell		56	116
Abby Patel		19	86
Abby Perez		19	170
Abigail Patterson		76	117
Abigail Patterson		76	117
Abigail Perry		76	122
Abigail Peterson		76	92
Abigail Powell		76	116

Testing Common Table Expressions

A CTE can be tested independently of the main query if it does not have nesting (reference to a previous CTE). The following screen snapshot displays the execution of the first CTE SELECT query.

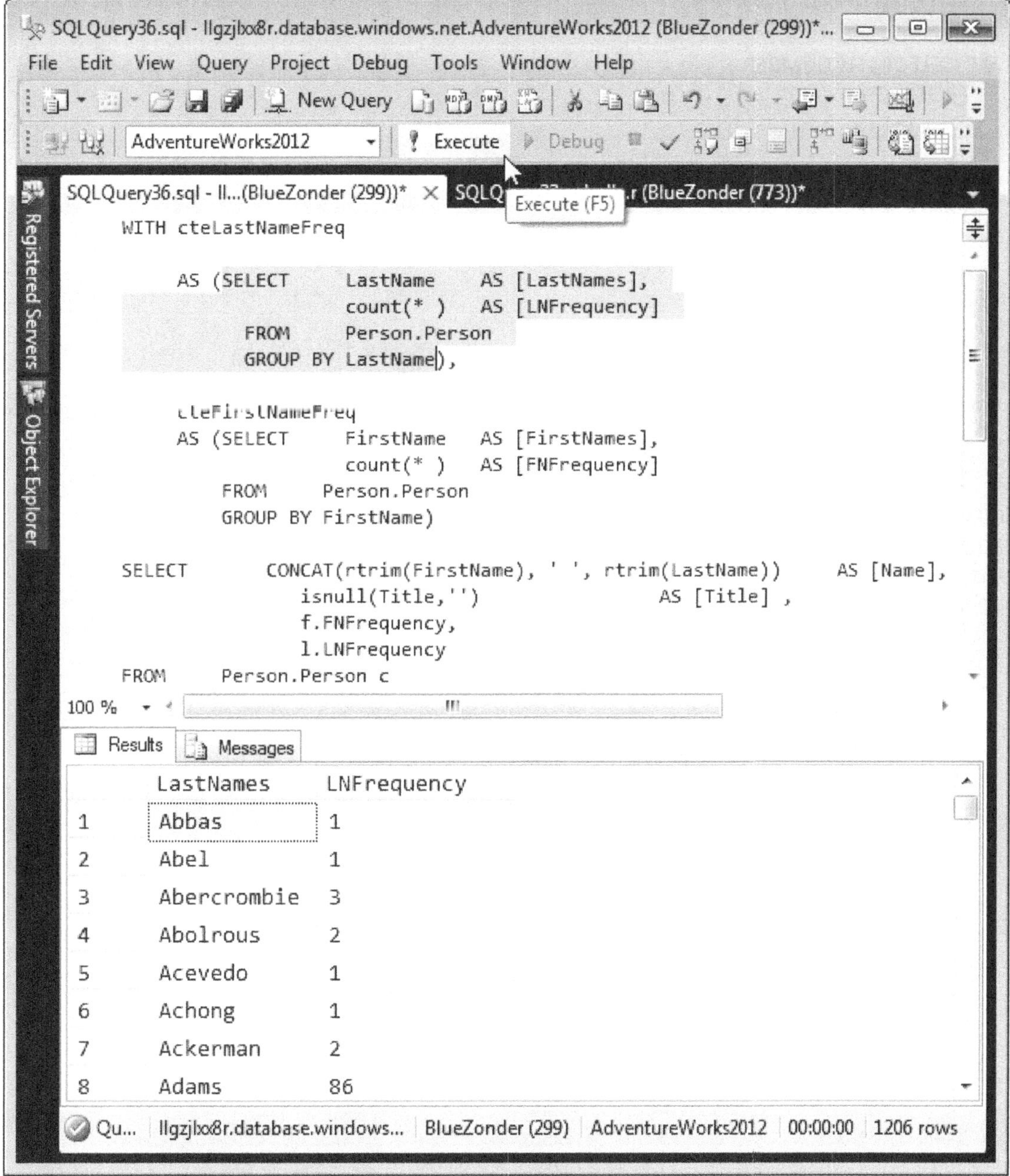
SQLQuery36.sql - llgzjlxx8r.database.windows.net.AdventureWorks2012 (BlueZonder (299))*...
File Edit View Query Project Debug Tools Window Help
New Query
AdventureWorks2012
Execute
Debug
Execute (F5)
SQLQuery36.sql - ll...(BlueZonder (299))*
Registered Servers
Object Explorer
WITH cteLastNameFreq
AS (SELECT LastName AS [LastNames],
count(*) AS [LNFrequency]
FROM Person.Person
GROUP BY LastName),
cteFirstNameFreq
AS (SELECT FirstName AS [FirstNames],
count(*) AS [FNFrequency]
FROM Person.Person
GROUP BY FirstName)
SELECT CONCAT(rtrim(FirstName), ' ', rtrim(LastName)) AS [Name],
isnull(Title,'') AS [Title] ,
f.FNFrequency,
l.LNFrequency
FROM Person.Person c
100 %
Results
Messages
LastNames LNFrequency
1 Abbas 1
2 Abel 1
3 Abercrombie 3
4 Abolrous 2
5 Acevedo 1
6 Achong 1
7 Ackerman 2
8 Adams 86
Qu...
llgzjlxx8r.database.windows...
BlueZonder (299)
AdventureWorks2012
00:00:00
1206 rows

Nested CTEs Queries

CTEs can be nested by reference to a previous CTE like a table.

```
;WITH CTE1
   AS (SELECT 1 AS NUMBER
      UNION ALL
      SELECT 1),
   CTE2
   AS (SELECT 1 AS NUMBER
      FROM   CTE1 x,
            CTE1 y),
   CTE3
   AS (SELECT 1 AS NUMBER
      FROM   CTE2 x,
            CTE2 y),
   CTE4
   AS (SELECT 1 AS NUMBER
      FROM   CTE3 x,
            CTE3 y),
   CTE8BIT
   AS (SELECT ROW_NUMBER()
              OVER(ORDER BY NUMBER) AS INTSequence
      FROM   CTE4)
SELECT *
FROM   CTE8BIT
ORDER BY INTSequence;
-- (256 row(s) affected) - Partial results.
```

INTSequence
241
242
243
244
245
246
247
248
249
250
251
252
253
254
255
256

CTE nesting: cteLastSalary has a nested reference to cteLastSalaryChange

```
USE AdventureWorks2012;

WITH cteLastSalaryChange
   AS (SELECT      BusinessEntityID                    AS EmployeeID,
                   Max(RateChangeDate)                 AS ChangeDate
     FROM    HumanResources.EmployeePayHistory    GROUP BY BusinessEntityID),

   cteLastSalary
   AS (SELECT      eph.BusinessEntityID                AS EmployeeID,      Rate
     FROM   HumanResources.EmployeePayHistory eph
          INNER JOIN cteLastSalaryChange lsc
           ON lsc.EmployeeID = eph.BusinessEntityID
             AND lsc.ChangeDate = eph.RateChangeDate)

-- SELECT * FROM cteLastSalary  -- for testing & debugging

SELECT TOP 1 FORMAT( Rate, 'c', 'en-US') AS SecondHighestPayRate
FROM    (SELECT   TOP 2 Rate     FROM    cteLastSalary    ORDER BY Rate DESC) a    -- Derived table
ORDER BY Rate ASC;
```

SecondHighestPayRate
$84.13

Testing Nested CTEs

Nested CTEs can be tested independently of the main query the following way.

```
USE AdventureWorks2012;
WITH cteLastSalaryChange
   AS (SELECT      BusinessEntityID                    AS EmployeeID,
                   Max(RateChangeDate)                 AS ChangeDate
     FROM    HumanResources.EmployeePayHistory
     GROUP BY BusinessEntityID),
   cteLastSalary
   AS (SELECT      eph.BusinessEntityID                AS EmployeeID,
                   Rate
     FROM   HumanResources.EmployeePayHistory eph
          INNER JOIN cteLastSalaryChange lsc
           ON lsc.EmployeeID = eph.BusinessEntityID
             AND lsc.ChangeDate = eph.RateChangeDate)
SELECT * FROM cteLastSalary  -- for testing & debugging
```

In Query Editor, uncomment the testing line, select (highlight) the top part of the query and execute it

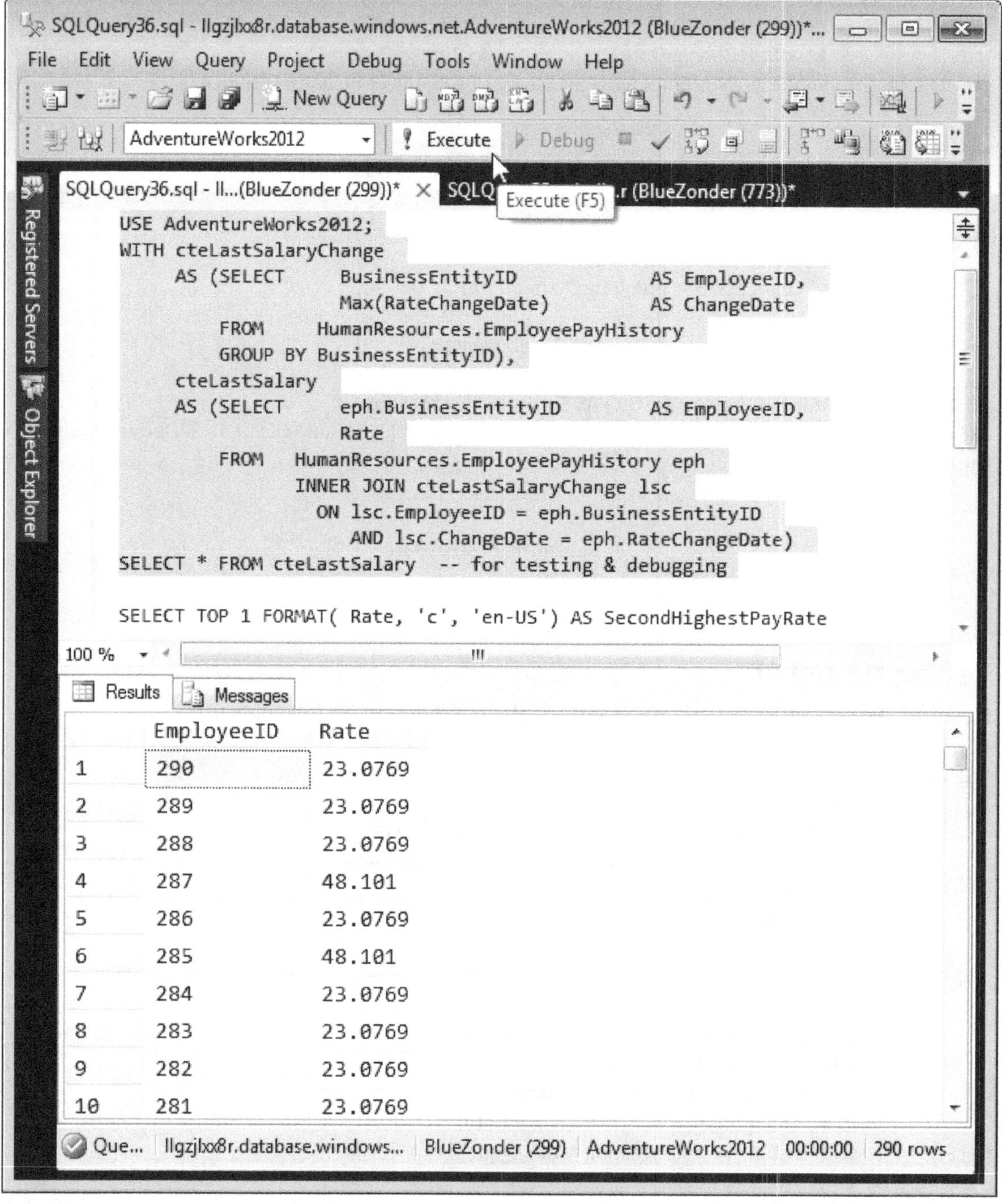
SQLQuery36.sql - llgzjlxx8r.database.windows.net.AdventureWorks2012 (BlueZonder (299))*...
File Edit View Query Project Debug Tools Window Help
New Query
AdventureWorks2012
Execute
Debug
Execute (F5)
SQLQuery36.sql - ll...(BlueZonder (299))*
SQLQ
.r (BlueZonder (773))*
Registered Servers
Object Explorer
USE AdventureWorks2012;
WITH cteLastSalaryChange
AS (SELECT BusinessEntityID AS EmployeeID,
Max(RateChangeDate) AS ChangeDate
FROM HumanResources.EmployeePayHistory
GROUP BY BusinessEntityID),
cteLastSalary
AS (SELECT eph.BusinessEntityID AS EmployeeID,
Rate
FROM HumanResources.EmployeePayHistory eph
INNER JOIN cteLastSalaryChange lsc
ON lsc.EmployeeID = eph.BusinessEntityID
AND lsc.ChangeDate = eph.RateChangeDate)
SELECT * FROM cteLastSalary -- for testing & debugging
SELECT TOP 1 FORMAT(Rate, 'c', 'en-US') AS SecondHighestPayRate
100 %
Results
Messages
EmployeeID Rate
1 290 23.0769
2 289 23.0769
3 288 23.0769
4 287 48.101
5 286 23.0769
6 285 48.101
7 284 23.0769
8 283 23.0769
9 282 23.0769
10 281 23.0769
Que... llgzjlxx8r.database.windows... BlueZonder (299) AdventureWorks2012 00:00:00 290 rows

Recursive CTEs for Tree Hierarchy Processing

Recursive CTEs are one of the most exciting new features introduced with SQL Server 2005. They allow tree processing, such as organizational charts or bill of materials parts assembly, as well as generating sets of data without tables. The following recursive CTE generates 1 million integers all by itself. The query execution time is 10 seconds as it can be seen in the lower right.

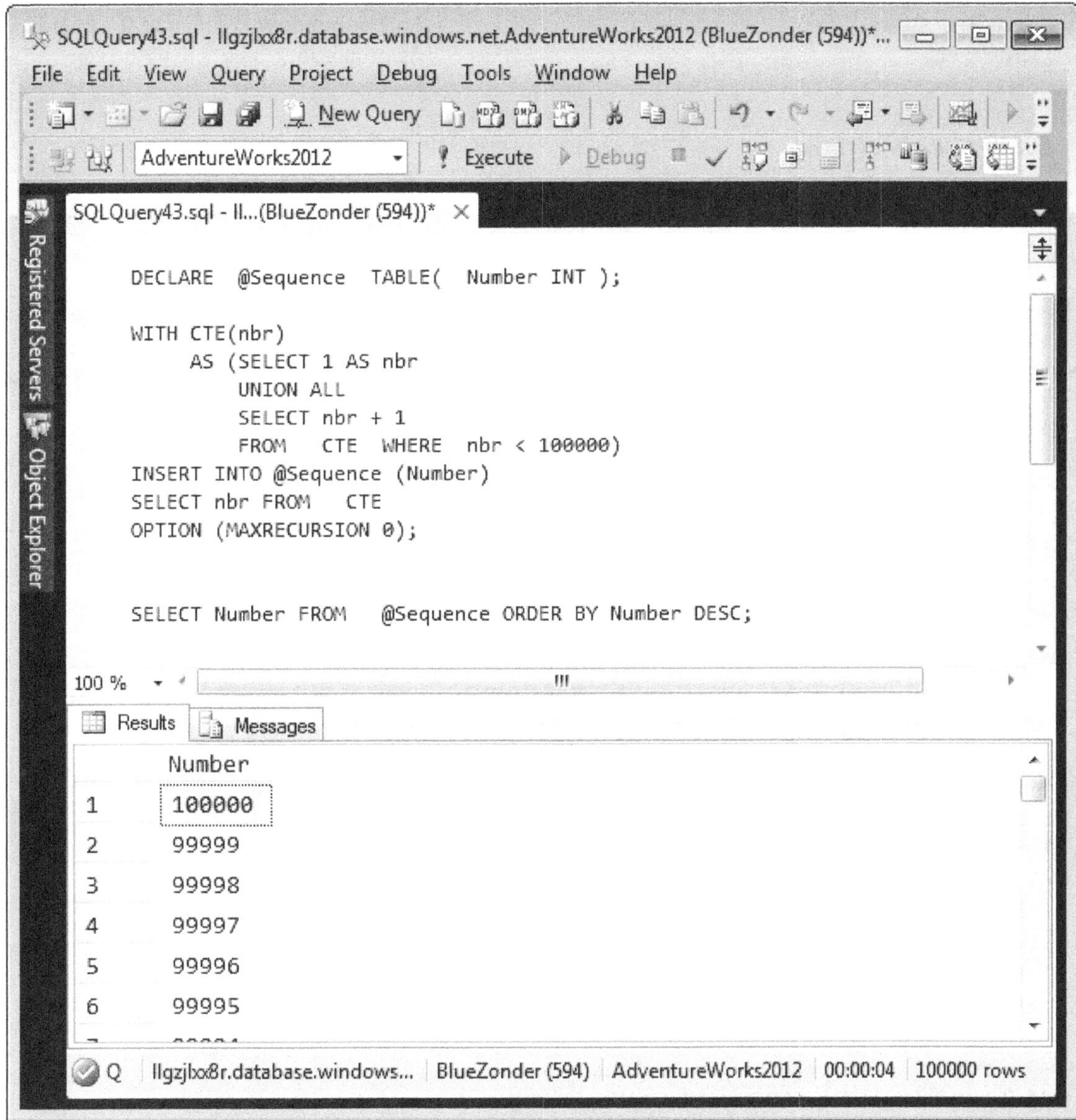

Recursive Generation of Date & Month Sequences

Date sequence can be generated without a calendar table (Note: generally it is helpful to have a calendar table in the database) using recursive CTE.

```
DECLARE @StartDate date = '20160701', @Range smallint = 1000;

WITH cteSEQ ( SeqNo) as
(
    SELECT 0                                    -- Anchor member
    UNION ALL                                   -- Assemble set
    SELECT SeqNo + 1                            -- Recursive member
    FROM cteSEQ
    WHERE SeqNo < @Range
)
SELECT TOP 10 [DATE]=DATEADD(day, SeqNo, @StartDate)
FROM cteSEQ
OPTION ( MAXRECURSION 0);
GO
```

DATE
2016-07-01
2016-07-02
2016-07-03
2016-07-04
2016-07-05
2016-07-06
2016-07-07
2016-07-08
2016-07-09
2016-07-10

```
-- Month sequence generation
DECLARE @StartDate date = '20160701', @Range smallint = 100;
WITH cteSEQ ( SeqNo) as
(
    SELECT 0                                    -- Anchor member
    UNION ALL                                   -- Assemble set
    SELECT SeqNo + 1                            -- Recursive member
    FROM cteSEQ
    WHERE SeqNo < @Range
)
SELECT TOP 3 [DATE]=DATEADD(month, SeqNo, @StartDate)
FROM cteSEQ  OPTION ( MAXRECURSION 0);
```

Generate Month Names in Different Languages

The following query can be used to generate month names in any of the SQL Server 2012 supported languages.

```
SET language Spanish;  -- Se cambió la configuración de idioma a Español.
;WITH CTE AS
(   SELECT    1 MonthNo, CONVERT(DATE, '19000101') MonthFirst
    UNION ALL
    SELECT    MonthNo+1, DATEADD(Month, 1, MonthFirst)
    FROM  CTE
    WHERE Month(MonthFirst) < 12    )
SELECT  MonthNo AS MonthNumber,  DATENAME(MONTH, MonthFirst) AS MonthName
FROM  CTE
ORDER BY MonthNo;
SET language English; -- Changed language setting to us_english.
```

```
SET language Hungarian;  -- Nyelvi beállítás átállítva a következőre: magyar.
;WITH CTE AS
(   SELECT    1 MonthNo, CONVERT(DATE, '19000101') MonthFirst
    UNION ALL
    SELECT    MonthNo+1, DATEADD(Month, 1, MonthFirst)
    FROM  CTE
    WHERE Month(MonthFirst) < 12    )
SELECT  MonthNo AS MonthNumber,  DATENAME(MONTH, MonthFirst) AS MonthName
FROM  CTE
ORDER BY MonthNo;
SET language English; -- Changed language setting to us_english.
```

MonthNumber	MonthName
1	Enero
2	Febrero
3	Marzo
4	Abril
5	Mayo
6	Junio
7	Julio
8	Agosto
9	Septiembre
10	Octubre
11	Noviembre
12	Diciembre

MonthNumber	MonthName
1	január
2	február
3	március
4	április
5	május
6	június
7	július
8	augusztus
9	szeptember
10	október
11	november
12	december

Graphical Organizational Chart of AdventureWorks Cycles

T-SQL recursive CTE query generates the entire company chart of AdventureWorks Cycles. The anchor term is Ken Sanchez CEO with ManagerID as NULL. Everybody else in the company has a ManagerID which is not NULL.

```
USE AdventureWorks2012;

WITH cteEmployeeTree
   AS (SELECT     Root.EmployeeName,  Root.ManagerName,
                  Root.EmployeeNode, Root.ManagerNode,
                  CONVERT(VARCHAR(MAX),Root.PathSequence) AS PathLabel
      FROM  (SELECT EmployeeName = CONCAT(p.FirstName, SPACE(1), p.LastName),
             ManagerName = convert(VARCHAR(128),''),
             e.OrganizationNode AS EmployeeNode,
             e.OrganizationNode.GetAncestor(1) AS ManagerNode,
             char(64 + ROW_NUMBER()  OVER(ORDER BY e.BusinessEntityID)) AS PathSequence
          FROM  HumanResources.Employee e
             INNER JOIN Person.Person p
              ON e.BusinessEntityID = p.BusinessEntityID
          WHERE  e.OrganizationNode.GetAncestor(1) IS NULL) Root              -- Anchor/root term
(above)
      UNION ALL                                           -- Build a set
      SELECT      Branch.EmployeeName,                    -- Recursive term (below)
                  Branch.ManagerName,
                  Branch.EmployeeNode, Branch.ManagerNode,
                  PathLabel = Branch.PathLabel + CONVERT(VARCHAR(MAX),  Branch.PathSequence)
      FROM  (SELECT EmployeeName = CONCAT(p.FirstName, SPACE(1), p.LastName),
            ManagerName = CONVERT(VARCHAR(128),CONCAT(pm.FirstName, SPACE(1), pm.LastName)),
             e.OrganizationNode AS EmployeeNode,
             e.OrganizationNode.GetAncestor(1) AS ManagerNode,
             cte.PathLabel,
             PathSequence = char(64 + ROW_NUMBER()  OVER(ORDER BY e.BusinessEntityID))
          FROM  cteEmployeeTree cte
             INNER JOIN HumanResources.Employee e
              ON e.OrganizationNode.GetAncestor(1) = cte.EmployeeNode
             INNER JOIN Person.Person p
              ON e.BusinessEntityID = p.BusinessEntityID
             INNER JOIN HumanResources.Employee em
              ON em.OrganizationNode = e.OrganizationNode.GetAncestor(1)
             INNER JOIN Person.Person pm
              ON em.BusinessEntityID = pm.BusinessEntityID) Branch)
-- Outer / main query
SELECT   CONCAT(REPLICATE(CHAR(9), LEN(PathLabel)-1),  -- tabs for indenting
                  EmployeeName) AS EmployeeName
FROM     cteEmployeeTree  ORDER BY PathLabel;
```

The resulting organizational chart was generated by Word as tabs (CHAR(9)) were converted to table columns (partial results).

EmployeeName				
Ken Sánchez				
	Terri Duffy			
		Roberto Tamburello		
			Rob Walters	
			Gail Erickson	
			Jossef Goldberg	
			Dylan Miller	
				Diane Margheim
				Gigi Matthew
				Michael Raheem
			Ovidiu Cracium	
				Thierry D'Hers
				Janice Galvin
			Michael Sullivan	
			Sharon Salavaria	
	David Bradley			
		Kevin Brown		
		John Wood		
		Mary Dempsey		
		Wanida Benshoof		
		Terry Eminhizer		
		Sariya Harnpadoungsataya		
		Mary Gibson		
		Jill Williams		
	James Hamilton			
		Peter Krebs		
			Jo Brown	
				Guy Gilbert
				Mark McArthur
				Britta Simon
				Margie Shoop
				Rebecca Laszlo
				Annik Stahl
				Suchitra Mohan
				Brandon Heidepriem
				Jose Lugo
				Chris Okelberry
				Kim Abercrombie
				Ed Dudenhoefer
			JoLynn Dobney	
				Bryan Baker
				James Kramer

Chain of Command Recursive Query

Find all ancestors (superiors) of a tree node(employee), all the up to the root of the tree (CEO in this instance).

```
USE AdventureWorks2012; DECLARE @EmployeeID INT = 100;
WITH CTE(Name, EmployeeNode, ManagerNode, Level)
   AS (SELECT      CONCAT(FirstName,' ', LastName),
                   OrganizationNode,   OrganizationNode.GetAncestor(1),  0 AS Level
      FROM   HumanResources.Employee AS E
         INNER JOIN Person.Person AS P
              ON P.BusinessEntityID = E.BusinessEntityID
      WHERE  E.BusinessEntityID = @EmployeeID
      UNION ALL
      SELECT       CONCAT(P.FirstName,' ', P.LastName),
                   HRE.OrganizationNode,   HRE.OrganizationNode.GetAncestor(1),  Level + 1
      FROM   HumanResources.Employee AS HRE
         INNER JOIN Person.Person AS P
              ON P.BusinessEntityID = HRE.BusinessEntityID
         INNER JOIN CTE AS E
              ON ManagerNode = HRE.OrganizationNode)
SELECT STUFF((SELECT CONCAT(', ', Name)
        FROM   CTE      ORDER  BY Level
        FOR XML PATH('')), 1, 2, '') AS [Chain of Command];
```

Chain of Command
Lolan Song, Kok-Ho Loh, Peter Krebs, James Hamilton, Ken Sánchez

Graphical Bill of Materials for Mountain-100 Silver, 44 Bike

T-SQL query will generate bill of materials (assembly) listing for Mountain-100 Silver, 44 mountain bike. The AdventureWorks2012 database image for Mountain-100 Silver, 44 in Production.ProductPhoto table.

```
USE AdventureWorks2012;
DECLARE         @StartProductID int         = 773,          -- Mountain-100 Silver, 44
                @CheckDate datetime          = '20080201';

  WITH cteBOM(ProductAssemblyID, ComponentID, ComponentName,   RecursionLevel)
  AS (
    SELECT b.ProductAssemblyID, b.ComponentID, p.Name,   0
         FROM Production.BillOfMaterials b
          INNER JOIN Production.Product p
            ON b.ComponentID = p.ProductID
    WHERE       b.ProductAssemblyID = @StartProductID
                AND @CheckDate >= b.StartDate
                AND @CheckDate <= ISNULL(b.EndDate, @CheckDate)     -- Anchor/root member (above)
    UNION ALL                                                        -- Build a set
    SELECT      b.ProductAssemblyID, b.ComponentID, p.Name,          -- Recursive member (below)
                RecursionLevel + 1
    FROM cteBOM c
      INNER JOIN Production.BillOfMaterials b
        ON b.ProductAssemblyID = c.ComponentID
      INNER JOIN Production.Product p
        ON b.ComponentID = p.ProductID
    WHERE       @CheckDate >= b.StartDate          AND @CheckDate <= ISNULL(b.EndDate, @CheckDate)   )
-- Outer/main query
  SELECT CONCAT(REPLICATE(CHAR(9), RecursionLevel),  -- Generate indents with tab character
                (SELECT Name FROM Production.Product WHERE ProductID=ProductAssemblyID)) AS PartName,
                ComponentName
         FROM cteBOM    GROUP BY  RecursionLevel,ProductAssemblyID,ComponentName
  ORDER BY      RecursionLevel, ProductAssemblyID,ComponentName    OPTION (MAXRECURSION 10);
-- (87 row(s) affected)
```

Partial graphical bill of materials for the mountain bike

PartName	ComponentName			
Mountain-100 Silver, 44	Chain			
Mountain-100 Silver, 44	Front Brakes			
Mountain-100 Silver, 44	Front Derailleur			
Mountain-100 Silver, 44	HL Bottom Bracket			
Mountain-100 Silver, 44	HL Crankset			
Mountain-100 Silver, 44	HL Headset			
Mountain-100 Silver, 44	Rear Brakes			
Mountain-100 Silver, 44	Rear Derailleur			
	HL Mountain Seat Assembly	HL Mountain Seat/Saddle		
	HL Mountain Seat Assembly	Pinch Bolt		
	HL Mountain Seat Assembly	Seat Lug		
	HL Crankset	Chainring Nut		
	HL Crankset	Freewheel		
	HL Crankset	HL Crankarm		
	HL Bottom Bracket	BB Ball Bearing		
	HL Bottom Bracket	HL Shell		
		BB Ball Bearing	Bearing Ball	
		BB Ball Bearing	Cone-Shaped Race	
		Top Tube	Metal Sheet 2	
		HL Fork	Blade	
		HL Fork	Fork Crown	
		HL Fork	Fork End	
		HL Fork	Steerer	
			Blade	Metal Sheet 5
			Fork End	Metal Sheet 2
			Fork Crown	Metal Sheet 5
			Steerer	Metal Sheet 6

PIVOT Operator to Transform Rows Into Columns

The PIVOT operator, new to SQL Server 2005, can be used to create pivot table also called cross tabulation (crosstab). The data to be PIVOTed is generated by a CTE.

```
USE AdventureWorks2012;
;WITH CTE    AS (SELECT  YEAR           = YEAR(orderDate),
                         QUARTER        = DatePart(qq,OrderDate),
                         Sales          = Sum(TotalDue)
    FROM    Sales.SalesOrderHeader   GROUP BY YEAR(OrderDate), DatePart(qq,OrderDate))
SELECT * FROM CTE;
```

YEAR	QUARTER	Sales
2007	4	14886562.6775
2006	3	11555907.1472
2007	1	7492396.3224
2007	2	9379298.7027
2006	1	6562121.6796
2006	4	9397824.1785
2008	3	56178.9223
2007	3	15413231.8434
2005	3	5203127.8807
2008	1	12744940.3554
2005	4	7490122.7457
2008	2	16087078.2305
2006	2	6947995.43

PIVOT operator takes the data from the CTE source, aggregates it and transforms it to columns.

```
;WITH CTE    AS (SELECT  YEAR           = YEAR(orderDate),
                         QUARTER        = DatePart(qq,OrderDate),
                         Sales          = Sum(TotalDue)
    FROM    Sales.SalesOrderHeader   GROUP BY YEAR(OrderDate), DatePart(qq,OrderDate)    )
SELECT    YEAR
               ,FORMAT ([1], 'c','en-US') AS Q1
               ,FORMAT ([2], 'c','en-US') AS Q2
               ,FORMAT ([3], 'c','en-US') AS Q3
               ,FORMAT ([4], 'c','en-US') AS Q4
FROM    (SELECT * FROM CTE) AS PivotInput
    PIVOT    (SUM(Sales)  FOR QUARTER IN ( [1],[2],[3],[4] ) ) AS PivotOutput  ORDER BY YEAR;
```

YEAR	Q1	Q2	Q3	Q4
2005	NULL	NULL	$5,203,127.88	$7,490,122.75
2006	$6,562,121.68	$6,947,995.43	$11,555,907.15	$9,397,824.18
2007	$7,492,396.32	$9,379,298.70	$15,413,231.84	$14,886,562.68
2008	$12,744,940.36	$16,087,078.23	$56,178.92	NULL

Recompiling the vSalesPersonSalesByFiscalYears View

The OrderDate years in Sales.SalesOrderHeader were advanced 4 years from AdventureWorks2008 to AdventureWork2012. Therefore we recompile the view to take the year shift into account.

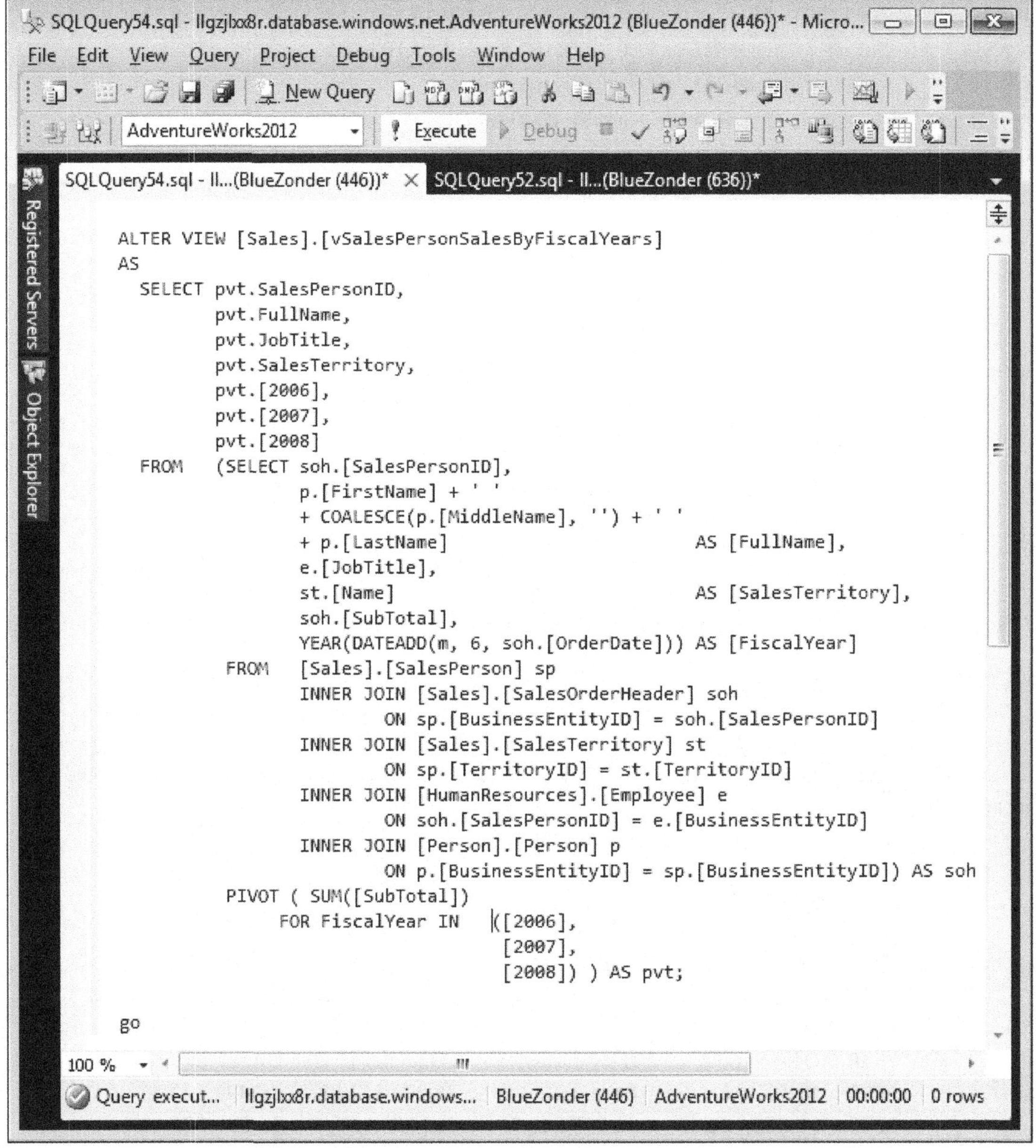

```
ALTER VIEW [Sales].[vSalesPersonSalesByFiscalYears]
AS
  SELECT pvt.SalesPersonID,
         pvt.FullName,
         pvt.JobTitle,
         pvt.SalesTerritory,
         pvt.[2006],
         pvt.[2007],
         pvt.[2008]
  FROM   (SELECT soh.[SalesPersonID],
                 p.[FirstName] + ' '
                 + COALESCE(p.[MiddleName], '') + ' '
                 + p.[LastName]                     AS [FullName],
                 e.[JobTitle],
                 st.[Name]                          AS [SalesTerritory],
                 soh.[SubTotal],
                 YEAR(DATEADD(m, 6, soh.[OrderDate])) AS [FiscalYear]
          FROM   [Sales].[SalesPerson] sp
                 INNER JOIN [Sales].[SalesOrderHeader] soh
                         ON sp.[BusinessEntityID] = soh.[SalesPersonID]
                 INNER JOIN [Sales].[SalesTerritory] st
                         ON sp.[TerritoryID] = st.[TerritoryID]
                 INNER JOIN [HumanResources].[Employee] e
                         ON soh.[SalesPersonID] = e.[BusinessEntityID]
                 INNER JOIN [Person].[Person] p
                         ON p.[BusinessEntityID] = sp.[BusinessEntityID]) AS soh
          PIVOT ( SUM([SubTotal])
               FOR FiscalYear IN ([2006],
                                  [2007],
                                  [2008]) ) AS pvt;

go
```

UNPIVOT Crosstab View Results

The vSalesPersonSalesByFiscalYears view is a crosstab listing of sales person (rows) and sales by year (columns). The UNPIVOT operation transforms the year columns into rows.

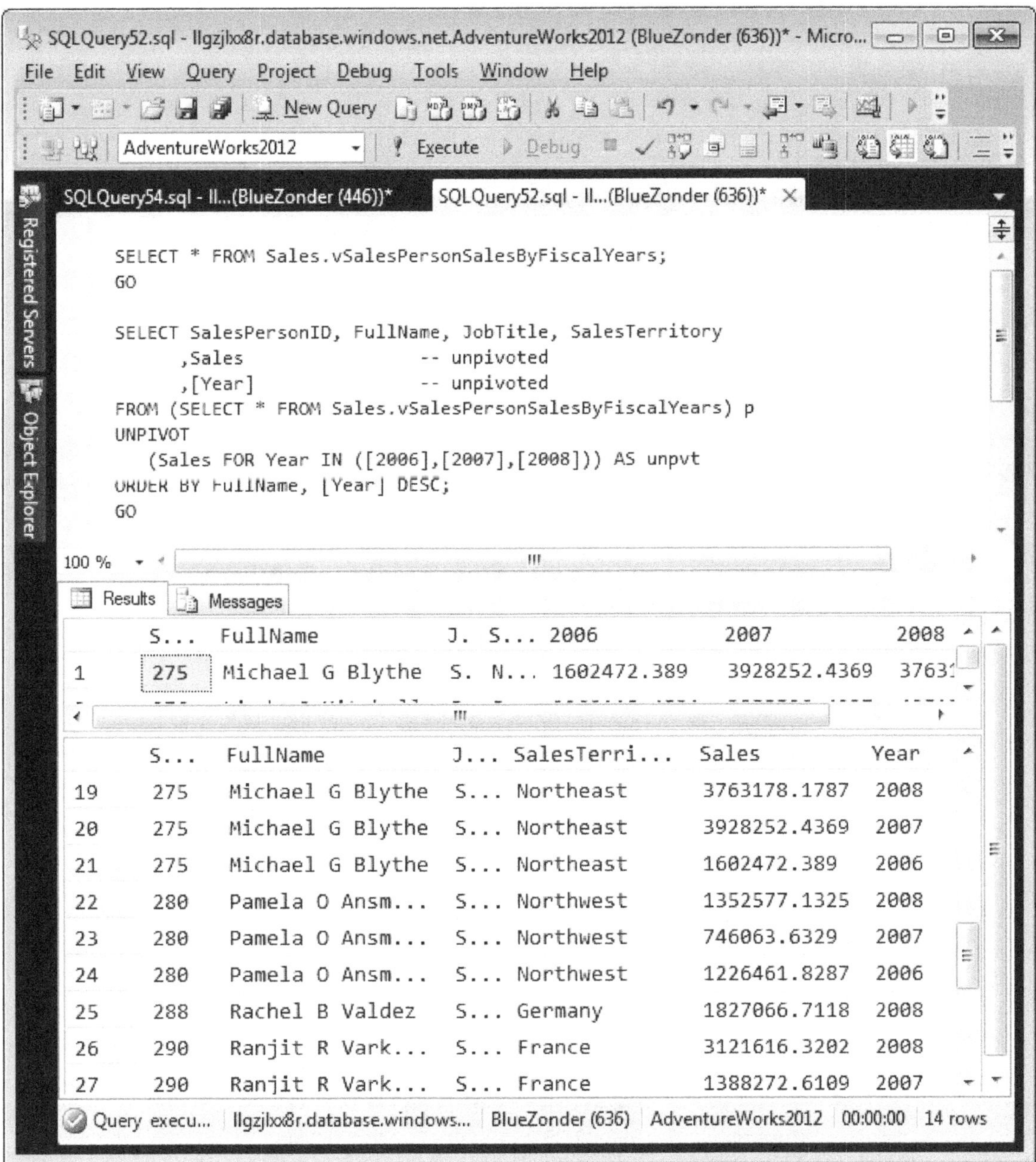
SQLQuery52.sql - llgzjlxx8r.database.windows.net.AdventureWorks2012 (BlueZonder (636))* - Micro...
File Edit View Query Project Debug Tools Window Help
New Query
AdventureWorks2012
Execute
Debug
SQLQuery54.sql - Il...(BlueZonder (446))*
SQLQuery52.sql - Il...(BlueZonder (636))*
Registered Servers
Object Explorer
SELECT * FROM Sales.vSalesPersonSalesByFiscalYears;
GO
SELECT SalesPersonID, FullName, JobTitle, SalesTerritory
,Sales -- unpivoted
,[Year] -- unpivoted
FROM (SELECT * FROM Sales.vSalesPersonSalesByFiscalYears) p
UNPIVOT
(Sales FOR Year IN ([2006],[2007],[2008])) AS unpvt
ORDER BY FullName, [Year] DESC;
GO
100 %
Results
Messages
S... FullName J. S... 2006 2007 2008
1 275 Michael G Blythe S. N... 1602472.389 3928252.4369
S... FullName J... SalesTerri... Sales Year
19 275 Michael G Blythe S... Northeast 3763178.1787 2008
20 275 Michael G Blythe S... Northeast 3928252.4369 2007
21 275 Michael G Blythe S... Northeast 1602472.389 2006
22 280 Pamela O Ansm... S... Northwest 1352577.1325 2008
23 280 Pamela O Ansm... S... Northwest 746063.6329 2007
24 280 Pamela O Ansm... S... Northwest 1226461.8287 2006
25 288 Rachel B Valdez S... Germany 1827066.7118 2008
26 290 Ranjit R Vark... S... France 3121616.3202 2008
27 290 Ranjit R Vark... S... France 1388272.6109 2007
Query execu... llgzjlxx8r.database.windows... BlueZonder (636) AdventureWorks2012 00:00:00 14 rows

Using Subquery in Column List of SELECT

A subquery can be used in the column list of a SELECT statement.

```
USE Northwind;
GO
```

```
;WITH CTE AS
(
 SELECT ShipCity,
        CONVERT(DATE, OrderDate)                                      AS OrderDate,
        (SELECT CONVERT(DATE, MAX(OrderDate))  FROM dbo.Orders)       AS CurrentOrderDate,
        DATEDIFF(dd,OrderDate,(SELECT MAX(OrderDate) FROM dbo.Orders)) AS DeltaDays,
        ROW_NUMBER() OVER (PARTITION BY ShipCity
                           ORDER BY OrderDate DESC)                   AS RN
 FROM dbo.Orders
)

SELECT TOP 20 ShipCity, OrderDate, CurrentOrderDate, DeltaDays
FROM CTE
WHERE RN=1    ORDER BY DeltaDays DESC;
GO
```

ShipCity	OrderDate	CurrentOrderDate	DeltaDays
Walla Walla	1997-05-22	1998-05-06	349
Elgin	1997-09-08	1998-05-06	240
Montréal	1997-10-30	1998-05-06	188
Reims	1997-11-12	1998-05-06	175
Caracas	1997-12-18	1998-05-06	139
Lille	1997-12-22	1998-05-06	135
Vancouver	1998-01-01	1998-05-06	125
Kirkland	1998-01-08	1998-05-06	118
Strasbourg	1998-01-12	1998-05-06	114
Lyon	1998-01-23	1998-05-06	103
San Francisco	1998-02-12	1998-05-06	83
Luleå	1998-03-04	1998-05-06	63
Barcelona	1998-03-05	1998-05-06	62
Cowes	1998-03-06	1998-05-06	61
Resende	1998-03-09	1998-05-06	58
Leipzig	1998-03-12	1998-05-06	55
Bergamo	1998-03-16	1998-05-06	51
Münster	1998-03-23	1998-05-06	44
Nantes	1998-03-24	1998-05-06	43
Versailles	1998-03-24	1998-05-06	43

CHAPTER 16: Modify Content - INSERT, UPDATE, DELETE & MERGE

INSERT VALUES - Table Value Constructor

T-SQL scripts illustrate the use of INSERT VALUES with Table Value Constructor (a list of values). Because the text columns are defined as nvarchar the string literals are prefixed with "N" indicating UNICODE literal. Since only Latin letters used, the "N" can be omitted.

```
USE AdventureWorks2012;
CREATE TABLE dbo.Department (DepartmentID smallint IDENTITY(1,1) PRIMARY KEY,
 Name dbo.Name NOT NULL, GroupName dbo.Name NOT NULL, ModifiedDate datetime NOT NULL);
-- The following statement is necessary because of the IDENTITY property
SET IDENTITY_INSERT dbo.Department ON;
GO
INSERT dbo.Department (DepartmentID, Name, GroupName, ModifiedDate) VALUES
(1, N'Engineering', N'Research and Development', getdate()),
(2, N'Tool Design', N'Research and Development', getdate()),
(3, N'Sales', N'Sales and Marketing', getdate()),
(4, N'Marketing', N'Sales and Marketing', getdate()),
(5, N'Purchasing', N'Inventory Management', getdate()),
(6, N'Research and Development', N'Research and Development', getdate()),
(7, N'Production', N'Manufacturing', getdate()),
(8, N'Production Control', N'Manufacturing', getdate()),
(9, N'Human Resources', N'Executive General and Administration', getdate()),
(10, N'Finance', N'Executive General and Administration', getdate()),
(11, N'Information Services', N'Executive General and Administration', getdate()),
(12, N'Document Control', N'Quality Assurance', getdate()),
(13, N'Quality Assurance', N'Quality Assurance', getdate()),
(14, N'Facilities and Maintenance', N'Executive General and Administration', getdate()),
(15, N'Shipping and Receiving', N'Inventory Management', getdate()),
(16, N'Executive', N'Executive General and Administration',getdate());
GO
SET IDENTITY_INSERT dbo.Department OFF;
GO
SELECT TOP 4 * FROM dbo.Department ORDER BY DepartmentID;
```

DepartmentID	Name	GroupName	ModifiedDate
1	Engineering	Research and Development	2016-08-02 06:35:44.623
2	Tool Design	Research and Development	2016-08-02 06:35:44.623
3	Sales	Sales and Marketing	2016-08-02 06:35:44.623
4	Marketing	Sales and Marketing	2016-08-02 06:35:44.623

INSERT VALUES - Ye Olde Way

T-SQL scripts illustrate the INSERT VALUES for single row insert, the only available method prior to SQL Server 2008.

```
USE AdventureWorks2012;
GO
```

```
CREATE TABLE Shift(
	ShiftID tinyint IDENTITY(1,1) NOT NULL,
	Name dbo.Name NOT NULL,
	StartTime time(7) NOT NULL,
	EndTime time(7) NOT NULL,
	ModifiedDate datetime NOT NULL,
	CONSTRAINT PK_Shift_ShiftID PRIMARY KEY CLUSTERED (ShiftID ASC) );
GO
```

```
SET IDENTITY_INSERT Shift ON;			-- To force insert into ShiftID
```

```
INSERT Shift (ShiftID, Name, StartTime, EndTime, ModifiedDate)
VALUES (1, N'Day', CAST(0x0700D85EAC3A0000 AS Time), CAST(0x07001882BA7D0000 AS Time),
CAST(0x0000921E00000000 AS DateTime))
INSERT Shift (ShiftID, Name, StartTime, EndTime, ModifiedDate)
VALUES (2, N'Evening', CAST(0x07001882BA7D0000 AS Time), CAST(0x070058A5C8C00000 AS Time),
getdate());
INSERT Shift (ShiftID, Name, StartTime, EndTime, ModifiedDate)
VALUES (3, N'Night', CAST(0x070058A5C8C00000 AS Time), CAST(0x0700D85EAC3A0000 AS Time),
CURRENT_TIMESTAMP);
GO
```

```
SET IDENTITY_INSERT Shift OFF;
```

```
ALTER TABLE Shift ADD  CONSTRAINT DF_Shift_ModifiedDate  DEFAULT (getdate()) FOR ModifiedDate
GO
```

```
SELECT * FROM Shift ORDER BY ShiftID;
GO
```

ShiftID	Name	StartTime	EndTime	ModifiedDate
1	Day	07:00:00.0000000	15:00:00.0000000	2002-06-01 00:00:00.000
2	Evening	15:00:00.0000000	23:00:00.0000000	2018-08-20 19:31:02.293
3	Night	23:00:00.0000000	07:00:00.0000000	2018-08-20 19:31:02.293

```
DROP TABLE Shift;
GO
```

INSERT SELECT

INSERT SELECT Literal List with UNION

T-SQL scripts demonstrate the insertion of literal records (rows) using INSERT SELECT.

```
USE AdventureWorks2012;
CREATE TABLE dbo.Department (DepartmentID smallint IDENTITY(1,1) PRIMARY KEY,
  Name dbo.Name NOT NULL,  GroupName dbo.Name NOT NULL, ModifiedDate datetime NOT NULL);
-- The following statement is necessary because of the IDENTITY property
SET IDENTITY_INSERT dbo.Department ON;
GO
INSERT dbo.Department (DepartmentID, Name, GroupName, ModifiedDate)
SELECT 1, N'Engineering', N'Research and Development', CURRENT_TIMESTAMP  UNION
SELECT 2, N'Tool Design', N'Research and Development', CURRENT_TIMESTAMP  UNION
SELECT 3, N'Sales', N'Sales and Marketing', CURRENT_TIMESTAMP  UNION
SELECT 4, N'Marketing', N'Sales and Marketing', CURRENT_TIMESTAMP  UNION
SELECT 5, N'Purchasing', N'Inventory Management', CURRENT_TIMESTAMP  UNION
SELECT 6, N'Research and Development', N'Research and Development', CURRENT_TIMESTAMP  UNION
SELECT 7, N'Production', N'Manufacturing', CURRENT_TIMESTAMP  UNION
SELECT 8, N'Production Control', N'Manufacturing', CURRENT_TIMESTAMP  UNION
SELECT 9, N'Human Resources', N'Executive General and Administration', CURRENT_TIMESTAMP  UNION
SELECT 10, N'Finance', N'Executive General and Administration', CURRENT_TIMESTAMP  UNION
SELECT 11, N'Information Services', N'Executive General and Administration', CURRENT_TIMESTAMP
UNION
SELECT 12, N'Document Control', N'Quality Assurance', CURRENT_TIMESTAMP  UNION
SELECT 13, N'Quality Assurance', N'Quality Assurance', CURRENT_TIMESTAMP  UNION
SELECT 14, N'Facilities and Maintenance', N'Executive General and Administration',
CURRENT_TIMESTAMP  UNION
SELECT 15, N'Shipping and Receiving', N'Inventory Management', CURRENT_TIMESTAMP  UNION
SELECT 16, N'Executive', N'Executive General and Administration', CURRENT_TIMESTAMP;
GO
SET IDENTITY_INSERT dbo.Department OFF;
GO
SELECT TOP 4 * FROM dbo.Department ORDER BY DepartmentID;
GO
```

DepartmentID	Name	GroupName	ModifiedDate
1	Engineering	Research and Development	2016-08-02 06:35:44.623
2	Tool Design	Research and Development	2016-08-02 06:35:44.623
3	Sales	Sales and Marketing	2016-08-02 06:35:44.623
4	Marketing	Sales and Marketing	2016-08-02 06:35:44.623

```
-- Cleanup
DROP TABLE tempdb.dbo.Department;
```

INSERT SELECT from Table

T-SQL script demonstrates table population with table SELECT.

```
USE AdventureWorks2012;
CREATE TABLE dbo.Department (DepartmentID smallint IDENTITY(1,1) PRIMARY KEY,
  Name dbo.Name NOT NULL,  GroupName dbo.Name NOT NULL, ModifiedDate datetime NOT NULL);
-- The following statement is necessary because of the IDENTITY property
SET IDENTITY_INSERT dbo.Department ON;
GO
INSERT dbo.Department (DepartmentID, Name, GroupName, ModifiedDate)
SELECT TOP 15 DepartmentID, Name, GroupName, ModifiedDate
FROM HumanResources.Department  ORDER BY DepartmentID;
GO
-- (15 row(s) affected)
SELECT TOP 4 * FROM dbo.Department ORDER BY DepartmentID;
```

DepartmentID	Name	GroupName	ModifiedDate
1	Engineering	Research and Development	2016-08-02 06:35:44.623
2	Tool Design	Research and Development	2016-08-02 06:35:44.623
3	Sales	Sales and Marketing	2016-08-02 06:35:44.623
4	Marketing	Sales and Marketing	2016-08-02 06:35:44.623

SCOPE_IDENTITY() for Last-Inserted IDENTITY Value

The last inserted IDENTITY value can be returned with the SCOPE_IDENTITY() or @@IDENTITY system function (variable). SCOPE_IDENTITY() is better choice since it is within the current connection scope. @@IDENTITY is at server level. The best choice though is the OUTPUT clause.

```
INSERT dbo.Department (DepartmentID, Name, GroupName, ModifiedDate)
SELECT TOP 1 DepartmentID, Name, GroupName, ModifiedDate
FROM HumanResources.Department  ORDER BY DepartmentID DESC;
GO
-- (1 row(s) affected)
```

Alternate is SELECT @@IDENTITY; @@ variables are system variables.

```
DECLARE @LastID INT = SCOPE_IDENTITY();
SELECT @LastID;  -- 16
```

```
SET IDENTITY_INSERT dbo.Department OFF;
GO
```

```
-- Cleanup
DROP TABLE tempdb.dbo.Department;
```

INSERT with Subset of Columns

Only the required columns must be present in the INSERT column list. A column with default or NULL property can be omitted. In the next T-SQL script, ModifiedDate is filled by default with getdate().

```
USE AdventureWorks2012;
CREATE TABLE dbo.Department (DepartmentID smallint IDENTITY(1,1) PRIMARY KEY,
 Name dbo.Name NOT NULL,  GroupName dbo.Name NOT NULL, ModifiedDate datetime NOT NULL);

ALTER TABLE dbo.Department ADD CONSTRAINT DF_Dept_ModDate
DEFAULT getdate() FOR ModifiedDate;
GO
SET IDENTITY_INSERT dbo.Department ON;
GO
INSERT dbo.Department (DepartmentID, Name, GroupName)
SELECT DepartmentID, Name, GroupName  FROM HumanResources.Department;
GO  -- (16 row(s) affected)
SELECT TOP 4 * FROM dbo.Department ORDER BY DepartmentID;
```

DepartmentID	Name	GroupName	ModifiedDate
1	Engineering	Research and Development	2016-08-02 06:35:44.623
2	Tool Design	Research and Development	2016-08-02 06:35:44.623
3	Sales	Sales and Marketing	2016-08-02 06:35:44.623
4	Marketing	Sales and Marketing	2016-08-02 06:35:44.623

Capturing Last-Inserted IDENTITY Set Values with OUTPUT

When more than one row is inserted with one statement, the OUTPUT clause can be used to capture the list of just inserted IDENTITY values.

```
DECLARE @LastInserted TABLE (ID INT);
INSERT dbo.Department (DepartmentID, Name, GroupName)
        OUTPUT inserted.DepartmentID INTO @LastInserted
SELECT DepartmentID+1000, Name, GroupName  FROM HumanResources.Department;
SELECT TOP 5 * FROM @LastInserted ORDER BY ID;
GO
```

ID
1001
1002
1003
1004
1005

```
SET IDENTITY_INSERT dbo.Department OFF;
DROP TABLE tempdb.dbo.Department;
```

INSERT EXEC Stored Procedure

Data can be directly inserted from the execution of a user-defined stored procedure or system procedure. We create a table and a stored procedure, then perform INSERT EXEC.

```
USE AdventureWorks2012;
IF OBJECT_ID ('dbo.EmployeeSales', 'U') IS NOT NULL    DROP TABLE dbo.EmployeeSales;
IF OBJECT_ID ('dbo.uspGetEmployeeSales', 'P') IS NOT NULL    DROP PROCEDURE uspGetEmployeeSales;
CREATE TABLE dbo.EmployeeSales
 (
   BusinessEntityID          INT NOT NULL PRIMARY KEY,
   LastName                  VARCHAR(40) NOT NULL,
   SalesDollars              MONEY NOT NULL,
   DataSource                VARCHAR(20) NOT NULL
 );
GO

CREATE PROCEDURE dbo.uspGetEmployeeSales AS
 BEGIN
    SELECT          e.BusinessEntityID, c.LastName, sp.SalesYTD, 'PROCEDURE'
    FROM   HumanResources.Employee AS e
        INNER JOIN Sales.SalesPerson AS sp
             ON e.BusinessEntityID = sp.BusinessEntityID
        INNER JOIN Person.Person AS c
             ON e.BusinessEntityID = c.BusinessEntityID
    WHERE  e.BusinessEntityID > 280      ORDER  BY    e.BusinessEntityID,    c.LastName;
 END;
GO

--INSERT...EXECUTE user-defined stored procedure
INSERT EmployeeSales EXECUTE uspGetEmployeeSales;

SELECT * FROM   EmployeeSales;
```

BusinessEntityID	LastName	SalesDollars	DataSource
281	Ito	2458535.6169	PROCEDURE
282	Saraiva	2604540.7172	PROCEDURE
283	Campbell	1573012.9383	PROCEDURE
284	Mensa-Annan	1576562.1966	PROCEDURE
285	Abbas	172524.4512	PROCEDURE
286	Tsoflias	1421810.9242	PROCEDURE
287	Alberts	519905.932	PROCEDURE
288	Valdez	1827066.7118	PROCEDURE
289	Pak	4116871.2277	PROCEDURE
290	Varkey Chudukatil	3121616.3202	PROCEDURE

Insert Into A Table Via The Direct Execution Of An SQL Query With The EXEC Command

```
SELECT Population = count(*)  FROM   dbo.EmployeeSales;
```

Population
10

```
--INSERT...EXECUTE('string') example
INSERT EmployeeSales
EXECUTE ('        SELECT e.BusinessEntityID, c.LastName,      sp.SalesYTD, ''EXEC SQL STRING''
                  FROM HumanResources.Employee AS e         INNER JOIN Sales.SalesPerson AS sp
                  ON e.BusinessEntityID = sp.BusinessEntityID        INNER JOIN Person.Person AS c
                  ON e.BusinessEntityID = c.BusinessEntityID
                  WHERE e.BusinessEntityID BETWEEN 270 and 280
                  ORDER BY e.BusinessEntityID, c.LastName ');
GO
-- (7 row(s) affected)
```

Inserted number of rows can be captured for later use. **Capture must be done immediately after the monitored statement.** Any following statement will change @@ROWCOUNT value.

```
DECLARE @InsertCount int = @@ROWCOUNT;
SELECT @InsertCount;  -- 7
GO
```

```
SELECT * FROM   dbo.EmployeeSales ORDER BY BusinessEntityID ;
```

BusinessEntityID	LastName	SalesDollars	DataSource
274	Jiang	559697.5639	EXEC SQL STRING
275	Blythe	3763178.1787	EXEC SQL STRING
276	Mitchell	4251368.5497	EXEC SQL STRING
277	Carson	3189418.3662	EXEC SQL STRING
278	Vargas	1453719.4653	EXEC SQL STRING
279	Reiter	2315185.611	EXEC SQL STRING
280	Ansman-Wolfe	1352577.1325	EXEC SQL STRING
281	Ito	2458535.6169	PROCEDURE
282	Saraiva	2604540.7172	PROCEDURE
283	Campbell	1573012.9383	PROCEDURE
284	Mensa-Annan	1576562.1966	PROCEDURE
285	Abbas	172524.4512	PROCEDURE
286	Tsoflias	1421810.9242	PROCEDURE
287	Alberts	519905.932	PROCEDURE
288	Valdez	1827066.7118	PROCEDURE
289	Pak	4116871.2277	PROCEDURE
290	Varkey Chudukatil	3121616.3202	PROCEDURE

INSERT EXEC System Procedure

Data can be inserted into a table by the execution of a system procedure. We create a test table with SELECT INTO FROM OPENQUERY. We can also create the table manually if we know the data type of columns. SQL Server 2012 script. sp_who is not supported in Windows Azure SQL Database.

```
-- DATA ACCESS must be turned on at YOURSERVER SQL Server instance
SELECT TOP(0) * INTO #SPWHO       FROM OPENQUERY(YOURSERVER, 'exec sp_who');
 -- will not work with sp_who2 due to duplicate column name
```

```
/* Table created
CREATE TABLE [dbo].[#SPWHO](
        [spid] [smallint] NOT NULL,
        [ecid] [smallint] NOT NULL,
        [status] [nchar](30) NOT NULL,
        [loginame] [nvarchar](128) NULL,
        [hostname] [nchar](128) NOT NULL,
        [blk] [char](5) NULL,
        [dbname] [nvarchar](128) NULL,
        [cmd] [nchar](16) NOT NULL,
        [request_id] [int] NOT NULL
); */
```

```
INSERT #SPWHO   EXEC sp_who;
```

The blk column contains blocking spid if any. A large update for example may block other queries until it completes. The spid of the current session is @@SPID.

```
SELECT * FROM  #SPWHO
GO -- (42 row(s) affected) - Partial results.
```

spid	ecid	status	loginame	hostname	blk	dbname	cmd	request_id
21	0	background	sa		0	master	TASK MANAGER	0
22	0	background	sa		0	master	CHECKPOINT	0
23	0	sleeping	sa		0	master	TASK MANAGER	0
24	0	background	sa		0	master	BRKR TASK	0
25	0	sleeping	sa		0	master	TASK MANAGER	0
26	0	sleeping	sa		0	master	TASK MANAGER	0
27	0	sleeping	sa		0	master	TASK MANAGER	0
28	0	sleeping	sa		0	master	TASK MANAGER	0
29	0	sleeping	sa		0	master	TASK MANAGER	0
30	0	sleeping	sa		0	master	TASK MANAGER	0
40	0	background	sa		0	master	BRKR TASK	0
42	0	background	sa		0	master	BRKR TASK	0
43	0	background	sa		0	master	BRKR TASK	0
51	0	sleeping	YOURSERVER \Owner	YOURSERVER	0	AdventureWorks2012	AWAITING COMMAND	0
52	0	sleeping	NT SERVICE\SQLSERVERAGENT	YOURSERVER	0	msdb	AWAITING COMMAND	0

```
DROP TABLE #SPWHO
GO
```

INSERT Only New Rows Omit the Rest

INSERT only new records. If record exists, do nothing. Note: **DELETE will not rollback IDENTITY current value.** Therefore with repeated testing, the IDENTITY current value will roll ahead.

```
USE AdventureWorks2012;
SELECT COUNT(*) FROM HumanResources.Department;          -- 16
SELECT COUNT(*) FROM dbo.Department;                     -- 16
```

```
-- All rows exists, no new row insertion
INSERT HumanResources.Department (Name, GroupName)
SELECT Name, GroupName
FROM dbo.Department D
WHERE NOT EXISTS (      SELECT * FROM HumanResources.Department DD  -- Correlated subquery
                        WHERE D.Name = DD.Name    AND D.GroupName = DD.GroupName);
GO -- (0 row(s) affected)
```

```
-- Prefix Name with "ZZZ", 16 successful new inserted rows
INSERT HumanResources.Department (Name, GroupName)
SELECT CONCAT('ZZZ', Name), GroupName
FROM dbo.Department D
WHERE NOT EXISTS (      SELECT * FROM HumanResources.Department DD
            WHERE DD.Name = CONCAT('ZZZ', D.Name)    AND DD.GroupName = D.GroupName);
GO -- (16 row(s) affected)
```

```
DELETE TOP ( 7 ) HumanResources.Department WHERE Name LIKE ('ZZZ%');       -- (7 row(s) affected)
```

```
-- Only 7 rows will be inserted since the rest are duplicates
INSERT HumanResources.Department (Name, GroupName)
SELECT CONCAT('ZZZ', Name), GroupName
FROM dbo.Department D
WHERE NOT EXISTS (      SELECT * FROM HumanResources.Department DD
                  WHERE DD.Name = CONCAT('ZZZ', D.Name)    AND DD.GroupName = D.GroupName);
GO  -- (7  row(s) affected)
```

```
SELECT * FROM HumanResources.Department;    -- (32 row(s) affected)  -- Partial results;
GO
```

DepartmentID	Name	GroupName	ModifiedDate
16	Executive	Executive General and Administration	2002-06-01 00:00:00.000
65	ZZZEngineering	Research and Development	2018-08-13 08:32:43.133

```
DELETE HumanResources.Department
WHERE Name LIKE ('ZZZ%');           -- (16 row(s) affected)
```

```
SELECT COUNT(*) FROM HumanResources.Department;          -- 16
```

DELETE - A Dangerous Operation

DELETE is a logged operation. DELETE may be slow from large table with indexes due to index reorganization.

> Warning: **DELETE is a dangerous operation since it removes data. Protection: regular database backup and/or creating a copy of the table prior to DELETE.**

```
CREATE TABLE #SalesOrderDetail(
        SalesOrderID int NOT NULL,
        SalesOrderDetailID int  NOT NULL,
        CarrierTrackingNumber nvarchar(25) NULL,
        OrderQty smallint NOT NULL,
        ProductID int NOT NULL,
        SpecialOfferID int NOT NULL,
        UnitPrice money NOT NULL,
        UnitPriceDiscount money NOT NULL,
        LineTotal  money NOT NULL,
        rowguid uniqueidentifier NOT NULL,
        ModifiedDate datetime NOT NULL);
GO
```

```
INSERT #SalesOrderDetail   SELECT *  FROM [Sales].[SalesOrderDetail];    -- (121317 row(s) affected)
```

```
-- Increase table population 8 fold
INSERT #SalesOrderDetail  SELECT * FROM #SalesOrderDetail;
GO 3
/* Beginning execution loop
(121317 row(s) affected)
(242634 row(s) affected)
(485268 row(s) affected)  Batch execution completed 3 times.  Execution time: 14 seconds    */
```

```
CREATE INDEX idxSOD on #SalesOrderDetail (SalesOrderID, ProductID);
-- Command(s) completed successfully. Execution time: 00:00:04
```

```
SELECT COUNT(*) FROM #SalesOrderDetail;  -- 970536
```

```
-- Delete even SalesOrderID records
DELETE FROM #SalesOrderDetail WHERE SalesOrderID % 2 = 0;
-- (490648 row(s) affected)  - Execution time - 00:00:14
```

```
SELECT COUNT(*) FROM #SalesOrderDetail;  -- 479888
```

TRUNCATE TABLE & DBCC CHECKIDENT

TRUNCATE TABLE command is very fast since it is minimally logged. It also resets IDENTITY column to (1,1). Warning: **TRUNCATE is a dangerous operation since it removes all the data in a table**. Protection: regular database backup and/or creating a copy of the table prior to TRUNCATE .

```
SELECT COUNT(*) FROM #SalesOrderDetail; -- 479888
```

```
TRUNCATE TABLE #SalesOrderDetail;
-- Command(s) completed successfully. Execution time: 00:00:00
```

```
SELECT COUNT(*) FROM #SalesOrderDetail; -- 0
GO
```

```
DROP TABLE #SalesOrderDetail;
GO -- Command(s) completed successfully
```

On-Premises SQL Server 2012 Script - No equivalent in Azure SQL

```
-- Create new test table with SELECT INTO
USE tempdb;
SELECT * INTO SOD FROM Sales.SalesOrderDetail;
GO -- (121317 row(s) affected)
```

```
-- Next IDENTITY value will be 121318.
DBCC CHECKIDENT ("dbo.SOD");
/* Checking identity information: current identity value '121317', current column value '121317'.
DBCC execution completed. If DBCC printed error messages, contact your system administrator. */
```

```
TRUNCATE TABLE SOD;
GO
-- Command(s) completed successfully.
```

```
-- IDENTITY is reset
DBCC CHECKIDENT ("dbo.SOD");
/* Checking identity information: current identity value 'NULL', current column value 'NULL'.
DBCC execution completed. If DBCC printed error messages, contact your system administrator. */
```

```
EXEC sp_help SOD;
GO
-- Partial results.
```

Identity	Seed	Increment	Not For Replication
SalesOrderDetailID	1	1	0

Reseeding IDENTITY - Not in Azure SQL- Slated for future addition

```
-- Without this command, it may not start at 1
DBCC CHECKIDENT ("SOD", RESEED, 1);
```

```
-- Populate the table with 5 rows
INSERT INTO SOD
        ([SalesOrderID]
        ,[CarrierTrackingNumber]
        ,[OrderQty]
        ,[ProductID]
        ,[SpecialOfferID]
        ,[UnitPrice]
        ,[UnitPriceDiscount]
        ,[LineTotal]
        ,[rowguid]
        ,[ModifiedDate])
 SELECT   TOP (5)
         [SalesOrderID]
        ,[CarrierTrackingNumber]
        ,[OrderQty]
        ,[ProductID]
        ,[SpecialOfferID]
        ,[UnitPrice]
        ,[UnitPriceDiscount]
        ,[LineTotal]
        ,[rowguid]
        ,[ModifiedDate]
FROM Sales.SalesOrderDetail;
GO
-- (5 row(s) affected)
```

```
-- Next value assigned is 6
DBCC CHECKIDENT ("dbo.SOD");
/*Checking identity information: current identity value '5', current column value '5'.
DBCC execution completed. If DBCC printed error messages, contact your system administrator. */
```

```
SELECT * FROM SOD;
-- (5 row(s) affected) - Partial results.
```

SalesOrderID	SalesOrderDetailID	CarrierTrackingNumber	OrderQty	ProductID	SpecialOfferID	UnitPrice	UnitPriceDiscount	LineTotal
43659	1	4911-403C-98	1	776	1	2024.994	0.00	2024.994000
43659	2	4911-403C-98	3	777	1	2024.994	0.00	6074.982000
43659	3	4911-403C-98	1	778	1	2024.994	0.00	2024.994000
43659	4	4911-403C-98	1	771	1	2039.994	0.00	2039.994000
43659	5	4911-403C-98	1	772	1	2039.994	0.00	2039.994000

UPDATE - A Complex Operation

UPDATE changes data content at a row and column level (cell). It is a logged operation: deleted row contains previous data, inserted row contains new data. Warning: UPDATE is a dangerous operation since it changes the data in a table. Protection: regular database backup and/or creating a copy of the table prior to UPDATE with SELECT INTO.

Some UPDATEs are reversible, such as some calculated UPDATE, others may be irreversible.

Checking Cardinality & Changes by UPDATE Prior to Execution

Since UPDATE is replaces previous data, it is very important to check prior to execution that is works correctly. It is quite simple to convert UPDATE into a checking SELECT. We intend to UPDATE the SalesYTD column with the last day sales for each salesperson.

```
USE AdventureWorks2012;
SELECT   sp.BusinessEntityID, SalesYTD,
                  [NewSalesYTD]=SalesYTD
            + (SELECT SUM(SODa.SubTotal)
            FROM   Sales.SalesOrderHeader AS SODa
            WHERE  CONVERT(date,SODa.OrderDate) = CONVERT(date,(SELECT MAX(OrderDate)
             FROM   Sales.SalesOrderHeader AS SODb
             WHERE
                 SODb.SalesPersonID = SODa.SalesPersonID))
                 AND sp.BusinessEntityID =   SODa.SalesPersonID
            GROUP  BY SODa.SalesPersonID)
FROM Sales.SalesPerson sp  ORDER BY sp.BusinessEntityID;
GO
```

BusinessEntityID	SalesYTD	NewSalesYTD
274	559697.5639	597350.4859
275	3763178.1787	4133185.161
276	4251368.5497	4534079.5941
277	3189418.3662	3527404.588
278	1453719.4653	1599132.4735
279	2315185.611	2548077.4756
280	1352577.1325	1503691.0098
281	2458535.6169	2678660.7921
282	2604540.7172	3030519.8258
283	1573012.9383	1714964.9067
284	1576562.1966	1719945.1917
285	172524.4512	176721.5652
286	1421810.9242	1649155.9058
287	519905.932	520578.226
288	1827066.7118	1962768.1658
289	4116871.2277	4556655.2802
290	3121616.3202	3240852.6195

ANSI Style UPDATE

T-SQL supports ANSI UPDATE, in addition T-SQL supports the FROM clause in UPDATE.

```
USE AdventureWorks2012;
UPDATE Sales.SalesPerson
SET    SalesYTD = SalesYTD
           + (SELECT SUM(SODa.SubTotal)
             FROM   Sales.SalesOrderHeader AS SODa
             WHERE  CONVERT(date,SODa.OrderDate) =
                    CONVERT(date,(SELECT MAX(OrderDate)
              FROM   Sales.SalesOrderHeader AS SODb
              WHERE
                 SODb.SalesPersonID = SODa.SalesPersonID))
                 AND Sales.SalesPerson.BusinessEntityID =   SODa.SalesPersonID
             GROUP  BY SODa.SalesPersonID);
GO
-- (17 row(s) affected)
```

```
SELECT BusinessEntityID, SalesQuota, SalesYTD, SalesLastYear
FROM Sales.SalesPerson
ORDER BY BusinessEntityID;
GO
```

BusinessEntityID	SalesQuota	SalesYTD	SalesLastYear
274	NULL	597350.4859	0.00
275	300000.00	4133185.161	1750406.4785
276	250000.00	4534079.5941	1439156.0291
277	250000.00	3527404.588	1997186.2037
278	250000.00	1599132.4735	1620276.8966
279	300000.00	2548077.4756	1849640.9418
280	250000.00	1503691.0098	1927059.178
281	250000.00	2678660.7921	2073505.9999
282	250000.00	3030519.8258	2038234.6549
283	250000.00	1714964.9067	1371635.3158
284	300000.00	1719945.1917	0.00
285	NULL	176721.5652	0.00
286	250000.00	1649155.9058	2278548.9776
287	NULL	520578.226	0.00
288	250000.00	1962768.1658	1307949.7917
289	250000.00	4556655.2802	1635823.3967
290	250000.00	3240852.6195	2396539.7601

UPDATE from Table in Another Database - OPSS

UPDATE can be performed with data from a second database. ZorigAdventureWorks2012 is an original read-only copy of the AdventureWorks2012 database. The "Z" prefix is to force it to the end of alphabetical database list in SSMS Object Explorer.

```
UPDATE Sales.SalesPerson
        SET SalesYTD = (
                                SELECT SalesYTD
                                FROM ZorigSales.SalesPerson sp
                                WHERE sp.BusinessEntityID =
Sales.SalesPerson.BusinessEntityID
                        );
GO
```

```
SELECT  BusinessEntityID,
        SalesQuota,
        SalesYTD,
        SalesLastYear
FROM Sales.SalesPerson
ORDER BY BusinessEntityID;
GO
```

BusinessEntityID	SalesQuota	SalesYTD	SalesLastYear
274	NULL	559697.5639	0.00
275	300000.00	3763178.1787	1750406.4785
276	250000.00	4251368.5497	1439156.0291
277	250000.00	3189418.3662	1997186.2037
278	250000.00	1453719.4653	1620276.8966
279	300000.00	2315185.611	1849640.9418
280	250000.00	1352577.1325	1927059.178
281	250000.00	2458535.6169	2073505.9999
282	250000.00	2604540.7172	2038234.6549
283	250000.00	1573012.9383	1371635.3158
284	300000.00	1576562.1966	0.00
285	NULL	172524.4512	0.00
286	250000.00	1421810.9242	2278548.9776
287	NULL	519905.932	0.00
288	250000.00	1827066.7118	1307949.7917
289	250000.00	4116871.2277	1635823.3967
290	250000.00	3121616.3202	2396539.7601

UPDATE Syntax Challenges

The UPDATE statement in SQL has perplexing and potentially confusing syntax. Typically mastered by expert DBA-s and SQL developers, and the rest of the database community uses it in an insecure manner: never sure if it works as intended. Simple T-SQL examples demonstrate some of the issues with the UPDATE syntax and offer solutions.

First we create a new table for experimentation from the AdventureWorks2012 database and perform a demo inner join UPDATE on the new table.

```
CREATE TABLE Product(	ProductID int NOT NULL PRIMARY KEY,
		ProductName nvarchar(50) NOT NULL,
		Cost money NOT NULL,
		ListPrice money NOT NULL,
		Color nvarchar(15) NULL,
		ModifiedDate DATE		);

INSERT Product
SELECT ProductID,
    Name,
    StandardCost,
    ListPrice,
    Color,
    ModifiedDate
FROM   Production.Product WHERE  ListPrice > 0.0  AND Color IS NOT NULL;
GO                                    -- (245 row(s) affected)
```

```
SELECT TOP 5 * FROM Product  ORDER BY ProductID DESC;
```

ProductID	ProductName	Cost	ListPrice	Color	ModifiedDate
999	Road-750 Black, 52	343.6496	539.99	Black	2008-03-11
998	Road-750 Black, 48	343.6496	539.99	Black	2008-03-11
997	Road-750 Black, 44	343.6496	539.99	Black	2008-03-11
993	Mountain-500 Black, 52	294.5797	539.99	Black	2008-03-11
992	Mountain-500 Black, 48	294.5797	539.99	Black	2008-03-11

We shall proceed and update ALL (no WHERE clause) the rows in the Product table. We increase the ListPrice by 5%.

```
UPDATE Product      SET ListPrice = ListPrice * 1.05;  -- (245 row(s) affected)
```

In this instance a reversible UPDATE. But not always.

```
UPDATE Product      SET ListPrice = ListPrice / 1.05;
-- (245 row(s) affected)
```

UPDATE with INNER JOIN

The UPDATE uses a table alias from the FROM clause.

```
SELECT TOP 2 * FROM Product  WHERE Color = 'Yellow' ORDER BY ProductID DESC;
```

ProductID	ProductName	Cost	ListPrice	Color	ModifiedDate
976	Road-350-W Yellow, 48	1082.51	1700.99	Yellow	2008-03-11
975	Road-350-W Yellow, 44	1082.51	1700.99	Yellow	2008-03-11

```
UPDATE p  SET   p.ModifiedDate = DATEADD(HH,1,awp.ModifiedDate)
FROM   Product p    INNER JOIN Production.Product awp
                    ON p.ProductID = awp.ProductID  AND  awp.Size LIKE '4%' ;
-- (91 row(s) affected)
```

Capturing Affected Rows with @@ROWCOUNT

When we have to know the number of updated rows, it is best to capture it into local variable and use it from there in the program logic.

```
DECLARE @UpdatedRows  int;    -- capture @@ROWCOUNT for subsequent  use in the program

UPDATE p  SET    p.ModifiedDate = DATEADD(mm,1,awp.ModifiedDate)
FROM   Product p
   INNER JOIN Production.Product awp    ON p.ProductID = awp.ProductID
WHERE  p.Color = 'Yellow' ;
-- (36 row(s) affected)

SET @UpdatedRows = @@ROWCOUNT;

SELECT @@ROWCOUNT;                -- @@ROWCOUNT already changed
-- 1
SELECT TOP 5 * FROM Product  WHERE Color = 'Yellow' ORDER BY ProductID DESC;

SELECT @@ROWCOUNT;                -- @@ROWCOUNT changed again
-- 5
SELECT @UpdatedRows;              -- local variable kept the UPDATE count
-- 36
```

ProductID	ProductName	Cost	ListPrice	Color	ModifiedDate
976	Road-350-W Yellow, 48	1082.51	1700.99	Yellow	2008-04-11
975	Road-350-W Yellow, 44	1082.51	1700.99	Yellow	2008-04-11
974	Road-350-W Yellow, 42	1082.51	1700.99	Yellow	2008-04-11
973	Road-350-W Yellow, 40	1082.51	1700.99	Yellow	2008-04-11
965	Touring-3000 Yellow, 62	461.4448	742.35	Yellow	2008-04-11

UPDATE with Common Table Expression

UPDATE can be issued through a CTE to UPDATE the underlying table, Product in this case. Prices are increased 5% for products with over $1,000.00 list price.

```
SELECT TOP 5 * FROM Product  WHERE ListPrice > 1000.0 ORDER BY ProductID DESC;
GO
```

ProductID	ProductName	Cost	ListPrice	Color	ModifiedDate
976	Road-350-W Yellow, 48	1082.51	1700.99	Yellow	2008-04-11
975	Road-350-W Yellow, 44	1082.51	1700.99	Yellow	2008-04-11
974	Road-350-W Yellow, 42	1082.51	1700.99	Yellow	2008-04-11
973	Road-350-W Yellow, 40	1082.51	1700.99	Yellow	2008-04-11
972	Touring-2000 Blue, 54	755.1508	1214.85	Blue	2008-03-11

```
;WITH CTE
   AS (SELECT Price = ListPrice
      FROM   Product
      WHERE  ListPrice > 1000.0)
UPDATE CTE
SET    Price = Price * 1.05
GO
-- (86 row(s) affected)
```

```
SELECT TOP 5 * FROM Product  WHERE ListPrice > 1000.0 ORDER BY ProductID DESC;
```

ProductID	ProductName	Cost	ListPrice	Color	ModifiedDate
976	Road-350-W Yellow, 48	1082.51	1786.0395	Yellow	2008-04-11
975	Road-350-W Yellow, 44	1082.51	1786.0395	Yellow	2008-04-11
974	Road-350-W Yellow, 42	1082.51	1786.0395	Yellow	2008-04-11
973	Road-350-W Yellow, 40	1082.51	1786.0395	Yellow	2008-04-11
972	Touring-2000 Blue, 54	755.1508	1275.5925	Blue	2008-03-11

Similar data modification with ANSI SQL UPDATE.

```
UPDATE Product
SET   ListPrice = (SELECT p8.ListPrice * 1.05
            FROM   Production.Product p8    WHERE  Product.ProductID = p8.ProductID)
WHERE  EXISTS (SELECT *  FROM   Production.Product p8
         WHERE  Product.ProductID = p8.ProductID    AND Product.ListPrice > 1000.0);
```

Four Methods of UPDATE with GROUP BY Query

UPDATE can be done a few ways with GROUP BY aggregates.

```
CREATE TABLE dbo.ProductColor(   Color nvarchar(15) NOT NULL PRIMARY KEY,
                                 ItemCount int NOT NULL);
INSERT INTO ProductColor
SELECT Color=ISNULL(Color,'N/A'), ItemCount=0
FROM Production.Product  GROUP BY Color;                    -- (10 row(s) affected)
```

```
SELECT * FROM ProductColor
GO
```

Color	ItemCount
N/A	0
Black	0
Blue	0
Grey	0
Multi	0
Red	0
Silver	0
Silver/Black	0
White	0
Yellow	0

ANSI UPDATE

```
UPDATE ProductColor
SET ItemCount = (SELECT ProductColorCount FROM  (SELECT Color=ISNULL(Color, 'N/A'),
                ProductColorCount=COUNT(*)
                 FROM Production.Product
                 GROUP BY Color) cg WHERE  ProductColor.Color = cg.Color)
GO -- (10 row(s) affected)
```

FROM Clause UPDATE with Derived Table

```
UPDATE pc   SET pc.ItemCount = cg.ProductColorCount
FROM ProductColor pc
INNER JOIN (SELECT Color=ISNULL(Color, 'N/A'), ProductColorCount=COUNT(*)
        FROM Production.Product GROUP BY Color) cg
ON pc.Color = cg.Color;
-- (10 row(s) affected)
```

FROM Clause UPDATE with CTE

```
;WITH CTE AS (SELECT Color=ISNULL(Color, 'N/A'), ProductColorCount=COUNT(*)
        FROM Production.Product
        GROUP BY Color)
UPDATE pc
SET pc.ItemCount = CTE.ProductColorCount
FROM ProductColor pc
INNER JOIN CTE
ON pc.Color = CTE.Color;
GO
-- (10 row(s) affected)
```

CTE UPDATE

```
;WITH CTE AS (SELECT * FROM ProductColor pc
        INNER JOIN (SELECT ColorPrd=ISNULL(Color, 'N/A'), ProductColorCount=COUNT(*)
        FROM Production.Product
        GROUP BY Color) cg
                        ON pc.Color = cg.ColorPrd)
UPDATE CTE SET CTE.ItemCount = CTE.ProductColorCount;
GO
-- (10 row(s) affected)
```

```
SELECT * FROM ProductColor;
GO
```

Color	ItemCount
N/A	248
Black	93
Blue	26
Grey	1
Multi	8
Red	38
Silver	43
Silver/Black	7
White	4
Yellow	36

```
DROP TABLE tempdb.dbo.ProductColor;
```

MERGE for Combination INSERT, UPDATE or DELETE

The MERGE statement can be used to INSERT, UPDATE and/or DELETE all in one statement.

```
USE AdventureWorksDWAZ2008R2;
```

```
CREATE TABLE dbo.FactResellerSalesTest(                    -- First test table
        ResellerKey int NOT NULL,  OrderDateKey int NOT NULL,
        ProductKey int NOT NULL, OrderQuantity smallint NULL,
        SalesAmount money NULL,
        PRIMARY KEY (ResellerKey, OrderDateKey, ProductKey));
```

```
INSERT FactResellerSalesTest
SELECT TOP (5000) ResellerKey, OrderDateKey, ProductKey, OrderQuantity, SalesAmount
FROM   dbo.FactResellerSales  ORDER BY OrderDateKey ;
GO   -- (5000 row(s) affected)
```

```
CREATE TABLE dbo.ResellerSalesTransaction(                 -- Second test table
        ResellerKey int NOT NULL,        OrderDateKey int NOT NULL,
        ProductKey int NOT NULL,         OrderQuantity smallint NULL,
        SalesAmount money NULL,
        PRIMARY KEY (ResellerKey, OrderDateKey, ProductKey));
```

```
INSERT INTO ResellerSalesTransaction
SELECT TOP (8000) ResellerKey, OrderDateKey, ProductKey, OrderQuantity, SalesAmount
FROM   FactResellerSales ;  -- (8000 row(s) affected)
```

```
DELETE rsc
FROM   ResellerSalesTransaction rsc
    JOIN (SELECT TOP 1000 *
        FROM   ResellerSalesTransaction
        ORDER  BY ResellerKey DESC) x
      ON x.ResellerKey = rsc.ResellerKey ;
go
-- (1001 row(s) affected)
```

```
UPDATE TOP (6000) ResellerSalesTransaction
SET    SalesAmount = SalesAmount * 1.1 ;
go
-- (6000 row(s) affected)
```

MERGE is a very powerful statement

```
SELECT TOP (10) *
FROM   FactResellerSalesTest
ORDER  BY ResellerKey,        OrderDateKey,         ProductKey ;
go
```

ResellerKey	OrderDateKey	ProductKey	OrderQuantity	SalesAmount
1	20050801	270	1	183.9382
1	20050801	275	1	356.898
1	20050801	285	1	178.5808
1	20050801	314	2	4293.924
1	20050801	317	1	874.794
1	20050801	319	2	1749.588
1	20050801	324	2	838.9178
1	20050801	326	1	419.4589
1	20050801	328	1	419.4589
1	20050801	332	2	838.9178

```
SELECT BeforeFactCount=COUNT(*)
FROM   FactResellerSalesTest ;
-- 5000
```

```
-- Ready for the MERGE (update if exists,  insert otherwise)
MERGE FactResellerSalesTest AS fact
USING (SELECT *
     FROM   ResellerSalesTransaction) AS feed
ON ( fact.ProductKey = feed.ProductKey
   AND fact.ResellerKey = feed.ResellerKey
   AND fact.OrderDateKey = feed.OrderDateKey )
WHEN MATCHED THEN
  UPDATE SET fact.OrderQuantity +=  feed.OrderQuantity,
          fact.SalesAmount +=  feed.SalesAmount
WHEN NOT MATCHED THEN
  INSERT (ResellerKey,
        OrderDateKey,
        ProductKey,
        OrderQuantity,
        SalesAmount)
  VALUES (feed.ResellerKey,
        feed.OrderDateKey,
        feed.ProductKey,
        feed.OrderQuantity,
        feed.SalesAmount);
go   -- (6999 row(s) affected)
```

Checking results after MERGE

```
SELECT TOP (10) *
FROM   FactResellerSalesTest ORDER BY    ResellerKey,    OrderDateKey,    ProductKey;
```

ResellerKey	OrderDateKey	ProductKey	OrderQuantity	SalesAmount
1	20050801	270	2	386.2702
1	20050801	275	2	749.4858
1	20050801	285	2	375.0197
1	20050801	314	4	9017.2404
1	20050801	317	2	1837.0674
1	20050801	319	4	3674.1348
1	20050801	324	4	1761.7274
1	20050801	326	2	880.8637
1	20050801	328	2	880.8637
1	20050801	332	4	1761.7274

```
SELECT AfterFactCount=COUNT(*)   FROM   FactResellerSalesTest;
go
-- 7647

DROP TABLE ResellerSalesTransaction;  DROP TABLE FactResellerSalesTest;
go
```

Using MERGE Instead of UPDATE

MERGE statement can be used in the UPDATE only mode to replace UPDATE. Use the FactResellerSalesTest and ResellerSalesTransaction tables, created & populated the same way as in the previous demonstration.

```
USE tempdb;
```

```
SELECT COUNT(*) FROM FactResellerSalesTest;                    -- 5000
SELECT COUNT(*) FROM ResellerSalesTransaction;                 -- 8000
```

```
-- Alter the test data
DELETE rsc
FROM   ResellerSalesTransaction rsc
     INNER JOIN (SELECT TOP 1000 * FROM   ResellerSalesTransaction
          ORDER  BY ResellerKey DESC) x   -- subquery inner join
       ON x.ResellerKey = rsc.ResellerKey;
GO --(1010 row(s) affected)
```

```
UPDATE TOP (6000) ResellerSalesTransaction SET SalesAmount = SalesAmount * 1.1;
GO -- (6000 row(s) affected)
```

```
SELECT BeforeFactCount=COUNT(*) FROM   FactResellerSales;
GO -- 5000
```

```
-- Ready for the MERGE UPDATE only mode
MERGE FactResellerSalesTest AS fact
USING (SELECT * FROM   ResellerSalesTransaction) AS feed
ON ( fact.ProductKey = feed.ProductKey
   AND fact.ResellerKey = feed.ResellerKey
   AND fact.OrderDateKey = feed.OrderDateKey )
WHEN MATCHED THEN
  UPDATE SET fact.OrderQuantity = fact.OrderQuantity + feed.OrderQuantity,
        fact.SalesAmount = fact.SalesAmount + feed.SalesAmount;
GO -- 4352 row(s) affected)
```

```
SELECT AfterFactCount=COUNT(*) FROM   FactResellerSalesTest;
GO -- 5000
```

```
DROP TABLE ResellerSalesTransaction;  DROP TABLE FactResellerSalesTest;
```

CHAPTER 17: Transact-SQL Programming Review

IF...ELSE Conditional

IF... ELSE is a step toward a bona fide programming language.

```
DECLARE @StringNumber varchar(32) ;
SET @StringNumber = '12,000,000';
IF EXISTS( SELECT * WHERE ISNUMERIC(@StringNumber) = 1)
        PRINT 'VALID NUMBER: ' + @StringNumber
ELSE    PRINT 'INVALID NUMBER: ' + @StringNumber;
GO
-- VALID NUMBER: 12,000,000
```

```
DECLARE @StringNumber varchar(32) = '12,000:000';

IF EXISTS( SELECT * WHERE ISNUMERIC(@StringNumber) = 1)
        PRINT CONCAT('VALID NUMBER: ' , @StringNumber)
ELSE    PRINT CONCAT('INVALID NUMBER: ', @StringNumber);
GO
-- INVALID NUMBER: 12,000:000
```

```
DECLARE @StringDate varchar(32);

SET @StringDate = '2017-03-15 18:50';

IF EXISTS( SELECT * WHERE ISDATE(@StringDate) = 1)
        PRINT 'VALID DATE: ' + @StringDate
ELSE    PRINT 'INVALID DATE: ' + @StringDate;
GO
-- Result: VALID DATE: 2017-03-15 18:50
```

```
DECLARE @StringDate varchar(32) = '20116-03-15 18:50';
IF EXISTS( SELECT * WHERE ISDATE(@StringDate) = 1)
        PRINT CONCAT('VALID DATE: ', @StringDate)
ELSE    PRINT CONCAT('INVALID DATE: ', @StringDate);
-- Result: INVALID DATE: 20116-03-15 18:50
```

WHILE Looping - UPDATE in Batches

WHILE looping can be used to break down large transaction to small batches. Executing in small batches is safer and does not block other OLTP transactions for a long time. Blocking can be seen by running sp_who (SQL Server 2012 feature) system stored procedure. Another way is using DMV query.

Blog: **Finding Blocking Queries in SQL Azure**
http://blogs.msdn.com/b/sqlazure/archive/2010/08/13/10049896.aspx

UPDATE of 121,317 rows is batched to 13 batches of 10,000 or less.

```
USE AdventureWorks2012; CREATE TABLE SOD(SalesOrderID int, SalesOrderDetailID int  PRIMARY KEY,
         CarrierTrackingNumber nvarchar(25), OrderQty smallint,ProductID int,SpecialOfferID int,
         UnitPrice money,UnitPriceDiscount money,LineTotal numeric(38, 6),rowguid uniqueidentifier,
         ModifiedDate datetime);
INSERT INTO SOD SELECT * FROM Sales.SalesOrderDetail ORDER BY SalesOrderDetailID;
--(121317 row(s) affected)
```

```
WHILE (2 > 1)   -- Infinite loop until BREAK is issued
 BEGIN
  UPDATE TOP ( 10000 ) SOD
  SET   UnitPriceDiscount = 0.08,  ModifiedDate = CONVERT(DATE, getdate())
  WHERE  ModifiedDate < CONVERT(DATE, getdate());

  IF @@ROWCOUNT = 0       BEGIN        BREAK;        END
  -- 1 second delay
  -- Very important for other (if any)  OLTP transactions execution (cease blocking for 1 sec)
  WAITFOR DELAY '00:00:01'
 END; -- WHILE
GO                                              -- Execution time: 00:00:16
```

(10000 row(s) affected)
(10000 row(s) affected)
(10000 row(s) affected)
(10000 row(s) affected)
(10000 row(s) affected)
(10000 row(s) affected)
(10000 row(s) affected)
(10000 row(s) affected)
(10000 row(s) affected)
(10000 row(s) affected)
(10000 row(s) affected)
(10000 row(s) affected)
(1317 row(s) affected)
(0 row(s) affected)

```
DROP TABLE tempdb.dbo.SOD
```

WHILE Loop Usage in Cursors

Transact-SQL logic will visit all databases on the current SQL Server instance using a cursor. NOTE: **cursor solutions do not scale well, first choice is set-based logic if appropriate.** SQL Server 2012 T-SQL script.

```
DECLARE @CurrentDB sysname;
DECLARE AllDBCursor CURSOR  STATIC LOCAL FOR
        SELECT  name FROM    MASTER.dbo.sysdatabases
        WHERE   name NOT IN ('master','tempdb','model','msdb') ORDER BY name;
OPEN AllDBCursor;
FETCH  AllDBCursor INTO @CurrentDB;
WHILE (@@FETCH_STATUS = 0) -- loop through all db-s
 BEGIN
/***** PROCESSING (like BACKUP database)  *****/
        PRINT @CurrentDB;
        FETCH  AllDBCursor   INTO @CurrentDB;
 END;  CLOSE AllDBCursor; DEALLOCATE AllDBCursor;
```

```
/*.... AdventureWorks
AdventureWorks2008
AdventureWorks2012
AdventureWorksDW2012  .... */
```

Transact-SQL script demonstrates a subcategory cursor.

```
USE AdventureWorks2012;
DECLARE curSubcategory CURSOR STATIC LOCAL  FOR          -- declare cursor
        SELECT ProductSubcategoryID, Subcategory=Name
        FROM Production.ProductSubcategory ORDER BY Subcategory;
DECLARE @Subcategory varchar(40), @PSID int
OPEN curSubcategory
FETCH NEXT FROM curSubcategory INTO @PSID, @Subcategory  -- fetch cursor
WHILE (@@fetch_status = 0)                  -- cursor fetch_status
BEGIN -- begin cursor loop
/***** USER DEFINED PROCESSING CODE HERE  *****/
        DECLARE @Msg varchar(128);
  SELECT @Msg = CONCAT('ProductSubcategory info: ', @Subcategory,' ',CONVERT(varchar, @PSID));
        PRINT @Msg;
FETCH NEXT FROM curSubcategory INTO @PSID, @Subcategory;  -- fetch cursor
END; -- end cursor loop
CLOSE curSubcategory;   DEALLOCATE curSubcategory;
```

```
/* ... ProductSubcategory info: Bike Stands 27
ProductSubcategory info: Bottles and Cages 28
ProductSubcategory info: Bottom Brackets 5  ... */
```

T-SQL Transaction

Transact-SQL language has been extended with features beyond ANSI SQL such as variables, IF... ELSE and WHILE. **"Transact" refers to the capability to execute business transactions which require the synchronized update of tables as one or none at all.**

DELETE from 2 Tables with TRANSACTION Control

DELETE PRIMARY KEY rows from PK table and related FOREIGN KEY rows from FK table in a single transaction. NOTE: Deleting lots of rows may interfere with online access in an ecommerce database.

Alternate method: define tables with CASCADE ON DELETE action.

```
BEGIN TRANSACTION
```

```
-- First delete from FOREIGN KEY table
DELETE OmegaFK
FROM Omega AS OmegaFK
  INNER JOIN Delta AS DeltaPK
    ON DeltaPK.ColApk = OmegaFK.ColBfk
WHERE DeltaPK.ColApk = {single value A} ;
```

```
IF @@ERROR <> 0
BEGIN
        ROLLBACK TRANSACTION;
        RAISERROR('FK delete failed.', 10, 1);
END
-- if no error, delete from PRIMARY KEY table
ELSE
        DELETE
        FROM Delta
        WHERE ColApk = = {single value A};
```

```
-- Commit transaction only if both DELETE-s succeeded
IF @@ERROR <> 0
BEGIN
        ROLLBACK TRANSACTION;
        RAISERROR('PK delete failed.', 10, 1);
ELSE
        COMMIT TRANSACTION;
```

Stored Procedure with Input & Output Parameters

A stored procedure usually returns a table-like result set from the SELECT(s) in the stored procedure. Scalar value can also be returned with the OUTPUT option.

```
USE AdventureWorks2012;
GO
CREATE PROCEDURE uspQuarterSales      @StartYear INT,      @TotalSales MONEY OUTPUT
AS
 BEGIN -- sproc definition
  SET NOCOUNT ON -- turn off rows affected messages
  SELECT @TotalSales = SUM(SubTotal)
  FROM  Sales.SalesOrderHeader   WHERE OrderDate >= DATEADD(YY,@StartYear-1900,'19000101')

  SELECT  YEAR = YEAR(OrderDate),
        COALESCE(FORMAT(SUM(CASE
              WHEN DATEPART(QQ,OrderDate) = 1 THEN SubTotal
                            END),'c','en-US'),'') AS 'Q1',
        COALESCE(FORMAT(SUM(CASE
              WHEN DATEPART(QQ,OrderDate) = 2 THEN SubTotal
                            END),'c','en-US'),'') AS 'Q2',
        COALESCE(FORMAT(SUM(CASE
              WHEN DATEPART(QQ,OrderDate) = 3 THEN SubTotal
                            END),'c','en-US'),'') AS 'Q3',
        COALESCE(FORMAT(SUM(CASE
              WHEN DATEPART(QQ,OrderDate) = 4 THEN SubTotal
                            END),'c','en-US'),'') AS 'Q4'
  FROM   Sales.SalesOrderHeader soh
  WHERE  OrderDate >= DATEADD(YY,@StartYear-1900,'19000101')
  GROUP BY YEAR(OrderDate)    ORDER BY YEAR(OrderDate);
 END; -- sproc definition
GO
```

```
-- Execute stored procedure with INPUT/OUTPUT parameters
DECLARE @TotSales money
EXEC uspQuarterSales 2007, @TotSales OUTPUT;
SELECT TotalSales = FORMAT(@TotSales,'c','en-US');
```

YEAR	Q1	Q2	Q3	Q4
2007	$6,679,873.80	$8,357,874.88	$13,681,907.05	$13,291,381.43
2008	$11,398,376.28	$14,379,545.19	$50,840.63	

TotalSales
$67,839,799.27

Dynamic SQL Stored Procedure to REBUILD Indexes

The following dynamic SQL stored procedure uses database metadata to loop through all tables in the database, assemble and execute the index REBUILD command.

```
USE AdventureWorks2012;
GO
```

```
CREATE PROC sprocAllTablesIndexREBUILD
AS
 BEGIN
    DECLARE @DatabaseName SYSNAME = DB_NAME(),
        @TableName    VARCHAR(256);
    DECLARE @DynamicSQL NVARCHAR(max) = CONCAT('DECLARE cursorForAllTables CURSOR FOR
                SELECT CONCAT(QUOTENAME(TABLE_SCHEMA),''.'', QUOTENAME(TABLE_NAME))
                                AS TABLENAME    FROM ', @DatabaseName,
        '.INFORMATION_SCHEMA.TABLES WHERE   TABLE_TYPE = ''BASE TABLE''');
     BEGIN
       EXEC sp_executeSQL
         @DynamicSQL; -- create tables cursor
       OPEN cursorForAllTables;

       FETCH NEXT FROM cursorForAllTables INTO @TableName;
       WHILE ( @@FETCH_STATUS = 0 )
        BEGIN
          SET @DynamicSQL = CONCAT('ALTER INDEX ALL ON ', @TableName,
                  ' REBUILD; ' );
          PRINT @DynamicSQL;  -- test & debug
          EXEC sp_executeSQL
            @DynamicSQL;
          FETCH NEXT FROM cursorForAllTables INTO @TableName;
        END; -- cursor WHILE
       CLOSE cursorForAllTables;   DEALLOCATE cursorForAllTables;
    END;
 END; -- sproc
GO
-- Command(s) completed successfully.
```

```
-- Index REBUILD for all tables in database
EXEC sprocAllTablesIndexREBUILD;
-- Execution time: 00:00:26
/*
ALTER INDEX ALL ON [Production].[BillOfMaterials] REBUILD;
ALTER INDEX ALL ON [Production].[Culture] REBUILD;
....  */
```

User-Defined Functions

Table-Valued Functions

A table-valued function returns a table variable, therefore, it has to be invoked like it were a table in a query. T-SQL table-valued function creates a table from a delimited string of values.

```
CREATE FUNCTION dbo.ufnSplitDelimitedString ( @StringList VARCHAR(MAX),    @Delimiter CHAR(1))
RETURNS @TableList TABLE(ID int identity(1,1), StringLiteral VARCHAR(128))
BEGIN
    IF @StringList = '' RETURN;
    IF @Delimiter = ''
    BEGIN
      WITH Split AS                                   -- Recursive CTE
          ( SELECT CharOne=LEFT(@StringList,1),R=RIGHT(@StringList,len(@StringList)-1)
            UNION ALL
            SELECT LEFT(R,1), R=RIGHT(R, len(R)-1)
            FROM Split    WHERE LEN(R)>0  )               -- End of CTE
      INSERT @TableList
      SELECT CharOne FROM Split     OPTION ( MAXRECURSION 0);
      RETURN;
    END; -- IF
   DECLARE @XML xml=CONCAT('<root><csv>',replace(@StringList,@Delimiter,'</csv><csv>'),
                           '</csv></root>');
    INSERT @TableList
    SELECT rtrim(ltrim(replace(Word.value('.','nvarchar(128)'),char(10),'')))     AS ListMember
    FROM @XML.nodes('/root/csv') AS WordList(Word);
RETURN;
END; -- FUNCTION
GO
```

```
SELECT * FROM dbo.ufnSplitDelimitedString ('New York, California, Arizona, Texas, Toronto, Grand
Canyon, Yosemite,   Yellowstone, Niagara Falls, Belgium, Denmark, South Africa, Sweden', ',');
```

ID	StringLiteral
1	New York
2	California
3	Arizona
4	Texas
5	Toronto
6	Grand Canyon
7	Yosemite
8	Yellowstone
9	Niagara Falls
10	Belgium
11	Denmark
12	South Africa
13	Sweden

Table-Valued Function for PRIME Numbers Generation

Transact-SQL table-valued function generates prime numbers up to the input parameter limit.

```
USE AdventureWorks2012;
GO

CREATE FUNCTION ufnPrimeNumbers ( @Stop INT)
RETURNS @Result TABLE  (Prime INT)
BEGIN
WITH CTE ( SeqNo)
   AS (SELECT 0
      UNION ALL
      SELECT SeqNo + 1
      FROM   CTE
      WHERE  SeqNo < @Stop)
INSERT @Result
SELECT PrimeNo = N2.SeqNo
FROM   CTE N1
     INNER JOIN CTE N2
   ON  N2.SeqNo % N1.SeqNo > 0
     AND N2.SeqNo % 2 > 0
     AND N1.SeqNo < N2.SeqNo
     AND N2.SeqNo > 1
     AND N1.SeqNo >= 1
GROUP  BY N2.SeqNo
HAVING ( N2.SeqNo - COUNT(*) ) = 2
OPTION ( MAXRECURSION 0);
RETURN ;
END;
GO
```

```
SELECT * FROM dbo.ufnPrimeNumbers (1000);
GO
-- (167 row(s) affected) - Partial results.
```

Prime
3
5
7
11
13
17
19
23
29
31

Inline Functions

An inline user-defined function, returns table, can be used as a parameterized view.

```
USE AdventureWorks2012
GO
```

```
CREATE FUNCTION Sales.ufnStaffSalesByFiscalYear (@OrderYear INT)
RETURNS TABLE  AS
RETURN
SELECT
        CONVERT(date, soh.OrderDate)                                          AS OrderDate
      ,CONCAT(p.FirstName, ' ', COALESCE(p.MiddleName, ''), ' ', p.LastName)  AS FullName
      ,e.JobTitle
      ,st.Name                                                                AS SalesTerritory
      ,FORMAT(soh.SubTotal, 'c', 'en-US')                                     AS SalesAmount
      ,YEAR(DATEADD(mm, 6, soh.OrderDate))                                    AS FiscalYear
FROM Sales.SalesPerson sp
      INNER JOIN Sales.SalesOrderHeader soh
            ON sp.BusinessEntityID = soh.SalesPersonID
      INNER JOIN Sales.SalesTerritory st
            ON sp.TerritoryID = st.TerritoryID
      INNER JOIN HumanResources.Employee e
            ON soh.SalesPersonID = e.BusinessEntityID
      INNER JOIN Person.Person p
            ON p.BusinessEntityID = sp.BusinessEntityID
WHERE         soh.OrderDate >= datefromparts(@OrderYear, 1, 1)
          AND soh.OrderDate < dateadd(yy,1, datefromparts(@OrderYear, 1, 1));
GO
-- Command(s) completed successfully.
```

```
SELECT * FROM Sales.ufnStaffSalesByFiscalYear (2007)
ORDER BY FullName, CONVERT(money, SalesAmount) DESC;     -- SalesAmount (string) does not sort correctly
--( 1476  row(s) affected)  -- Partial results.
```

OrderDate	FullName	JobTitle	SalesTerritory	SalesAmount	FiscalYear
2007-08-01	David R Campbell	Sales Representative	Northwest	$101,609.29	2008
2007-07-01	David R Campbell	Sales Representative	Northwest	$93,397.64	2008
2007-04-01	David R Campbell	Sales Representative	Northwest	$75,104.65	2007
2007-07-01	David R Campbell	Sales Representative	Northwest	$74,149.95	2008
2007-04-01	David R Campbell	Sales Representative	Northwest	$73,963.26	2007
2007-08-01	David R Campbell	Sales Representative	Northwest	$71,283.24	2008
2007-09-01	David R Campbell	Sales Representative	Northwest	$66,871.84	2008
2007-01-01	David R Campbell	Sales Representative	Northwest	$63,864.71	2007
2007-11-01	David R Campbell	Sales Representative	Northwest	$63,339.26	2008
2007-10-01	David R Campbell	Sales Representative	Northwest	$60,519.95	2008

Scalar Functions

A scalar user-defined function returns a scalar value. It can be used in a query wherever a single value is required.

```
USE AdventureWorks2012;
GO
CREATE FUNCTION dbo.ufnNumberToEnglish (@Number INT)
RETURNS VARCHAR(1024)   AS
 BEGIN
    DECLARE @Below20 TABLE      ( ID   INT IDENTITY ( 0, 1 ),    Word VARCHAR(32) );
    DECLARE @Tens TABLE   (  ID   INT IDENTITY ( 2, 1 ),    Word VARCHAR(32) );
    INSERT @Below20  (Word)
    VALUES('Zero'), ('One'),('Two'),  ('Three'), ('Four'), ('Five'), ('Six'), ('Seven'), ('Eight'),
        ('Nine'), ('Ten'),  ('Eleven'),  ('Twelve'), ('Thirteen'),  ('Fourteen'),  ('Fifteen'),
        ('Sixteen'), ('Seventeen'), ('Eighteen'), ('Nineteen');
    INSERT @Tens
    VALUES('Twenty'),   ('Thirty'), ('Forty'),  ('Fifty'),  ('Sixty'),  ('Seventy'),  ('Eighty'), ('Ninety');
    DECLARE @English VARCHAR(1024) = (SELECT CASE
            WHEN @Number = 0 THEN ''
            WHEN @Number BETWEEN 1 AND 19
                    THEN (SELECT Word FROM   @Below20 WHERE  ID = @Number)
            WHEN @Number BETWEEN 20 AND 99 THEN
      CONCAT((SELECT Word FROM   @Tens
WHERE  ID = @Number / 10), '-', dbo.ufnNumberToEnglish(@Number%10))
       WHEN @Number BETWEEN 100 AND 999 THEN CONCAT((
          dbo.ufnNumberToEnglish(@Number / 100) ), ' Hundred ',
dbo.ufnNumberToEnglish(@Number%100))
      WHEN @Number BETWEEN 1000 AND 999999 THEN CONCAT((
         dbo.ufnNumberToEnglish(@Number / 1000) ), ' Thousand ',
dbo.ufnNumberToEnglish(@Number%1000))
     WHEN @Number BETWEEN 1000000 AND 999999999 THEN CONCAT((
        dbo.ufnNumberToEnglish(@Number / 1000000) ), ' Million ',
dbo.ufnNumberToEnglish(@Number%1000000))
      ELSE ' INVALID INPUT'   END);
    SELECT @English = RTRIM(@English);
    SELECT @English = RTRIM(LEFT(@English, len(@English) - 1))    WHERE  RIGHT(@English, 1) = '-';
    RETURN ( @English );                                    END;
GO  -- Command(s) completed successfully.
```

```
SELECT dbo.ufnNumberToEnglish (9999);  -- Nine Thousand Nine Hundred Ninety-Nine
```

```
SELECT dbo.ufnNumberToEnglish (1000001);  -- One Million One
```

```
SELECT dbo.ufnNumberToEnglish (7777777);
-- Seven Million Seven Hundred Seventy-Seven Thousand Seven Hundred Seventy-Seven
```

Dynamic PIVOT Script

Static PIVOT has pretty limited role since it has to be changed when data changes effects the PIVOT range. Dynamic SQL makes PIVOT data driven. Instead of hard-wired columns, dynamic PIVOT builds the columns from the data dynamically.

```
USE AdventureWorks2012;
GO
```

```
DECLARE @OrderYear AS TABLE
 (
   YYYY INT NOT NULL PRIMARY KEY
 );
DECLARE @DynamicSQL AS NVARCHAR(4000) ;

INSERT INTO @OrderYear
SELECT DISTINCT YEAR(OrderDate)
FROM   Sales.SalesOrderHeader;

DECLARE @ReportColumnNames AS NVARCHAR(MAX),  @IterationYear    AS INT;

SET @IterationYear = (SELECT MIN(YYYY)      FROM   @OrderYear);
SET @ReportColumnNames = N'';

-- Assemble pivot list dynamically
WHILE ( @IterationYear IS NOT NULL )
 BEGIN
    SET @ReportColumnNames = @ReportColumnNames + N','
                  + QUOTENAME(CAST(@IterationYear AS NVARCHAR(10)));
     SET @IterationYear = (SELECT MIN(YYYY)
                  FROM   @OrderYear
                  WHERE  YYYY > @IterationYear);
 END;

SET @ReportColumnNames = SUBSTRING(@ReportColumnNames, 2,
                LEN(@ReportColumnNames));

PRINT @ReportColumnNames; -- [2005],[2006],[2007],[2008]

SET @DynamicSQL = CONCAT(N'SELECT * FROM (SELECT [Store (Freight Summary)]=s.Name,
        YEAR(OrderDate) AS OrderYear,  Freight = convert(money, convert(varchar, Freight))
        FROM Sales.SalesOrderHeader soh
        INNER JOIN Sales.Customer c ON c.CustomerID = soh.CustomerID
        INNER JOIN Sales.Store s ON c.StoreID = s.BusinessEntityID) as Header
        PIVOT (SUM(Freight)    FOR OrderYear IN(', @ReportColumnNames,N'))  AS Pvt ORDER BY 1;');
-- T-SQL script continued
```

```
-- T-SQL script continued
PRINT @DynamicSQL; -- Testing & debugging
/* SELECT * FROM (SELECT [Store (Freight Summary)]=s.Name,
        YEAR(OrderDate) AS OrderYear,  Freight = convert(money, convert(varchar, Freight))
        FROM Sales.SalesOrderHeader soh
        INNER JOIN Sales.Customer c ON c.CustomerID = soh.CustomerID
        INNER JOIN Sales.Store s ON c.StoreID = s.BusinessEntityID) as Header
        PIVOT (SUM(Freight)    FOR OrderYear IN([2005],[2006],[2007],[2008]))  AS Pvt ORDER BY 1;     */
-- Execute dynamic sql
EXEC sp_executesql  @DynamicSQL;
GO  -- (633 row(s) affected) - Partial results.
```

Store (Freight Summary)	2005	2006	2007	2008
A Bike Store	921.55	1637.24	NULL	NULL
A Great Bicycle Company	142.08	114.34	15.24	NULL
A Typical Bike Shop	976.61	1529.08	NULL	NULL
Acceptable Sales & Service	12.58	25.17	NULL	NULL

INSERT, UPDATE & DELETE through a View

Underlying table can be modified through a view, thus adding flexibility to security access since a view can be permissioned independently of the table.

```
USE AdventureWorks2012;
```

```
CREATE TABLE Product
   (ID INT PRIMARY KEY, ProductName nvarchar(50), ListPrice money, ModifiedDate date);
INSERT Product
SELECT ProductID, Name, ListPrice, ModifiedDate FROM Production.Product;
GO -- (504 row(s) affected)
CREATE VIEW vProduct AS SELECT * FROM Product;
GO
UPDATE vProduct SET ModifiedDate = '2018-01-01';
GO -- (504 row(s) affected)
INSERT vProduct VALUES (2000, 'Three-Wheeler Bike', $999.99, getdate());
GO -- (1 row(s) affected)
DELETE TOP (10) FROM vProduct;
GO -- (10 row(s) affected)
SELECT TOP (1) * FROM Product;  -- 322 Chainring          0.00      2018-01-01 00:00:00.000
GO
DROP VIEW dbo.vProduct;
DROP TABLE dbo.Product;
GO
```

Sensitive Data Audit Trigger

Triggers can be used to track sensitive data changes into an audit table. The OUTPUT clause is an alternative, but not exactly equivalent.

```
USE Payroll;
GO
```

```
CREATE TRIGGER uTrgEmployeeUpdate
ON Employee
AFTER UPDATE
AS
  IF ( Update(Salary)
      OR Update(SSN) )
    BEGIN
      INSERT INTO CorpSecurityEmployeeAudit
              (auditlogtype,
               auditEmployeeDeptID,
               auditEmployeeID,
               auditEmployeeSalary,
               auditEmployeeSSN,
               auditUpdatedBy)
      SELECT 'PREVIOUSDATA',
          DeptID,
          EmployeeID,
          Salary,
          SSN,
          User_name()
      FROM   DELETED

      INSERT INTO CorpSecurityEmployeeAudit
              (auditlogtype,
               auditEmployeeDeptID,
               auditEmployeeID,
               auditEmployeeSalary,
               auditEmployeeSSN,
               auditUpdatedBy)
      SELECT 'NEWDATA',
          DeptID,
          EmployeeID,
          Salary,
          SSN,
          User_name()
      FROM   INSERTED
    END;
GO
```

Automatic Timestamp Trigger

Whenever the Person.Contact is updated, the ModifiedDate will be updated to current time by the update after trigger. NOTE: disable/drop other update triggers on this table, if any, for the test.

```
USE AdventureWorks2012;
GO
```

```
CREATE TRIGGER uTrgPersonTimestamp
ON Person.Person
FOR UPDATE
AS
  BEGIN
   IF TRIGGER_NESTLEVEL() > 1      RETURN;
    UPDATE Person.Person  SET    Person.Person.ModifiedDate = CURRENT_TIMESTAMP
    FROM   Person.Person p
           INNER JOIN INSERTED i
             ON p.BusinessEntityID = i.BusinessEntityID
  END
GO
-- (1 row(s) affected)

SELECT *
FROM   Person.Person
WHERE  FirstName = 'Kim'    AND MiddleName = 'B'      AND LastName = 'Abercrombie'
GO
-- ModifiedDate: 2004-02-10 00:00:00.000

-- Updating a column will automatically update the ModifiedDate
UPDATE Person.Person              SET    MiddleName = 'B'
WHERE  FirstName = 'Kim'    AND MiddleName = 'B'     AND LastName = 'Abercrombie'
GO

SELECT *
FROM   Person.Person WHERE  FirstName = 'Kim'    AND MiddleName = 'B'    AND LastName =
'Abercrombie'
GO
-- ModifiedDate: 2018-08-11 07:22:01.157

-- Cleanup
DROP TRIGGER Person.uTrgPersonTimestamp
```

Recursive Product Assembly

Recursive Common Table Expression (CTE) is used to assemble a bike frame based on the BillOfMaterials table.

```
USE AdventureWorks2012;
```

```
DECLARE @ProductID int = 831;
WITH CTE(AssemblyID, ComponentID, PerAssemblyQty,  AssemblyLevel) AS
(       SELECT bom0.ProductAssemblyID, bom0.ComponentID, bom0.PerAssemblyQty,
                0 AS AssemblyLevel
        FROM Production.BillOfMaterials AS bom0
        WHERE bom0.ProductAssemblyID = @ProductID
                AND bom0.EndDate is null
        UNION ALL
        SELECT bom.ProductAssemblyID, bom.ComponentID, p.PerAssemblyQty,
                AssemblyLevel + 1
        FROM Production.BillOfMaterials AS bom
                INNER JOIN CTE AS p
                        ON bom.ProductAssemblyID = p.ComponentID   AND bom.EndDate is null   )
SELECT pp.Name AS ProductName, AssemblyID, ComponentID,
        p.Name AS AssemblyName, PerAssemblyQty, AssemblyLevel
FROM CTE
        INNER JOIN Production.Product AS p
                ON CTE.ComponentID = p.ProductID
        INNER JOIN Production.Product AS pp
                ON CTE.AssemblyID = pp.ProductID
ORDER BY AssemblyLevel, AssemblyID, ComponentID;
```

ProductName	AssemblyID	ComponentID	AssemblyName	PerAssemblyQty	AssemblyLevel
ML Mountain Frame - Black, 44	831	324	Chain Stays	2.00	0
ML Mountain Frame - Black, 44	831	325	Decal 1	2.00	0
ML Mountain Frame - Black, 44	831	326	Decal 2	1.00	0
ML Mountain Frame - Black, 44	831	327	Down Tube	1.00	0
ML Mountain Frame - Black, 44	831	399	Head Tube	1.00	0
ML Mountain Frame - Black, 44	831	492	Paint - Black	8.00	0
ML Mountain Frame - Black, 44	831	532	Seat Stays	4.00	0
ML Mountain Frame - Black, 44	831	533	Seat Tube	1.00	0
ML Mountain Frame - Black, 44	831	534	Top Tube	1.00	0
ML Mountain Frame - Black, 44	831	803	ML Fork	1.00	0
Chain Stays	324	486	Metal Sheet 5	2.00	1
Down Tube	327	483	Metal Sheet 3	1.00	1
Head Tube	399	485	Metal Sheet 4	1.00	1
Seat Stays	532	484	Metal Sheet 7	4.00	1
Seat Tube	533	478	Metal Bar 2	1.00	1
Top Tube	534	482	Metal Sheet 2	1.00	1
ML Fork	803	316	Blade	1.00	1
ML Fork	803	331	Fork End	1.00	1
ML Fork	803	350	Fork Crown	1.00	1
ML Fork	803	531	Steerer	1.00	1
Blade	316	486	Metal Sheet 5	1.00	2
Fork End	331	482	Metal Sheet 2	1.00	2
Fork Crown	350	486	Metal Sheet 5	1.00	2
Steerer	531	487	Metal Sheet 6	1.00	2

Percent on Base Calculation

When deriving percent on base, we need to calculate the overall total in a single value subquery to use it as denominator in the percentile calculation.

```
USE AdventureWorks2012;
```

```
SELECT YEAR(OrderDate) AS [Year],
    FORMAT(SUM(TotalDue),'c0','en-US') AS YearTotal,
    FORMAT(SUM(TotalDue) /
        (SELECT SUM(TotalDue) FROM Sales.SalesOrderHeader),'p0') AS Percentile
FROM Sales.SalesOrderHeader
GROUP BY YEAR(OrderDate)
ORDER BY YEAR ASC;
```

Year	YearTotal	Percentage
2005	$12,693,251	10 %
2006	$34,463,848	28 %
2007	$47,171,490	38 %
2008	$28,888,198	23 %

Adding a Grand Total line with ROLLUP.

```
SELECT COALESCE(CONVERT(varchar,YEAR(OrderDate)), 'Grand Total') AS [Year],
    FORMAT(SUM(TotalDue),'c0','en-US') AS [SalesTotal],
    FORMAT(SUM(TotalDue) /
        (SELECT SUM(TotalDue) FROM Sales.SalesOrderHeader),'p0') AS Percentage
FROM Sales.SalesOrderHeader
GROUP BY YEAR(OrderDate)
        WITH ROLLUP
ORDER BY YEAR ASC;
```

Year	SalesTotal	Percentage
2005	$12,693,251	10 %
2006	$34,463,848	28 %
2007	$47,171,490	38 %
2008	$28,888,198	23 %
Grand Total	$123,216,786	100 %

CHAPTER 18: Exporting & Importing Data - On-Premises SS 2012

Saving a T-SQL Script as .sql File

Any T-SQL script can be saved as .sql file. One easy way is saving from Management Studio Query Editor. Here is the script we will save.

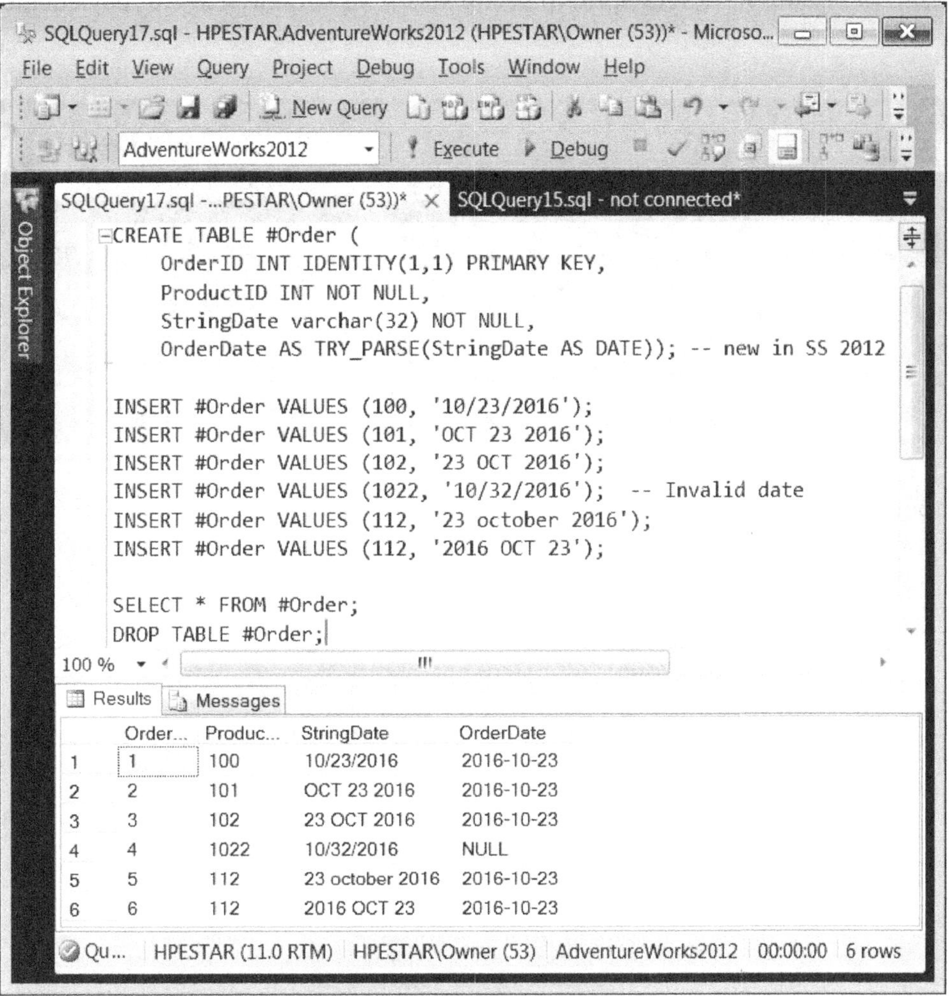

Click on File, click on Save .. As, choose a path and enter the file name for the script. To load it back: click on File, click on Open File, locate file in Open File dialog pop-up.

Executing a .sql Script File Using SQLCMD

The SQLCMD command line utility can be used to execute a .sql script file typically with the -i (input) and -o (output) options. **Note: with any of the Command Prompt utilities the command line should not be broken with carriage return or line feed (CR/LF), it has to be one long line.**

```
SQLCMD -S"HPESTAR" -Uyourlogin -Psecret007 -i "f:\data\sql\tryparsedemo.sql" -
o"f:\data\result\tryparsedemo.txt"
```

"HPESTAR" is the name of the SQL Server. With Windows authentication:

```
SQLCMD -S"HPESTAR"  -i "f:\data\sql\tryparsedemo.sql" -o"f:\data\result\tryparsedemo.txt"
```

```
Command Prompt
Microsoft Windows [Version 6.1.7601]
Copyright (c) 2009 Microsoft Corporation.  All rights reserved.

C:\Users\Owner>SQLCMD -S"HPESTAR"  -i "f:\data\sql\tryparsedemo.sql" -o"f:\data\
result\tryparsedemo.txt"

C:\Users\Owner>_
```

The output file collects warnings, messages, errors and results.

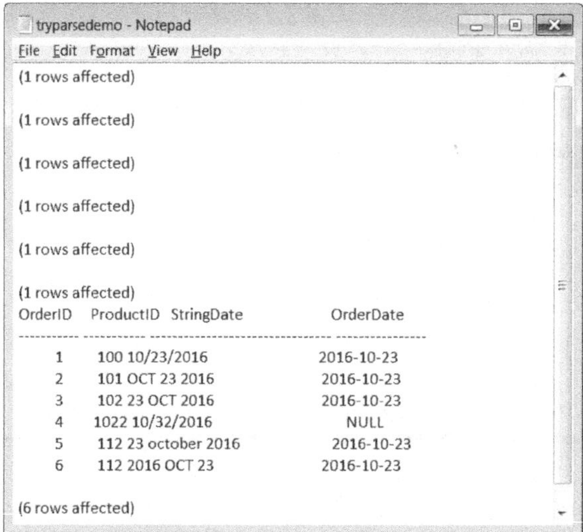

tryparsedemo - Notepad

File Edit Format View Help

(1 rows affected)

(1 rows affected)

(1 rows affected)

(1 rows affected)

(1 rows affected)

(1 rows affected)

OrderID	ProductID	StringDate	OrderDate
1	100	10/23/2016	2016-10-23
2	101	OCT 23 2016	2016-10-23
3	102	23 OCT 2016	2016-10-23
4	1022	10/32/2016	NULL
5	112	23 october 2016	2016-10-23
6	112	2016 OCT 23	2016-10-23

(6 rows affected)

Making a T-SQL Script Rerunnable

It takes special attention to make a T-SQL script re-executable as many times as desired. A CREATE VIEW script can only be executed once.

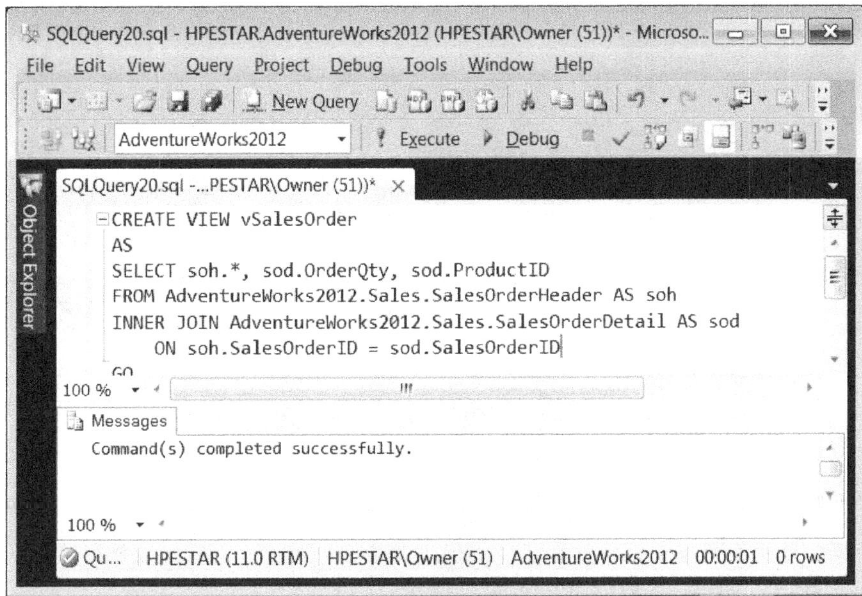

Repeat execution gives an error.

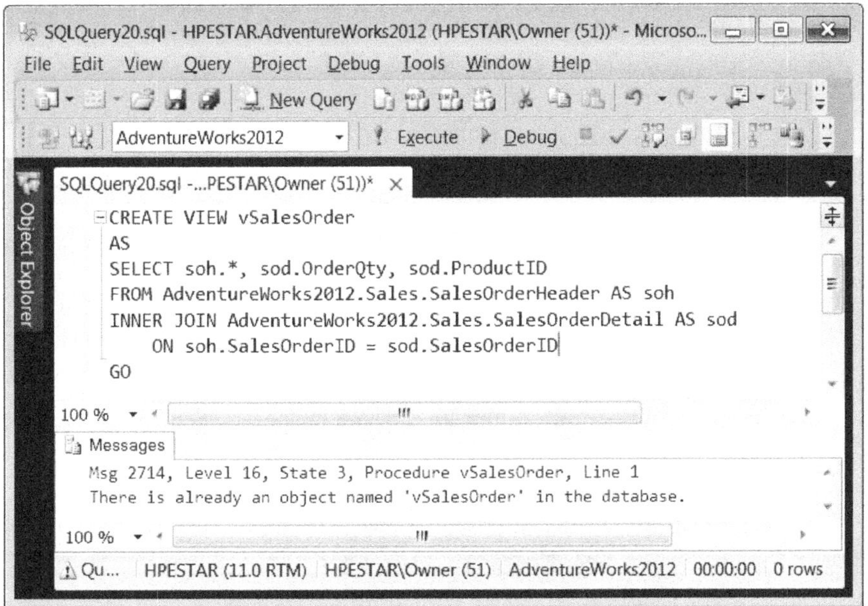

IF...ELSE Conditional Way to Make a Script Rerunnable

IF...ELSE is frequently the solution to prepare a rerunnable script. In this instance, first we check if the view exists. If it doesn't exist, we just go ahead and create it. If indeed it exists, we drop it first, then create it again.

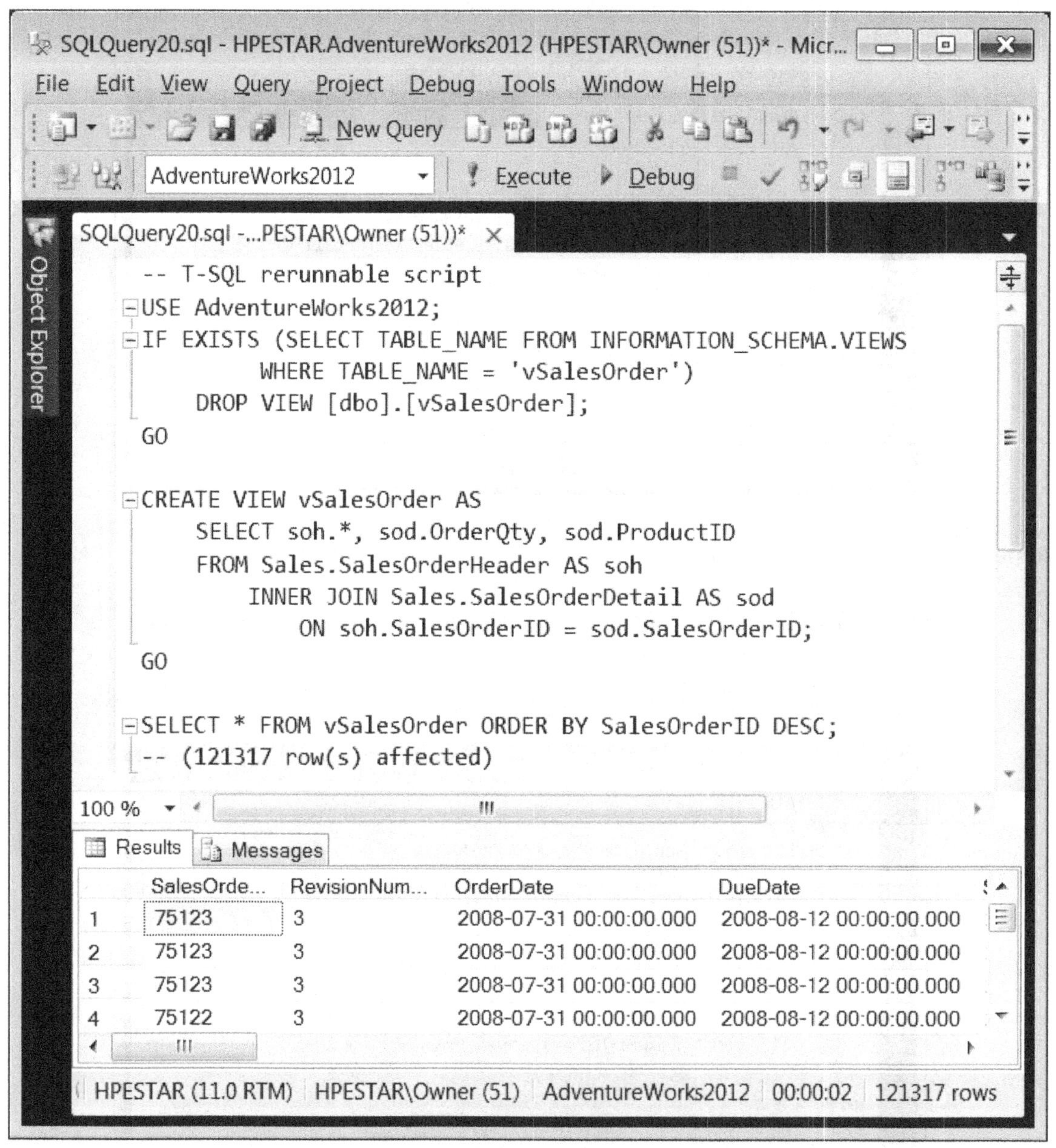

```
-- T-SQL rerunnable script
USE AdventureWorks2012;
IF EXISTS (SELECT TABLE_NAME FROM INFORMATION_SCHEMA.VIEWS
        WHERE TABLE_NAME = 'vSalesOrder')
    DROP VIEW [dbo].[vSalesOrder];
GO

CREATE VIEW vSalesOrder AS
    SELECT soh.*, sod.OrderQty, sod.ProductID
    FROM Sales.SalesOrderHeader AS soh
        INNER JOIN Sales.SalesOrderDetail AS sod
            ON soh.SalesOrderID = sod.SalesOrderID;
GO

SELECT * FROM vSalesOrder ORDER BY SalesOrderID DESC;
-- (121317 row(s) affected)
```

	SalesOrde...	RevisionNum...	OrderDate	DueDate
1	75123	3	2008-07-31 00:00:00.000	2008-08-12 00:00:00.000
2	75123	3	2008-07-31 00:00:00.000	2008-08-12 00:00:00.000
3	75123	3	2008-07-31 00:00:00.000	2008-08-12 00:00:00.000
4	75122	3	2008-07-31 00:00:00.000	2008-08-12 00:00:00.000

bcp Usage for Exporting & Importing Data

bcp (Bulk Copy Program) is a command line utility for moving data. The Production.Product table is exported to a flat file with bcp using Windows authentication.

For SQL Server authentication, add the "-Uyourlogin -Pyourpasswrd" parameters. **Note: the command must be one long line without breaks.**

```
Command Prompt
Microsoft Windows [Version 6.1.7601]
Copyright (c) 2009 Microsoft Corporation.  All rights reserved.

C:\Users\Owner>bcp AdventureWorks2012.Production.Product out F:\data\export\prod
uctz.txt -w -T -S"HPESTAR"

Starting copy...
SQLState = S1000, NativeError = 0
Error = [Microsoft][SQL Server Native Client 11.0]Warning: BCP import with a for
mat file will convert empty strings in delimited columns to NULL.

504 rows copied.
Network packet size (bytes): 4096
Clock Time (ms.) Total     : 125    Average : (4032.00 rows per sec.)

C:\Users\Owner>_
```

The **results of a query execution** can be exported with bcp as well using the queryout option. Rule is the same, no carriage return or line feed in the command no matter how long is it. The command can be edited in SSMS Query Editor and pasted into Command Prompt with Right Mouse Click Paste. CTRL-V does not work.

```
Command Prompt

C:\Users\Owner>bcp "SELECT * from AdventureWorks2012.HumanResources.Department"
queryout F:\data\export\departmentz.txt -w -T -S"HPESTAR"

Starting copy...

16 rows copied.
Network packet size (bytes): 4096
Clock Time (ms.) Total     : 453    Average : (35.32 rows per sec.)

C:\Users\Owner>_
```

Importing Data with the bcp Utility

Importing is very similar to exporting. For better control though it is necessary to use a format file. First we create an empty table for the data.

```
use tempdb;
select  TOP 0 * into product1 from Production.Product;
go
```

We are ready to execute the bcp import command.

```
Command Prompt

C:\Users\Owner>bcp tempdb.dbo.product1 in F:\data\export\productz.txt -w -T -S"H
PESTAR"

Starting copy...

504 rows copied.
Network packet size (bytes): 4096
Clock Time (ms.) Total     : 312     Average : (1615.38 rows per sec.)

C:\Users\Owner>
```

Checking the results.

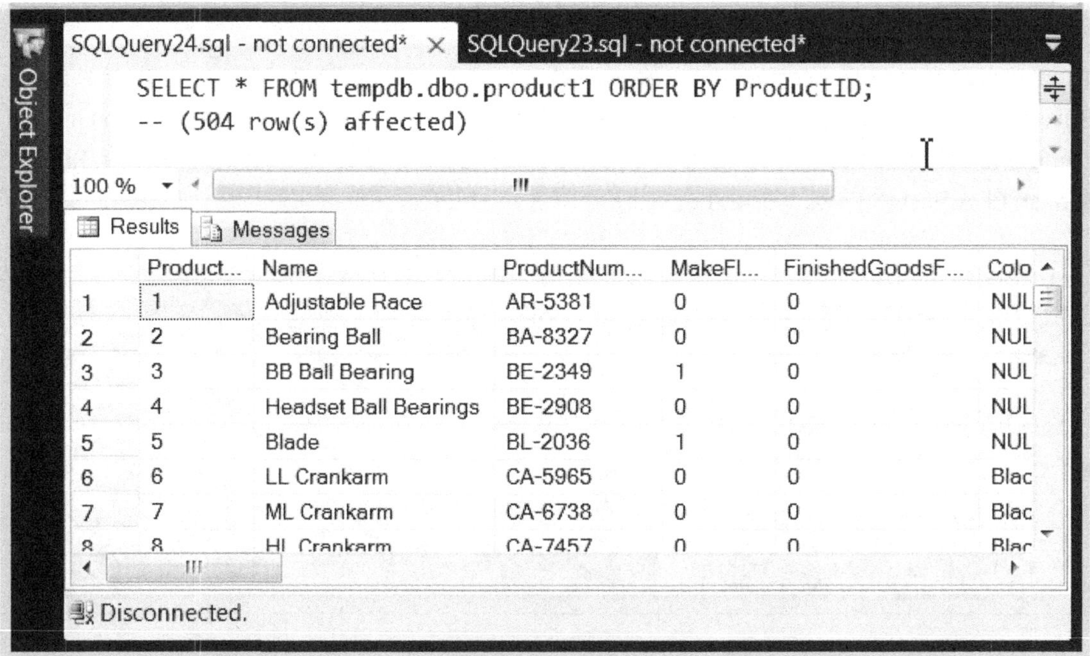

	Product...	Name	ProductNum...	MakeFl...	FinishedGoodsF...	Colo
1	1	Adjustable Race	AR-5381	0	0	NUL
2	2	Bearing Ball	BA-8327	0	0	NUL
3	3	BB Ball Bearing	BE-2349	1	0	NUL
4	4	Headset Ball Bearings	BE-2908	0	0	NUL
5	5	Blade	BL-2036	1	0	NUL
6	6	LL Crankarm	CA-5965	0	0	Blac
7	7	ML Crankarm	CA-6738	0	0	Blac
8	8	HL Crankarm	CA-7457	0	0	Blac

Exporting Data with SQL Server Import and Export Wizard

We will export a view query results to a new Excel worksheet. The SELECT query returns 8,914 rows from the vPersonDemographics view.

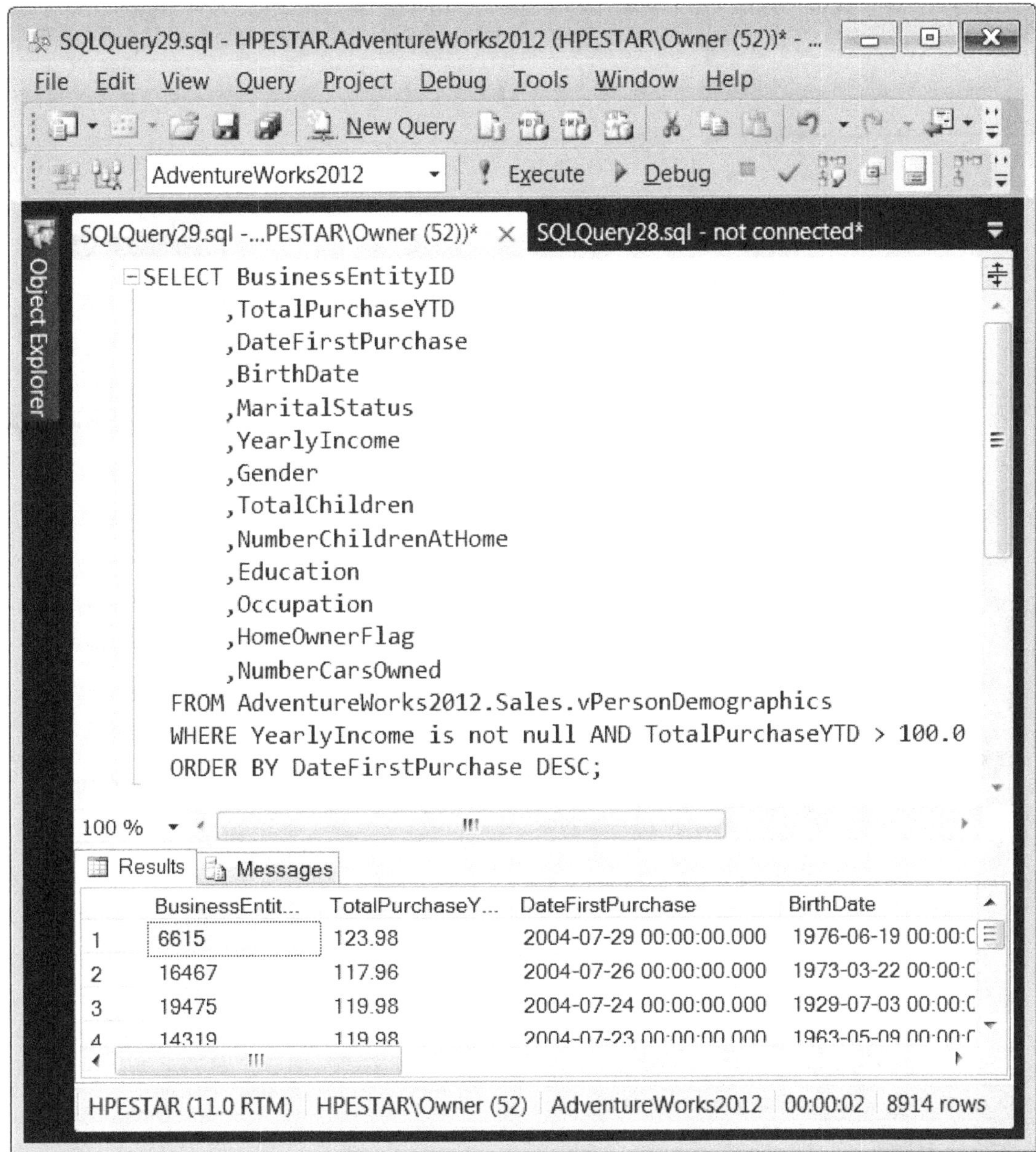

SQLQuery29.sql - HPESTAR.AdventureWorks2012 (HPESTAR\Owner (52))* - ...
File Edit View Query Project Debug Tools Window Help
New Query
AdventureWorks2012
Execute Debug
SQLQuery29.sql -...PESTAR\Owner (52))*
SQLQuery28.sql - not connected*
Object Explorer
SELECT BusinessEntityID
,TotalPurchaseYTD
,DateFirstPurchase
,BirthDate
,MaritalStatus
,YearlyIncome
,Gender
,TotalChildren
,NumberChildrenAtHome
,Education
,Occupation
,HomeOwnerFlag
,NumberCarsOwned
FROM AdventureWorks2012.Sales.vPersonDemographics
WHERE YearlyIncome is not null AND TotalPurchaseYTD > 100.0
ORDER BY DateFirstPurchase DESC;
100 %
Results
Messages
BusinessEntit... TotalPurchaseY... DateFirstPurchase BirthDate
1 6615 123.98 2004-07-29 00:00:00.000 1976-06-19 00:00:0
2 16467 117.96 2004-07-26 00:00:00.000 1973-03-22 00:00:0
3 19475 119.98 2004-07-24 00:00:00.000 1929-07-03 00:00:0
HPESTAR (11.0 RTM) HPESTAR\Owner (52) AdventureWorks2012 00:00:02 8914 rows

Starting the SSIS Import and Export Wizard

We start the SSIS Import/Export Wizard by a Right Click on the database in Object Explorer. It does not matter much if we choose Import Data or Export data since it only presets the destination or source pages respectively.

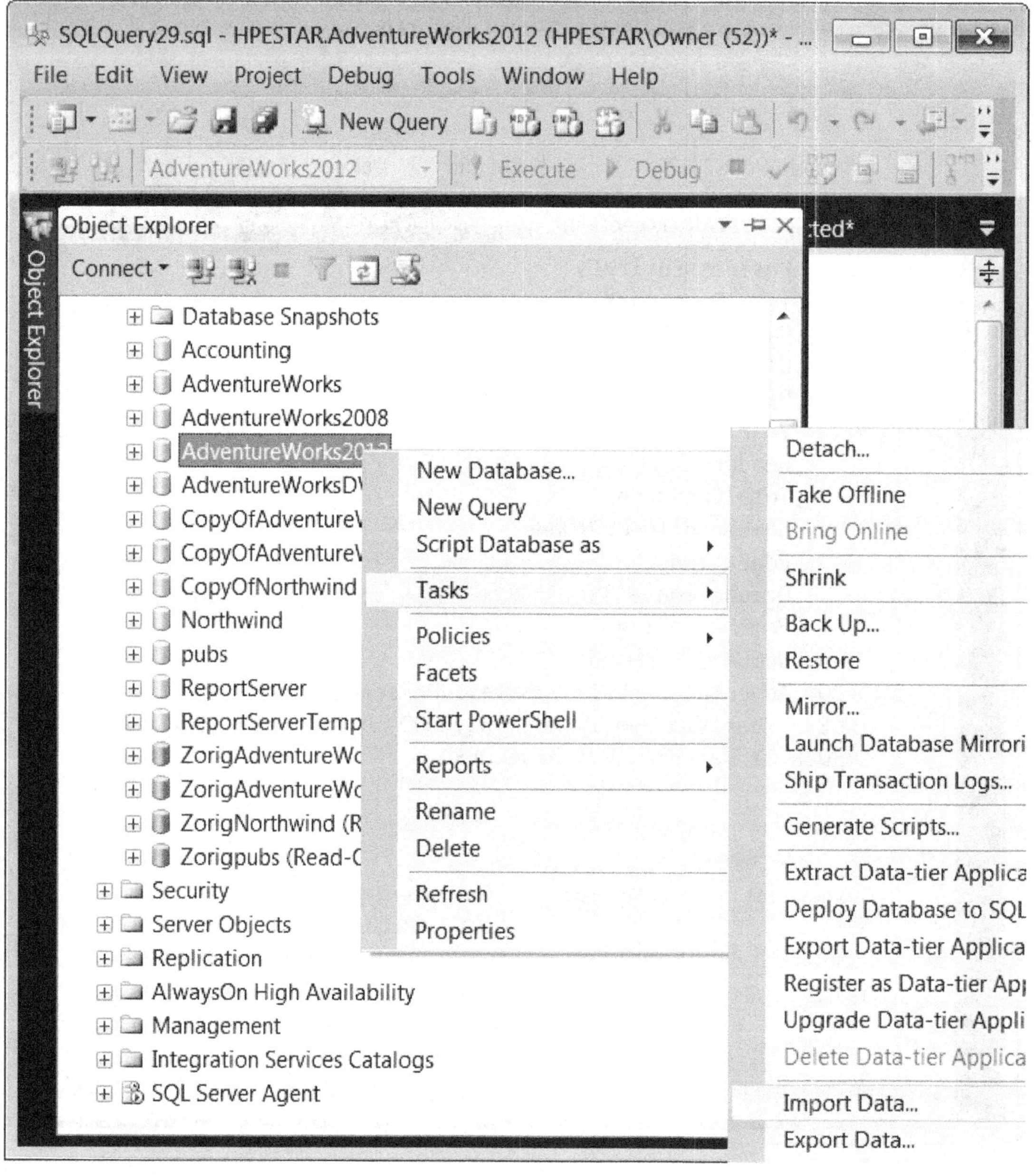

Optional Wizard Starting Welcome Screen

There is a checkmark option on the bottom to turn it off.

Configuring the Data Source Page

The data source is a database, therefore the server and database must be set up on this page.

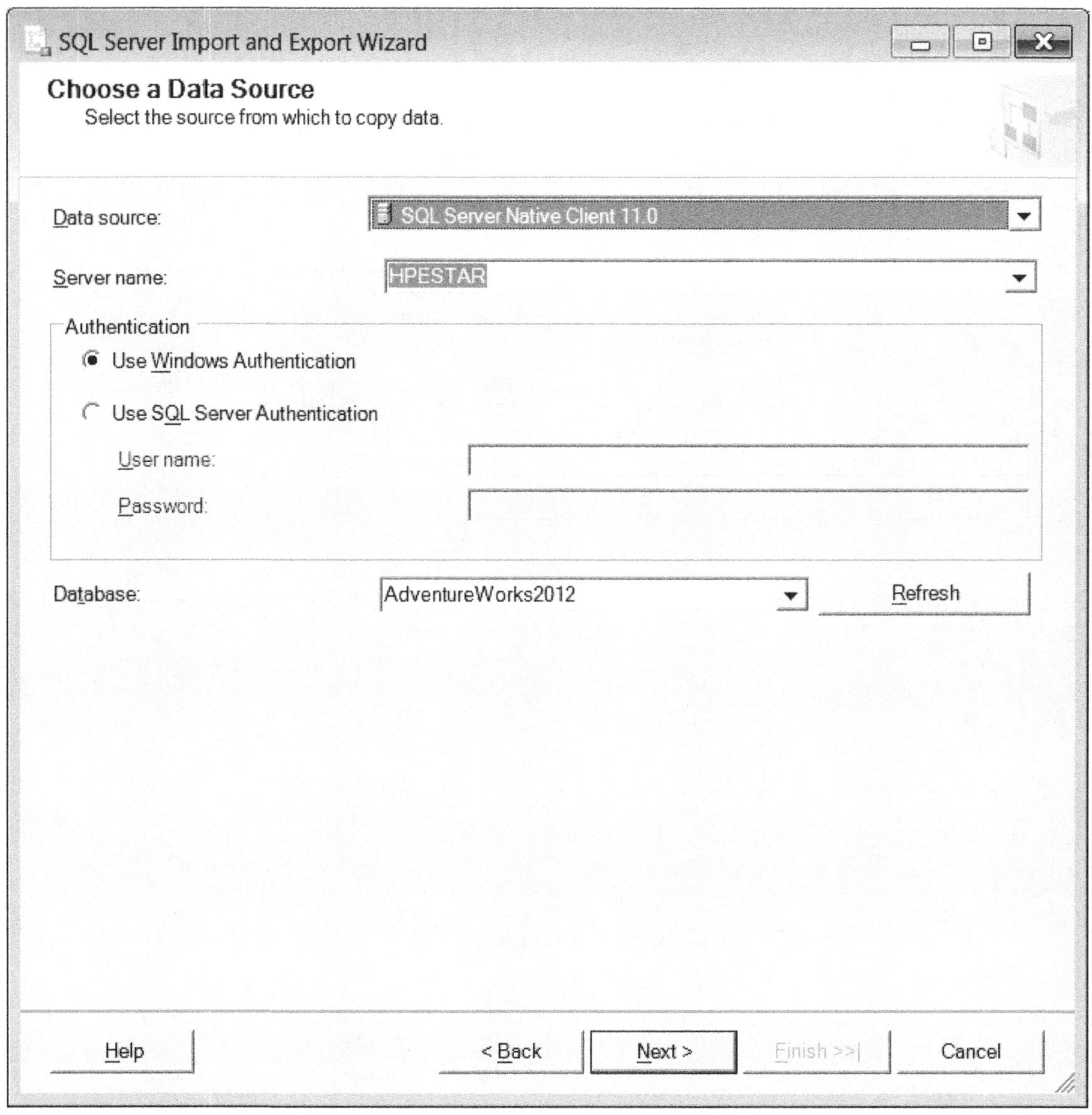

Configuring the Destination Page

The destination is a new Excel worksheet. Path & name must be given.

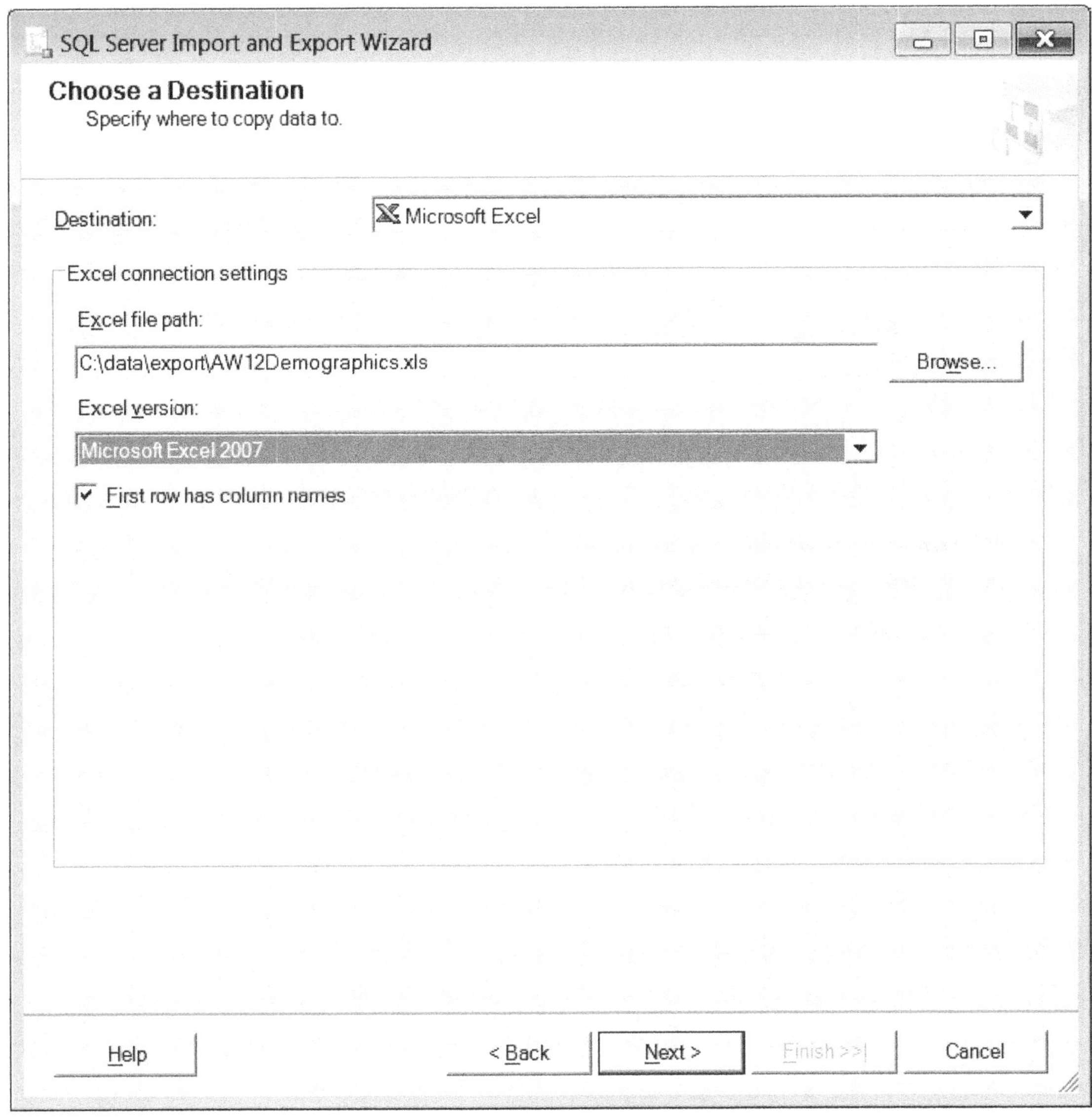

Specifying Table/View or Query Source

The Wizard logic branches based on what radio button we choose. If the choose table/view source, the next dialog box offers the entire list of tables/views in the database for checkmark selection.

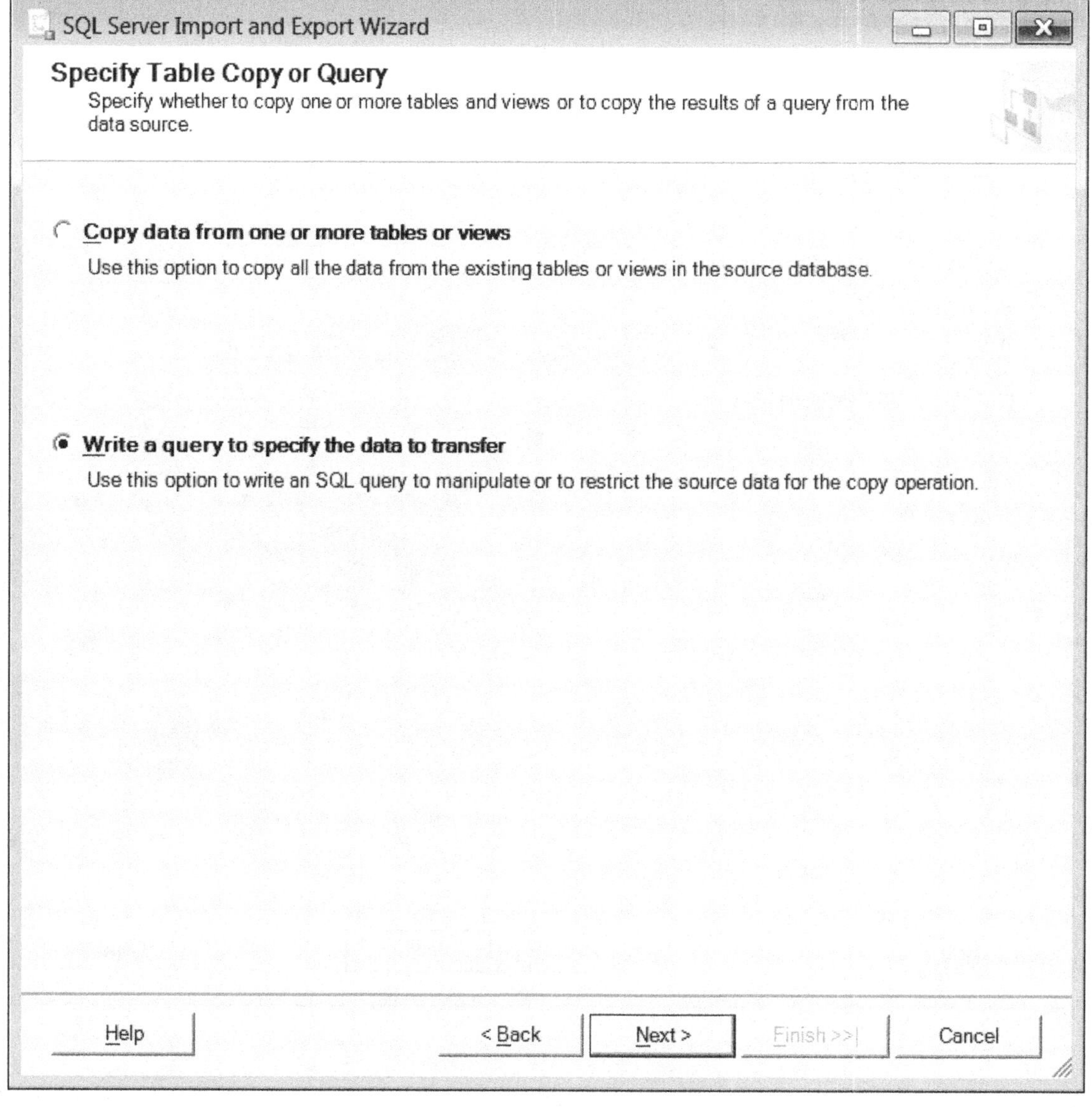

Entering the Query Source

We should use a tested query in order to avoid a failure in the execution of the generated SSIS package. Parse option is available for syntax checking.

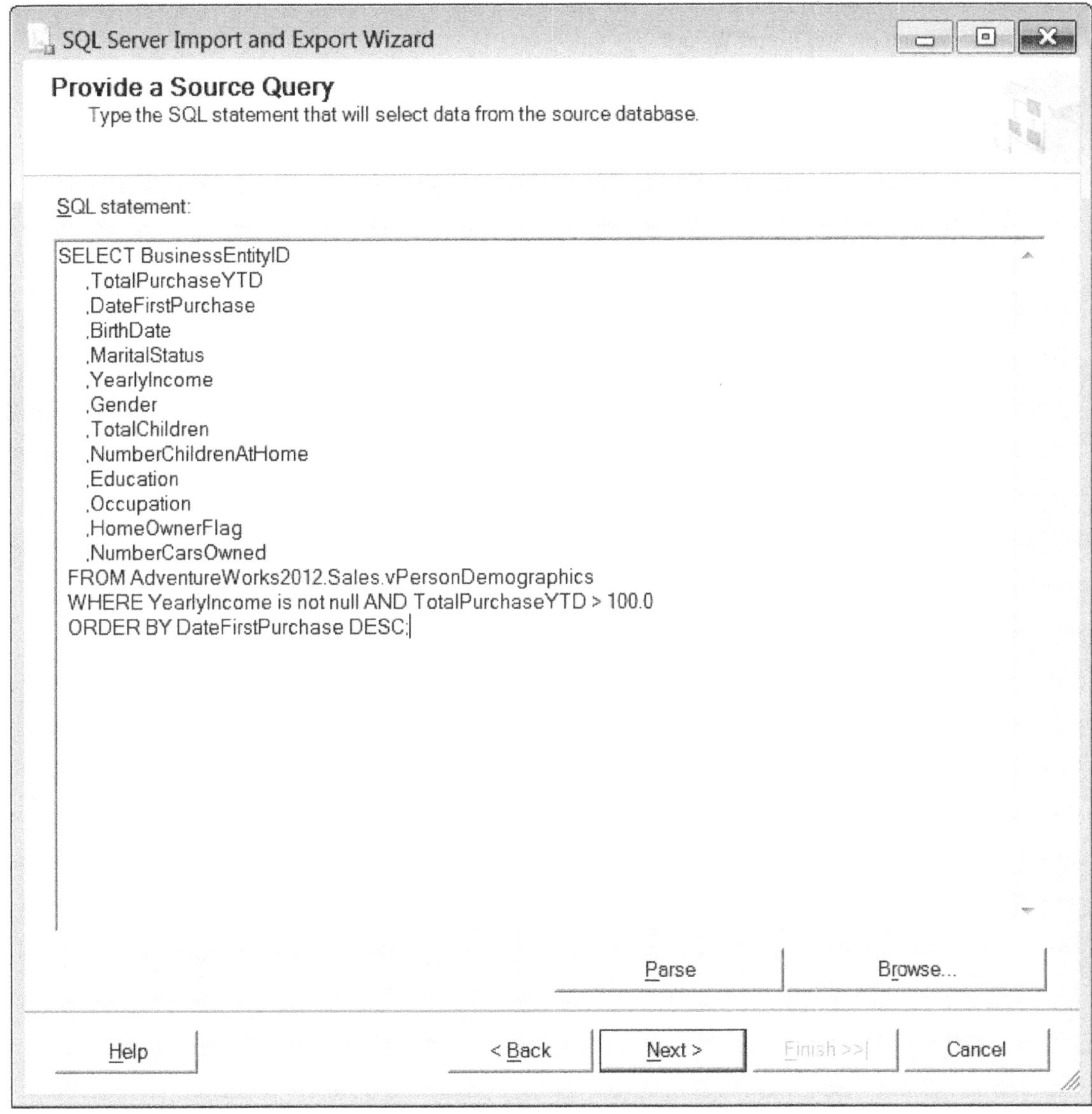

Option to Edit Mappings & Review Data

If you trust the Wizard, you can just click "Next". Otherwise, you can edit column mappings and review the data.

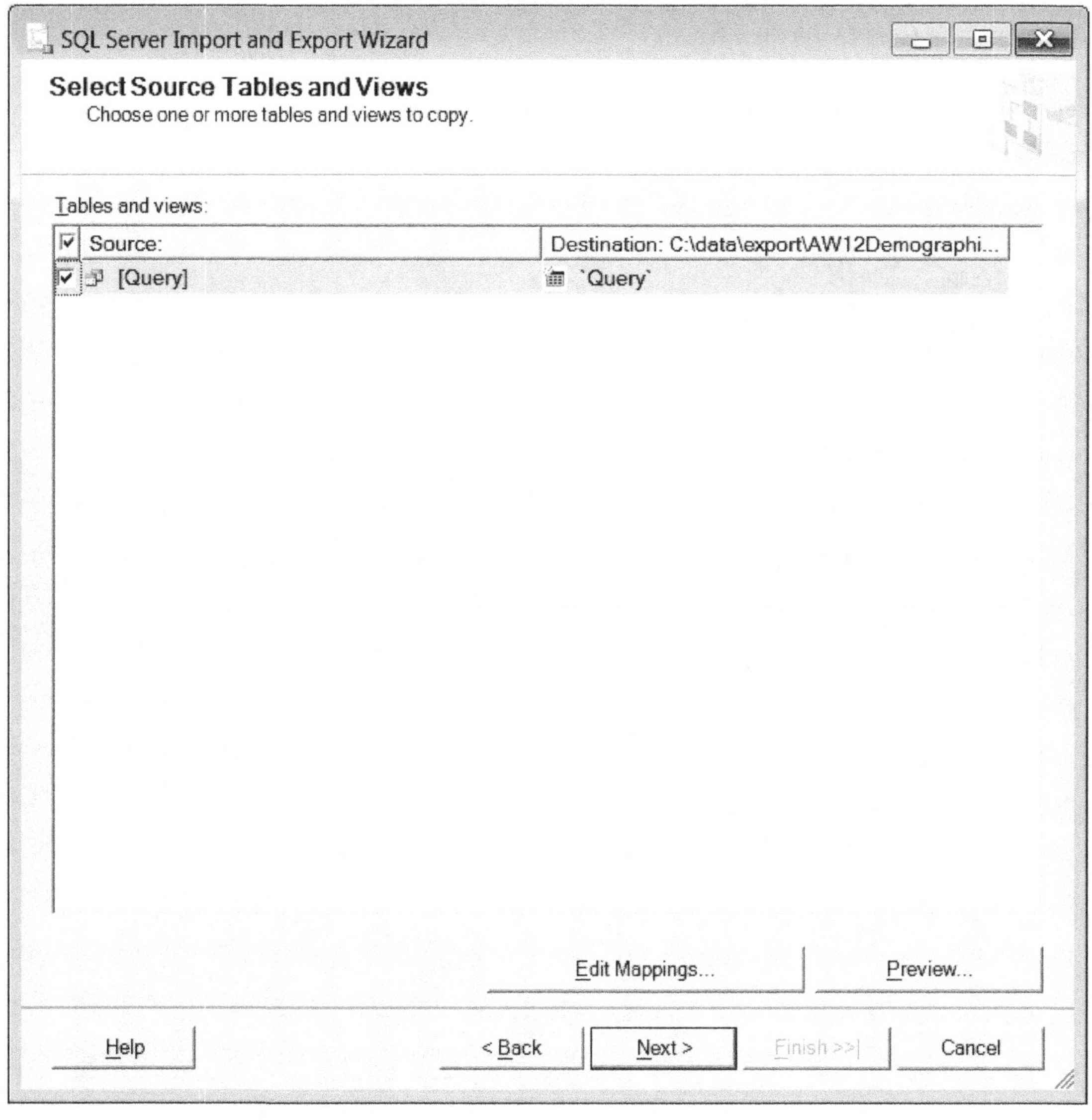

Edit Mappings & Preview

The next Wizard screen offers popup windows for editing the column mappings, changing the CREATE TABLE SQL and preview the data. We don't perform any change.

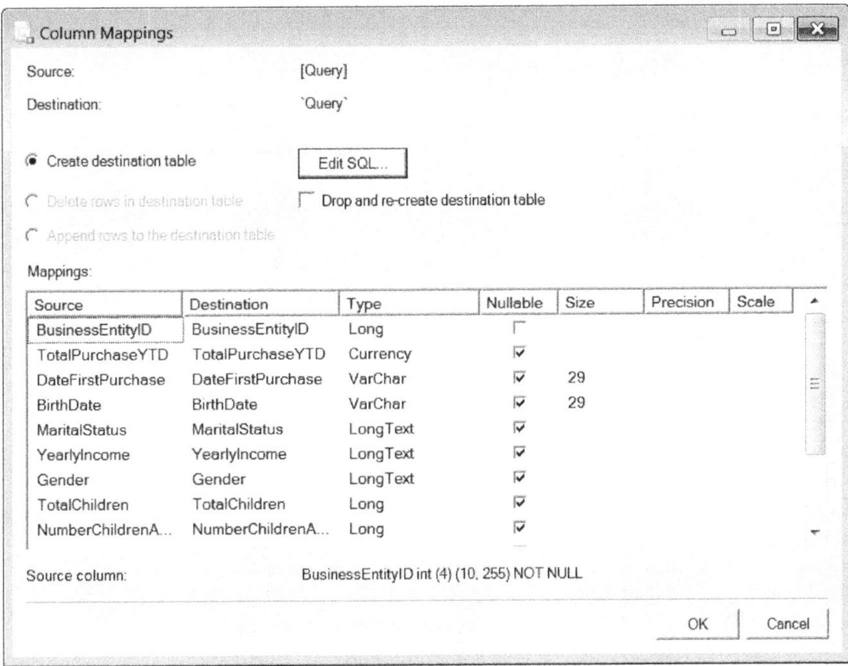

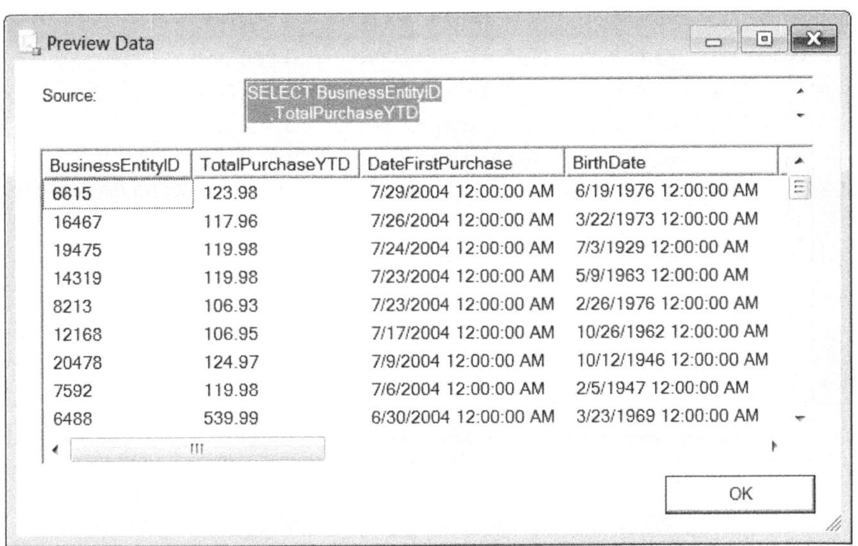

Review Data Type Mappings

Column data mappings can be reviewed in detail on this dialog box.

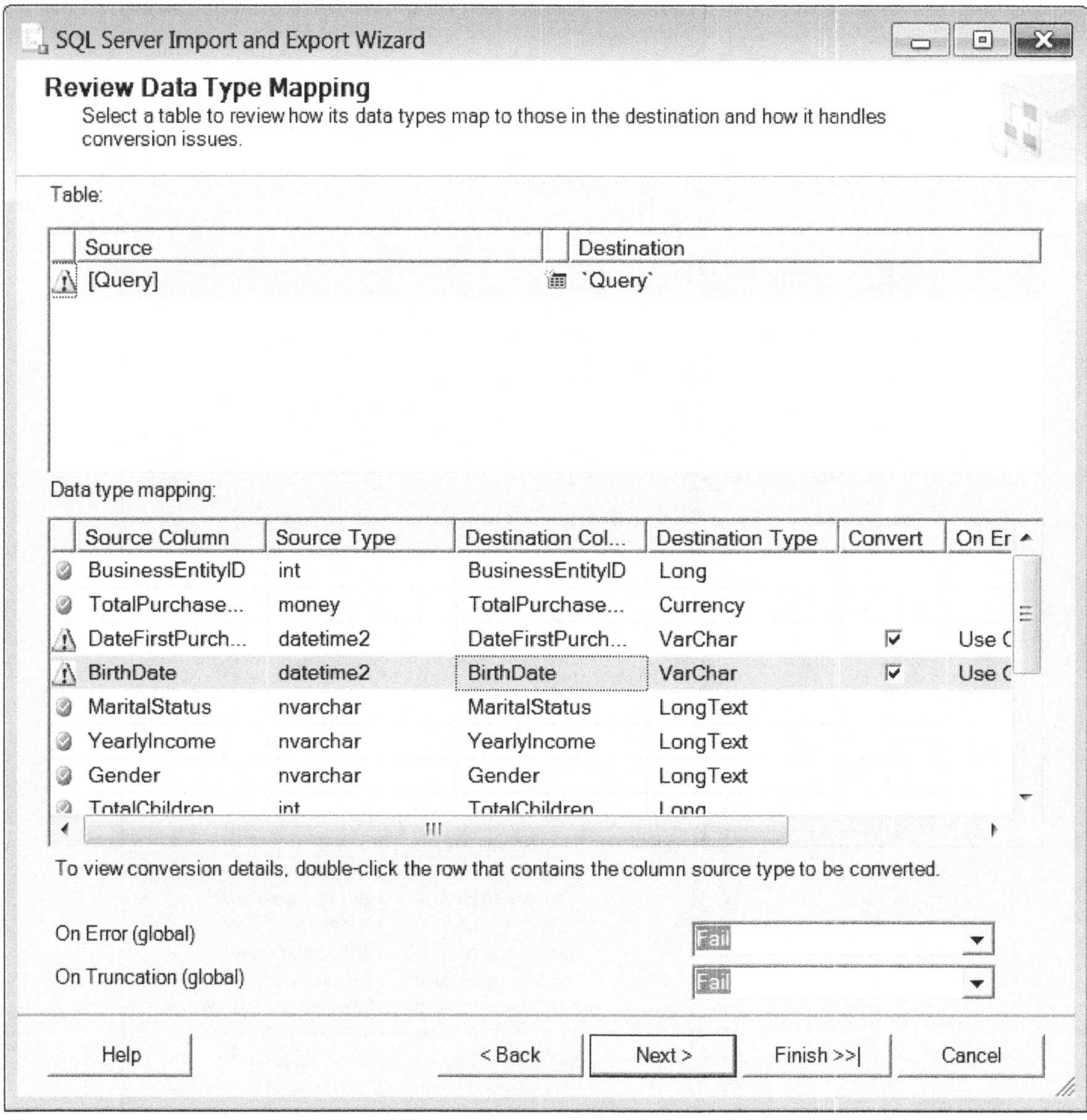

Save and/or Run Package

The Wizard generated SSIS package can be saved for future use or enhancements. If we run it immediately without saving, it will just go away after execution.

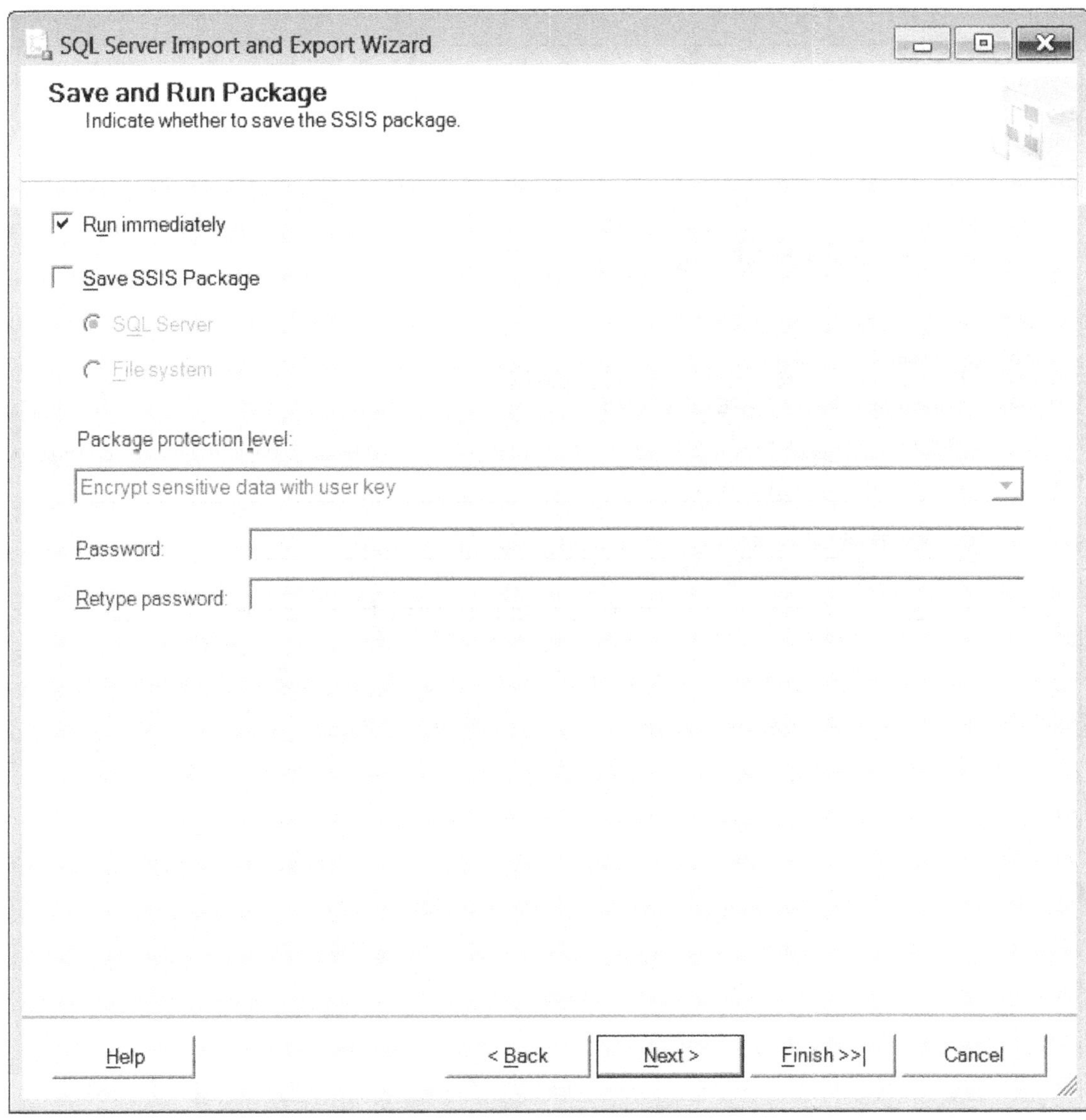

Verification Screen before Execution

At this point we still can go back and make changes should it be necessary. Once we click on Finish and we did not checkmark Save, the package will execute and goes away on success or failure.

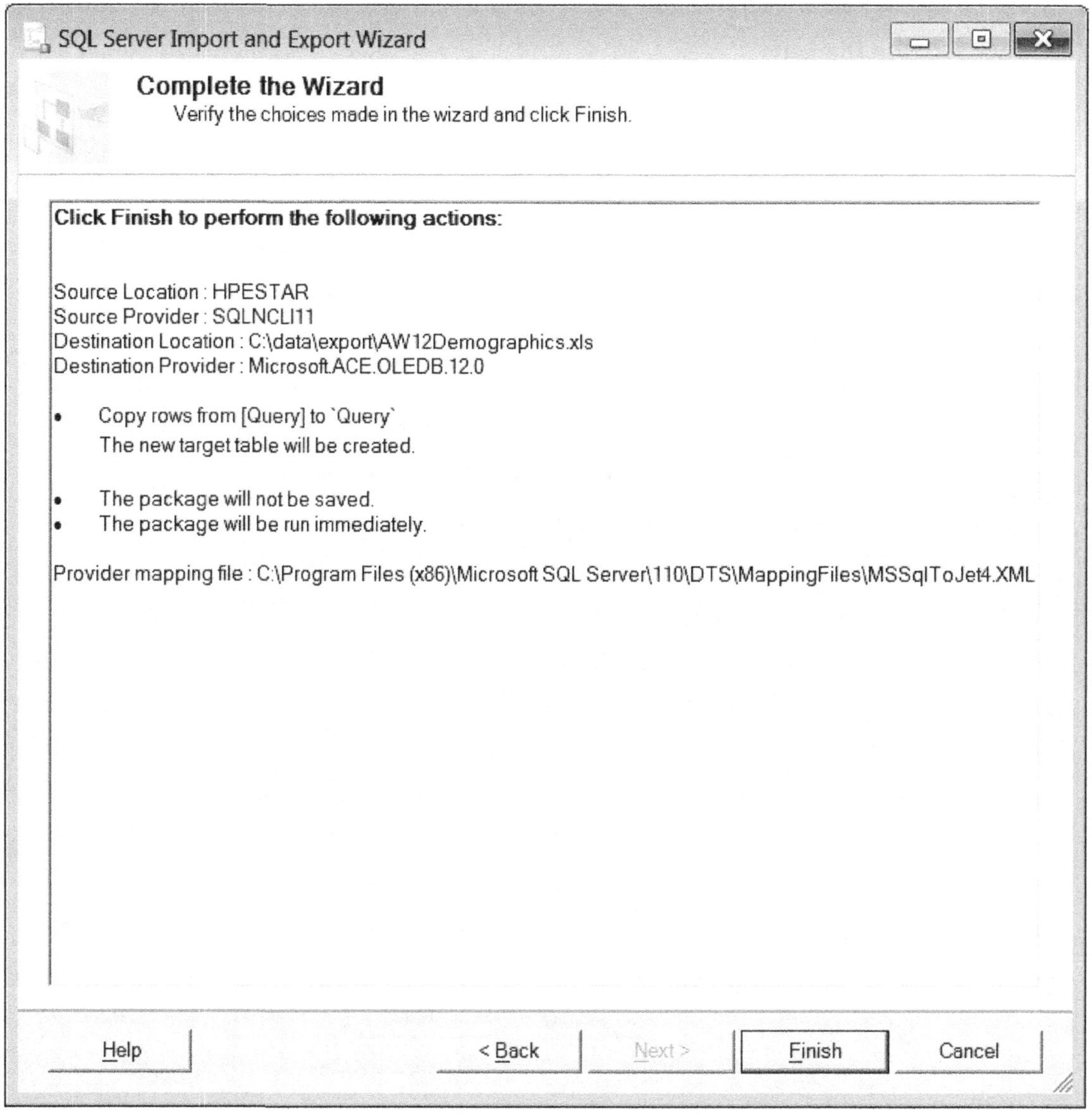

Execution Results Screen

If there are errors in the execution of the package, they will show in this window. The current Wizard generated SSIS package executed successfully.

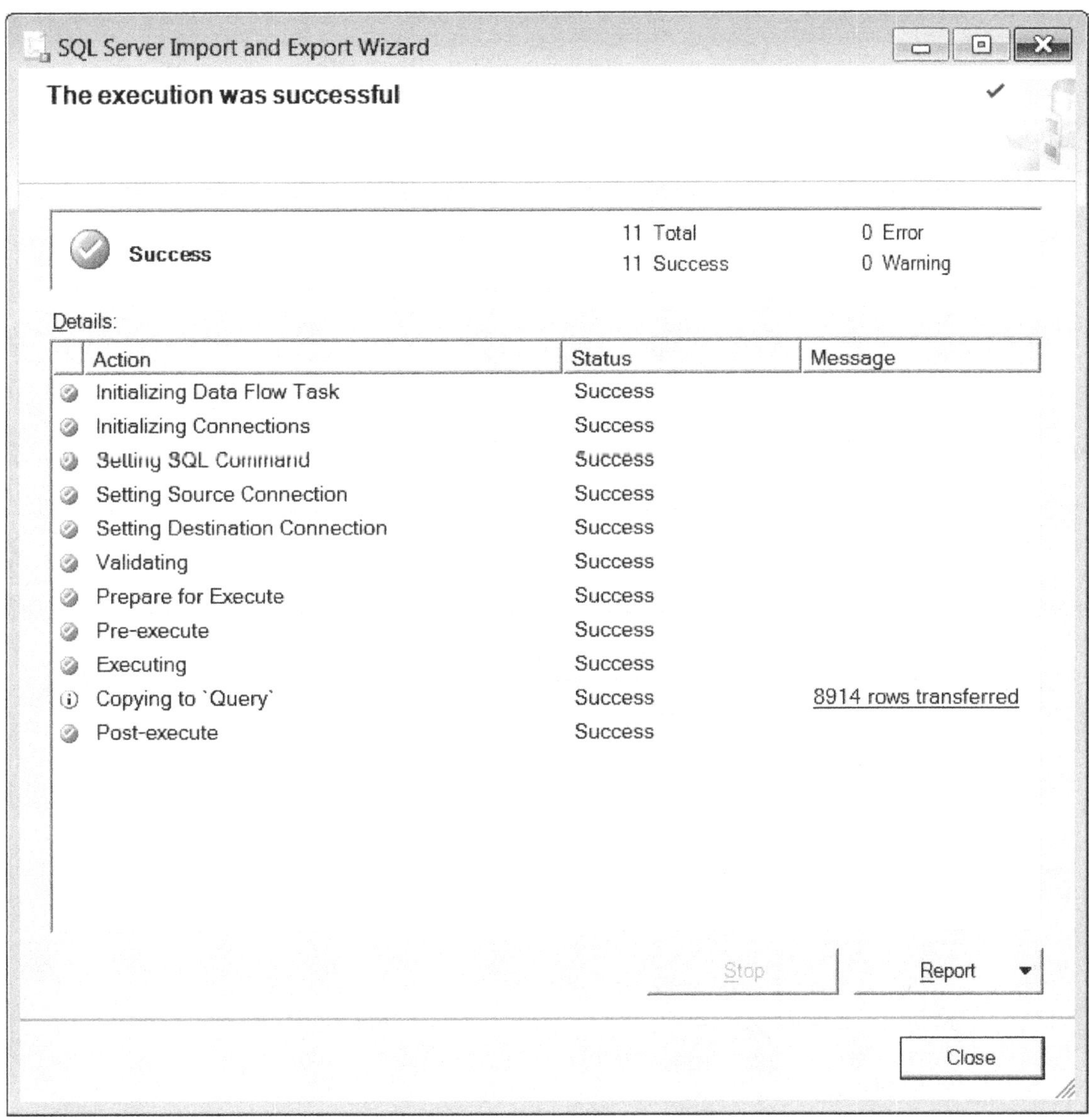

Checking Results in Excel

If the double click on the destination filename, the transferred data is displayed by Excel.

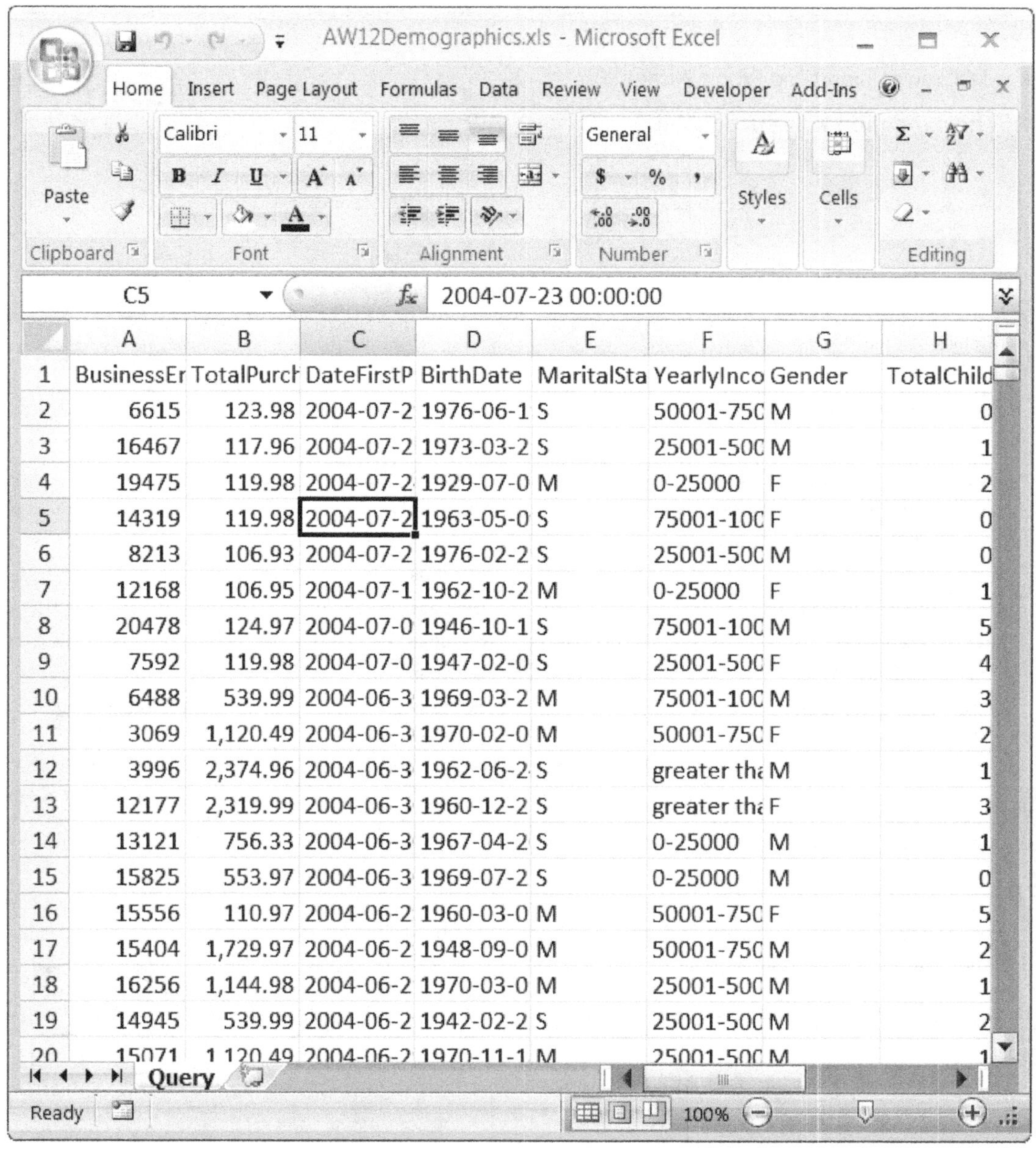

	A	B	C	D	E	F	G	H
1	BusinessEr	TotalPurch	DateFirstP	BirthDate	MaritalSta	YearlyInco	Gender	TotalChild
2	6615	123.98	2004-07-2	1976-06-1	S	50001-750	M	0
3	16467	117.96	2004-07-2	1973-03-2	S	25001-500	M	1
4	19475	119.98	2004-07-2	1929-07-0	M	0-25000	F	2
5	14319	119.98	2004-07-2	1963-05-0	S	75001-100	F	0
6	8213	106.93	2004-07-2	1976-02-2	S	25001-500	M	0
7	12168	106.95	2004-07-1	1962-10-2	M	0-25000	F	1
8	20478	124.97	2004-07-0	1946-10-1	S	75001-100	M	5
9	7592	119.98	2004-07-0	1947-02-0	S	25001-500	F	4
10	6488	539.99	2004-06-3	1969-03-2	M	75001-100	M	3
11	3069	1,120.49	2004-06-3	1970-02-0	M	50001-750	F	2
12	3996	2,374.96	2004-06-3	1962-06-2	S	greater tha	M	1
13	12177	2,319.99	2004-06-3	1960-12-2	S	greater tha	F	3
14	13121	756.33	2004-06-3	1967-04-2	S	0-25000	M	1
15	15825	553.97	2004-06-3	1969-07-2	S	0-25000	M	0
16	15556	110.97	2004-06-2	1960-03-0	M	50001-750	F	5
17	15404	1,729.97	2004-06-2	1948-09-0	M	50001-750	M	2
18	16256	1,144.98	2004-06-2	1970-03-0	M	25001-500	M	1
19	14945	539.99	2004-06-2	1942-02-2	S	25001-500	M	2
20	15071	1,120.49	2004-06-2	1970-11-1	M	25001-500	M	1

Importing Data with SQL Server Import and Export Wizard

Importing with the Wizard is very similar to the exporting process. We are going to import the just created AW12Demographics.xls Excel worksheet into a new database table. We start the Wizard the same as for export. First we configure the source as Excel worksheet.

Specify Data Source

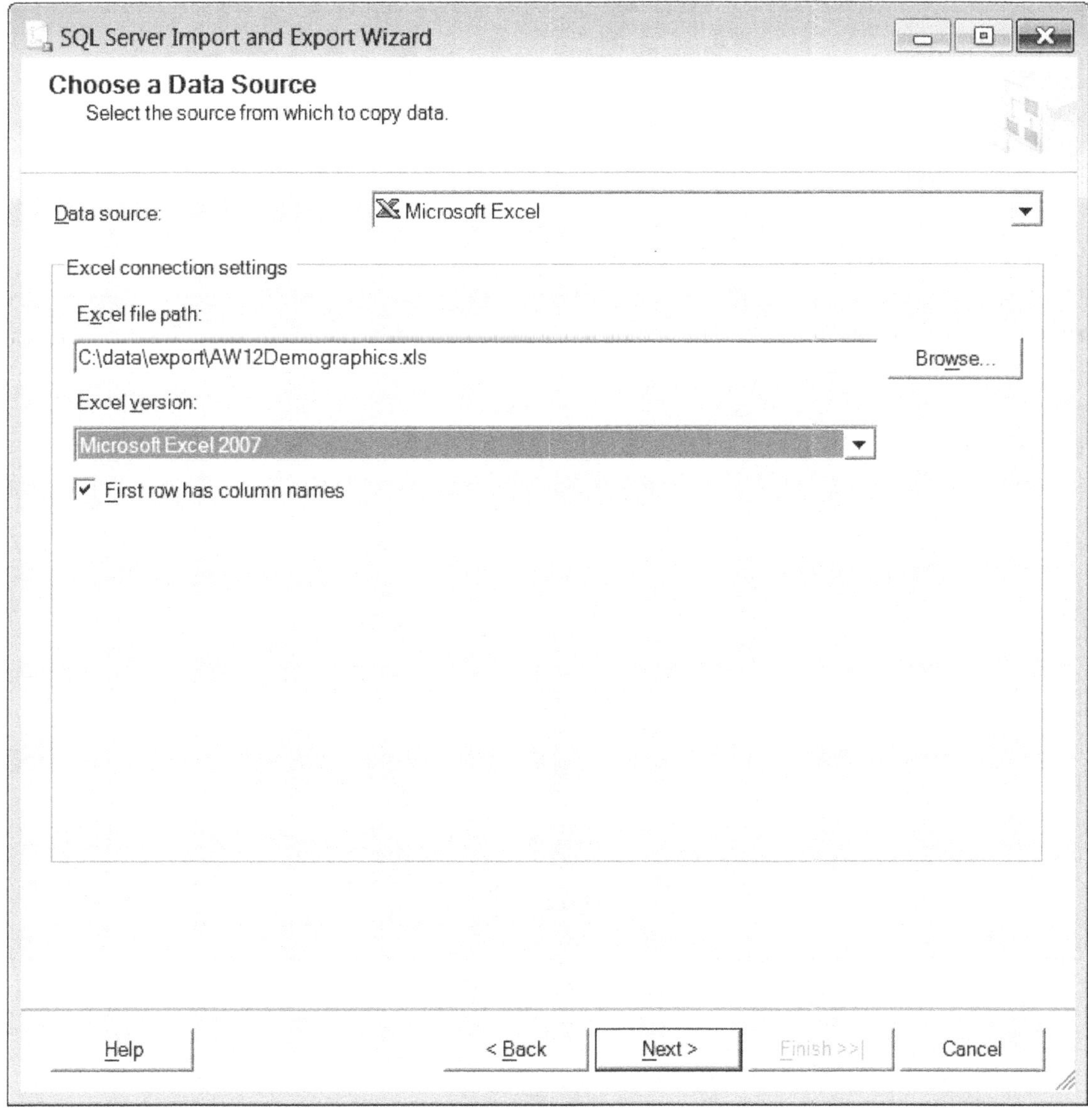

Specify Data Destination as Database

AdventureWorks2012 is the destination for the data movement.

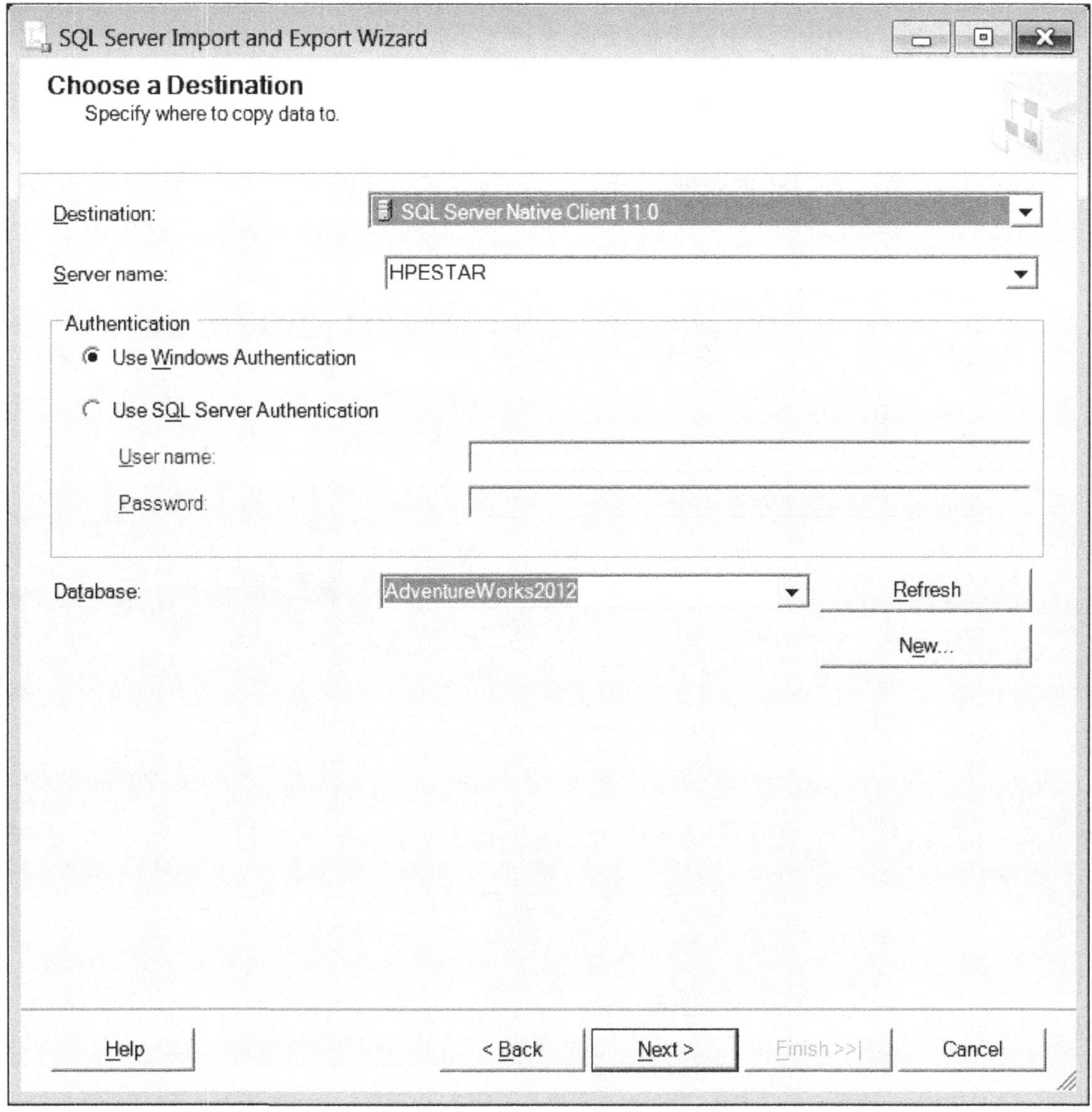

Excel Worksheet Source Is Considered a Table

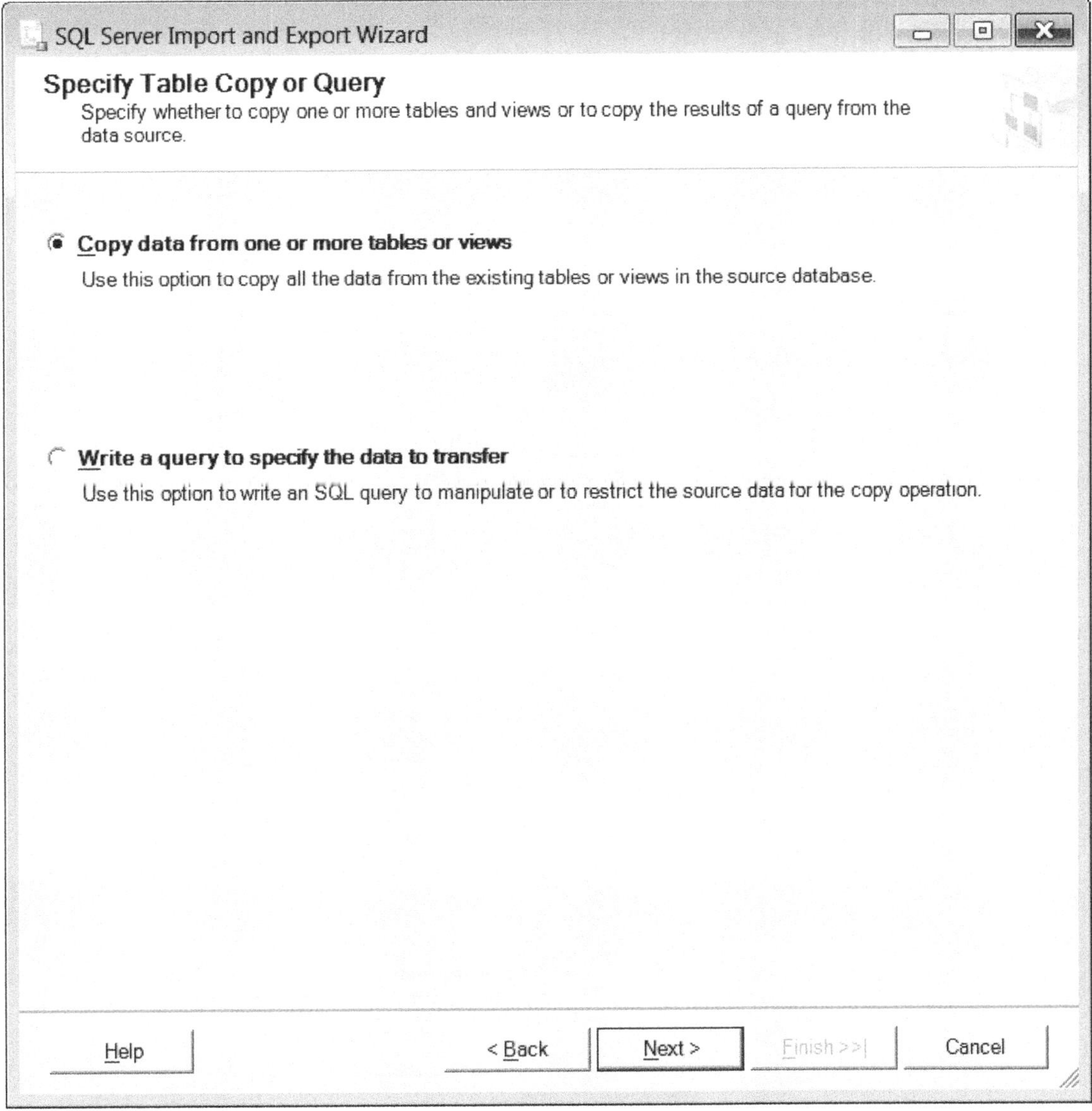

Select Excel Sheet and Assign Database Table Name

All the data is on the 'Query' sheet.

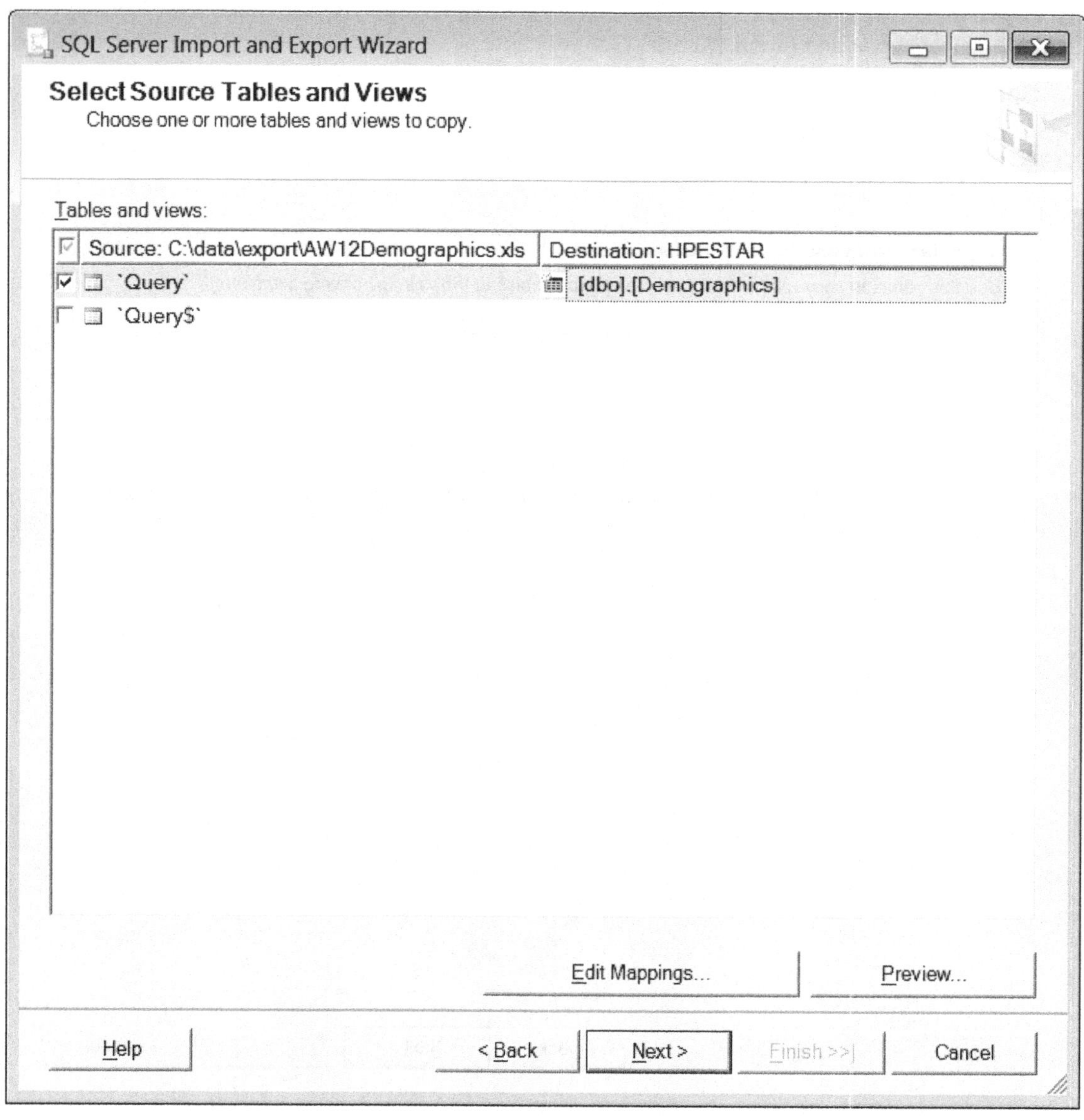

Column Mappings & CREATE TABLE Edit Panels

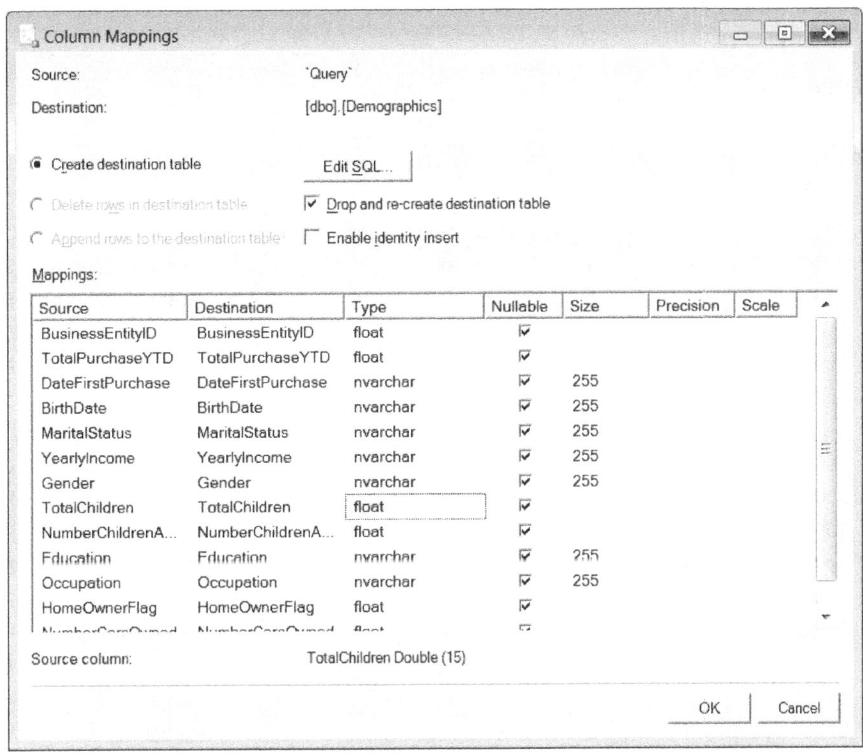

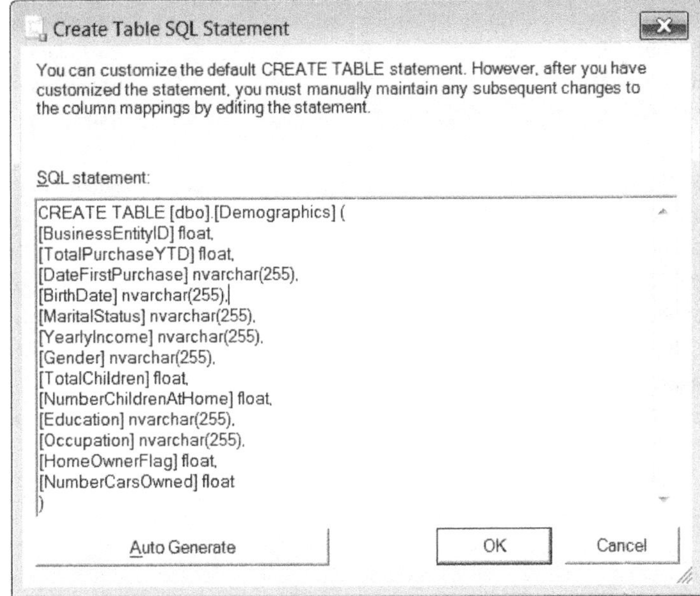

Source Data Inspection with Preview Data

This is a very important step. If the data does not look correct here, it will not be correct in the database table either.

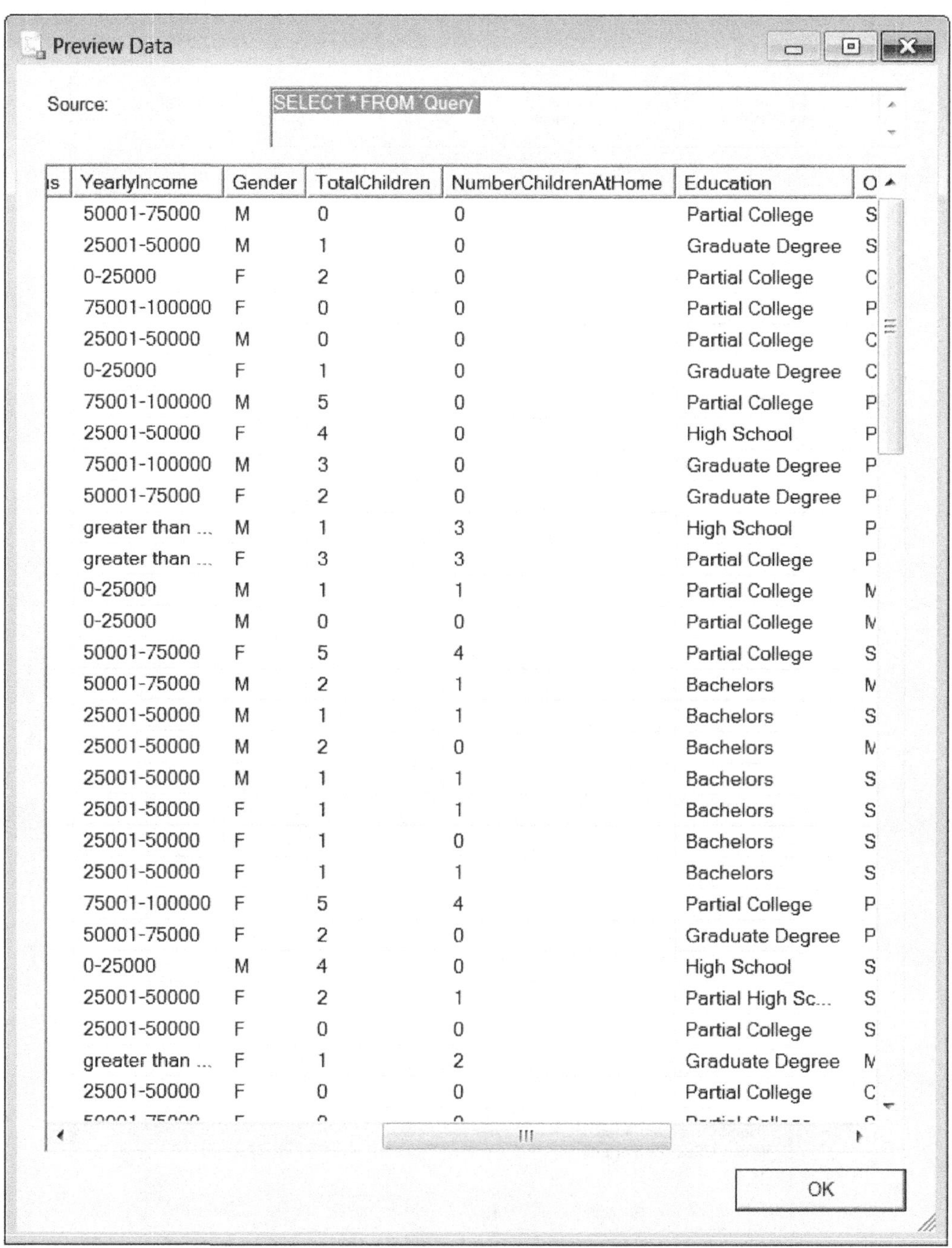

Preview Data

Source: SELECT * FROM `Query`

YearlyIncome	Gender	TotalChildren	NumberChildrenAtHome	Education	O
50001-75000	M	0	0	Partial College	S
25001-50000	M	1	0	Graduate Degree	S
0-25000	F	2	0	Partial College	C
75001-100000	F	0	0	Partial College	P
25001-50000	M	0	0	Partial College	C
0-25000	F	1	0	Graduate Degree	C
75001-100000	M	5	0	Partial College	P
25001-50000	F	4	0	High School	P
75001-100000	M	3	0	Graduate Degree	P
50001-75000	F	2	0	Graduate Degree	P
greater than ...	M	1	3	High School	P
greater than ...	F	3	3	Partial College	P
0-25000	M	1	1	Partial College	M
0-25000	M	0	0	Partial College	M
50001-75000	F	5	4	Partial College	S
50001-75000	M	2	1	Bachelors	M
25001-50000	M	1	1	Bachelors	S
25001-50000	M	2	0	Bachelors	M
25001-50000	M	1	1	Bachelors	S
25001-50000	F	1	1	Bachelors	S
25001-50000	F	1	0	Bachelors	S
25001-50000	F	1	1	Bachelors	S
75001-100000	F	5	4	Partial College	P
50001-75000	F	2	0	Graduate Degree	P
0-25000	M	4	0	High School	S
25001-50000	F	2	1	Partial High Sc...	S
25001-50000	F	0	0	Partial College	S
greater than ...	F	1	2	Graduate Degree	M
25001-50000	F	0	0	Partial College	C

OK

Indicate Saving and/or Run the SSIS Package

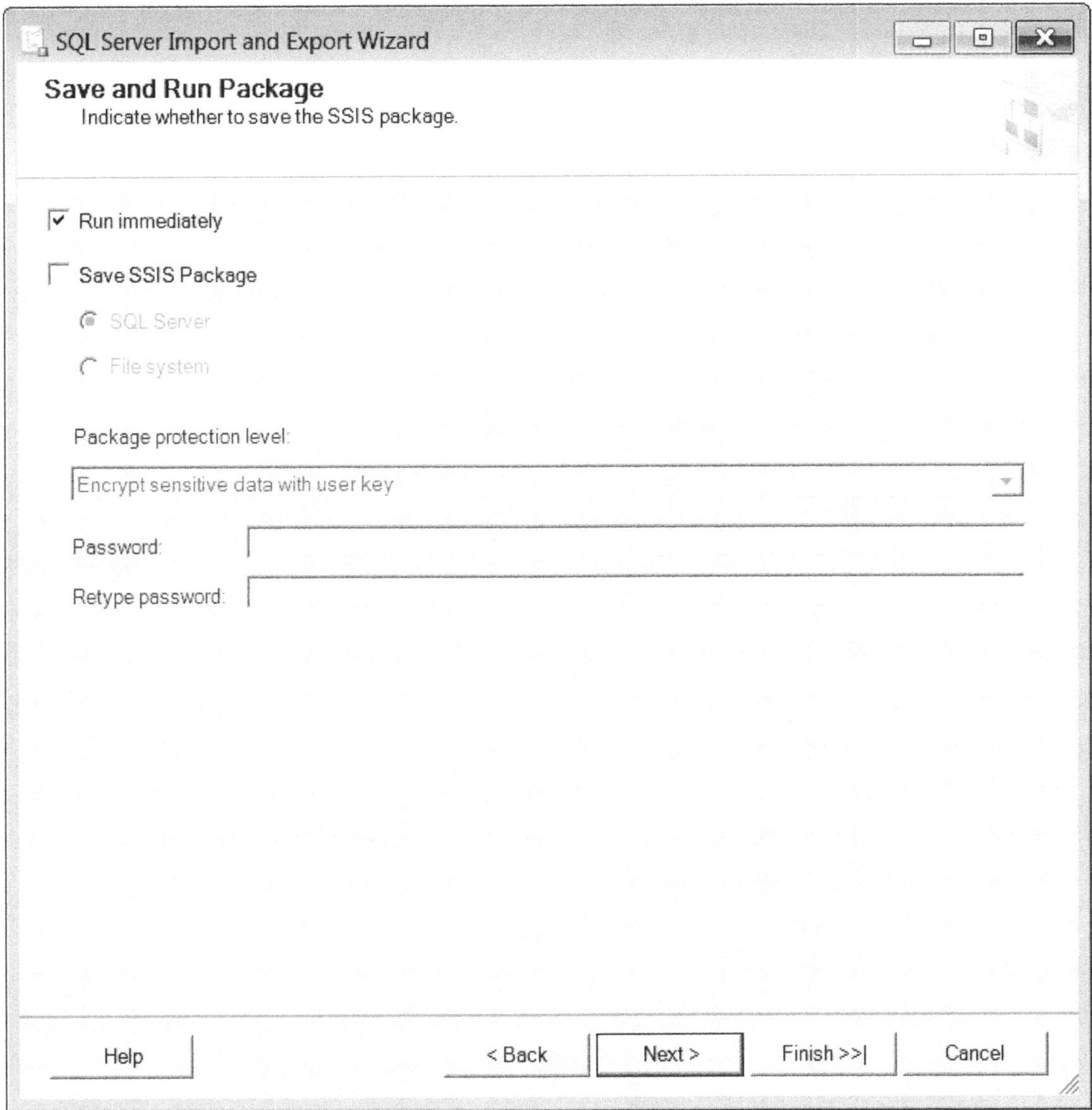

The Final Release Screen for Execution

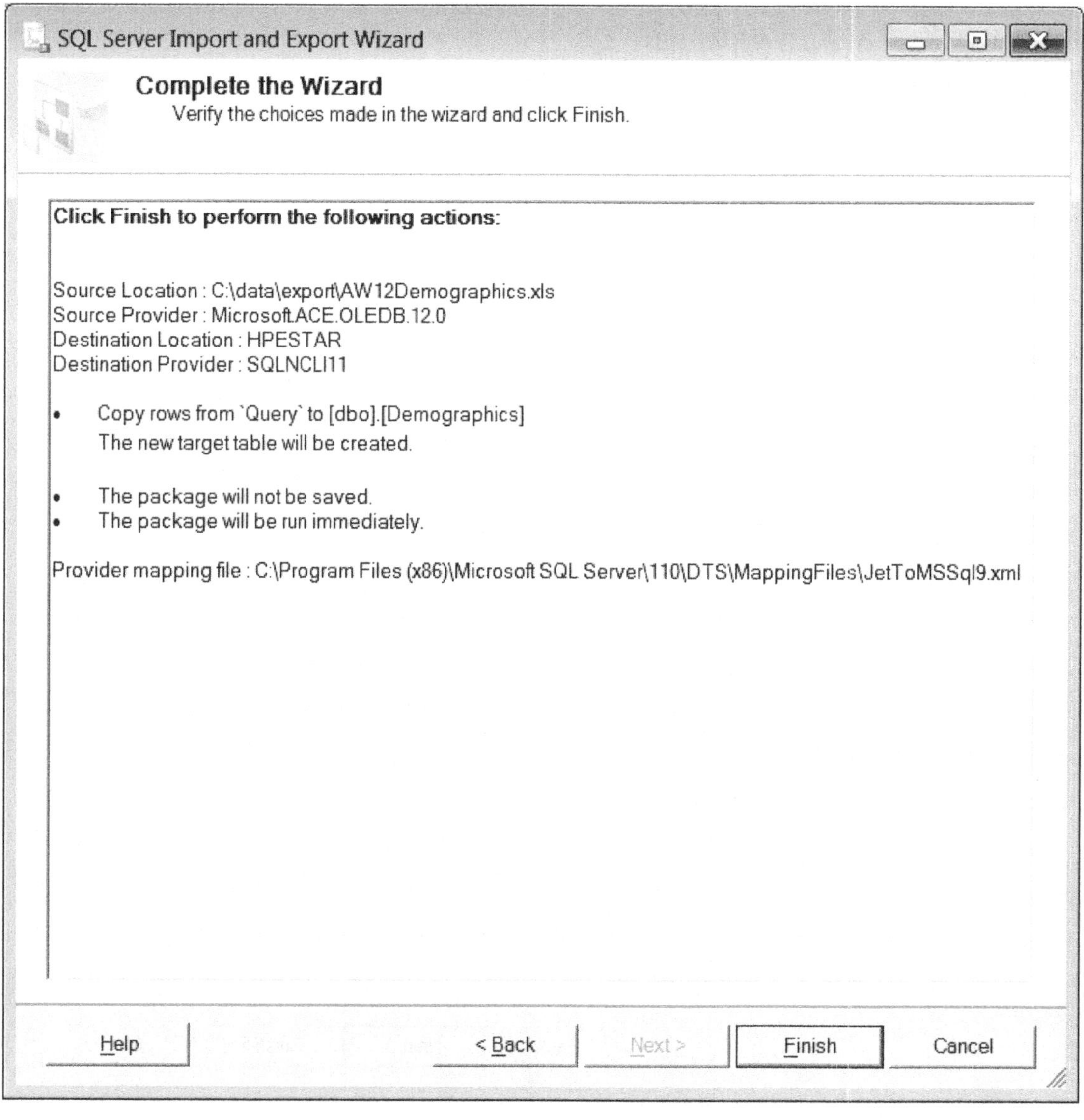

SQL Server Import and Export Wizard
Complete the Wizard
Verify the choices made in the wizard and click Finish.
Click Finish to perform the following actions:
Source Location : C:\data\export\AW12Demographics.xls
Source Provider : Microsoft.ACE.OLEDB.12.0
Destination Location : HPESTAR
Destination Provider : SQLNCLI11
• Copy rows from `Query` to [dbo].[Demographics]
The new target table will be created.
• The package will not be saved.
• The package will be run immediately.
Provider mapping file : C:\Program Files (x86)\Microsoft SQL Server\110\DTS\MappingFiles\JetToMSSql9.xml
Help
< Back
Next >
Finish
Cancel

Successful Execution Screen

In case of errors, hyperlink to errors will display.

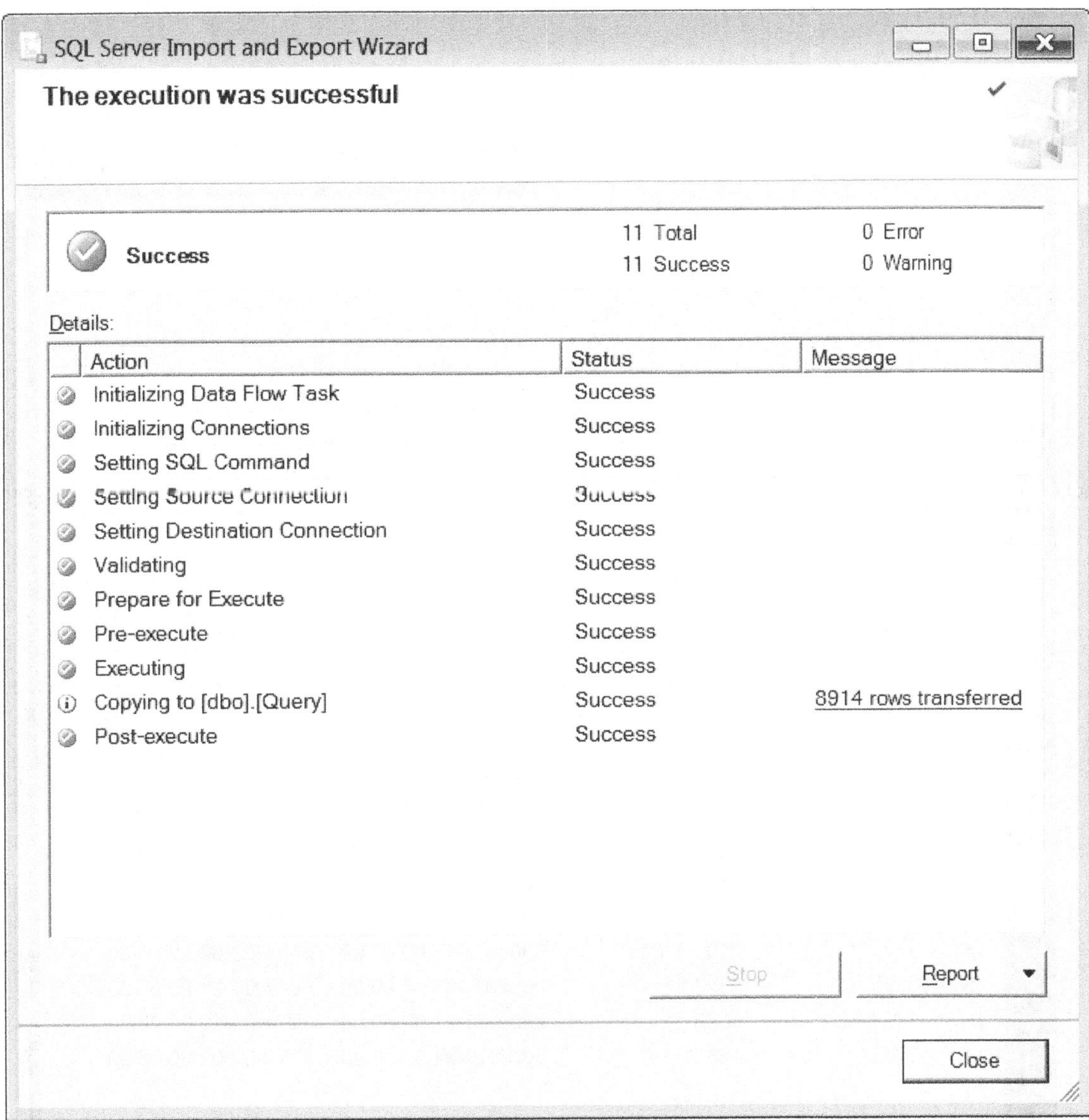

Check New Table in Database

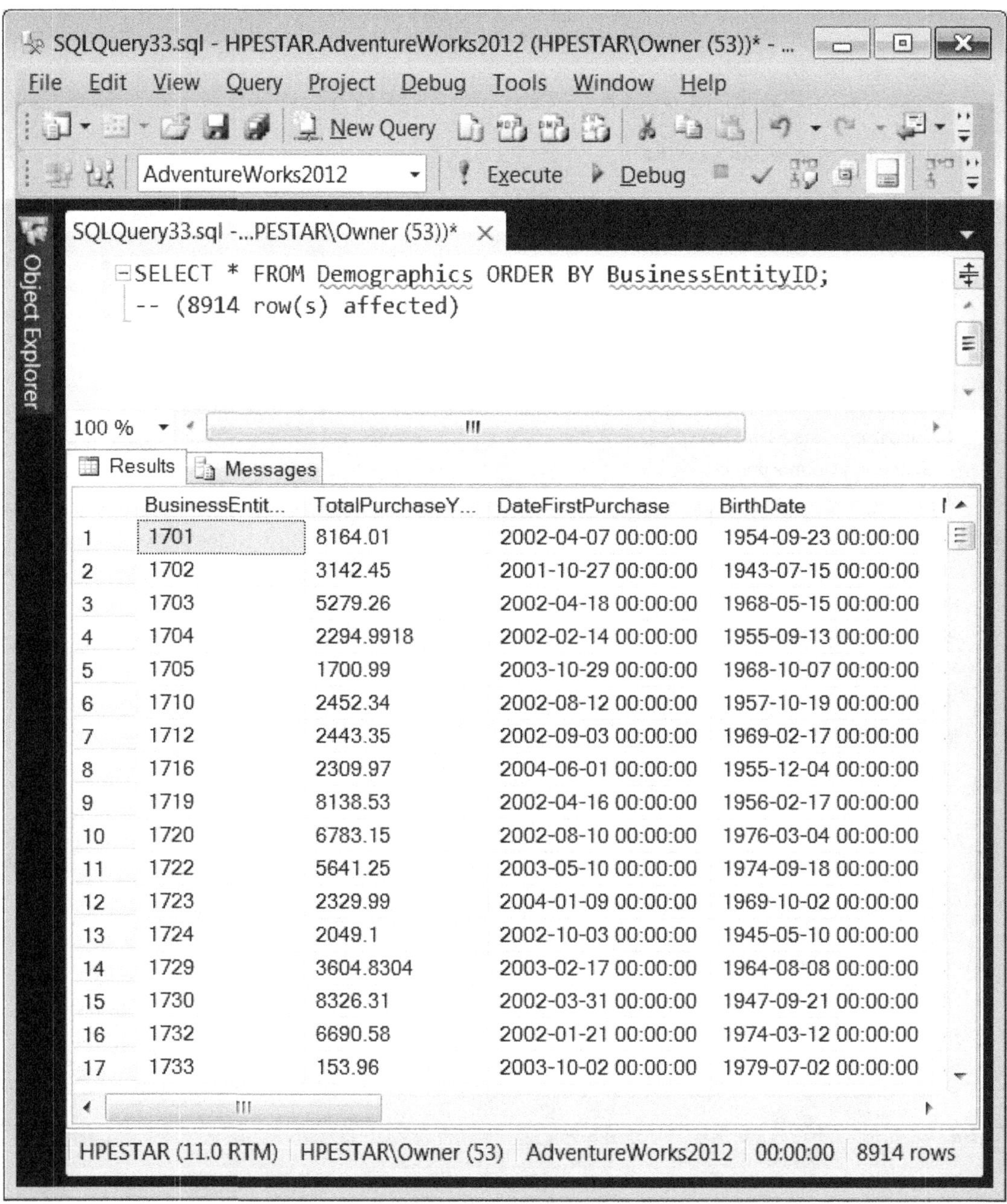
SQLQuery33.sql - HPESTAR.AdventureWorks2012 (HPESTAR\Owner (53))* - ...
File Edit View Query Project Debug Tools Window Help
New Query
AdventureWorks2012
Execute
Debug
Object Explorer
SQLQuery33.sql -...PESTAR\Owner (53))*
SELECT * FROM Demographics ORDER BY BusinessEntityID;
-- (8914 row(s) affected)
100 %
Results
Messages
BusinessEntit... TotalPurchaseY... DateFirstPurchase BirthDate
1 1701 8164.01 2002-04-07 00:00:00 1954-09-23 00:00:00
2 1702 3142.45 2001-10-27 00:00:00 1943-07-15 00:00:00
3 1703 5279.26 2002-04-18 00:00:00 1968-05-15 00:00:00
4 1704 2294.9918 2002-02-14 00:00:00 1955-09-13 00:00:00
5 1705 1700.99 2003-10-29 00:00:00 1968-10-07 00:00:00
6 1710 2452.34 2002-08-12 00:00:00 1957-10-19 00:00:00
7 1712 2443.35 2002-09-03 00:00:00 1969-02-17 00:00:00
8 1716 2309.97 2004-06-01 00:00:00 1955-12-04 00:00:00
9 1719 8138.53 2002-04-16 00:00:00 1956-02-17 00:00:00
10 1720 6783.15 2002-08-10 00:00:00 1976-03-04 00:00:00
11 1722 5641.25 2003-05-10 00:00:00 1974-09-18 00:00:00
12 1723 2329.99 2004-01-09 00:00:00 1969-10-02 00:00:00
13 1724 2049.1 2002-10-03 00:00:00 1945-05-10 00:00:00
14 1729 3604.8304 2003-02-17 00:00:00 1964-08-08 00:00:00
15 1730 8326.31 2002-03-31 00:00:00 1947-09-21 00:00:00
16 1732 6690.58 2002-01-21 00:00:00 1974-03-12 00:00:00
17 1733 153.96 2003-10-02 00:00:00 1979-07-02 00:00:00
HPESTAR (11.0 RTM) HPESTAR\Owner (53) AdventureWorks2012 00:00:00 8914 rows

Exporting Database Table to Excel

The Wizard sequence is very similar to exporting query results. We shall export Sales.SalesOrderHeader table.

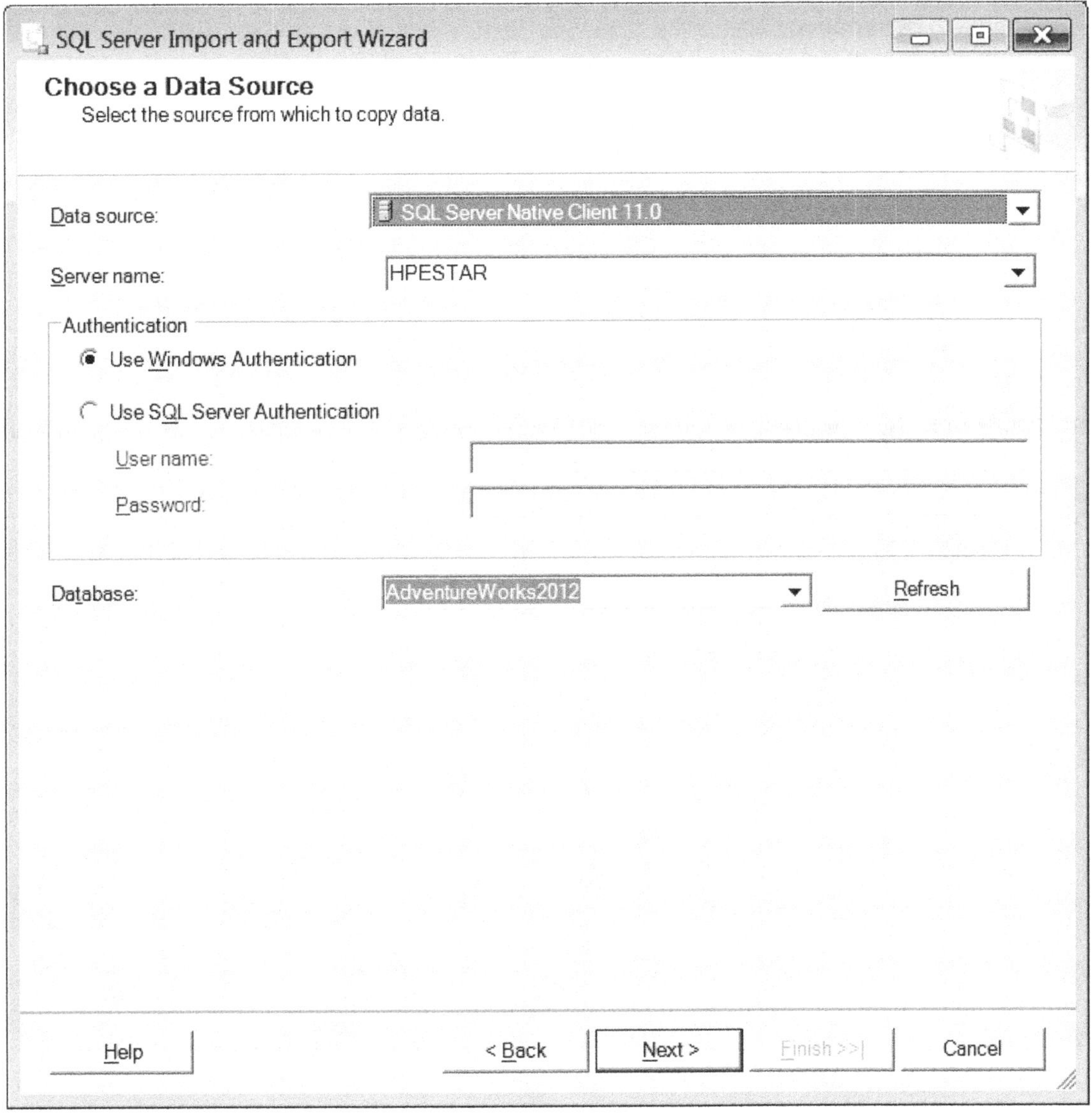

Specify Destination

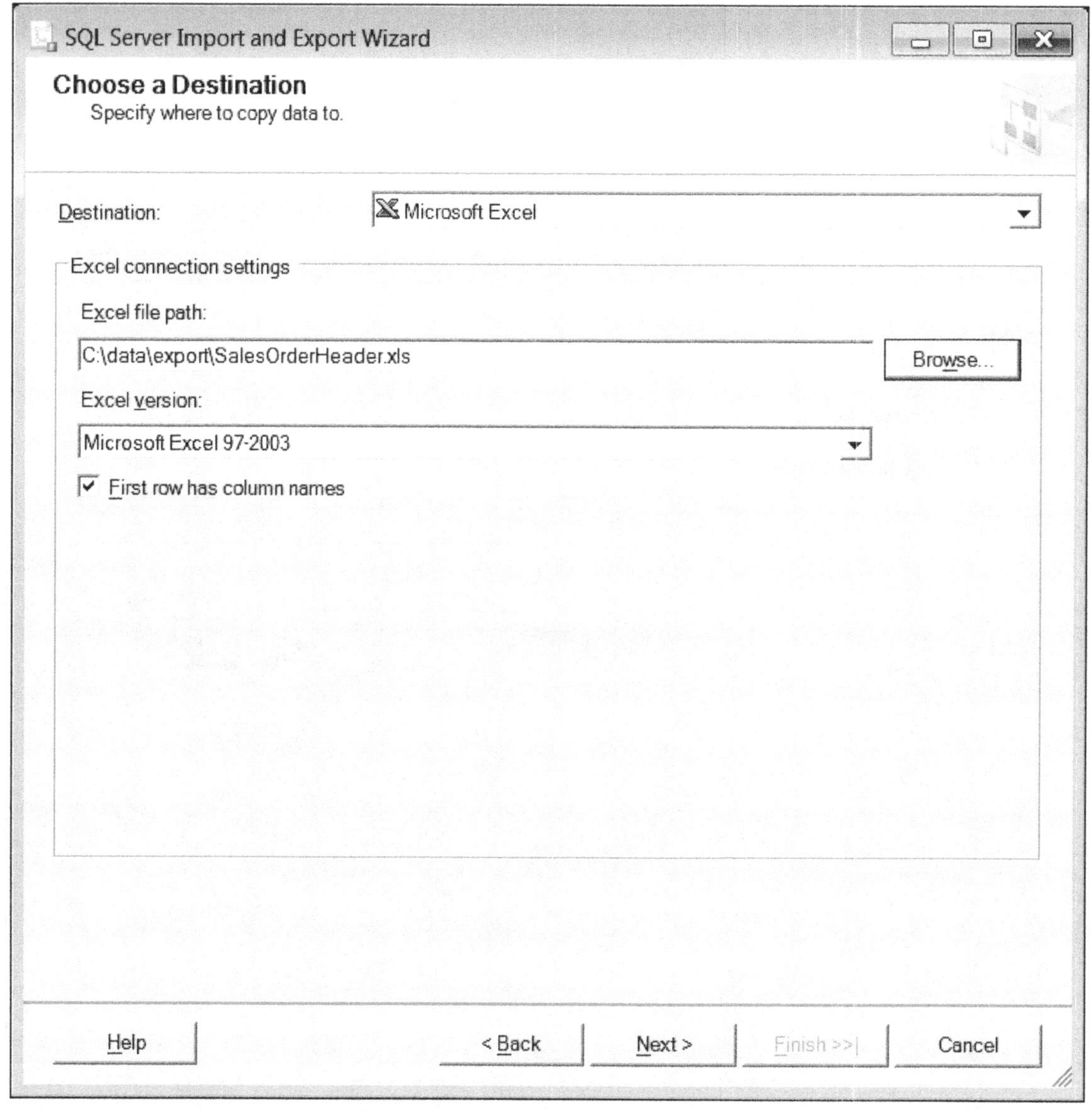

Choose Table Copy or Query

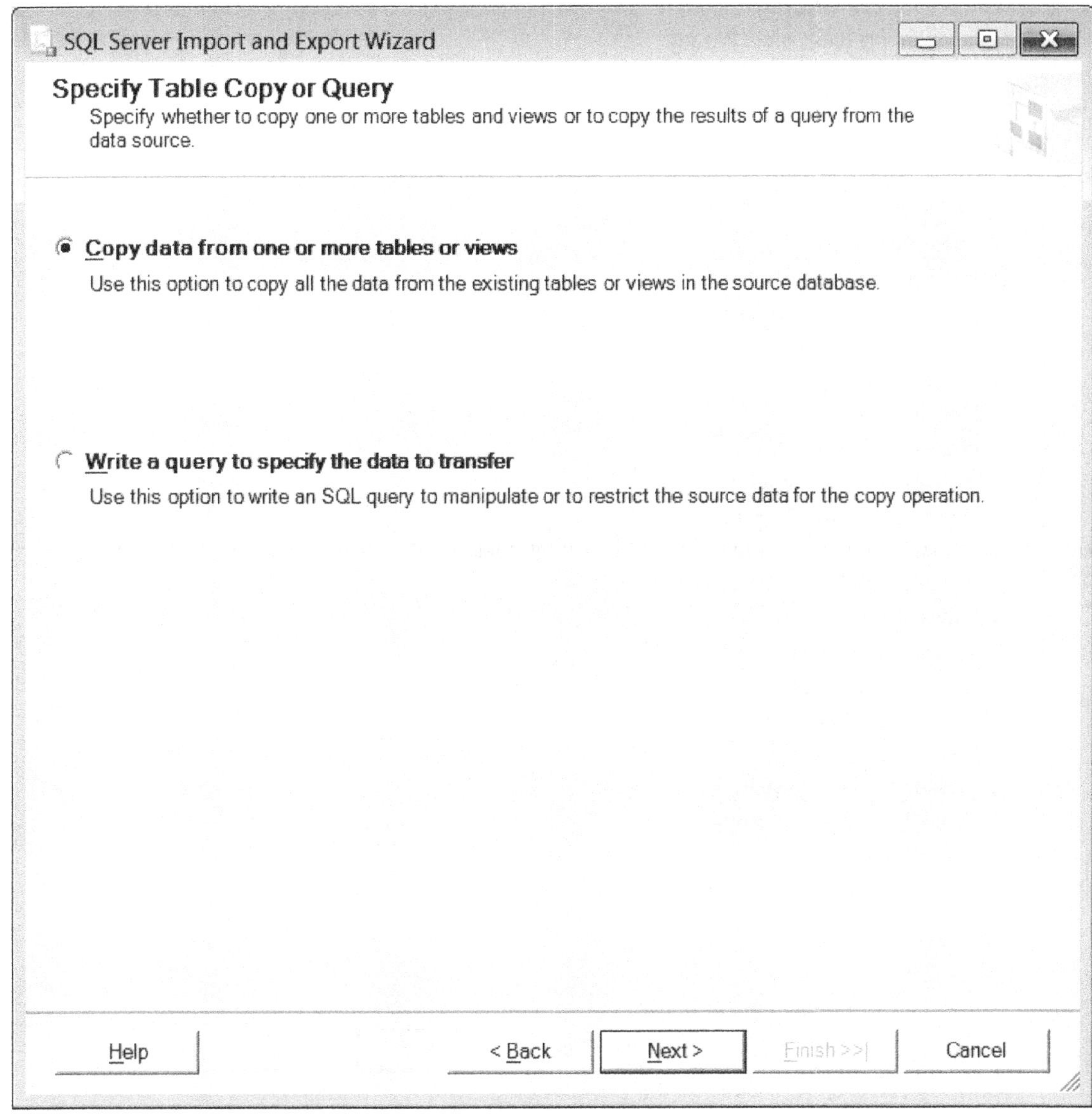

Checkmark Source Table

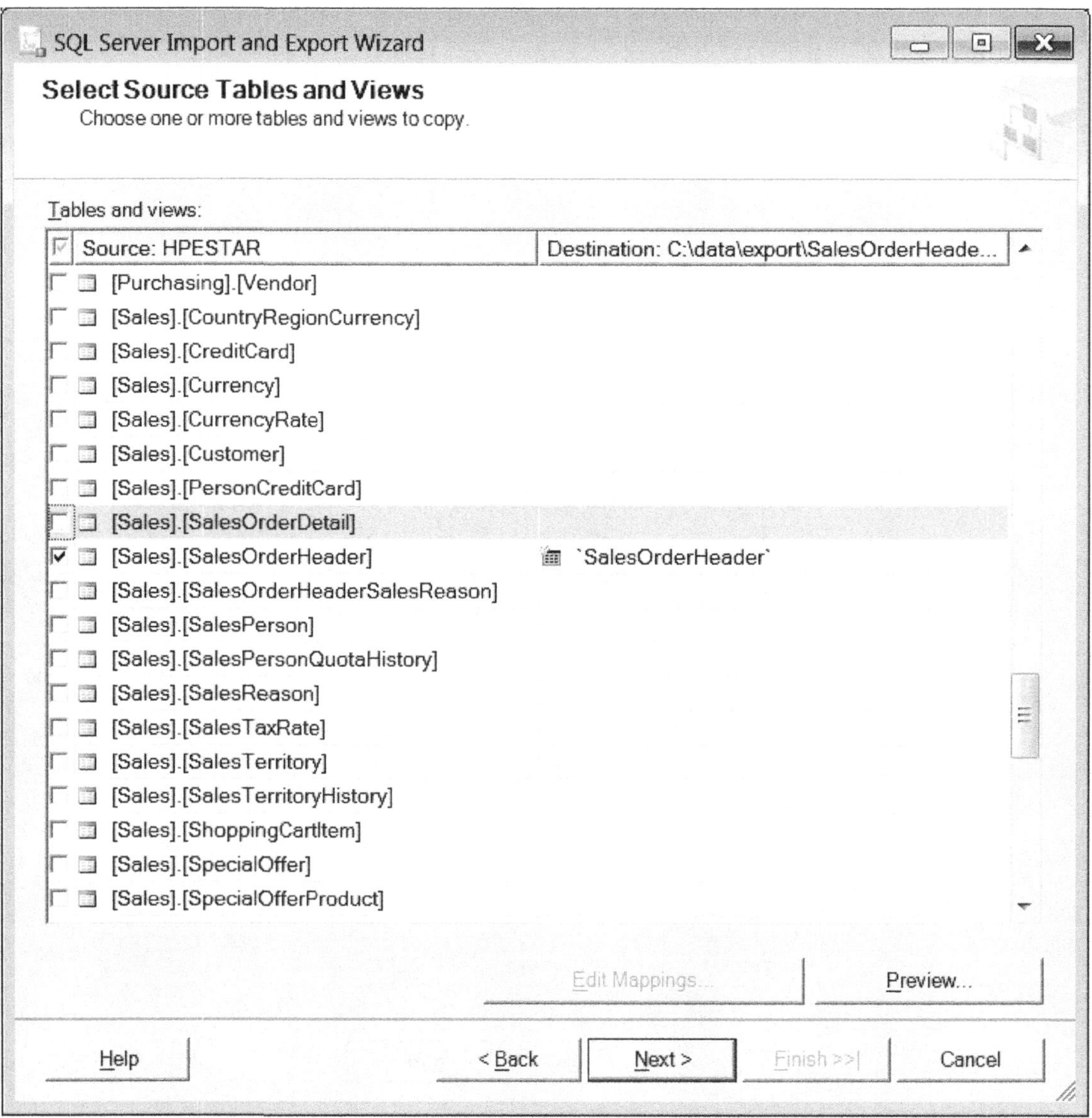

Check Data Type Mapping

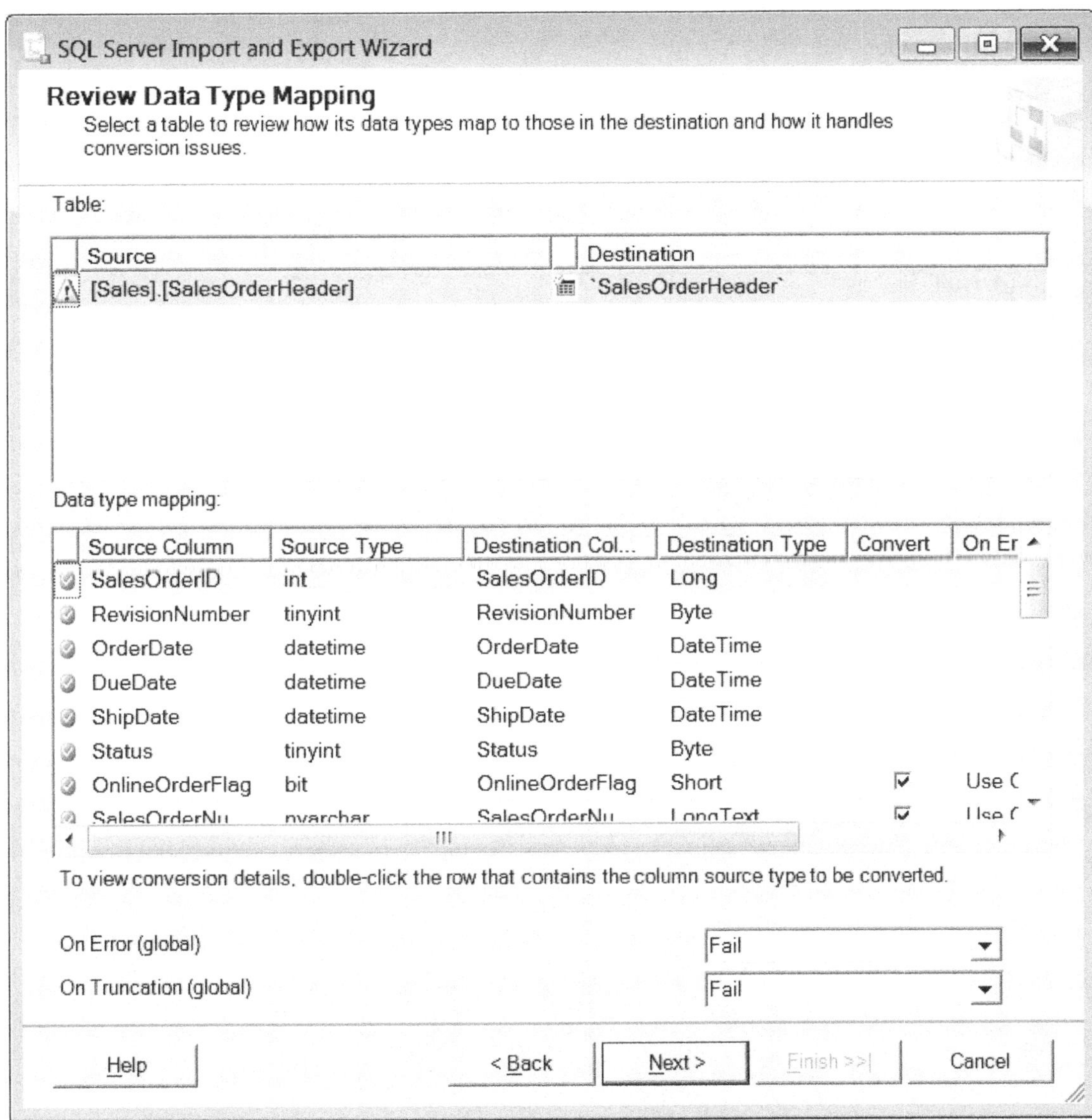

Save and/or Run Package

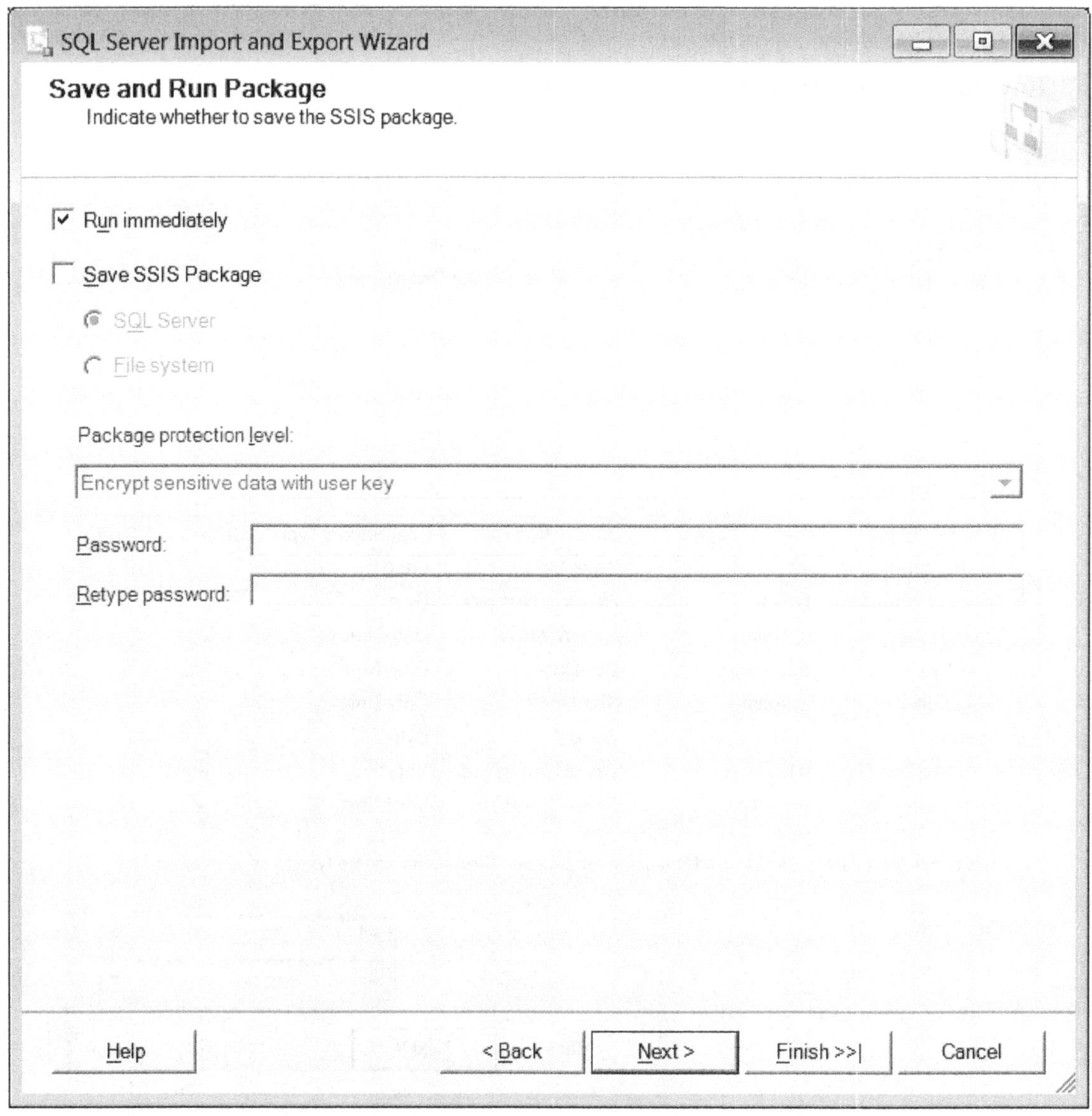

Complete the Wizard

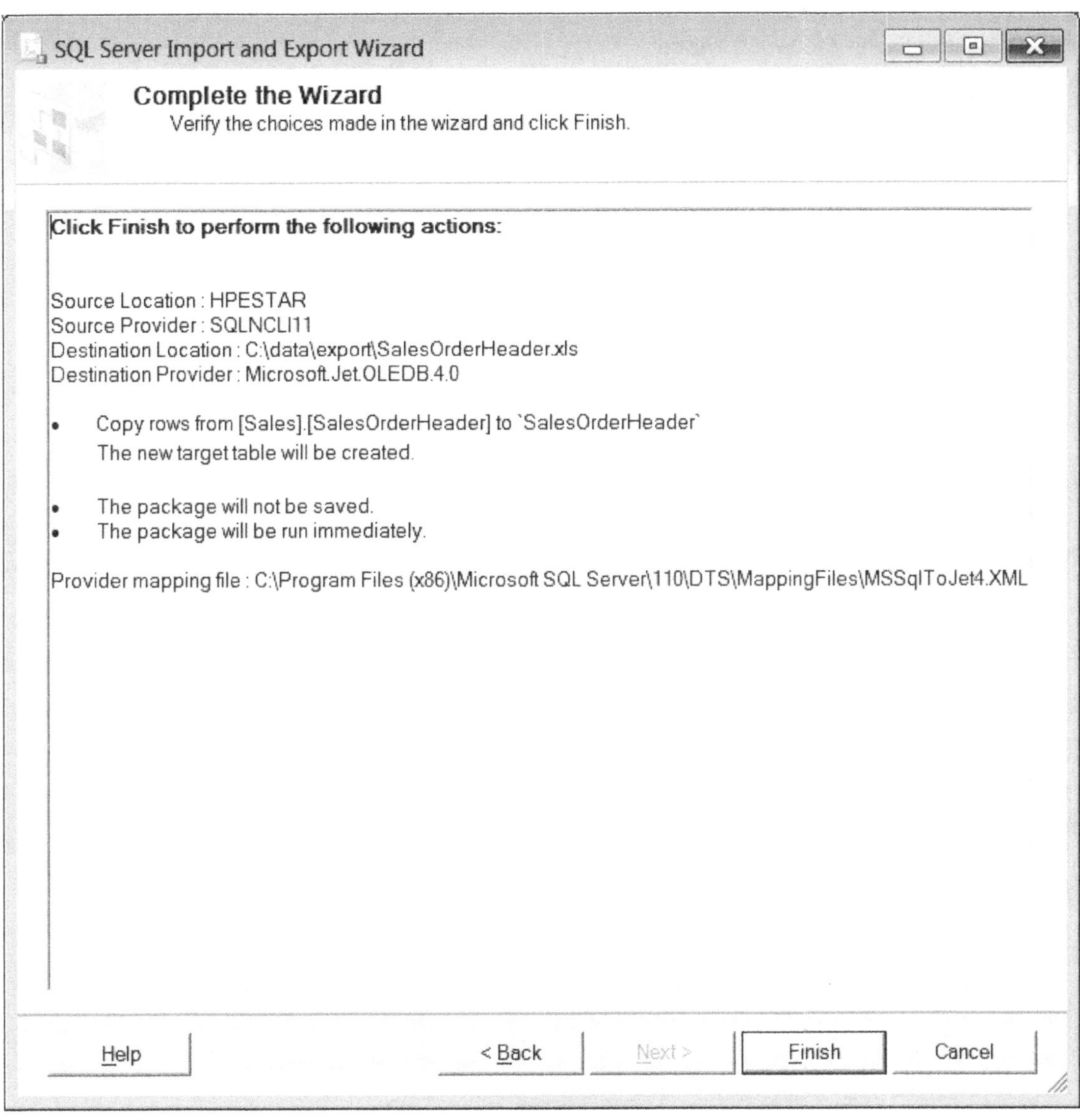

Successful Execution Screen

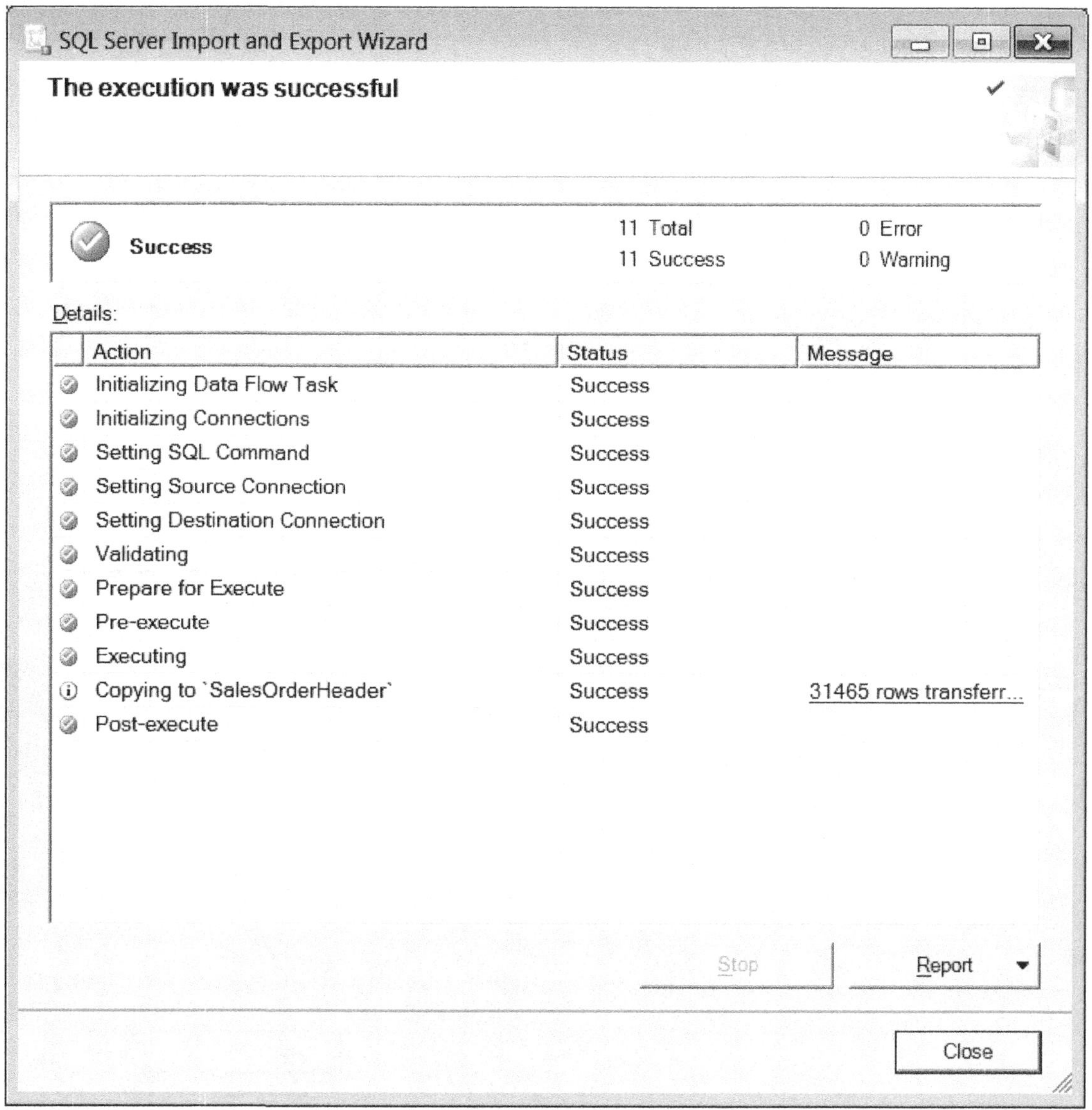

Check File in Folder and Data in Excel

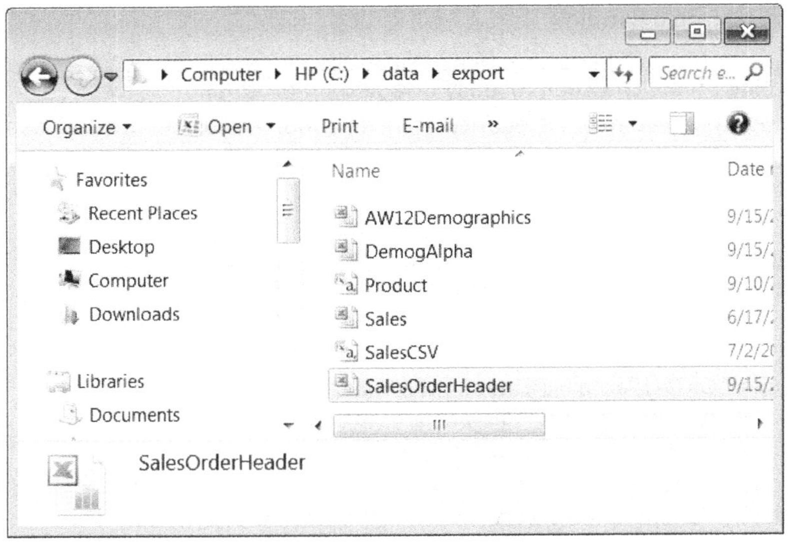

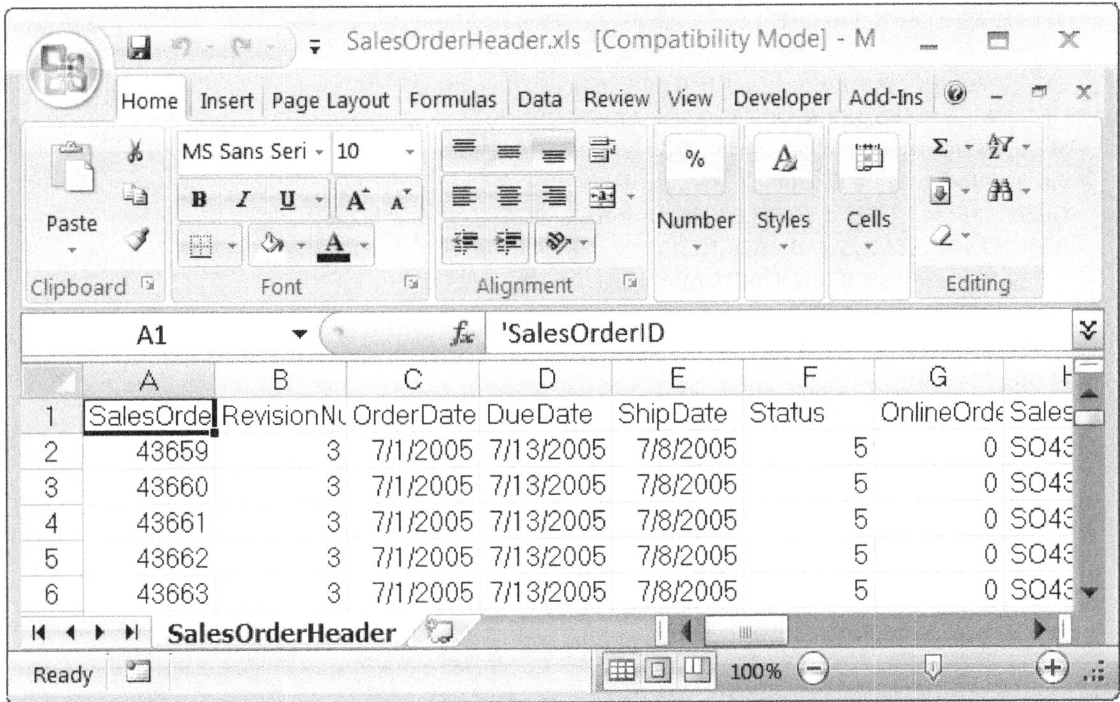

Exporting Data Directly into a Flat File

There is no equivalent of BULK INSERT, however, with xp_cmdshell & ECHO commands we can export data directly into a flat file.

> Security blog on xp_cmdshell (usually disabled on production server):
> http://blogs.msdn.com/b/sqlsecurity/archive/2008/01/10/xp-cmdshell.aspx .

```
USE AdventureWorks;
GO
CREATE PROC uspWeeklySupplierSummary  @FilePath VARCHAR(100) AS  BEGIN
  DECLARE  @Line NVARCHAR(1000), @Command NVARCHAR(2000) ,@Return INT;
  DECLARE  @VendorID   INT,   @VendorName NVARCHAR(50), @ProductName NVARCHAR(50);
  SET @Line = '******** SUPPLIERS PRODUCTS REPORT ********';
  SET @Command = CONCAT('echo ', @Line , ' >>', @FilePath);
  EXEC @Return = master..xp_cmdshell  @Command, no_output;
  DECLARE curVendor CURSOR FAST_FORWARD FOR
  SELECT   VendorID, Name  FROM  Purchasing.Vendor  WHERE   CreditRating = 1   ORDER BY VendorID;
  OPEN curVendor  FETCH NEXT FROM curVendor  INTO @VendorID,  @VendorName;
  WHILE @@FETCH_STATUS = 0       BEGIN
    SET @Line = '. '; SET @Command = CONCAT('echo ', @Line,' >>', @FilePath);
    EXEC @Return = master..xp_cmdshell  @Command, no_output;
    SET @Line = '***** Products From Supplier: ' + @VendorName;
    SET @Command = CONCAT('echo ', @Line, ' >>', @FilePath);
    EXEC @Return = master..xp_cmdshell  @Command, no_output
    DECLARE curProduct CURSOR FAST_FORWARD FOR
    SELECT v.Name  FROM   Purchasing.ProductVendor pv INNER JOIN Production.Product v
    ON  pv.ProductID = v.ProductID   AND pv.VendorID = @VendorID;
    OPEN curProduct; FETCH NEXT FROM curProduct INTO @ProductName;
    IF @@FETCH_STATUS <> 0    BEGIN
      SET @Line = '*** NO PRODUCTS AVAILABLE AT THIS TIME *** ';
      SET @Command = CONCAT('echo ', @Line,' >>', @FilePath);
      EXEC @Return = master..xp_cmdshell  @Command,  no_output;
     END;
    WHILE @@FETCH_STATUS = 0   BEGIN
      SET @Line = CONCAT( SPACE(1), @ProductName );
      SET @Command = CONCAT('echo ', @Line,' >>',@FilePath);
      EXEC @Return = master..xp_cmdshell  @Command,  no_output;
      FETCH NEXT FROM curProduct   INTO @ProductName;
     END;   CLOSE curProduct;  DEALLOCATE curProduct;
    FETCH NEXT FROM curVendor  INTO @VendorID, @VendorName;
   END ;    CLOSE curVendor;    DEALLOCATE curVendor;
 END
GO
```

```
EXEC uspWeeklySupplierSummary   'F:\data\export\SUPPWeek31.txt' ;
```

Command Prompt Commands List by HELP

Command Prompt commands can be used for data transport as well including COPY & XCOPY. We can get the entire command list by typing the "HELP" command. It is like a time machine back to the programming style of 1960-s.

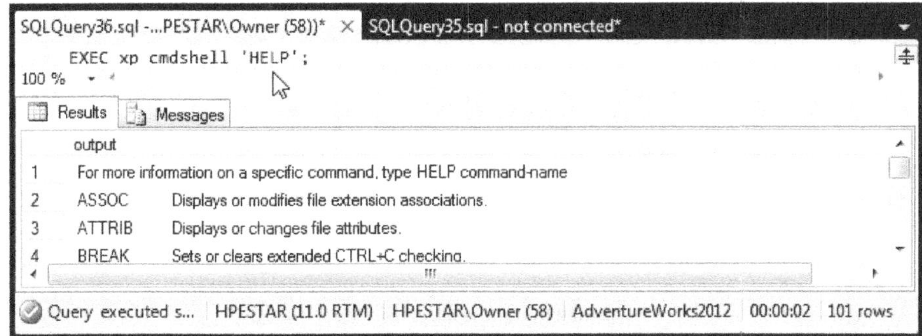

Command List

ASSOC	Displays or modifies file extension associations.
ATTRIB	Displays or changes file attributes.
BREAK	Sets or clears extended CTRL+C checking.
BCDEDIT	Sets properties in boot database to control boot loading.
CACLS	Displays or modifies access control lists (ACLs) of files.
CALL	Calls one batch program from another.
CD	Displays the name of or changes the current directory.
CHCP	Displays or sets the active code page number.
CHDIR	Displays the name of or changes the current directory.
CHKDSK	Checks a disk and displays a status report.
CHKNTFS	Displays or modifies the checking of disk at boot time.
CLS	Clears the screen.
CMD	Starts a new instance of the Windows command interpreter.
COLOR	Sets the default console foreground and background colors.
COMP	Compares the contents of two files or sets of files.
COMPACT	Displays or alters the compression of files on NTFS partitions.
CONVERT	Converts FAT volumes to NTFS. You cannot convert the current drive.
COPY	Copies one or more files to another location.
DATE	Displays or sets the date.
DEL	Deletes one or more files.
DIR	Displays a list of files and subdirectories in a directory.
DISKCOMP	Compares the contents of two floppy disks.
DISKCOPY	Copies the contents of one floppy disk to another.
DISKPART	Displays or configures Disk Partition properties.
DOSKEY	Edits command lines, recalls Windows commands, and creates macros.
DRIVERQUERY	Displays current device driver status and properties.
ECHO	Displays messages, or turns command echoing on or off.
ENDLOCAL	Ends localization of environment changes in a batch file.
ERASE	Deletes one or more files.
EXIT	Quits the CMD.EXE program (command interpreter).
FC	Compares two files or sets of files, and displays the differences between them.
FIND	Searches for a text string in a file or files.

FINDSTR	Searches for strings in files.
FOR	Runs a specified command for each file in a set of files.
FORMAT	Formats a disk for use with Windows.
FSUTIL	Displays or configures the file system properties.
FTYPE	Displays or modifies file types used in file extension associations.
GOTO	Directs the Windows command interpreter to a labeled line in a batch program.
GPRESULT	Displays Group Policy information for machine or user.
GRAFTABL	Enables Windows to display an extended character set in graphics mode.
HELP	Provides Help information for Windows commands.
ICACLS	Display, modify, backup, or restore ACLs for files and directories.
IF	Performs conditional processing in batch programs.
LABEL	Creates, changes, or deletes the volume label of a disk.
MD	Creates a directory.
MKDIR	Creates a directory.
MKLINK	Creates Symbolic Links and Hard Links
MODE	Configures a system device.
MORE	Displays output one screen at a time.
MOVE	Moves one or more files from one directory to another directory.
OPENFILES	Displays files opened by remote users for a file share.
PATH	Displays or sets a search path for executable files.
PAUSE	Suspends processing of a batch file and displays a message.
POPD	Restores the previous value of the current directory saved by PUSHD.
PRINT	Prints a text file.
PROMPT	Changes the Windows command prompt.
PUSHD	Saves the current directory then changes it.
RD	Removes a directory.
RECOVER	Recovers readable information from a bad or defective disk.
REM	Records comments (remarks) in batch files or CONFIG.SYS.
REN	Renames a file or files.
RENAME	Renames a file or files.
REPLACE	Replaces files.
RMDIR	Removes a directory.
ROBOCOPY	Advanced utility to copy files and directory trees
SET	Displays, sets, or removes Windows environment variables.
SETLOCAL	Begins localization of environment changes in a batch file.
SC	Displays or configures services (background processes).
SCHTASKS	Schedules commands and programs to run on a computer.
SHIFT	Shifts the position of replaceable parameters in batch files.
SHUTDOWN	Allows proper local or remote shutdown of machine.
SORT	Sorts input.
START	Starts a separate window to run a specified program or command.
SUBST	Associates a path with a drive letter.
SYSTEMINFO	Displays machine specific properties and configuration.
TASKLIST	Displays all currently running tasks including services.
TASKKILL	Kill or stop a running process or application.
TIME	Displays or sets the system time.
TITLE	Sets the window title for a CMD.EXE session.
TREE	Graphically displays the directory structure of a drive or path.
TYPE	Displays the contents of a text file.
VER	Displays the Windows version.
VERIFY	Tells Windows whether to verify that your files are written correctly to a disk.
VOL	Displays a disk volume label and serial number.
XCOPY	Copies files and directory trees.
WMIC	Displays WMI information inside interactive command shell.

CHAPTER 19: Ensuring Data Integrity in the Enterprise

Why is Data Integrity Paramount

A business or organization can only operate efficiently with good quality data. Computers were the real engine of economic progress since the 1950-s. Without computers, we would pretty much be at post Second World War level. Computers work with data and produce data. As the saying goes: garbage in, garbage out. Therefore it is our job as database designers, database developers and database administrators to ensure the data integrity in a database. What are the sources of the bad data? They can be data feeds received from various sources, data entry by people, and bugs in database or application programming. The best way to minimize bugs is putting each piece of new software through rigorous quality assurance (QA) process. To prevent bad data getting into the database there are a number of possibilities: table design, constraints, stored procedures, triggers and application software.

At the lowest level, constraints make up the guarding force over data integrity. The default constraint is different from the rest: it provides predefined default value if no value is provided for a cell (a column in a row), it does not give an error message.

```
USE AdventureWorks2012;
SELECT          ConstraintType = type_desc,  [Count] = COUNT(*)
FROM sys.objects
WHERE type_desc in      (
                        'CHECK_CONSTRAINT',
                        'DEFAULT_CONSTRAINT',
                        'FOREIGN_KEY_CONSTRAINT',
                        'PRIMARY_KEY_CONSTRAINT',
                        'UNIQUE_CONSTRAINT'
                        )
GROUP BY type_desc  ORDER BY type_desc;
```

ConstraintType	Count
CHECK_CONSTRAINT	91
DEFAULT_CONSTRAINT	166
FOREIGN_KEY_CONSTRAINT	99
PRIMARY_KEY_CONSTRAINT	92
UNIQUE_CONSTRAINT	13

Entity Integrity

Entity Integrity defines a row as a unique entity for a particular table. The main enforcing mechanisms are: NOT NULL constraint and unique index. PRIMARY KEY implies not null, and unique index automatically created. In the Production.Product table ProductID is the INT IDENTITY PRIMARY KEY, Name & ProductNumber are NATURAL KEYs and rowguid is a system generated unique key. All four keys are not null and all have unique index defined. The implication is that we can use any of 4 columns for row identification. However, ProductID INT (4 bytes) column is the most efficient row (record) identifier.

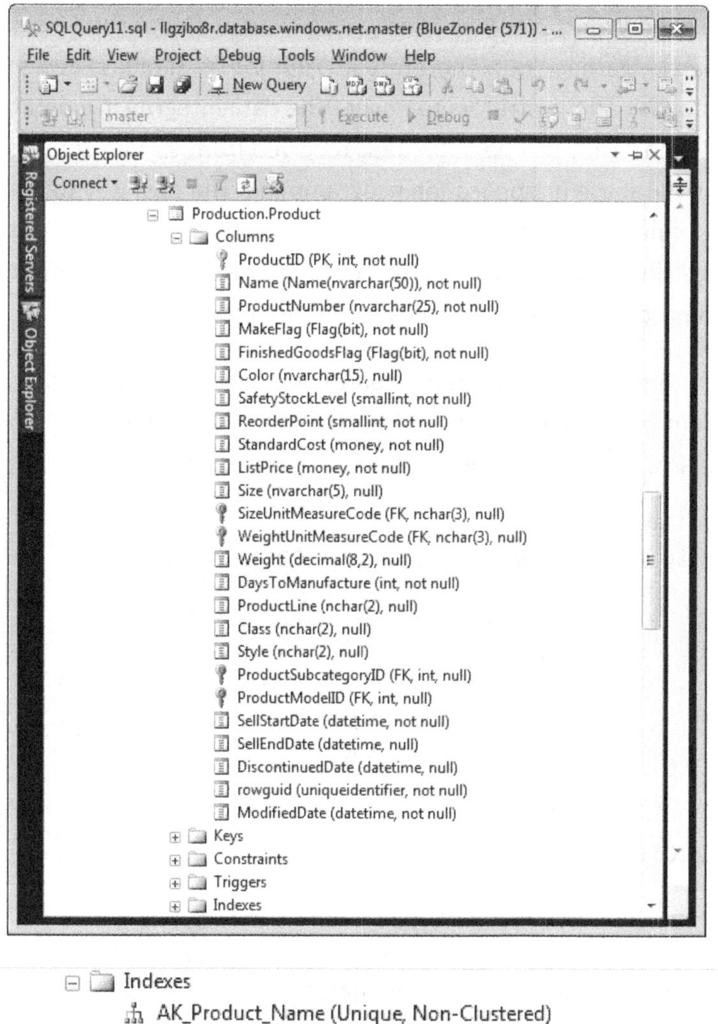

How to Remove Duplicates in a Table

The best way to prevent duplicates is by placing a UNIQUE KEY or unique index on the unique column(s). PRIMARY KEY & UNIQUE KEY constraints automatically create a unique index on the key column(s). If the entire row is a duplicate, removal is real simple with the DISTINCT clause.

```
SELECT DISTINCT * FROM T1;
GO
```

If duplicates are only in one or more columns, then duplicates removal is fairly easy with the ROW_NUMBER method, it is more involved with the GROUP BY method (prior to SQL Server 2005). We create and populate the Product test table for the demonstration.

```
USE AdventureWorks2012;
CREATE TABLE dbo.Product(ProductID int PRIMARY KEY, ProductName nvarchar(50) NOT NULL,
        ProductNumber nvarchar(25) NOT NULL, ListPrice numeric(20, 4) NULL );
```

```
INSERT Product
SELECT          ProductID,          Name,          ProductNumber,
                ListPrice = ListPrice + 1.00
FROM Production.Product    WHERE ListPrice > 0.0;    -- (304 row(s) affected)
```

```
-- Unique index prevents duplicates
CREATE UNIQUE INDEX idxProd ON Product(ProductName, ProductNumber);
GO
```

```
 -- Try to insert  duplicates on ProductName & ProductNumber
INSERT INTO Product
SELECT          TOP (100) ProductID=CONVERT(int, ProductID) + 1000,
                ProductName = Name, ProductNumber,
                ListPrice = ListPrice + 2.00
FROM   Production.Product
WHERE ListPrice > 0.0 ORDER BY NEWID();
GO
/*  Msg 2601, Level 14, State 1, Line 2
Cannot insert duplicate key row in object 'dbo.Product' with unique index 'idxProd'.
The duplicate key value is (Fender Set - Mountain, FE-6654).
The statement has been terminated.  */
```

```
DROP INDEX Product.idxProd;
GO
```

Rows with Duplicates Can Be Numbered in Ordered or Random Manner

```
-- Insert  100 duplicates on ProductName & ProductNumber
INSERT INTO Product
SELECT        TOP (100) ProductID=CONVERT(int, ProductID) + 1000,
              ProductName = Name, ProductNumber,   ListPrice = ListPrice + 2.00
FROM  Production.Product
WHERE ListPrice > 0.0
ORDER BY NEWID();
GO
```

```
-- Quantify duplicates with GROUP BY query
SELECT ProductName, ProductNumber, [Count] = count(*)
FROM Product
GROUP BY ProductName, ProductNumber
        HAVING count(*) > 1
ORDER BY ProductName, ProductNumber;
GO -- (100 row(s) affected) - Partial results.
```

ProductName	ProductNumber	Count
Bike Wash - Dissolver	CL-9009	2
Classic Vest, L	VE-C304-L	2
Classic Vest, S	VE-C304-S	2
Front Brakes	FB-9873	2
Full-Finger Gloves, M	GL-F110-M	2

```
-- Quantify duplicates with ROW_NUMBER OVER - we don't care about duplicates ordering
;WITH CTE AS (
   SELECT RN=ROW_NUMBER() OVER (PARTITION BY ProductName, ProductNumber
   ORDER BY NEWID() ),  ProductName, ProductNumber
   FROM Product)
SELECT * FROM CTE WHERE RN > 1
ORDER BY ProductName, ProductNumber;
GO -- (100 row(s) affected) - Partial results.
```

RN	ProductName	ProductNumber
2	Bike Wash - Dissolver	CL-9009
2	Classic Vest, L	VE-C304-L
2	Classic Vest, S	VE-C304-S
2	Front Brakes	FB-9873
2	Full-Finger Gloves, M	GL-F110-M

Remove Duplicates with CTE & ROW_NUMBER OVER PARTITION BY

```
-- To removal of duplicates is real easy with CTE & ROW_NUMBER
;WITH CTE AS (
    SELECT RN=ROW_NUMBER() OVER (PARTITION BY ProductName, ProductNumber
    ORDER BY NEWID()),  ProductName, ProductNumber    FROM Product)
DELETE CTE  WHERE RN > 1;
GO -- (100 row(s) affected)
```

```
-- Test for duplicates again
SELECT ProductName, ProductNumber, [Count] = count(*)
FROM Product  GROUP BY ProductName, ProductNumber  HAVING count(*) > 1
ORDER BY ProductName, ProductNumber;
GO -- (0 row(s) affected)
```

```
SELECT COUNT(*) FROM Product;  -- 304
GO
```

Remove Duplicates with GROUP BY

```
-- Insert  duplicates on ProductName & ProductNumber
INSERT INTO Product     SELECT      TOP (100) ProductID=CONVERT(int, ProductID) + 2000,
                        ProductName = Name, ProductNumber,     ListPrice = ListPrice + 2.00
FROM  Production.Product  WHERE ListPrice > 0.0  ORDER BY NEWID();
GO
```

```
-- Sample of conflicting data - It is a business decision what to keep
SELECT TOP (4) * FROM Product WHERE ProductNumber IN
    ( SELECT ProductNumber FROM Product   GROUP BY ProductNumber HAVING count(*) > 1    )
ORDER BY ProductNumber;
```

ProductID	ProductName	ProductNumber	ListPrice
992	Mountain-500 Black, 48	BK-M18B-48	540.9900
1992	Mountain-500 Black, 48	BK-M18B-48	541.9900
993	Mountain-500 Black, 52	BK-M18B-52	540.9900
1993	Mountain-500 Black, 52	BK-M18B-52	541.9900

```
-- Assume it does not matter which duplicate to keep: any ProductID and any ListPrice OK
SELECT ProductID=MIN(ProductID), ProductName, ProductNumber, ListPrice=MIN(ListPrice)
FROM Product GROUP BY ProductName, ProductNumber ORDER BY ProductID;
GO  -- (304 row(s) affected)
```

Domain Integrity

A domain defines the possible values for a column. Domain Integrity rules enforce the validity data in a column:

Data type	table design
Data length	table design
Nullability	table design
Collation	table design
Allowable values	check constraints - table design
Default value	default constraints - table design

CHECK constraint is used for simple rules such as OrderQty > 0. UDF CHECK constraints can be used for complex rules. In addition, at the development phase, triggers, stored procedures and client-side application software can be developed to enforce Domain Integrity.

Server-side CHECK constraints are the most desirable. Client-side Domain Integrity enforcement is the least desirable. However, it may happen that there is no database expert on the project and developers feel more confident programming data validity rules in the application software. Ultimately what counts is valid data in the database. Usually big-budget projects can do everything the right way due to the availability of expert-level resources in all areas of the software development project. Basic table definition data from INFORMATION_SCHEMA views.

```
SELECT          COLUMN_NAME, ORDINAL_POSITION, DATA_TYPE, IS_NULLABLE,
                CHARACTER_MAXIMUM_LENGTH, COLLATION_NAME, COLUMN_DEFAULT
FROM INFORMATION_SCHEMA.COLUMNS WHERE TABLE_NAME = 'SalesOrderHeader';
```

COLUMN_NAME	ORDINAL_POSITION	DATA_TYPE	IS_NULLABLE	CHARACTER_MAXIMUM_LENGTH	COLLATION_NAME	COLUMN_DEFAULT
SalesOrderID	1	int	NO	NULL	NULL	NULL
RevisionNumber	2	tinyint	NO	NULL	NULL	((0))
OrderDate	3	datetime	NO	NULL	NULL	(getdate())
DueDate	4	datetime	NO	NULL	NULL	NULL
ShipDate	5	datetime	YES	NULL	NULL	NULL
tatus	6	tinyint	NO	NULL	NULL	((1))
OnlineOrderFlag	7	bit	NO	NULL	NULL	((1))
SalesOrderNumber	8	nvarchar	NO	25	SQL_Latin1_General_CP1_CI_AS	NULL
PurchaseOrderNumber	9	nvarchar	YES	25	SQL_Latin1_General_CP1_CI_AS	NULL
AccountNumber	10	nvarchar	YES	15	SQL_Latin1_General_CP1_CI_AS	NULL
CustomerID	11	int	NO	NULL	NULL	NULL
SalesPersonID	12	int	YES	NULL	NULL	NULL
TerritoryID	13	int	YES	NULL	NULL	NULL
BillToAddressID	14	int	NO	NULL	NULL	NULL
ShipToAddressID	15	int	NO	NULL	NULL	NULL
ShipMethodID	16	int	NO	NULL	NULL	NULL
CreditCardID	17	int	YES	NULL	NULL	NULL
CreditCardApprovalCode	18	varchar	YES	15	SQL_Latin1_General_CP1_CI_AS	NULL
CurrencyRateID	19	int	YES	NULL	NULL	NULL
SubTotal	20	money	NO	NULL	NULL	((0.00))
TaxAmt	21	money	NO	NULL	NULL	((0.00))
Freight	22	money	NO	NULL	NULL	((0.00))
TotalDue	23	money	NO	NULL	NULL	NULL
Comment	24	nvarchar	YES	128	SQL_Latin1_General_CP1_CI_AS	NULL
rowguid	25	uniqueidentifier	NO	NULL	NULL	(newid())
ModifiedDate	26	datetime	NO	NULL	NULL	(getdate())

Domain Integrity Summary Display with sp_help

The sp_help system procedure provides a convenient way to display a summary of Domain Integrity definitions for a table.

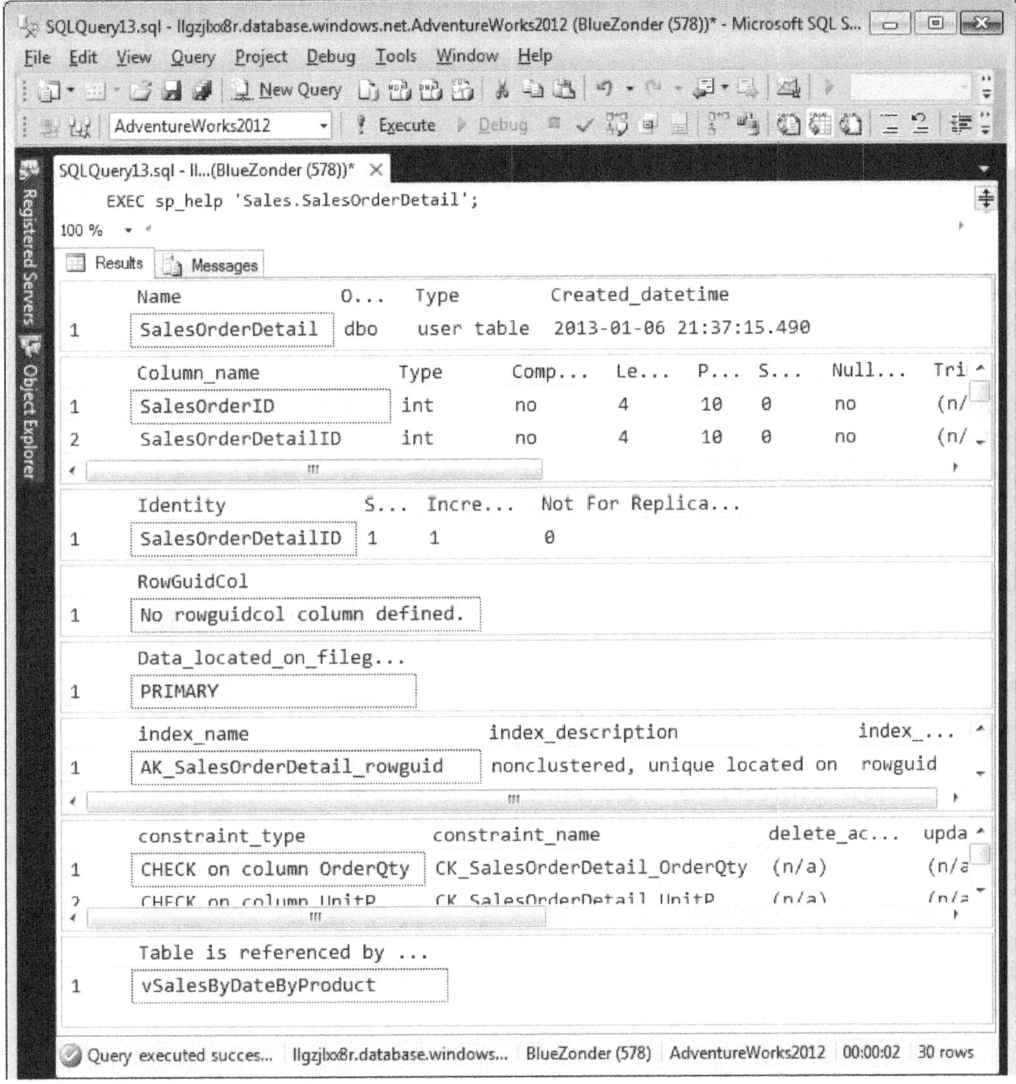

We can query "sys" system views metadata for column definition as well.

```
SELECT * FROM sys.columns   WHERE object_name(object_id) = 'PurchaseOrderHeader'
ORDER BY column_id;   -- (13 row(s) affected) - Partial results.
```

object_id	name	column_id	system_type_id	user_type_id	max_length	precision	scale	collation_name
946102411	PurchaseOrderID	1	56	56	4	10	0	NULL

THE COLUMNPROPERTY() Function

The COLUMNPROPERTY() function can be used for programmatic discovery of column properties. Script to generate SELECT queries for all properties.

```
USE AdventureWorks2012;
GO
```

```
DECLARE @Parms TABLE (Property varchar(32))
INSERT  @Parms VALUES
('AllowsNull'), ('ColumnId'),
('FullTextTypeColumn'), ('IsComputed'),
('IsCursorType'), ('IsDeterministic'),
('IsFulltextIndexed'), ('IsIdentity'),
('IsIdNotForRepl'), ('IsIndexable'),
('IsOutParam'), ('IsPrecise'),
('IsRowGuidCol'), ('IsSystemVerified'),
('IsXmlIndexable'), ('Precision'),
('Scale'), ('StatisticalSemantics'),
('SystemDataAccess'), ('UserDataAccess'),
('UsesAnsiTrim'), ('IsSparse'),
('IsColumnSet')
SELECT CONCAT('SELECT COLUMNPROPERTY( OBJECT_ID(''Person.Person''), ''LastName'', ''',
                   Property, ''') AS [', Property, '];')
FROM @Parms
GO  -- Partial results.
```

```
SELECT COLUMNPROPERTY( OBJECT_ID('Person.Person'), 'LastName', 'AllowsNull') AS [AllowsNull];
SELECT COLUMNPROPERTY( OBJECT_ID('Person.Person'), 'LastName', 'ColumnId') AS [ColumnId];
SELECT COLUMNPROPERTY( OBJECT_ID('Person.Person'), 'LastName', 'FullTextTypeColumn') AS [FullTextTypeColumn];
SELECT COLUMNPROPERTY( OBJECT_ID('Person.Person'), 'LastName', 'IsComputed') AS [IsComputed];
SELECT COLUMNPROPERTY( OBJECT_ID('Person.Person'), 'LastName', 'IsCursorType') AS [IsCursorType];
```

Executing the queries, the column properties are returned one by one.

	AllowsNull
1	0

	ColumnId
1	7

	FullTextTypeColumn
1	0

	IsComputed
1	0

	IsCursorType
1	0

Column List Using System Views & Data Dictionary

We can combine sys. system views with data dictionary description to get a valuable list when working with domain integrity. On-premises SQL Server 2012 query. sys.extended_properties system view is not supported in Azure SQL.

```
USE AdventureWorks2012;
SELECT SCHEMA_NAME(T.schema_id)   AS SchemaName,
    T.name                        AS TableName,
    C.name                        AS ColumnName,
    TP.name                       AS ColumnType,
    C.max_length                  AS ColumnLength,
    COALESCE(EP.value, Space(1))  AS ColumnDesc
FROM   sys.tables AS T
    INNER JOIN sys.columns AS C
        ON T.object_id = C.object_id
    INNER JOIN sys.types AS TP
        ON  C.system_type_id = TP.user_type_id
    LEFT JOIN sys.extended_properties AS EP
        ON EP.major_id = T.object_id
          AND EP.minor_id = C.column_id
ORDER  BY SchemaName,  TableName,  ColumnName;
GO
-- (643 row(s) affected) - Partial Results.
```

SchemaName	TableName	ColumnName	ColumnType	ColumnLength	ColumnDesc
Sales	SalesOrderDetail	SpecialOfferID	int	4	Promotional code. Foreign key to SpecialOffer.SpecialOfferID.
Sales	SalesOrderDetail	UnitPrice	money	8	Selling price of a single product.
Sales	SalesOrderDetail	UnitPriceDiscount	money	8	Discount amount.
Sales	SalesOrderHeader	AccountNumber	nvarchar	30	Financial accounting number reference.
Sales	SalesOrderHeader	BillToAddressID	int	4	Customer billing address. Foreign key to Address.AddressID.
Sales	SalesOrderHeader	Comment	nvarchar	256	Sales representative comments.
Sales	SalesOrderHeader	CreditCardApprovalCode	varchar	15	Approval code provided by the credit card company.
Sales	SalesOrderHeader	CreditCardID	int	4	Credit card identification number. Foreign key to CreditCard.CreditCardID.
Sales	SalesOrderHeader	CurrencyRateID	int	4	Currency exchange rate used. Foreign key to CurrencyRate.CurrencyRateID.
Sales	SalesOrderHeader	CustomerID	int	4	Customer identification number. Foreign key to Customer.BusinessEntityID.
Sales	SalesOrderHeader	DueDate	datetime	8	Date the order is due to the customer.
Sales	SalesOrderHeader	Freight	money	8	Shipping cost.
Sales	SalesOrderHeader	ModifiedDate	datetime	8	Date and time the record was last updated.
Sales	SalesOrderHeader	OnlineOrderFlag	bit	1	0 = Order placed by sales person. 1 = Order placed online by customer.
Sales	SalesOrderHeader	OrderDate	datetime	8	Dates the sales order was created.

Declarative Referential Integrity

Referential Integrity refers to ensuring that relationships between tables remain consistent. Declarative means it is part of table setup, not in programming objects like stored procedure. When one table attempts to create a FOREIGN KEY to another (PK) table, Referential Integrity requires that the primary key value exists in the referenced (PK) table. The optional cascading update & cascading delete ensure that changes made to the primary table are reflected in the linked referencing (FK) table. For example, if a row is deleted in the primary table, then all referencing rows are automatically deleted in the linked (FK) table when ON DELETE CASCADE is set. All three Referential Integrity constraint actions are demonstrated by the following script.

```
USE AdventureWorks2012;

-- Create 2 test tables with PK-FK relationship
CREATE TABLE Product (
        ProductID INT PRIMARY KEY,
        ProductName varchar(50) UNIQUE,
        ProductNumber varchar(20) UNIQUE,
        ListPrice MONEY);
GO
```

```
-- First we test without the DELETE CASCADE action
CREATE TABLE OrderDetail (
        SalesOrderID INT,
        SalesOrderDetailID INT,
        PRIMARY KEY (SalesOrderID, SalesOrderDetailID),
        OrderQty INT ,
        ProductID INT REFERENCES Product(ProductID)  -- ON DELETE CASCADE
);
```

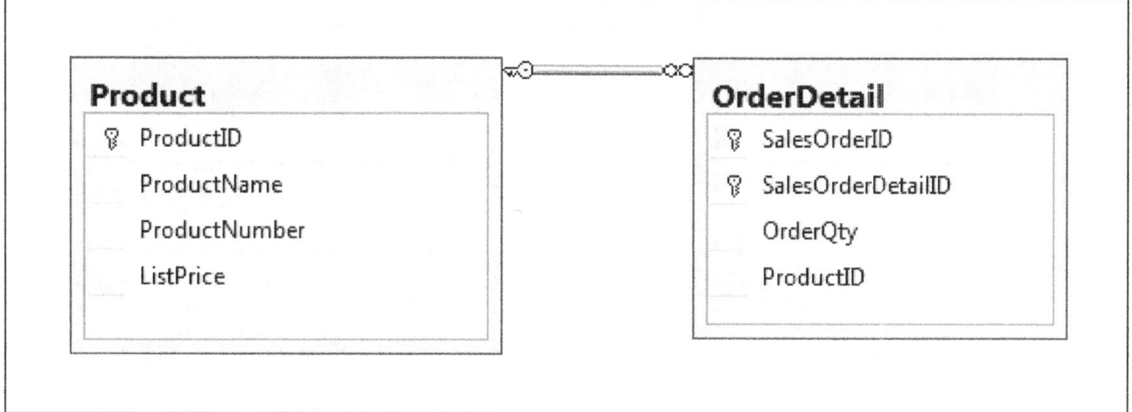

FOREIGN KEY Constraint Protects Two Ways

```
-- Populate test tables
INSERT Product
SELECT ProductID, Name, ProductNumber, ListPrice
FROM Production.Product
ORDER BY ProductID;
GO
--(504 row(s) affected)
```

```
INSERT OrderDetail
SELECT      SalesOrderID,
            SalesOrderDetailID,
            OrderQty,
            ProductID
FROM Sales.SalesOrderDetail
ORDER BY SalesOrderID, SalesOrderDetailID;
GO
-- (121317 row(s) affected)
```

```
-- Attempting to insert into FK table a reference to a non-existing (PK) ProductID
INSERT OrderDetail
SELECT      SalesOrderID = 100000,
            SalesOrderDetailID = 1000000,
            OrderQty = 5,
            ProductID = 2000
GO
/* Msg 547, Level 16, State 0, Line 4
The INSERT statement conflicted with the FOREIGN KEY constraint
"FK__OrderDeta__Produ__226010D3". The conflict occurred in database
"AdventureWorks2012", table "dbo.Product", column 'ProductID'.
The statement has been terminated.*/
```

```
-- Attempting to delete from  PK table a ProductID which is referenced from the FK table
DELETE Product WHERE ProductID = 800;
GO
/* Msg 547, Level 16, State 0, Line 1
The DELETE statement conflicted with the REFERENCE constraint
"FK__OrderDeta__Produ__226010D3". The conflict occurred in database
"AdventureWorks2012", table "dbo.OrderDetail", column 'ProductID'.
The statement has been terminated.*/
```

ON DELETE CASCADE Action Causes DELETE Chain Reaction

```
-- Change FOREIGN KEY: specify ON DELETE CASCADE option
-- Lookup FK constraints name
SELECT * FROM INFORMATION_SCHEMA.REFERENTIAL_CONSTRAINTS;
```

CONSTRAINT_CATALOG	CONSTRAINT_SCHEMA	CONSTRAINT_NAME	UNIQUE_CONSTRAINT_CATALOG	UNIQUE_CONSTRAINT_SCHEMA	UNIQUE_CONSTRAINT_NAME	MATCH_OPTION	UPDATE_RULE	DELETE_RULE
tempdb	dbo	FK__OrderDeta__Produ__0A9D95DB	tempdb	dbo	PK__Product__B40CC6ED66641298	SIMPLE	NO ACTION	NO ACTION

```
BEGIN TRANSACTION
GO
ALTER TABLE dbo.OrderDetail  DROP CONSTRAINT FK__OrderDeta__Produ__0A9D95DB;
GO
ALTER TABLE dbo.Product SET (LOCK_ESCALATION = TABLE)
GO
COMMIT TRANSACTION -- Command(s) completed successfully.
```

```
BEGIN TRANSACTION;
GO
ALTER TABLE dbo.OrderDetail  ADD CONSTRAINT FK__OrderDeta__Produ__0A9D95DB
FOREIGN KEY (ProductID)  REFERENCES dbo.Product (ProductID) ON DELETE  CASCADE;
GO
ALTER TABLE dbo.OrderDetail SET (LOCK_ESCALATION = TABLE);
GO
COMMIT TRANSACTION;  -- Command(s) completed successfully.
```

```
SELECT * FROM INFORMATION_SCHEMA.REFERENTIAL_CONSTRAINTS;
```

CONSTRAINT_CATALOG	CONSTRAINT_SCHEMA	CONSTRAINT_NAME	UNIQUE_CONSTRAINT_CATALOG	UNIQUE_CONSTRAINT_SCHEMA	UNIQUE_CONSTRAINT_NAME	MATCH_OPTION	UPDATE_RULE	DELETE_RULE
tempdb	dbo	FK__OrderDeta__Produ__0A9D95DB	tempdb	dbo	PK__Product__B40CC6ED66641298	SIMPLE	NO ACTION	CASCADE

```
SELECT COUNT(*) FROM OrderDetail;
GO  -- 121317
```

```
-- Cascading DELETE: first DELETE all referencing FK records, then DELETE PK record
DELETE Product WHERE ProductID = 800;
GO
-- (1 row(s) affected)
```

```
SELECT COUNT(*) FROM OrderDetail;
GO  -- 120822
```

FOREIGN KEY Constraints Represent the Only Connections Among Tables

While we talk about linked tables in functional terms such as master/header-detail, parent-child, dimension-fact, junction, etc., **there is only a single way to connect tables: FOREIGN KEY references PRIMARY KEY in another table**. We are going to demonstrate it in a grand manner: we will create 290 tables with the names of all the employees of AdventureWorks Cycles (fictional) company in a new test database. We shall connect all of them with FOREIGN KEY constraints: employee (FK table) references manager (PK table). SQL Server 2012 demo.

```
USE master;
GO
CREATE DATABASE AWOrgChart;
GO
```

```
USE AWOrgChart;
GO
```

```
DECLARE @SQL NVARCHAR(max) = '';

WITH CTE (ID, Emp, Mgr, MgrNode)  -- CTE with column names
   AS
(     SELECT E.BusinessEntityID,
           Emp=CONCAT(P.FirstName, SPACE(1), P.LastName),
           NULL,
           NULL
      FROM   HumanResources.Employee E
           INNER JOIN Person.Person P
                ON E.BusinessEntityID = P.BusinessEntityID
      WHERE  E.OrganizationNode = 0x                              -- Root node
      UNION
      SELECT E.BusinessEntityID,
          CONCAT(P.FirstName, SPACE(1), P.LastName)                  AS Emp,
          CONCAT(PP.FirstName, SPACE(1), PP.LastName)                AS Mgr,
          E.OrganizationNode.GetAncestor(1)                          AS SuperNode
      FROM   HumanResources.Employee E
           INNER JOIN Person.Person P
                ON E.BusinessEntityID = P.BusinessEntityID
           INNER JOIN HumanResources.Employee EE
                ON ( EE.OrganizationNode =  E.OrganizationNode.GetAncestor(1) )
           INNER JOIN Person.Person PP
                ON EE.BusinessEntityID = PP.BusinessEntityID)
```

```
-- T-SQL script continued.
SELECT @SQL = CONCAT(@SQL, CONCAT('CREATE TABLE ', QUOTENAME(Emp),
                    '( ID INT PRIMARY KEY ,',
                        ' MgrID INT ',
                            CASE
            WHEN Mgr IS NOT NULL THEN CONCAT(' REFERENCES ',
                            QUOTENAME(Mgr),    '(ID)')
            ELSE ''   END, '); '))
FROM   CTE;

PRINT @SQL;  -- Partial text.
```

CREATE TABLE [Ken Sánchez](ID INT PRIMARY KEY , MgrID INT);
CREATE TABLE [Terri Duffy](ID INT PRIMARY KEY , MgrID INT REFERENCES [Ken Sánchez](ID));
CREATE TABLE [Roberto Tamburello](ID INT PRIMARY KEY , MgrID INT REFERENCES [Terri Duffy](ID));
CREATE TABLE [Rob Walters](ID INT PRIMARY KEY , MgrID INT REFERENCES [Roberto Tamburello](ID));
CREATE TABLE [Gail Erickson](ID INT PRIMARY KEY , MgrID INT REFERENCES [Roberto Tamburello](ID));
CREATE TABLE [Jossef Goldberg](ID INT PRIMARY KEY , MgrID INT REFERENCES [Roberto Tamburello](ID));
CREATE TABLE [Dylan Miller](ID INT PRIMARY KEY , MgrID INT REFERENCES [Roberto Tamburello](ID));
CREATE TABLE [Diane Margheim](ID INT PRIMARY KEY , MgrID INT REFERENCES [Dylan Miller](ID));
CREATE TABLE [Gigi Matthew](ID INT PRIMARY KEY , MgrID INT REFERENCES [Dylan Miller](ID));
CREATE TABLE [Michael Raheem](ID INT PRIMARY KEY , MgrID INT REFERENCES [Dylan Miller](ID));
CREATE TABLE [Ovidiu Cracium](ID INT PRIMARY KEY , MgrID INT REFERENCES [Roberto Tamburello](ID));
CREATE TABLE [Thierry D'Hers](ID INT PRIMARY KEY , MgrID INT REFERENCES [Ovidiu Cracium](ID));

The functional meaning of Terry Duffy "references" Ken Sanchez: Duffy reports to Sanchez.

```
EXEC sp_executeSQL @SQL;  -- Dynamic SQL execution: create 290 linked tables
GO
```

```
-- USE master;
DROP DATABASE AWOrgChart;
```

Diagram Tool Can Be Used for Organizational Charts

We can use the diagram tool in the AWOrgChart database as an orgchart tool. We add a chosen table to the diagram, for example, [Ken Sanchez]. With the right click menu, we add related tables, set view to table name only & arrange selection. The result is orgchart with the CEO and executive managers.

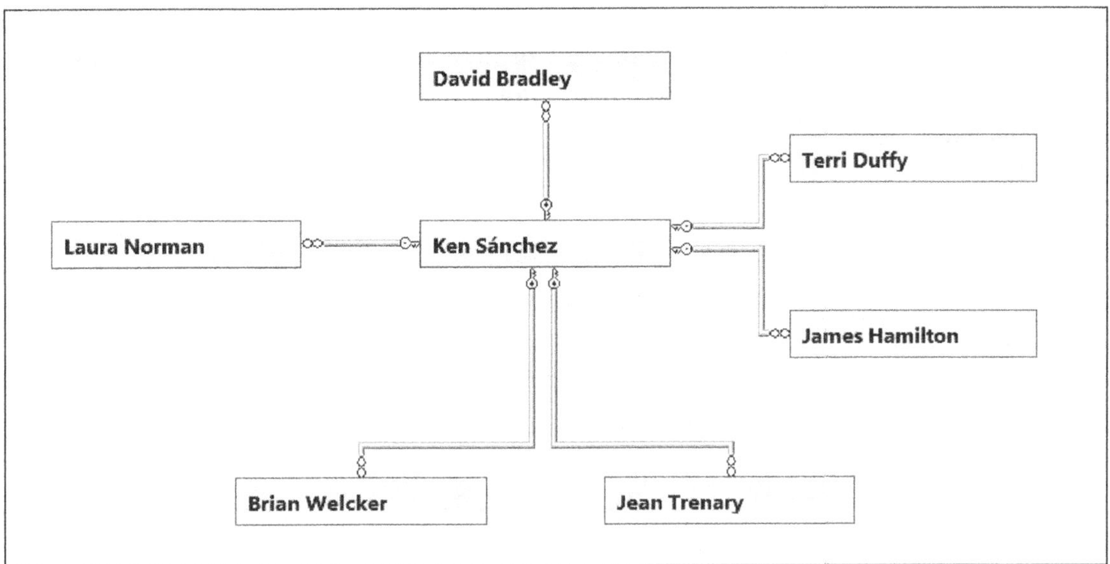

Orgchart starting with [David Hamilton]. Hamilton reports to Krebs (Gold Key).

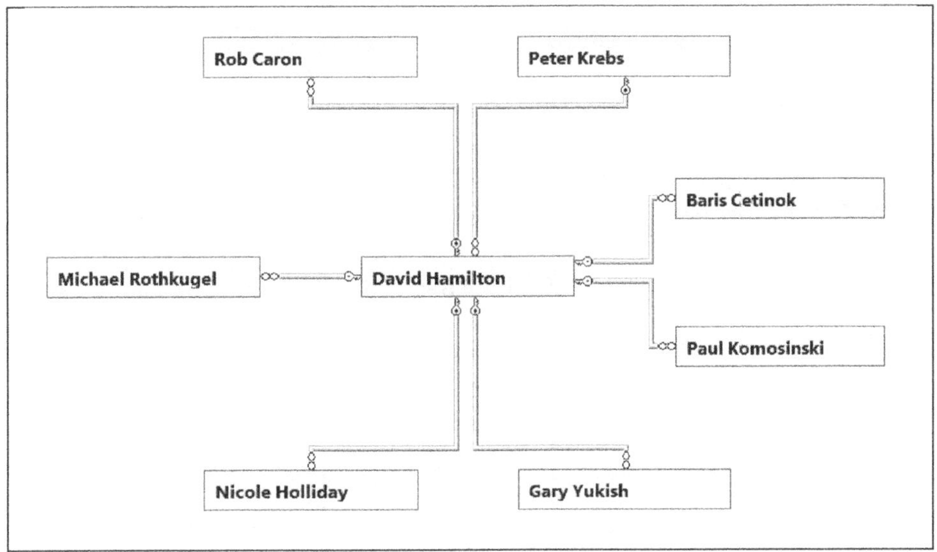

Enterprise-Level Business Rules Enforcement

Enterprise-Level Business Rules can be enforced by stored procedures & triggers on the server-side and application programs on the client-side. While stored procedures & application programs can be used to implement a complex set of business rules, they can only effect the current application. Stored procedure or application cannot catch an UPDATE transaction, for example, coming from a legacy application nobody dares to touch at the IT department. In a way stored procedure can be configured to perform after-the-fact near-real-time updates for recently posted data: configure the stored procedure as SQL Server Agent job and schedule it to run each minute.

Special Role of Triggers

Triggers, on the other hand, can catch, for example, an INSERT to the ProductPrice table, wherever it is coming from; current in-house application software, old in-house application, another profit-center of the enterprise application or 3rd party software package. An example for an enterprise business rule: convert foreign currency pricing to USD in the INSERT record to ProductPrice using the latest conversion rates from the ForeignExchange table. A constraint cannot be used to implement such a rule, a trigger can. Trigger code almost as flexible as stored procedure code. Triggers can also be used for cross-database referential integrity enforcement. While triggers are compiled into one database, they can access tables in another database. Because of their omnipotent nature, triggers are frequently misapplied as fix-it-all tools.

> WARNING
> Triggers are high maintenance database objects. Triggers are not for junior staff.
> Dropped/disabled triggers do not "COMPLAIN": **stealth** behavior.

Triggers are just like silent workhorses. They can be forgotten after months of operation since they don't have to be called explicitly from the client-side application programs, they are event launched on the server-side. DDL trigger can be applied to guard DML triggers, but then someone or something has to guard the DDL trigger as well. On the other hand, a dropped stored procedure causes user error ("complains"). Dropped trigger can cause user error also, but the error cannot easily be traced back the trigger.

The following update trigger will prevent last name update from new software, old software, other department's software or even 3rd party software package.

```
CREATE TRIGGER trgEmployee  ON Employee FOR UPDATE AS
   IF (UPDATE(LastName))                    BEGIN
     RAISERROR ('Last name cannot be changed', 16, 1);   ROLLBACK TRAN;    RETURN;    END
GO
```

Product Reorder Trigger

The UPDATE trigger is attached to the Products table. It fires whenever there is an UPDATE for the table, no matter what kind of software application from what part of the world executed the UPDATE statement. **A trigger should never return a result set**. However, there is no error if we try to return a result set with a SELECT statement just like in a stored procedure. For testing & debugging purposes we can return results.

```
USE Northwind
GO
```

```
-- Logging table for product reorder notices
CREATE TABLE Reorder (
        ID INT IDENTITY(1,1) PRIMARY KEY,
        Message varchar(256),
        CreateDate datetime default (CURRENT_TIMESTAMP));
GO
```

```
IF EXISTS (select * from sys.objects where type='TR' and name = 'trgProductReorder')
        DROP TRIGGER trgProductReorder
GO
```

```
CREATE TRIGGER trgProductReorder
ON Products FOR UPDATE
AS
 BEGIN
   SET NOCOUNT ON;
   DECLARE @MsgText    varchar(128),    @QtyOnHand    int,   @ReorderLevel int;
   SELECT @MsgText = CONCAT('Please place a reorder  for ',  Rtrim(ProductName))
   FROM   inserted;

   SELECT @QtyOnHand = UnitsInStock,   @ReorderLevel = ReorderLevel   FROM   inserted;

   IF @QtyOnHand < @ReorderLevel
        INSERT Reorder  (Message)       SELECT @MsgText;

 --select * from deleted -- for testing &debugging only
 --select * from inserted
 --select @MsgText
 END
GO
```

A Trigger Should Never Return A Result Set Like A Stored Procedure

Check Data Manipulation Language (DML) trigger existence with sp_helptrigger system procedure.

```
EXEC sp_helptrigger Products ;
GO
```

trigger_name	trigger_owner	isupdate	isdelete	isinsert	isafter	isinsteadof	trigger_schema
trgProductReorder	dbo	1	0	0	1	0	dbo

```
-- Test trigger
/* For demonstration purposes, the debugging statements in trigger were uncommented */
UPDATE Products
	SET	UnitsInStock = 10
	WHERE	ProductID = 77;
GO
```

SQL Server UPDATE is implemented as complete deleted (old) and inserted (new) rows. Even if 1 byte updated, a complete row deleted and complete row inserted generated for logging.

deleted table row:

ProductID	ProductName	SupplierID	CategoryID	QuantityPerUnit	UnitPrice	**UnitsInStock**	UnitsOnOrder	ReorderLevel	Discontinued
77	Original Frankfurter grüne Soße	12	2	12 boxes	13.00	**50**	0	15	0

inserted table row:

ProductID	ProductName	SupplierID	CategoryID	QuantityPerUnit	UnitPrice	**UnitsInStock**	UnitsOnOrder	ReorderLevel	Discontinued
77	Original Frankfurter grüne Soße	12	2	12 boxes	13.00	**10**	0	15	0

```
SELECT * FROM	Reorder;
GO
```

ID	Message	CreateDate
1	Please place a reorder for Original Frankfurter grüne Soße	2016-11-25 06:06:45.043

```
DROP TRIGGER trgProductReorder;
DROP TABLE Reorder;
```

Trigger Examples In AdventureWorks2012

List of triggers in the sample database. parent_object_id is the object_id of the trigger parent table. SELF-JOIN is required to get the parent information.

```
USE AdventureWorks2012;
SELECT
   o.name                                                    AS TriggerName,
   SCHEMA_NAME(po.schema_id)                                 AS TableSchema,
   OBJECT_NAME(o.parent_object_id)                           AS TableName,
   OBJECTPROPERTY( o.object_id, 'ExecIsUpdateTrigger')       AS [isupdate],
   OBJECTPROPERTY( o.object_id, 'ExecIsDeleteTrigger')       AS [isdelete],
   OBJECTPROPERTY( o.object_id, 'ExecIsInsertTrigger')       AS [isinsert],
   OBJECTPROPERTY( o.object_id, 'ExecIsAfterTrigger')        AS [isafter],
   OBJECTPROPERTY( o.object_id, 'ExecIsInsteadOfTrigger')    AS [isinsteadof],
   OBJECTPROPERTY( o.object_id, 'ExecIsTriggerDisabled')     AS [disabled]
FROM sys.objects AS o
        INNER JOIN sys.objects AS po     ON o.parent_object_id = po.object_id
WHERE o.[type] = 'TR'  ORDER BY TableSchema, TableName, TriggerName;
```

TriggerName	TableSchema	TableName	isupdate	isdelete	isinsert	isafter	isinsteadof	disabled
dEmployee	HumanResources	Employee	0	1	0	0	1	0
iuPerson	Person	Person	1	0	1	1	0	0
iWorkOrder	Production	WorkOrder	0	0	1	1	0	0
uWorkOrder	Production	WorkOrder	1	0	0	1	0	0
iPurchaseOrderDetail	Purchasing	PurchaseOrderDetail	0	0	1	1	0	0
uPurchaseOrderDetail	Purchasing	PurchaseOrderDetail	1	0	0	1	0	0
uPurchaseOrderHeader	Purchasing	PurchaseOrderHeader	1	0	0	1	0	0
dVendor	Purchasing	Vendor	0	1	0	0	1	0
iduSalesOrderDetail	Sales	SalesOrderDetail	1	1	1	1	0	0
uSalesOrderHeader	Sales	SalesOrderHeader	1	0	0	1	0	0

Alternate method of obtaining all triggers information.

```
SELECT * FROM sys.triggers ORDER BY name; -- Partial results.
```

name	object_id	parent_class	parent_class_desc	parent_id	type	type_desc
ddlDatabaseTriggerLog	261575970	0	DATABASE	0	TR	SQL_TRIGGER
dEmployee	1739153241	1	OBJECT_OR_COLUMN	1237579447	TR	SQL_TRIGGER
dVendor	1851153640	1	OBJECT_OR_COLUMN	766625774	TR	SQL_TRIGGER
iduSalesOrderDetail	1819153526	1	OBJECT_OR_COLUMN	1154103152	TR	SQL_TRIGGER
iPurchaseOrderDetail	1771153355	1	OBJECT_OR_COLUMN	850102069	TR	SQL_TRIGGER
iuPerson	1755153298	1	OBJECT_OR_COLUMN	1765581328	TR	SQL_TRIGGER
iWorkOrder	1867153697	1	OBJECT_OR_COLUMN	846626059	TR	SQL_TRIGGER
uPurchaseOrderDetail	1787153412	1	OBJECT_OR_COLUMN	850102069	TR	SQL_TRIGGER
uPurchaseOrderHeader	1803153469	1	OBJECT_OR_COLUMN	946102411	TR	SQL_TRIGGER
uSalesOrderHeader	1835153583	1	OBJECT_OR_COLUMN	1266103551	TR	SQL_TRIGGER
uWorkOrder	1883153754	1	OBJECT_OR_COLUMN	846626059	TR	SQL_TRIGGER

Trigger Can Be Modified in Object Explorer

A trigger can be scripted into a new Query Editor window. After changing the "CREATE" to "ALTER", it can be modified and compiled.

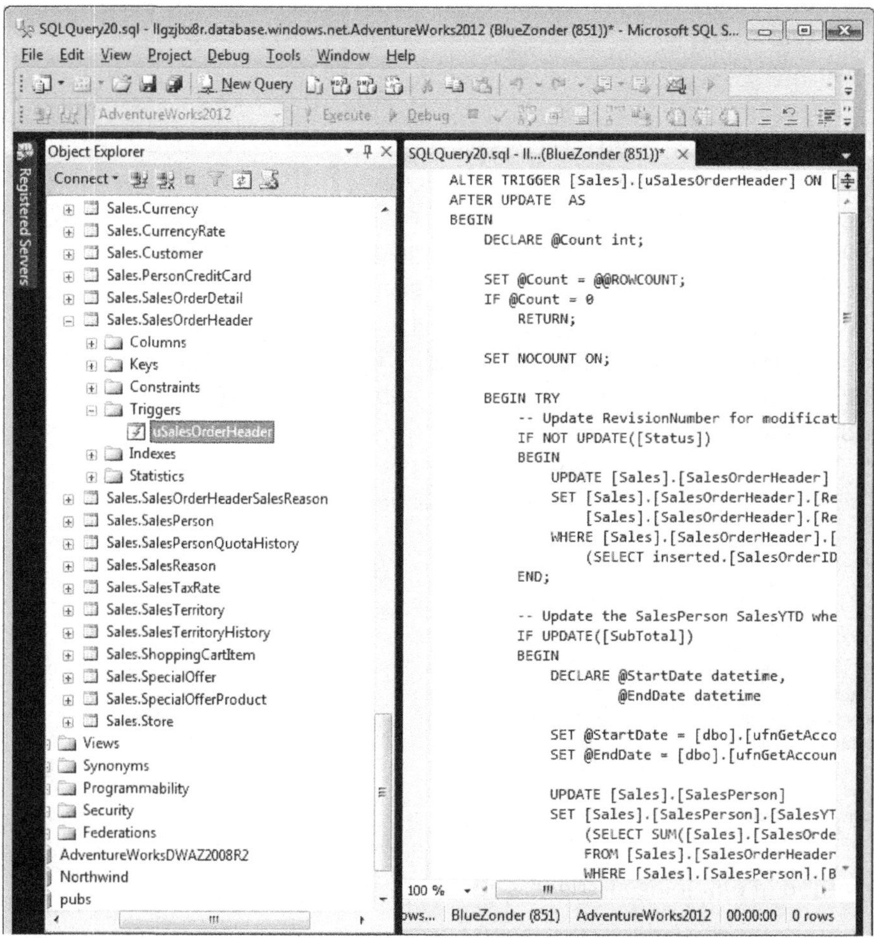

Programmatic way to get trigger definition.

```
SELECT OBJECT_DEFINITION( object_id('Person.iuPerson'));
```

CREATE TRIGGER [Person].[iuPerson] ON [Person].[Person]
AFTER INSERT, UPDATE NOT FOR REPLICATION AS
BEGIN
DECLARE @Count int;
SET @Count = @@ROWCOUNT;
IF @Count = 0 RETURN;
SET NOCOUNT ON;
IF UPDATE([BusinessEntityID]) OR UPDATE([Demographics])

Business Intelligence in the Enterprise - On-premises Demo

SQL Server Analysis Services (SSAS), SQL Server Integration Services (SSIS) & SQL Server Reporting Services (SSRS) are the server side Business Intelligence software components. Easy to remember associations: SSAS: OLAP cubes and more, SSIS: ETL (extract, transform, load) data transfer system & SSRS: traditional reports, interactive & OLAP reports. SQL Server Data Tools (SSDT) provides 3 customized templates as design environments.

SSRS: Designing Complex Interactive Reports

SSDT report design environment: product catalog in the report design editor.

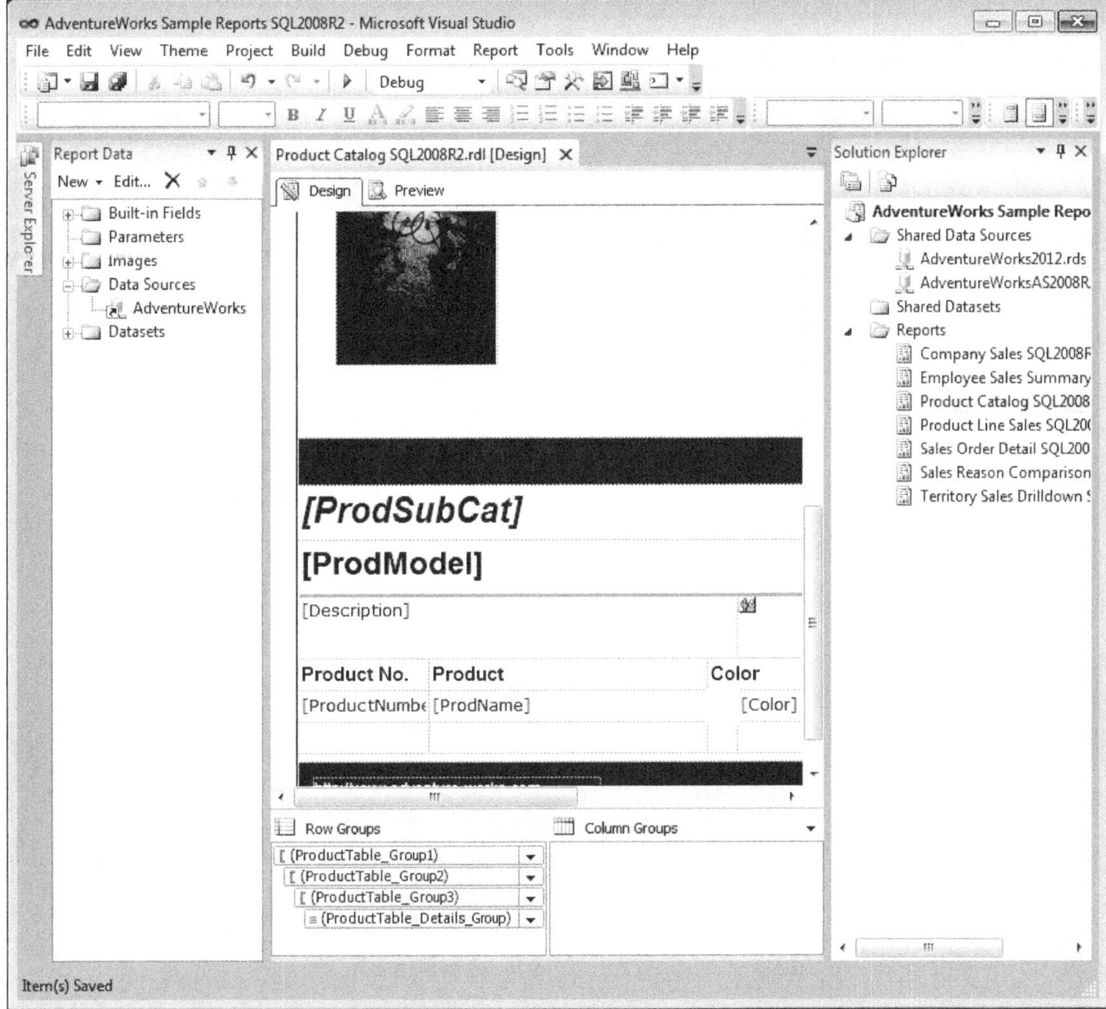

Previewing the Report Design

The product catalog is interactive with a drill down directory on the left which is based on the Production.ProductCategory and Production.ProductSubcategory tables. The Product, ProductSubcategory & ProductCategory tables form a hierarchy which is neatly exploited in the product catalog report. What makes the report design environment extremely powerful that you can try the look & feel of a report just by clicking a tab and staying in the studio environment. The product images are from the ProductPhoto table(in Management Studio we cannot see the images, only the binary code).

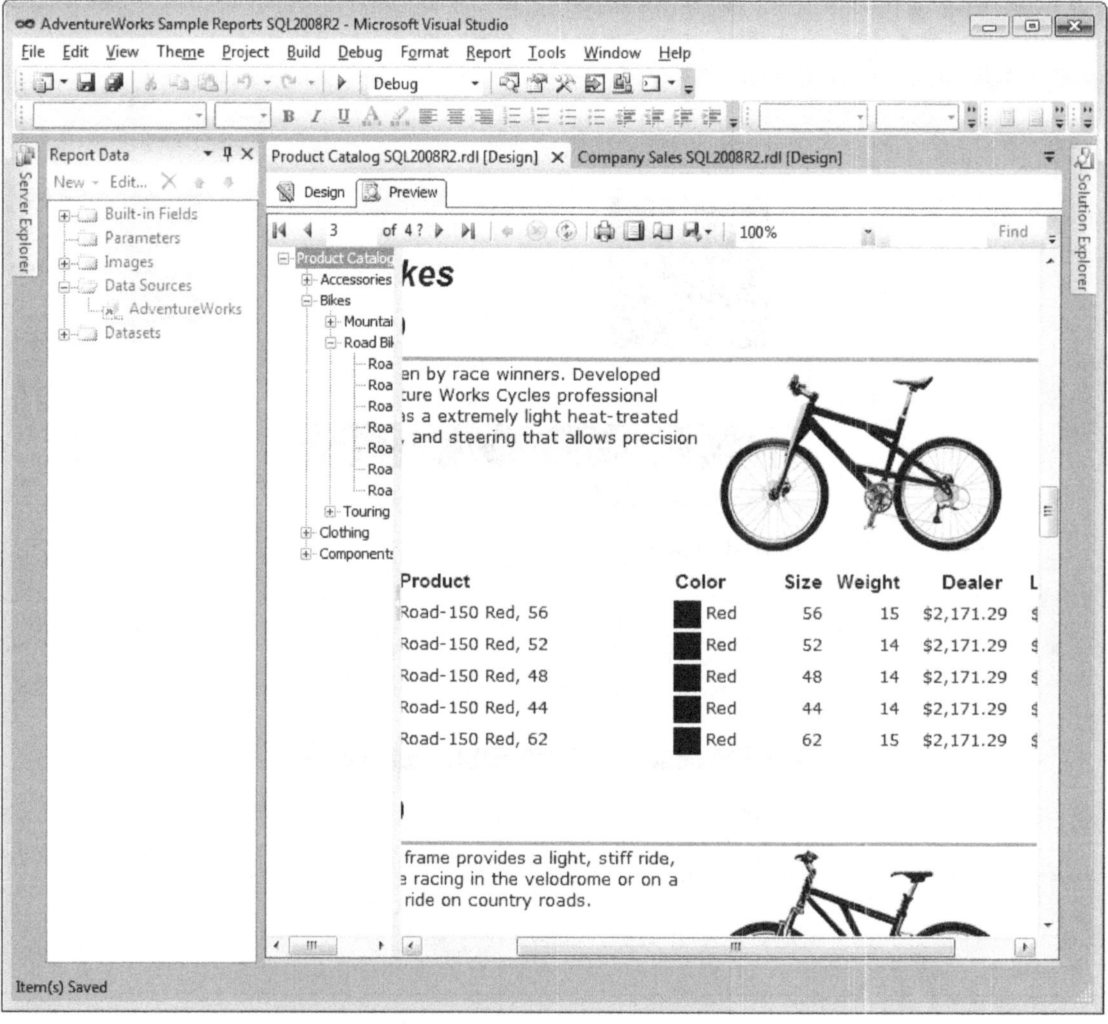

Detailed Preview of AWC Product Catalog

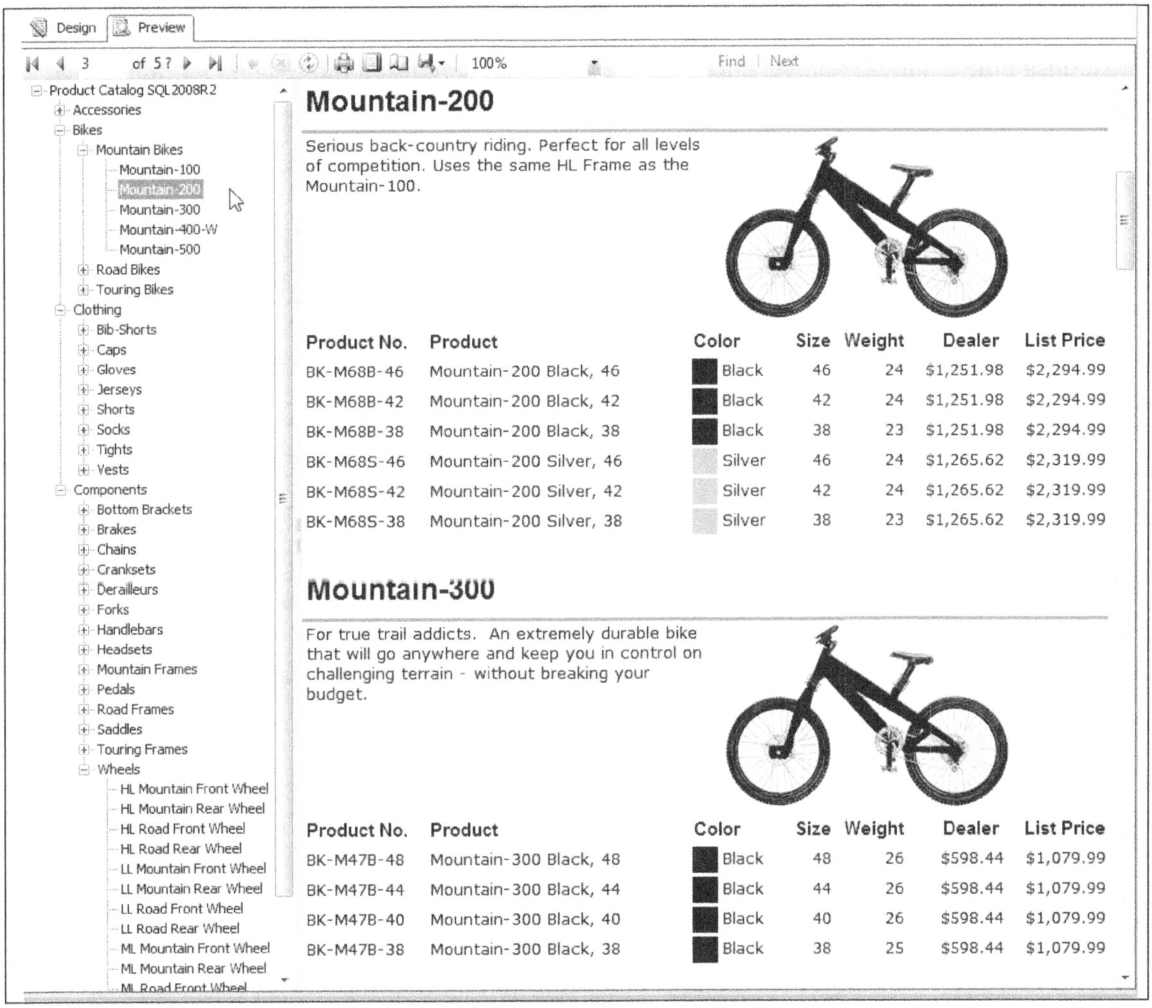

Design | Preview

3 of 5 ? | 100% | Find | Next

- Product Catalog SQL2008R2
  - Accessories
  - Bikes
    - Mountain Bikes
      - Mountain-100
      - Mountain-200
      - Mountain-300
      - Mountain-400-W
      - Mountain-500
    - Road Bikes
    - Touring Bikes
  - Clothing
    - Bib-Shorts
    - Caps
    - Gloves
    - Jerseys
    - Shorts
    - Socks
    - Tights
    - Vests
  - Components
    - Bottom Brackets
    - Brakes
    - Chains
    - Cranksets
    - Derailleurs
    - Forks
    - Handlebars
    - Headsets
    - Mountain Frames
    - Pedals
    - Road Frames
    - Saddles
    - Touring Frames
    - Wheels
      - HL Mountain Front Wheel
      - HL Mountain Rear Wheel
      - HL Road Front Wheel
      - HL Road Rear Wheel
      - LL Mountain Front Wheel
      - LL Mountain Rear Wheel
      - LL Road Front Wheel
      - LL Road Rear Wheel
      - ML Mountain Front Wheel
      - ML Mountain Rear Wheel
      - ML Road Front Wheel

Mountain-200

Serious back-country riding. Perfect for all levels of competition. Uses the same HL Frame as the Mountain-100.

Product No.	Product	Color	Size	Weight	Dealer	List Price
BK-M68B-46	Mountain-200 Black, 46	Black	46	24	$1,251.98	$2,294.99
BK-M68B-42	Mountain-200 Black, 42	Black	42	24	$1,251.98	$2,294.99
BK-M68B-38	Mountain-200 Black, 38	Black	38	23	$1,251.98	$2,294.99
BK-M68S-46	Mountain-200 Silver, 46	Silver	46	24	$1,265.62	$2,319.99
BK-M68S-42	Mountain-200 Silver, 42	Silver	42	24	$1,265.62	$2,319.99
BK-M68S-38	Mountain-200 Silver, 38	Silver	38	23	$1,265.62	$2,319.99

Mountain-300

For true trail addicts. An extremely durable bike that will go anywhere and keep you in control on challenging terrain - without breaking your budget.

Product No.	Product	Color	Size	Weight	Dealer	List Price
BK-M47B-48	Mountain-300 Black, 48	Black	48	26	$598.44	$1,079.99
BK-M47B-44	Mountain-300 Black, 44	Black	44	26	$598.44	$1,079.99
BK-M47B-40	Mountain-300 Black, 40	Black	40	26	$598.44	$1,079.99
BK-M47B-38	Mountain-300 Black, 38	Black	38	25	$598.44	$1,079.99

SSAS: Designing Multi-Dimensional Cubes

SSAS cubes contain millions of pre-calculated answers just waiting for the question like: what was the net revenue in Florida for the 3rd Quarter of 2016? Since the answer is ready, the response time is sub-second. AS cubes are derived from dimension tables and fact tables in a data warehouse database.

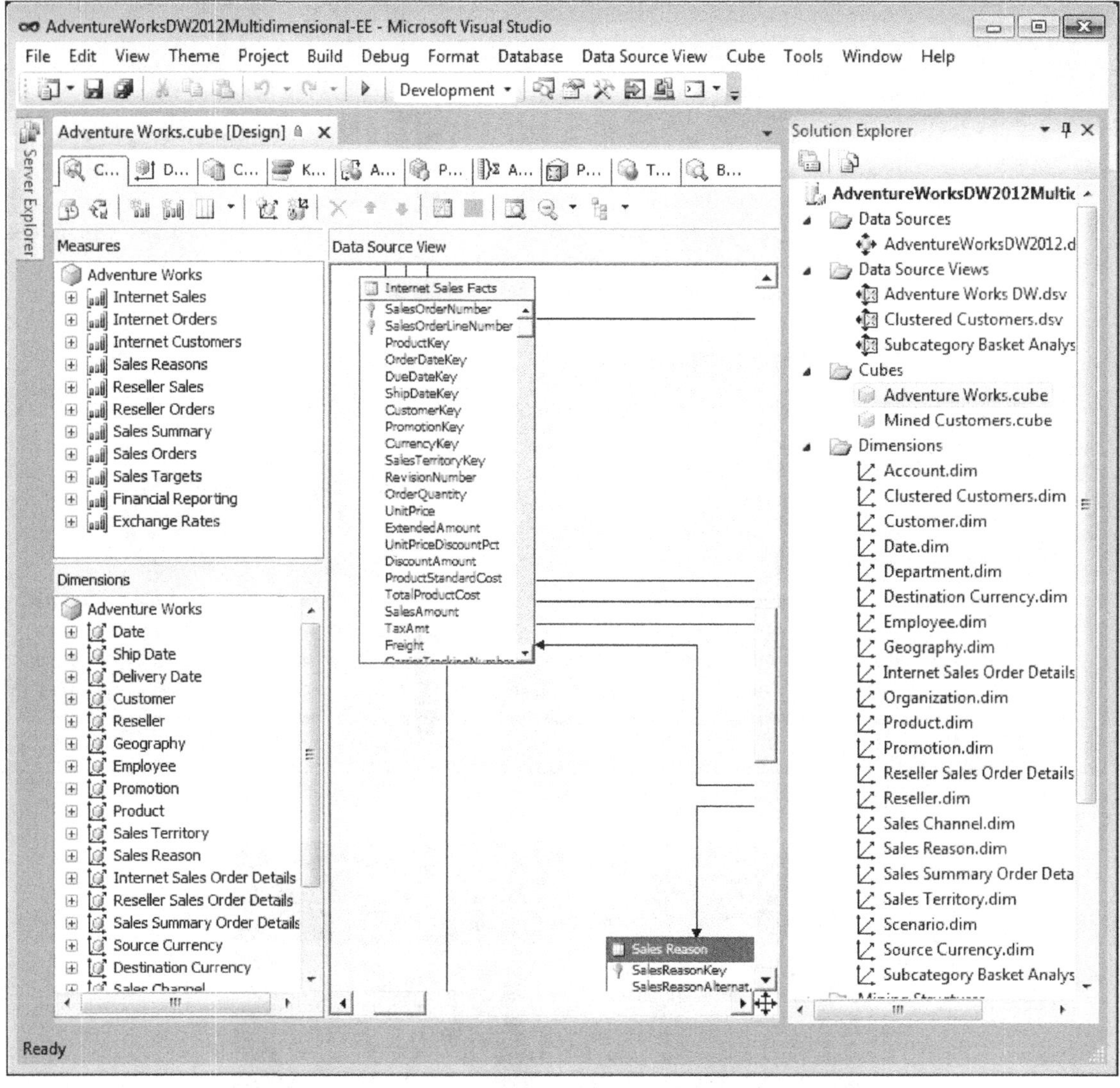

Test OLAP Analysis Services Cube Design with Browser

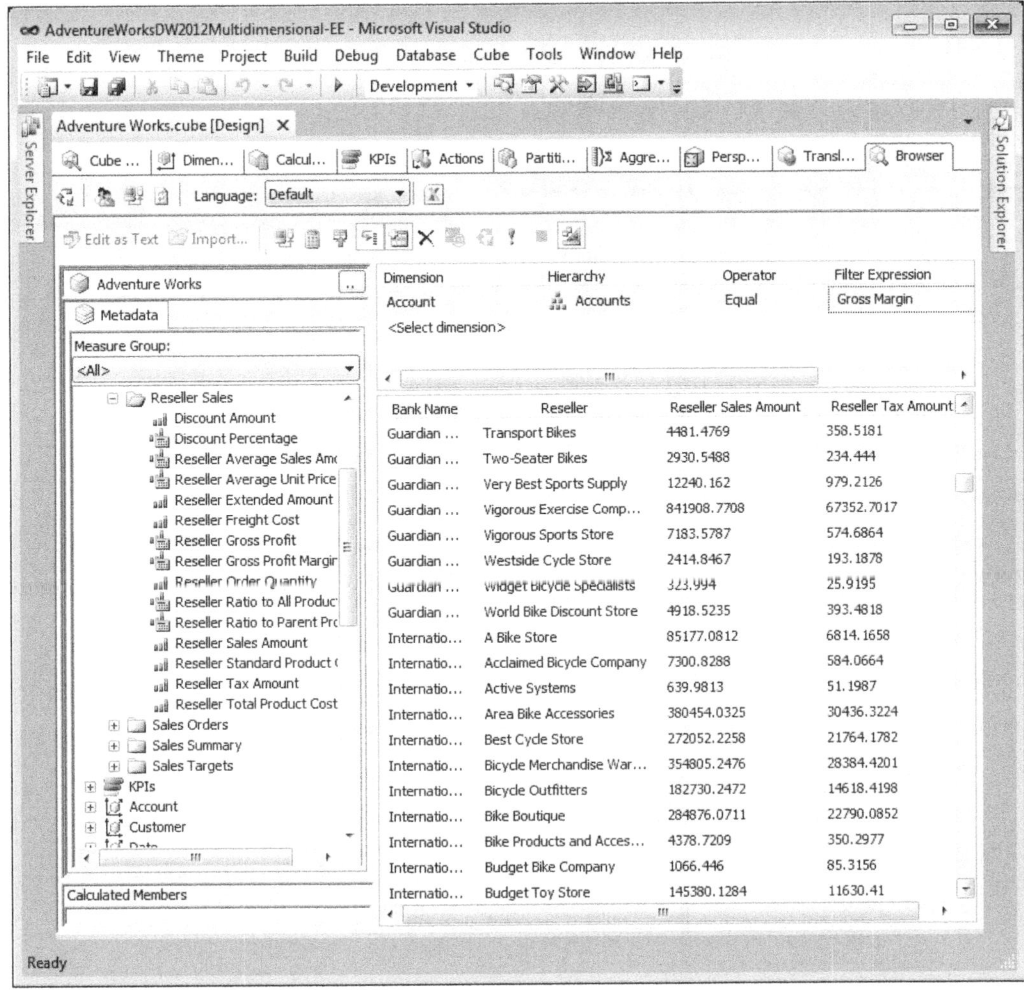

Dimension Usage Display

Cube Structure | Dimension Usage | Calculations | KPIs | Actions | Partitions | Aggregations | Perspectives | Translations | Browser

Dimensions	Measure Groups: Internet Sales	Internet Orders	Internet Customers	Sales Reasons	Reseller S
Date	Date	Date	Date		Date
Date (Ship Date)	Date	Date	Date		Date
Date (Delivery Date)	Date	Date	Date		Date
Customer	Customer	Customer	Customer		

Browsing Multidimensional Cube in Management Explorer

In Object Explorer we can connect to Analysis Server and browse the available multidimensional cubes.

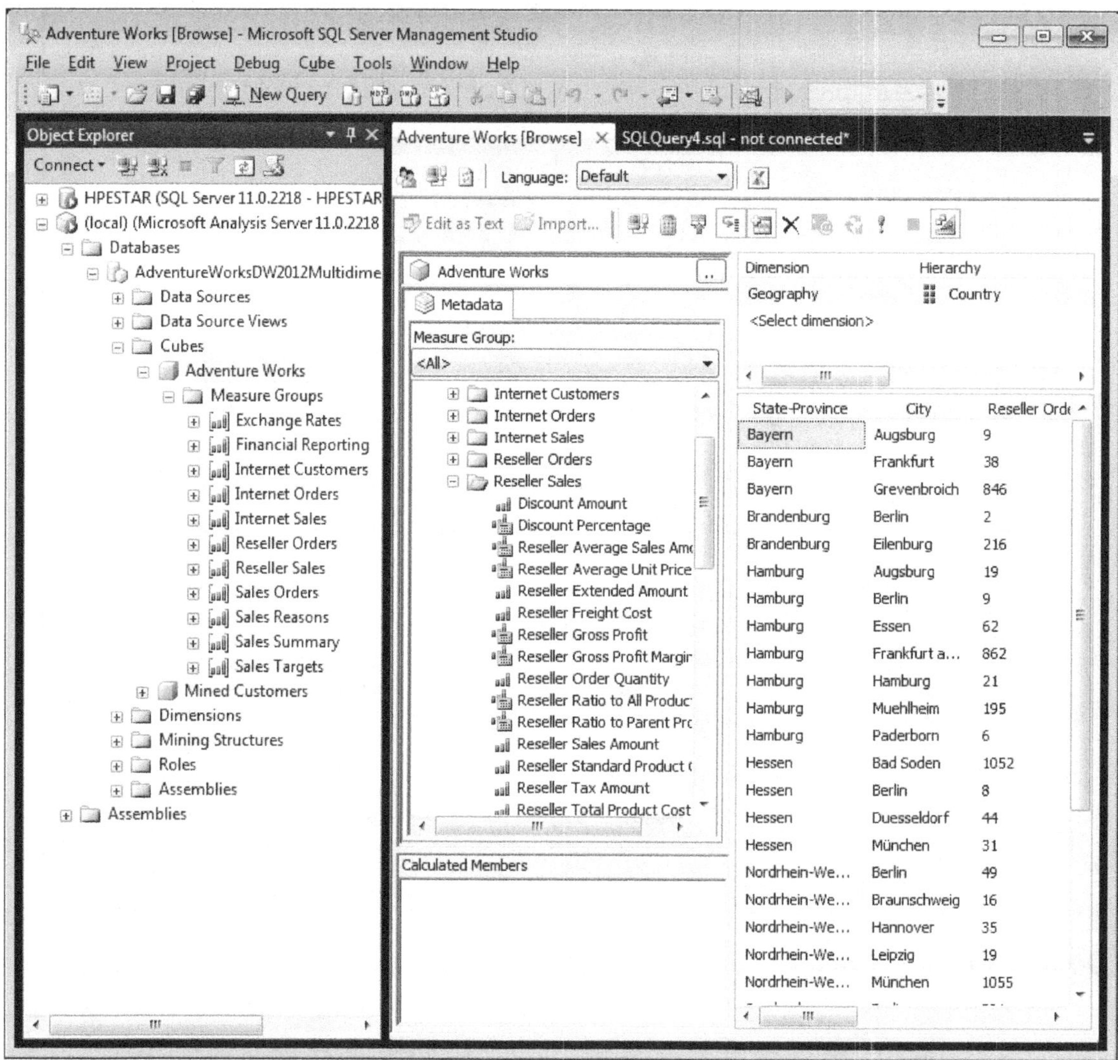

```
USE AdventureWorksDW2012;
-- Searching data warehouse database metadata for table objects
SELECT  CONCAT(schema_name(O.schema_id),'.', O.NAME) AS ObjectName,
        O.TYPE AS ObjectType,     C.NAME AS ColumnName
FROM sys.objects O INNER JOIN sys.columns C ON O.OBJECT_ID = C.OBJECT_ID
WHERE  O.type='U' AND O.NAME LIKE '%sales%' AND C.NAME LIKE '%price%'
ORDER BY ObjectName, ColumnName;   -- Partial results.
-- dbo.FactInternetSales    U         UnitPrice
```

Excel PivotTable Report Using AS Cube Datasource

Excel can use as datasource SQL Server database and Analysis Services database(bottom image). Actually PivotTable is a very good match for browsing multidimensional cubes since the underlying concepts are very similar: summary data tabulations by dimensions.

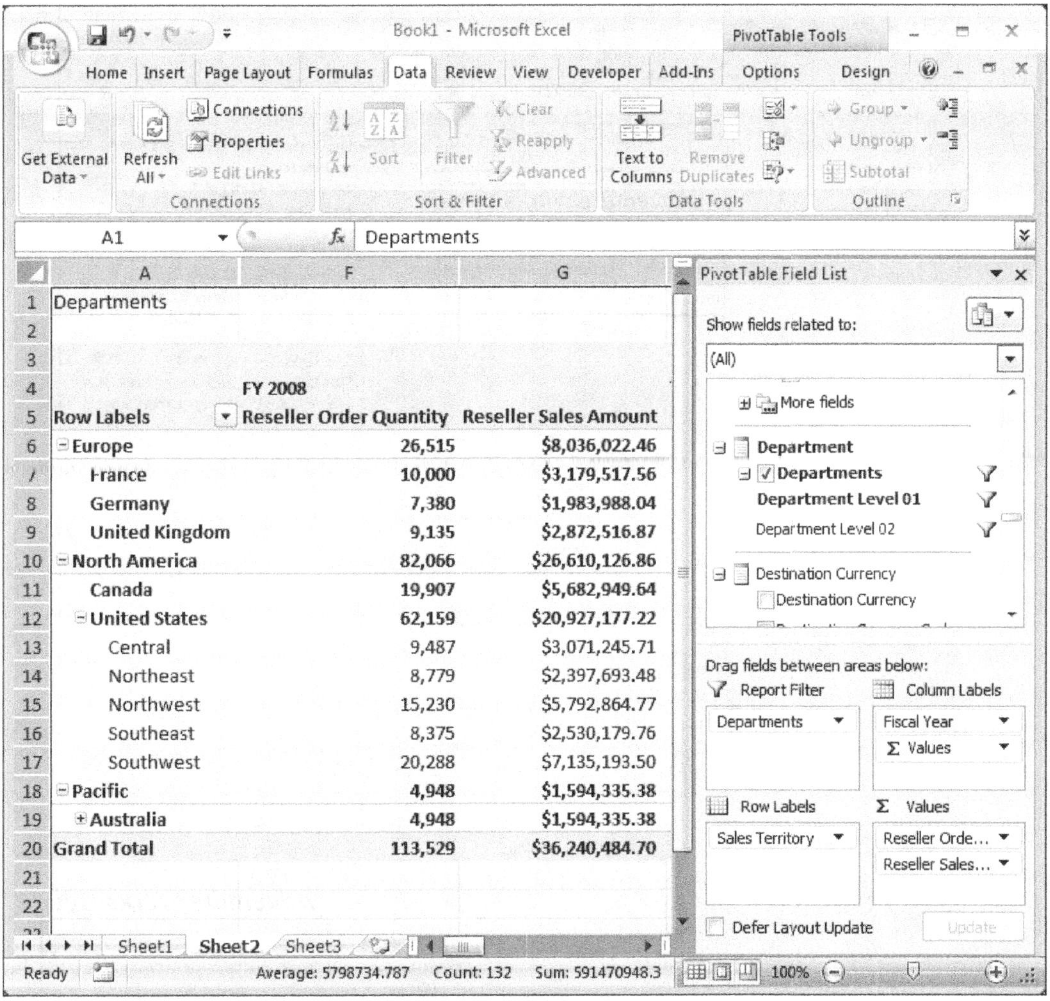

Departments		
	FY 2008	
Row Labels	Reseller Order Quantity	Reseller Sales Amount
Europe	26,515	$8,036,022.46
France	10,000	$3,179,517.56
Germany	7,380	$1,983,988.04
United Kingdom	9,135	$2,872,516.87
North America	82,066	$26,610,126.86
Canada	19,907	$5,682,949.64
United States	62,159	$20,927,177.22
Central	9,487	$3,071,245.71
Northeast	8,779	$2,397,693.48
Northwest	15,230	$5,792,864.77
Southeast	8,375	$2,530,179.76
Southwest	20,288	$7,135,193.50
Pacific	4,948	$1,594,335.38
Australia	4,948	$1,594,335.38
Grand Total	113,529	$36,240,484.70

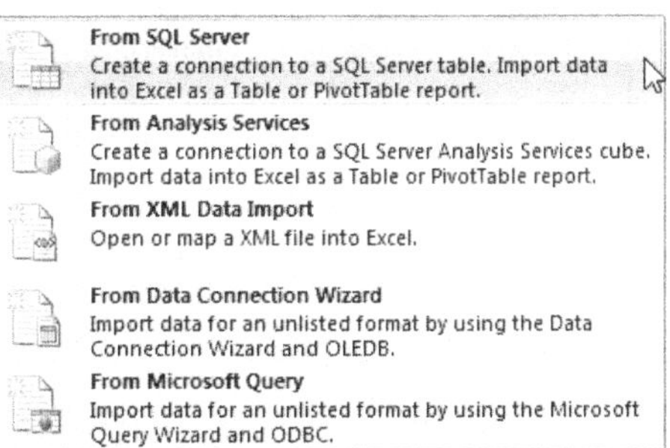
From SQL Server
Create a connection to a SQL Server table. Import data into Excel as a Table or PivotTable report.
From Analysis Services
Create a connection to a SQL Server Analysis Services cube. Import data into Excel as a Table or PivotTable report.
From XML Data Import
Open or map a XML file into Excel.
From Data Connection Wizard
Import data for an unlisted format by using the Data Connection Wizard and OLEDB.
From Microsoft Query
Import data for an unlisted format by using the Microsoft Query Wizard and ODBC.

Sales Reason Comparison Report Based on AS Cube

The Sales Reason Comparison report (converted to 2012) is based on the multidimensional AdventureWorksAS AS cube. Design mode and report segment in preview mode.

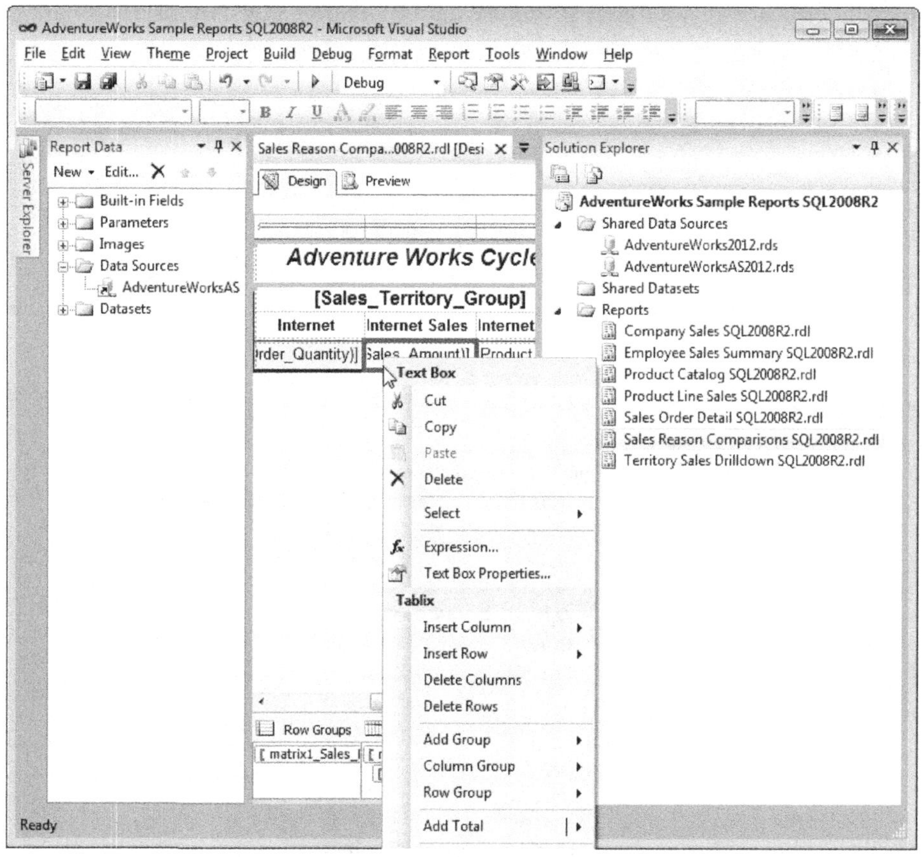

1 of 1 100% Find | Next

Adventure Works Cyc

Sales Reason	Europe			North America		
	Internet Orders	Internet Sales Amount	Internet Total Product Cost	Internet Orders	Internet Sales Amount	Interr Prod
Manufacturer	$352	$1,206,594	$733,050	$803	$2,765,552	$
On Promotion	$1,118	$2,009,804	$1,182,740	$1,298	$2,217,191	$
Other	$111	$65,666	$39,932	$109	$62,743	
Price	$2,275	$3,586,028	$2,120,140	$2,630	$4,158,322	$
Quality	$316	$1,130,733	$686,129	$718	$2,569,198	$
Review	$226	$436,477	$250,168	$319	$578,245	

SSIS: Enterprise Level Data Integration

SSIS is an enterprise level data integration and data transformation software tool. Transmit (clean, transformed) data from different data sources to the database and vice versa. The Data Flow editor in SSDT for an SSIS sample project.

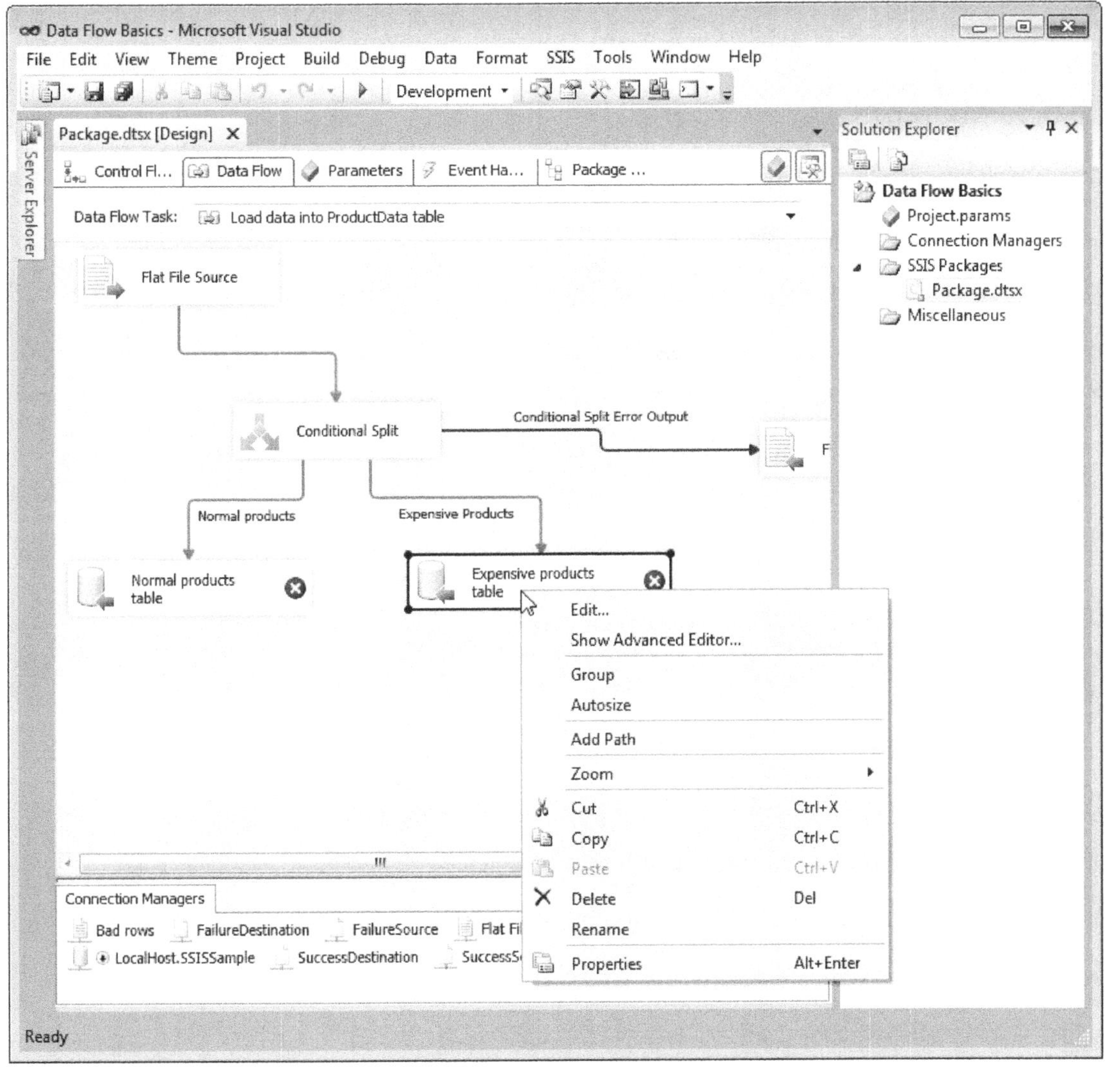

Full-Text Index & Full-Text Search - On-Premises SS

Full-Text Search (not supported in Azure SQL) in SQL Server 2012 allows users and application programs, such as C#, to execute Full-Text Search queries against text-based data in SQL Server 2012 tables. Prior to running full-text search queries on a table, full-text catalog and full-text indexes on table text column(s) must be created.

```
USE AdventureWorks2012;
SELECT * INTO dbo.JobCandidate FROM HumanResources.JobCandidate; ; -- (13 row(s) affected)
GO
CREATE UNIQUE INDEX idxHRJC ON JobCandidate(JobCandidateID);
CREATE FULLTEXT CATALOG HRFullText AS DEFAULT;
CREATE FULLTEXT INDEX ON JobCandidate(Resume) KEY INDEX idxHRJC WITH STOPLIST = SYSTEM;
GO
```

```
SELECT JobCandidateID FROM JobCandidate WHERE CONTAINS(Resume, ' "production line" ');      -- 2
```

```
SELECT JobCandidateID FROM JobCandidate WHERE CONTAINS(Resume, ' "C#" ');      -- 3
```

```
SELECT JobCandidateID FROM JobCandidate WHERE CONTAINS (Resume, ' "machin*" ' );      -- 1, 7
```

```
SELECT * FROM CONTAINSTABLE(JobCandidate, Resume, 'ISABOUT ("mach*",
     tool WEIGHT(0.9), automatic WEIGHT(0.1)   ) ' );
```

KEY	RANK
1	51
7	22

```
SELECT jc.JobCandidateID, x.* FROM JobCandidate jc
          INNER JOIN  CONTAINSTABLE(JobCandidate, Resume, 'ISABOUT ("mach*",
                    tool WEIGHT(0.9), automatic WEIGHT(0.1)  ) ' ) x  ON x.[KEY] = jc.JobCandidateID;
```

JobCandidateID	KEY	RANK
1	1	51
7	7	22

```
SELECT JobCandidateID FROM JobCandidate WHERE CONTAINS(Resume, '(ingénierie NEAR expérimenté)');  -- 7
```

```
SELECT JobCandidateID FROM JobCandidate WHERE CONTAINS(Resume, '(visual and basic)');  -- 3
```

```
SELECT JobCandidateID FROM JobCandidate WHERE CONTAINS(Resume, '(visual or basic)'); -- 2, 3
```

```
SELECT JobCandidateID FROM JobCandidate WHERE CONTAINS (Resume,'FORMSOF(INFLECTIONAL,"computer")'); -- 1
GO
```

```
DROP TABLE dbo.JobCandidate;
DROP FULLTEXT CATALOG HRFullText;
GO
```

CHAPTER 19: Ensuring Data Integrity in the Enterprise

CHAPTER 20: Performance Optimization Techniques

Optimization Basics

Optimization revolves around techniques for the reduction of the resource requirements to carry out an operation such as a SELECT query. There are two ways to do optimization:

- Engineering the query / script the optimal way
- Creating indexes on the tables

In both instances the usual objective is "reads" (logical 8K page reads) reduction. While the final objective is the "duration" reduction, that measure involves blocking as well so it is not as reliable as the "reads" measure. Using the first software engineering technique, we aim to eliminate unneeded operations or find a replacement which is less resource intensive. The second indexing technique is purely "reads" reduction in focus, we are not changing the query or the script. T-SQL has 2 statistics commands for taking basic performance measures. For even tests, we don't want to use cache memory (fast), but only disk (slow). A "cold" execute of a query may take 8 seconds, while the next (using cache) 1 second only.

```
USE AdventureWorks2012;

SET STATISTICS IO ON; SET STATISTICS TIME ON;
        EXEC uspGetBillOfMaterials 801, '2008-01-05';
SET STATISTICS TIME OFF; SET STATISTICS IO OFF;  -- Messages
```

```
DBCC execution completed. If DBCC printed error messages, contact your system administrator.
SQL Server parse and compile time:
  CPU time = 0 ms, elapsed time = 0 ms.

 SQL Server Execution Times:
  CPU time = 0 ms,  elapsed time = 0 ms.
Table 'Product'. Scan count 0, logical reads 178, physical reads 3, read-ahead reads 0, lob logical reads 0, lob physical reads 0, lob read-ahead reads 0.
Table 'BillOfMaterials'. Scan count 90, logical reads 181, physical reads 4, read-ahead reads 0, lob logical reads 0, lob physical reads 0, lob read-ahead reads 0.
Table 'Worktable'. Scan count 2, logical reads 510, physical reads 0, read-ahead reads 0, lob logical reads 0, lob physical reads 0, lob read-ahead reads 0.

 SQL Server Execution Times:
  CPU time = 16 ms,  elapsed time = 6 ms.

 SQL Server Execution Times:
  CPU time = 16 ms,  elapsed time = 6 ms.
```

No Disk IO Needed When All Pages for a Query Are in Buffer Cache

When we execute a query shortly after the previous execution, most pages may still be on cache memory, thus reduction in the need for (slow) disk io. SQL Server 2012 feature. Azure SQL is a more complex environment, it may or may not work the same way.

```
USE AdventureWorks2012;
SET STATISTICS IO ON;
SET STATISTICS TIME ON;
        EXEC uspGetBillOfMaterials 801, '2008-01-05';
SET STATISTICS TIME OFF;  SET STATISTICS IO OFF;
GO -- Messages
```

```
SQL Server parse and compile time:
   CPU time = 0 ms, elapsed time = 0 ms.

 SQL Server Execution Times:
   CPU time = 0 ms,  elapsed time = 0 ms.
Table 'Product'. Scan count 0, logical reads 178, physical reads 0, read-ahead reads 0, lob logical reads 0, lob physical reads 0, lob read-ahead reads 0.
Table 'BillOfMaterials'. Scan count 90, logical reads 181, physical reads 0, read-ahead reads 0, lob logical reads 0, lob physical reads 0, lob read-ahead reads 0.
Table 'Worktable'. Scan count 2, logical reads 510, physical reads 0, read-ahead reads 0, lob logical reads 0, lob physical reads 0, lob read-ahead reads 0.

 SQL Server Execution Times:
   CPU time = 0 ms,  elapsed time = 2 ms.

 SQL Server Execution Times:
   CPU time = 0 ms,  elapsed time = 2 ms.
```

We can see that physical reads have been eliminated, hence the faster execution. Note, however, timing will vary due to server activities. Therefore, to obtain good measurements we should average over multiple executions, for example 3, 11 or 31. When we monitor a similar execution sequence in SQL Server Profiler, we can see that the logical reads (Reads) were the same but the execution was faster (2 milliseconds) the second time due to the lack of disk io (physical reads). Note: STATISTICS IO and Profiler are 2 different piece of software, hence the difference in figures.

CPU	Reads	Writes	Duration
0	1096	0	7
0	1096	0	2

Optimizing a Query by Reengineering

Less fancy way of saying is rewriting the query. Consider an INNER JOIN query with a view which may look simple until we look at the view underlying code. The database engine has to expand the view definition "on the fly" and develop a plan for the more complex query.

```
USE [AdventureWorks2012]
GO
```

```
SET STATISTICS IO ON;
SET STATISTICS TIME ON;
SELECT  LTRIM(CONCAT(ISNULL(Title,''),SPACE(1), FullName))          AS SalesPerson,
        JobTitle, SalesTerritory, FORMAT([2008],'c0','en-US')       AS [2008]
FROM [Sales].[vSalesPersonSalesByFiscalYears] VSP
  INNER JOIN Person.Person P
    ON CONCAT(FirstName, ' ', MiddleName, ' ', LastName) = VSP.FullName
ORDER BY [2008] DESC;
SET STATISTICS TIME OFF;  SET STATISTICS IO OFF;
```

SalesPerson	JobTitle	SalesTerritory	2008
Linda C Mitchell	Sales Representative	Southwest	$4,251,369
Jae B Pak	Sales Representative	United Kingdom	$4,116,871
Michael G Blythe	Sales Representative	Northeast	$3,763,178
Jillian Carson	Sales Representative	Central	$3,189,418
Ranjit R Varkey Chudukatil	Sales Representative	France	$3,121,616
José Edvaldo Saraiva	Sales Representative	Canada	$2,604,541
Shu K Ito	Sales Representative	Southwest	$2,458,536
Tsvi Michael Reiter	Sales Representative	Southeast	$2,315,186
Rachel B Valdez	Sales Representative	Germany	$1,827,067
Mr. Tete A Mensa-Annan	Sales Representative	Northwest	$1,576,562
David R Campbell	Sales Representative	Northwest	$1,573,013
Garrett R Vargas	Sales Representative	Canada	$1,453,719
Lynn N Tsoflias	Sales Representative	Australia	$1,421,811
Pamela O Ansman-Wolfe	Sales Representative	Northwest	$1,352,577

```
DBCC execution completed. If DBCC printed error messages, contact your system administrator.

(14 row(s) affected)
Table 'Worktable'. Scan count 0, logical reads 0, physical reads 0, read-ahead reads 0, lob logical reads 0, lob physical reads 0, lob read-ahead reads 0.
Table 'SalesOrderHeader'. Scan count 5, logical reads 865, physical reads 2, read-ahead reads 784, lob logical reads 0, lob physical reads 0, lob read-ahead reads 0.
Table 'Employee'. Scan count 0, logical reads 28, physical reads 1, read-ahead reads 0, lob logical reads 0, lob physical reads 0, lob read-ahead reads 0.
Table 'Person'. Scan count 5, logical reads 4240, physical reads 2, read-ahead reads 3817, lob logical reads 0, lob physical reads 0, lob read-ahead reads 0.
Table 'SalesTerritory'. Scan count 0, logical reads 28, physical reads 1, read-ahead reads 0, lob logical reads 0, lob physical reads 0, lob read-ahead reads 0.
Table 'SalesPerson'. Scan count 0, logical reads 34, physical reads 1, read-ahead reads 0, lob logical reads 0, lob physical reads 0, lob read-ahead reads 0.
Table 'Worktable'. Scan count 0, logical reads 0, physical reads 0, read-ahead reads 0, lob logical reads 0, lob physical reads 0, lob read-ahead reads 0.

 SQL Server Execution Times:
   CPU time = 172 ms,  elapsed time = 1162 ms.
```

JOIN on INT Columns Faster Than on nvarchar Strings

Our suspicion is that JOINing on nvarchar fields may be improved if we replace it with JOIN on INT columns (4 bytes). Actually, we are in luck, it is just an easy rewrite of the query.

```
USE [AdventureWorks2012]
GO
```

```
SET STATISTICS IO ON;
SET STATISTICS TIME ON;
SELECT LTRIM(CONCAT(ISNULL(Title,''),SPACE(1), FullName))            AS SalesPerson,
        JobTitle, SalesTerritory, FORMAT([2008],'c0','en-US')        AS [2008]
FROM [Sales].[vSalesPersonSalesByFiscalYears] VSP
 INNER JOIN Person.Person P
   ON P.BusinessEntityID = VSP.SalesPersonID ORDER BY [2008] DESC;
SET STATISTICS TIME OFF; SET STATISTICS IO OFF;
GO
```

```
DBCC execution completed. If DBCC printed error messages, contact your system administrator.

(14 row(s) affected)
Table 'Person'. Scan count 0, logical reads 90, physical reads 2, read-ahead reads 0, lob logical reads 0, lob physical reads 0, lob read-ahead reads 0.
Table 'SalesOrderHeader'. Scan count 14, logical reads 12333, physical reads 9, read-ahead reads 352, lob logical reads 0, lob physical reads 0, lob read-ahead reads 0.
Table 'Employee'. Scan count 0, logical reads 28, physical reads 2, read-ahead reads 0, lob logical reads 0, lob physical reads 0, lob read-ahead reads 0.
Table 'SalesTerritory'. Scan count 0, logical reads 28, physical reads 1, read-ahead reads 0, lob logical reads 0, lob physical reads 0, lob read-ahead reads 0.
Table 'SalesPerson'. Scan count 1, logical reads 2, physical reads 1, read-ahead reads 0, lob logical reads 0, lob physical reads 0, lob read-ahead reads 0.

 SQL Server Execution Times:
   CPU time = 16 ms,  elapsed time = 68 ms.
```

When we compare the statistics we observe the elimination of 2 worktables and we reduced the "reads" on the Person table by the more efficient JOIN. The low CPU in the Profiler comparison screenshot indicative of the simpler JOIN. Even though the total "reads" are higher, the indexed INT JOIN proves to be quite advantageous over varchar JOIN as reflected in the lower CPU figure. SQL Profiler tracing is an on-premises SQL Server 2012 feature.

CPU	Reads	Writes	Duration
0	0	0	0
236	5314	0	1144
0	0	0	0
78	14194	0	302

Examining the Actual Execution Plan

There are two execution plan which can be turned by clicking on the corresponding icons: estimated and actual. The execution plan can be helpful with missing indexes and improvement considerations. Understanding a complex execution plan requires extensive studying and experience.

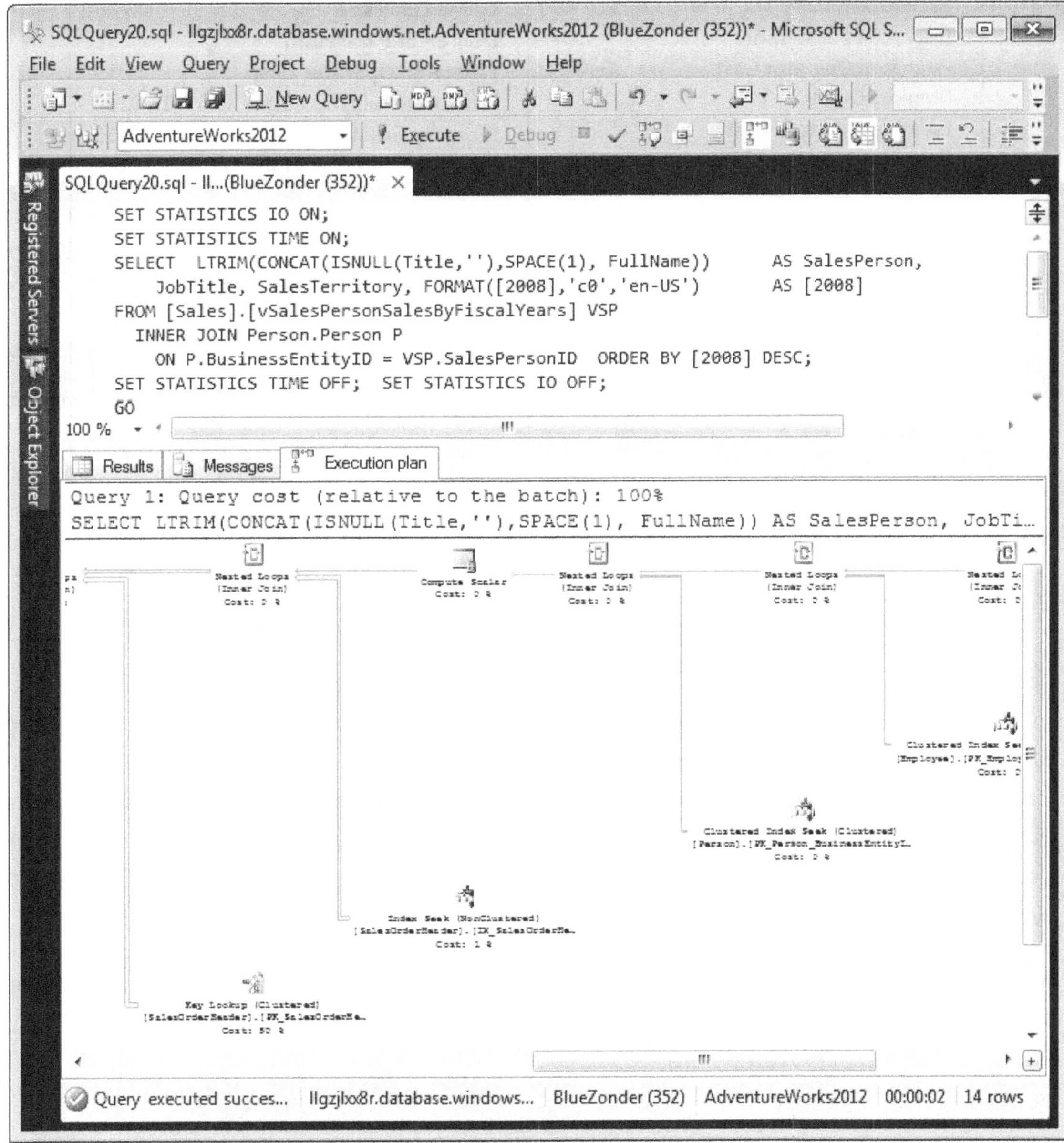

Comparing Execution Plan Cost Summary Pop-ups

When hovering with the mouse over the SELECT on the left side of the execution plan, a cost summary panel pops up.

SELECT		SELECT	
Cached plan size	120 KB	Cached plan size	96 KB
Degree of Parallelism	4	Degree of Parallelism	1
Estimated Operator Cost	0 (0%)	Estimated Operator Cost	0 (0%)
Memory Grant	1018816	Estimated Subtree Cost	1.60204
Estimated Subtree Cost	15132.9	Memory Grant	7352
Estimated Number of Rows	2608890	Estimated Number of Rows	1306.27

Statement

```
SELECT LTRIM(CONCAT(ISNULL
(Title,''),SPACE(1), FullName)) AS
SalesPerson,
JobTitle, SalesTerritory, FORMAT
([2008],'c0','en-US') AS [2008]
FROM [Sales].
[vSalesPersonSalesByFiscalYears] VSP
  INNER JOIN Person.Person P
    ON CONCAT(FirstName, ' ',
MiddleName, ' ', LastName) =
VSP.FullName
ORDER BY [2008] DESC;
```

Statement

```
SELECT LTRIM(CONCAT(ISNULL
(Title,''),SPACE(1), FullName)) AS
SalesPerson,
JobTitle, SalesTerritory, FORMAT
([2008],'c0','en-US') AS [2008]
FROM [Sales].
[vSalesPersonSalesByFiscalYears] VSP
  INNER JOIN Person.Person P
    ON P.BusinessEntityID =
VSP.SalesPersonID
ORDER BY [2008] DESC;
```

Side by side comparison of the cost panels shows dramatic differences. Cost of 15,132 versus 1.6 are simply shocking. The example powerfully illustrates the challenges in query optimization whereby relatively simple rewrite may result in huge performance improvement. We cannot say much about the optimization state of a query just by looking at cost. Only when we compare it to a different version of the query we can say if worsened, improved or much improved. We can also notice the huge difference in rows: 2.6 million vs. 1,300. Memory requirement for the nvarchar JOIN is over a million grants, while only 7 thousands for the INT JOIN.

Poorly written query not only slow in execution but very resource intensive as well, therefore it slows down other queries executing simultaneously. Hence the need to optimize queries especially frequently executed ones.

An extreme bad query can bring down the mightiest server to its "knees". We can see why just by looking at this very simple example with bad and good INNER JOINs.

Optimizing with Multi Statements Query Using Temporary Tables

Assume that the fast INT JOIN is not available. Another technique: instead of a single statement query multi statements since we have more control over the execution plan. In the current example we are forcing the optimizer to evaluate the view query first and store the results into a temporary table. Note: messages shows the long (real) name of #VSP temporary table, personalized to this connection.

```
SET STATISTICS IO ON;
SET STATISTICS TIME ON;
```

```
CREATE TABLE #VSP(SalesPersonID int NULL, FullName nvarchar(152) NULL,
        JobTitle nvarchar(50) NOT NULL, SalesTerritory nvarchar(50) NOT NULL,
        [2006] money NULL,     [2007] money NULL,     [2008] money NULL );
INSERT #VSP SELECT  *  FROM Sales.vSalesPersonSalesByFiscalYears;
```

```
SELECT  LTRIM(CONCAT(ISNULL(Title,''),SPACE(1), FullName))            AS SalesPerson,
        JobTitle, SalesTerritory, FORMAT([2008],'c0','en-US')          AS [2008]
FROM #VSP   INNER JOIN Person.Person P
   ON CONCAT(FirstName, ' ', MiddleName, ' ', LastName) = #VSP.FullName
ORDER BY [2008] DESC;
SET STATISTICS TIME OFF;  SET STATISTICS IO OFF;
GO
DROP TABLE #VSP
```

Messages

```
DBCC execution completed. If DBCC printed error messages, contact your system administrator.
Table 'SalesOrderHeader'. Scan count 14, logical reads 12452, physical reads 9, read-ahead reads 352, lob logical reads 0, lob physical reads 0, lob read-ahead reads 0.
Table 'Person'. Scan count 0, logical reads 42, physical reads 2, read-ahead reads 0, lob logical reads 0, lob physical reads 0, lob read-ahead reads 0.
Table 'Employee'. Scan count 0, logical reads 28, physical reads 2, read-ahead reads 0, lob logical reads 0, lob physical reads 0, lob read-ahead reads 0.
Table 'SalesTerritory'. Scan count 0, logical reads 28, physical reads 1, read-ahead reads 0, lob logical reads 0, lob physical reads 0, lob read-ahead reads 0.
Table 'SalesPerson'. Scan count 1, logical reads 2, physical reads 1, read-ahead reads 0, lob logical reads 0, lob physical reads 0, lob read-ahead reads 0.

(14 row(s) affected)

(1 row(s) affected)

 SQL Server Execution Times:
   CPU time = 94 ms,  elapsed time = 362 ms.
SQL Server parse and compile time:
   CPU time = 0 ms, elapsed time = 70 ms.
SQL Server parse and compile time:
   CPU time = 0 ms, elapsed time = 236 ms.

(14 row(s) affected)
Table 'Person'. Scan count 1, logical reads 3826, physical reads 0, read-ahead reads 3817, lob logical reads 0, lob physical reads 0, lob read-ahead reads 0.
Table 'Worktable'. Scan count 1, logical reads 42166, physical reads 0, read-ahead reads 0, lob logical reads 0, lob physical reads 0, lob read-ahead reads 0.
Table '#VSP___________________________________________________________________________________000000000074'. Scan count
1, logical reads 1, physical reads 0, read-ahead reads 0, lob logical reads 0, lob physical reads 0, lob read-ahead reads 0.

(1 row(s) affected)

 SQL Server Execution Times:
   CPU time = 266 ms,  elapsed time = 832 ms.
```

Obstacle: Worktable 42K "reads" Cannot Be Decreased

This course of action is not as good as the JOIN on the INT (integer) keys. Yet the combination of costs came down to 6, a reasonable figure relatively speaking. The Estimated Number of Rows are "reasonable" as well, just like the Memory Grants.

CPU	Reads	Writes	Duration
125	15849	3	1155
203	42536	123	356

SELECT INTO

Cached plan size	120 KB
Degree of Parallelism	1
Estimated Operator Cost	0 (0%)
Estimated Subtree Cost	1.6378
Estimated Number of Rows	1306.27

Statement

```
SELECT * INTO #VSP FROM [Sales].
[vSalesPersonSalesByFiscalYears];
```

SELECT

Cached plan size	32 KB
Degree of Parallelism	1
Estimated Operator Cost	0 (0%)
Memory Grant	1024
Estimated Subtree Cost	4.18429
Estimated Number of Rows	19972

Statement

```
SELECT LTRIM(CONCAT(ISNULL
(Title,''),SPACE(1), FullName)) AS
SalesPerson,
JobTitle, SalesTerritory, FORMAT
([2008],'c0','en-US') AS [2008]
FROM #VSP
  INNER JOIN Person.Person P
    ON #VSP.FullName = CONCAT
(FirstName, ' ', MiddleName, ' ',
LastName)
ORDER BY [2008] DESC;
```

The 42K "reads" is huge, in this case on an internal work table which is outside our direct control, however, indirectly we may be able to influence it. The common goal of optimization is "reads" reduction usually with indexing if the query is engineered correctly. With indexing we may be able to bring down the reads to 500 or even 50.

Optimizing with Covering Index

We can achieve miracles in query optimization with indexing but at a cost: index represents an overhead since it slows down some operations such as INSERT or DELETE and it has to be maintained. First we add a computed column to the Person.Person table, them create a "covering" index on it which includes the Title used in the SELECT clause. Note: computed column and covering index are "luxury" items which are used to support **business critical queries** only. In a covering index all columns are present in the index for the query as keys or included column. **Note: there is no "free lunch" with indexing only tradeoff**. Covering index tends to be wide and may slow down other than the target queries.

```
ALTER TABLE Person.Person ADD FullName
        AS CONCAT(FirstName, ' ', MiddleName, ' ', LastName)        PERSISTED;
GO
--Command(s) completed successfully.
```

```
CREATE INDEX idxFullName
                on Person.Person(FullName) INCLUDE (Title);
GO
-- Command(s) completed successfully.
```

```
-- DROP INDEX Person.Person.idxFullName;
```

The new query using the new column in the INNER JOIN:

```
SELECT  LTRIM(CONCAT(ISNULL(Title,''),SPACE(1), #VSP.FullName))        AS SalesPerson,
        JobTitle, SalesTerritory, FORMAT([2008],'c0','en-US')           AS [2008]
FROM #VSP
 INNER JOIN Person.Person P
  ON P.FullName = #VSP.FullName
```

The result is simply amazing: the 42K "reads" on the work table is gone. The 123 "writes" are gone as well. Duration is not a stable measure because it includes blocking as well. If there is no blocking duration is proportionally higher with higher CPU, Reads & Writes.

CPU	Reads	Writes	Duration
140	15802	1	551
16	81	0	117

Optimizing with Indexing

The general rule is that all JOIN keys and WHERE condition columns should be indexed. Since PRIMARY KEY is automatically indexed, the rule means that all FOREIGN KEYs should be indexed since that is not automatic.

```
USE AdventureWorks2012;
CREATE TABLE dbo.SOD(SalesOrderID int, SalesOrderDetailID int,
        CarrierTrackingNumber nvarchar(25), OrderQty smallint,
        ProductID int,    SpecialOfferID int, UnitPrice money,
        UnitPriceDiscount money, LineTotal numeric(38, 6),
        rowguid uniqueidentifier, ModifiedDate datetime );
GO
```

```
CREATE CLUSTERED INDEX idxSOD on SOD (SalesOrderID);
GO
```

```
INSERT INTO SOD SELECT SalesOrderID,SalesOrderDetailID,CarrierTrackingNumber
    ,OrderQty,ProductID,SpecialOfferID,UnitPrice,UnitPriceDiscount
    ,LineTotal,rowguid, ModifiedDate
FROM Sales.SalesOrderDetail;
GO -- (121317 row(s) affected)
```

```
INSERT SOD SELECT * FROM SOD;  -- increase size of table by duplicating itself
GO 5
/* Beginning execution loop
(121317 row(s) affected)
(242634 row(s) affected)
(485268 row(s) affected)
(970536 row(s) affected)
(1941072 row(s) affected)
Batch execution completed 5 times.      Time: 00:01:42   */
```

```
SELECT FORMAT(COUNT(*), '###,###,###') FROM SOD;  -- 3,882,144
```

```
SELECT  COUNT(*)  FROM Product;     -- 504
GO
```

The Larger the Table the More Benefits of Indexing

```
SET STATISTICS IO ON; SET STATISTICS TIME ON;
        SELECT * FROM SOD INNER JOIN Product P
                ON SOD.ProductID = P.ProductID      WHERE P.ProductID = 800;
SET STATISTICS TIME OFF;   SET STATISTICS IO OFF;
GO
```

```
DBCC execution completed. If DBCC printed error messages, contact your system administrator.

(15840 row(s) affected)
Table 'SOD'. Scan count 5, logical reads 54796, physical reads 0, read-ahead reads 1719, lob logical reads 0, lob physical reads 0, lob read-ahead reads 0.
Table 'Product'. Scan count 1, logical reads 14, physical reads 0, read-ahead reads 0, lob logical reads 0, lob physical reads 0, lob read-ahead reads 0.
Table 'Worktable'. Scan count 0, logical reads 0, physical reads 0, read-ahead reads 0, lob logical reads 0, lob physical reads 0, lob read-ahead reads 0.

 SQL Server Execution Times:
   CPU time = 483 ms,  elapsed time = 845 ms.
```

```
CREATE  INDEX idxPrd ON SOD(ProductID);
CREATE UNIQUE INDEX idxPrd ON Product(ProductID);
GO
```

```
SET STATISTICS IO ON;  SET STATISTICS TIME ON;
        SELECT * FROM SOD INNER JOIN Product P
                ON SOD.ProductID = P.ProductID      WHERE P.ProductID = 800;
SET STATISTICS TIME OFF;   SET STATISTICS IO OFF;
GO
```

```
DBCC execution completed. If DBCC printed error messages, contact your system administrator.
SQL Server parse and compile time:
   CPU time = 0 ms, elapsed time = 2 ms.

(15840 row(s) affected)
Table 'SOD'. Scan count 1, logical reads 210, physical reads 0, read-ahead reads 206, lob logical reads 0, lob physical reads 0, lob read-ahead reads 0.
Table 'Product'. Scan count 0, logical reads 3, physical reads 0, read-ahead reads 0, lob logical reads 0, lob physical reads 0, lob read-ahead reads 0.

(1 row(s) affected)

 SQL Server Execution Times:
   CPU time = 47 ms,  elapsed time = 517 ms.
```

Clustered Index for Business Critical Query Support

Clustered index (a requirement on Azure SQL tables) is another "luxury" item in optimization since there can only be one on a table and 0 to many nonclustered indexes. In this example nonclustered index does some improvement, but not significant. Cleanup commands for the indexing example script.

```
-- DROP INDEX SOD.idxPrd; DROP INDEX Product.idxPrd;
DROP TABLE SOD; DROP TABLE Product;
```

SQL Profiler statistics on the sequence of batches we sent to the server from SSMS Query Editor.

SQL Server Profiler - [Untitled - 1 (HPESTAR)]

File Edit View Replay Tools Window Help

TextData	CPU	Reads	Writes	Duration	SPID	EventClass
USE tempdb;	0	0	0	0	53	SQL:BatchCompleted
SELECT [SalesOrderID] ,CONVE...	218	3327	672	782	53	SQL:BatchCompleted
INSERT SOD SELECT * FROM SOD; -...	796	496577	2968	832	53	SQL:BatchCompleted
INSERT SOD SELECT * FROM SOD; -...	1685	1026720	3103	1700	53	SQL:BatchCompleted
INSERT SOD SELECT * FROM SOD; -...	3354	2086787	6433	3505	53	SQL:BatchCompleted
INSERT SOD SELECT * FROM SOD; -...	6645	4207017	12832	6709	53	SQL:BatchCompleted
INSERT SOD SELECT * FROM SOD; -...	13229	8447507	25504	13339	53	SQL:BatchCompleted
/* Beginning execution loop (121...	719	55189	9	249	53	SQL:BatchCompleted
DBCC DROPCLEANBUFFERS; SET STATI...	732	57035	1	1182	53	SQL:BatchCompleted
CREATE CLUSTERED INDEX idxPrd ON ...	15398	133236	51211	13607	53	SQL:BatchCompleted
DBCC DROPCLEANBUFFERS; SET STATI...	109	225	0	497	53	SQL:BatchCompleted
-- DROP INDEX SOD.idxPrd -- DROP...	16	480	0	147	53	SQL:BatchCompleted

We can see the reads of 57,035 decreased to 225 after creating the indexes. Not only we speeded up this query but other queries as well by decreasing the load on the server. The execution plan displays **table scan** prior to index creation.

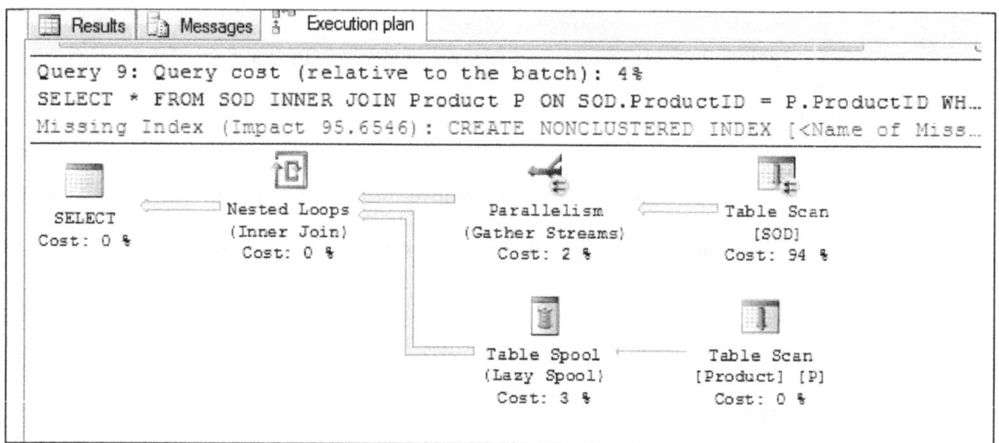

Execution Plan after Index Creation & Cost Comparison

The execution plan shows clustered index seek instead of table scan after index creation. Generally our aim with indexing is to replace table scan or index scan with index seek.

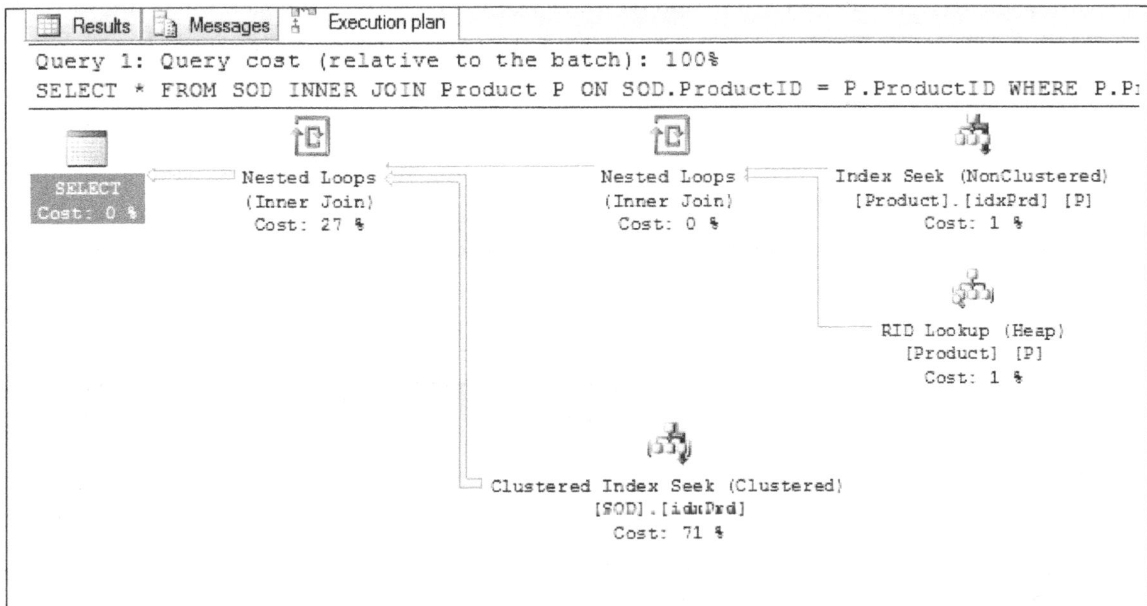

Cost comparison before and after index create reflects a very significant improvement in cost, roughly 200 fold.

SELECT (before index creation)

Cached plan size	56 KB
Degree of Parallelism	4
Estimated Operator Cost	0 (0%)
Estimated Subtree Cost	45.4362
Memory Grant	72
Estimated Number of Rows	15513.1

Statement

```
SELECT * FROM SOD INNER JOIN
Product P
        ON SOD.ProductID = P.ProductID
    WHERE P.ProductID = 800;
```

SELECT (after index creation)

Cached plan size	56 KB
Degree of Parallelism	1
Estimated Operator Cost	0 (0%)
Estimated Subtree Cost	0.247049
Estimated Number of Rows	15840

Statement

```
SELECT * FROM SOD INNER JOIN Product
P
        ON SOD.ProductID = P.ProductID
    WHERE P.ProductID = 800;
```

Non-SARGable Predicates Force Index Scan

The term SARGable stands for Search ARGument ABLE. It means the WHERE clause OR join ON clause predicate written such a way that the database engine can use the index on the column. Basically means if we form an expression with the indexed column, index scan will be performed instead of index seek, in other words, index will not be used to speed up the query. The (SOD.ProductID +1 - 1) expression in the ON clause causes clustered index scan. The relative query costs are 1% (SARGable) and 99% (non-SARGable) in the batches of 2 queries, which is reflected in the execution times.

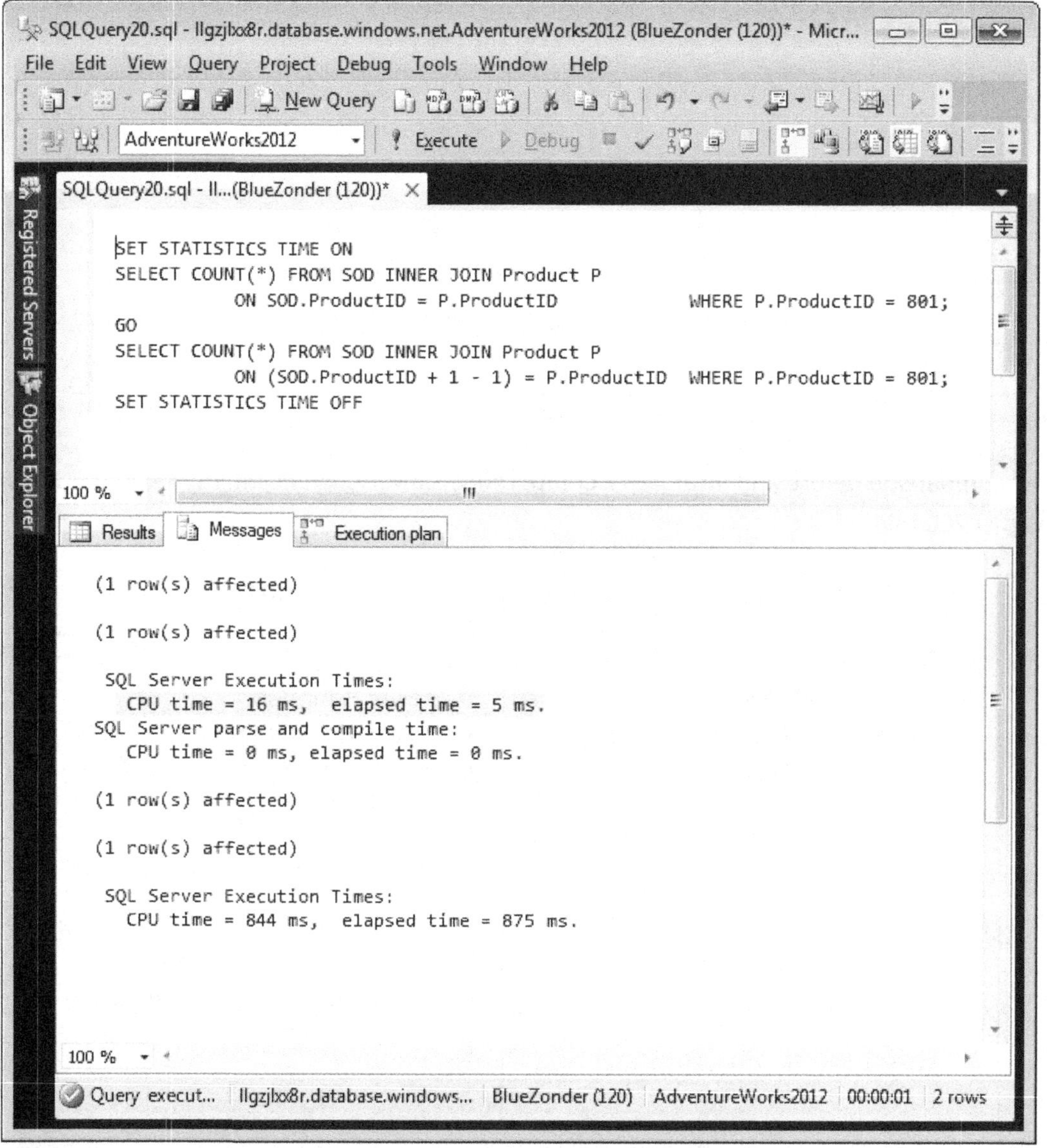

SQLQuery20.sql - llgzjbx8r.database.windows.net.AdventureWorks2012 (BlueZonder (120))* - Micr...
File Edit View Query Project Debug Tools Window Help
New Query
AdventureWorks2012
Execute Debug
SQLQuery20.sql - ll...(BlueZonder (120))*
SET STATISTICS TIME ON
SELECT COUNT(*) FROM SOD INNER JOIN Product P
ON SOD.ProductID = P.ProductID WHERE P.ProductID = 801;
GO
SELECT COUNT(*) FROM SOD INNER JOIN Product P
ON (SOD.ProductID + 1 - 1) = P.ProductID WHERE P.ProductID = 801;
SET STATISTICS TIME OFF
100 %
Results Messages Execution plan
(1 row(s) affected)
(1 row(s) affected)
SQL Server Execution Times:
CPU time = 16 ms, elapsed time = 5 ms.
SQL Server parse and compile time:
CPU time = 0 ms, elapsed time = 0 ms.
(1 row(s) affected)
(1 row(s) affected)
SQL Server Execution Times:
CPU time = 844 ms, elapsed time = 875 ms.
100 %
Query execut... llgzjbx8r.database.windows... BlueZonder (120) AdventureWorks2012 00:00:01 2 rows
Registered Servers
Object Explorer

WHERE Clause SARGable Predicate Construction

It is a challenge to remember all the time to make the predicate SARGable. Frequently, so much easier to make it non-SARGable.

```
YEAR(OrderDate) = 2016 AND MONTH(OrderDate) = 10                          -- non-SARGable
OrderDate >= '2016-10-01' AND OrderDate < DATEADD(MM,1, '2016-10-01') -- SARGable
```

```
ISNULL(Color,'Blue') = 'Blue'                    -- Non-SARGable
Color = 'Blue' or Color is NULL                  -- SARGable
```

The payoff can be great as shown by the previous SARGable & non-SARGable examples, duration in msec.

CPU	Reads	Writes	Duration
125	223	0	668
1527	51451	0	11497

Clustered Index Seek (Clustered)

Scanning a particular range of rows from a clustered index.

Physical Operation	Clustered Index Seek
Logical Operation	Clustered Index Seek
Actual Execution Mode	Row
Estimated Execution Mode	Row
Storage	RowStore
Actual Number of Rows	15840
Actual Number of Batches	0
Estimated Operator Cost	0.174279 (71%)
Estimated I/O Cost	0.156698
Estimated CPU Cost	0.017581
Estimated Subtree Cost	0.174279
Number of Executions	1
Estimated Number of Executions	1
Estimated Number of Rows	15840
Estimated Row Size	112 B
Actual Rebinds	0
Actual Rewinds	0
Ordered	True
Node ID	54

Object
[tempdb].[dbo].[SOD].[idxPrd]
Output List
[tempdb].[dbo].[SOD].SalesOrderID, [tempdb].[dbo].[SOD].SalesOrderDetailID, [tempdb].[dbo].[SOD].CarrierTrackingNumber, [tempdb].[dbo].[SOD].OrderQty, [tempdb].[dbo].[SOD].ProductID, [tempdb].[dbo].[SOD].SpecialOfferID, [tempdb].[dbo].[SOD].UnitPrice, [tempdb].[dbo].[SOD].UnitPriceDiscount, [tempdb].[dbo].[SOD].LineTotal, [tempdb].[dbo].[SOD].rowguid, [tempdb].[dbo].[SOD].ModifiedDate
Seek Predicates
Seek Keys[1]: Prefix: [tempdb].[dbo].[SOD].ProductID = Scalar Operator((800))

Clustered Index Scan (Clustered)

Scanning a clustered index, entirely or only a range.

Physical Operation	Clustered Index Scan
Logical Operation	Clustered Index Scan
Actual Execution Mode	Row
Estimated Execution Mode	Row
Actual Number of Rows	15840
Actual Number of Batches	0
Estimated I/O Cost	37.8224
Estimated Operator Cost	39.9576 (97%)
Estimated CPU Cost	2.13526
Estimated Subtree Cost	39.9576
Number of Executions	4
Estimated Number of Executions	1
Estimated Number of Rows	15840
Estimated Row Size	112 B
Actual Rebinds	0
Actual Rewinds	0
Ordered	False
Node ID	58

Predicate
([tempdb].[dbo].[SOD].[ProductID]+(1)-(1))=(800)
Object
[tempdb].[dbo].[SOD].[idxPrd]
Output List
[tempdb].[dbo].[SOD].SalesOrderID, [tempdb].[dbo].[SOD].SalesOrderDetailID, [tempdb].[dbo].[SOD].CarrierTrackingNumber, [tempdb].[dbo].[SOD].OrderQty, [tempdb].[dbo].[SOD].ProductID, [tempdb].[dbo].[SOD].SpecialOfferID, [tempdb].[dbo].[SOD].UnitPrice, [tempdb].[dbo].[SOD].UnitPriceDiscount, [tempdb].[dbo].[SOD].LineTotal, [tempdb].[dbo].[SOD].rowguid, [tempdb].[dbo].[SOD].ModifiedDate

Stored Procedure Parameter Sniffing & Prevention

When SQL Server database engine compiles a stored procedure, it may use the actual parameters supplied to prepare an execution plan. If the parameters are atypical, the plan may be slow for typical parameters. For consistent stored procedure performance parameter sniffing should be eliminated. A telltale sign of parameter sniffing when suddenly a stored procedure executes in 2 minutes, as an example, instead of the usual 10 seconds. *This is different when the first (cold from disk) execution of a stored procedure is much longer than the second & on (warm since pages in buffer memory) execution.* Parameter sniffing may show up also as 5 minutes execution in one environment (like application) and 2 seconds in another (like SSMS).

> Technet Article
> **Batch Compilation, Recompilation, and Plan Caching Issues in SQL Server 2005**
> http://technet.microsoft.com/en-us/library/cc966425.aspx

First prevention method: remap parameters to local variables and use those only.

```
USE AdventureWorks2012;
GO
CREATE PROCEDURE uspProductByColor @pcolor varchar(20)   AS BEGIN
        DECLARE @color varchar(20) = @pcolor;            -- remapping
        SET NOCOUNT ON;
        SELECT * FROM Production.Product WHERE Color = @color  ORDER BY name;    END
```

```
EXEC uspProductByColor 'Red';  -- 38 rows returned
```

Second prevention method: RECOMPILE stored procedure at each execution (for large procedure compilation time may be significant).

```
CREATE PROCEDURE uspProductByColor @pcolor varchar(20)
WITH RECOMPILE AS BEGIN  SET NOCOUNT ON;
  SELECT * FROM Production.Product WHERE Color = @pcolor    ORDER BY name;     END
```

Optimizing with MERGE

Single statement MERGE can perform better than multi statements INSERT/UPDATE/DELETE.

> Technet Article: **Optimizing MERGE Statement Performance**
> http://technet.microsoft.com/en-us/library/cc879317(v=sql.105).aspx

Stress Testing a View with Include Client Statistics Feature

Client Statistics feature can be turned by icon or right click drop-down menu option. It calculates averages for up to 10 trials. DBCC DROPCLEANBUFFERS equalizes the tests by purging thecached data pages from buffer memory. Note: server load will influence timings. Query drop-down has option to Reset Client Statistics. SQL Server 2012 feature.

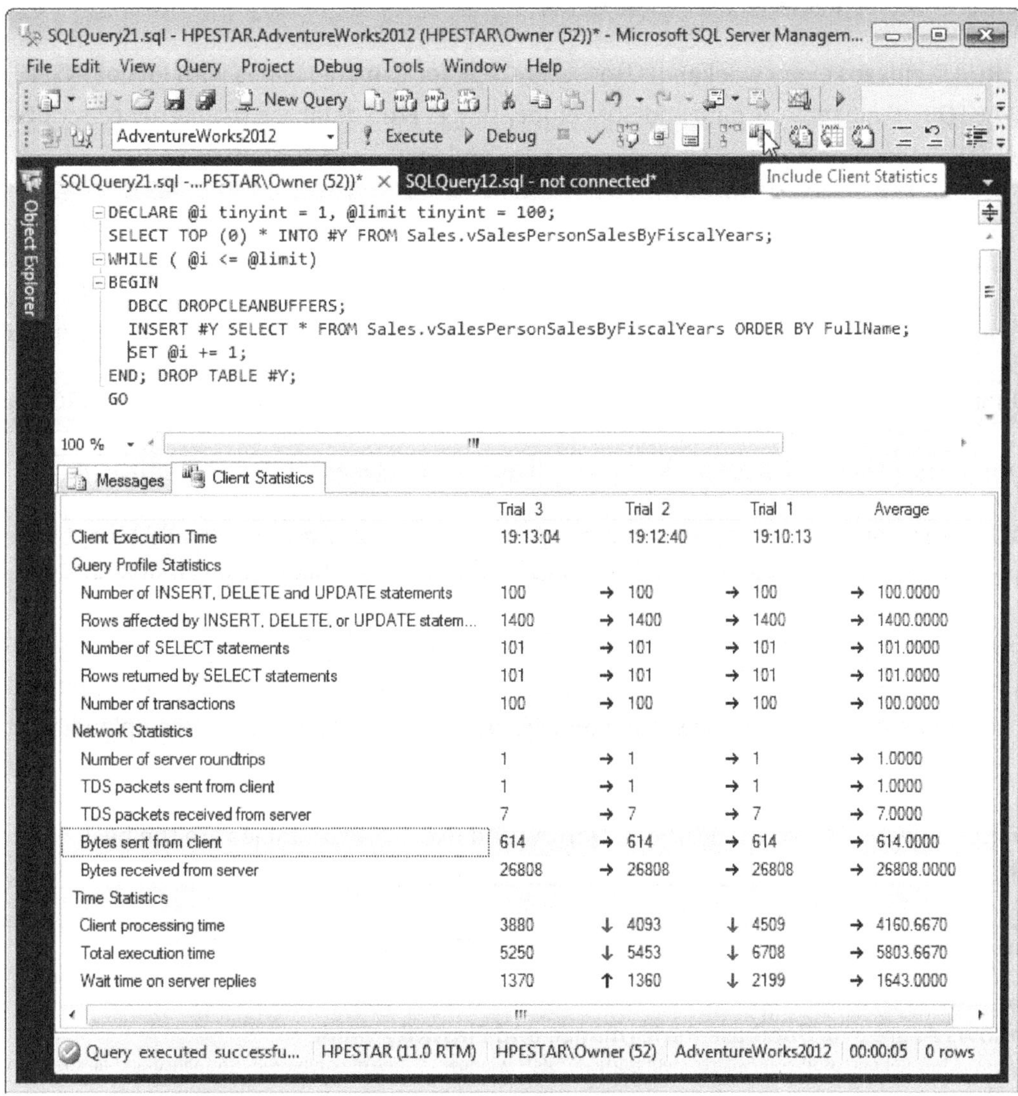

Maximum Capacity Specifications for SQL Server
http://msdn.microsoft.com/en-us/library/ms143432.aspx

8 Point Optimization Guide

Performance tuning and optimization are a huge topic. We only touch the tip of the iceberg. Nonetheless, the important elements of optimization can be summarized quite easily. It starts with prioritizing what is **business critical**, what is not. If 500 users are unhappy with a stored procedure, that is business critical. If one user is unhappy with a slow report, that is not business critical, unless that user is the CEO.

1. REBUILD indexes every weekend. Use FILLFACTOR for dynamic tables with lots of INSERTs. FILLFACTOR 70 means 70% data and 30% empty space. Free database maintenance scripts at http://ola.hallengren.com/ - SQL Server ... Index and Statistics Maintenance.

2. UPDATE STATISTICS every night. The database engine query optimizer uses the statistics to prepare efficient execution plans.

3. Eliminate missing indexes. All FOREIGN KEY & WHERE condition columns should be indexed.

4. Optimize all business critical queries. WHERE & ON clause predicates should be SARGable.

5. Examine execution plan for business critical queries to make sure they are efficient.

6. Optimize all business critical stored procedures. In a sproc all queries should be optimized and looping should be kept at an absolute minimum. Non-scalable cursors should be avoided.

7. Operational solutions for performance problems which cannot be readily resolved due to lack of resources. For example, external feed arrives 11AM every day and promptly uploaded in 1/2 hour thus slowing down the system and annoying users. Instead schedule uploading low use time like 11pm.

8. Database design should be efficient. Narrow and fixed row size tables are the best performant. Indexes also should be as narrow as possible.

Articles: **Troubleshoot and Optimize Queries with Windows Azure SQL Database**
http://social.technet.microsoft.com/wiki/contents/articles/1104.troubleshoot-and-optimize-queries-with-windows-azure-sql-database.aspx

Windows Azure SQL Database Performance and Elasticity Guide
http://social.technet.microsoft.com/wiki/contents/articles/3507.windows-azure-sql-database-performance-and-elasticity-guide.aspx

Improving Your I/O Performance
http://blogs.msdn.com/b/sqlazure/archive/2010/07/27/10043069.aspx

Improving SQL Server Performance
http://msdn.microsoft.com/en-us/library/ff647793.aspx

Object Explorer GUI REBUILD Indexes - On-premises SS 2012

The indexes can be rebuilt in SSMS Object Explorer using Graphical User Interface. **REBUILD indexes updates statistics as well.** T-SQL command syntax example:

```
ALTER INDEX ALL ON [Sales].[SalesOrderDetail] REBUILD WITH ( FILLFACTOR = 90);
```

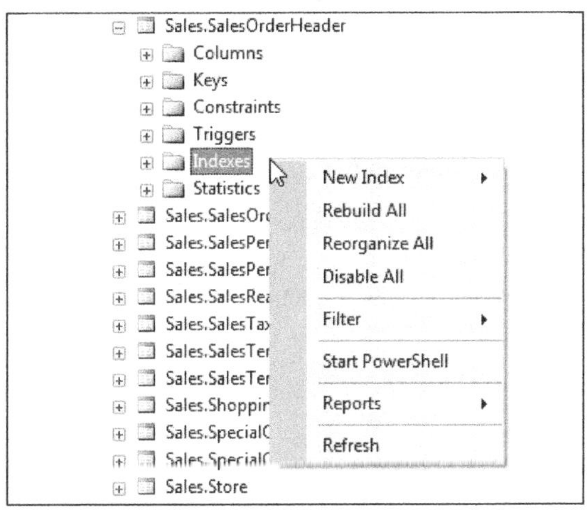

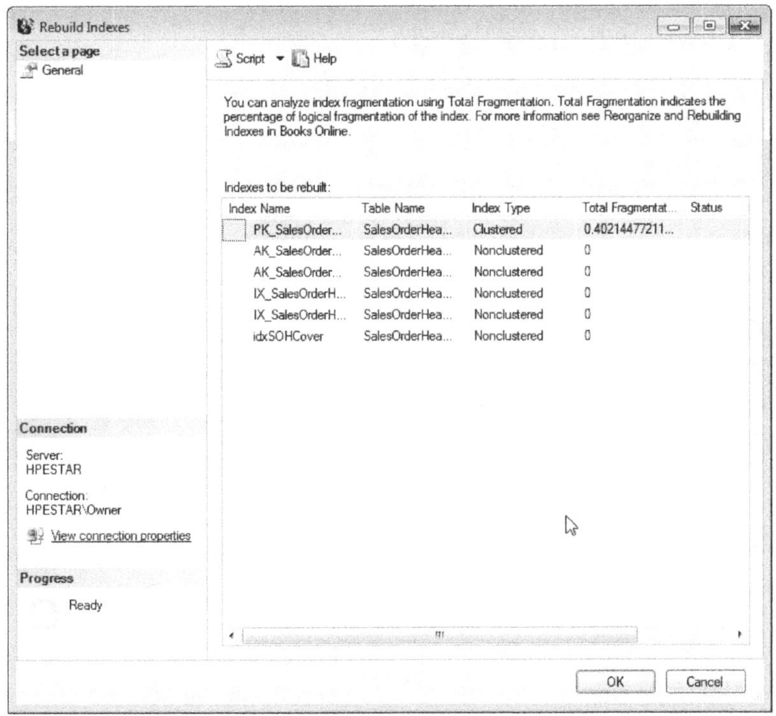

UPDATE STATISTICS on All Tables Stored Procedure

The UPDATE STATISTICS on all tables stored procedure has one parameter: the sample percent for scanning. Lower the number, faster the update. WITH FULLSCAN option does 100% sampling, it may be slow for large tables. Create & execute stored procedure script.

```
CREATE PROCEDURE sprocUpdateAllStats (@Sample int)  AS
BEGIN
DECLARE @SQL AS NVARCHAR(1024), @Table sysname, @Schema sysname;
DECLARE curAllTables CURSOR FOR
        SELECT TABLE_SCHEMA, TABLE_NAME
        FROM INFORMATION_SCHEMA.TABLES
        WHERE TABLE_TYPE='BASE TABLE'
        ORDER BY TABLE_SCHEMA, TABLE_NAME;
OPEN curAllTables;
FETCH NEXT FROM curAllTables
        INTO @Schema, @Table;

WHILE (@@FETCH_STATUS = 0)
BEGIN
 SET @SQL =     CONCAT('UPDATE STATISTICS ',
                QUOTENAME( @Schema),'.', QUOTENAME( @Table),
                ' WITH SAMPLE ', CONVERT(char(3), @sample), ' PERCENT;');
--              ' WITH FULLSCAN; ');
 PRINT @SQL;
 -- UPDATE STATISTICS [Sales].[Store] WITH SAMPLE 10 PERCENT;

 EXEC sp_executesql @SQL;

 FETCH NEXT FROM curAllTables
        INTO @Schema, @Table;
END -- while
 CLOSE curAllTables;  DEALLOCATE curAllTables;
END
GO
```

```
EXEC sprocUpdateAllStats 10;                    -- Execution time 00:00:27
```

Blocking of a Query by Another Query

SQL Server applies locks at the row, page and table level in order to maintain data integrity. If another query tries to operate on the locked part, it may get blocked. It is easy to see how blocking can degrade the performance of the server. We can simulate blocking. In connection 1 we execute and leave open a transaction. In connection 2 we execute a query which intends to operate on the locked table. The result is blocking of connection 2 query by connection 1 query.

```
-- Connection 1
BEGIN TRAN;
UPDATE HumanResources.Shift SET ModifiedDate = convert(datetime, ModifiedDate);
-- ROLLBACK TRAN;
```

```
-- Connection 2
BEGIN TRAN;
UPDATE HumanResources.Shift SET ModifiedDate = convert(datetime, ModifiedDate);
COMMIT TRAN;
```

Checking blocking by **sp_who** system procedure (exec sp_who in a 3rd connection) and **Activity Monitor** (right click on server menu). The Activity Monitor chart even shows the Head Blocker which is very helpful to trace the source of a blocking chain. A quick resolution is killing the head blocker (kill 55). Long term fix is making the blocking query efficient.

	spid	ecid	status	loginame	hostname	blk	dbname	cmd
36	52	0	runnable	HPES...	HPEST...	0	master	SELECT
37	53	0	sleeping	NT SE...	HPEST...	0	ReportServer	AWAITING COMMAND
38	54	0	sleeping	HPES...	HPEST...	0	master	AWAITING COMMAND
39	55	0	sleeping	HPES...	HPEST...	0	AdventureWorks2012	AWAITING COMMAND
40	56	0	sleeping	NT SE...	HPEST...	0	ReportServer	AWAITING COMMAND
41	57	0	suspended	HPES...	HPEST...	55	AdventureWorks2012	UPDATE

S..	U..	Login	Dat...	Tas...	Com...	Appl...	Wait Tim...	Wait...	Wait...	Blocked By	Head Blocker	Me...
51	1	HPESTA...	master			Microsoft...	0					
52	1	HPESTA...	master			Microsoft...	0					
53	1	NT SER...	ReportS...			Report S...	0					
54	1	HPESTA...	master	RUNNING	SELECT	Microsoft...	0					
55	1	HPESTA...	Adventur...			Microsoft...	0				1	
56	1	NT SER...	ReportS...			Report S...	0					
57	1	HPESTA...	Adventur...	SUSPEN...	UPDATE	Microsoft...	172568	LCK_M_U	keylock ...	55		

Activity Monitor - On-premises SS 2012

The Activity Monitor provides real time operational information in list and graphical chart formats based on operational DMV-s.

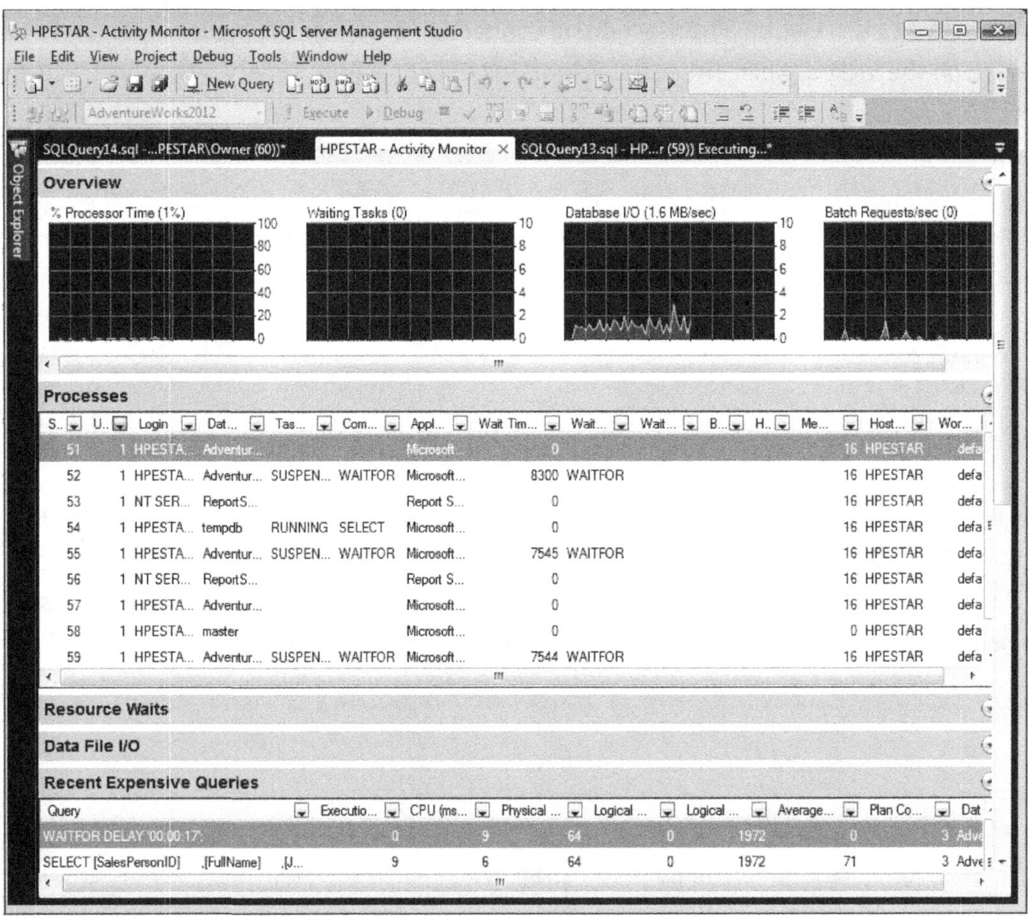

Operational Solutions for Performance Problems

Frequently real fix cannot be carried out quickly or at all for a performance issue due to software complexities and limited expert-level resources. In such a case we have to think about implementing operational solutions:

- Users complain about slow online reports. Setup reports as night jobs with automatic email distribution.
- Reports slow OLTP activities. Restore last night DB backup under new name as reporting DB. Usually, only a small fraction of reports need to be real-time.

Server & Database Standard Reports - On-premises SS 2012

The Server Standard Reports can be accessed via the right click on server drop-down menu in SSMS Object Explorer (top left). The Database Standard Reports can be accessed via the right click on database drop down menu (top right). The reports are based on Dynamic Management Views (DMV-s). They represent operational data since the last restart of the server. At the bottom, partial display of the Index Usage Statistics report.

Server Standard Reports	Database Standard Reports
Server Dashboard	Disk Usage
Configuration Changes History	Disk Usage by Top Tables
Schema Changes History	Disk Usage by Table
Scheduler Health	Disk Usage by Partition
Memory Consumption	Backup and Restore Events
Activity - All Blocking Transactions	All Transactions
Activity - All Cursors	All Blocking Transactions
Activity - Top Cursors	Top Transactions by Age
Activity - All Sessions	Top Transactions by Blocked Transactions Count
Activity - Top Sessions	Top Transactions by Locks Count
Activity - Dormant Sessions	Resource Locking Statistics by Objects
Activity - Top Connections	Object Execution Statistics
Top Transactions by Age	Database Consistency History
Top Transactions by Blocked Transactions Count	Index Usage Statistics
Top Transactions by Locks Count	Index Physical Statistics
Performance - Batch Execution Statistics	Schema Changes History
Performance - Object Execution Statistics	User Statistics
Performance - Top Queries by Average CPU Time	
Performance - Top Queries by Average IO	
Performance - Top Queries by Total CPU Time	
Performance - Top Queries by Total IO	
Service Broker Statistics	
Transaction Log Shipping Status	

⊟ HumanResources.Employee

Index Name	Index Type	# User Seeks	# User Scans	# User Updates
PK_Employee_BusinessEntityID	CLUSTERED	697	0	0

⊟ HumanResources.Shift

Index Name	Index Type	# User Seeks	# User Scans	# User Updates
PK_Shift_ShiftID	CLUSTERED	0	5	5

⊟ Person.Person

Server Dashboard - On-premises SS 2012

The Server Dashboard contains important high-level information about the server.

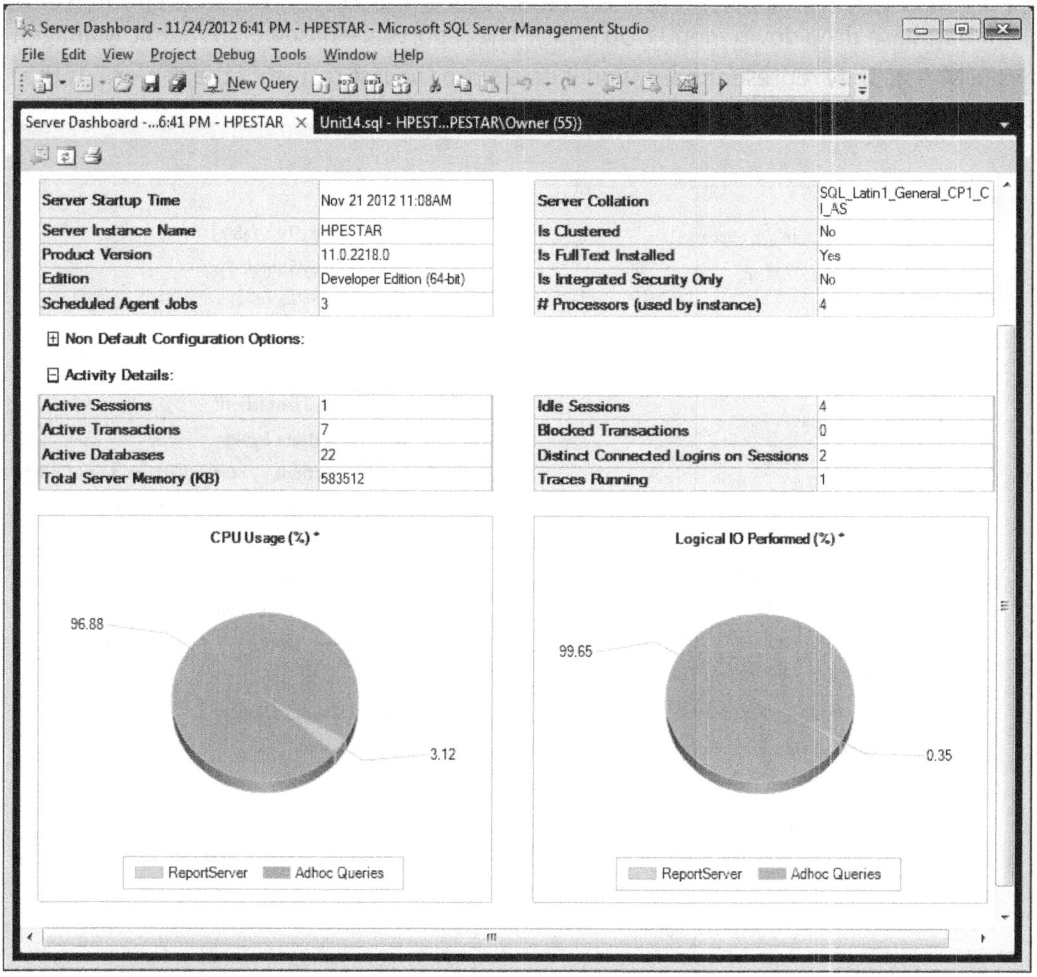

Server Dashboard - 11/24/2012 6:41 PM - HPESTAR - Microsoft SQL Server Management Studio

File Edit View Project Debug Tools Window Help

New Query

Server Dashboard -...6:41 PM - HPESTAR × Unit14.sql - HPEST...PESTAR\Owner (55))

Server Startup Time	Nov 21 2012 11:08AM	Server Collation	SQL_Latin1_General_CP1_CI_AS
Server Instance Name	HPESTAR	Is Clustered	No
Product Version	11.0.2218.0	Is FullText Installed	Yes
Edition	Developer Edition (64-bit)	Is Integrated Security Only	No
Scheduled Agent Jobs	3	# Processors (used by instance)	4

⊞ Non Default Configuration Options:

⊟ Activity Details:

Active Sessions	1	Idle Sessions	4
Active Transactions	7	Blocked Transactions	0
Active Databases	22	Distinct Connected Logins on Sessions	2
Total Server Memory (KB)	583512	Traces Running	1

CPU Usage (%) *

96.88

3.12

ReportServer Adhoc Queries

Logical IO Performed (%) *

99.65

0.35

ReportServer Adhoc Queries

Segment from Performance - Top Queries by Total CPU Time report.

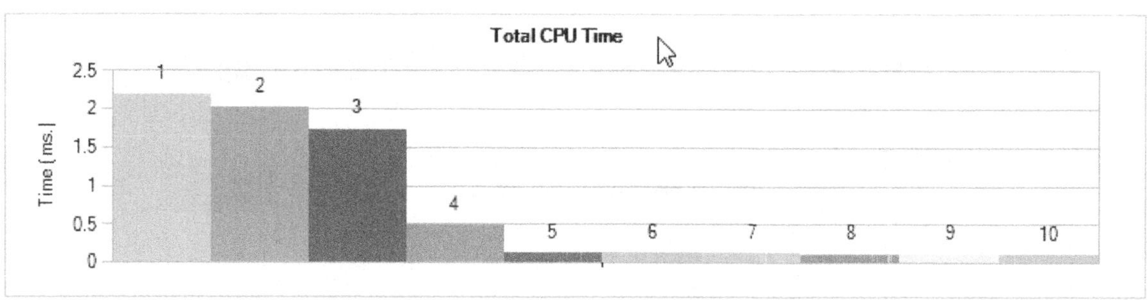

Batching Large INSERT, UPDATE & DELETE

Batch processing jobs best executed at low use time like night or weekend. Frequently, however, we may not have a choice, we have to run them during transactional activities. We can minimize conflict by breaking down a large job to small batches and providing 1 second or so wait time for other queries to execute. During that 1 second hundreds of short transactions may execute. DELETE from large tables may prove to be very slow due to restructuring of the index pages.

```
USE AdventureWorks2012;
CREATE TABLE #Product(ProductID INT, ProductName nvarchar(50),
 ProductNumber nvarchar(25), ListPrice smallmoney, Color nvarchar(15), Size nvarchar(5));
INSERT #Product SELECT ProductID, Name, ProductNumber, ListPrice, Color, Size
FROM Production.Product;  -- (504 row(s) affected)
GO
```

```
INSERT #Product SELECT * FROM #Product;  -- Double table rows at each execution
GO 12
/* ... (1032192 row(s) affected)  Batch execution completed 16 times. Execution time 00:00:20  */
```

```
SELECT FORMAT(COUNT(*),'###,###,###') FROM #Product;   -- 2,064,384
GO
```

```
CREATE CLUSTERED INDEX idxProductID  on #Product(ProductID);
GO -- Execution time 00:00:27
```

```
DECLARE @BatchSize int = 1000;
WHILE (@@ROWCOUNT > 0)   BEGIN     WAITFOR DELAY '00:00:01';
        DELETE TOP (@BatchSize) FROM #Product    WHERE ProductNumber = 'CA-5965';
END
GO   -- Execution time 00:00:07
/*1000 row(s) affected)
(1000 row(s) affected)
(1000 row(s) affected)
(1000 row(s) affected)
(96 row(s) affected)
(0 row(s) affected)  */
```

```
SELECT FORMAT(COUNT(*),'###,###,###') FROM #Product;   -- 2,060,288  -- 5 seconds
GO
DROP TABLE #Product;
```

Database Engine Tuning Advisor - On-Premises SQL Server

The Database Engine Tuning Advisor (DETA or DTA) provides indexing & statistics recommendations based on the supplied workload. A single query can be analyzed as well, right click Query drop-down menu.

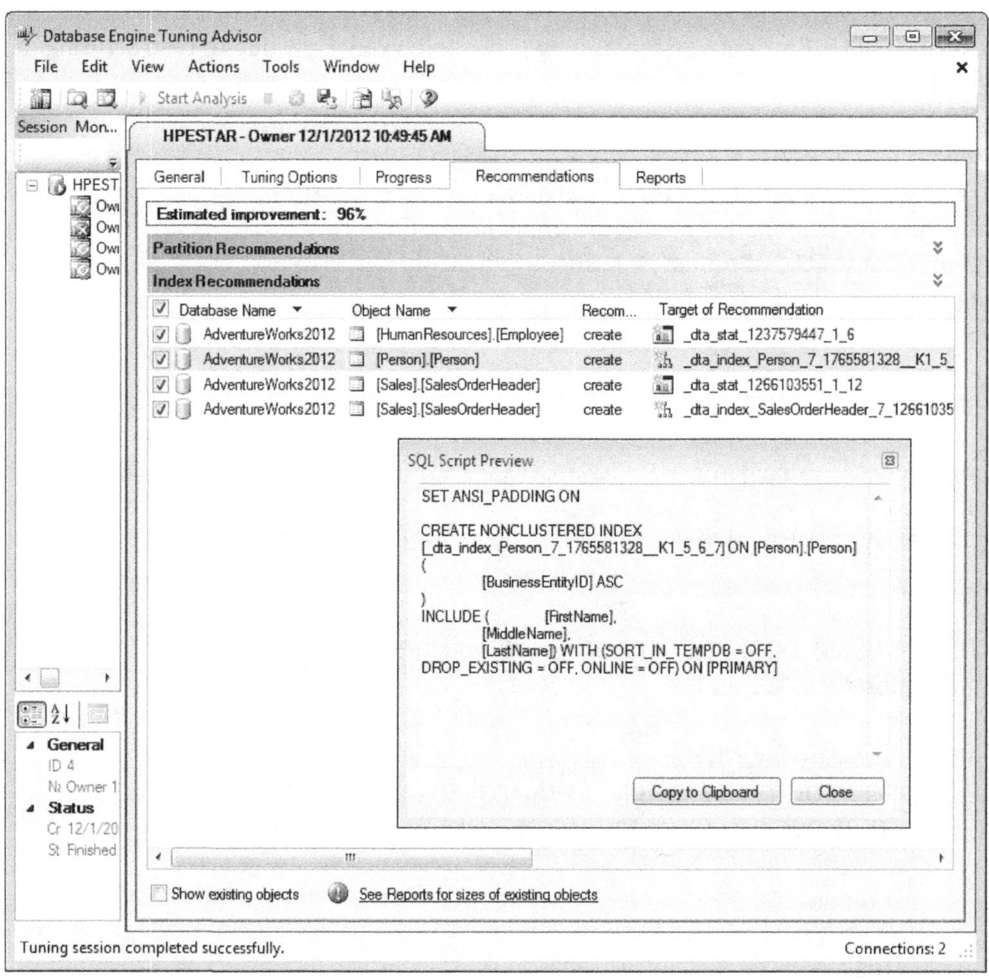

DBCC HELP Command

With the DBCC HELP command you can get syntax assistance with any of the DBCC commands, some of them related to optimization & performance tuning.

```
DBCC HELP (checkdb);
```

MSDN Article: **SQL Server Optimization**
http://msdn.microsoft.com/en-us/library/aa964133(v=sql.90).aspx

CHAPTER 21: Advanced T-SQL Querying & Programming

String Pattern Matching & Parsing

The CHARINDEX() function, PATINDEX() function and LIKE operator offer substring search in string functionality with some differences. Frequently, all 3 can be used for the same result.

The LIKE Operator

LIKE operator usage for numeric and alphanumeric differentiation.

```
USE AdventureWorks2012;
SELECT AddressID, City, StateProvinceID, PostalCode
FROM Person.Address WHERE PostalCode LIKE '%[^0-9]%';
-- (3644 row(s) affected) - Partial results.
```

AddressID	City	StateProvinceID	PostalCode
532	Ottawa	57	K4B 1S2
497	Burnaby	7	V5A 4X1
15272	Haney	7	V2W 1W2
14068	Cambridge	14	CB4 4BZ

```
SELECT AddressID, City, StateProvinceID, PostalCode
FROM Person.Address WHERE PostalCode NOT LIKE '%[^0-9]%';
-- (15970 row(s) affected) - Partial results.
```

AddressID	City	StateProvinceID	PostalCode
26916	Dunkerque	145	59140
28885	Lille	145	59000
708	Paris	161	75017
23902	Lieusaint	163	77127

Elaborate patterns can be formed from regular characters and wildcard characters. Underscore (_) matches any character.

```
DECLARE @Pattern varchar(20) = '[CFPS]___[eo]n'
SELECT DISTINCT LastName FROM Person.Person WHERE LastName  LIKE @Pattern;
-- Campen, Cannon, Carson,  Fulton, Patten, Slaven, Sutton
```

The CHARINDEX() Function

The CHARINDEX() function locates a substring within a string. A string with 2 hyphens (-) is split into 3 parts.

```
SELECT      ProductNumber,
            [Part1] = LEFT(ProductNumber,CHARINDEX('-',ProductNumber) - 1),
            [Part2] = SUBSTRING(ProductNumber,CHARINDEX('-',ProductNumber) + 1,
                      CHARINDEX('-',ProductNumber,CHARINDEX('-',
                      ProductNumber) + 1) - (CHARINDEX('-',ProductNumber) + 1)),
            [Part3] = RIGHT(ProductNumber,CHARINDEX('-',REVERSE(ProductNumber)) - 1)
FROM Production.Product
WHERE LEN(ProductNumber) - LEN(REPLACE(ProductNumber, '-','')) = 2;  -- 2 hyphens in string
-- (213 row(s) affected) - Partial results.
```

ProductNumber	Part1	Part2	Part3
BK-M18B-40	BK	M18B	40
BK-M18B-42	BK	M18B	42
BK-M18B-44	BK	M18B	44
BK-M18B-48	BK	M18B	48
BK-M18B-52	BK	M18B	52

Find the left part of a string before the comma. We get an error without the NULLIF function due to subtracting 1 from the LEN() result which may be 0 (zero).

```
SELECT Name, LEFT(Name,CHARINDEX(',',Name)-1) AS NamePrefix
FROM Production.Product ORDER BY Name;
/* Msg 537, Level 16, State 3, Line 1
Invalid length parameter passed to the LEFT or SUBSTRING function. */
```

```
SELECT ProductNumber,
       NamePrefix=LEFT(Name,COALESCE(NULLIF(CHARINDEX(',',Name)-1,-1),LEN(Name))),
       ProductName=Name
FROM Production.Product ORDER BY ProductName;
-- (504 row(s) affected) - Partial results;
```

ProductNumber	NamePrefix	ProductName
FR-T67Y-58	LL Touring Frame - Yellow	LL Touring Frame - Yellow, 58
FR-T67Y-62	LL Touring Frame - Yellow	LL Touring Frame - Yellow, 62
HB-T721	LL Touring Handlebars	LL Touring Handlebars
SA-T467	LL Touring Seat Assembly	LL Touring Seat Assembly

The PATINDEX() Function

The PATINDEX() function can be used for complex pattern searches.

```
use AdventureWorks2012;
```

```
select      [Name]                      AS ProductName,
            ProductNumber,
            [Description],
            ListPrice
from [Production].[Product] p
  inner join [Production].[ProductModelProductDescriptionCulture] pmpdc
     on p.ProductModelID = pmpdc.ProductModelID
  inner join  [Production].[ProductDescription] pd
     on pmpdc.ProductDescriptionID = pd.ProductDescriptionID
where patindex( '%mountain%innovative%', pd.[Description]) > 0
order by ProductNumber DESC;
-- (8 row(s) affected) - Partial results.
```

ProductName	ProductNumber	Description	ListPrice
Mountain-100 Silver, 48	BK-M82S-48	Top-of-the-line competition mountain bike. Performance-enhancing options include the innovative HL Frame, super-smooth front suspension, and traction for all terrain.	3399.99

Searching UNICODE Chinese text.

```
select [Name] AS ProductName, ProductNumber, [Description], ListPrice
from [Production].[Product] p
  inner join [Production].[ProductModelProductDescriptionCulture] pmpdc
     on p.ProductModelID = pmpdc.ProductModelID
  inner join  [Production].[ProductDescription] pd
     on pmpdc.ProductDescriptionID = pd.ProductDescriptionID
where patindex( N'%量的%快速%', pd.[Description]) > 0
order by ProductNumber DESC;
```

ProductName	ProductNumber	Description	ListPrice
HL Headset	HS-3479	高质量的一英寸无螺纹车头碗组具有油口，可确保快速润滑。	124.73

Complex pattern match with wildcards.

```
SELECT PATINDEX('%[A-T,0-9]%[Q,0-9]%[0-9]%','ZQZQXYZABC123');  --2
```

Composable DML - INSERT into 2 Tables with One Statement

Composable DML is new to SQL Server 2012. It expands the concept of SELECT subquery to INSERT/UPDATE/DELETE/MERGE operation using the OUTPUT clause with some restrictions.

```
USE AdventureWorks2012;
CREATE TABLE PurchaseOrderDetail(                -- Create 2 empty tables for testing
        PurchaseOrderID int NOT NULL,PurchaseOrderDetailID int NOT NULL,
        DueDate datetime NOT NULL,OrderQty smallint NOT NULL,
        ProductID int NOT NULL,UnitPrice money NOT NULL,LineTotal  money,
        ReceivedQty decimal(8, 2) NOT NULL,RejectedQty decimal(8, 2) NOT NULL,
        StockedQty  int,ModifiedDate datetime NOT NULL);
CREATE TABLE POD( PurchaseOrderID int NOT NULL,
        PurchaseOrderDetailID int NOT NULL,DueDate datetime NOT NULL,
        OrderQty smallint NOT NULL,ProductID int NOT NULL,
        UnitPrice money NOT NULL,LineTotal  money,ReceivedQty decimal(8, 2) NOT NULL,
       RejectedQty decimal(8, 2) NOT NULL,StockedQty  int,ModifiedDate datetime NOT NULL);
GO
CREATE CLUSTERED INDEX idxPOD1 on PurchaseOrderDetail(PurchaseOrderDetailID);
CREATE CLUSTERED INDEX idxPOD2 on POD(PurchaseOrderDetailID);
GO
```

```
INSERT PurchaseOrderDetail  OUTPUT inserted.*           -- Test query with OUTPUT
SELECT * FROM Purchasing.PurchaseOrderDetail
GO
-- (8845 row(s) affected)
```

```
TRUNCATE TABLE PurchaseOrderDetail;
GO
-- Command(s) completed successfully.
```

```
INSERT POD                                                  -- Composable DML
SELECT *  FROM (
        INSERT PurchaseOrderDetail      OUTPUT inserted.*
        SELECT * FROM Purchasing.PurchaseOrderDetail ) X ;
GO
```

```
SELECT COUNT(*) FROM POD;                                   -- 8845
SELECT COUNT(*) FROM PurchaseOrderDetail;                   -- 8845
GO
```

```
DROP TABLE POD;  DROP TABLE PurchaseOrderDetail;
```

Double Assignment Operator

The multiple value assignment operator allows more than one assignment for the same value.

```
USE AdventureWorks2012;
CREATE TABLE #DateSequence (ID INT, TestDate DATE);
INSERT #DateSequence
SELECT          SalesOrderID, ModifiedDate
FROM   Sales.SalesOrderHeader ;
go -- (31465 row(s) affected)
```

```
SELECT TOP 5 *
FROM   #DateSequence ;
go
```

ID	TestDate
43659	2005-07-08
43660	2005-07-08
43661	2005-07-08
43662	2005-07-08
43663	2005-07-08

```
-- Multiple assignment UPDATE
DECLARE @Date date = dateadd(day, 1, CURRENT_TIMESTAMP),
        @id   int = 0 ;
```

```
UPDATE #DateSequence
        SET     @id = ID = @id + 1,
                @Date = TestDate = dateadd (Day, -1, @Date);
go
```

```
SELECT TOP 5 * FROM   #DateSequence ORDER BY TestDate DESC;
go
```

ID	TestDate
1	2016-10-21
2	2016-10-20
3	2016-10-19
4	2016-10-18
5	2016-10-17

Running Total & MovingAverage Calculation

Running total support is a new feature of SQL Server 2012. OVER clause makes the RT calculation a breeze. SQL Server 2012 query.

```
USE AdventureWorks2012;
GO
```

```
SELECT SalesOrderID,
  FORMAT(TotalDue,'c0','en-US')                                    AS TotalDue,
  FORMAT(COUNT(TotalDue) OVER( ORDER BY SalesOrderID), '###,###') AS RunningCount,
  FORMAT(SUM(TotalDue) OVER( ORDER BY SalesOrderID), 'c0','en-US')  AS RunningTotal,
  FORMAT(AVG(TotalDue) OVER( ORDER BY SalesOrderID), 'c0','en-US')  AS MovingAvg
FROM Sales.SalesOrderHeader
WHERE OrderDate >='20080201'
        AND OrderDate < DATEADD(mm,1,'20080201')
ORDER BY SalesOrderID;
GO
-- (2032 row(s) affected) - Partial results.
```

SalesOrderID	TotalDue	RunningCount	RunningTotal	RunningAvg
63119	$247	1	$247	$247
63120	$234	2	$481	$240
63121	$187	3	$668	$223
63122	$213	4	$881	$220
63123	$16,320	5	$17,201	$3,440
63124	$36,462	6	$53,663	$8,944
63125	$9,603	7	$63,266	$9,038
63126	$2,298	8	$65,564	$8,196
63127	$8,870	9	$74,435	$8,271
63128	$21,805	10	$96,240	$9,624
63129	$1,691	11	$97,930	$8,903
63130	$4,355	12	$102,285	$8,524
63131	$97,929	13	$200,214	$15,401
63132	$38,158	14	$238,372	$17,027
63133	$36,926	15	$275,298	$18,353
63134	$8,597	16	$283,896	$17,743
63135	$1,872	17	$285,768	$16,810
63136	$41,760	18	$327,528	$18,196
63137	$987	19	$328,515	$17,290
63138	$5,344	20	$333,859	$16,693

Running Total with Subquery - Ye Olde Way

Calculating cumulative totals with subquery is quite inefficient, but it works.

```
USE AdventureWorks2012;
GO
```

```
DECLARE @Year INT = 2005, @Month INT = 7;
SELECT   RN = ROW_NUMBER()
              OVER(ORDER BY SalesOrderID),
      OrderDate = convert(CHAR(10),OrderDate,111), -- date formatting
      SalesOrderId,
      TotalDue = '$' + convert(VARCHAR,TotalDue,1), -- Currency formatting
      [Running Total] = '$' + convert(VARCHAR,
      (SELECT sum(TotalDue)
       FROM   Sales.SalesOrderHeader
       WHERE  SalesOrderID <= soh.SalesOrderID     -- Key predicate in the process
          AND year(OrderDate) = @Year
          AND month(OrderDate) = @Month),
                         1)
FROM     Sales.SalesOrderHeader soh
WHERE    year(OrderDate) = @Year
      AND month(OrderDate) = @Month
ORDER BY RN;
GO
-- (184 row(s) affected) - Partial results.
```

RN	OrderDate	SalesOrderId	TotalDue	Running Total
1	2005/07/01	43659	$23,153.23	$23,153.23
2	2005/07/01	43660	$1,457.33	$24,610.56
3	2005/07/01	43661	$36,865.80	$61,476.36
4	2005/07/01	43662	$32,474.93	$93,951.30
5	2005/07/01	43663	$472.31	$94,423.61
6	2005/07/01	43664	$27,510.41	$121,934.02
7	2005/07/01	43665	$16,158.70	$138,092.71
8	2005/07/01	43666	$5,694.86	$143,787.57
9	2005/07/01	43667	$6,876.36	$150,663.94
10	2005/07/01	43668	$40,487.72	$191,151.66
11	2005/07/01	43669	$807.26	$191,958.92
12	2005/07/01	43670	$6,893.25	$198,852.17
13	2005/07/01	43671	$9,153.61	$208,005.78
14	2005/07/01	43672	$6,895.41	$214,901.19
15	2005/07/01	43673	$4,216.03	$219,117.21

Running Total with Multiple Assignment UPDATE

Cumulative total can be generated a fast way using double assignment SET in UPDATE command. There are some restrictions such as no table partitioning. It should not be used in production unless there is a serious performance problem.

```
USE AdventureWorks2012;
```

```
DECLARE  @RunningTotal MONEY;
DECLARE  @Result  TABLE(
              SalesOrderID INT    NOT NULL    PRIMARY KEY,
              TotalDue     MONEY,
              RunningTotal MONEY
              );
SET @RunningTotal = 0.0;
INSERT INTO @Result
       (SalesOrderID,
        TotalDue)
SELECT   SalesOrderID,       TotalDue
FROM     Sales.SalesOrderHeader
ORDER BY SalesOrderID
-- (31465 row(s) affected)

UPDATE @Result
SET    @RunningTotal = RunningTotal = @RunningTotal + TotalDue;
-- (31465 row(s) affected)

SELECT   SalesOrderId,
         FORMAT(TotalDue,'c0','en-US')              AS TotalDue,
         FORMAT(RunningTotal, 'c0','en-US')         AS RunningTotal
FROM     @Result ORDER BY SalesOrderID;
GO
-- (31465 row(s) affected) -- Partial results.
```

SalesOrderId	TotalDue	RunningTotal
43659	$23,153	$23,153
43660	$1,457	$24,611
43661	$36,866	$61,476
43662	$32,475	$93,951
43663	$472	$94,424
43664	$27,510	$121,934
43665	$16,159	$138,093

Subtotal, Total & Grand Total GROUPING Function

It is a challenge to generate multi-level totals in T-SQL. The GROUPING() function tells us what level we are on in the GROUP BY summary.

```
USE AdventureWorks2012;
```

```
SELECT *
FROM   (SELECT COALESCE(CONVERT(VARCHAR, YEAR(OrderDate)), '')             AS YYYY,
        COALESCE(LEFT(CONVERT(VARCHAR, OrderDate, 111), 7), '')           AS MM,
        FORMAT(COUNT(*), '###,###')                                        AS ORDERS,
        FORMAT(SUM(TotalDue), 'c0', 'en-US')                               AS SALES,
        CASE    WHEN GROUPING(LEFT(CONVERT(VARCHAR, OrderDate, 111), 7)) = 0
            AND GROUPING(YEAR(OrderDate)) = 1 THEN 'SUBTOTAL'
         ELSE ''
        END                                                                AS GRPMM,
         CASE   WHEN GROUPING(YEAR(OrderDate)) = 0
            AND GROUPING(LEFT(CONVERT(VARCHAR, OrderDate, 111), 7)) =  1 THEN  'TOTAL'
         ELSE ''
        END                                                                AS GRPYY,
         CASE   WHEN GROUPING(LEFT(CONVERT(VARCHAR, OrderDate, 111), 7)) = 1
            AND GROUPING(YEAR(OrderDate)) = 1 THEN 'GRAND TOTAL'
         ELSE ''
        END                                                                AS GRPALL
     FROM  Sales.SalesOrderHeader
   GROUP  BY YEAR(OrderDate),  LEFT(CONVERT(VARCHAR, OrderDate, 111), 7) WITH CUBE) rpt
WHERE  GRPMM != ''  OR GRPYY != ''   OR GRPALL != ''
ORDER  BY CASE  WHEN GRPALL != '' THEN 3   WHEN GRPYY != '' THEN 2    ELSE 1  END,
      YYYY,  MM ;
```

YYYY	MM	ORDERS	SALES	GRPMM	GRPYY	GRPALL
	2008/01	1,946	$3,359,927	SUBTOTAL		
	2008/02	2,032	$4,662,656	SUBTOTAL		
	2008/03	2,109	$4,722,358	SUBTOTAL		
	2008/04	2,128	$4,269,365	SUBTOTAL		
	2008/05	2,386	$5,813,557	SUBTOTAL		
	2008/06	2,374	$6,004,156	SUBTOTAL		
	2008/07	976	$56,179	SUBTOTAL		
2005		1,379	$12,693,251		TOTAL	
2006		3,692	$34,463,848		TOTAL	
2007		12,443	$47,171,490		TOTAL	
2008		13,951	$28,888,198		TOTAL	
		31,465	$123,216,786			GRAND TOTAL

The GROUP BY Clause with GROUPING SETS

A GROUP BY clause that uses GROUPING SETS is equivalent to multiple GROUP BY queries combined with UNION ALL operator.

```
USE AdventureWorks2012;

SELECT T."Group"                                AS Continent,
    T.CountryRegionCode                         AS Country,
    S.Name                                      AS Dealer,
    CN.LastName                                 AS SalesStaff,
    FORMAT(SUM(TotalDue), 'c0','en-US')         AS N'TotalSales'
FROM   Sales.Customer C
    INNER JOIN Sales.Store S
        ON C.StoreID = S.BusinessEntityID
    INNER JOIN Sales.SalesTerritory T
        ON C.TerritoryID = T.TerritoryID
    INNER JOIN Sales.SalesOrderHeader H
        ON C.CustomerID = H.CustomerID
    LEFT JOIN Person.Person CN
        ON H.SalesPersonID = CN.BusinessEntityID
GROUP  BY GROUPING SETS( CUBE(T."Group", T.CountryRegionCode), S.Name, CN.LastName  )
ORDER  BY Continent, Country, Dealer, SalesStaff;
GO
-- (650 row(s) affected) - Partial results.
```

Continent	Country	Dealer	SalesStaff	TotalSales
NULL	NULL	Year-Round Sports	NULL	$197,777
NULL	NULL	Yellow Bicycle Company	NULL	$102,699
NULL	AU	NULL	NULL	$2,185,110
NULL	CA	NULL	NULL	$19,316,294
NULL	DE	NULL	NULL	$2,741,548
NULL	FR	NULL	NULL	$6,215,065
NULL	GB	NULL	NULL	$5,758,606
NULL	US	NULL	NULL	$72,049,624
Europe	NULL	NULL	NULL	$14,715,219
Europe	DE	NULL	NULL	$2,741,548
Europe	FR	NULL	NULL	$6,215,065
Europe	GB	NULL	NULL	$5,758,606
North America	NULL	NULL	NULL	$91,365,917
North America	CA	NULL	NULL	$19,316,294
North America	US	NULL	NULL	$72,049,624
Pacific	NULL	NULL	NULL	$2,185,110
Pacific	AU	NULL	NULL	$2,185,110

SELECT Top N from Each Group

Top 3 in each group is a very popular interview question.

```
USE AdventureWorks2012;
```

```
DECLARE @TopN tinyint = 3;
WITH cteBestSalesByProduct
   AS (SELECT ROW_NUMBER() OVER( PARTITION BY sod.ProductID
                ORDER BY Sum(sod.LineTotal) DESC)                AS  SeqNo,
        CONCAT(FirstName, SPACE(1), LastName)                    AS  [Name],
         p.Name                                                  AS ProductName,
        FORMAT(CONVERT(MONEY, Sum(sod.LineTotal)), 'c', 'en-US') AS TotalBySalesPerson,
        p.ProductNumber,
        sod.ProductID
     FROM   Sales.SalesOrderDetail AS sod
        INNER JOIN Production.Product AS p
            ON sod.ProductID = p.ProductID
        INNER JOIN Sales.SalesOrderHeader AS soh
            ON sod.SalesOrderID = soh.SalesOrderID
        INNER JOIN Person.Person AS pe
            ON soh.SalesPersonID = pe.BusinessEntityID
     WHERE  soh.SalesPersonID IS NOT NULL
     GROUP  BY        CONCAT(FirstName, SPACE(1), LastName),
                      sod.ProductID,
                      p.ProductNumber,
                      p.Name )
SELECT *
FROM   cteBestSalesByProduct cte
WHERE  SeqNo <= @TopN
ORDER  BY       ProductID,
                SeqNo;
-- (749 row(s) affected) - Partial results.
```

SeqNo	Name	ProductName	TotalBySalesPerson	ProductNumber	ProductID
1	Jae Pak	Women's Mountain Shorts, L	$19,385.51	SH-W890-L	869
2	Linda Mitchell	Women's Mountain Shorts, L	$15,371.85	SH-W890-L	869
3	Michael Blythe	Women's Mountain Shorts, L	$11,411.44	SH-W890-L	869
1	Jillian Carson	Water Bottle - 30 oz.	$936.04	WB-H098	870
2	Linda Mitchell	Water Bottle - 30 oz.	$833.59	WB-H098	870
3	Rachel Valdez	Water Bottle - 30 oz.	$758.01	WB-H098	870
1	Jillian Carson	Patch Kit/8 Patches	$163.51	PK-7098	873
2	Jae Pak	Patch Kit/8 Patches	$120.91	PK-7098	873
3	Ranjit Varkey Chudukatil	Patch Kit/8 Patches	$104.42	PK-7098	873

SELECT Top N from Each Group Ye Olde Way

SQL Server 2005 has introduced revolutionary enhancements including the OVER clause and recursive CTE-s. It was a bit cumbersome to program certain tasks prior to SS 2005.

```
USE AdventureWorks2012;  DECLARE @Top TINYINT = 3;                     -- TOP N products in each subcategory
SELECT Subcategory,    ProductName,   ProductID
FROM  ( SELECT PSC.Name                                               AS SubCategory,
          P1.Name                                                     AS ProductName,    P1.ProductID,
         (SELECT COUNT(*)
         FROM  Production.ProductSubcategory PSC    LEFT JOIN Production.Product P2
         ON P2.ProductSubcategoryID =        PSC.ProductSubcategoryID
         WHERE  P2.ProductSubcategoryID = P1.ProductSubcategoryID AND P2.ProductID <= P1.ProductID) AS RN
  FROM  Production.ProductSubcategory PSC    LEFT JOIN Production.Product P1
           ON P1.ProductSubcategoryID = PSC.ProductSubcategoryID  ) AS   X -- derived table
WHERE  RN <= @Top  ORDER  BY Subcategory,  ProductID; -- (90 row(s) affected) - Partial results.
```

UPDATE PRIMARY KEY & Connecting FK in a Transaction

Disable & Enable FOREIGN KEY Constraint

The update PRIMARY KEY task (with disable constraint & enable constraint) demonstrates the importance of transaction to protect the integrity of the database: it prevents the database left in a disarray if something goes wrong. Demo only! No reason to change surrogate PK ever!

```
USE AdventureWorks2012;
CREATE TABLE Subcategory(ProductSubcategoryID int, ProductCategoryID int, Name varchar(50));
CREATE CLUSTERED INDEX idxName on Subcategory(Name);  INSERT Subcategory
SELECT ProductSubcategoryID, ProductCategoryID, Name  FROM Production.ProductSubcategory; -- (37 row(s) affected)
GO
CREATE TABLE Product (ProductID int, Name varchar(50), ListPrice money, ProductSubcategoryID int);
CREATE CLUSTERED INDEX idxName on Product(Name);   INSERT Product
SELECT ProductID, Name, ListPrice, ProductSubcategoryID FROM Production.Product;  --(504 row(s) affected)
GO
ALTER TABLE Subcategory ALTER COLUMN ProductSubcategoryID INT NOT NULL;
ALTER TABLE Subcategory ADD CONSTRAINT pkSubcat PRIMARY KEY(ProductSubcategoryID);
ALTER TABLE Product ALTER COLUMN ProductID INT NOT NULL;
GO
ALTER TABLE Product ADD CONSTRAINT pkProd PRIMARY KEY(ProductID);
ALTER TABLE Product ADD CONSTRAINT fkSubcat FOREIGN KEY (ProductSubcategoryID)
REFERENCES Subcategory(ProductSubcategoryID);
GO
BEGIN TRAN
ALTER TABLE Product NOCHECK CONSTRAINT fkSubcat;      -- Disable constraint
UPDATE Subcategory SET ProductSubcategoryID = 999 WHERE ProductSubcategoryID = 8;  --(1 row(s) affected)
UPDATE Product SET ProductSubcategoryID = 999 WHERE ProductSubcategoryID = 8;       -- (3 row(s) affected)
ALTER TABLE Product CHECK CONSTRAINT fkSubcat;                       -- Enable constraint
COMMIT TRAN
GO
DROP TABLE Product; DROP TABLE Subcategory;
```

Table-Valued Parameters

Table-valued parameters were introduced with SQL Server 2008. They can be used to send parameters to SQL statement, stored procedure or function as next demonstrated.

```
USE AdventureWorks2012;
GO
```

```
-- Create new user-defined table data type
CREATE TYPE dbo.utpProdInfo AS TABLE(
	ProdID		int,
	ProdNbr		char(12),
	StandardCost	money,
	ListPrice		money,
	Color	char(16));
GO
```

```
-- Create user- defined table-valued function(UDF) with table-valued parameter
CREATE FUNCTION ufnColorGrouping (@Input dbo.utpProdInfo READONLY)
	RETURNS @Result TABLE (Color char(16), AvgListPrice money)
AS
BEGIN
 INSERT @Result
 SELECT Color, avg(ListPrice) FROM @Input
 GROUP BY Color
 RETURN
END;
GO
```

```
-- Create stored procedure with table-valued parameter
CREATE PROCEDURE uspPriceRange
			@Input dbo.utpProdInfo READONLY
AS
BEGIN
 SELECT Color,  MinPrice=format(min(ListPrice), 'c0','en-US'),
		MaxPrice=format(max(ListPrice), 'c0','en-US')
  FROM @Input
  GROUP BY Color
  ORDER BY MAX(ListPrice)  DESC
END;
GO
```

Among the TVP's Benefits: Simple but Powerful Modular Programming

```
-- Test TVF with table-valued parameter
DECLARE @PriceDetail dbo.utpProdInfo
INSERT @PriceDetail SELECT ProductID, ProductNumber, StandardCost, ListPrice, Color
        FROM Production.Product WHERE Color is not null;
```

```
SELECT * FROM ufnColorGrouping (@PriceDetail)
ORDER BY AvgListPrice DESC
```

Color	AvgListPrice
Red	1401.95
Yellow	959.0913
Blue	923.6792
Silver	850.3053
Black	725.121
Grey	125.00
Silver/Black	64.0185
Multi	59.865
White	9.245

```
-- Test stored procedure with table-valued parameter
DECLARE @PriceDetail dbo.utpProdInfo;
INSERT @PriceDetail SELECT ProductID, ProductNumber, StandardCost, ListPrice, Color
        FROM Production.Product WHERE Color is not null;
```

```
EXEC uspPriceRange @PriceDetail;
GO
```

Color	MinPrice	MaxPrice
Red	$35	$3,578
Silver	$0	$3,400
Black	$0	$3,375
Blue	$35	$2,384
Yellow	$54	$2,384
Grey	$125	$125
Multi	$9	$90
Silver/Black	$40	$81
White	$9	$10

```
-- Cleanup
DROP FUNCTION ufnColorGrouping;
DROP PROC uspPriceRange;
DROP TYPE dbo.utpProdInfo;
```

Creating Comma Delimited String from a Column

XML PATH is the most popular way of accomplishing it, but other methods available as well.

```
;WITH CTE AS (
SELECT   ps.[Name]                                                  AS Subcategory,
         Stuff((SELECT ', ' + Color AS [text()]
                FROM Production.Product p
                WHERE p.ProductSubcategoryID = ps.ProductSubcategoryID
                                    AND Color is not null
                GROUP BY Color ORDER BY Color
                FOR XML PATH ('')),1,1,'')                          AS ColorList,
         Stuff((SELECT ', ' + Size AS [text()]
                FROM Production.Product p
                WHERE p.ProductSubcategoryID = ps.ProductSubcategoryID
                                    AND Size is not null
                GROUP BY Size ORDER BY Size
                FOR XML PATH ('')),1,1,'')                          AS SizeList
FROM     Production.ProductSubcategory ps  )
SELECT * FROM CTE WHERE ColorList is not null AND SizeList is not null  ORDER BY Subcategory;
```

Subcategory	ColorList	SizeList
Bib-Shorts	Multi	L, M, S
Gloves	Black	L, M, S
Hydration Packs	Silver	70
Jerseys	Multi, Yellow	L, M, S, XL
Mountain Bikes	Black, Silver	38, 40, 42, 44, 46, 48, 52
Mountain Frames	Black, Silver	38, 40, 42, 44, 46, 48, 52
Road Bikes	Black, Red, Yellow	38, 40, 42, 44, 48, 52, 56, 58, 60, 62
Road Frames	Black, Red, Yellow	38, 40, 42, 44, 48, 52, 56, 58, 60, 62
Shorts	Black	L, M, S, XL
Socks	White	L, M
Tights	Black	L, M, S
Touring Bikes	Blue, Yellow	44, 46, 50, 54, 58, 60, 62
Touring Frames	Blue, Yellow	44, 46, 50, 54, 58, 60, 62
Vests	Blue	L, M, S

```
DECLARE @CSVList VARCHAR(MAX) = '';   -- Multiple variable assignment method
SELECT @CSVList = CONCAT(Color, ', ', @CSVList)
FROM (SELECT DISTINCT Color FROM Production.Product
                              WHERE Color is not null) x;
SELECT CommaDelimitedList=@CSVList;
-- Yellow, White, Silver/Black, Silver, Red, Multi, Grey, Blue, Black,
```

Configuring Comma Delimited Result Sets in SSMS

It requires special setup for CSV result sets when using Management Studio. This feature is applicable for the Results to Text mode.

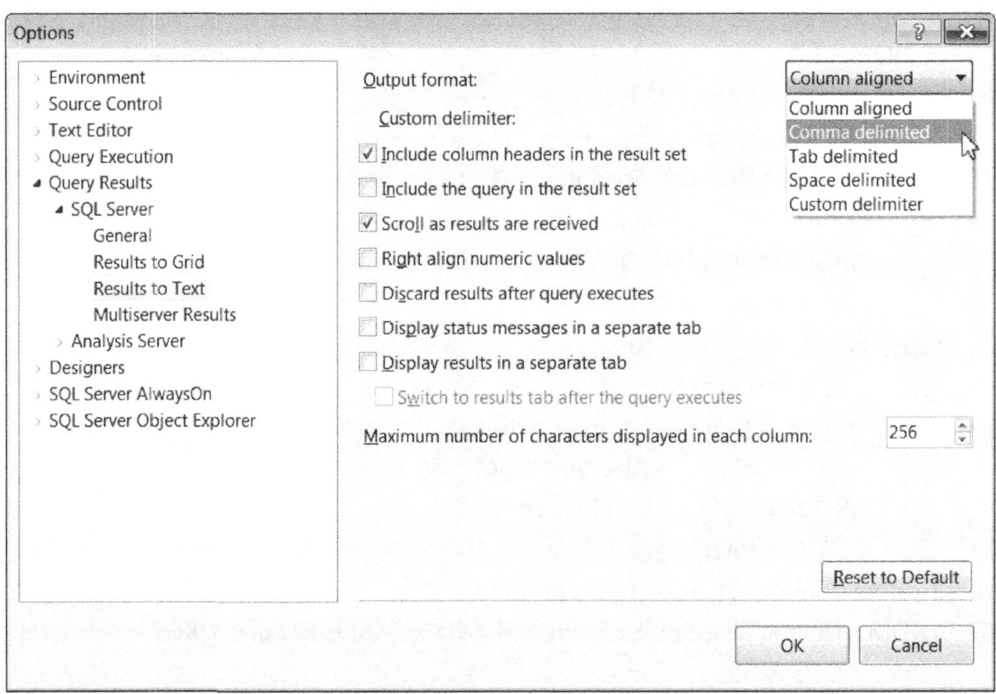

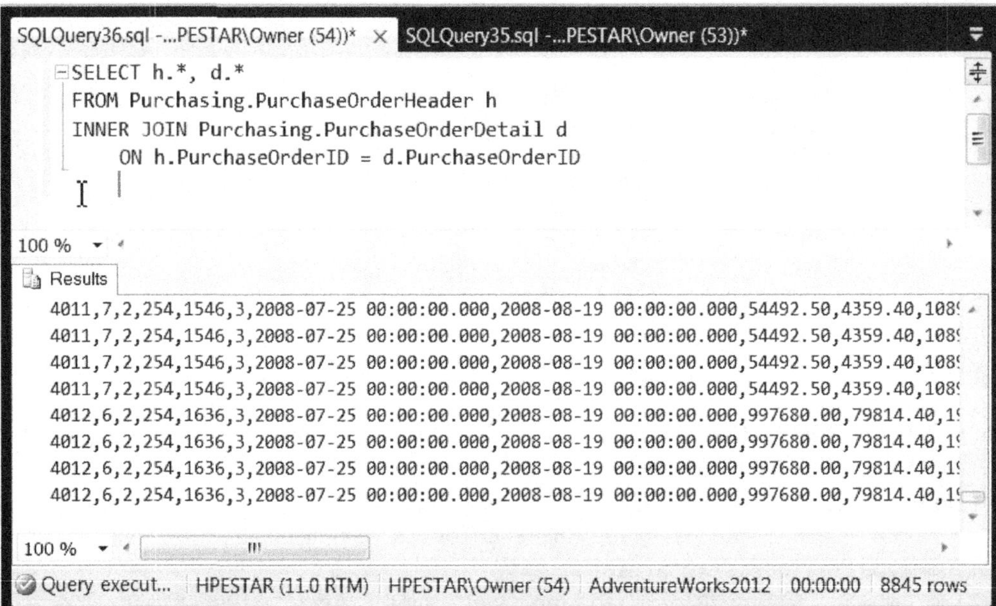

Nesting Cursors

Cursors should be avoided with a few exceptions: better performance (rare but happens) or cannot be done by set-based statements. Being new to set-based logic is not a good excuse for using cursors because they do not scale well. Single-level cursor example. SQL Server 2012 script.

SQLQuery33.sql - not connected* - Microsoft SQL Server Management Studio
File Edit View Query Project Debug Tools Window Help
New Query
AdventureWorks2012
Execute
Debug
SQLQuery33.sql - not connected*
SQLQuery32.sql - not connected*
USE master;
DECLARE @dbName sysname;
DECLARE AllDatabases CURSOR STATIC LOCAL FOR
SELECT name FROM MASTER.dbo.sysdatabases
WHERE name NOT IN ('master','tempdb','model','msdb') -- exclude
ORDER BY name;
OPEN AllDatabases; FETCH AllDatabases INTO @dbName;
WHILE (@@FETCH_STATUS = 0) -- loop through all db-s
BEGIN
/***** PROCESSING STARTS HERE *****/
PRINT @dbName;
/***** PROCESSING ENDS HERE *****/
FETCH AllDatabases INTO @dbName
END; -- while
CLOSE AllDatabases; DEALLOCATE AllDatabases;
100 %
Messages
Accounting
AdventureWorks
AdventureWorks2008
AdventureWorks2012
AdventureWorksDW2012
100 %
Disconnected.

Nested Cursors

Outer cursor over period Purchase Orders. Inner cursor over products ordered for each PO.

```
USE AdventureWorks2012;

DECLARE @StartTime datetime = Getdate();
DECLARE @IterationID INT,   @OrderDetail VARCHAR(max),   @ProductName VARCHAR(10);
DECLARE @Result TABLE  (  PurchaseOrderID INT, ProductList VARCHAR(max)  ) ;

DECLARE PurchaseOrdersInPeriod CURSOR STATIC LOCAL FOR     -- OUTER CURSOR declaration
 SELECT PurchaseOrderID   FROM   Purchasing.PurchaseOrderHeader
 WHERE  Year(OrderDate) = 2008  AND Month(OrderDate) = 2  ORDER  BY PurchaseOrderID;

OPEN PurchaseOrdersInPeriod; FETCH NEXT FROM PurchaseOrdersInPeriod INTO @IterationID;
PRINT 'OUTER LOOP START';
WHILE ( @@FETCH_STATUS = 0 ) -- sql cursor fetch_status
 BEGIN      SET @OrderDetail = SPACE(0);

   DECLARE POLineItems CURSOR STATIC LOCAL FOR                    -- INNER CURSOR declaration
    SELECT p.productNumber   FROM   Purchasing.PurchaseOrderDetail pd
        INNER JOIN Production.Product p  ON pd.ProductID = p.ProductID
    WHERE  pd.PurchaseOrderID = @IterationID ORDER  BY PurchaseOrderDetailID;

   OPEN POLineItems;  FETCH NEXT FROM POLineItems INTO @ProductName;
   PRINT 'INNER LOOP START';
   WHILE ( @@FETCH_STATUS = 0 )
    BEGIN           SET @OrderDetail = CONCAT(@OrderDetail, @ProductName,', ');
      FETCH NEXT FROM POLineItems INTO @ProductName;      PRINT 'INNER LOOP' ;
    END -- inner while
   CLOSE POLineItems;   DEALLOCATE POLineItems;

   SET @OrderDetail = LEFT(@OrderDetail, Len(@OrderDetail) - 1);  -- Truncate trailing comma
   INSERT INTO @Result   VALUES     (@IterationID,@OrderDetail);
   FETCH NEXT FROM PurchaseOrdersInPeriod INTO @IterationID ;    PRINT 'OUTER LOOP';
 END -- outer while
CLOSE PurchaseOrdersInPeriod; DEALLOCATE PurchaseOrdersInPeriod;

SELECT * FROM   @Result ORDER  BY PurchaseOrderID;   -- Results  (268 row(s) affected)

SELECT ExecutionMsec = Datediff(millisecond, @StartTime, Getdate());  -- Timing  653 msec
GO
```

Nested Cursor Loops Processing Partial Results

PurchaseOrderID	ProductList
1573	CR-7833
1574	RA-2345
1575	PB-6109
1576	CR-9981
1577	SD-2342, SD-9872
1578	PA-187B, PA-361R, PA-529S, PA-632U, PA-823Y
1579	SE-R581, SE-R908, SE-R995, SE-T312, SE-T762
1580	RF-9198
1581	RC-0291
1582	RM-M464, RM-M692
1583	TP-0923
1584	FC-3982, FL-2301
1585	RM-M464, RM-M692
1586	NI-9522
1587	FW-5160, FW-5800, FW-7160, FW-9160
1588	PD-M282, PD-M340
1589	HN-5400, HN-5811, HN-5818, HN-6320, HN-7161
1590	MS-2348, MS-6061, MT-1000
1591	KW-4091
1592	RM-R436, RM-R600

Set Based Operations Equivalent Code

```
DECLARE @StartTime datetime = CURRENT_TIMESTAMP;
SELECT poh.PurchaseOrderID,OrderDetail = Stuff((
                              -- correlated subquery
                              SELECT CONCAT(', ', ProductNumber) AS  [text()]
                               FROM  Purchasing.PurchaseOrderDetail pod
                                     INNER JOIN Production.Product p
                                      ON pod.ProductID = p.ProductID
                               WHERE  pod.PurchaseOrderID =  poh.PurchaseOrderID
                               ORDER  BY PurchaseOrderDetailID
                               FOR XML PATH ('')), 1, 1, '')
FROM   Purchasing.PurchaseOrderHeader poh
WHERE  Year(OrderDate) = 2008 AND Month(OrderDate) = 2
ORDER  BY PurchaseOrderID;
SELECT ExecutionMsec = Datediff(millisecond, @StartTime, Getdate())
-- Timing:  6 msec
```

Advanced Graphical Query Designer - On-Premises SS

While SSMS GUI query / view designer cannot handle very complex queries, it does a pretty good job with "normal" relational database queries.

Aliasing Tables in the Diagram Pane

We start with right click on the top table frame in the Diagram Pane.

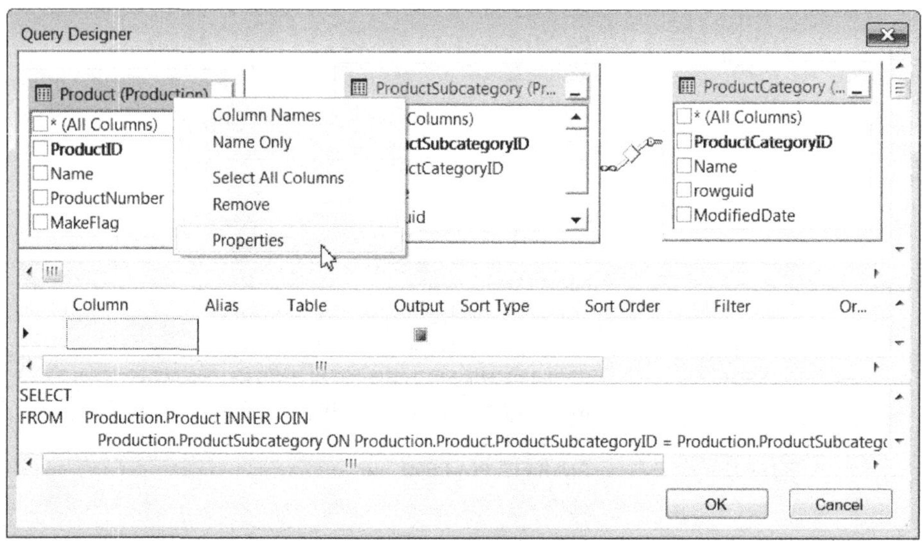

In the pop-up dialog box we enter the alias for the table.

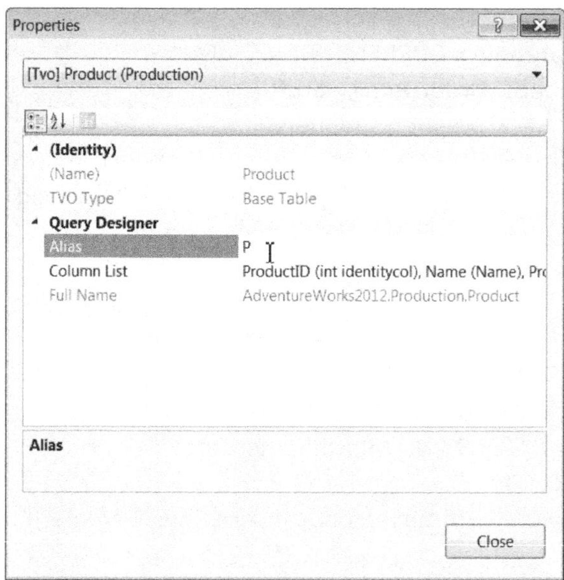

Specifying OUTER JOIN in Diagram Pane

To change the INNER JOIN to RIGHT JOIN, right click on the connection square in the middle and click on Properties.

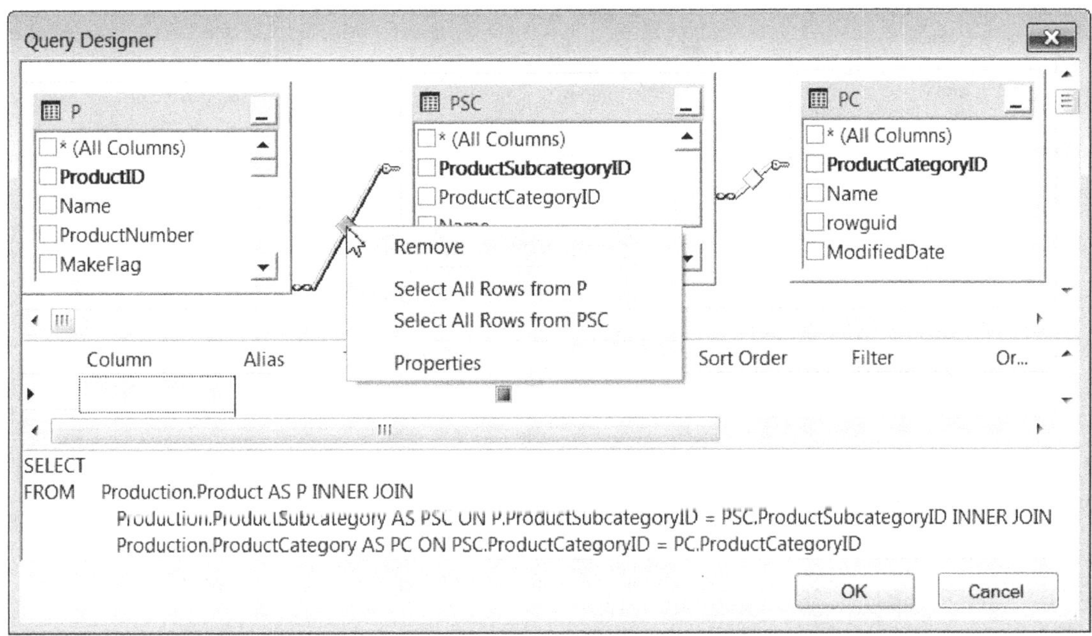

With checkmark selection we can specify LEFT JOIN, RIGHT JOIN or FULL JOIN.

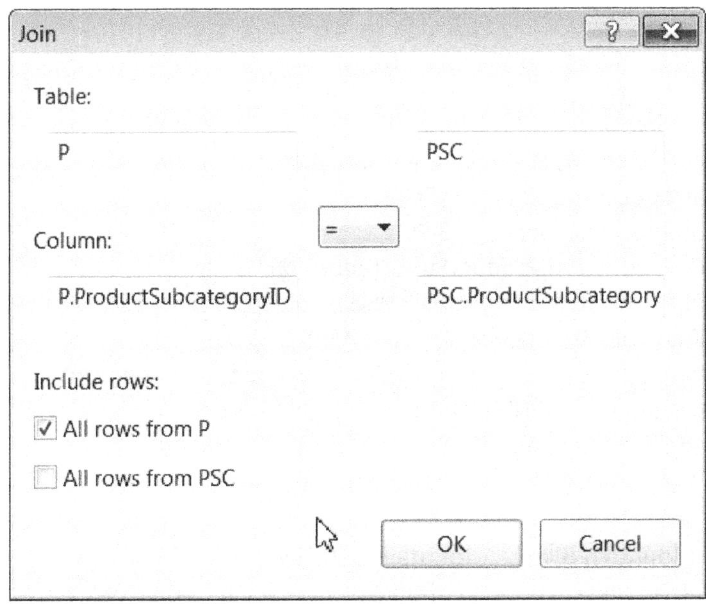

Query Designer Generated Query

This is the final graphical image in Query Designer prior to the exiting to Query Editor.

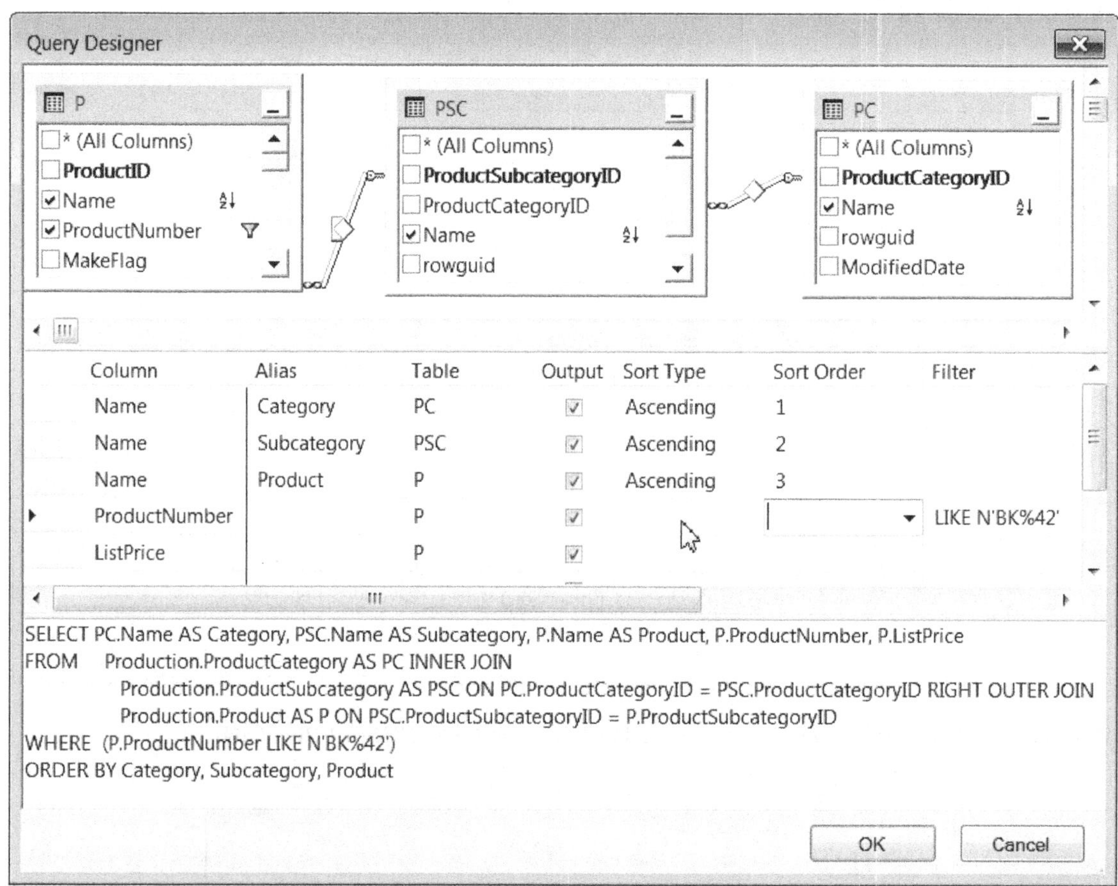


```
SELECT  PC.Name AS Category, PSC.Name AS Subcategory, P.Name AS Product,
                P.ProductNumber, P.ListPrice
FROM    Production.ProductCategory AS PC
        INNER JOIN Production.ProductSubcategory AS PSC
                ON PC.ProductCategoryID = PSC.ProductCategoryID
        RIGHT OUTER JOIN Production.Product AS P
                ON PSC.ProductSubcategoryID = P.ProductSubcategoryID
WHERE  (P.ProductNumber LIKE N'BK%42') ORDER BY Product, Subcategory, Category;
-- (9 row(s) affected) - Partial results.
```

Category	Subcategory	Product	ProductNumber	ListPrice
Bikes	Mountain Bikes	Mountain-500 Silver, 42	BK-M18S-42	564.99
Bikes	Road Bikes	Road-350-W Yellow, 42	BK-R79Y-42	1700.99

Template Explorer & Browser

The Template Explorer & Browser helps to start coding by providing a framework code with optional parameter replacements.

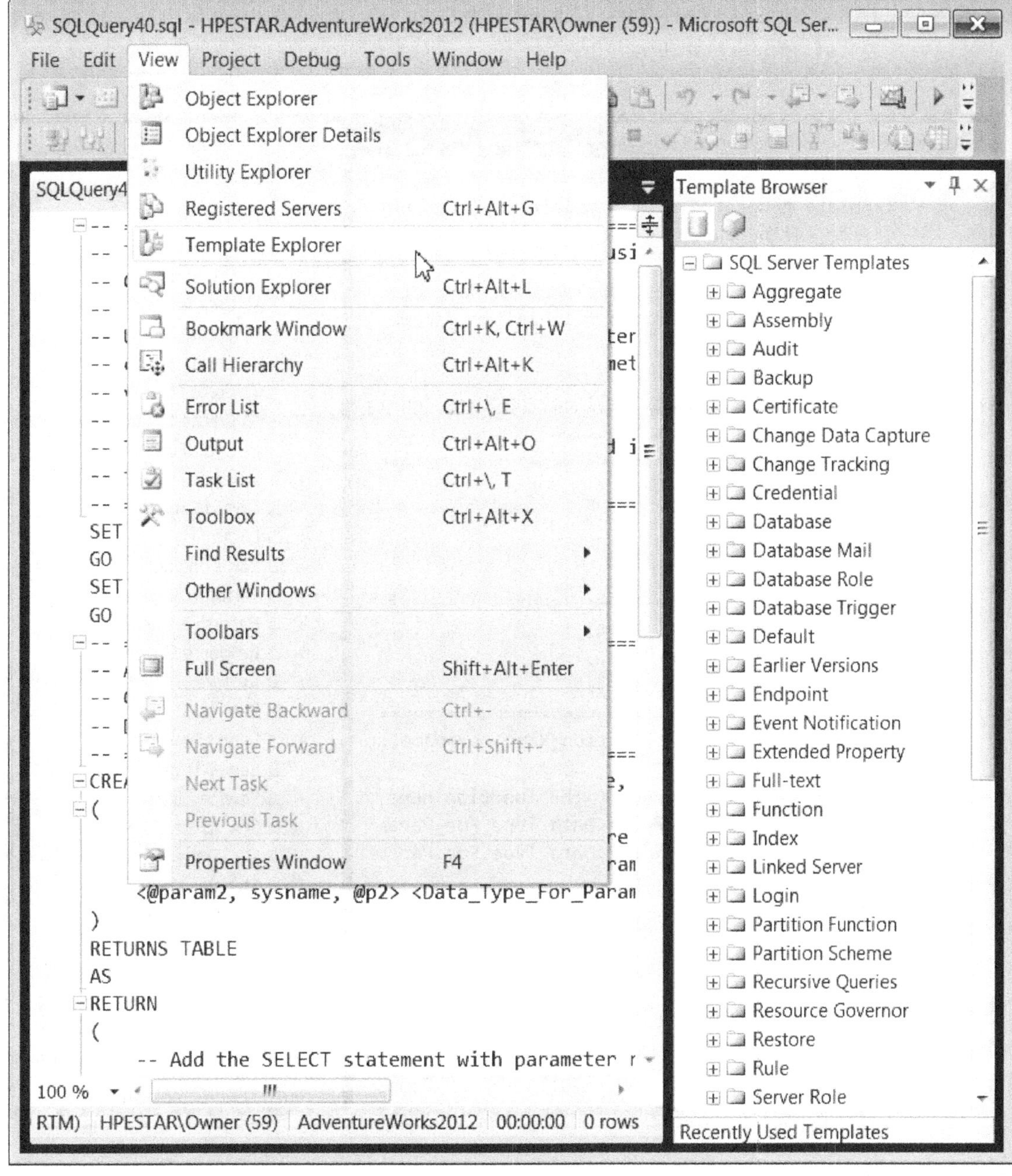

Create Inline Function Template

Double on the template name to get the starter code in a new Query Editor window.

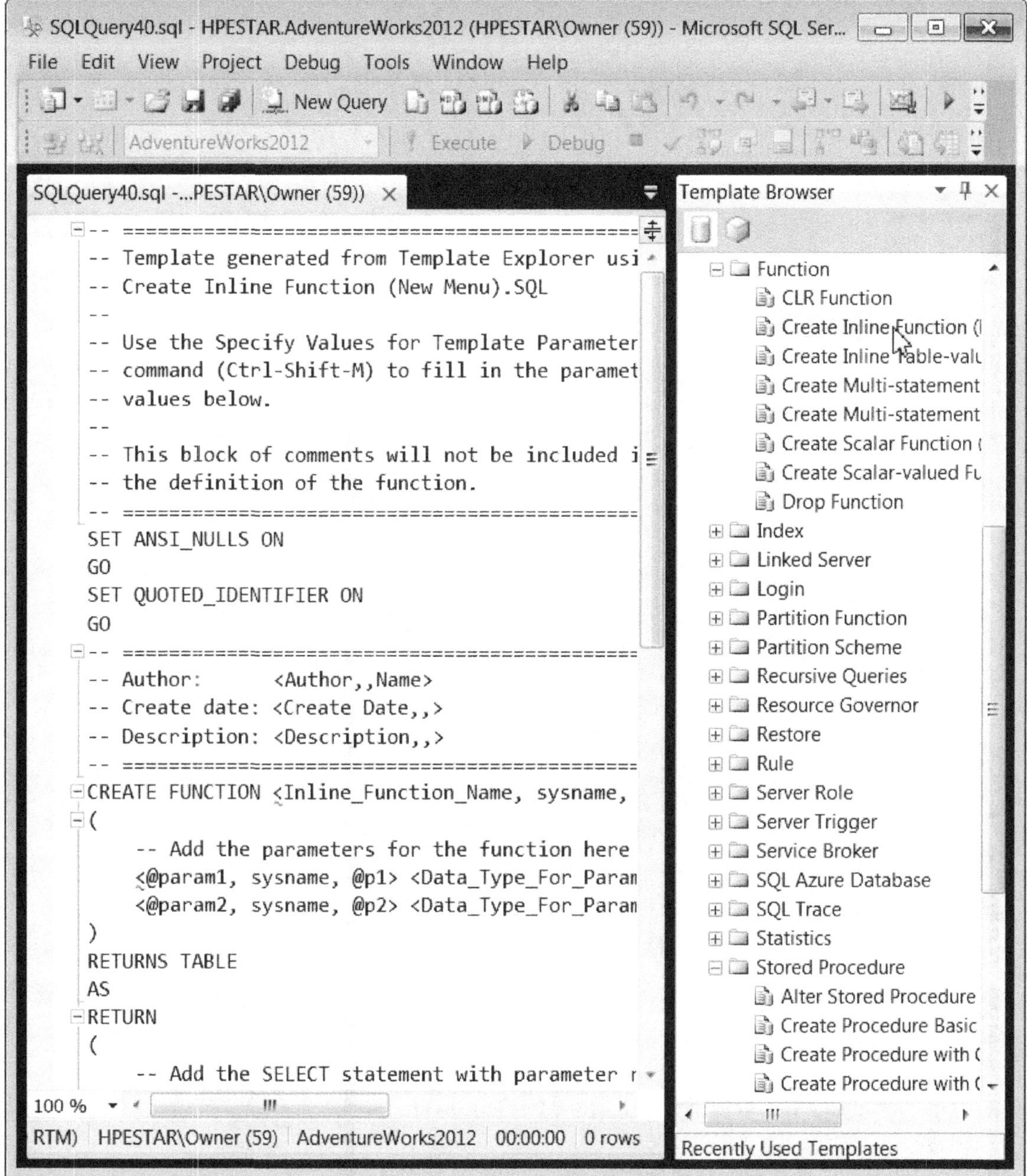

Template Parameters Specifications

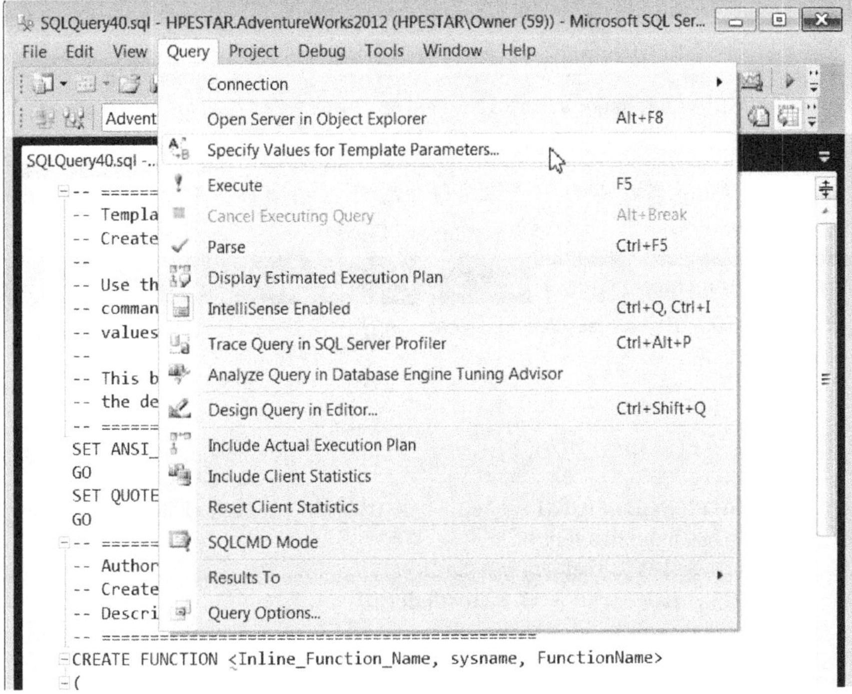

The values must be filled in for the parameter in the dialog box.

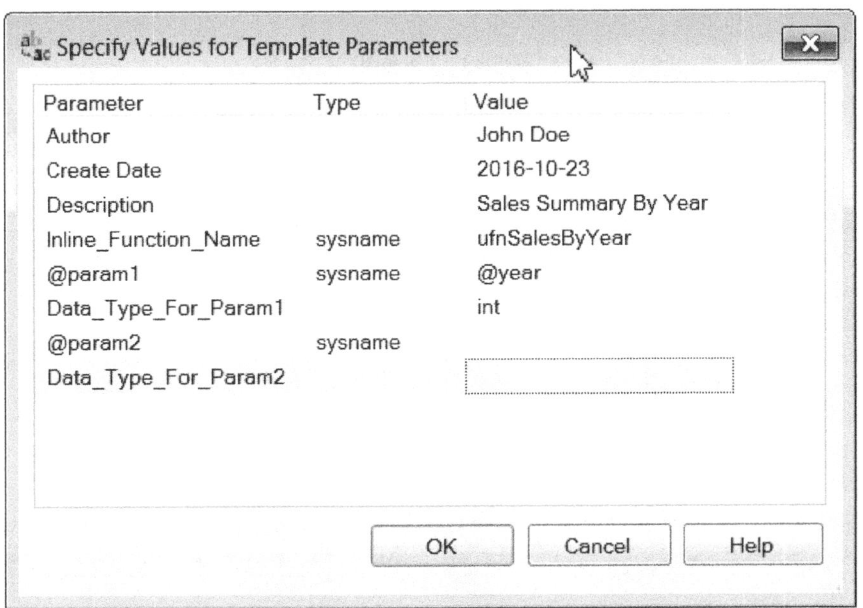

Completion of the Function by Entering the SELECT Query with Parameter

Inline user-defined function can be used as a make over for a view with accepting parameters feature.

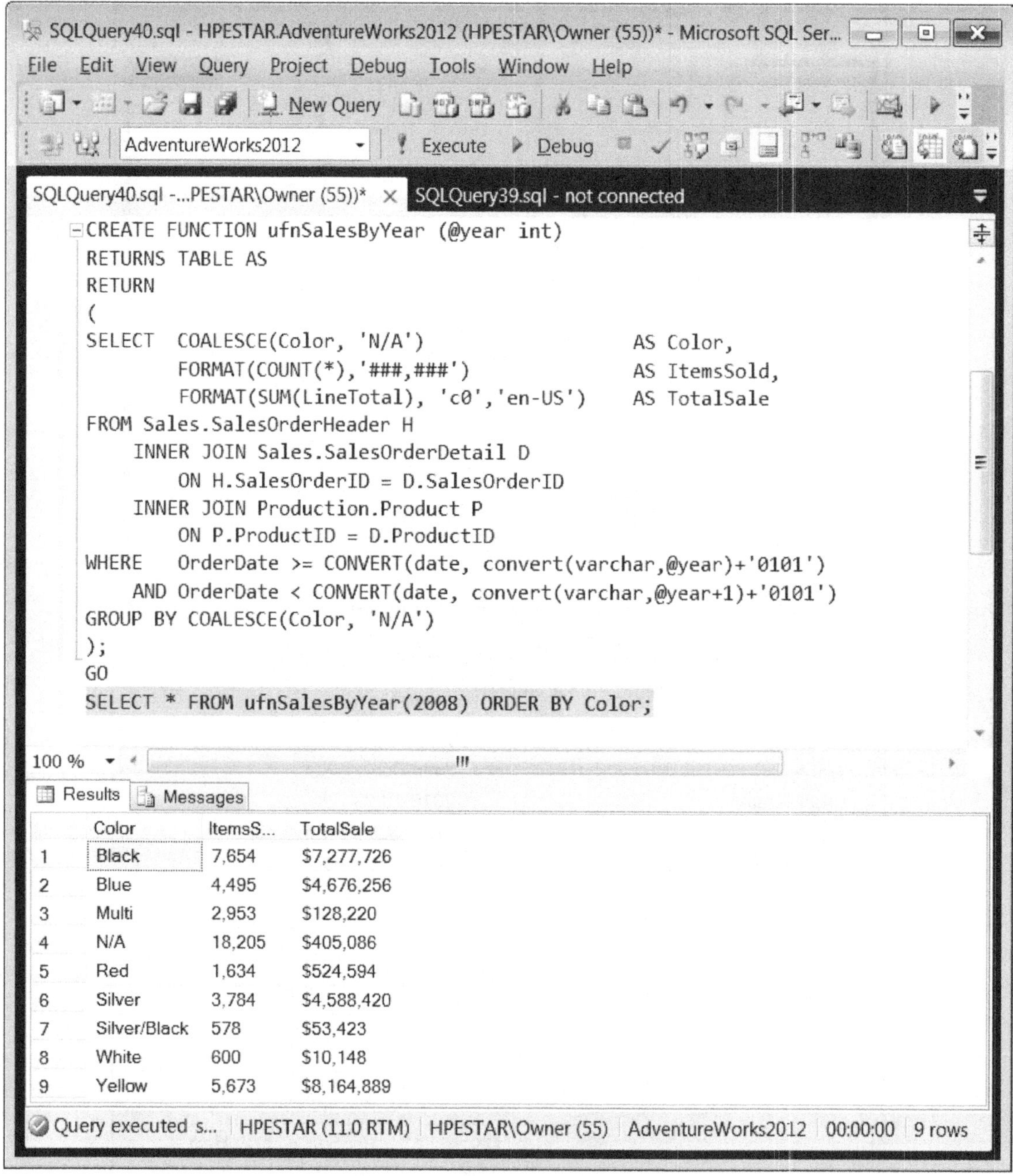
SQLQuery40.sql - HPESTAR.AdventureWorks2012 (HPESTAR\Owner (55))* - Microsoft SQL Ser...
File Edit View Query Project Debug Tools Window Help
New Query
AdventureWorks2012
Execute
Debug
SQLQuery40.sql -...PESTAR\Owner (55))*
SQLQuery39.sql - not connected
CREATE FUNCTION ufnSalesByYear (@year int)
RETURNS TABLE AS
RETURN
(
SELECT COALESCE(Color, 'N/A') AS Color,
FORMAT(COUNT(*),'###,###') AS ItemsSold,
FORMAT(SUM(LineTotal), 'c0','en-US') AS TotalSale
FROM Sales.SalesOrderHeader H
INNER JOIN Sales.SalesOrderDetail D
ON H.SalesOrderID = D.SalesOrderID
INNER JOIN Production.Product P
ON P.ProductID = D.ProductID
WHERE OrderDate >= CONVERT(date, convert(varchar,@year)+'0101')
AND OrderDate < CONVERT(date, convert(varchar,@year+1)+'0101')
GROUP BY COALESCE(Color, 'N/A')
);
GO
SELECT * FROM ufnSalesByYear(2008) ORDER BY Color;
100 %
Results
Messages
Color ItemsS... TotalSale
1 Black 7,654 $7,277,726
2 Blue 4,495 $4,676,256
3 Multi 2,953 $128,220
4 N/A 18,205 $405,086
5 Red 1,634 $524,594
6 Silver 3,784 $4,588,420
7 Silver/Black 578 $53,423
8 White 600 $10,148
9 Yellow 5,673 $8,164,889
Query executed s...
HPESTAR (11.0 RTM)
HPESTAR\Owner (55)
AdventureWorks2012
00:00:00
9 rows

PowerShell - On-Premises SQL Server

MSDN/Technet Blogs: **Windows Azure SQL Database Management with PowerShell**
http://blogs.msdn.com/b/windowsazure/archive/2013/02/07/windows-azure-sql-database-management-with-powershell.aspx
How to Manage Windows Azure SQL Database Servers Using Windows PowerShell
http://social.technet.microsoft.com/wiki/contents/articles/3804.how-to-manage-windows-azure-sql-database-servers-using-windows-powershell-en-us.aspx

In addition to executing sqlps in Command Prompt, we can enter PowerShell from SSMS Object Explorer via the right click drop-down menu. Entering the get-childitem command will list all the views in the path (directory).

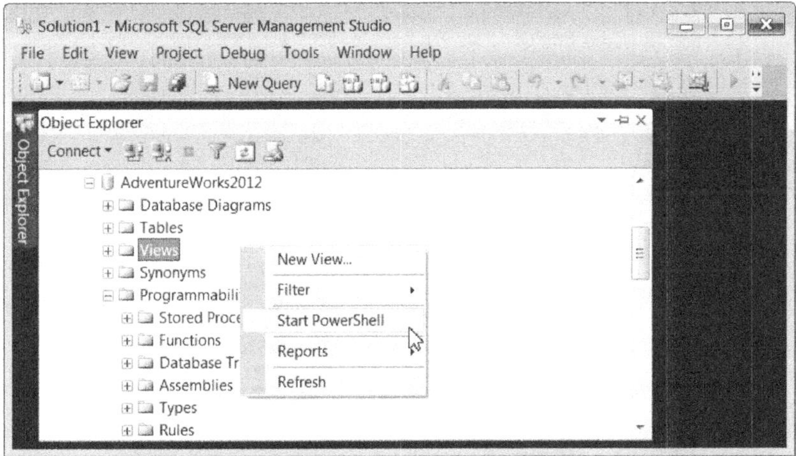

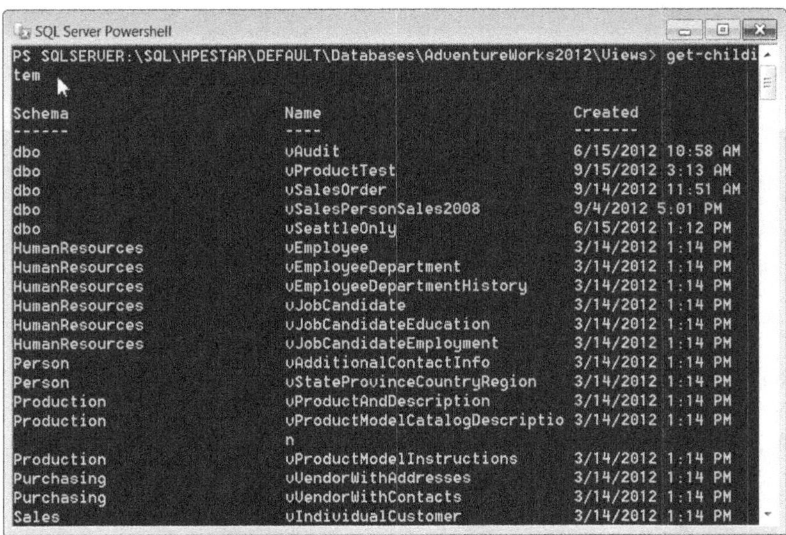

PowerShell Command List

The following command will list all the PowerShell commands.

```
get-command | out-file 'f:\temp\command.txt'
```

CommandType	Name	Definition
-----------	----	----------
Alias	%	ForEach-Object
Alias	?	Where-Object
Function	A:	Set-Location A:
Alias	ac	Add-Content
Cmdlet	Add-Computer	Add-Computer [-DomainName] <...
Cmdlet	Add-Content	Add-Content [-Path] <String[...
Cmdlet	Add-History	Add-History [[-InputObject] ...
Cmdlet	Add-Member	Add-Member [-MemberType] <PS...
Cmdlet	Add-PSSnapin	Add-PSSnapin [-Name] <String...
Cmdlet	Add-RoleMember	Add-RoleMember [-MemberName]...
Cmdlet	Add-SqlAvailabilityDatabase	Add-SqlAvailabilityDatabase ...
Cmdlet	Add-SqlAvailabilityGroupList...	Add-SqlAvailabilityGroupList...
Cmdlet	Add-Type	Add-Type [-TypeDefinition] <...
Alias	asnp	Add-PSSnapIn
Function	B:	Set-Location B:
Cmdlet	Backup-ASDatabase	Backup-ASDatabase [-BackupFi...
Cmdlet	Backup-SqlDatabase	Backup-SqlDatabase [-Databas...
Function	C:	Set-Location C:
Alias	cat	Get-Content
Alias	cd	Set-Location
Function	cd..	Set-Location ..
Function	cd\	Set-Location \
Alias	chdir	Set-Location
Cmdlet	Checkpoint-Computer	Checkpoint-Computer [-Descri...
Alias	clc	Clear-Content
Alias	clear	Clear-Host
Cmdlet	Clear-Content	Clear-Content [-Path] <Strin...
Cmdlet	Clear-EventLog	Clear-EventLog [-LogName] <S...
Cmdlet	Clear-History	Clear-History [[-Id] <Int32[...
Function	Clear-Host	$space = New-Object System.M...
Cmdlet	Clear-Item	Clear-Item [-Path] <String[]...
Cmdlet	Clear-ItemProperty	Clear-ItemProperty [-Path] <...
Cmdlet	Clear-Variable	Clear-Variable [-Name] <Stri...
Alias	clhy	Clear-History
Alias	cli	Clear-Item
Alias	clp	Clear-ItemProperty
Alias	cls	Clear-Host
Alias	clv	Clear-Variable
Alias	compare	Compare-Object
Cmdlet	Compare-Object	Compare-Object [-ReferenceOb...
Cmdlet	Complete-Transaction	Complete-Transaction [-Verbo...
Cmdlet	Connect-WSMan	Connect-WSMan [[-ComputerNam...
Cmdlet	ConvertFrom-Csv	ConvertFrom-Csv [-InputObjec...
Cmdlet	ConvertFrom-SecureString	ConvertFrom-SecureString [-S...
Cmdlet	ConvertFrom-StringData	ConvertFrom-StringData [-Str...
Cmdlet	Convert-Path	Convert-Path [-Path] <String...
Cmdlet	ConvertTo-Csv	ConvertTo-Csv [-InputObject]...
Cmdlet	ConvertTo-Html	ConvertTo-Html [[-Property] ...
Cmdlet	ConvertTo-SecureString	ConvertTo-SecureString [-Str...
Cmdlet	ConvertTo-Xml	ConvertTo-Xml [-InputObject]...
Cmdlet	Convert-UrnToPath	Convert-UrnToPath [-Urn] <St...
Alias	copy	Copy-Item
Cmdlet	Copy-Item	Copy-Item [-Path] <String[]>...
Cmdlet	Copy-ItemProperty	Copy-ItemProperty [-Path] <S...
Alias	cp	Copy-Item
Alias	cpi	Copy-Item
Alias	cpp	Copy-ItemProperty
Alias	cvpa	Convert-Path
Function	D:	Set-Location D:
Alias	dbp	Disable-PSBreakpoint
Cmdlet	Debug-Process	Debug-Process [-Name] <Strin...

Cmdlet	Decode-SqlName	Decode-SqlName [-SqlName] <S...
Alias	del	Remove-Item
Alias	diff	Compare-Object
Alias	dir	Get-ChildItem
Cmdlet	Disable-ComputerRestore	Disable-ComputerRestore [-Dr...
Cmdlet	Disable-PSBreakpoint	Disable-PSBreakpoint [-Break...
Function	Disable-PSRemoting	...
Cmdlet	Disable-PSSessionConfiguration	Disable-PSSessionConfigurati...
Cmdlet	Disable-SqlAlwaysOn	Disable-SqlAlwaysOn [[-Path]...
Cmdlet	Disable-WSManCredSSP	Disable-WSManCredSSP [-Role]...
Cmdlet	Disconnect-WSMan	Disconnect-WSMan [[-Computer...
Function	E:	Set-Location E:
Alias	ebp	Enable-PSBreakpoint
Alias	echo	Write-Output
Cmdlet	Enable-ComputerRestore	Enable-ComputerRestore [-Dri...
Cmdlet	Enable-PSBreakpoint	Enable-PSBreakpoint [-Id] <I...
Cmdlet	Enable-PSRemoting	Enable-PSRemoting [-Force] [...
Cmdlet	Enable-PSSessionConfiguration	Enable-PSSessionConfiguratio...
Cmdlet	Enable-SqlAlwaysOn	Enable-SqlAlwaysOn [[-Path] ...
Cmdlet	Enable-WSManCredSSP	Enable-WSManCredSSP [-Role] ...
Cmdlet	Encode-SqlName	Encode-SqlName [-SqlName] <S...
Cmdlet	Enter-PSSession	Enter-PSSession [-ComputerNa...
Alias	epal	Export-Alias
Alias	epcsv	Export-Csv
Alias	epsn	Export-PSSession
Alias	erase	Remove-Item
Alias	etsn	Enter-PSSession
Cmdlet	Exit-PSSession	Exit-PSSession [-Verbose] [-...
Cmdlet	Export-Alias	Export-Alias [-Path] <String...
Cmdlet	Export-Clixml	Export-Clixml [-Path] <Strin...
Cmdlet	Export-Console	Export-Console [[-Path] <Str...
Cmdlet	Export-Counter	Export-Counter [-Path] <Stri...
Cmdlet	Export-Csv	Export-Csv [-Path] <String> ...
Cmdlet	Export-FormatData	Export-FormatData [-InputObj...
Cmdlet	Export-ModuleMember	Export-ModuleMember [[-Funct...
Cmdlet	Export-PSSession	Export-PSSession [-Session] ...
Alias	exsn	Exit-PSSession
Function	F:	Set-Location F:
Alias	fc	Format-Custom
Alias	fl	Format-List
Alias	foreach	ForEach-Object
Cmdlet	ForEach-Object	ForEach-Object [-Process] <S...
Cmdlet	Format-Custom	Format-Custom [[-Property] <...
Cmdlet	Format-List	Format-List [[-Property] <Ob...
Cmdlet	Format-Table	Format-Table [[-Property] <O...
Cmdlet	Format-Wide	Format-Wide [[-Property] <Ob...
Alias	ft	Format-Table
Alias	fw	Format-Wide
Function	G:	Set-Location G:
Alias	gal	Get-Alias
Alias	gbp	Get-PSBreakpoint
Alias	gc	Get-Content
Alias	gci	Get-ChildItem
Alias	gcm	Get-Command
Alias	gcs	Get-PSCallStack
Alias	gdr	Get-PSDrive
Cmdlet	Get-Acl	Get-Acl [[-Path] <String[]>]...
Cmdlet	Get-Alias	Get-Alias [[-Name] <String[]...
Cmdlet	Get-AuthenticodeSignature	Get-AuthenticodeSignature [-...
Cmdlet	Get-ChildItem	Get-ChildItem [[-Path] <Stri...
Cmdlet	Get-Command	Get-Command [[-ArgumentList]...
Cmdlet	Get-ComputerRestorePoint	Get-ComputerRestorePoint [[-...
Cmdlet	Get-Content	Get-Content [-Path] <String[...
Cmdlet	Get-Counter	Get-Counter [[-Counter] <Str...
Cmdlet	Get-Credential	Get-Credential [-Credential]...
Cmdlet	Get-Culture	Get-Culture [-Verbose] [-Deb...
Cmdlet	Get-Date	Get-Date [[-Date] <DateTime>...
Cmdlet	Get-Event	Get-Event [[-SourceIdentifie...
Cmdlet	Get-EventLog	Get-EventLog [-LogName] <Str...
Cmdlet	Get-EventSubscriber	Get-EventSubscriber [[-Sourc...
Cmdlet	Get-ExecutionPolicy	Get-ExecutionPolicy [[-Scope...
Cmdlet	Get-FormatData	Get-FormatData [[-TypeName] ...
Cmdlet	Get-Help	Get-Help [[-Name] <String>] ...

Cmdlet	Get-History	Get-History [[-Id] <Int64[]>...
Cmdlet	Get-Host	Get-Host [-Verbose] [-Debug]...
Cmdlet	Get-HotFix	Get-HotFix [[-Id] <String[]>...
Cmdlet	Get-Item	Get-Item [-Path] <String[]> ...
Cmdlet	Get-ItemProperty	Get-ItemProperty [-Path] <St...
Cmdlet	Get-Job	Get-Job [[-Id] <Int32[]>] [-...
Cmdlet	Get-Location	Get-Location [-PSProvider <S...
Cmdlet	Get-Member	Get-Member [[-Name] <String[...
Cmdlet	Get-Module	Get-Module [[-Name] <String[...
Cmdlet	Get-PfxCertificate	Get-PfxCertificate [-FilePat...
Cmdlet	Get-Process	Get-Process [[-Name] <String...
Cmdlet	Get-PSBreakpoint	Get-PSBreakpoint [[-Script] ...
Cmdlet	Get-PSCallStack	Get-PSCallStack [-Verbose] [...
Cmdlet	Get-PSDrive	Get-PSDrive [[-Name] <String...
Cmdlet	Get-PSProvider	Get-PSProvider [[-PSProvider...
Cmdlet	Get-PSSession	Get-PSSession [[-ComputerNam...
Cmdlet	Get-PSSessionConfiguration	Get-PSSessionConfiguration [...
Cmdlet	Get-PSSnapin	Get-PSSnapin [[-Name] <Strin...
Cmdlet	Get-Random	Get-Random [[-Maximum] <Obje...
Cmdlet	Get-Service	Get-Service [[-Name] <String...
Cmdlet	Get-TraceSource	Get-TraceSource [[-Name] <St...
Cmdlet	Get-Transaction	Get-Transaction [-Verbose] [...
Cmdlet	Get-UICulture	Get-UICulture [-Verbose] [-D...
Cmdlet	Get-Unique	Get-Unique [-InputObject <PS...
Cmdlet	Get-Variable	Get-Variable [[-Name] <Strin...
Function	Get-Verb	...
Cmdlet	Get-WinEvent	Get-WinEvent [[-LogName] <St...
Cmdlet	Get-WmiObject	Get-WmiObject [-Class] <Stri...
Cmdlet	Get-WSManCredSSP	Get-WSManCredSSP [-Verbose] ...
Cmdlet	Get-WSManInstance	Get-WSManInstance [-Resource...
Alias	ghy	Get-History
Alias	gi	Get-Item
Alias	gjb	Get-Job
Alias	gl	Get-Location
Alias	gm	Get-Member
Alias	gmo	Get-Module
Alias	gp	Get-ItemProperty
Alias	gps	Get-Process
Alias	group	Group-Object
Cmdlet	Group-Object	Group-Object [[-Property] <O...
Alias	gsn	Get-PSSession
Alias	gsnp	Get-PSSnapIn
Alias	gsv	Get-Service
Alias	gu	Get-Unique
Alias	gv	Get-Variable
Alias	gwmi	Get-WmiObject
Alias	h	Get-History
Function	H:	Set-Location H:
Function	help	...
Alias	history	Get-History
Function	I:	Set-Location I:
Alias	icm	Invoke-Command
Alias	iex	Invoke-Expression
Alias	ihy	Invoke-History
Alias	ii	Invoke-Item
Cmdlet	Import-Alias	Import-Alias [-Path] <String...
Cmdlet	Import-Clixml	Import-Clixml [-Path] <Strin...
Cmdlet	Import-Counter	Import-Counter [-Path] <Stri...
Cmdlet	Import-Csv	Import-Csv [-Path] <String[]...
Cmdlet	Import-LocalizedData	Import-LocalizedData [-Bindi...
Cmdlet	Import-Module	Import-Module [-Name] <Strin...
Cmdlet	Import-PSSession	Import-PSSession [-Session] ...
Function	ImportSystemModules	...
Cmdlet	Invoke-ASCmd	Invoke-ASCmd [-Verbose] [-De...
Cmdlet	Invoke-Command	Invoke-Command [-ScriptBlock...
Cmdlet	Invoke-Expression	Invoke-Expression [-Command]...
Cmdlet	Invoke-History	Invoke-History [[-Id] <Strin...
Cmdlet	Invoke-Item	Invoke-Item [-Path] <String[...
Cmdlet	Invoke-PolicyEvaluation	Invoke-PolicyEvaluation [-Po...
Cmdlet	Invoke-ProcessCube	Invoke-ProcessCube [-Name] <...
Cmdlet	Invoke-ProcessDimension	Invoke-ProcessDimension [-Na...
Cmdlet	Invoke-ProcessPartition	Invoke-ProcessPartition [-Na...
Cmdlet	Invoke-Sqlcmd	Invoke-Sqlcmd [[-Query] <Str...

Cmdlet	Invoke-WmiMethod	Invoke-WmiMethod [-Class] <S...
Cmdlet	Invoke-WSManAction	Invoke-WSManAction [-Resourc...
Alias	ipal	Import-Alias
Alias	ipcsv	Import-Csv
Alias	ipmo	Import-Module
Alias	ipsn	Import-PSSession
Alias	ise	powershell_ise.exe
Alias	iwmi	Invoke-WMIMethod
Function	J:	Set-Location J:
Cmdlet	Join-Path	Join-Path [-Path] <String[]>...
Cmdlet	Join-SqlAvailabilityGroup	Join-SqlAvailabilityGroup [-...
Function	K:	Set-Location K:
Alias	kill	Stop-Process
Function	L:	Set-Location L:
Cmdlet	Limit-EventLog	Limit-EventLog [-LogName] <S...
Alias	lp	Out-Printer
Alias	ls	Get-ChildItem
Function	M:	Set-Location M:
Alias	man	help
Alias	md	mkdir
Alias	measure	Measure-Object
Cmdlet	Measure-Command	Measure-Command [-Expression...
Cmdlet	Measure-Object	Measure-Object [[-Property] ...
Cmdlet	Merge-Partition	Merge-Partition [-Name] <Str...
Alias	mi	Move-Item
Function	mkdir	...
Function	more	param([string[]]$paths)...
Alias	mount	New-PSDrive
Alias	move	Move-Item
Cmdlet	Move-Item	Move-Item [-Path] <String[]>...
Cmdlet	Move-ItemProperty	Move-ItemProperty [-Path] <S...
Alias	mp	Move-ItemProperty
Alias	mv	Move-Item
Function	N:	Set-Location N:
Alias	nal	New-Alias
Alias	ndr	New-PSDrive
Cmdlet	New-Alias	New-Alias [-Name] <String> [...
Cmdlet	New-Event	New-Event [-SourceIdentifier...
Cmdlet	New-EventLog	New-EventLog [-LogName] <Str...
Cmdlet	New-Item	New-Item [-Path] <String[]> ...
Cmdlet	New-ItemProperty	New-ItemProperty [-Path] <St...
Cmdlet	New-Module	New-Module [-ScriptBlock] <S...
Cmdlet	New-ModuleManifest	New-ModuleManifest [-Path] <...
Cmdlet	New-Object	New-Object [-TypeName] <Stri...
Cmdlet	New-PSDrive	New-PSDrive [-Name] <String>...
Cmdlet	New-PSSession	New-PSSession [[-ComputerNam...
Cmdlet	New-PSSessionOption	New-PSSessionOption [-Maximu...
Cmdlet	New-RestoreFolder	New-RestoreFolder [-Original...
Cmdlet	New-RestoreLocation	New-RestoreLocation [-File <...
Cmdlet	New-Service	New-Service [-Name] <String>...
Cmdlet	New-SqlAvailabilityGroup	New-SqlAvailabilityGroup [-N...
Cmdlet	New-SqlAvailabilityGroupList...	New-SqlAvailabilityGroupList...
Cmdlet	New-SqlAvailabilityReplica	New-SqlAvailabilityReplica [...
Cmdlet	New-SqlHADREndpoint	New-SqlHADREndpoint [-Name] ...
Cmdlet	New-TimeSpan	New-TimeSpan [[-Start] <Date...
Cmdlet	New-Variable	New-Variable [-Name] <String...
Cmdlet	New-WebServiceProxy	New-WebServiceProxy [-Uri] <...
Cmdlet	New-WSManInstance	New-WSManInstance [-Resource...
Cmdlet	New-WSManSessionOption	New-WSManSessionOption [-Pro...
Alias	ni	New-Item
Alias	nmo	New-Module
Alias	nsn	New-PSSession
Alias	nv	New-Variable
Function	O:	Set-Location O:
Alias	ogv	Out-GridView
Alias	oh	Out-Host
Cmdlet	Out-Default	Out-Default [-InputObject <P...
Cmdlet	Out-File	Out-File [-FilePath] <String...
Cmdlet	Out-GridView	Out-GridView [-InputObject <...
Cmdlet	Out-Host	Out-Host [-Paging] [-InputOb...
Cmdlet	Out-Null	Out-Null [-InputObject <PSOb...
Cmdlet	Out-Printer	Out-Printer [[-Name] <String...
Cmdlet	Out-String	Out-String [-Stream] [-Width...

Function	P:	Set-Location P:
Alias	popd	Pop-Location
Cmdlet	Pop-Location	Pop-Location [-PassThru] [-S...
Function	prompt	$(if (test-path variable:/PS...
Alias	ps	Get-Process
Alias	pushd	Push-Location
Cmdlet	Push-Location	Push-Location [[-Path] <Stri...
Alias	pwd	Get-Location
Function	Q:	Set-Location Q:
Alias	r	Invoke-History
Function	R:	Set-Location R:
Alias	rbp	Remove-PSBreakpoint
Alias	rcjb	Receive-Job
Alias	rd	Remove-Item
Alias	rdr	Remove-PSDrive
Cmdlet	Read-Host	Read-Host [[-Prompt] <Object...
Cmdlet	Receive-Job	Receive-Job [-Job] <Job[]> [...
Cmdlet	Register-EngineEvent	Register-EngineEvent [-Sourc...
Cmdlet	Register-ObjectEvent	Register-ObjectEvent [-Input...
Cmdlet	Register-PSSessionConfiguration	Register-PSSessionConfigurat...
Cmdlet	Register-WmiEvent	Register-WmiEvent [-Class] <...
Cmdlet	Remove-Computer	Remove-Computer [[-Credentia...
Cmdlet	Remove-Event	Remove-Event [-SourceIdentif...
Cmdlet	Remove-EventLog	Remove-EventLog [-LogName] <...
Cmdlet	Remove-Item	Remove-Item [-Path] <String[...
Cmdlet	Remove-ItemProperty	Remove-ItemProperty [-Path] ...
Cmdlet	Remove-Job	Remove-Job [-Id] <Int32[]> [...
Cmdlet	Remove-Module	Remove-Module [-Name] <Strin...
Cmdlet	Remove-PSBreakpoint	Remove-PSBreakpoint [-Breakp...
Cmdlet	Remove-PSDrive	Remove-PSDrive [-Name] <Stri...
Cmdlet	Remove-PSSession	Remove-PSSession [-Id] <Int3...
Cmdlet	Remove-PSSnapin	Remove-PSSnapin [-Name] <Str...
Cmdlet	Remove-RoleMember	Remove-RoleMember [-MemberNa...
Cmdlet	Remove-SqlAvailabilityDatabase	Remove-SqlAvailabilityDataba...
Cmdlet	Remove-SqlAvailabilityGroup	Remove-SqlAvailabilityGroup ...
Cmdlet	Remove-SqlAvailabilityReplica	Remove-SqlAvailabilityReplic...
Cmdlet	Remove-Variable	Remove-Variable [-Name] <Str...
Cmdlet	Remove-WmiObject	Remove-WmiObject [-Class] <S...
Cmdlet	Remove-WSManInstance	Remove-WSManInstance [-Resou...
Alias	ren	Rename-Item
Cmdlet	Rename-Item	Rename-Item [-Path] <String>...
Cmdlet	Rename-ItemProperty	Rename-ItemProperty [-Path] ...
Cmdlet	Reset-ComputerMachinePassword	Reset-ComputerMachinePasswor...
Cmdlet	Resolve-Path	Resolve-Path [-Path] <String...
Cmdlet	Restart-Computer	Restart-Computer [[-Computer...
Cmdlet	Restart-Service	Restart-Service [-Name] <Str...
Cmdlet	Restore-ASDatabase	Restore-ASDatabase [-Restore...
Cmdlet	Restore-Computer	Restore-Computer [-RestorePo...
Cmdlet	Restore-SqlDatabase	Restore-SqlDatabase [-Databa...
Cmdlet	Resume-Service	Resume-Service [-Name] <Stri...
Cmdlet	Resume-SqlAvailabilityDatabase	Resume-SqlAvailabilityDataba...
Alias	ri	Remove-Item
Alias	rjb	Remove-Job
Alias	rm	Remove-Item
Alias	rmdir	Remove-Item
Alias	rmo	Remove-Module
Alias	rni	Rename-Item
Alias	rnp	Rename-ItemProperty
Alias	rp	Remove-ItemProperty
Alias	rsn	Remove-PSSession
Alias	rsnp	Remove-PSSnapin
Alias	rv	Remove-Variable
Alias	rvpa	Resolve-Path
Alias	rwmi	Remove-WMIObject
Function	S:	Set-Location S:
Alias	sajb	Start-Job
Alias	sal	Set-Alias
Alias	saps	Start-Process
Alias	sasv	Start-Service
Alias	sbp	Set-PSBreakpoint
Alias	sc	Set-Content
Alias	select	Select-Object
Cmdlet	Select-Object	Select-Object [[-Property] <...

Cmdlet	Select-String	Select-String [-Pattern] <St...
Cmdlet	Select-Xml	Select-Xml [-XPath] <String>...
Cmdlet	Send-MailMessage	Send-MailMessage [-To] <Stri...
Alias	set	Set-Variable
Cmdlet	Set-Acl	Set-Acl [-Path] <String[]> [...
Cmdlet	Set-Alias	Set-Alias [-Name] <String> [...
Cmdlet	Set-AuthenticodeSignature	Set-AuthenticodeSignature [-...
Cmdlet	Set-Content	Set-Content [-Path] <String[...
Cmdlet	Set-Date	Set-Date [-Date] <DateTime> ...
Cmdlet	Set-ExecutionPolicy	Set-ExecutionPolicy [-Execut...
Cmdlet	Set-Item	Set-Item [-Path] <String[]> ...
Cmdlet	Set-ItemProperty	Set-ItemProperty [-Path] <St...
Cmdlet	Set-Location	Set-Location [[-Path] <Strin...
Cmdlet	Set-PSBreakpoint	Set-PSBreakpoint [-Script] <...
Cmdlet	Set-PSDebug	Set-PSDebug [-Trace <Int32>]...
Cmdlet	Set-PSSessionConfiguration	Set-PSSessionConfiguration [...
Cmdlet	Set-Service	Set-Service [-Name] <String>...
Cmdlet	Set-SqlAvailabilityGroup	Set-SqlAvailabilityGroup [[-...
Cmdlet	Set-SqlAvailabilityGroupList...	Set-SqlAvailabilityGroupList...
Cmdlet	Set-SqlAvailabilityReplica	Set-SqlAvailabilityReplica [...
Cmdlet	Set-SqlHADREndpoint	Set-SqlHADREndpoint [[-Path]...
Cmdlet	Set-StrictMode	Set-StrictMode -Version <Ver...
Cmdlet	Set-TraceSource	Set-TraceSource [-Name] <Str...
Cmdlet	Set-Variable	Set-Variable [-Name] <String...
Cmdlet	Set-WmiInstance	Set-WmiInstance [-Class] <St...
Cmdlet	Set-WSManInstance	Set-WSManInstance [-Resource...
Cmdlet	Set-WSManQuickConfig	Set-WSManQuickConfig [-UseSS...
Cmdlet	Show-EventLog	Show-EventLog [[-ComputerNam...
Alias	si	Set-Item
Alias	sl	Set-Location
Alias	sleep	Start-Sleep
Alias	sort	Sort-Object
Cmdlet	Sort-Object	Sort-Object [[-Property] <Ob...
Alias	sp	Set-ItemProperty
Alias	spjb	Stop-Job
Cmdlet	Split-Path	Split-Path [-Path] <String[]...
Alias	spps	Stop-Process
Alias	spsv	Stop-Service
Function	SQLSERVER:	Set-Location SQLSERVER:
Alias	start	Start-Process
Cmdlet	Start-Job	Start-Job [-ScriptBlock] <Sc...
Cmdlet	Start-Process	Start-Process [-FilePath] <S...
Cmdlet	Start-Service	Start-Service [-Name] <Strin...
Cmdlet	Start-Sleep	Start-Sleep [-Seconds] <Int3...
Cmdlet	Start-Transaction	Start-Transaction [-Timeout ...
Cmdlet	Start-Transcript	Start-Transcript [[-Path] <S...
Cmdlet	Stop-Computer	Stop-Computer [[-ComputerNam...
Cmdlet	Stop-Job	Stop-Job [-Id] <Int32[]> [-P...
Cmdlet	Stop-Process	Stop-Process [-Id] <Int32[]>...
Cmdlet	Stop-Service	Stop-Service [-Name] <String...
Cmdlet	Stop-Transcript	Stop-Transcript [-Verbose] [...
Cmdlet	Suspend-Service	Suspend-Service [-Name] <Str...
Cmdlet	Suspend-SqlAvailabilityDatabase	Suspend-SqlAvailabilityDatab...
Alias	sv	Set-Variable
Cmdlet	Switch-SqlAvailabilityGroup	Switch-SqlAvailabilityGroup ...
Alias	swmi	Set-WMIInstance
Function	T:	Set-Location T:
Function	TabExpansion	...
Alias	tee	Tee-Object
Cmdlet	Tee-Object	Tee-Object [-FilePath] <Stri...
Cmdlet	Test-ComputerSecureChannel	Test-ComputerSecureChannel [...
Cmdlet	Test-Connection	Test-Connection [-ComputerNa...
Cmdlet	Test-ModuleManifest	Test-ModuleManifest [-Path] ...
Cmdlet	Test-Path	Test-Path [-Path] <String[]>...
Cmdlet	Test-SqlAvailabilityGroup	Test-SqlAvailabilityGroup [[...
Cmdlet	Test-SqlAvailabilityReplica	Test-SqlAvailabilityReplica ...
Cmdlet	Test-SqlDatabaseReplicaState	Test-SqlDatabaseReplicaState...
Cmdlet	Test-WSMan	Test-WSMan [[-ComputerName] ...
Cmdlet	Trace-Command	Trace-Command [-Name] <Strin...
Alias	type	Get-Content
Function	U:	Set-Location U:
Cmdlet	Undo-Transaction	Undo-Transaction [-Verbose] ...
Cmdlet	Unregister-Event	Unregister-Event [-SourceIde...

Cmdlet	Unregister-PSSessionConfigur...	Unregister-PSSessionConfigur...
Cmdlet	Update-FormatData	Update-FormatData [[-AppendP...
Cmdlet	Update-List	Update-List [[-Property] <St...
Cmdlet	Update-TypeData	Update-TypeData [[-AppendPat...
Cmdlet	Use-Transaction	Use-Transaction [-Transacted...
Function	V:	Set-Location V:
Function	W:	Set-Location W:
Cmdlet	Wait-Event	Wait-Event [[-SourceIdentifi...
Cmdlet	Wait-Job	Wait-Job [-Id] <Int32[]> [-A...
Cmdlet	Wait-Process	Wait-Process [-Name] <String...
Alias	where	Where-Object
Cmdlet	Where-Object	Where-Object [-FilterScript]...
Alias	wjb	Wait-Job
Alias	write	Write-Output
Cmdlet	Write-Debug	Write-Debug [-Message] <Stri...
Cmdlet	Write-Error	Write-Error [-Message] <Stri...
Cmdlet	Write-EventLog	Write-EventLog [-LogName] <S...
Cmdlet	Write-Host	Write-Host [[-Object] <Objec...
Cmdlet	Write-Output	Write-Output [-InputObject] ...
Cmdlet	Write-Progress	Write-Progress [-Activity] <...
Cmdlet	Write-Verbose	Write-Verbose [-Message] <St...
Cmdlet	Write-Warning	Write-Warning [-Message] <St...
Function	X:	Set-Location X:
Function	Y:	Set-Location Y:
Function	Z:	Set-Location Z:

We can access help for a command just by typing "help" and the command name. "help" example for format-list.

```
help format-list
```

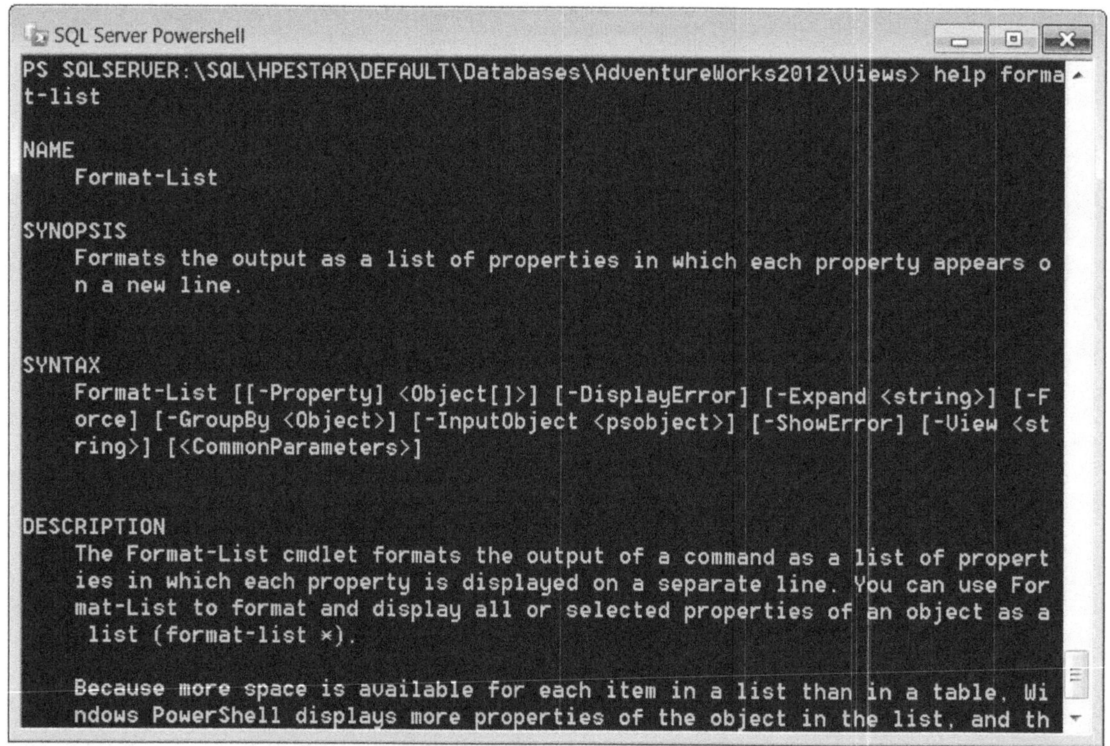

SQL Server Powershell
PS SQLSERVER:\SQL\HPESTAR\DEFAULT\Databases\AdventureWorks2012\Views> help forma
t-list
NAME
Format-List
SYNOPSIS
Formats the output as a list of properties in which each property appears o
n a new line.
SYNTAX
Format-List [[-Property] <Object[]>] [-DisplayError] [-Expand <string>] [-F
orce] [-GroupBy <Object>] [-InputObject <psobject>] [-ShowError] [-View <st
ring>] [<CommonParameters>]
DESCRIPTION
The Format-List cmdlet formats the output of a command as a list of propert
ies in which each property is displayed on a separate line. You can use For
mat-List to format and display all or selected properties of an object as a
list (format-list *).
Because more space is available for each item in a list than in a table, Wi
ndows PowerShell displays more properties of the object in the list, and th

TRY...CATCH Block With TRANSACTION

If the TRY is successful the transaction is committed, otherwise the transaction (previous statements if any) is rolled back and the error is logged into an errorlog table.

```
USE AdventureWorks2012; -- Create & configure table for testing
IF OBJECT_ID ('dbo.Product', 'U') IS NOT NULL DROP TABLE dbo.Product ;
CREATE TABLE Product(ID INT PRIMARY KEY, ProductName varchar(50),
        ListPrice smallmoney, ModifiedDate smalldatetime); INSERT Product
SELECT ProductID, Name, ListPrice, ModifiedDate FROM Production.Product WHERE ListPrice > 0; -- (304 row(s) affected)
GO
ALTER TABLE PRODUCT ADD CONSTRAINT uqProd UNIQUE (ProductName);
ALTER TABLE PRODUCT ADD CONSTRAINT dfProd DEFAULT (CURRENT_TIMESTAMP) FOR ModifiedDate;
ALTER TABLE PRODUCT ADD rowguid UNIQUEIDENTIFIER default(newid());
GO -- Command(s) completed successfully.
```

```
IF OBJECT_ID ('dbo.ErrorLogForTransactions', 'U') IS NOT NULL DROP TABLE dbo.ErrorLogForTransactions ;
CREATE TABLE ErrorLogForTransactions( ID INT IDENTITY(1,1) PRIMARY KEY,
      UserName sysname, TableName sysname, ErrorNumber sysname, ErrorSeverity sysname,
      ErrorState sysname, ErrorMessage nvarchar(1024), rowguid UNIQUEIDENTIFIER default(newid()),
      ModifiedDate datetime default (getdate()));
GO -- Command(s) completed successfully.
```

```
IF OBJECT_ID ('dbo.uspInsertNewProduct', 'P') IS NOT NULL DROP PROC dbo.uspInsertNewProduct ;
GO
CREATE PROCEDURE uspInsertNewProduct ( @NewProduct NVARCHAR(64), @Price SMALLMONEY) AS
BEGIN   DECLARE @TableName SYSNAME, @ErrorMessage NVARCHAR(1024);
  BEGIN TRY;   BEGIN TRANSACTION;
   SELECT @ErrorMessage = 'Duplicate insert failed', @TableName = 'Product';
   INSERT dbo.Product (ID, ProductName, ListPrice)
        SELECT max(ID)+1, @NewProduct, @Price FROM Product;   COMMIT TRANSACTION;
  END TRY
  BEGIN CATCH   ROLLBACK TRANSACTION;   INSERT dbo.ErrorLogForTransactions
          (UserName, TableName, ErrorNumber, errorSeverity, errorState, ErrorMessage)
          VALUES(suser_sname(),@TableName,ERROR_NUMBER(),ERROR_SEVERITY(),
           ERROR_STATE(),ERROR_MESSAGE());   RAISERROR (@ErrorMessage,16,1);   END CATCH
END
GO
```

```
EXEC uspInsertNewProduct 'xDelta SmartPhone', 999.99;          -- Valid INSERT
```

```
DECLARE @NewProduct varchar(64) = (SELECT TOP(1) ProductName FROM Product), @Price SMALLMONEY = 999.99;
EXEC uspInsertNewProduct @NewProduct, @Price;          -- Invalid INSERT - duplicate name
GO -- Msg 50000, Level 16, State 1, Procedure uspInsertNewProduct, Line 10 Duplicate insert failed
```

```
SELECT * FROM ErrorLogForTransactions;
```

ID	UserName	TableName	ErrorNumber	ErrorSeverity	ErrorState	ErrorMessage	ModifiedDate
1	BlueZonder	Product	2627	14	1	Violation of UNIQUE KEY constraint 'uqProd'. Cannot insert duplicate key in object 'dbo.Product'. The duplicate key value is (All-Purpose Bike Stand).	2016-12-09 13:35:23.687

SET TRANSACTION ISOLATION LEVEL Command

Note: Distributed transactions are not supported among Azure SQL databases.

The syntax for setting isolation level:

SET TRANSACTION ISOLATION LEVEL

{ READ UNCOMMITTED

| READ COMMITTED

| REPEATABLE READ

| SNAPSHOT

| SERIALIZABLE } [;]

Preparation for demonstrating levels. We have to use 2 connections to represent 2 users of the database. First we create a test table.

```
USE AdventureWorks2012; -- Create & configure table for testing
IF OBJECT_ID ('dbo.Product', 'U') IS NOT NULL DROP TABLE dbo.Product ;
CREATE TABLE Product(ProductID INT PRIMARY KEY, ProductName varchar(50),
        ListPrice smallmoney, Color varchar(15), ModifiedDate smalldatetime); INSERT Product
SELECT ProductID, Name, ListPrice, Color, ModifiedDate FROM Production.Product; -- (504 row(s) affected)
```

In connection 1 we simulate a large (slow) transaction on the Product table.

```
BEGIN TRAN;
SELECT StartTime = CURRENT_TIMESTAMP;
UPDATE Product SET ListPrice=ListPrice * 1.05;
WAITFOR DELAY '00:00:20'; -- 20 sec delay to keep transaction pending
ROLLBACK TRAN;
SELECT FinishTime = CURRENT_TIMESTAMP;
```

In connection 2 we test the isolation levels. We start execution after connection 1 started.

```
SET TRANSACTION ISOLATION LEVEL READ UNCOMMITTED
SELECT StartTime = CURRENT_TIMESTAMP;
SELECT TOP (2) * FROM Product ORDER BY ListPrice DESC;
SELECT FinishTime = CURRENT_TIMESTAMP;
```

READ UNCOMMITTED Isolation Level - Dirty Reads

The SELECT with TOP started 4 seconds later after the UPDATE, yet it finished immediately without waiting for the UPDATE transaction to come to a conclusion (ROLLBACK or COMMIT).

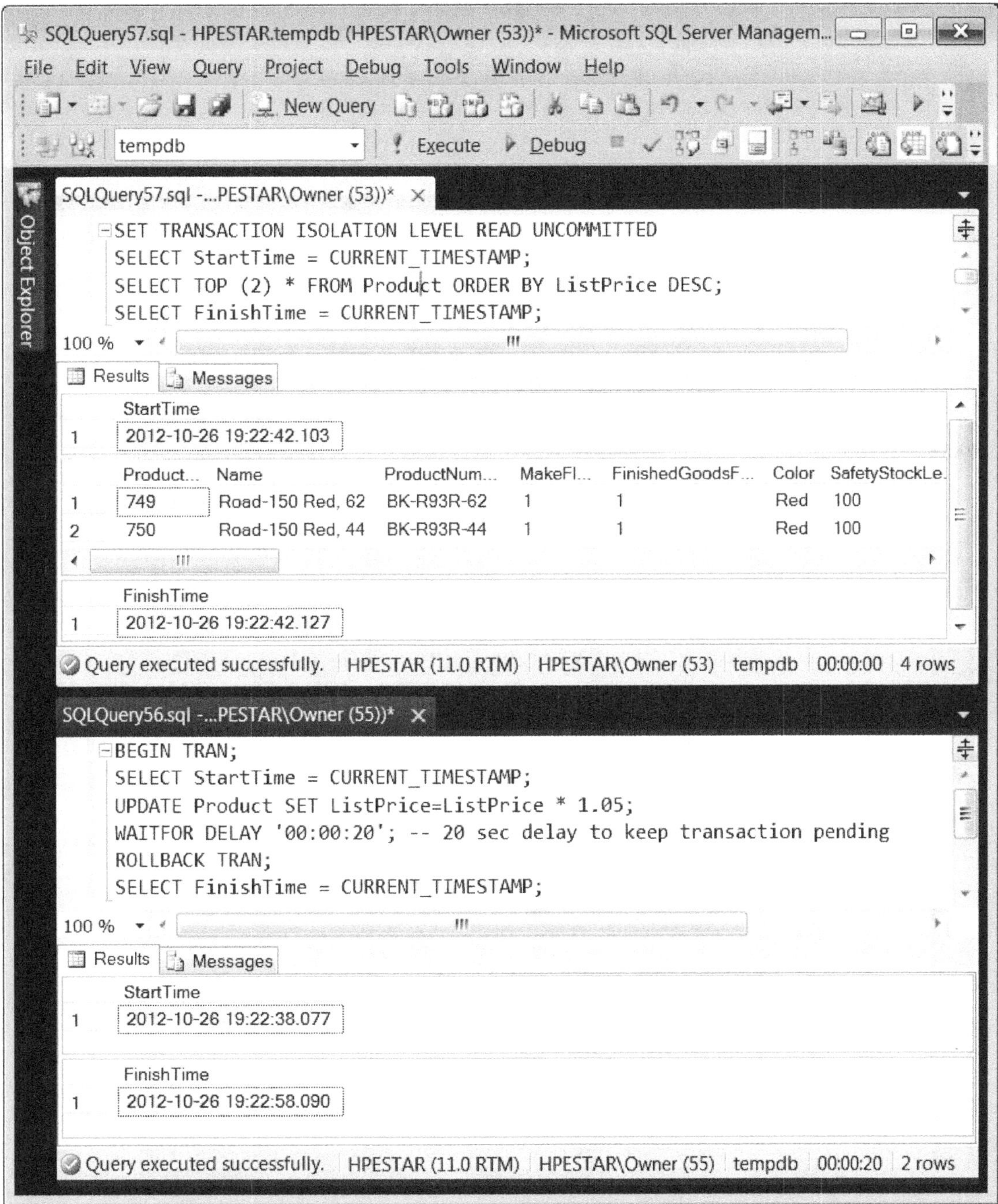
SQLQuery57.sql - HPESTAR.tempdb (HPESTAR\Owner (53))* - Microsoft SQL Server Managem...
File Edit View Query Project Debug Tools Window Help
New Query
tempdb
Execute
Debug
SQLQuery57.sql -...PESTAR\Owner (53))*
SET TRANSACTION ISOLATION LEVEL READ UNCOMMITTED
SELECT StartTime = CURRENT_TIMESTAMP;
SELECT TOP (2) * FROM Product ORDER BY ListPrice DESC;
SELECT FinishTime = CURRENT_TIMESTAMP;
100 %
Results
Messages
StartTime
1 2012-10-26 19:22:42.103
Product... Name ProductNum... MakeFl... FinishedGoodsF... Color SafetyStockLe.
1 749 Road-150 Red, 62 BK-R93R-62 1 1 Red 100
2 750 Road-150 Red, 44 BK-R93R-44 1 1 Red 100
FinishTime
1 2012-10-26 19:22:42.127
Query executed successfully. HPESTAR (11.0 RTM) HPESTAR\Owner (53) tempdb 00:00:00 4 rows
SQLQuery56.sql -...PESTAR\Owner (55))*
BEGIN TRAN;
SELECT StartTime = CURRENT_TIMESTAMP;
UPDATE Product SET ListPrice=ListPrice * 1.05;
WAITFOR DELAY '00:00:20'; -- 20 sec delay to keep transaction pending
ROLLBACK TRAN;
SELECT FinishTime = CURRENT_TIMESTAMP;
100 %
Results
Messages
StartTime
1 2012-10-26 19:22:38.077
FinishTime
1 2012-10-26 19:22:58.090
Query executed successfully. HPESTAR (11.0 RTM) HPESTAR\Owner (55) tempdb 00:00:20 2 rows
Object Explorer

READ COMMITTED Isolation Level - Default for SQL Server

The SELECT query waits until the exclusive lock is removed by the UPDATE transaction. To prevent such a wait, frequently the NOLOCK hint (dirty reads) is used.

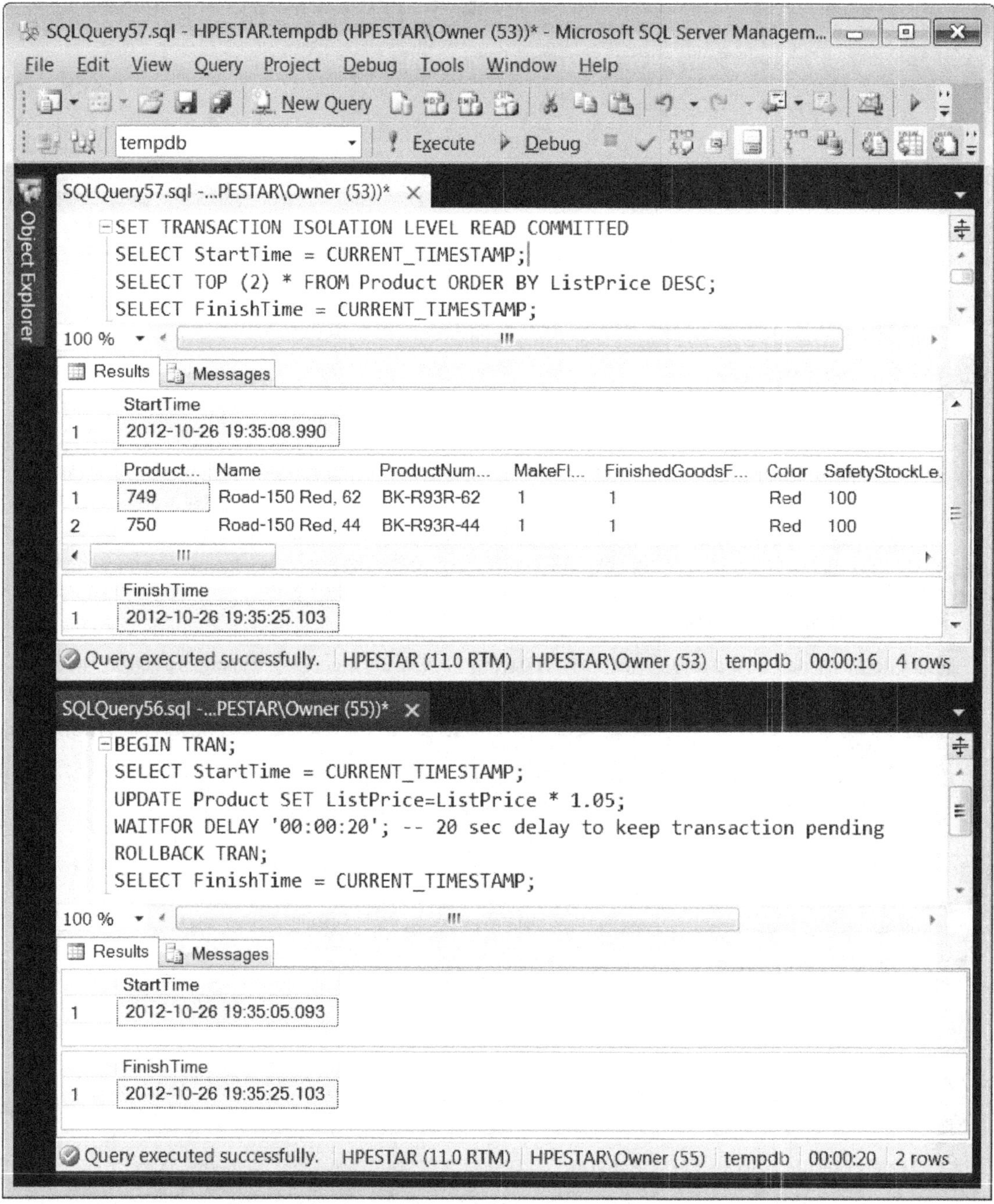

REPEATABLE READ Isolation Level

The UPDATE (transaction by itself) must wait until the exclusive lock is released by the 2 SELECT statements transaction. The ListPrice changed after the COMMIT transaction.

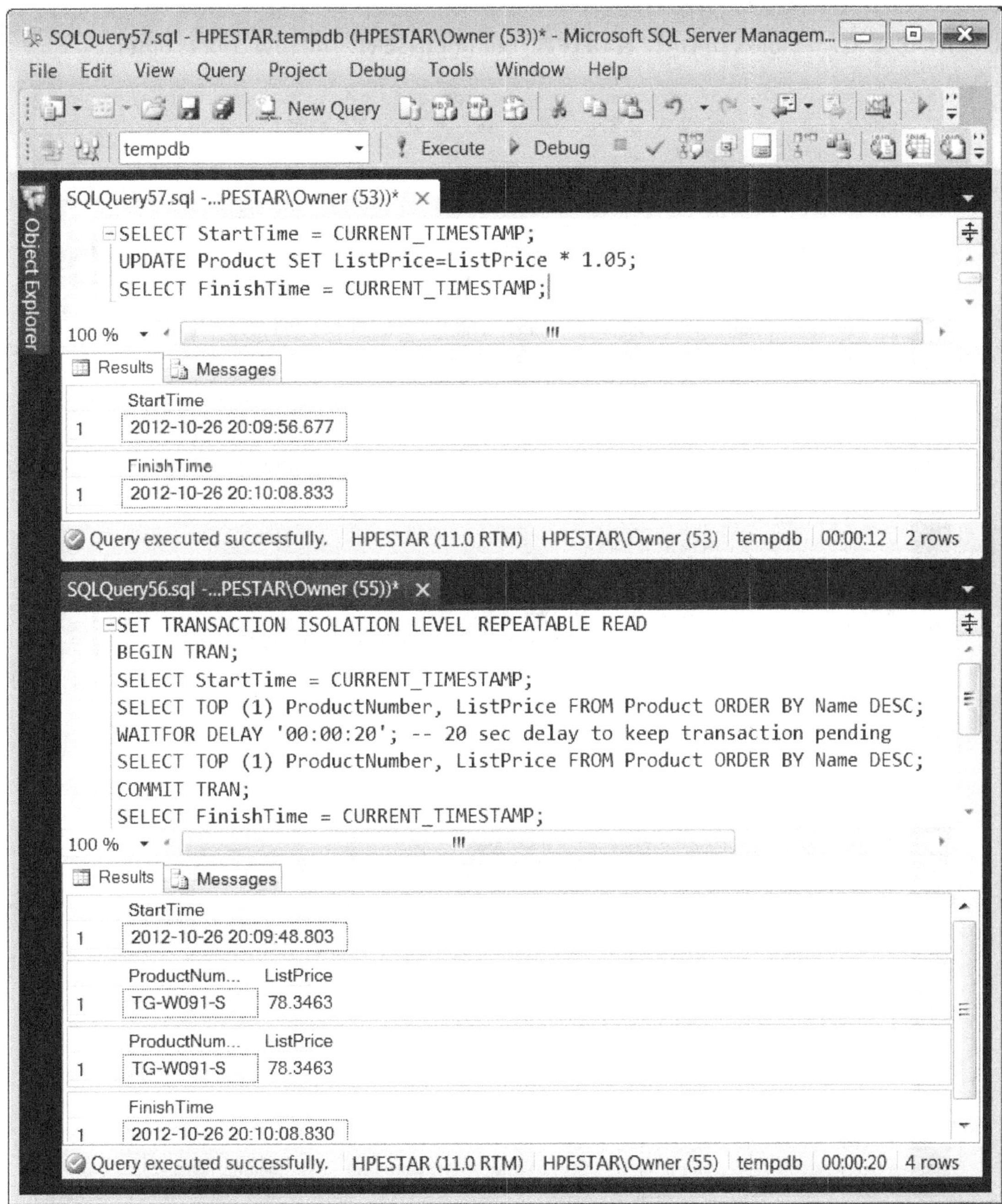
SQLQuery57.sql - HPESTAR.tempdb (HPESTAR\Owner (53))* - Microsoft SQL Server Managem...
File Edit View Query Project Debug Tools Window Help
New Query
tempdb
Execute
Debug
SQLQuery57.sql -...PESTAR\Owner (53))*
SELECT StartTime = CURRENT_TIMESTAMP;
UPDATE Product SET ListPrice=ListPrice * 1.05;
SELECT FinishTime = CURRENT_TIMESTAMP;
100 %
Results
Messages
StartTime
1 2012-10-26 20:09:56.677
FinishTime
1 2012-10-26 20:10:08.833
Query executed successfully. HPESTAR (11.0 RTM) HPESTAR\Owner (53) tempdb 00:00:12 2 rows
SQLQuery56.sql -...PESTAR\Owner (55))*
SET TRANSACTION ISOLATION LEVEL REPEATABLE READ
BEGIN TRAN;
SELECT StartTime = CURRENT_TIMESTAMP;
SELECT TOP (1) ProductNumber, ListPrice FROM Product ORDER BY Name DESC;
WAITFOR DELAY '00:00:20'; -- 20 sec delay to keep transaction pending
SELECT TOP (1) ProductNumber, ListPrice FROM Product ORDER BY Name DESC;
COMMIT TRAN;
SELECT FinishTime = CURRENT_TIMESTAMP;
100 %
Results
Messages
StartTime
1 2012-10-26 20:09:48.803
ProductNum... ListPrice
1 TG-W091-S 78.3463
ProductNum... ListPrice
1 TG-W091-S 78.3463
FinishTime
1 2012-10-26 20:10:08.830
Query executed successfully. HPESTAR (11.0 RTM) HPESTAR\Owner (55) tempdb 00:00:20 4 rows

Redefining the Product table without IDENTITIY & testing it

```
DROP TABLE tempdb.dbo.Product;
SELECT ID = CONVERT(INT, ProductID), Name, ProductNumber, ListPrice, Color
INTO tempdb.dbo.Product FROM Production.Product;
```

REPEATABLE READ blocks UPDATE & DELETE, but not INSERT. The row counts differ.

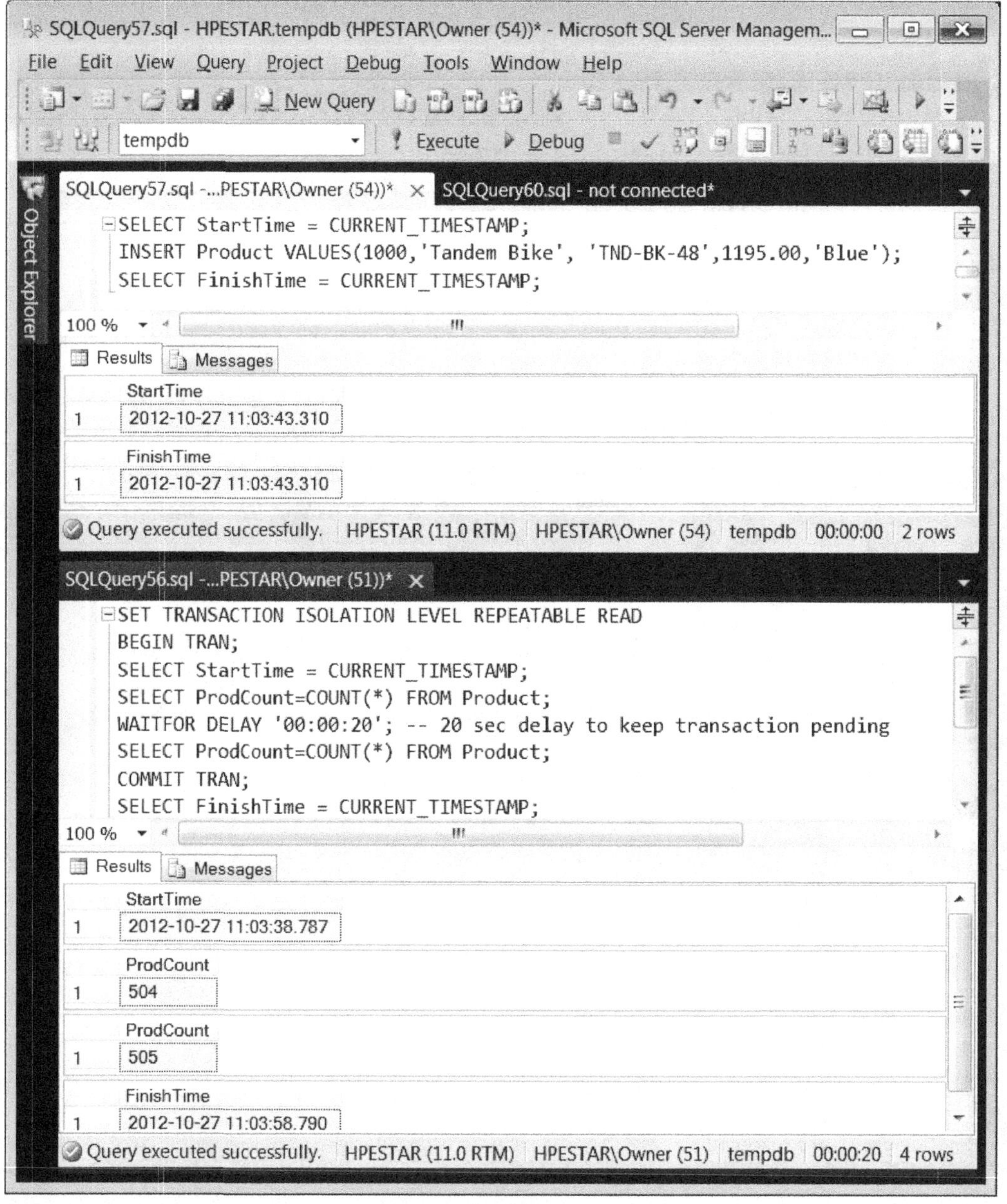
SQLQuery57.sql - HPESTAR.tempdb (HPESTAR\Owner (54))* - Microsoft SQL Server Managem...
File Edit View Query Project Debug Tools Window Help
New Query
tempdb
Execute Debug
Object Explorer
SQLQuery57.sql -...PESTAR\Owner (54))*
SQLQuery60.sql - not connected*
SELECT StartTime = CURRENT_TIMESTAMP;
INSERT Product VALUES(1000,'Tandem Bike', 'TND-BK-48',1195.00,'Blue');
SELECT FinishTime = CURRENT_TIMESTAMP;
100 %
Results
Messages
StartTime
1 2012-10-27 11:03:43.310
FinishTime
1 2012-10-27 11:03:43.310
Query executed successfully. HPESTAR (11.0 RTM) HPESTAR\Owner (54) tempdb 00:00:00 2 rows
SQLQuery56.sql -...PESTAR\Owner (51))*
SET TRANSACTION ISOLATION LEVEL REPEATABLE READ
BEGIN TRAN;
SELECT StartTime = CURRENT_TIMESTAMP;
SELECT ProdCount=COUNT(*) FROM Product;
WAITFOR DELAY '00:00:20'; -- 20 sec delay to keep transaction pending
SELECT ProdCount=COUNT(*) FROM Product;
COMMIT TRAN;
SELECT FinishTime = CURRENT_TIMESTAMP;
100 %
Results
Messages
StartTime
1 2012-10-27 11:03:38.787
ProdCount
1 504
ProdCount
1 505
FinishTime
1 2012-10-27 11:03:58.790
Query executed successfully. HPESTAR (11.0 RTM) HPESTAR\Owner (51) tempdb 00:00:20 4 rows

SERIALIZABLE Isolation Level

SERIALIZABLE isolation level blocks INSERT as well in addition to blocking UPDATE & DELETE. The row counts are the same.

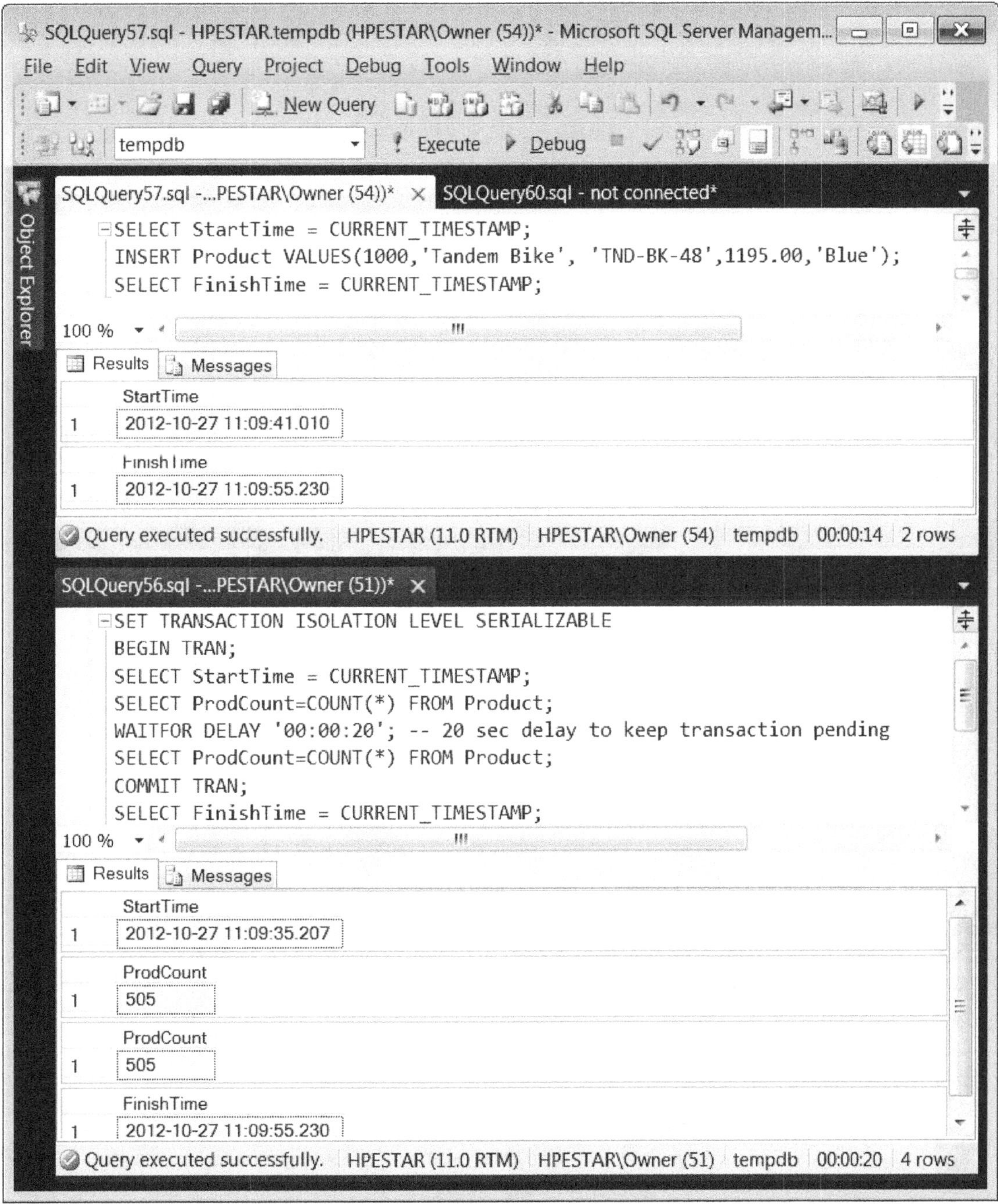

SNAPSHOT Isolation Level

SNAPSHOT isolation produces the same results as SERIALIZABLE without blocking INSERT (same for UPDATE &DELETE).

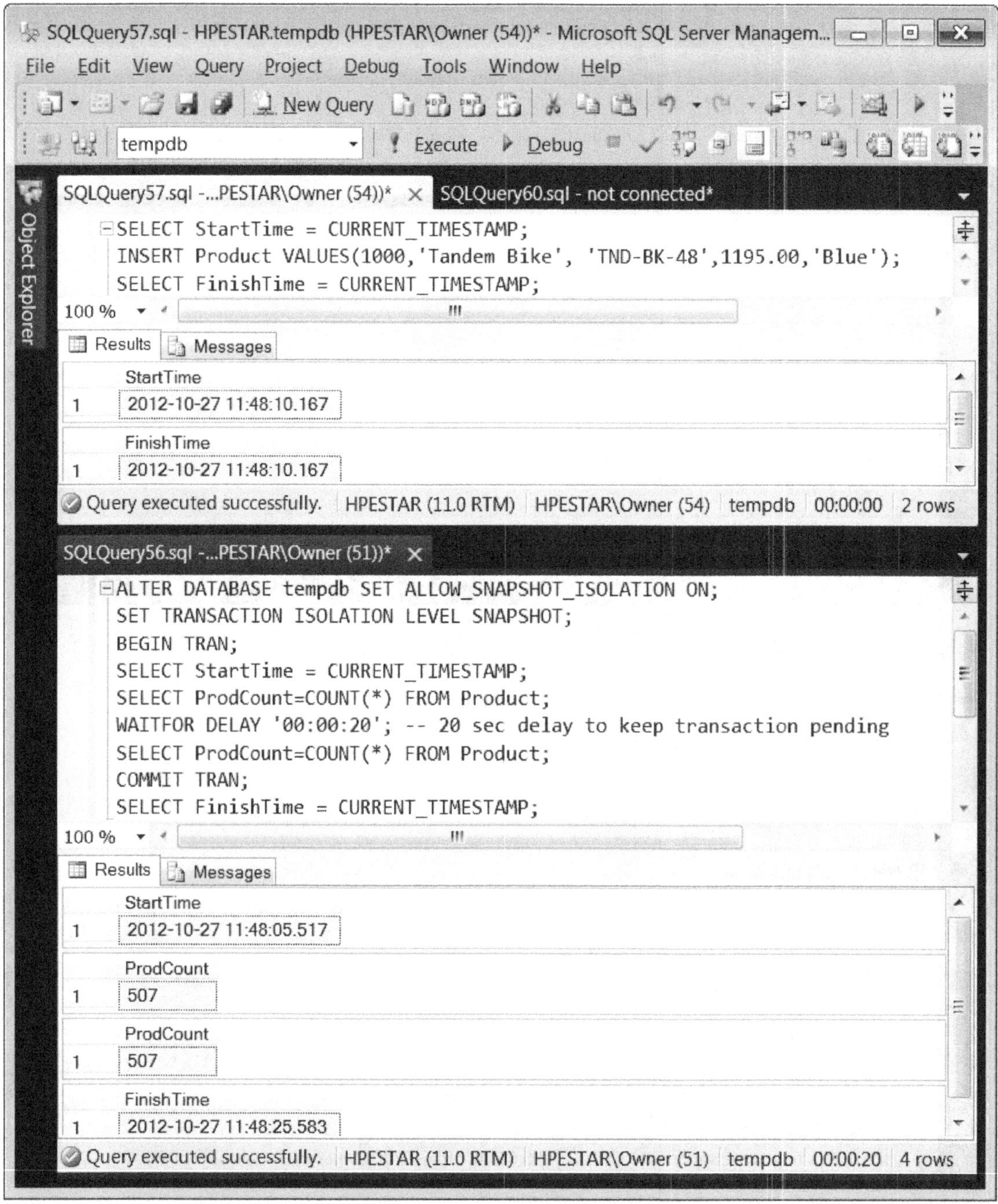

Tabular Summary of Isolation Levels

DBCC command returns the isolation level property for the database among other database options. SQL Server 2012 query.

```
USE tempdb; DBCC USEROPTIONS;  /* (13 row(s) affected)
DBCC execution completed. If DBCC printed error messages, contact your system administrator. */
```

Set Option	Value
textsize	2147483647
language	us_english
dateformat	mdy
datefirst	7
......	
isolation level	**read committed**

DMV Query of Current Session Isolation Level

```
SELECT session_id, CASE transaction_isolation_level WHEN 0 THEN 'Unspecified'
WHEN 1 THEN 'ReadUncommitted' WHEN 2 THEN 'ReadCommitted' WHEN 3 THEN 'RepeatableRead'
WHEN 4 THEN 'Serializable' WHEN 5 THEN 'Snapshot' END AS transaction_isolation_level
FROM sys.dm_exec_sessions where session_id = @@SPID;                -- 329     ReadCommitted
```

Dirty Reads & Phantom Reads

Dirty Reads: reading uncommitted data; there is no guarantee that data read will ever be committed.

Phantom Reads: data working with in the first connection changed by another transaction in the second connection since first read. Subsequent reads of the data in the first connection same transaction could be different.

Isolation level	Dirty read	Nonrepeatable read	Phantom read
Read uncommitted	Yes	Yes	Yes
Read committed	No	Yes	Yes
Repeatable read	No	No	Yes
Serializable	No	No	No
Snapshot	No	No	No

INSERT Data Into Parent-Child Tables in One Transaction

The business meaning of transaction: either insert successfully to both tables or do nothing, return an error. First we prepare the test data to be inserted in two test tables by CREATE TABLE and INSERT SELECT to populate.

```
USE AdventureWorks2012
GO
CREATE TABLE #SOH(OrderDate datetime ,
   DueDate datetime,ShipDate datetime,Status tinyint,OnlineOrderFlag bit,
          PurchaseOrderNumber varchar(25), AccountNumber nvarchar(15),
          CustomerID int ,SalesPersonID int , TerritoryID int ,
          BillToAddressID int ,ShipToAddressID int ,ShipMethodID int ,
          CreditCardID int ,CreditCardApprovalCode varchar(15) ,CurrencyRateID int ,
          SubTotal money ,TaxAmt money ,Freight money ,Comment nvarchar(128) );
CREATE TABLE #SOD(CarrierTrackingNumber nvarchar(25),OrderQty smallint,
          ProductID int,       SpecialOfferID int,  UnitPrice money,    UnitPriceDiscount money );
GO
DECLARE @SourceSOID int = 51522;
INSERT #SOH SELECT          OrderDate
            ,DueDate ,ShipDate,Status,OnlineOrderFlag,PurchaseOrderNumber
          ,AccountNumber,CustomerID,SalesPersonID,TerritoryID,BillToAddressID
          ,ShipToAddressID,ShipMethodID,CreditCardID,CreditCardApprovalCode
          ,CurrencyRateID,SubTotal,TaxAmt,Freight,Comment
 FROM Sales.SalesOrderHeader WHERE SalesOrderID = @SourceSOID;   -- (1 row(s) affected)

INSERT #SOD SELECT          CarrierTrackingNumber,OrderQty,ProductID,SpecialOfferID,UnitPrice,UnitPriceDiscount
FROM Sales.SalesOrderDetail
WHERE SalesOrderID = @SourceSOID;
GO  -- (6 row(s) affected)
```

```
SELECT * FROM #SOH;
```

```
/* SalesOrderID OrderDate          DueDate          ShipDate          Status OnlineOrderFlag PurchaseOrderNumber     AccountNumber
CustomerID  SalesPersonID TerritoryID BillToAddressID ShipToAddressID ShipMethodID CreditCardID CreditCardApprovalCode CurrencyRateID
SubTotal         TaxAmt           Freight          Comment
------------ ----------------------- ----------------------- ----------------------- ------ --------------- ------------------------- --------------- ----------- ------------- ----------- ---------------
--------------- ------------ ------------ --------------------- -------------- -------------------- -------------------- --------------------- ---------------
50701     2007-06-01 00:00:00.000 2007-06-13 00:00:00.000 2007-06-08 00:00:00.000 5    0        PO2407199018         10-4020-000225  29882
279     5      933        933       5        12808      56789Vi66226        NULL       777.2902          73.4748           22.9609          NULL*/
```

```
SELECT * FROM #SOD;
GO
```

SalesOrderID	SalesOrderDetailID	CarrierTrackingNumber	OrderQty	ProductID	SpecialOfferID	UnitPrice	UnitPriceDiscount
50701	34412	B67A-4C0A-B3	1	843	1	15.00	0.00
50701	34413	B67A-4C0A-B3	1	726	1	202.332	0.00
50701	34414	B67A-4C0A-B3	1	722	1	183.9382	0.00
50701	34415	B67A-4C0A-B3	4	855	1	53.994	0.00
50701	34416	B67A-4C0A-B3	2	813	1	65.6018	0.00
50701	34417	B67A-4C0A-B3	1	716	1	28.8404	0.00

ROLLBACK Does Not Roll Back Everything

ROLLBACK has no effect on IDENTITY seed, table variable or writing to a flat file. The implication is that IDENTITY column will have gaps where ROLLBACKs happened. With RAISERROR we return an error flag to the calling application program.

```
BEGIN TRANSACTION

DECLARE @Insert TABLE(ID INT); DECLARE @Error INT; DECLARE @ID INT;

INSERT INTO Sales.SalesOrderHeader(OrderDate
        ,DueDate ,ShipDate,Status,OnlineOrderFlag,PurchaseOrderNumber
        ,AccountNumber,CustomerID,SalesPersonID,TerritoryID,BillToAddressID
        ,ShipToAddressID,ShipMethodID,CreditCardID,CreditCardApprovalCode
        ,CurrencyRateID,SubTotal,TaxAmt,Freight,Comment )
OUTPUT inserted.SalesOrderID INTO @Insert(ID)  -- This is the PRIMARY KEY value
SELECT * FROM #SOH; -- (1 row(s) affected)

SET @Error = @@ERROR;
IF @Error <>0 BEGIN
        ROLLBACK TRANSACTION;
        RAISERROR ('An error occured inserting Sales.SalesOrderHeader',12,1);   END
ELSE BEGIN

SELECT * FROM @Insert; -- debugging   -- 75124

SELECT @ID = ID FROM @Insert;  -- FOREIGN KEY value

INSERT Sales.SalesOrderDetail ( SalesOrderID,
        CarrierTrackingNumber, OrderQty, ProductID, SpecialOfferID,
        UnitPrice, UnitPriceDiscount)
SELECT @ID, * FROM #SOD;  -- (6 row(s) affected)

SET @Error = @@ERROR;
IF @Error <>0 BEGIN
  ROLLBACK TRANSACTION;
  RAISERROR ('An error occured inserting Sales.SalesOrderDetail',12,1);
 END
ELSE
        COMMIT TRAN;
END
GO
```

Optimistic Concurrency Control

A table can have only one rowversion(formerly timestamp) column which is used for version-stamping rows. The value in the rowversion column is updated automatically every time a row in the table inserted or updated. Of course this means we cannot use it as a PRIMARY KEY, because we may get many FK orphans quickly if updates are performed on other columns. When a row is modified in a table, the timestamp is updated with the current database timestamp value obtained from the @@DBTS function.

Rowversion is the synonym for timestamp starting with SQL Server 2005. It is an 8 bytes unique binary key within the database. A quick demo of rowversion data type follows. **Rowversion values may not be consecutive.** Since all the columns in the demo table have default values, we can use the DEFAULT VALUES clause for INSERT.

```
USE AdventureWorks2012;
GO
```

```
CREATE TABLE Alpha ( ID int IDENTITY(1,1) PRIMARY KEY,
        Number int default(datepart(ss,CURRENT_TIMESTAMP)),
        String varchar(16) default(datename(dw, CURRENT_TIMESTAMP)),
        ModifiedDate date default(CURRENT_TIMESTAMP),
        RowStamp rowversion);
GO
```

```
INSERT Alpha DEFAULT VALUES;
GO 100
```

```
SELECT TOP(5) * FROM Alpha ORDER BY ID;
GO
```

ID	Number	String	ModifiedDate	RowStamp
1	43	Sunday	2012-10-28	0x0000000000000840
2	43	Sunday	2012-10-28	0x0000000000000841
3	43	Sunday	2012-10-28	0x0000000000000842
4	43	Sunday	2012-10-28	0x0000000000000843
5	43	Sunday	2012-10-28	0x0000000000000844

The rowversion (timestamp) starts changing as soon as the transaction begins. If the transaction is rolled back, it returns to the original value.

The main purpose is row versioning in multi user environment, in other words concurrency checking. The users may be humans or computer programs.

Pessimistic Concurrency Control vs. Optimistic

Pessimistic concurrency means locking the data at the row, page, or table level and don't allow anyone to modify it until the target user is done modifying the data and saving it back into the database. Trouble with this method: it may take a few minutes for the target user to update a record during which period other users may be prevented from doing their work (locked out from the table by blocking). If the target user called away for a meeting for example in the middle of data entry, you need to unlock the table by a timeout mechanism in order to prevent damaging disruption to data access by other users.

Optimistic concurrency means reading a record in a table and displaying it for the target user, but not locking it. Other users can read and modify the record at anytime while the target user is performing the manual update on the computer screen. When the target user releases the record for database update you need to check if someone changed it in between the initial read and the release (like 1-5 minutes). Usually this is not a problem due to the work distribution among staff (business process organization), nevertheless you have to program for it to avoid conflicting updates and damage to database integrity.

Assume you are a developer and developing a program in Visual Basic to update the name and address table of customers. There will be 100 staff member who can perform this application function. How can you be sure that while target staff Alpha typing in the change, staff Beta is not changing the same row?

Here is what you can do:

- Read the name and address table including the rowversion. You display the info to the user for update and save the rowversion.
- Certain amount of time later, like 2 minutes, the user presses the submit button after changes were typed in.
- You open a transaction with Begin Transaction.
- You read the rowversion of the name and address row.
- You compare the current rowversion to the saved rowversion.
- If the rowversions are same, you update the row and commit the transaction.
- If rowversions are different, you roll back the transaction and notify the user about the fact that the data was changed by someone else. You can let then the user decide what to do or follow the appropriate company business rule for data entry conflict resolution.

This is pretty common practice in multi-user environment. The alternate would be to examine a datetime column, or the entire row which is more processing intensive and less reliable as well due to potential blocking.

Example Showing rowversion (formerly timestamp) in Action

```
USE AdventureWorks2012;

CREATE TABLE Star
 (
        StarID                  INT IDENTITY PRIMARY KEY,           -- SURROGATE PK
        FirstName               VARCHAR(25),
        LastName                VARCHAR(30),
        UNIQUE (LastName, FirstName),                                -- NATURAL KEY
        ModifiedDate            DATE default( CURRENT_TIMESTAMP),
        VERSIONSTAMP            ROWVERSION
 );
go

-- Populate table
INSERT Star     (FirstName, LastName)
VALUES          ('Tom', 'Jones'),
                ('Jessica', 'Simpson'),
                ('Luciano', 'Pavarotti'),
                ('Stevie',  'Brock'),
                ('Christina', 'Aguilera'),
                ('Frank', 'Sinatra'),
                ('Doris', 'Day'),
                ('Elvis', 'Presley');
go

SELECT * FROM   Star ORDER BY StarID;
go
```

StarID	FirstName	LastName	ModifiedDate	VERSIONSTAMP
1	Tom	Jones	2018-11-07	0x00000000000007E0
2	Jessica	Simpson	2018-11-07	0x00000000000007E1
3	Luciano	Pavarotti	2018-11-07	0x00000000000007E2
4	Stevie	Brock	2018-11-07	0x00000000000007E3
5	Christina	Aguilera	2018-11-07	0x00000000000007E4
6	Frank	Sinatra	2018-11-07	0x00000000000007E5
7	Doris	Day	2018-11-07	0x00000000000007E6
8	Elvis	Presley	2018-11-07	0x00000000000007E7

Simulation of Conflicting Updates of the Same Record

```
-- Temporary table to store current record version
CREATE TABLE #semaphore
 (
   ID                    INT IDENTITY(1, 1) PRIMARY KEY,
   StartVersion          BIGINT,
   PK                    INT
 );
```

```
INSERT INTO #semaphore (StartVersion, PK)
SELECT VERSIONSTAMP,  StarID
FROM   Star
WHERE  StarID = 1;
```

```
SELECT * FROM #semaphore;
```

ID	StartVersion	PK
1	2016	1

```
-- We send the info to "our" application user;  user is making changes on the app form;
SELECT StarID, FirstName, LastName
FROM Star
WHERE StarID = 1;
```

```
-- SIMULATION: somebody else updating the same record meanwhile
-- Execute the following UPDATE statement in a different SSMS connection
/*******************************************************
UPDATE Star
SET     FirstName = 'Celine',
        LastName = 'Dion'
WHERE  StarID = 1
*******************************************************/
```

```
SELECT StarID, FirstName, LastName FROM Star WHERE StarID = 1;
```

StarID	FirstName	LastName
1	Celine	Dion

We Envelope the UPDATE Attempt into a Transaction

```
-- We are attempting to update, but cannot because current version is different
BEGIN TRANSACTION
```

```
IF (SELECT StartVersion
    FROM   #semaphore
    WHERE PK=1 )
       =
   (SELECT VERSIONSTAMP
    FROM   Star
    WHERE  StarID = 1)
  BEGIN
      UPDATE Star
      SET    FirstName = 'Julia',
             LastName = 'Roberts'
      WHERE  StarID = 1
      COMMIT TRANSACTION
  END
ELSE
  BEGIN
      ROLLBACK TRANSACTION
      PRINT 'ROLLBACK - UPDATE CONFLICT'
      RAISERROR ('Star update conflict.',10,0)
  END;
```

```
/* Messages
ROLLBACK - UPDATE CONFLICT
Star update conflict.   */
```

RAISERROR returns error flag to application. The application will follow a business rule to handle the exception.

Xquery Examples

The XML data type has the following methods for exposing the data: Query, Value, Exist, Modify, and Nodes.

The query() Method

The query() method takes an XQuery expression that evaluates to a list of XML nodes and allows the extraction of fragments of an XML document. The result is an instance of untyped XML. First we create xml data with the FOR XML AUTO clause, then query it.

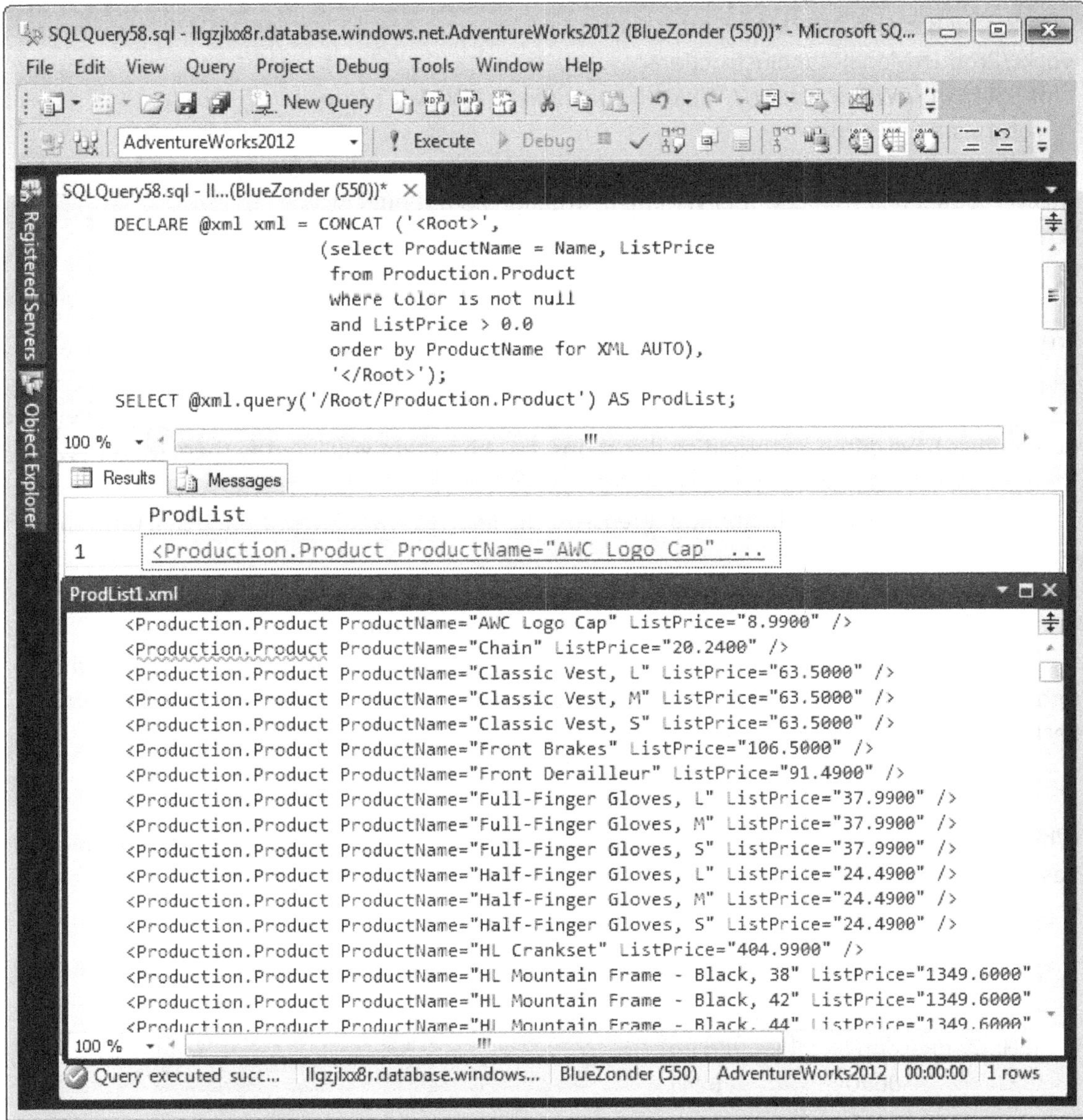

The query() Method Retrieves Assembly Instructions from XML Column

inst is a derived table representing the inner query which retrieves information from the ProductModel table XML column. The outer query formats and filters the data to return the final result set.

```
USE AdventureWorks2012;
SELECT ProductModelID,
       rtrim(ltrim(convert(nvarchar(max),[Procedure]))) AS [Procedure]
FROM
(SELECT ProductModelID,Instructions.query(
' declare namespace AWPMMI="http://schemas.microsoft.com/sqlserver/2004/07/adventure-works/ProductModelManuInstructions";
  for $Step in /AWPMMI:root/AWPMMI:Location[1]/AWPMMI:step
    return string($Step)'
) AS [Procedure]
FROM Production.ProductModel WHERE Instructions is not null) inst
WHERE ProductModelID = 53;
GO
```

ProductModelID	Procedure
53	
Visually examine the pedal spindles to determine left and right pedals. The left and right pedals have different threading directions. It is important you identify them correctly.	
Apply a small amount of grease to the left pedal and thread the pedal onto the left crank arm by hand.	
If the threads do not turn easily, back the spindle out and re-start.	
Securely tighten the spindle against the crank arm using a small wrench.	
Apply a small amount of grease to the right pedal and thread the pedal onto the right crank arm by hand. If the threads do not turn easily, back the spindle out and re-start. Securely tighten the spindle against the crank arm using a small wrench.	
Inspect per specification FI-520.	

When we examine the Procedure string with convert(varbinary(max), ...), we can see that it has next line (hex 0A) an leading spaces (hex 20) imbedded for formatting purposes. We can check the size of XML data with the DATALENGTH() function:

```
select  MinLen = min(datalength(resume)),  MaxLen = max(datalength(resume)),
        AvgLen = avg(datalength(resume))
from HumanResources.JobCandidate;
-- 3931          9080          6241
```

value() Method

The value() method performs an XQuery against the XML and returns a scalar value.

```
DECLARE @xmlDoc xml =' <root><MP3List><MP3ListID>99</MP3ListID></MP3List> </root>';
SELECT @xmlDoc.value('(/root//MP3List/MP3ListID/text())[1]','nvarchar(32)' );  -- 99
```

nodes() Method

The nodes() method shreds an XML data type instance into relational data. It returns a rowset. In the XML resume example, each column returned as scalar value.

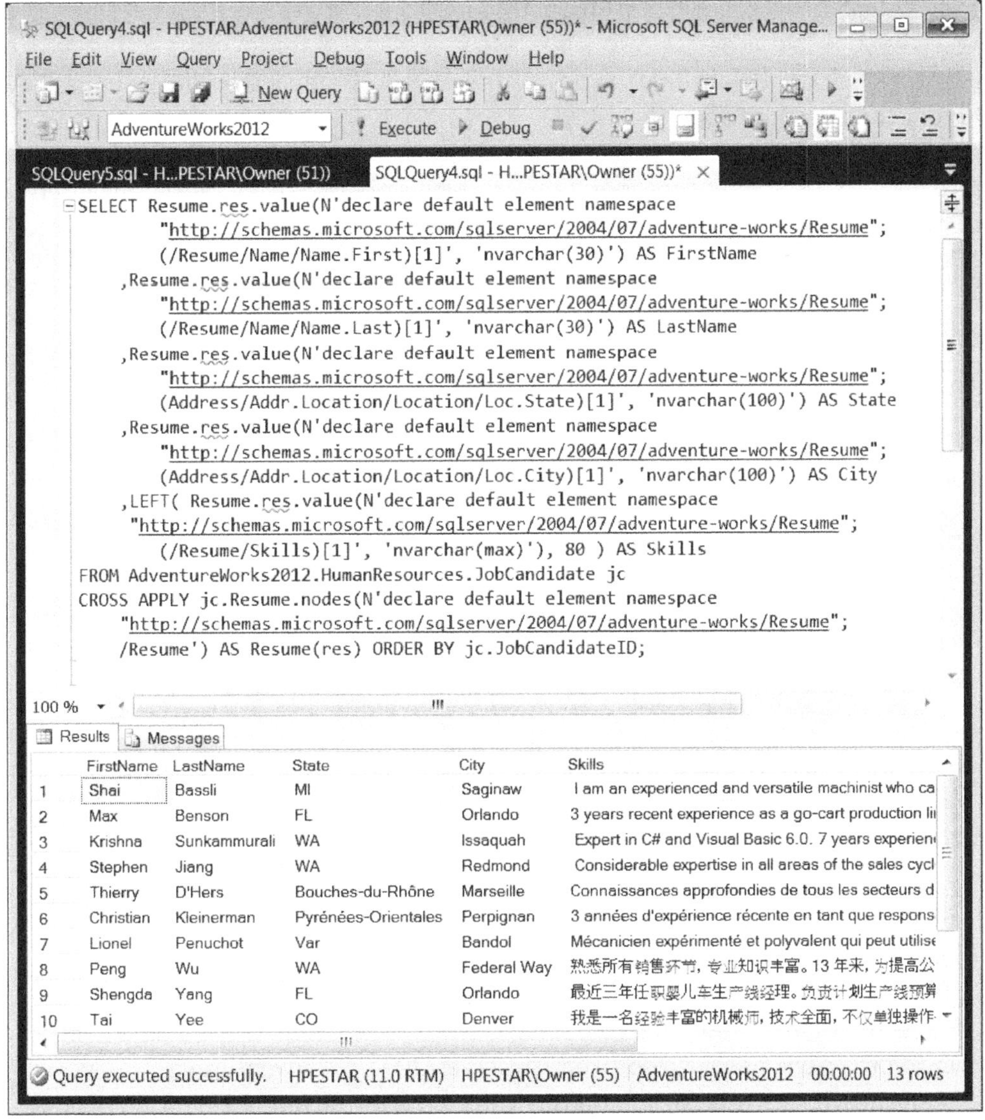

SQLQuery4.sql - HPESTAR.AdventureWorks2012 (HPESTAR\Owner (55))* - Microsoft SQL Server Manage...
File Edit View Query Project Debug Tools Window Help
New Query
AdventureWorks2012 Execute Debug
SQLQuery5.sql - H...PESTAR\Owner (51))
SQLQuery4.sql - H...PESTAR\Owner (55))*
SELECT Resume.res.value(N'declare default element namespace
"http://schemas.microsoft.com/sqlserver/2004/07/adventure-works/Resume";
(/Resume/Name/Name.First)[1]', 'nvarchar(30)') AS FirstName
,Resume.res.value(N'declare default element namespace
"http://schemas.microsoft.com/sqlserver/2004/07/adventure-works/Resume";
(/Resume/Name/Name.Last)[1]', 'nvarchar(30)') AS LastName
,Resume.res.value(N'declare default element namespace
"http://schemas.microsoft.com/sqlserver/2004/07/adventure-works/Resume";
(Address/Addr.Location/Location/Loc.State)[1]', 'nvarchar(100)') AS State
,Resume.res.value(N'declare default element namespace
"http://schemas.microsoft.com/sqlserver/2004/07/adventure-works/Resume";
(Address/Addr.Location/Location/Loc.City)[1]', 'nvarchar(100)') AS City
,LEFT(Resume.res.value(N'declare default element namespace
"http://schemas.microsoft.com/sqlserver/2004/07/adventure-works/Resume";
(/Resume/Skills)[1]', 'nvarchar(max)'), 80) AS Skills
FROM AdventureWorks2012.HumanResources.JobCandidate jc
CROSS APPLY jc.Resume.nodes(N'declare default element namespace
"http://schemas.microsoft.com/sqlserver/2004/07/adventure-works/Resume";
/Resume') AS Resume(res) ORDER BY jc.JobCandidateID;
100 %
Results Messages
FirstName LastName State City Skills
1 Shai Bassli MI Saginaw I am an experienced and versatile machinist who ca
2 Max Benson FL Orlando 3 years recent experience as a go-cart production li
3 Krishna Sunkammurali WA Issaquah Expert in C# and Visual Basic 6.0. 7 years experien
4 Stephen Jiang WA Redmond Considerable expertise in all areas of the sales cycl
5 Thierry D'Hers Bouches-du-Rhône Marseille Connaissances approfondies de tous les secteurs d
6 Christian Kleinerman Pyrénées-Orientales Perpignan 3 années d'expérience récente en tant que respons
7 Lionel Penuchot Var Bandol Mécanicien expérimenté et polyvalent qui peut utilise
8 Peng Wu WA Federal Way 熟悉所有销售环节，专业知识丰富。13 年来，为提高公
9 Shengda Yang FL Orlando 最近三年任职婴儿车生产线经理。负责计划生产线预算
10 Tai Yee CO Denver 我是一名经验丰富的机械师，技术全面，不仅单独操作
Query executed successfully. HPESTAR (11.0 RTM) HPESTAR\Owner (55) AdventureWorks2012 00:00:00 13 rows

exist() Method

The exist() method returns bit 1 (true) if the XQuery expression returns at least one XML node.

Bike models are listed if <Summary> element is included in XML ProductDescription.

```
SELECT      Name                                    AS ModelName,
            CatalogDescription.query('
declare namespace pd="http://schemas.microsoft.com/sqlserver/2004/07/adventure-
works/ProductModelDescription";
  <Product
     ProductModelID= "{ sql:column("ProductModelID") }"
     />
')                                                  AS ProductModelID
FROM Production.ProductModel
WHERE CatalogDescription.exist('
  declare namespace  pd="http://schemas.microsoft.com/sqlserver/2004/07/adventure-
works/ProductModelDescription";
   /pd:ProductDescription[(pd:Summary)]'
  ) = 1
ORDER BY ModelName;
GO
```

ModelName	ProductModelID
Mountain-100	<Product ProductModelID="19" />
Mountain-500	<Product ProductModelID="23" />
Road-150	<Product ProductModelID="25" />
Road-450	<Product ProductModelID="28" />
Touring-1000	<Product ProductModelID="34" />
Touring-2000	<Product ProductModelID="35" />

The CatalogDescription XML data for ProductModelID 23

```
<?xml-stylesheet href="ProductDescription.xsl" type="text/xsl"?>
<p1:ProductDescription
xmlns:p1="http://schemas.microsoft.com/sqlserver/2004/07/adventure-
works/ProductModelDescription"
xmlns:wm="http://schemas.microsoft.com/sqlserver/2004/07/adventure-
works/ProductModelWarrAndMain" xmlns:wf="http://www.adventure-
```

```
works.com/schemas/OtherFeatures" xmlns:html="http://www.w3.org/1999/xhtml"
ProductModelID="23" ProductModelName="Mountain-500">
 <p1:Summary>
  <html:p>Suitable for any type of riding, on or off-road.
                        Fits any budget. Smooth-shifting with a comfortable ride.
            </html:p>
 </p1:Summary>
 <p1:Manufacturer>
  <p1:Name>AdventureWorks</p1:Name>
  <p1:Copyright>2002</p1:Copyright>
  <p1:ProductURL>HTTP://www.Adventure-works.com</p1:ProductURL>
 </p1:Manufacturer>
 <p1:Features>Product highlights include:
        <wm:Warranty><wm:WarrantyPeriod>1
year</wm:WarrantyPeriod><wm:Description>parts and
labor</wm:Description></wm:Warranty><wm:Maintenance><wm:NoOfYears>3
years</wm:NoOfYears><wm:Description>maintenance contact available through
dealer</wm:Description></wm:Maintenance><wf:wheel>Stable, durable wheels suitable for
novice riders.</wf:wheel><wf:saddle>Made from synthetic leather and features gel padding for
increased comfort.</wf:saddle><wf:pedal><html:b>Expanded platform</html:b> so you can
ride in any shoes; great for all-around riding.</wf:pedal><wf:crankset> Super rigid spindle.
</wf:crankset><wf:BikeFrame>Our best value frame utilizing the same, ground-breaking
technology as the ML aluminum frame.</wf:BikeFrame></p1:Features>
 <!-- add one or more of these elements... one for each specific product in this product model --
>
 <p1:Picture>
  <p1:Angle>front</p1:Angle>
  <p1:Size>small</p1:Size>
  <p1:ProductPhotoID>1</p1:ProductPhotoID>
 </p1:Picture>
 <!-- add any tags in <specifications> -->
 <p1:Specifications> These are the product specifications.
         <Height>Varies</Height> Centimeters.
         <Material>Aluminum Alloy</Material><Color>Available in all
colors.</Color><ProductLine>Mountain
bike</ProductLine><Style>Unisex</Style><RiderExperience>Novice to Intermediate
riders</RiderExperience></p1:Specifications>
</p1:ProductDescription>
```

modify() Method

The modify() method modifies the contents of an XML document. It can only be used in the SET statement or the SET clause of an UPDATE statement for tables with XML columns.

```
DECLARE @XML xml = '<Root>
 <Picture>
  <Angle>front</Angle>
  <Size>small</Size>
  <ProductPhotoID>1</ProductPhotoID>
 </Picture>      </Root>';          SELECT @XML;
```

```
<Root><Picture><Angle>front</Angle><Size>small</Size><ProductPhotoID>1</ProductPhotoID
></Picture></Root>
```

```
-- update angle
SET @XML.modify('
 replace value of (/Root/Picture/Angle[1]/text())[1]
 with    "side" ');          SELECT @XML;
```

```
<Root><Picture><Angle>side</Angle><Size>small</Size><ProductPhotoID>1</ProductPhotoID>
</Picture></Root>
```

```
-- update size
SET @XML.modify('
 replace value of (/Root/Picture/Size[1]/text())[1]
 with    "medium" ');    SELECT @XML;
```

```
<Root><Picture><Angle>side</Angle><Size>medium</Size><ProductPhotoID>1</ProductPhotoI
D></Picture></Root>
```

```
-- update productphotoid
SET @XML.modify('
 replace value of (/Root/Picture/ProductPhotoID[1]/text())[1]
 with    "99" ');          SELECT @XML;
```

```
<Root><Picture><Angle>side</Angle><Size>medium</Size><ProductPhotoID>99</ProductPhot
oID></Picture></Root>
```

Insert (XML DML)

Insert(XML DML) inserts one or more nodes as child nodes or siblings of the target node.

```
DECLARE @XML xml = '<Root>
 <Picture ID = "4">
  <Angle>front</Angle>
  <Size>small</Size>
  <ProductPhotoID>1</ProductPhotoID>
 </Picture>       </Root>';
SELECT @XML;
```

```
<Root>
 <Picture ID="4">
  <Angle>front</Angle>
  <Size>small</Size>
  <ProductPhotoID>1</ProductPhotoID>
 </Picture>
</Root>
```

```
SET @XML.modify('insert  <Picture ID = "1">
  <Angle>front</Angle>
  <Size>large</Size>
  <ProductPhotoID>45</ProductPhotoID>
 </Picture> as first    into   (/Root)[1] ');
SELECT @XML;
```

```
<Root>
 <Picture ID="1">
  <Angle>front</Angle>
  <Size>large</Size>
  <ProductPhotoID>45</ProductPhotoID>
 </Picture>
 <Picture ID="4">
  <Angle>front</Angle>
  <Size>small</Size>
  <ProductPhotoID>1</ProductPhotoID>
 </Picture>
</Root>
```

Delete (XML DML)

The delete(XML DML) deletes nodes from an XML instance.

```
DECLARE @XML xml = '<Root>
<Picture ID = "1">
  <Angle>front</Angle>
  <Size>large</Size>
  <ProductPhotoID>45</ProductPhotoID>
 </Picture>
 <Picture ID = "4">
  <Angle>front</Angle>
  <Size>small</Size>
  <ProductPhotoID>1</ProductPhotoID>
 </Picture>
  <Picture ID = "8">
  <Angle>above</Angle>
  <Size>small</Size>
  <ProductPhotoID>12</ProductPhotoID>
 </Picture>      </Root>';
```

```
SET @XML.modify('
 delete /Root/Picture[@ID=4]  ');
```

```
SELECT @XML;
```

```
<Root>
  <Picture ID="1">
    <Angle>front</Angle>
    <Size>large</Size>
    <ProductPhotoID>45</ProductPhotoID>
  </Picture>
  <Picture ID="8">
    <Angle>above</Angle>
    <Size>small</Size>
    <ProductPhotoID>12</ProductPhotoID>
  </Picture>
</Root>
```

Working with hierarchyid Data Type

Orgchart Based on AdventureWorks2012

Let's take a look at the hierarchyid and related data in the Employee table first.

```
USE AdventureWorks2012;
```

```
SELECT TOP(20) BusinessEntityID, NationalIdNumber, OrganizationNode, OrganizationLevel,
           OrgNodeText=CONVERT(varchar, OrganizationNode),  JobTitle
FROM HumanResources.Employee  ORDER BY OrganizationNode;
```

BusinessEntityID	NationalIdNumber	OrganizationNode	OrganizationLevel	OrgNodeText	JobTitle
1	295847284	0x	0	/	Chief Executive Officer
2	245797967	0x58	1	/1/	Vice President of Engineering
3	509647174	0x5AC0	2	/1/1/	Engineering Manager
4	112457891	0x5AD6	3	/1/1/1/	Senior Tool Designer
5	695256908	0x5ADA	3	/1/1/2/	Design Engineer
6	998320692	0x5ADE	3	/1/1/3/	Design Engineer
7	134969118	0x5AE1	3	/1/1/4/	Research and Development Manager
8	811994146	0x5AE158	4	/1/1/4/1/	Research and Development Engineer
9	658797903	0x5AE168	4	/1/1/4/2/	Research and Development Engineer
10	879342154	0x5AE178	4	/1/1/4/3/	Research and Development Manager
11	974026903	0x5AE3	3	/1/1/5/	Senior Tool Designer
12	480168528	0x5AE358	4	/1/1/5/1/	Tool Designer
13	486228782	0x5AE368	4	/1/1/5/2/	Tool Designer
14	42487730	0x5AE5	3	/1/1/6/	Senior Design Engineer
15	56920285	0x5AE7	3	/1/1/7/	Design Engineer
16	24756624	0x68	1	/2/	Marketing Manager
17	253022876	0x6AC0	2	/2/1/	Marketing Assistant
18	222969461	0x6B40	2	/2/2/	Marketing Specialist
19	52541318	0x6BC0	2	/2/3/	Marketing Assistant
20	323403273	0x6C20	2	/2/4/	Marketing Assistant

```
-- Convert text node to hierarchyid
SELECT CONVERT(hierarchyid, '/3/1/22/4/');  -- 0x7AF07610
```

Inline User-Defined Function OrgChart at Any Level

We can easily wrap the company orgchart logic into a parameterized function to get the orgchart for any executive or manager in the company.

```
CREATE FUNCTION ufnOrgChart ( @OrganizationNode hierarchyid )
RETURNS TABLE AS RETURN
(WITH cteOrgChart(ManagerID, EmployeeID, EmployeeLevel)
  AS (SELECT OrganizationNode,
          OrganizationNode,
          0
      FROM   HumanResources.Employee
      WHERE  OrganizationNode = @OrganizationNode
      UNION ALL
      SELECT e.OrganizationNode.GetAncestor(1),
          e.OrganizationNode,
          EmployeeLevel+1
      FROM   HumanResources.Employee e
          INNER JOIN cteOrgChart d
           ON e.OrganizationNode.GetAncestor(1) = d.EmployeeID)
SELECT   Employee = CONCAT(replicate(CHAR(9),(EmployeeLevel)), P.LastName, ', ',
                                   P.FirstName)
FROM     cteOrgChart OC
      INNER JOIN HumanResources.Employee E
       ON OC.EmployeeID = E.OrganizationNode
      INNER JOIN Person.Person P
       ON E.BusinessEntityID = P.BusinessEntityID  );
GO
```

```
SELECT * FROM ufnOrgChart (0x84);  -- (29 row(s) affected) - Partial Results.
```

Employee			
Norman, Laura			
	Barreto de Mattos, Paula		
	Liu, David		
	Kahn, Wendy		
	Barber, David		
		Word, Sheela	
			Sandberg, Mikael
			Rao, Arvind
			Meisner, Linda
			Ogisu, Fukiko

hierarchyid System Functions

Specialized system hierarchyid functions available to deal with hierarchyid data.

```
SELECT      BusinessEntityID, JobTitle,
            OrganizationNode,
            OrganizationLevel,
            OrganizationNode.ToString()              AS TextOrgNode,
            OrganizationNode.GetLevel()              AS NodeLevel,
            OrganizationNode.GetAncestor(1)          AS Ancestor,
            OrganizationNode.IsDescendantOf(0x58)    AS [0x58 Descendant]
FROM HumanResources.Employee
ORDER BY TextOrgNode;
 -- (290 row(s) affected) - Partial results.
```

BusinessEntityID	JobTitle	OrganizationNode	OrganizationLevel	TextOrgNode	NodeLevel	Ancestor	0x58 Descendant
1	Chief Executive Officer	0x	0	/	0	NULL	0
2	Vice President of Engineering	0x58	1	/1/	1	0x	1
3	Engineering Manager	0x5AC0	2	/1/1/	2	0x58	1
4	Senior Tool Designer	0x5AD6	3	/1/1/1/	3	0x5AC0	1
5	Design Engineer	0x5ADA	3	/1/1/2/	3	0x5AC0	1
6	Design Engineer	0x5ADE	3	/1/1/3/	3	0x5AC0	1
7	Research and Development Manager	0x5AE1	3	/1/1/4/	3	0x5AC0	1
8	Research and Development Engineer	0x5AE158	4	/1/1/4/1/	4	0x5AE1	1
9	Research and Development Engineer	0x5AE168	4	/1/1/4/2/	4	0x5AE1	1
10	Research and Development Manager	0x5AE178	4	/1/1/4/3/	4	0x5AE1	1
11	Senior Tool Designer	0x5AE3	3	/1/1/5/	3	0x5AC0	1
12	Tool Designer	0x5AE358	4	/1/1/5/1/	4	0x5AE3	1
13	Tool Designer	0x5AE368	4	/1/1/5/2/	4	0x5AE3	1
14	Senior Design Engineer	0x5AE5	3	/1/1/6/	3	0x5AC0	1
15	Design Engineer	0x5AE7	3	/1/1/7/	3	0x5AC0	1
16	Marketing Manager	0x68	1	/2/	1	0x	0
17	Marketing Assistant	0x6AC0	2	/2/1/	2	0x68	0
18	Marketing Specialist	0x6B40	2	/2/2/	2	0x68	0
19	Marketing Assistant	0x6BC0	2	/2/3/	2	0x68	0
20	Marketing Assistant	0x6C20	2	/2/4/	2	0x68	0
21	Marketing Specialist	0x6C60	2	/2/5/	2	0x68	0
22	Marketing Specialist	0x6CA0	2	/2/6/	2	0x68	0
23	Marketing Specialist	0x6CE0	2	/2/7/	2	0x68	0
24	Marketing Specialist	0x6D10	2	/2/8/	2	0x68	0

Sort Outline Numbering with hierarchyid

Certain sorts which are obvious to us, due to our Human Intelligence, are a challenge in traditional SQL programming due to lack of tree/hierarchy structure processing. Such a case is outline numbers which are easily convertible to hierarchyid, hence the simple solution.

```
CREATE TABLE #OutlineNumber   (Nbr Varchar(64));
INSERT #OutlineNumber Values
 ('1'), ('1.1'), ('1.1.1'), ('1.1.9'), ('1.1.10'), ('1.1.11'), ('2'), ('2.1'), ('2.1.1'), ('10.1.2'), ('11.1.9');
SELECT * FROM #OutlineNumber ORDER BY Nbr;
```

Nbr	
1	
1.1	
1.1.1	
1.1.10	
1.1.11	
1.1.9	out of order
10.1.2	out of order
11.1.9	out of order
2	
2.1	
2.1.1	

```
-- Sorting on hierarchyid by converting outline string with "/" replaces "."  & "/" prefix, suffix
SELECT *, [HierarchyID].ToString() AS TextHierarchyID FROM
  (SELECT *, CONVERT(hierarchyid, CONCAT('/',REPLACE(Nbr, '.', '/') ,'/')) AS [HierarchyID]
   FROM #OutlineNumber) x /* derived table */ ORDER BY HierarchyID;
```

Nbr	HierarchyID	TextHierarchyID
1	0x58	/1/
1.1	0x5AC0	/1/1/
1.1.1	0x5AD6	/1/1/1/
1.1.9	0x5AE980	/1/1/9/
1.1.10	0x5AEA80	/1/1/10/
1.1.11	0x5AEB80	/1/1/11/
2	0x68	/2/
2.1	0x6AC0	/2/1/
2.1.1	0x6AD6	/2/1/1/
10.1.2	0xAAB680	/10/1/2/
11.1.9	0xAEBA60	/11/1/9/

Dynamic SQL PIVOT

Dynamic SQL PIVOT transposes rows into columns based on dynamic data. Dynamic PIVOT contrasts hard-wired PIVOT. Prior to coding the dynamic SQL, write out & test the static query.

> Database security article: Dynamic SQL & SQL Injection:
> http://blogs.msdn.com/b/raulga/archive/2007/01/04/dynamic-sql-sql-injection.aspx

We need the following data-driven column header list of years:

[2005], [2006], [2007], [2008]

We need the following static PIVOT query to be generated dynamically:

```
SELECT * FROM (SELECT [Store (Freight Summary)] = S.Name,
                YEAR(OrderDate) AS OrderYear, Freight
FROM    Sales.SalesOrderHeader SOH
INNER JOIN Sales.Customer C ON SOH.CustomerID = C.CustomerID
INNER JOIN Sales.Store S ON C.StoreID = S.BusinessEntityID) as Header
PIVOT (SUM(Freight) FOR OrderYear IN( [2005], [2006], [2007], [2008])) AS Pvt ORDER BY 1;
-- (633 row(s) affected) - Partial results.
```

Store (Freight Summary)	2005	2006	2007	2008
Sensible Sports	NULL	NULL	364.2076	472.8672
Separate Parts Corporation	1243.1035	4883.5698	2493.3725	NULL
Serious Cycles	4868.9888	3511.0184	354.9403	NULL
Seventh Bike Store	831.2495	4329.8166	4866.4755	2024.7107
Sharp Bikes	912.9061	549.7834	NULL	NULL
Sheet Metal Manufacturing	NULL	6050.2523	9169.2709	3328.5167
Shipping Specialists	NULL	NULL	NULL	12.9692
Showcase for Cycles	NULL	NULL	35.2509	6.2386
Simple Bike Parts	87.9217	100.5808	31.1732	29.8886
Sixth Bike Store	426.1619	1346.1144	79.9409	NULL
Sleek Bikes	NULL	NULL	3407.692	2364.0185
Small Bike Accessories Shop	NULL	NULL	1116.6658	992.0197
Small Bike Shop	2359.1319	5277.5806	3681.3405	2216.5242
Small Cycle Store	152.3481	989.9408	801.0264	553.2965
Social Activities Club	177.3895	52.9214	9.7198	29.8886
Solid Bike Parts	1134.6482	1535.374	372.4571	NULL
Some Discount Store	2499.3443	733.0964	38.0211	1.1373
South Bike Company	NULL	NULL	1043.9713	837.2011
Spa and Exercise Outfitters	NULL	94.3411	3777.5336	2441.4004

Dynamic SQL PIVOT: Dealer Freight Cost by Year

```
USE AdventureWorks2012;

DECLARE  @OrderYear  AS  TABLE( YYYY INT    NOT NULL    PRIMARY KEY  )
DECLARE  @DynamicSQL  AS NVARCHAR(MAX)

INSERT INTO @OrderYear
SELECT DISTINCT YEAR(OrderDate)  FROM   Sales.SalesOrderHeader

DECLARE  @ReportColumnNames  AS NVARCHAR(MAX),     @IterationYear     AS INT
SET @IterationYear = (SELECT MIN(YYYY) FROM   @OrderYear)
SET @ReportColumnNames = N''

-- Assemble pivot list dynamically
WHILE (@IterationYear IS NOT NULL)
 BEGIN
  SET @ReportColumnNames = CONCAT(@ReportColumnNames, N', ',
   QUOTENAME(CAST(@IterationYear AS NVARCHAR(10))))
  SET @IterationYear = (SELECT MIN(YYYY)
              FROM   @OrderYear    WHERE  YYYY > @IterationYear)
 END

SET @ReportColumnNames =
SUBSTRING(@ReportColumnNames,2,LEN(@ReportColumnNames))

PRINT @ReportColumnNames

-- Assemble final code
SET @DynamicSQL = CONCAT(N'SELECT * FROM
                         (SELECT [Store (Freight Summary)]=S.Name,
                         YEAR(OrderDate) AS OrderYear,  Freight
FROM     Sales.SalesOrderHeader SOH
INNER JOIN Sales.Customer C ON SOH.CustomerID = C.CustomerID
INNER JOIN Sales.Store S ON C.StoreID = S.BusinessEntityID) as Header
PIVOT (SUM(Freight)
FOR OrderYear IN(', @ReportColumnNames, N'))  AS Pvt ORDER BY 1;')

PRINT @DynamicSQL; -- Testing & debugging

EXEC sp_executesql @DynamicSQL;
```

Date Range Programming with Datetime Column

The time portion of a datetime column presents a big problem ("midnight bug") when looking for a time range of records (rows). The equal operator picks up only the midnight records, nothing beyond as demonstrated. Similar issue for the BETWEEN operator. Best solution is to use DATE (SQL Server2008) if time portion is of no interest. With datetime we cannot assume that the time portion is 00:00:00.000 since it may have been changed unintentionally.

```
USE AdventureWorks2012;
CREATE TABLE #SOH(SalesOrderID int,RevisionNumber tinyint,OrderDate datetime,
        DueDate datetime,ShipDate datetime, Status tinyint,OnlineOrderFlag bit,
        SalesOrderNumber nvarchar(25),PurchaseOrderNumber varchar(20),AccountNumber varchar(15),
        CustomerID int,SalesPersonID int,TerritoryID int,BillToAddressID int,
        ShipToAddressID int,ShipMethodID int,CreditCardID int,
        CreditCardApprovalCode varchar(15),  CurrencyRateID int,SubTotal money,
        TaxAmt money,Freight money,TotalDue money,Comment nvarchar(128),
        rowguid uniqueidentifier,ModifiedDate datetime);
INSERT #SOH SELECT * FROM Sales.SalesOrderHeader; -- Create test table
GO -- (31465 row(s) affected)
SELECT COUNT(SalesOrderID), MAX(OrderDate) FROM #SOH WHERE OrderDate = '2008-02-01';
-- 244      2008-02-01 00:00:00.000
SELECT COUNT(SalesOrderID), MAX(OrderDate) FROM #SOH
WHERE OrderDate BETWEEN '2008-02-01' AND '2008-02-01';
-- 244      2008-02-01 00:00:00.000
-- Advance order date 1 second passed midnight
UPDATE #SOH SET OrderDate = dateadd(ss, 1, OrderDate) WHERE OrderDate = '2008-02-01';
-- (244 row(s) affected)
-- Due to the non-zero time portion, no equal match
SELECT COUNT(SalesOrderID), MAX(OrderDate) FROM #SOH WHERE OrderDate = '2008-02-01';
-- 0        NULL
-- The BETWEEN operator also fails
SELECT COUNT(SalesOrderID), MAX(OrderDate) FROM #SOH
WHERE OrderDate BETWEEN '2008-02-01' AND '2008-02-01';
-- 0        NULL
-- A safe way to get all the sales - not the best performant if there is index on OrderDate
SELECT COUNT(SalesOrderID), MAX(OrderDate) FROM #SOH
WHERE YEAR(OrderDate)=2008 AND MONTH(OrderDate) = 2 AND DAY(OrderDate) = 1;
--244       2008-02-01 00:00:01.000
-- Another way to get all sales - no performance issue in case of index on OrderDate
SELECT COUNT(SalesOrderID), MAX(OrderDate) FROM #SOH
WHERE OrderDate >= '2008-02-01' AND OrderDate < DATEADD(dd,1,'2008-02-01');
-- 244      2008-02-01 00:00:01.000
-- Using the BETWEEN operator - performance issue in case of index on OrderDate
SELECT COUNT(SalesOrderID), MAX(OrderDate) FROM #SOH
WHERE CONVERT(DATE, OrderDate) BETWEEN '2008-02-01' AND '2008-02-01';
-- 244      2008-02-01 00:00:01.000
GO
DROP TABLE #SOH;
GO;
```

The BETWEEN Operator for DATE & DATETIME Ranges

```
-- BETWEEN dates implementation for datetime OrderDate
DECLARE @StartDate datetime ='20080201', @EndDate datetime = '20080205';
SELECT OrderCount=COUNT(*) FROM Sales.SalesOrderHeader
WHERE OrderDate >= @StartDate and OrderDate < DATEADD(DD,1,@EndDate);
GO
-- 502
```

```
-- BETWEEN dates implementation for datetime OrderDate using DATE data type
DECLARE @StartDate date ='20080201', @EndDate date = '20080205';
SELECT OrderCount=COUNT(*) FROM Sales.SalesOrderHeader
WHERE OrderDate >= @StartDate and OrderDate < DATEADD(DD,1,@EndDate);
GO
-- 502
```

```
-- Past midnight and next midnight
SELECT  dateadd(dd, datediff(dd, 0, CURRENT_TIMESTAMP)+0, 0),
        dateadd(dd, 1+datediff(dd, 0, CURRENT_TIMESTAMP)+0, 0)
-- 2016-10-23 00:00:00.000    2016-10-24 00:00:00.000
```

```
-- Orders for today (date range 1 day)
SELECT * FROM Sales.SalesOrderHeader
WHERE OrderDate >= dateadd(dd, datediff(dd, 0, CURRENT_TIMESTAMP)+0, 0)
 AND OrderDate <  dateadd(dd, 1+datediff(dd, 0, CURRENT_TIMESTAMP)+0, 0)
GO
```

```
-- Create a copy of the PurchaseOrderHeader (similar to SalesOrderHeader) table
CREATE TABLE #POH(PurchaseOrderID int,RevisionNumber tinyint,Status tinyint,
        EmployeeID int,VendorID int,ShipMethodID int,OrderDate datetime,ShipDate datetime,
        SubTotal money,TaxAmt money,Freight money,TotalDue money,ModifiedDate datetime);
INSERT #POH SELECT * FROM Purchasing.PurchaseOrderHeader;  -- (4012 row(s) affected)
```

```
-- Purchase order count for the entire month of MARCH 2008
SELECT COUNT(*) FROM #POH WHERE OrderDate >='2008-03-01  00:00:00.000'
            AND OrderDate < '2008-04-01  00:00:00.000'
-- 313
```

```
-- Equivalent datetime or date comparison queries
SELECT COUNT(*) FROM #POH WHERE OrderDate >='2008-03-01' AND OrderDate < '2008-04-
01'
-- 313
```

BETWEEN for Date Ranges cont.

```
-- SQL date between - performance issue due to CAST if OrderDate is indexed
SELECT COUNT(*) FROM #POH WHERE
        CAST(OrderDate AS DATE) BETWEEN '2008-03-01' AND '2008-03-31';
-- 313
```

```
-- SQL datetime between with explicit inclusive lower and upper limits
/***** WORKS BUT NOT BEST PRACTICES *****/
SELECT COUNT(*) FROM #POH WHERE OrderDate
BETWEEN '2008-03-01 00:00:00.000' AND '2008-03-31 23:59:59.997'; -- 313
```

```
/***** NOT BEST PRACTICES - WRONG RESULT IF TIME PART IS NOT 12:00AM *****/
SELECT COUNT(*) FROM #POH WHERE OrderDate
        BETWEEN '2008-03-01 00:00:00.000' AND '2008-03-31 00:00:00.000' ; --313
SELECT COUNT(*) FROM #POH WHERE OrderDate BETWEEN '2008-03-01' AND '2008-03-31';
-- 313
/********************************************************************/
```

```
-- TIME PART assumed to be 12:00AM = 00:00:00.000 if not specified
SELECT COUNT(*) FROM #POH WHERE OrderDate BETWEEN '2008-01-02' AND '2008-01-07';
-- 60
UPDATE TOP(1) #POH SET OrderDate = DATEADD (second, 1, OrderDate)
        WHERE  OrderDate='2008-01-07';          -- (1 row(s) affected)
-- The 1 second passed midnight record is no longer included in the BETWEEN range
SELECT COUNT(*) FROM #POH WHERE OrderDate BETWEEN '2008-01-02' AND '2008-01-07';
-- 59
```

```
-- BETWEEN is inclusive operator - it includes the limits
SELECT COUNT(*) FROM #POH WHERE OrderDate
        BETWEEN '2008-01-02 00:00:00.000' AND '2008-01-07 00:00:00.000';  -- 59
```

```
-- Include midnight and midnight+1 sec records for 2008-01-07
SELECT COUNT(*) FROM #POH WHERE OrderDate
        BETWEEN '2008-01-02 00:00:00.000' AND '2008-01-07 00:00:01.000'; -- 60
```

```
-- Date range query - good performance if OrderDate indexed ( SARGABLE)
SELECT [Sales]=COUNT(*) FROM Purchasing.PurchaseOrderHeader
WHERE OrderDate >= CONVERT(DATE,'20080301')
        AND OrderDate < CONVERT(DATE,'20080316');
-- 137
```

4-Week 13 Month Calendar

The Christian (Gregorian, Western) calendar, used in most parts of the World, has been introduced by Pope Gregory in 1582. It appears to be irregular due to using 12 months instead of 13 months. While 13 month calendars were proposed in the past, its urgency rapidly increasing due to the expansion of Business Intelligence. 4 weeks 13 months calendar totals to 364 days, almost on the mark!

```
SELECT 4 * 7 * 13  -- 364
```

To include the remaining 1 or 2 (leap year) days, we have to make the last week of the year longer with 1 or 2 days, tentatively named **Earthday** and **Starday**. Each month starts with Monday. Therefore, each year starts with Monday. The new month is tentatively called **Undecimber** after undecim, Latin for 11. This naming follows the Latin number sequence starting with September (septem Latin for 7). The year ends two ways:

- Friday, Saturday, Sunday, Earthday (Undecimber 29)
- Friday, Saturday, Sunday, Earthday, Starday (Undecimber 30) - leap year
- January 1 is Monday in each year
- Each month calendar identical with Undecimber having an extra day or two

```
DECLARE @4week13month TABLE( ID INT IDENTITY(1,1),
 Mon char(3), Tue char(3), Wed char(3), Thu char(3), Fri char(3), Sat char(3), Sun char(3));
INSERT @4week13month VALUES ('MON', 'TUE', 'WED', 'THU', 'FRI', 'SAT', 'SUN'),
('1','2','3','4','5','6','7'), ('8','9','10','11','12','13','14'),
('15','16','17','18','19','20','21'),('22','23','24','25','26','27','28');
SELECT * FROM @4week13month ORDER BY ID;
```

MON	TUE	WED	THU	FRI	SAT	SUN
1	2	3	4	5	6	7
8	9	10	11	12	13	14
15	16	17	18	19	20	21
22	23	24	25	26	27	28

The SQL significance of such a calendar is immense: week can be used in GROUP BY summaries just like month. Currently week-based analysis is misaligned with month-based analysis. Some businesses do use 13-month calendars for business analysis and reporting.

The **benefits of 13 month calendar** are presented at:
http://en.wikipedia.org/wiki/International_Fixed_Calendar

DDL Trigger on DATABASE CREATE

DDL trigger carries out action, in this instance just sending a message, when a new database is created. The screenshot segment shows the DDL trigger listing in SSMS Object Explorer. SQL Server 2012 demo. Server-Scoped Triggers are not supported in Azure SQL.

```
USE master;
GO
CREATE TRIGGER trgNewDatabase
ON ALL SERVER  FOR CREATE_DATABASE  AS
BEGIN
DECLARE @database sysname, @event_data XML = EVENTDATA()
 SET @database = @event_data.value('(/EVENT_INSTANCE/DatabaseName)[1]', 'sysname')
 RAISERROR( 'trgNewDatabase DDL trigger message: %s DB has been created', 16,1, @database)
END
GO -- Command(s) completed successfully.
```

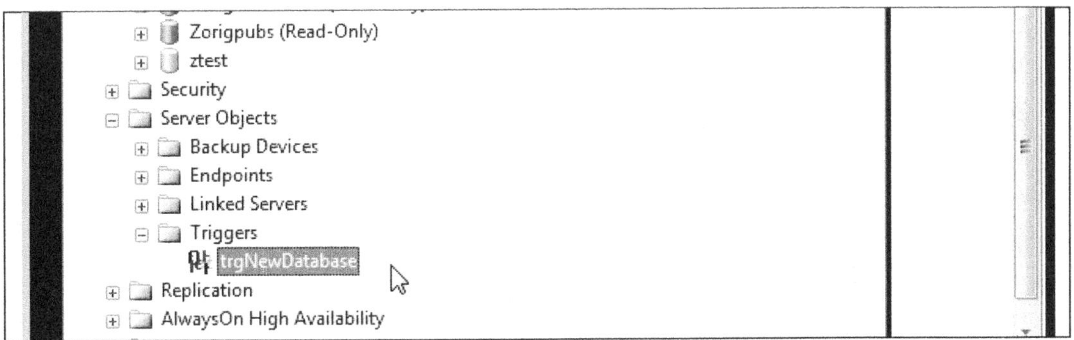


```
CREATE DATABASE zTest1;
GO  /* Messages
Msg 50000, Level 16, State 1, Procedure trgNewDatabase, Line 10
trgNewDatabase DDL trigger message: zTest1 DB has been created */
```

```
DROP DATABASE zTest1;
GO -- Command(s) completed successfully.
```

```
DROP TRIGGER [trgNewDatabase] ON ALL SERVER
GO -- Command(s) completed successfully.
```

Spatial Data Types: Geometry & Geography

The POLYGON & STLength() Functions

The geometry data type and geography data type are used for spatial and mapping applications. The geometry data type can store polygons. The perimeter of a polygon can be calculated by the STLength() spatial function and the polygon itself can be visualized in Management Studio Spatial results.

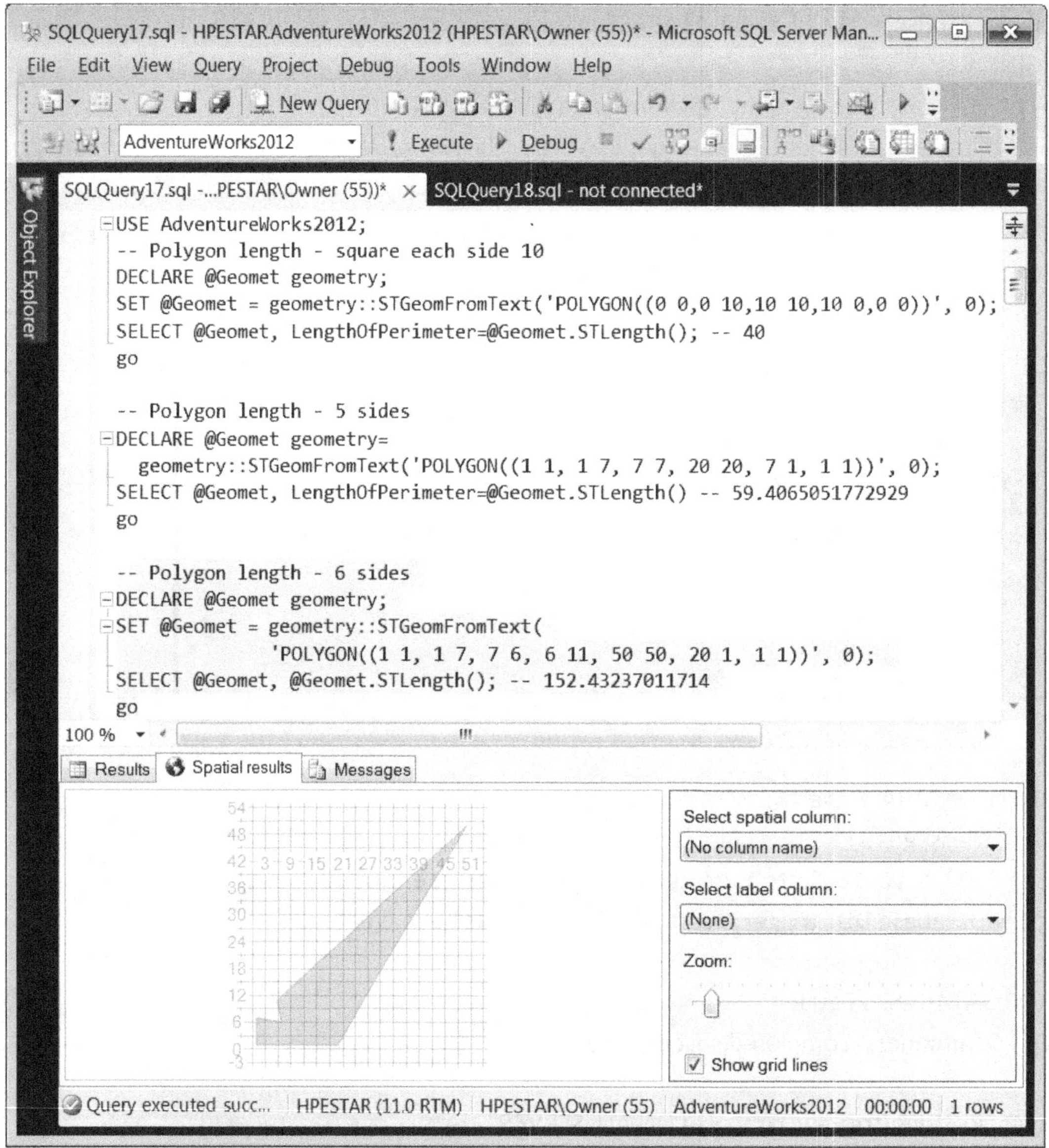

```
USE AdventureWorks2012;
-- Polygon length - square each side 10
DECLARE @Geomet geometry;
SET @Geomet = geometry::STGeomFromText('POLYGON((0 0,0 10,10 10,10 0,0 0))', 0);
SELECT @Geomet, LengthOfPerimeter=@Geomet.STLength(); -- 40
go

-- Polygon length - 5 sides
DECLARE @Geomet geometry=
  geometry::STGeomFromText('POLYGON((1 1, 1 7, 7 7, 20 20, 7 1, 1 1))', 0);
SELECT @Geomet, LengthOfPerimeter=@Geomet.STLength() -- 59.4065051772929
go

-- Polygon length - 6 sides
DECLARE @Geomet geometry;
SET @Geomet = geometry::STGeomFromText(
              'POLYGON((1 1, 1 7, 7 6, 6 11, 50 50, 20 1, 1 1))', 0);
SELECT @Geomet, @Geomet.STLength(); -- 152.43237011714
go
```

Polygon Difference & Intersection

The STDifference() and STIntersection functions will calculate the difference and intersection of two polygons. The example is for a small square inside a bigger square. The difference is displayed in Spatial results which is the dark area. The intersection coincidentally is the white small square.

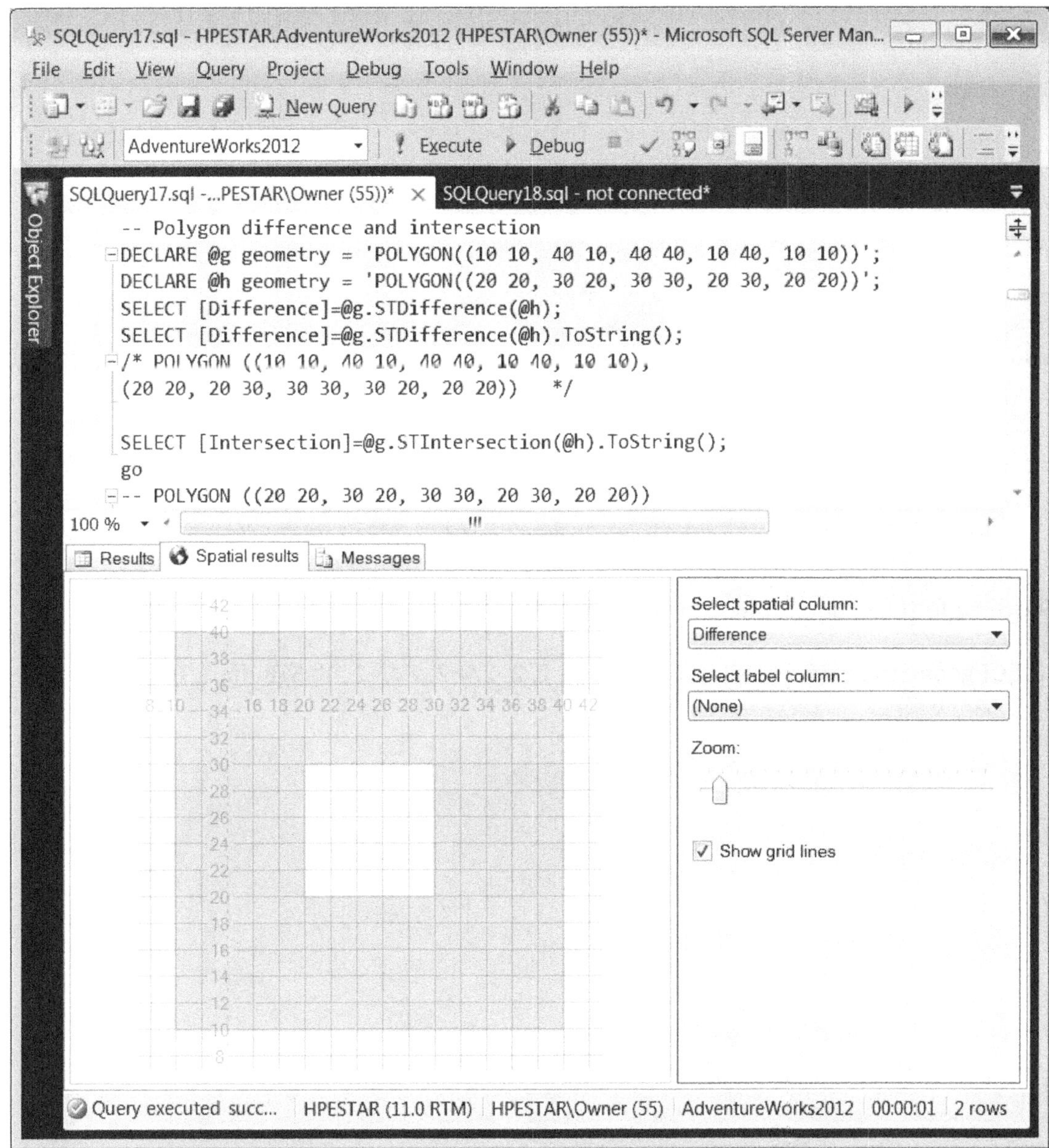

SQLQuery17.sql - HPESTAR.AdventureWorks2012 (HPESTAR\Owner (55))* - Microsoft SQL Server Man...
File Edit View Query Project Debug Tools Window Help
New Query
AdventureWorks2012
Execute
Debug
Object Explorer
SQLQuery17.sql -...PESTAR\Owner (55))*
SQLQuery18.sql - not connected*
-- Polygon difference and intersection
DECLARE @g geometry = 'POLYGON((10 10, 40 10, 40 40, 10 40, 10 10))';
DECLARE @h geometry = 'POLYGON((20 20, 30 20, 30 30, 20 30, 20 20))';
SELECT [Difference]=@g.STDifference(@h);
SELECT [Difference]=@g.STDifference(@h).ToString();
/* POLYGON ((10 10, 40 10, 40 40, 10 40, 10 10),
(20 20, 20 30, 30 30, 30 20, 20 20)) */
SELECT [Intersection]=@g.STIntersection(@h).ToString();
go
-- POLYGON ((20 20, 30 20, 30 30, 20 30, 20 20))
100 %
Results
Spatial results
Messages
Select spatial column:
Difference
Select label column:
(None)
Zoom:
Show grid lines
Query executed succ...
HPESTAR (11.0 RTM)
HPESTAR\Owner (55)
AdventureWorks2012
00:00:01
2 rows

Geometry Area & CIRCULARSTRING Functions

```
-- Area of a polygon - triangle
DECLARE @Geomet geometry;
SET @Geomet = geometry::STGeomFromText('POLYGON((3 3,40 40, 80 3, 3 3))', 0);
SELECT @Geomet, AreaOfPolygon=@Geomet.STArea();
GO
-- 1424.5
```

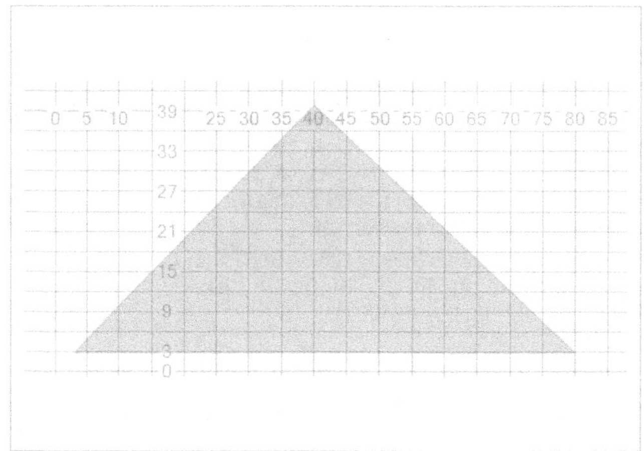

The STBuffer() function "draws" the thick border.

```
SELECT geometry::Parse('CIRCULARSTRING(-2 2, 2 -2, 4 2, 2 4, -2 2)').STBuffer(.3);
```

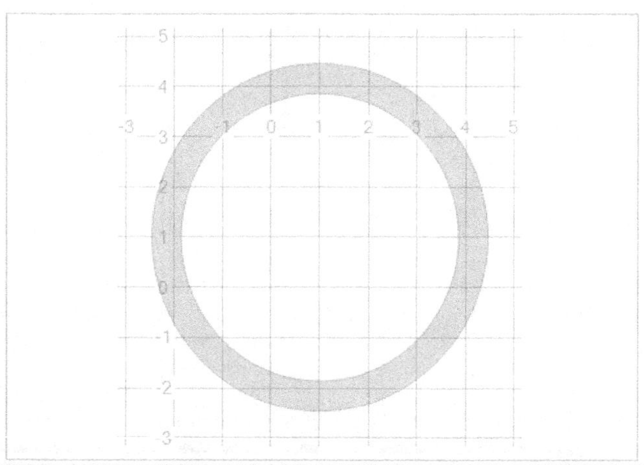

Working with geometry Data in Tables

```
IF OBJECT_ID ( 'dbo.GeometryTest', 'U' ) IS NOT NULL     DROP TABLE dbo.GeometryTest;
go
```

```
create table GeometryTest
(
        GeometryTestID int identity(1,1) primary key,
        Geom geometry ,
        GeomText as Geom.STAsText(),                    -- computed column
        GeomDim as Geom.STDimension());                  -- computed column
go
```

```
insert GeometryTest (Geom) values
        (geometry::STPointFromText ( 'POINT (85 115)',0)),
        (geometry::STPointFromText ( 'POINT (100 100)',0)),
        (geometry::STGeomFromText ('LINESTRING (70 70, 30 150,  150 150)', 0)),
        (geometry::STGeomFromText ('POLYGON ((0 0, 300 0, 300 300, 0 300, 0 0))', 0));
```

```
select * from GeometryTest
go
```

GeometryTestID	Geom	GeomText	GeomDim
1	0x00000000010C00000000004055400000000000C05C40	POINT (85 115)	0
2	0x00000000010C00000000000059400000000000005940	POINT (100 100)	0
3	0x0000000001040300000000000000008051400000000000008051400000000000003E400000000000C062400000000000C062400000000000C06240010000000100000000010000000FFFFFFFF0000000002	LINESTRING (70 70, 30 150, 150 150)	1
4	0x000000000104050000000000000000000000000000000000000000000000C0724000000000000000000000000000C072400000000000C0724000000000000000000000000000C0724000000000000000000000000000000000000000000000000100000002000000000100000000FFFFFFFF0000000003	POLYGON ((0 0, 300 0, 300 300, 0 300, 0 0))	2

```
declare @gmtry1 geometry,  @gmtry2 geometry, @combo geometry;
select @gmtry1 = Geom from GeometryTest where GeometryTestID=3
select @gmtry2 = Geom from GeometryTest where GeometryTestID=4
select @combo = @gmtry1.STIntersection(@gmtry2)
select Intersection = @Combo.STAsText();
go
```

Intersection
LINESTRING (150 150, 30 150, 70 70)

The geography Data Type in Map Application

Locating address in a rectangular Earth region based on the Person.Address table geo SpatialLocation column data.

```
USE AdventureWorks2012;
```

```
DECLARE @Rectangle geography;
SET @Rectangle = geography::STGeomFromText(
        'POLYGON((-50.0 50.0, -90.0 50.0, -90.0 25.0, -50.0 25.0, -50.0 50.0))',
                    4326);
SELECT          s.BusinessEntityID
                ,s.Name                         AS Dealer
                ,a.AddressLine1
                ,a.City
                ,sp.StateProvinceCode
                ,a.PostalCode
 FROM Sales.Store s
        INNER JOIN Person.BusinessEntityAddress bea
                        ON s.BusinessEntityID =bea.BusinessEntityID
        INNER JOIN Person.Address a
                        ON bea.AddressID = a.AddressID
        INNER JOIN Person.StateProvince sp
                        ON a.StateProvinceID = sp.StateProvinceID
WHERE  a.SpatialLocation.STIntersects(@Rectangle) = 1
         ORDER BY Dealer;
GO  -- (240 row(s) affected) - Partial results.
```

BusinessEntityID	Dealer	AddressLine1	City	StateProvinceCode	PostalCode
2051	A Bicycle Association	6405 Erie Blvd. Hills Plaza	De Witt	NY	13214
354	Acclaimed Bicycle Company	830 Highway 499 So	Mcdonough	GA	30253
836	Active Cycling	Indian Mound Mall	Heath	OH	43056
1916	Active Life Toys	55 Standish Court	Mississauga	ON	L5B 3V4
1936	Active Transport Inc.	225200 Miles Ave.	North Randall	OH	44128
366	Activity Center	Factory Stores Of America	Crossville	TN	38555
1046	Better Bike Shop	42525 Austell Road	Austell	GA	30106
878	Bicycle Outfitters	Cherry Grove Plaza	Cincinnati	OH	45202
422	Bike Boutique	Polaris Town Center	Columbus	OH	43215
1924	Bike Products and Accessories	Regency Hilltop Shopping Cntr	Virginia Beach	VA	23451
698	Bike Rims Company	Edgewater Mall	Biloxi	MS	39530
622	Bikes and Motorbikes	22580 Free Street	Toronto	ON	M4B 1V7
424	Bikes Anyone?	Ames Plaza	Saugus	MA	01906
1162	Bikes for Kids and Adults	9900 Ronson Drive	Etobicoke	ON	M9W 3P3
510	Bikes for Two	63 West Beaver Creek	Richmond Hill	ON	L4E 3M5

Surveying Spatial Locations in Person.Address with TABLESAMPLE

Since the limit is 5000 for Spatial results graphics, we use TABLESAMPLE random sampling. The outline of the Unites States is clearly visible in the spatial graphics. 4810 dots and partial results.

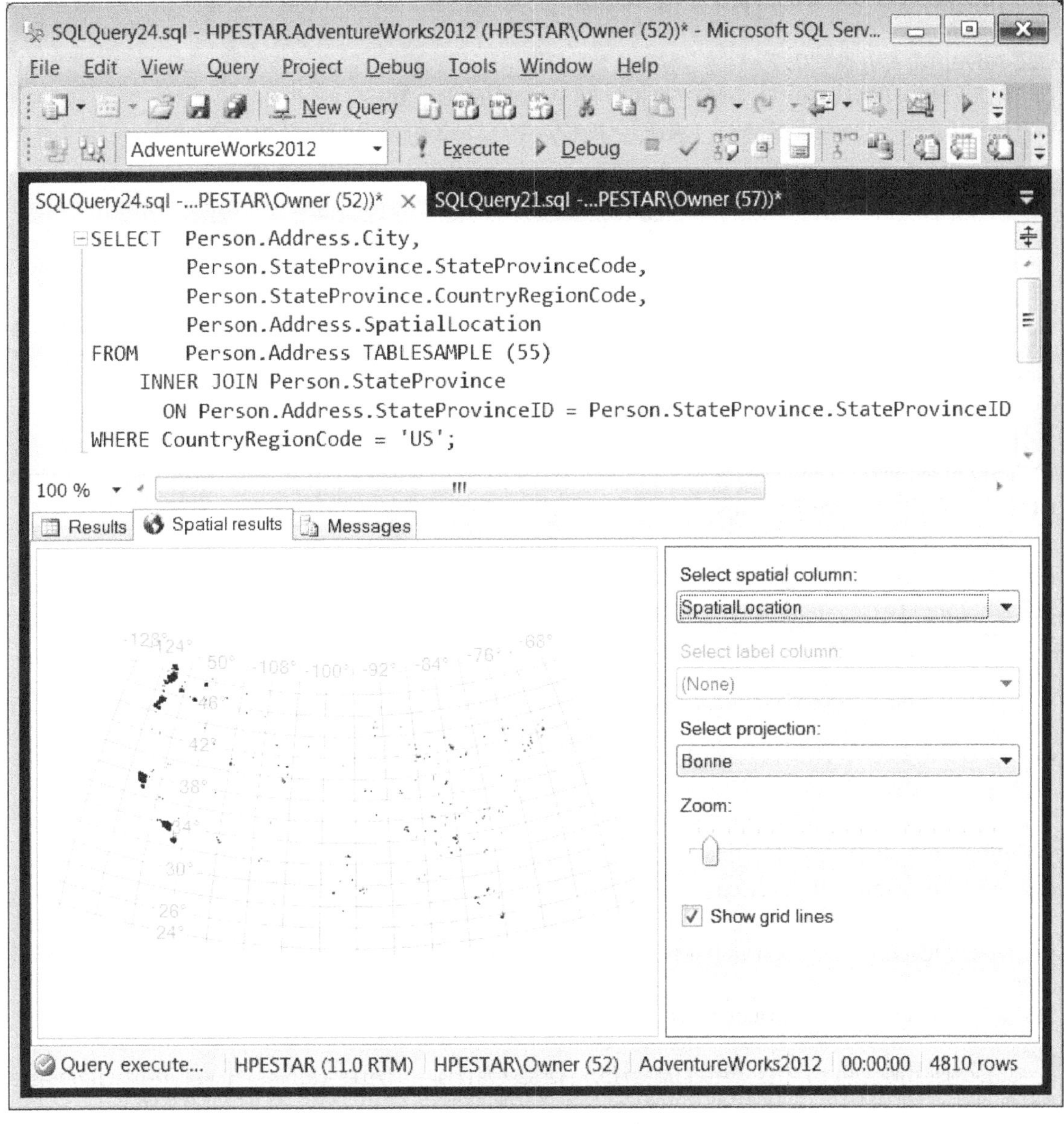

City	StateProvinceCode	CountryRegionCode	SpatialLocation
Concord	CA	US	0xE6100000010CA18642EB19FF4240E84C0794157B5EC0
Seattle	WA	US	0xE6100000010CCC2A6CCDCBCA474094427543D1995EC0
Torrance	CA	US	0xE6100000010C943F7FEBB1E440402956F3FF52A05DC0
Woodburn	OR	US	0xE6100000010CBF692502648C4640839FE7AD54AB5EC0
Puyallup	WA	US	0xE6100000010C827BF9CD1598474096246A5843935EC0

Data Encryption & Decryption

Data encryption is an important part of keeping sensitive data, such as credit card numbers, safe. When we encrypt successively, the encrypted string varies. SQL Server 2012 script. EncryptByCert is not supported in Azure SQL.

```
USE AdventureWorks2012;
CREATE CERTIFICATE CertQ  ENCRYPTION BY PASSWORD = '007SkyFall$'
WITH SUBJECT ='CertQ',  START_DATE = '2012/01/01', EXPIRY_DATE = '2016/01/01';

DECLARE  @CypherText VARBINARY(MAX);
SET @CypherText = EncryptByCert(Cert_ID('CertQ'),'United States of America');
SELECT  @CypherText;
/*
0xDFAD2CABDDD07E75A74722CECF799B4AADBFE704D29F366DBF6F22C229E7EB6D94BC082BB2DFC7795C1AA92F7452D0AE2EF91
A2356B22F8508E37F7BC440CF926BC89C0FFCBBB04DF75206F2C6282FE87756D2003F40D738F92499674749BA8C9204A3BCAC9A7
8366939786A8D4E421DC71289E9D9D8140678EFD329BB5D7822
*/
SELECT Decyphered = CONVERT(VARCHAR(256),DecryptByCert(Cert_ID('CertQ'),
@CypherText,N'007SkyFall$'));
GO  -- United States of America

DECLARE  @CypherText VARBINARY(MAX);
SET @CypherText = EncryptByCert(Cert_ID('CertQ'),'United States of America');
SELECT  @CypherText;
/*
0x77E17C2A7B30E68B3AA5792400842FBDA19E121F8BEFCF787F3C6F68D720CC6B992BBF1C27168CC7B5592359437494BF1F719FF
67A1B5131C5AA69EEEA539DC5AA261BBAEDC12201BDC2EC1E31280FD0B76E8773CDB57582BE857F24FD86997582ACFAE07028A9
0A0FA9D29A69FB53FC24261828F53884636A4452597A18A908
*/
SELECT Decyphered = CONVERT(VARCHAR(256), DecryptByCert(Cert_ID('CertQ'),
@CypherText,N'007SkyFall$'));
GO  -- United States of America

DECLARE  @CypherText VARBINARY(MAX), @cleartext varchar(256)='Yellowstone National Park ID, MT
,WY';
SET @CypherText = EncryptByCert(Cert_ID('CertQ'), @cleartext);  SELECT  @CypherText;
/*
0x386D15B848B3200CA2F0FD1341550AD16C61A19B71D2A14256B8C281249B5F9471EEB9C81DE9FA21CBE4602E099E1F7F363923
B8E0BF2960CAF13824D5EE0E852BA0B156532D50B336377648C6580BDFEB85453F34D722038FF6F7BD695343617E39E68259B05D
65F686CE63A68CFC795D86F94ADC75D0974882721A5083842C
*/
SELECT Decyphered = CONVERT(VARCHAR(256),DecryptByCert(Cert_ID('CertQ'),
@CypherText,N'007SkyFall$'));
GO  -- Yellowstone National Park ID, MT ,WY
```

Database Backup - On-Premises SQL Server

Full Database Backup with Verification

Full database backup and verify script for the AdventureWorks2012 database.

```
USE master;
GO
-- Backup database
BACKUP DATABASE [AdventureWorks2012] TO  DISK = N'F:\data\backup\AW2012.bak' WITH
NAME = N'AdventureWorks2012-Full DB Backup', STATS = 5;
GO
-- Verify database backup
DECLARE @backupSetId as int;
SELECT @backupSetId = position from msdb..backupset where
database_name=N'AdventureWorks2012' and backup_set_id=(select max(backup_set_id) from
msdb..backupset where database_name=N'AdventureWorks2012' );

IF @backupSetId is null begin raiserror(N'Verify failed. Backup info for DB
"AdventureWorks2012" not found.', 16, 1) end;

RESTORE VERIFYONLY FROM  DISK = N'F:\data\backup\AW2012.bak' WITH  FILE =
@backupSetId,  NOUNLOAD,  NOREWIND;
GO
```

```
/* Messages
5 percent processed.
10 percent processed.
15 percent processed.
.......
95 percent processed.
Processed 27920 pages for database 'AdventureWorks2012', file 'AdventureWorks2012_Data' on file 1.
Processed 80 pages for database 'AdventureWorks2012', file 'FSAlpha' on file 1.
Processed 2 pages for database 'AdventureWorks2012', file 'AdventureWorks2012_Log' on file 1.
100 percent processed.
BACKUP DATABASE successfully processed 28002 pages in 7.931 seconds (27.582 MB/sec).

The backup set on file 1 is valid.   */
```

Full Database Backup with Datestamp in Filename

```
DECLARE @BackupPathFile nvarchar(256)
 = N'f:\data\backup\AW2012_' + CONVERT(varchar, CURRENT_TIMESTAMP, 112) + '.BAK'
PRINT @BackupPathFile  -- f:\data\backup\AW2012_20121114.BAK
BACKUP DATABASE [AdventureWorks2012] TO  DISK = @BackupPathFile
```

Backup of a Single Table

Here is the list of options available.

- SELECT * INTO table2 FROM table1
- SSMS Script Wizard generates script with INSERTs
- SSMS execute SELECT query & the save the output to a file
- bcp table to a file
- SS Import/Export Wizard - export table to a table or file

The first one is the easiest, the last one is the most flexible. We have to pay attention that the export is reversible. For example, if we use CSV format then the strings should be enclosed in double quotes for example in order not to conflict with commas used for column separation. Execute the query.

```
SELECT * FROM Production.Product ORDER BY ProductNumber;
```

On upper left corner in results, right click, save results as, .csv (comma delimited). Sounds safe. But it is not because the some product names contain commas. That makes the data export irreversible, and probably useless for any application.

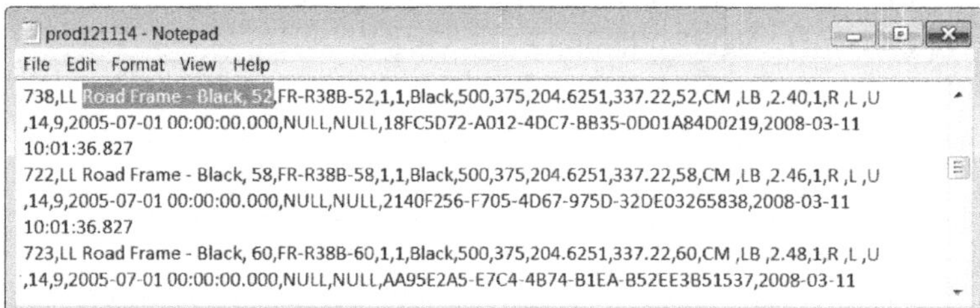

The SS Import & Export Wizard has option to specify Text qualifier for flat file destination.

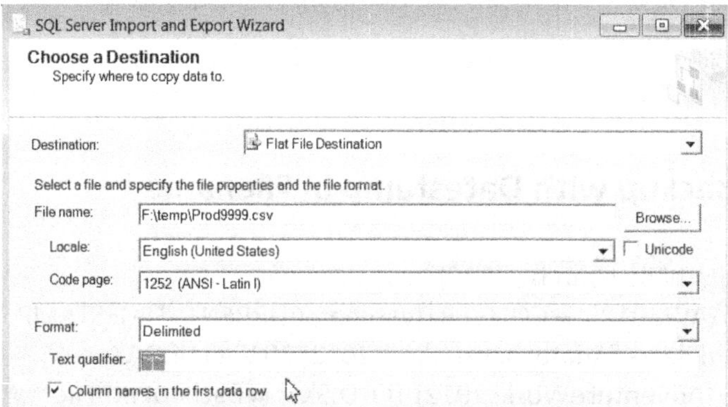

Setting SSMS Query Options to Include Double Quotes with Strings

There is a query option in SSMS setting to set double quote as text qualifier when saving in csv format. Click on Query, click on Query Options. Configure as shown.

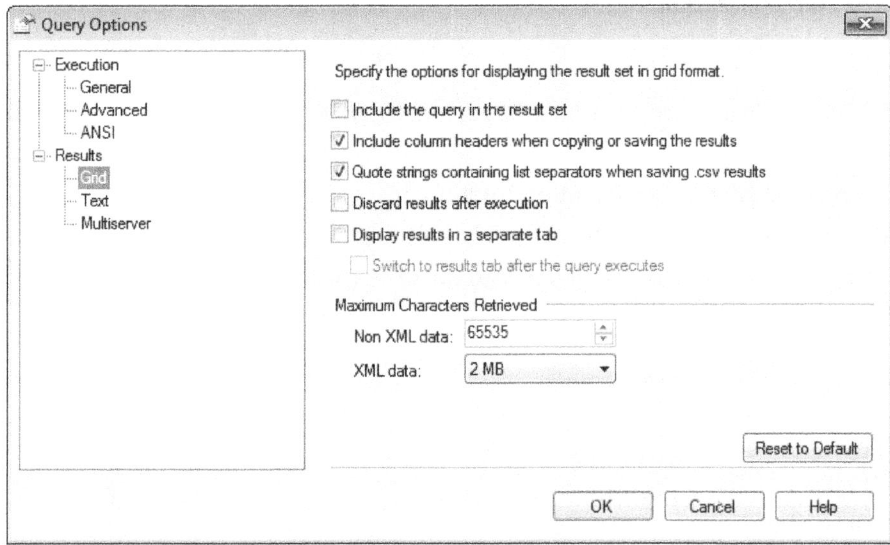

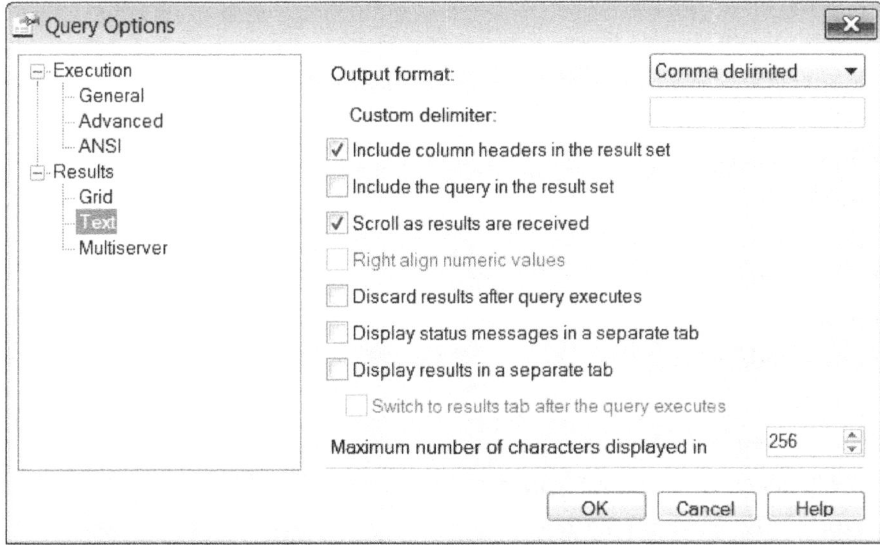

The output will be proper csv file.

793,"Road-250 Black, 44",BK-R89B-44,1,1,Black,100,75,1554.9479,2443.35,44,CM ,LB ,14.77,4,R ,H ,U ,2,26,2006-07-01 00:00:00.000,NULL,NULL,1FF419B5-52AF-4F7E-AEAE-4FEC5E99DE35,2008-03-11 10:01:36.827

Database Restore - On-Premises SQL Server

To restore a database backup to a new database we have to indicate the location (path & name) of the database files. FILE=1 refers to the first backup set in AW2012.BAK. A backup file can contain more than one backup.

```
USE [master]
RESTORE DATABASE [rptAdventureWorks2012] FROM  DISK = N'f:\data\backup\AW2012.BAK'
WITH  FILE = 1,
MOVE N'FSAlpha' TO N'F:\data\db\data\FSAlpha',
MOVE N'AdventureWorks2012_Data' TO N'F:\data\db\data\AdventureWorks2012_Data.mdf',
MOVE N'AdventureWorks2012_Log' TO N'F:\data\db\log\AdventureWorks2012_log.ldf',
NOUNLOAD,  STATS = 5
GO
```

```
/* Messages
5 percent processed.
10 percent processed.
15 percent processed.
.....
55 percent processed.
60 percent processed.
65 percent processed.
70 percent processed.
75 percent processed.
80 percent processed.
85 percent processed.
90 percent processed.
95 percent processed.
100 percent processed.
Processed 27920 pages for database 'rptAdventureWorks2012', file
'AdventureWorks2012_Data' on file 1.
Processed 2 pages for database 'rptAdventureWorks2012', file 'AdventureWorks2012_Log' on
file 1.
Processed 81 pages for database 'rptAdventureWorks2012', file 'FSAlpha' on file 1.

RESTORE DATABASE successfully processed 28002 pages in 25.375 seconds (8.621 MB/sec). */
```

Restore of a Single Table

Restoring a table can be tricky. When exporting a table, basically the data content goes, and some metadata such as column names. SELECT INTO copies the data, column names, data types, sizes and the IDENTITY property if any. Constraints and indexes are not exported. Before restoring, the current table should be emptied. DELETE and TRUNCATE are not exactly the same. TRUNCATE is faster due to minimal logging. TRUNCATE also resets the IDENTITY SEED.

```
SELECT * INTO tempdb.dbo.Product
FROM Production.Product;
GO  - (504 row(s) affected)
```

```
use tempdb;
CREATE UNIQUE INDEX idxProd on Product(Name);
GO
```

```
DELETE Product;  -- (504 row(s) affected)
DBCC CHECKIDENT(Product);
/*Checking identity information: current identity value '999', current column value 'NULL'.
DBCC execution completed. If DBCC printed error messages, contact your system
administrator.*/
```

```
TRUNCATE TABLE Product;
GO
DBCC CHECKIDENT(Product);
GO
/*Checking identity information: current identity value 'NULL', current column value 'NULL'.
DBCC execution completed. If DBCC printed error messages, contact your system
administrator.*/
```

```
-- Restore the content of table
INSERT Product
SELECT *
FROM Production.Product;
/*Msg 8101, Level 16, State 1, Line 1
An explicit value for the identity column in table 'Product' can only be specified when a column
list is used and IDENTITY_INSERT is ON.*/
```

Repopulating Table with IDENTITY Column - On-Premises SQL Server

IDENTITY is an obstacle in moving back the original data. We have to set the IDENTITY_INSERT flag and we have to specify all the columns in the INSERT statement. After repopulating we have to check if IDENTITY is seeded at the right value and rebuild the out-of-shape index.

```
SET IDENTITY_INSERT Product ON;
GO
INSERT INTO [dbo].[Product]
        ([ProductID],[Name]
        ,[ProductNumber],[MakeFlag]
        ,[FinishedGoodsFlag],[Color]
        ,[SafetyStockLevel],[ReorderPoint]
        ,[StandardCost],[ListPrice]
        ,[Size],[SizeUnitMeasureCode]
        ,[WeightUnitMeasureCode],[Weight]
        ,[DaysToManufacture],[ProductLine]
        ,[Class] ,[Style]
        ,[ProductSubcategoryID],[ProductModelID]
        ,[SellStartDate],[SellEndDate]
        ,[DiscontinuedDate],[rowguid],[ModifiedDate])
SELECT *
FROM Production.Product;
GO
-- (504 row(s) affected)
SET IDENTITY_INSERT Product OFF;
```

```
DBCC CHECKIDENT(Product) ;
GO
/*Checking identity information: current identity value '999', current column value '999'.
DBCC execution completed. If DBCC printed error messages, contact your system
administrator.*/
```

```
ALTER INDEX [idxProd] ON [dbo].[Product] REBUILD;
```

A good strategy is to save the table script with all related item scripts onto a disk .sql file.

That way we isolate table definition with constraints, defaults and indexes from table content.

Database Maintenance Plan Wizard - On-Premises SS

The SQL Server Maintenance Plan Wizard is an SSMS Object Explorer GUI tool to prepare a partial or complete maintenance plan for a database(s).

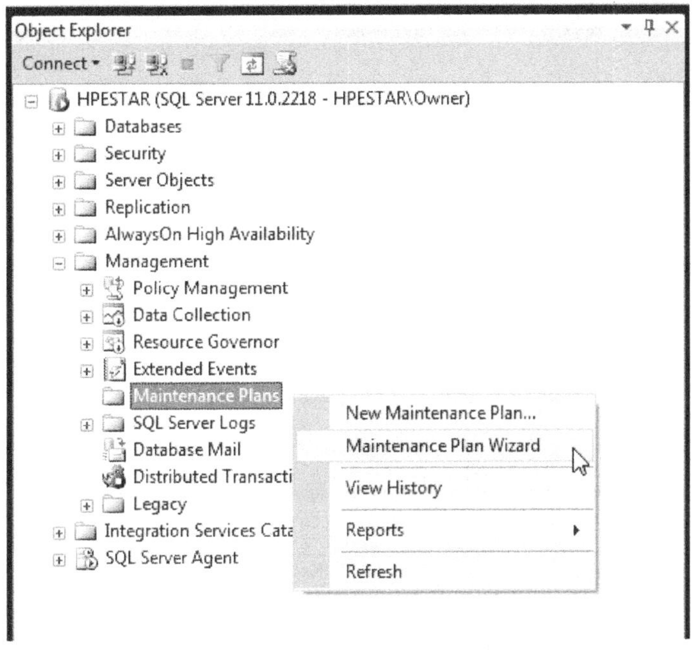

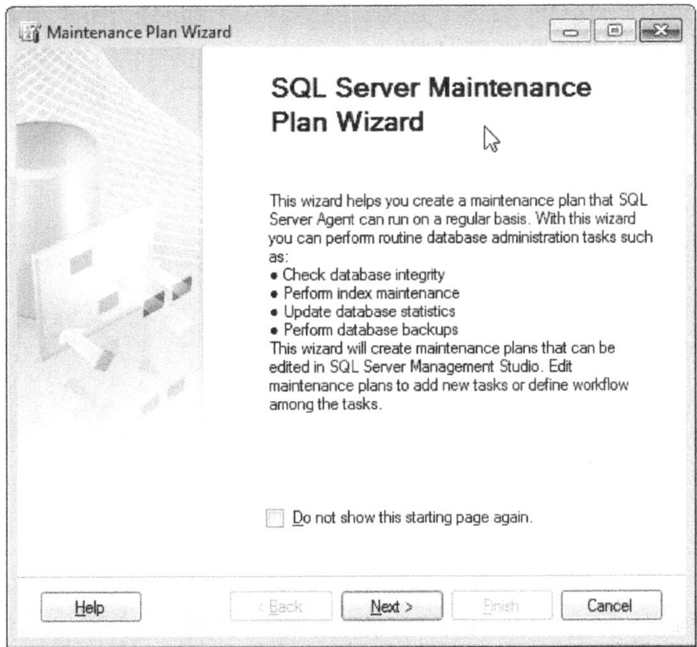

Follow the Plan Wizard Step by Step

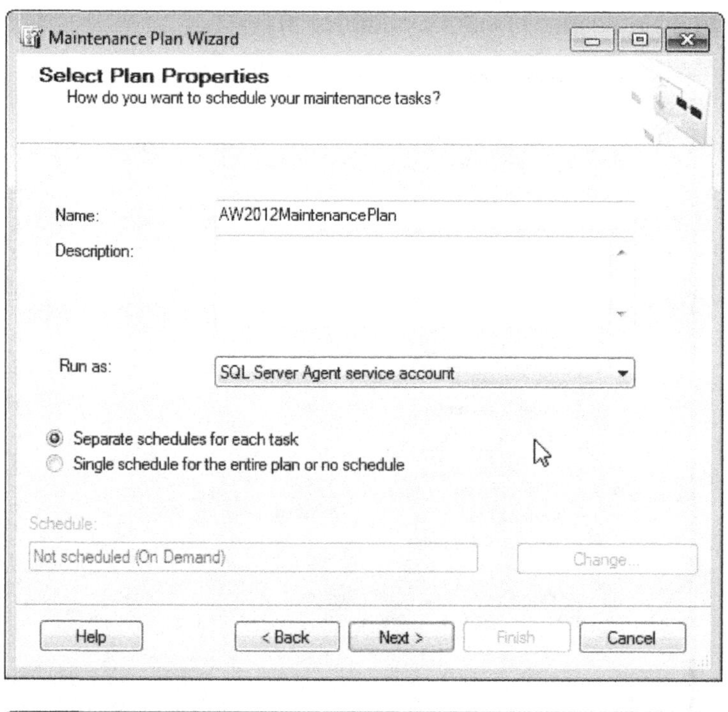

Maintenance Plan Wizard

Select Maintenance Tasks

Which tasks should this plan perform?

Select one or more maintenance tasks:

- [x] Check Database Integrity
- [ ] Shrink Database
- [ ] Reorganize Index
- [x] Rebuild Index
- [ ] Update Statistics
- [ ] Clean Up History
- [ ] Execute SQL Server Agent Job
- [x] Back Up Database (Full)
- [ ] Back Up Database (Differential)
- [ ] Back Up Database (Transaction Log)
- [x] Maintenance Cleanup Task

The Rebuild task reorganizes data on the data and index pages by rebuilding indexes. This improves performance of index scans and seeks. This task also optimizes the distribution of data and free space on the index pages, allowing faster future growth.

Help | < Back | Next > | Finish | Cancel

One or More Databases Can Be Specified, Schedule Setup

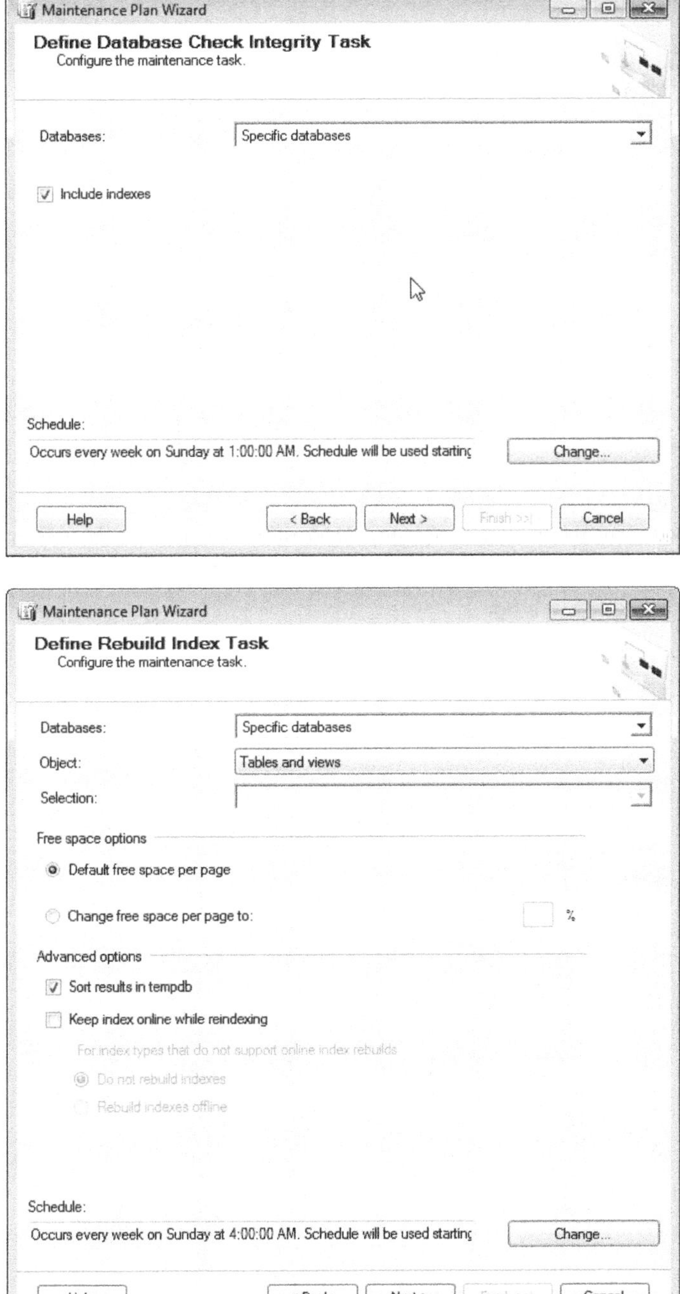

Full Database Backup Specifications

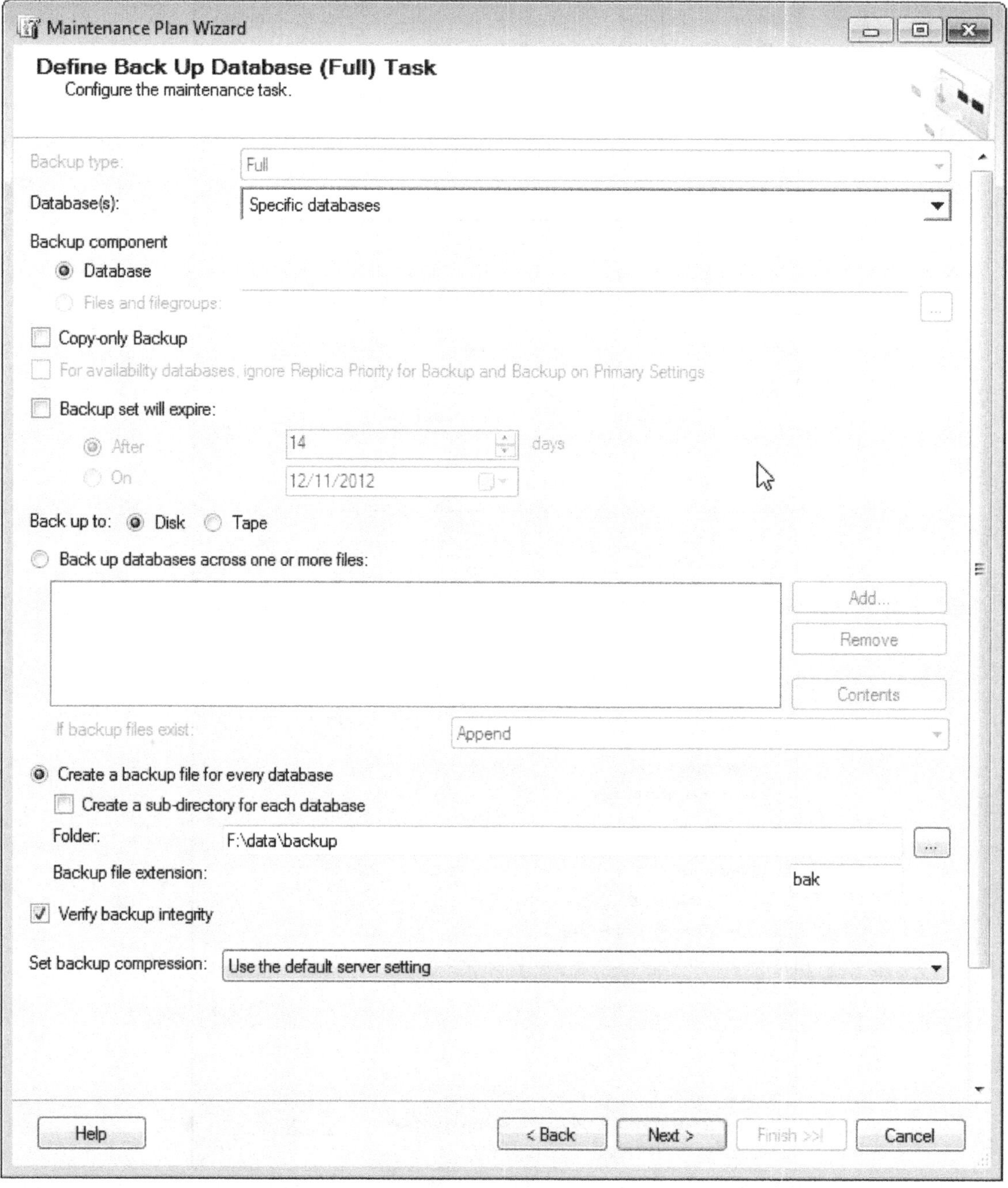

Create the Maintenance Plan & Schedule the Jobs

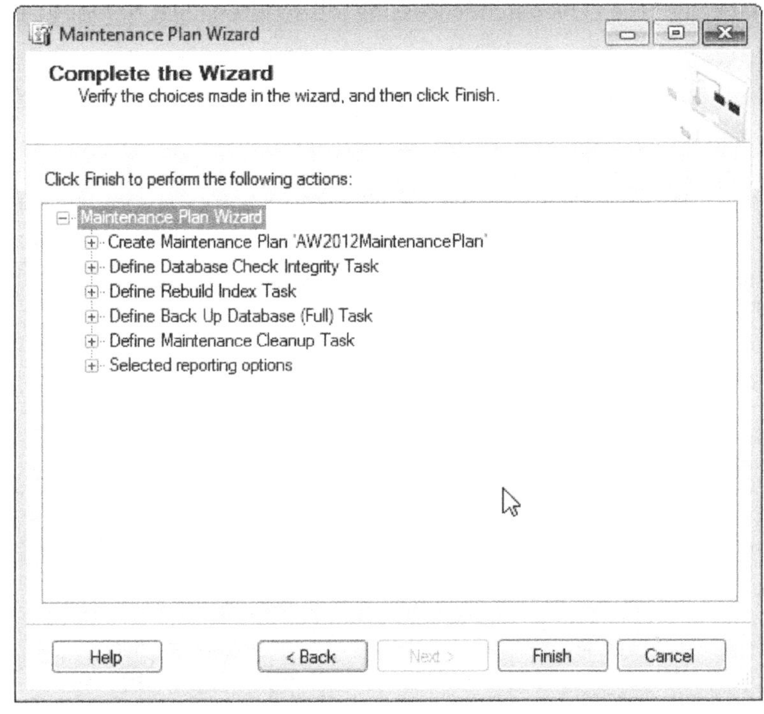

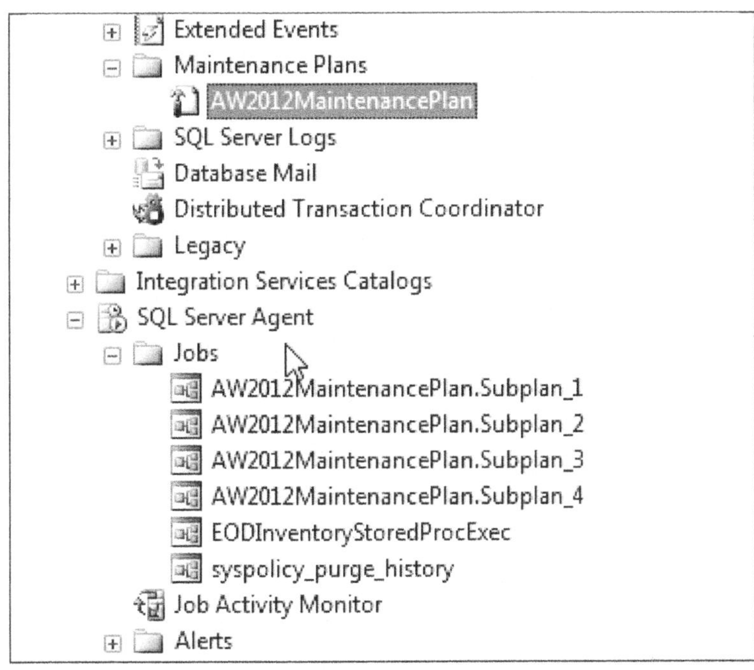

Configure Stored Procedure As SS Agent Job & Schedule

SSMS Object Explorer GUI editor can be used to setup a new job with schedule. It can also be done programmatically. The EOWBatchProcessing job scripted. SQL Server 2012 script.

```
USE [msdb];
GO
```

```
BEGIN TRANSACTION
DECLARE @ReturnCode INT; SELECT @ReturnCode = 0;
IF NOT EXISTS (SELECT name FROM msdb.dbo.syscategories WHERE name=N'Database Maintenance' AND category_class=1)
BEGIN

EXEC @ReturnCode = msdb.dbo.sp_add_category @class=N'JOB', @type=N'LOCAL', @name=N'Database Maintenance'
IF (@@ERROR <> 0 OR @ReturnCode <> 0) GOTO QuitWithRollback
END

DECLARE @jobId BINARY(16)

EXEC @ReturnCode = msdb.dbo.sp_add_job @job_name=N'EOWBatchProcessing',
                    @enabled=1,                    @notify_level_eventlog=0,
                    @notify_level_email=0,         @notify_level_netsend=0,
                    @notify_level_page=0,          @delete_level=0,
                    @description=N'Process all end of week jobs.',      @category_name=N'Database Maintenance',
                    @owner_login_name=N'HPESTAR\Owner',                 @job_id = @jobId OUTPUT
IF (@@ERROR <> 0 OR @ReturnCode <> 0) GOTO QuitWithRollback

EXEC @ReturnCode = msdb.dbo.sp_add_jobstep @job_id=@jobId, @step_name=N'EOWInventory',
                    @step_id=1,                    @cmdexec_success_code=0,
                    @on_success_action=1,          @on_success_step_id=0,
                    @on_fail_action=2,             @on_fail_step_id=0,
                    @retry_attempts=0,             @retry_interval=0,
                    @os_run_priority=0, @subsystem=N'TSQL',             @command=N'exec uspInventoryEOW;',
                    @database_name=N'AdventureWorks2018',               @flags=0
IF (@@ERROR <> 0 OR @ReturnCode <> 0) GOTO QuitWithRollback

EXEC @ReturnCode = msdb.dbo.sp_update_job @job_id = @jobId, @start_step_id = 1
IF (@@ERROR <> 0 OR @ReturnCode <> 0) GOTO QuitWithRollback

EXEC @ReturnCode = msdb.dbo.sp_add_jobschedule @job_id=@jobId, @name=N'EOWProcessingSATAM',
                    @enabled=1,                    @freq_type=8,
                    @freq_interval=65,             @freq_subday_type=1,
                    @freq_subday_interval=0,       @freq_relative_interval=0,
                    @freq_recurrence_factor=1,     @active_start_date=20181127,
                    @active_end_date=99991231,     @active_start_time=40000,
                    @active_end_time=235959,       @schedule_uid=N'0610654b-da58-46ff-9a96-39d69a0686a1'
IF (@@ERROR <> 0 OR @ReturnCode <> 0) GOTO QuitWithRollback

EXEC @ReturnCode = msdb.dbo.sp_add_jobserver @job_id = @jobId, @server_name = N'(local)'
IF (@@ERROR <> 0 OR @ReturnCode <> 0) GOTO QuitWithRollback
COMMIT TRANSACTION
GOTO EndSave
QuitWithRollback:
  IF (@@TRANCOUNT > 0) ROLLBACK TRANSACTION
EndSave:
GO
```

BULK INSERT Command - On-Premises SQL Server

BULK INSERT is a T-SQL command which corresponds to bcp "in" action for uploading a file into a database table. The command includes an optional format file. Generally it is a good idea to use format file with BULK INSERT and bcp for more reliable and successful data transfer.

Format File Generation with bcp

Format file can be created manually by an editor or automatically by bcp. Execute at Command Prompt as one line with no breaks to create a non-XML format file:

```
bcp HumanResources.Department format nul -T -n -f f:\data\bcpdemo\hrdept.fmt
```

The generated format file:

```
11.0
4
1   SQLSMALLINT   0   2    ""  1   DepartmentID   ""
2   SQLNCHAR      2   100  ""  2   Name           SQL_Latin1_General_CP1_CI_AS
3   SQLNCHAR      2   100  ""  3   GroupName      SQL_Latin1_General_CP1_CI_AS
4   SQLDATETIME   0   8    ""  4   ModifiedDate   ""
```

11.0 refers to SQL Server 2012 internal version number.

Export Data with bcp Format File Option

We use the format file for exporting the data at Command Prompt.

```
bcp HumanResources.Department out  f:\data\bcpdemo\hrdept.txt  -f
f:\data\bcpdemo\hrdept.fmt  -T
```

This is how the exported data looks in Notepad:

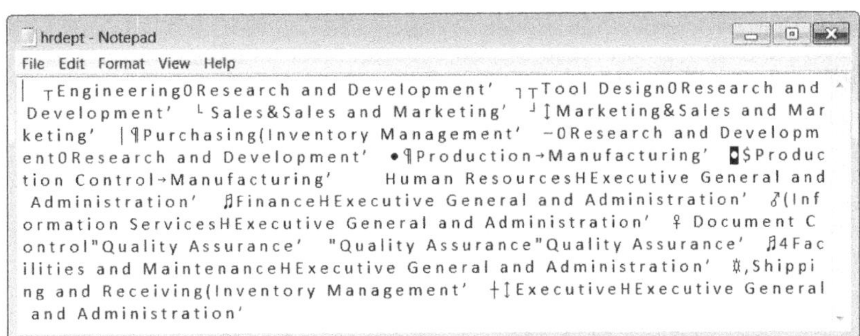

Import Data with BULK INSERT Format File Option

The same format file can be used to import the data into the database with BULK INSERT. First we create an empty table for the data import.

```
USE tempdb;
SELECT TOP(0)
          [DepartmentID] = CONVERT(INT, DepartmentID) --prevent IDENTITY inheritance
         ,[Name]
         ,[GroupName]
         ,[ModifiedDate]
INTO Department
FROM [AdventureWorks2012].[HumanResources].[Department];
GO
-- (0 row(s) affected)
```

```
BULK INSERT Department
         FROM 'f:\data\bcpdemo\hrdept.txt'
         WITH (FORMATFILE = 'f:\data\bcpdemo\hrdept.fmt');
GO
-- (16 row(s) affected)
```

```
SELECT TOP (3) * FROM Department ORDER BY NEWID();
GO
```

DepartmentID	Name	GroupName	ModifiedDate
14	Facilities and Maintenance	Executive General and Administration	2002-06-01 00:00:00.000
15	Shipping and Receiving	Inventory Management	2002-06-01 00:00:00.000
3	Sales	Sales and Marketing	2002-06-01 00:00:00.000

We can use the -n native mode for exporting data and DATAFILETYPE for importing.

```
bcp HumanResources.Shift out f:\temp\shift.txt -n -T
```

```
CREATE TABLE [Shift](
         [ShiftID] [tinyint]  NOT NULL,
         [Name] [dbo].[Name] NOT NULL,
         [StartTime] [time](7) NOT NULL,
         [EndTime] [time](7) NOT NULL,
         [ModifiedDate] [datetime] NOT NULL,
);
```

```
BULK INSERT Shift     FROM 'f:\temp\shift.txt'     WITH (DATAFILETYPE='native');
```

Importing & Exporting Images - OPSS

Importing & exporting images and other binary large objects (BLOB) requires special techniques. We use OPENROWSET BULK method to import an image.

SQLQuery29.sql - HPESTAR.AdventureWorks2012 (HPESTAR\Owner (54))* - Microsoft SQL Server Ma...
File Edit View Query Project Debug Tools Window Help
New Query
AdventureWorks2012
Execute
Debug
SQLQuery29.sql -...PESTAR\Owner (54))*
SQLQuery27.sql -...PESTAR\Owner (53))*
USE AdventureWorks2012;
GO
-- Create image warehouse for storing images in database
CREATE TABLE dbo.PhotoLand (
PhotoLandID INT IDENTITY (1 , 1) PRIMARY KEY,
ImageName VARCHAR(100) UNIQUE,
Photo VARBINARY(MAX),
ModifiedDate datetime default (CURRENT_TIMESTAMP));
GO
-- Insert image name
INSERT INTO dbo.PhotoLand ([ImageName]) VALUES ('ALASKALODGE.JPG');
-- (1 row(s) affected)
DECLARE @ID INT = SCOPE_IDENTITY(); -- get last identity inserted
UPDATE dbo.PhotoLand
SET Photo = (SELECT *
FROM OPENROWSET(BULK 'f:\data\images\ALASKALODGE.JPG',
SINGLE_BLOB) AS x)
WHERE PhotoLandID = @ID;
GO
--(1 row(s) affected)
-- Check table population
SELECT * FROM dbo.PhotoLand;
GO
100 %
Results
Messages
PhotoLand... ImageName Photo ModifiedDate
1 1 ALASKALODGE.JPG 0xFFD8FFE000104A464946000102000... 2012-11-12 16:52:03.727
Query executed success...
HPESTAR (11.0 RTM)
HPESTAR\Owner (54)
AdventureWorks2012
00:00:00
1 rows

Exporting Image with bcp

The bcp command can be used to export an image. In the following demo, it is executed from xp_cmdshell. **NOTE: on most production servers the xp_cmdshell option is disabled due to security concerns.**

```
DECLARE @Command NVARCHAR(4000);

-- Keep the command on ONE LINE - here it wraps around
SET @Command = 'bcp "SELECT Photo FROM dbo.PhotoLand WHERE PhotoLandID=1" queryout
"F:\temp\ALASKALODGE.jpg" -T -n' ;

PRINT @Command -- debugging

EXEC xp_cmdshell @Command;
GO
/*NULL
Starting copy...
NULL
1 rows copied.
Network packet size (bytes): 4096
Clock Time (ms.) Total     : 203    Average : (4.93 rows per sec.)
NULL */
```

Building a bcp Format File Interactively for Image Export

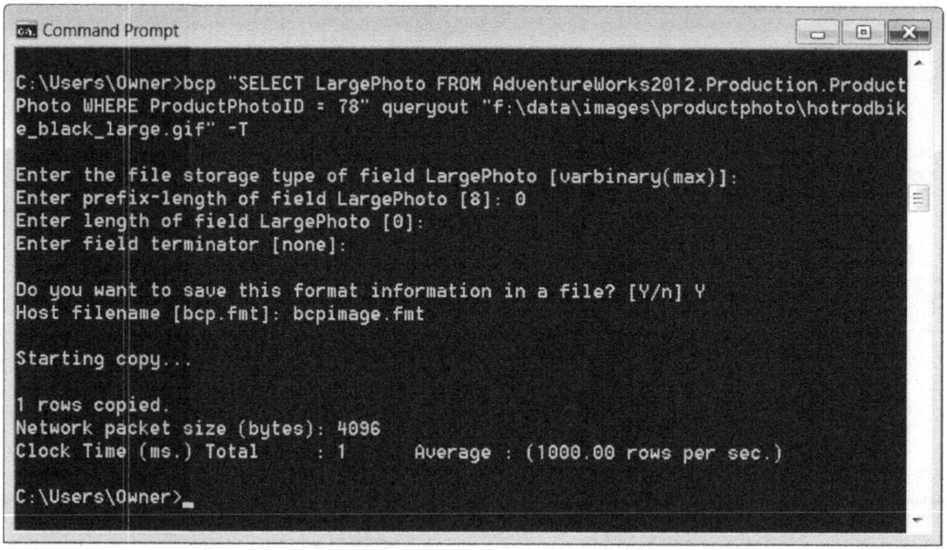

```
C:\Users\Owner>bcp "SELECT LargePhoto FROM AdventureWorks2012.Production.Product
Photo WHERE ProductPhotoID = 78" queryout "f:\data\images\productphoto\hotrodbik
e_black_large.gif" -T

Enter the file storage type of field LargePhoto [varbinary(max)]:
Enter prefix-length of field LargePhoto [8]: 0
Enter length of field LargePhoto [0]:
Enter field terminator [none]:

Do you want to save this format information in a file? [Y/n] Y
Host filename [bcp.fmt]: bcpimage.fmt

Starting copy...

1 rows copied.
Network packet size (bytes): 4096
Clock Time (ms.) Total     : 1      Average : (1000.00 rows per sec.)

C:\Users\Owner>_
```

Exporting All Images from Table

The content of the previously created bcp format file.

```
11.0
1
1     SQLBINARY       0     0     ""  1     LargePhoto          ""
```

T-SQL script for exporting all images to the file system from Production.ProductPhoto table LargePhoto column.

```
USE AdventureWorks2012;
GO
```

```
DECLARE @Command   VARCHAR(4000),  @PhotoID  INT,  @ImageFileName VARCHAR(128) ;
DECLARE PHOTOcursor CURSOR  FOR
        SELECT ProductPhotoID,   LargePhotoFileName  FROM   Production.ProductPhoto
        WHERE  LargePhotoFileName != 'no_image_available_large.gif';

OPEN PHOTOcursor FETCH NEXT FROM PHOTOcursor INTO @PhotoID,  @ImageFileName;

WHILE (@@FETCH_STATUS = 0) -- Cursor loop
 BEGIN
-- No carriage return or new line in bcp command string!
  SET @Command = CONCAT('bcp "SELECT LargePhoto FROM Production.ProductPhoto WHERE
ProductPhotoID = ',
  convert(VARCHAR,@PhotoID) + '" queryout "f:\data\images\productphoto\',
  @ImageFileName,'" -T -f "f:\data\images\bcpimage.fmt" ');

  PRINT @Command -- debugging
  EXEC xp_cmdshell @Command, no_output;

  FETCH NEXT FROM PHOTOcursor  INTO @PhotoID,    @ImageFileName;
 END;  -- cursor loop

CLOSE PHOTOcursor; DEALLOCATE PHOTOcursor;
GO
```

Product Photo Icons in the ProductPhoto Folder

The folder contains 100 exported product photos. The photos cannot be visualized in SSMS. but in the file system or SSRS reports. The following is a partial list of image icons.

In SSIS the Export Column & Import Column Transformations can be used for exporting and importing a set of images to and from folders.

FOR XML Clause

A SELECT query returns results as a table-like rowset. With a FOR XML clause the results are returned in XML format.

FOR XML RAW

The FOR XML RAW mode generates a single <row> element per row in the rowset that is returned by the SELECT statement. Tree structure can be generated by nesting queries.

```
SELECT *
FROM HumanResources.Shift
ORDER BY ShiftID
FOR XML RAW;
```


```
<row ShiftID="1" Name="Day" StartTime="07:00:00" EndTime="15:00:00" ModifiedDate="2002-06-01T00:00:00" />
<row ShiftID="2" Name="Evening" StartTime="15:00:00" EndTime="23:00:00" ModifiedDate="2002-06-01T00:00:00" />
<row ShiftID="3" Name="Night" StartTime="23:00:00" EndTime="07:00:00" ModifiedDate="2002-06-01T00:00:00" />
```


FOR XML AUTO

The FOR XML AUTO mode generates nesting in the resulting XML by using heuristics based on the way the SELECT statement is specified. You have minimal control over the shape of the XML generated. Tree structure can be generated by nesting queries.

```
SELECT *
FROM HumanResources.Shift
ORDER BY ShiftID
FOR XML AUTO;
```


```
<HumanResources.Shift ShiftID="1" Name="Day" StartTime="07:00:00" EndTime="15:00:00" ModifiedDate="2002-06-01T00:00:00" />
<HumanResources.Shift ShiftID="2" Name="Evening" StartTime="15:00:00" EndTime="23:00:00" ModifiedDate="2002-06-01T00:00:00" />
<HumanResources.Shift ShiftID="3" Name="Night" StartTime="23:00:00" EndTime="07:00:00" ModifiedDate="2002-06-01T00:00:00" />
```

FOR XML EXPLICIT

The FOR XML EXPLICIT mode allows extensive control over the shape of the XML document. Attributes and elements can be freely combined in deciding the shape of the XML document. One of the options with XML EXPLICIT is the ELEMENT directive. The UNION ALL operator is used to assemble the tag and data information.

```
SELECT          1               AS Tag,
                NULL            AS Parent,
                ProductNumber AS [ProductHeader!1!ProdNo],
                NULL             AS [ProductDetail!2!ProductName!ELEMENT],
                NULL            AS [ProductDetail!2!ListPrice!ELEMENT],
                NULL            AS [ProductDetail!2!Color!ELEMENT],
                NULL            AS [ProductDetail!2!Size!ELEMENT]
FROM   Production.Product P WHERE ProductSubcategoryID is not NULL
UNION ALL
SELECT          2,
                1,
                ProductNumber,
                Name,
                 ListPrice,
                Color,
                 Size
FROM   Production.Product P  WHERE ProductSubcategoryID is not NULL
ORDER BY [ProductHeader!1!ProdNo], Tag   FOR XML EXPLICIT;
-- (590 row(s) affected) - Partial results.
```

```
<ProductHeader ProdNo="BK-M68B-46">
  <ProductDetail>
    <ProductName>Mountain-200 Black, 46</ProductName>
    <ListPrice>2294.9900</ListPrice>
    <Color>Black</Color>
    <Size>46</Size>
  </ProductDetail>
</ProductHeader>
<ProductHeader ProdNo="BK-M68S-38">
  <ProductDetail>
    <ProductName>Mountain-200 Silver, 38</ProductName>
    <ListPrice>2319.9900</ListPrice>
    <Color>Silver</Color>
    <Size>38</Size>
  </ProductDetail>
</ProductHeader>
```

FOR XML PATH

The FOR XML PATH mode together with the nested FOR XML query capability provides the flexibility of the EXPLICIT mode in a simpler manner. The example lists sales orders with detail line and header information.

SQLQuery38.sql - HPESTAR.AdventureWorks2012 (HPESTAR\Owner (56))* - Microsoft SQL Server M...
File Edit View Query Project Debug Tools Window Help
New Query
AdventureWorks2012
Execute
Debug
SQLQuery38.sql -...PESTAR\Owner (56))*
SQLQuery40.sql -...PESTAR\Owner (57))*
SELECT TOP(100) S.Name AS '@Reseller',
CONCAT(P.LastName, ', ', P.FirstName) AS '@ContactName',
SOH.SalesOrderID AS '@SalesOrderID',
SOD.SalesOrderDetailID AS 'SOD/SalesOrderDetailID',
SOD.OrderQty AS 'SOD/OrderQty',
SOD.ProductID AS 'SOD/ProductID',
SOD.UnitPrice AS 'SOD/UnitPrice',
SOD.LineTotal AS 'SOD/LineTotal'
FROM Sales.SalesOrderHeader AS SOH
INNER JOIN Sales.SalesOrderDetail AS SOD
ON SOH.SalesOrderID = SOD.SalesOrderID
INNER JOIN Sales.Customer AS C ON SOH.CustomerID = C.CustomerID
INNER JOIN Person.Person AS P ON C.PersonID = P.BusinessEntityID
INNER JOIN Sales.Store AS S ON C.StoreID = S.BusinessEntityID
ORDER BY SOH.SalesOrderID, SalesOrderDetailID
FOR XML PATH('SalesOrderLine'), ROOT('SalesOrdersReceived');
100 %
Results
Messages
XML_F52E2B61-18A1-11d1-B105-00805F49916B
1 <SalesOrdersReceived><SalesOrderLine Reseller="B...
Query executed succe...
HPESTAR (11.0 RTM)
HPESTAR\Owner (56)
AdventureWorks2012
00:00:00
14 rows
XML_F52E2B61-18A...805F49916B25.xml
<SalesOrdersReceived>
<SalesOrderLine Reseller="Better Bike Shop" ContactName="Hendergart, James" Sal
<SOD>
<SalesOrderDetailID>1</SalesOrderDetailID>
<OrderQty>1</OrderQty>
<ProductID>776</ProductID>
<UnitPrice>2024.9940</UnitPrice>
<LineTotal>2024.994000</LineTotal>
</SOD>
</SalesOrderLine>
<SalesOrderLine Reseller="Better Bike Shop" ContactName="Hendergart, James" Sal
100 %

Concatenation Loop With XML PATH

The FOR XML PATH clause makes it possible to do program looping within a query without requiring multiple statements. One way is to implement it as a correlated subquery.

```
Use AdventureWorks2012;
Go
```

```
SELECT   PM.Name AS Model
         ,(SELECT CONCAT(P.Name, ', ')
          FROM Production.Product AS P   WHERE P.ProductModelID = PM.ProductModelID
          ORDER BY P.Name FOR XML PATH('') ) AS ProductLineup
FROM Production.ProductModel AS PM ORDER BY Model;
-- (128 row(s) affected) - Partial result.
```

Model	ProductLineup
All-Purpose Bike Stand	All-Purpose Bike Stand,
Bike Wash	Bike Wash - Dissolver,
Cable Lock	Cable Lock,
Chain	Chain,
Classic Vest	Classic Vest, L, Classic Vest, M, Classic Vest, S,
Cycling Cap	AWC Logo Cap,
Fender Set - Mountain	Fender Set - Mountain,
Front Derailleur	Front Derailleur,
Full-Finger Gloves	Full-Finger Gloves, L, Full-Finger Gloves, M, Full-Finger Gloves, S,

A popular solution for the trailing comma issue is making it leading comma and taking it out from the first position with the STUFF function. Since the product name may contain commas, we use "|" as string list delimiter.

```
SELECT  PM.Name AS Model
        ,LTRIM(RTRIM(STUFF((SELECT CONCAT('| ', P.Name)
         FROM Production.Product AS P   WHERE P.ProductModelID = PM.ProductModelID
         ORDER BY P.Name FOR XML PATH('') ), 1, 1, ''))) AS ProductLineup
FROM Production.ProductModel AS PM
ORDER BY Model;
-- (128 row(s) affected) - Partial result.
```

Model	ProductLineup
ML Mountain Frame	ML Mountain Frame - Black, 40| ML Mountain Frame - Black, 44| ML Mountain Frame - Black, 48

Interesting T-SQL Scripts

Challenging String Manipulations

```
-- Displaying hidden characters (whitespace) in a string; TAB character appears as space;
DECLARE @text varchar(64) = 'New'+char(9)+'York'+char(9)+'City'+char(9);
SELECT @text, CONVERT(varbinary(64), @text);
-- New York City 0x4E657709596F726B094369747909
```

```
-- Working with SUBSTRING & ASCII functions
SELECT      TOP (5)
            ProductNumber,
            MiddleOfString     =     SUBSTRING(ProductNumber,4,5),
            SecondChar         =     SUBSTRING(ProductNumber,2,1),
            ASCIIValue         =     ASCII(SUBSTRING(ProductNumber,2,1))
FROM Production.Product  ORDER BY NEWID();
```

ProductNumber	MiddleOfString	SecondChar	ASCIIValue
FR-R72R-44	R72R-	R	82
BK-R89B-48	R89B-	K	75
HN-4402	4402	N	78
LJ-1220	1220	J	74
BA-8327	8327	A	65

```
-- Compare empty string and NULL string
DECLARE @NullString varchar(32) = NULL, @EmptyString varchar(32)= '';
```

```
SELECT LEN(@EmptyString); SELECT LEN(@NullString);   -- 0  NULL
```

```
SELECT DATALENGTH(@EmptyString); SELECT DATALENGTH(@NullString);  -- 0  NULL
```

```
-- Testing for empty string and null string
SELECT 'Miami' WHERE @EmptyString = '';  SELECT 'Miami' WHERE @NullString is null;
-- Miami Miami
```

```
SELECT 'Miami' WHERE LEN(@EmptyString)=0;  SELECT 'Miami' WHERE LEN(@NullString) = 0;
-- Miami  (0 row(s) affected)
```

```
SELECT @EmptyString + @NullString+'Vegas';                    -- NULL
```

```
SELECT CONCAT(@EmptyString,@NullString, 'Vegas');             -- Vegas
```

Date & Datetime Manipulations

```
-- Count business days for a date range
CREATE FUNCTION ufnWeekDaysCount ( @DateStart DATETIME, @DateEnd DATETIME)
RETURNS INT AS BEGIN
   IF ( @DateStart IS NULL OR @DateEnd IS NULL )
     RETURN ( 0 )
   DECLARE @i INT = 0;
   WHILE ( @DateStart <= @DateEnd ) BEGIN
      SET @i = @i + CASE
               WHEN datename(dw, @DateStart) IN ( 'Saturday', 'Sunday' )
               THEN 0  ELSE 1  END
      SET @DateStart = @DateStart + 1
     END -- while
   RETURN ( @i )
 END -- function
GO
```

```
SELECT dbo.ufnWeekDaysCount('2016-01-01', '2016-12-31');     -- 261
```

```
-- YEAR(), MONTH(), DATENAME() functions in aggregate query
SELECT YEAR         = YEAR(OrderDate),
       MONTH        = MONTH(OrderDate),
       MMM          = UPPER(left(DATENAME(MONTH,OrderDate),3)),
        Sales       = FORMAT(sum(TotalDue),'c0','en-US'),
       OrderCount   = COUNT(* )
FROM    Sales.SalesOrderHeader
GROUP BY     YEAR(OrderDate), MONTH(OrderDate), DATENAME(MONTH,OrderDate)
ORDER BY     YEAR, MONTH;
GO -- (37 row(s) affected) - Partial results.
```

YEAR	MONTH	MMM	Sales	OrderCount
2008	5	MAY	$5,813,557	2386
2008	6	JUN	$6,004,156	2374

```
-- Month start/end is easy with EOMONTH() - Find month ending weekday
SELECT DATEADD(DD,1,EOMONTH(GETDATE(),-2) )     AS FirstDayOfPreviousMonth,
       EOMONTH(GETDATE(),-1)                    AS LastDayOfPreviousMonth
-- 2016-11-01   2016-11-30
```

```
SELECT DATENAME(DW, EOMONTH(CURRENT_TIMESTAMP)) -- Monday
```

Find Sprocs, Triggers, Functions & Views Where Column is Used

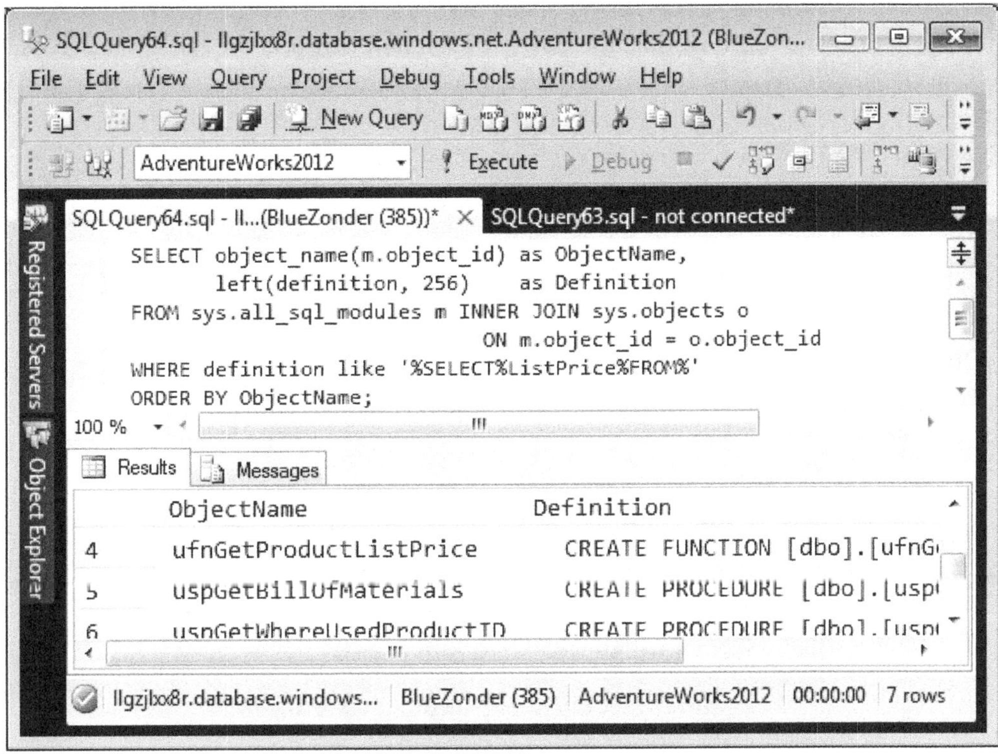

Designing the Query in GUI Query Designer - On-Premises SQL Server

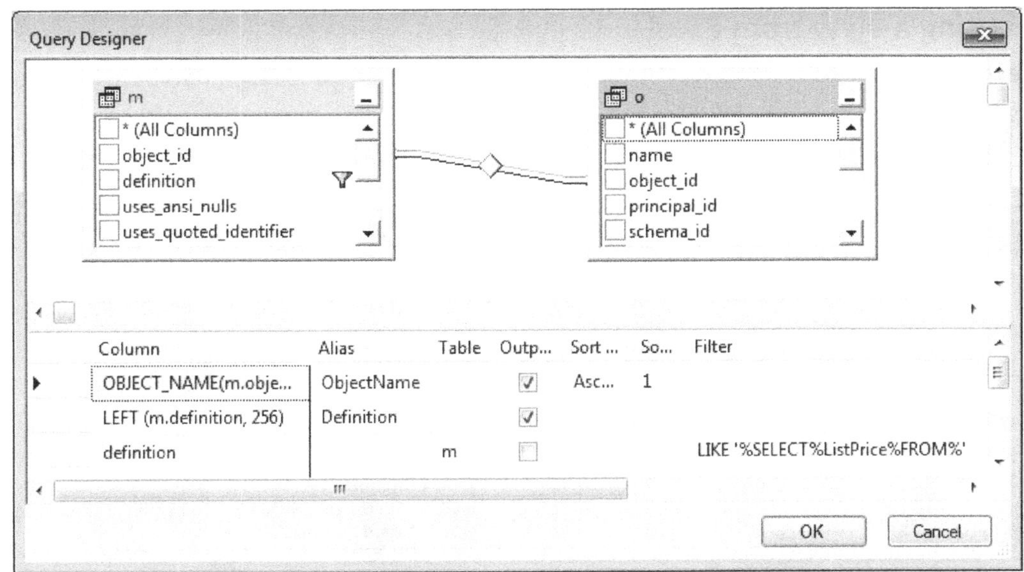

Transforming Dynamic SQL Result Set into a View

A view is "clean", a dynamic SQL script can be pretty "messy". By wrapping dynamic SQL into a view, we get the best of both worlds: the power of dynamic SQL and the table-like access to a view. SQL Server 2012 script.

```
USE AdventureWorks2012;
GO
CREATE PROC sprocListDepartment AS   BEGIN
DECLARE @SQL nvarchar(max) =
 'SELECT DepartmentID, Name, GroupName FROM HumanResources.Department ORDER BY
DepartmentID DESC';
EXEC sp_executeSQL @SQL;
END
GO
```

```
CREATE VIEW vDepartment AS
SELECT * FROM OPENQUERY( HPESTAR, 'exec dbo.sprocListDepartment WITH RESULT SETS  ((ID
int, Department varchar(50), GroupName varchar(50)))');
GO
```

```
SELECT * FROM vDepartment;     -- (16 row(s) affected)
```

Accessing a View from Excel

A view can be accessed from Excel by logging in to SQL Server, choosing a database and picking the view.

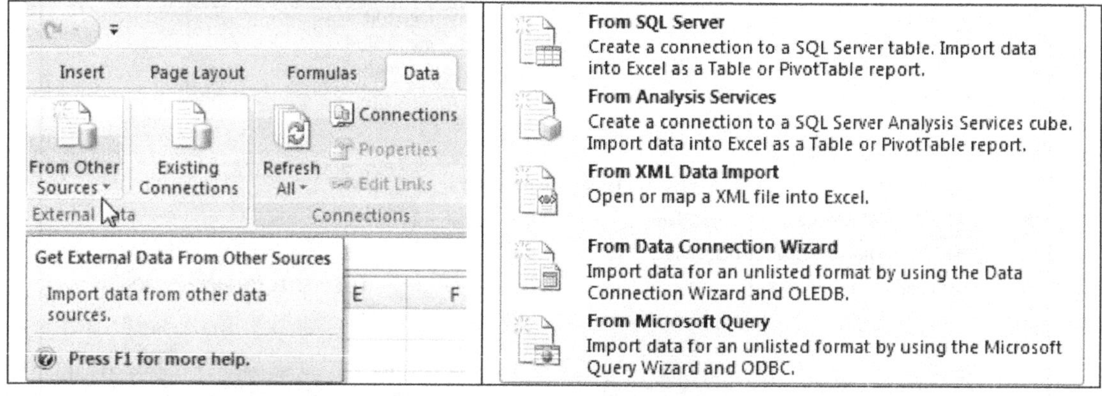
Insert
Page Layout
Formulas
Data
From Other Sources
Existing Connections
Refresh All
Connections
Properties
Edit Links
External Data
Connections
Get External Data From Other Sources
Import data from other data sources.
Press F1 for more help.
E
F
From SQL Server
Create a connection to a SQL Server table. Import data into Excel as a Table or PivotTable report.
From Analysis Services
Create a connection to a SQL Server Analysis Services cube. Import data into Excel as a Table or PivotTable report.
From XML Data Import
Open or map a XML file into Excel.
From Data Connection Wizard
Import data for an unlisted format by using the Data Connection Wizard and OLEDB.
From Microsoft Query
Import data for an unlisted format by using the Microsoft Query Wizard and ODBC.

After Login the Data Connection Wizard Guides Us Through

The Data Connection Wizard requires network access and login to SQL Server.

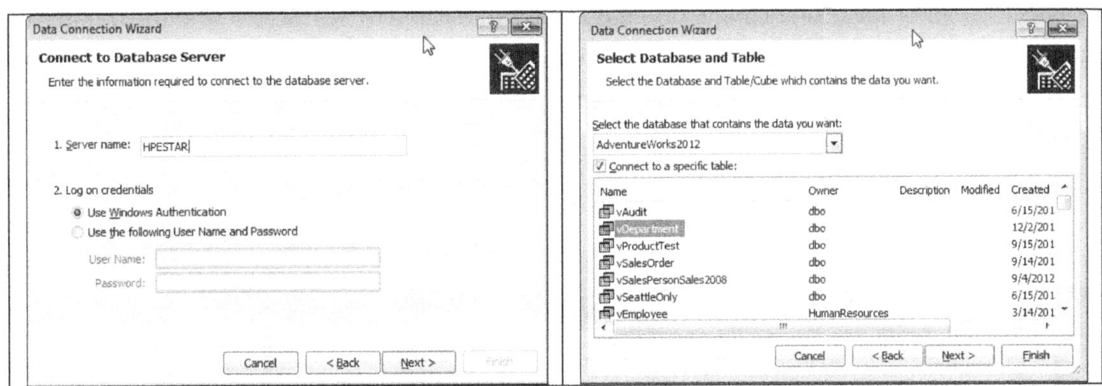

The next popop window offers radio button selection for: Table, PivotTable and PivotChart & PivotTable; choosing Table.

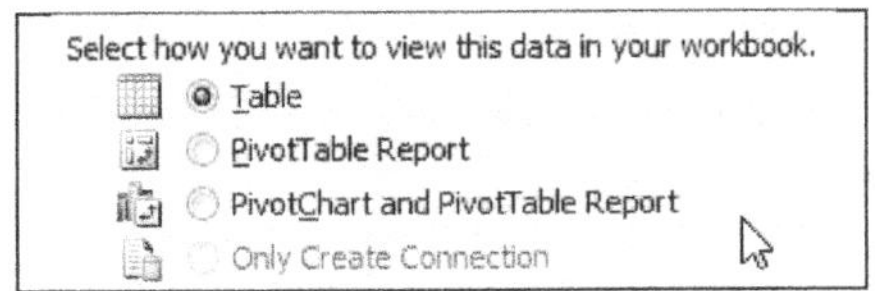

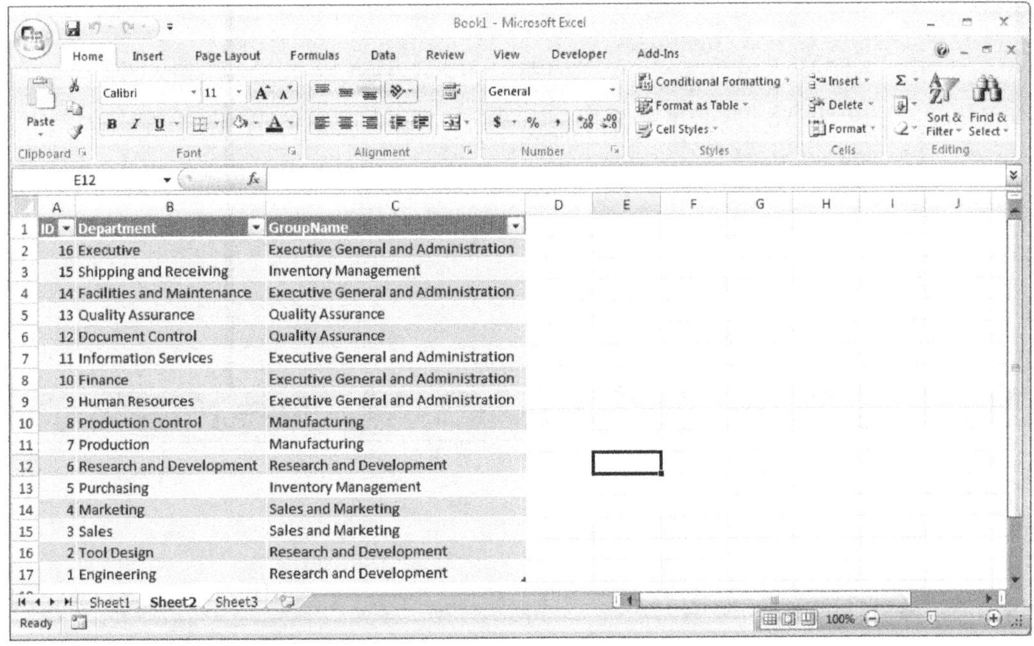

ID	Department	GroupName
16	Executive	Executive General and Administration
15	Shipping and Receiving	Inventory Management
14	Facilities and Maintenance	Executive General and Administration
13	Quality Assurance	Quality Assurance
12	Document Control	Quality Assurance
11	Information Services	Executive General and Administration
10	Finance	Executive General and Administration
9	Human Resources	Executive General and Administration
8	Production Control	Manufacturing
7	Production	Manufacturing
6	Research and Development	Research and Development
5	Purchasing	Inventory Management
4	Marketing	Sales and Marketing
3	Sales	Sales and Marketing
2	Tool Design	Research and Development
1	Engineering	Research and Development

Querying the Database from a Client C# Program

The general program logic for SQL Server database access is very similar for other languages such as C++, VB or Java. First connection has to be established to SQL Server and the database, then a SQL query or stored procedure execution command is sent to the server, and finally the server returns a result set which has to be processed in a C# loop. SQL Server 2012 connection.

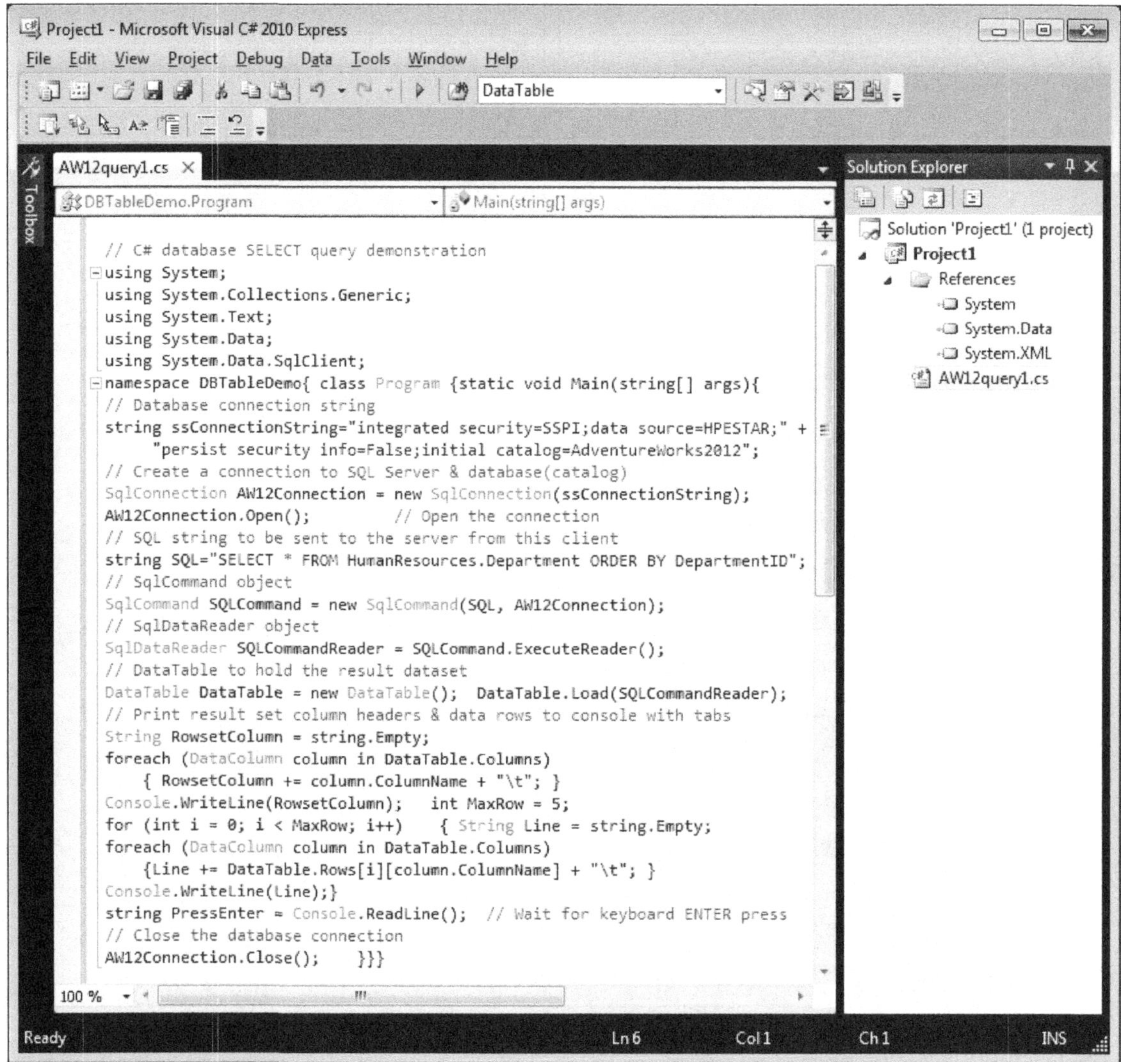

C# Code Listing

```
// C# database SELECT query demonstration
using System;
using System.Collections.Generic;
```

```
using System.Text;
using System.Data;
using System.Data.SqlClient;
namespace DBTableDemo{ class Program {static void Main(string[] args){
// Database connection string
string ssConnectionString="integrated security=SSPI;data source=HPESTAR;" +
    "persist security info=False;initial catalog=AdventureWorks2012";
// Create a connection to SQL Server & database(catalog)
SqlConnection AW12Connection = new SqlConnection(ssConnectionString);
AW12Connection.Open();        // Open the connection
// SQL string to be sent to the server from this client
string SQL="SELECT * FROM HumanResources.Department ORDER BY DepartmentID";
// SqlCommand object
SqlCommand SQLCommand = new SqlCommand(SQL, AW12Connection);
// SqlDataReader object
SqlDataReader SQLCommandReader = SQLCommand.ExecuteReader();
// DataTable to hold the result dataset
DataTable DataTable = new DataTable();  DataTable.Load(SQLCommandReader);
// Print result set column headers & data rows to console with tabs
String RowsetColumn = string.Empty;
foreach (DataColumn column in DataTable.Columns)
   { RowsetColumn += column.ColumnName + "\t"; }
Console.WriteLine(RowsetColumn);   int MaxRow = 5;
for (int i = 0; i < MaxRow; i++)    { String Line = string.Empty;
foreach (DataColumn column in DataTable.Columns)
   {Line += DataTable.Rows[i][column.ColumnName] + "\t"; }
Console.WriteLine(Line);}
string PressEnter = Console.ReadLine();  // Wait for keyboard ENTER press
// Close the database connection
AW12Connection.Close();    }}}
```

Console Image with Data Display from HumanResources.Department

```
file:///C:/Users/Owner/AppData/Local/Temporary Projects/Project1/bin/Debug/Project1.EXE
DepartmentID    Name    GroupName       ModifiedDate
1       Engineering     Research and Development        6/1/2002 12:00:00 AM

2       Tool Design     Research and Development        6/1/2002 12:00:00 AM

3       Sales   Sales and Marketing     6/1/2002 12:00:00 AM
4       Marketing       Sales and Marketing     6/1/2002 12:00:00 AM
5       Purchasing      Inventory Management    6/1/2002 12:00:00 AM
```

C# Connection to Windows Azure SQL Database

Only the connection string is different, the rest of the sample C# program is the same. Change "llgzjlxx8r" to your server, "BlueZonder" to your login and "AdventureWorks2012" to your database.

```
// Database connection string
string ssConnectionString="Server=tcp:llgzjlxx8r.database.windows.net;" +
"Database=AdventureWorks2012;Uid=BlueZonder@llgzjlxx8r;Pwd=yourazuresqlpassword;Encrypt=yes;";
```

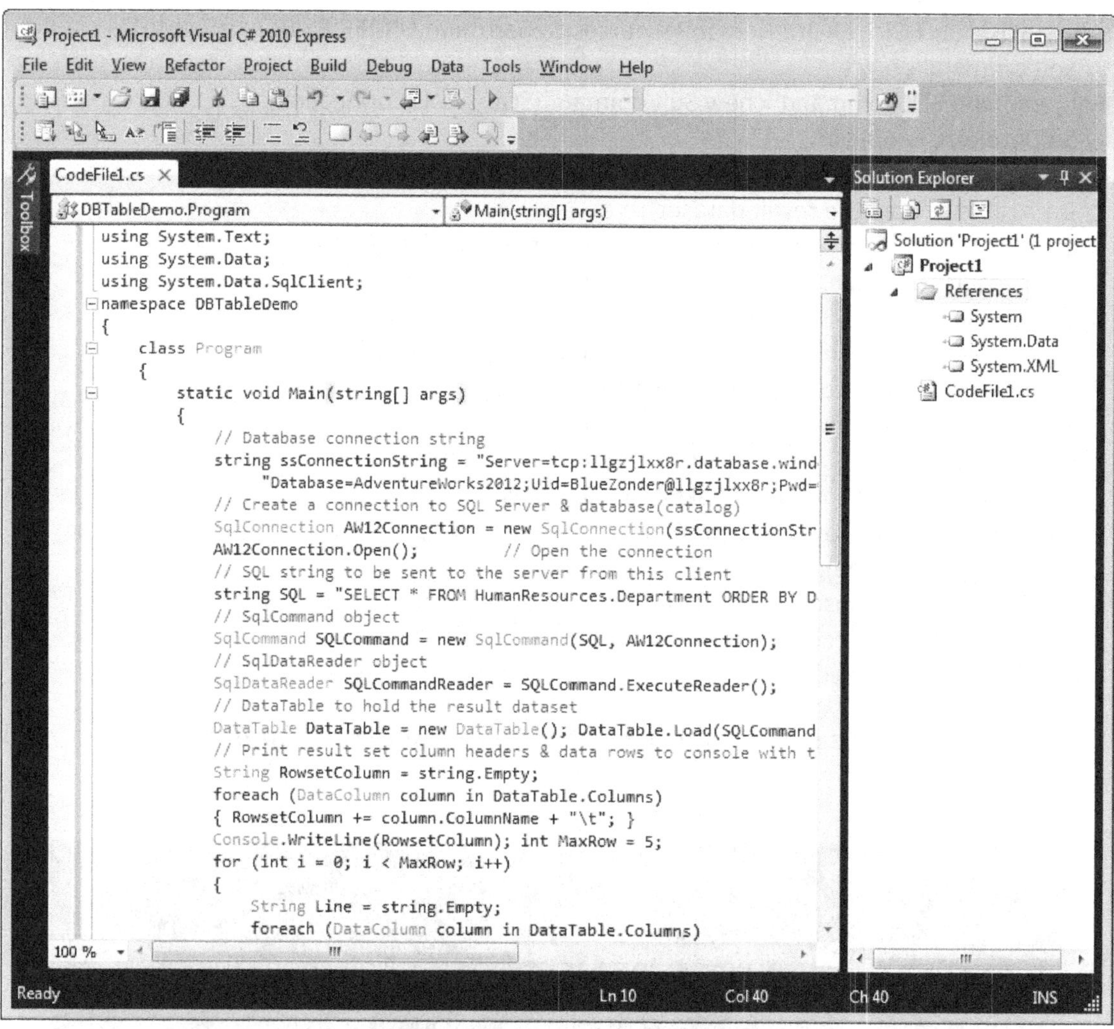

APPENDIX A: Job Interview Questions

Selected Database Design Questions

D1. What is your approach to database design?
D2. Some of our legacy databases are far from 3NF. Can you work in such an environment?
D3. Can UNIQUE KEY be used instead of PRIMARY KEY?
D4. Can a FOREIGN KEY be NULL?
D5. Can a PRIMARY KEY be NULL?
D6. Can a PRIMARY KEY be based on non-clustered unique index?
D7. Do you implement OrderQty > 0 condition as a CHECK constraint or in the application software?
D8. What is a heap?
D9. Can a table have 2 IDENTITY columns, 2 FOREIGN KEYs, 2 PRIMARY KEYs and 2 clustered indexes?
D10. Should each table have a NATURAL KEY or is INT IDENTITY PK sufficient?
D11. How can you prevent entry of "U.S", "USA", etc. instead of "United States" into Country column?
D12. How would you implement ManagerID in an Employee table with EmployeeID as PRIMARY KEY?
D13. How would you implement the relationship between OrderMaster and OrderDetail tables?
D14. Product table has the Color column. Would you create a Color table & change column to ColorID FK?
D15. Can you insert directly into an IDENTITY column?
D16. Which one is better? Composite PRIMARY KEY on NATURAL KEY, or INT IDENTITY PRIMARY KEY & UNIQUE KEY on NATURAL KEY?
D17. What is the lifetime of a temporary table?
D18. How many different ways can you connect tables in a database?
D19. How would you connect the Vehicle and Owner tables?
D20. Can you have the same table names in different schemas?

Selected Database Programming Questions

P1. Write a query to list all departments with employee count based on the Department column of Employee table.
P2. Same as above but the Employee table has the DepartmentID column.
P3. Write an INSERT statement for a new "Social Technology" department with GroupName "Sales & Marketing".
P4. Same query es in P2, but the new department should be included even though no employees yet.
P5. Write a query to generate 1000 sequential numbers without a table.
P6. Write a query with SARGable predicate to list all orders from OrderMaster received on 2016-10-23. OrderDate is datetime.
P7. Write a query to add a header record DEPARTMENTNAME to the departments listing from the Department table. If there are 20 departments, the result set should have 21 records.
P8. Make the previous query a derived table in an outer SELECT * query
P9. Write an ORDER BY clause for the previous query with CASE expression to sort DEPARTMENTNAME as first record and alphabetically descending from there on.
P10. Same as above with the IIF conditional.
P11. The table-valued dbo.ufnSplitCSV splits a comma delimited string (input parameter). The Product table has some ProductName-s with comma(s). Write a CROSS APPLY query to return ProductName-s with comma and each split string value from the UDF as separate line. ProductName should repeat for each split part.

ProductName	SplitPart
Full-Finger Gloves, L	Full-Finger Gloves
Full-Finger Gloves, L	L

P12. You need the inserted lines count 10 lines down following the INSERT statement. What should be the statement immediately following the INSERT statement?
P13. What is the result of the second query? What is it called?
SELECT COUNT_BIG(*) FROM Sales.SalesOrderDetail; -- 121317
SELECT COUNT_BIG(*) FROM Sales.SalesOrderDetail x, Sales.SalesOrderDetail y;
P14. Declare & Assign the string variable @Text varchar(32) the literal '2016/10/23 10:20:12' without the "/" and ":".
P15. You want to add a parameter to a frequently used view. What is the workaround?
P16. When converting up to 40 characters string, can you use varchar instead of varchar(40)?
P17. Can you roll back IDENTITY seeds and table variables with ROLLBACK TRANSACTION?
P18. How do you decide where to place the clustered index?
P19. What is the simplest solution for the collation error: "Cannot resolve collation conflict..."?
P20. Which system table can be used for integer sequence up to 2^12 values?
P21. Can you use SELECT INTO in Azure SQL?

This page is intentionally left blank.

This page is intentionally left blank.

APPENDIX B: Job Interview Answers

Selected Database Design Answers

D1. I prefer 3NF design due to high database developer productivity and low maintenance cost.
D2. I did have such projects in the past. I can handle them. Hopefully, introduce some improvements.
D3. Partially yes since UNIQUE KEYs can be FK referenced, fully no. Every table should a PRIMARY KEY.
D4. Yes.
D5. No.
D6. Yes. The default is clustered unique index. Only unique index is required.
D7. CHECK constraint. A server-side object solution is more reliable than code in application software.
D8. A table without clustered index. Database engine generally works better if a table has clustered index.
D9. No, yes, no, no.
D10. A table should be designed with NATURAL KEY(s). INT IDENTITY PK is not a replacement for NK.
D11. Lookup table with UDF CHECK Constraint. UDF checks the Lookup table for valid entries.
D12. ManagerID as a FOREIGN KEY referencing the PRIMARY KEY of the same table; self-referencing.
D13. OrderID PRIMARY KEY of OrderMaster. OrderID & LineItemID composition PK of OrderDetail. OrderID of OrderDetail FK to OrderID of OderMaster.
D14. Yes. It makes sense for color to be in its own table.
D15. No. Only if you SET IDENTITY_INSERT tablename ON.
D16. Meaningless INT IDENTITY PRIMARY KEY with UNIQUE KEY ON NATURAL KEY is better.
D17. Until the temporary table is dropped or connection(session)/stored procedure ends.
D18. There is only one way: FOREIGN KEY constraint.
D19. With the OwnerVehicleXref junction table reflecting many-to-many relationship.
D20. Yes. A table is identified by SchemaName.TableName . dbo is the default schema.

Selected Database Programming Answers

P1. SELECT Department, Employees=COUNT(*) FROM Employee GROUP BY Department ORDER BY Department;
P2. SELECT d.Department, Employees = COUNT(EmployeeID) FROM Employee e INNER JOIN Department d ON e.DepartmentID = d.DepartmentID GROUP BY d.Department ORDER BY Department;
P3. INSERT Department (Name, GroupName) VALUES ('Social Technology', 'Sales & Marketing');
P4. SELECT d.Department, Employees = COUNT(EmployeeID) FROM Employee e RIGHT JOIN Department d ON e.DepartmentID = d.DepartmentID GROUP BY d.Department ORDER BY Department;
P5. ;WITH Seq AS (SELECT SeqNo = 1 UNION ALL SELECT SeqNo+1 FROM Seq WHERE SeqNo < 100) SELECT * FROM Seq;
P6. SELECT * FROM OrderMaster WHERE OrderDate >='20161023' AND OrderDate < DATEADD(DD,1,'20161023');
P7. SELECT AllDepartments = 'DEPARTMENTNAME' UNION SELECT Department FROM Department;
P8. SELECT * FROM (SELECT AllDepartments = 'DEPARTMENTNAME' UNION SELECT Name FROM HumanResources.Department) x
P9. ORDER BY CASE WHEN AllDepartments = 'DEPARTMENTNAME' THEN 1 ELSE 2 END, AllDepartments DESC;
P10. ORDER BY IIF(AllDepartments = 'DEPARTMENTNAME', 1 , 2), AllDepartments DESC;
P11. SELECT ProductName, S.SplitPart FROM Product P CROSS APPLY dbo.ufnSplitCSV (Name) S WHERE ProductName like '%,%';
P12. DECLARE @InsertedCount INT = @@ROWCOUNT;
P13. 121317*121317; Cartesian product.
P14. DECLARE @Text varchar(32) = REPLACE(REPLACE ('2016/10/23 10:20:12', '/', SPACE(0)), ':', SPACE(0));
P15. Table-valued INLINE user-defined function.
P16. varchar(40). It is a good idea to specify the length always. The default is 30.
P17. No. ROLLBACK has no effect on IDENTITY seeds or table variables. If an INSERT advanced the IDENTITY seed by 5 during the rollbacked transaction, it will stay that way after the ROLLBACK. It means a gap in the IDENTITY sequence.
P18. Business critical queries are the determining factor in placing the clustered index. Clustered index speeds up range queries.
P19. Place "COLLATE DATABASE_DEFAULT" on the right side of the expression.
P20. spt_values table. `SELECT N = number FROM master.dbo.spt_values WHERE type='P' ORDER BY N;`
P21. No. You have to use CREATE TABLE and INSERT SELECT to populate.

INDEX of Windows Azure SQL Database Programming & Design

Index of the Most Important Topics

(

(.bacpac, 66

.

.sql script file, 566

@

@@DATEFIRST, 444
@@IDENTITY, 528
@@ROWCOUNT, 531
@@SPID, 532

3

3NF, 255
3-Part Name, 332
3-part Naming, 90

4

4-part name, 332
4-Week 13 Month Calendar, 730

A

a derived table, 505
a unique index, 466
Accent sensitive, 187
Accessing a View from Excel, 764
accessories, 1
Activity Monitor, 658
administration, 181
Administration Tools, 93
AdventureWorks, 1
AdventureWorks2008, 19
AdventureWorks2012, 20
AdventureWorksDW2012, 17, 18
aggregate, 107
aggregation, 8
Alberto Ferrari, 231
alphanumeric field, 475
ALTER TABLE, 198
American, 442
Amsterdam, 443
Analysis Services, 113, 627
analytic functions, 395
ancestors, 518
ANSI, 442
ANSI Date literal, 442
ANSI SQL UPDATE, 542
ANSI Style UPDATE, 538
ANSI UPDATE, 538
Arizona, 555
Ascii, 475
ASCII, 185
assignment, 667
assignment operator, 667
attribute, 13
Australia, 474
AVG(ListPrice), 95

B

BACKUP & RESTORE, 90
BACKUP DATABASE, 66
backup filename with datestamp, 66
backup history query, 34

Backup of a Single Table, 740
batch, 125
Batch processing, 661
bcp, 569
BEGIN TRANSACTION, 552
Berlin, 443
BETWEEN, 475
BETWEEN Operator, 728
bill of materials, 519
billing, 91
BillOfMaterials, 563
binary number, 185
Binary String, 185
bit, 185
blocking, 532, 657
BOL, 84
Bond, 274
Books Online, 84
Boolean, 185
brackets, 182
Brazil, 506
British, 443
browse, 632
B-tree, 159
bugs, 607
BULK INSERT, 751
business critical, 654
Business Rules, 622

C

C# Program, 766
cache memory, 637
Calendar table, 491
California, 555
CamelCase, 181
Canada, 474
cardinality, 419
Cardinality of CROSS JOIN, 427
cardinality of DISTINCT, 450
Cardinality of OUTER JOINs, 424
carriage return, 569
Cartesian explosion, 427
Cartesian Product, 419
CASE, 102, 475
Case insensitive, 187
case sensitive sort, 456
CAST, 442
category, 23, 97
Category, 10
Century, 480
CEO, 516
Chain of Command, 518
Character String, 185
CHARINDEX, 96, 447
CHECK constraint, 612
CHECKPOINT, 532
CHOOSE(), 388
chronological order, 429
Cinderella syndrom, 452
CIRCULARSTRING, 734
client, 115
client software, 125
Client Statistics, 653
Client-Server, 153
clustered index, 345, 346
Clustered index, 161, 204, 648
COALESCE, 447
COLLATE clause, 378
COLLATE DATABASE_DEFAULT, 187
collation, 187, 378
Collation, 612
collation_name, 186
column alias, 404
column properties, 376
columnstore index, 318
Columnstore Index, 317
comma delimited string, 98
Command Prompt, 605
COMMIT TRANSACTION, 552
Common Table Expression, 428
compatibility level, 324
Composable DML, 666
composite, 277
composite index, 159
composite PRIMARY KEY, 204, 345
composite **UNIQUE KEY**, 345
Compressed Index, 301
compression, 300
computed columns, 280

computer geeks, 6
CONCAT(), 388
Concatenation, 760
Connecting to Azure SQL Server, 88
connection, 152, 657
constants, 95
context-sensitive, 133
Conversion, 477
CONVERT(), 477
COPY, 605
copy with headers, 123
correlated subqueries, 504
correlated subquery, 499
cost panels, 642
COUNT, 177
COUNT(), 177
COUNT(*), 375
COUNT_BIG(), 177
covering index, 159, 645
create a view, 417
Create clustered index, 54
CREATE DATABASE, 324
Create Partition Wizard, 316
CREATE SCHEMA, 190
credit card, 738
CROSS JOIN, 427, 428
cross tabulation, 521
cross-reference, 269
Cross-reference, 12
crosstab, 521
crosstab listing, 523
CSV, 98
CTE, 110, 507
culture parameter, 381
currency format, 431
current session, 532
Cursors, 679

D

DATA ACCESS, 532
Data compression, 295
Data Compression Wizard, 302
Data Connection Wizard, 765
Data Dictionary, 12, 284
Data Modeling, 183
data type, 102
Data Types, 185
data warehouse, 630
Data Warehouse, 17, 317
data warehouse query, 18
data warehousing, 17
Database backup, 66
Database Backup, 739
Database Design Standards, 320
database engine, 181, 639
Database Engine Tuning Advisor, 662
Database Maintenance Plan Wizard, 745
database modeling, 227
Database Restore, 742
Database security, 725
DATABASEPROPERTYEX, 380
DATALENGTH(), 9
data-tier application, 79
Date Only, 482
Date sequence, 514
DATEFIRST, 444
dateformat, 443
DATEFROMPARTS(), 390
DATENAME(), 494
DATEPART(), 493
datetime2, 185
DATETIMEFROMPARTS(), 390
datetimeoffset, 185
DBCC CHECKIDENT, 535
DBCC HELP, 662
DBCC USEROPTIONS, 446
dbo, 172
DDL Trigger, 731
dealer network, 1
debugging, 125
decompress, 295
Decryption, 738
default instance, 63
default schema, 428
Deferred Name Resolution Process, 129
Delete (XML DML), 720
DELETE CASCADE, 205, 618
Delete Tables, 232
Demographic, 12

denormalization, 257
DENSE_RANK, 176
Dependency, 94
dependency chart, 362
derived table, 97
Design tools, 94
developer productivity, 221
diagram, 3
Diagram Design, 220
dimension tables, 17, 630
Dirty Reads, 699
disable constraint, 674
Display Line numbers, 143
DISTINCT, 101
Distributed transactions, 698
distributor, 1
DMF, 31
DMV, 31
dmy, 443
Domain Integrity, 612
drill-down, 30
DROP COLUMN, 384
DROP TABLE, 200
drop-down, 207
DSN, 64
duplicate, 609
duplicates, 101
duplicates removal, 609
duration, 637
Dynamic Management Functions, 31
Dynamic Management Views, 31
Dynamic PIVOT, 725
dynamic SQL, 764
Dynamic SQL, 725
dynamic tables, 654

E

eadability, 221
ECHO, 604
ecommerce, 552
empty string, 98
enable constraint, 674
Encryption, 738
end of batch, 179
English, 443
Enterprise-Level, 622
Entity integrity, 608
EOMONTH(), 391
EQUI-JOIN, 400
Error handling, 125
error message, 127, 151
Error Message, 248
Español, 515
European, 442
Exact Numerics, 185
Excel, 121, 764
EXCEPT operator, 109
exec sp_who, 532
Execute, 115
execution errors, 129
execution plan, 641, 642, 649
exist() Method, 716
export, 571
Exporting All Images, 755
expression, 221
expressions, 95

F

fact tables, 17, 630
Federation, 316
Federations, 308
File, 118
FILESTREAM, 289
FileTable, 289
filter, 7
firewall rule, 40
FIRST_VALUE(), 395
Fixed length, 185
Flat File, 121
floating point, 185
FOR XML AUTO, 757
FOR XML Clause, 757
FOR XML EXPLICIT, 758
FOR XML PATH, 759
FOR XML RAW, 757
FOREIGN KEY, 341
FOREIGN KEY constraint, 619
FORMAT, 97, 319

format file, 752
FORMAT(), 387
frames and parts, 1
France, 102, 475
Frequency, 449
FULL JOIN, 426
FULLSCAN, 656
full-text index, 357
Full-text index is not supported, 44
Fulltext Indexes, 232
full-text search, 357
Full-Text Search, 636

G

Generate Change Script, 236
geography, 186
Geography, 732
geometry, 186
Geometry, 732
German, 492
Germany, 475
Globally Unique Identifier, 185
GO, 115
gold key, 211
gourmet food, 1
graphical, 134
Gregorian, 730
Grid, 116
GROUPING(), 671
GUI, 113
GUID, 185
Guidelines and Limitations, 84

H

HAVING clause, 108
HAVING count(*), 95
heap, 204
Hex, 481
hierarchical, 267
hierarchyid, 19, 110, 185, 186, 268, 721
hierarchyid functions, 723
Hijri date, 479
Hong Kong, 443
Horizontal Partitioning, 316
Hovering, 150, 151
Hungarian, 492
Hungarian naming, 181

I

Identifier, 181
identifiers, 181
IDENTITY SEED, 743
IIF, 472
IIF(), 390
Implementation Hierarchy, 286
implicit conversion, 123
implicit looping, 11
import, 585
index, 159
index scan, 649
index seek, 649
indexed view, 165
Information Services, 5
INFORMATION_SCHEMA, 177, 350
INFORMATION_SCHEMA.TABLES, 177
Inline Function, 686
inline user-defined function, 557
INNER JOIN, 97, 683
inner query, 499
Insert (XML DML), 719
INSERT Data, 706
INSERT EXEC, 530
INSERT SELECT, 527
INSERT VALUES, 525, 526
Installing Books On Line, 84
Integration Services, 113, 627
IntelliSense, 125, 150
internal storage, 481
international standard, 479
INTERSECT operator, 109
interview question, 673
INVALID DATE, 490
Invalid object name, 248
invalid table reference, 129
ISDATE(), 490
ISNUMERIC, 96

ISO 8601 format, 479
ISO date time, 442
ISO string date formats, 188

J

Japanese, 443
JOIN keys, 221
JOIN on non-key columns, 29
JOIN predicate, 406
junction table, 27, 269, 339

K

Ken Sanchez, 516
keyword, 354

L

LAG(), 394
LANGUAGE Turkish, 492
Last Word of a String, 474
LAST_VALUE(), 395
Latin, 525
Latin1_General_CS_AI, 456
LEAD(), 394
leading space, 9
leading zeros, 319
LEFT, 447
LEFT JOIN, 421
Leipzig, 475
LEN(), 9
less than JOIN, 411
LIKE operator, 663
line feed, 569
linked server, 64
list price, 23
literals, 95
local variable, 179
logical data model, 183
London, 25
Lookup table, 12
Lookup Tables, 275
Los Angeles, 475
LTRIM(), 9

M

Madrid, 506
magyar, 515
maintenance, 181
major key, 109
Major sort key, 410
management portal, 84, 92
Management Studio, 113
Managing Azure SQL server, 84
many-to-many JOIN, 413, 414
master system database, 31
master-detail tables, 271
MAX(OrderQty), 104
Maximum Capacity Specifications, 653
maximum storage size, 185
mdy, 429, 443
meaningful names, 181
MERGE, 652
Messages, 125
metadata, 12, 177, 365
metadata query, 287
Miami, 475
midnight, 727
midnight bug, 452, 727
MIN(OrderQty), 104
minor key, 109
Minor sort key, 410
missing indexes, 654
model database, 33
modify() Method, 718
money, 185
Moscow, 443
Mountain-100, 100
msdb, 34
Msg 10053, 91
multidimensiona, 632
multidimensional, 634
multi-level totals, 671
multi-part identifier, 151
multiple WHERE conditions, 440
multiplication table, 428
München, 475

N

named instance, 63
NATURAL KEY, 346
nchar, 186
Nested CTEs, 511
New York, 443
New York City, 447
newid(), 102
NEWID(), 349
NEWSEQUENTIALID(), 349
Niagara Falls, 555
NOLOCK, 700
nonclustered index, 648
nonclustered PRIMARY KEY, 204
non-correlated subquery, 505
Nondeterministic, 480
nondeterministic CTE, 434
Northwind, 24
not null, 95, 198, 265, 290, 323, 325, 331, 390, 421, 426, 466, 470
ntelliSense, 145
ntext, 186
NTILE, 176
NULL, 13
Nullability, 612
NULLIF, 447
numbering, 415
nvarchar, 186, 380

O

Object Explorer Details, 354
OBJECT_DEFINITIION(), 355
OFFSET FETCH, 393
OLAP reports, 627
OLTP, 1, 17
OLTP query, 21
ON, 5
ON clause, 412
On Line Transaction Processing, 1
On-premises SQL Server, XXX
OPENQUERY, 532
OPSS2012, XXX
Optimistic Concurrency Control, 708
Optimization, 637
optimizer, 643
ORDER BY, 5
ORDER by newid(), 14
ORDER BY NEWID(), 102
Organizational Chart, 516
orgchart, 722
outer query, 499
Outline Numbering, 724
OUTPUT clause, 529, 666
OVER clause, 104, 674

P

pad, 319
Padding with leading zeros, 319
PAGE-LEVEL compression, 296
parameter sniffing, 652
parameterized view, 557
paramount, 401
parent table, 625
Parent-Child Tables, 706
PARSE(), 381
partially supported T-SQL, 84
partially supported T-SQL statements, 84
partition, 107
Partition, 316
PARTITION BY, 100
Partition Function, 308
Partitioned Table, 308
Pascal case, 181
PATINDEX, 495
PATINDEX string function, 495
PATINDEX(), 665
pattern match, 665
Pattern Matching, 495
performance improvement, 642
Pessimistic Concurrency Control, 709
PIVOT Operator, 521
PivotChart, 765
PivotTable, 633, 765
Plan Caching, 652
Polish, 492
POLYGON, 732

populated table, 198
Portland, 475
PowerShell, 689
PowerShell commands, 690
PowerShell script, 356
predicate, 106, 651
prefix, 447
prime numbers, 556
prioritizing, 654
product photos, 756
Product table, 21
productivity, 181
Profiler, 156, 638
Programming Standards, 320
project team, 320
pubs, 24

Q

Quality Assurance, 5
queries, 156
query, 1, 177
Query Designer, 134, 340, 684
Query Editor, 113
query optimization, 257, 645
query performance, 295, 318
query() Method, 713
queryout, 569
Queso, 97
QUOTENAME(), 379
Quotient, 1

R

RAISERROR, 707
random sort, 102
range query, 346
RANK, 176
ranking functions, 104
READ UNCOMMITTED, 699
readability, 221
reads, 637
real, 186
Recursive, 563
Recursive CTEs, 513
Recursive Query, 518
red squiggly, 152
red wave underlining, 150
relationship diagram, 341
relationships, 220
REPEATABLE READ, 701
Reporting Services, 113, 627
rerunnable script, 568
reserved keywords, 455
Restore of a Single Table, 743
Results to File, 120
Results to Text, 119
REVERSE, 448
reverse engineer, 229
reversible UPDATE, 540
RIGHT, 453
RIGHT JOIN, 422
right-click, 207
Rio de Janeiro, 443
Road Bikes, 14
ROLLBACK, 707
ROLLBACK TRANSACTION, 552
row count, 375
ROWGUIDCOL, 22
ROW-LEVEL compression, 297
rowversion, 710
RTRIM(), 9
Running total, 668
runtime, 129
Russian, 492

S

SalesOrderHeader, 20
sample database, 1
SARGable, 106, 650, 651
scalar user-defined function, 558
schema, 190, 191
SCHEMA_NAME(), 191
SCOPE_IDENTITY(), 528
scripting options, 363
search box, 354
Seattle, 25, 475
Security, 604

SELECT INTO, 90, 457, 473, 474, 477
SELECT statement, 5
self-join, 413
SELF-JOIN, 625
semi-structured data, 338
SERIALIZABLE Isolation, 703
Server Dashboard, 660
session, 152
SET LANGUAGE, 444
SET TRANSACTION ISOLATION LEVEL, 698
set-based logic, 679
Shard, 308
signed integer, 185
Single-valued SQL queries, 11
single-valued subquery, 503
smalldatetime, 185
smallint, 185
smallmoney, 185
SNAPSHOT Isolation, 704
software engineering, 637
software engineers, 320
Software standards, 320
soundex(), 15
South Africa, 555
sp_addextendedproperty, 284
sp_dropextendedproperty, 284
sp_help, 365
sp_helpconstraints, 287
sp_helpdb, 364
sp_helptext, 250, 365
sp_rename, 199
sp_updateextendedproperty, 285
sp_who2, 532
Spain, 506
Spanish, 492
Spatial Data Types, 732
Spatial Indexes, 232
SQL, i, ii, 1, 5, 12, 24, 29, 30, 31, 33, 34, 113, 180, 181, 182, 183, 185, 188, 189, 190, 191, 193, 198, 200, 247, 257, 268, 289, 290, 291, 294, 295, 317, 320, 324, 383, 385, 386, 387, 388, 389, 390, 391, 402, 407, 415, 420, 424, 426, 427, 429, 437, 440, 441, 443, 444
SQL Azure version, 40
SQL Data Synch, 91
SQL Database Migration Wizard, 86
SQL Injection, 725
SQL Server 2005, 1, 507
SQL Server 2008 R2, 358
SQL Server Agent, 90
SQL Server Analysis Services, 627
SQL Server Data Tools, 627
SQL Server instance, 62
SQL Server Profiler, 156
sql_variant, 186
SQLCMD, 566
sqlps, 689
square brackets, 182
SSAS, 113, 627
SSDT, 627
SSIS, 113, 627
SSIS Import/Export Wizard, 572
SSMS, 113
SSMS Object Explorer, 63
SSRS, 113, 627
staging tables, 223
standard cost, 23
Standard Reports, 659
star schema, 18
stealth, 170
stealth behavior, 622
STLength(), 732
Stock, 274
stored procedure, 393
String Date Format, 443
String literal, 22
string literals, 443
structured programming, 110
STUFF, 479
STUFF(), 98
style number, 477
subcategory, 23
Subcategory, 10
subquery, 97
SUBSTRING, 453
SUM, 448
Summary of Isolation Levels, 705
Sweden, 102, 555
Sybase, 24
synonym, 476

syntax errors, 128, 129
sys.bandwidth_usage, 91
sys.database_usage, 91
sys.objects, 180, 348
sys.sql_modules, 371
syscomments, 371
syslanguages, 445
sysname, 186
system databases, 30
system tables, 180, 357
system views, 157, 159, 167, 170, 180, 182, 357
systems analyst, 286

T

table alias, 505
table designer, 376
table editor, 374
table population, 528
table scan, 649
Table Value Constructor, 525
Table variable, 179
TABLESAMPLE, 737
Table-valued parameters, 675
tabs, 517
Technet Article, 652
tempdb, 35
Template Explorer, 685
temporal, 442
temporary table, 643
Temporary table, 35
Texas, 555
Text, 118
THEN, 475
THROW, 389
TIES, 100
tinyint, 185
titles table, 28
Tokyo, 443
TOP 10, 100
TOP clause, 100, 439
TOP n by group, 112
Toronto, 555
Touring-1000, 1
trailing spaces, 9
transaction, 697, 706
Transaction, 706
TRANSACTION ISOLATION LEVEL, 698
translate, 275
transport-level error, 91
tree hierarchy, 19
trigger, 622
TRY...CATCH Block, 697
TRY_CAST, 385
TRY_CONVERT(), 383, 385
TRY_PARSE(), 386

U

UDF CHECK constraint, 369
UK-Style, 443
underscore, 181
UNICODE, 185, 264
UNICODE Chinese, 665
UNION ALL, 111, 506
unique, 101
UNIQUE, 346
unique index, 204, 609
UNIQUE KEY, 346
uniqueidentifier, 185
UNIQUEIDENTIFIER, 349
United Kingdom, 474
United States, 474
UNPIVOT, 523
unsupported T-SQL, 84
unsupported T-SQL statements, 84
update PRIMARY KEY, 674
UPDATE STATISTICS, 654
us_english, 515
USE dbname, 89
user-defined function, 688
US-Style, 443

V

Valid Range, 496
value() Method, 715
varbinary, 185
varchar, 185

Variable-length, 185
version-stamping, 185
Vertical Partitioning, 316
violation of 3NF, 345
Visio Forward Engineer Addin, 231
Visual Studio, 113

W

WHEN, 475
WHERE clause, 99
WHERE condition, 11, 646
wildcard, 5, 354
window function, 104
Windows Azure SQL Database, 64
WITH CUBE, 99
WITH RESULT SETS, 396
WITH ROLLUP, 99
with xp_cmdshell, 604
worksheet, 123, 124
writes, 645

X

xml, 185
XML data, 338
XML Indexes, 232
XML PATH, 98, 760
XML PATH clause, 98
xp_cmdshell, 604
Xquery, 713

Y

ydm, 443
YEAR(OrderDate), 20
Yellowstone, 555
ymd, 442, 443
YYYYMMDD, 442

This page is intentionally left blank.

Made in the USA
Coppell, TX
10 January 2024